*f*P

THE FREE PRESS

New York London Toronto Sydney Singapore

THE POPULATION OF THE UNITED STATES

THIRD EDITION

Douglas L. Anderton

University of Massachusetts at Amherst

Richard E. Barrett

University of Illinois at Chicago

Donald J. Bogue

University of Chicago

with statistical assistance of
Alison Kadlec Donta

and additional textboxes by
Pamela R. Davidson
Alison Kadlec Donta
Karla L. Egan
Susan Hautaniemi
Erin Leahey
John Michael Oakes
Janet Tonner-Wagner

THE FREE PRESS
A Division of Simon & Schuster Inc.
1230 Avenue of the Americas
New York, NY 10020

Manufactured in the United States of America

10   9   8   7   6   5   4   3   2   1

Library of Congress Cataloging-in-Publication Data

Anderton, Douglas L.
    The population of the United States /
  Douglas L. Anderton, Richard Barrett, Donald J. Bogue. — 3rd ed.
      p.   cm.
    Previous ed. entered under Donald J. Bogue.
    Includes index.
    1. United States—Population.   2. United States—Census, 1990.
I. Bogue, Donald Joseph.   II. Barrett, Richard Edward.
III. Title.
HB3505.B63   1997
304.6'2'0973—DC21   96–48990
                                              CIP

ISBN 0–684–82774–3

CONTENTS

PREFACE AND ACKNOWLEDGMENTS

Much of the history of a nation is recorded in its population censuses, surveys, and vital registration systems. The single most influential address ever given by an American historian, Frederick Jackson Turner's "The Closing of the American Frontier" (1893), is based on an analysis of data from the Census of 1890. Just as the inhabitants of the United States seem drawn to sports wherein achievement can be quantified (such as the baseball hitter's batting average or the basketball player's shooting percentage), they also increasingly demand quantification from other aspects of life. Polls (and candidate's poll standings) are now the story as much as the ideas or characteristics of the candidates themselves. Ronald Reagan made good use of the so-called "misery index" (the unemployment rate added to the rate of monetary inflation) to unseat Jimmy Carter as President in 1980; Robert Dole based much of his 1996 campaign against Bill Clinton on a reported rise in drug use among adolescents as reported in government social surveys.

What is perhaps less well known is that almost all of these measures, from political polls to unemployment rates to the Consumer Price Index to surveys of drug use, are dependent on accurate and current measures of many characteristics of the population. Population data themselves contain a high percentage of the factual data available about present social and economic conditions. They, in turn, form the basis of systems by which the population can be stratified and sampled efficiently. The survival of the United States and the collapse from within of the Soviet Union in the second half of the twentieth century may well be due, in part, to the latter's failure to take censuses and surveys and to adjust and fine-tune industrial and agricultural policies in the light of social, economic and political realities. Throughout the Cold War, the average American could, by visiting his or her public library, learn more useful information about the United States than any member of the Politburo could ever discover about the U.S.S.R. The available population data on the United States is a huge natural resource, even though it is seldom recognized as such.

Members of almost all professions find it necessary to use population data from various sources to make decisions, interpret change, and anticipate the future in their particular sphere of interest. Familiarity with population facts and figures is becoming an increasingly essential part of the training of students at the secondary, college and post-secondary levels. Given the tremendous amount of information released each year, keeping up with population trends can be a difficult task. The sheer volume of population statistics and their increasing multiplicity of sources may lead many to give up and leave these topics to experts.

This volume is intended to be of service to all who find they need to know the fundamental facts of population growth, its composition and distribution in the United States, and to understand the implication of these facts for the present and the future. It is written in the belief that a large number of people need and want a comprehensive statement of this type within the covers of a single book-and that such a book does not exist. This kind of book should not be over-simplified by the omission of basic information; hence the large number of tables and charts. Insofar as possible, we have attempted to spare the interested reader who may lack specific demographic training the many technical details having little effect on a correct understanding of the results. The authors are convinced that a quantitative knowledge of population trends in the United States is so essential to people in so many fields (and so many nations) that it cannot be kept within a select 'priesthood' of demographic experts.

Our aim has been to produce a book that is complete enough in historical detail that the reader need only consult other sources for more specialized topics. We have tried to select the most cogent information from all available sources, to summarize it in easy-to-use statistical tables, and to provide a comprehensive exposition of the fundamental details that the reader must understand to make good use of the data presented. In general, any reader who understands percentages and simple algebra and who is willing to work his or her way systematically through a chapter's text and tables should be able to understand almost all of the material presented here.

There are four principal ways in which this book can be used:

- **As a reference work** for anyone—from corporate executives and government workers to high school and college students writing research papers—who wishes to learn about a particular topic. The detailed index, bibliographies at the end of each chapter, and technical appendices where appropriate will all be valuable to such users. The authors also recognize that, for many, this volume is not the last word, but is instead a jumping-off point. For that reason, each chapter stresses the sources of specific kinds of population data, their degree of comparability over time, and where they can be obtained at present. Appendix 2-3 includes a list of major government and scholarly Internet web-sites from which the reader can obtain current and past U.S. demographic data.

- **As an update** for people who have followed U.S. population trends for some time, but who have not had a recent opportunity to "put it all together" to arrive at an up-to-date integrated understanding. Special care has been taken to present time series for statistics appearing in annual publications. Some users may disagree with particular interpretations, but will appreciate the convenience of having data spanning many years from scattered sources compiled in one text.

- **As a textbook** for students undergoing pre-professional and professional training at a more sophisticated level than the usual "population problems" approach. Basic concepts are defined in a separate Definition Box in each chapter, thereby making them available but not forcing informed readers to interrupt their reading of the text to review them. Given the scope of this text the bibliographies with each chapter are selective rather than comprehensive. They provide guidance in further readings that students of population trends may find of assistance and insight beyond the materials presented in the respective chapter.

- **As an introduction to the United States population**, primarily for international readers seeking to become better acquainted with this nation. Such readers usually lack access to the population materials found in U.S. libraries. Consulting U.S. Bureau of the Census publications such as the annual *Statistical Abstract of the United States* or *Historical Statistics of the United States from Colonial Times to the Present* (1970) provide a highly incomplete set of statistical tables with no explanatory text. Readers of the present volume will learn about the increasingly diverse population of Americans, how they earn their living, their living conditions, and many of their social and economic problems and accomplishments as reflected in population statistics.

This volume is in no sense a government publication, even though the vast preponderance of the data presented here are government statistics. Neither the Bureau of the Census nor any other branch of the U.S. government has ever written such an introduction to the population of the United States. In fact, less interpretive material on the U.S. population is available for the 1990 Census than for the 1980 Census. This situation is unlikely to change in the near future; the publication of interpretations of the broader meanings of U.S. demographic trends by government experts appears to be another casualty of the ideological warfare of the last decade in Washington. We pretend no Olympian objectivity, but after introducing the reader to the key concepts in the study of the topics in each chapter, we have tried to use these demographic data to tell what has gone on, and why.

As the authors prepared each chapter, they often discovered a very different picture of life in the United States than can be gleaned by a perusal of news magazines, policy journals, or even scholarly works. An in-depth analysis of detailed census tables and survey results assembled over time is a little like William Least Heat Moon's *Blue Highways*: a journey over America's less-traveled roads that avoids the interstate highways where every place tends to look alike. Each chapter emphasizes population diversity across social groups and includes data on the current regional variation in population characteristics so that readers can contrast these with national trends over time. Indeed, much of the text's vitality derives from the excitement of discovering the detailed, diverse and ever changing character of the United States population.

This volume has also been able to draw upon a number of important advances in demographic methodology to provide new insights beyond earlier editions. The development of the first large-scale national panel survey that included detailed information on poverty, wealth and participation in government support and welfare programs (the Survey of Income and Program Participation, SIPP) in the 1980s was a major breakthrough in the study of the demography of social stratification. The many health surveys of the National Center for Health Statistics now provide a much clearer picture of the nation's health and the utilization of health resources. The continuity in the government's definition of racial minorities and the identification of the Hispanic population over the past two decades means that we can have some confidence that we are measuring real differences (or changes in differences) between such groups over time.

In a work that tries to interpret history, the reader deserves some clues as to the provenance of the work. A book with the title *The Population of the United States* was published by Donald J. Bogue in 1959. This volume provided detailed data and interpretations for the years immediately preceding and following World War II. An entirely new book with the same title by the same author (assisted by George W. Rumsey, Odalia Ho, David Hartmann, and Albert Woolbright) was published in 1985, and concentrated on data from the 1960s through 1984. This 1996 volume uses much the same style as the 1985 volume, but every chapter, table, and bibliography was re-written in light of new data, demographic trends and interpretations of these trends. The overall structure of the text was also reworked to address current population issues and policy interests in the United States.

Douglas Anderton and Richard Barrett are responsible for the majority of the chapters in this volume. Donald Bogue crafted a critical chapter in the present text and, more importantly, deserves the credit for the vision to attempt such an ambitious project (and complete it twice in the past). Many people assisted in the completion of what seems, in retrospect, a Herculean task. Many of these are acknowledged on the title page to this volume. The invaluable assistance of Alison Donta in compiling and formatting tables and graphics for the text cannot be overstated. Karen Mason provided copy editing for the text, and George Rumsey and Matthew Perry set our words into final print form. Irene Tse assisted Donald Bogue in preparing Chapter 8.

In a task which is so thoroughly absorbing and demanding, our spouses, families and colleagues have endured some hardships alongside us. To Terri, Teresa and all the others, we owe a special debt of gratitude for your support.

THE SIZE AND GROWTH OF THE UNITED STATES POPULATION

The population residing in the United States as we enter the middle of this decade (January 1, 1995) is estimated to be about 261.6 million persons. Since the census of 1990 the population has grown by 5.2 percent (12.9 million persons). Most of this gain in population is from natural increase (births minus deaths). During the previous year, 1994, natural increase accounted for two-thirds of the population increase in the United States. International immigrants and individuals returning from abroad accounted for the other one-third of population growth. These figures, however, represent a comparatively small share of the earth's inhabitants and of the earth's population growth. Only about 4.6 percent of the world's people live in the United States, and the United States' share of the world's population has declined steadily, from approximately 6.0 percent in 1950. The land area of the United States (916,660 thousand hectares or 3,539,289 square miles) is a larger proportion of the earth's total land area than is its population. The United States constitutes 7.0 percent of the land area of the world.

The population estimated by the United Nations for each nation, region, and continent of the world, across selected dates since 1950 and projected to 2025, is reported in Table 1-1. These earlier estimates for the United States population differ only slightly from the latest Census Bureau estimates above. Since the breakup of the USSR, only two nations—China and India—have populations larger than that of the United States. China's population is 4.7 times larger, and India's is 3.5 times larger, than the size of the U.S. population. Together the five most populous nations (China, India, United States, Indonesia, and Brazil) contain nearly one-half (48.5 percent) of the estimated number of people in the world. The population in most of these countries has grown faster over the past half decade than has that of the United States.

The United States has not yet doubled the population it had in 1950, but will reach that point early in the next century. All of the other five most populous nations have more than doubled their populations over this period. Brazil's population has more than trebled over this period and both China and India will have tripled their population of 1950 early in the coming century. In 1995, ten countries had a population of over 100 million compared to only four countries (including the USSR) in 1950. Sixty-five more countries have a population between 10 million and 100 million. In 1950 less than half as many countries had a population of over 10 million.

The density of settlement in the United States—287 persons per 1,000 hectares or 74.4 per square mile—is slightly higher than the world average. Population density is also increasing fairly rapidly in the United States. Ten years ago, in 1985, there were only 251 persons per 1,000 hectares or 65 per square mile. However, the United States is less densely settled than the twenty-five other largest nations except the Russian Federation and Brazil. Population densities are reported in Table 1-1 for each continent and nation. This table also notes, in terms of 1,000 hectare units (approximately 3.86 square statute miles each), the estimated land area of each continent, region, and country. However, because of adverse climate, hostile topography, and lack of resources, much of the world's land is virtually uninhabited. So, densities computed in terms of total land area are only very crude measures of the relation of population to natural resources.

U. S. Growth in Comparison with the World and with Other Nations

Population trends in the United States can be better appreciated if they are viewed from the perspective of population growth throughout the world given by the

Chapter 1 Definitions
THE SIZE AND GROWTH OF THE UNITED STATES POPULATION

Each chapter of this book contains a "definition box," wherein demographic concepts and terms not defined in previous chapters are defined or explained. This avoids needless reading for those familiar with demographic terminology. The index specifies the page on which each item is defined.

Population Size. The total number of inhabitants of a specified area at a specified date.

Resident Population. The population living within the national boundaries, including military personnel stationed there. This is the definition used in most discussions and for the official census count.

Total Population. The total population includes population abroad (armed forces and federal civilian employees and their dependents stationed abroad, crews of merchant vessels, and U.S. civilian citizens living abroad).

Civilian Population. For many purposes it is preferable to exclude the armed forces stationed within the nation from the resident population and define the resident civilian population only.

Census Enumeration. An organized campaign to count the number of inhabitants residing within a specified area as of a specified date, enumerating their demographic, social, and economic characteristics in the process.

Population Density. The total population size divided by the total land area, in either square miles or square kilometers.

Population Change. Increase or decrease in population size between two dates.

Intercensal Population Change. Increase or decrease in population size between two censuses.

Intercensal Rate of Change. Percentage increase or decrease in population between two censuses.

Average Annual Rate of Change. The average percentage increase or decrease per annum required to account for the population change between two dates.

Components of Population Change. Births, deaths, immigration, and emigration.

Reproductive Change (Natural Increase). Births minus deaths.

Demographic Balancing Equation. Addition of the components of change between two censuses to the total of the earlier census in order to estimate the population count of the later census.

Error of Closure. Difference between the expected count, resulting from use of the demographic balancing equation, and the actual count at the later census.

Midyear Population. Estimate of population as of July 1 of a given year. Usually computed by averaging estimates of population at beginning and end of the calendar year.

Crude Birth Rate. Number of births during a year per 1,000 midyear population in that year.

Crude Death Rate. Number of deaths during a year per 1,000 midyear population in that year.

Net Migration Rate. Amount of net migration during a year per 1,000 midyear population in that year.

Population Projection. Estimate of what the population will be at a future date, based on the current population structure and assumptions about the future course of birth, death, and migration rates.

Sex Ratio. The number of males per 100 or per 1,000 females. This ratio may be computed for age groups, race groups, births, or any other trait or combinations of traits subclassified by sex.

Dependency Ratio. Number of persons under age fifteen or over sixty-five per 100 population aged 15-64. Some demographers employ age under twenty instead of under fifteen in computing this ratio.

Age Pyramid. A diagram illustrating the age and sex composition of a population. Single-year or five-year age groups are stacked successively atop each other, beginning with the youngest age. Number (or percent) of the total population is used as the horizontal scale. Male population is plotted on the left and female population on the right side of the diagram.

Birth Cohort. A subpopulation born in a particular year or set of years which therefore are the same age group and pass through the life cycle together. Their progress may be charted by following them at successively older ages in consecutive censuses or enumerations.

annual growth rates in Table 1-1. It is estimated that as of 1995, the world contained approximately 5.76 billion inhabitants. Both the rate at which world population is growing (1.69 percent a year) and the amount by which it is growing (approaching 95 million a year) are striking. The world has acquired 36 percent of its total present population in the last twenty-five years alone; 3.23 billion of the 5.76 billion has been added since 1950. However, a trend toward slower growth is under way and is expected to continue. The population estimates for the year 2025, as projected by the United Nations, and the estimated annual growth rates from 1995 to 2025, are reported in Table 1-1. A world population of 8.47 billion in 2025 is predicted. This predicted increase is higher than that which the United Nations predicted ten years ago. And, this increase is in sharp contrast to the slow population growth over the many thousands of years that elapsed between the origin of humankind and the middle of the seventeenth century, before the human species numbered even 500 million. Some demographers expect world population

growth to become zero about the year 2100, with a total world population of 10 billion to 12 billion. Opinions concerning the potentially devastating effects of such population growth and the promise which such growth might bring to human development are varied and hotly contested among demographers.

The great "population explosion," with each decade witnessing an ever growing increase in the number of people, resulted from the fact that death rates have declined faster, and by greater amounts, than birth rates. Nations all over the world are benefiting from modern knowledge of medicine and public health. The incidence of infectious diseases that once killed off infants, children, and young adults before they had a chance to marry and reproduce have been greatly reduced. As a result a much greater proportion of the infants who are born survive to age forty or older, to marry and have children. Meanwhile, birth rates have declined much more slowly than death rates and are still high enough to produce a substantial increase.

Race. Race, as used by the Census Bureau, reflects self-identification of the racial group to which persons most closely identify and categories reflect influences of racial and national origin and sociocultural groups. Basic categories include White (including Canadian, German, Arab, etc.); Black (including African American, Black Puerto Rican, Jamaican, West Indian, etc.); American Indian, Eskimo and Aleut; Asian (including Chinese, Japanese, Asian Indian, etc.) or Pacific Islander (including Hawaiian, Samoan, Guamanian, etc.) and Other Race. More detailed racial definitions and discussions are provided in the Definition Box for Chapter 9.

Hispanic. Persons of Hispanic origin in the 1990 Census are those who were self-identified as one of the specific Hispanic categories (i.e. Mexican, Puerto Rican, Cuban) or those who indicated they were of Other Spanish/Hispanic origin. Where ambiguities were encountered interviewers asked for the group which best described origin or descent. The 1990 Census data are generally comparable to 1980 despite minor differences in wording. These data are not directly comparable to 1970 Spanish origin data but are presented alongside this data as the best available for historical purposes (see Chapter 9 Definition Box for more detail).

Regions and Divisions. Four regions and nine divisions are commonly used by demographers and the Census Bureau to amplify the geographic breakdown of population characteristics and the geographic composition of the population itself. These units are composed of states and are generally contiguous but somewhat arbitrary. They have no legal standing.

Place. In 1990, place includes census designated places and incorporated places. Each place is assigned both a four-digit census code and a five-digit FIPS code which are both unique within states. Both the census and FIPS codes are assigned based on alphabetical order within states.

Census Designated Place (CDP). CDPs comprise densely-settled concentrations of population that are identifiable by name, but are not legally incorporated places. Their boundaries, which usually coincide with visible features or the boundary of an adjacent incorporated place, have no legal status, nor do these places have elected officials.

Incorporated Place. In 1990 Census data, incorporated places are those reported to the Census Bureau as legally in existence on January 1, 1990 under the laws of their respective states as cities, boroughs, towns, and villages, with the following exceptions: the towns in the New England States, New York, and Wisconsin, and the boroughs in New York are recognized as minor civil divisions for census purposes; the boroughs in Alaska are county equivalents.

Urban and Rural. As defined for the 1990 Census, urban comprises all territory, population, and housing units in urbanized areas and in places of 2,500 or more persons outside urbanized areas. Territory, population, and housing units not classified as urban are classified as rural. The urban and rural classification cuts across other divisions; for example, there is generally both urban and rural territory within both metropolitan and nonmetropolitan areas.

Urbanized Area. The Census Bureau delineates urbanized areas to provide a better separation of urban and rural territory, population, and housing in the vicinity of large places. An urbanized area comprises one or more places (central place) and the adjacent densely settled surrounding territory (urban fringe) that together have a minimum of 50,000 persons. The urban fringe generally consists of contiguous territory having a density of at least 1,000 persons per square mile.

Metropolitan Area. The concept of a metropolitan area (MA) is one of a large population center, together with adjacent communities that have a high degree of economic and social integration with that center. Some MAs are defined around two or more centers. Each MA must contain either a place with a minimum population of 50,000 or a Census Bureau-defined urbanized area and a total MA population of a least 100,000 (75,000 in New England). Each MA comprises one or more central counties and may include one or more outlying counties that have close economic and social relationships with the central counties. In New England, MAs are composed of cities and towns rather than whole counties. The territory, population, and housing units in MAs are referred to as metropolitan. Those located outside MAs are referred to as nonmetropolitan.

Metropolitan Statistical Area (MSA). These are relatively freestanding MAs and are not closely associated with other MAs or are surrounded by nonmetropolitan counties. The title of an MSA contains the name of its largest central city and up to two additional city names. Generally, a city with a population of 250,000 or more is an MSA title.

The United States is a typical "More Developed Country." Its birth rates and death rates are slightly lower than the averages for more developed countries. However, its growth rates are higher than many nations of Europe (several of which have birth rates almost equal to their death rates, and are near or actually in a zero-growth situation). As Table 1-1 suggests, a nearly zero-growth situation now exists in the Russian Federation, Germany, Sweden, Norway, Finland, Denmark, the United Kingdom, Austria, Belgium, Hungary, and Switzerland. Given the present trends, it is unlikely (but not impossible) that the United States will have a zero-growth reproductive situation in the early decades of the next century. Yet, the annual growth rate forecast for the United States from 1995 to 2025 is relatively small compared to the countries of the world other than those near zero growth.

The History of Population Growth

The recent population growth in the United States can also be more readily appreciated when viewed in light of the nation's historical growth and the dynamic factors underlying population growth. The chapters of section II in this text examine the dynamic factors of population growth and change in great detail. The present section summarizes the historical character of population growth over the entire history of the United States. The population of the American colonies and settlements that eventually became the United States, with decennial increases and rates of increase, have been estimated as shown in Table 1-2. By 1690, the population of the United States was just over 200,000. In the next hundred years it rose to nearly 19 times that, or to 3.9 million by 1790. In the next one hundred years it rose again nearly 16-fold to 63 million by 1890. Again in the past one hundred years leading to 1990, the population of the U.S. rose nearly fourfold to nearly a quarter of a billion. The rate of the nation's growth has declined, but the numbers of individuals added each decade has appreciably decreased only during times of war (mostly due to drops in immigration) and in the recent decades since the contraceptive revolution.

Table 1-1. Population, Growth Rate, Land Area, and Population Density for Countries Over 10 Million Population in 1995: 1950, 1970, 1990, 1995, and 2025

| Country | Population (in millions) | | | | | Average annual growth rate | | Land area (in 1,000 hectares) | Density (per 1,000 hectares) |
	1950	1970	1990	1995	2025	1990-1995	1995-2025		1995
World total	2,524.62	3,695.58	5,295.30	5,759.28	8,472.45	1.69	1.30	13,041,713	442
China	556.61	838.40	1,153.47	1,238.32	1,539.76	1.43	0.73	932,641	1,328
India	368.46	552.47	846.19	931.04	1,393.87	1.93	1.35	297,319	3,131
United States	152.27	204.88	249.98	263.14	322.01	1.03	0.68	916,660	287
Indonesia	80.02	122.21	184.28	201.48	283.32	1.80	1.14	181,157	1,112
Brazil	52.84	95.32	149.04	161.38	219.67	1.60	1.03	845,651	191
Russian Federation	—	—	148.28	149.74	—	0.20	—	1,699,580	88
Pakistan	38.48	65.71	118.12	134.97	259.56	2.70	2.20	77,088	1,751
Bangladesh	40.57	68.28	113.68	128.25	223.25	2.44	1.86	13,017	9,853
Nigeria	33.23	56.35	108.54	126.93	285.82	3.18	2.74	91,077	1,394
Japan	83.63	104.33	123.54	125.88	127.03	0.38	0.03	37,652	3,343
Mexico	26.89	51.19	84.49	93.67	137.48	2.08	1.29	190,869	491
Germany	49.99	60.70	79.48	81.26	83.88	0.44	0.11	34,931	2,326
Viet Nam	30.09	43.13	66.69	73.81	116.96	2.05	1.55	32,549	2,268
Philippines	20.86	37.54	62.44	69.26	105.15	2.09	1.40	29,817	2,323
Iran, Islamic Republic	16.91	28.36	58.27	66.72	144.63	2.75	2.61	163,600	408
Turkey	20.81	35.32	55.99	62.03	92.88	2.07	1.35	76,963	806
Egypt	20.46	32.82	52.43	58.52	93.54	2.22	1.58	99,545	588
Thailand	20.97	36.50	54.68	58.27	72.26	1.28	0.72	51,089	1,141
United Kingdom	50.62	55.48	57.41	58.09	60.25	0.24	0.12	24,160	2,404
Ethiopia	16.25	25.45	49.83	58.04	130.67	3.10	2.74	110,100	527
Italy	46.77	53.57	57.66	57.91	56.24	0.09	-0.10	29,406	1,969
France	41.74	50.67	56.72	57.77	60.79	0.37	0.17	55,010	1,050
Ukraine	—	—	51.89	52.39	—	0.19	—	60,355	868
Myanmar	—	—	41.83	46.55	75.60	2.16	1.63	65,754	708
Korea, Republic	20.36	31.92	21.77	45.18	50.29	15.72	0.36	9,873	4,576
Zaire	14.18	21.64	37.39	43.81	104.53	3.22	2.94	226,760	193
South Africa	13.86	22.36	37.96	42.74	73.21	2.40	1.81	122,104	350
Spain	27.87	33.78	38.96	39.28	40.61	0.16	0.11	49,944	786
Poland	24.82	32.66	38.18	38.74	43.79	0.29	0.41	30,442	1,273
Colombia	11.60	20.80	32.30	35.10	49.36	1.68	1.14	103,870	338
Argentina	17.15	23.75	32.32	34.26	45.51	1.17	0.95	273,669	125
Tanzania	8.21	13.30	25.99	30.74	74.17	3.41	2.98	88,604	347
Sudan	9.32	14.09	25.20	28.96	60.60	2.82	2.49	237,600	122
Algeria	8.75	13.75	24.96	28.58	51.83	2.75	2.00	238,174	120
Canada	13.74	21.41	26.64	28.54	38.36	1.39	0.99	922,097	31
Morocco	8.95	15.13	25.06	28.26	47.48	2.43	1.74	44,630	633
Afghanistan	8.25	12.34	16.56	28.20	45.83	11.23	1.63	65,209	432
Kenya	6.42	11.25	23.59	27.89	63.83	3.41	2.80	56,969	490
Yugoslavia (former)	16.35	20.37	23.81	24.11	26.08	0.25	0.26	25,540	944
Korea, Democratic People's Republic	9.74	13.89	21.77	23.92	33.34	1.90	1.11	12,041	1,987
Peru	7.99	13.46	21.55	23.85	37.35	2.05	1.51	128,000	186
Romania	16.31	20.36	23.21	23.51	26.27	0.26	0.37	23,034	1,021
Uzbekistan	—	—	20.51	22.83	—	2.17	—	42,540	537
Nepal	8.31	11.42	19.57	22.12	40.06	2.48	2.00	13,680	1,617
Venezuela	5.14	10.96	19.32	21.48	32.67	2.14	1.41	88,205	244
Iraq	5.16	9.36	18.08	21.22	46.26	3.25	2.63	43,737	485
Uganda	5.16	9.81	17.56	20.41	45.93	3.05	2.74	19,955	1,023
Malaysia	6.25	10.86	17.89	20.13	31.27	2.39	1.48	32,855	613
Sri Lanka	7.68	12.51	17.22	18.35	24.74	1.28	1.00	6,463	2,839
Australia	8.22	12.55	17.09	18.34	25.21	1.42	1.07	764,444	24
Saudi Arabia	3.20	5.75	14.87	17.61	40.43	3.44	2.81	214,969	82
Ghana	4.37	8.61	15.02	17.45	37.99	3.04	2.63	22,754	767
Kazakhstan	—	—	16.74	17.44	—	0.82	—	266,980	65
Mozambique	5.71	8.14	14.20	16.36	36.29	2.87	2.69	78,409	209
Czechoslovakia (former)	12.39	14.36	15.66	15.88	17.92	0.28	0.40	12,536	1,267

Table 1-1. Population, Growth Rate, Land Area, and Population Density for Countries Over 10 Million Population in 1995: 1950, 1970, 1990, 1995, and 2025 (continued)

Country	Population (in millions)					Average annual growth rate		Land area (in 1,000 hectares)	Density (per 1,000 hectares)
	1950	1970	1990	1995	2025	1990-1995	1995-2025		1995
Netherlands	10.11	13.03	14.94	15.50	17.67	0.74	0.44	3,392	4,570
Syrian Arab Republic	3.50	6.26	12.36	14.78	35.25	3.64	2.94	18,392	804
Cote d'Ivoire	2.67	5.34	11.98	14.40	37.94	3.75	3.28	31,800	453
Chile	6.09	9.37	13.17	14.24	19.77	1.57	1.10	74,880	190
Madagascar	4.56	6.80	12.01	14.16	33.75	3.35	2.94	58,154	243
Yemen	3.32	4.84	11.68	13.90	34.24	3.54	3.05	52,797	263
Cameroon	—	—	11.52	13.28	29.26	2.88	2.67	46,540	285
Ecuador	3.31	5.96	10.55	11.82	18.64	2.30	1.53	27,684	427
Zimbabwe	2.42	5.31	9.95	11.54	22.89	3.01	2.31	38,667	298
Malawi	2.70	4.51	9.58	11.30	24.92	3.36	2.67	9,408	1,201
Cuba	5.86	8.58	10.61	11.09	12.99	0.89	0.53	10,982	1,010
Angola	4.12	5.59	9.19	11.07	26.62	3.79	2.97	124,670	89
Mali	3.43	5.36	9.21	10.80	24.58	3.24	2.78	122,019	89
Guatemala	2.96	5.35	9.20	10.62	21.67	2.91	2.41	10,843	979
Hungary	9.34	10.35	10.55	10.47	10.40	-0.15	-0.02	9,234	1,134
Burkina Faso	—	—	8.99	10.35	22.63	2.86	2.64	27,380	378
Belarus	—	—	10.26	10.31	—	0.10	—	20,760	497
Greece	7.57	8.79	10.12	10.25	10.10	0.26	-0.05	12,890	795
Somalia	1.91	2.79	8.68	10.17	23.40	3.22	2.82	62,734	162
Belgium	8.64	9.64	9.97	10.03	9.91	0.12	-0.04	3,023	3,318

Source: United Nations, "World Resources 1994-95," Tables 16.1 and 17.1, "Demographic Indicators of Countries: Estimates and Projections as Assessed in 1980," (1950 and 1970 data), Oxford University Press, New York, 1994 and 1982.

The first census, taken in 1790, must be the starting point for any detailed analysis, but even the data provided by the first several censuses are much too sparse and incomplete to answer all significant questions. By considering the conditions that must have given rise to the events and trends that emerged, however, it is possible to build up a fairly complete and reliable history of population growth in terms of the components of this growth. Broadly speaking, the nation has passed through five distinct phases of growth and is now in a sixth. Each phase represents a distinctive combination of the components of reproductive change and net migration.

1. *Colonial and Early National Phase, 1620-1830.* High rates of reproductive change with initially high and then lower rates of net immigration characterized the colonial period. In the early part of the period, birth rates were extremely high, approaching the maximum of which human populations are biologically capable. Migrants to the New World appear to have considered children an economic asset in conquering the wilderness. Marriage occurred at an earlier age in America than in Europe, which meant that each married couple experienced a longer period of childbearing. In much of Europe deaths were almost as numerous as births, whereas death rates in America were only moderate, and permitted a rapid population growth. The high fertility of this population enabled the colonies to grow at an almost unprecedented

rate for more than two centuries. Meanwhile, immigrants from Europe continued to enter the colonies. While America was in this phase, its growth from natural increase is assumed to have been about 3 percent per annum from 1650 to 1820.

During the last portion of this phase, 1770 to 1830, the rate of immigration from abroad appears to have declined. The insecurity and uncertainty created by the Revolutionary War, the establishment of the Republic, and the British blockade of Napoleonic Europe tended to reduce temporarily the flow of migrants from abroad. Meanwhile the rate of reproductive growth continued to be very high. Thompson and Whelpton estimate that at the beginning of the nineteenth century there were about 55 births and 25 deaths per 1,000 residents annually, which means that the United States had a net annual reproductive gain of 30 per 1,000, or 3 percent per annum. Such a high rate of growth attracted worldwide attention. When Thomas Malthus looked for proof that the human species tended to increase geometrically, he found it in the population of the newly established United States. Even though the net immigration from abroad had declined to a comparatively low point toward the end of the period, the decline had no seriously depressing effect upon population growth.

2. *Frontier and Early Urbanization Phase, 1830-1910.* Large but rapidly declining rates of reproductive increase and a very large volume of immigration from

Table 1-2. Estimated Population of the American Colonies 1630-1780 and Population of the United States at Each Decennial Census: 1790-1990

Year	Population	Increase over preceding decade Number	Increase over preceding decade Percent	Average annual rate of increase
1990	248,709,873	22,164,068	9.8	0.94
1980	226,545,805	23,243,774	11.4	1.09
1970	203,302,031	23,978,856	13.4	1.26
1960	179,323,175	27,997,377	18.5	1.71
1950	151,325,798	19,161,229	14.5	1.36
1940	132,164,569	8,961,945	7.3	0.70
1930	123,202,624	17,181,087	16.2	1.51
1920	106,021,537	13,793,041	15.0	1.40
1910	92,228,496	16,016,328	21.0	1.93
1900	76,212,168	13,232,402	21.0	1.93
1890	62,979,766	12,790,557	25.5	2.30
1880	50,189,209	11,630,838	30.2	2.67
1870	38,558,371	7,115,050	22.6	2.06
1860	31,443,321	8,251,445	35.6	3.09
1850	23,191,876	6,128,523	35.9	3.12
1840	17,063,353	4,202,651	32.7	2.87
1830	12,860,702	3,222,249	33.4	2.93
1820	9,638,453	2,398,572	33.1	2.90
1810	7,239,881	1,931,398	36.4	3.15
1800	5,308,483	1,379,269	35.1	3.05
1790	3,929,214	1,148,845	41.3	3.52
1780	2,780,369	632,293	29.4	2.61
1770	2,148,076	554,451	34.8	3.03
1760	1,593,625	422,865	36.1	3.13
1750	1,170,760	265,197	29.3	2.60
1740	905,563	276,118	43.9	3.70
1730	629,445	163,260	35.0	3.05
1720	466,185	134,474	40.5	3.46
1710	331,711	80,823	32.2	2.83
1700	250,888	40,516	19.3	1.78
1690	210,372	58,865	38.9	3.34
1680	151,507	39,572	35.4	3.07
1670	111,935	36,877	49.1	4.08
1660	75,058	24,690	49.0	4.07
1650	50,368	23,734	89.1	6.58
1640	26,634	21,988	473.3	19.08
1630	4,646	—	—	—

Source: U.S. Bureau of the Census, "General Population Characteristics," 1990 Census of Population, Table 1, "Number of Inhabitants," 1980 Census of Population, Table 8, "Historical Statistics of the United States," Series Z 1-19, U.S. Government Printing Office, Washington, D.C., 1992, 1983, and 1960.

abroad characterized the second phase. The rapid growth of commerce and industry following the War of 1812 created almost unlimited opportunities for incoming migrants. Land was plentiful and easily obtained. During each decade except the first, 1830-40, the nation grew by about 5 percent as a result of immigration alone. In four of the decades the decennial rate due to net immigration was 8.3 percent or more, as the United States took Europe's surplus population. Meanwhile, the average annual rate of reproductive change was declining steadily and rapidly from the high point it had reached about 1800. It fell from about 2.9 percent in the 1830-40 decade to about 1.3 percent in the 1900-10 decade. This was a decline of 1.6 points, or more than half, in the span of eighty years. This precipitous drop represents a narrowing of the gap between birth rates and death rates.

During this period, the germ theory of disease, epidemic control, antiseptic surgery, regulation of the water supply and waste disposal, better care of the sick, and greater interest in public health all began to exert a measurable influence on mortality. Their combined effect was to lower the death rate considerably. In turn, because the population is known to have halved its rate of reproductive increase and to have enjoyed lower death rates during the sixty years between 1830 and 1890, the inference that birth rates were reduced drastically over that period is inescapable. Our grandparents and great-grandparents reduced their fertility within a remarkably short time, and without the efficient devices available today. They seem to have lowered their birth rates by means of later marriages and the use of simple techniques which avoided, or at least postponed, pregnancy. The period during which this drastic reduction in fertility took place was also the period during which the population became industrialized and urbanized. And, it has been generally assumed that birth control practices began in the cities and slowly diffused throughout the whole population, hence that urbanization and industrialization have been factors underlying this fertility decline. However, there is evidence that birth rates fell as rapidly in early American rural communities as they did in the cities. Birth rates appear to have dropped in rural New England even before 1800, and the decline in rural birth rates traveled westward as the land filled up.

3. *Early Twentieth Century Phase, 1900-1925.* Moderate and almost constant rates of reproductive increase were combined with declining immigration. This phase overlaps the one preceding it in that the rate of reproductive increase began to be steady at the turn of the century, but immigration did not begin to decline until after 1910.

Figure 1-1. Components of Population Change: 1910-2050

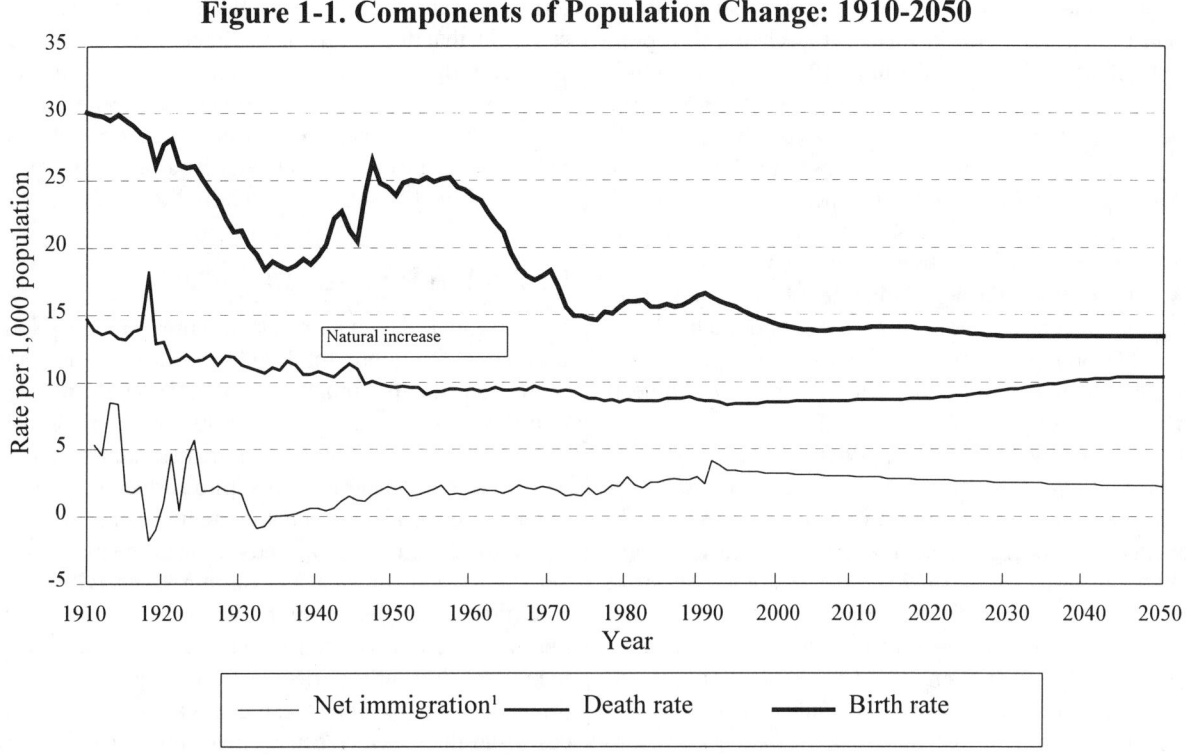

[1] From 1911-1939, represents the total of alien immigrants plus citizens arrived minus emigrants and citizens departed.
Source: Data from 1940 on from CPS data, birth and death rate data prior to 1940 from "Historical Statistics of the U.S.," and
immigration data prior to 1940 from U.S. Immigration and Naturalization Service data.

More factual data are available for evaluating the trends of this period than for previous periods. Figure 1-1 presents the estimates of the actual birth and death rates from 1910 through the mid-1990's and for projections to the year 2050, from which more exact measurements of annual and decennial growth can be made. In order to interpret year-to-year changes in the components, it is customary to express them as rates per 1,000 population as of July 1 of the calendar year to which they refer. These are called crude rates. Thus:

Crude birth rate (CBR) = (Births during year / Midyear population) x 1,000

Crude death rate (CDR) = (Deaths during year / Midyear population) x 1,000

Net immigration rate = (Immigrants minus emigrants / Midyear population) x 1,000

The annual growth rate or natural increase for a year is equal to CBR minus CDR, plus or minus net immigration. During this period of 1900-1925, for example, both birth and death rates appear to have been declining moderately and at about the same rate such that natural increase remained relatively constant as the immigration rate fluctuated more erratically.

With the exception of a temporary fluctuation during and after World War I, the birth rate appears to have leveled off from its previous steep decline and to have paralleled the more gradual decline of the death rate. Except for 1918, when there was an influenza epidemic, death rates continued to decline. In this phase immigration from abroad slowed until it was about one-third of the average for the preceding period. In 1924 Congress passed the National Origins Quota Act restricting immigration to a small quota for each foreign country. This combination of growth components resulted in national growth rates that were very moderate in comparison with those of the past; they were still very rapid in comparison with the rates in much of the world, however, and would be considered excessive if applied to a large population for any prolonged period.

4. *Post-World War I Phase, 1925-40.* A precipitous decline in birth rates and very low immigration marked the fourth phase. In 1919 birth rates had suffered a sharp but temporary decline because of the number of men who were overseas with the armed forces. In 1920 and 1921 birth rates increased abruptly as the armed forces were demobilized. Shortly thereafter, about 1925, birth rates began to decline again very rapidly—as rapidly, in fact, as they had at any time during the 1800s. In less than

ten years the birth rate fell by more than 10 per 1,000 (see Figure 1-1), and then leveled off. It reached its low point in 1933 and remained there until 1939, at which time it made a moderate upswing. This sharp decline was attributed in part to the Great Depression. Also because of the depression, immigration from abroad shrank to very low levels. The fertility decline preceded the economic collapse of 1929. It may have begun as a compensating reaction to the wave of births immediately following World War I and then, through coincidence, may have been strengthened and prolonged by the economic hardships of the Depression. It may also have been a resumption of the steady downward trend that characterized the years from 1830 to 1900.

5. *World War II and Postwar "Baby Boom" Phase, 1940-57.* Moderately high rates of reproductive increase were combined with moderate immigration. An unexpected upsurge in population growth began about 1940 and lasted until 1957. Its cause was a rise in the birth rate (see Table 1-2 and Figure 1-1). Just how dramatic it was, as a reversal of the direction of trends in fertility and reproduction that had prevailed for at least a century and a quarter, may be more fully appreciated when it is viewed from the perspective of the nation's previous growth history.

The reproductive change between 1940 and 1957 was sharply higher than the very small rate of growth from 1925 to 1940 (see Figure 1-1). Yet the nation did not return to the levels of rapid population growth of the nineteenth century in terms of either immigration or reproductive change. The rate of reproductive increase between 1940 and 1957 was quite similar to the rates that prevailed in the decades between 1890 and 1930. The difference was that the earlier rates were applied to a base of moderately high but declining birth and death rates, whereas the 1940 to 1957 rate of reproductive change was based upon very low death rates and moderately high birth rates. It is evident that the baby boom was a major deviation from more than a century of declining fertility. Immigration also increased to a moderate level, largely explained by the entrance of refugees from World War II and the Korean War and of brides of servicemen who married overseas.

6. *Contemporary "Baby Bust" and "Boomer Echo" Phase, 1957-95.* The present is characterized by low rates of reproductive increase and moderate immigration. Just as suddenly as it began its upsurge, the American birth rate began to decline in 1957, and by 1965 it had returned to the pre-boom level. The decline continued, and in 1976 the crude birth rate reached an all-time low of 14.5 per 1,000. Throughout the 1980-90 decade birth rates fluctuated between approximately 15.0 and 17.0, ending the decade on the higher end of this range. Part of this resurgent fertility is an echo effect reflecting both baby boomers of childbearing age deciding to have children before it is too late and their older children entering into childbearing ages. Projections reflect the assumption that this fertility rise will be short-lived. Meanwhile, immigration totals have sustained a moderate level, partially as a result of immigration of refugees from Vietnam, Cuba, Haiti, and Central America. There has also been a major influx of legal and illegal immigrants from less developed countries, especially Mexico.

Projected Population Growth

By making what appear to be reasonable assumptions about the future trends in births, deaths, and net immigration, demographers prepare "population projections," which estimate or predict future population size. The U.S. Bureau of the Census makes such projections and revises them periodically as new perspectives are obtained on trends in the components of growth. Table 1-3 shows the growth projected for the future under "low," "medium," and "high" growth assumptions. All these assumptions presume that mortality rates will decline and that immigration will continue to be realistically within the range of recent experience. Accordingly, these recent projections are for somewhat higher growth than was forecast from the previous census in 1980. The chief variation is in assumptions about the future course of fertility. Some demographers expect another return to higher fertility (but not another baby boom). Others expect birth rates to decline even below the low level reached in 1976. Under the "medium" growth, or most likely projection, the population will continue to grow to reach about 276 million in the year 2000, 300 million in 2010 and about 392 million by 2050. If birth rates and net immigration are low and death rates improve very little, the popula-

Table 1-3. Projections of the Total United States Population: 1995-2050 [numbers in thousands]

Year	Projection series		
	Low	Medium	High
1995	262,051	263,434	264,715
2000	270,259	276,241	281,957
2005	276,316	288,286	299,941
2010	281,180	300,431	319,536
2020	289,553	325,942	363,213
2030	292,902	349,993	410,991
2040	290,351	371,505	463,579
2050	285,502	392,031	522,098

Source: U.S. Bureau of the Census, Current Population Reports," Population Projections of the United States, by Age, Sex, Race, and Hispanic Origin: 1993 to 2050," Table C, Series P-25 Number 1104, U.S. Government Printing Office, Washington, D.C., 1993.

Citizenship

by Alison Kadlec Donta

There are six ways to become a citizen of the United States. Most U.S. citizens are such because they were born in the United States. Persons born abroad to a citizen parent(s) are also citizens. A third way to become a citizen is by naturalization in a court exercising naturalization jurisdiction, and a fourth method is by derivation after birth through the naturalization of one's parent or parents. Citizenship can also be granted by application of an adoptive parent or parents for an adopted child. Finally, legislation has been passed that collectively naturalizes persons born in Guam, Puerto Rico, the Virgin Islands, and the Commonwealth of Northern Mariana Islands.

Citizenship in the United States is granted either through the Constitution or through laws enacted by Congress. The Immigration and Nationality Act was passed by Congress in 1952 and amended most recently in 1995 (P.L. 104-8). In most cases, before an alien can apply for and petition for naturalization, he or she must be 18 years old after having been admitted for lawful permanent residence for five years and have been physically present in the U.S. for periods totaling more than half that time. He or she must also live in the state in which the petition will be filed for six months prior to the submission of the petition. Before a person can become naturalized, he or she must be able speak, read, and write English and have an understanding of the Constitution, history, and government of the United States.

In 1990, citizens comprised 95.3% of the United States population. While 92.1% of those were native-born, another 3.2% were naturalized citizens. This is the highest proportion of non-citizens in the country since 1930, when 94.9% of the population were citizens (88.4% native and 6.5% naturalized). The accompanying table further illustrates the trends in citizenship status since 1920, the first year in which citizenship status was as-

Nativity and Citizenship of the U.S. Population: 1920-1990

| Year | Native | Foreign born | |
		Naturalized citizen	Not a citizen
1990	92.1	3.2	4.7
1980	93.8	3.1	3.1
1970	95.2	3.1	1.7
1960	94.6	—	—
1950	93.1	5.0	1.9
1940	91.2	5.5	3.3
1930	88.4	6.5	5.1
1920	86.8	6.1	7.0

Source: U.S. Bureau of the Census, "General Social and Economic Characteristics: United States Summary," 1990 Census of Population, Table 143, and 1980 Census of Population, Table 99, and "Historical Statistics of the United States," Series C 181-194, U.S. Government Printing Office, Washington, D.C., 1993, 1983, and 1975.

sessed by the census for the entire population. The proportion of the population that was native-born was 86.8% in 1920 and reached its peak in 1970, when 95.2% of the population was native-born. Since 1970, this segment of the population has been declining; the proportion of the population that is naturalized has remained relatively steady, and the proportion of non-citizens is increasing. There was a 232.3% increase in the number of non-citizens between 1970 and 1990.

At the same time, there has also been a change in the proportion of foreign-born persons who are citizens. In 1920, there were 87.3 naturalized citizens for every 100 non-citizens. Beginning in 1930, however, that ratio was reversed. In that year, there were 126 naturalized citizens for every non-citizen among the foreign-born. The greatest ratio between citizens and non-citizens was 271.6:100 in 1950. Since then, the trend has reversed, and in 1990 there were only 67.9 naturalized citizens per 100 non-citizens among the foreign-born population. This may represent a greater influx of foreign-born persons during the 1980s, a backlog of naturalization applications, a waiting list for submitting naturalization petitions, and a decreasing number of foreign-born persons who choose to apply for citizenship. This can also be explained through an examination of the source of many recent immigrants. The largest number of foreign-born persons during this past decade came from North America (44.1%) and from Asia (32.3%). In addition, persons from North America, particularly from Mexico and Central America, were less likely to be citizens than foreign-born persons in general. Of the total foreign-born population in 1990, 40.5% were citizens while only 29.3% of the total North American foreign-born were citizens. Addition-

ally, only 22.6% of those who came from Mexico and 20.7% of those who originated in Central America were citizens. Of those who were born in Asia, 40.8% were citizens in 1990.

In 1990, citizenship status in the United States also varies by region of residence. While 92.1% of the total population was native-born, a higher proportion of those living in the Midwest and the South were native-born. Conversely, only 89.7% of those living in the Northeast and 85.2% of those living in the West were native-born. The division with the highest proportion of native-born residents was the East South Central while the Pacific division had the lowest proportion of native-born population. Similarly, the Pacific is the division with the highest proportion of non-citizens. This 12% of the population that is composed of non-citizens in the Pacific is followed by 5.9% in the Middle Atlantic division. These numbers are explained, in part, by the influx of immigrants to large metropolitan areas such as Los Angeles and New York City. By contrast, only 0.6% of the population of the more rural East South Central division are non-citizens.

Nativity and Citizenship of the U.S. Population, by Region and Division: 1990

| Region and division | Total | Native | Foreign born | |
			Naturalized citizen	Not a citizen
United States	100.0	92.1	3.2	4.7
Northeast region	100.0	89.7	4.9	5.4
New England	100.0	92.1	3.8	4.1
Middle Atlantic	100.0	88.9	5.3	5.9
Midwest region	100.0	96.4	1.8	1.8
East North Central	100.0	95.8	2.1	2.1
West North Central	100.0	98.0	1.0	1.0
South region	100.0	94.6	2.1	3.2
South Atlantic	100.0	93.7	2.6	3.6
East South Central	100.0	99.0	0.5	0.6
West South Central	100.0	93.6	2.2	4.1
West region	100.0	85.2	5.0	9.8
Mountain	100.0	94.8	2.2	3.0
Pacific	100.0	81.8	6.0	12.2

Source: U.S. Bureau of the Census, "Social and Economic Characteristics: United States Summary," 1990 Census of Population, U.S. Government Printing Office, Washington, D.C., 1993, Table 143.

Additional Sources:

Committee on the Judiciary of the House of Representatives. Immigration and Nationality Act. 104th Congress 1st Session, Serial No. 1. Washington, D.C.: U.S. Government Printing Office, 1995.

U.S. Bureau of the Census. Historical Statistics of the United States: Colonial Times to 1970. Washington, D.C.: U.S. Government Printing Office, 1975.

_____. General Social and Economic Characteristics: United States Summary. 1980 Census of Population. Washington, D.C.: U.S. Government Printing Office, 1983.

_____. Social and Economic Characteristics: United States Summary. 1990 Census of Population. Washington, D.C.: U.S. Government Printing Office, 1993.

U.S. Department of Justice. Basic Guide to Naturalization and Citizenship. Washington, D.C.: U.S. Government Printing Office, 1990.

tion in 2010 can be as much as 19 million less; if fertility rises slightly above replacement, death rates fall a great deal, and net immigration is large, the population in 2010 can be as high as 19 million more than the medium growth projection. Long-term forecasts are notoriously inaccurate. Accordingly, by 2050 the range between the low and high growth projections is almost 236 million, or as much as 90 percent of the current population of the United States.

Population Composition

Treating population simply as numbers of people is a necessary first step, but for the purposes of population study it is not sufficient. Population characteristics are no less important than numbers of inhabitants. The chapters in sections III and IV of this text present detailed information on the social (e.g. race, sex, age, living arrangements, education) and economic (e.g. employment, occupation, income, poverty) composition of the United States population. This chapter provides a short summary of what demographers consider to be the most basic composition characteristics (i.e. race, sex and age) of the U.S. population.

Racial Composition

In the 1990 Census all persons were asked to classify themselves as belonging to one of a large number of race categories (see Chapter 9 Definition Box for details). The resulting data therefore show how the respondents identified themselves by race, as they interpreted the census question. The categories obviously are not a scientific classification of distinctive, genetically determined biological stocks. It is, rather, a set of categories deemed to be important for social, economic, and administrative purposes in one or more of the fifty states. Because the 1990 Census was primarily one of self-enumeration, and because public ideas of what constitute categories of race probably are subject to great variation, the data may have substantial response errors. For example, many respondents who should have classified themselves as white (especially non-black Hispanics) apparently regarded the question as one about nationality, and when they did not find their nation of origin mentioned, simply marked "other." Similarly, there is evidence to indicate that many individuals developed a new sense of self-identity as Native Americans between the 1980 and 1990 censuses. All of these ambiguities are then further amplified by concerns from one census to another as to the adequacy of coverage for various racial or ethnic groups (see Chapter 2). And, of course, racial classifications have changed in substance and in significance over any significant historical period. In the interests of accuracy, this text uses the categories provided by the census (e.g. black) rather than other designations (e.g. African-American) which various groups have proposed for self-identification but

which do not correspond to available data and are even more ambiguous in self-identification.

Table 1-4 presents the changing U.S. racial composition for several major racial categories from 1790 to 1990. After those identifying themselves as white, blacks are the second largest racial group in the United States. The percentage of the population which is black has increased steadily over the past fifty years. When the nation was founded, and for its first half-century, almost one resident in five was black (preponderantly slaves). When the importation of slaves was forbidden and as the floodgates of immigration from Europe were opened, this proportion declined by almost half. Its lowest point was reached in 1930. During the most recent half-century, higher black than white fertility, and a reduction in immigration from abroad, has caused the proportion of blacks to climb. By mid-decade, i.e. 1995, blacks constituted nearly 13 percent of the United States population (nearly what it was in 1880.) Were it not for the continuing inflow of white and other race immigrants from Latin America and other nations the proportion would climb more quickly toward the 1790 figure because of the substantially higher fertility among black than among white residents.

Because of a steady and comparatively large inflow of immigrants from Latin America, the Hispanic population has also come to constitute an important minority in the United States. This group includes Mexicans, Puerto Ricans, Cubans, and persons with origins in other Latin American nations or Spain. Residents of Brazilian or Portuguese origin are not generally included. However, historical comparisons are confounded by the changing treatment of this category across censuses (see Chapter 9 Definition Box). And, it is important to note that the Hispanic classification of the population is not racial but ethnic (linguistic and cultural). If, nonetheless, Hispanics were included alongside the racial categories of Table 1-4, this group would rank as the third largest population group. Both whites and blacks can be classified as Hispanic, but there are relatively few Hispanic blacks (roughly 3/4 million) and non-black Hispanics (approximately 11.5 million) are still a smaller group than black non-Hispanics. It is widely assumed that the rapid inflow of migrants from Latin America will continue beyond the turn of the century, unless special legal measures are taken to curtail it. Because it is now the third largest group in the population and still growing rapidly, throughout this book special attention will be given to the Hispanic, as well as the black, population in comparisons with the majority white population. Following the convention of demographers, and the Census Bureau, this text provides separate tabulation of Hispanics, occasionally identifying white or non-white Hispanics as suits the substance of any particular discussion.

Notwithstanding the history of slavery in the United States, no racial group has suffered more from the ag-

Table 1-4. Racial Composition of the Population of the United States: 1790 to 1990

Year	Number, in thousands							Percent distribution			Percent change since previous decade		
	White	Black	American Indian	Japanese	Chinese	Filipino	Other	White	Black	Other	White	Black	Other
1990	199,686	29,986	1,959¹	848	1,645	1,408	13,179	80.9	12.2	6.9	6.0	13.2	46.2
1980	188,372	26,495	1,364	701	806	775	8,033	83.1	11.7	5.2	6.0	17.3	305.1
1970	177,749	22,580	793	591	435	343	721	87.5	11.1	1.4	11.9	19.6	78.1
1960	158,832	18,872	524	464	237	176	218	88.6	10.5	0.9	17.5	25.4	43.1
1950	135,150	15,045	357	326	150	123	175	89.3	9.9	0.7	14.2	16.9	20.2
1940	118,358	12,866	345	285	106	99	106	89.6	9.7	0.7	7.2	8.2	2.8
1930	110,396	11,892	343	279	102	108	83	89.6	9.7	0.7	16.3	13.6	39.7
1920	94,904	10,464	244	221	85	27	78	89.5	9.9	0.6	16.0	6.5	11.4
1910	81,812	9,829	277	153	94	3	61	88.7	10.7	0.6	22.3	11.3	15.3
1900	66,869	8,834	237	86	119	—	68	87.7	11.6	0.7	21.4	18.0	42.5
1890	55,101	7,489	249	2	107	—	…	87.5	11.9	0.6	27.0	13.8	108.1
1880	43,403	6,581	66	…	106	—	…	86.5	13.1	0.3	29.2	34.9	91.1
1870	33,589	4,880	26	…	64	—	…	87.1	12.7	0.2	24.8	9.9	13.9
1860	26,923	4,442	44	…	35	—	…	85.6	14.1	0.3	37.7	22.1	—
1850	19,553	3,639	—	—	—	—	—	84.3	15.7	—	37.7	26.6	—
1840	14,196	2,874	—	—	—	—	—	83.2	16.8	—	34.7	23.5	—
1830	10,537	2,328	—	—	—	—	—	81.9	18.1	—	33.9	31.4	—
1820	7,867	1,772	—	—	—	—	—	81.6	18.4	—	34.2	28.6	—
1810	5,862	1,378	—	—	—	—	—	81.0	19.0	—	36.1	37.5	—
1800	4,306	1,002	—	—	—	—	—	81.1	18.9	—	35.8	32.4	—
1790	3,172	757	—	—	—	—	—	80.7	19.3	—	—	—	—

¹ Includes Eskimo and Aleut.

Source: U.S. Bureau of the Census, "General Population Characteristics," 1990 Census of Population, Table 3, 1980 Census of Population, Table 40, and "Historical Statistics of the United States," Series A 91-104, U.S. Government Printing Office, Washington, D.C., 1992, 1983, and 1975.

gressive colonization of this country by others than native American Indians. American Indians appeared to be almost an endangered group at the close of the Civil War (1870), with only 26,000 reported in the census. The enumeration of this group at the various censuses has been erratic and, until 1960, incomplete. In recent censuses the group has increased to a more substantial size, showing phenomenal growth. The self-identification method of enumerating race introduced in 1980, when almost a doubling of the American Indian population within a decade was recorded, may have contributed to many individuals entering this category which were not previously classified in this group. Some people have said that light-skinned black residents (many of whom have Indian blood) who report themselves as American Indian may account for part of the growth. Others have argued that the self-identification may have been abused by those who wished to express solidarity or personal affiliation with American Indians regardless of any blood relation. In the 1980 and 1990 censuses other native Americans were added to this category which now includes the Eskimo and Aleut populations.

The Chinese population entered the United States in a wave that lasted from 1870 to 1900. Chinese laborers provided inexpensive labor for such massive projects as the Pacific side of the transcontinental railroad. However, as early as the 1870s the federal government erected legal barriers to exclude Chinese immigrants, and a similar policy of exclusion was applied to Japanese immigrants after 1907. Once established, each of these populations has grown by natural increase as well as by additional migration. Both Chinese and Japanese groups have increased in size at a rapid rate since World War II. The Chinese population has nearly doubled each of the past three decades while the Japanese population has increased relatively slowly. Both fertility and recent Chinese immigration (including that in the face of the imminent reversion of Hong Kong to Chinese control) have fueled the recent growth of the Chinese population. The Filipino population, which began entering the nation in large numbers in the 1920s, has grown especially rapidly since 1950. Like the Chinese population, it has nearly doubled in each of the past three decades. Many other Asian groups have had substantial migrations to the United States, primarily since 1960, including most notably the Koreans, Vietnamese and Asian Indians. These groups are, however, still relatively small population groups compared to those in Table 1-4. More detailed racial groups are discussed in later chapters devoted to racial composition.

Increasing racial diversity will characterize the changing composition of the United States population in the foreseeable future. In 1990, whites actually constituted nearly the same percentage of the population as they did in 1790. This majority dominance has, however, declined from the levels it reached in 1930, and the rising

percentage of the population in other racial groups will, in all likelihood, continue apace in the early part of the next century. Racial groups other than blacks and whites have increased from less than one percent of the population in 1960 to nearly seven percent in 1990. Hispanics and Asians and Pacific Islanders (APIs) are the fastest growing of the major racial and ethnic groups in the United States. It is the continuing rise of these other racial groups, and to a lesser extent blacks, which will generate an even more diverse national population in the future.

Age and Sex Composition

The age and sex structure of the United States population in 1990 is readily seen in a population pyramid such as that in Figure 1-2. The pyramid, with males on the left and females on the right side, shows the size of the population of each sex at each age. The general narrowing of the pyramid toward the older ages reflects the mortality of the population as it ages. The width of the pyramid's base reflects the relative size of very young individuals, and hence of the level of fertility in the population. As Figure 1-3 indicates, high fertility and high mortality regimes in less developed countries will characteristically have a very pyramidal composition. In contrast, more developed countries with lower fertility and lower mortality will have a more columnar population pyramid. The United States population in Figure 1-2 is in transition between these two situations. The larger bulge in the middle of the pyramid reflects the aging of high fertility 'baby boom' cohorts through the population. At younger ages the lower fertility of the population is evident in smaller cohorts. At older ages the relatively low mortality is evident in the survival of relatively large cohorts into older ages, with dramatic mortality effects confined to the very oldest age groups. (For an analysis of United States population by age composition, cohort and life cycle effects, see Chapter 10.)

The population pyramid also shows less dramatic differences in the population's sex composition. Females outnumber males in the United States, as in almost all other industrialized nations. In 1990, 48.7 percent of the population was male and 51.3 percent was female. It is conventional to express a population's sex composition in terms of the sex ratio, or the number of males per 100 females. The sex ratio for the United States in 1990 was 95.1 males per 100 females, up slightly from 94.5 in 1980.

Several factors influence the sex ratio of a population. First, among live-born white and Asian infants, males outnumber females in a ratio of about 106 to 100 (the black sex ratio at birth is about 102). Because of this initial preponderance of males at birth, the sex ratio of the population would always be higher than 100 if it were not for other factors. The greater number of males in the very youngest cohorts is evident in Figure 1-2. Second, this initially high sex ratio is gradually reduced by death

Figure 1-2. Distribution of the U.S. Population, by Age and Sex: 1990

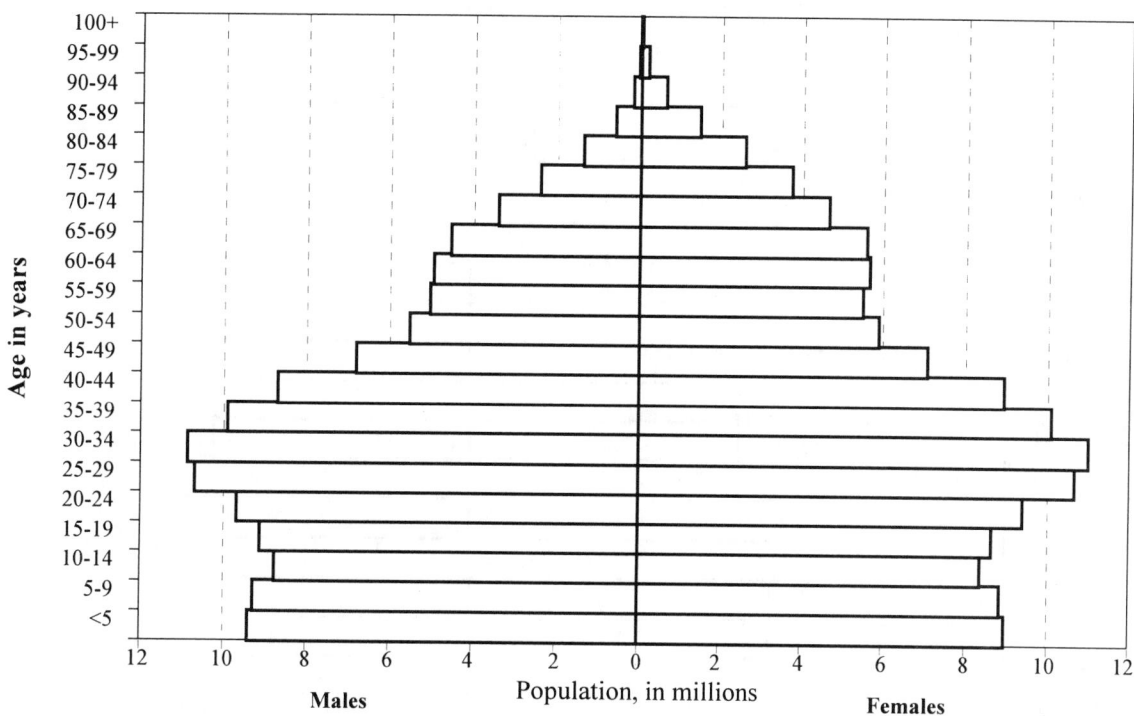

Source: 1990 U.S. Census data.

rates, which are higher for boys than for girls, and for men than for women. At about age thirty, the preponderance of males due to sex ratio at birth is counterbalanced by differential mortality. At the very oldest ages the greater survivorship of women is clearly apparent in Figure 1-2. Third, throughout the nineteenth century and until 1910, immigration to the United States was predominantly male. During the past half-century, however, the situation has been reversed, and more females than males have entered the United States legally. Thus, immigration is now contributing to the low sex ratio in the nation. Finally, because the armed forces have been preponderantly male, expansion in the size of these forces overseas reduces the sex ratio of the population residing in the United States. Loss of armed forces in combat makes a part of this a permanent reduction. In times of comparative peace, more recent cohorts' war losses have not significantly influenced population composition.

In addition to these effects on the sex ratio, many censuses have undercounted (to some extent) young men between the ages of twenty and thirty-five, in comparison with the enumeration of women for the same ages. Yet, in earlier centuries censuses tended to undercount young women under the ages of twenty-five. The effects of under-enumeration do not alter the sex ratio, but only the reported or estimated sex ratio.

Throughout the nation's history until the year 1950, males had outnumbered females in the white population by a considerable margin. The sex ratio of the black population has been consistently below 100 and lower than that of the white population since 1840. The sex ratio for the Hispanic population is considerably above the average for the general population. However, there is much variation among its subgroups and sex-selectivity in migration profoundly affects Hispanic sex ratios.

The age composition of the population reflected in Figure 1-2 is clearly more striking than differences in sex ratios. The age structure of the population is directly determined by trends in fertility, mortality and immigration. The declining fertility of recent years, with the sizable exception of the baby boom cohort, have impacted many aspects of daily life and popular culture in the United States (see Chapter 10). The tremendous strides in reduction of mortality and the subsequently growing elderly population, especially as the baby boom cohort ages, is a subject of considerable policy concern (see Chapter 7). Overall, migrants tend to be more heavily comprised of working age adults and have less of an impact on age structures than general fertility and mortality trends.

Age statistics are used frequently to compute a measure of the dependency load that the population of working age must carry. The dependency load, comprising children, youth, and people of retirement age, is measured approximately by the "dependency ratio," defined as the ratio of the number of persons under fifteen or over sixty-five years of age to the number in the 15-64 age

Figure 1-3. Comparative Population Distributions of More Developed and Less Developed Regions of World, by Age and Sex: 1990

More Developed Regions

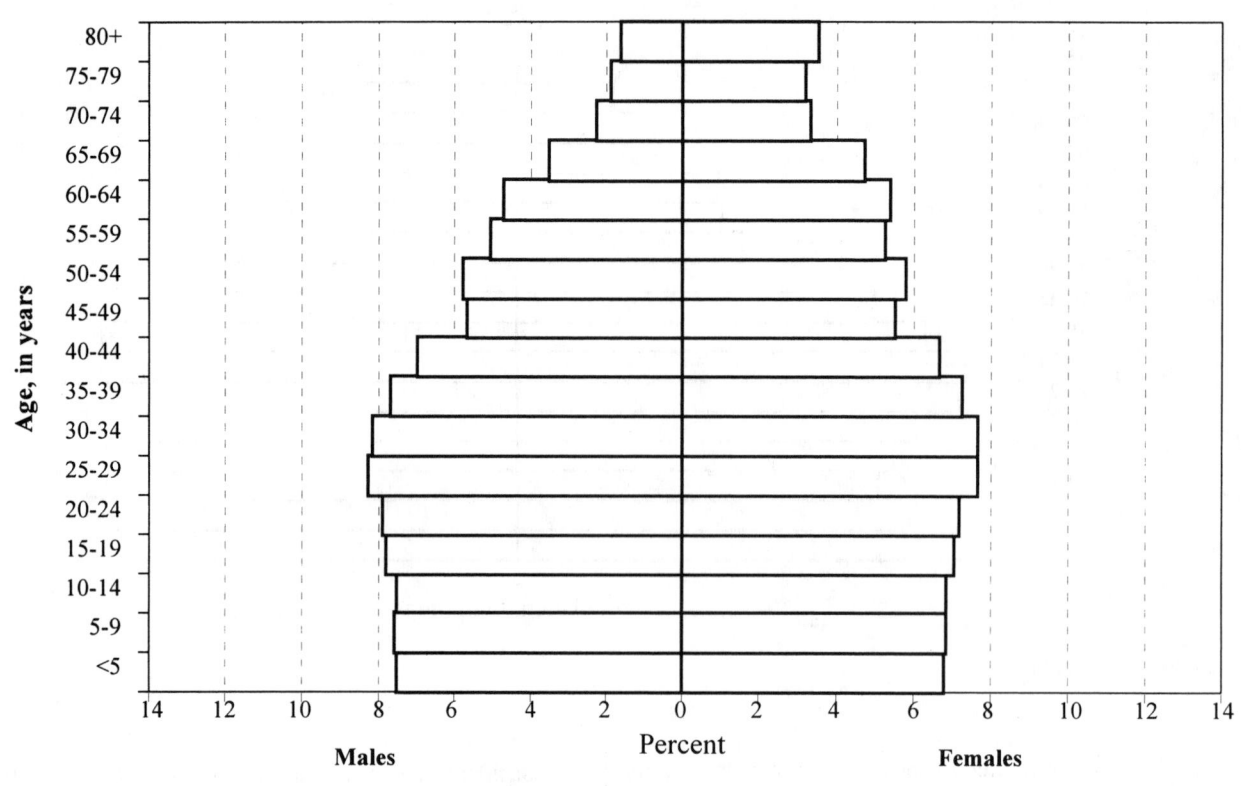

Less Developed Regions

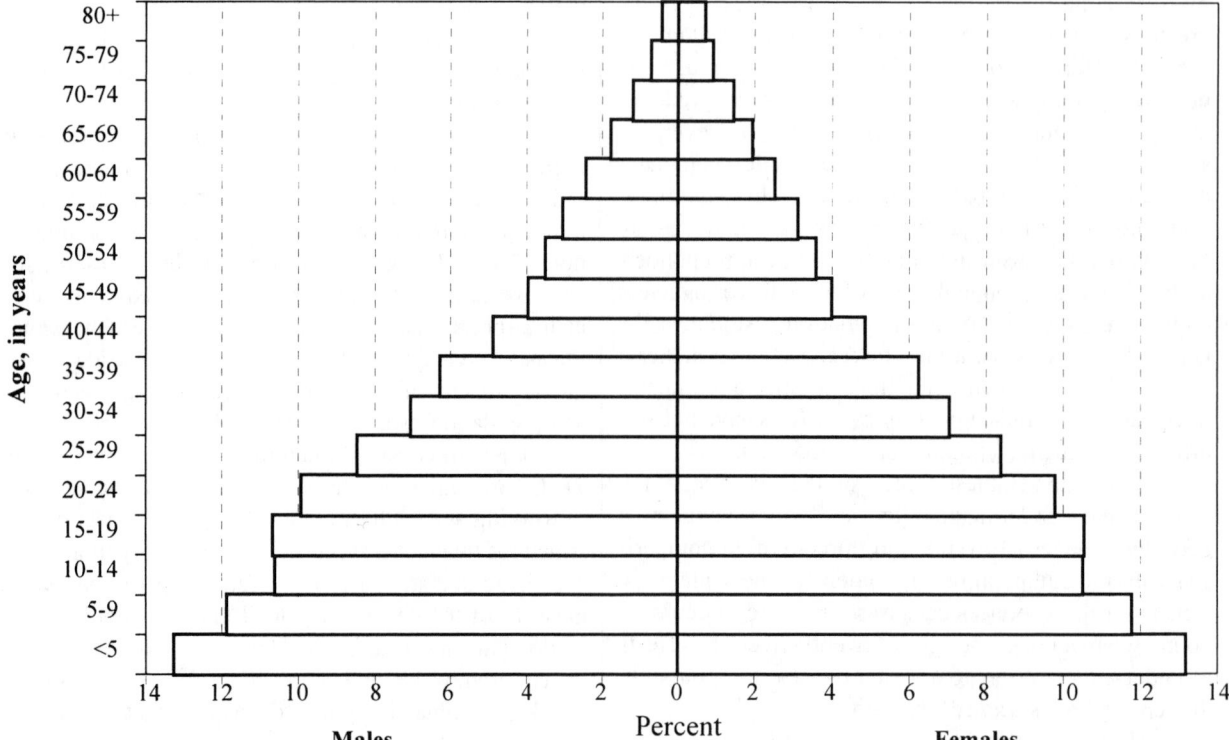

Source: 1992 United Nations data.

Table 1-5. Percent of Population in Youth or Old Age and Dependency Ratio, by Race: 1800-1990

Year	All races Percent <15 years	All races Percent 65 and over	All races Dependency ratio	White Percent <15 years	White Percent 65 and over	White Dependency ratio	Black Percent <15 years	Black Percent 65 and over	Black Dependency ratio
1990	21.7	12.6	51.7	20.1	13.9	51.6	26.9	8.4	54.4
1980	22.6	11.3	51.3	21.3	12.2	50.3	28.7	7.9	57.7
1970	28.5	9.9	62.3	27.6	10.3	61.0	35.4	6.9	73.3
1960	31.1	9.2	67.5	30.3	9.6	66.4	37.6	6.2	77.9
1950	26.9	8.1	53.8	26.3	8.4	53.3	31.8	5.8	60.3
1940	25.0	6.8	46.6	24.5	7.1	46.1	30.1	4.8	53.6
1930	29.4	5.4	53.4	29.0	5.7	53.1	32.4	3.1	55.0
1920	31.8	4.7	57.5	31.5	4.8	57.1	34.9	3.2	61.6
1910	32.1	4.3	57.3	31.5	4.5	56.2	37.4	3.0	67.8
1900	34.5	4.1	62.7	33.8	4.2	61.3	40.0	3.0	75.2
1890	35.6	3.9	65.2	34.7	4.0	63.2	42.7	2.8	83.7
1880	38.1	3.4	70.9	37.1	3.6	68.6	—	—	—
1870	39.2	3.0	73.0	38.7	3.1	71.8	43.0	2.5	83.7
1860	40.6	—	68.3[1]	40.0	—	66.7[1]	44.4	—	79.7[1]
1850	41.5	—	71.1[1]	40.9	—	69.3[1]	44.8	—	81.0[1]
1840	—	—	—	43.7	—	77.6[1]	—	—	—
1830	—	—	—	45.0	—	81.8[1]	—	—	—
1820	—	—	—	48.9[2]	—	95.7[1]	—	—	—
1810	—	—	—	50.0[2]	—	100.1[1]	43.0	—	75.4[1]
1800	—	—	—	50.1[2]	—	100.4[1]	—	—	—

[1] For explanation of this calculation, see Donald Bogue, "Population in the United States," Free Press, New York, 1985, Table 2-12.
[2] 0 to 15 years old.

Source: U.S. Bureau of the Census, "General Population Characteristics," 1990 Census of Population, Table 13, 1980 Census of Population, Table 44, and "Historical Statistics of the United States, Part I," (Series A 119-134), U.S. Government Printing Office, Washington, D.C., 1992, 1983, and 1975.

group, multiplied by 100. This is not a measure of the number of persons each worker must support in addition to himself. However, it is a rough indication of the average number of dependents that each 100 adult persons would be required to support and care for if the load were equally divided among the adult population, and if all persons under fifteen and over sixty-five were dependent, and no one between fifteen and sixty-four was dependent. None of these conditions is met completely, and the degree to which they are approximated varies from one population to another, and over time, within the same population. Nevertheless, in the absence of more detailed information with which to estimate actual dependence, this ratio is useful for making general comparisons.

The dependency ratios for the United States, for selected dates since 1800, are shown in Table 1-5 for the total population, and separately for whites and blacks. Note that there was a relatively steady decline in the total dependency ratio from 1800 until 1940 (with the exception of the data for 1870). Because of the baby boom, it rose between 1940 and 1960, and then declined through 1980. In 1990 the rising elderly population has caused a slight resurgence in the dependency ratio once again. Note, however, that this rise is not evidenced in the black population. As an example, the dependency load in 1990 for the white population (51.6) was just over one-half as large as in 1800. Because a higher proportion of persons under fifteen and over sixty-five were economically active in the nineteenth and early twentieth centuries, the decline of the actual dependency load was not as great as indicated by the index. Nevertheless, these statistics may be used to illustrate the general magnitude of the decline in dependency, and the time pattern of that decline.

The decline in dependency over the 190-year period from 1800 to 1990 consisted of a net balance between two opposing trends: a drop in the dependency load for the youth, and a rise in the dependency load for the aged. As is evident in Figure 1-3, this corresponds to the transition from the high youth dependency load of a high fertility, less developed country to the higher elderly dependency ratio of a more developed country with lower mortality. One direct result of fertility control is an almost immediate lessening of the overall burden of dependency, since such control lowers the large burden of

Table 1-6. Age and Sex Composition of Nations with 10 Million or More Inhabitants: 1995

Country	Percent distribution			Dependency ratio			M:F sex ratio	
	Less than 15 years	15 to 65 years	66 years and over	Total	Youth <15 years	Aged >65 years	Urban	Rural
World total	31.9	61.6	6.5	0.62	0.52	0.11	—	—
China	27.3	66.4	6.3	0.51	0.41	0.09	1.04	1.04
India	34.9	60.3	4.9	0.66	0.58	0.08	1.12	1.04
United States	21.9	65.5	12.6	0.53	0.33	0.19	0.93	1.00
Indonesia	33.4	62.2	4.4	0.61	0.54	0.07	0.96[2]	1.09[2]
Brazil	32.2	62.7	5.2	0.60	0.51	0.08	0.96[2]	1.09[2]
Russian Federation[1]	23.0	67.0	10.0	0.49	0.34	0.15	—	—
Pakistan	43.6	53.4	2.9	0.87	0.82	0.05	1.15	1.09
Bangladesh	40.3	56.7	3.0	0.76	0.71	0.05	1.19	1.04
Nigeria	47.0	50.4	2.6	0.98	0.93	0.05	1.08	0.95
Japan	16.8	69.2	13.9	0.44	0.24	0.20	0.97	0.95
Mexico	36.0	60.0	4.0	0.67	0.60	0.07	0.95	1.03
Germany	17.1	68.1	14.8	0.47	0.25	0.22	0.91	0.94
Viet Nam	37.0	58.1	4.9	0.72	0.64	0.08	1.06	0.92
Philippines	38.4	58.3	3.3	0.72	0.66	0.06	0.95	1.04
Iran, Islamic Republic	45.9	50.3	3.8	0.99	0.91	0.08	1.05	1.04
Turkey	33.7	61.5	4.8	0.63	0.55	0.08	1.10	0.98
Egypt	37.9	57.9	4.2	0.73	0.65	0.07	1.05	1.04
Thailand	29.2	66.3	4.5	0.51	0.44	0.07	0.96	1.00
United Kingdom	19.7	64.7	15.6	0.55	0.30	0.24	0.95	1.03
Ethiopia	46.5	50.7	2.8	0.97	0.92	0.06	0.87	1.02
Italy	15.4	69.0	15.6	0.45	0.22	0.23	—	—
France	19.8	65.3	14.9	0.53	0.30	0.23	0.93	1.00
Ukraine[1]	21.0	67.0	12.0	0.49	0.31	0.18	—	—
Myanmar	37.4	58.5	4.1	0.71	0.64	0.07	0.99	0.98
Korea, Republic	23.3	71.3	5.4	0.40	0.33	0.08	0.99	1.02
Zaire	48.1	49.0	2.8	1.04	0.98	0.06	1.03	0.95
South Africa	37.5	58.5	4.0	0.71	0.64	0.07	1.01	0.93
Spain	17.0	68.3	14.7	0.46	0.25	0.22	0.96	1.02
Poland	23.5	65.6	10.9	0.52	0.36	0.17	0.93	1.00
Colombia	32.9	62.6	4.5	0.60	0.53	0.07	0.91	1.14
Argentina	28.3	62.1	9.6	0.61	0.46	0.15	0.95	1.16
Tanzania	48.0	49.6	2.5	1.02	0.97	0.05	1.08	0.94
Sudan	44.5	52.6	2.9	0.90	0.85	0.06	1.14	1.01
Algeria	41.4	55.2	3.4	0.81	0.75	0.06	0.98	1.00
Canada	20.7	67.3	12.0	0.49	0.31	0.18	0.94	1.06
Morocco	38.7	57.4	3.9	0.74	0.67	0.07	1.01	1.00
Afghanistan	40.0	57.4	2.6	0.74	0.70	0.05	1.06[3]	1.05[3]
Kenya	47.4	49.7	2.9	1.01	0.95	0.06	1.22	0.95
Yugoslavia (former)	21.6	67.8	10.6	0.47	0.32	0.16	0.95	1.00
Korea, Dem. People's Republic	29.1	66.3	4.6	0.51	0.44	0.07	—	—
Peru	35.5	60.4	4.1	0.66	0.59	0.07	1.00[2]	1.04[2]
Romania	22.2	66.4	11.3	0.50	0.33	0.17	0.96	0.98
Uzbekistan[1]	41.0	55.0	4.0	0.82	0.75	0.07	—	—
Nepal	43.1	53.8	3.2	0.86	0.80	0.06	1.15	1.04
Venezuela	34.7	61.1	4.1	0.64	0.57	0.07	1.00[2]	1.15[2]
Iraq	43.8	53.3	3.0	0.88	0.82	0.06	1.08	1.00
Uganda	48.7	48.9	2.4	1.04	1.00	0.05	1.16	0.96

Table 1-6. Age and Sex Composition of Nations with 10 Million or More Inhabitants: 1995 (continued)

Country	Percent distribution			Dependency ratio			M:F sex ratio	
	Less than 15 years	15 to 65 years	66 years and over	Total	Youth <15 years	Aged >65 years	Urban	Rural
Malaysia	37.9	58.2	3.9	0.72	0.65	0.07	1.01	1.00
Sri Lanka	30.3	63.8	5.9	0.57	0.47	0.09	1.10	1.02
Australia	21.7	66.8	11.6	0.50	0.32	0.17	0.97	1.12
Saudi Arabia	42.0	55.3	2.7	0.81	0.76	0.05	—	—
Ghana	45.3	51.8	2.9	0.93	0.87	0.06	—	—
Kazakhstan[1]	32.0	62.0	6.0	0.61	0.52	0.10	—	—
Mozambique	44.9	51.9	3.3	0.93	0.87	0.06	1.14	0.93
Czechoslovakia (former)	20.9	67.0	12.1	0.49	0.31	0.18	0.93	0.97
Netherlands	18.6	68.3	13.0	0.46	0.27	0.19	0.97	1.03
Syrian Arab Republic	47.6	49.6	2.8	1.02	0.96	0.06	1.08	1.02
Cote d'Ivoire	49.0	48.4	2.6	1.07	1.01	0.05	—	—
Chile	30.5	63.2	6.4	0.58	0.48	0.10	0.94	1.19
Madagascar	45.7	51.4	2.9	0.95	0.89	0.06	0.97	1.01
Yemen	49.3	48.3	2.4	1.07	1.02	0.05	1.11	0.90
Cameroon	44.0	52.4	3.6	0.91	0.84	0.07	1.08	0.96
Ecuador	37.1	58.9	4.0	0.70	0.63	0.07	0.97	1.06
Zimbabwe	44.6	52.6	2.8	0.90	0.85	0.05	1.14	0.91
Malawi	49.2	48.2	2.6	1.07	1.02	0.05	1.16	0.91
Cuba	23.2	67.8	9.0	0.47	0.34	0.13	0.97	1.12
Angola	47.1	50.0	2.9	1.00	0.94	0.06	—	—
Mali	47.4	50.0	2.5	1.00	0.95	0.05	0.97	0.95
Guatemala	44.3	52.2	3.5	0.92	0.85	0.07	0.95	1.08
Hungary	18.5	67.7	13.9	0.48	0.27	0.21	0.92	0.96
Burkina Faso	44.9	52.0	3.1	0.92	0.86	0.06	—	—
Belarus[1]	23.0	66.0	11.0	0.52	0.35	0.17	—	—
Greece	17.3	67.2	15.4	0.49	0.26	0.23	0.94	1.00
Somalia	47.5	49.8	2.7	1.01	0.95	0.05	—	—
Belgium	18.0	66.4	15.7	0.51	0.27	0.24	0.95	1.01

[1] Data are from 1990.

[2] Excludes Indian jungle population.

[3] Excludes nomads.

Source: United Nations, "World Resources 1994-95," Tables 16.1, 16.2, and 16.6, Oxford University Press, New York, 1994.

youth dependency. In fact, the result is a temporary situation in which the dependency load is unusually light. This is to some extent true for the baby boom cohort and the declining fertility since this cohort. There are fewer children and many adults, and there is a delay in the increase in the ratio of older persons to adults in the 15-64 age groups. Later, when the aging process passes the spate of adult workers into the older ages, the dependency ratio will tend to rise somewhat, provided the fertility level remains low. That slight rise is evidenced in 1990.

As serious as the aging of the American population might be, discussing it as if it were an extremely severe social problem is somewhat out of perspective. A really onerous dependency load is borne by nations where high death rates remove children of all ages before they have a chance to make a productive contribution. As a result of demographic processes the United States population has, for more than a century, borne a smaller dependency load than most populations of the world have been carrying. Table 1-6 presents the percentages of young, working age and elderly populations for nations with 10 million or more inhabitants. The table also presents dependency ratios, and sex ratios for both urban and rural areas. Among the ten largest national populations seven countries have higher dependency ratios than the United States. Japan has the lowest dependency, followed by the Russian Federation and then the United States. Japan clearly reflects the population of a more developed country with the lowest youth dependency ratio and highest elderly dependency ratio among these countries. Pakistan, Bangladesh and Nigeria all reflect the patterns of high youth dependency and very low elderly dependency common to less developed countries. The low overall dependency ratio for China reflects the combined impact of radically lowered fertility and a still somewhat higher mortality. Not surprisingly, the highest dependency ratios in the world are in the high fertility countries of Africa (e.g. Kenya, Zaire, Uganda, Cote d'Ivoire, Somalia) and some high fertility Middle Eastern countries (e.g. Syrian Arab Republic, Yemen).

Most nations of Western Europe have an age composition roughly similar to that of the more developed nations, having lower proportions of children and youth and higher proportions of those in old age than are found in most other parts of the world. Differences between the age composition of the United States and most nations of Western Europe result from lower birth rates and a longer period of declining births in Western Europe than in the United States. Since 1985, however, the United States has achieved lower dependency ratios than several European countries which had previously lower dependency (e.g. France, United Kingdom). Part of this recent decline in dependency in the United States is because the offspring of the baby boom are predominantly in the working ages of life.

In developed countries differences in urban and rural sex ratios are small and generally random. However, in many developing countries the sex ratio in urban areas is much higher, reflecting the migration of males into urban areas to seek employment to send money back to their family, bring their family to live with them later, or form a new family after they are secure. This pattern is true in four of the ten largest countries: India, Bangladesh, Pakistan and Nigeria. As migration theorists have known for some time, this pattern is notable in many African countries (e.g. Kenya, Uganda, Sudan, Mozambique, Zimbabwe, etc.).

Projected Future Growth

By making what appear to be reasonable assumptions about the future trends in births, deaths, and net immigration, demographers prepare "population projections," which estimate or predict future population size. The U.S. Bureau of the Census makes such projections and revises them periodically as new perspectives are obtained on trends in the components of growth. To illustrate the full range of possibilities, the Census Bureau makes several alternative projections assuming high, medium and low growth rates. Tables 1-7A through 1-7F show the growth projected for selected racial groups of the United States population from 1995 through the year 2050 under the medium growth assumptions. As with all projections, those in more recent years are made with

greater confidence than are projections to far distant years. These assumptions presume that mortality rates will continue to decline. Life expectancy is assumed to increase from 75.9 years in 1993 to 82.6 years in 2050. This mortality decline has been modified downward recently, including some negating effects of AIDS. Some demographers expect another return to higher fertility (but not another baby boom). Others expect birth rates to decline even below the low level reached in 1976. In the middle series of population projections, however, the U.S. Bureau of the Census expects fertility to coast along at about the same age specific levels as in 1990 (see Chapter 6) for most groups with the exception of a 15 percent decline in fertility rates between 1995 and 2050 for those of Hispanic origin and the non-Hispanic Asian and Pacific Islander population. Immigration is assumed to remain constant at 1990 levels (see Chapter 8) over the projection period.

Under this "medium growth" or "most likely" projection of the U.S. Bureau of the Census the population will continue to grow to reach about 276 million in the year 2000 and about 300 million in 2010. Note that these forecasted increases are greater than those anticipated when projections were made in 1985. Ten years ago the projected population for 2000 was only 268 million. And, the population was projected to reach 300 million by 2025, fifteen years later than the current projections.

Throughout the remaining chapters of this book, attention will be paid to the implications of these projections of growth both for population composition and for internal distribution. While growth rates are expected to be modest in comparison with the nineteenth century and the "baby boom" periods, the absolute population increase will be substantial under all three assumptions for the remainder of this century, because these low rates apply to what has become a very large population.

Future Changes in Age Composition

As the population is projected forward to the year 2050 there are also profound changes in the age structure of the population. Figure 1-4 illustrates these changes from the data in Table 1-7A. Due to the relatively low fertility assumptions made in the medium growth projections, there are declining percentages of the population at younger ages and increasing proportions in older age groups. With the additional assumption of a continuing decline in mortality, the proportion in older age groups is amplified. Yet, the elderly dependency ratio is actually projected to decrease until after 2010 when large aging cohorts age past 64 and into the retirement ages. For the rest of the next half century the elderly dependency ratio will be considerably higher, according to these projections.

The persons born during the baby boom (1945-57) are thirty-eight to fifty years of age in 1995. These are

Table 1-7A. Population Projection for All Races: 1995-2050
[numbers in thousands]

Age	1995	2000	2010	2030	2050
Total	263,434	276,241	300,431	349,993	392,031
Under 5 years	20,181	19,431	20,017	22,689	25,382
Under 1 year	3,963	3,862	4,099	4,579	5,130
1 year	3,957	3,836	4,013	4,515	5,056
2 years	3,998	3,862	3,980	4,514	5,052
3 years	4,114	3,891	3,948	4,510	5,042
4 years	4,150	3,980	3,978	4,572	5,101
5 to 9 years	19,116	20,531	19,722	22,794	25,222
5 years	3,963	4,016	3,957	4,568	5,085
6 years	3,838	4,047	3,938	4,555	5,054
7 years	3,800	4,093	3,943	4,564	5,050
8 years	3,629	4,052	3,799	4,394	4,847
9 years	3,886	4,324	4,085	4,713	5,186
10 to 14 years	18,939	19,972	20,724	23,423	25,650
10 years	3,789	4,157	4,120	4,732	5,194
11 years	3,794	3,982	4,083	4,660	5,104
12 years	3,809	3,935	4,111	4,658	5,099
13 years	3,754	3,942	4,177	4,684	5,123
14 years	3,793	3,956	4,234	4,689	5,130
15 to 19 years	17,790	19,819	22,398	23,536	25,897
15 years	3,654	3,872	4,308	4,704	5,152
16 years	3,548	3,943	4,359	4,683	5,133
17 years	3,596	4,040	4,487	4,744	5,215
18 years	3,382	3,870	4,514	4,600	5,071
19 years	3,610	4,094	4,730	4,804	5,326
20 to 24 years	18,473	17,947	20,976	22,398	25,313
25 to 29 years	19,294	18,370	19,757	21,470	24,659
30 to 34 years	22,376	19,867	18,422	22,102	24,803
35 to 39 years	22,215	22,695	19,263	23,115	24,316
40 to 44 years	19,935	22,428	20,396	21,925	23,423
45 to 49 years	16,873	19,530	22,431	20,504	22,266
50 to 54 years	13,351	16,640	21,668	18,432	22,071
55 to 59 years	11,050	13,047	18,845	18,557	22,367
60 to 64 years	10,191	10,643	15,707	18,872	20,553
65 to 69 years	10,099	9,594	11,944	20,132	18,859
70 to 74 years	8,864	8,957	9,034	17,852	15,769
75 to 79 years	6,668	7,507	7,378	13,966	14,510
80 to 84 years	4,419	4,931	5,779	9,382	12,078
85 years and over	3,598	4,333	5,869	8,843	18,893
85 to 89 years	2,317	2,692	3,534	4,919	9,283
90 to 94 years	976	1,193	1,667	2,416	5,779
95 to 99 years	253	373	598	1,032	2,623
100 years and over	52	75	170	477	1,208

Source: U.S. Bureau of the Census, Current Population Reports, "Population Projections of the United States, by Age, Sex, Race, and Hispanic Origin: 1993 to 2050," U.S. Government Printing Office, Washington, D.C, 1993, Table 2.

Table 1-7B. Projection for the White Population: 1995-2050
  [numbers in thousands]

Age	1995	2000	2010	2030	2050
Total	218,334	226,267	240,297	267,457	285,591
Under 5 years	15,841	14,945	14,893	16,073	17,216
Under 1 year	3,087	2,945	3,036	3,222	3,462
1 year	3,102	2,944	2,986	3,197	3,433
2 years	3,141	2,973	2,963	3,201	3,431
3 years	3,247	3,005	2,944	3,205	3,427
4 years	3,263	3,078	2,964	3,248	3,463
5 to 9 years	15,154	16,012	14,775	16,294	17,146
5 years	3,120	3,116	2,954	3,253	3,454
6 years	3,037	3,158	2,954	3,262	3,448
7 years	3,018	3,196	2,957	3,268	3,439
8 years	2,890	3,175	2,851	3,147	3,296
9 years	3,089	3,368	3,060	3,365	3,509
10 to 14 years	15,009	15,627	15,606	16,710	17,277
10 years	3,009	3,240	3,094	3,383	3,514
11 years	3,015	3,113	3,077	3,338	3,456
12 years	3,014	3,075	3,087	3,313	3,422
13 years	2,975	3,094	3,151	3,339	3,444
14 years	2,995	3,105	3,197	3,337	3,442
15 to 19 years	14,116	15,581	17,126	16,862	17,550
15 years	2,881	3,029	3,256	3,342	3,450
16 years	2,816	3,097	3,321	3,349	3,466
17 years	2,852	3,178	3,429	3,396	3,529
18 years	2,692	3,053	3,481	3,315	3,463
19 years	2,875	3,225	3,639	3,461	3,641
20 to 24 years	14,772	14,199	16,276	16,219	17,464
25 to 29 years	15,618	14,551	15,369	15,636	17,177
30 to 34 years	18,409	15,983	14,346	16,359	17,494
35 to 39 years	18,407	18,586	15,093	17,410	17,246
40 to 44 years	16,674	18,553	16,301	16,709	16,734
45 to 49 years	14,387	16,339	18,361	15,800	16,144
50 to 54 years	11,465	14,196	17,969	14,303	16,355
55 to 59 years	9,509	11,200	15,810	14,610	16,985
60 to 64 years	8,846	9,139	13,403	15,179	15,820
65 to 69 years	8,890	8,297	10,217	16,567	14,672
70 to 74 years	7,932	7,923	7,781	14,991	12,461
75 to 79 years	6,019	6,735	6,440	11,896	11,696
80 to 84 years	4,016	4,484	5,172	8,195	10,093
85 years and over	3,271	3,917	5,357	7,646	16,061
85 to 89 years	2,118	2,452	3,203	4,326	7,991
90 to 94 years	882	1,075	1,499	2,089	4,968
95 to 99 years	229	327	521	866	2,193
100 years and over	43	63	135	365	908

Source: U.S. Bureau of the Census, Current Population Reports, "Population Projections of the
  United States, by Age, Sex, Race, and Hispanic Origin: 1993 to 2050," U.S. Government
  Printing Office, Washington, D.C, 1993, Table 2.

Table 1-7C. Projection for the Black Population: 1995-2050
[numbers in thousands]

Age	1995	2000	2010	2030	2050
Total	33,117	35,469	40,224	50,596	61,586
Under 5 years	3,243	3,214	3,518	4,277	5,171
Under 1 year	645	653	731	879	1,060
1 year	635	639	708	856	1,034
2 years	637	637	698	849	1,026
3 years	654	634	686	839	1,015
4 years	672	652	695	856	1,036
5 to 9 years	3,981	3,302	3,369	4,167	5,031
5 years	639	650	684	845	1,023
6 years	603	645	671	830	1,004
7 years	591	654	672	832	1,005
8 years	552	646	642	795	959
9 years	596	707	699	864	1,040
10 to 14 years	2,900	3,141	3,442	4,211	5,038
10 years	575	675	694	856	1,029
11 years	573	632	679	836	1,002
12 years	587	623	688	843	1,008
13 years	569	604	684	834	996
14 years	595	607	696	842	1,004
15 to 19 years	2,762	3,057	3,649	4,218	5,028
15 years	579	600	712	853	1,015
16 years	550	604	709	840	999
17 years	561	620	725	847	1,008
18 years	520	593	732	824	982
19 years	552	639	770	855	1,023
20 to 24 years	2,692	2,668	3,185	3,795	4,608
25 to 29 years	2,625	2,597	2,829	3,427	4,225
30 to 34 years	2,850	2,638	2,580	3,339	4,078
35 to 39 years	2,754	2,873	2,629	3,392	3,937
40 to 44 years	2,334	2,737	2,639	3,070	3,673
45 to 49 years	1,762	2,248	2,744	2,750	3,355
50 to 54 years	1,360	1,706	2,553	2,438	3,190
55 to 59 years	1,127	1,305	2,096	2,378	3,126
60 to 64 years	997	1,065	1,558	2,306	2,760
65 to 69 years	919	938	1,171	2,352	2,452
70 to 74 years	710	748	826	1,862	1,868
75 to 79 years	511	571	624	1,310	1,576
80 to 84 years	324	336	401	687	1,066
85 years and over	268	3,226	413	615	1,405
85 to 89 years	163	186	217	311	666
90 to 94 years	78	94	115	163	402
95 to 99 years	20	37	55	82	202
100 years and over	7	10	25	58	135

Source: U.S. Bureau of the Census, Current Population Reports, "Population Projections of the United States, by Age, Sex, Race, and Hispanic Origin: 1993 to 2050," U.S. Government Printing Office, Washington, D.C, 1993, Table 2.

**Table 1-7D. Projection for the American Indian, Eskimo, and Aleut
Population: 1995-2050 [numbers in thousands]**

Age	1995	2000	2010	2030	2050
Total	2,226	2,380	2,719	3,473	4,346
Under 5 years	222	215	252	303	373
Under 1 year	43	44	53	63	77
1 year	42	43	50	60	74
2 years	42	43	50	60	74
3 years	47	43	50	60	74
4 years	48	43	49	60	74
5 to 9 years	225	229	239	298	370
5 years	47	43	49	60	75
6 years	45	43	48	59	73
7 years	44	43	48	59	74
8 years	43	48	46	58	72
9 years	46	51	49	62	77
10 to 14 years	231	248	247	319	392
10 years	46	51	49	63	78
11 years	46	49	48	62	77
12 years	46	49	49	64	79
13 years	47	50	50	65	80
14 years	45	49	50	65	79
15 to 19 years	194	229	252	309	372
15 years	43	48	50	65	79
16 years	40	48	49	63	76
17 years	39	47	49	63	76
18 years	35	43	51	58	69
19 years	36	43	53	60	72
20 to 24 years	185	185	238	280	339
25 to 29 years	177	183	219	254	319
30 to 34 years	187	173	180	232	303
35 to 39 years	175	181	175	231	286
40 to 44 years	152	171	165	223	263
45 to 49 years	121	143	167	193	227
50 to 54 years	91	113	150	153	198
55 to 59 years	72	84	123	140	187
60 to 64 years	57	65	95	124	170
65 to 69 years	47	50	68	119	141
70 to 74 years	37	40	50	100	105
75 to 79 years	25	31	37	76	90
80 to 84 years	16	19	26	50	69
85 years and over	14	21	36	69	142
85 to 89 years	8	12	17	29	54
90 to 94 years	4	6	10	19	40
95 to 99 years	1	3	6	11	25
100 years and over	0	1	3	10	23

Source: U.S. Bureau of the Census, Current Population Reports, "Population Projections of the
United States, by Age, Sex, Race, and Hispanic Origin: 1993 to 2050," U.S. Government
Printing Office, Washington, D.C, 1993, Table 2.

Table 1-7E. Projection for the Asian and Pacific Islander Population: 1995-2050 [numbers in thousands]

Age	1995	2000	2010	2030	2050
Total	9,756	12,125	17,191	28,467	40,508
Under 5 years	876	1,056	1,354	2,036	2,622
Under 1 year	188	219	279	416	532
1 year	179	210	268	402	516
2 years	177	210	269	404	520
3 years	165	209	269	406	525
4 years	166	208	269	408	529
5 to 9 years	757	989	1,339	2,036	2,677
5 years	156	207	270	410	534
6 years	153	201	266	404	528
7 years	148	200	266	405	532
8 years	145	183	259	394	521
9 years	156	198	278	423	561
10 to 14 years	800	955	1,430	2,183	2,942
10 years	159	191	283	430	574
11 years	160	188	279	425	569
12 years	161	189	287	438	590
13 years	163	194	291	445	603
14 years	157	195	290	445	605
15 to 19 years	719	952	1,372	2,147	2,948
15 years	151	195	290	445	607
16 years	142	194	280	432	592
17 years	144	195	283	438	602
18 years	135	180	251	404	557
19 years	147	187	268	428	590
20 to 24 years	823	895	1,276	2,105	2,903
25 to 29 years	874	1,039	1,340	2,153	2,937
30 to 34 years	931	1,073	1,316	2,172	2,928
35 to 39 years	880	1,055	1,366	2,082	2,847
40 to 44 years	775	968	1,291	1,923	2,753
45 to 49 years	603	800	1,159	1,761	2,540
50 to 54 years	435	625	996	1,538	2,329
55 to 59 years	343	459	817	1,430	2,069
60 to 64 years	290	374	651	1,263	1,803
65 to 69 years	244	309	487	1,093	1,594
70 to 74 years	185	246	377	899	1,335
75 to 79 years	114	170	278	683	1,148
80 to 84 years	64	91	180	450	850
85 years and over	44	69	163	513	1,286
85 to 89 years	28	43	96	253	571
90 to 94 years	12	18	43	145	369
95 to 99 years	3	7	17	73	203
100 years and over	1	2	6	43	143

Source: U.S. Bureau of the Census, Current Population Reports, "Population Projections of the United States, by Age, Sex, Race, and Hispanic Origin: 1993 to 2050," U.S. Government Printing Office, Washington, D.C, 1993, Table 2.

Table 1-7F. Projection for the Hispanic Population: 1995-2050
  [numbers in thousands]

Age	1995	2000	2010	2030	2050
Total	26,798	31,166	40,525	62,810	88,071
Under 5 years	3,090	3,293	3,983	5,716	7,429
Under 1 year	625	674	833	1,173	1,517
1 year	612	661	807	1,149	1,491
2 years	606	655	792	1,138	1,479
3 years	632	650	777	1,126	1,468
4 years	616	653	774	1,129	1,474
5 to 9 years	2,644	3,232	3,721	5,478	7,166
5 years	586	649	763	1,118	1,461
6 years	540	644	753	1,108	1,448
7 years	525	639	745	1,098	1,436
8 years	483	640	709	1,046	1,369
9 years	509	661	752	1,108	1,451
10 to 14 years	2,387	2,846	3,654	5,344	7,022
10 years	495	633	749	1,102	1,444
11 years	473	578	732	1,076	1,411
12 years	477	559	724	1,060	1,392
13 years	471	540	725	1,057	1,392
14 years	471	536	724	1,048	1,383
15 to 19 years	2,233	2,624	3,709	5,175	6,903
15 years	461	523	725	1,042	1,378
16 years	441	512	725	1,034	1,372
17 years	444	531	735	1,041	1,387
18 years	434	514	752	1,008	1,351
19 years	454	544	772	1,050	1,415
20 to 24 years	2,316	2,489	3,339	4,871	6,663
25 to 29 years	2,494	2,488	3,019	4,531	6,274
30 to 34 years	2,527	2,657	2,815	4,420	6,072
35 to 39 years	2,165	2,609	2,731	4,300	5,709
40 to 44 years	1,729	2,221	2,788	3,775	5,273
45 to 49 years	1,310	1,725	2,631	3,285	4,789
50 to 54 years	964	1,321	2,197	2,911	4,478
55 to 59 years	767	969	1,717	2,720	4,229
60 to 64 years	640	765	1,303	2,670	3,613
65 to 69 years	546	627	939	2,471	3,108
70 to 74 years	409	510	698	1,937	2,597
75 to 79 years	261	371	533	1,402	2,260
80 to 84 years	175	215	381	899	1,884
85 years and over	141	203	367	906	2,602
85 to 89 years	90	123	216	482	1,324
90 to 94 years	39	56	98	255	767
95 to 99 years	9	20	40	115	350
100 years and over	2	4	13	53	161

Source: U.S. Bureau of the Census, Current Population Reports, "Population Projections of the
  United States, by Age, Sex, Race, and Hispanic Origin: 1993 to 2050," U.S. Government
  Printing Office, Washington, D.C, 1993, Table 2.

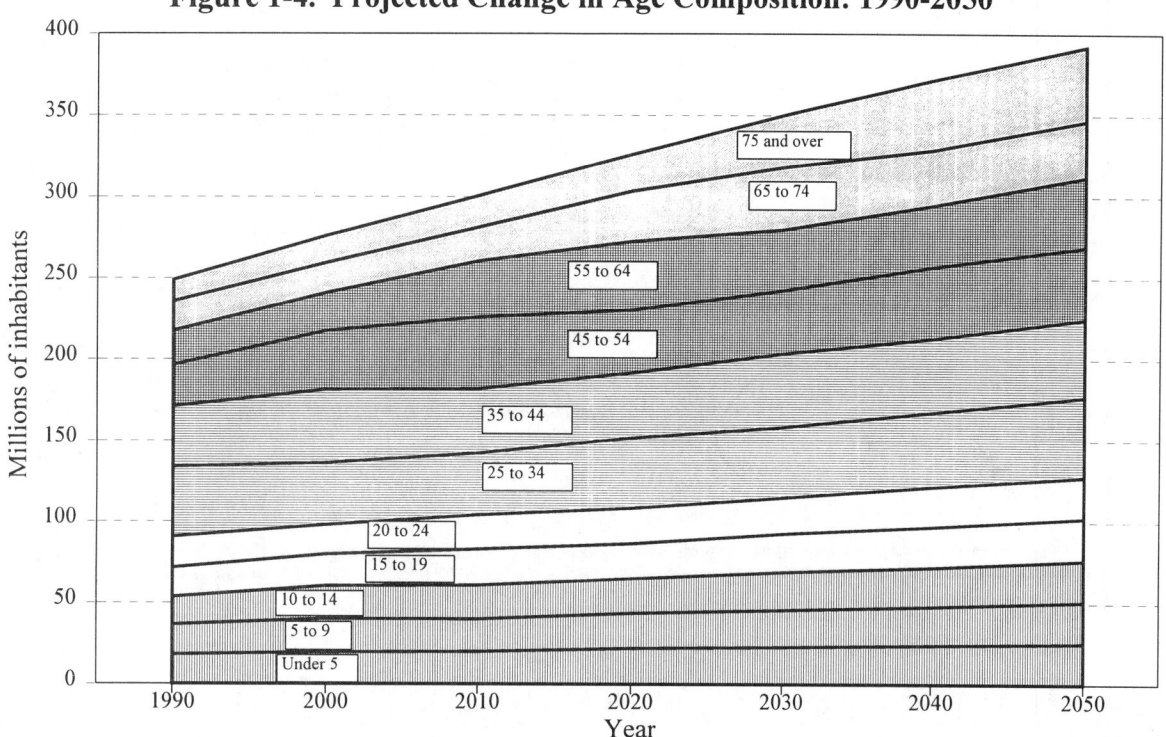

Figure 1-4. Projected Change in Age Composition: 1990-2050

Source: 1990 U.S. Census data and 1993 CPS projections.

ages of declining fertility but vigorous labor force participation. For the remainder of this century the baby boom generation will comprise the core of the work force, but will contribute little to fertility. The "baby bust" generation, born since 1957 (and especially since 1960) are twenty to thirty-five years of age in 1985. They will place much more modest demands for expansion on the labor force than did the baby boom generation. If conditions of near full employment exist, the pressure for women to join the labor force may be stronger than ever, which could have an additional depressing effect on fertility. As the "baby bust" generation passes peak childbearing years, the number of births can be expected to sink, even though birth rates may remain the same. The small bulge of "baby boom echo" babies born since 1975 are eighteen years of age or younger in 1995.

The smaller cohorts of persons born during the Great Depression and the strong fertility decline of the 1920s will be entering retirement age between 1990 and 2010. As a result, the expansion of the elderly population will be moderate. Growth in the old age population will come more from increased longevity, not larger cohorts entering old age. But, beginning about 2010-15, the large cohorts born during the baby boom will begin to reach retirement. The number and proportion of persons over sixty-five years of age will skyrocket, especially if assumptions of increased longevity materialize.

Future Race Composition of the Population

Given higher fertility rates and immigration, most minority groups are projected to increase at a faster rate between 1995 and 2050 than is the white population. The increase in the white population across these years is projected to be nearly 31 percent (over 67 million). Increase among blacks will be nearly 85 percent, approaching a doubling of the population (or over 28 million). Similarly, the American Indian, Eskimo and Aleut combined population is projected to increase by over 95 percent (or over 2.1 million). Projected growth among the Asian and Pacific Islander population is even more dramatic with a projected increase of over 315 percent (nearly 32 million), more than quadrupling the size of this population at present. Only slightly less dramatic is the projected increase in the Hispanic population between 1995 and 2050. Hispanics are projected to increase by 228 percent (just over 61 million), more than tripling their present population.

Another way to see the change these projections forecast for the United States population is to consider the composition of the population now and that projected in 2050. At present the white population is approximately 83 percent of the total United States population. In 1995 the black population is approximately 12.6 percent and

Table 1-8. United States Population, by Region, Division, and State: 1790 to 1990

Region, division, and state	1890	1900	1910	1920	1930	1940	1950	1960	1970	1980	1990
United States, total	62,979,766	76,212,168	92,228,496	106,021,537	123,202,624	132,164,569	151,325,798	179,323,175	203,302,031	226,545,805	248,709,873
Northeast region	17,406,969	21,046,695	25,868,573	29,662,053	34,427,091	35,976,777	39,477,986	44,677,819	49,060,514	49,135,283	50,809,229
New England	4,700,749	5,592,017	6,552,681	7,400,909	8,166,341	8,437,290	9,314,453	10,509,367	11,847,245	12,348,493	13,206,943
Middle Atlantic	12,706,220	15,454,678	19,315,892	22,261,144	26,260,750	27,539,487	30,163,533	34,168,452	37,213,269	36,786,790	37,602,286
Midwest region	22,410,417	26,333,004	29,888,542	34,019,792	38,594,100	40,143,332	44,460,762	51,619,139	56,590,294	58,865,670	59,668,632
East North Central	13,478,305	15,985,581	18,250,621	21,475,543	25,297,185	26,626,342	30,399,368	36,225,024	40,262,747	41,682,217	42,008,942
West North Central	8,932,112	10,347,423	11,637,921	12,544,249	13,296,915	13,516,990	14,061,394	15,394,115	16,327,547	17,183,453	17,659,690
South region	20,028,059	24,523,527	29,389,330	33,125,803	37,857,633	41,665,901	47,197,088	54,973,113	62,812,980	75,372,362	85,445,930
South Atlantic	8,857,922	10,443,480	12,194,895	13,990,272	15,793,589	17,823,151	21,182,335	25,971,732	30,628,826	35,959,123	43,566,853
East South Central	6,429,154	7,547,757	8,409,901	8,893,307	9,887,214	10,778,225	11,477,181	12,050,126	12,808,077	14,666,423	15,176,284
West South Central	4,740,983	6,532,290	8,784,534	10,242,224	12,176,830	13,064,525	14,537,572	16,951,255	19,326,077	23,746,816	26,702,793
West region	3,134,321	4,308,942	7,082,051	9,213,889	12,323,800	14,378,559	20,189,962	28,053,104	34,838,243	43,172,490	52,786,082
Mountain	1,213,935	1,674,657	2,633,517	3,336,101	3,701,789	4,150,003	5,074,998	6,855,060	8,289,901	11,372,785	13,658,776
Pacific	1,920,386	2,634,285	4,448,534	5,877,788	8,622,011	10,228,556	15,114,964	21,198,044	26,548,342	31,799,705	39,127,306
New England											
Maine	661,086	694,466	742,371	768,014	797,423	847,226	913,774	969,265	993,722	1,124,660	1,227,928
New Hampshire	376,530	411,588	430,572	443,083	465,293	491,524	533,242	606,921	737,681	920,610	1,109,252
Vermont	332,422	343,641	355,956	352,428	359,611	359,231	377,747	389,881	444,732	511,456	562,758
Massachusetts	2,238,947	2,805,346	3,366,416	3,852,356	4,249,614	4,316,721	4,690,514	5,148,578	5,689,170	5,737,037	6,016,425
Rhode Island	345,506	428,556	542,610	604,397	687,497	713,346	791,896	859,488	949,723	947,154	1,003,464
Connecticut	746,258	908,420	1,114,756	1,380,631	1,606,903	1,709,242	2,007,280	2,535,234	3,032,217	3,107,576	3,287,116
Middle Atlantic											
New York	6,003,174	7,268,894	9,113,614	10,385,227	12,588,066	13,479,142	14,830,192	16,782,304	18,241,391	17,558,072	17,990,455
New Jersey	1,444,933	1,883,669	2,537,167	3,155,900	4,041,334	4,160,165	4,835,329	6,066,782	7,171,112	7,364,823	7,730,188
Pennsylvania	5,258,113	6,302,115	7,665,111	8,720,017	9,631,350	9,900,180	10,498,012	11,319,366	11,800,766	11,863,895	11,881,643
East North Central											
Ohio	3,672,329	4,157,545	4,767,121	5,759,394	6,646,697	6,907,612	7,946,627	9,706,397	10,657,423	10,797,630	10,847,115
Indiana	2,192,404	2,516,462	2,700,876	2,930,390	3,238,503	3,427,796	3,934,224	4,662,698	5,195,392	5,490,224	5,544,159
Illinois	3,826,352	4,821,550	5,638,591	6,485,280	7,630,654	7,897,241	8,712,176	10,081,158	11,110,285	11,426,518	11,430,602
Michigan	2,093,890	2,420,982	2,810,173	3,668,412	4,842,325	5,256,106	6,371,766	7,823,194	8,881,826	9,262,078	9,295,297
Wisconsin	1,693,330	2,069,042	2,333,860	2,632,067	2,939,006	3,137,587	3,434,575	3,951,777	4,417,821	4,705,767	4,891,769
West North Central											
Minnesota	1,310,283	1,751,394	2,075,708	2,387,125	2,563,953	2,792,300	2,982,483	3,413,864	3,806,103	4,075,970	4,375,099
Iowa	1,912,297	2,231,853	2,224,771	2,404,021	2,470,939	2,538,268	2,621,073	2,757,537	2,825,368	2,913,808	2,776,755
Missouri	2,679,185	3,106,665	3,293,335	3,404,055	3,629,367	3,784,664	3,954,653	4,319,813	4,677,623	4,916,686	5,117,073
North Dakota	190,983	319,146	577,056	646,872	680,845	641,935	619,636	632,446	617,792	652,717	638,800
South Dakota	348,600	401,570	583,888	636,547	692,849	642,961	652,740	680,514	666,257	690,768	696,004
Nebraska	1,062,656	1,066,300	1,192,214	1,296,372	1,377,963	1,315,834	1,325,510	1,411,330	1,485,333	1,569,825	1,578,385
Kansas	1,428,108	1,470,495	1,690,949	1,769,257	1,880,999	1,801,028	1,905,299	2,178,611	2,249,071	2,363,679	2,477,574

Table 1-8. United States Population, by Region, Division, and State: 1790 to 1990 (continued)

Region, division, and state	1880	1870	1860	1850	1840	1830	1820	1810	1800	1790
United States, total	50,189,209	38,558,371	31,443,321	23,191,876	17,063,353	12,860,702	9,638,453	7,239,881	5,308,483	3,929,214
Northeast region	14,507,407	12,298,730	10,594,268	8,626,851	6,761,082	5,542,381	4,359,916	3,486,675	2,635,576	1,968,040
New England	4,010,529	3,487,924	3,135,283	2,728,116	2,234,822	1,954,717	1,660,071	1,471,973	1,233,011	1,009,408
Middle Atlantic	10,496,878	8,810,806	7,458,985	5,898,735	4,526,260	3,587,664	2,699,845	2,014,702	1,407,565	958,632
Midwest region	17,364,111	12,981,111	9,096,716	5,403,595	3,351,542	1,610,473	859,305	292,107	51,006	—
East North Central	11,206,668	9,124,517	6,926,884	4,523,260	2,924,728	1,470,018	792,719	272,324	51,006	—
West North Central	6,157,443	3,856,594	2,169,832	880,335	426,814	140,455	66,586	19,783	—	—
South region	16,516,568	12,288,020	11,133,361	8,982,612	6,950,729	5,707,848	4,419,232	3,461,099	2,621,901	1,961,174
South Atlantic	7,597,197	5,853,610	5,364,703	4,679,090	3,925,299	3,645,752	3,061,063	2,674,891	2,286,494	1,851,806
East South Central	5,585,151	4,404,445	4,020,991	3,363,271	2,575,445	1,815,969	1,190,489	708,590	335,407	109,368
West South Central	3,334,220	2,029,965	1,747,667	940,251	449,985	246,127	167,680	77,618	—	—
West region	1,801,123	990,510	618,976	178,818	—	—	—	—	—	—
Mountain	653,119	315,385	174,923	72,927	—	—	—	—	—	—
Pacific	1,148,004	675,125	444,053	105,891	—	—	—	—	—	—
New England										
Maine	648,936	626,915	628,279	583,169	501,793	399,455	298,335	228,705	151,719	96,540
New Hampshire	346,991	318,300	326,073	317,976	284,574	269,328	244,161	214,460	183,858	161,885
Vermont	332,288	330,551	315,098	314,120	291,948	280,652	235,981	217,895	154,465	85,425
Massachusetts	1,783,085	1,457,351	1,231,066	994,514	737,699	610,408	523,287	472,040	422,845	378,787
Rhode Island	276,531	217,353	174,620	147,545	108,830	97,199	83,059	76,931	69,122	68,825
Connecticut	622,700	537,454	460,147	370,792	309,978	297,675	275,248	261,942	251,002	237,946
Middle Atlantic										
New York	5,082,871	4,382,759	3,880,735	3,097,394	2,428,921	1,918,608	1,372,812	959,049	589,051	340,120
New Jersey	1,131,116	906,096	672,035	489,555	373,306	320,823	277,575	245,562	211,149	184,139
Pennsylvania	4,282,891	3,521,951	2,906,215	2,311,786	1,724,033	1,348,233	1,049,458	810,091	602,365	434,373
East North Central										
Ohio	3,198,062	2,665,260	2,339,511	1,980,329	1,519,467	937,903	581,434	230,760	45,365	—
Indiana	1,978,301	1,680,637	1,350,428	988,416	685,866	343,031	147,178	24,520	5,641	—
Illinois	3,077,871	2,539,891	1,711,951	851,470	476,183	157,445	55,211	12,282	—	—
Michigan	1,636,937	1,184,059	749,113	397,654	212,267	31,639	8,896	4,762	—	—
Wisconsin	1,315,497	1,054,670	775,881	305,391	30,945	—	—	—	—	—
West North Central										
Minnesota	780,773	439,706	172,023	6,077	—	—	—	—	—	—
Iowa	1,624,615	1,194,020	674,913	192,214	43,112	—	—	—	—	—
Missouri	2,168,380	1,721,295	1,182,012	682,044	383,702	140,455	66,586	19,783	—	—
North Dakota	36,909	2,405	—	—	—	—	—	—	—	—
South Dakota	98,268	11,776	4,837	—	—	—	—	—	—	—
Nebraska	452,402	122,993	28,841	—	—	—	—	—	—	—
Kansas	996,096	364,399	107,206	—	—	—	—	—	—	—

Table 1-8. United States Population, by Region, Division, and State: 1790 to 1990 (continued)

Region, division, and state	1990	1980	1970	1960	1950	1940	1930	1920	1910	1900	1890
South Atlantic											
Delaware	666,168	594,338	548,104	446,292	318,085	266,505	238,380	223,003	202,322	184,735	168,493
Maryland	4,781,468	4,216,975	3,923,897	3,100,698	2,343,001	1,841,244	1,631,526	1,449,661	1,295,346	1,188,044	1,042,390
District of Columbia	606,900	638,333	756,668	763,956	802,178	663,091	486,869	437,571	331,069	278,718	230,392
Virginia	6,187,358	5,346,818	4,651,448	3,966,949	3,318,680	2,677,773	2,421,851	2,309,187	2,061,612	1,854,184	1,655,980
West Virginia	1,793,477	1,949,644	1,744,237	1,860,421	2,005,552	1,901,974	1,729,205	1,463,701	1,221,119	958,800	762,794
North Carolina	6,628,637	5,881,766	5,084,411	4,556,155	4,061,929	3,571,623	3,170,276	2,559,123	2,206,287	1,893,810	1,617,949
South Carolina	3,486,703	3,121,820	2,590,713	2,382,594	2,117,027	1,899,804	1,738,765	1,683,724	1,515,400	1,340,314	1,151,149
Georgia	6,478,216	5,463,105	4,587,930	3,943,116	3,444,578	3,123,723	2,908,506	2,895,832	2,609,121	2,216,331	1,837,353
Florida	12,937,926	9,746,324	6,791,418	4,951,560	2,771,305	1,897,414	1,468,211	968,470	752,619	528,542	391,422
East South Central											
Kentucky	3,685,296	3,660,777	3,220,711	3,038,156	2,944,806	2,845,627	2,614,589	2,416,630	2,289,905	2,147,174	1,858,635
Tennessee	4,877,185	4,591,120	3,926,018	3,567,089	3,291,718	2,915,841	2,616,556	2,337,885	2,184,789	2,020,616	1,767,518
Alabama	4,040,587	3,893,888	3,444,354	3,266,740	3,061,743	2,832,961	2,646,248	2,348,174	2,138,093	1,828,697	1,513,401
Mississippi	2,573,216	2,520,638	2,216,994	2,178,141	2,178,914	2,183,796	2,009,821	1,790,618	1,797,114	1,551,270	1,289,600
West South Central											
Arkansas	2,350,725	2,286,435	1,923,322	1,786,272	1,909,511	1,949,387	1,854,482	1,752,204	1,574,449	1,311,564	1,128,211
Louisiana	4,219,973	4,205,900	3,644,637	3,257,022	2,683,516	2,363,880	2,101,593	1,798,509	1,656,388	1,381,625	1,118,588
Oklahoma	3,145,585	3,025,290	2,599,463	2,328,284	2,233,351	2,336,434	2,396,040	2,028,283	1,657,155	790,391	258,657
Texas	16,986,510	14,229,191	11,198,655	9,579,677	7,711,194	6,414,824	5,824,715	4,663,228	3,896,542	3,048,710	2,235,527
Mountain											
Montana	799,065	786,690	694,409	674,767	591,024	559,456	537,606	548,889	376,053	243,329	142,924
Idaho	1,006,749	943,935	713,015	667,191	588,637	524,873	445,032	431,866	325,594	161,772	88,548
Wyoming	453,588	469,557	332,416	330,066	290,529	250,742	225,565	194,402	145,965	95,531	62,555
Colorado	3,294,394	2,889,964	2,209,596	1,753,947	1,325,089	1,123,296	1,035,791	939,629	799,024	539,700	413,249
New Mexico	1,515,069	1,302,894	1,017,055	951,023	681,187	531,818	423,317	360,350	327,301	195,310	160,282
Arizona	3,665,228	2,718,215	1,775,399	1,302,161	749,587	499,261	435,573	334,162	204,354	122,931	88,243
Utah	1,722,850	1,461,037	1,059,273	890,627	688,862	550,310	507,847	449,396	373,351	276,749	210,779
Nevada	1,201,833	800,493	488,738	285,278	160,083	110,247	91,058	77,407	81,875	42,335	47,355
Pacific											
Washington	4,866,692	4,132,156	3,413,244	2,853,214	2,378,963	1,736,191	1,563,396	1,356,621	1,141,990	518,103	357,232
Oregon	2,842,321	2,633,105	2,091,533	1,768,687	1,521,341	1,089,684	953,786	783,389	672,765	413,536	317,704
California	29,760,021	23,667,902	19,971,069	15,717,204	10,586,223	6,907,387	5,677,251	3,426,861	2,377,549	1,465,053	1,213,398
Alaska	550,043	401,851	302,583	226,167	128,643	72,524	59,278	55,036	64,356	63,592	32,052
Hawaii	1,108,229	964,691	769,913	632,772	499,794	422,770	368,300	255,881	191,874	154,001	----

Table 1-8. United States Population, by Region, Division, and State: 1790 to 1990 (continued)

Region, division, and state	1880	1870	1860	1850	1840	1830	1820	1810	1800	1790
South Atlantic										
Delaware	146,608	125,015	112,216	91,532	78,085	76,748	72,749	72,674	64,273	59,096
Maryland	934,943	780,894	687,049	583,034	470,019	447,040	407,350	380,546	341,548	319,728
District of Columbia	177,824	131,700	75,080	51,687	33,745	30,261	23,336	15,471	8,144	—
Virginia	1,512,565	1,225,163	1,219,630	1,119,348	1,025,227	1,044,054	938,261	877,683	807,557	691,737
West Virginia	618,457	442,014	376,688	302,313	224,537	176,924	136,808	105,469	78,592	55,873
North Carolina	1,399,750	1,071,361	992,622	869,039	753,419	737,987	638,829	555,500	478,103	393,751
South Carolina	995,577	705,606	703,708	668,507	594,398	581,185	502,741	415,115	345,591	289,073
Georgia	1,542,180	1,184,109	1,057,286	906,185	691,392	516,823	340,989	252,433	162,686	82,948
Florida	269,493	187,748	140,424	87,445	54,477	34,730	—	—	—	—
East South Central										
Kentucky	1,648,690	1,321,011	1,155,684	982,405	779,828	687,917	564,317	406,511	220,955	73,677
Tennessee	1,542,359	1,256,520	1,109,801	1,002,717	829,210	681,904	422,823	261,727	105,602	35,691
Alabama	1,262,505	996,992	964,201	771,677	590,756	309,527	127,901	9,046	1,250	—
Mississippi	1,131,597	827,922	791,305	606,526	375,651	136,621	75,448	31,306	7,600	—
West South Central										
Arkansas	802,525	484,471	435,450	209,897	97,574	30,388	14,273	1,062	—	—
Louisiana	939,946	726,915	708,002	517,762	352,411	215,739	153,407	76,556	—	—
Oklahoma	—	—	—	—	—	—	—	—	—	—
Texas	1,591,749	818,579	604,215	212,592	—	—	—	—	—	—
Mountain										
Montana	39,159	20,595	—	—	—	—	—	—	—	—
Idaho	32,610	14,999	—	—	—	—	—	—	—	—
Wyoming	20,789	9,118	—	—	—	—	—	—	—	—
Colorado	194,327	59,864	34,277	—	—	—	—	—	—	—
New Mexico	119,565	91,874	93,516	61,547	—	—	—	—	—	—
Arizona	40,440	9,658	—	—	—	—	—	—	—	—
Utah	143,963	86,786	40,273	11,380	—	—	—	—	—	—
Nevada	62,266	42,491	6,857	—	—	—	—	—	—	—
Pacific										
Washington	75,116	23,955	11,594	1,201	—	—	—	—	—	—
Oregon	174,768	90,923	52,465	12,093	—	—	—	—	—	—
California	864,694	560,247	379,994	92,597	—	—	—	—	—	—
Alaska	33,426	—	—	—	—	—	—	—	—	—
Hawaii	—	—	—	—	—	—	—	—	—	—

Source: U.S. Bureau of the Census, "General Population Characteristics," 1990 Census of Population, Table 251, and "Number of Inhabitants: U.S. Summary," 1980 Census of Population, Table 8, U.S. Government Printing Office, Washington, D.C., 1992 and 1983.

Table 1-9. Decennial Rates of Change in Population, by Region, Division, and State: 1790 to 1990

Region, division, and state	Change 1980 to 1990		Percent change								
	Population	Percent	1970 to 1980	1960 to 1970	1950 to 1960	1940 to 1950	1930 to 1940	1920 to 1930	1910 to 1920	1900 to 1910
United States, total	22,164,068	9.8	11.4	13.4	18.5	14.5	7.3	16.2	15.0	21.0
Northeast region	1,673,946	3.4	0.2	9.8	13.2	9.7	4.5	16.1	14.7	22.9
New England	858,450	7.0	4.2	12.7	12.8	10.4	3.3	10.3	12.9	17.2
Middle Atlantic	815,496	2.2	-1.1	8.9	13.3	9.5	4.9	18.0	15.2	25.0
Midwest region	802,962	1.4	4.0	9.6	16.1	10.8	4.0	13.4	13.8	13.5
East North Central	326,725	0.8	3.5	11.1	19.2	14.2	5.3	17.8	17.7	14.2
West North Central	476,237	2.8	5.2	6.1	9.5	4.0	1.7	6.0	7.8	12.5
South region	10,073,568	13.4	20.0	14.3	16.5	13.3	10.1	14.3	12.7	19.8
South Atlantic	7,607,730	21.2	17.4	17.9	22.6	18.8	12.9	12.9	14.7	16.8
East South Central	509,861	3.5	14.5	6.3	5.0	6.5	9.0	11.2	5.7	11.4
West South Central	2,955,977	12.4	22.9	14.0	16.6	11.3	7.3	18.9	16.6	34.5
West region	9,613,592	22.3	23.9	24.2	38.9	40.4	16.7	33.8	30.1	64.4
Mountain	2,285,991	20.1	37.2	20.9	35.1	22.3	12.1	11.0	26.7	57.3
Pacific	7,327,601	23.0	19.8	25.2	40.2	47.8	18.6	46.7	32.1	68.9
New England										
Maine	103,268	9.2	13.2	2.5	6.1	7.9	6.2	3.8	3.5	6.9
New Hampshire	188,642	20.5	24.8	21.5	13.8	8.5	5.6	5.0	2.9	4.6
Vermont	51,302	10.0	15.0	14.1	3.2	5.2	-0.1	2.0	-1.0	3.6
Massachusetts	279,388	4.9	0.8	10.5	9.8	8.7	1.6	10.3	14.4	20.0
Rhode Island	56,310	5.9	-0.3	10.5	8.5	11.0	3.8	13.7	11.4	26.6
Connecticut	179,540	5.8	2.5	19.6	26.3	17.4	6.4	16.4	23.9	22.7
Middle Atlantic										
New York	432,383	2.5	-3.7	8.7	13.2	10.0	7.1	21.2	14.0	25.4
New Jersey	365,365	5.0	2.7	18.2	25.5	16.2	2.9	28.1	24.4	34.7
Pennsylvania	17,748	0.1	0.5	4.3	7.8	6.0	2.8	10.5	13.8	21.6
East North Central										
Ohio	49,485	0.5	1.3	9.8	22.1	15.0	3.9	15.4	20.8	14.7
Indiana	53,935	1.0	5.7	11.4	18.5	14.8	5.8	10.5	8.5	7.3
Illinois	4,084	...	2.8	10.2	15.7	10.3	3.5	17.7	15.0	16.9
Michigan	33,219	0.4	4.3	13.5	22.8	21.2	8.5	32.0	30.5	16.1
Wisconsin	186,002	4.0	6.5	11.8	15.1	9.5	6.8	11.7	12.8	12.8
West North Central										
Minnesota	299,129	7.3	7.1	11.5	14.5	6.8	8.9	7.4	15.0	18.5
Iowa	-137,053	-4.7	3.1	2.5	5.2	3.3	2.7	2.8	8.1	-0.3
Missouri	200,387	4.1	5.1	8.3	9.2	4.5	4.3	6.6	3.4	6.0
North Dakota	-13,917	-2.1	5.7	-2.3	2.1	-3.5	-5.7	5.3	12.1	80.8
South Dakota	5,236	0.8	3.7	-2.1	4.3	1.5	-7.2	8.8	9.0	45.4
Nebraska	8,560	0.5	5.7	5.2	6.5	0.7	-4.5	6.3	8.7	11.8
Kansas	113,895	4.8	5.1	3.2	14.3	5.8	-4.3	6.3	4.6	15.0

Hispanics are approximately 10.2 percent of the total population. By 2050 whites will constitute only 73 percent of the population. At that time, projections are that blacks will comprise 15.7 percent, and Hispanics (who can be of any race) 22.5 percent of the population. The American Indian, Eskimo and Aleut combined population will rise from approximately 0.8 percent to 1.1 percent of the population while Asian and Pacific Islanders will rise from roughly 3.7 to 10.3 percent of the population over the same period. While the white population will continue to be a substantial majority, the diversity of the population will be dramatically increased over these years if the population projections are borne out.

States, Regions and the Geographic Distribution of the Population

Because the United States is a union of states, there are both legal and administrative reasons why as much information should be provided for each state as for the nation, insofar as resources and data permit. In addition, over the history of the United States the territory included in the country and number of states have expanded dramatically. The distribution of the population across this vast territory has had equally dramatic changes over time. Indeed, this country is now so large and geographically

Table 1-9. Decennial Rates of Change in Population, by Region, Division, and State: 1790 to 1990 (continued)

Region, division, and state	Percent change										
	1890 to 1900	1880 to 1890	1870 to 1880	1860 to 1870	1850 to 1860	1840 to 1850	1830 to 1840	1820 to 1830	1810 to 1820	1800 to 1810	1790 to 1800
United States, total	21.0	25.5	30.2	22.6	35.6	35.9	32.7	33.4	33.1	36.4	35.1
Northeast region	20.9	20.0	18.0	16.1	22.8	27.6	22.0	27.1	25.0	32.3	33.9
New England	19.0	17.2	15.0	11.2	14.9	22.1	14.3	17.7	12.8	19.4	22.2
Middle Atlantic	21.6	21.0	19.1	18.1	26.5	30.3	26.2	32.9	34.0	43.1	46.8
Midwest region	17.5	29.1	33.8	42.7	68.3	61.2	108.1	87.4	194.2	472.7	—
East North Central	18.6	20.3	22.8	31.7	53.1	54.7	99.0	85.4	191.1	433.9	—
West North Central	15.8	45.1	59.7	77.7	146.5	106.3	203.9	110.9	236.6	—	—
South region	22.4	21.3	34.4	10.4	23.9	29.2	21.8	29.2	27.7	32.0	33.7
South Atlantic	17.9	16.6	29.8	9.1	14.7	19.2	7.7	19.1	14.4	17.0	23.5
East South Central	17.4	15.1	26.8	9.5	19.6	30.6	41.8	52.5	68.0	111.3	206.7
West South Central	37.8	42.2	64.3	16.2	85.9	109.0	82.8	46.8	116.0	—	—
West region	37.5	74.0	81.8	60.0	246.1	—	—	—	—	—	—
Mountain	38.0	85.9	107.1	80.3	139.9	—	—	—	—	—	—
Pacific	37.2	67.3	70.0	52.0	319.3	—	—	—	—	—	—
New England											
Maine	5.0	1.9	3.5	-0.2	7.7	16.2	25.6	33.9	30.4	50.7	57.2
New Hampshire	9.3	8.5	9.0	-2.4	2.5	11.7	5.7	10.3	13.8	16.6	13.6
Vermont	3.4	...	0.5	4.9	0.3	7.6	4.0	18.9	8.3	41.1	80.8
Massachusetts	25.3	25.6	22.4	18.4	23.8	34.8	20.9	16.6	10.9	11.6	11.6
Rhode Island	24.0	24.9	27.2	24.5	18.4	35.6	12.0	17.0	8.0	11.3	0.4
Connecticut	21.7	19.8	15.9	16.8	24.1	19.6	4.1	8.1	5.1	4.4	5.5
Middle Atlantic											
New York	21.1	18.1	16.0	12.9	25.3	27.5	26.6	39.8	43.1	62.8	73.2
New Jersey	30.4	27.7	24.8	34.8	37.3	31.1	69.1	-20.4	13.0	16.3	14.7
Pennsylvania	19.9	22.8	21.6	21.2	25.7	34.1	27.9	28.5	29.5	34.5	38.7
East North Central											
Ohio	13.2	14.8	-63.9	278.9	18.1	30.3	62.0	61.3	152.0	408.7	—
Indiana	14.8	10.8	17.7	24.5	36.6	44.1	99.9	133.1	500.2	334.7	—
Illinois	26.0	24.3	21.2	48.4	101.1	78.8	202.4	185.2	349.5	—	—
Michigan	15.6	27.9	38.2	58.1	88.4	87.3	570.9	255.7	86.8	—	—
Wisconsin	22.2	28.7	24.7	35.9	154.1	886.9	—	—	—	—	—
West North Central											
Minnesota	33.7	67.8	77.6	155.6	2,730.7	—	—	—	—	—	—
Iowa	16.7	17.7	36.1	76.9	251.1	345.8	—	—	—	—	—
Missouri	16.0	23.6	26.0	45.6	73.3	77.8	173.2	110.9	236.6	—	—
North Dakota	67.1	417.4	1,434.7	—	—	—	—	—	—	—	—
South Dakota	15.2	254.7	734.5	143.5	—	—	—	—	—	—	—
Nebraska	0.3	134.9	267.8	326.5	—	—	—	—	—	—	—
Kansas	3.0	43.4	173.4	239.9	—	—	—	—	—	—	—

diverse that many regions, or even states, are virtually countries unto themselves. Thus the fifty states are primary areal subdivisions for the study of population distribution. For a combination of reasons involving differences in geography, economy, and history, and the characteristics of the inhabitants, the states tend to be clustered into regions of coterminous states. Two such regional systems of delimitation are in common use: the nine geographic divisions, which in turn can be combined to form four geographic regions (see Chapter 2 for more details). Table 1-8 presents the decennial population of these regions, divisions and all fifty states and the District of Columbia for the two hundred years since 1790. Table 1-9 provides the decennial rates of change in popu-

lation for the same geographic areas over the same period. Many of the present states did not even exist as a part of the United States in 1790. Thus, comparisons across states and regions reflect the addition of both population and territories.

Since 1970, there has been very little growth in the Northeast region (3.6% increase). Similarly, there has been very little growth in the North Central region (5.4%) and very little since 1980 (1.4%). Almost all of the population growth over the past two decades has been concentrated in the South (36.0%) and in the West (51.5%). Since 1980 the fastest growing region has clearly been the West (22.3%) and within that region the Pacific division has grown slightly more (23.0%) than the Mountain division

Table 1-9. Decennial Rates of Change in Population, by Region, Division, and State: 1790 to 1990 (continued)

Region, division, and state	Change 1980 to 1990 Population	Change 1980 to 1990 Percent	Percent change 1970 to 1980	1960 to 1970	1950 to 1960	1940 to 1950	1930 to 1940	1920 to 1930	1910 to 1920	1900 to 1910
South Atlantic										
Delaware	71,830	12.1	8.4	22.8	40.3	19.4	11.8	6.9	10.2	9.5
Maryland	564,493	13.4	7.5	26.5	32.3	27.3	12.9	12.5	11.9	9.0
District of Columbia	-31,433	-4.9	-15.6	-1.0	-4.8	21.0	36.2	11.3	32.2	18.8
Virginia	840,540	15.7	14.9	17.3	19.5	23.9	10.6	4.9	12.0	11.2
West Virginia	-156,167	-8.0	11.8	-6.2	-7.2	5.4	10.0	18.1	19.9	27.4
North Carolina	746,871	12.7	15.7	11.6	12.2	13.7	12.7	23.9	16.0	16.5
South Carolina	364,883	11.7	20.5	8.7	12.5	11.4	9.3	3.3	11.1	13.1
Georgia	1,015,111	18.6	19.1	16.4	14.5	10.3	7.4	0.4	11.0	17.7
Florida	3,191,602	32.7	43.5	37.2	78.7	46.1	29.2	51.6	28.7	42.4
East South Central										
Kentucky	24,519	0.7	13.7	6.0	3.2	3.5	8.8	8.2	5.5	6.6
Tennessee	286,065	6.2	16.9	10.1	8.4	12.9	11.4	11.9	7.0	8.1
Alabama	146,699	3.8	13.1	5.4	6.7	8.1	7.1	12.7	9.8	16.9
Mississippi	52,578	2.1	13.7	1.8	-0.0	-0.2	8.7	12.2	-0.4	15.8
West South Central										
Arkansas	64,290	2.8	18.9	7.7	-6.5	-2.0	5.1	5.8	11.3	20.0
Louisiana	14,073	0.3	15.4	11.9	21.4	13.5	12.5	16.9	8.6	19.9
Oklahoma	120,295	4.0	16.4	11.6	4.3	-4.4	-2.5	18.1	22.4	109.7
Texas	2,757,319	19.4	27.1	16.9	24.2	20.2	10.1	24.9	19.7	27.8
Mountain										
Montana	12,375	1.6	13.3	2.9	14.2	5.6	4.1	-2.1	46.0	54.5
Idaho	62,814	6.7	32.4	6.9	13.3	12.1	17.9	3.0	32.6	101.3
Wyoming	-15,969	-3.4	41.3	0.7	13.6	15.9	11.2	16.0	33.2	52.8
Colorado	404,430	14.0	30.8	26.0	32.4	18.0	8.4	10.2	17.6	48.0
New Mexico	212,175	16.3	28.1	6.9	39.6	28.1	25.6	17.5	10.1	67.6
Arizona	947,013	34.8	53.1	36.3	73.7	50.1	14.6	30.3	63.5	66.2
Utah	261,813	17.9	37.9	18.9	29.3	25.2	8.4	13.0	20.4	34.9
Nevada	401,340	50.1	63.8	71.3	78.2	45.2	21.1	17.6	-5.5	93.4
Pacific										
Washington	734,536	17.8	21.1	19.6	19.9	37.0	11.1	15.2	18.8	120.4
Oregon	209,216	7.9	25.9	18.3	16.3	39.6	14.2	21.8	16.4	62.7
California	6,092,119	25.7	18.5	27.1	48.5	53.3	21.7	65.7	44.1	62.3
Alaska	148,192	36.9	32.8	33.8	75.8	77.4	22.3	7.7	-14.5	1.2
Hawaii	143,538	14.9	25.3	21.7	26.6	18.2	14.8	43.9	33.4	24.6

(20.1%). The South Atlantic division is the only other area of the country to experience a similar rate of growth over the past decade (21.2%).

In the past decade the ten fastest growing state populations have been in the states of Nevada, Alaska, Arizona, Florida, California, New Hampshire, Texas, Georgia, Utah, and Washington, in order of percentage population increase between 1980 and 1990. This list is less dominated by the Sunbelt states than was the increase between 1970 and 1980. Five areas which lost population over the same decade were the states (or districts) of West Virginia, the District of Columbia, Iowa, Wyoming, and North Dakota. Followed by Illinois, Pennsylvania, Louisiana, Nebraska, Ohio and Kentucky, these form the ten slowest growing states (and one district) over the decade between the 1980 and 1990 census. Overall, the population growth between the 1980 and 1990 census was lower and more unevenly distributed than that of the prior decade, an era dominated by the massive Sunbelt migra-

tion of the 1970's.

The migration trends underlying changes in regional and state populations over the last decade are discussed in further detail in Chapter 8 of this text. Readers should, however, be cautious in interpreting the growth rates for the 1980-1970 decade for population subgroups such as those at the state level. The error of closure, or coverage, is believed to be different for these two censuses (see Chapter 2) and part of the difference in state population totals across the decade may reflect these differences in coverage.

Table 1-9 shows that the West region, especially the Pacific division, has grown at rates roughly double those of the nation for every decade since 1850. The Northeast, by contrast, has managed to grow only at rates well below the national level in most decades, arriving at near zero growth in the period from 1970 to 1980, but with an increasing growth rate for the past decade. This changing trend may reflect a decline in the continual out-

Table 1-9. Decennial Rates of Change in Population, by Region, Division, and State: 1790 to 1990 (continued)

Region, division, and state	Percent change										
	1890 to 1900	1880 to 1890	1870 to 1880	1860 to 1870	1850 to 1860	1840 to 1850	1830 to 1840	1820 to 1830	1810 to 1820	1800 to 1810	1790 to 1800
South Atlantic											
Delaware	9.6	14.9	17.3	11.4	22.6	17.2	1.7	5.5	0.1	13.1	8.8
Maryland	14.0	11.5	19.7	13.7	17.8	24.0	5.1	9.7	7.0	11.4	6.8
District of Columbia	21.0	29.6	35.0	75.4	45.3	53.2	11.5	29.7	50.8	90.0	—
Virginia	12.0	9.5	23.5	0.5	9.0	9.2	-1.8	11.3	6.9	8.7	16.7
West Virginia	25.7	23.3	39.9	17.3	24.6	34.6	26.9	29.3	29.7	34.2	40.7
North Carolina	17.1	15.6	30.7	7.9	14.2	15.3	2.1	15.5	15.0	16.2	21.4
South Carolina	16.4	15.6	41.1	0.3	5.3	12.5	2.3	15.6	21.1	20.1	19.6
Georgia	20.6	19.1	30.2	12.0	16.7	31.1	33.8	51.6	35.1	55.2	96.1
Florida	35.0	45.2	43.5	33.7	60.6	60.5	56.9	—	—	—	—
East South Central											
Kentucky	15.5	12.7	24.8	14.3	17.6	26.0	13.4	21.9	38.8	84.0	199.9
Tennessee	14.3	14.6	22.7	13.2	10.7	20.9	21.6	61.3	61.6	147.8	195.9
Alabama	20.8	-99.9	26.6	3.4	24.9	30.6	90.9	142.0	1,313.9	623.7	—
Mississippi	20.3	14.0	36.7	4.6	30.5	61.5	175.0	81.1	141.0	311.9	—
West South Central											
Arkansas	16.3	40.6	65.6	11.3	107.5	115.1	221.1	112.9	1,244.0	—	—
Louisiana	23.5	19.0	29.3	2.7	36.7	46.9	63.4	40.6	100.4	—	—
Oklahoma	205.6	—	—	—	—	—	—	—	—	—	—
Texas	36.4	40.4	94.5	35.5	184.2	—	—	—	—	—	—
Mountain											
Montana	70.3	265.0	90.1	—	—	—	—	—	—	—	—
Idaho	82.7	171.5	117.4	—	—	—	—	—	—	—	—
Wyoming	52.7	200.9	128.0	—	—	—	—	—	—	—	—
Colorado	30.6	112.7	224.6	74.6	—	—	—	—	—	—	—
New Mexico	21.9	34.1	30.1	-1.8	51.9	—	—	—	—	—	—
Arizona	39.3	118.2	318.7	—	—	—	—	—	—	—	—
Utah	31.3	46.4	65.9	115.5	253.9	—	—	—	—	—	—
Nevada	-10.6	-23.9	46.5	519.7	—	—	—	—	—	—	—
Pacific											
Washington	45.0	375.6	213.6	106.6	865.4	—	—	—	—	—	—
Oregon	30.2	81.8	92.2	73.3	333.8	—	—	—	—	—	—
California	20.7	40.3	54.3	47.4	310.4	—	—	—	—	—	—
Alaska	98.4	-4.1	—	—	—	—	—	—	—	—	—
Hawaii	—	—	—	—	—	—	—	—	—	—	—

Source: U.S. Bureau of the Census, "General Population Characteristics," 1990 Census of Population, Table 251, and "Number of Inhabitants: U.S. Summary," 1980 Census of Population, Table 8, U.S. Government Printing Office, Washington, D.C., 1992 and 1983.

ward migration to the West region. The North Central region grew rapidly during its settlement (1800-1900) but has consistently grown less than the nation during every decade of this century. As a result, the North Central has now displaced the Northeast as the slowest growing region of the country.

The South, which as a region grew only at average rates or below until 1960, has grown more rapidly than the nation since. It has had a mixed internal pattern of growth. The South Atlantic division has a higher rate of growth in the past decade than any division other than the Pacific. Florida has led this South Atlantic growth at least since 1830, the first year census data were collected for Florida. The relatively high growth between 1970 and 1980 in several South Atlantic states (e.g. South Carolina, North Carolina, West Virginia) has leveled off somewhat between 1980 and 1990.

Figure 1-5 shows the percentage of the population in each sub-region over the past two centuries. From 1790 through 1870 the principal changes in population distribution were due to the rapid settlement of the North Central regions of the country. During this period the percentage of the population in the Middle Atlantic division kept pace while the percentages in the South Atlantic and in the New England divisions declined relative to the more rapidly growing areas of the country. For the next century, between 1870 and 1970, the similar rapid settlement of the West (i.e. Pacific and Mountain) along with the West South Central sub-region has led to a relative decrease in the percentage of the population in the Midwest region. Until 1970 the Middle Atlantic managed to grow at a sufficient rate to nearly maintain its percentage share of the country's population. The decline in the New England share of population has been a steady, but slow,

Figure 1-5. Percent Distribution of Population, by Division: 1790-1990

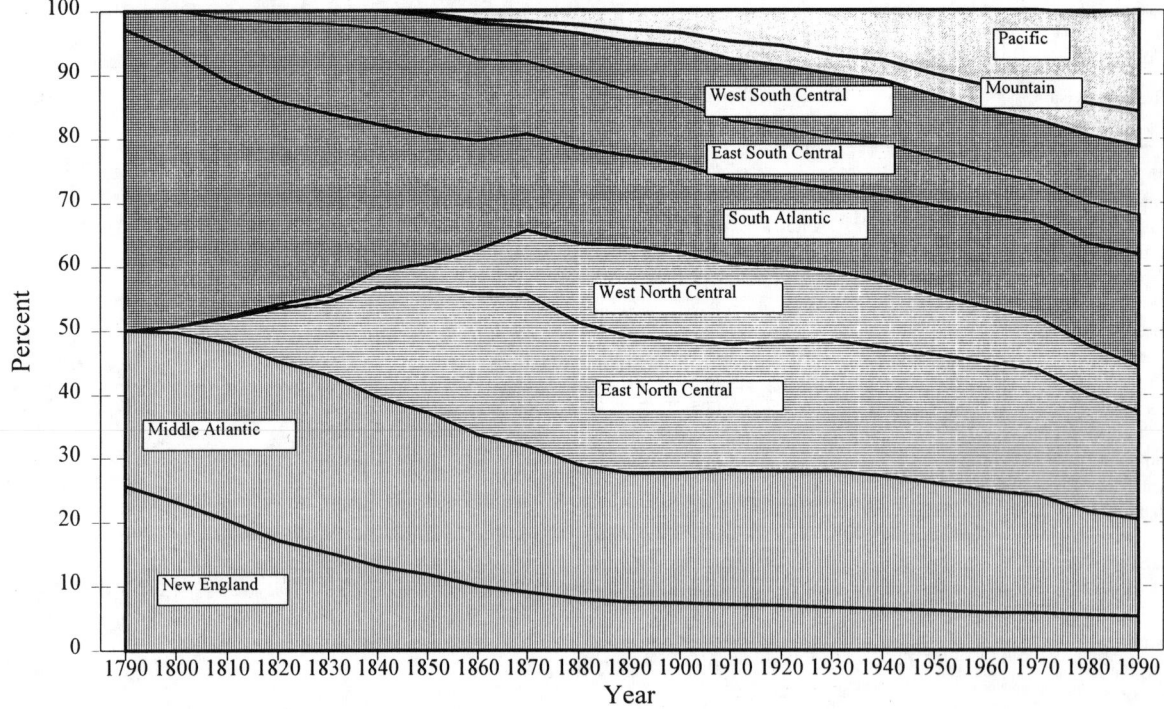

Source: 1790 to 1990 U.S. Census data.

decrease. However, since 1970 the Middle Atlantic division and Midwest region have decreased in population share due to continuing greater growth in the West region and West South Central division along with resurgent South Atlantic division growth.

There is little question, given current migration trends, that the West and South will continue to grow in their population shares. However, parts of the South and West may have an eventually limited growth potential in the short run in response to limited natural resources, including fresh water. Table 1-10 provides information on the land area, inland water and population density of regions, all fifty states and the District of Columbia for decennial years since 1800. The ratio of inland water to land for the United States as a whole is approximately 14.1 square land miles to each square mile of inland water. This ratio of land to water is 8.55 in the Northeast, 10.70 in the North Central, 17.83 in the South and 15.52 in the West. In the Mountain division of the West region there is a staggering ratio of 114.27 square miles of land area to each square mile of inland water. New Mexico has 518.65 square miles of land to each square mile of inland water. The relatively low population density of this region (i.e. 16 persons per square mile for the Mountain West and 12.5 for New Mexico) reflects not only regional settlement histories, but is also influenced by the limited settlement possibilities associated with natural resources, especially water scarcity.

Settlement histories and current fertility rates sub-

stantially influence the age structure of different regions and their likely course in the future. As Table 1-11 shows, the more recently settled West region, which maintains higher than average fertility rates (see Chapter 6), has the greatest percentage of population under fourteen years of age and the lowest percentages over 65 years of age. Utah, with its notably high fertility associated with the Mormon religion, has the highest percentage of children 5 to 14 years of age. However, Alaska has a slightly higher proportion of those under five years of age (10.0 percent) than does Utah (9.8 percent). Both Alaska and Utah are predicted to maintain extraordinarily high percentages of those under 14 years of age into the year 2020. Not surprisingly, Florida, which is a retirement destination for many senior citizens, has the highest percentage of population over 65 years of age. By the year 2020, one of every four Floridians is predicted to be over 65 years old.

Urban-Rural Residence

A highly useful classification for studying population distribution is one that separates city dwellers from country dwellers. The separation is achieved by setting up a definition of the residential places that are to be considered urban and classifying the rest as rural. In the United States, with the mass use of automobiles and a highway system that permits a wide choice of locations for residence in relation to any given place of work, urban and rural localities shade into each other as more of a

Table 1-10. 1990 Area, and Population Density, by Region, Division, and State: Selected Years 1800 to 1990

Region, division, and state	1990 area [in square miles]			Population per square miles of land area								
	Total	Land	Inland water	1990	1980	1970	1960	1950	1940	1900	1850	1800
United States, total	3,787,319	3,536,338	250,980	70.3	64.0	57.5	50.6	50.7	44.2	25.6	7.9	6.1
Northeast region	181,248	162,274	18,974	313.1	301.9	300.5	273.4	242.6	221.1	129.3	53.0	16.2
New England	71,997	62,812	9,185	210.3	196.0	188.2	166.8	147.8	133.9	88.7	43.3	19.6
Middle Atlantic	109,251	99,462	9,789	378.1	368.9	371.0	340.2	302.4	276.0	155.0	59.1	14.1
Midwest region	821,762	751,519	70,243	79.4	76.3	75.3	68.6	59.1	53.4	35.0	7.2	—
East North Central	301,369	243,539	57,831	172.5	170.9	164.9	148.2	124.6	109.1	69.6	18.5	0.2
West North Central	520,393	507,980	12,412	34.8	33.8	32.2	30.3	27.7	26.6	20.4	1.7	—
South region	919,945	871,070	48,875	98.1	86.3	71.9	62.8	54.1	47.7	28.1	10.3	3.0
South Atlantic	293,002	266,220	26,782	163.6	138.5	114.9	97.1	79.4	66.8	39.1	17.5	8.6
East South Central	183,414	178,616	4,798	85.0	82.0	71.6	67.2	64.2	60.3	42.2	18.8	1.9
West South Central	443,530	426,234	17,295	62.6	55.6	45.2	39.5	34.0	30.6	15.3	2.2	—
West region	1,864,363	1,751,475	112,888	30.1	24.6	19.9	16.0	11.5	8.2	2.5	0.1	—
Mountain	863,613	856,121	7,492	16.0	13.3	9.7	8.0	5.9	4.9	2.0	0.1	—
Pacific	1,000,750	895,354	105,397	43.7	35.5	29.8	23.8	16.9	11.4	2.9	0.1	—
New England												
Maine	35,387	30,865	4,523	39.8	36.3	32.1	31.3	29.4	27.3	23.2	19.5	5.1
New Hampshire	9,351	8,969	382	123.7	102.4	81.7	67.2	59.1	54.5	45.6	35.2	20.4
Vermont	9,615	9,249	366	60.8	55.2	48.0	42.0	40.7	38.7	37.7	34.4	16.9
Massachusetts	10,555	7,838	2,717	767.6	733.3	727.0	657.3	596.2	545.9	349.0	123.7	52.6
Rhode Island	1,545	1,045	500	960.3	897.8	905.4	819.3	748.5	674.2	401.6	138.3	64.8
Connecticut	5,544	4,845	698	678.4	637.8	623.7	520.6	409.7	348.9	188.5	76.9	52.1
Middle Atlantic												
New York	54,471	47,224	7,247	381.0	370.6	381.4	350.6	309.3	281.2	152.5	65.0	12.4
New Jersey	8,722	7,419	1,303	1,042.0	986.2	953.5	805.5	642.8	553.1	250.7	65.2	28.1
Pennsylvania	46,058	44,820	1,239	265.1	264.3	262.4	251.4	233.1	219.8	140.6	51.6	13.4
East North Central												
Ohio	44,828	40,953	3,875	264.9	263.3	260.1	236.6	193.8	168.0	102.1	48.6	1.1
Indiana	36,420	35,870	550	154.6	152.8	143.9	128.8	108.7	94.7	70.1	27.5	...
Illinois	57,918	55,593	2,325	205.6	205.3	199.3	180.4	155.8	141.2	86.1	15.2	—
Michigan	96,705	56,809	39,896	163.6	162.6	156.3	137.7	111.7	92.2	42.1	6.9	—
Wisconsin	65,499	54,314	11,186	90.1	86.5	81.1	72.6	62.8	57.3	37.4	5.5	—
West North Central												
Minnesota	86,943	79,617	7,326	55.0	51.2	48.0	43.1	37.3	34.9	21.7	...	—
Iowa	56,276	55,875	401	49.7	52.1	50.5	49.2	46.8	45.3	40.2	3.5	—
Missouri	69,709	68,898	811	74.3	71.3	67.8	62.6	57.1	54.6	45.2	9.9	—
North Dakota	70,704	68,994	1,710	9.3	9.4	8.9	9.1	8.8	9.2	4.5	—	—
South Dakota	77,121	75,896	1,225	9.2	9.1	8.7	9.0	8.5	8.4	5.2	—	—
Nebraska	77,358	76,878	481	20.5	20.5	19.4	18.4	17.3	17.2	13.9	—	—
Kansas	82,282	81,823	459	30.3	28.9	27.5	26.6	23.2	21.9	18.0	—	—

Table 1-10. 1990 Area, and Population Density, by Region, Division, and State: Selected Years 1800 to 1990 (continued)

Region, division, and state	1990 area [in square miles]			Population per square miles of land area								
	Total	Land	Inland water	1990	1980	1970	1960	1950	1940	1900	1850	1800
South Atlantic												
Delaware	2,489	1,955	535	340.8	307.6	276.5	225.2	160.8	134.7	94.0	46.6	32.7
Maryland	12,407	9,775	2,632	489.2	428.7	396.7	313.5	237.1	184.2	119.5	58.6	34.4
District of Columbia	68	62	7	9,884.4	10,132.3	12,404.4	12,523.9	13,159.5	10,870.3	3,972.3	891.2	156.6
Virginia	42,777	39,598	3,179	156.3	134.7	116.9	99.6	83.2	67.1	46.1	22.1	13.7
West Virginia	24,231	24,087	145	74.5	80.8	72.5	77.2	83.3	79.0	39.9	—	—
North Carolina	53,821	48,718	5,103	136.1	120.4	104.2	93.2	82.7	72.7	38.9	17.8	9.8
South Carolina	32,008	30,111	1,897	115.8	103.4	85.7	78.7	69.9	62.1	44.0	21.9	11.3
Georgia	59,441	57,919	1,522	111.9	94.1	79.0	67.8	58.9	53.4	37.7	15.4	1.5
Florida	65,758	53,997	11,761	239.6	180.0	125.6	91.5	51.1	35.0	9.6	1.6	—
East South Central												
Kentucky	40,411	39,732	679	92.8	92.3	81.2	76.2	73.9	70.9	53.4	24.4	5.5
Tennessee	42,146	41,220	927	118.3	111.6	95.0	86.2	78.8	69.5	48.5	24.1	2.5
Alabama	52,423	50,750	1,673	79.6	76.7	67.9	64.2	59.9	55.5	35.7	15.0	—
Mississippi	48,434	46,914	1,520	54.8	53.4	46.9	46.0	46.1	46.1	33.5	13.1	0.3
West South Central												
Arkansas	53,182	52,075	1,107	45.1	43.9	37.0	34.2	36.3	37.0	25.0	4.0	—
Louisiana	51,844	43,566	8,277	96.9	94.5	81.1	72.2	59.4	52.3	30.4	11.4	—
Oklahoma	69,903	68,659	1,244	45.8	44.1	37.2	33.8	32.4	33.7	11.4	—	—
Texas	268,601	261,914	6,687	64.9	54.3	42.7	36.4	29.3	24.3	11.6	0.8	—
Mountain												
Montana	147,046	145,556	1,490	5.5	5.4	4.8	4.6	4.1	3.8	1.7	—	—
Idaho	83,574	82,751	823	12.2	11.5	8.6	8.1	7.1	6.3	1.9	—	—
Wyoming	97,818	97,105	714	4.7	4.8	3.4	3.4	3.0	2.6	0.9	—	—
Colorado	104,100	103,729	371	31.8	27.9	21.3	16.9	12.8	10.8	5.2	—	—
New Mexico	121,598	121,365	234	12.5	10.7	8.4	7.8	5.6	4.4	1.6	—	—
Arizona	114,006	113,642	364	32.3	23.9	15.7	11.5	6.6	4.4	1.1	0.3	—
Utah	84,904	82,168	2,736	21.0	17.8	12.9	10.8	8.4	6.7	3.4	—	—
Nevada	110,567	109,806	761	10.9	7.3	4.4	2.6	1.5	1.0	0.4	...	—
Pacific												
Washington	71,302	66,581	4,721	73.1	62.1	51.3	42.8	35.6	25.9	7.8	—	—
Oregon	98,386	96,003	2,383	29.6	27.4	21.7	18.4	15.8	11.3	4.3	—	—
California	163,707	155,973	7,734	190.8	151.4	127.7	100.4	67.5	44.1	9.5	0.6	—
Alaska	656,424	570,374	86,050	1.0	0.7	0.5	0.4	0.2	0.1	0.1	—	—
Hawaii	10,932	6,423	4,508	172.5	150.1	119.8	98.5	78.0	66.0	24.0	—	—

Source: U.S. Bureau of the Census, "Population and Housing Unit Counts," 1990 Census of Population and Housing, Table 22, and "Number of Inhabitants: U.S. Summary," 1980 Census of Population, Table A1-5, U.S. Government Printing Office, Washington, D.C., 1993 and 1983.

Table 1-11. Percent Distribution of Age, by Region, Division, and State: 1990, 2000, and 2020

Region, division, and state	1990				2000				2020			
	Under 5 years	5 to 14 years	15 to 64 years	65 years and over	Under 5 years	5 to 14 years	15 to 64 years	65 years and over	Under 5 years	5 to 14 years	15 to 64 years	65 years and over
United States, total	7.3	14.0	65.4	12.5	7.0	14.7	65.5	12.8	6.7	13.2	63.7	16.4
Northeast region	6.9	12.8	66.6	13.8	6.5	14.2	65.3	14.1	6.2	12.5	64.4	16.9
New England	7.0	12.6	67.1	13.4	6.2	13.9	65.9	14.0	5.9	11.9	64.7	17.5
Middle Atlantic	6.9	12.9	66.4	13.9	6.6	14.2	65.1	14.1	6.3	12.7	64.3	16.7
Midwest region	7.4	14.7	65.0	13.0	6.9	14.7	65.3	13.1	6.7	13.4	63.7	16.2
East North Central	7.4	14.5	65.5	12.6	7.0	14.7	65.4	12.8	6.8	13.5	63.9	15.9
West North Central	7.4	15.0	63.7	13.9	6.7	14.6	65.0	13.7	6.5	13.2	63.1	17.1
South region	7.1	13.9	64.4	12.4	6.9	14.4	65.6	13.1	6.4	12.7	63.4	17.5
South Atlantic	7.0	13.2	66.4	13.4	6.5	13.9	65.4	14.3	6.0	12.0	62.7	19.2
East South Central	7.0	14.7	65.5	12.7	6.8	14.4	65.9	12.9	6.3	12.8	64.0	17.0
West South Central	7.3	14.5	60.6	10.6	7.6	15.3	65.8	11.2	7.2	13.9	64.0	14.9
West region	8.0	14.7	66.4	10.9	7.8	15.4	65.8	10.9	7.5	14.1	63.8	14.6
Mountain	8.1	16.0	64.7	11.2	7.6	15.5	65.5	11.4	7.1	13.9	63.0	16.0
Pacific	7.9	14.2	67.0	10.9	7.9	15.4	65.9	10.8	7.6	14.1	64.1	14.1
New England	7.0	12.6	67.1	13.4	6.2	13.9	65.9	14.0	5.9	11.9	64.7	17.5
Maine	7.0	14.1	65.6	13.3	5.8	13.6	66.5	14.1	5.6	12.1	64.0	18.3
New Hampshire	7.6	13.7	67.4	11.3	6.1	14.3	67.5	12.1	5.9	12.0	65.2	16.9
Vermont	7.3	14.2	66.7	11.8	6.4	14.2	67.2	12.2	6.2	12.5	64.6	16.7
Massachusetts	6.9	12.1	67.5	13.6	6.1	13.8	66.0	14.2	5.8	11.5	65.3	17.4
Rhode Island	6.7	12.3	66.1	15.0	6.0	13.5	65.3	15.1	6.0	11.8	64.3	17.9
Connecticut	6.9	12.3	67.2	13.6	6.5	14.2	64.9	14.4	6.3	12.5	63.8	17.4
Middle Atlantic	6.9	12.9	66.4	13.9	6.6	14.2	65.1	14.1	6.3	12.7	64.3	16.7
New York	7.0	12.9	67.0	13.1	6.8	14.4	65.5	13.3	6.6	12.8	64.7	15.8
New Jersey	6.9	12.6	67.2	13.4	6.7	14.6	65.0	13.7	6.4	13.1	64.2	16.3
Pennsylvania	6.7	13.0	64.9	15.4	6.1	13.8	64.5	15.6	5.9	12.1	63.8	18.2
East North Central	7.4	14.5	65.5	12.6	7.0	14.7	65.4	12.8	6.8	13.5	63.9	15.9
Ohio	7.2	14.4	65.4	13.0	6.6	14.3	65.5	13.5	6.4	13.0	64.0	16.7
Indiana	7.2	14.7	65.5	12.6	6.8	14.5	65.9	12.8	6.5	13.2	64.2	16.2
Illinois	7.4	14.3	65.7	12.6	7.2	14.9	65.4	12.4	7.1	13.8	64.3	14.8
Michigan	7.6	14.6	65.9	11.9	7.4	15.3	65.0	12.4	7.2	14.3	63.2	15.2
Wisconsin	7.4	14.9	64.4	13.3	6.5	14.6	65.6	13.2	6.2	12.9	63.6	17.3
West North Central	7.4	15.0	63.7	13.9	6.7	14.6	65.0	13.7	6.5	13.2	63.1	17.1
Minnesota	7.7	15.1	64.7	12.5	6.7	14.7	66.1	12.5	6.4	13.0	63.6	16.9
Iowa	7.0	14.9	62.8	15.3	6.5	14.1	64.4	15.0	6.2	12.8	63.0	17.9
Missouri	7.2	14.4	64.3	14.0	6.6	14.4	64.9	14.1	6.3	13.0	63.2	17.5
North Dakota	7.5	15.8	62.5	14.3	6.2	14.3	64.9	14.6	6.4	13.5	63.8	16.3
South Dakota	7.8	16.4	61.1	14.7	7.3	15.7	63.1	13.9	7.3	14.8	61.4	16.5
Nebraska	7.6	15.4	62.8	14.1	6.9	14.9	64.3	13.8	6.7	13.7	62.8	16.8
Kansas	7.6	15.2	63.4	13.8	7.3	14.7	64.5	13.5	7.1	13.7	62.7	16.5

Table 1-11. Percent Distribution of Age, by Region, Division, and State: 1990, 2000, and 2020 (continued)

Region, division, and state	1990 Under 5 years	5 to 14 years	15 to 64 years	65 years and over	2000 Under 5 years	5 to 14 years	15 to 64 years	65 years and over	2020 Under 5 years	5 to 14 years	15 to 64 years	65 years and over
South Atlantic	7.0	13.2	66.4	13.4	6.5	13.9	65.4	14.3	6.0	12.0	62.7	19.2
Delaware	7.3	13.5	67.0	12.1	6.9	14.2	65.9	13.0	6.5	12.7	63.9	16.8
Maryland	7.5	13.2	68.5	10.8	7.3	15.0	66.4	11.3	7.0	13.7	64.5	14.8
District of Columbia	6.2	10.1	70.9	12.8	5.2	9.7	71.5	13.6	5.7	9.1	71.7	13.7
Virginia	7.2	13.3	68.8	10.7	6.6	14.1	67.9	11.4	6.1	12.4	65.8	15.7
West Virginia	5.9	14.2	64.9	15.0	5.9	13.1	49.6	31.4	5.5	11.9	64.1	18.5
North Carolina	6.9	13.2	67.7	12.1	6.4	14.0	66.6	13.1	5.9	11.9	64.1	18.1
South Carolina	7.4	14.6	66.6	11.4	6.9	14.5	66.3	12.2	6.4	12.8	64.0	16.8
Georgia	7.6	14.7	67.6	10.1	7.1	15.1	67.3	10.4	6.7	13.3	65.0	15.0
Florida	6.6	12.1	63.0	18.3	5.9	12.8	61.7	19.6	5.4	10.7	58.3	25.6
East South Central	7.0	14.7	65.5	12.7	6.8	14.4	65.9	12.9	6.3	12.8	64.0	17.0
Kentucky	6.8	14.7	65.9	12.7	6.7	14.0	66.6	12.8	6.2	12.6	64.3	16.9
Tennessee	6.8	13.9	66.6	12.7	6.3	13.8	67.0	12.9	5.8	11.9	64.8	17.5
Alabama	7.0	14.7	65.4	12.9	7.2	14.8	64.8	13.2	6.7	13.6	63.0	16.7
Mississippi	7.6	16.5	63.4	12.5	7.3	15.3	64.7	12.7	6.5	13.6	63.3	16.6
West South Central	7.3	14.5	60.6	10.6	7.6	15.3	65.8	11.2	7.2	13.9	64.0	14.9
Arkansas	7.0	14.9	63.2	14.9	6.6	14.4	64.1	14.9	6.1	12.7	61.9	19.3
Louisiana	7.9	16.6	64.3	11.1	7.6	15.4	65.5	11.5	7.3	14.4	64.0	14.3
Oklahoma	7.2	15.1	64.2	13.5	6.6	14.6	65.4	13.4	6.3	13.4	63.8	16.4
Texas	8.2	15.8	65.9	10.1	7.9	15.5	66.2	10.4	7.5	14.0	64.4	14.2
Mountain	8.1	16.0	64.7	11.2	7.6	15.5	65.5	11.4	7.1	13.9	63.0	16.0
Montana	7.4	16.1	63.2	13.3	6.8	14.8	65.7	12.7	6.7	13.7	63.3	16.2
Idaho	8.0	17.9	62.1	12.0	7.8	16.1	65.0	11.1	7.1	14.6	62.9	15.4
Wyoming	7.7	17.5	64.4	10.4	7.5	15.3	67.4	9.8	7.6	14.9	66.4	11.1
Colorado	7.7	14.6	67.7	10.0	6.8	14.4	68.7	10.2	6.3	12.5	65.9	15.3
New Mexico	8.3	16.7	64.3	10.8	8.1	16.8	63.9	11.2	7.7	15.5	61.8	15.0
Arizona	8.0	14.7	64.2	13.1	7.4	15.5	63.0	14.0	6.9	13.4	60.1	19.6
Utah	9.8	21.3	60.1	8.7	9.7	18.3	63.2	8.8	9.0	17.2	61.7	12.1
Nevada	7.7	13.4	68.3	10.6	7.0	13.6	68.6	10.8	6.4	11.7	66.3	15.6
Pacific	7.9	14.2	67.0	10.9	7.9	15.4	65.9	10.8	7.6	14.1	64.1	14.1
Washington	7.5	14.6	66.1	11.8	6.9	14.8	67.1	11.1	6.5	13.1	64.8	15.6
Oregon	7.1	14.5	64.7	13.8	6.8	14.4	66.1	12.7	6.6	13.3	63.6	16.6
California	8.1	14.1	67.3	10.5	8.2	15.6	65.6	10.6	7.9	14.3	64.0	13.8
Alaska	10.0	17.3	68.7	4.1	9.3	17.6	68.7	4.4	9.6	17.0	67.3	6.1
Hawaii	7.5	14.0	67.2	11.3	8.0	14.2	65.8	12.0	7.4	13.4	64.7	14.4

Source: U.S. Bureau of the Census, "General Population Characteristics," 1990 Census of Population, Table 251 and Current Population Reports, "Population Projections for States, by Age, Sex, Race, and Hispanic Origin: 1993 to 2020," Series P-25, No. 1111, Table 4, U.S. Government Printing Office, Washington, D.C., 1992 and 1994.

continuum than two clearly demarcated categories. Whatever dividing line is placed between the two is therefore arbitrary. Before 1950 the U.S. Bureau of the Census defined urban population as the residents of incorporated places numbering 2,500 or more inhabitants in that particular census. Suburban overflow across city boundaries into contiguous unincorporated territory prompted the Census Bureau for the 1950 census to use the term "urbanized areas," defined as the city plus its "urban fringe" with a total population (in 1980 and 1990) of 50,000 persons. This urban fringe is the contiguous closely settled surrounding suburban territory. A population density of at least 1,000 persons per square mile is the principal criterion for establishing the urbanized area boundaries. However, the boundaries are also drawn to include contiguous or enclosed urban land use areas not intended primarily for residence (e.g. industrial parks, railroad yards, storage areas and so forth), even though the density may be below 1,000 persons per square mile. In addition, extended cities created by city annexations of rural territory were identified in the 1970, 1980 and 1990 censuses with the rural portions of these city populations being classified as rural rather than included in urban population totals.

Throughout the history of the United States internal and international migration has tended to favor relocation of the population to urban centers of growth. At the time of World War I the population of the country became one with a majority of residents located in urban areas. During the decade between 1970 and 1980 the nearly parallel growth of the rural population was heralded by some as a reversal of the nearly steady trend toward a more urban population. However, in the past decade urban populations have again resumed their more rapid growth (see Chapter 8). As Table 1-12 shows, the percentage of the population classified as urban rose in the Midwest, South and West over the past decade. Only in the Northeast did the percentage of urban population continue to decline. In the past century the population has increased from approximately 1 out of 3 residents living in urban areas to a situation where 3 of every 4 residents now live in an urban area. This represents dramatic and innumerable changes for the majority of this country's residents in the lifestyles, cultural influences, economic opportunities, daily circumstances, employment, etc., available to them.

Substantial regional differences have characterized urbanization. In part, this again reflects the timing of settlement and differences in historical settlement patterns. In 1990, for example, the East South Central division remains the area with the lowest percentage of urban residents, constituting a slim majority of only 56.2 percent compared to the total population's urban proportion of 75.2 percent, or the West region's 86.3 percent. Several states have less than a majority of urban residents. Vermont's urban population, 33.2 percent, is roughly that

of the country as a whole more than one hundred years ago. Maine, South Dakota, West Virginia and Mississippi also have less than a majority percentage of urban residents. Even in those states with substantial majorities of urban residents, not all have seen a reversal in the decline of the proportion of urban residents in recent years. In New England, for example, only Connecticut and Massachusetts increased their percentage urban over the past decade and now have a greater percentage urban population than in 1960. Every state in the Middle Atlantic division continued to experience a decline in percentage urban between 1980 and 1990. Meanwhile, every other state in the country experienced either urban growth or relatively minor declines in the percentage of urban population.

Figure 1-6 shows the regional patterns in urban growth. Despite the common trend, it is clear that the Northeast saw a leveling off of urban growth as long ago as the 1930 census. The clearly exceptional urban nature of growth in the West, which is influenced by such historical and geographic factors as centralized highway and water systems, is evident in the continual rise in that region's urban population. The West is arguably the only region which does not show a leveling of urban growth trends at somewhere between 70 and 80 percent urban over the past few decades.

Size of Place

Urban places range in size from small cities of 2,500 to New York City's 7.3 million persons. Within rural areas there are thousands of villages and towns of various sizes, all with less than 2,500 inhabitants. Table 1-13 provides a detailed report of this distribution of urban and rural sizes of place, both for 1990 and 1980.

There was an increase in the percentage of population in urbanized areas and in central cities between 1980 and 1990. Only the percentage population in central cities of 500,000 to 999,999 residents declined over the decade among all central cities. This decrease was also greater than the increase in larger cities, indicating the shift is not simply an artifact due to increases in city size over the decade. Meanwhile, the percentage of population in the urban fringe decreased in every place of 10,000 or more residents, was constant in places of 5,000 to 9,999 residents and increased in the smallest places of between 2,500 and 4,999 residents. The percentage of the population who were other urban residents living outside urban areas also decreased across all sizes of place. This decline is less dramatic, however, than a similar decrease of nearly ten percent during the 1970 to 1980 decade.

Reversing the patterns of the earlier decade, and returning to patterns which have been historically more typical, the percentage of population living in rural areas decreased between 1980 and 1990. These changes were, however, not dramatic and appear more as a leveling in

Table 1-12. Percent of Population Classified as Urban, by Region, Division, and State: 1850-1990[1]

Region, division, and state	1990	1980	1970	1960	1950	1940	1930	1920	1910	1900	1890	1880	1870	1860	1850
United States, total	75.2	73.7	73.6	69.9	64.0	56.5	56.1	51.2	45.6	39.6	35.1	28.2	25.7	19.8	15.3
Northeast region	78.9	79.2	80.6	80.2	79.5	76.6	77.6	75.5	71.8	66.1	59.0	50.8	44.3	35.7	26.5
New England	74.4	75.1	76.6	76.4	76.2	76.1	77.3	75.9	73.3	68.6	61.6	52.4	44.4	36.6	28.8
Middle Atlantic	80.5	80.6	81.8	81.4	80.5	76.8	77.7	75.4	71.2	65.2	58.0	50.2	44.2	35.4	25.5
Midwest region	71.7	70.5	71.6	68.7	64.1	58.4	57.9	52.3	45.1	38.6	33.1	24.2	20.8	13.9	9.2
East North Central	74.0	73.3	74.8	73.0	69.7	65.5	66.4	60.8	52.7	45.2	37.9	27.5	21.6	14.1	9.0
West North Central	66.3	63.9	63.7	58.8	52.0	44.3	41.8	37.7	33.2	28.5	25.8	18.2	18.9	13.4	10.3
South region	68.6	66.9	64.8	58.5	48.6	36.7	34.1	28.1	22.5	18.0	16.3	12.2	12.2	9.6	8.3
South Atlantic	69.4	67.1	64.1	57.2	49.1	38.8	36.1	31.0	25.4	21.4	19.5	14.9	14.4	11.5	9.8
East South Central	56.2	55.7	54.7	48.4	39.1	29.4	28.1	22.4	18.7	15.0	12.7	8.4	8.8	5.9	4.2
West South Central	74.5	73.4	72.7	67.7	55.6	39.8	36.4	29.0	22.3	16.2	15.1	12.5	13.3	12.3	15.1
West region	86.3	83.9	83.1	77.7	69.5	58.8	58.4	51.8	47.9	39.9	37.0	30.2	25.8	16.0	6.4
Mountain	79.7	76.4	73.1	67.1	54.9	42.7	39.4	36.5	35.9	32.3	29.3	21.6	12.3	10.1	6.2
Pacific	88.6	86.6	86.2	81.1	74.4	64.9	66.6	60.5	55.0	44.7	41.9	35.2	32.1	18.4	6.4
New England															
Maine	44.6	47.5	50.8	51.3	51.7	40.5	40.3	39.0	35.3	33.5	28.1	22.6	21.0	16.6	13.5
New Hampshire	51.0	52.2	56.4	58.3	57.5	57.6	58.7	56.5	51.8	46.7	39.3	30.0	26.2	22.1	17.1
Vermont	32.2	33.8	32.2	38.5	36.4	34.3	33.0	31.2	27.8	22.1	15.2	10.0	6.9	2.0	1.9
Massachusetts	84.3	83.8	84.6	83.6	84.4	89.4	90.2	90.0	89.0	86.0	82.0	74.7	66.7	59.6	50.7
Rhode Island	86.0	87.0	87.1	86.4	84.3	91.6	92.4	91.9	91.0	88.3	85.3	82.0	74.6	63.3	55.6
Connecticut	79.1	78.8	78.4	78.3	77.6	67.8	70.4	67.8	65.6	59.9	50.9	41.9	33.0	26.5	16.0
Middle Atlantic															
New York	84.3	84.6	85.7	85.4	85.5	82.8	83.6	82.7	78.9	72.9	65.1	56.4	50.0	39.3	28.2
New Jersey	89.4	89.0	88.9	88.6	86.6	81.6	82.6	79.9	76.4	70.6	62.6	54.4	43.7	32.7	17.6
Pennsylvania	68.9	69.3	71.5	71.6	70.5	66.5	67.8	65.1	60.4	54.7	48.6	41.6	37.3	30.8	23.6
East North Central															
Ohio	74.1	73.3	75.3	73.4	70.2	66.8	67.8	63.8	55.9	48.1	41.1	32.2	25.6	17.1	12.2
Indiana	64.9	64.2	64.9	62.4	59.9	55.1	55.5	50.6	42.4	34.3	26.9	19.5	14.7	8.6	4.5
Illinois	84.6	83.3	83.2	80.7	77.6	73.6	73.9	67.9	61.7	54.3	44.9	30.6	23.5	14.3	7.6
Michigan	70.5	70.7	74.0	73.4	70.7	65.7	68.2	61.1	47.2	39.3	34.9	24.8	20.1	13.3	7.3
Wisconsin	65.7	64.2	65.9	63.8	57.9	53.5	52.9	47.3	43.0	38.2	33.2	24.1	19.6	14.4	9.4
West North Central															
Minnesota	69.9	66.9	66.5	62.2	54.2	49.8	49.0	44.1	41.0	34.1	33.8	19.1	16.1	9.4	...
Iowa	60.6	58.6	57.2	53.0	47.7	42.7	39.6	36.4	30.6	25.6	21.2	15.2	13.1	8.9	5.1
Missouri	68.7	68.1	70.1	66.6	61.5	51.8	51.2	46.6	42.3	36.3	32.0	25.2	25.0	17.2	11.8
North Dakota	53.3	48.8	44.3	35.2	26.6	20.6	16.6	13.6	11.0	7.3	5.6	—	—	—	—
South Dakota	50.0	46.4	44.6	39.3	33.2	24.6	18.9	16.0	13.1	10.2	8.2	—	—	—	—
Nebraska	66.1	62.9	61.5	54.3	46.9	39.1	35.3	31.3	26.1	23.7	27.4	18.0	18.0	...	—
Kansas	69.1	66.7	66.1	61.0	52.1	41.9	38.8	34.8	29.1	22.4	18.9	14.2	14.2	9.4	—

Table 1-12. Percent of Population Classified as Urban, by Region, Division, and State: 1850-1990¹ (continued)

Region, division, and state	1990	1980	1970	1960	1950	1940	1930	1920	1910	1900	1890	1880	1870	1860	1850
South Atlantic															
Delaware	73.0	70.6	72.2	65.6	62.6	52.3	51.7	54.2	48.0	46.4	42.2	33.4	24.7	18.9	15.3
Maryland	81.3	80.3	76.6	72.7	69.6	59.3	59.8	60.0	50.8	49.8	47.6	40.2	37.8	34.0	32.3
District of Columbia	100.0	100.0	100.0	100.0	100.0	100.0	100.0	100.0	100.0	100.0	100.0	90.0	91.6	93.0	93.6
Virginia	69.4	66.0	63.2	55.6	47.0	35.3	32.4	29.2	23.1	18.3	17.1	12.5	11.9	9.5	8.0
West Virginia	36.1	36.2	39.1	38.2	34.6	28.1	28.4	25.2	18.7	13.1	10.7	8.7	8.1	5.3	3.8
North Carolina	50.4	48.0	45.5	39.5	33.7	27.3	25.5	19.2	14.4	9.9	7.2	3.9	3.4	2.5	2.4
South Carolina	54.6	54.1	48.3	41.2	36.7	24.5	21.3	17.5	14.8	12.8	10.1	7.5	8.6	6.9	7.3
Georgia	63.2	62.4	60.3	55.3	45.3	34.4	30.8	25.1	20.6	15.6	14.0	9.4	8.4	7.1	4.3
Florida	84.8	84.3	81.7	73.9	65.5	55.1	51.7	36.5	29.1	20.3	19.8	10.0	8.1	4.1	...
East South Central															
Kentucky	51.8	50.9	52.3	44.5	36.8	29.8	30.6	26.2	24.3	21.8	19.2	15.2	14.8	10.4	7.5
Tennessee	60.9	60.4	59.1	52.3	44.1	35.2	34.3	26.1	20.2	16.2	13.5	7.5	7.5	4.2	2.2
Alabama	60.4	60.0	58.6	54.8	43.8	30.2	28.1	21.7	17.3	11.9	10.1	5.4	6.3	5.1	4.6
Mississippi	47.1	47.3	44.5	37.7	27.9	19.8	16.9	13.4	11.5	7.7	5.4	3.1	4.0	2.6	1.8
West South Central															
Arkansas	53.5	51.6	50.0	42.8	33.0	22.0	20.6	16.6	12.9	8.5	6.5	4.0	2.6	0.9	...
Louisiana	68.1	68.6	66.5	63.3	54.8	41.5	39.7	34.9	30.0	26.5	25.4	25.5	27.9	26.1	26.0
Oklahoma	67.7	67.3	68.0	62.9	51.0	37.6	34.3	26.5	19.2	7.4	3.7	—	—	—	—
Texas	80.3	79.6	79.7	75.0	62.7	45.4	41.0	32.4	24.1	17.1	15.6	9.2	6.7	4.4	3.6
Mountain															
Montana	52.5	52.9	53.4	50.2	43.7	37.8	33.7	31.3	35.5	34.7	27.1	17.8	15.1	—	—
Idaho	57.4	54.0	54.1	47.5	42.9	33.7	29.1	27.6	21.5	6.2		...	...	—	—
Wyoming	65.0	62.7	60.5	56.8	49.8	37.3	31.1	29.4	29.6	28.8	34.3	29.6	...	—	—
Colorado	82.4	80.6	78.5	73.7	62.7	52.6	50.2	48.2	50.3	48.3	45.0	31.4	11.9	13.9	—
New Mexico	73.0	72.1	69.8	65.9	50.2	33.2	25.2	18.0	14.2	14.0	6.2	5.5	5.2	5.0	7.4
Arizona	87.5	83.8	79.6	74.5	55.5	34.8	34.4	36.1	31.0	15.9	9.4	17.3	33.4	—	—
Utah	87.0	84.4	80.4	74.9	65.3	55.5	52.4	48.0	46.3	38.1	35.7	23.4	18.4	20.5	—
Nevada	88.3	85.3	80.9	70.4	57.2	39.3	37.8	19.7	16.3	17.0	33.8	31.1	16.6	...	—
Pacific															
Washington	76.4	73.5	73.4	68.1	63.2	53.1	56.6	54.8	53.0	40.8	35.6	9.5	...	—	...
Oregon	70.5	67.9	67.1	62.2	53.9	48.8	51.3	49.8	45.6	32.2	27.9	14.8	9.1	5.5	...
California	92.6	91.3	90.9	86.4	80.7	71.0	73.3	67.9	61.8	52.3	48.6	42.9	37.2	20.7	7.4
Alaska	67.5	64.3	56.9	37.9	26.6	24.0	13.2	5.6	9.5	24.5	...	—	—	—	—
Hawaii	89.0	86.5	83.1	76.5	69.0	62.5	53.7	36.1	30.7	25.5	...	—	—	—	—

¹ From 1950 based on current definition, prior to 1950 from previous urban definition.

Source: U.S. Bureau of the Census, "Population and Housing Unit Counts," 1990 Census of Population and Housing, Table 25, and "Number of Inhabitants: U.S. Summary," 1980 Census of Population, Table 13, U.S. Government Printing Office, Washington, D.C., 1993 and 1983.

Table 1-13. Population of the United States, by Size of Place: 1980 and 1990

Urban and rural areas, by size of place	1990			1980		
	Places	Population	Percent distribution	Places	Population	Percent distribution
United States	23,435	248,709,873	100.0	22,529	226,545,805	100.0
Urban	9,421	187,053,487	75.2	8,765	167,050,992	73.7
Inside urbanized areas	5,483	158,258,878	63.6	4,938	139,170,683	61.4
Central cities	549	78,847,406	31.7	431	67,035,302	29.6
1,000,000 or more	8	19,952,631	8.0	6	17,530,248	7.7
500,000 to 999,999	15	10,107,184	4.1	16	10,834,121	4.8
250,000 to 499,999	41	14,585,006	5.9	33	11,900,309	5.3
100,000 to 249,999	97	14,602,452	5.9	82	12,295,543	5.4
50,000 to 99,999	177	12,274,504	4.9	125	8,649,031	3.8
Less than 50,000	211	7,325,629	2.9	169	5,826,050	2.6
Urban fringe	4,934	79,411,472	31.9	4,507	72,135,381	31.8
Places of 2,500 or more	4,023	62,775,855	25.2	3,491	58,212,417	25.7
100,000 or more	39	5,100,382	2.1	36	4,976,800	2.2
50,000 to 99,999	178	11,752,941	4.7	165	11,137,456	4.9
25,000 to 49,999	443	15,118,958	6.1	424	14,539,729	6.4
10,000 to 24,999	1,167	18,482,502	7.4	1,087	17,232,991	7.6
5,000 to 9,999	1,200	8,679,826	3.5	1,108	7,900,939	3.5
2,500 to 4,999	996	3,641,246	1.5	671	2,424,502	1.1
Places of less than 2,500	911	1,078,903	0.4	1,016	1,260,246	0.6
2,000 to 2,499	162	362,540	0.1	183	406,475	0.2
1,500 to 1,999	159	276,809	0.1	210	367,921	0.2
1,000 to 1,499	192	240,177	0.1	238	297,473	0.1
Less than 1,000	398	199,377	0.1	385	188,377	0.1
Other urban	—	15,556,714	6.3	—	12,662,718	5.6
Outside urbanized areas	3,938	28,794,609	11.6	3,827	27,880,309	12.3
25,000 or more	121	3,917,665	1.6	118	3,773,752	1.7
10,000 to 24,999	652	9,907,357	4.0	642	9,708,035	4.3
5,000 to 9,999	1,135	7,909,614	3.2	1,073	7,455,198	3.3
2,500 to 4,999	2,030	7,059,973	2.8	1,994	6,943,324	3.1
Rural	14,014	61,656,386	24.8	13,764	59,494,813	26.3
Places of 1,000 to 2,499	4,424	7,050,858	2.8	4,434	7,037,840	3.1
2,000 to 2,499	931	2,074,977	0.8	918	2,048,678	0.9
1,500 to 1,999	1,378	2,381,156	1.0	1,318	2,280,677	1.0
1,000 to 1,499	2,115	2,594,725	1.0	2,198	2,708,485	1.2
Places of less than 1,000	9,590	3,801,051	1.5	9,330	3,863,470	1.7
Other rural	—	50,804,477	20.4	—	48,593,503	21.4

Source: U.S. Bureau of the Census, "Population and Housing Unit Counts," 1990 Census of Population and Housing, Table 8, and "Number of Inhabitants: U.S. Summary," 1980 Census of Population, Table 4, U.S. Government Printing Office, Washington, D.C., 1993 and 1983.

Figure 1-6. Percent of Population Classified as Urban, by Region: 1790-1990

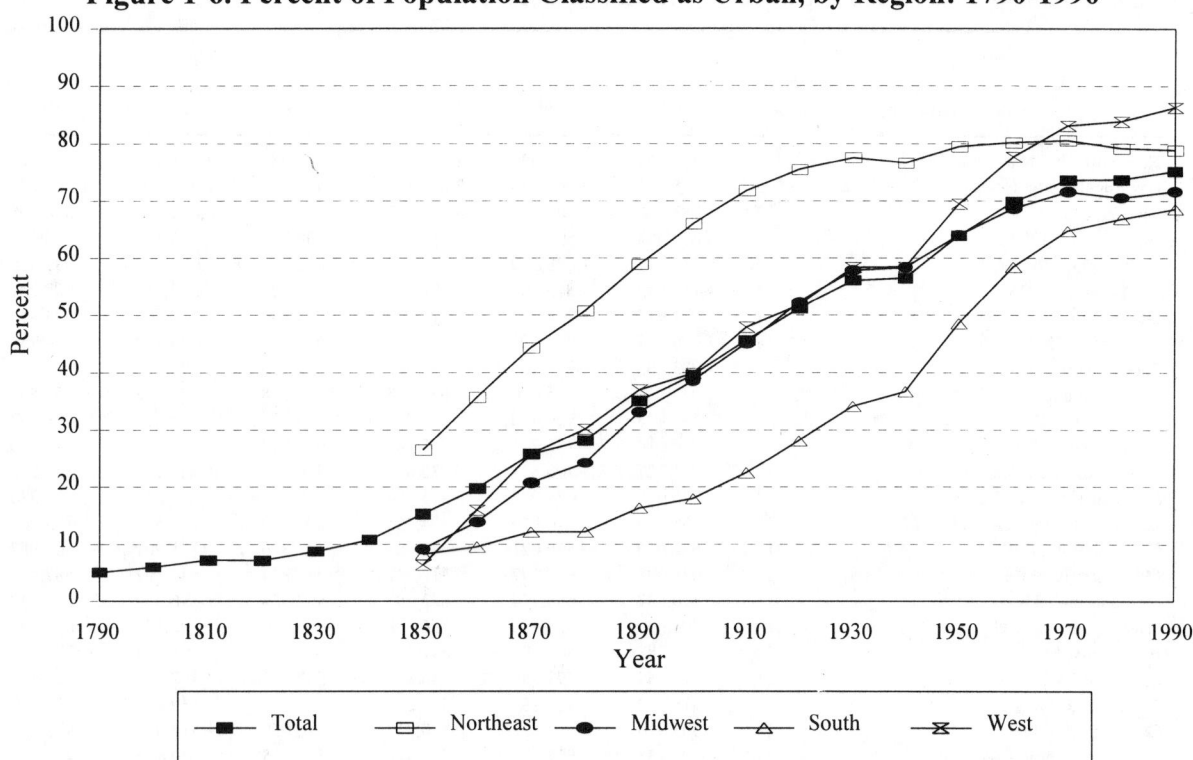

Source: 1790-1990 U.S. Census data.

urban to rural population ratios during the decade than any dramatic change. The largest decline in the rural population was in the rural population outside of designated places. The persistently decreasing population in rural areas and small places reflects a declining role of the small town in American life. Some social scientists have emphasized the mythical character of the small town in American popular culture. However, the sheer magnitude of the decline in small towns and rural life in the United States over the past half century is not a trend which is, or should be, easily dismissed. Our way of life has clearly changed over the past century and a new character of life has emerged in growing urban centers as we move into the coming century.

It is important to remember that some of the largest urban centers in the United States have not grown dramatically over the past fifty years while others have experienced explosive growth. In Table 1-14 the population of the top fifty incorporated places in the United States is given for each census over the past half century from 1790 to 1990. Three of the top five incorporated places are actually smaller than they were fifty years ago. New York, Chicago and Philadelphia have all lost population more recently and have experienced a net loss of population over the past half century. These three cities are also the only cities in the United States which had over one million in population a century ago. At that time, no other United States city was even over one half million in popu-

lation size. Many of the major cities in 1890, such as Boston, Baltimore and St. Louis, are no longer among the very largest cities in the country.

Not surprisingly, those major incorporated places among the top fifty which have lost population over the more recent past tend to be those settled in the more distant past, those in deindustrializing areas of the country, those precluded from growth through annexation, and those in the states which have either grown less rapidly or have lost population in the recent past. By contrast, among the top five incorporated places, Los Angeles and Houston have both experienced tremendous, even explosive, growth over the past half century, part of which comes from annexation of new areas. The most rapidly-growing of the top ten incorporated places are Houston, San Diego, Dallas, Phoenix and San Antonio, all southwestern and Pacific, or what have been called 'sun belt,' cities. Many of these western cities have been centers of immigration, of the development of new industries and of growth through annexation, and are located in states which have generally experienced high rates of population growth over the past half century.

Metropolitan Areas

In order to acknowledge the metropolitanized aspect of the economy and to provide separate statistics for areas which are under direct metropolitan dominance, the

Table 1-14. Population of the Top 50 Incorporated Places: 1790-1990

Incorporated place	1990 population rank	1990	1980	1970	1960	1950	1940
New York city, NY	1	7,322,564	7,071,639	7,895,563	7,781,984	7,891,957	7,454,995
Los Angeles city, CA	2	3,485,398	2,968,528	2,811,801	2,479,015	1,970,358	1,504,277
Chicago city, IL	3	2,783,726	3,005,072	3,369,357	3,550,404	3,620,962	3,396,808
Houston city, TX	4	1,630,553	1,595,138	1,233,535	938,219	596,163	384,514
Philadelphia city, PA	5	1,585,577	1,688,210	1,949,996	2,002,512	2,071,605	1,932,334
San Diego city, CA	6	1,110,549	875,538	697,741	573,224	334,387	203,341
Detroit city, MI	7	1,027,974	1,203,368	1,514,063	1,670,144	1,849,568	1,623,452
Dallas city, TX	8	1,006,877	904,599	844,401	679,684	434,462	294,734
Phoenix city, AZ	9	983,403	789,704	584,303	439,170	106,818	65,414
San Antonio city, TX	10	935,933	785,940	654,153	587,718	408,442	253,854
San Jose city, CA	11	782,248	629,400	459,913	204,196	95,280	68,457
Baltimore city, MD	12	736,014	786,741	905,787	939,024	949,708	859,100
Indianapolis (remainder), IN	13	731,327	700,807	736,856	476,258	427,173	386,972
San Fransisco city, CA	14	723,959	678,974	715,674	740,316	775,357	634,536
Jacksonville city (remainder), FL	15	635,230	540,920	504,265	201,030	204,517	173,065
Columbus city, OH	16	632,910	565,021	540,025	471,316	375,901	306,087
Milwaukee city, WI	17	628,088	636,297	717,372	741,324	637,392	587,472
Memphis city, TN	18	610,337	646,174	623,988	497,524	396,000	292,942
Washington city, DC	19	606,900	638,432	756,668	763,956	802,178	663,091
Boston city, MA	20	574,283	562,994	641,071	697,197	801,444	770,816
Seattle city, WA	21	516,259	493,846	530,831	557,087	467,591	368,302
El Paso city, TX	22	515,342	425,259	322,261	276,687	130,485	96,810
Cleveland city, OH	23	505,616	573,822	750,879	876,050	914,808	878,336
New Orleans city, LA	24	496,938	557,927	593,471	627,525	570,445	494,537
Nashville-Davidson (remainder), TN	25	488,374	455,651	426,029	154,563	174,307	167,402
Denver city, CO	26	467,610	492,686	514,678	493,887	415,786	322,412
Austin city, TX	27	465,622	345,890	253,539	186,545	132,459	87,930
Fort Worth city, TX	28	447,619	385,164	393,455	356,268	278,778	117,662
Oklahoma City city, OK	29	444,719	404,014	368,164	324,253	243,504	204,424
Portland city, OR	30	437,319	368,148	379,967	372,676	373,628	305,394
Kansas City city, MO	31	435,146	448,028	507,330	475,539	456,622	399,178
Long Beach city, CA	32	429,433	361,498	358,879	344,168	250,767	164,271
Tucson city, AZ	33	405,390	330,537	262,933	212,892	45,454	35,752
St. Louis city, MO	34	396,685	452,801	622,236	750,026	856,796	816,048
Charlotte city, NC	35	395,934	315,474	241,420	201,564	134,042	100,899
Atlanta city, GA	36	394,017	425,022	495,039	487,455	331,314	302,288
Virginia Beach city, VA	37	393,069	262,199	172,106	8,091	5,390	2,600
Albuquerque city, NM	38	384,736	332,920	244,501	201,189	96,815	35,449
Oakland city, CA	39	372,242	339,337	361,561	367,548	384,575	302,163
Pittsburg city, PA	40	369,879	423,959	520,089	604,332	676,806	671,659
Sacramento city, CA	41	369,365	275,741	257,105	191,667	137,572	105,958
Minneapolis city, MN	42	368,383	370,951	434,400	482,872	521,718	492,370
Tulsa city, OK	43	367,302	360,919	330,350	261,685	182,740	142,157
Honolulu CDP, HI	44	365,272	365,048	324,871	294,194	248,034	179,326
Cincinnati city, OH	45	364,040	385,409	453,514	502,550	503,998	455,610
Miami city, FL	46	358,548	346,681	334,859	291,688	249,276	172,172
Fresno city, CA	47	354,202	217,491	165,655	133,929	91,669	60,685
Omaha city, NE	48	335,795	313,939	346,929	301,598	251,117	223,844
Toledo city, OH	49	332,943	354,635	383,062	318,003	303,616	282,349
Buffalo city, NY	50	328,123	357,870	462,768	532,759	580,132	575,901

Table 1-14. Population of the Top 50 Incorporated Places: 1790-1990 (continued)

Incorporated place	1930	1920	1910	1900	1890	1880	1870
New York city, NY	6,930,446	5,620,048	4,766,883	3,437,202	2,507,414	1,911,698	1,478,103
Los Angeles city, CA	1,238,048	576,673	319,198	102,479	50,395	11,183	5,728
Chicago city, IL	3,376,438	2,701,705	2,185,283	1,698,575	1,099,850	503,185	298,977
Houston city, TX	292,352	138,276	78,800	44,633	27,557	16,513	9,382
Philadelphia city, PA	1,950,961	1,823,779	1,549,008	1,293,697	1,046,964	847,170	647,022
San Diego city, CA	147,995	74,361	39,578	17,700	16,159	2,637	2,300
Detroit city, MI	1,568,662	993,678	465,766	285,704	205,876	116,340	79,577
Dallas city, TX	260,475	158,976	92,104	42,638	38,067	10,358	—
Phoenix city, AZ	48,118	29,053	11,134	5,544	3,152	—	—
San Antonio city, TX	231,542	161,379	96,614	53,321	37,673	20,550	12,256
San Jose city, CA	57,651	39,642	28,946	21,500	18,060	12,567	9,089
Baltimore city, MD	804,874	733,826	558,485	508,957	434,439	332,313	267,354
Indianapolis (remainder), IN	364,161	314,194	233,650	169,614	105,436	75,056	48,244
San Fransisco city, CA	634,394	506,676	416,912	342,782	298,997	233,959	149,473
Jacksonville city (remainder), FL	129,549	91,558	57,699	28,429	17,201	7,650	6,912
Columbus city, OH	290,564	237,031	181,511	125,560	88,150	51,647	31,274
Milwaukee city, WI	578,249	457,147	373,857	285,315	204,468	115,587	71,440
Memphis city, TN	253,143	162,351	131,105	102,320	64,495	33,592	40,226
Washington city, DC	486,869	437,571	331,069	278,718	188,932	147,293	109,199
Boston city, MA	781,188	748,060	670,585	560,892	448,477	362,839	250,526
Seattle city, WA	365,583	315,312	237,194	80,671	42,837	3,533	1,107
El Paso city, TX	102,421	77,560	39,279	15,906	10,338	736	—
Cleveland city, OH	900,429	796,841	560,663	381,768	261,353	160,416	92,829
New Orleans city, LA	458,762	387,219	339,075	287,104	242,039	216,090	191,418
Nashville-Davidson (remainder), TN	153,866	118,342	110,364	80,865	76,168	43,350	25,865
Denver city, CO	287,861	256,491	213,381	133,859	106,713	35,629	4,759
Austin city, TX	53,120	34,876	29,860	22,258	14,575	11,013	4,428
Fort Worth city, TX	163,447	106,482	73,312	26,688	23,076	6,663	—
Oklahoma City city, OK	185,389	91,295	64,205	10,037	4,151	—	—
Portland city, OR	301,815	258,288	207,214	90,426	46,385	17,577	8,293
Kansas City city, MO	399,746	324,410	248,381	163,752	132,716	55,785	32,260
Long Beach city, CA	142,032	55,593	17,809	2,252	564	—	—
Tucson city, AZ	32,506	20,292	13,193	7,531	5,150	7,007	3,224
St. Louis city, MO	821,960	772,897	687,029	575,238	451,770	350,518	310,864
Charlotte city, NC	82,675	46,338	34,014	18,091	11,557	7,094	4,473
Atlanta city, GA	270,366	200,616	154,839	89,872	65,533	37,409	21,789
Virginia Beach city, VA	1,719	846	320	—	—	—	—
Albuquerque city, NM	26,570	15,157	11,020	6,238	3,785	—	—
Oakland city, CA	284,063	216,261	150,174	66,960	48,682	34,555	10,500
Pittsburg city, PA	669,817	588,343	533,905	321,616	238,617	156,389	86,076
Sacramento city, CA	93,750	65,908	44,696	29,282	26,386	21,420	16,283
Minneapolis city, MN	464,356	380,582	301,408	202,718	164,738	46,887	13,066
Tulsa city, OK	141,258	72,075	18,182	1,390	—	—	—
Honolulu CDP, HI	137,582	83,327	52,183	39,306	22,907	—	—
Cincinnati city, OH	451,160	401,247	363,591	325,902	296,908	255,139	216,239
Miami city, FL	110,637	29,571	5,471	1,681	—	—	—
Fresno city, CA	52,513	45,086	24,892	12,470	10,818	1,112	—
Omaha city, NE	214,006	191,601	124,096	102,555	140,452	30,518	16,083
Toledo city, OH	290,718	243,164	168,497	131,822	81,434	50,137	31,854
Buffalo city, NY	573,076	506,775	423,715	352,387	255,664	155,134	117,714

Table 1-14. Population of the Top 50 Incorporated Places: 1790-1990 (continued)

Incorporated place	1860	1850	1840	1830	1820	1810	1800	1790
New York city, NY	1,174,779	696,115	391,114	242,278	152,056	119,734	79,216	49,401
Los Angeles city, CA	4,385	1,610	—	—	—	—	—	—
Chicago city, IL	112,172	29,963	4,470	—	—	—	—	—
Houston city, TX	4,845	2,396	—	—	—	—	—	—
Philadelphia city, PA	565,529	121,376	93,665	80,462	63,802	53,722	41,220	28,522
San Diego city, CA	731	—	—	—	—	—	—	—
Detroit city, MI	45,619	21,019	9,102	2,222	1,422	—	—	—
Dallas city, TX	—	—	—	—	—	—	—	—
Phoenix city, AZ	—	—	—	—	—	—	—	—
San Antonio city, TX	8,235	3,488	—	—	—	—	—	—
San Jose city, CA	—	—	—	—	—	—	—	—
Baltimore city, MD	212,418	169,054	102,313	80,620	62,738	46,555	26,514	135,003
Indianapolis (remainder), IN	18,611	8,091	2,692	—	—	—	—	—
San Fransisco city, CA	56,802	3,477	—	—	—	—	—	—
Jacksonville city (remainder), FL	2,118	1,045	—	—	—	—	—	—
Columbus city, OH	18,554	17,882	6,048	2,435	—	—	—	—
Milwaukee city, WI	45,246	20,061	1,712	—	—	—	—	—
Memphis city, TN	22,623	8,841	—	—	—	—	—	—
Washington city, DC	61,122	40,001	23,364	18,826	13,247	8,208	3,210	—
Boston city, MA	177,840	136,881	93,383	61,392	43,298	33,787	24,937	18,320
Seattle city, WA	—	—	—	—	—	—	—	—
El Paso city, TX	—	—	—	—	—	—	—	—
Cleveland city, OH	43,417	17,034	6,071	1,076	606	—	—	—
New Orleans city, LA	168,675	116,375	102,193	46,082	27,176	17,242	—	—
Nashville-Davidson (remainder), TN	16,988	10,165	6,929	5,566	—	—	345	—
Denver city, CO	4,749	—	—	—	—	—	—	—
Austin city, TX	3,494	629	—	—	—	—	—	—
Fort Worth city, TX	—	—	—	—	—	—	—	—
Oklahoma City city, OK	—	—	—	—	—	—	—	—
Portland city, OR	2,874	—	—	—	—	—	—	—
Kansas City city, MO	4,418	—	—	—	—	—	—	—
Long Beach city, CA	—	—	—	—	—	—	—	—
Tucson city, AZ	—	—	—	—	—	—	—	—
St. Louis city, MO	160,773	77,860	16,469	4,977	—	—	—	—
Charlotte city, NC	2,265	1,065	—	—	—	—	—	—
Atlanta city, GA	9,554	2,572	—	—	—	—	—	—
Virginia Beach city, VA	—	—	—	—	—	—	—	—
Albuquerque city, NM	—	—	—	—	—	—	—	—
Oakland city, CA	1,543	—	—	—	—	—	—	—
Pittsburg city, PA	49,221	46,601	21,115	12,568	7,243	4,768	1,565	—
Sacramento city, CA	13,785	6,820	—	—	—	—	—	—
Minneapolis city, MN	2,564	—	—	—	—	—	—	—
Tulsa city, OK	—	—	—	—	—	—	—	—
Honolulu CDP, HI	—	—	—	—	—	—	—	—
Cincinnati city, OH	161,044	115,435	46,338	24,831	9,642	2,540	—	—
Miami city, FL	—	—	—	—	—	—	—	—
Fresno city, CA	—	—	—	—	—	—	—	—
Omaha city, NE	1,883	—	—	—	—	—	—	—
Toledo city, OH	13,768	3,829	1,222	—	—	—	—	—
Buffalo city, NY	81,129	42,261	18,213	8,668	2,095	1,508	—	—

Source: U.S. Bureau of the Census, "Population and Housing Unit Counts," 1990 Census of Population and Housing, U.S. Government
   Printing Office, Washington, D.C., 1993, Table 46.

Bureau of the Census began, in 1950, to define metropolitan areas. The definition and terminology designating such areas has changed slightly across censuses since that time. Metropolitan areas are usually one or more whole counties containing the central city (metropolis) and extending into the hinterland sufficiently far to encompass the immediate area of trade, commuting, and the "zone of daily influence." The current definition for Metropolitan Statistical Areas, or MSAs, is provided in the Definition Box.

The number and population of MSAs (and Consolidated MSAs, or CMSAs) by population size-class in 1990 is presented for 1990, 1980 and 1970 in Table 1-15. There are currently 268 MSAs and CMSAs in the United States, of which nearly half are less than 250,000 in population and of which only 40 have over a million residents. These forty largest MSAs, however, include over two-thirds of the entire metropolitan population over the two decades since 1970. Just as the population has become more urbanized and dominated by urban centers, these largest MSAs represent a concentration of metropolitan influence over a large portion of the country's population in a relatively few geographic places in the country. In fact, nearly a majority of the metropolitan population, and well over a third of the entire United States population, reside in just 15 MSAs with an average of over 2.5 million residents each.

The dominance of the largest MSAs can be expected to continue into the near future. Despite a relatively small increase in the population of these areas during the 1970 to 1980 decade, only the very smallest MSAs of less than 250,000 residents lagged behind in population growth during the more recent decade of 1980 to 1990. If the size of larger MSAs increases as uniformly as it has over the recent decades there may be a slow rise in the number of the dominant MSAs in the country. However, in the short run, it may be equally likely that population redistribution to the largest of these MSAs will continue to concentrate population among the largest of the MSAs and restrict any growth in the number of such MSAs.

The regional character of growth in the metropolitan population gives reason to suspect that substantial processes of change are at work behind the apparent stability of metropolitan areas. In Table 1-16 the metropolitan and nonmetropolitan populations are broken down by region and state for the past three censuses spanning two decades. Not surprisingly, the greatest gains in metropolitan population have been in those regions of the South and West which have experienced the greatest population growth. Metropolitan growth in the South has, however, slowed its pace considerably while there has been only a very slight downturn in that of the West. The greatest growth in nonmetropolitan population has been in the Pacific and New England divisions. This growth reverses a decline in New England but represents a longstanding continuing pattern of general population growth in the West. The fastest growth of metropolitan population occurred in Nevada during the 1980 to 1990 decade and in Idaho during the 1970 to 1980 decade. Meanwhile, the fastest growth in nonmetropolitan population occurred in Alaska during the 1980 to 1990 decade (followed closely by Nevada and Hawaii) and in Wyoming during the 1970 to 1980 decade (followed closely by Hawaii and Nevada).

Projections of Regional and State Populations

Taking into account recent trends, the Bureau of

Table 1-15. Number and Population of Metropolitan Areas, by Population Size-Class in 1990: 1970-1990

Population size-class in 1990	Number in 1990	Population 1990		Population 1980		Population 1970		Population percent change	
		Number in millions	Percent in each class	Number in millions	Percent in each class	Number in millions	Percent in each class	1980-1990	1970-1980
Total	268	197.7	100.0	176.9	100.0	159.6	100.0	11.8	10.8
1,000,000 or more	40	132.9	67.2	118.7	67.1	109.4	68.5	12.0	8.5
2,500,000 or more	15	94.1	47.6	84.3	47.7	79.0	49.5	11.6	6.7
1,000,000 to 2,499,999	25	38.8	19.6	34.4	19.4	30.4	19.0	12.8	13.2
250,000 to 999,999	96	46.4	23.5	41.2	23.3	35.5	22.2	12.6	16.1
500,000 to 999,999	33	24.3	12.3	21.4	12.1	18.2	11.4	13.6	17.6
250,000 to 499,999	63	22.0	11.1	19.8	11.2	17.3	10.8	11.1	14.5
100,000 to 249,999	110	16.6	8.4	15.2	8.6	13.0	8.1	9.2	16.9
Less than 100,000	22	1.9	1.0	1.8	1.0	1.7	1.1	5.6	5.9

Table header: **CMSAs and MSAs[1]**

[1] CMSA=consolidated metropolitan statistical area and MSA=metropolitan statistical area as defined by the U.S. Office of Management and Budget, June 30, 1993

Source: U.S. Bureau of the Census, "Statistical Abstract of the United States: 1994," U.S. Government Printing Office, Washington, D.C., 1994, Table No. 40.

Table 1-16. Metropolitan[1] and Nonmetropolitan Area Population, by Region, Division, and State: 1970-1990

Region, division, and state	Metropolitan population					Nonmetropolitan population				
	Population, in thousands			Percent change		Population, in thousands			Percent change	
	1990	1980	1970	1980-1990	1970-1980	1990	1980	1970	1980-1990	1970-1980
United States, total	197,725	176,893	156,085	11.8	13.3	50,985	49,649	47,217	2.7	5.2
Northeast region	45,455	44,047	43,890	3.2	0.4	5,354	5,090	5,171	5.2	-1.6
New England	11,127	10,470	9,822	6.3	6.6	2,080	1,878	2,026	10.8	-7.3
Middle Atlantic	34,328	33,576	34,068	2.2	-1.4	3,274	3,212	3,145	1.9	2.1
Midwest region	43,691	42,557	40,487	2.7	5.1	15,978	16,310	16,103	-2.0	1.3
East North Central	33,391	33,031	31,621	1.1	4.5	8,618	8,652	8,642	-0.4	0.1
West North Central	10,300	9,526	8,867	8.1	7.4	7,360	7,658	7,461	-3.9	2.6
South region	63,092	53,634	42,387	17.6	26.5	22,354	21,733	20,426	2.9	6.4
South Atlantic	34,294	28,226	22,051	21.5	28.0	9,273	8,732	8,628	6.2	1.2
East South Central	8,563	8,057	7,018	6.3	14.8	6,613	6,609	5,790	0.1	14.1
West South Central	20,235	17,351	13,318	16.6	30.3	6,468	6,392	6,008	1.2	6.4
West region	45,487	36,655	29,320	24.1	25.0	7,299	6,516	5,518	12.0	18.1
Mountain	9,605	7,645	5,155	25.6	48.3	4,054	3,726	3,135	8.8	18.9
Pacific	35,882	29,010	24,165	23.7	20.0	3,245	2,790	2,383	16.3	17.1
New England										
Maine	443	405	365	9.4	11.0	785	721	628	8.9	14.8
New Hampshire	659	535	404	23.2	32.4	450	386	333	16.6	15.9
Vermont	152	133	99	14.3	34.3	411	378	346	8.7	9.2
Massachusetts	5,788	5,530	5,266	4.7	5.0	229	207	423	10.6	-51.1
Rhode Island	938	886	868	5.9	2.1	65	61	82	6.6	-25.6
Connecticut	3,148	2,982	2,819	5.6	5.8	140	126	213	11.1	-40.8
Middle Atlantic										
New York	16,515	16,144	16,795	2.3	-3.9	1,475	1,414	1,447	4.3	-2.3
New Jersey	7,730	7,365	7,171	5.0	2.7	...	...	...	—	—
Pennsylvania	10,083	10,067	10,102	0.2	-0.3	1,799	1,798	1,698	0.1	5.9
East North Central										
Ohio	8,826	8,791	8,565	0.4	2.6	2,021	2,007	2,092	0.7	-4.1
Indiana	3,962	3,885	3,551	2.0	9.4	1,582	1,605	1,644	-1.4	-2.4
Illinois	9,574	9,461	9,125	1.2	3.7	1,857	1,967	1,986	-5.6	-1.0
Michigan	7,698	7,719	7,361	-0.3	4.9	1,598	1,543	1,521	3.6	1.4
Wisconsin	3,331	3,176	3,019	4.9	5.2	1,561	1,530	1,399	2.0	9.4
West North Central										
Minnesota	3,011	2,674	2,434	12.6	9.9	1,364	1,402	1,373	-2.7	2.1
Iowa	1,200	1,198	1,154	0.2	3.8	1,577	1,716	1,671	-8.1	2.7
Missouri	3,491	3,314	3,170	5.3	4.5	1,626	1,603	1,508	1.4	6.3
North Dakota	257	234	196	9.8	19.4	381	418	422	-8.9	-0.9
South Dakota	221	194	155	13.9	25.2	475	497	512	-4.4	-2.9
Nebraska	787	728	650	8.1	12.0	791	842	835	-6.1	0.8
Kansas	1,333	1,184	1,109	12.6	6.8	1,145	1,180	1,140	-3.0	3.5

Table 1-16. Metropolitan[1] and Nonmetropolitan Area Population, by Region, Division, and State: 1970-1990 (continued)

Region, division, and state	Metropolitan population					Nonmetropolitan population				
	Population, in thousands			Percent change		Population, in thousands			Percent change	
	1990	1980	1970	1980-1990	1970-1980	1990	1980	1970	1980-1990	1970-1980
South Atlantic										
Delaware	553	496	386	11.5	28.5	113	98	162	15.3	-39.5
Maryland	4,439	3,920	3,668	13.2	6.9	343	297	255	15.5	16.5
District of Columbia	607	638	757	-4.9	-15.7	…	…	…	—	—
Virginia	4,773	3,966	3,279	20.3	21.0	1,414	1,381	1,373	2.4	0.6
West Virginia	748	796	683	-6.0	16.5	1,045	1,155	1,061	-9.5	8.9
North Carolina	4,376	3,749	2,755	16.7	36.1	2,253	2,131	2,330	5.7	-8.5
South Carolina	2,423	2,114	1,504	14.6	40.6	1,064	1,006	1,087	5.8	-7.5
Georgia	4,352	3,507	2,807	24.1	24.9	2,127	1,956	1,781	8.7	9.8
Florida	12,023	9,039	6,213	33.0	45.5	915	708	578	29.2	22.5
East South Central										
Kentucky	1,780	1,735	1,550	2.6	11.9	1,906	1,925	1,671	-1.0	15.2
Tennessee	3,298	3,045	2,630	8.3	15.8	1,579	1,546	1,296	2.1	19.3
Alabama	2,710	2,560	2,274	5.9	12.6	1,331	1,334	1,171	-0.2	13.9
Mississippi	776	716	564	8.4	27.0	1,798	1,805	1,653	-0.4	9.2
West South Central										
Arkansas	1,040	963	730	8.0	31.9	1,311	1,323	1,193	-0.9	10.9
Louisiana	3,160	3,125	2,439	1.1	28.1	1,060	1,082	1,205	-2.0	-10.2
Oklahoma	1,870	1,724	1,432	8.5	20.4	1,276	1,301	1,127	-1.9	15.4
Texas	14,166	11,539	8,716	22.8	32.4	2,821	2,686	2,483	5.0	8.2
Mountain										
Montana	191	189	169	1.1	11.8	608	598	525	1.7	13.9
Idaho	296	257	112	15.2	129.5	711	687	601	3.5	14.3
Wyoming	134	141	108	-5.0	30.6	319	329	225	-3.0	46.2
Colorado	2,686	2,326	1,772	15.5	31.3	608	563	438	8.0	28.5
New Mexico	842	675	456	24.7	48.0	673	628	562	7.2	11.7
Arizona	3,106	2,264	1,323	37.2	71.1	559	453	453	23.4	0.0
Utah	1,336	1,128	822	18.4	37.2	387	333	238	16.2	39.9
Nevada	1,014	666	394	52.3	69.0	188	135	94	39.3	43.6
Pacific										
Washington	4,036	3,366	2,752	19.9	22.3	830	766	661	8.4	15.9
Oregon	1,985	1,799	1,415	10.3	27.1	858	834	676	2.9	23.4
California	28,799	22,907	19,241	25.7	19.1	961	760	730	26.4	4.1
Alaska	226	174	126	29.9	38.1	324	227	176	42.7	29.0
Hawaii	836	763	631	9.6	20.9	272	202	139	34.7	45.3

[1] In 1990 and 1980, metropolitan refers to 250 metropolitan statistical areas (MSAs) and 18 consolidated metropolitan statistical areas (CMSAs) and in 1970, metropolitan refers to 263 MSAs and 20 CMSAs as defined by the U.S. Office of Management and Budget, June 30, 1993 and June 30, 1989 respectively.

Source: U.S. Bureau of the Census, "Statistical Abstract of the United States: 1994," Table No. 41 and "Statistical Abstract of the United States: 1990," Table No. 35, U.S. Government Printing Office, Washington, D.C., 1994 and 1990.

Table 1-17. Estimate and Projections of the Resident Population of Regions, Divisions, and States: 1990-2020 [numbers in thousands]

Region, division, and state	Population 1990	Population projections 2000	Population projections 2010	Population projections 2020	Percent change 1990 to 2000	Percent change 2000 to 2010	Percent change 2010 to 2020	Components of change 1990-2000 Natural increase	Components of change 1990-2000 Net migration	Components of change 2000-2010 Natural increase	Components of change 2000-2010 Net migration	Components of change 2010-2020 Natural increase	Components of change 2010-2020 Net migration
United States, total	249,391	276,241	300,431	325,942	10.8	8.8	8.5	17,707	8,794	14,698	8,794	15,779	8,792
Northeast region	50,837	51,885	53,301	55,352	2.1	2.7	3.8	2,302	-1,386	1,252	-6	1,475	414
New England	13,204	13,217	13,754	14,527	0.1	4.1	5.6	597	-615	274	210	341	377
Middle Atlantic	37,633	38,668	39,547	40,824	2.8	2.3	3.2	1,707	-769	977	-215	1,134	36
Midwest region	59,781	63,837	66,332	68,984	6.8	3.9	4.0	3,548	341	2,863	-542	2,955	-543
East North Central	42,091	44,806	46,258	47,799	6.5	3.2	3.3	2,585	14	1,990	-651	2,050	-658
West North Central	17,690	19,031	20,074	21,185	7.6	5.5	5.5	965	326	871	110	904	117
South region	85,734	97,241	107,385	117,498	13.4	10.4	9.4	5,880	5,545	4,594	20,282	4,463	5,248
South Atlantic	43,732	50,004	55,321	60,610	14.3	10.6	9.6	2,503	3,760	1,566	3,566	1,391	3,656
East South Central	15,210	16,762	17,941	19,078	10.2	7.0	6.3	843	686	613	523	531	535
West South Central	26,791	30,476	34,124	37,809	13.8	12.0	10.8	2,534	1,099	2,414	1,194	2,540	1,056
West region	53,039	63,277	73,412	84,109	19.3	16.0	14.6	5,976	4,298	5,989	4,064	6,887	3,679
Mountain	13,734	16,889	19,094	21,147	23.0	13.1	10.8	1,428	1,690	1,470	685	1,533	445
Pacific	39,305	46,388	54,318	62,961	18.0	17.1	15.9	4,547	2,610	4,518	3,382	5,354	3,234
New England													
Maine	1,229	1,240	1,309	1,400	0.9	5.6	7.0	37	-30	16	47	17	68
New Hampshire	1,108	1,165	1,280	1,399	5.1	9.9	9.3	59	...	35	75	39	76
Vermont	564	592	623	658	5.0	5.2	5.6	31	-3	22	5	24	8
Massachusetts	6,012	5,950	6,097	6,363	-1.0	2.5	4.4	252	-342	104	22	133	117
Rhode Island	1,004	998	1,034	1,090	-0.6	3.6	5.4	36	-47	15	17	25	29
Connecticut	3,287	3,271	3,412	3,617	-0.5	4.3	6.0	177	-187	81	46	106	85
Middle Atlantic													
New York	18,002	18,237	18,546	19,111	1.3	1.7	3.0	1,030	-877	688	-412	774	-235
New Jersey	7,734	8,135	8,562	9,058	5.2	5.2	5.8	386	43	202	194	244	221
Pennsylvania	11,897	12,296	12,438	12,656	3.4	1.2	1.8	292	70	86	8	116	52
East North Central													
Ohio	10,866	11,453	11,659	11,870	5.4	1.8	1.8	533	17	358	-182	332	-160
Indiana	5,557	6,045	6,286	6,488	8.8	4.0	3.2	317	169	244	-19	228	-48
Illinois	11,452	12,168	12,652	13,218	6.3	4.0	4.5	784	-100	643	-2,680	714	-175
Michigan	9,312	9,759	10,033	10,377	4.8	2.8	3.4	697	-276	530	-277	571	-253
Wisconsin	4,904	5,381	5,629	5,846	9.7	4.6	3.9	253	209	218	14	206	-14
West North Central													
Minnesota	4,386	4,824	5,127	5,426	10.0	6.3	5.8	298	126	262	24	267	5
Iowa	2,780	2,930	2,981	3,038	5.4	1.7	1.9	103	39	93	-49	90	-44
Missouri	5,125	5,437	5,760	6,123	6.1	5.9	6.3	232	63	181	125	183	155
North Dakota	638	643	676	719	0.8	5.1	6.4	30	-26	30	1	37	4
South Dakota	698	770	815	863	10.3	5.8	5.9	43	26	50	-8	57	-11
Nebraska	1,581	1,704	1,793	1,885	7.8	5.2	5.1	83	36	83	...	87	-1
Kansas	2,481	2,722	2,922	3,130	9.7	7.3	7.1	174	63	171	24	184	16

Table 1-17. Estimate and Projections of the Resident Population of Regions, Divisions, and States: 1990-2020 [numbers in thousands] (continued)

Region, division, and state	Population 1990	Population projections 2000	Population projections 2010	Population projections 2020	Percent change 1990 to 2000	Percent change 2000 to 2010	Percent change 2010 to 2020	Components of change 1990-2000 Natural increase	Components of change 1990-2000 Net migration	Components of change 2000-2010 Natural increase	Components of change 2000-2010 Net migration	Components of change 2010-2020 Natural increase	Components of change 2010-2020 Net migration
South Atlantic													
Delaware	669	759	815	871	13.5	7.4	6.9	41	47	28	26	24	28
Maryland	4,797	5,322	5,782	6,289	10.9	8.6	8.8	399	144	296	149	327	163
District of Columbia	605	537	577	636	-11.2	7.4	10.2	24	-99	16	28	26	36
Virginia	6,206	7,048	7,728	8,388	13.6	9.6	8.5	442	403	312	345	294	339
West Virginia	1,795	1,840	1,842	1,852	2.5	0.1	0.5	16	13	-5	1	-13	12
North Carolina	6,650	7,617	8,341	9,014	14.5	9.5	8.1	372	595	221	471	174	465
South Carolina	3,501	3,932	4,311	4,685	12.3	9.6	8.7	242	184	163	204	143	213
Georgia	6,507	7,637	8,553	9,426	17.4	12.0	10.2	555	565	464	439	450	398
Florida	13,003	15,313	17,372	19,449	17.8	13.4	12.0	412	1,908	51	1,906	-36	2,001
East South Central													
Kentucky	3,691	3,989	4,160	4,313	8.1	4.3	3.7	183	99	133	26	109	27
Tennessee	4,892	5,538	6,007	6,434	13.2	8.5	7.1	236	404	168	286	135	270
Alabama	4,050	4,485	4,856	5,231	10.7	8.3	7.7	261	179	196	164	194	164
Mississippi	2,577	2,750	2,918	3,100	6.7	6.1	6.2	163	4	117	47	93	77
West South Central													
Arkansas	2,355	2,578	2,782	3,005	9.5	7.9	8.0	95	120	65	130	53	156
Louisiana	4,227	4,478	4,808	5,193	5.9	7.4	8.0	338	-105	295	32	299	70
Oklahoma	3,151	3,382	3,683	4,020	7.3	8.9	9.2	141	58	127	165	134	192
Texas	17,058	20,039	22,850	25,592	17.5	14.0	12.0	1,960	1,030	1,927	868	2,053	641
Mountain													
Montana	801	920	996	1,071	14.9	8.3	7.5	48	66	53	19	57	14
Idaho	1,013	1,290	1,454	1,600	27.3	12.7	10.0	105	174	121	40	124	17
Wyoming	455	522	596	658	14.7	14.2	10.4	38	30	48	26	58	6
Colorado	3,311	4,059	4,494	4,871	22.6	10.7	8.4	303	430	299	126	297	65
New Mexico	1,522	1,823	2,082	2,338	19.8	14.2	12.3	161	135	166	83	189	58
Arizona	3,682	4,437	5,074	5,713	20.5	14.4	12.6	336	402	297	321	308	305
Utah	1,732	2,148	2,462	2,749	24.0	14.6	11.7	298	115	342	-25	358	-74
Nevada	1,218	1,691	1,935	2,145	38.8	14.4	10.9	141	339	147	98	144	61
Pacific													
Washington	4,896	6,070	7,025	7,960	24.0	15.7	13.3	407	761	420	515	458	448
Oregon	2,858	3,404	3,876	4,367	19.1	13.9	12.7	171	368	188	274	215	261
California	29,883	34,888	41,085	47,953	16.7	17.8	16.7	3,735	1,348	3,659	2,535	4,389	2,467
Alaska	554	699	781	866	26.2	11.7	10.9	99	44	121	-39	140	-56
Hawaii	1,114	1,327	1,551	1,815	19.1	16.9	17.0	134	91	134	99	150	117

Source: U.S. Bureau of the Census, Current Population Reports, "Population Projections for States, by Age, Sex, Race, and Hispanic Origin: 1993 to 2020," Tables 1 and 2, U.S. Government Printing Office, Washington, D.C., 1992 and 1994.

the Census has prepared projections of the future population of each state. The projections are reported for regions, subregions and states for the year 2000, 2010 and 2020 alongside the 1990 census population in Table 1-17. These projections correspond to the medium assumptions in Table 1-3, discussed above. Projections are also broken down into the components of population change due to natural increase (births minus deaths) and net migration. The total population of the United States is forecast to grow from roughly 250 million in 1990 to just over 300 million by the year 2010 and to roughly 326 million by the year 2020. For the three decades following the 1990 Census the forecast percentage increase in the population declines from 10.8 percent growth between 1990 and 2000, to 8.8 and then 8.5 percent in the decades leading up to 2020. The contribution of natural increase to this growth is forecast to decline and then rise, in both absolute terms and relative to growth from migration. For the current decade, growth from natural increase is forecast to be twice that of migration. This figure is forecast to fall to roughly 1.7 times that of migration between 2000 and 2010, and then rise slightly to 1.8 times that of migration during the 2010 and 2020 decades. Again, readers should beware of the many changes which might alter these forecast growth figures.

Within regions, New England is the only region forecast to have negative growth from net migration in the present decade. This loss of population through migration is forecast to slowly abate, but to remain at a slight loss in the coming decade of 2000 to 2010 and becoming only slightly positive in the next decade between 2010 and 2020. Meanwhile, the Midwest is forecast to have an increasing net loss of population due to out-migration over the first two decades of the new century. Percentage population growth is expected to decline, or remain nearly stable, across all regions and divisions of the country except for the Northeast. The slightly rising percentage growth in the Northeast parallels the decline in the loss of population due to negative net migration and a slight rise in natural increase forecast for the decade from 2010 to 2020. Despite this rise in the percentage growth in the Northeast, the most rapidly growing areas are clearly still forecast to remain in the South and West.

Among states, those with most rapid growth between 1990 and the year 2000 are forecast to be Nevada, Idaho, Alaska, Utah, Washington, Colorado and Arizona. Only Montana and Wyoming are forecast to experience significantly less than a 20 percent growth rate over this decade among the states of the West. In the first decade of the new century, 2000 to 2010, the role of Pacific rim and Hispanic migration is clearly reflected in the forecasts for a growth of more than 15 percent for only the three states of Hawaii, California and Washington. In the following decade, 2010 to 2020, these same three states are forecast to remain those with the highest percentage growth.

Conclusion

The data in this introduction provide only a brief, if informative, glimpse of the United States population. In the remaining chapters of this book, greater attention will be paid to even more detailed analysis of the general population composition and demographic trends in the United States population. Throughout, we emphasize the use of a wide variety of the most recently available demographic data (see Chapter 2 for an overview of data resources). However, respect for the long-term historical patterns of change at work in the population is equally important to appreciate the significance of demographic trends and to avoid historical judgements based upon only a short period of experience. Therefore, wherever appropriate, the history of the United States population and historically available data are also emphasized. The analysis of long-term trends of population growth always raises questions concerning the effects of population growth and resources for the population in the future. We devote a special introductory chapter to these more general environmental and resource concerns (see Chapter 3).

Following the three introductory chapters, this text details the demographic components and behaviors affecting the dynamics of population growth, and the relationship of these demographic phenomena to the socially and culturally defined groups which make up the United States population. Section II contains chapters devoted to mortality, nuptiality, fertility, health and migration. The social composition of the population is further elaborated in detailed chapters on race and ethnicity, age and gender, families and households, and school enrollment and educational attainment, in Section III. Finally, Section IV presents the detailed economic characteristics of the population with chapters on the labor force and employment, occupation and industry, and on income, poverty and wealth of the population. Through these chapters the reader will gain insight into the population of the United States, its history and its projected future as we enter into the new century.

Bibliography

Ahlburg, Dennis A. "The Census Bureau's New Projections of the U.S. Population." Population and Development Review 19(1993):159-74.

Anderson, Margo. The American Census: A Social History. New Haven: Yale University Press. 1988.

Baldassare, Mark. Trouble in Paradise: The Suburban Transformation in America. New York: Columbia University Press. 1986.

Beale, Calvin L., and Johnson, Kenneth M. "The Rural Rebound Revisited." American Demographics 17(1995):46-55.

Bean, Frank, and Tienda, Marta. The Hispanic Population of the United States. New York: Russell Sage Foundation. 1987.

Bogue, Donald J. Principles of Demography. (Chapter 7, "Population Composition: The Demographic Variables.") New York: John Wiley and Sons, 1969.

Bogue, Donald J., Arriaga, Eduardo A., and Anderton, Douglas L. Readings in Population Research Methodology. Volumes I-VIII. Chicago: Social Development Center Press/UNFPA, 1993.

Bouvier, Leon F. and De Vita, Carol J. The Baby Boom--Entering Midlife. PRB Bulletin 46(3). Washington, D.C.: Population Reference Bureau, 1991.

Bradbury, Katherine L., Downs, Anthony, and Small, Kenneth A. Urban Decline and the Future of American Cities. Washington D.C.: Brookings Institution Press. 1982.

Cafferty, Pastora San Juan, Chiswick, Barry, Greeley, Andrew M., and Sullivan, Teresa A. The Dilemma of American Immigration: Beyond the Golden Door. New Brunswick: Transaction Press. 1983.

Coale, Ansley J., and Zelnick, Melvin. New Estimates of Fertility and Population in the U. S. Princeton, NJ: Princeton University Press, 1963.

Cisneros, Henry G. (ed.). Interwoven Destinies: Cities and the Nation. New York: Norton. 1993.

De Vita, Carol J. United States at Mid-Decade. PRB Bulletin 50(4). Washington, D.C.: Population Reference Bureau, 1995.

Dogan, Mattei, and Kasarda, John D. (eds.) The Metropolis Era: A World of Giant Cities. Newbury Park: Sage Press. 1988.

Dublin, Louis I. (ed.). The American People: Studies in Population. Philadelphia: The American Academy of Political and Social Science, 1936.

Easterlin, Richard A. "Long Swings in the United States Demographic and Economic Growth: Some Findings in Historical Pattern." Demography 2 (1965):490-507.

_____. Birth and Fortune: The Impact of Numbers on Personal Welfare. Chicago: University of Chicago Press. 1987.

_____, Shaeffer, Christine M., and Macunovich, Diane J. "Will the Baby Boomers Be Less Well Off Than Their Parents? Income, Wealth, and Family Circumstances Over the Life Cycle in the United States." Population and Development Review 19(1993): 497-522.

Farley, Reynolds. Blacks and Whites: Narrowing the Gap? Cambridge: Harvard University Press. 1984.

_____ (ed.). State of the Union: America in the 1990s. Vols. I-II. New York: Russell Sage Foundation, 1995.

Frey, William H. Metropolitan America: Beyond the Transition. PRB Bulletin 45(2). Washington, D.C.: Population Reference Bureau, 1990.

_____, and Farley, Reynolds. "Latino, Asian, and Black Segregation in U.S. Metropolitan Areas: Are Multiethnic Metros Different?" Demography 33(1996):35-50.

_____, and Speare, Alda, Jr. "The Revival of Metropolitan Population Growth in the United States: An Assessment of Findings from the 1990 Census." Population and Development Review 18(1992):129-46.

Fuguitt, Glenn V., and Brown, David L. "Residential Preferences and Population Redistribution: 1972-1988." Demography 27(1990):589-600.

Gober, Patricia. Americans on the Move. PRB Bulletin 48(3). Washington, D.C.: Population Reference Bureau, 1993.

Haupt, Arthur, and Kane, Thomas. United States Population Handbook, 3rd edition. Washington, D.C.: Population Reference Bureau, 1991.

Hauser, Philip M. Population Perspectives. (Chapter 2, "The United States Population Explosion: The Facts.") New Brunswick, NJ: Rutgers University Press, 1960.

Jaynes, Gerald David, and Williams, Robert M. Jr. (eds). A Common Destiny: Blacks and American Society. Washington D.C.: National Academy of Sciences. 1989.

Kreps, Juanita M. Economics of a Stationary Population. A Report to the National Science Foundation. Washington, D.C.: U.S. Government Printing Office, 1977.

Lieberson, Stanley. Ethnic Patterns in American Cities. New York: The Free Press, 1963.

_____. A Piece of the Pie: Blacks and White Immigrants Since 1880. Berkeley: University of California Press. 1980.

Long, Larry H., and DeAre, Diana. "U.S. Population Redistribution: A Perspective on the Nonmetropolitan Turnaround." Population and Development Review 14(1988):433-50.

Lorimer, Frank, Winston, Ellen, and Kiser, Louise K. Foundations of American Population Policy. (Chapter 2, "Population Trends in the United States.") New York: Harper and Brothers, 1940.

Macunovich, Diane J., Esterline, Richard A., Crimmins, Eileen M., and Shaeffer, Christine M. "Echoes of the Baby Boom and Bust." Demography 32(1995):17-28.

Martin, Phillip, and Midgley, Elizabeth. Immigration to the United States: Journey to an Uncertain Destination. PRB Bulletin 49(2). Washington, D.C.: Population Reference Bureau, 1994.

Massey, Douglas S., and Denton, Nancy A. American Apartheid: Segregation and the Making of the Underclass. Cambridge: Harvard University Press, 1993.

Massey, Douglas S., and Singer, Audrey. "New Estimates of Undocumented Mexican Migration and the Probability of Apprehensions." Demography 32(1995):203-14.

National Resources Committee. The Problems of a Changing Population. (Chapter 1, "The Trend of Population.") Washington, D.C.: U.S. Government Printing Office, 1938.

O'Hare, William P. America's Minorities—The Demographics of Diversity. PRB Bulletin 47(4). Washington, D.C.: Population Reference Bureau, 1992.

O'Malley, Sharon. "The Rural Rebound." American Demographics 16(1994):24-31.

Portes, Alejandro, and Rumbaut, Ruben. Immigrant America: A Portrait. Berkeley: University of California Press. 1990.

President's Research Committee on Social Trends. Recent Social Trends in the United States. New York: McGraw-Hill. 1933.

Preston, Samuel H. "Children and the Elderly: Divergent Paths for America's Dependents." Demography 21(1984):435-57.

Rogers, Andrei, and Woodward, Jennifer. "The Sources of Regional Elderly Population Growth: Migration and Aging-in-place." The Professional Geographer 40(1988):450-59.

Rusk, David. Cities without Suburbs. Washington D.C.: Woodrow Wilson Center Press, 1995.

Taeuber, Conrad, and Taeuber, Irene B. The Changing Population of the United States. New York: John Wiley and Sons, 1958.

Taeuber, Irene B., and Taeuber, Conrad. People of the United States in the 20th Century. (Chapter I, "Increase, Expansion, and Concentration," Chapter IV, "Age: Formation, Structure, Differentiation" and Chapter XI, "Population Change.") Washington, D.C.: U.S. Bureau of the Census, 1971.

Thompson, W.S., and Whelpton, P.K. Population Trends in the United States. New York: McGraw-Hill, 1933.

Treas, Judith. Older Americans in the 1990s and Beyond. PRB Bulletin 50(2). Washington, D.C.: Population Reference Bureau, 1995.

U.S. Bureau of the Census. General Population Characteristics, 1990 Census of Population. Washington D.C.: U.S. Government Printing Office, 1992.

_____. Historical Statistics of the United States, Part I, (Series A 119-134). Washington D.C.: U.S. Government Printing Office, 1975.

_____. Household and Family Characteristics: March 1990 and 1989. Current Population Reports, Series P-20 No. 447. Washington D.C.: U.S. Government Printing Office, 1990.

_____. Marital Status and Living Arrangements: March 1990. Current Population Characteristics, Series P-20 No 450. Washington, D.C.: U.S. Government Printing Office, 1991.

_____. Poverty in the United States: 1991. Current Population Reports, Series P-60 No. 181. Washington, D.C.: U.S. Government Printing Office, 1992.

_____. Population Projections of the United States, by Age, Race, and Hispanic Origin: 1993 to 2050. Current Population Reports, Series P-25 No. 1104. Washington, D.C.: U.S. Government Printing Office, 1993.

_____. Statistical Abstract of the United States: 1994. Washington D.C.: U.S. Government Printing Office, 1994.

Wilson, William J. The Declining Significance of Race. Chicago: University of Chicago Press, 1980.

_____. The Truly Disadvantaged: The Inner City, the Underclass, and Public Policy. Chicago: University of Chicago Press. 1987.

2

SOURCES OF UNITED STATES POPULATION DATA

Understanding population data from the United States also requires an understanding of their sources. This is necessary to gauge the validity and reliability of the data, and to decide what kinds of data can be combined in different ways. The Bureau of the Census and other federal agencies have often been in the forefront of developing innovative techniques of measuring and analyzing social and economic data, so this task can give insights into the history of social science as well.

Constraints on the U.S. Census

Most federal agencies that keep statistics operate under a set of constraints seldom found in other nations. There is a tradition of voluntary compliance: most government agencies (and the Congress that directly oversees their operations) prefer to use normative rather than coercive means in collecting data, and to appeal to the respondents' sense of patriotism and cooperation with the government rather than threatening retribution for noncompliance.

Americans are also highly mobile; they move frequently within a large land mass. Even if the United States had ever had a system of household or individual registration with local police authorities similar to that found in many other nations, it probably would have been largely ineffective in generating much useful data. Since the United States has never had such a system of continuous household registration, social statisticians have had to develop other means for measuring population characteristics.

In fact, many of the methodologies developed for intercensal population estimation, population projection and survey sampling were innovations developed by U.S. government statisticians and their private-sector and academic colleagues precisely because there were legal, cul-

tural and other barriers to collecting large amounts of data from the entire population on a continuous basis. An incapacity or inability to perform in one area can lead to innovation in others.

Since the late 1930s, government statisticians have developed an interlocking set of methodologies for measuring the characteristics of the population. Decennial censuses measure the detailed characteristics of the population. The detailed measurement of characteristics of different areas has permitted the development of large-scale sample surveys (usually utilizing stratified random or cluster samples) that can measure changes in the characteristics of the population at more frequent intervals. These are the samples most commonly used by government and private surveys. They provide a high degree of sampling efficiency at very low cost, because relatively few individuals must be sampled. What is sometimes forgotten (especially by those who suggest that the U.S. Census could be replaced by a survey) is that it would be very difficult to construct any national, state or local stratified sampling frame without census data on the population as a whole.

The United States population is also highly diverse, and spread across a huge and varied land area: local conditions or characteristics are often very different from national or regional ones. As a result, there is a constant tension between the need for national-level survey data at frequent intervals (which may miss local variations) and for locally-specific census data at infrequent intervals (which may miss rapid changes in social and economic conditions). The solution has been an overlapping system of censuses and surveys. In general, frequent surveys show national or regional trends, and decennial censuses provide the local detail.

More use is made of federal government statistics by other levels of government, private industry and schol-

Chapter 2 Definitions
SOURCES OF UNITED STATES POPULATION DATA

Administrative Records. Birth, death, marriage, tax and other records created during the operations of federal, state and local government agencies. Such records may be used to estimate intercensal demographic rates and as a means of evaluating data collected in the census.

Apportionment. The U.S. Census is used as the basis of dividing up the 435 seats in the House of Representatives every ten years on the basis of the total population. Insofar as possible, each congressional district is supposed to have the same population size. Public Law 94-171 requires that the Bureau of the Census report local population totals to the states by January 1 of the year following the census.

Census. A survey in which information is collected from every unit (person, housing unit, company, etc.) in the survey universe; in other words, a 100-percent sample. Ideally, censuses should be universal (counting everyone), periodic (taken at regular intervals), simultaneous (counting everyone at the same time), and individual (recording data for persons as well as for households or families).

Confidentiality. The legal requirement that the Census Bureau hold answers to census and survey questions in strict confidence, and to publish no data that allows the identification of particular persons, housing units, or business establishments.

Economic Censuses. Periodic and comprehensive canvasses of industrial and business activities.

Enumeration. The counting of all members of a population. A census taker is called an enumerator.

Family. A householder and one or more other persons living in the same household who are related by birth, marriage or adoption.

Group Quarters. Non-household dwellings of two types: a) institutional, such as hospitals or prisons, and b) non-institutional, such as rooming houses or group homes (of 9 residents or more).

Household. All persons who occupy a housing unit.

Long Form (Sample data). The longer version of the census administered to about one out of every six households in 1990.

Nonsampling Error. Error arising in any stage of data collection and processing of census data, including enumeration errors, respondents' failure to give correct answers, varying interpretation of questions, nonresponse, undercount, and machine and clerical errors. These errors are largely unrelated to sampling error.

Population. The number of inhabitants of an area, including undocumented aliens.

Post-Enumeration Survey (PES). A large-scale survey taken soon after the 1990 Census. Using a capture-recapture design, it was used to estimate the amount of undercount, overcount and mis-count of the population in the original census count.

Public-Use Microdata Sample (PUMS). Computerized sample files of randomly chosen and non-identifiable individuals and housing units that have been made available to non-governmental researchers after each census since 1940.

Sampling Error. The unavoidable error associated with a statistical estimate based on a sample rather than an entire population. Population estimates based on data from the long (sample) form of the census are affected by sampling error, but those based on data from the short form (complete count) are not; however, both kinds of estimates can be affected by non-sampling error.

Short Form (Complete count data). The form of the census administered to all households that contains fewer questions.

Summary Tape Files (STFs). Summary tabulations of population and housing data from both the complete and sample census counts that are made available on computer tape and CD-ROM.

Undercount. The error in census data that results from the failure to count some persons or housing units in the census. It is one component of non-sampling error.

ZIP Code. An areal unit developed by the U.S. Postal Service for sorting mail. ZIP codes have little or no relationship to most units of census geography, although some census data are classified by ZIP codes.

---

ars than in almost any other nation. These well-informed constituencies leave federal statisticians with less real power than their opposite numbers in most other nations. In the United States, there are powerful, influential outside groups evaluating the kind and quality of federal statistics. This has had both positive and negative effects on the development of the census and on the federal statistical system in general.

Many statisticians and demographers within the United States government identify strongly with scholarly groups and professional organizations whose memberships include those inside and outside the government, a phenomenon found in few other nations. Over the past sixty years, there has been a constant give-and-take among professional demographers and statisticians inside and outside the various federal bureaucracies about ways to improve efficiency and coverage and to reduce the bias in federal statistical efforts. Since 1985, for example, the papers delivered at the Bureau of the Census'

Annual Research Conference by inside and outside experts are remarkable for their honest and frequently unsparing criticism of Bureau policies, statistical methods and assumptions.

Data Sources for Federal Statistics

This chapter discusses the current state of federal statistical resources on the United States population and related topics. It addresses the three key sources of demographic data at the federal level:

(a) censuses of population and housing, and of economic activity and establishments;

(b) major demographic and social surveys; and

(c) vital statistics and administrative records.

While these three topics are discussed separately, the reader should be aware that much of the information that he or she is presented with daily is often a sophisticated combination of data from all of these sources. For example, a statistic on the projected longevity of the U.S. population may include census data on the current and future age distribution of the population, vital statistics data on rates of death by age, race, sex and cause, and survey data on the current rates of smoking and other risky behaviors among different population groups. What can be done with the whole of the statistical system is often far greater than the sum of what can be done with its different parts, so it is important to have at least a superficial idea of how the different statistical systems fit together. The multiplicity of data sources is also frequently responsible for some of our disagreements about the degree of seriousness of different social and economic problems and the effects of various government programs on them.

Censuses of Population and Housing and Economic Activity and Establishments

A census is an effort at a total enumeration of a population. Censuses are usually held periodically, and the federal government has recently tried to conduct establishment censuses at equal intervals of time, just as it does with the Census of Population and Housing. The federal government has generally made data from censuses available through rapid publication following the census.

There are two major types of censuses in the United States: the census of population and housing, and the various censuses of establishments. The former uses the household (or residential dwelling unit) as its primary unit of counting. Individuals are enumerated within households. Households are assigned to various geographic units, some defined by pre-existing local government administration and some by statistical concepts used by the Bureau of the Census.

Censuses of establishments, also conducted by the Bureau of the Census, use different economic or administrative units as their basic unit. Most provide no information on individuals or households; instead, only aggregated information on categories of individuals (usually employees) in different establishments is collected. There are other "surveys" of establishments which are so large that they are essentially censuses. For example, the Equal Employment Opportunity Commission's biennial EEO-6 "Higher Education Staff Information Survey" is essentially a census of 3,000 colleges and universities covering 95 percent of all employees in higher education.

The Census of Population and Housing

The United States census is the oldest continuously-operating system of population data collection in the world. Beginning in 1790, it has recorded information on population and other topics every ten years. For over half of that time, it was run by a makeshift bureaucratic organization that was assembled shortly before the administration of the census and disbanded soon after the last tabulations were made.

During the late nineteenth and twentieth centuries, the Census Bureau and other government agencies concerned with counting and estimating the characteristics of various parts of the population have also been responsible for many scientific and technological advances that are now used in many fields. The wide availability and relatively unbiased nature of data provided by the Census Bureau has also served as a model of information collection and dissemination for many nations.

Since 1940, the decennial census has been a Census of Population and Housing. It has attempted to record information on every person, household and dwelling unit, occupied and unoccupied, within the nation's borders. It has recorded many aspects of the family relationships (if any) between these persons, and also data on the physical and financial condition of the dwelling unit itself. The "census form" which records these different kinds of information changes from decade to decade. Questions may be added or dropped, or the possible categories of answers may change. The census form must be approved by the Congress, and Congress appropriates the funds for administration of the federal census. Hence these changes in questions are often an interesting barometer of the important political questions of the day and of the power of various interest groups to keep questions on or off the census, or to have questions (or response categories) worded in certain ways.

Since the birth of American demography in the 1920s and 1930s, data derived from U.S. census forms have been a major touchstone for demographers, sociologists and social historians. Researchers have tracked the major demographic forces: the urbanization of the population, the black migration to the North, the Baby Boom and later Baby Bust, and the gradual aging of the population. Data from census forms are also rich sources of information on the life of ordinary Americans. For example, in 1940, 76 percent of all households were married-couple ones, 15 percent had a female householder, and 9 percent had a male householder. By 1990, the aging of the population and changing patterns of marriage and divorce resulted in married-couple households falling to 55 percent of all households and female householder and male householder households rising to 28 percent and 17 percent of all households, respectively. Changes in the responses to questions about the conditions of housing and housing amenities can shed more light on how everyday life differed between generations.

Design of the 1990 Census of Population and Housing

The Census of Population and Housing has a hybrid research design. The 1980 and 1990 census forms

The 2000 Census

The outline of the proposed plan for the U.S. Census in the year 2000 is now known. Overall, it will resemble the 1990 Census, but there will be some significant changes. The planned content of the 2000 Census form is very similar to that used in 1990, except that it will be easier to fill out. There may be changes in how racial and Hispanic categories are defined. There may also be major changes in how the census is administered.

In 2000, the Bureau of the Census plans to try to achieve a 90 percent count of the population. Counting the last few percent of the population is very expensive on a per-person basis, so the Bureau plans to use a 10 percent sample of the remaining 10 percent of the population to complete the enumeration phase. These estimation techniques will be based on the Post Enumeration Survey (PES) of the 1990 Census and large-scale government surveys. The aim is to produce a "one-number" census that will be a count of the population that is both accurate and defensible from statistical and legal points of view. These plans have proceeded within the Census Bureau despite the Supreme Court decision stating that the Secretary of Commerce was within his legal mandate in deciding not to statistically adjust the 1990 decennial census for differential undercount. The sampling strategy has also been endorsed by the American Statistical Association's Census 2000 Blue Ribbon Panel on the Census and two panels from the National Research Council's Committee on National Statistics. Nonetheless,

strong political opposition to the use of statistical methods in adjusting enumerations has been voiced by several states and congressmen before the House of Representatives' Government Reform and Oversight Committee.

The second major change in the 2000 Census will be that the sample part of the census (the "long form"), which was administered to about one out of every six American families in 1990, will now be split into a number of sample forms. Each of these long forms will now be shorter and easier to answer, which may increase response rates. Yet since any particular question on the long form will be asked of fewer people in a given area, the confidence intervals for these questions will be wider. Hence long form questions for local areas will be less exact, and estimates or projections for these areas may suffer.

In the past, the Bureau of the Census made no effort to reach most individuals or households except through the home delivery of census forms through the mail, or by having census takers come to their dwellings. Now, the Bureau plans to send an introductory letter and multiple copies of the census form (to those who failed to fill out the first form) to improve response rates.

The Bureau also plans to have census forms available at a number of locations (such as community centers or stores) and to encourage people to pick up and fill out census forms if they think that they have been missed. Use of telephone response or filling in the census questionnaire via the Internet is also un-

der consideration. The Bureau of the Census feels that the possibility of an overcount (due to one person filling out more than one census form, or several members of the same household filling out multiple census forms) is much less of a problem than missing individuals and households due to inaccurate and incomplete lists of addresses. Further, advances in data processing and computer technology should make it relatively easy to find and correct cases of overcount in the months following the census.

Special attention will be paid to previously undercounted groups, including mobile populations, those in unusual housing situations, and linguistically isolated groups. Spanish-language census questionnaires will be mailed to heavily Hispanic neighborhoods, and the help of local officials will be enlisted to try to find missing dwelling units and residents. There will be no effort to count the homeless on the streets where they reside (formerly called "S-Night"); instead, they will be counted where they receive various services. The Post-Enumeration Survey will be integrated with the census to produce a "one number" census and, the Bureau hopes, avert controversies similar to those surrounding undercounts in the 1990 Census.

Bibliography

Billard, Lynne. "Some of Our Responsibilities as Statisticians—The Census Report." Amstat News, No. 235, Oct. 1996: 10-13.

Edmonston, Barry, and Schultze, Charles (eds.). Modernizing the U.S. Census. Washington, D.C.: National Academy Press. 1994.

Panel to Evaluate Alternative Census Methods. A Census that Mirrors America. Washington, D.C.: National Academy Press. 1993.

Steffy, Duane L., and Bradburn, Norman (eds.). Counting People in the Information Age. Washington, D.C.: National Academy Press. 1994.

began by asking that the census form be filled out by the household member "in whose name the home is owned or rented." If there was no such person, any adult household member could put himself or herself in column 1. (See Technical Appendix 2-1 for an abridged example of the 1990 U. S. Census Form.) All other household members were then to be listed in succeeding columns, with no specification given as to their order. Thus the census uses a respondent strategy for the person filling out the census questionnaire (in that this person is providing information about himself or herself), and an informant strategy (in that this person is providing information about others) for all other household members.

Long Forms and Short Forms of the Census

Not all census forms are the same. Since 1940, the Census Bureau has used different kinds of census forms in the Census of Population and Housing to provide an

in-depth look at certain topics which may not need to be asked of the entire population. In recent censuses these forms have been limited to two forms, the "short form" and the "long form." For the census in the year 2000, however, the Bureau of the Census is planning to return to the 1940 strategy of using several types of "long form" questionnaires focusing on different topics to supplement the "short form" administered to all households (see this chapter's first Textbox, "The Year 2000 Census").

In the 1990 Census short form, seven questions were asked about each person living in the household, and seven questions were asked about the condition of the dwelling unit. In the "long form" version of the questionnaire, 33 questions were asked about every person in the household (including all of the short form's seven personal questions) and 26 questions were asked about the dwelling unit (including the same seven questions asked in the short form). A randomly selected sample of about

Table 2-1. Population Items Covered[1] on U.S. Censuses: 1940-1990

Item Covered	1940	1950	1960	1970	1980	1990
Demographic Characteristics						
Age	X	X	X	X	X	X
Sex	X	X	X	X	X	X
Color or race	X	X	X	X	X	X
American Indian Tribe				X	X	X
Spanish/Hispanic origin				S	X	X
Relationship to head of houshold/family or householder	X	X	X	X	X	X
Education						
School attendance	X	S	S	S	X	S
Educational attainment	X	S	S	S	X	S
Public or private school			S	S	X	S
Vocational training				S		
Marriage and fertility						
Marital status	X	X	X	X	X	X
Number of years married		S				
Age at or date of first marriage	S		S	S	S	
Married more than once	S	S	S	S	S	
If remarried, was first marriage ended by death?					S	
Number of years widowed, divorced, or separated		S				
Number of children ever born to mother	S	S	S	S	S	
Veteran status						
Veteran status	S	S	S	S	S	S
Wife or widow of veteran	S					
If child of veteran, is father dead?	S					
If veteran, time of active duty					S	S
Present and past residence						
Farm residence	X	X	S	X	S	S
Farm residence in a previous year	X	S				
Place of residence in a previous year	X	S	S	S	S	S
Years moved to present residence			S	S		
Economic characteristics						
Industry	X	X	S	S	S	S
Occupation	X	X	S	S	S	S
Class of worker	X	X	S	S	S	S
Employment status	X	X	S	S	S	S
Duration of unemployment	X	S				
Year last worked			S	S	S	S
Weeks worked in preceding year	X	S	S	S	S	S
Hours worked in preceding week	X	S	S	S	S	S
Activity 5 years ago				S	S	
Industry 5 years ago				S		
Occupation 5 years ago				S		
Class of worker 5 years ago				S		
Income	X	S	S	S	S	S
Place of work			S	S	S	S
Means of transportation to work			S	S	S	S
Social Security registration and deductions	S					
Ill or disabled				S	S	S
Duration of disability				S		
Immigration, ancestry, and citizenship						
Place of birth	X	X	S	S	S	S
Place of birth of parents	S	S	S	S		
Citizenship	X	X	X	S	S	S
If foreign-born, year of immigraton				S	S	S
Language used at home	S		S	S	S	S
Ancestry/ethnic origin					S	S

[1] X=question asked of all census respondents. S=question asked of a sample of all census respondents. Kinds of samples and proportions of the population sampled varied between censuses.

Source: Data for 1980 and 1990 taken from the U.S. Census long forms; data for 1940-70 taken from U.S. Bureau of the Census, "Census '80: Continuing the Factfinder Tradition," U.S. Government Printing Office, Washington, D.C., 1980, pp. 434-43.

one out of every six households (a higher proportion in rural areas, a lower proportion in densely-populated urban areas) received the long form of the census, and the other five received the short form of the 1990 Census. The abridged version of the official 1990 U.S. Census Form given in Technical Appendix 2-1 is a long-form questionnaire.

Many of the questions on the 1990 Census were similar to those asked in other recent censuses. Table 2-1 shows the major population topics covered in complete and sample census questionnaires between 1940 and 1990. In many cases (particularly between the 1940, 1950 and 1960 censuses) questions were moved from the complete enumeration to the sample questionnaire because it was shown that a) a tabulation of the responses to the question was not needed for small areas, and b) the sample size (usually between 15 and 20 percent of the population) was so large that any sample answer had a very narrow confidence interval, and hence was a reliable estimate of this particular characteristic of the population. While similar questions may be asked from census to census, the response categories may differ considerably. Response categories on questions such as dollar amounts of income or rent, relationship to head of household or householder, or race have changed a great deal over time.

Census Undercounts

It is well known that the U.S. censuses have never been complete counts of the population. What is in more dispute is whether various groups in the population (certain racial minorities, age groups, the homeless, and so on) were less likely than others to be enumerated, hence giving an inaccurate picture of the population.

There are two current methods of estimating the census undercount: demographic analysis and dual-system estimate (DSE). In demographic analysis, data from a prior census is combined with birth, death and net international migration data from succeeding years to estimate the expected size of the population at the time of the next census. Table 2-2 shows the estimates of the size of the net undercount by race and age between 1940 and 1990. The estimates of the undercount of censuses from 1940 to 1990 suggest that a) the undercount decreased progressively from 1940 to 1980, with an increase between 1980 and 1990; b) the undercount of blacks was about 3-5 percent higher than for non-blacks in each census; and c) there has been a slow increase in the undercount of males (relative to females) in censuses between 1940 and 1990.

The other method of measuring the undercount is called the dual system estimate. Soon after the 1990 Census was taken, a separate group of enumerators were dispatched to take an intensive, large-scale survey of certain key sample areas. This Post Enumeration Survey (PES) focused on areas which were suspected of having been undercounted; enumerators made special efforts to find everyone on target blocks and in target households. The PES allowed Census Bureau analysts to discover who was undercounted (missed households or individuals), miscounted (counted in the wrong household or locality), or over-counted (households or individuals counted on two or more census forms).

Since the 1990 Post Enumeration Survey was the largest and most

Table 2-2. Demographic Analysis Estimate of Net Undercount for Censuses, by Race and Sex: 1940-1990 [percent]

Race and sex	1940	1950	1960	1970	1980	1990
Total	5.4	4.1	3.1	2.7	1.2	1.8
Male	5.8	4.4	3.5	3.4	2.2	2.8
Female	5.0	3.8	2.7	2.0	0.3	0.9
Non-black	5.0	3.8	2.7	2.2	0.8	1.3
Male	5.2	3.8	2.9	2.7	1.5	2.0
Female	4.9	3.7	2.4	1.7	0.1	0.6
Black	8.4	7.5	6.6	6.5	4.5	5.7
Male	10.9	9.7	8.8	9.1	7.5	8.5
Female	6.0	5.4	4.4	4.0	1.7	3.0

Source: Robinson, J.G., Gupta, P.D., and Woodrow, R.A., "Estimation of Population Coverage in the 1990 United States Census based on Demographic Analysis," Journal of the American Statistical Association 88(1993):1065

Table 2-3. Dual-system Estimate Undercounts[1], by Race-ethnicity and Housing Tenure Status: 1990 [percent]

Race-ethnicity	Total	Owner	Non-owner
Non-Hispanic white and other	0.7	-0.3	3.1
Black	4.6	2.3	6.5
Hispanic	5.0	1.8	7.4
Asian/Pacific Islander	2.4	-1.4	7.0
Reservation Indian	12.2	—	—

[1] Any figure that is negative indicates an overcount of the population in that category.

Source: Passell, J.S., "Comment," Journal of the American Statistical Association 88(1993): 1074-77.

comprehensive survey of its kind ever taken, its findings are important, but cannot be compared to similar small-scale efforts in prior years. Table 2-3 gives the estimates of undercounts by race, Hispanic origin and tenure of housing unit derived from the dual-system estimate method (i.e. comparing the original 1990 Census and the PES).

Overall, the dual-system estimate of the 1990 Census undercount was 1.6 percent, and the demographic analysis undercount estimate (Table 2-2) was 1.8 percent. Considering that these two estimates were made using completely different methodologies, there is a remarkable degree of congruence between them. In addition, the similarity in the pattern of undercount of various sub-populations (a far higher rate of undercount of blacks as mea-

sured by either method) suggests that both methods are measuring true patterns of undercount in the 1990 Census.

Because the Post Enumeration Survey was conducted in localities throughout the United States, it is possible to use the dual system estimate method to compute the undercount in each state. (One drawback of the demographic analysis method is that it can estimate the population undercount only of the entire United States, not of any of its constituent parts.) Table 2-4 shows that there was considerable variation in the undercount of population in the nation's regions, divisions and states. The undercount was far larger, both in percent and absolute terms, in the South and West regions. The highest

Table 2-4. Estimates of Underenumeration in the 1990 Census, by Region, Division, and State [numbers in thousands]

Region, division, and state	Census population	Post-enumeration survey population (revised)	Estimated population undercount	Percent undercount
United States, total	248,710	252,713	4,003	1.584
Northeast region	50,809	51,236	427	0.833
New England	13,207	13,283	76	0.572
Middle Atlantic	37,602	37,953	351	0.925
Midwest region	59,669	60,082	413	0.687
East North Central	42,009	42,321	312	0.737
West North Central	17,660	17,761	101	0.569
South region	85,446	87,280	1,834	2.101
South Atlantic	43,566	44,449	883	1.987
East South Central	15,176	15,452	276	1.786
West South Central	26,703	27,379	676	2.469
West region	52,786	54,115	1,329	2.456
Mountain	13,659	13,976	317	2.268
Pacific	39,127	40,139	1,012	2.521
New England				
Maine	1,228	1,237	9	0.728
New Hampshire	1,109	1,119	10	0.894
Vermont	563	569	6	1.054
Massachusetts	6,016	6,045	29	0.480
Rhode Island	1,003	1,005	2	0.199
Connecticut	3,287	3,308	21	0.635
Middle Atlantic				
New York	17,990	18,262	272	1.489
New Jersey	7,730	7,774	44	0.566
Pennsylvania	11,882	11,917	35	0.294
East North Central				
Ohio	10,847	10,922	75	0.687
Indiana	5,544	5,572	28	0.503
Illinois	11,431	11,544	113	0.979
Michigan	9,295	9,361	66	0.705
Wisconsin	4,892	4,922	30	0.610
West North Central				
Minnesota	4,375	4,394	19	0.432
Iowa	2,777	2,788	11	0.395
Missouri	5,117	5,149	32	0.621
North Dakota	639	643	4	0.622
South Dakota	696	703	7	0.996
Nebraska	1,578	1,589	11	0.692
Kansas	2,478	2,495	17	0.681

Table 2-4. Estimates of Underenumeration in the 1990 Census, by Region, Division, and State [numbers in thousands] (continued)

Region, division, and state	Census population	Post-enumeration survey population (revised)	Estimated population undercount	Percent undercount
South Atlantic				
Delaware	666	678	12	1.770
Maryland	4,781	4,882	101	2.069
District of Columbia	607	628	21	3.344
Virginia	6,187	6,314	127	2.011
West Virginia	1,793	1,819	26	1.429
North Carolina	6,629	6,753	124	1.836
South Carolina	3,487	3,559	72	2.023
Georgia	6,478	6,619	141	2.130
Florida	12,938	13,197	259	1.963
East South Central				
Kentucky	3,685	3,746	61	1.628
Tennessee	4,877	4,964	87	1.753
Alabama	4,041	4,113	72	1.751
Mississippi	2,573	2,629	56	2.130
West South Central				
Arkansas	2,351	2,392	41	1.714
Louisiana	4,220	4,314	94	2.179
Oklahoma	3,146	3,203	57	1.780
Texas	16,987	17,470	483	2.765
Mountain				
Montana	799	818	19	2.323
Idaho	1,007	1,029	22	2.138
Wyoming	454	464	10	2.155
Colorado	3,294	3,364	70	2.081
New Mexico	1,515	1,563	48	3.071
Arizona	3,665	3,754	89	2.371
Utah	1,723	1,753	30	1.711
Nevada	1,202	1,231	29	2.356
Pacific				
Washington	4,867	4,958	91	1.835
Oregon	2,842	2,896	54	1.865
California	29,760	30,595	835	2.729
Alaska	550	561	11	1.961
Hawaii	1,108	1,129	21	1.860

Source: Hogan, Howard, "The 1990 Post-enumeration Survey: Operations and Results," Journal of the American Statistical Association 88(1993):1047-60.

percentage undercount was in the Pacific Division of the West region. This was largely due to a very high rate of undercount in California (2.73 percent). Texas, with a rate of 2.77 percent, also had a very high rate of undercount, as did New Mexico (3.07 percent), the District of Columbia (3.34 percent), Arizona (2.37 percent), and Nevada (2.36 percent). Several states had very low rates of undercount, including Rhode Island (0.20 percent), Pennsylvania (0.29 percent), Iowa (0.40 percent) and Minnesota (0.43 percent).

Several factors appear to contribute to high or low undercount rates in different states, regions and localities. To some extent, states with high Hispanic proportions in their populations also have high undercount rates. However, work by Jeffrey Passell indicates that social class may play a major part here as well. Renters are far more likely than homeowners to be undercounted, and the high proportion of renters among Hispanics may account for their high rates of undercount. The black population, especially the black, male, urban population aged 20-29 is also frequently heavily undercounted. The data in this table also show that there was a significant degree of undercount in less-urbanized Southern and Western states as well.

The Census Bureau reported the 1990 original count data for purposes of the reapportionment of seats in the U.S. House of Representatives between states as well as for redistricting electoral districts within states. It has also used the original counts for a number of other purposes, including making population projections, computing vital statistics rates, and so on. Yet most of the Census Bureau's statisticians and many outside experts are convinced that the estimates of the undercount derived from the Post Enumeration Survey give a much closer estimate of the "true" population size, at least down to the level of states and metropolitan areas. By 1994, the Census Bureau had begun to use adjusted estimates of population size and distribution derived from the PES as the basis for projecting characteristics of the population (such as the number of Americans in poverty) derived from sample surveys such as the Current Population Survey.

Nonsampling Errors in Census Data

The U.S. Bureau of the Census is one of the very few organizations that releases estimates of what proportion of its respondents answered its questions in an incorrect way. Using the PES, Census researchers have been able to estimate the proportion of respondents who answer different questions incorrectly. Typically, between about 1 and 2 percent of all respondents answer questions incorrectly for themselves or for others in their households (see Appendix C, "Accuracy of the Data," in almost any volume of census data from the 1990 Census). For only a few questions (number of children ever born, ancestry, place of birth, or type of residence [urban/rural])

does the rate of error rise above 2 percent. Thus when using census data it is possible to include this source of non-sampling error into the calculation of standard errors for the population.

Censuses of Economic Activity and Establishments

While the Census of Population and Housing is by far the best-known of the federal government's data collection efforts, it also conducts a variety of other censuses that generate useful data on the population and economy. Most of these censuses are relatively little-known because they are censuses of establishments (i.e. farms, factories, units of government, and so on) and not of individuals or households. Frequently workers at an establishment are unaware that such a census is underway because the census forms are filled out by accountants or personnel managers who have access to the kind of data needed to complete such a census. These censuses generate economic or personnel data that are widely used by those measuring economic and social activity in various sectors of the economy.

These establishment censuses are generally taken more frequently than the Census of Population and Housing, and in years other than those ending in zero (which is reserved for the decennial census). The current establishment censuses and the frequency with which they have been taken are the:

Census of Manufacturing and Mineral Industries: The Census Bureau conducts both censuses and surveys of manufacturing and mineral industries on such topics as employment, inventories, capital expenditures, ownership and control, and products shipped. The census of manufacturing covers industries in Standard Industrial Classification (SIC) codes 20-39, and the census of mineral industries covers activities in SIC codes 10, 12, 13 and 14. Data are available for the 50 states, the District of Columbia, Puerto Rico and some outlying areas; they are generally available down to the metropolitan area or county level. In 1810-1900, these censuses were taken every 10 years (no census in 1830); in 1905-19, every 5 years; in 1919-39, every 2 years; in 1947, 1954, 1958, 1963, 1967, 1972, 1977, 1982, 1987, and every year hereafter in years ending in a 2 or 7.

Census of Agriculture: This census asks questions about the amount of acreage of different crops, livestock and poultry, use of fertilizer, machinery and equipment, characteristics of the farm operator, and many other topics. These data are available at the state (and outlying areas and Puerto Rico) and county level. In 1840-1920, the Census of Agriculture was taken every 10 years; in 1920-74, every 5 years; in 1954-74, in years ending in 4 or 9; in 1978 and 1982; then for years ending 2 or 7 thereafter.

Census of Transportation: Beginning in 1880, the

Census Bureau began to record statistics on rail and water transportation in the decennial census. Since 1963 the Census Bureau has administered a transportation census at five-year intervals. This census now has two parts: a census of establishments in the transportation industry and a survey on the characteristics of trucks used in this industry. Topics covered include revenues, number of employees, commodities carried, vehicle size, fuel economy of vehicles, and so on. Data are available for the 50 states and the District of Columbia as well as for some metropolitan areas. Rail and water transportation censuses were taken in 1880 and 1890; water transportation censuses in 1906, 1916, and 1926; in 1907 the Census of Express Business; the National Travel Survey in 1957. The first Census of Transportation was in 1963, then in 1977 and in subsequent years ending in 2 or 7.

Census of Construction and Housing: From 1967 on, the Census Bureau has collected data on the construction industries in a separate census (prior to this, construction and housing questions had usually been included in either the Census of Population or the Census of Business). This census includes data on establishments building houses, roads, or engaged in trades such as electrical or plumbing work (SIC Codes 15, 16 and 17). Data include number of employees, worker hours, class of construction, etc., and are available for states and major metropolitan areas. This census was first taken as part of the Census of Business in 1930, 1935, and 1939. The first Census of Transportation was in 1967, then in subsequent years ending in 2 or 7.

Census of Retail Trade: This mailed-out census covers the sale of merchandise and services to the general public for individual or household consumption; it includes questions about kind of business, payroll, sales, legal form of organization, and so on. Data are available for all states, the District of Columbia, Puerto Rico and most outlying areas for counties, metropolitan areas, incorporated areas of 2,500 or more persons or 5-digit ZIP codes. Again, this census was first taken as part of the Census of Business in 1929, 1933, 1935, 1939, 1948, 1954, 1958, 1963, and 1967. It was taken as an independent census in 1972, 1977, 1982, 1987, 1992, and for years ending in 2 or 7 thereafter.

Census of Wholesale Trade: This census covers the sale of merchandise to retailers and others who are not end-users; it includes sales to institutions, to farmers for farm use, and to governments. Topics covered are similar to those found on the Census of Retail Trade, as is the geographic availability of data. Taken as part of the Census of Business in 1929, 1933, 1935, 1939, 1948, 1954, 1958, 1963, and 1967, this census has been taken as an independent census in 1972, 1977, 1982, 1987, 1992, and for years ending in 2 or 7 thereafter.

Census of Service Industries: This census includes businesses that provide repairs, accommodations, education, amusements and other services. This census began

as part of the Census of Business in 1933, and is now a mail-out census. Data are available for the same general topics and geographic units as are available for the Census of Retail Trade. Again, this census was taken as part of the Census of Business in 1933, 1935, 1939, 1948, 1954, 1958, 1963, and 1967. It has been taken as an independent census in 1972, 1977, 1982, 1987, and 1992, and for years ending in 2 or 7 thereafter.

Census of Governments: While this census dates back to 1840, it began again in modern form in 1957. It covers characteristics and descriptions of local governments, taxable property and property tax rates, governmental employment, government finances (including debt), and similar topics. Data are usually available for states, municipalities, townships, school districts, special districts, and so on. Taken as a Census of Schools and Pupils in 1840, then as a Census of Governments taken every ten years between 1850 and 1942; since 1957, this census has been taken in every year ending in a 2 or 7.

In 1987, there were also the Economic Census of Outlying Areas; the Enterprise Statistics Program; the Survey of Minority-owned Business Enterprises, and the Survey of Women-owned Businesses. The 1992 Economic Censuses also cover communications, utilities, and the financial, insurance and real estate industries.

How Data From United States Censuses Are Reported

Most analyses of U.S. census data are not conducted at the national level, but rather at some lower level of geography. Because census data (particularly data from the Census of Population and Housing) are reported in a number of different ways, it is important to have a basic understanding of the different systems of geography used by the Census Bureau and by other federal agencies.

Census Geography

The Census Bureau has divided the United States into a complete and exhaustive set of areal units for use in the compilation of census data. These units are organized on a general set of principles:

1. Census areas are generally hierarchical: each smaller unit usually fits entirely within the next larger one in the hierarchy. There are several major hierarchies. However, there are important exceptions, and sometimes what appear to be lower-level units are split between two or more higher- level units.

2. Census areas are contiguous: with a few minor exceptions (such as islands), no parts of a census geographic unit are separated by another census geographic unit.

3. The Census Bureau supplies information for both governmental units and for statistical units, i.e. geographic entities that the Bureau has invented for descriptive or administrative reasons.

4. The Census Bureau's statistical units, especially those that measure the degree of urbanization of an area, attempt to measure the current pattern of settlement and density, the degree of homogeneity of the area, and its degree of functional integration. As a result, the boundaries of some statistical units change frequently.

5. For a variety of historical and political reasons, the Bureau of the Census' definitions of governmental and statistical units can vary depending upon the region of the country. Data from Alaska, Hawaii and the New England states are particularly prone to be classified differently than those from other regions.

6. The Bureau of the Census is not the only branch of the government that creates statistical areas. The well-known Metropolitan Statistical Areas (MSAs), for example, are created according to standards of the Office of Management of the Budget (OMB).

Census areas change relatively frequently between censuses as certain areas achieve the size or degree of urbanization necessary for promotion to a new census category. For example, previously non-metropolitan counties may become part of a Metropolitan Statistical Area. Sometimes administrative or governmental units change, such as when North Dakota returned to the use of Minor Civil Divisions (MCDs, usually the equivalent of townships) rather than continuing to use Census County Divisions.

The Census Bureau or other government agencies may also change their definition of what constitutes their own statistical units from census to census, so it is often necessary to trace the history of a unit through definition, nomenclature and boundary changes. Metropolitan areas, for example, were called Standard Metropolitan Statistical Areas (SMSAs) in 1980, but were known as Metropolitan Statistical Areas (MSAs) in the 1990 Census, even though their definitions were substantially the same.

The Hierarchy of Census Geographic Units

Figure 2-1 shows how the United States is divided into four Census Regions (Northeast, South, North Central and West) and how each of these regions is divided into two or three Census Divisions. The distribution of states across regions and divisions is listed in Figure 2-2.

For the 1990 Census, the Bureau of the Census provided printed reports and data in other media for 57 state-equivalent areas of the United States: the 50 states, the District of Columbia, and the six so-called outlying areas of the United States: American Samoa, Guam, Commonwealth of the Northern Marianas Islands, Republic of Palau, Puerto Rico, and the Virgin Islands of the United States.

Hierarchies of Units Within States

Below the state level, there are several distinct geographical classification systems used by the Census Bureau. These hierarchies are:

(1) Incorporated or Census Designated Places;
(2) Consolidated Cities;
(3) Non-metropolitan Counties;
(4) Metropolitan Counties;
(5) Zip Codes;
(6) Congressional and Voting Districts; and
(7) School Districts.

There are also two distinct urban/rural hierarchies that are organized on two different principles: urban/rural as defined by size of place, and urban/rural as defined by inclusion in a metropolitan area. The current definitions of these areal units for 1990 can be found in Appendix A of any census volume of any state. Since 1990 Census Bureau publications provide little help in showing how these units fit together, this topic will be discussed here. Finally, American Indian and Alaska Native Areas are not treated in these hierarchies because of their inherent complexity (they sometimes overlap with other geographic units).

Table 2-5 gives exact numbers or estimates of the number of units (i.e. nationwide totals) in 1990. Figure 2-3 shows the principal hierarchical relationships between units in the three major hierarchies used by the Census Bureau in providing data: the State/County hierarchy (A), the Metropolitan Area hierarchy (B), and the Urban/Rural hierarchy (C).

A. The state and non-metropolitan/metropolitan county hierarchy

This hierarchy is a mix between governmental units (the boxes in the figure) and geographic statistical units (the ovals in the figure):

1. *Incorporated or Census Designated Places:* The Census Bureau reports population and housing data for two kinds of recognized urban groupings: Incorporated Places, which are legally recognized urban entities with governmental powers (usually towns, villages, and so on, but differing from state to state), and Census Designated Places, which are also densely settled concentrations of populations with identifiable names, but which have no legal governmental standing.

Incorporated or Census Designated Places can exist outside of or overlap county boundaries. For example, the city of Elgin, Illinois (an incorporated place) had 15,400 of its population in Cook County and 77,010 in Kane County in 1990.

2. *Consolidated Cities:* These areal units are among the most poorly defined of census terms. Basically, they are units of "local government for which the functions of an incorporated place and its county or minor civil division have merged." These units are generally excluded from hierarchical listings of areal or governmental units, but may be appended to the end. They do not have a place in the normal hierarchy of metropolitan areas (census tracts, etc.) or units below Minor Civil Divisions (MCDs).

Figure 2-1. Map of Census Regions and Divisions

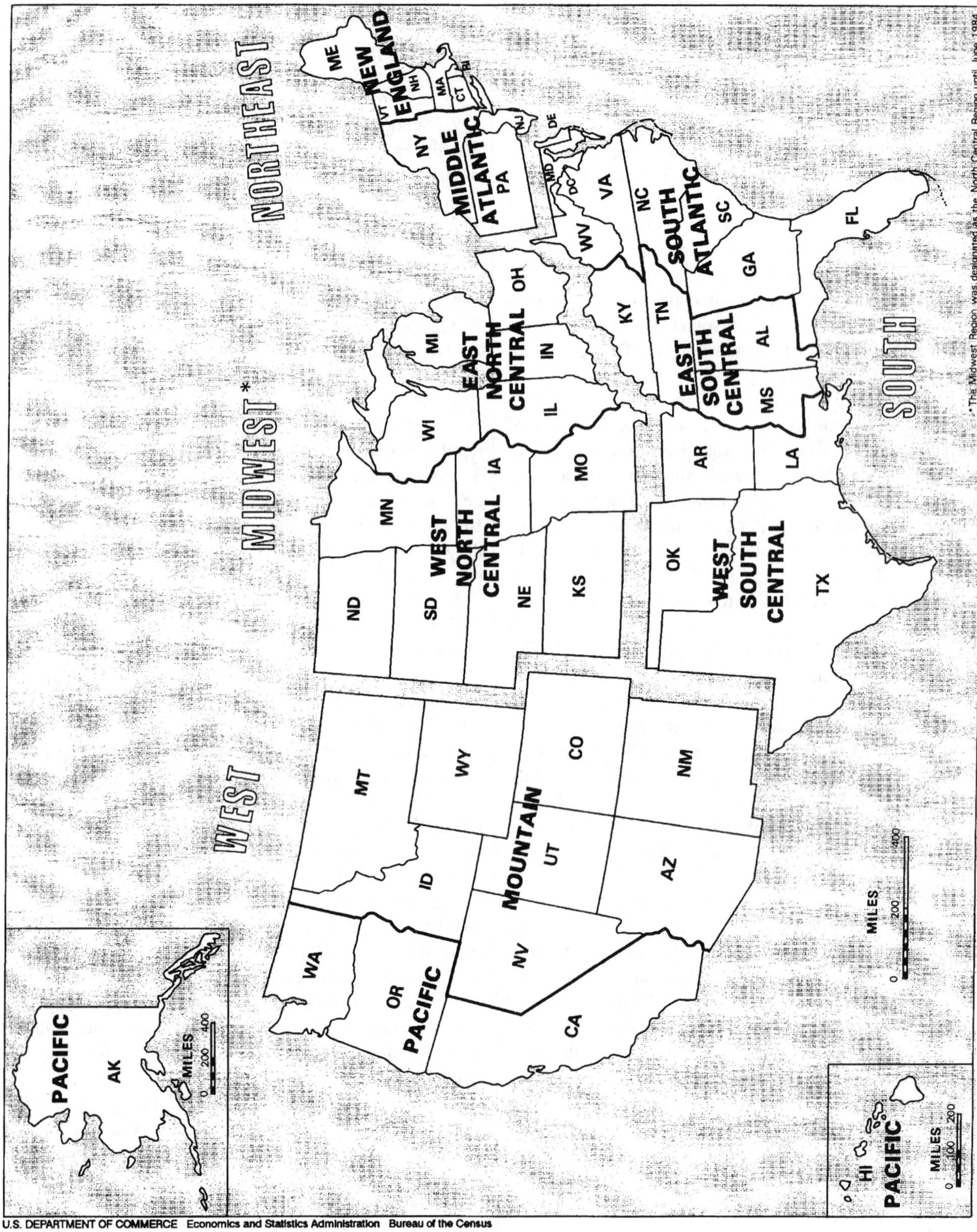

Figure 2-2. The Distribution of States by Census Regions and Divisions: 1990

Northeast Region		Midwest Region	
New England Division	**Middle Atlantic Division**	**East North Central Division**	**West North Central Division**
Connecticut	New Jersey	Illinois	Iowa
Maine	New York	Indiana	Kansas
Massachusetts	Pennsylvania	Michigan	Minnesota
New Hampshire		Ohio	Missouri
Vermont		Wisconsin	Nebraska
Rhode Island			North Dakota
			South Dakota
South Region		**West Region**	
South Atlantic Division	**East South Central Division**	**Mountain Division**	**Pacific Division**
Delaware	Alabama	Arizona	Alaska
District of Columbia	Kentucky	Colorado	California
Florida	Mississippi	Idaho	Hawaii
Georgia	Tennessee	Montana	Oregon
Maryland		Nevada	Washington
North Carolina	**West South Central Division**	New Mexico	
South Carolina	Arkansas	Utah	
Virginia	Louisiana	Wyoming	
West Virginia	Oklahoma		
	Texas		

Source: 1990 U.S. Census information.

3. *Non-metropolitan Counties:* The non-metropolitan county hierarchy uses the basic building block of sub-state governance, the county. Depending upon their degree of urbanization, the Census Bureau classifies all counties in the United States as either metropolitan or non-metropolitan.

Within all non-metropolitan counties, the Census Bureau has two kinds of geographic sub-units. In 28 states, there are legal entities with governmental powers (and non-overlapping geographic areas of governance) that have been designated as Minor Civil Divisions. These MCDs include units with such designations as towns, townships, supervisor's districts, precincts, and even plantations. In nine of these 28 states, there are counties that contain one or more areas that are not included within MCDs. The Census Bureau designates these portions of such counties as unorganized territories.

In 22 other states, no such sub-county governmental bodies exist, so the Census Bureau (in conjunction with local authorities) created Census County Divisions (CCDs) as statistical sub-county units for which different data are collected. Thus, depending on the state, all sub-county units will either be MCDs (or unorganized territories) or CCDs.

Below the MCDs and the CCDs, the Census Bureau collects information on Block Numbering Areas, small statistical areas of MCDs or CCDs in non-metropolitan coun-

ties. The constituent parts of block numbering areas are block groups, which in turn are divided into blocks. One key advance of the 1990 Census over its predecessors is that the United States is now finally divided into blocks in rural as well as in urban areas, and block data are now available throughout the country.

Neither Incorporated Places nor Census Designated Places (often referred to just as places) are in the County/MCD or CCD hierarchy. It is frequently possible to have a city or a village split between several counties or county subdivisions. For example, the incorporated place of Womac City, Illinois (pop. 1,492 in 1990) is split between Brookside Township (an MCD) in Clinton County (645 people), Centralia Township (another MCD) in Marion County (721 people), and Irvington Township (a third MCD) in Washington County (126 people). Similarly, there is no necessary match between units of the sub-county hierarchy (MCDs or CCDs, block numbering areas, block groups and blocks) and Census Designated Places. In addition, the boundaries of Census Designated Places (CDPs) often change considerably between censuses, depending on patterns and levels of urban growth, while the state/county hierarchy system has changed relatively little over the past several censuses.

4. *Metropolitan Counties:* The metropolitan area hierarchy (see Figure 2-3, Part B) used in the 1990 Census is part of a broader, evolving system of metropolitan clas-

Figure 2-3. Geographic Hierarchies of 1990 U.S. Census Data

Hierarchy A: Non-Metropolitan Counties

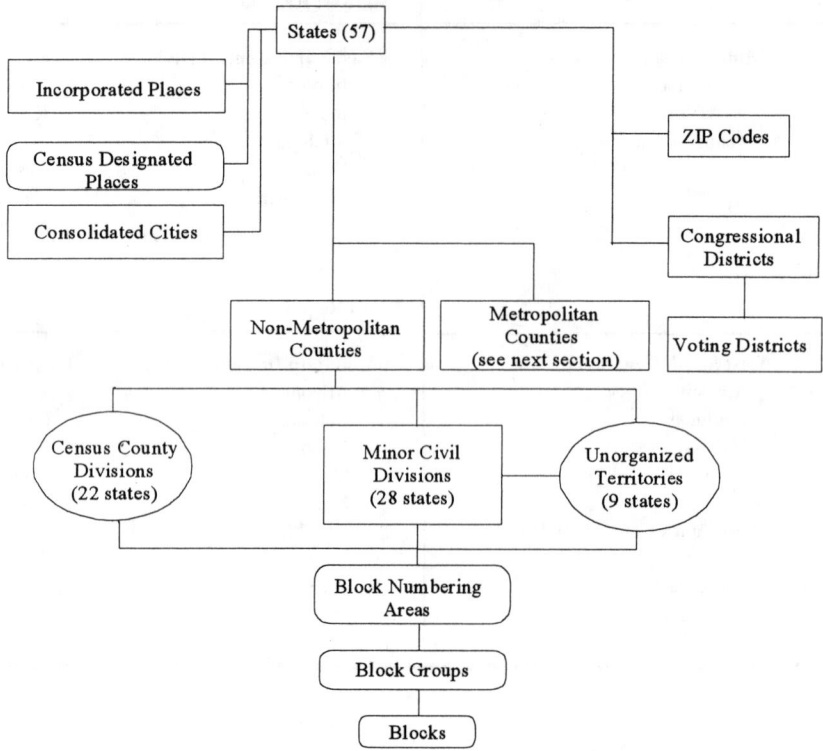

Hierarchy B: Metropolitan Counties

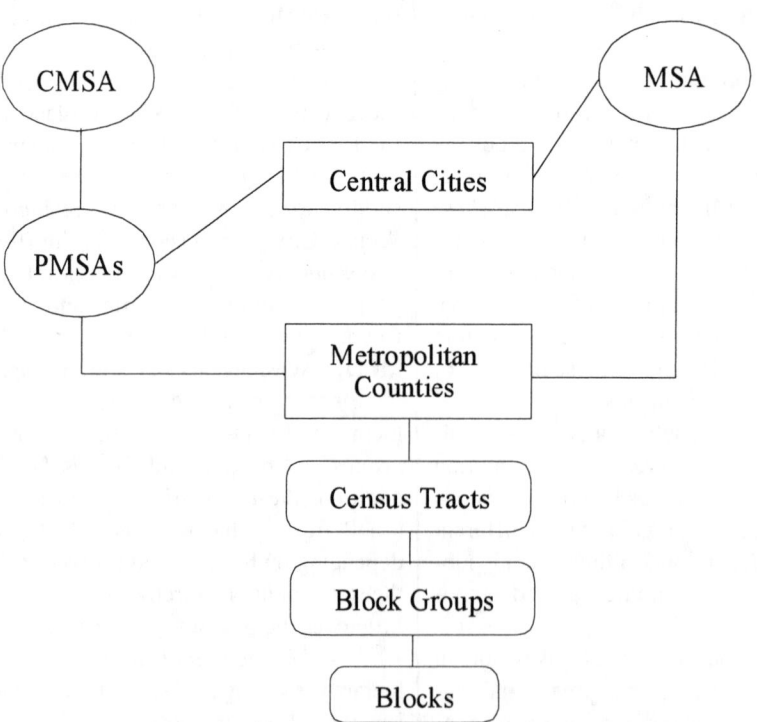

Figure 2-3. Geographic Hierarchies of 1990 U.S. Census Data (continued)

Hierarchy C, Part 1: Urban/Rural by Size of Place

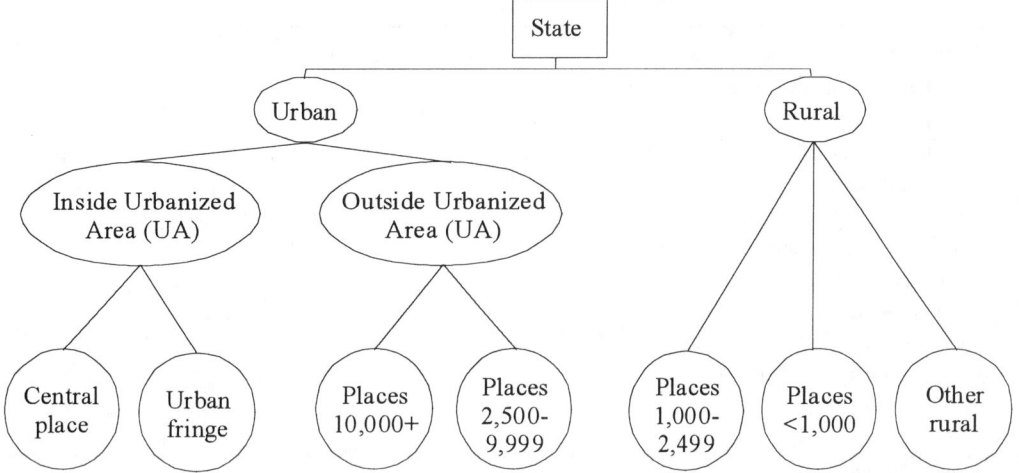

Hierarchy C, Part 2: Urban/Rural by Metropolitan Area Status

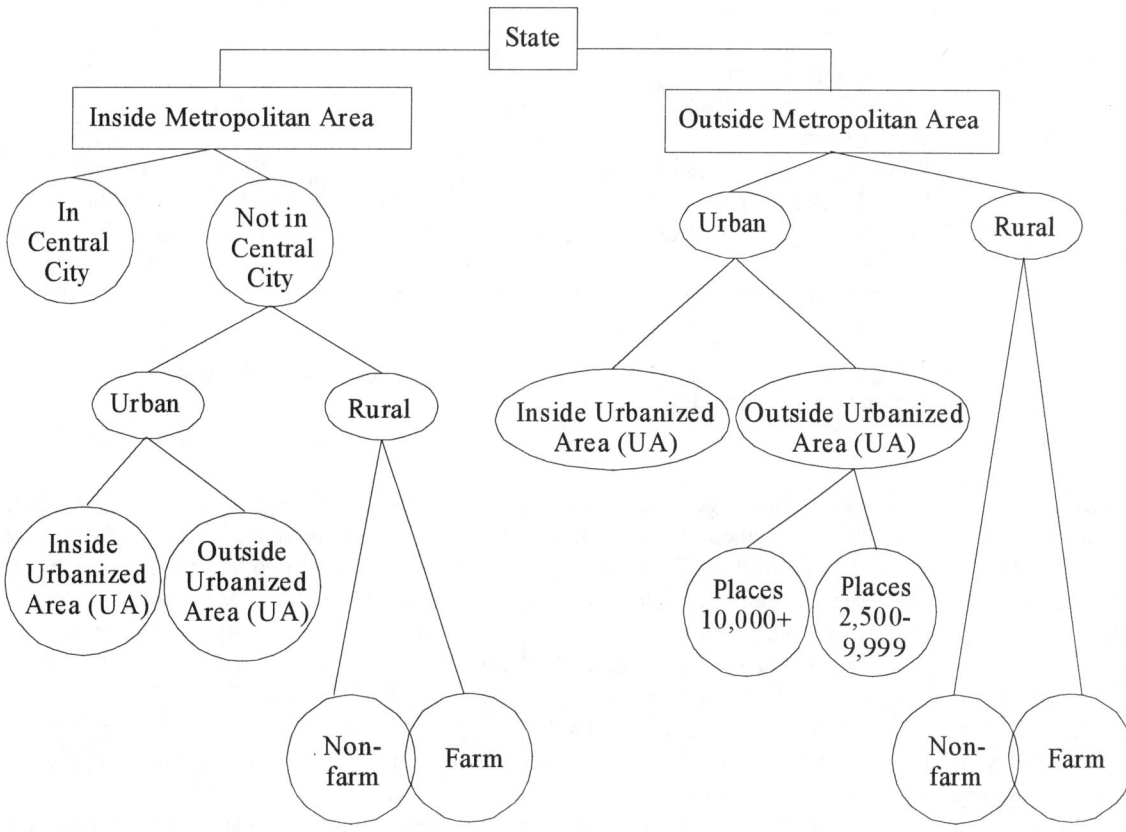

Source: U.S. Census information.

Table 2-5. Number of Geographic Entities in the United States Census: 1980 and 1990

Entities	1980	1990
Legal/administrative entities		
States and equivalent entities	57	57
States	50	50
District of Columbia	1	1
Outlying areas	6	6
Counties and equivalent areas	3,231	3,248
Minor Civil Divisions (MCDs)	30,450	30,386
Incorporated places	19,176	19,365
Consolidated cities	—	6
Congressional Districts (CDs)	435	435
Voting Districts (VTDs)	36,361	148,872
School districts	16,075	14,442
ZIP codes	37,000[1]	29,469
Statistical entities		
Regions	4	4
Divisions	9	9
Metropolitan Area (MA) designations		
Standard Metropolitan Statistical Areas (SMSAs)	323	—
Metropolitan Statistical Areas (MSAs)	—	268
Standard Consolidated Statistical Areas (SCSAs)	17	—
Primary Metropolitan Statistical Areas (PMSAs)	—	73
Consolidated Metropolitan Statistical Areas (CMSAs)	—	21
Urbanized areas	373	405
County subdivisions		
Census County Divisions (CCDs)	5,512	5,903
Unorganized territories	274	282
Census Designated Places (CDPs)	3,733	4,423
Census tracts	43,691	50,690
Block Numbering Areas (BNAs)	3,423	11,586
Block Groups (BGs)	156,163	229,196
Enumeration Districts (EDs)	102,235	now BGs
Blocks	2,473,679	7,017,425

[1] Estimated.

Source: U.S. Bureau of the Census, "A Guide to State and Local Census Geography," U.S. Government Printing Office, Washington, D.C., 1993, pp. 14-5.

sification used by a number of federal agencies. There is an official set of standards as to what constitutes a "metropolitan area" and its classification in the hierarchy. These standards include such factors as population size, degree of social and economic integration of the urban area, whether it has one or more clear nuclei, and so on. The problem for census data users is that the federal definitions and classification standards have shifted considerably from year to year. There was a major shift in the federal classification system of metropolitan areas in the 1980s, so that the terminology of the urban hierarchy is quite different for the 1980 and 1990 censuses.

Briefly, the federal government uses counties as the building blocks of Metropolitan Areas (except in New England, where metropolitan areas are composed of cities and towns). Basically, a Metropolitan Area (MA) must have a place (typically a city) with a population of at least 50,000, and a total population for the area of 100,000 or more (75,000 or more in New England). It is comprised of one or more central counties, and may include outlying counties that have a close relationship with the central county.

Metropolitan areas are either Metropolitan Statistical Areas (MSAs), or Consolidated Metropolitan Statistical Areas (CMSAs). The largest place in either an MSA or a CMSA is designated as the central city. In general, metropolitan areas with more than one million people qualify as CMSAs. These units are further subdivided into one or more Primary Metropolitan Statistical Areas (PMSAs). In most PMSAs, the key central city is also designated.

How does this system differ from the 1980 metropolitan hierarchy? The new CMSA is very similar to the 1980 Standard Consolidated Statistical Area (SCSA), which was also at the top of the urban hierarchy. In 1980, however, there was no distinction between 1990's MSAs (i.e. smaller, independent metropolitan areas) and PMSAs (the component cities that make up the huge belts of urbanized America, such as the Chicago, Los Angeles or New York areas); instead, all of these cities were considered to be Standard Metropolitan Statistical Areas (SMSAs). Thus a 1980 SMSA may be either a 1990 PMSA or MSA.

In both 1980 and 1990, metropolitan areas included whole counties. Once a county was included in a metropolitan area, all of its area was divided into census tracts. Unlike the boundaries of census-designated places, the boundaries of census tracts change very little over time. In addition, while census tracts are built at the county level, their small size usually means that such geographic entities as the central cities within metropolitan areas do not run across the boundaries of census tracts. As a result, many of the geographic problems, noted in the previous section, of mixing data from census-designated places with MCDs, etc., are not a major hindrance to data collection or manipulation in metropolitan areas.

How do the different units described above in the State/Non-metropolitan County and Metropolitan Area hierarchies compare in terms of average population size? Obviously, non-metropolitan counties, MSAs, PMSAs and CMSAs differ greatly with respect to average size, with the latter two units almost always being much larger. Below that level, however, there is some degree of equivalence between census tracts and block numbering areas; the former average about 4,000 people nationwide, and the latter have a somewhat smaller population.

Block groups in both the State/County and Metropolitan Area hierarchies average about 1,000 people; the difference here is that block groups in rural areas cover much larger areas due to lower population densities. Blocks in Metropolitan Areas average about 85 people, while blocks in the State/County hierarchy usually have about 30 people. While these population figures can vary widely (a block in a non-metropolitan county that happens to include a trailer park could have far more than 30 people, for example), these numbers should give a rough idea of the size-equivalent units in metropolitan and non-metropolitan areas.

5. *ZIP Codes:* ZIP Codes are geographic units that exist for the convenience of and at the pleasure of the United States Postal Service. As the Census Bureau succinctly puts it, ZIP codes "usually do not have clearly identifiable boundaries, often serve a continually changing area, are changed periodically to meet postal requirements, and do not cover all the land area of the United States" (1990 Census, Illinois CPH-5-15, A-13). While ZIP code areas usually do not cross state boundaries, there are exceptions, such as 82423 (in both Wyoming and Montana) or 81324 (straddling the Utah-Colorado border).

ZIP codes can be almost any size: the one-block square in Chicago upon which the Sears Tower rests comprises two ZIP codes. Potential users should remember that the census data will be for 1990 ZIP codes, and it may be very time consuming to trace later (or earlier) changes in boundaries. Of course, many marketing companies will use this ZIP code data to classify and cluster ZIP code areas for direct mail and other business purposes, so corrected data may be available from private vendors. It is also possible to link some "ZIP+4" data (a subunit of a ZIP code usually comprising the dwelling units on one side of a city block) to census data for the same area.

6. *Congressional Districts:* The application of census data to the reapportionment of congressional districts is, of course, the major constitutional responsibility of the decennial census. Under Public Law 94-171, these data (simple counts by age, race and Hispanic origin for the population aged 18 years and over) were the first to be delivered by the Census Bureau in January, 1991.

The Census Bureau provides simple descriptive statistics on the population for all congressional districts and, where states have requested them, on other kinds of voting districts as well. However, since these counts are for the congressional and voting districts circa 1990, they will have little to do with the new voting districts redrawn for elections in 1992 and later. Again, congressional and voting districts often do not match any of the units in the other areal hierarchies described here.

7. *School Districts:* The Bureau of the Census also provides information from the decennial census to school districts that request it. Since school districts frequently cut across political, administrative and statistical unit boundaries, this set of units is an entirely separate one from the other hierarchies and does not cover the entire area of the United States.

B. The urban/rural hierarchy
    The urban/rural hierarchy is a complex one, because the delineation of urban and rural places overlaps with the definitions of both places and metropolitan areas. "The urban and rural classification cuts across the other hierarchies; for example, there is generally both urban and rural territory within both metropolitan and non-metropolitan areas" (U.S. Census Bureau, 1990, *General Population Characteristics,* Illinois: A-11).

The Urban/Rural Hierarchy by Size of Place: There

The Future of Federally Sponsored Statistical Surveys

by Alison Kadlec Donta

Although it compiles data on one of the largest and most complex nations in the world, the current United States statistical system is also one of the most decentralized. Today it consists of eleven separate statistical agencies in nine different cabinet departments. In addition, there are over 70 other government agencies with large statistical programs. At the same time, the group that coordinates this system is one of the smallest in the world. Since 1947, the number of people assigned to statistical policy and coordination fell from 65 to 5 although the budget for statistics has increased 19 times over that same time period. The Office of Management and Budget (OMB) reported a 1994 federal budget for statistics of under $2.7 billion which represented less than 0.2% of the national budget. Many federal agencies have recently had budget cuts and are facing additional ones in the future. Amidst these austere times, the federal social surveys will try to meet the demands of the upcoming century. Some changes are necessary if this statistical system is to meet the challenges of the future which include accurately documenting a growing and more complex population, and facing the increasing technological capacity of the nation as a whole.

There are currently several bills before the U.S. Congress to restructure the system, relocate key agencies, and reallocate programs and budgets. The options are to centralize the entire system or to better organize the current decentralized system. A Central Statistical Bureau has been proposed which would be made up of the Bureau of Labor Statistics, the Bureau of Economic Analysis, the Bureau of the Census, and the Statistical Policy Division currently in the OBM. This system, presided over by a Chief Statistician, would represent a move toward a centralized and more efficient statistical system which could serve to eliminate, among other things, duplication of data across surveys. At the same time, opponents of this plan fear that the change to a centralized system would lead to excess bureaucracy and be too costly in this era of downsizing government. Alternatively, it would be possible to develop a National Statistical Law which would create uniform policies and standards to be followed by all the participating statistical agencies still within a decentralized framework.

One attempt at centralization has already been proposed by the Department of Health and Human Services (HHS) to integrate, coordinate, and consolidate health surveys. This Survey Integration Plan is designed to create cross-agency surveys to meet common goals. When completed, this proposal will integrate data efforts of the National Center for Health Statistics (NCHS), the Agency for Health Care Policy and Research (AHCPR), and the Health Care Financing Administration (HCFA). Benefits of this more centralized system include more efficient survey sampling, enhanced analytic capabilities of all HHS surveys by allowing direct linkage of questionnaire data, and more flexibility to meet the growing public health data demands in the future. Although the Survey Integration Plan is not yet complete, there has already been the linkage of the National Health Interview Survey and National Medical Expenditures Panel Survey samples. This HHS plan may serve as an example that the entire U.S. statistical system could emulate if the decision is made to move toward centralization.

Different agencies within the U.S. statistical system are already making changes to respond to the demands of the future. Although facing a 20% reduction in sample size in upcoming years, the Current Population Survey (CPS) has also redesigned its survey questionnaire as of January 1994 in order to elicit more detailed and accurate employment data. At the same time, the CPS has introduced Computer Assisted Personal Interviewing (CAPI) in which CPS field interviewers use lap-top computers with an interactive version of the new questionnaire to record responses and feed the information back to a central data source.

The U.S. Bureau of the Census is currently testing its new American Community Survey (ACS), a yearly survey of a sample of U.S. households. The ACS will serve to supplement data produced by the decennial census and the yearly CPS. It will be a continuous measurement program which will provide moving averages to better track longitudinal trends. The ACS was tested at four sites in 1996 and will be expanded in 1997.

Another way the federal social surveys of population are rising to the challenges of the future is to place an increasing emphasis on electronic means of data dispersion (see Appendix 2-3). In 1996, the U.S. Bureau of the Census introduced a prototype of the Data Access and Dissemination System (DADS). This system, when complete, will be available through the Internet and house much of the data produced by the Census Bureau in upcoming years. Users will be able to access record-level census data for extraction and tabulation in an interactive system. It will be possible to create desired tables by choosing variables of interest such as race, Hispanic origin, marital status, geographic region, and labor force status.

Part of the DADS system that is already in use is the Federal Electronic Research and Review Extraction Tool (FERRET), currently available through the Internet. To date, FERRET has data from the CPS and Survey of Income and Program Participation (SIPP) available. In the near future, data from the American Housing Survey (AHS), the National Science Foundation (NSF), and the National Center for Health Statistics (NCHS) will be added.

As the United States moves into the 21st century, there will be an increasing demand for more detailed and accessible data from the public, the business world, and government agencies. Several ideas have already been implemented to provide the timely and accurate data needed now and in the future, and still others are under current development. The questions still remain, however, whether the U.S. statistical system will face the 21st century as a newly formatted centralized system or as a better organized decentralized system operated by various government and private agencies, and whether or not the new system will be able to maintain data quality and continuity through these major transitions.

Additional Sources:

Bonnen, James T. "The Politics of Statistical Reform: A Cautionary Tale, 1978-1980." Chance 9(1996):17-26.

Hunter, Edward L, and Arnett, Ross III. "Survey 'Reinventing' at Health and Human Services." Chance 9(1996):54-57.

National State Data Center. Annual Meeting notes and materials. October, 1996.

Norwood, Janet L. "The Winds of Change: Opportunity or Disaster—the U.S. Federal Statistics." Chance 9(1996):50-52.

U.S. Bureau of the Census. Bureau of the Census Home Page. Http://www.census.gov, 1996.

are two hierarchies for the classification of urban and rural data (see Figure 2-3, Part C). The first hierarchy, Urban/Rural by Size of Place, divides up areal units within each state on the basis of the size of place. By definition, a densely settled area that has a population of 50,000 or more is called an urbanized area, and the entire population within that area is urban. Within such urbanized areas, the population is further categorized into the central place and the urban fringe. Outside of urbanized areas, urban populations can also exist; they are classified into areas with populations of 10,000 or more, and those with populations of 2,500 to 9,999 people. Thus the urban population is really broken down into two major classifications and four sub-classifications, which are ordered by population size and degree of urban complexity.

The rural classification by size of place is simpler. It classifies areas into a) places of 1,000 to 2,499 people, b) places of less than 1,000 people, and c) other rural. This last category can refer to both rural populations living outside of recognized places and also to the rural portion of "extended cities" (cities which have a significant rural section within their boundaries). The break between places of less than 1,000 people and "other rural" category is new; in 1980 these two categories were combined.

The Urban/Rural Hierarchy by Metropolitan Status: The 1990 Census has also seen a much more complex designation of how urban and rural areas are distributed between metropolitan and non-metropolitan counties. In census statistics, states are divided into parts inside and outside of metropolitan areas (i.e. by county, since that is the basic building block of metropolitan areas).

Inside metropolitan areas, areas are either inside or outside the central city. The central city population is entirely urban. Outside of the central city, however, the population can be urban or rural (remember, the definition of metropolitan does not mean an entire county must have an urban character). Further, this non-central city urban component is further subdivided into inside urbanized area and outside urbanized area categories. Thus within a metropolitan area, there are four possible levels of urbanity: in the central city, outside the central city but within the urbanized area, beyond the urbanized area but still urban, and rural.

Outside of metropolitan areas, it is also possible for areas to be either urban or rural. Non-metropolitan urban areas are divided between those inside and outside of urbanized areas, and the latter category is further subdivided into places with populations of 10,000 or more and those with from 2,500 to 9,999 people. This classification scheme is much more complex than in 1980, when non-metropolitan areas were simply divided into their urban and rural elements.

Finally, disregarding the principle of non-overlapping geographic units within hierarchies, the census further classifies the rural population (whether inside or outside of metropolitan areas) as farm or non-farm. This categorization has nothing to do with geography; it is based on whether a household living on a farm sold $1,000 or more of agricultural products in 1989. The populations of those households were called farm; everyone else in the rural area (including, perhaps, their next-door neighbors) were classified as the non-farm population. The ovals designating these farm and non-farm statistical units in Figure 2-3, Part C overlap to remind the reader that these are not geographically exclusive units.

Clearly, there is considerable geographic overlap between the size of place and metropolitan status urban/rural hierarchies. However, they are conceptually distinct, have different kinds of census data available for their constituent units, and can be used for different purposes.

Reporting Individual and Household-level Census Data

Census data are reported in three major modes: reports on population, reports on housing, and reports that combine population and housing characteristics. Some of these reports are based on 100-percent (short-form) data; some are based on sample (long-form) data, and some are based on a mixture of data from both sources.

Census data are available for units ranging from the entire United States down to small areas such as census tracts, block groups, or even blocks. In order to preserve confidentiality, the Bureau of the Census has established certain minimum numbers (called thresholds) of households or individuals with certain identifiable characteristics. If the number of households or individuals with these characteristics falls below this threshold (usually between 250 and 1,000), then the Bureau employs suppression, whereby parts of data are not released. In the 1990 Census the Bureau also used confidentiality edits, whereby certain characteristics of households or individuals were "swapped" with similar neighbors to make it even more difficult to identify them individually.

Census Data Available in Printed Form

For the last several censuses, the Bureau of the Census has published printed volumes of population and housing results for the United States as a whole and for every state. The state volumes also contain data on metropolitan areas, counties, places and various other units in the statistical and administrative hierarchies mentioned above. In general, however, the cost of printing means that data on only very general topics are available for small areal units. The five key printed volumes that are available for every state and for the nation as a whole from the 1990 Census are:

CP-1. General Population Characteristics

CP-2. Social and Economic Characteristics

CPH-5. Summary Social, Economic and Housing Characteristics.

CH-1. General Housing Characteristics.
CH-2. Detailed Housing Characteristics.

In addition to these 1990 Census volumes on different areas of the United States, the Bureau of the Census also published a variety of studies on such specific topics as the foreign-born, ancestry groups, racial minorities, how housing is financed, and so on.

Census Data Available in Electronic Form

Since 1970, the Bureau of the Census has made electronic data from the census available to outside researchers. Initially, these were in the form of magnetic tapes, and were called Summary Tape Files (STFs). For data on areas, these STFs are essentially huge tables where different population characteristics are cross-tabulated by different levels of census geography. The Summary Tape Files can compress huge amounts of data onto magnetic tape; they are also much easier to convert into input files for computer-based statistical analysis programs. The data from each state are found on a separate Summary Tape File, and the data from some large states are so extensive that they require a multiple-tape STF.

Another kind of data of primary interest to scholars is the Public Use Microdata Sample (PUMS). In 1990, two random samples of households (a 5 percent sample and a 1 percent sample of the U.S. population) were taken from the households that filled out the long form of the census. These data were put on computer tape and also made available to outside researchers. These 12.5 and 2.5 million person samples of all long-form characteristics are tremendous resources to those with an interest in how population characteristics are distributed at the household or individual level. Recently, similar public use microdata samples have been made available for a 1-per-1,000 household sample for all censuses between 1940 and 1990 (see Appendix 2-3, under "CIESIN U.S. Demography Homepage").

The Bureau of the Census is now in the process of providing both printed and electronic data in new media. It is already sending data and reports to major research libraries in the form of CD-ROMs, and much intercensal data (for instance, data from the Current Population Survey) are now available over the Internet. A considerable amount of data from the 1990 and prior censuses are available via the Internet from several of the data archives listed in Appendix 2-3.

Vital Statistics Registration

Throughout the twentieth century there has been a move towards a consolidation of vital statistics registration kept at state or city levels to broader regions, eventually including the entire United States. During the nineteenth century, national statistics on natality (births), mortality (deaths), nuptiality (marriages) and divorces were based on responses to questions included in the decen-

nial censuses. However, it was recognized that obtaining vital statistics from the decennial censuses had serious deficiencies.

By 1880, a "death registration area" of New Jersey, Massachusetts, the District of Columbia and several other large cities was established, and by 1933 all states were included in it. A national birth registration area was established in 1915, and by 1933 it included all 48 states (the territory of Hawaii was added in 1929, and the territory of Alaska in 1950). Since 1942, statistics on fetal deaths have been collected; the National Center for Health Statistics (NCHS) now collects data on all fetal deaths that occur 20 weeks or more after gestation (and data on earlier fetal deaths in some states). Data on marriage and divorce have never been as complete as for mortality or natality. The federal government began to collect state data on these topics in 1917-21. By 1988 (the latest year for which federal statistics are available), the Marriage Registration Area (MRA) used by the NCHS included 42 states and the District of Columbia, and the Divorce Registration Area (DRA) included 31 states and the District of Columbia. These registration areas covered about 81 percent of all marriages and 49 percent of all divorces in the United States in 1988.

The National Vital Statistics Registration System

Two important parts of the establishment of a national vital statistics registration system have been getting states to collect data in a similar way and to report data in a timely manner. In recent years, this has meant getting states to cooperate in submitting computer data tapes that are organized in a similar fashion. Information on births and deaths have been collected on national standard certificates since 1900; the latest revisions of these forms were in 1989. The standard certificates of marriage and of divorce, dissolution of marriage or annulment have been used since 1955, with revisions in 1968 and 1978 (see Appendix 2-2 for examples of the current versions of these certificates).

In recent years, researchers at the NCHS, the Centers for Disease Control and Prevention (CDC) and other agencies have begun to combine or abstract vital statistics data to form new data sets. There is now a national linked file of live births and infant deaths that allows researchers to study the characteristics of infant mortality at the individual level. The Bureau of Criminal Justice Statistics has recently abstracted a file of the ages of about 400,000 U.S. murder victims and their killers from the years 1976-1992 from the national mortality statistics and other sources. The National Institute for Occupational Safety and Health compiles the National Traumatic Occupational Fatalities (NTOF) Surveillance System based on information taken from death certificates.

How Vital Statistics Data Are Reported

Vital statistics are reported annually in the *Vital Statistics of the United States*, published by the Centers for Disease Control and Prevention of the Public Health Service. These data are available as both counts of events and as rates, and are broken down by various areas (states, metropolitan areas, and so on) and by characteristics (race of the decedent, birth parity, age of the person marrying, whether children were involved in the divorce, etc.). Appendix 2-2 gives a brief introduction to the items on each of the certificates and how they are reported. These data are also available in electronic form as public use data tapes from the National Technical Information Service for 1968 and subsequent years for natality, mortality and marriage statistics, and for 1982 and subsequent years for fetal death statistics.

Major Demographic and Social Surveys

Various U.S. government agencies cooperate on a number of social and demographic surveys of the population. Topics include such varied subjects as family income, fertility, patterns of cigarette smoking among youth, farm family health hazards, frequency of contacts with their children among the elderly, and a host of others. These surveys are taken as frequently as once a month or at intervals of several years. Because they are often special-purpose surveys, their sampling frames may differ; in many cases they attempt to measure the characteristics of relatively small subpopulations of special interest. What follows is not a description of every government survey, but rather a precis of the more important surveys and examples of some of the more useful specialized surveys.

1. The Current Population Survey (CPS)

The Current Population Survey is the most important source of information on the United States population between censuses. In the early 1990s it was taken in 729 sample areas in the 50 states and the District of Columbia, and typically covered about 60,000 households. In every month it included a number of questions about employment and unemployment from which Bureau of Labor Statistics analysts derived monthly employment and unemployment rates. In each month, other questions were "piggy-backed" on this questionnaire: March for the annual demographic file, June for fertility expectations, October for school enrollment, and so on. A list of these topics and their distribution across months and years is given in Table 2-6.

Between 1967 and 1993, the CPS survey questionnaire and its method of administration remained the same. In January 1994, the CPS underwent several dramatic changes. Changes were introduced in the questions re-lating to the definition of work, multiple job-holding, hours worked, earnings, unemployment status, and other topics. The sampling process was changed: many households are now interviewed using computer-assisted telephone interviewing (CATI), and a portion of the overall sample is chosen using the random digit dialing (RDD) method. In addition, interviewers now use laptop computers to ask questions and record answers, rather than using a printed questionnaire. In this computer-assisted personal interviewing (CAPI) method, interviewers send data back to the Bureau of the Census using a telephone modem at the end of each day. Due to the complexity of the CPS questions and their many possible answers, one remarkable upshot of this new process is that there is no paper version of the new CPS questionnaire.

In addition to the changes in the questionnaire and the survey methodology in January 1994, the Bureau of the Census also decided to use the Post Enumeration Survey-adjusted population as the basis for the estimation of sample characteristics. From January 1994 on, the CPS unemployment rate has experienced a minor rise because the population that was missed in the original count but covered in the PES adjustment tended to be younger and more heavily minority, groups with higher rates of unemployment.

Three major series of reports on the U.S. population are derived from Current Population Survey and census data:

P-20, Population Characteristics: Statistics on school enrollment, marital status, mobility, fertility and so on are given in these annual (biennial for voting registration and participation) reports.

P-23, Special Studies: This series of reports includes studies of methodology and special reports on computer use, women, family life, migration, and other topics.

P-60, Consumer Income: This series includes occasional studies on money income of families, poverty, and experiments with different ways of analyzing consumer income, poverty, effects of taxes, and so on.

2. Survey of Income Program Participation (SIPP)

The SIPP is another large-scale national survey; it differs from the CPS in that respondents stay in the survey over a period of time. This allows for a more complete analysis of the behavior of individuals and households over time, and a better specification of the correlates or causes of different kinds of behavior. Various "waves" of the sample in over 200 Primary Sampling Units (consisting of counties or adjacent groups of counties) are asked questions at different intervals. Some are asked the same questions several times; the successive responses on household income, for example, allow for the computation of how many people are moving into and out of poverty as the nation's economic situation changes (see the "Pov-

Table 2-6. Current Population Survey Topics by Month and Year

Survey month and topic	Years collected	Years available
January		
Job finding	1973	1973
Job tenure and occupational mobility	1973, 1978, 1981, 1983, 1987, 1991	1973, 1978, 1981, 1983, 1987, 1991
Displaced workers	1984, 1986, 1988, 1990, 1992	1984, 1986, 1988, 1990, 1992
Job training	1983, 1984, 1991	1983, 1984, 1991
Tobacco use	1993	—
Housing tenure/children	1972, 1974-1977	1972, 1974-1977
February		
Unemployment compensation	1990, 1993	1990
March		
Demographic data	1968-1993	1968-1993
CPS/Social Security summary earnings exact match	1978	1978
After-tax money income estimates	1981-1986	1981-1986
Value of noncash benefits	1980, 1982-1986	1980, 1982-1986
April		
Volunteer work	1974	1974
Food stamp participation	1975-1977	1975-1977
Swine flu immunization	1977	—
Child support and alimony payments	1979, 1982, 1984, 1986, 1988, 1990, 1992	1979, 1982, 1984, 1986, 1988, 1990
Immigration	1983	1983
Veterans	1985	1985
Employee benefits	1993	—
May		
Multiple job holding and premium pay	1969-1981, 1985, 1989, 1991	1969-1981, 1985, 1989, 1991
Adult education	1969, 1972, 1975, 1978, 1981, 1984	1978, 1981, 1984
Private household workers	1971	1971
Post-secondary schol enrollment	1974	1974
Job search of the unemployed	1976	1976
Job search of the employed	1977	1977
Pension/retirement plan coverage	1979, 1983, 1988	1979, 1983, 1988
Shift work/flexitime	1980, 1981, 1985, 1989, 1991	1980, 1981, 1985, 1989, 1991
Employee benefits	1988	1988
Volunteer workers	1989	1989
Unemployment compensation	1989	1989
Tobacco use	1993	—
June		
Fertility and birth expectations	1973-1988, 1990, 1992	1973-1977, 1979-1988, 1990
Immigration	1986, 1988, 1991	1986, 1988, 1991
Marriage and birth history	1971, 1975, 1980, 1985, 1990	1975, 1980, 1985, 1990
Child care	1977, 1982	1977, 1982
Marital history	1985, 1990	1985, 1990
Emigration	1988, 1991	—
Unemployment compensation	1993	—

erty" section of Chapter 15). Other groups of questions on special topics (or "modules") are asked in different waves of the survey; for example, a survey on Americans with Disabilities was asked of 30,000 SIPP households in the sixth wave of 1990 and the third wave of 1991.

SIPP data are used to produce the Census Bureau's Series P-70, Household Economic Studies. Beginning in 1984, these reports looked at different economic and health assistance programs in the context of the income and poverty levels of the respondents to the survey. The SIPP data are particularly valuable because their questions allow for a much more fine-grained examination of the effects of different government programs on the lives of participants. In addition, the structure of the SIPP interviews allows the researcher to follow the same individual over a period of time, which means that the dynamic features of social processes (such as who is climbing out of or dropping into poverty over time) can be measured in a more accurate way. Other Bureau of the Census analytic series such as Series P-60, Consumer Income, are starting to integrate Current Population Survey and SIPP data in order to give a clearer picture of trends in income and poverty. The SIPP data are also available as public use computer tapes.

3. American Housing Survey

This large-scale survey, collected by the Bureau of the Census for the Department of Housing and Urban Development, is designed to provide an annual

Table 2-6. Current Population Survey Topics by Month and Year (continued)

Survey month and topic	Years collected	Years available
July		
Survey of languages	1975	1975
Telephone availablility	1984-1993	1984-1993
Emigration	1987	—
Housing tenure/children	1977, 1978	1977, 1978
August		
Food stamp participants	1977	1977
School lunch program participants	1977	1977
Smoking	1967-1968	1967-1968
Retiree health insurance	1988	1988
Unemployment compensation	1989, 1993	1989
September		
Immunization	1969, 1977-1985	1969, 1977-1985
Smoking	1985, 1989, 1990, 1992	1985, 1989, 1990
Tobacco use	1992	—
Veterans	1989, 1991, 1993	1989, 1991
October		
School enrollment	1968-1993	1968-1993
Recent college graduates	1971-1972	—
Post-secondary school enrollment	1973	1973
November		
Voting	Every 2 years since 1968	1972-1990(even years)
Ethnic background and literacy	1969, 1979, 1989	1969, 1979, 1989
Multiple job holding	1970	—
Private household workers	1974	1974
Telephone availability	1983-1993	1983-1992
Veterans	1987	1987
Immigration/emigration/language	1989	1989
Unemployment compensation	1989, 1993	1989
December		
Farm wage workers	1971-1977, 1979-1987(odd years)	1975-1987(odd years)
Food stamp participation	1975	1975
Child care	1984	1984
GED recipiency	1986	—
Receipt of pension bnefits	1989	1989

Source: U.S. Bureau of the Census, "Census Catalog and Guide: 1996," U.S. Government Printing Office, Washington, D.C., 1996, Figure 34.

supplement and update to the housing data obtained from the decennial census. It also includes more extensive data on housing conditions (including neighborhood characteristics) not included on the census. Two other quarterly surveys provide data on the current characteristics of the rental and home ownership markets. National-level data are available from this survey, as well as occasional "Housing Profile" data for selected metropolitan areas.

4. National Survey of Family Growth

Five NSFG surveys (in 1973, 1976, 1982-3, 1988, and 1993) have been conducted. The first two surveys covered about 10,000 ever-married women aged 15-44 years; the last three surveys each included more than 8,000 women aged 15-44 years regardless of marital status. Questions included on the 1973 and 1976 surveys considered marital and pregnancy histories, use of contracep-

tive methods, and so on. The 1982-3 survey added questions on sex education and sexually-transmitted diseases, and the last two versions included questions about AIDS, cohabitation and adoption. The 1988 respondents were reinterviewed in 1990. Public use data tapes for all years except 1990 are available from the National Technical Information Service.

5. National Health Interview Survey

This large-scale sample survey is composed of modules of questions on topics including illnesses, injuries, impairments, chronic conditions, and demographic background characteristics of respondents. Some of the modules are repeated, while others are asked only infrequently.

This is an ongoing survey that is conducted throughout the year. In each year, there are typically 40,000-50,000 households and about 110,000-125,000 individuals who fall into the sample. Data from the 1980s and early 1990s are available on computer tape and CD-ROM; both over-all survey data and data from particular modules are available.

6. The National Longitudinal Surveys

The NLS are a set of surveys, sponsored by the Bureau of Labor Statistics, which have gathered longitudinal information on a variety of socioeconomic characteristics including labor force experiences for cohorts of American men and women. Cohort surveys of older men (i.e. age 45-59 in 1966) ceased in 1990 and those of young men (i.e. aged 14-24 in 1966) ceased in 1981. Continuing cohort studies include those for mature women (i.e. aged 30-44 in 1967), young women (i.e. aged 14-24 in 1968), youth (i.e. aged 14-22 in 1979) and children (i.e. aged 0-22 in 1986).

NLS data has been used to study school-to-work transitions, life course work experiences, marriage and labor interactions, occupational choices and labor force retraining, and retirement patterns among other demographic behaviors. Data are weighted to achieve representation of all Americans born into the given cohort. Sampling procedures insure representation of non-whites, youth, women and the economically disadvantaged.

7. The Panel Study of Income Dynamics

The PSID is conducted by the Institute for Social Research at the University of Michigan. Since 1968 the PSID has collected a variety of income and labor force data for a representative sample of individuals and households in which they reside. The data are similar to some Current Population Survey items. Key among the data available are detailed work histories and labor force status throughout the year. These panel data also include a variety of related demographic characteristics for both individuals and families including marital status and family composition.

In 1968 the PSID began with a sample of white and black households. Members formed new households and the sample had grown to over 7,300 households by 1990. In that year the PSID sample was augmented by the addition of over 2,000 Latino households.

Administrative Statistics and Their Uses

The U.S. government also produces a number of different kinds of administrative data which are of great use to demographers. These data are continuously produced and collected by different government bureaucracies as they carry out their administrative functions. These sources are often used in the field of applied demography, but even in the mainstream areas of mortality, fertility and migration we are in many senses as much dependent upon administrative statistics as we are on data from censuses and surveys. What follows is not an exhaustive list of administrative statistics at the federal level (and state and local administrative statistics are widely used by demographers as well), but rather a sampling of sources.

1. Immigration Statistics

Immigration statistics are collected by the Immigration and Naturalization Service from both entry visas (submitted by those entering the United States) and change of immigration status forms (used by non-citizens already within the United States). These statistics include data on country of origin, visa and citizenship status, and a number of socioeconomic variables describing the immigrants. It is important to remember that no attempt has been made to measure *emigration* (the migration of population to areas outside the United States) since 1957. The Immigration and Naturalization Service publishes an annual *Statistical Yearbook*, and also makes data available via electronic media.

2. Surveillance, Epidemiology and End Results Survey

As cancer became an increasingly prevalent cause of death, and as life-style and environmental factors began to be increasingly recognized to play causal roles in cancer, the U.S. government began to get involved in organizing data on cancer incidence. While state-wide cancer incidence registries have been found in states like Connecticut as far back as the 1930s, a concerted effort to pull together national-level estimates of cancer incidence took place only in the 1970s and 1980s.

The National Cancer Institute's Surveillance, Epidemiology and End Results (SEER) program integrates data from 11 population-based registries of cancerous tumors from throughout the United States. These registries include only patients who were residents of these 11 areas at the time that their cancer was diagnosed; the population figures used to determine incidence rates were calculated by the U.S. Census Bureau.

SEER data are computed from hospital-based "tumor registries" built up from the biopsies of individual patients. Once they are classified according to kind of tumor and stage of growth, place of residence of the patient and various demographic characteristics, the data are transferred to the National Cancer Institute.

SEER data are published for 11 regions of the United States. Since the diagnosis and definition of tumors in each region corresponds to international standards, the SEER data can be compared to the extensive cancer data now available from a number of other nations.

3. National Hospital Discharge Survey

Since 1964, short-stay, non-federal hospitals have

been surveyed in order to see why patients were hospitalized. This survey has changed considerably in terms of its sampling frame and coverage of hospitals over the past thirty years. By 1992, the NHDS included 494 participating hospitals, and the records of 274,000 patients were examined.

By examining these medical records, the reasons for admission, length of stay, diagnoses, operations, and a number of other medical characteristics can be discovered. The NHDS also includes a number of demographic and social characteristics of these patients as well. Annual results from the NHDS are available in printed and electronic form from the National Center for Health Statistics.

4. National Notifiable Diseases Surveillance System

The NNDSS is a national passive surveillance system of 52 major infectious diseases designated by the Council of State and Territorial Epidemiologists and reported to the Centers for Disease Control and Prevention (CDC). Data are collected through the National Electronic Telecommunications System for Surveillance (NETSS) and other means. These data are collected by health personnel and laboratory workers, reported to state or local health departments, and then reported to the CDC. It is known that the reporting of many diseases through this system is a significant underestimate of their true incidence.

The CDC publishes state-based data on the incidence of major infectious diseases on a weekly basis in *Morbidity and Mortality Weekly Report*. In addition, it publishes an annual, the *Summary of Notifiable Diseases, United States*. These data are also available in electronic form from the CDC.

5. Department of Labor and Bureau of Labor Statistics Surveys

The previous section mentioned several specific surveys supported by the BLS. The Labor Department has, however, an enormous variety of ongoing administrative and survey programs with rich labor and economic detail. Among the major Department of Labor surveys are the following:

The Current Employment Statistics (CES) program collects data on employment, work hours and earnings from a sample of almost 400,000 establishments each month. Advance employment statistics for wage and salary workers on the payroll of nonagricultural establishments are published in *The Employment Situation* and additional detail follows later in *Employment and Earnings*. CES data excludes several groups included in the Current Population Survey, including the self-employed, agriculturally employed, private household and unpaid family workers, etc.

The Covered Employment and Wages (ES-202) program is one of several major collaborations between the Bureau of Labor Statistics and State Employment Security Agencies (SESAs). This program produces a comprehensive enumeration of employment and wage information for workers covered by state unemployment insurance laws providing a nearly comprehensive survey of payroll employment. The information available from the survey includes establishments, employment, and quarterly wages by industry and ownership sector.

The Occupational Employment Statistics (OES) are compiled by the Bureau of Labor Statistics, again using data provided by State Employment Security Agencies (SESAs). This survey covers workers in approximately 725,000 non-farm establishments in over 400 industries across all states and several territories of the United States. The survey runs on a three-year cycle with manufacturing industries interviewed every third year and non-manufacturing industries interviewed in the intervening two years. The data provide for occupational employment estimates by industry at detailed geographic levels of analysis.

The Unemployment Insurance Claims (UI) statistics are compiled by the Employment and Training Administration in the Department of Labor from data provided by State Employment Security Agencies (SESAs) to enumerate persons filing claims, filing first claims, denied benefits rights, eligible but not filing, etc. About 90 percent of United States workers are covered within the UI program.

6. Equal Employment Opportunity Commission Survey Program (2)

Several survey reports from the Equal Employment Opportunity Commission are so substantial as to deserve consideration alongside the other major administrative data resources of this section.

EEO-1, the Employer Information Report, covers private employers with 100 or more employees (about 50 percent of all private employment). The most recent survey covered 43 million workers employed by 45,000 employers. This survey was taken in 1966, 1970, 1975, and 1978-93, and is now taken annually.

EEO-3, the Local Union Report, covers local referral unions. The most recent survey covered 2,000 unions and 1.2 million members. The survey was taken in 1970, 1972, 1974, 1976, 1979, 1983, 1984, 1986, 1988, 1990 and 1992 and is now taken biennially.

EEO-4, the State and Local Government Information Report, covers state and local government employees (excluding school districts). The latest survey covered 6.0 million employees in 5,000 units of government (93 percent of state or local employment). The survey was taken in 1973-76, 1979, 1980, 1981, 1983-91 and 1993. It is now taken biennially.

EEO-5, the Elementary-Secondary Staff Information Report, covers teachers and staff in elementary and secondary public school districts. The latest survey included 3.7 employees in 4,500 school districts (90 percent of public school employment). The survey was taken in 1980, 1982, 1984, 1986, 1988, 1990 and 1992; and is now taken biennially.

EEO-6, the Higher Education Staff Information Report, covers teachers and staff in colleges and universities (public and private). The latest survey covered 2.5 million employees in 3,000 institutions (95 percent of employees in higher education). The survey was taken in 1975, 1979, 1981, 1983, 1985, 1987, 1989, and 1991. It is now taken biennially.

Conclusion

This chapter has attempted to show how the decennial census, the source we usually think of when we want "population data," is enmeshed in a much broader statistical effort by many government agencies at the local, state and federal levels. Many of these efforts at data collection would be seriously handicapped or impossible without the census. On the other hand, the continuous collection of data through vital statistics registers and the large-scale national surveys are invaluable in measuring how much (and what parts) of the population is missed by the census, and how the census can be improved in the future.

During the 1970s, Denis Johnston of the Office of Management of the Budget and an interagency team of statisticians prepared and published three reports on the "social indicators" of American society. However, since that time there has been little effort at integrating the increasing amount of quantitative information available on this nation's population. Instead, there has been a tendency (especially in the health field) towards the development of specialized data sets that measure narrow problems, with little attention to the big picture. Yet the breakthroughs in information-retrieval technologies (personal computers, inexpensive CD-ROMs, data available over the Internet) mean that those who need data on the population and its characteristics can now obtain such information more easily than ever before. What the user now needs to know are what the sources and organization of different kinds of data are. This chapter and the following ones may provide a road map to the sources of information, as well as a guide to how such data are organized.

This chapter has emphasized major data collection efforts undertaken by government agencies, or with their support, on a relatively regular basis. It is also important to note that several figures and tables throughout this text are drawn from more incidental or sporadic special-purpose surveys. As demographic topics and policy issues come to the fore, such special surveys are often a necessary and invaluable supplement to the regular data collection efforts which provide the bulk of our knowledge concerning the population of the United States.

Bibliography

Advisory Committee on Problems of Census Enumeration (National Research Council). America's Uncounted People. Washington, D.C.: National Academy of Sciences. 1972.

Alonso, William, and Starr, Paul (eds.). The Politics of Numbers. New York: Russell Sage Foundation. 1987.

Anderson, Margo. The American Census: A Social History. New Haven: Yale University Press. 1988.

Barrett, Richard E. Using the 1990 Census for Research. Thousand Oaks, CA: Sage Publications. 1994.

Bogue, Donald J. The Population of the United States: Historical Trends and Future Projections. New York: Free Press. 1985.

Choldin, Harvey. Looking for the Last Percent: The Controversy over Census Undercounts. Rutgers, NJ: Rutgers University Press. 1994.

Cohany, Sharon R., Polivka, Anne E., and Rothgeb, Jennifer M. "Revisions in the Current Population Survey Effective January 1994." Employment and Earnings, February (1994): 13-37.

Eckler, A. Ross. The Bureau of the Census. New York: Praeger. 1972.

Eriksen, Eugene P., Estrada, Leobardo F., Tukey, John W., and Wolter, Kirk M. Report on the 1990 Decennial Census and the Post-Enumeration Survey. Submitted to the Secretary of the U.S. Department of Commerce, 21 June 1991.

Federman, Maya, Garner, Theresa I., Short, Kathleen, Cutter, W. Bowman IV, Kiely, John, Levine, David, McGoug, Duane, and McMillen, Marilyn. "What Does it Mean to be Poor in America?" Monthly Labor Review 119(1996): 3-17.

Halacy, Dan. Census: 190 Years of Counting America. New York: Elsevier/Nelson Books. 1980.

Hogan, Howard. "The 1990 Post-Enumeration Survey: Operations and Results." Journal of the American Statistical Association 88(1993):1047-60.

Jenkins, Robert M. Procedural History of the 1940 Census of Housing and Population. Madison, WI: University of Wisconsin Press. 1985.

Koo, D., Wetterhall, S.F. "History and Current Status of the National Notifiable Diseases Surveillance System." Journal of Health Management Practice 2(1996):4-10.

Marx, Robert W. Census Geography. Alexandria, VA: American Chamber of Commerce Researchers Association. 1990.

Mitroff, Ian I., Mason, Richard O., and Barabba, Vincent P. The 1980 Census: Policymaking amid Turbulence. Lexington, MA: Lexington Books. 1983.

Myers, Dowell. Analysis with Local Census Data: Portraits of Change. Boston: Academic Press. 1992.

Passel, Jeffrey S. "Comment." Journal of the American Statistical Association 88,423 (1993):1074-77.

Polivka, Anne E., and Rothgeb, Jennifer M. "Redesigning the CPS Questionnaire." Monthly Labor Review 116(1993): 10-28.

Raymondo, James C. Population Estimation and Projection: Methods for Marketing, Demographic and Planning Personnel. New York: Quorum. 1992.

Robinson, J.G, Gupta, P.D., and Woodrow, R.A. "Estimation of Population Coverage in the 1990 United States Census Based on Demographic Analysis." Journal of the American Statistical Association 88(1993):1065.

Scott, Ann Herbert. Census, U.S.A.: Fact-finding for the American people, 1790-1970. New York: Seabury. 1968.

U.S. Bureau of the Census. Historical Statistics of the United States: Colonial Times to 1970. Washington, D.C.: U.S. Government Printing Office. 1975.

_____. Census '80: Continuing the Factfinder Tradition. Washington, D.C.: U.S. Government Printing Office. 1980.

_____. Census of Population and Housing: Public Use Microdata Samples, Technical Documentation. Washington, D.C.: Bureau of the Census. 1983.

_____. 1980 Census of Population and Housing. Evaluation and Research Reports. The Coverage of Population in the 1980 Census. PHC80-E4. Washington, D.C.: U.S. Bureau of the Census. 1988.

_____. Hidden Treasures! Census Bureau Data and Where to Find It. Washington, D.C.: Bureau of the Census. 1990.

_____. Population of Metropolitan Areas and Component Geography: 1990 and 1980 (6-30-90 Definitions). 1990 CPH-L-10. Washington, D.C.: U.S. Department of Commerce. 1991.

_____. Maps and More: Your Guide to Census Bureau Geography. Washington, D.C.: Bureau of the Census. 1992.

_____. 1990 Census of Population and Housing: Guide. Part A. Text. Washington, D.C.: U.S. Government Printing Office. 1992.

_____. 1990 Census of Population and Housing: Public Use Microdata Samples: United States, Technical Documentation. Washington, D.C.: U.S. Bureau of the Census. 1992.

_____. Americans with Disabilities: 1991-92; Data from the Survey of Income and Program Participation. John M. McNeil. Current Population Reports, Household Economic Studies, P70-33. 1993.

_____. A Guide to State and Local Census Geography. Washington, D.C.: U.S. Government Printing Office. 1993.

_____. 1990 Census of Population and Housing. Part B. Glossary. Washington, D.C.: U.S. Government Printing Office. 1993

_____. Census Catalog and Guide: 1996. Washington, D.C.: U.S. Government Printing Office. 1996.

_____. Statistical abstract of the United States: 1995. Washington, D.C.: U.S. Government Printing Office. 1996.

U.S. General Accounting Office. Decennial Census: 1990 Results Show Need for Fundamental Reform (GAO/GDD-92-94, June 9, 1992). Washington, D.C.: United States General Accounting Office. 1992.

_____. Formula Programs: Adjusted Census Data Would Redistribute Small Percentage of Funds to States (GAO/GDD-92-12, Nov. 7, 1991). Washington, D.C.: United States Government Accounting Office. 1991.

_____. 1990 Census: Reported Net Undercount Obscured Magnitude of Error (GAO/GDD-91-113, Aug. 22, 1991). Washington, D.C.: United States General Accounting Office. 1991.

U.S. Public Health Service. Directory of Minority Health Data Resources of the Public Health Service. Washington, D.C.: U.S. Department of Health and Human Services, Public Health Service, Office of Minority Health. 1992.

Appendix 2-1
1990 U.S. Census Form (Long Form)

CENSUS '90

OFFICIAL 1990
U.S. CENSUS FORM

Thank you for taking time to complete and return this census questionnaire. It's important to you, your community, and the Nation.

The law requires answers but guarantees privacy.

By law (Title 13, U.S. Code), you're required to answer the census questions to the best of your knowledge. However, the same law guarantees that your census form remains confidential. For 72 years--or until the year 2062--only Census Bureau employees can see your form. No one else--no other government body, no police department, no court system or welfare agency--is permitted to see this confidential information under any circumstances.

How to get started--and get help.

Start by listing on the next page the names of all the people who live in your home. Please answer all questions with a black lead pencil. You'll find detailed instructions for answering the census in the enclosed guide. If you need additional help, call the toll-free telephone number to the left, near your address.

Please answer and return your form promptly.

Complete your form and return it by April 1, 1990 in the postage-paid envelope provided. Avoid the inconvenience of having a census taker visit your home.

Again, thank you for answering the 1990 Census.
Remember: Return the completed form by April 1, 1990.

Para personas de habla hispana --
(For Spanish-speaking persons)

Si usted desea un cuestionario del censo en español, llame sin cargo alguno al siguiente número: **1-800-CUENTAN**
(o sea 1-800-283-6826)

U.S. Department of Commerce
BUREAU OF THE CENSUS

FORM **D-2**

OMB No. 0607-0628
Approval Expires 07/31/91

The 1990 census must count every person at his or her "usual residence." This means the place where the person lives and sleeps most of the time.

1a. List on the numbered lines below the name of each person living here on Sunday, April 1, including all persons staying here who have no other home. If EVERYONE at this address is staying here temporarily and usually lives somewhere else, follow the instructions given in question 1b below.

Include

- Everyone who usually lives here such as family members, housemates and roommates, foster children, roomers, boarders, and live-in employees
- Persons who are temporarily away on a business trip, on vacation, or in a general hospital
- College students who stay here while attending college
- Persons in the Armed Forces who live here
- Newborn babies still in the hospital
- Children in boarding schools below the college level
- Persons who stay here most of the week while working even if they have a home somewhere else
- Persons with no other home who are staying here on April 1

Do NOT include

- Persons who usually live somewhere else

- Persons who are away in an institution such as a prison, mental hospital, or a nursing home
- College students who live somewhere else while attending college
- Persons in the Armed Forces who live somewhere else

- Persons who stay somewhere else most of the week while working

Print last name, first name, and middle initial for each person. Begin on line 1 with the household member (or one of the household members) in whose name this house or apartment is owned, being bought, or rented. If there is no such person, start on line 1 with any adult household member.

	LAST	FIRST	INITIAL		LAST	FIRST	INITIAL
1				**7**			
2				**8**			
3				**9**			
4				**10**			
5				**11**			
6				**12**			

1b. If EVERYONE is staying here only temporarily and usually lives somewhere else, list the name of each person on the numbered lines above, fill this circle ⟶ ○ and print their usual address below. DO NOT PRINT THE ADDRESS LISTED ON THE FRONT COVER.

House number	Street or road/Rural route and box number	Apartment number

City	State	ZIP Code

County or foreign country	Names of nearest intersecting streets or roads

NOW PLEASE OPEN THE FLAP TO PAGE 2 AND ANSWER ALL QUESTIONS FOR THE FIRST 7 PEOPLE LISTED. USE A BLACK LEAD PENCIL ONLY.

	PERSON 1	PERSON 2
Please fill one column for each person listed in Question 1a on page 1.	Last name First name ___ Middle initial	Last name First name ___ Middle initial

2. How is this person related to PERSON 1?

Fill ONE circle for each person.

If **Other relative** of person in column 1, fill circle and print exact relationship, such as mother-in-law, grandparent, son-in-law, niece, cousin, and so on.

Person 1: START in this column with the household member (or one of the members) in whose name the home is owned, being bought, or rented.

If there is no such person, start in this column with any adult household member.

■

Person 2:

If a RELATIVE of Person 1:
- ○ Husband/wife   ○ Brother/sister
- ○ Natural-born   ○ Father/mother
  or adopted   ○ Grandchild
  son/daughter   ○ Other relative ⌐
- ○ Stepson/
  stepdaughter

If NOT RELATED to Person 1:
- ○ Roomer, boarder,   ○ Unmarried
  or foster child   partner
- ○ Housemate, ■   ○ Other
  roommate   nonrelative

3. Sex

Fill ONE circle for each person.

Person 1: ○ Male   ○ Female

Person 2: ○ Male   ○ Female

4. Race

Fill ONE circle for the race that the person considers himself/herself to be.

If **Indian (Amer.)**, print the name of the enrolled or principal tribe. ⟶

If **Other Asian or Pacific Islander (API)**, print one group, for example: Hmong, Fijian, Laotian, Thai, Tongan, Pakistani, Cambodian, and so on. ⟶

If **Other race**, print race ⟶

Person 1:
- ○ White
- ○ Black or Negro
- ○ Indian (Amer.) (Print the name of the enrolled or principal tribe.) ⌐
- ○ Eskimo
- ○ Aleut

Asian or Pacific Islander (API)
- ○ Chinese   ○ Japanese
- ○ Filipino ■   ○ Asian Indian
- ○ Hawaiian   ○ Samoan
- ○ Korean   ○ Guamanian
- ○ Vietnamese   ○ Other API ⌐
- ○ Other race (Print race) ⌐

Person 2:
- ○ White
- ○ Black or Negro
- ○ Indian (Amer.) (Print the name of the enrolled or principal tribe.) ⌐
- ○ Eskimo
- ○ Aleut

Asian or Pacific Islander (API)
- ○ Chinese   ○ Japanese
- ○ Filipino ■   ○ Asian Indian
- ○ Hawaiian   ○ Samoan
- ○ Korean   ○ Guamanian
- ○ Vietnamese   ○ Other API ⌐
- ○ Other race (Print race) ⌐

5. Age and year of birth.

a. Print each person's age at last birthday. Fill in the matching circle below each box.

b. Print each person's year of birth and fill the matching circle below each box.

Person 1:

a. Age

| 0 ○ 0 ○ 0 ○ |
| 1 ○ 1 ○ 1 ○ |
| 2 ○ 2 ○ |
| 3 ○ 3 ○ |
| 4 ○ 4 ○ ■ |
| 5 ○ 5 ○ |
| 6 ○ 6 ○ |
| 7 ○ 7 ○ |
| 8 ○ 8 ○ |
| 9 ○ 9 ○ |

b. Year of birth

| 1 ● 8 ○ 0 ○ 0 ○ |
| 9 ○ 1 ○ 1 ○ |
| 2 ○ 2 ○ |
| 3 ○ 3 ○ |
| 4 ○ 4 ○ |
| 5 ○ 5 ○ |
| 6 ○ 6 ○ |
| 7 ○ 7 ○ |
| 8 ○ 8 ○ |
| 9 ○ 9 ○ |

Person 2:

a. Age

| 0 ○ 0 ○ 0 ○ |
| 1 ○ 1 ○ 1 ○ |
| 2 ○ 2 ○ |
| 3 ○ 3 ○ |
| 4 ○ 4 ○ ■ |
| 5 ○ 5 ○ |
| 6 ○ 6 ○ |
| 7 ○ 7 ○ |
| 8 ○ 8 ○ |
| 9 ○ 9 ○ |

b. Year of birth

| 1 ● 8 ○ 0 ○ 0 ○ |
| 9 ○ 1 ○ 1 ○ |
| 2 ○ 2 ○ |
| 3 ○ 3 ○ |
| 4 ○ 4 ○ |
| 5 ○ 5 ○ |
| 6 ○ 6 ○ |
| 7 ○ 7 ○ |
| 8 ○ 8 ○ |
| 9 ○ 9 ○ |

6. Marital status

Fill ONE circle for each person.

Person 1:
- ○ Now married   ○ Separated
- ○ Widowed   ○ Never married
- ○ Divorced

Person 2:
- ○ Now married   ○ Separated
- ○ Widowed   ○ Never married
- ○ Divorced

7. Is this person of Spanish/Hispanic origin?

Fill ONE circle for each person.

If **Yes, other Spanish/Hispanic**, print one group. ⟶

Person 1:
- ○ No (not Spanish/Hispanic)
- ○ Yes, Mexican, Mexican-Am., Chicano
- ○ Yes, Puerto Rican ■
- ○ Yes, Cuban
- ○ Yes, other Spanish/Hispanic
  (Print one group, for example: Argentinean, Colombian, Dominican, Nicaraguan, Salvadoran, Spaniard, and so on.) ⌐

Person 2:
- ○ No (not Spanish/Hispanic)
- ○ Yes, Mexican, Mexican-Am., Chicano
- ○ Yes, Puerto Rican
- ○ Yes, Cuban
- ○ Yes, other Spanish/Hispanic
  (Print one group, for example: Argentinean, Colombian, Dominican, Nicaraguan, Salvadoran, Spaniard, and so on.) ⌐

FOR CENSUS USE ⟶

Person 1: ○ ○

Person 2: ○ ○

PERSON 7

st name

st name   Middle Initial

a RELATIVE of Person 1:

- ○ Husband/wife   ○ Brother/sister
- ○ Natural-born   ○ Father/mother
  or adopted   ○ Grandchild
  son/daughter   ○ Other relative ⌐
- ○ Stepson/
  stepdaughter

NOT RELATED to Person 1:

- ○ Roomer, boarder,   ○ Unmarried
  or foster child   partner
- ○ Housemate,   ○ Other
  roommate ■   nonrelative

- ○ Male   ○ Female

- ○ White
- ○ Black or Negro
- ○ Indian (Amer.) (Print the name of the
  enrolled or principal tribe.) ⌐

- ○ Eskimo
- ○ Aleut

Asian or Pacific Islander (API)

- ○ Chinese   ○ Japanese
- ○ Filipino ■   ○ Asian Indian
- ○ Hawaiian   ○ Samoan
- ○ Korean   ○ Guamanian
- ○ Vietnamese   ○ Other API ⌐

- ○ Other race (Print race) ◢

Age	b. Year of birth
	1

○ 0	○ 0	○ 0	1 ● 8	○ 0	○ 0	○ 0	○ 0
○ 1	○ 1	○ 0	9 ○ 1	○ 0	○ 1	○ 1	○ 0
2 ○	2 ○	0	2 ○	2 ○	0
3 ○	3 ○	0	3 ○	3 ○	0
4 ○	4 ○ ■	0	4 ○	4 ○	0
5 ○	5 ○	0	5 ○	5 ○	0
6 ○	6 ○	0	6 ○	6 ○	0
7 ○	7 ○	0	7 ○	7 ○	0
8 ○	8 ○	0	8 ○	8 ○	0
9 ○	9 ○	0	9 ○	9 ○	0

- ○ Now married   ○ Separated
- ○ Widowed   ○ Never married
- ○ Divorced

- ○ No (not Spanish/Hispanic)
- ○ Yes, Mexican, Mexican-Am., Chicano
- ○ Yes, Puerto Rican ■
- ○ Yes, Cuban
- ○ Yes, other Spanish/Hispanic
  (Print one group, for example: Argentinean,
  Colombian, Dominican, Nicaraguan,
  Salvadoran, Spaniard, and so on.) ⌐

- ○
- ○

NOW PLEASE ANSWER QUESTIONS H1a— H26 FOR YOUR HOUSEHOLD

H1a. Did you leave anyone out of your list of persons for Question 1a on page 1 because you were not sure if the person should be listed — for example, someone temporarily away on a business trip or vacation, a newborn baby still in the hospital, or a person who stays here once in a while and has no other home?

- ○ Yes, please print the name(s)   ○ No
  and reason(s). ⌐

_____

b. Did you include anyone in your list of persons for Question 1a on page 1 even though you were not sure that the person should be listed — for example, a visitor who is staying here temporarily or a person who usually lives somewhere else?

- ○ Yes, please print the name(s)   ○ No
  and reason(s). ⌐

_____

H2. Which best describes this building? Include all apartments, flats, etc., even if vacant.

- ○ A mobile home or trailer
- ○ A one-family house detached from any other house
- ○ A one-family house attached to one or more houses
- ○ A building with 2 apartments
- ○ A building with 3 or 4 apartments
- ○ A building with 5 to 9 apartments
- ○ A building with 10 to 19 apartments
- ○ A building with 20 to 49 apartments
- ○ A building with 50 or more apartments
- ○ Other

H3. How many rooms do you have in this house or apartment? Do NOT count bathrooms, porches, balconies, foyers, halls, or half-rooms.

- ○ 1 room ■   ○ 4 rooms   ○ 7 rooms
- ○ 2 rooms   ○ 5 rooms   ○ 8 rooms
- ○ 3 rooms   ○ 6 rooms   ○ 9 or more rooms

H4. Is this house or apartment —

- ○ Owned by you or someone in this household with a mortgage or loan?
- ○ Owned by you or someone in this household free and clear (without a mortgage)?
- ○ Rented for cash rent?
- ○ Occupied without payment of cash rent?

If this is a ONE-FAMILY HOUSE —

H5a. Is this house on ten or more acres?

- ○ Yes   ○ No

b. Is there a business (such as a store or barber shop) or a medical office on this property?

- ○ Yes   ○ No   ■

Answer only if you or someone in this household OWNS OR IS BUYING this house or apartment —

H6. What is the value of this property; that is, how much do you think this house and lot or condominium unit would sell for if it were for sale?

○ Less than $10,000	○ $70,000 to $74,999
○ $10,000 to $14,999	○ $75,000 to $79,999
○ $15,000 to $19,999	○ $80,000 to $89,999
○ $20,000 to $24,999	○ $90,000 to $99,999
○ $25,000 to $29,999	○ $100,000 to $124,999
○ $30,000 to $34,999	○ $125,000 to $149,999
○ $35,000 to $39,999	○ $150,000 to $174,999
○ $40,000 to $44,999	○ $175,000 to $199,999
○ $45,000 to $49,999	○ $200,000 to $249,999
○ $50,000 to $54,999	○ $250,000 to $299,999
○ $55,000 to $59,999	○ $300,000 to $399,999
○ $60,000 to $64,999	○ $400,000 to $499,999
○ $65,000 to $69,999	○ $500,000 or more

Answer only if you PAY RENT for this house or apartment —

H7a. What is the monthly rent?

○ Less than $80	○ $375 to $399
○ $80 to $99	○ $400 to $424
○ $100 to $124	○ $425 to $449
○ $125 to $149	○ $450 to $474
○ $150 to $174	○ $475 to $499
○ $175 to $199	○ $500 to $524
○ $200 to $224	○ $525 to $549 ■
○ $225 to $249	○ $550 to $599
○ $250 to $274	○ $600 to $649
○ $275 to $299	○ $650 to $699
○ $300 to $324	○ $700 to $749
○ $325 to $349	○ $750 to $999
○ $350 to $374	○ $1,000 or more

b. Does the monthly rent include any meals?

- ○ Yes   ○ No

FOR CENSUS USE

A. Total persons	B. Type of unit	D. Months vacant	G. DO	ID

A. Total persons

○ I ○
2 2
3
4 ■
5
6
7
8
9

B. Type of unit

Occupied	Vacant
○ First form	○ Regular
○ Cont'n	○ Usual home elsewhere

C1. Vacancy status

- ○ For rent   ○ For seas/
- ○ For sale only   rec/occ
- ○ Rented or   ○ For migrant
  sold, not   workers
  occupied   ○ Other vacant

C2. Is this unit boarded up?

- ○ Yes   ○ No

D. Months vacant

- ○ Less than 1   ○ 6 up to 12
- ○ 1 up to 2   ○ 12 up to 24
- ○ 2 up to 6   ○ 24 or more

E. Complete after

- ○ LR ○ TC ○ QA
- ○ P/F ○ RE ○ I/T   JIC 1
- ○ MV ○ ED ○ EN ■

- ○ P0 ○ P3 ○ P6
- ○ P1 ○ P4 ○ 1A   JIC 2
- ○ P2 ○ P5 ○ SM ○

F. Cov.

- ○ 1b ○ 1a ○ 7 ○ H1

G. DO / ID

0	0	0	0	0	0	0	0	0	0
1	1	1	1	1	1	1	1	1	1
2	2	2	2	2	2	2	2	2	2
3	3	3	3	3	3	3	3	3	3
4	4	4	4	4	4	4	4	4	4
5	5	5	5	5	5	5	5	5	5
6	6	6	6	6	6	6	6	6	6
7	7	7	7	7	7	7	7	7	7
8	8	8	8	8	8	8	8	8	8
9	9	9	9	9	9	9	9	9	9

ge 4

H8. When did the person listed in column 1 on page 2 move into this house or apartment?

- ○ 1989 or 1990
- ○ 1985 to 1988
- ○ 1980 to 1984
- ○ 1970 to 1979
- ○ 1960 to 1969
- ○ 1959 or earlier

H9. How many bedrooms do you have; that is, how many bedrooms would you list if this house or apartment were on the market for sale or rent?

- ○ No bedroom
- ○ 1 bedroom
- ○ 2 bedrooms
- ○ 3 bedrooms
- ○ 4 bedrooms
- ○ 5 or more bedrooms

H10. Do you have COMPLETE plumbing facilities in this house or apartment; that is, 1) hot and cold piped water, 2) a flush toilet, and 3) a bathtub or shower?

- ○ Yes, have all three facilities
- ○ No

H11. Do you have COMPLETE kitchen facilities; that is, 1) a sink with piped water, 2) a range or cookstove, and 3) a refrigerator?

- ○ Yes
- ○ No

H12. Do you have a telephone in this house or apartment?

- ○ Yes
- ○ No

H13. How many automobiles, vans, and trucks of one-ton capacity or less are kept at home for use by members of your household?

- ○ None
- ○ 1
- ○ 2
- ○ 3
- ○ 4
- ○ 5
- ○ 6
- ○ 7 or more

H14. Which FUEL is used MOST for heating this house or apartment?

- ○ Gas: from underground pipes serving the neighborhood
- ○ Gas: bottled, tank, or LP
- ○ Electricity
- ○ Fuel oil, kerosene, etc.
- ○ Coal or coke
- ○ Wood
- ○ Solar energy
- ○ Other fuel
- ○ No fuel used

H15. Do you get water from —

- ○ A public system such as a city water department, or private company?
- ○ An individual drilled well?
- ○ An individual dug well?
- ○ Some other source such as a spring, creek, river, cistern, etc.?

H16. Is this building connected to a public sewer?

- ○ Yes, connected to public sewer
- ○ No, connected to septic tank or cesspool
- ○ No, use other means

H17. About when was this building first built?

- ○ 1989 or 1990
- ○ 1985 to 1988
- ○ 1980 to 1984
- ○ 1970 to 1979
- ○ 1960 to 1969
- ○ 1950 to 1959
- ○ 1940 to 1949
- ○ 1939 or earlier
- ○ Don't know

H18. Is this house or apartment part of a condominium?

- ○ Yes
- ○ No

If you live in an apartment building, skip to H20.

H19a. Is this house on less than 1 acre?

- ○ Yes — *Skip to H20*
- ○ No

b. In 1989, what were the actual sales of all agricultural products from this property?

- ○ None
- ○ $1 to $999
- ○ $1,000 to $2,499
- ○ $2,500 to $4,999
- ○ $5,000 to $9,999
- ○ $10,000 or more

H20. What are the yearly costs of utilities and fuels for this house or apartment?
If you have lived here less than 1 year, estimate the yearly cost.

a. Electricity

$ .00
Yearly cost — Dollars

OR

- ○ Included in rent or in condominium fee
- ○ No charge or electricity not used

b. Gas

$ .00
Yearly cost — Dollars

OR

- ○ Included in rent or in condominium fee
- ○ No charge or gas not used

c. Water

$ .00
Yearly cost — Dollars

OR

- ○ Included in rent or in condominium fee
- ○ No charge

d. Oil, coal, kerosene, wood, etc.

$ .00
Yearly cost — Dollars

OR

- ○ Included in rent or in condominium fee
- ○ No charge or these fuels not used

INSTRUCTION:

Answer questions H21 TO H26, if this is a one-family house, a condominium, or a mobile home that someone in this household OWNS OR IS BUYING; otherwise, go to page 6.

H21. What were the real estate taxes on THIS property last year?

$ _____ .00
Yearly amount — Dollars

OR

○ None

H22. What was the annual payment for fire, hazard, and flood insurance on THIS property?

$ _____ .00
Yearly amount — Dollars

OR

○ None

H23a. Do you have a mortgage, deed of trust, contract to purchase, or similar debt on THIS property?

○ Yes, mortgage, deed of trust, or similar debt ⎫
○ Yes, contract to purchase ⎬ Go to H23b
○ No — *Skip to H24a* ⎭

b. How much is your regular monthly mortgage payment on THIS property? Include payment only on first mortgage or contract to purchase.

$ _____ .00
Monthly amount — Dollars

OR

○ No regular payment required — *Skip to H24a*

c. Does your regular monthly mortgage payment include payments for real estate taxes on THIS property?

○ Yes, taxes included in payment
○ No, taxes paid separately or taxes not required

d. Does your regular monthly mortgage payment include payments for fire, hazard, or flood insurance on THIS property?

○ Yes, insurance included in payment
○ No, insurance paid separately or no insurance

H24a. Do you have a second or junior mortgage or a home equity loan on THIS property?

○ Yes
○ No — *Skip to H25*

b. How much is your regular monthly payment on all second or junior mortgages and all home equity loans?

$ _____ .00
Monthly amount — Dollars

OR

○ No regular payment required

Answer ONLY if this is a CONDOMINIUM —

H25. What is the monthly condominium fee?

$ _____ .00
Monthly amount — Dollars

Answer ONLY if this is a MOBILE HOME —

H26. What was the total cost for personal property taxes, site rent, registration fees, and license fees on this mobile home and its site last year? Exclude real estate taxes.

$ _____ .00
Yearly amount — Dollars

Please turn to page 6.

PERSON 1

Last name | First name | Middle initial

8. In what U.S. State or foreign country was this person born?

(Name of State or foreign country; or Puerto Rico, Guam, etc.)

9. Is this person a CITIZEN of the United States?

- ○ Yes, born in the United States — *Skip to 11*
- ○ Yes, born in Puerto Rico, Guam, the U.S. Virgin Islands, or Northern Marianas
- ○ Yes, born abroad of American parent or parents
- ○ Yes, U.S. citizen by naturalization
- ○ No, not a citizen of the United States

10. When did this person come to the United States to stay?

- ○ 1987 to 1990
- ○ 1985 or 1986
- ○ 1982 to 1984
- ○ 1980 or 1981
- ○ 1975 to 1979
- ○ 1970 to 1974
- ○ 1965 to 1969
- ○ 1960 to 1964
- ○ 1950 to 1959
- ○ Before 1950

11. At any time since February 1, 1990, has this person attended regular school or college?
Include only nursery school, kindergarten, elementary school, and schooling which leads to a high school diploma or a college degree.

- ○ No, has not attended since February 1
- ○ Yes, public school, public college
- ○ Yes, private school, private college

12. How much school has this person COMPLETED?
Fill ONE circle for the highest level COMPLETED or degree RECEIVED. If currently enrolled, mark the level of previous grade attended or highest degree received.

- ○ No school completed
- ○ Nursery school
- ○ Kindergarten
- ○ 1st, 2nd, 3rd, or 4th grade
- ○ 5th, 6th, 7th, or 8th grade
- ○ 9th grade
- ○ 10th grade
- ○ 11th grade
- ○ 12th grade, NO DIPLOMA
- ○ HIGH SCHOOL GRADUATE - high school DIPLOMA or the equivalent (For example: GED)
- ○ Some college but no degree
- ○ Associate degree in college - Occupational program
- ○ Associate degree in college - Academic program
- ○ Bachelor's degree (For example: BA, AB, BS)
- ○ Master's degree (For example: MA, MS, MEng, MEd, MSW, MBA)
- ○ Professional school degree (For example: MD, DDS, DVM, LLB, JD)
- ○ Doctorate degree (For example: PhD, EdD)

13. What is this person's ancestry or ethnic origin?
(See instruction guide for further information.)

(For example: German, Italian, Afro-Amer., Croatian, Cape Verdean, Dominican, Ecuadoran, Haitian, Cajun, French Canadian, Jamaican, Korean, Lebanese, Mexican, Nigerian, Irish, Polish, Slovak, Taiwanese, Thai, Ukrainian, etc.)

14a. Did this person live in this house or apartment 5 years ago (on April 1, 1985)?

- ○ Born after April 1, 1985 — *Go to questions for the next person*
- ○ Yes — *Skip to 15a*
- ○ No

b. Where did this person live 5 years ago (on April 1, 1985)?

(1) Name of U.S. State or foreign country

(If outside U.S., print answer above and skip to 15a.)

(2) Name of county in the U.S.

(3) Name of city or town in the U.S.

(4) Did this person live inside the city or town limits?

- ○ Yes
- ○ No, lived outside the city/town limits

15a. Does this person speak a language other than English at home?

- ○ Yes
- ○ No — *Skip to 16*

b. What is this language?

(For example: Chinese, Italian, Spanish, Vietnamese)

c. How well does this person speak English?

- ○ Very well
- ○ Well
- ○ Not well
- ○ Not at all

16. When was this person born?

- ○ Born before April 1, 1975 — *Go to 17a*
- ○ Born April 1, 1975 or later — *Go to questions for the next person*

17a. Has this person ever been on active-duty military service in the Armed Forces of the United States or ever been in the United States military Reserves or the National Guard? If service was in Reserves or National Guard only, see instruction guide.

- ○ Yes, now on active duty
- ○ Yes, on active duty in past, but not now
- ○ Yes, service in Reserves or National Guard only — *Skip to 18*
- ○ No — *Skip to 18*

b. Was active-duty military service during —
Fill a circle for each period in which this person served.

- ○ September 1980 or later
- ○ May 1975 to August 1980
- ○ Vietnam era (August 1964—April 1975)
- ○ February 1955—July 1964
- ○ Korean conflict (June 1950—January 1955)
- ○ World War II (September 1940—July 1947)
- ○ World War I (April 1917—November 1918)
- ○ Any other time

c. In total, how many years of active-duty military service has this person had?

Years

18. Does this person have a physical, mental, or other health condition that has lasted for 6 or more months and which —

a. Limits the kind or amount of work this person can do at a job?

- ○ Yes
- ○ No

b. Prevents this person from working at a job?

- ○ Yes
- ○ No

19. Because of a health condition that has lasted for 6 or more months, does this person have any difficulty —

a. Going outside the home alone, for example, to shop or visit a doctor's office?

- ○ Yes
- ○ No

b. Taking care of his or her own personal needs, such as bathing, dressing, or getting around inside the home?

- ○ Yes
- ○ No

If this person is a female —

20. How many babies has she ever had, not counting stillbirths? Do not count her stepchildren or children she has adopted.

None 1 2 3 4 5 6 7 8 9 10 11 12 or more
○ ○ ○ ○ ○ ○ ○ ○ ○ ○ ○ ○ ○

21a. Did this person work at any time LAST WEEK?

- ○ Yes — Fill this circle if this person worked full time or part time. (Count part-time work such as delivering papers, or helping without pay in a family business or farm. Also count active duty in the Armed Forces.)
- ○ No — Fill this circle if this person did not work, or did only own housework, school work, or volunteer work. — *Skip to 25*

b. How many hours did this person work LAST WEEK (at all jobs)? Subtract any time off; add overtime or extra hours worked.

Hours

22. At what location did this person work LAST WEEK?
If this person worked at more than one location, print where he or she worked most last week.

a. Address (Number and street)

(If the exact address is not known, give a description of the location such as the building name or the nearest street or intersection.)

b. Name of city, town, or post office

c. Is the work location inside the limits of that city or town?

- ○ Yes
- ○ No, outside the city/town limits

d. County

e. State   **f. ZIP Code**

23a. How did this person usually get to work LAST WEEK? If this person usually used more than one method of transportation during the trip, fill the circle of the one used for most of the distance.

- ○ Car, truck, or van
- ○ Bus or trolley bus
- ○ Streetcar or trolley car
- ○ Subway or elevated
- ○ Railroad
- ○ Ferryboat
- ○ Taxicab
- ○ Motorcycle
- ○ Bicycle
- ○ Walked
- ○ Worked at home → *Skip to 28*
- ○ Other method

If "car, truck, or van" is marked in 23a, go to 23b. Otherwise, skip to 24a.

b. How many people, including this person, usually rode to work in the car, truck, or van LAST WEEK?

- ○ Drove alone
- ○ 2 people
- ○ 3 people
- ○ 4 people
- ○ 5 people
- ○ 6 people
- ○ 7 to 9 people
- ○ 10 or more people

24a. What time did this person usually leave home to go to work LAST WEEK?

[ ] ○ a.m. ○ p.m.

b. How many minutes did it usually take this person to get from home to work LAST WEEK?

[ ] Minutes — *Skip to 28*

25. Was this person TEMPORARILY absent or on layoff from a job or business LAST WEEK?

- ○ Yes, on layoff
- ○ Yes, on vacation, temporary illness, labor dispute, etc.
- ○ No

26a. Has this person been looking for work during the last 4 weeks?

- ○ Yes
- ○ No — *Skip to 27*

b. Could this person have taken a job LAST WEEK if one had been offered?

- ○ No, already has a job
- ○ No, temporarily ill
- ○ No, other reasons (in school, etc.)
- ○ Yes, could have taken a job

27. When did this person last work, even for a few days?

- ○ 1990
- ○ 1989
- ○ 1988
- ○ 1985 to 1987
} *Go to 28*
- ○ 1980 to 1984
- ○ 1979 or earlier
- ○ Never worked
} *Skip to 32*

28-30. CURRENT OR MOST RECENT JOB ACTIVITY. Describe clearly this person's chief job activity or business last week. If this person had more than one job, describe the one at which this person worked the most hours. If this person had no job or business last week, give information for his/her last job or business since 1985.

28. Industry or Employer

a. For whom did this person work? If now on active duty in the Armed Forces, fill this circle → ○ and print the branch of the Armed Forces.

[ ] (Name of company, business, or other employer)

b. What kind of business or industry was this? Describe the activity at location where employed.

[ ] (For example: hospital, newspaper publishing, mail order house, auto engine manufacturing, retail bakery)

c. Is this mainly — Fill ONE circle

- ○ Manufacturing
- ○ Wholesale trade
- ○ Retail trade
- ○ Other (agriculture, construction, service, government, etc.)

29. Occupation

a. What kind of work was this person doing?

[ ] (For example: registered nurse, personnel manager, supervisor of order department, gasoline engine assembler, cake icer)

b. What were this person's most important activities or duties?

[ ] (For example: patient care, directing hiring policies, supervising order clerks, assembling engines, icing cakes)

30. Was this person — Fill ONE circle

- ○ Employee of a PRIVATE FOR PROFIT company or business or of an individual, for wages, salary, or commissions
- ○ Employee of a PRIVATE NOT-FOR-PROFIT, tax-exempt, or charitable organization
- ○ Local GOVERNMENT employee (city, county, etc.)
- ○ State GOVERNMENT employee
- ○ Federal GOVERNMENT employee
- ○ SELF-EMPLOYED in own NOT INCORPORATED business, professional practice, or farm
- ○ SELF-EMPLOYED in own INCORPORATED business, professional practice, or farm
- ○ Working WITHOUT PAY in family business or farm

31a. Last year (1989), did this person work, even for a few days, at a paid job or in a business or farm?

- ○ Yes
- ○ No — *Skip to 32*

b. How many weeks did this person work in 1989? Count paid vacation, paid sick leave, and military service.

[ ] Weeks

c. During the weeks WORKED in 1989, how many hours did this person usually work each week?

[ ] Hours

32. INCOME IN 1989 — Fill the "Yes" circle below for each income source received during 1989. Otherwise, fill the "No" circle. If "Yes," enter the total amount received during 1989.

For income received jointly, see instruction guide.

If exact amount is not known, please give best estimate.

If net income was a loss, write "Loss" above the dollar amount.

a. Wages, salary, commissions, bonuses, or tips from all jobs — Report amount before deductions for taxes, bonds, dues, or other items.

- ○ Yes
- ○ No
$[ ].00
Annual amount — Dollars

b. Self-employment income from own nonfarm business, including proprietorship and partnership — Report NET income after business expenses.

- ○ Yes →
- ○ No
$[ ].00
Annual amount — Dollars

c. Farm self-employment income — Report NET income after operating expenses. Include earnings as a tenant farmer or sharecropper.

- ○ Yes →
- ○ No
$[ ].00
Annual amount — Dollars

d. Interest, dividends, net rental income or royalty income, or income from estates and trusts — Report even small amounts credited to an account.

- ○ Yes →
- ○ No
$[ ].00
Annual amount — Dollars

e. Social Security or Railroad Retirement

- ○ Yes →
- ○ No
$[ ].00
Annual amount — Dollars

f. Supplemental Security Income (SSI), Aid to Families with Dependent Children (AFDC), or other public assistance or public welfare payments

- ○ Yes →
- ○ No
$[ ].00
Annual amount — Dollars

g. Retirement, survivor, or disability pensions — Do NOT include Social Security.

- ○ Yes →
- ○ No
$[ ].00
Annual amount — Dollars

h. Any other sources of income received regularly such as Veterans' (VA) payments, unemployment compensation, child support, or alimony — Do NOT include lump-sum payments such as money from an inheritance or the sale of a home.

- ○ Yes →
- ○ No
$[ ].00
Annual amount — Dollars

33. What was this person's total income in 1989? Add entries in questions 32a through 32h; subtract any losses. If total amount was a loss, write "Loss" above amount.

- ○ None OR $[ ].00
Annual amount — Dollars

Please turn to the next page and answer the questions for Person 2 on page 2. If this is the last person listed in question 1a on page 1, go to the back of the form

Technical Appendix 2-2
Part A: Registration and Tabulation of Natality Statistics

The following is an abstract of Section 4 (Technical Appendix) of the Vital Statistics of the United States, 1992, Volume I-Natality. It describes the procedures by which these data are collected and tabulated.

Definition of Live Birth

Every product of conception that gives a sign of life after birth, regardless of the length of the pregnancy, is considered a live birth. This concept is embraced by the definition set forth by the World Health Organization as follows:

Live birth is the complete expulsion or extraction from its mother of a product of conception, irrespective of the duration of pregnancy, which, after such separation, breathes or shows any other evidence of life, such as the beating of the heart, pulsation of the umbilical cord, or definite movement of voluntary muscles, whether or not the umbilical cord has been cut or the placenta is attached; each product of such a birth is considered liveborn.

Birth-Registration Area

At present the birth-registration system of the United States covers the fifty states, the District of Columbia, Puerto Rico, the U.S. Virgin Islands, Guam, American Samoa, and the Commonwealth of the Northern Marianas. However, in the statistical tabulations, United States refers only to the aggregate of the fifty states and the District of Columbia. Tabulations for Puerto Rico, the Virgin Islands, and Guam are shown separately.

The national birth-registration area was established in 1915, and completed in 1933. The organized territories of Hawaii and Alaska were admitted in 1929 and 1950, respectively. (Additional states were admitted as the required completeness of registration and other requirements were achieved.) The original birth-registration area of 1915 consisted of ten states and the District of Columbia.

Because of the growth of the area for which data have been collected and tabulated, a national series of geographically comparable data prior to 1933 can be obtained only by estimation. These estimates include adjustments for underregistration as well as for states not in the birth-registration area before 1933.

Natality Statistics

Natality statistics are based on information provided by the individual states. After 1985, statistics for all states and the District of Columbia are based on information derived from computer data tapes coded by the states and provided to the National Center for Health Statistics (NCHS) through the Vital Statistics Cooperative Program (VSCP). The Center receives these tapes from the registration offices of each state, the District of Columbia, and New York City.

Standard Certificate of Live Birth

The Standard Certificate of Live Birth, issued by the Public Health Service, has served for many years as the principal means of attaining uniformity in the content of the documents used to collect information on births in the United States. It has been modified in each state to the extent required by the particular needs of the state, or by special provisions of the state vital statistics law. However, the certificates of most states conform closely to the content of the Standard Certificate.

The first standard certificate of birth was developed in 1900; it has been revised periodically since then. Effective January 1, 1989, a revised U.S. Standard Certificate of Live Birth (see the figure) replaced the 1978 revision. This revision provides a wide variety of new information on maternal and infant health characteristics, and represents a significant departure from previous versions in both content and format. The most significant change was the use of checkboxes to obtain detailed medical and health information about mother and child.

The reformatted items include "Medical Risk Factors for this Pregnancy," " Complications of Labor and/or Delivery," and "Congenital Anomalies of the Child." For each of these items at least 15 specific conditions have been identified. Several new items have been added to the revised certificate, including items on alcohol and tobacco use during pregnancy, obstetric procedures, weight gain during pregnancy, method of delivery, and abnormal conditions of the newborn. Another modification was the addition of a Hispanic identifier for the mother and father. The revised certificate also includes more detail on the birth attendant and the place of birth.

CLASSIFICATION OF DATA

1. Classification by Occurrence and Residence: Natality tabulations for states and other areas within the United States are by place of residence unless otherwise specified in the tables. Births to U.S. residents occurring outside this country are not reallocated to the United States. In tabulations by place of residence, births occurring within the United States to U.S. citizens and to resident aliens are allocated to the usual place of residence of the mother in the United States as reported on the birth certificate. Beginning in 1970, births to nonresidents of the United States occurring in the United States are excluded from these tabulations.

Incomplete residence—Beginning in 1973 where only the state of residence is reported with no city or country specified, and the state named is different from the state of occurrence, the birth is allocated to the largest city of the state of residence. For years prior to 1973, such births were allocated to the exact place of occurrence.

2. Race or National Origin: The categories for race are "White," "Black," "American Indian" (including Aleuts and Eskimos), "Chinese," "Japanese," "Hawaiian," "Filipino," and "Other Asian or Pacific Islander" (including Asian Indian). Before 1992 there was an "Other" category, which is now combined with the "Not Stated" category. Before 1978 the category "Other Asian and Pacific Islander" was not identified separately but included with the "Other" races.

TYPE/PRINT IN PERMANENT BLACK INK FOR INSTRUCTIONS SEE HANDBOOK

CHILD

U.S. STANDARD
CERTIFICATE OF LIVE BIRTH

LOCAL FILE NUMBER

BIRTH NUMBER

1. CHILD'S NAME *(First, Middle, Last)*

2. DATE OF BIRTH *(Month, Day, Year)*

3. TIME OF BIRTH

N

4. SEX

5. CITY, TOWN, OR LOCATION OF BIRTH

6. COUNTY OF BIRTH

7. PLACE OF BIRTH: ☐ Hospital   ☐ Freestanding Birthing Center
   ☐ Clinic/Doctor's Office   ☐ Residence
   ☐ Other *(Specify)* _____

8. FACILITY NAME *(If not institution, give street and number)*

CERTIFIER/ ATTENDANT

DEATH UNDER ONE YEAR OF AGE
Enter State File Number of death certificate for this child

9. I certify that this child was born alive at the place and time and on the date stated.

Signature ▶

10. DATE SIGNED *(Month, Day, Year)*

11. ATTENDANT'S NAME AND TITLE *(If other than certifier) (Type/Print)*

Name _____

☐ M.D.   ☐ D.O.   ☐ C.N.M.   ☐ Other Midwife
☐ Other *(Specify)*

12. CERTIFIER'S NAME AND TITLE *(Type/Print)*

Name _____

☐ M.D.   ☐ D.O.   ☐ Hospital Admin.   ☐ C.N.M.   ☐ Other Midwife
☐ Other *(Specify)*

13. ATTENDANT'S MAILING ADDRESS *(Street and Number or Rural Route Number, City or Town, State, Zip Code)*

14. REGISTRAR'S SIGNATURE
▶

15. DATE FILED BY REGISTRAR *(Month, Day, Year)*

MOTHER

16a. MOTHER'S NAME *(First, Middle, Last)*

16b. MAIDEN SURNAME

17. DATE OF BIRTH *(Month, Day, Year)*

18. BIRTHPLACE *(State or Foreign Country)*

19a. RESIDENCE—STATE

19b. COUNTY

19c. CITY, TOWN, OR LOCATION

19d. STREET AND NUMBER

19e. INSIDE CITY LIMITS? *(Yes or no)*

20. MOTHER'S MAILING ADDRESS *(If same as residence, enter Zip Code on*

FATHER

21. FATHER'S NAME *(First, Middle, Last)*

22. DATE OF BIRTH *(Month, Day, Year)*

23. BIRTHPLACE *(State or Foreign Country)*

INFORMANT

24. I certify that the personal information provided on this certificate is correct to the best of my knowledge and belief.

Signature of Parent or Other Informant ▶

INFORMATION FOR MEDICAL AND HEALTH USE ONLY

MOTHER

FATHER

25. OF HISPANIC ORIGIN? (Specify No or Yes—If yes, specify Cuban, Mexican, Puerto Rican, etc.)

26. RACE—American Indian, Black, White, etc. (Specify below)

27. EDUCATION *(Specify only highest grade completed)*

| | Elementary/Secondary (0-12) | College (1-4 or 5 + |

25a. ☐ No   ☐ Yes
Specify:

26a.

27a.

25b. ☐ No   ☐ Yes
Specify:

26b.

27b.

MULTIPLE BIRTHS
Enter State File Number for Mate(s)
LIVE BIRTH(S)

FETAL DEATH(S)

28. PREGNANCY HISTORY
(Complete each section)

LIVE BIRTHS (Do not include this child)		OTHER TERMINATIONS (Spontaneous and induced at any time after conception)
28a. Now Living	28b. Now Dead	28d.
Number _____	Number _____	Number _____
☐ None	☐ None	☐ None
28c. DATE OF LAST LIVE BIRTH *(Month, Year)*		28e. DATE OF LAST OTHER TERMINATION *(Month, Year)*

29. MOTHER MARRIED? (At birth, conception, or any time between) (Yes or no)

30. DATE LAST NORMAL MENSES BEGAN *(Month, Day, Year)*

31. MONTH OF PREGNANCY PRENATAL CARE BEGAN—First, Second, Third, etc. *(Specify)*

32. PRENATAL VISITS—Total Number *(If none, so state)*

33. BIRTH WEIGHT *(Specify unit)*

34. CLINICAL ESTIMATE OF GESTATION *(Week*

35a. PLURALITY—Single, Twin, Triplet, etc. *(Specify)*

35b. IF NOT SINGLE BIRTH—Born First, Second, Third, etc. *(Specify)*

36. APGAR SCORE

| 36a. 1 Minute | 36b. 5 Minutes |

37a. MOTHER TRANSFERRED PRIOR TO DELIVERY? ☐ No   ☐ Yes   If Yes, enter name of facility transferred from:

37b. INFANT TRANSFERRED? ☐ No   ☐ Yes   If Yes, enter name of facility transferred to:

U.S. Standard Certificate of Live Birth: 1989 Revision

SECTION 4 — TECHNICAL APPENDIX — PAGE 3

38a. MEDICAL RISK FACTORS FOR THIS PREGNANCY
(Check all that apply)

- Anemia (Hct. <30/Hgb. <10) .... 01 ☐
- Cardiac disease .... 02 ☐
- Acute or chronic lung disease .... 03 ☐
- Diabetes .... 04 ☐
- Genital herpes .... 05 ☐
- Hydramnios/Oligohydramnios .... 06 ☐
- Hemoglobinopathy .... 07 ☐
- Hypertension, chronic .... 08 ☐
- Hypertension, pregnancy-associated .... 09 ☐
- Eclampsia .... 10 ☐
- Incompetent cervix .... 11 ☐
- Previous infant 4000+ grams .... 12 ☐
- Previous preterm or small-for-gestational-age infant .... 13 ☐
- Renal disease .... 14 ☐
- Rh sensitization .... 15 ☐
- Uterine bleeding .... 16 ☐
- None .... 00 ☐
- Other _____ 17 ☐
  (Specify)

38b. OTHER RISK FACTORS FOR THIS PREGNANCY
(Complete all items)

- Tobacco use during pregnancy .... Yes ☐ No ☐
  Average number cigarettes per day _____
- Alcohol use during pregnancy .... Yes ☐ No ☐
  Average number drinks per week _____
- Weight gained during pregnancy _____ lbs.

39. OBSTETRIC PROCEDURES
(Check all that apply)

- Amniocentesis .... 01 ☐
- Electronic fetal monitoring .... 02 ☐
- Induction of labor .... 03 ☐
- Stimulation of labor .... 04 ☐
- Tocolysis .... 05 ☐
- Ultrasound .... 06 ☐
- None .... 00 ☐
- Other _____ 07 ☐
  (Specify)

40. COMPLICATIONS OF LABOR AND/OR DELIVERY
(Check all that apply)

- Febrile (>100°F. or 38°C.) .... 01 ☐
- Meconium, moderate/heavy .... 02 ☐
- Premature rupture of membrane (>12 hours) .... 03 ☐
- Abruptio placenta .... 04 ☐
- Placenta previa .... 05 ☐
- Other excessive bleeding .... 06 ☐
- Seizures during labor .... 07 ☐
- Precipitous labor (<3 hours) .... 08 ☐
- Prolonged labor (>20 hours) .... 09 ☐
- Dysfunctional labor .... 10 ☐
- Breech/Malpresentation .... 11 ☐
- Cephalopelvic disproportion .... 12 ☐
- Cord prolapse .... 13 ☐
- Anesthetic complications .... 14 ☐
- Fetal distress .... 15 ☐
- None .... 00 ☐
- Other _____ 16 ☐
  (Specify)

41. METHOD OF DELIVERY *(Check all that apply)*

- Vaginal .... 01 ☐
- Vaginal birth after previous C-section .... 02 ☐
- Primary C-section .... 03 ☐
- Repeat C-section .... 04 ☐
- Forceps .... 05 ☐
- Vacuum .... 06 ☐

42. ABNORMAL CONDITIONS OF THE NEWBORN
(Check all that apply)

- Anemia (Hct. <39/Hgb. <13) .... 01 ☐
- Birth injury .... 02 ☐
- Fetal alcohol syndrome .... 03 ☐
- Hyaline membrane disease/RDS .... 04 ☐
- Meconium aspiration syndrome .... 05 ☐
- Assisted ventilation <30 min .... 06 ☐
- Assisted ventilation ≥30 min .... 07 ☐
- Seizures .... 08 ☐
- None .... 00 ☐
- Other _____ 09 ☐
  (Specify)

43. CONGENITAL ANOMALIES OF CHILD
(Check all that apply)

- Anencephalus .... 01 ☐
- Spina bifida/Meningocele .... 02 ☐
- Hydrocephalus .... 03 ☐
- Microcephalus .... 04 ☐
- Other central nervous system anomalies .... 05 ☐
  (Specify)
- Heart malformations .... 06 ☐
- Other circulatory/respiratory anomalies .... 07 ☐
  (Specify)
- Rectal atresia/stenosis .... 08 ☐
- Tracheo-esophageal fistula/Esophageal atresia .... 09 ☐
- Omphalocele/Gastroschisis .... 10 ☐
- Other gastrointestinal anomalies .... 11 ☐
  (Specify)
- Malformed genitalia .... 12 ☐
- Renal agenesis .... 13 ☐
- Other urogenital anomalies .... 14 ☐
  (Specify)
- Cleft lip/palate .... 15 ☐
- Polydactyly/Syndactyly/Adactyly .... 16 ☐
- Club foot .... 17 ☐
- Diaphragmatic hernia .... 18 ☐
- Other musculoskeletal/integumental anomalies .... 19 ☐
  (Specify)
- Down's syndrome .... 20 ☐
- Other chromosomal anomalies .... 21 ☐
  (Specify)
- None .... 00 ☐
- Other _____ 22 ☐
  (Specify)

PHS-T-002
REV. 1/89

U.S. Standard Certificate of Live Birth: 1989 Revision (Continued)

Beginning with the 1989 data year, birth data are tabulated primarily by race of mother. In 1988 and prior years the race or national origin shown in tabulation was that of the newborn child. The race of the child was determined for statistical purposes by an algorithm based on the race of the mother and father as reported on the birth certificate. When the parents were of the same race, the race of the child was the same as that of the parents. When the parents were of different races and one parent was white, the child was assigned to the race of the other parent. When the parents were of different races and neither parent was white, the child was assigned to the race of the father, with one exception—if either parent was Hawaiian, the child was assigned to Hawaiian. If the race was missing for one parent, the child was assigned the race of the parent for whom it was reported.

Nearly all statistics by race or national origin for the United States as a whole in 1962 and 1963 are affected by a lack of information for New Jersey. Birth rates by race for those years are computed on a population base which excludes New Jersey.

3. Age of Mother or Father: Beginning in 1989 an item on the birth certificate asks for "Date of Birth" for each parent. In previous years, "Age (at time of this birth)" was requested. Not all states have revised this item for 1989, and therefore the age of mother either is derived from the reported month and year of birth or coded as stated on the certificate.

Age-specific birth rates shown in this report are based on populations of women by age, which are prepared by the U.S. Bureau of the Census. In census years the census decennial counts are used. In intercensal years, estimates of the population of women by age are published in the Current Population Reports of the U.S. Bureau of the Census.

Not stated age of mother—Beginning in 1964 birth records with age of mother not stated have been allocated according to the age appearing on the record previously processed for a mother of identical color and having the same total-birth order (total of fetal deaths and live births).

Age of father is derived from the reported date of birth or coded as stated on the birth certificate. Information on age of father is often missing on birth certificates of children born to unmarried mothers, greatly inflating the number of "not stated" in all tabulations by age of father.

4. Live-Birth Order and Parity: Birth order and parity classifications refer to the total number of live births the mother has had, including the birth in the latest year. Fetal deaths are excluded.

Birth order indicates what number the present birth represents, e.g., a baby born to a mother who has had two previous live births (even if one or both are not now living) has a birth order of three.

Parity indicates how many live births a mother has had. Before delivery a mother having her first baby has a parity of zero and a mother having her third baby has a parity of two. After delivery the mother of a baby who is a first live birth has a parity of one and the mother of a baby who is a third live birth has a parity of three.

5. Dates of Last Live Birth and Last Fetal Death: Date of last live birth and date of last fetal death were added to the Standard Certificate of Live Birth in 1968 for the purpose of providing information on child spacing and pregnancy intervals. Tabulations on these items were presented for the first time in 1969.

6. Educational Attainment: Data on the educational attainment of both parents were collected beginning in 1968. The educational attainment of either parent is defined as "the number of years of school completed." Only those years completed in "regular" schools are counted.

7. Marital Status: Beginning with 1980 data, national estimates of births to unmarried women are derived from two sources. In 1992 marital status was reported directly on the birth certificates of 44 states and the District of Columbia. In the remaining six states marital status is inferred from a comparison of the child's and parents' surnames. This procedure represents a substantial departure from the method used before 1980 to prepare national estimates of births to unmarried women, which assumed that the incidence of births to unmarried women in states with no direct question on marital status was the same as the incidence in reporting states in the same geographic division.

8. Place of Delivery and Attendant at Birth: The 1989 revision of the U.S. Standard Certificate of Live Birth includes separate categories for freestanding birthing centers, the mother's residence, and clinic or doctor's office as place of birth. In previous years place of birth was classified simply as either "In hospital" or "Not in hospital." Births occurring in hospitals, institutions, clinics, centers, or homes were included in the category "In hospital." In this context the word "homes" does not refer to the mother's residence but to an institution, such as a home for unmarried women. Birthing centers were included in either category, depending on each state's assessment of the facility. Beginning in 1989 births occurring in clinics and in birthing centers not attached to a hospital are classified as "Not in hospital."

Beginning in 1975 the attendant at birth and place of delivery were coded independently, primarily to permit the identification of the person in attendance at hospital deliveries. The 1989 certificate includes separate classifications for "M.D." (Doctor of Medicine), "D.O." (Doctor of Osteopathy), "C.N.M." (certified nurse midwife), "Other midwife," and "Other" attendants.

9. Birth Weight: In some areas birth weight is reported in terms of pounds and ounces rather than in grams. However, the metric system has been used in tabulating and presenting the statistics to facilitate comparison with data published by other groups. For purposes of classification, infants weighing 2,500 grams or less at birth are considered to be of low birth weight.

10. Period of Gestation: The period of gestation is defined as beginning with the first day of the last normal menstrual period (LMP) and ending with the day of the birth. The LMP is used as the initial date because it can be more accurately determined than the date of conception, which usually occurs 2 weeks after the LMP. Births occurring before 37 completed weeks of gestation are considered to be "preterm" or "premature" for purposes of classification. At 37-41 weeks gestation, births are considered to be "term," and at 42 completed weeks and over, "postterm." These distinctions are according to the ICD-9 (*Ninth*

Revision of the International Lists of Diseases and Causes of Death) definitions.

11. Month Pregnancy Care Began: For those records in which the name of the month is entered for this item, instead of first, second, third, and so forth, the month of the pregnancy in which prenatal care began is determined from the month named and the month last normal menses began.

12. Number of Prenatal Visits: Tabulations of the number of prenatal visits were presented for the first time in 1972. Beginning in 1989 these data were collected from the birth certificates of all states.

13. Apgar Score: One- and 5-minute Apgar scores were added to the U.S. Standard Certificate of Live Birth in 1978 to evaluate the condition of the infant at 1 and 5 minutes after birth. The Apgar score is a useful measure of the need for resuscitation and a predictor of the infant's chances of surviving the first year of life. It is a summary measure of the infant's condition based on heart rate, respiratory effort, muscle tone, reflex irritability, and color.

14. Tobacco and alcohol use during pregnancy: The checkbox format allows for classification of a mother as a smoker or drinker during pregnancy and for reporting the average number of cigarettes smoked per day or drinks consumed per week.

15. Weight gain during pregnancy: Weight gain is reported in pounds; a loss of weight is reported as zero gain.

16. Medical risk factors for this pregnancy: In 1992 this item, which includes 16 specific medical risk factors, was included on the birth certificates of all states and the District of Columbia. Three states, however, did not include all factors on their birth certificates.

17. Obstetric procedures: This item includes six specific obstetric procedures; it was reported by all states and the District of Columbia.

18. Complications of labor and/or delivery: This includes 15 specific complications and permits the designation of more than one complication. All states and the District of Columbia included this item on their birth certificates; however, not all of the complications were reported by all states.

19. Method of Delivery: The choices include vaginal delivery, with the additional options of forceps, vacuum, and vaginal birth after a previous Caesarian section (VBAC), a well as the choice of primary or repeat Caesarian. In 1992 this information was collected from the birth certificates of all states and the District of Columbia.

QUALITY OF DATA

While vital statistics data are useful for a variety of administrative and scientific purposes, they cannot be correctly interpreted unless various qualifying factors and methods of classification are taken into account.

Most of the factors limiting the use of data arise from imperfections in the original records or from the impracticability of tabulating these data in very detailed categories. These defects should not be ignored, but their existence does not vitiate the value of the data for most general purposes.

Completeness of Registration

It is estimated that 99.3 percent of all births occurring in the United States in 1992 were registered; for white births registration was 99.4 percent complete and for all other births, 98.6 percent complete. These estimates are based on the results of the 1964-68 test of birth-registration completeness according to place of delivery (in or out of hospital) and race and on the 1989 proportions of births in these categories.

Population bases used in the computation of rates and other measures

Natality rates are computed on the basis of population statistics prepared by the U.S. Bureau of the Census. For 1940, 1950, 1960, 1970, 1980, and 1990, they are based on the population enumerated as of April 1 in the censuses of those years. Rates for all other years are based on an estimated midyear (July 1) population for the respective year. Birth rates for the United States, individual states, and metropolitan areas are based on the total resident populations of the respective areas. Except as noted these populations exclude the Armed Forces abroad but include the Armed Forces stationed in each area.

The U.S. Bureau of the Census has conducted extensive research to evaluate the coverage of the U.S. population (including undercount, overcount, and misstatement of age, race, and sex) in the last five decennial censuses. These studies indicate that there is differential coverage in the censuses among population subgroups; that is, some age, race, and sex groups are more completely enumerated than others. If adjustments were made for persons who were not counted in the census of population, the size of the denominators would generally increase and the rates would be smaller than without adjustment.

Enumeration of white females in the childbearing ages was at least 97 percent complete for all ages. Among black women, the undercount ranged up to 5 percent. Generally, females in the childbearing ages were more completely enumerated than males for similar race-age groups.

Part B: Registration and Tabulation of Mortality Statistics

The information provided below is an annotated extract of Section 7, "Technical Appendix" to the annual reports of Vital Statistics of the United States. Volume II-Mortality. The report for 1992 was used in preparing this part of the Appendix. Procedures are presented here as those in effect for the 1990s, which differ in minor respects from procedures for earlier decades. For a full history of changes in definitions and procedures, readers should consult earlier volumes of the mortality series.

Death and Fetal-Death Statistics

Mortality statistics for 1992 are, as for all previous years except 1972, based on information from records of all deaths occurring in the United States. Fetal-death statistics for every year are based on all reports of fetal deaths received by the National Center for Health Statistics (NCHS).

The United States death-registration system and the fetal-death registration system covers the fifty states, the District of Columbia, New York City (which is independent of New York state for the purposes of death registration), Puerto Rico, the Virgin Islands, Guam, American Samoa, and the Commonwealth of the Northern Marianas. Tabulations for Guam and Puerto Rico are shown separately, and data are not included for American Samoa or the Commonwealth of the Northern Marianas.

Standard Certificates and Reports

The U.S. Standard Certificate of Death and the U.S. Standard Report of Fetal Death, issued by the Public Health Service, have served for many years as the principal means of attaining uniformity in the content of the documents used to collect information on these events. They have been modified in each state to the extent necessitated by the particular needs of the state or by special provisions of the state vital statistics law. However, the certificates or reports of most states conform closely in content and arrangement to the standards.

The Standard Certificate of Death, first issued in 1900, has been revised periodically by the national vital statistics agency in consultation with state health officers and registrars; federal agencies concerned with vital statistics; national, state, and county medical societies; and others working in such fields as public health, social welfare, demography, and insurance. This revision procedure has assured careful evaluation of each item in terms of its current and future usefulness for registration, identification, legal, medical, and research purposes. New items have been added where necessary, and old items have been modified to ensure better reporting, or in some cases have been dropped when their usefulness appeared to be limited. The current versions of the two certificates were recommended for state use beginning on January 1, 1989 (see the examples shown here).

Classification of Data

The principal value of vital statistics data is realized through the presentation of rates, which are computed by relating the vital events of a class to the population of a similarly defined class. Vital statistics and population statistics must therefore be classified according to similarly defined systems and tabulated in comparable groups. Even when the variables common to both, such as geographic area, age, race, and sex, have been similarly classified and tabulated, differences between the enumeration method of obtaining population data and the registration method of obtaining vital statistics data may result in significant discrepancies.

1. Classification by Occurrence and Residence: Tabulations for the United States and specified geographic areas in this report are by place of residence unless stated as by place of occurrence. Deaths of nonresidents of the United States are not included in tables by place of residence. The Metropolitan Statistical Areas (MSAs) and the Primary Metropolitan Statistical Areas (PMSAs) are those established by the Office of Management of the Budget as of April 1, 1990.

2. Race: As of 1992, deaths are classified by the following racial groups: white, black, American Indian, Chinese, Hawaiian, Japanese, Filipino, and Other Asian or Pacific Islander. Beginning in 1992 all records coded as "other races" (0.01 percent of total deaths) were assigned to the specified race of the previous record. Mortality data for Filipino and Other Asian and Pacific Islander were shown for the first time in 1979. The white category includes, in addition to persons reported as white, those reported as Mexican, Puerto Rican, Cuban, and all other Caucasians. The American Indian category includes American, Alaskan, Canadian, Eskimo and Aleut. If a mixture of races other than white is given (except Hawaiian), the entry is coded to the first race listed. This procedure for coding the first race listed has been used since 1969. Before 1969 if the entry for race was a mixture of black and any other race except Hawaiian, the entry was coded to black.

3. Hispanic origin: Mortality statistics for the Hispanic-origin population are based on information for those states and the District of Columbia that included items on the death certificate to identify Hispanic or ethnic origin of decedents. Data for 1992 were obtained from all states and the District of Columbia except Hew Hampshire and Oklahoma, which were excluded because their death certificates did not include an item to identify Hispanic or ethnic origin.

4. Marital Status: Mortality statistics by marital status are tabulated separately for never married, married, widowed, and divorced, and have been published annually since 1979 (as well as in the volumes for 1949-51 and 1959-61).

5. Educational Attainment: Beginning with the 1989 data year, mortality data on educational attainment were tabulated from information reported on the death certificate.

6. Place of Death and Status of the Decedent: Mortality data by place of death have been published annually since 1979 (also in 1958).

7. Mortality by month and date of death: Deaths by month have been tabulated and published in the annual volume for each year since 1900. Date of death, first published in 1972, allows for the analysis of the frequency distribution of deaths by selected causes by day of the week, and to identify holidays with peak numbers of deaths from specified causes.

TYPE/PRINT IN PERMANENT BLACK INK FOR INSTRUCTIONS SEE OTHER SIDE AND HANDBOOK

U.S. STANDARD
CERTIFICATE OF DEATH

LOCAL FILE NUMBER

STATE FILE NUMBER

NAME OF DECEDENT: For use by physician or institution

DEPARTMENT OF HEALTH AND HUMAN SERVICES – PUBLIC HEALTH SERVICE – NATIONAL CENTER FOR HEALTH STATISTICS – 1989 REVISION

DECEDENT

1. DECEDENT'S NAME (First, Middle, Last)
2. SEX
3. DATE OF DEATH (Month, Day, Year)

4. SOCIAL SECURITY NUMBER
5a. AGE–Last Birthday (Years)
5b. UNDER 1 YEAR — Months | Days
5c. UNDER 1 DAY — Hours | Minutes
6. DATE OF BIRTH (Month, Day, Year)
7. BIRTHPLACE (City and State or Foreign Country)

8. WAS DECEDENT EVER IN U.S. ARMED FORCES? (Yes or no)
9a. PLACE OF DEATH (Check only one; see instructions on other side)
HOSPITAL: ☐ Inpatient ☐ ER/Outpatient ☐ DOA   OTHER: ☐ Nursing Home ☐ Residence ☐ Other (Specify)

9b. FACILITY NAME (If not institution, give street and number)
9c. CITY, TOWN, OR LOCATION OF DEATH
9d. COUNTY OF DEATH

10. MARITAL STATUS—Married, Never Married, Widowed, Divorced (Specify)
11. SURVIVING SPOUSE (If wife, give maiden name)
12a. DECEDENT'S USUAL OCCUPATION (Give kind of work done during most of working life. Do not use retired.)
12b. KIND OF BUSINESS/INDUSTRY

13a. RESIDENCE—STATE
13b. COUNTY
13c. CITY, TOWN, OR LOCATION
13d. STREET AND NUMBER

13e. INSIDE CITY LIMITS? (Yes or no)
13f. ZIP CODE
14. WAS DECEDENT OF HISPANIC ORIGIN? (Specify No or Yes - If yes, specify Cuban, Mexican, Puerto Rican, etc.) ☐ No ☐ Yes Specify:
15. RACE—American Indian, Black, White, etc. (Specify)
16. DECEDENT'S EDUCATION (Specify only highest grade completed) Elementary/Secondary (0-12) | College (1-4 or 5 +)

PARENTS

17. FATHER'S NAME (First, Middle, Last)
18. MOTHER'S NAME (First, Middle, Maiden Surname)

INFORMANT

19a. INFORMANT'S NAME (Type/Print)
19b. MAILING ADDRESS (Street and Number or Rural Route Number, City or Town, State, Zip Code)

DISPOSITION

20a. METHOD OF DISPOSITION ☐ Burial ☐ Cremation ☐ Removal from State ☐ Donation ☐ Other (Specify) _____
20b. PLACE OF DISPOSITION (Name of cemetery, crematory, or other place)
20c. LOCATION—City or Town, State

21a. SIGNATURE OF FUNERAL SERVICE LICENSEE OR PERSON ACTING AS SUCH ▶
21b. LICENSE NUMBER (of Licensee)
22. NAME AND ADDRESS OF FACILITY

PRONOUNCING PHYSICIAN ONLY

SEE DEFINITION ON OTHER SIDE

ITEMS 24-26 MUST BE COMPLETED BY PERSON WHO PRONOUNCES DEATH

Complete items 23a-c only when certifying physician is not available at time of death to certify cause of death.
23a. To the best of my knowledge, death occurred at the time, date, and place stated. Signature and Title ▶
23b. LICENSE NUMBER
23c. DATE SIGNED (Month, Day, Year)

24. TIME OF DEATH M
25. DATE PRONOUNCED DEAD (Month, Day, Year)
26. WAS CASE REFERRED TO MEDICAL EXAMINER/CORONER? (Yes or no)

CAUSE OF DEATH

SEE INSTRUCTIONS ON OTHER SIDE

27. PART I. Enter the diseases, injuries, or complications that caused the death. Do not enter the mode of dying, such as cardiac or respiratory arrest, shock, or heart failure. List only one cause on each line.
Approximate Interval Between Onset and Death

IMMEDIATE CAUSE (Final disease or condition resulting in death) ➔ a. _____
DUE TO (OR AS A CONSEQUENCE OF):

Sequentially list conditions, if any, leading to immediate cause. Enter UNDERLYING CAUSE (Disease or injury that initiated events resulting in death) LAST
b. _____
DUE TO (OR AS A CONSEQUENCE OF):
c. _____
DUE TO (OR AS A CONSEQUENCE OF):
d. _____

PART II. Other significant conditions contributing to death but not resulting in the underlying cause given in Part I.
28a. WAS AN AUTOPSY PERFORMED? (Yes or no)
28b. WERE AUTOPSY FINDINGS AVAILABLE PRIOR TO COMPLETION OF CAUSE OF DEATH? (Yes or no)

29. MANNER OF DEATH
☐ Natural ☐ Pending Investigation
☐ Accident
☐ Suicide ☐ Could not be Determined
☐ Homicide
30a. DATE OF INJURY (Month, Day, Year)
30b. TIME OF INJURY M
30c. INJURY AT WORK? (Yes or no)
30d. DESCRIBE HOW INJURY OCCURRED

30e. PLACE OF INJURY—At home, farm, street, factory, office building, etc. (Specify)
30f. LOCATION (Street and Number or Rural Route Number, City or Town, State)

CERTIFIER

SEE DEFINITION ON OTHER SIDE

31a. CERTIFIER (Check only one)
☐ CERTIFYING PHYSICIAN (Physician certifying cause of death when another physician has pronounced death and completed Item 23) To the best of my knowledge, death occurred due to the cause(s) and manner as stated.
☐ PRONOUNCING AND CERTIFYING PHYSICIAN (Physician both pronouncing death and certifying to cause of death) To the best of my knowledge, death occurred at the time, date, and place, and due to the cause(s) and manner as stated.
☐ MEDICAL EXAMINER/CORONER On the basis of examination and/or investigation, in my opinion, death occurred at the time, date, and place, and due to the cause(s) and manner as stated.

31b. SIGNATURE AND TITLE OF CERTIFIER
31c. LICENSE NUMBER
31d. DATE SIGNED (Month, Day, Year)

32. NAME AND ADDRESS OF PERSON WHO COMPLETED CAUSE OF DEATH (ITEM 27) (Type/Print)

REGISTRAR

33. REGISTRAR'S SIGNATURE ▶
34. DATE FILED (Month, Day, Year)

PHS-T-003

U.S. Standard Certificate of Death

TYPE/PRINT IN PERMANENT BLACK INK FOR INSTRUCTIONS SEE HANDBOOK

U.S. STANDARD
REPORT OF FETAL DEATH

STATE FILE NUMBER

1. FACILITY NAME (If not institution, give street and number)

2. CITY, TOWN, OR LOCATION OF DELIVERY | 3. COUNTY OF DELIVERY | 4. DATE OF DELIVERY (Month, Day, Year) | 5. SEX OF FETUS

PARENTS

6a. MOTHER'S NAME (First, Middle, Last) | 6b. MAIDEN SURNAME | 7. DATE OF BIRTH (Month, Day, Year)

8a. RESIDENCE-STATE | 8b. COUNTY | 8c. CITY, TOWN, OR LOCATION | 8d. STREET AND NUMBER

8e. INSIDE CITY LIMITS? (Yes or no) | 8f. ZIP CODE | 9. FATHER'S NAME (First, Middle, Last) | 10. DATE OF BIRTH (Month, Day, Year)

11. OF HISPANIC ORIGIN? (Specify No or Yes—If yes, specify Cuban, Mexican, Puerto Rican, etc.) | 12. RACE—American Indian, Black, White, etc. (Specify below) | 13. EDUCATION (Specify only highest grade completed) Elementary/Secondary (0-12) / College (1-4 or 5+) | 14. OCCUPATION AND BUSINESS/INDUSTRY (Worked during last year) Occupation / Business/Industry

MOTHER
11a. ☐ No ☐ Yes Specify: | 12a. | 13a. | 14a. | 14b.

FATHER
11b. ☐ No ☐ Yes Specify: | 12b. | 13b. | 14c. | 14d.

MULTIPLE BIRTHS Enter State File Number for Mate(s) LIVE BIRTH(S) FETAL DEATH(S)

15. PREGNANCY HISTORY (Complete each section)

LIVE BIRTHS | OTHER TERMINATIONS (Spontaneous and induced at any time after conception)

15a. Now Living Number ____ ☐ None | 15b. Now Dead Number ____ ☐ None | 15d. (Do not include this fetus) Number ____ ☐ None

15c. DATE OF LAST LIVE BIRTH (Month, Year) | 15e. DATE OF LAST OTHER TERMINATION (Month, Year)

16. MOTHER MARRIED? (At delivery, conception, or any time between) (Yes or no)

17. DATE LAST NORMAL MENSES BEGAN (Month, Day, Year)

18. MONTH OF PREGNANCY PRENATAL CARE BEGAN—First, Second, Third, etc. (Specify) | 19. PRENATAL VISITS—Total Number (If none, so state)

20. WEIGHT OF FETUS (Specify Unit) | 21. CLINICAL ESTIMATE OF GESTATION (Weeks)

22a. PLURALITY—Single, Twin, Triplet, etc. (Specify) | 22b. IF NOT SINGLE BIRTH—Born First, Second, Third, etc. (Specify)

MEDICAL AND HEALTH INFORMATION

23a. MEDICAL RISK FACTORS FOR THIS PREGNANCY (Check all that apply)

Anemia (Hct. < 30/Hgb. < 10) .... 01 ☐
Cardiac disease .... 02 ☐
Acute or chronic lung disease .... 03 ☐
Diabetes .... 04 ☐
Genital herpes .... 05 ☐
Hydramnios/Oligohydramnios .... 06 ☐
Hemoglobinopathy .... 07 ☐
Hypertension, chronic .... 08 ☐
Hypertension, pregnancy-associated .... 09 ☐
Eclampsia .... 10 ☐
Incompetent cervix .... 11 ☐
Previous infant 4000+ grams .... 12 ☐
Previous preterm or small-for-gestational-age infant .... 13 ☐
Renal disease .... 14 ☐
Rh sensitization .... 15 ☐
Uterine bleeding .... 16 ☐
None .... 00 ☐
Other _____ (Specify) .... 17 ☐

23b. OTHER RISK FACTORS FOR THIS PREGNANCY (Complete all items)

Tobacco use during pregnancy .... Yes ☐ No ☐
Average number cigarettes per day ____
Alcohol use during pregnancy .... Yes ☐ No ☐
Average number drinks per week ____
Weight gained during pregnancy ____ lbs.

24. OBSTETRIC PROCEDURES (Check all that apply)

Amniocentesis .... 01 ☐
Electronic fetal monitoring .... 02 ☐
Induction of labor .... 03 ☐
Stimulation of labor .... 04 ☐
Tocolysis .... 05 ☐
Ultrasound .... 06 ☐
None .... 00 ☐
Other _____ (Specify) .... 07 ☐

25. COMPLICATIONS OF LABOR AND/OR DELIVERY (Check all that apply)

Febrile (>100°F. or 38°C.) .... 01 ☐
Meconium, moderate/heavy .... 02 ☐
Premature rupture of membrane (>12 hours) .... 03 ☐
Abruptio placenta .... 04 ☐
Placenta previa .... 05 ☐
Other excessive bleeding .... 06 ☐
Seizures during labor .... 07 ☐
Precipitous labor (< 3 hours) .... 08 ☐
Prolonged labor (>20 hours) .... 09 ☐
Dysfunctional labor .... 10 ☐
Breech/Malpresentation .... 11 ☐
Cephalopelvic disproportion .... 12 ☐
Cord prolapse .... 13 ☐
Anesthetic complications .... 14 ☐
Fetal distress .... 15 ☐
None .... 00 ☐
Other _____ (Specify) .... 16 ☐

26. METHOD OF DELIVERY (Check all that apply)

Vaginal .... 01 ☐
Vaginal birth after previous C-section .... 02 ☐
Primary C-section .... 03 ☐
Repeat C-section .... 04 ☐
Forceps .... 05 ☐
Vacuum .... 06 ☐
Hysterotomy/Hysterectomy .... 07 ☐

27. CONGENITAL ANOMALIES OF FETUS (Check all that apply)

Anencephalus .... 01 ☐
Spina bifida/Meningocele .... 02 ☐
Hydrocephalus .... 03 ☐
Microcephalus .... 04 ☐
Other central nervous system anomalies (Specify) _____ .... 05 ☐
Heart malformations .... 06 ☐
Other circulatory/respiratory anomalies (Specify) _____ .... 07 ☐
Rectal atresia/stenosis .... 08 ☐
Tracheo esophageal fistula/Esophageal atresia .... 09 ☐
Omphalocele/Gastroschisis .... 10 ☐
Other gastrointestinal anomalies (Specify) _____ .... 11 ☐
Malformed genitalia .... 12 ☐
Renal agenesis .... 13 ☐
Other urogenital anomalies (Specify) _____ .... 14 ☐
Cleft lip/palate .... 15 ☐
Polydactyly/Syndactyly/Adactyly .... 16 ☐
Club foot .... 17 ☐
Diaphragmatic hernia .... 18 ☐
Other musculoskeletal/integumental anomalies (Specify) _____ .... 19 ☐
Down's syndrome .... 20 ☐
Other chromosomal anomalies (Specify) _____ .... 21 ☐
None .... 00 ☐
Other _____ (Specify) .... 22 ☐

CAUSE OF FETAL DEATH

28. Enter only one cause per line for a, b, and c.

PART I. Fetal or maternal condition directly causing fetal death.

IMMEDIATE CAUSE
a. _____ | Specify Fetal or Maternal

DUE TO (OR AS A CONSEQUENCE OF):

Fetal and/or maternal conditions, if any, giving rise to the immediate cause(s), stating the underlying cause last.

b. _____ | Specify Fetal or Maternal

DUE TO (OR AS A CONSEQUENCE OF):

c. _____ | Specify Fetal or Maternal

PART II. Other significant conditions of fetus or mother contributing to fetal death but not resulting in the underlying cause given in Part I.

29. FETUS DIED BEFORE LABOR, DURING LABOR OR DELIVERY, UNKNOWN (Specify)

30. ATTENDANT'S NAME AND TITLE (Type/Print)
Name _____
☐ M.D. ☐ D.O. ☐ C.N.M. ☐ Other Midwife
☐ Other (Specify) _____

31. NAME AND TITLE OF PERSON COMPLETING REPORT (Type/Print)
Name _____
Title _____

PHS-T-007

DEPARTMENT OF HEALTH AND HUMAN SERVICES — PUBLIC HEALTH SERVICE — NATIONAL CENTER FOR HEALTH STATISTICS — 1989 REVISION

U.S. Standard Report of Fetal Death

8. Report of an autopsy: Beginning in 1972, all registration areas requested information on the death certificate as to whether an autopsy had been performed. For 1992 autopsies were reported on 224,071 death certificates, 10.3 percent of the total.

9. Cause of Death: Since 1949 cause-of-death statistics have been based on the underlying cause of death, which is defined as "(a) the disease or injury which initiated the train of events leading directly to death, or (b) the circumstances of the accident or violence which produced the fatal injury."

For each death the underlying cause is selected from an array of conditions reported in the medical certification section on the death certificate. This section provides a format for entering the cause of death sequentially. The conditions are translated into medical codes through the use of the classification structure and the selection and modification rules contained in the applicable revision of the *International Classification of Diseases* (ICD), published by the World Health Organization (WHO).

Tabulation lists—Beginning with the data year 1979, the cause-of-death statistics published by NCHS have been classified according to the Ninth Revision of the *International Classification of Diseases* (ICD-9). In addition to specifying that ICD-9 should be used, WHO also recommends how the data should be tabulated to promote international comparability.

Five lists of causes have been developed for tabulation and publication of mortality data in NCHS publications: the Each-Cause List, List of 282 Selected Causes of Death, List of 72 Selected Causes of Death, List of 61 Selected Causes of Infant Death, and List of 34 Selected Causes of Death. These lists were designed to be as comparable as possible with the NCHS list used under the Eighth Revision (ICD-8).

HIV: Beginning with the data for 1987, changes were made in these lists to accommodate the introduction in the United States of new categories *042-*044 for Human immunodeficiency virus (HIV) infection. The changes are described in the Technical Appendix from *Vital Statistics of the United States, 1987.* The asterisks appearing before the categories indicate that these codes are not part of ICD-9.

Ill-defined conditions: Although deaths occur for which it is impossible to determine the underlying cause (ICD-9 Nos. 780-799, Symptoms, signs and ill-defined conditions), this proportion indicates the care and consideration given to the certification by the medical certifier. In 1992 a record low of 1.1 percent of all reported deaths in the United States were assigned to this category, the same as in 1991.

10. Infant deaths: Infant death is defined as a death under one year of age; it excludes fetal deaths.

Fetal Deaths

In May of 1950 WHO recommended the following definition of fetal death be adopted for international use:

Death prior to the complete expulsion or extraction from its mother of a product of conception, irrespective of the duration of pregnancy; the death is indicated by the fact that after such separation, the fetus does not breathe or show any other evidence of life such as beating of the heart, pulsation of the umbilical cord, or definite movement of voluntary muscles.

The term "fetal death" was defined on an all-inclusive basis to end confusion arising from the use of such terms as stillbirth, spontaneous abortion, and miscarriage. Shortly thereafter, this definition was adopted by NCHS as the nationally recommended standard. All registration areas except Puerto Rico have definitions similar to the standard definition. Puerto Rico has no formal definition.

As another step towards increasing comparability of data on fetal deaths for different countries, WHO recommended that for statistical purposes fetal deaths be classified as early, intermediate, and late. These groups are: less than 20 completed weeks of gestation (early fetal deaths, Group I); 20 completed weeks of gestation but less than 28 weeks (intermediate fetal deaths, Group II); 28 completed weeks of gestation and over (late fetal deaths, Group III). Fetal deaths with gestation periods not classifiable in Groups I, II, or III are listed as Group IV.

Until 1939 the nationally recommended procedure for registration of a fetal death required the filing of a live-birth certificate and a death certificate. In 1939 a separate Standard Certificate of Stillbirth (fetal death) was created to replace the former procedure. This was revised in 1949, 1956, 1968, 1978, and 1989. The form shown here is the latest 1989 U.S. Standard Report of Fetal Death. States vary considerably with regard to the period of gestation: 7 states require reporting fetal deaths at all periods of gestation, but most of the others require only reporting fetal deaths at beyond 20 weeks (or a fetal weight of 350-500 grams). Underreporting of fetal deaths is most likely to occur in the earlier part of the required reporting period for each state.

Perinatal Mortality

Beginning with the data year 1979, perinatal mortality data for the United States and for each state have been published. Because birthweight and gestational age are not reported on death certificates in the United States, the NCHS was unable to adopt WHO recommendations on how perinatal deaths should be defined. NCHS instead uses three definitions of perinatal mortality:
• Perinatal Definition I: fetal deaths of 28 weeks of gestation or more and infant deaths under 7 days;
• Perinatal Definition II: fetal deaths of 20 weeks of gestation or more and infant deaths under 28 days; and
• Perinatal Definition III: fetal deaths of 20 weeks or more of gestation and infant deaths under 7 days. Because states have different requirements regarding the gestational age at which fetal deaths must be reported, some states may have more complete reporting of perinatal mortality than others.

Population Bases

The death rates are computed on the basis of population statistics published or made available by the U.S. Bureau of the Census. Rates for 1940, 1950, 1960, 1970, 1980 and 1990 are based on the populations enumerated as of April 1 in the censuses of those years. Rates for all other years are based on the estimated midyear (July 1) population for the respective years. These populations exclude the Armed Forces abroad but include the Armed Forces stationed in each area.

Part C: Registration and Tabulation of Marriage and Divorce Statistics

The material reported below was extracted from Section 4, Technical Appendix, of Volume III, Vital Statistics of the United States: 1988 (Marriage and Divorce). The reader is referred to the full report for a complete account of the effort to develop a vital statistics reporting system for marriages and divorces comparable in scope and quality to the one used for births and deaths.

Data on marriages and divorces and on the persons involved for the states that constitute the marriage registration area (MRA) and the divorce registration area (DRA) are based on information from two sources. For some states, samples of records are drawn by the National Center for Health Statistics (NCHS) from microfilm copies of the original certificates received from the state registration offices. Other states submit computer tapes to NCHS through the Vital Statistics Cooperative Program (VSCP). For these states the complete file is used. Statistical data for 1988 for marriages and divorces were provided to the VSCP by nine states- Illinois, Missouri, Nebraska, New Hampshire, New York (except New York City marriages), Rhode Island, South Carolina, Vermont, and Virginia. States participating in the VSCP for marriage data only were Florida, Maine, Montana, and Wisconsin.

Marriage and divorce statistics for the United States, for the registration areas, and for individual states are limited to events occurring during the year and registered within the specified area. All tabulations are by place of occurrence and include events occurring to non-residents. Marriages or divorces of members of the Armed Forces or other U.S. nationals that occur outside the United States are excluded. "United States" refers to the fifty states and the District of Columbia. Alaska has been included in the U.S. tabulations since 1959 and Hawaii since l960. Data for Puerto Rico and the Virgin Islands were compiled for 1988 and preceding years except 1966-69 and 1972; these data are processed separately from the rest of the MRA or DRA.

Nationwide Counts

In 1988 the total counts of marriages by state and county were obtained from central files of marriage records for 47 states and from the District of Columbia. The total count of marriages for New York City was obtained from a 100-percent sample of microfilmed marriage certificates. In the states without central marriage files—Arizona, New Mexico and Oklahoma—counts were obtained from counties by state officials and reported to NCHS.

Beginning with final marriage statistics for 1978, non-licensed (confidential) marriages registered in California are included in national and geographic totals and rates. Section 4213 of the California Civil Code allows unmarried couples who have been living together to be married confidentially without obtaining a marriage license or health certificate. In 1972 this section was amended to require county clerks to keep sealed records of these marriages and periodically to report the total number to the California State Department of Health Services.

Total counts of divorces by state and county include decrees of absolute divorce and of annulment as well as decrees of marriage dissolution introduced in many states in the 1970s. These counts are obtained from central files of 46 states and from the District of Columbia. Either local or state officials provided the county totals for the four states without central files of divorce records. Local officials in Indiana and New Mexico supplied the county totals. State officials in Arizona and Oklahoma obtained the county totals and forwarded them to NCHS.

Data from Registration Areas

Registration areas for the collection of marriage and divorce statistics were established in 1957 and 1958, respectively. These areas include states with adequate programs for collecting marriage and divorce statistics. Criteria for participation in the registration areas are
1. A central file of marriage or divorce records.
2. A statistical report form conforming closely in content to the Standard License and Certificate of Marriage or Standard Certificate of Divorce, Dissolution of Marriage, or Annulment.
3. Regular reporting to the state office by all local areas in which marriages or divorces are recorded.
4. Tests for completeness and accuracy of marriage or divorce registration and completeness of reporting of items in the records carried out in cooperation with NCHS.

In 1988 the MRA comprised 42 states, the District of Columbia, Puerto Rico, the Virgin Islands, and the independent registration area of New York City. The DRA included 31 states, the District of Columbia and the Virgin Islands.

In the statistical tabulations in 1988, the *marriage registration area* refers only to the 42 states and the District of Columbia. The *divorce registration area* refers only to the 31 states and the District of Columbia. Marriages in the MRA accounted for 81 percent of all marriages in the United States in 1988 (77 percent excluding California nonlicensed marriages), and divorces in the DRA accounted for 49 percent of all divorces.

Standard Certificates

The U.S. Standard License and Certificate of Marriage and the U.S. Standard Certificate of Divorce, Dissolution of Marriage or Annulment (see examples here) , issued by the Public Health Service, serve as the principal means of obtaining comparable data from documents used to collect information on marriages and divorces in the United States. Model reporting forms were first recommended to the states in 1954 for adoption January 1, 1955, and stood without revision through 1967. Revisions of the standard certificates were made for use beginning January 1, 1968, and January 1, 1978.

Each state and independent registration area determines the form and content of its vital records. Consequently, the records vary in certain details. Although modified in each state as required by the particular needs or by special provisions of the state vital statistics law, the marriage and divorce certificates of most states in the MRA and DRA conform closely to the standard certificates.

U.S. Standard License and Certificate of Marriage

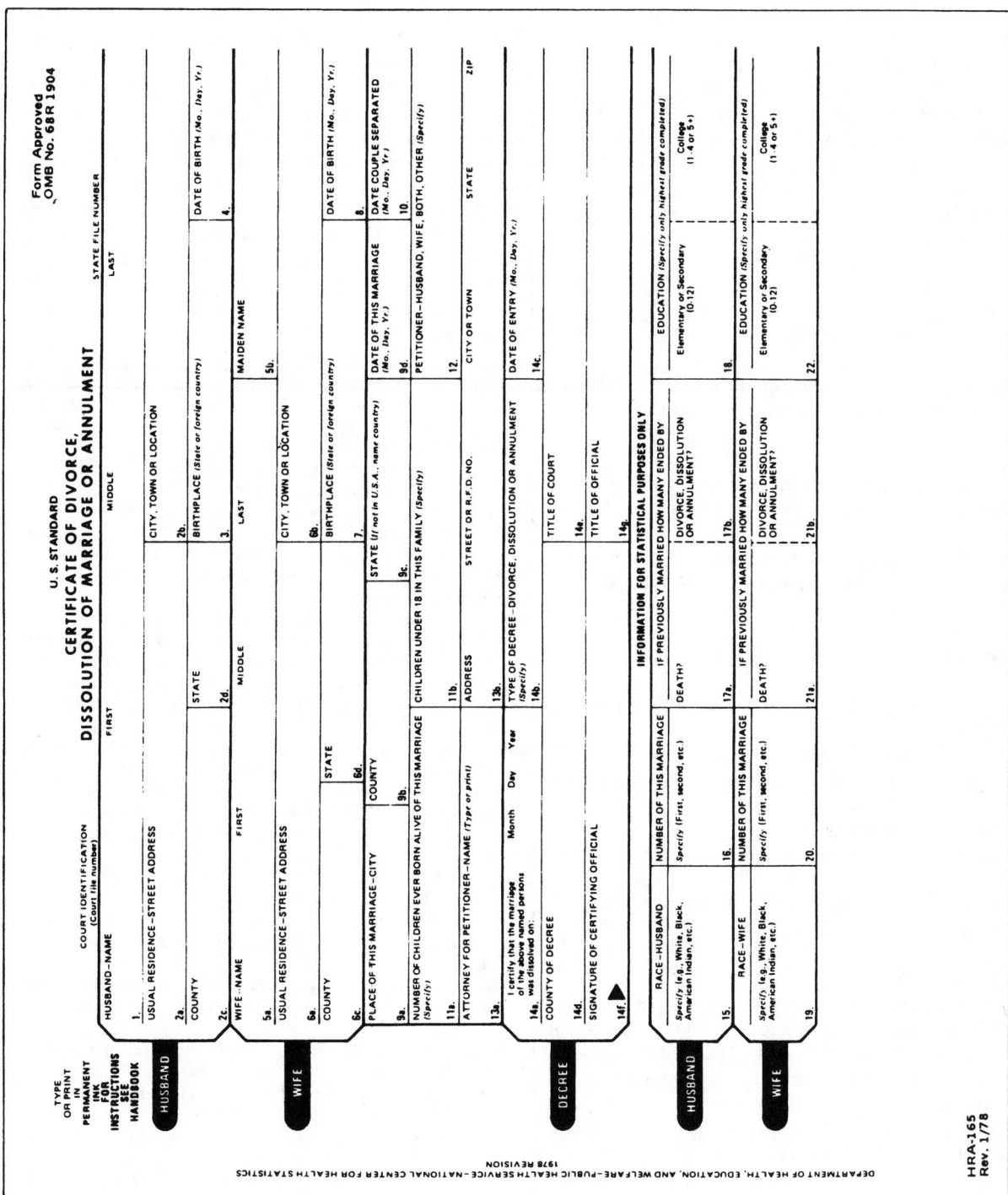

U.S. Standard Certificate of Divorce, Dissolution of Marriage or Annulment

Characteristics of Marriages and Divorces

The following is a brief summary of the important items asked on the marriage certificate and the number of states and registration areas that asked the item in 1988:

1. Date of marriage; date of birth and age at marriage of bride and groom; state of marriage; and state of residence of bride and groom: All states that were in the MRA and the District of Columbia reported these items.
2. State of birth of the bride and groom: All 42 states in the MRA reported; the District of Columbia did not.
3. Type of ceremony: The District of Columbia and 39 states reported this.
4. Race: Reported by 34 states, but not by the District of Columbia.
5. Education: Reported by 23 states.
6. Previous marital status: All MRA areas except Iowa reported.
7. Number of this marriage: Reported by all MRA areas except Iowa.
8. Marriage order: Reported by all MRA areas except Iowa.
9. Date last marriage ended: Reported by all MRA areas except Iowa.

The following items about the characteristics of divorcing spouses were reported by states and areas in the DRA in 1988:

1. Date of divorce, number of children under 18, date of birth or age at decree of husband and wife; state of divorce; and state of residence: Reported by all 31 states and the District of Columbia.
2. State of marriage: Reported by 30 states and the District of Columbia.
3. Number of children born alive of this marriage: Reported by 25 states.
4. Date couple separated: Reported by 21 states.
5. Number of this marriage: Reported by 30 states and the District of Columbia.
6. Education: Reported by 21 states.
7. Race: Reported by 27 states and the District of Columbia.
8. If previously married, how many ended by death; if previously married, how many ended by divorce: Reported by 30 states and the District of Columbia.

Percents and Rates

Rates for 1940, 1950, and 1970, 1980 and 1990 are based on the population enumerated as of April 1 in the censuses of those years. Rates for all other years are based on the estimated rnidyear (July 1) population for the respective years. Rates are based on population estimates including Armed Forces stationed in the United States but excluding Armed Forces abroad, except divorce rates for 1941-46, which are based on populations including Armed Forces abroad. Since 1980, rates by previous marital status have been based on the unmarried population 15 years of age and over rather than 14 years and over, which had been the standard until 1980.

Children Involved in Divorces

To obtain national estimates for 1970 through 1978, the average number of children under eighteen years of age per decree for the DRA was multiplied by the national divorce total.

From 1965 to 1969 the average number of children per decree was computed for the sixteen states that had reported children with a satisfactory degree of completeness in 1965 (Alaska, Hawaii, Idaho, Iowa, Kansas, Michigan, Missouri, Montana, Nebraska, Ohio, Oregon, South Dakota, Tennessee, Virginia, Wisconsin, and Wyoming) and the national divorce total was multiplied by this average.

The race of a child involved in a divorce is inferred from the race of the husband and wife. When spouses are both in the same racial category, the child is assigned to that category. When the husband is white and the wife is not, the child is assigned to the wife's race. When the husband is not white, the child is assigned to the husband's race. When the race of only one spouse is stated, the child is assigned to the stated race. When the race of both spouses is not stated, the child is assigned to race not stated.

References

Centers for Disease Control and Prevention, Public Health Service. Vital Statistics of the United States, 1992. Volume I-Natality. Washington, D.C.: U.S. Department of Health and Human Services. 1996.

Centers for Disease Control and Prevention, Public Health Service. Technical Appendix from Vital Statistics of the United States, 1992. Volume II- Mortality. Washington, D.C.: U.S. Department of Health and Human Services. 1996.

Centers for Disease Control and Prevention, Public Health Service. Vital Statistics of the United States, 1988. Volume III- Marriage and Divorce. Washington, D.C.: U.S. Department of Health and Human Services. 1996.

Grove, RD, Hetzel AM. Vital Statistics in the United States, 1940-60. National Center for Health Statistics. Washington, D.C.: Public Health Service. 1968.

Heuser, R. Fertility tables for birth cohorts by color: United States, 1917-73. Washington, D.C.: National Center for Health Statistics. 1976.

Hoyert, D.L. "Effect on mortality rates of the 1989 change in tabulating race." Vital and Health Statistics 20(25). 1994.

Linder, FE, Grove, RD. Vital Statistics in the United States, 1900-40. Washington, D.C.: National Office of Vital Statistics. 1947.

National Center for Health Statistics. Model State Vital Statistics Act and Model State Vital Statistics Regulations. Washington, D.C.: Public Health Service. 1995.

National Office of Vital Statistics. Births and birth rates in the entire United States, 1909 to 1948. Vital Statistics- Special Reports; Vol. 33 no. 8. Washington, D.C.: Public Health Service. 1950.

Sorlie, P.D., E. Rogot, and N.J. Johnson. "Validity of demographic characteristics on the death certificate." Epidemiology 3(2):181-4. 1992.

U.S. Bureau of the Census. Test of birth-registration completeness, 1964 to 1968. 1970 Census of Population and Housing: PHC (E)-2. Evaluation and Research Program. Washington, D.C.: Department of Commerce. 1973.

_____. U.S. population estimates, by age, sex, race and Hispanic origin, 1980-91. Current Population Reports; series P-25, no. 1095. Washington, D.C.: U.S. Department of Commerce. 1992.

World Health Organization. Manual of the International Statistical Classification of Diseases, Injuries and Causes of Death, based on the recommendations of the Ninth Revision Conference, 1975. Geneva: World Health Organization. 1977.

Appendix 2-3

Internet Sources of U.S. Census, Vital Statistics and Survey Data

Over the past several years there has been a virtual explosion in the amount of U.S. government census, survey and vital statistics data available on-line through the Internet. Typically these data are available directly through the World-Wide Web or through Gopher systems that allow the user to download large files. The data are usually available as reports or summary tables; in some cases, the original data can be obtained as well.

Some of the more important sources of on-line data (either the homepages of major agencies or of the data sources themselves) are listed below. Various search engines (such as Lycos, Inktomi, Magellan, etc.) can also be used to search for such sites. While it is possible that some of these sites may change their homepage addresses in the future, specifying the name of the desired agency or the desired data source for a search engine should permit one to track down the current location of the homepage.

U.S. GOVERNMENT SOURCES OF CURRENT DATA:

U.S. Bureau of the Census Homepage:

http://www.census.gov/

This homepage is the basic introduction to the U.S. Bureau of the Census, the current state of planning for the 2000 Census, various press releases, subscription information, and so on. It has links to many other major sources of U.S. Census data.

U.S. Bureau of the Census User Manual:

http://www.census.gov/main/www/man_main.html

This site gives more specific information on the use of census data, Bureau of the Census policies, how census data are made available (print media, CD-ROM, over the Internet), and other topics.

U.S. Bureau of the Census TIGER Homepage:

http://tiger.census.gov/

The TIGER (Topographically Integrated Geographic Encoding and Referencing) system is the huge electronic map of every block in the United States developed for the 1990 Census and updated since then. This homepage provides extensive information on this important part of the U.S. Census, and on current and future developments in this field. One part of this remarkable homepage can produce maps of any area of the United States at different levels of aggregation in a few seconds, and also provide the accompanying census data; see the "U.S. Gazetteer" at *http://www.census.gov/cgi-bin/gazetteer*

Current Population Survey (CPS)

http://www.census.gov/hhes/cpsdesc.html

A description of the monthly data from the current versions of the CPS is available at this site. The historical data from earlier CPS is available through CIESIN (see below).

American Housing Survey (AHS)

http://www.census.gov/pub/hhes/www/ahs.html

These data are from a sample of about 50,000 housing units surveyed at a two-year interval by the Bureau of the Census for the Department of Housing and Urban Development.

Survey of Income Program Participation (SIPP)

http://www.census.gov/hhes/sippdesc.html

This site describes the data available from the SIPP, the largest government panel survey of social and economic conditions of families and the government programs designed to aid them.

Bureau of Labor Statistics Homepage:

http://stats.bls.gov/blshome.html

This homepage gives an extensive menu of sites for current social (especially labor) and economic data, including unemployment rates and Consumer Price Index information.

National Longitudinal Surveys (NLS)

http://stats.bls.gov:80/nlshome.htm

The NLS are a set of panel surveys that have gathered information on the labor market experiences of six groups of American men and women of different ages. Four of these groups are still being surveyed; the latest data are from 1994 or 1995.

Consumer Expenditure Survey

http://stats.bls.gov:80/csxhome.htm

This quarterly survey of about 5,000 consumer units (similar to households) provides information on the purchasing patterns of the U.S. population.

National Center for Health Statistics Homepage:

http://www.cdc.gov/nchswww/nchshome.htm

This is the homepage through which to start searches for vital statistics data, including current data on births, deaths, marriages, infant mortality, and other topics. This homepage provides useful information and e-mail contacts on the current major surveys of American health.

Centers for Disease Control and Prevention (CDC) Homepage

http://www.cdc.gov/

The CDC is the major clearinghouse for information on the current prevalence of disease and various health conditions and efforts at their control and prevention.

National Health Interview Survey

http://www.cdc.gov/nchswww/nhis.htm

This continuous nationwide sample survey (usually covering about 60,000 households per year) includes questions on illnesses, injuries, impairments, chronic conditions, utilization of health resources, and other health topics.

National Health and Nutrition Examination Survey (NHANES III)

http://ftp.cdc.gov/nchswww/nhanes.htm

This 1988-94 survey examined the health condition of about 30,000 persons in order to estimate the national prevalence of selected diseases and risk factors. This third survey in a series (the others were in 1971-74 and 1976-80) includes measurement of serum cholesterol and blood pressure levels. It oversampled children aged 2-35 months, persons 70 years of age and over, blacks and Mexican Americans.

National Center for Education Statistics (NCES) Homepage

http://www.ed.gov/NCES/index.html

The NCES is the major source of educational statistics in the U.S.; these include data from population surveys, surveys of educational establishments and various kinds of administrative data.

National Household Education Survey

http://www.ed.gov/NCES/nhes

This survey, conducted in 1993, had two different parts. About 11,000 parents of 3- to 7-year olds responded to the School Readiness component, and 12,700 parents of children in grades 3 through 12 and 6,500 youths in grades 6 through 12 answered the School Safety and Discipline part of the survey.

High School and Beyond Survey

http://www.ed.gov/NCES/surveys/hsb.html

This longitudinal survey tracks about 15,000 persons who were high school sophomores or seniors in 1980; the most recent follow-up survey was in 1992-93. Recent follow-up survey questions have included those on completed levels of education and income.

Bureau of Criminal Justice Statistics Homepage

http://www.ojp.usdoj.gov/bjs

The Bureau of Criminal Justice Statistics collects data from a number of surveys and from administrative sources, including the Uniform Crime Reports.

National Crime Victimization Survey

http://www.ojp.usdoj.gov/bjs/cvict.htm#ncvs

Residents of a national sample of 60,000 households are interviewed seven times over three years on their experiences with crime (both reported and unreported) over the past few months.

DATA ARCHIVES OF U.S. CENSUS AND SURVEY STATISTICS:

Inter-University Consortium for Political and Social Research (ICPSR)

http://www.icpsr.umich.edu/

Located at the Institute of Social Research at the University of Michigan, ICPSR is a membership-based, non-profit scholarly organization with the most extensive archive of social science data in the world. These include vast U.S. census data holdings, including many decennial censuses, many of the surveys mentioned in this chapter, the City and County Data Books, and a limited supply of foreign census materials.

Missouri State Census Data Center Gopher Site:

gopher://gopher.coin.missouri.edu:70/11/reference/census/about

This site has data from the 1980 and 1990 censuses (with computed rates of change between the censuses) for different demographic variables at state and county levels. See also *gopher://gopher.coin.missouri.edu:70/11/reference/census/us*

University of Michigan Gopher Site:

gopher://una.hh.lib.umich.edu:70/11/census

In addition to data on Michigan and other areas from recent censuses, this site has references to other electronic data sources on U.S. demography. Also includes indices of useful telephone numbers at the U.S. Bureau of the Census.

Integrated Public Use Microdata Samples—IPUMS Homepage:

http://www.hist.umn.edu/~ipums/

This University of Minnesota historical census archive contains 23 public use microdata samples of the United States population between 1850 and 1990.

Lawrence Berkeley National Laboratory Homepage:

http://cedr.lbl.gov/mdocs/LBL_census.html

This site at the University of California at Berkeley may have the most extensive data sets on recent censuses ever assembled; it includes over 300 gigabytes of demographic data from the 1970s and 1980s. If you need small area data on anywhere in the U.S., this is one place to find it.

CIESIN U.S. Demography Homepage:

http://www.ciesin.org/datasets/us-demog/us-demog-home.html

CIESIN (Consortium for International Earth Science Information Network) is a NASA-sponsored data bank of information on oceanography, meteorology, and the like, but it contains important census data as well. Its crown jewel is a set of samples from the Public Use Microdata Samples for every census since 1940 (usually a 1 per 1,000 sample of the population), and the software (Ulysses) to allow Internet users to generate crosstabulations from these data. This source also has much recent data from the Current Population Surveys. This is a tremendous resource for anyone with an interest in recent American social or economic history.

Other Sources

An increasing number of other university libraries and organizations are putting their census data online, but some have restrictions on access. See, for example, the archived census data at the University of Southern California at *http://www.usc.edu/userserv/consult/statistics/help/census/*

POPULATION RESOURCES AND CHALLENGES IN THE 21ST CENTURY

As we face the coming century, the many changing demographic behaviors and composition of the United States population raise both hopes and concerns. Throughout the rest of this volume demographic behaviors and trends are covered in considerable detail. This chapter raises some of the larger issues confronting the population for discussion in more general terms. There is no attempt to resolve these complex issues nor to pretend that our demographic crystal ball is capable of forecasting trends accurately into the distant future. It is, however, important to place the more narrowly demographic material within this volume in the larger context of social, political, economic and environmental concerns which are related to population growth and composition.

Our Changing Age Structure

Basic population trends presented in the introductory chapter to this volume illustrate the significance of declining fertility, declining mortality, and the changing age structure of the United States population. The aging of the population is one major demographic trend with impacts which are echoed and elaborated on in many of the chapters to follow. There are very general questions associated with the changing composition of the United States population spread throughout these chapters. How "old" is the United States population in a comparative international perspective? What is happening to the ratio of laborers to consumers, children to parents, and what do these changing patterns of dependency foretell for the future? Are age groups or cohorts becoming new minorities within the United States which are increasingly residentially segregated or pitted against each other in economic terms? These are just a few of the many questions

raised by the profoundly changing age structure of the United States population.

The Changing Age Distribution in International Perspective

While it may seem that the U.S. population will be aging rapidly over the next quarter century, in comparison to other large nations, the process may be much less disruptive than elsewhere. In 1994, the U.S. ranked third among all nations in the number of persons over age 65 (see Table 3-1). Between 1994 and 2020, the number of elderly in the U.S. will rise from 33.169 million to 53.348 million. While this is a significant rise (an increase of 60.8 percent), it is dwarfed by the increases in the number of elderly in a number of large Third World nations. In that same time period, China's elderly population will rise from 71 million to more than 168 million (an increase of 136.8 percent), and India's will increase from 36 million to almost 88 million (a rise of 142 percent). As Table 3-1 shows, the world's elderly will be increasingly concentrated among the large Third World nations (such as Brazil and Indonesia) rather than among the aging European nations.

The degree of disruption that the aging of the population may cause is linked to the rate at which this aging is taking place and the social and institutional changes that are needed to take care of the elderly. As will be shown in Chapter 15, the elderly in the United States are actually quite well-off, especially in comparison to many other age groups in the population. Institutional structures for the provision of medical and other forms of care (Medicare, nursing homes, Meals on Wheels, and so on) are also well-established. Probably the greatest resource of the U.S. elderly is their interest in public affairs and their high

**Table 3-1. The Twelve Nations with the Largest Number of
Persons Age 65 and Over: 1994 and Projection for 2020**

Country/area	Rank		Population age 65 and over (in thousands)	
	1994	2020	1994	2020
China, mainland	1	1	71,073	168,318
India	2	2	36,282	87,797
United States	3	3	33,169	53,348
Russia	4	5	17,384	26,050
Japan	5	4	17,140	32,231
Germany	6	7	12,476	18,551
Italy	7	9	9,259	13,012
United Kingdom	8	11	9,175	12,018
France	9	10	8,924	12,969
Ukraine	10	13	7,155	9,917
Brazil	11	8	7,098	18,084
Indonesia	12	6	6,875	19,476

Source: U.S. Bureau of the Census, Current Population Reports, "65+ in the
United States," Series P-23, Number 190, U.S. Government Printing Office,
Washington, D.C., 1996, Table 2-7.

rate of political participation, especially in terms of voting. Politicians are well aware that attempts to cut back on benefits for the elderly can be political suicide. Since almost all Americans expect to be among this elderly population themselves, there is broad support for programs like medical care for the elderly.

In China, by contrast, care for the elderly may become a major problem. There is no government-sponsored system of saving for the elderly in rural China; the burden falls almost entirely on younger family members. In urban areas, there are retirement systems, but with the decline in state-sector employment such generous retirement programs may become far less common, or the benefits may not keep up with the rate of inflation. In most urban (and some rural) areas where the family planning regulations of the 1980s and 1990s were successful in establishing the "one-child family," the population pyramid in 2020 may have a very strange shape. By that time, a married couple in their thirties or forties may have the primary responsibility for three or four aging parents (not to mention any surviving grandparents) as well as their children. The "accelerated demographic transition" found in many East Asian nations will give them much less time to adapt their social, cultural and institutional structures to the burden of a rapidly aging population.

Population Trends and Changing Inequities

Population trends in the United States have an intimate relationship to the social inequities which exist within the country. As the population of the United States ages, becomes more diverse, has smaller family sizes, is more likely to live out of marriage or in non-traditional households, is more likely to depend upon two wage earners, etc., the distribution of wealth in the country is impacted in various ways. The life courses experienced by the individuals of the United States population have changed radically over the past half century. And, since 1967 when the Census Bureau began reporting on the income distribution of households, there has been growing income inequality (see Chapter 15). These inequities grew slowly until the 1980s when a sudden increase in income inequality was experienced. Then, from 1987 through 1992 income inequality seemed to have reached a plateau. However, since that time, inequality has experienced another large increase. Unfortunately, changes in survey methodology in 1993 confound the interpretation of this latest increase. Inequities in the income distribution and trends in income inequality are amplified if current social programs are discounted and income-in-kind benefits and gains are included as income (see Chapter 15). Figure 3-1 shows the percentage of aggregate income received by income quintiles for 1995 using such a definition. Excluding government payments the lowest income quintile accounts for less than one percent, while the highest income quintile accounts for more than half of all aggregate income received.

Income inequality is, of course, only one measurement of the inequities in our society. For example, according to the National Center for Education Statistics, the population of the United States is more unevenly divided

Figure 3-1. Percentage of Aggregate Income[1] Received by Income Quintiles: 1995

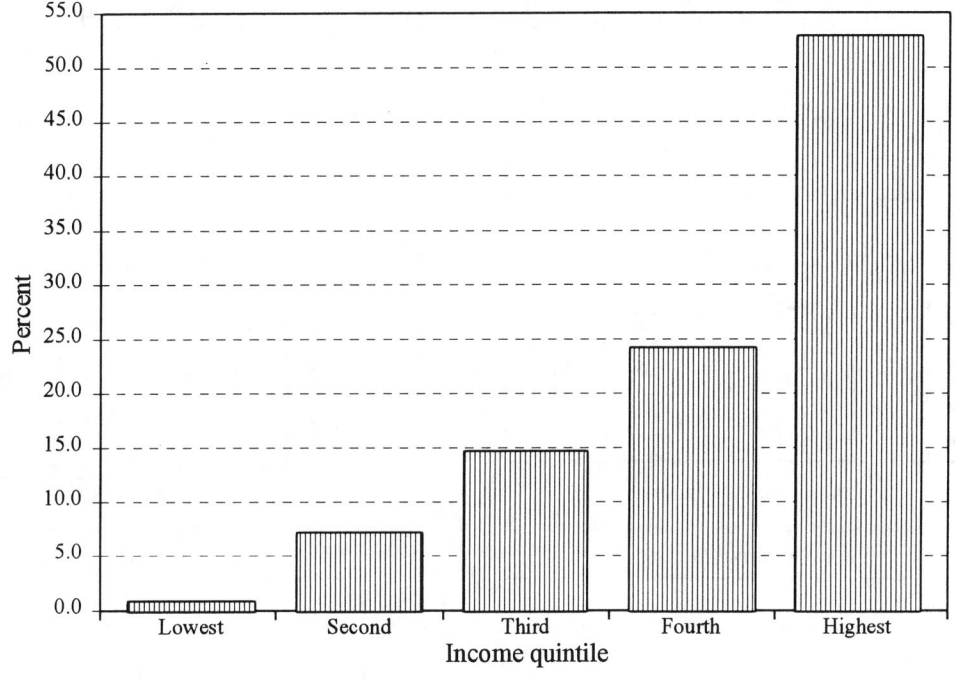

[1] Income Definition 4 which is the current measure of income (Definition 1) less government cash transfers plus capital gains and employee health benefits.
Source: 1995 U.S. Bureau of the Census data.

across the highest and lowest levels of literacy than most countries. Among a variety of countries studied, only Sweden had a greater proportion of its population score at the highest levels of literacy than the U.S. population. However, only Poland had a greater percentage of its population score at the lowest levels of literacy. Similarly, there are considerable differences in the quality of residential environments across the population. As of the 1990 Census, 1 in every 5 United States residents lived in poverty areas (i.e. tracts or block numbering areas where at least 20 percent of the population was below poverty levels). Not all of these individuals are themselves poor. They share, however, the many social impacts of living in a poverty area. Differential access to health care services, access to quality schooling, abilities to relocate, access to high wage job markets, and many similar inequities have been found within various regions of the United States.

The Environment and the Socially Disadvantaged

A new concern with poverty areas has been voiced over more specifically environmental risks and burdens imposed upon socially disadvantaged populations. Throughout the history of the United States the poor, minorities, and recent immigrants have found themselves relegated to the degraded neighborhoods of major United States cities. Quality of housing, ambient air pollution,

lead paint, open waterways, railroads and highways, urban crime, etc. are but some of the risks which are disproportionately borne by those who are limited in residential choices by larger social patterns of inequity. As the great European migrations have been replaced by, largely, Third World immigration and the historical internal migration of United States' minorities into the urban centers, the composition of those who bear such burdens has shifted to minorities and the working poor. And, as women and children have swelled the ranks of poverty they too have become more vulnerable to such environmental inequities.

Much of the concern over environmental inequities in recent years has been over the location of locally unwanted land uses (e.g. Superfund sites, hazardous waste treatment-storage-disposal facilities, chemical industries, landfills, etc.) in neighborhoods with higher concentrations of socially disadvantaged populations. For example, Figure 3-2 shows the percentage of census tract populations which are black, Hispanic, below the poverty level for a family of four, and receiving public assistance by the distance from commercial hazardous waste facilities. While these facilities are not necessarily sited directly in disadvantaged neighborhoods they appear to be located in industrial areas which in turn are more likely to be nearby neighborhoods in which socially disadvantaged populations are concentrated. Beyond the focused issue of where industrial facilities are sited, there is a more complex

Figure 3-2. Percentages of Select Minority and Disadvantaged Populations by Distance to Nearest Commercial Hazardous Waste (TSDF) Facility[1]: 1990

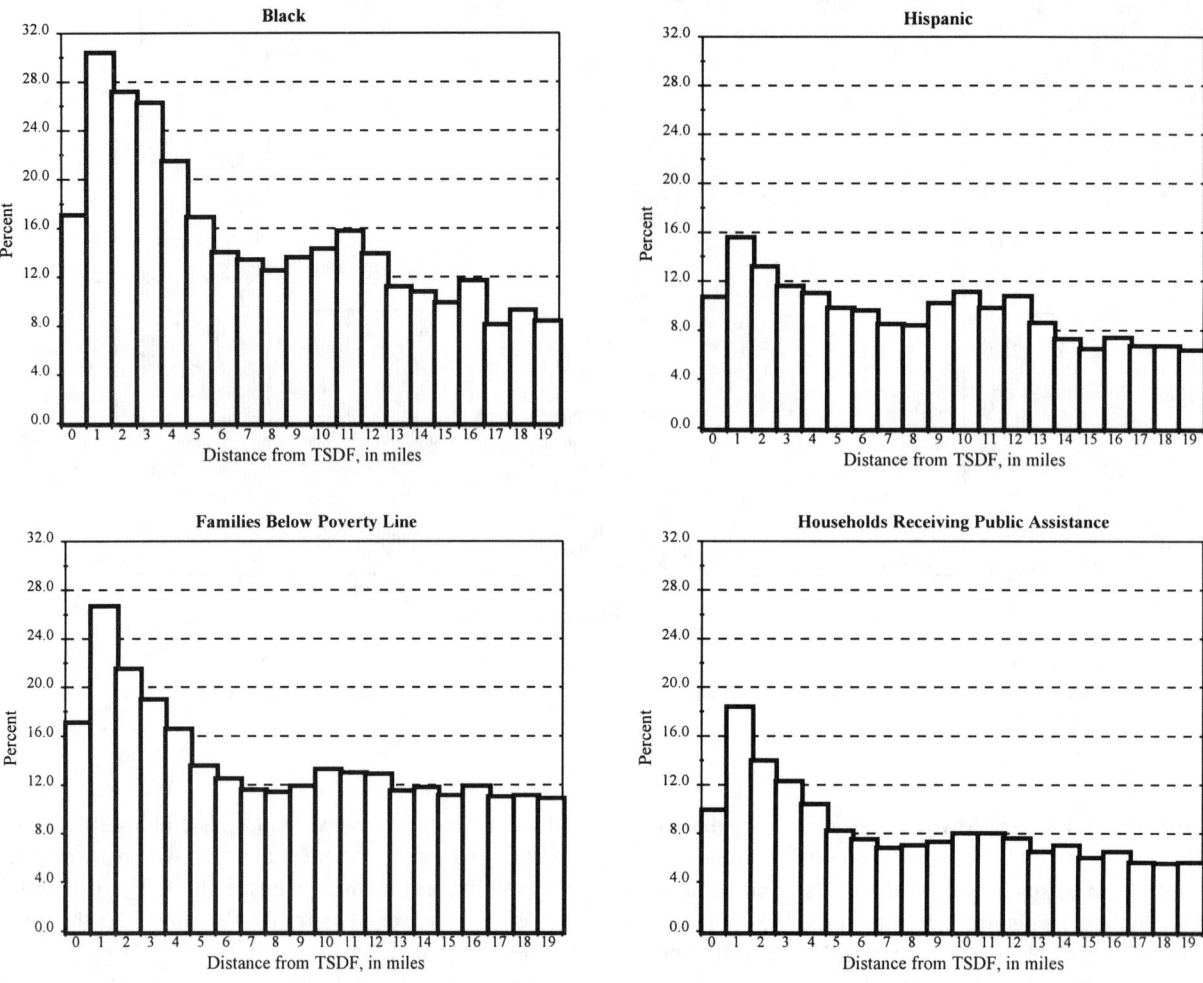

[1] Commercial TSDFs are Treatment, Storage, and Disposal Facilities which process over 50% of off-site waste for a fee.
Source: 1990 Social and Demographic Research Institute data.

history of residential patterns in which disadvantaged neighborhoods are both concentrated and plagued by lower quality housing, inadequate social services, urban crime, etc. (see Chapter 8 Textbox).

The Demographics of Poverty and Social Welfare

In contrast to income trends in the 1980s, more of the United States population experienced decreasing, rather than increasing, incomes. According to data from the Survey of Income and Program Participation, 40.4 percent of the population experienced an income decline between 1991 and 1992 while 37.2 percent of the population experienced gains of equivalent magnitude. Declining incomes and rising inequality have been clearly reflected in the composition of poverty (see Chapter 15) and are clearly impacted by differential marital and different labor force

experiences among different segments of society (see Chapters 13 and 14). Poverty rates are lower among those with high educational attainment, and far higher in families with female householders living with children and no husband present; and children, more than adults, tend to be the victims of poverty.

Using longitudinal data from the Survey of Income and Program Participation it is also possible to look more narrowly at long-term poverty. Over 1992 and 1993, 4.8 percent of the entire population was poor for the entire 24 months. This percentage of long-term poverty was 2.5 percent of non-Hispanic whites but 15.1 percent of blacks and 10.3 percent of Hispanics. Of those under 18 years of age 8.3 percent were poor the entire 24 months, while only 3.2 percent of those aged 18 to 64, and 4.9 percent of those over 65, experienced long-term poverty. The percentage of long-term poverty was highest (21.9 percent, or more than 1 of every 5) among families with a female house-

Changes in Participation in Public Assistance Programs

by Pamela R. Davidson

Today, there are at least 75 federal programs that offer assistance to the economically disadvantaged. Out of these, means-tested programs utilize income and asset thresholds to determine eligibility for benefits and provide cash and non-cash assistance to participants. The major means-tested programs include Aid to Families with Dependent Children (AFDC), General Assistance, and Supplemental Security Income (SSI) that provide cash benefits; and food stamps, Medicaid, and housing assistance that offer non-cash benefits. In 1993, estimates from the Survey of Income and Program Participation (SIPP) determined that of the estimated 258 million civilians living in the United States, approximately 36 million persons or 1 in 7 women and men received public assistance from the major means-tested government programs. This constitutes 14.0% of the total population, an increase from 11.4% in 1987-88.

In general, poverty and its correlates represent the best indicators of program participation. Whereas 57.3 percent of individuals with incomes below the poverty line were program participants in 1993, the same is true for only 6.5% of all individuals with higher incomes. Since children have a high likelihood of living in poverty, it is not surprising to find that recipients of means-tested assistance are usually children. Almost one quarter of all children under 18 years of age received means-tested assistance compared with 10.0% of persons 18 years of age and older. Families headed by single females relied on major means-assisted programs to a greater degree than other types of households. Whereas 42.9% of female-headed households participated in means-assisted programs, only 7.7% of households headed by married couples did so. There are other disparities in program participation that appear to be related to poverty and its correlates. A greater proportion of blacks receive public assistance from means-tested programs than do whites. In 1993, 1 in 3 blacks and 1 in 10 whites received means-tested assistance. Program participation is closely related to educational attainment, with persons 18 and over without a high school diploma significantly more likely to participate (23.6%) than persons with at least a high school diploma. Finally, central city residents are approximately twice as likely to be means-tested program participants than both non-central city and non-metropolitan residents.

The Survey of Income and Program Participation (SIPP) has collected information on the federal government program participation of individuals and households since 1983 on a subannual basis. Estimated first quarter household participation averages across the various programs reveal a similar trend: average household participation declined during the mid-eighties during a period of economic recovery. As the U.S. economy began to sink into recession beginning in 1988, participation rates began to steadily increase. For example, in 1984, 19.2% of households participated in some type of government assistance program. This proportion decreased to a low of 17.9% in 1987 but had increased again to 20.4% by 1992. An exception to this pattern is participation in the food stamps program. There, noticeable increases did not occur until the early nineties.

Program participation can be either short-term or long-term. In 1993, 20.2 million individuals or 8.3% of the total population were long-term participants in means-tested assistance programs, meaning they had participated in all 24 months of 1991 and 1992. This represents a substantial increase compared with the previous two-year period when 7.6% of the total population were long-term participants. In contrast to this increase in absolute numbers, the median length of time participants received benefits from means-tested programs has remained at approximately 8 months. This represents an increase since the late eighties when the median spell duration was 6.4 months. There are differences in median participation spells across the programs. During the 1990s, AFDC recipients increased their median participation length from 7.4 to 8.5 months, a decrease from the 10.4 months duration in 1987. Developments in the median length of participation in the food stamps program followed the opposite path, decreasing during the 1990s from 8.8 to 8.0 months, after increasing from a low of 7 months in 1987 to the median participation spell of 6.9 months in 1987.

In 1993, individuals who were not employed had the highest median length of time in means-tested public assistance programs (16.7 months). This was followed by female heads-of-household and blacks with median participation lengths of 13.1 and 13.3 months, respectively. Characteristic of the 1987-88 period is the absence of large divergences in average duration. Individuals who were not employed had the highest average duration (8.9 months) and children had the lowest (4.9 months). The average participation spell in all other categories ranged between 5 and 7 months. Moreover, in 1987 there was close to no difference in average participation duration between those above and below the poverty line. This situation is clearly different from that in 1993 in which those with incomes below the poverty line had participation spells

Average Monthly Program Participation, All Means-tested Programs: 1987-1993

Characteristics	1987-88	1990-91	1992-93
Total	11.4	11.5	14.0
Race-ethnicity			
White	8.0	8.4	10.6
Black	33.7	32.2	35.5
Hispanic	22.1	24.9	28.9
Age			
Under 18 years	18.3	18.8	23.7
18 to 64 years	8.3	8.3	10.0
Household type			
Married couple	6.2	6.1	7.7
Female-headed	37.4	37.2	42.9
Educational attainment			
No high school diploma	20.8	20.9	23.6
High school graduate	7.3	7.9	10.1
Some college	2.9	3.3	4.1
Residence			
Metropolitan	10.6	11.0	13.3
Central city	17.0	17.3	19.8
Outside central city	6.0	6.8	8.8
Nonmetropolitan	14.3	13.3	16.2
Poverty status			
Ratio less than 1.0	54.3	52.8	57.3
Ratio 1.0 or above	4.8	5.4	6.5

Source: U.S. Bureau of the Census, Current Population Reports, "Who Gets Assistance?" Series P-70, No. 58, Table A, and "Program Participation: 1990 to 1992," Series P-70, No. 41, Tables B, D, E, F, H, and II, U.S. Government Printing Office, Washington, D.C., 1996 and 1997.

Average Monthly Household Participation in Means-tested Government Programs: 1984-1992

		Households receiving benefits						
Year	All households	Total	AFDC	SSI	School meals	Food stamps	Medicaid	Housing
Monthly average								
1992	93,473	19,063	4,171	3,723	7,989	7,573	10,224	4,446
1991	93,313	18,203	4,051	3,593	7,461	6,814	9,652	4,836
1990	91,776	16,690	3,523	3,239	6,841	5,939	8,348	4,576
1989	91,394	16,408	3,744	3,388	6,825	5,787	8,104	4,575
1988	89,858	16,741	3,318	3,496	6,855	5,996	7,882	4,488
1987	88,131	15,793	3,717	3,075	5,924	6,230	7,707	3,883
1986	87,134	16,422	3,753	3,107	6,278	6,588	7,593	4,172
1985	85,228	—	3,536	2,990	—	5,999	7,277	3,751
1984	83,643	16,052	3,876	2,880	5,896	6,462	7,593	3,615
Percent of households								
1992	100.0	20.4	4.5	4.0	8.5	8.1	10.9	4.8
1991	100.0	19.5	4.3	3.9	8.0	7.3	10.3	5.2
1990	100.0	18.2	3.8	3.5	7.5	6.5	9.1	5.0
1989	100.0	18.0	4.1	3.7	7.5	6.3	8.9	5.0
1988	100.0	18.6	3.7	3.9	7.6	6.7	8.8	5.0
1987	100.0	17.9	4.2	3.5	6.7	7.1	8.7	4.4
1986	100.0	18.8	4.3	3.6	7.2	7.6	8.7	4.8
1985	100.0	—	4.1	3.5	—	7.0	8.5	4.4
1984	100.0	19.2	4.6	3.4	7.0	7.7	9.1	4.3

Source: U.S. Bureau of the Census, Current Population Reports, "Monitoring the Economic Health of American Households," Series P-70, No. 35, U.S. Government Printing Office, Washington, D.C., 1994, Table 5.

Median Duration of Program Participation: 1987-1993

	All programs			AFDC			Food stamps		
Characteristics	1987-88	1990-91	1992-93	1987-88	1990-91	1992-93	1987-88	1990-91	1992-93
Total	6.4	7.9	7.7	10.4	7.5	8.5	6.9	8.8	8.0
Race-ethnicity									
White	6.4	7.8	7.3	7.1	8.3	7.3	5.4	7.8	7.2
Black	6.7	8.7	13.3	11.3	14.0	13.8	15.2	13.9	13.3
Hispanic	7.2	10.2	9.3	7.9	15.3	7.5	7.5	10.5	9.5
Age									
Under 18 years	4.9	7.4	7.2	8.0	12.5	10.0	7.5	9.5	8.5
18 to 64 years	6.4	8.1	7.8	7.3	9.1	7.8	5.8	7.9	7.5
Houshold type									
Married couple	5.4	7.3	6.3	4.9	7.0	5.0	5.4	7.9	6.7
Female-headed	6.8	11.4	13.1	13.7	11.5	12.3	10.5	15.5	11.5
Employment status									
Employed									
Full-time	5.2	6.3	5.4	3.8	3.5	3.7	3.9	5.7	4.2
Part-time	6.7	8.2	7.5	3.9	6.1	7.0	4.5	6.5	7.2
Unemployed	4.9	7.6	9.0	5.8	7.3	6.1	4.2	7.2	7.8
Not employed	8.9	11.9	16.7	10.3	14.7	11.5	9.7	11.9	12.8
Poverty Status									
Ratio less than 1.0	7.3	10.6	11.5	9.3	12.1	9.6	7.8	10.6	9.8
Ratio 1.0 or above	7.0	4.2	6.0	4.8	6.7	5.5	3.9	6.0	5.9

Source: U.S. Bureau of the Census, Current Population Reports, "Who Gets Assistance?" Series P-70, No. 58, Table B, and "Program Participation: 1990 to 1992," Series P-70, No. 41, Tables B3, D2, E2, and 12, U.S. Government Printing Office, Washington, D.C., 1996 and 1997.

that were nearly twice as long than for those above the poverty line.

The median length of children's participation has remained relatively stable in the nineties for major means-tested programs. In AFDC and food stamps programs, children have experienced a noticeable decrease in the median spell length beginning in 1990. In contrast, single mothers increased their median length of participation in both means-tested programs in general and the AFDC program in particular. Female-headed households were able to decrease their average participation spells in the food stamps program to 11.5 months, although this average still remains higher than the average 10.5 months in 1987. While part-time employees reduced their median participation rates in the aggregate, they increased their median participation lengths in AFDC and food stamp programs.

State-specific caseload data and the National Integrated Quality Control System's monthly sample of cases compiled by the Department of Health and Human Services on participation in AFDC extend further back in time than the SIPP data. Record data show a dramatic increase in participation in AFDC between 1970 and 1993. During this period, the number of participants almost doubled from 7.4 million to 14.1 million individuals. As the figure illustrates, this constitutes an increase from 3.6 to 5.5 percent of the total resident population. At the same time, the number of children receiving AFDC increased by close to 74% from 1.9 million in 1970 to 5.0 million individuals in 1993. This represents an increase from 7.1 percent of total resident children ages 19 and under to 12.9 percent. Most of this increase took place between 1970 and 1975 when the number of AFDC children and total recipients increased by between 44 and 49 percent. Thereafter, the rate of increase was slower. After 1989, the number of participant children and total recipients began to climb again, increasing by about 30 percent between 1989 and 1993. Participation is projected to increase at a slower but steady rate until the turn of the century, reaching 15.6 million total recipients and 10.7 million children in 1999.

Caseload data show important shifts in the demographic characteristics of AFDC participants. The average family size

of AFDC recipients shrank from 4.0 persons in 1969 to 2.9 persons in 1992. The percentage of participating households reporting no father in the home increased from 85% 1979 to 89% in 1992. This increase was accompanied by a decreased percentage of families reporting earnings. The percentage of families with earnings decreased from 14.6% in 1975 and 12.8% in 1979 to 5.7% in 1983. The decrease in the percentage of mothers reporting a full-time job during that same period was much more rapid, from 8.7% in 1979 to 1.5% in 1983. While access to earnings decreased, AFDC participants received increasingly smaller benefits. In 1970, the average monthly benefit per family was $675 (after adjusting for inflation). By 1993, this amount had fallen to $373, a 45 percent reduction. At the same time, participation of AFDC households in the food stamp or donated food program increased by 65 percent (from 52.9% to 87.3%), with one third of that increase taking place between 1973 and 1983 alone. In contrast, participation in public housing by AFDC recipients decreased from 12.8% in 1969 to 9.2% 1992. Participation in SSI decreased from 3.0% of AFDC families in 1986 to 1.3% in 1992. Moreover, it is estimated that while in 1979 means-tested benefits pulled 30.0% of single-parent families out of poverty, that percentage decreased to only 15.1% in 1983 and 17.6% in 1992. In contrast, for married couples, this percentage remained fairly constant across the entire time range (between 15 and 19 percent) with only a temporary decrease in 1983.

Additional Sources:

Gibbons, Sam M. Green Book: Overview of Entitlement Programs. Committee on Ways and Means, U.S. House of Representatives, Washington, D.C. July(1994).

Ryscavage, Paul. Monitoring the Economic Health of American Households: Average Monthly Estimates of Income, Labor Force Activity, Program Participation, and Health Insurance. U.S. Bureau of the Census, Current Population Reports, P-70-35. Washington, D.C.: U.S. Government Printing Office. 1994.

Shea, Martina. Dynamics of Well-Being: Program Participation, 1990 to 1992. U.S. Bureau of the Census, Current Population Reports, P-70-41. Washington, D.C.: U.S. Government Printing Office. 1995.

Tin, Jan. Dynamics of Economic Well-Being: Program Participation, 1992 to 1993. Who Gets Assistance? U.S. Bureau of the Census, Current Population Reports, P-70-58. Washington, D.C.: U.S. Government Printing Office July(1996).

Percent of the Population Receiving AFDC Benefits: 1970-1999[1]

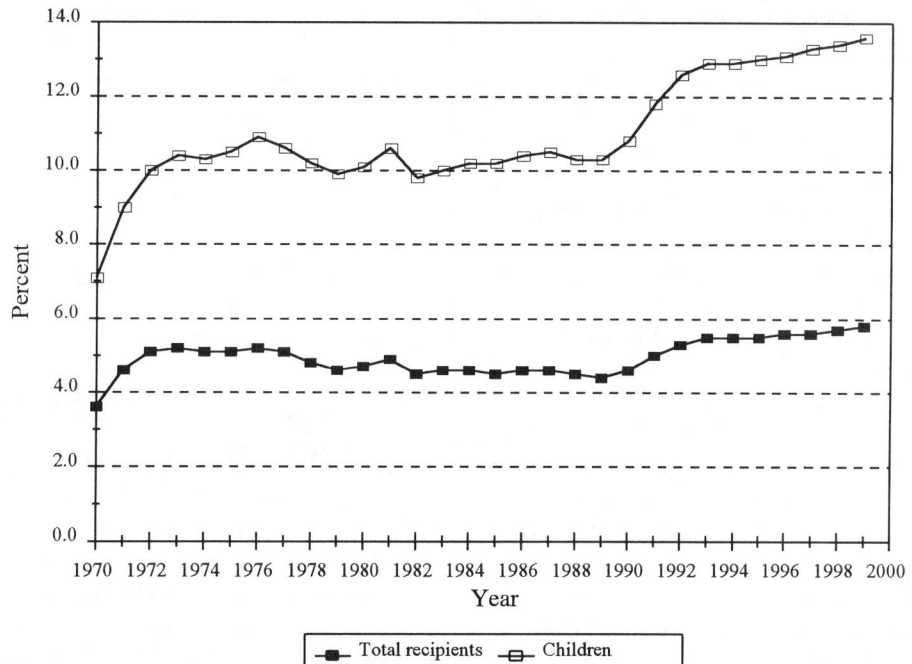

[1] Values for 1994-1999 are administration projections under current law.
Source: 1970-1993 Office of Financial Management, Administration for Children and Families data.

holder, no spouse present and with related children under 18 years of age.

These data also provide some indication of the transitions into and out of poverty over the same period (see Table 3-2). More than 1 in 5 (21.6 percent) of those who were poor in 1992 were not by 1993. Only 3.0 percent of the non-poor became poor over the same year. Nonetheless, the number of those becoming poor was roughly five percent greater than those becoming non-poor. Among children the transition out of poverty is lower than for the total poor population (17.7 percent) and the transition into poverty is higher (4.0 percent). In terms of a net difference in the numbers of children entering and leaving poverty, however, roughly six percent more children left poverty status than entered it over these two years.

The demographics of poverty and those of various groups receiving different forms of public assistance (see Textbox) are much stereotyped and misunderstood. Disproportionately women and children have risen to comprise ever more of the poor within the United States over the past half century.

Working Mothers, Single Mothers and the Wage Gap

Many of the most interesting and profound demographic changes in recent decades focus on the changing nature of women's lives. The contraceptive revolution and fertility decline have had a profound impact on childbearing and child rearing expectations over the life course. Women's entry into the labor force has surely affected both other demographic behaviors and the distribution of wealth in the United States. Despite labor saving technologies working women continue to carry the large bulk of domestic burdens and yet continue to earn less than comparable worth in the labor market (see Textbox). Women are also facing increased periods of their life in which they are required to be economically independent. Increasing divorce, decreasing marriage and remarriage trends, advancing age of widowhood with nonetheless increasing years spent as a widow, all illustrate the demographic changes which have increased the economic burdens of independence upon women for greater periods of their life. At the same time, the two-wage earner family has become more of an economic standard or necessity.

Next to high educational attainment, being married and living with a spouse is the most important factor in avoiding poverty (see Chapter 15). Rising divorce rates, single parenthood, delay of marriage and similar trends (see Chapters 5, 6 and 11) have contributed dramatically to the rising proportion of women and children living in poverty. At the same time, some of these trends, such as the gloomy marriage prospects for older highly educated women, have been often overstated and misunderstood (see Textbox). Nonetheless, the strong possibility of an increasing social division or inequity centered on the eco-

Table 3-2. Transitions Into and Out of Poverty, by Age, Sex, and Race-ethnicity: 1992-1993

Characteristics and poverty status in 1992	Total (in thousands)	Poverty status in 1993	
		Poor	Nonpoor
Total	246,176	11.9	88.1
Poor	28,986	78.4	21.6
Nonpoor	217,190	3.0	97.0
Race-ethnicity			
White	205,614	9.2	90.8
Poor	18,838	74.3	25.7
Nonpoor	186,776	2.6	97.4
Black	30,963	29.4	70.6
Poor	8,754	86.8	13.2
Nonpoor	22,210	6.7	93.3
Hispanic	23,202	26.7	73.3
Poor	5,729	81.6	18.4
Nonpoor	17,473	8.6	91.4
Age			
Under 18 years	64,777	19.0	81.0
Poor	12,416	82.3	17.7
Nonpoor	52,361	4.0	96.0
18 to 64 years	152,848	9.4	90.6
Poor	14,101	73.9	26.1
Nonpoor	138,747	2.8	97.2
65 years and over	28,550	9.4	90.6
Poor	2,470	85.0	15.0
Nonpoor	26,081	2.2	97.8
Sex			
Male	119,339	10.4	89.6
Poor	12,230	76.9	23.1
Nonpoor	107,109	2.8	97.2
Female	126,836	13.3	86.7
Poor	16,756	79.5	20.5
Nonpoor	110,081	3.2	96.8

Source: U.S. Bureau of the Census, "Dynamics of Economic Well-being: Poverty, 1992 to 1993," http:/www.census.gov, 1996, Table 5.

nomic hardships of women living out of wedlock contrasted to those of men or couples' earnings potential is one which should be of grave concern as we enter the next century.

Disinvestment in Our Children: the Long-Term Effects

The growing proportion of children among the poor has profound social ramifications. The rise of children in poverty is, at the same time, only one indication of the ways in which government austerity has failed, or disinvested in, children. Inadequate social programs, educational resources, health care, etc., bear largely upon the young. Demographic trends have amplified the inequality of wealth across generations as more of the elderly live

Technology, Women's Labor, and Compensation

by Susan Hautaniemi

Historically, technological changes influenced women to enter the labor force in two ways. Mechanization of many processes, particularly cloth production, both decreased the time women spent in producing goods for family use and eliminated sources of income derived from producing for the market. In addition, in an effort to drive down labor costs, industrialists developed new machinery meant to replace skilled male laborers with unskilled female labor. Both the loss of income from home production and the lowering of male wages worked to induce women to take jobs outside the home.

Changes in domestic technologies, many of which are revealed in the census, also made women's labor force participation possible. Particularly before 1940, running a home was a time-intensive occupation for American families, and most of the burden fell on women. Homes dependent on coal, coke or wood made up 78 percent of all dwellings in 1940. These fuels require constant maintenance of heating equipment, and, because they are inherently dirty, increase the amount of cleaning that must be done. By 1990, less than 5 percent of all homes were dependent on these energy sources, and 77 percent of all homes used clean and low-maintenance fuels like electricity or utility-supplied natural gas. In 1940, daily shopping was necessary for many families, since only 44 percent of all homes had mechanical refrigeration; another 27 percent used ice, and in 29 percent of all homes there was no means of keeping food or beverages cold. Only a decade later, by 1950, 80 percent of homes had mechanical refrigeration.

Well into this century, sewing, mending, washing and ironing the family's clothing required at least two days of hard labor per week. Water had to be drawn, carried, heated on wood or coal stoves, and later carried out again. Laundry had to be scrubbed, boiled, wrung, rinsed, hung to dry and ironed using heavy flatirons heated on the stove. This, in addition to maintaining fires and cooking three meals each day, not only required that women work seven long days a week, but also meant that their work was physically taxing. The small electric motor and the provision of running water were the two developments that had the most influence in decreasing the arduous nature of household work. Between 1925 and 1955 public water supplies in the United States more than doubled.

The current high rates of labor force participation among women with children would not have been possible without these labor-saving devices. The labor force participation rate of women has steadily increased from 16% in 1890 to over 58% in 1990 (see Chapter 13), with most of the change accounted for by a dramatic increase in married women's participation rates. Yet, special purpose surveys and studies which go beyond the limits of census data reveal that these technological advances have not led to an appreciable decrease in the number of hours spent in housework, due to increased standards of cleanliness, more material possessions to be cared for, and increased emphasis on mother-intensive child rearing which began in the middle of the nineteenth century.

Household tasks have consumed approximately 50 hours per week since at least 1926, and are still largely performed by women. Even in dual-earner households, time spent by husbands accounts for only 35%, while their wives contribute 65% of the time devoted to household tasks (see Table 1). Husbands who are at home during the day while their wives are working tend to do more traditionally female tasks than other males, and a smaller gap in earnings is correlated with a smaller gap in time devoted to housework. However, increased housework associated with children falls more to wives than to husbands. Furthermore, women do more household tasks than men, regardless of their marital status, with the greatest gap between husbands and wives (17.83 hours per week and 36.67 hours per week, respectively) and cohabiting couples (19.16 and 31.12, respectively). Adult sons living at home spend the least time doing household chores (14.93 hours per week); their time spent on housework increases to only 19% (or slightly less than 3 hours) when they marry. Gender stereotypes seem to be holding, with husbands spending more time than wives in only two areas: car maintenance and outside maintenance. These patterns are apparently set early; while an adult daughter living at home reduces housework, an adult son increases a woman's housework. Of all living situations, only males who are widowed or divorced spend more time on housework than adult daughters living at home (the lowest group for women). So, while technology allowed women's labor force participation to increase by making housework easier, it did not appreciably change the domestic division of labor.

Although women are more likely to work, continue to spend more time with housework, and make up an increasingly greater percentage of the workforce, they also continue to earn less in employment than men. Persistence of pay inequity

Female Earnings as a Percent of Male Earnings: 1970-1990

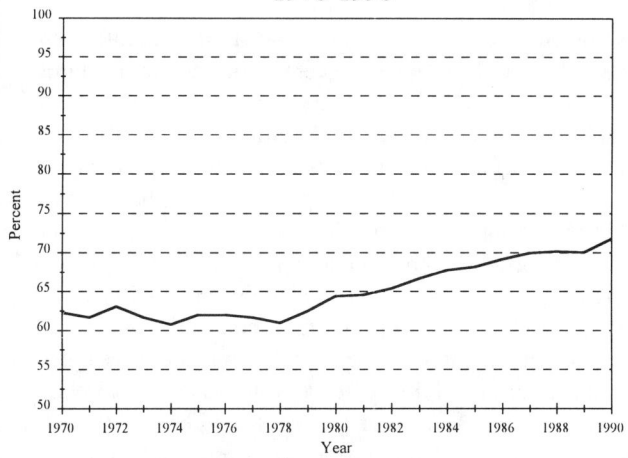

Female Earnings as a Percent of Male Earnings: Selected Years 1914-1990

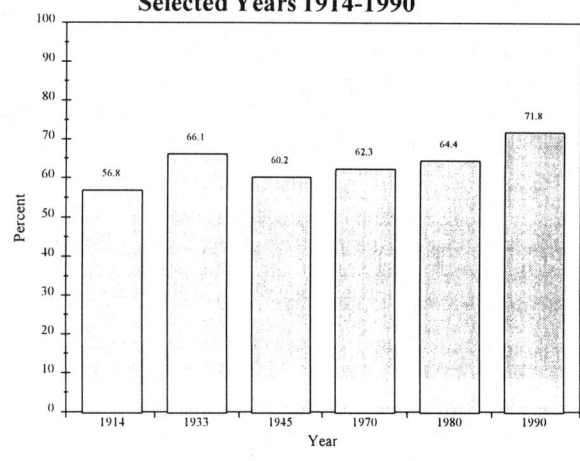

arises partly because women continue to be clustered in low-skill, low-paying jobs. The census of 1950 was the first one in which "servant" was not the most frequently returned occupation for employed women. In 1990, the greatest percentage of women were employed in technical, sales and administrative support occupations (44%), with only 3.7% of them technicians. However, women also generally receive less compensation when they hold the same jobs as men (see Chapter 14). Even during the "Rosie the Riveter" war years, women production workers earned only 60-70 % of what their male counterparts did. Women's earnings relative to men's were nearly as high in 1934 (68.8%), in 1948 (68.6%) and in 1985 (68.2%) as they are now. Today, women in many professions earn substantially less than men in the same profession, with women having a slight advantage over men when employed as apprentices and child care workers, and near equity in some other occupational categories (see Chapter 14).

Women's earnings as a percentage of men's earnings range between a low of 55.2% in 1942 to 71.8% in 1990. Figure 1 shows male and female earnings for selected years: 1914 is the first year for which data are available; 1933 was the year of highest unemployment during the Depression, 1945 was the peak of wartime production, and 1970 and 1980 captured the influx of working women coinciding with the women's movement. Data are not available for the years 1948 through 1966 and 1968. There have also been changes in the reporting of relative wage information over time. Although the overall trend shows an increase in women's earnings relative to men's, there is a great deal of fluctuation, with a gain of nearly 10 percentage points between 1914 and the Depression, followed by a 6 point loss from 1933 to 1945. This loss was not recouped until after 1980, with a gain of slightly less than 6 percentage points from the Depression to the present, and a gain of only 7.4 percentage points in the last decade.

Figure 2 graphs female earnings as a percentage of male earnings for the past two decades. Women's wage position relative to men's has improved, with less fluctuation since 1980. However, it remains to be seen whether another loss in relative earnings, as seen in the past, will prevent women from reaching compensation parity with men. Furthermore, a recent study found that over 50% of the remaining wage gap between white men and women cannot be accounted for by differences in employment history or on-the-job training. Without significant changes in gender norms, it seems doubtful that women will earn as much as men in the near future. It also seems likely that women will continue to bear the brunt of the "double shift," working both professional and domestic jobs, regardless of their living arrangements or employment status.

Additional Sources:

Abel, Marjorie, and Folbre, Nancy. "A Methodology for Revising Estimates." Historical Methods 23(1990): 167-76.

Baxandall, Rosalyn, Gordon, Linda, and Reverby, Susan (eds.). America's Working Women. New York: Random House. 1976.

Kessler-Harris, Alice. Out to Work. Oxford: Oxford University Press. 1982.

Presser, Harriet B. "Employment Schedules, Gender, and Household Labor." American Sociological Review 59(1994): 348-64.

South, Scott J., and Spitze, Glenna. "Housework in Marital and Nonmarital Households." American Sociological Review 59(1994): 327-47.

Wellington, Alison J. "The Male/Female Wage Gap among Whites: 1976 and 1985." American Sociological Review 59(1994): 839-48.

Mean Hours per Week Spent on Household Tasks by Dual-earner Married Couples: 1987-1988

Household Task	Husband	Wife
Number of respondents	1,845	1,845
Mean hours, total	17.8	32.5
Female tasks	6.7	25.1
Preparing meals	2.4	8.6
Washing dishes and cleaning up after meals	1.9	5.3
Cleaning house	1.7	7.0
Washing, ironing, and mending clothes	0.7	4.2
Male tasks	7.3	1.6
Outdoor tasks or other housework maintenance tasks	5.3	1.4
Automobile maintenance and repair	2.0	0.2
Neutral tasks	3.8	5.8
Shopping for groceries and other household goods	1.3	2.7
Paying bills and keeping financial records	1.3	1.6
Driving household members to work, school, other activities	1.1	1.6

Source: Presser, H.B., "Employment Schedules, Gender, and Household Labor," American Sociological Review 59(1994):348-64, Table 1.

Female Earnings as a Percent of Male Earnings

	1990	1980	1970	1945	1933	1914
Earnings	71.8	64.4	62.3	60.2	66.1	56.8

Source: 1990 data from U.S. Bureau of Labor Statistics, "Employment and Earnings: January 1991," Table 54; 1980 data from "Handbook of Labor Statistics: 1985," Table 41; 1970 data from "Handbook of Labor Statistics: 1980," Table 60; and 1914-1945 data from U.S. Bureau of the Census, "Historical Statistics of the United States: Colonial Times to 1957," Table D 669-684, U.S. Government Printing Office, Washington, D.C., 1991, 1989, 1980, 1960.

longer with a greater share of the wealth among older generations than in the past.

The disinvestment in children is particularly short-sighted given research which demonstrates early investment is critical to the future life course of the next generation. The relationship between early investment in children and subsequent criminal activities is merely one example of such effects. The High/Scope Foundation's Perry Preschool study in Michigan presented evidence that the number of later lifecourse "chronic lawbreakers" was reduced by up to 80 percent among children who received child care similar to Head Start along with family "coaching" visitations. The savings in crime costs alone were nearly $150,000 per child in the High/Scope study. The Syracuse University Family Development Study similarly

shows that child delinquency over a 10 year follow-up period was reduced by 90 percent among children of families receiving quality childhood programs for children through five years of age. Preventing one child from becoming a criminal has been estimated to have savings as great as $1.5 million. Similar programs have been shown effective at later stages of adolescence as well. The Quantum Opportunities program in five United States cities cut the risk of arrest during high school years by 50 percent through a high school program of counseling, academic support and community service. Similar studies suggest that even after an initial offense, youth and family investment can cut the risk of subsequent offenses by up to half. The RAND Corporation's attempt to determine the cost-effectiveness of various early interventions (see

Table 3-3. Cost-effectiveness of Early Interventions for Crime Prevention After 30 Years: 1996

Program costs and benefits	Intervention			
	Home visit/ day care	Parent training	Graduation incentives	Delinquent supervision
Cost per participant	$29,400	$3,000	$12,520	$10,000
Net present value of cost per participant	$26,290	$3,000	$11,816	$10,000
Serious crimes prevented per participant	0.59	0.71	4.16	0.99
Net present value of serious crimes prevented per participant	0.30	0.47	3.05	0.72
Dollars per serious crime prevented	$89,035	$6,351	$3,881	$13,899
Serious crimes per million dollars spent	11	157	258	72

Source: Greenwood, Peter W., Model, Karyn E., Rydell, C. P., and Chiesa, James, "Diverting Children from a Life of Crime: Measuring Costs and Benefits," http:/www.rand.org/publications/MR/MR699, 1996, Table 3.

Table 3-3) found that some programs resulted in prevention of a serious crime within the following 30 years for as little as under four thousand dollars' investment in youth services. Even the most expensive intervention (under $90,000) studied would be cost effective in comparison with the costs of serious crime and incarceration.

The return value on programmatic child investment in terms of subsequent educational and labor force gains is similarly borne out by a variety of studies. Unfortunately, the intergenerational nature of these effects will not be fully borne out within the generation which has chosen to curtail such programs. Only after the neglected youth of this century become young adults in the coming one will the full cost of such generational investment decisions be known.

Diversity in the Population: Source of Strength or Weakness

Due to the growth of minority populations, a high rate of immigration, and changing norms which pit respect for cultural diversity against older visions of assimilative national solidarity, the United States population is increasingly diverse in both demographic and cultural composition. Some in our society view rising diversity as both a sign and a source of cultural vitality and strength. Others may fear that diversity represents the "balkanization" of the United States and a growing potential source of divisiveness or political turmoil.

Internationally, the late twentieth century has seen the breakup of some large states (e.g. the USSR) along largely ethnic lines. It has also witnessed the growing integration of others (e.g. the European Union) in efforts to overcome borders of the past. And, still other countries with diverse populations have strong ethnic strains within their borders which have caused periodic turmoil and are yet to be resolved (e.g. China). Some of the bloodiest of recent global conflicts have been along heavily ethnic lines bordering on wars of genocide (e.g. Bosnia, Burundi). At a national level, and in light of recent history, it is not unreasonable to view ethnic sub-nationalism with some fear and suspicion as a major source of weakness and potential conflict.

The United States, however, is a unique country with a history that confounds many of those from nations in which ethnic turmoil has arisen. Despite the fact that concentrations of minority populations often contribute to urban unrest and political tensions throughout the country, the patterns of ethnic diversity are unquestionably more complex than those which have promoted turmoil abroad. There are strong patterns of residential segregation in many metropolitan areas of the United States (see Textbox, Chapter 8). But, there is a decreasing regional concentration of blacks, the country's largest minority group. While Mexicans are predominantly immigrating to key border areas (e.g. California, Texas, etc.) they are migrating in large numbers to many other states as well. Asian immigrants are concentrating into a number of key states but are not segregating themselves into distinct neighborhoods as heavily as might be anticipated, and, like Hispanics, are suburbanizing rapidly. Finally, the lines of diversity in the United States may be sharp at times, but they are not monolithic ones pitting one minority against a majority in a singular course of domination. There are a variety of ethnic groups throughout the United States with more, and less, distinctive cultural identities. This country has also witnessed ethnic divisions throughout its history and part of its strength in avoiding divisiveness may lie in the fact that, however categorized, the majority population is itself woven from a historical web of diversity and processes of accommodation.

To what extent will the increasing diversity of the United States population serve as an engine of dynamic change or a source of divisiveness and weakness? Undoubtedly a large part of the answer to these concerns lies in the extent to which we allow inequalities to overlap

Probabilities of Marriage Among Older Women and Economic Consequences of Divorce

by Erin Leahey

One of the most highly publicized demographic trends of the past decade has been the supposed decline in marriage possibilities for women between the ages of 25 and 50. The steepness of the decline has been hotly debated: one study found that a woman's chance of marrying dropped precipitously after age 25, so that by age 45, a never-married, college-educated woman has a negligible (.0003 percent) chance of ever marrying (see Exter 1987 for a review of the unpublished study). In contrast, the Census Bureau assumed a more gradual decline in the probability of marriage, reporting that a 45-year-old never-married, college-educated woman has a 10 percent chance of marrying by age 65. What are we to believe?

Certainly, there are some indications of a general decline in marriage. For example, delays in marriage are mirrored in median age of first marriage, which increased from 20.2 in 1995 to 24.4 in 1992 for women, and from 22.6 to 26.5 for men in that same time period. Marital instability is also high as evidenced in the growing divorce rate: only 3.6 percent of women aged 35-44 were divorced in 1950, whereas 14.8 percent were classified as divorced in 1990. And fewer women in all age groups are married now as compared to a few decades ago (see Chapter 5).

Despite some general evidence of marriage decline, the prospects of marriage for older, professional women are not as dim as initially believed. Rates of first marriage for women aged 25-34 with some college education increased from 1972 to 1987. And for all women aged 25-43, rate of first marriage increased from 1979 to 1987. These changes contradict the widespread impression of increasing hopelessness for older, well-educated women who seek to marry. There appears to be little support for the supposedly drastic reduction of marriage opportunities for older, educated women (Qian & Preston 1993).

Although the reduced chances of marriage for older professional women may have been overstated, there has nevertheless been a general decline in marriage over the past few decades. The factors contributing to the decline are varied and debated. Economists cite the decreasing gains to marriage for women as they attain higher levels of education, enter the labor force in greater numbers, and increasingly earn higher wages relative to men (Van Der Klaauw 1996). Social change and modernization also replaced many of the functions once carried out by families, thus reducing the necessity of marriage and early family formation. In addition, "older unmarried individuals remain unmarried in large measure because they do not desire to marry" (South 1993 p.364). The sex ratio, particularly the proportion of unmarried women to unmarried men within age groups, may also influence marriage possibilities. Availability of a potential spouse improved for most women between 1972 and 1987. However, college-educated women, whose economic independence may permit them to set higher standards for potential spouses, saw a decline in the availability of eligible partners. When this decline of eligible spouses is taken into consideration, the marriage rates for college-educated women actually decline more sharply than the statistics demonstrate.

Although older professional women may achieve greater economic independence through their education and commitment to work, they are even more likely to earn comparably less than men within their occupations (see Chapter 15). It appears that singlehood at any age has economic consequences for women.

Change[1] in Marriage Rates for Women, by Age and Educational Attainment: 1979-1987

| Age | Educational attainment | | |
	Less than high school	High school graduate	Some college
17 to 19 years	0.54	0.52	0.72
20 to 24 years	0.77	1.02	0.87
25 to 29 years	1.02	1.37	1.34
30 to 34 years	1.34	2.26	1.12
35 to 43 years	0.86	1.46	1.24

[1] Ratio of 1987 marriage rate to 1979 marriage rate.

Source: Qian, Z, and Preston, S.H., "Changes in American Marriage, 1972 to 1987: Availability and Forces of Attraction by Age and Education," American Sociological Review 58 (1993): 482-95, Table 1.

Change[1] in Availability of Potential Spouses for Women, by Age and Educational Attainment: 1972-1987

| Age | Educational attainment | | |
	Less than high school	High school graduate	Some college
17 to 19 years	1.26	1.34	1.16
20 to 24 years	1.10	1.08	1.07
25 to 29 years	1.07	1.07	0.99
30 to 34 years	1.04	1.12	0.83
35 to 43 years	1.03	1.19	0.97

[1] Ratio of predicted 1987 marriage rate to 1972 marriage rate.

Source: Qian, Z, and Preston, S.H., "Changes in American Marriage, 1972 to 1987: Availability and Forces of Attraction by Age and Education," American Sociological Review 58 (1993): 482-95, Table 1.

Divorce and increasingly lower probabilities of remarriage also have an economic impact on women. It is widely agreed that women fare worse economically after divorce than men, although it is unclear whether recent changes in divorce legislation increase the gender disparity. Women in longer marriages and those with higher incomes experience the greatest drop in their post-divorce standards of living (Weitzman 1996). Thus divorce can have drastic consequences even for well-educated, professional women. Although the consequences of divorce are not as unequal as once supposed, women on average experience a 27% decline in standard of living after divorce, and men experience a 10% increase (Peterson 1996).

Additional Sources:

Exter, Thomas. "How To Figure Your Chances of Getting Married." American Demographics 9(1987): 50.

Peterson, Richard. "A Re-evaluation of the Economic Consequences of Divorce." American Sociological Review 61(1996).

Peterson, Richard. "Statistical Errors, Faulty Conclusions, Misguided Policy: Reply to Weitzman." American Sociological Review 61(1996).

South, Scott J. "Racial and Ethnic Differences in The Desire To Marry." Journal of Marriage and The Family 55(1993): 357-70.

Van Der Klaauw. "Female Labour Supply and Marital Status Decisions: A Life Cycle Model." Review of Economic Studies 63(1996): 199-235.

Weitzman, Lenore. "The Economic Consequences of Divorce Are Still Unequal: Comment on Peterson." American Sociological Review 61(1996).

Qian, Zhenchao, and Preston, Samuel. "Changes in American Marriage, 1972 to 1987: Availability and Forces of Attraction by Age and Education." American Sociological Review 58(1993): 482-95.

with ethnic identities. To the extent that we allow particular ethnic or cultural groups to become marginalized, subject to inflammatory prejudice, or economically disadvantaged, the likelihood that these conflicts will generate violent group conflicts along ethnic lines will rise. Some analysts, like Douglas S. Massey, foresee the coming of an "age of extremes," with spatial concentrations of affluence and poverty, especially in urban areas. Yet other researchers see some decreases in residential racial segregation in recent years.

Population and Natural Resources

Humankind possesses the powerful, and perhaps dangerous, conscious ability to consider itself as apart from, and master over, its environment. It is this instrumental consciousness which has led to the tremendous advances of the human race over the relatively recent geologic past. It is to this consciousness that we owe most of the relative health, amenities, security and comfort which most of the population of the United States now enjoys. Despite the disease, hunger and poverty which remain within our society, few would trade their current life for one of even greater squalor in the past.

At the same time, there is no question as to the ability of the human race to abuse and neglect its physical environment. Mortality places limits upon our lives and the rapid course of technological change, complexity of ecological systems, and uncertain knowledge of the repercussions of our own actions all limit our abilities to be custodians of the future environment despite our best intentions. And, of course, simplistic ideologies of a "pure" free market system in which each need strive only for his or her own immediate gratification promote far less than our best intentions as environmental custodians.

Perhaps the most cited demographic theory in history is that of Thomas Robert Malthus who, in 1798, laid forth an argument that the power of the human race to reproduce exceeds the power of the earth to produce subsistence for ever-growing numbers. In Malthus' pessimistic view, population growth would likely go unchecked by preventive reasons alone to the point at which the population would confront positive checks from immiseration, mortality and starvation. Despite the crude historical nature of Malthus' specific arguments, the basic notion he advanced—that individuals cannot or will not act individually of their own reason to check population growth before ecological disasters occur—remains the cornerstone of ecological concerns in the United States as well as abroad. Many contemporary population ecologists and demographers echo this basic theme (e.g. Paul Ehrlich, Dennis Meadows, and Jeremy Rifkin).

Karl Marx and Friedrich Engels were young men at the time Malthus died in 1834. As Malthus was formulating his dire demographic predictions in face of the rising age of industrialism, Marx and Engels were formulating the notion that the effects of growing density, the distribution of wealth, and the apparently increasing immiseration of the population were primarily determined by the kind of social organization a population developed. Within the labor theory of value developed by Marx and Engels, population is a resource or form of wealth in its own right. If society could be properly organized then relative wealth might increase, and society would benefit, rather than suffer, from population growth. Again, many of the contemporary social scientists who argue that population growth concerns are overstated by some ecologists echo the basic themes of this classical argument. The central premises that social organization, rather than population growth, is responsible for problems associated with population density (espoused, e.g., by Betsy Hartmann) and that higher fertility represents a resource rather than threat to our betterment (Julian Simon, Ben Wattenberg) have defenders equally ardent as those of any population ecologist.

Part of the difficulty in both simplistic views of population growth is their attempt to forecast well beyond the predictable horizon. If one believes that limits to technology and resources exist then there are certainly some ultimate limits to growth. Yet, if one believes such limits are far distant or largely surmountable then present concern for them is hardly warranted. Both arguments are all too frequently made as grand theories or simply expressions of belief systems beyond present knowledge. Both suffer from the reality that all forecasts grow increasingly uncertain with their distance from past experience and knowledge of the present.

Yet, in a practical sense, the net costs and benefits of each additional birth depend heavily upon the social organization and technology over the life course of the individual born. For the near future these conditions are foreseeable. The impact of the current population and likely population growth can be seen clearly within the prevailing social context without resorting to the distant and uncertain future. It is enough to look to the present to see the growing evidence that our current social organization, technology and population have wreaked havoc upon some parts of our environment to our own detriment. It is equally certain that in many current circumstances, near-term high rates of population growth can increase human misery. In many cases, such as declining biodiversity, we can clearly witness environmental impacts which merit cautious respect despite their uncertain implications for the future. Yet, it is clear that many environmental impacts have not been so unmanageable nor dire as some quarters have suggested. In fact, it is again sufficient to look at current data and recent historical trends to demonstrate that a number of environmental conditions have actually improved over the recent periods of population growth.

Without wading into the details of this pervasive debate, which is well beyond the scope of this text, it is

Figure 3-3. Water Withdrawals per Day, by End Use: 1940-1990

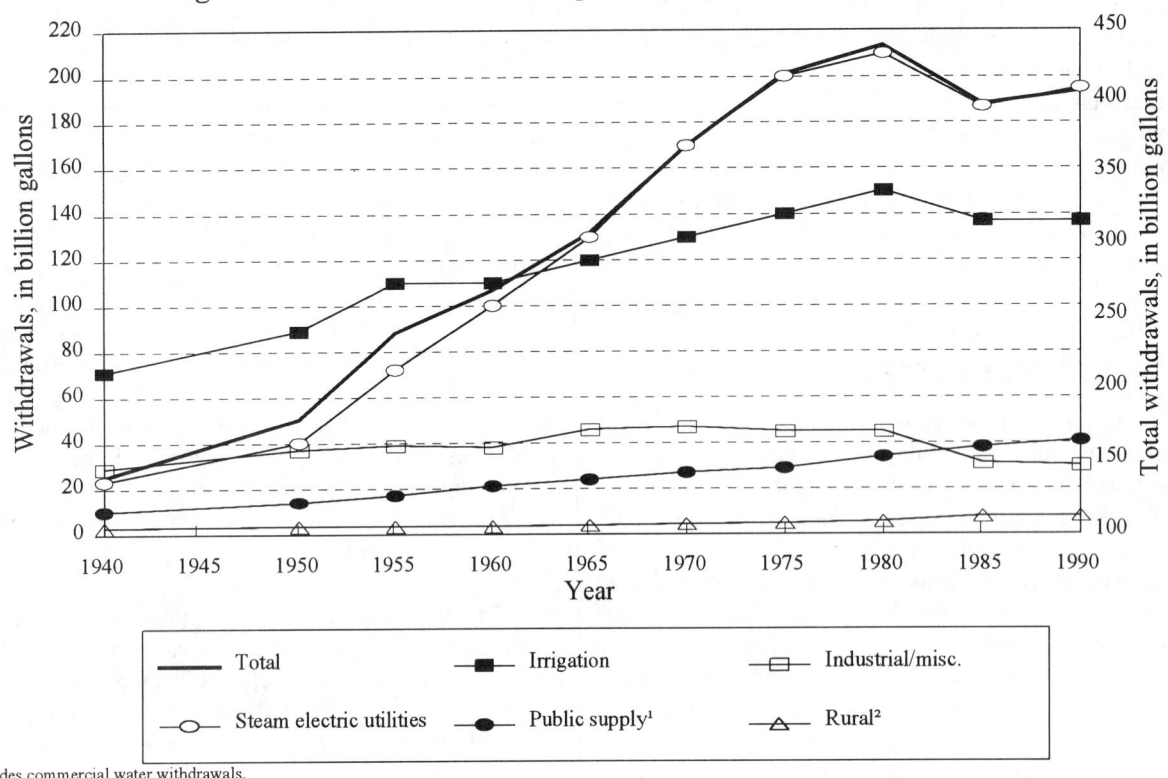

[1] Includes commercial water withdrawals.
[2] Rural farm and nonfarm household and garden use, and water for farm stock and dairies.
Source: 1940-1960 U.S. Senate Committee on National Water Resources data and 1965-1990 U.S. Geologic Survey data.

Table 3-4. National Ambient Water Quality in Rivers and Streams--Violation Rate: 1980-1994

Pollutant	Violation level	1980	1985	1988	1989	1990	1991	1992	1993	1994
Fecal coliform bacteria	Above 200 cells per 100 ml	31	28	22	30	26	15	28	31	29
Dissolved oxygen	Below 5 mg per liter	5	3	2	3	2	2	2	...	...
Phosphorus, total	Above 1.0 mg per liter	4	3	4	2	3	2	2	2	4
Lead, dissolved	Above 50 micrograms per liter	...	...	...	...	...	...	...	—	—
Cadmium, dissolved	Above 10 micrograms per liter	1	...	...	...	...	...	...	—	—

Source: U.S. Bureau of the Census, "Statistical Abstract of the United States: 1995," U.S. Government Printing Office, Washington, D.C., 1995,
    Table No. 371.

important to recognize that the United States population is enmeshed within the global environment and is a major player, often culprit, in the light of these globally oriented arguments. In this section we intend to focus only upon the most immediate and significant major ecological topics related to global population growth. Our emphasis is not on the far distant future carrying capacity of planet Earth but on the situation of the United States and the world at the start of the twenty-first century.

Water Quality

As populations grow, and both industrial and agricultural uses of water intensify, the amount of water used by society increases rapidly. Yet, water is a resource which is an increasingly scarce and environmentally limited re-source. Not surprisingly, populations which live on the "hydrological margin" are more common in the Third World, where greater amounts of water are devoted to agriculture and farming practices such as overgrazing, overcutting of woodlands and technologically limited agricultural methods that all intensify these water demands. Water quality is also generally poor in the Third World if United States water quality standards were to be applied.

Over 70 percent of all water worldwide, and over 33.5 percent of that in the United States, is used for agricultural purposes. The percentage of water in the United States used for agriculture has declined to a third of all withdrawals in 1990 from over half of all withdrawals in 1940. At the same time, the total amount of water withdrawn for irrigation has nearly doubled (see Figure 3-3). Per capita water consumption in this country reached a peak in 1975 and has declined since. Clearly technological improvements in water management have some potential to relieve immediate water scarcities.

Before a condition of chronic scarcity is reached, dry season shortages and declining water quality are indicators of growing population pressure on water supplies. There are unquestionably regional dry season shortages of water in the United States at present. Despite massive water projects over the past half century in the Western states there are still relatively regular water shortages as the population has grown rapidly in those areas of the country and improvements in controlling water usage have been minimal. However, there is also evidence to indicate substantial improvements in water quality over the recent past. Legislation, public awareness, changes in industrial and municipal activities, and technological innovations have all contributed to improved water quality. Although water quality violations in rivers and streams can vary from year to year, the general recent pattern has been for a decline in the most common violations (see Table 3-4). Increasing regional shortages appears to be one of the most pressing water quality issues in the near term for the United States population.

Air Quality

Much of the United States population might tend to associate poor air quality with industry and automobiles. However, air quality is again generally poor in Third World countries if the air quality standards of industrialized nations are employed. By contrast, most measures of urban air quality in industrialized countries have shown improvement over the recent past. As Figure 3-4 shows, the ratio of ambient air pollution concentrations in the United States to the prevailing air quality standards has declined appreciably for carbon monoxide and lead. Several other major pollutants have either declined or held nearly level over these same years including ozone, sulfur dioxide, particulate matter, and nitrogen dioxide. Emissions of carbon dioxide, lead, sulfur dioxide, and volatile organic compounds were at a peak in 1970 and have declined since. Particulate matter had higher concentrations in the 1950s and has declined since (see Table 3-5). Particulate matter emissions, however, along with those of nitrogen dioxide have not appreciably declined over the past quarter of a century.

The greatest single source of emissions of particulates, sulfur dioxide and nitrogen dioxide is stationary sources of fuel combustion. All but particulates and carbon monoxide are heavily concentrated in electric utility and industrial emissions. Particulates and carbon monoxide are equally distributed across residential combustion (e.g. woodstoves and oil furnaces). Highway vehicles are also major contributors to these common pollutants. Vehicles account for over a quarter of all lead emissions, nearly two thirds of all carbon monoxide emissions, and over a third of all nitrogen oxide emissions. Despite improving ambient air quality it is clear that considerable room for technological improvement still remains within the United States.

Land Use

Land is considered an essentially renewable resource despite relatively rare occasions of permanently damaged land areas and such regional issues as topsoil losses or degradation. Up through the first half of the twentieth century worldwide demands for increased agricultural productivity to feed the world's growing populations were largely addressed through bringing new lands under cultivation. This rapid expansion of lands under cultivation was by no means limited to the New World.

Bringing land under cultivation has potentially serious environmental consequences. One of the grave concerns with current patterns of land use is the biological diversity loss through deforestation. In the United States alone, an estimated 50 million hectares of wetlands, among the most productive and regenerative ecosystems, have been drained over the past 150 years. In total, between a quarter and a half of the entire world's wetlands have been lost to date. And, while the area under grassland and pasturage is more stable throughout the world, the quality of these lands has been substantially altered as some of the best pasturage is plowed up for croplands and limited diversity domestic livestock has replaced indigenous animal life. The near disappearance of bison and antelope from the United States' plains have their dramatic counterparts throughout the world.

Table 3-6 gives the percentage distribution of land cover and uses by state as of 1992 (excluding Alaska and the District of Columbia). Nearly a fifth of all surface area is federal land. These federal lands are largely in just a few Western states (i.e. Arizona, California, Colorado, Idaho, Montana, Nevada, New Mexico, Oregon, Utah and Wyoming). Over 85 percent of Nevada and over 65 percent of Utah land is federal. Developed non-federal land is, in contrast, concentrated in Eastern seaboard states and those with large urban populations. Again, a relatively small number of states account for a large proportion of all developed lands (i.e. California, Florida, Georgia, Illinois, Michigan, New York, North Carolina, Ohio, Pennsylvania and Texas). Croplands and pasturage are heavily concentrated in the farm belt states which share concentrations of range land with the Western states. Perhaps the most surprising land use pattern to many readers is the fact that forest lands are heavily concentrated in the Eastern United States. Excluding Alaska, it is Georgia, Alabama, New York, Mississippi, Michigan and Pennsylvania that lead the states with total amounts of forest land, rather than the states of the Rocky Mountains or Sierra Nevada range.

Most of us believe that federal lands are those which are held in a collective trust for the future and which are

Figure 3-4. National Ambient Air Pollutant Concentration Ratios: 1985-1993

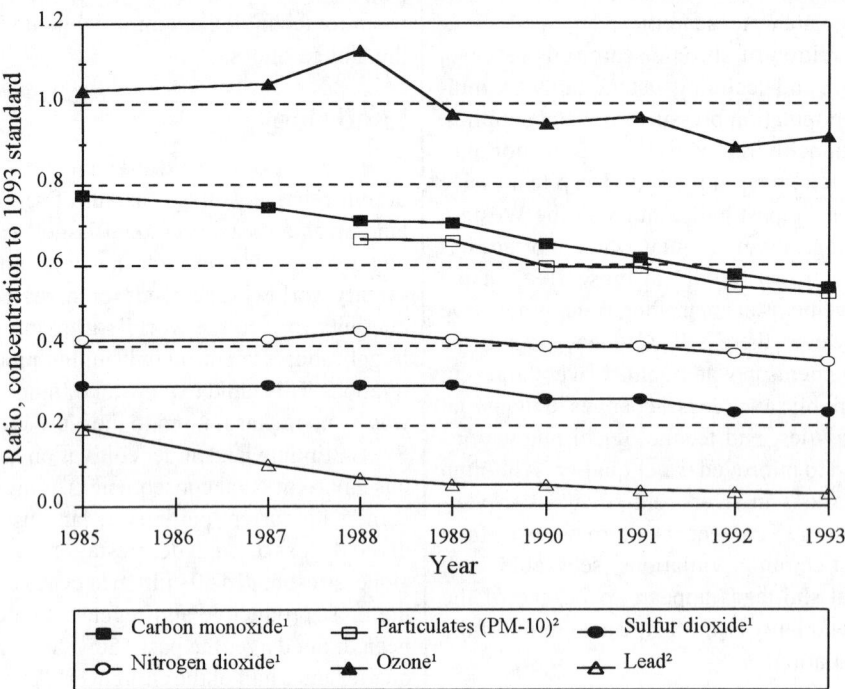

[1] In parts per million.
[2] In micrograms per cubic meter of air.
Source: 1985-1993 U.S. Environmental Protection Agency data.

Table 3-5. National Air Pollutant Emissions: 1940-1993 [in thousands of tons]

Year[1]	Particulates (PM-10)	PM-10, fugitive dust	Sulfur dioxide	Nitrogen dioxide	Volatile organic compounds	Carbon monoxide	Lead
1993	3,688	41,801	21,888	23,402	23,312	97,208	4,885
1992	3,676	44,953	21,592	22,991	23,020	96,368	4,741
1991	3,902	49,127	22,149	22,977	23,508	99,898	5,020
1990	4,229	44,929	22,261	23,192	24,276	103,753	5,635
1989	3,661	53,323	22,653	23,250	23,731	100,806	6,099
1988	3,697	59,975	22,535	23,221	24,961	106,100	6,464
1987	3,630	42,131	22,085	22,386	24,338	105,117	6,840
1986	3,679	49,940	22,361	22,409	24,826	108,070	7,296
1985	3,676	44,701	23,148	22,853	25,417	112,072	20,124
1984	6,126	—	23,396	23,172	25,572	114,262	42,217
1983	5,849	—	22,471	22,364	24,607	115,334	49,232
1980	6,928	—	25,813	23,281	25,893	115,625	74,956
1970	12,838	—	31,096	20,625	30,646	128,079	219,471
1960	15,558	—	22,245	14,581	24,322	103,777	—
1950	17,133	—	22,384	10,403	20,856	98,785	—
1940	15,956	—	19,954	7,568	17,118	90,865	—

[1] Data for 1990-1993 are preliminary.

Source: U.S. Environmental Protection Agency, "National Air Pollutant Emission Trends, 1900-1993," Office of Air Quality Planning and Standards, Research Triangle Park, NC, 1994, Tables 3.1-3.6 and A.1-A.6.

Table 3-6. Land Cover/Use, by State: 1992 [total in thousands of acres, other values as percents]

State	Total surface area[1]	Federal	Nonfederal Total	Developed[2]	Rural Total	Crop land	Pasture land	Range land	Forest land	Minor cover/use
Total	1,940,011	21.0	76.4	4.8	71.7	19.7	6.5	20.6	20.4	4.6
United States	1,937,678	21.1	76.4	4.7	71.7	19.7	6.5	20.6	20.4	4.6
Alabama	33,091	2.8	94.3	6.2	88.1	9.5	11.4	0.2	63.4	3.6
Arizona	72,960	41.5	58.1	1.9	56.2	1.6	0.1	44.2	6.5	3.8
Arkansas	34,040	9.4	87.6	3.9	83.7	22.7	16.8	0.5	41.9	1.8
California	101,572	46.1	52.1	4.9	47.2	9.9	1.1	16.9	14.6	4.7
Colorado	66,618	35.9	63.4	2.5	60.9	13.4	1.9	35.3	5.6	4.6
Connecticut	3,212	0.5	95.1	25.4	69.7	7.1	3.4	...	54.8	4.4
Delaware	1,309	2.5	92.7	15.7	77.0	38.1	2.0	...	27.0	9.9
Florida	37,545	10.1	81.0	12.4	68.6	8.0	11.6	9.2	33.0	6.8
Georgia	37,702	5.5	91.8	8.2	83.6	13.7	8.2	...	57.6	4.1
Hawaii	4,093	10.6	88.4	4.2	84.3	6.7	2.2	22.6	36.2	16.6
Idaho	53,481	62.3	36.5	1.1	35.4	10.5	2.3	12.5	7.5	2.6
Illinois	36,061	1.4	96.4	8.6	87.8	66.8	7.7	...	9.5	3.9
Indiana	23,159	2.1	96.2	9.0	87.2	58.3	8.1	...	15.7	5.1
Iowa	36,016	0.5	98.2	4.9	93.2	69.4	10.3	...	5.4	8.2
Kansas	52,658	1.2	97.8	3.8	94.0	50.4	4.4	29.9	2.5	6.8
Kentucky	25,862	4.6	92.7	6.4	86.4	19.7	22.7	...	39.9	4.1
Louisiana	30,561	4.1	86.3	5.8	80.5	19.5	7.4	0.7	42.4	10.4
Maine	21,290	0.8	91.7	3.3	88.4	2.1	0.5	...	82.5	3.3
Maryland	6,695	2.5	90.1	16.4	73.8	25.0	8.1	...	35.3	5.3
Massachusetts	5,302	1.7	91.3	24.7	66.6	5.1	3.2	...	52.4	5.8
Michigan	37,457	8.5	88.2	9.8	78.4	24.0	6.3	...	41.7	6.4
Minnesota	54,017	6.3	87.2	4.5	82.7	39.5	6.1	...	25.6	11.5
Mississippi	30,521	5.7	91.7	4.4	87.3	18.8	13.3	...	51.7	3.7
Missouri	44,606	4.5	93.5	5.2	88.3	29.9	26.7	0.3	26.1	5.2
Montana	94,109	28.8	69.8	1.2	68.6	16.0	3.6	39.1	5.5	4.4
Nebraska	49,507	1.5	97.2	2.5	94.7	38.9	4.2	45.8	1.6	4.3
Nevada	70,759	85.2	14.2	0.6	13.6	1.1	0.4	11.1	0.5	0.5
New Hampshire	5,938	12.6	83.4	9.5	73.9	2.4	1.7	...	66.2	3.7
New Jersey	4,984	3.2	91.3	31.9	59.4	13.0	3.2	...	35.4	7.7
New Mexico	77,819	35.2	64.5	1.1	63.4	2.4	0.3	51.1	5.9	3.6
New York	31,429	0.7	94.8	9.6	85.2	17.9	9.5	...	54.7	3.1
North Carolina	33,708	7.3	84.5	10.5	74.0	17.7	6.0	...	47.4	2.9
North Dakota	45,250	4.3	93.2	3.0	90.3	54.7	2.6	22.8	0.9	9.2
Ohio	26,451	1.4	97.0	13.5	83.5	45.1	8.6	...	25.0	4.8
Oklahoma	44,772	2.7	94.7	4.2	90.5	22.5	17.2	31.4	15.6	3.7
Oregon	62,127	52.0	46.9	1.8	45.1	6.1	3.1	15.1	19.1	1.8
Pennsylvania	28,997	2.4	95.9	11.8	84.1	19.3	8.0	...	52.8	3.9
Rhode Island	776	0.5	85.3	24.5	60.8	3.2	3.1	...	50.6	3.9
South Carolina	19,912	5.8	90.2	9.3	80.9	15.0	6.0	...	54.9	5.1
South Dakota	49,354	5.9	92.1	2.3	89.8	33.3	4.4	44.4	1.1	6.6
Tennessee	26,972	5.1	91.7	8.0	83.7	18.0	19.1	...	42.9	3.6
Texas	170,756	1.9	95.9	4.8	91.0	16.6	9.8	55.1	5.8	3.7
Utah	54,336	65.5	31.0	1.0	30.0	3.3	1.2	18.5	3.0	4.0
Vermont	6,153	6.0	89.7	5.3	84.5	10.3	5.7	...	67.3	1.2
Virginia	26,091	9.2	87.3	8.4	78.9	11.1	13.2	...	51.9	2.7
Washington	43,608	28.6	68.6	4.2	64.4	15.5	3.1	12.6	28.8	4.5
West Virginia	15,508	7.7	91.2	4.4	86.7	5.9	10.4	...	67.9	2.5
Wisconsin	35,938	5.1	91.1	6.6	84.6	30.1	8.2	...	37.3	8.9
Wyoming	62,598	48.0	51.1	0.9	50.3	3.6	1.4	41.6	1.6	2.1
Caribbean	2,334	3.9	94.7	17.4	77.3	15.7	30.5	6.2	22.3	2.5

[1] Includes water area not shown separately.

[2] Includes urban and built-up areas in units of 10 acres or greater, and rural transportation

Source: U.S. Department of Agriculture, Soil Conservation Service, and Iowa State University, Statistical Laboratory, "Summary Report, 1992 National Resources Inventory," as cited in U.S. Bureau of the Census, "Statistical Abstract of the United States: 1995," U.S. Government Printing Office, Washington, D.C., 1995, Table No. 365.

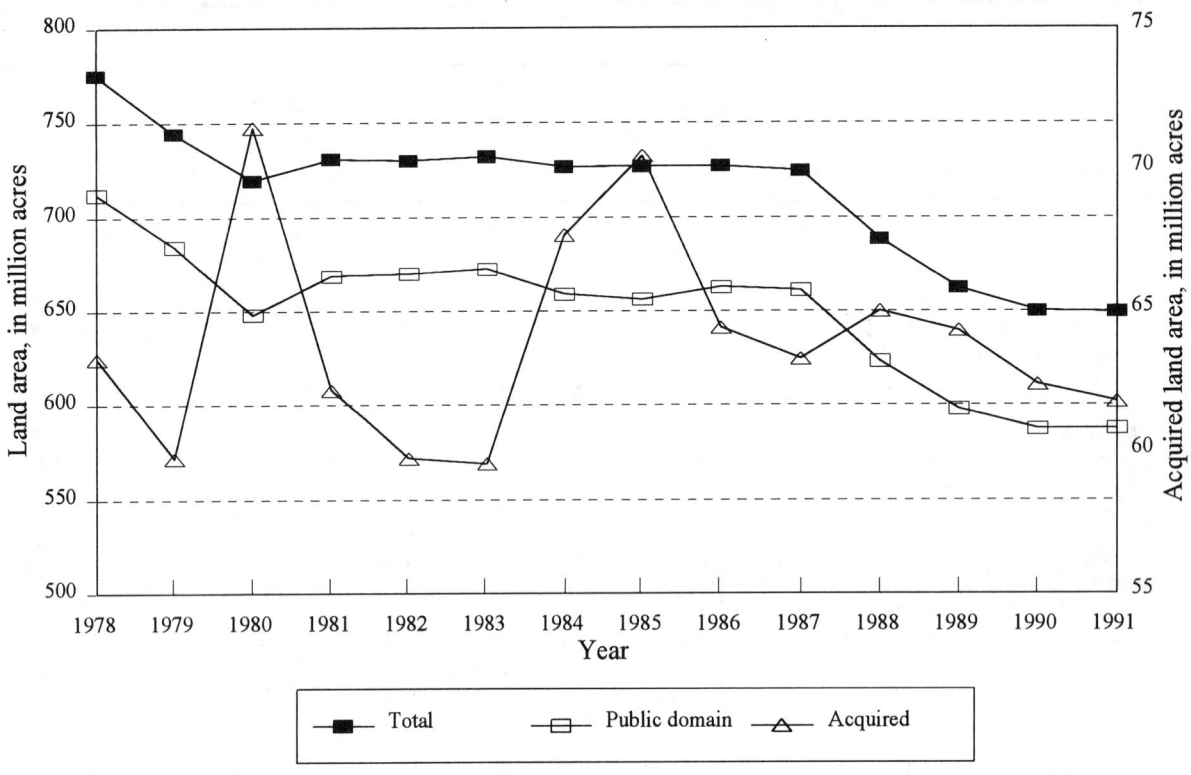

Figure 3-5. Area[1] and Acquisition of Federal Lands: 1978-1991

[1] Owned by the federal government.
Source: 1978-1991 U.S. Department of the Interior data.

Table 3-7. Endangered Threatened Animal and Plant Species: 1994

Type of species	Endangered[1]				Threatened[2]			
	Total	U.S. only	U.S and foreign	Foreign only	Total	U.S. only	U.S and foreign	Foreign only
Mammals	307	36	19	252	31	6	3	22
Birds	228	58	17	153	16	8	8	...
Reptiles	79	8	6	65	33	15	4	14
Amphibians	14	6		8	5	4	1	...
Fishes	78	62	5	11	36	30	6	...
Snails	15	14		1	7	7	...	...
Clams	53	50	1	2	6	6	...	...
Crustaceans	14	14			3	3	...	...
Insects	23	16	3	4	9	9	...	...
Arachnids	4	4	...	...	...	...	...	...
Plants	416	404	11	1	90	76	12	2

[1] One in danger of becoming extinct throughout all or a significant part of its natural range.

[2] One likely to become endangered in the forseeable future.

Source: U.S. Fish and Wildlife Service, "Endangered Species Technical Bulletin," Volume 19(1994):20.

being expanded with each new publicized acquisition. However, the publicity accorded acquisitions and the relative silence associated with federal property dispositions offer a misleading impression. As Figure 3-5 shows, despite the fact that acquisitions over the period from 1978 to 1991 remained relatively stable, the land held in public domain steadily shrank in size. As the federal government sells or opens up more public lands the collective resource represented by these lands has, in fact, steadily diminished. Whether collective purposes are best served by public domain properties, privatization of land, or selective exchange favoring strategic acquisitions has been, historically, a heated political issue. As population pressures increase upon the land mass of the United States it is, however, important that we not suffer the misimpression that our public domain is an increasing land resource with each acquisition.

Biodiversity

The expansion of cropland and pasturage worldwide has resulted in a vast loss of native habitat for the variety of species which make up the genetic stock of the planet. The loss of habitat is especially problematic because of the dense and exclusive concentrations of many species in relatively small habitat ranges. For example, in Madagascar 60 percent of the documented plant (9,500) and animal (190,000) species are endemic only in the island's eastern forest, of which 90 percent has already disappeared. Just 10,000 square kilometers of South Af-

rica contain 6,000 plant species of which 70 percent are endemic to the area and at least 2,000 of which are threatened. The potential loss of biodiversity represented by these extreme cases is still understated given the restriction of our knowledge to documented species. The vast genetic potential of these reserves is unknown and barely accessible to our rapidly expanding biological and genetic technology.

Although biodiversity is less concentrated in many habitats of North America, there are 346 mammal species in the United States of which 27 percent are endemic and 8 percent are threatened; 650 bird species of which 11 percent are endemic and 7 percent threatened; and 19,473 plant species of which 21 percent are endemic and 12 percent are threatened. That is, more than one of every ten species in the United States were threatened with extinction as of 1990. Table 3-7 provides more recent data from 1994 detailing the numbers of threatened and endangered species and identifying whether they are endemic only to the U.S. or to foreign habitats as well.

Resource Stocks

Many known world resource reserves have greatly expanded, rather than contracted, over the past half century (e.g. aluminum, copper, iron, lead, etc.). The price of many of these resources has also declined when adjusted for real dollar values. The issues of expanding known reserves and stable or declining prices, it is often argued, demonstrate that scarcity is not an issue with these non-

Table 3-8. Forest and Timberland Area, Sawtimber, and Stock: 1987, 1990, and Percent Change 1987-1992

| Year and region | Total forest land | Timberland, ownership (in mil. acres) | | | | Sawtimber, net volume (in bil. bd ft) | | Growing stock, net volume (in bil. cu. ft) | |
		Total	Federally owned/ managed	State, county, municipal	Private	Total	Softwood	Total	Softwood
1992, total	737	490	97	35	358	2,992	2,047	786	450
North	168	158	11	19	127	540	137	207	51
South	212	199	16	4	179	842	389	251	103
Rocky Mountains	140	63	40	3	20	415	397	110	101
Pacific Coast	217	70	30	8	32	1,196	1,124	218	195
1987, total	731	485	97	34	354	2,853	2,040	766	453
North	165	154	11	19	124	459	126	190	48
South	203	197	16	4	177	781	388	245	106
Rocky Mountains	142	61	39	3	20	411	394	108	100
Pacific Coast	220	72	31	8	32	1,202	1,132	223	199
Percent change 1987-1992	0.8	1.0	...	2.9	1.1	4.9	0.3	2.6	-0.7
North	1.8	2.6	...	...	2.4	17.6	8.7	8.9	6.3
South	4.4	1.0	...	...	1.1	7.8	0.3	2.4	-2.8
Rocky Mountains	-1.4	3.3	2.6	...	...	1.0	0.8	1.9	1.0
Pacific Coast	-1.4	-2.8	-3.2	...	...	-0.5	-0.7	-2.2	-2.0

Source: U.S. Forest Service, "Forest Resources of the United States, 1992," as cited in U.S. Bureau of the Census, "Statistical Abstract of the United States: 1995," U.S. Government Printing Office, Washington, D.C., 1995, Table No. 1148.

Figure 3-6. Recovered Paper Utilization and Recovery Rates: 1970-1994

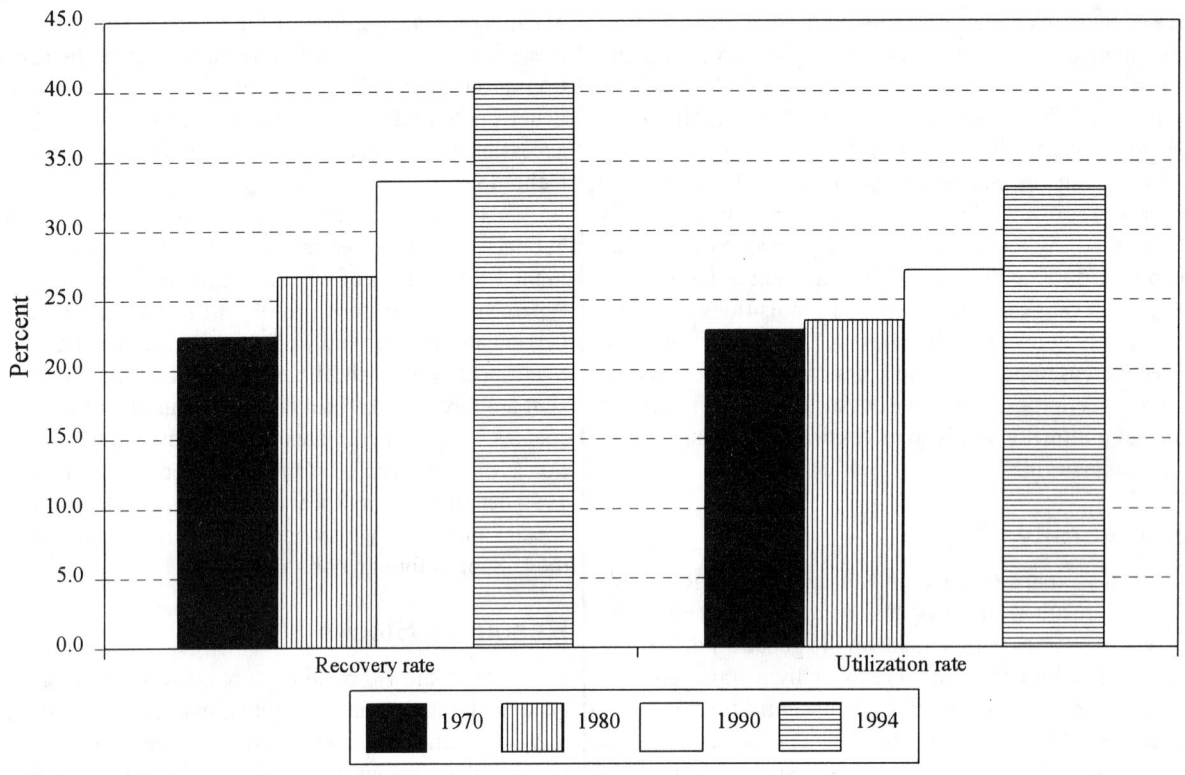

Source: 1970-1994 American Forest and Paper Association data.

renewable resources. Of course, real reserves (rather than known ones) are not expanding in anthropometric time and prices may react to scarcity only after the fact. Nonetheless, there is a clear case that for many natural resources, expanding known reserves and improved usage technology place scarcity of these resources on the far horizon at the least.

In the United States the management of renewable resources and efforts at reuse are gaining further in the drive to improve resource usage. Table 3-8 shows the regional change in forest lands and board foot lumber production between 1987 and 1992. Forested land has increased overall at the same time that total production has increased. The northern and southern secondary growth forests have increased while those in the Rocky Mountains and Pacific coast states have declined slightly. This table does not elaborate the controversial issues surrounding the logging of old growth or primary forests. At the same time that forested land appears to be slightly increasing or nearly stable, recycling and recovery of pulp products has increased dramatically. Figure 3-6 graphs the recovered utilization rate (i.e. the ratio of recovered paper utilized in production to paper and board mill production) and the recovery rate (i.e. the ratio of total recovered paper to new supply) for paper products over the

past three and a half decades. The recovery rate and recovered utilization rate for paper products have increased substantially across these years and especially within the past decade.

Fisheries constitute another potentially renewable resource which has attracted considerable concern over possible depletion and local scarcities. Figure 3-7 shows the total quantity and price per pound for the domestic catch from 1970 through 1993. The quantity of the catch has increased dramatically over recent years despite concerns over depletion. And, while the price has increased more or less consistently up to 1988, it has fallen considerably since that time as quantity has risen sharply. Figure 3-8 illustrates the more localized scarcity concerns over major fisheries. This figure shows the catch in millions of pounds from specific United States ports with more than 100 million pounds in any year from 1985 through 1993. Most of these fisheries are in Alaska and have expanded rapidly accounting for the rise in production over the past few years. At the same time, the long- standing fisheries of the Eastern seaboard, the Gulf and even California have dramatically declining catches over recent years. While catches have expanded over these years there is clearly concern over the depletion of traditional fisheries in United States waters.

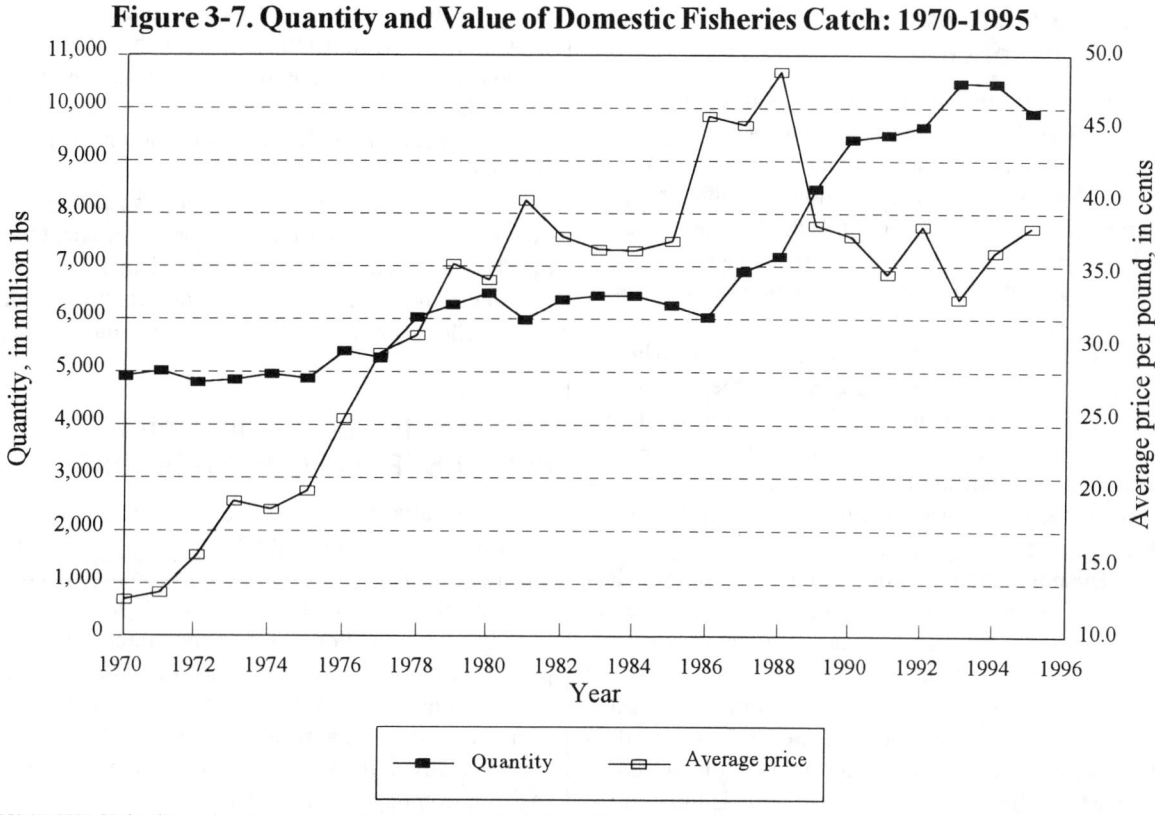

Figure 3-7. Quantity and Value of Domestic Fisheries Catch: 1970-1995

Source: 1970-1995 U.S. National Oceanic and Atmospheric Administration, National Marine Fisheries Service data.

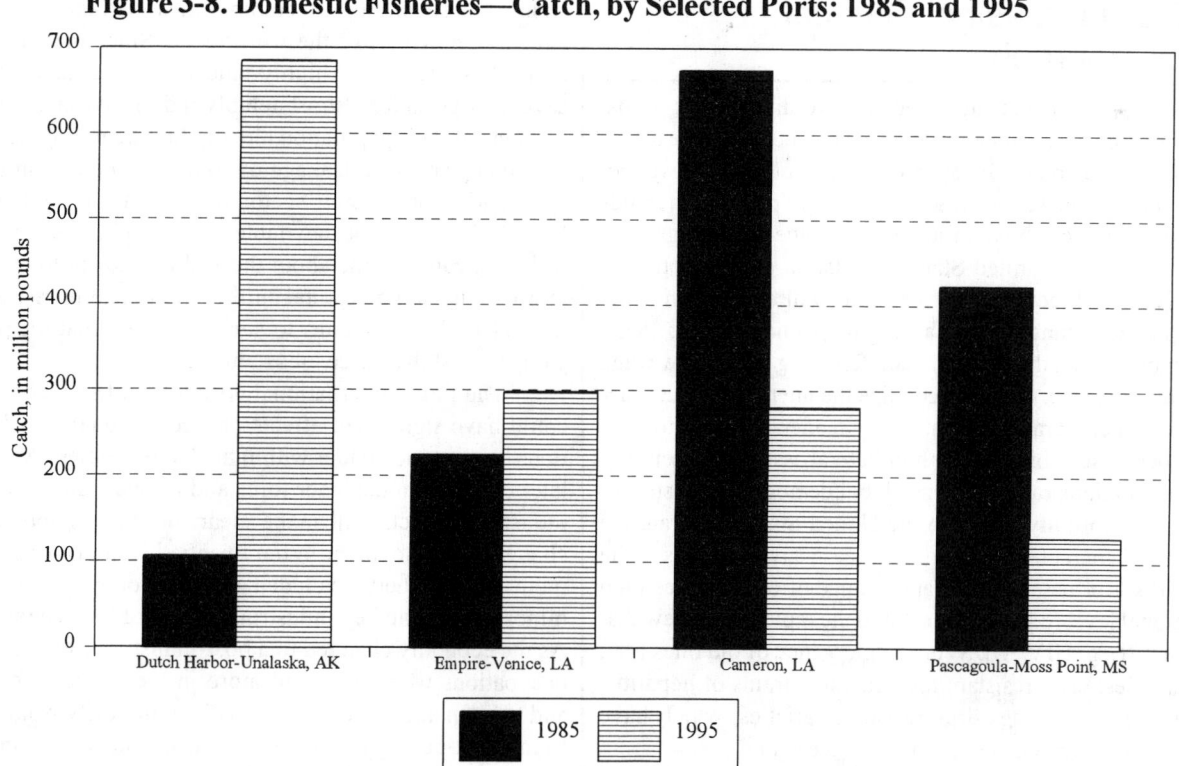

Figure 3-8. Domestic Fisheries—Catch, by Selected Ports: 1985 and 1995

Source: 1985 and 1995 U.S. National Oceanic and Atmospheric Administration, National Marine Fisheries Service data.

Population Growth and the Quality of Life

It is more difficult to quantify issues surrounding the quality of life in the United States and the possible impact of population growth upon the pursuit of life, liberty and happiness. Crime, pollution, crowding, etc., are often pointed to as indicators of declining quality of life for most United States citizens. At the same time, the continual growth of the urban population of the country (see Chapters 1 and 8) hardly bespeaks a population fleeing the horrors of urban density or urban threats to health and security. Urban crowding certainly does bring new challenges to governmental and social structures and does indeed alter the quality of individuals' lives. There is, however, every indication that our population is equally attracted to the features, services and social systems which urban centers provide.

The population growth of the United States is less rapid than that in most countries of the world. Nonetheless, the population's growth has accelerated considerably over the life of the country and declining fertility has not led the United States to a zero population growth state. Features of life will inevitably be altered by increased density as we move into the coming century. A larger issue, however, for the United States population is likely to be that of deciding how to adjust to more rapid growth and significant demographic trends in other sectors of the world.

Our Increasingly Global Demography

With increasing frequency we discuss our global economy or specifically global events such as ozone depletion in the upper atmosphere. Less frequently do we recognize the increasingly global nature of population trends and behavior. Yet, an increasing range of demographic trends in the United States population are impacted, or even the direct result of, international events. In some specific instances which are highly publicized (e.g. illegal immigration, the flight of manufacturing jobs to low wage countries, etc.) we do recognize the international character of demographic events. Our tendency is still to consider these as bilateral, or multilateral, issues between specific nations rather than as global demographic issues.

Mortality trends in the United States illustrate the global character of changing disease environments in the virtual, or complete, disappearance of old diseases on a global level (e.g. smallpox), and the rapid rise of new diseases (e.g. HIV/AIDS) or re-emergence of old ones (e.g. measles, drug-resistant tuberculosis, strains of hepatitis, etc.) in sometimes drug-resistant varieties, which have become global health problems once again.

Migration also illustrates the globalization of demographic trends. Much of the recent migration to the United States has been the result of international crises abroad. Global economic divisions create much of the incentive for both legal and illegal immigration. And, a large proportion of the change in our occupational and industrial labor force has been linked to the globalization of industries and markets.

Can a nation, even a powerful one such as the United States, develop policies that can control or adapt to such events in a structured way? Or are we increasingly subject to the forces of a global domain larger than our national policies, or even multinational agreements, can govern?

Where is the Locus of Control over U.S. Population Problems?

Several aspects of U.S. demography appear to be the result of major international trends. The first is that the post-industrial, service-based economy is now becoming buffeted by the same currents of globalization that have had such a major effect on manufacturing over the past three decades. With advanced global communications systems, there is no reason why insurance claims cannot be processed almost as easily in Ireland as in Chicago, or why software cannot be written and tested as easily in Bombay as in Palo Alto.

As a result, many service jobs may become just as linked to swings and shifts in the patterns of international trade and finance as manufacturing jobs are today. The potential for the disruption (company closures, downsizing, and so on) of local communities and families may shift to a new part of the workforce. Since the United States has a relatively highly-paid workforce, and since several large nations (most notably India) have large proportions of their population already literate in English, it would appear that a leakage of some service jobs in the information-processing sector outward to these Third World nations may be inevitable. There appears relatively little that can be done about these shifts except to try to improve the human capital and technological infrastructure of the United States to such an extent that highly-paid, high-skill service jobs remain here.

The future international portability of service jobs could have significant effects on occupational distributions by race and gender within the United States. As the later chapters on the labor force and its occupational and industrial aspects will make clear, the most important change in employment in the twentieth century was the inclusion of hitherto excluded groups (women and racial minorities) in the key industrial sectors of the economy. As the economy changed to a post-industrial form, these occupations were more and more in the service sector, and women and minorities (especially minority women) found well-paying jobs there. While the incomes of men (especially those without much education or those in the manufacturing sector) stagnated, women's incomes rose,

Table 3-9. Travel to and from the United States, by U.S. Residents and Foreign Travelers: 1985-1995 [numbers in thousands]

Group of travelers	1985	1992[1]	1995[1] (projection)
Total U.S. residents--travel abroad	34,715	44,623	47,419
To Canada	11,558	12,252	12,920
To Mexico	10,461	16,381	15,759
Total overseas	12,696	15,990	18,740
To Europe	6,780	8,043	—
To Latin America	3,592	4,749	—
To other countries	2,324	3,198	—
Foreign travelers to the U.S.	25,399	39,539	42,983
From Canada	10,721	18,598	17,095
From Mexico	7,141	8,258	10,410
From overseas	7,537	17,791	20,440
From Europe	2,905	8,262	9,717
From Latin America	1,795	3,255	4,198
From other countries	2,897	6,274	6,525
Foreign travelers coming for pleasure trips[2]	6,609	13,418	17,155
U.S. net travel and passenger payments[3]			
Receipts from foreign travelers	22.17	58.31	76.49
Payments by U.S. travelers	31.04	37.35	44.83
Net balance of payments	-8.87	20.96	31.66

[1] Information on foreign travelers coming for pleasure trips is from 1990 and 1994; information on U.S. net travel and passenger payments is from 1990 and 1995.

[2] Foreign travelers coming for pleasure trips are computed for years ending on September 20.

[3] Balance of payments, in billions of dollars, computed in current U.S. dollars.

Source: U.S. Bureau of the Census, "Statistical Abstract of the United States, 1996," U. S. Government Printing Office, Washington, D.C., 1996, Tables 429, 430, 431, and 432.

both in a relative and an absolute sense.

Yet the internationalization of service jobs could threaten American women's gains in employment and in income. By the late 1980s, computer-based word processing and voice mail had replaced the need for secretaries and receptionists in many organizations. It is possible that in the near future, someone transferred to Cheyenne, Wyoming and looking for a house there will deal over the Internet with a "local" real estate agent who is actually based in Birmingham (in either Alabama or Great Britain). Since industries such as real estate have a high proportion of women workers (who often like the flexible hours and local nature of the job), these changes could have a significant effect on the job market for women.

Trade, Tourism, and Immigration

The second trend over which the United States may have relatively little control is international immigration. For a variety of reasons, it is not clear whether it would be possible to stop the large-scale migration into the United States (much of it from Mexico) that has taken place over the past three decades. Even if there was a real political will to do so (and it is not clear that such a will exists), it might prove to be very difficult and disruptive to prevent large-scale immigration.

Immigration is but one part of a much larger skein of increased international contact. Over the past decade, the United States has become a major destination of international travelers, whether for business or pleasure. In 1985, about 34.7 million Americans traveled abroad, but only 12.7 million went overseas (beyond Canada and Mexico; see Table 3-9). By 1995, the number of U.S. residents going overseas had risen by almost 50 percent, to a projected figure of 18.7 million. The rise in international travel to the United States has been even more striking. In 1985, there were 7.5 million foreign travelers from overseas (excluding Mexicans and Canadians) who visited the United States; by 1995, the projected number is 20.4 million, a more than two-fold increase. Foreign travel to the

United States for pleasure played a very significant role here: those taking pleasure trips increased from 6.6 million to 17.2 million between 1985 and 1994.

The economic impact of foreign tourism is also important. In 1985, the United States ran a large net deficit: its 34.7 million visitors to other nations spent 8.9 billion dollars more than did the 25.4 million foreign travelers to the United States. Yet by 1995, the United States will have a projected 31.7 billion dollar net surplus in tourism and travel income as the 43 million foreign visitors outspend the 47 million U.S. residents who visit other countries.

There is little indication that these trends (which have not come at a time when the dollar was weak relative to foreign currencies) will change markedly in coming years. More and more U.S. jobs will be linked to foreign trade and tourism, and this, more than anything else, will act to dampen the rise of xenophobia here. For better or worse, the United States is still seen as the nation of the future, and the rise of the worldwide youth culture (many of whose adherents are now in their forties and fifties) is linked to American cultural idioms. From the point of view of demography and human ecology, the United States is, in many ways, the cultural metropolis for the emerging middle classes and educational elites in many nations, and this almost guarantees a high amount of interchange of people and ideas between the metropolis and smaller centers in the hinterlands.

In the future, international contact may be affected more by the workings of international markets than by adherence to political blocs or to prior historical and cultural linkages. Such market linkages could mean that the nations with which the United States has connections would more closely reflect their population sizes. The world's regions and nations are predicted to grow at quite dissimilar rates over the next three decades (Table 3-10). Regions like sub-Saharan Africa or the Near East will double in size, while the growth rate in the more developed countries will taper off from 0.6 percent per year in 1990-2000 to only 0.2 percent per year in 2010-2020.

Of course, in terms of trade with and tourism to the United States, the future per capita incomes of these nations will also be important. The slackening of population growth in many of today's Third World nations (especially in Asia) may be both a cause and a consequence of rising incomes, and may have important consequences for further linkages with the United States. A world of 7.6 billion people by the year 2020 will almost certainly have need of North America's large food exports, but the rapid growth of a large urban middle class in a number of nations (including China and India) during the next several decades could also provide new markets for a variety of other U.S. products.

The Internationalization of Mortality

William McNeill and others have identified the ex-

istence of a "world disease pool" in Mediterranean Europe and elsewhere by the late Middle Ages. In essence, the emergence of urban centers and the growth of trade between these towns and cities led to the more rapid transmission of epidemic diseases than ever before. Because the victims of these diseases usually either died from them or became immune, the frequency of epidemics of particular diseases declined, while the overall frequency of epidemics may have increased. In addition, the mortality rate of diseases may have declined. Highly virulent diseases tend to be self-limiting because they frequently kill their hosts before the hosts can pass them on. Within the world disease pool, virulent diseases tended to become endemic, less virulent childhood diseases.

Yet these endemic diseases had the capability to become epidemic diseases when they came into contact with populations that lacked immunity to them. Most of the European settlers who came to North America had their origins in areas of Europe that had become part of the world disease pool, while the American Indian population had little or no immunity to many of these diseases. This "epidemiological fifth column" played a particularly important part in depopulating the original peoples of the lands east of the Mississippi, Hawaii and other parts of the current United States.

United States public health authorities have had to contend with a number of epidemic and endemic diseases: cholera in the nineteenth century, the influenza epidemic of 1918-19, and outbreaks of diphtheria, plague, polio, and so on. Yet the development of antibiotics, vaccinations and reporting systems have led to complacency on the part of much of the U.S. population about the dangers of epidemic and endemic disease.

Over the last five centuries, the part of the world that had cities, trade, explorers, and colonizing forces usually posed much more of a threat to the isolated, largely rural populations of the rest of the world. Yet there are a set of modern conditions that may be leading to a historic reversal of this balance.

Relatively isolated areas of the world which may have been long afflicted by local diseases that can be shared by both human and animal hosts are now in better contact with the rest of the world. The classic cases here (and now the stuff of the new generation of hi-tech horror films) are the Ebola and Marburg viruses, which have recorded case-fatality rates of 25-90 percent in various outbreaks. Rodents throughout the world are afflicted with hantaviruses; areas of the Western part of the United States (particularly prairie dog communities) are reservoirs of plague, as are many other world regions. What has changed is that higher human population densities may be putting more people in contact with these animal hosts, and better transport facilities now allow those infected with even highly virulent diseases to come into contact with more potential human agents of transmission.

The communist states of the former Soviet Union,

Table 3-10. Population Size and Growth Rates for World Regions: 1990-2020

World region or nation	Population size (midyear, in millions)				Average annual percent growth		
	1990	2000	2010	2020	1990-2000	2000-10	2010-20
World	5,282	6,091	6,862	7,600	1.7	1.2	1.0
Less developed countries	4,139	4,903	5,634	6,351	2.0	1.4	1.2
More developed countries	1,142	1,189	1,228	1,249	0.6	0.3	0.2
Africa	624	807	1,009	1,230	2.6	2.2	2.0
Sub-Saharan	504	659	831	1,022	2.7	2.3	2.1
Ethiopia	48	63	81	101	—	—	—
Nigeria	86	117	157	205	—	—	—
North Africa	120	149	178	207	2.1	1.8	1.5
Near East	134	175	223	276	2.7	2.4	2.1
Asia	2,989	3,448	3,852	4,219	1.4	1.1	0.9
China	1,154	1,276	1,364	1,438	—	—	—
India	856	1,013	1,156	1,289	—	—	—
Indonesia	188	219	250	276	—	—	—
Pakistan	114	141	171	199	—	—	—
Philippines	65	81	97	113	—	—	—
Latin American and the Caribbean	443	517	584	643	1.6	1.2	1.0
Mexico	85	103	120	136	—	—	—
North America	277	307	333	361	1.0	0.8	0.8
United States	250	277	301	326	—	—	—
Canada	27	30	33	35	—	—	—
Oceania	27	30	34	37	1.4	1.1	0.9

Source: U.S. Bureau of the Census, "World Population Profile: 1996," Report WP/96, U.S. Government Printing Office, Washington, D.C., 1996, Tables A-2 and A-4.

Eastern Europe and China may have had their shortcomings from the point of view of human rights and economic development, but they were good at one thing: immobilizing large numbers of people through a combination of internal passports and security police measures. This led to the rapid decline of epidemic disease and a good administrative basis on which to attack various endemic diseases as well. These states were able to make striking improvements in their life expectancies while doing little to improve the nutritional status of the population or its access to high-technology medical care.

The demise of the communist states in the Soviet Union and Eastern Europe and the internal changes in China have had several key results. State responsibility for funding public health and monitoring its progress has declined greatly. Due to differential rates of economic development between areas, ethnic conflict and internal disorders, internal and international migration (now largely unmonitored by public health authorities) has greatly increased.

These changes may have several effects on mortality. Diseases such as influenza will spread more rapidly, increasing death rates among the old. Sexually-transmitted diseases will increase, leading to higher death rates from AIDS and hepatitis B (usually much later, from liver cancer). Lack of funds to screen blood supplies and a lack of disposable needles will result in increased fatality rates from hepatitis C and other diseases.

As immunization rates decline (due to lack of funds, administrative capability and high rates of migration) below the "herd immunity" level, outbreaks of "old" diseases may occur. Diphtheria, controlled for over 30 years in the former Soviet Union, began in the Russian Federation in 1990 and spread to all but one of the New Independent States by 1994. Large numbers of adults (more than 70 percent of all cases were among those 15 years and over) who were thought to be protected by childhood immunization were victims of the disease. This is not a problem confined to this area: researchers estimate that among adults in developed nations aged 20 and over, between 20 and 60 percent are susceptible to this disease.

At least for some "old" diseases, high rates of childhood immunization alone may not provide protection for adults. In a world of global trade and tourism, it will probably prove impossible to erect walls (between our nations or our neighborhoods) against new or old infectious diseases, and the magic bullet of immunization may not provide complete, lifetime protection. Cain's biblical question "Am I my brother's keeper?" may turn out, from an epidemiological perspective, to be an enlightened form of self-interest.

Both in these states and in much of the Third World, the expense and lack of drugs are leading to the partial treatment of many infectious diseases. In the Third World, many antibiotics are available as over-the-counter drugs. People there (and here) often take the drugs until they begin to feel better, or until their money runs out. Such a process can result in diseases becoming resistant to various kinds of antibiotics. In essence, there is now a worldwide, unintended, unsupervised medical experiment being conducted to develop drug-resistant diseases. This process is also underway in the United States: since 1989 there have been many cases of drug-resistant tuberculosis, and these new strains of the disease can pose serious risks to the health personnel treating such patients.

While the emphasis here has been on health risks that may move from other nations to the United States, the process is a two-way street. As the U.S. market for tobacco wanes (see the Textbox in Chapter 4, "Cigarette Smoking and Mortality"), the U.S. has becoming a major exporter of cigarettes to other nations. Asia, where increases in income among its population make disposable income available for this new form of addiction, is seen as a major new market. Asian women, who have traditionally had low rates of smoking, are seen as a particular target, especially if cigarette smoking can be marketed as part of the modern woman's image . Thus the U.S. may make a major contribution to raising international death rates from lung cancer, heart disease, emphysema and other smoking-related diseases.

Conclusions

The emphasis of this volume is again on the population of the United States. Yet, in considering demographic trends within the United States it is important to remind ourselves of the increasing integration of the national population with a global community. Whether we are concerned with population growth, changing composition, environmental quality, economic trends, migration, disease, or indeed with any aspect of the United States population, these data must be understood in the context of worldwide trends, markets, and environs. If there is one clear trend which overlaps all of the demographic topics addressed within this volume it is the increasing relevance of the global theater to the United States population. Although subsequent chapters emphasize the national character of the population and demographic issues within the United States, frequent reference to international comparisons are provided. As global data continues to improve in scope and quality such comparisons will become only more relevant to an understanding of national demographic issues.

Bibliography

Ahlburg, Dennis A. "The Census Bureau's New Projections of the U.S. Population." Population and Development Review 19(1993):159-74.

Atkinson, A.B., Rainwater, L., and Smeeding, T.M. Income Distribution in the OECD Countries: Evidence from the Luxembourg Income Study. Paris: Organisation for Economic Development and Cooperation. 1995.

Bellah, Robert R., Madsen, Richard, Swindler, A., Sullivan, W., and Tipton, S. Habits of the Heart: Individualism and Commitment in American Life. Berkeley, CA: University of California Press. 1985.

Briggs, Vernon M., Jr., and Moore, Stephen. Still an Open Door? U.S. Immigration Policy and the American Economy. Washington, D.C.: American University Press. 1994.

Burkhauser, Richard V., and Slisbury, Dallas L. (eds.). Pensions in a Changing Economy. Washington, D.C.: Employee Benefit Research Institute. 1993.

Casper, Lynne M., McLanahan, Sara, and Garfinkel, Irwin. "The Gender Poverty Gap: What We Can Learn from Other Countries." American Sociological Review 59(1994):594-605.

Cohen, Joel E. How Many People Can the Earth Support? New York: W.W. Norton & Company. 1995.

_____. "Maximum Occupancy." American Demographics 18(1996): 44-51.

Colombo, Bernardo, Demeny, Paul, and Perutz, Max F. Resources and Population: Natural, Institutional, and Demographic Dimensions of Development. Oxford: Clarendon Press. 1996.

Ehrlich, Paul R. The Population Bomb. New York: Ballantine Books. 1978.

Falkenmark, Malin, and Widstrand, Carl. "Population and Water Resources: A Delicate Balance." Population Bulletin 47(1992): 2-35.

Farley, Reynolds. State of the Union: America in the 1990s. New York: Russell Sage Foundation. 1995.

_____. The New American Reality: Who We Are, How We Got Here, Where We Are Going. New York: Russell Sage Foundation. 1996.

Goode, William J. The World Changes in Divorce Patterns. New Haven, CT: Yale University Press. 1993.

Greenwood, Peter W., Model, Karyn E., Rydell, C.P., and Chiesa, James. "Diverting Children from a Life of Crime: Measuring Costs and Benefits." Http://www.rand.org/publications/MR/MR699. 1996.

Hartmann, Betsy, and Boyce, James K. Needless Hunger: Voices from a Bangladesh Village. San Francisco: Institute for Food and Development Policy. 1982.

Hernandez, Donald J. America's Children: Resources from Family, Government and the Economy. New York: Russell Sage Foundation. 1996.

Lamm, Richard, and Imhoff, Gary. The Immigration Time-Bomb: The Fragmenting of America. New York: Truman Talley Books, E.P. Dutton. 1985.

Lipset, Seymour Martin. American Exceptionalism: A Double-Edged Sword. New York: W.W. Norton. 1996.

Malthus, Thomas Robert. An Essay on the Principle of Population. Anthony Flew (ed.). Baltimore: Penguin Books. 1970.

Massey, Douglas S. "The Age of Extremes: Concentrated Affluence and Poverty in the Twenty-First Century." Demography 33(1996):395-412.

Meadows, Donella H., Meadows, Dennis L., Randers, Jørgen, and Behrens, William W. II. The Limits to Growth. New York: Universe Books. 1972.

Miller, John J. (ed.). Strangers at Our Gate: Immigration in the 1990s. Washington, D.C.: Manhattan Institute. 1994.

Mortality and Morbidity Weekly Report. "Diphtheria Epidemic—Newly Independent States of the Former Soviet Union, 1990-1994." 44(1995): 177-81.

_____. "Update: Diphtheria Epidemic—New Independent States of the Former Soviet Union, January 1995- March 1996." 45 (1996): 693-97.

Peterson, Peter G. "Will America Grow Up Before It Grows Old?" Atlantic Monthly May(1996): 55-86.

Population Reference Bureau. Population and Water Resources: A Delicate Balance.

Reich, Robert S. The Work of Nations: Preparing Ourselves for 21st-Century Capitalism. New York: Alfred A. Knopf. 1991.

Repetto, Robert. "Population, Resources, Environment: An Uncertain Future." Population Bulletin 42(1993): 2-43.

Rieff, David. The Exile: Cuba in the Heart of Miami. New York: Simon and Schuster. 1993.

_____. Los Angeles: Capital of the Third World. New York: Simon and Schuster. 1993.

Rifkin, Jeremy. Entropy: A New World View. New York: Bantam Books. 1980.

Roberts, Sam. Who We Are: A Portrait of America Based on the Latest U.S. Census. New York: Times Books. 1993.

Simon, Julian L. Theory of Population and Economic Growth. New York: Basil Blackwell Inc. 1986.

Spain, Daphne, and Bianchi, Suzanne. Balancing Act: Motherhood, Marriage and Employment Among American Women. New York: Russell Sage Foundation. 1996.

Ungar, Sanford J. Fresh Blood: The New American Immigrants. New York: Simon and Schuster. 1995.

United Nations Children's Fund (UNICEF). The State of the World's Children. New York: Oxford University Press for UNICEF. 1994.

U.S. Bureau of the Census. "Dynamics of Economic Well-being: Poverty, 1992 to 1993." Http:/www.census.gov. 1996.

_____. The Impact of HIV/AIDS on World Population. Washington, D.C.: Government Printing Office. 1994.

_____. "Income 1995." Http:/www.census.gov. 1996.

_____. Population Characteristics: Marital Status and Living Arrangements, March 1993. Current Population Reports. Washington, D.C.: U.S. Government Printing Office. 1994.

_____. Report WP/96. World Population Profile: 1996. Washington, D.C.: Government Printing Office. 1996.

_____. Special Studies: 65+ in the United States. Current Population Reports, P23-190. Washington, D.C.: Government Printing Office. 1996.

_____. Statistical Abstracts of the United States: 1995. Washington, D.C.: U.S. Government Printing Office. 1995.

_____. "Statistical Abstract of the United States: 1996." Washington, D.C.: U.S. Government Printing Office, 1996.

U.S. Environmental Protection Agency. "National Air Pollutant Emission Trends, 1900-1993." Research Triangle Park, NC: Office of Air Quality Planning and Standards. 1994.

U.S. Fish and Wildlife Service. "Endangered Species Technical Bulletin" 19(1994): 20.

U.S. National Oceanic and Atmospheric Administration, National Marine Fisheries Service. "Fisheries of the United States: 1995." Silver Spring, MD: U.S. National Oceanic and Atmospheric Administration. 1996

_____. "Fisheries of the United States: 1975." Silver Spring, MD: U.S. National Oceanic and Atmospheric Administration. 1976.

_____. "Fisheries of the United States: 1985." Silver Spring, MD: U.S. National Oceanic and Atmospheric Administration. 1986.

Wattenburg, Ben. The Birth Dearth: What Happens When People in Free Countries Don't Have Enough Babies. New York: Pharos Books. 1987.

World Resources Institute. World Resources, 1994-95. New York: Oxford University Press. 1994.

Yaukey, David. Demography: The Study of Human Population. New York: St. Martin's Press. 1985.

4

MORTALITY

Mortality has, paradoxically, the best- and worst-developed theories among the major topics of demography. William H. McNeill and other historical demographers have shown how epidemic diseases of the ancient Old World evolved into a European "world disease pool" of endemic diseases that colonial settlers to America brought with them to visit (once again in epidemic fashion) upon the native peoples. During the nineteenth century, death rates in the United States were high, especially in urban areas, due to the prevalence of epidemic and endemic diseases.

The history of mortality in the United States and other nineteenth-century industrializing nations is the story of a progressively decreasing rate of death. Omran and other researchers developed the theory of the "epidemiological transition;" first epidemic diseases are controlled, then inroads are made into endemic diseases, and finally most deaths become due to chronic conditions or non-infectious diseases such as cancer or cardiovascular and cerebrovascular diseases. Death rates change from being high and unstable to becoming low and stable. The major arguments among historical demographers are not about if the decline took place (all agree it did), but rather about the timing of the decline (the nineteenth-century records are less conclusive here) and whether it was due to better medical techniques, general improvements in public health, or improvements in living standards and nutrition.

The gradual decline in the death rate throughout the nineteenth century sped up during the first fifty years of the twentieth century. Because death has been seen as an important event at the societal and personal level, we have good records on it throughout most of the United States during the twentieth century. As Figure 4-1 shows, the overall crude death rate had already fallen from about 17 per 1,000 population per year (less than half the CDR found

in many traditional nations) in 1900 to below 10 per 1,000 by 1950. Nonwhite death rates had an even steeper decline during this half-century, dropping from about 25 per 1,000 to slightly less than 10 per 1,000. In terms of the application of the general theory of the epidemiologic transition to the United States, the period from 1900 captures the end of the period of receding epidemics and pandemics (ending with the worldwide influenza pandemic of 1918-19), the era of declining endemic diseases (from 1920 to about 1950), and the era of chronic and man-made diseases (from about 1950 to the present).

Yet this general theory of the effects of the changing nature of disease in modern societies (and in the United States in particular) has failed to explain the continuing large disparities in the risks of death between social classes and racial groups. Building on the work of Antonovsky and Hauser and Kitagawa in the late 1960s, a number of researchers have documented these mortality differentials. Researchers have also made a better delineation of the distribution of the causes of death in the United States, and of the measurement of the contributions of these causes to the risks of death.

While we understand how the epidemiologic transition took place in the United States in the aggregate, we know relatively little about how many of the more mundane aspects of this process affected the risks of death for individuals. For example, it is clear that various forms of immunization played a key role in the decline in infectious diseases, but there has been surprisingly little scholarly interest in the social and economic differentials in immunization coverage, or how immunization led to the decline in these death rates (see Chapter 7). The same is true about the relative availability of antibiotics (a major reason for the decline in the death rate after 1940) to various population groups and its effect on differential declines in mortality.

Chapter 4 Definitions
MORTALITY

Crude Death Rate (CDR). The number of annual deaths per 1,000 midyear population in a given year. This rate may be computed separately for each sex, for specific races, or for each geographic area of a nation. Also called "general death rate" or simply the "death rate."

Age-Specific Mortality Rate (ASMR). The number of annual deaths at a given age per 1,000 midyear population of that age. Deaths and population usually are grouped into 5-year or 10-year age groups, except for the two youngest age groups, which are computed as ages under age 1 and from age 1 to under age 5 years. Also called Age-Specific Death Rates (ASDR).

Age- and Sex-Specific Mortality Rates. Age-specific death rates computed separately for each sex.

Death Probability. The proportion of persons alive at a given birth date who will die before reaching the end of that year of life. These probabilities are derived from age-specific death rates in order to compute life tables. Also called "age-specific mortality rate" or "proportion dying at age (x)."

Life Table. A statistical procedure for summarizing mortality rates for a particular date. A hypothetical cohort of 100,000 persons is assumed to be subject to the age-specific death probabilities observed for an actual population during the particular time period. The number who would die at each age and who would survive to be exposed to death at later ages is computed. From such statistics, it is possible to compute life expectancy. Such life tables are termed "cross-sectional" or "period" life tables. Generational life tables may also be computed, using the age-specific mortality probabilities of real cohorts.

Life Expectancy. The average number of additional years of life a person will live if he or she is exposed for an entire remaining lifetime to the age-specific death probabilities of a given year, derived from a life table. Life expectancy can be computed for any age (x).

Life Expectancy at Birth (°e0). Life expectancy of a person at age 0 (birth), derived from a life table for a specific year. This is the best single summary measure of the overall effect of mortality on a population.

Standard Population. An age-specific population distribution used to norm mortality rates so that different populations or the same population over time can be compared through indirect standardization.

Age-adjusted Mortality Rates. Age-specific mortality rates computed using a standard population.

Cause of Death. The disease or event that caused death. Causes are categorized and assigned according to internationally-established coding procedures. World Health Organization regulations specify that cause of death be categorized according to the current revision of the International Statistical Classification of Diseases, Injuries, and Causes of Death (see Appendix 2-2).

Cause-Specific Death Rates. The annual number of deaths from a given cause per 100,000 midyear population. Cause-specific rates may be reported for age groups, by sex, race, or other categories.

Infant Mortality Rate (IMR). The annual number of deaths to infants under one year of age, computed per 1,000 or per 100,000 live births in the same year. This rate is similar to, but not identical with, the age-specific death rate for age 0-1.

Neonatal Mortality Rate. Annual number of deaths to infants under 28 days of life per 100,000 live births during the year. It is commonly (not wholly correctly) assumed that deaths during the first month of life are caused primarily by factors relating to physiology, prenatal care, and delivery.

Postneonatal Mortality Rate. Annual number of deaths to infants from 28 days to 365 days of life per 100,000 live births during the year. It is commonly (not wholly correctly) assumed that deaths during this period are caused by environmental, nutritional, and health care conditions. The neonatal mortality rate plus the postneonatal mortality rate equals the infant mortality rate.

Fetal Mortality Rate. The annual number of fetal deaths with stated or presumed gestation of 20 weeks or more divided by the sum of live births plus fetal deaths, stated per 1,000 live births plus fetal deaths.

Perinatal Mortality Rate. The sum of all late fetal deaths (those with a stated or presumed gestational age of 28 weeks or more) plus infant deaths within 7 days of birth divided by the sum of live births plus late fetal deaths, stated per 1,000 live births.

Maternal Mortality Rate (MMR). Annual number of deaths to women as a result of childbirth (i.e. assigned to causes of deaths related to complications of pregnancy, childbirth and the puerperium) per 100,000 live births in that year.

Years of Potential Life Lost (YPLL). A life table-based measure of the amount of premature mortality in a population from birth to age 65 years.

Similarly, while there are great disparities in the risks of death by sex, race, and social class, it has proven surprisingly difficult to show how social stratification influences the distribution of causes of death among individuals. The emergence of homelessness in the 1980s, of increasing disparities in income distribution and of increased rates of homicide and suicide among certain subpopulations over the past decade has shown that there is no overarching paradigm that can explain how and why the risks of death in modern America are distributed between social groups. The theory of the epidemiological transition tended to imply that once death rates dropped to very low levels, the only job left would be to concentrate on bringing subpopulations with higher death rates down to the lower levels found among the general population.

It is not clear that we can make this kind of optimistic assumption today.

Finally, the emergence of infectious diseases such as AIDS and the re-emergence of new forms of old diseases (such as drug-resistant tuberculosis) have made us more aware that Mother Nature has a few more tricks up her sleeve for our species. It has also shown that the study of U.S. mortality cannot be conducted in a vacuum (which the current literature on this topic largely assumes). Mortality trends in other nations will continue to affect our understanding and perception of U.S. death rates, both in terms of the international transmission of infectious diseases and in the degree to which we see certain kinds of deaths as "excess mortality" rather than as part of the natural order of things. Nations such as Sweden or Japan, which have reached very low mortality rates at all but the oldest ages, also give us a yardstick by which we can measure our own efforts at controlling death.

Overview

Mortality in the United States is low and declining. Two summary measures of the force of mortality upon a population, the crude death rate (CDR) and the expectation of life at birth (identified by the symbol e(0,0)), are reported in Tables 4-1 and 4-2 respectively, and illustrated graphically in Figures 4-1 and 4-2. (For explanations of CDR and expectation of life at birth, see this chapter's Definitions Box). In both tables, measures are provided for each sex and for white and black or nonwhite populations for selected years in this century. Because death is concentrated at older ages, the crude death rate is strongly affected by a population's age composition. Although the CDR is useful in understanding a population's growth rate, expectation of life at birth is a more precise measure of mortality.

Tables 4-1 and 4-2 and Figures 4-1 and 4-2 show the following:

1. The CDR in 1991 stood at 8.6 per 1,000 population, and life expectancy at birth was 75.5 years. Because of a changing age composition (i.e. an aging population), the CDR has declined by only one point since 1950, yet life expectancy has risen by more than seven years.

2. Between 1970 and 1985, the United States was in a phase of modest improvement in life expectancy. This was preceded by a decade of only a slight improvement, which caused speculation at the time that some biological maximum length of life was being approached. Since 1985, there has been a slower rate of improvement in life expectancy.

3. Mortality decline has not been steady and uniform. There were periods of more rapid improvement in mortality conditions spanning 1900-15, 1940-50, and 1970-85, with periods of slower improvement between.

4. Male mortality has been consistently higher than female mortality. As of 1991 male life expectancy was 6.9 years less than (only 91 percent of) that of females.

5. Black mortality has been consistently higher than white mortality. In 1991, the life expectancy of the white population was 4.8 years (6 percent) higher than that of the black population.

6. Year-to-year fluctuations in death rates were common occurrences before World War I (especially with the influenza epidemic of 1918). With the passage of time, these fluctuations have diminished.

7. Both race and sex have important effects on differences in life expectancy. Sex differences in life expectancy peaked about 1975 (at 7.8 years); in 1991 they were 6.9 years. Black-white differences in life expectancy narrowed throughout the twentieth century until 1985, but this race differential has widened to 6.2 years by 1991.

The gap in life expectancy between black and white males (8.3 years in 1991) is particularly large, and is due to the decline in black male life expectancy since 1985.

All of these points will be explored in considerable detail in this chapter.

The Measurement of Mortality

There are several ways to measure mortality, each of which reveals different aspects of the degree of risk that populations or individuals run from exposure to this natural phenomenon. In this chapter, five major measures of mortality will be used:

Crude Death Rates: The first and most familiar rate is the crude death rate. It is well-known even to non-demographers that the risks of death are very differentially distributed by age; hence the crude death rate is not a very accurate measure of the state of mortality in a population, or when comparing two or more populations. For example, a number of Third World nations with poor systems of medical care have crude death rates below those of many advanced industrialized states; this is because they have a large proportion of their population in the younger age groups, where few die in any one year. A hallmark of a nation that has successfully controlled death and disease is that many more people survive to the oldest age groups, where, paradoxically, they tend to inflate the crude death rate (which accounts for the lack of change in the U.S. crude death rate between 1950 and 1991).

Category-Specific and Age-and-Category-Specific Death Rates: Since the crude death rate is such a poor measure of mortality conditions, it is essential to break this aggregate measure into its component parts. This is done by examining the characteristics of the overall population and the decedents with those same characteristics, and computing the risks of death to population subgroups in a time interval. There are two basic ways that this can be done, but they are conceptually the same.

The first is to compute mortality rates for groups by demographic characteristics, such as age-specific mortality rates (ASMRs), sex-specific death rates, and so on. These can also be combined into age-and-category-specific mortality rates, such as the computation of the mortality rate for black women aged 15-19 years in 1992.

The second kind of category-specific or age-and-category-specific mortality rate is the **cause-specific** mortality rate. In essence, this rate is just a special case of the category-specific rate; it simply uses the cause of death given on the death certificate as the category to which to assign the decedent. Again, cause-specific death rates can be (and usually are) combined with other kinds of demographic categories: thus the mortality rate of white men aged 50-54 from heart disease in 1991 is computed by using only white men aged 50-54 who died of this disease in 1991 as the numerator and all white men 50-54 in 1991 as the denominator.

Table 4-1. Crude Death Rates[1], by Race and Sex: 1900-1991[2]

Year	Total			White			Nonwhite			Black			Ratios	
	Total	Male	Female	Total	Male	Female	Total	Male	Female	Total	Male	Female	Male to female	Nonwhite to white
1991	8.6	9.1	8.1	8.9	9.3	8.5	7.3	8.4	6.3	8.6	10.0	7.4	1.12	0.82
1990	8.6	9.2	8.1	8.9	9.3	8.5	7.4	8.5	6.3	8.7	10.1	7.5	1.14	0.83
1985	8.8	9.5	8.1	9.0	9.6	8.4	7.4	8.6	6.4	8.5	9.9	7.3	1.17	0.82
1980	8.8	9.8	7.9	8.9	9.8	8.1	7.9	9.4	6.6	8.8	10.3	7.3	1.24	0.89
1975	8.8	10.0	7.6	8.9	10.0	7.8	8.2	9.9	6.7	8.8	10.6	7.3	1.32	0.92
1970	9.5	10.9	8.1	9.5	10.9	8.1	9.4	11.2	7.8	10.0	11.9	8.3	1.35	0.99
1965	9.4	10.9	8.0	9.4	10.9	8.0	9.7	11.2	8.2	10.1	11.6	8.6	1.36	1.03
1960	9.5	11.0	8.1	9.5	11.0	8.0	10.1	11.5	8.7	10.4	11.8	9.1	1.36	1.06
1955	9.3	10.8	7.9	9.2	10.7	7.8	10.0	11.3	8.8	—	—	—	1.37	1.09
1950	9.6	11.1	8.2	9.5	10.9	8.0	11.2	12.5	9.9	—	—	—	1.35	1.18
1945	10.6	12.6	8.8	10.4	12.5	8.6	11.9	13.5	10.5	—	—	—	1.43	1.14
1940	10.8	12.0	9.5	10.4	11.6	9.2	13.8	15.1	12.6	—	—	—	1.26	1.33
1935	10.9	12.0	9.9	10.6	11.6	9.5	14.3	15.6	13.0	—	—	—	1.21	1.35
1930	11.3	12.3	10.4	10.8	11.7	9.8	16.3	17.4	15.3	—	—	—	1.18	1.51
1925	11.7	12.4	10.9	11.1	11.8	10.4	17.4	18.2	16.6	—	—	—	1.14	1.57
1920	13.0	13.4	12.6	12.6	13.0	12.1	17.7	17.8	17.5	—	—	—	1.06	1.40
1915	13.2	14.0	12.3	12.9	13.7	12.0	20.2	20.8	19.5	—	—	—	1.14	1.57
1910	14.7	15.6	13.7	14.5	15.4	13.6	21.7	22.3	21.0	—	—	—	1.14	1.50
1905	15.9	16.7	15.0	15.7	16.5	14.8	25.5	26.8	24.3	—	—	—	1.11	1.62
1900	17.2	17.9	16.5	17.0	17.7	16.3	25.0	25.7	24.4	—	—	—	1.08	1.47

[1] Per 1,000 population.

[2] Values for 1900-1930 are based on death-registration states which increased in number from 10 states and D.C. in 1900 to the entire coterminous U.S. in 1933.

Source: National Center for Health Statistics, "Vital Statistics of the United States: 1991, Volume II–Mortality Part A," National Center for Health Statistics, Hyattsville, MD, 1996, Table 1-2.

Table 4-2. Estimated Average Length of Life, in Years, by Race and Sex: 1900-1991[1]

Year	Total			White			Nonwhite			Black			Ratios	
	Total	Male	Female	Total	Male	Female	Total	Male	Female	Total	Male	Female	Male to female	Nonwhite to white
1991	75.5	72.0	78.9	76.3	72.9	79.6	71.5	67.3	75.5	69.3	64.6	73.8	0.91	0.94
1990	75.4	71.8	78.8	76.1	72.7	79.4	71.2	67.0	75.2	69.1	64.5	73.6	0.91	0.94
1985	74.7	71.1	78.2	75.3	71.8	78.7	71.0	67.0	74.8	69.3	65.0	73.4	0.91	0.94
1980	73.7	70.0	77.4	74.4	70.7	78.1	69.5	65.3	73.6	68.1	63.8	72.5	0.90	0.93
1975	72.6	68.8	76.6	73.4	69.5	77.3	68.0	63.7	72.4	66.8	62.4	71.3	0.90	0.93
1970	70.8	67.1	74.7	71.7	68.0	75.6	65.3	61.3	69.4	64.1	60.0	68.3	0.90	0.91
1965	70.2	66.8	73.8	71.1	67.6	74.8	64.3	61.2	67.6	—	—	—	0.91	0.90
1960	69.7	66.6	73.1	70.6	67.4	74.1	63.6	61.1	66.3	—	—	—	0.91	0.90
1955	69.6	66.7	72.8	70.5	67.4	73.7	63.7	61.4	66.1	—	—	—	0.92	0.90
1950	68.2	65.6	71.1	69.1	66.5	72.2	60.8	59.1	62.9	—	—	—	0.92	0.88
1945	65.9	63.6	67.9	66.8	64.4	69.5	57.7	56.1	59.6	—	—	—	0.94	0.86
1940	62.9	60.8	65.2	64.2	62.1	66.6	53.1	51.5	54.9	—	—	—	0.93	0.83
1935	61.7	59.9	63.9	62.9	61.0	65.0	53.1	51.3	55.2	—	—	—	0.94	0.84
1930	59.7	58.1	61.6	61.4	59.7	63.5	48.1	47.3	49.2	—	—	—	0.94	0.78
1925	59.0	57.6	60.6	60.7	59.3	62.4	45.7	44.9	46.7	—	—	—	0.95	0.75
1920	54.1	53.6	54.6	54.9	54.4	55.6	45.3	45.5	45.2	—	—	—	0.98	0.83
1915	54.5	52.5	56.8	55.1	53.1	57.5	38.9	37.5	40.5	—	—	—	0.92	0.71
1910	50.0	48.4	51.8	50.3	48.6	52.0	35.6	33.8	37.5	—	—	—	0.93	0.71
1905	48.7	47.3	50.2	49.1	47.6	50.6	31.3	29.6	33.1	—	—	—	0.94	0.64
1900	47.3	46.3	48.3	47.6	46.6	48.7	33.0	32.5	33.5	—	—	—	0.96	0.69

[1] Values for 1900-1930 are based on death-registration states.

Source: National Center for Health Statistics, "Vital Statistics of the United States: 1991, Volume II--Mortality Part A," National Center for Health Statistics, Hyattsville, MD, 1996, Table 6-5.

Figure 4-1. Trends in Crude Death Rates, by Race: 1900-1991

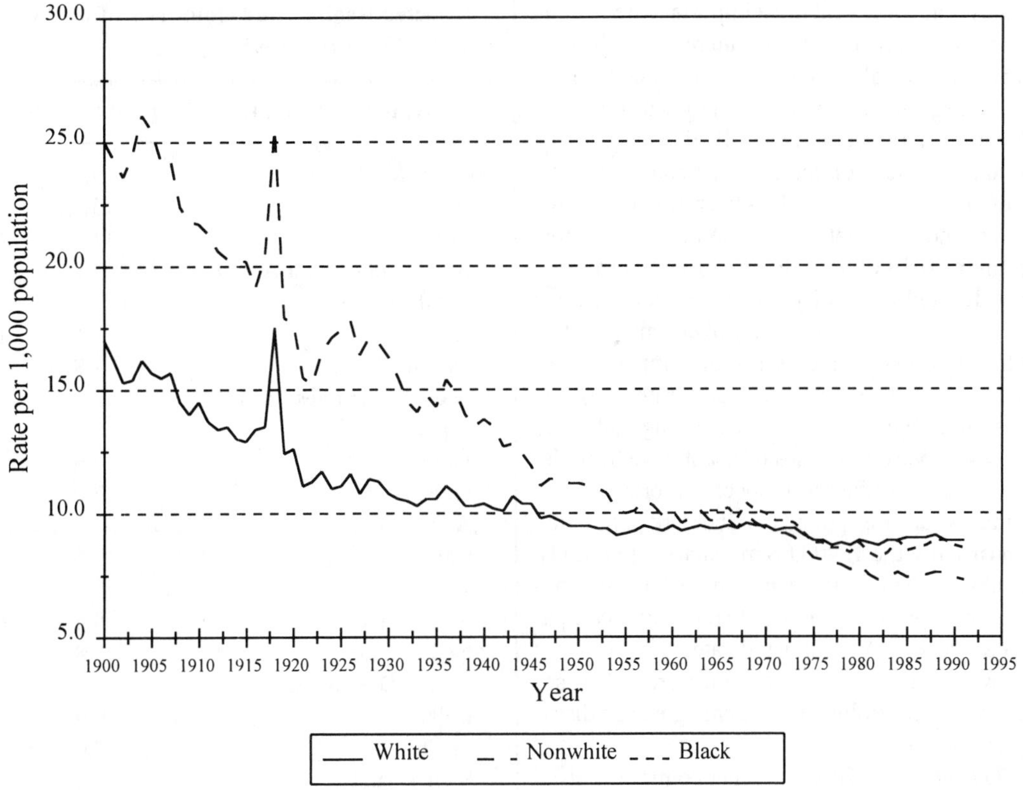

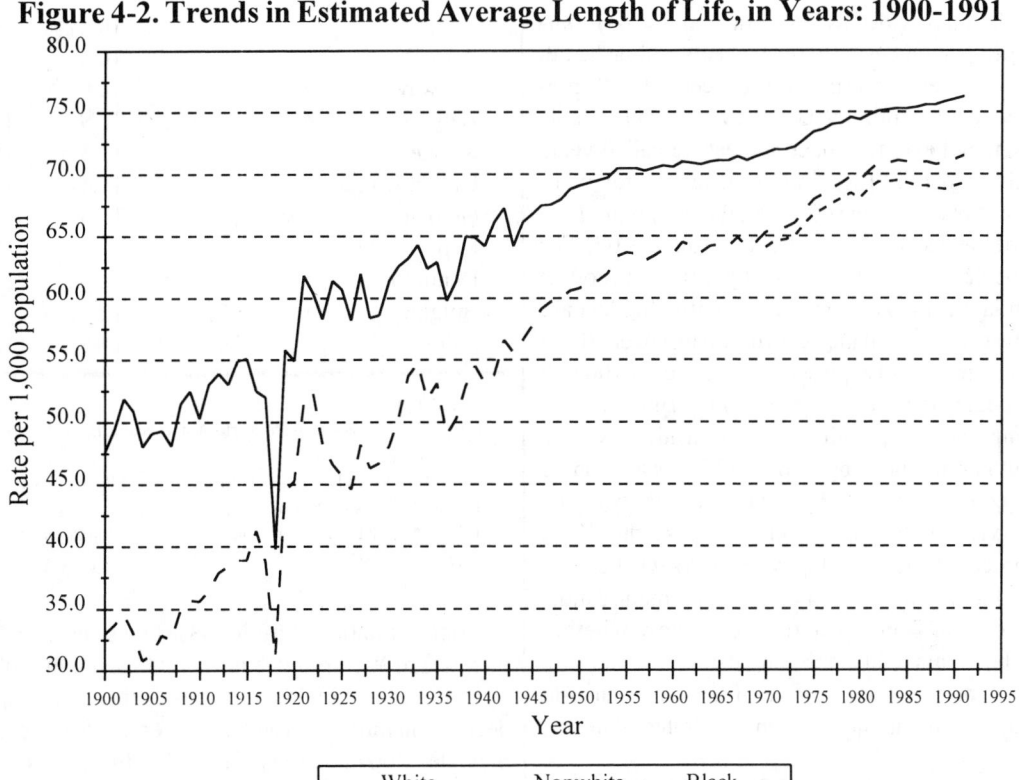

Source: 1900-1991 NCHS data.

Figure 4-2. Trends in Estimated Average Length of Life, in Years: 1900-1991

Source: 1900-1991 NCHS data.

The most important category into which to divide mortality rates is age; the next most important are sex and (in the United States) race. Because there are such striking differences in mortality rates between these different demographic categories, the majority of tables dealing with mortality rates in this chapter will also divide the subpopulation's mortality rates by these characteristics. The ratios of mortality rates (such as the ratio of the black to white infant mortality rate) will also be used to show differences in the risks of mortality to different groups.

Age-Adjusted Mortality Rates: Because the age composition of a population can vary over time, it is frequently difficult to make much sense of comparisons of crude or summed cause-specific mortality rates between widely-separated years. For this reason, age-adjusted mortality rates for various causes of death have been developed. In these rates, the cause-specific mortality rates from individual years are applied to a standard population distribution (usually the 1940 U.S. population pyramid); the total deaths are then summed and divided by this standard population to produce a mortality rate that is comparable between years. Age-adjusted rates are a way of showing how the risks of death from different diseases are changing while controlling for the changing age distribution of the population.

Life Expectancy: This is another commonly-used measure of the risk of mortality. Life expectancy is a measure of the mean number of years of life remaining to a population sharing certain characteristics (the total population, populations divided by sex or race, and so on) computed on a per-person basis: In recent years, public health specialists have become especially concerned with premature or avoidable mortality. Using a variant of life-table techniques, they have developed a measure called years of potential life lost (YPLL). In this technique, for every death that occurs before age 65 years, the midpoint of the age group of the decedent is subtracted from age 65. For example, the death of a person 15-24 years of age counts as 45 potential years lost. Years of potential life lost are computed by summing all the years of life lost over all age groups under age 65, and expressing it as a rate per 100,000 population under 65 years of age. The YPLL measure can also be computed for specific causes of death as well as for different population subgroups. YPLL is a valuable tool in analyzing the effects of premature mortality on the potential survival of the population. In a sense, the YPLL is the reciprocal of life expectancy: it shows what causes of death are having the greatest effect on premature mortality, and comparisons over time can show whether progress is being made in combating them.

This chapter will use all five of these measures in analyzing the change in mortality in the United States.

International Comparisons of Crude Death Rates

The pattern of change in the Crude Death Rate across

Table 4-3. Crude Death Rates[1] for the United States and Selected Regions and Countries of the World: 1950-55, 1970-75, and 1990-95

Region and country	1990-95	1970-75	1950-55
World, total	9.3	11.7	10.6
Africa	13.7	19.2	15.6
Europe	11.2	10.1	10.7
North and Central America[2]	7.8	9.2	9.1
South America[2]	7.1	9.7	8.2
Asia	8.4	11.4	—
Oceania	7.8	9.6	8.8
Selected countries			
Cuba	6.8	6.6	6.4
Israel	6.9	7.1	7.3
Iceland	7.0	7.0	7.0
Australia	7.4	8.5	8.0
Canada	7.6	7.4	7.6
Japan	7.6	6.6	6.7
New Zealand	8.4	8.4	8.0
Netherlands	8.8	8.3	8.9
UNITED STATES	8.8	9.2	9.2
Ireland	9.0	11.0	9.8
Spain	9.0	8.3	8.4
Switzerland	9.4	9.0	10.3
Greece	9.8	8.6	9.9
France	9.8	10.6	10.9
Italy	9.9	9.8	9.8
Finland	10.3	9.5	10.0
Austria	10.8	12.8	12.8
Norway	10.9	10.0	10.8
Belgium	10.9	12.1	12.2
Sweden	11.3	10.4	11.8
United Kingdom	11.4	11.7	12.3
Germany	11.6	12.4	—
Kenya	11.7	17.3	—
Denmark	12.0	10.0	11.0
Bulgaria	12.7	9.7	10.3
Zaire	14.5	18.9	—

[1] Per 1,000 population.

[2] In 1950-55, categories were North America and Latin America.

Source: The World Resources Institute, "World Resources 1996-97," Oxford University Press, New York, 1996, Table 8.3; 1950-55 data from United Nations, "Demographic Indicators of Countries," United Nations, New York, 1982.

a variety of nations (Table 4-3) shows some of the complexities of attempting to interpret this measure of mortality. Between 1950-55 and 1970-75, there were significant declines in mortality (and increases in life expectancy) in most developed nations. However, there were few large decreases in the crude death rate in these countries; in a few nations, the CDR actually increased. By 1990-95, the situation is even more confusing: the two countries with the longest expectation of life, Japan and Sweden, had both experienced significant increases in their CDRs. Nations that had declines in their CDRs between 1970-75 and 1990-95 usually had significant increases in life expectancy, moderately high fertility, or, as is also the case in the United States, significant in-migration of young, healthy people.

Sources of Mortality Data

The principal source of statistical information about deaths is the annual report, *Vital Statistics of the United States:Mortality (Volume II)*, published by the National Center for Health Statistics (NCHS). That report is made up of two parts, each bound separately: Part A contains detailed analytical tables for each of the major mortality topics pertaining primarily to the nation as a whole; Part B presents mortality statistics in geographical detail.

Mortality statistics presented here are based on information obtained directly from copies of certificates of death or coded from those certificates, received from the registration office of each state. In addition, NCHS publishes summary mortality statistics in its Monthly Vital Statistics Report. An annual issue in this series presents advance yearly totals pending the release (after a delay of three or four years) of the final volume of vital statistics. The reader may update the analysis of this chapter by consulting these sources. The *Statistical Abstract of the United States* provides an up-to-date summary of some of this information. Appendix 2-2 provides more information about these data, as well as examples of the U.S. Standard Certificate of Death and the U.S. Standard Report of Fetal Death. U.S. death certificates have undergone periodic revisions (the most recent one in 1989), as has the International Classification of Causes of Death (now in its ninth revision, ICD-9).

Seasonality of Mortality

Deaths in the United States are not evenly distributed throughout the year. In 1900, there were about 21 percent more deaths in January than in the average month, and this trend continued in muted form throughout the late winter and spring. The six months between January and June, 1900 accounted for 53.7 percent of all deaths in that year. By 1990, deaths had shifted to a heavier concentration in the colder months: January still had 21 percent more deaths than the average month, but the October-March period accounted for 52.4 percent of all annual deaths.

The seasonality of deaths is largely linked to seasonal variations in disease, and, in earlier years, to seasonal swings in births and the accompanying high neonatal mortality. The higher number of deaths in colder months in 1990 was due to the vulnerability of the increasing number of elderly persons to influenza epidemics and pulmonary diseases. In general, the monthly and seasonal variation in deaths due to epidemic diseases has been decreasing, and most endemic diseases or chronic conditions have little or no seasonality. Some non-disease causes of death are seasonal (drownings are more likely to occur in the summer, as are heat-related deaths), but these comprise only a small proportion of all deaths. The aging population in the future could result in an even higher death rate in the colder months, but the increasing rates of immunization among the elderly and a great drop in deaths from influenza and pneumonia since 1970 may further dampen these seasonal or monthly swings.

Age Pattern of Mortality

Age-specific mortality rates (ASMR, see Definition Box; also called age-specific death rates, ASDR) show a characteristic curve of the type shown in Table 4-4 and Figure 4-3. The ASMR is high for the first year of life, then falls to a very low level for ages one to about forty-four years. Thereafter, the rate rises with increasing age until it becomes very high at the oldest ages. This general shape is characteristic of the age-curves of the death rates of all human populations under normal conditions. However, there can be great variation in the height of the curve from one population to another or at different times for the same population.

The Historical Decline in Age-Specific Mortality, 1900-1980

The schedule of age-specific mortality rates in the United States for 1900, 1940 and 1990 shows that the decline in mortality rates has not been evenly distributed among age groups (Table 4-5). There has been a most remarkable reduction in the death rate for infants under one year of age. The rate for this group in 1900 was 162.4; it declined to 64.9 in 1940, and to 9.7 per 1,000 by 1990. There were also impressive declines in mortality at ages up to 35-44 years between 1900 and 1940. Although the size of the 1900-40 decline was smaller for the intermediate ages (because the rates are normally lower at these ages), the percentage declines at these ages were also striking, especially for children.

The gains during the four decades after 1900 were primarily at below age fifty-five. None of the age groups at 55 and over had more than a 20 percent decline in mortality between 1900 and 1940, a period when the declines of the younger age groups ranged from 85.4 to 29.3 percent.

The gains during the 40 years between 1940 and 1980 have been at all ages, but with significant improvements at below 1 year of life and above 55 years. The ASMR of those age 85 and above stood at 260.9 per 1,000 in 1900, and at 235.7 in 1940; yet by 1980 it had fallen to 159.8 (a 9.7 percent decline during 1900-40, and a 32.2 percent decline during 1940-80). The decline in the ASMR for the 75-84 year age group was even more impressive

Table 4-4. Age-specific Mortality Rates[1], by Race and Sex: 1900-1991

Year, race, and sex	Total	Under 1 year	1 to 4 years	5 to 14 years	15 to 24 years	25 to 34 years	35 to 44 years	45 to 54 years	55 to 64 years	65 to 74 years	75 to 84 years	85 years and over
All races, total												
1991	8.6	9.2	0.5	0.2	1.0	1.4	2.2	4.7	11.8	26.2	58.9	151.1
1990	8.6	9.7	0.5	0.2	1.0	1.4	2.2	4.7	12.0	26.5	60.1	153.3
1985	8.8	10.9	0.5	0.3	0.9	1.2	2.1	5.2	12.9	28.6	64.0	157.1
1980	8.8	12.9	0.6	0.3	1.2	1.4	2.3	5.8	13.5	29.9	66.9	159.8
1975	8.8	16.0	0.7	0.4	1.2	1.4	2.7	6.5	14.8	31.8	70.3	156.6
1970	9.5	21.4	0.8	0.4	1.3	1.6	3.1	7.3	16.6	35.8	80.0	163.4
1960	9.5	27.0	1.1	0.5	1.1	1.5	3.0	7.6	17.4	38.2	87.5	198.6
1950	9.6	33.0	1.4	0.6	1.3	1.8	3.6	8.5	19.0	41.0	93.3	202.0
1940	10.8	54.9	2.9	1.0	2.0	3.1	5.2	10.6	22.3	48.0	112.0	235.7
1930	11.3	69.0	5.6	1.7	3.3	4.7	6.8	12.2	24.0	51.4	112.7	228.0
1920	13.0	92.3	9.9	2.6	4.9	6.8	8.1	12.2	23.6	52.5	118.9	248.3
1910	14.7	131.8	14.0	2.9	4.5	6.5	9.0	13.7	26.2	55.6	122.2	250.3
1900	17.2	162.4	19.8	3.9	5.9	8.2	10.2	15.0	27.2	56.4	123.3	260.9
All races, male												
1991	9.1	10.2	0.5	0.3	1.5	2.0	3.1	6.1	15.2	34.4	76.9	178.0
1990	9.2	10.8	0.5	0.3	1.5	2.0	3.1	6.1	15.5	34.9	78.9	180.6
1985	9.5	12.2	0.6	0.3	1.4	1.9	2.8	6.7	17.1	38.6	85.0	186.1
1980	9.8	14.3	0.7	0.4	1.7	2.0	3.0	7.7	18.2	41.1	88.2	188.0
1975	10.0	17.9	0.8	0.4	1.7	2.0	3.5	8.6	20.2	44.1	91.5	181.3
1970	10.9	24.1	0.9	0.5	1.9	2.2	4.0	9.6	22.8	48.7	100.1	178.2
1960	11.0	30.6	1.2	0.6	1.5	1.9	3.7	9.9	23.1	49.1	101.8	211.9
1950	11.1	37.3	1.5	0.7	1.7	2.2	4.3	10.7	24.0	49.3	104.3	216.4
1940	12.0	61.9	3.1	1.2	2.3	3.4	5.9	12.5	26.2	54.2	121.3	246.4
1930	12.3	77.0	6.0	1.9	3.5	4.9	7.5	13.6	26.6	55.8	119.1	236.7
1920	13.4	103.6	10.3	2.8	4.8	6.4	8.2	12.6	24.6	54.5	122.1	253.0
1910	15.6	145.5	14.6	3.0	4.8	6.9	10.0	15.2	28.7	58.7	127.4	255.8
1900	17.9	179.1	20.5	3.8	5.9	8.2	10.7	15.7	28.7	59.3	128.3	268.8
All races, female												
1991	8.1	8.0	0.4	0.2	0.5	0.7	1.4	3.4	8.7	19.8	48.0	140.7
1990	8.1	8.6	0.4	0.2	0.5	0.7	1.4	3.4	8.8	19.9	48.8	142.7
1985	8.1	9.5	0.4	0.2	0.5	0.7	1.4	3.8	9.3	21.0	51.6	145.5
1980	7.9	11.4	0.5	0.2	0.6	0.8	1.6	4.1	9.3	21.4	54.4	147.5
1975	10.0	15.5	0.7	0.4	1.6	1.7	3.0	7.9	19.4	43.4	92.7	185.6
1970	10.9	21.1	0.8	0.5	1.7	1.8	3.4	8.8	22.0	48.1	101.0	185.5
1960	11.0	26.9	1.0	0.5	1.4	1.6	3.3	9.3	22.3	48.5	103.0	217.5
1950	10.9	34.0	1.4	0.7	1.5	1.9	3.8	9.8	23.0	48.6	105.3	221.2
1940	11.6	56.7	2.8	1.1	2.0	2.8	5.1	11.4	25.2	54.0	122.0	251.4
1930	11.7	71.5	5.5	1.8	3.0	4.1	6.5	12.3	25.5	55.1	119.2	237.6
1920	13.0	98.1	9.8	2.7	4.2	5.9	7.7	12.0	24.2	54.2	122.5	253.6
1910	15.4	143.0	14.2	3.0	4.7	6.7	9.7	15.0	28.4	58.6	127.6	257.9
1900	17.7	175.9	20.2	3.8	5.8	8.1	10.6	15.5	28.5	59.1	128.2	269.2
White, male												
1991	9.3	8.6	0.5	0.3	1.3	1.8	2.7	5.4	14.4	33.5	76.4	180.2
1990	9.3	9.0	0.5	0.3	1.3	1.8	2.7	5.5	14.7	34.0	78.4	182.7
1985	9.6	10.6	0.5	0.3	1.3	1.6	2.4	6.1	16.3	37.7	84.9	189.8
1980	9.8	12.3	0.7	0.4	1.7	1.7	2.6	7.0	17.3	40.4	88.3	179.2
1975	10.0	15.5	0.7	0.4	1.6	1.7	3.0	7.9	19.4	43.4	92.7	185.6
1970	10.9	21.1	0.8	0.5	1.7	1.8	3.4	8.8	22.0	48.1	101.0	185.5
1960	11.0	26.9	1.0	0.5	1.4	1.6	3.3	9.3	22.3	48.5	103.0	217.5
1950	10.9	34.0	1.4	0.7	1.5	1.9	3.8	9.8	23.0	48.6	105.3	221.2
1940	11.6	56.7	2.8	1.1	2.0	2.8	5.1	11.4	25.2	54.0	122.0	251.4
1930	11.7	71.5	5.5	1.8	3.0	4.1	6.5	12.3	25.5	55.1	119.2	237.6
1920	13.0	98.1	9.8	2.7	4.2	5.9	7.7	12.0	24.2	54.2	122.5	253.6
1910	15.4	143.0	14.2	3.0	4.7	6.7	9.7	15.0	28.4	58.6	127.6	257.9
1900	17.7	175.9	20.2	3.8	5.8	8.1	10.6	15.5	28.5	59.1	128.2	269.2

Table 4-4. Age-specific Mortality Rates[1], by Race and Sex: 1900-1991 (continued)

Year, race, and sex	Total	Under 1 year	1 to 4 years	5 to 14 years	15 to 24 years	25 to 34 years	35 to 44 years	45 to 54 years	55 to 64 years	65 to 74 years	75 to 84 years	85 years and over
White, female												
1991	8.5	6.6	0.4	0.2	0.5	0.6	1.2	3.1	8.2	19.1	47.5	141.9
1990	8.5	6.9	0.4	0.2	0.5	0.6	1.2	3.1	8.2	19.2	48.4	144.0
1985	8.4	8.0	0.4	0.2	0.5	0.6	1.2	3.4	8.7	20.3	51.1	147.5
1980	8.1	9.6	0.5	0.2	0.6	0.7	1.4	3.7	8.8	20.7	52.6	149.8
1975	7.8	11.9	0.6	0.3	0.6	0.7	1.7	4.1	9.3	21.4	57.9	147.5
1970	8.1	16.1	0.7	0.3	0.6	0.8	1.9	4.6	10.1	24.7	67.0	159.8
1960	8.0	20.1	0.9	0.3	0.5	0.9	1.9	4.6	10.8	27.8	77.0	194.8
1950	8.0	25.7	1.1	0.5	0.7	1.1	2.4	5.5	12.9	32.4	84.8	196.8
1940	9.2	43.6	2.4	0.8	1.4	2.2	3.7	7.5	16.8	41.5	104.8	235.0
1930	9.8	56.0	4.8	1.4	2.5	3.6	5.2	9.2	19.9	46.0	107.6	225.1
1920	12.1	76.1	9.0	2.3	4.3	6.5	7.3	10.9	21.7	49.9	116.4	247.0
1910	13.6	115.2	13.0	2.8	4.1	5.9	7.7	11.8	23.4	52.2	117.8	248.1
1900	16.3	142.6	18.7	3.8	5.6	8.1	9.6	14.0	25.5	53.4	118.9	256.7
Nonwhite, male												
1991	8.4	15.9	0.8	0.4	2.3	3.5	5.6	10.0	21.3	42.3	81.6	157.6
1990	8.5	18.1	0.8	0.4	2.2	3.5	5.6	10.2	22.2	43.5	83.2	160.8
1985	8.6	19.4	0.8	0.4	1.6	3.0	5.1	10.9	24.4	46.6	86.2	151.6
1980	9.4	23.5	1.0	0.4	2.0	3.6	5.9	13.1	26.1	47.5	86.9	157.7
1975	9.9	29.7	1.1	0.6	2.4	4.4	7.2	14.5	27.6	50.4	79.6	138.6
1970	11.2	40.2	1.4	0.7	3.0	5.0	8.7	16.5	30.5	54.7	89.8	114.1
1960	11.5	51.9	2.1	0.8	2.1	3.9	7.3	15.5	31.5	56.6	86.6	152.4
1950	12.5	59.9	2.7	1.0	2.9	5.0	8.6	18.6	34.8	57.9	90.3	160.2
1940	15.1	101.2	5.3	1.6	5.0	8.5	13.2	24.5	39.5	56.5	108.8	199.7
1930	17.4	122.3	10.0	2.7	7.8	12.1	17.0	26.3	40.4	67.3	117.6	228.5
1920	17.8	167.7	15.0	3.7	9.9	12.2	14.4	20.1	31.1	60.2	116.0	247.1
1910	22.3	257.6	30.1	5.4	10.0	12.6	17.5	24.8	38.7	66.3	113.8	174.1
1900	25.7	369.3	43.4	7.8	11.8	12.5	14.2	24.7	42.1	71.6	131.4	249.3
Nonwhite, female												
1991	6.3	12.9	0.6	0.2	0.6	1.3	2.5	5.3	12.0	25.2	52.7	127.2
1990	6.3	14.8	0.6	0.3	0.6	1.3	2.4	5.4	12.5	25.5	53.1	128.6
1985	6.4	16.0	0.7	0.3	0.6	1.2	2.3	5.8	13.5	27.0	56.8	127.2
1980	6.6	19.4	0.8	0.3	0.7	1.4	2.9	6.9	14.2	28.6	58.6	119.2
1975	6.7	24.9	0.9	0.3	0.8	1.6	3.6	7.8	15.8	31.8	52.7	108.5
1970	7.8	31.7	1.2	0.4	1.1	2.2	4.9	9.8	18.9	36.8	63.9	102.9
1960	8.7	40.7	1.7	0.5	1.1	2.6	5.5	11.4	24.1	39.8	67.1	128.7
1950	9.9	47.5	2.3	0.8	2.2	3.9	7.5	15.5	27.6	46.1	70.6	133.7
1940	12.6	77.4	4.4	1.4	5.0	7.4	11.7	21.1	35.7	46.3	84.1	159.7
1930	15.3	97.9	8.7	2.6	8.2	11.1	15.3	25.2	41.4	60.0	91.4	187.2
1920	17.5	131.1	14.2	3.9	10.8	13.5	16.0	23.4	35.8	60.4	106.4	221.2
1910	21.0	221.4	26.6	5.9	10.5	11.6	16.4	24.3	38.2	61.9	93.9	177.9
1900	24.4	299.5	43.5	10.1	11.2	11.7	15.6	23.9	42.1	66.4	113.2	195.8

[1] Per 1,000 population.

Source: 1980-1991 data from National Center for Health Statistics, "Vital Statistics of the United States: 1991, Volume II--Mortality Part A," National Center for Health Statistics, Hyattsville, MD, 1996, Table 1-4; 1950-1975 data from National Center for Health Statistics, "Monthly Vital Statistics Report," Volume 31, No. 13, 1983, Table 6; and data prior to 1950 from Bogue, Donald, "The Population of the United States," The Free Press, New York, 1985, Table 5-4.

Figure 4-3. Change in Age-specific Mortality Rates: 1900, 1940, and 1990

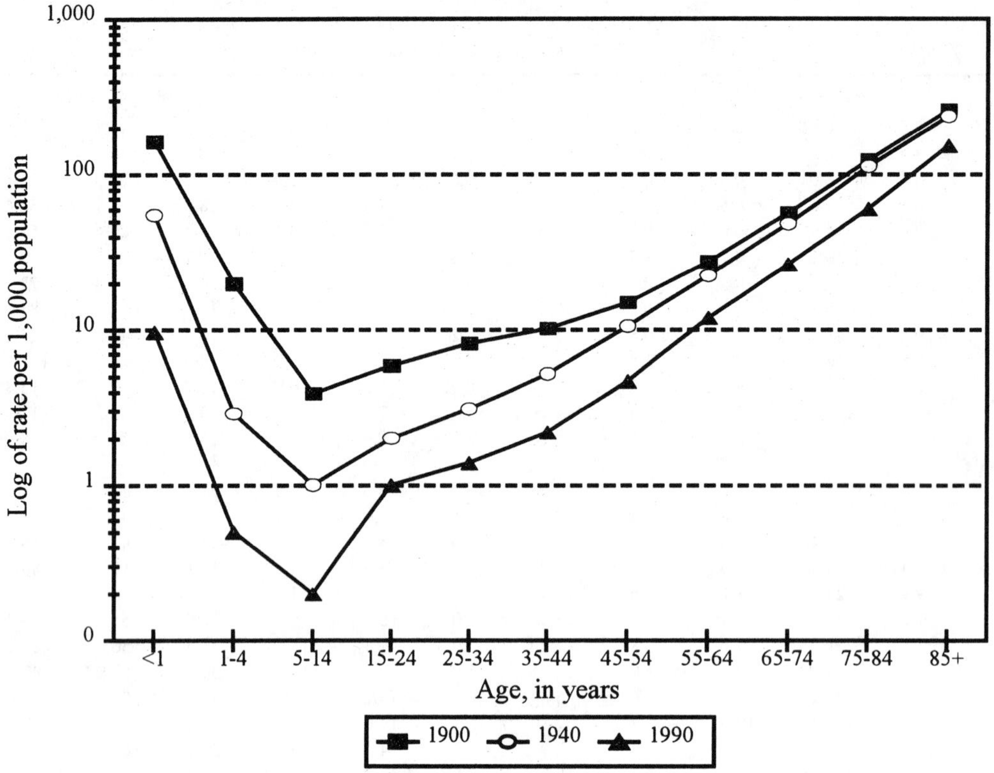

Source: 1900, 1940, and 1990 National Center for Health Statistics data.

Table 4-5. Absolute and Relative Decline in Age-specific Mortality Rates: 1900-40, 1940-80, and 1980-91

Age	Decline in rate			Percent decline		
	1980-91	1940-80	1900-40	1980-91	1940-80	1900-40
All ages	-0.2	-2.0	-6.4	-2.3	-18.5	-37.2
Under 1 year	-3.7	-42.0	-107.5	-28.7	-76.5	-66.2
1 to 4 years	-0.1	-2.3	-16.9	-16.7	-79.3	-85.4
5 to 14 years	-0.1	-0.7	-2.9	-33.3	-70.0	-74.4
15 to 24 years	-0.2	-0.8	-3.9	-16.7	-40.0	-66.1
25 to 34 years	...	-1.7	-5.1	...	-54.8	-62.2
35 to 44 years	-0.1	-2.9	-5.0	-4.3	-55.8	-49.0
45 to 54 years	-1.1	-4.8	-4.4	-19.0	-45.3	-29.3
55 to 64 years	-1.7	-8.8	-4.9	-12.6	-39.5	-18.0
65 to 74 years	-3.7	-18.1	-8.4	-12.4	-37.7	-14.9
75 to 84 years	-8.0	-45.1	-11.3	-12.0	-40.3	-9.2
85 years and over	-8.7	-75.9	-25.2	-5.4	-32.2	-9.7

Source: 1980 and 1991 data from National Center for Health Statistics, "Vital Statistics of the
    United States: 1991, Volume II--Mortality Part A," National Center for Health Statistics,
    Hyattsville, MD, 1996, Table 1-4; 1900 and 1940 data from Bogue, Donald, "The Population
    of the United States," The Free Press, New York, 1985, Table 5-4.

Table 4-6. Male to Female Ratios in Mortality Rates, by Race: 1900-1991

Year and race	Total	Under 1 year	1 to 4 years	5 to 14 years	15 to 24 years	25 to 34 years	35 to 44 years	45 to 54 years	55 to 64 years	65 to 74 years	75 to 84 years	85 years and over
All races												
1991	1.12	1.28	1.25	1.50	3.00	2.86	2.21	1.79	1.75	1.74	1.60	1.27
1990	1.14	1.26	1.25	1.50	3.00	2.86	2.21	1.79	1.76	1.75	1.62	1.27
1985	1.17	1.28	1.50	1.50	2.80	2.71	2.00	1.76	1.84	1.84	1.65	1.28
1980	1.24	1.25	1.40	2.00	2.83	2.50	1.88	1.88	1.96	1.92	1.62	1.27
1975	1.00	1.15	1.14	1.00	1.06	1.18	1.17	1.09	1.04	1.02	0.99	0.98
1970	1.00	1.14	1.13	1.00	1.12	1.22	1.18	1.09	1.04	1.01	0.99	0.96
1960	1.00	1.14	1.20	1.20	1.07	1.19	1.12	1.06	1.04	1.01	0.99	0.97
1950	1.02	1.10	1.07	1.00	1.13	1.16	1.13	1.09	1.04	1.01	0.99	0.98
1940	1.03	1.09	1.11	1.09	1.15	1.21	1.16	1.10	1.04	1.00	0.99	0.98
1930	1.05	1.08	1.09	1.06	1.17	1.20	1.15	1.11	1.04	1.01	1.00	1.00
1920	1.03	1.06	1.05	1.04	1.14	1.08	1.06	1.05	1.02	1.01	1.00	1.00
1910	1.01	1.02	1.03	1.00	1.02	1.03	1.03	1.01	1.01	1.00	1.00	0.99
1900	1.01	1.02	1.01	1.00	1.02	1.01	1.01	1.01	1.01	1.00	1.00	1.00
White												
1991	1.09	1.30	1.25	1.50	2.60	3.00	2.25	1.74	1.76	1.75	1.61	1.27
1990	1.09	1.30	1.25	1.50	2.60	3.00	2.25	1.77	1.79	1.77	1.62	1.27
1985	1.14	1.33	1.25	1.50	2.60	2.67	2.00	1.79	1.87	1.86	1.66	1.29
1980	1.21	1.28	1.40	2.00	2.83	2.43	1.86	1.89	1.97	1.95	1.68	1.20
1975	1.28	1.30	1.17	1.33	2.67	2.43	1.76	1.93	2.09	2.03	1.60	1.26
1970	1.35	1.31	1.14	1.67	2.83	2.25	1.79	1.91	2.18	1.95	1.51	1.16
1960	1.38	1.34	1.11	1.67	2.80	1.78	1.74	2.02	2.06	1.74	1.34	1.12
1950	1.36	1.32	1.27	1.40	2.14	1.73	1.58	1.78	1.78	1.50	1.24	1.12
1940	1.26	1.30	1.17	1.38	1.43	1.27	1.38	1.52	1.50	1.30	1.16	1.07
1930	1.19	1.28	1.15	1.29	1.20	1.14	1.25	1.34	1.28	1.20	1.11	1.06
1920	1.07	1.29	1.09	1.17	0.98	0.91	1.05	1.10	1.12	1.09	1.05	1.03
1910	1.13	1.24	1.09	1.07	1.15	1.14	1.26	1.27	1.21	1.12	1.08	1.04
1900	1.09	1.23	1.08	1.00	1.04	1.00	1.10	1.11	1.12	1.11	1.08	1.05
Nonwhite												
1991	1.33	1.23	1.33	2.00	3.83	2.69	2.24	1.89	1.78	1.68	1.55	1.24
1990	1.35	1.22	1.33	1.33	3.67	2.69	2.33	1.89	1.78	1.71	1.57	1.25
1985	1.34	1.21	1.14	1.33	2.67	2.50	2.22	1.88	1.81	1.73	1.52	1.19
1980	1.42	1.21	1.25	1.33	2.86	2.57	2.03	1.90	1.84	1.66	1.48	1.32
1975	1.48	1.19	1.22	2.00	3.00	2.75	2.00	1.86	1.75	1.58	1.51	1.28
1970	1.44	1.27	1.17	1.75	2.73	2.27	1.78	1.68	1.61	1.49	1.41	1.11
1960	1.32	1.28	1.24	1.60	1.91	1.50	1.33	1.36	1.31	1.42	1.29	1.18
1950	1.26	1.26	1.17	1.25	1.32	1.28	1.15	1.20	1.26	1.26	1.28	1.20
1940	1.20	1.31	1.20	1.14	1.00	1.15	1.13	1.16	1.11	1.22	1.29	1.25
1930	1.14	1.25	1.15	1.04	0.95	1.09	1.11	1.04	0.98	1.12	1.29	1.22
1920	1.02	1.28	1.06	0.95	0.92	0.90	0.90	0.86	0.87	1.00	1.09	1.12
1910	1.06	1.16	1.13	0.92	0.95	1.09	1.07	1.02	1.01	1.07	1.21	0.98
1900	1.05	1.23	1.00	0.77	1.05	1.07	0.91	1.03	1.00	1.08	1.16	1.27

Source: 1980-1991 data from National Center for Health Statistics, "Vital Statistics of the United States: 1991, Volume II--Mortality Part A," National Center for Health Statistics, Hyattsville, MD, 1996, Table 1-4; 1950-1975 data from National Center for Health Statistics, "Monthly Vital Statistics Report," Volume 31, No. 13, 1983, Table 6; and data prior to 1950 from Bogue, Donald, "The Population of the United States," The Free Press, New York, 1985, Table 5-4.

Figure 4-4. Sex Differentials in Mortality, by Race: 1940 and 1990

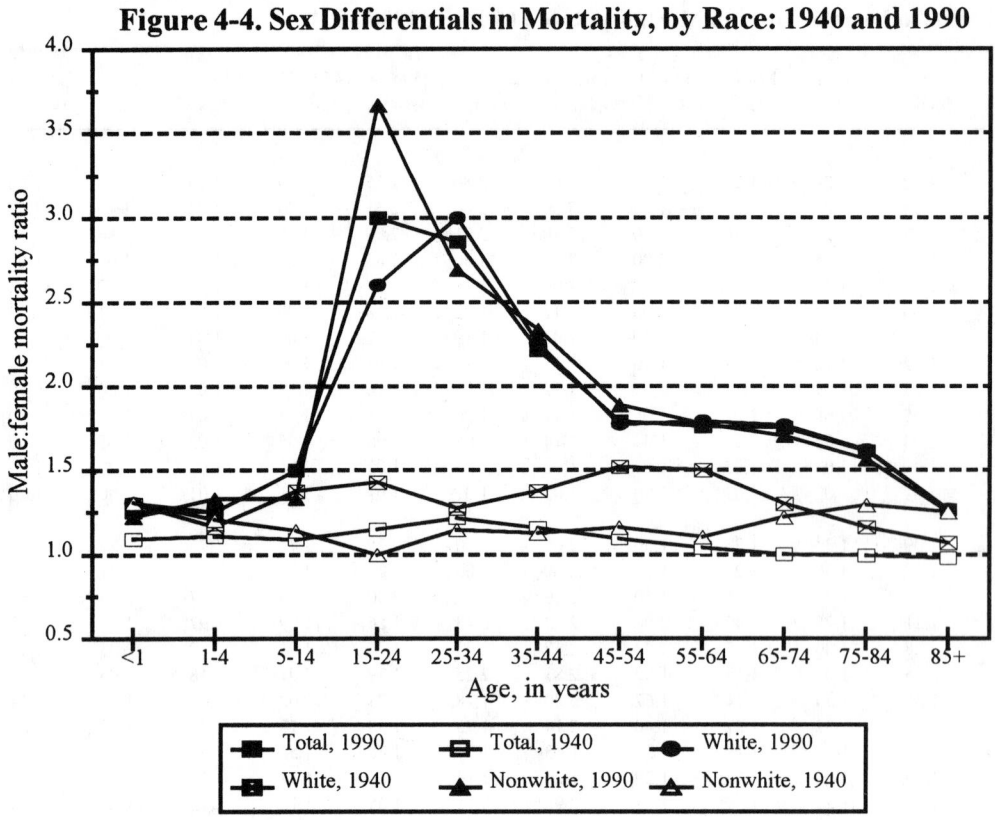

Source: 1940 and 1990 National Center for Health Statistics data.

over this later era: while this group's mortality had declined by only about 10 percent from 1900 to 1940 (from 123.3 to 112.0), it dropped to only about half of the 1940 level (to 66.9) by 1980.

Recent Declines in
Age-Specific Mortality, 1980-91

During both the 1900-1940 and 1940-80 periods, children and young and middle-aged adults experienced the greatest declines in their risks of death. This was unexpected, in a way, because the age groups between 1 and 54 years already had the lowest death rates in 1900. Yet by the 1980-91 era, this pattern changed: those aged under one year to 24 years had the largest declines in death rates, followed by those aged 45 to 84 years. Those at ages 25-44 had little or no decline in death over this decade.

Age Patterns of Mortality
Differentials by Sex and Race

In all low-mortality nations, the death rate of males is higher at every age than that of females, although the amount of difference can vary considerably between groups and over time. This sex differential in age-specific mortality is shown in Table 4-6 and graphed in Figure 4-4.

Around 1900, the age-specific mortality rates of men and women were similar at all ages, and the sex ratio of mortality hovered around 1.0. By 1940, with the decline in maternal mortality (see below) and growing death rates from cardiovascular diseases (which afflict more men), the 34-64 year age group of whites had the largest sex differential in mortality. The nonwhite sex ratio of mortality showed only a minor increase between 1900 and 1940, probably because of a very high maternal mortality rate and because nonwhite (at that time almost entirely black) men were confined to unskilled, active jobs that, paradoxically, gave them some measure of protection against cardiovascular disease.

In the half-century after 1940, the sex differential increased greatly at all but the youngest ages for whites and nonwhites. In addition, the largest sex differentials in mortality shifted to younger ages. By 1991, the nonwhite sex differential had climbed to a historic high of 3.83 at age 15-24 years, and the white ratio had risen to 3.00 at age 25-34 years. For both whites and nonwhites, it was at least twice as dangerous to be a male as a female at ages 15-44 after 1985.

Yet the changes in the sex ratios of mortality are not entirely unidirectional. Among whites, the sex ratios peaked during the 1960-75 period for those under 1 year, at 5-24 years, and at 45-74 years. However, the white sex

Figure 4-5. Race Differential in Mortality, by Sex: 1940 and 1990

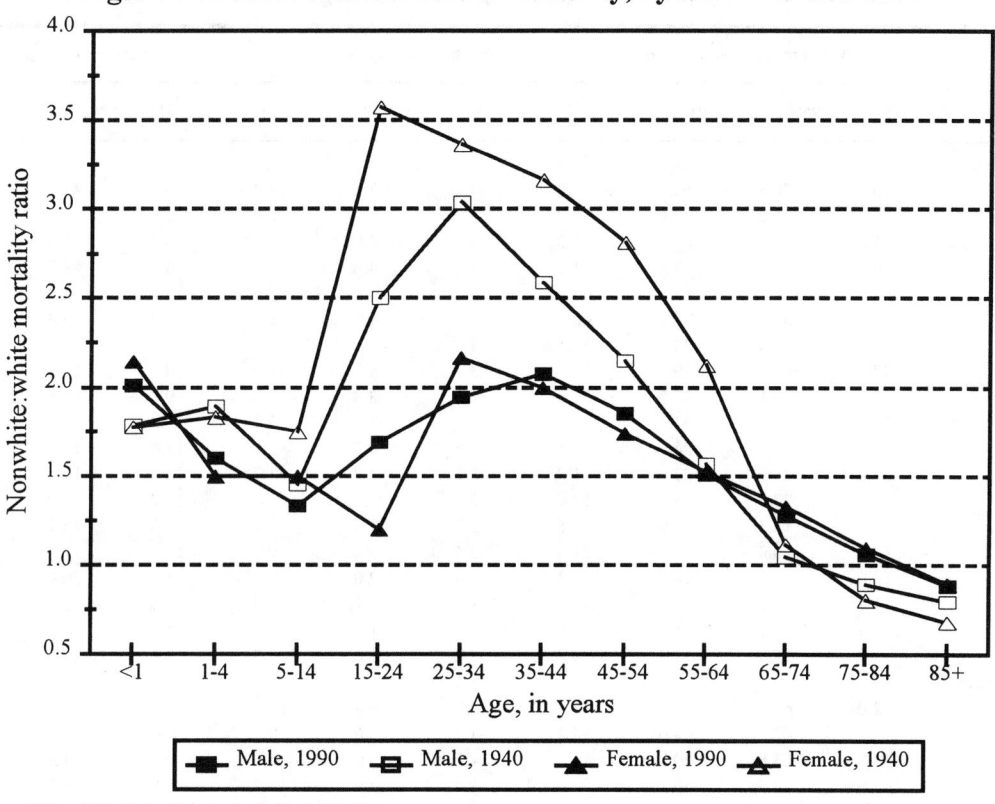

Source: 1940 and 1990 National Center for Health Statistics data.

ratio of mortality appears to be still climbing for those aged 1-4 and 75 years and over. For nonwhites, the peak sex ratio of mortality was reached during 1960-75 for those under 1 year of age, but at all other ages the ratio is continuing to climb.

The race differential (between whites and nonwhites) in mortality has dropped considerably since 1940 (Table 4-4 and Figure 4-5), but it continues to be high. In 1940, nonwhite men and women aged 15-54 years had death rates that were at least twice as high as those of their white counterparts. The ASMR of nonwhite males aged 15-44 years was at least three times that of white males of the same ages.

By 1990, these racial death ratios had declined at most ages, although certain anomalies exist. For example, the ratio of white-to-nonwhite infant deaths has actually risen slightly during the past fifty years, as has the death ratio of those over 65 years. Demographers have debated for many years whether the low mortality rates of nonwhites at the oldest ages in 1940 and other years were not real, but rather were due to exaggeration of ages on death certificates or poor coverage of death registration in the nonwhite population. The latest studies on the so-called "black-white crossover effect" of mortality rates at the oldest ages suggest that it is a statistical fluke rather than a real pattern of mortality.

While considerable media attention is given to the high death rates of young nonwhite men and boys, Figure 4-5 shows that the highest race differential is found among males aged 25-54 years. The "excess mortality" of the twelve-year-old black youth who is shot makes the front page or the eleven o'clock television news; the death of his father from heart disease and his uncle from diabetes will barely make the obituary pages. There is a remarkable similarity in the race differentials in mortality between the two sexes in 1990; yet while both black men and women have made progress on closing the gap with whites over the past fifty years, black women (especially those at age 15-54 years) have gained more ground on white women.

Life Expectancy

The life table technique for analyzing mortality can estimate the average number of years remaining to be lived by any person who has survived to a particular age. Table 4-2 provides data on life expectancy at birth in the United States at selected years between 1900-02 and 1991 for different race-sex groups, but the life table has more specific uses than this aggregate measure of risk of death. It can also answer such questions as, "How many years do black or white men who have just retired on their sixty-fifth birthdays have to live in the state of retirement?" Tables 4-7A

Table 4-7A. Average Number of Years of Life Remaining at Selected Ages, by Sex: All Races, 1900-1991

Age, race, and sex	Average number of years				Absolute change (in years)			Percent change		
	1991	1969-71	1939-41	1900-02	1971-91	1941-71	1902-41	1971-91	1941-71	1902-41
All races, total										
Birth	75.5	70.8	63.6	49.2	4.7	7.2	14.4	6.6	11.3	29.3
1 year	75.2	71.2	65.8	55.2	4.0	5.4	10.6	5.6	8.2	19.2
5 years	71.3	67.4	62.5	55.0	3.9	4.9	7.5	5.8	7.8	13.6
10 years	66.4	62.6	57.8	51.1	3.8	4.8	6.7	6.1	8.3	13.1
15 years	61.5	57.7	53.1	46.8	3.8	4.6	6.3	6.6	8.7	13.5
20 years	56.8	53.0	48.5	42.8	3.8	4.5	5.7	7.2	9.3	13.3
25 years	52.1	48.4	44.1	39.1	3.7	4.3	5.0	7.6	9.8	12.8
30 years	47.4	43.7	39.7	35.5	3.7	4.0	4.2	8.5	10.1	11.8
35 years	42.7	39.1	35.3	31.9	3.6	3.8	3.4	9.2	10.8	10.7
40 years	38.1	34.5	31.0	28.3	3.6	3.5	2.7	10.4	11.3	9.5
45 years	33.6	30.1	26.9	24.8	3.5	3.2	2.1	11.6	11.9	8.5
50 years	29.2	25.9	23.0	21.3	3.3	2.9	1.7	12.7	12.6	8.0
55 years	24.9	22.0	19.3	17.9	2.9	2.7	1.4	13.2	14.0	7.8
60 years	21.0	18.3	15.9	14.8	2.7	2.4	1.1	14.8	15.1	7.4
65 years	17.4	15.0	12.8	11.9	2.4	2.2	0.9	16.0	17.2	7.6
70 years	14.0	12.0	10.0	9.3	2.0	2.0	0.7	16.7	20.0	7.5
75 years	11.1	9.3	7.6	7.1	1.8	1.7	0.5	19.4	22.4	7.0
80 years	8.4	7.1	5.7	5.3	1.3	1.4	0.4	18.3	24.6	7.5
85 years	6.2	5.3	4.3	4.0	0.9	1.0	0.3	17.0	23.3	7.5
All races, male										
Birth	72.0	67.0	61.6	47.9	5.0	5.4	13.7	7.5	8.8	28.6
1 year	71.8	67.6	64.0	54.4	4.2	3.6	9.6	6.2	5.6	17.6
5 years	67.9	63.8	60.8	54.2	4.1	3.0	6.6	6.4	4.9	12.2
10 years	63.0	59.0	56.1	50.4	4.0	2.9	5.7	6.8	5.2	11.3
15 years	58.1	54.1	51.4	46.1	4.0	2.7	5.3	7.4	5.3	11.5
20 years	53.4	49.5	46.9	42.0	3.9	2.6	4.9	7.9	5.5	11.7
25 years	48.9	45.1	42.5	38.4	3.8	2.6	4.1	8.4	6.1	10.7
30 years	44.3	40.5	38.1	34.8	3.8	2.4	3.3	9.4	6.3	9.5
35 years	39.8	36.0	33.8	31.2	3.8	2.2	2.6	10.6	6.5	8.3
40 years	35.3	31.5	29.6	27.7	3.8	1.9	1.9	12.1	6.4	6.9
45 years	30.9	27.2	25.5	24.1	3.7	1.7	1.4	13.6	6.7	5.8
50 years	26.6	23.1	21.7	20.7	3.5	1.4	1.0	15.2	6.5	4.8
55 years	22.5	19.4	18.2	17.4	3.1	1.2	0.8	16.0	6.6	4.6
60 years	18.7	16.0	15.0	14.3	2.7	1.0	0.7	16.9	6.7	4.9
65 years	15.3	13.0	12.1	11.5	2.3	0.9	0.6	17.7	7.4	5.2
70 years	12.2	10.4	9.5	9.0	1.8	0.9	0.5	17.3	9.5	5.6
75 years	9.5	8.1	7.2	6.8	1.4	0.9	0.4	17.3	12.5	5.9
80 years	7.2	6.3	5.4	5.1	0.9	0.9	0.3	14.3	16.7	5.9
85 years	5.3	4.7	4.1	3.8	0.6	0.6	0.3	12.8	14.6	7.9
All races, female										
Birth	78.9	74.6	65.9	50.7	4.3	8.7	15.2	5.8	13.2	30.0
1 year	78.5	75.0	67.7	56.1	3.5	7.3	11.6	4.7	10.8	20.7
5 years	74.7	71.2	64.4	55.8	3.5	6.8	8.6	4.9	10.6	15.4
10 years	69.7	66.3	59.7	51.9	3.4	6.6	7.8	5.1	11.1	15.0
15 years	64.8	61.4	55.0	47.6	3.4	6.4	7.4	5.5	11.6	15.5
20 years	59.9	56.6	50.4	43.6	3.3	6.2	6.8	5.8	12.3	15.6
25 years	55.1	51.8	45.9	39.9	3.3	5.9	6.0	6.4	12.9	15.0
30 years	50.3	47.0	41.4	36.3	3.3	5.6	5.1	7.0	13.5	14.0
35 years	45.5	42.3	37.0	32.7	3.2	5.3	4.3	7.6	14.3	13.1
40 years	40.7	37.6	32.7	29.1	3.1	4.9	3.6	8.2	15.0	12.4
45 years	36.0	33.1	28.5	25.4	2.9	4.6	3.1	8.8	16.1	12.2
50 years	31.5	28.8	24.4	21.8	2.7	4.4	2.6	9.4	18.0	11.9
55 years	27.1	24.6	20.5	18.4	2.5	4.1	2.1	10.2	20.0	11.4
60 years	22.9	20.6	16.9	15.2	2.3	3.7	1.7	11.2	21.9	11.2
65 years	19.1	16.8	13.6	12.2	2.3	3.2	1.4	13.7	23.5	11.5
70 years	15.4	13.4	10.6	9.6	2.0	2.8	1.0	14.9	26.4	10.4
75 years	12.1	10.3	8.0	7.3	1.8	2.3	0.7	17.5	28.8	9.6
80 years	9.1	7.7	6.0	5.5	1.4	1.7	0.5	18.2	28.3	9.1
85 years	6.5	5.6	4.5	4.1	0.9	1.1	0.4	16.1	24.4	9.8

Table 4-7B. Average Number of Years of Life Remaining at Selected Ages, by Sex: White, 1900-1991

Age, race, and sex	Average number of years				Absolute change (in years)			Percent change		
	1991	1969-71	1939-41	1900-02	1971-91	1941-71	1902-41	1971-91	1941-71	1902-41
White, total										
Birth	76.3	71.6	64.9	—	4.7	6.7	—	6.6	10.3	—
1 year	75.9	71.9	66.9	—	4.0	5.0	—	5.6	7.5	—
5 years	72.0	68.1	63.5	—	3.9	4.6	—	5.7	7.2	—
10 years	67.0	63.3	58.8	—	3.7	4.5	—	5.8	7.7	—
15 years	62.1	58.4	54.1	—	3.7	4.3	—	6.3	7.9	—
20 years	57.4	53.7	49.5	—	3.7	4.2	—	6.9	8.5	—
25 years	52.6	49.0	44.9	—	3.6	4.1	—	7.3	9.1	—
30 years	47.9	44.3	40.4	—	3.6	3.9	—	8.1	9.7	—
35 years	43.2	39.6	35.9	—	3.6	3.7	—	9.1	10.3	—
40 years	38.5	35.0	31.5	—	3.5	3.5	—	10.0	11.1	—
45 years	33.9	30.5	27.3	—	3.4	3.2	—	11.1	11.7	—
50 years	29.5	26.2	23.3	—	3.3	2.9	—	12.6	12.4	—
55 years	25.2	22.2	19.5	—	3.0	2.7	—	13.5	13.8	—
60 years	21.2	18.5	16.0	—	2.7	2.5	—	14.6	15.6	—
65 years	17.5	15.1	12.8	—	2.4	2.3	—	15.9	18.0	—
70 years	14.1	12.0	10.0	—	2.1	2.0	—	17.5	20.0	—
75 years	11.1	9.3	7.6	—	1.8	1.7	—	19.4	22.4	—
80 years	8.4	7.0	5.6	—	1.4	1.4	—	20.0	25.0	—
85 years	6.1	5.2	4.2	—	0.9	1.0	—	17.3	23.8	—
White, male										
Birth	72.9	67.9	62.8	48.2	5.0	5.1	14.6	7.4	8.1	30.3
1 year	72.5	68.3	65.0	54.6	4.2	3.3	10.4	6.1	5.1	19.0
5 years	68.7	64.6	61.7	54.4	4.1	2.9	7.3	6.3	4.7	13.4
10 years	63.7	59.7	57.0	50.6	4.0	2.7	6.4	6.7	4.7	12.6
15 years	58.8	54.8	52.3	46.3	4.0	2.5	6.0	7.3	4.8	13.0
20 years	54.1	50.2	47.8	42.2	3.9	2.4	5.6	7.8	5.0	13.3
25 years	49.5	45.7	43.3	38.5	3.8	2.4	4.8	8.3	5.5	12.5
30 years	44.9	41.1	38.8	34.9	3.8	2.3	3.9	9.2	5.9	11.2
35 years	40.3	36.4	34.4	31.3	3.9	2.0	3.1	10.7	5.8	9.9
40 years	35.8	31.9	30.0	27.7	3.9	1.9	2.3	12.2	6.3	8.3
45 years	31.3	27.5	25.9	24.2	3.8	1.6	1.7	13.8	6.2	7.0
50 years	26.9	23.3	22.0	20.8	3.6	1.3	1.2	15.5	5.9	5.8
55 years	22.7	19.5	18.3	17.4	3.2	1.2	0.9	16.4	6.6	5.2
60 years	18.9	16.1	15.1	14.4	2.8	1.0	0.7	17.4	6.6	4.9
65 years	15.4	13.0	12.1	11.5	2.4	0.9	0.6	18.5	7.4	5.2
70 years	12.3	10.4	9.4	9.0	1.9	1.0	0.4	18.3	10.6	4.4
75 years	9.5	8.1	7.2	6.8	1.4	0.9	0.4	17.3	12.5	5.9
80 years	7.2	6.2	5.4	5.1	1.0	0.8	0.3	16.1	14.8	5.9
85 years	5.3	4.6	4.0	3.8	0.7	0.6	0.2	15.2	15.0	5.3
White, female										
Birth	79.6	75.5	67.3	51.1	4.1	8.2	16.2	5.4	12.2	31.7
1 year	79.1	75.7	68.9	56.4	3.4	6.8	12.5	4.5	9.9	22.2
5 years	75.2	71.9	65.6	56.0	3.3	6.3	9.6	4.6	9.6	17.1
10 years	70.2	67.0	60.9	52.2	3.2	6.1	8.7	4.8	10.0	16.7
15 years	65.3	62.1	56.1	47.8	3.2	6.0	8.3	5.2	10.7	17.4
20 years	60.4	57.2	51.4	43.8	3.2	5.8	7.6	5.6	11.3	17.4
25 years	55.6	52.4	46.8	40.1	3.2	5.6	6.7	6.1	12.0	16.7
30 years	50.7	47.6	42.2	36.4	3.1	5.4	5.8	6.5	12.8	15.9
35 years	45.9	42.8	37.7	32.8	3.1	5.1	4.9	7.2	13.5	14.9
40 years	41.1	38.1	33.3	29.2	3.0	4.8	4.1	7.9	14.4	14.0
45 years	36.4	33.5	28.9	25.5	2.9	4.6	3.4	8.7	15.9	13.3
50 years	31.8	29.1	24.7	21.9	2.7	4.4	2.8	9.3	17.8	12.8
55 years	27.3	24.9	20.7	18.4	2.4	4.2	2.3	9.6	20.3	12.5
60 years	23.1	20.8	17.0	15.2	2.3	3.8	1.8	11.1	22.4	11.8
65 years	19.2	16.9	13.6	12.2	2.3	3.3	1.4	13.6	24.3	11.5
70 years	15.5	13.4	10.5	9.6	2.1	2.9	0.9	15.7	27.6	9.4
75 years	12.1	10.2	7.9	7.3	1.9	2.3	0.6	18.6	29.1	8.2
80 years	9.1	7.6	5.9	5.5	1.5	1.7	0.4	19.7	28.8	7.3
85 years	6.5	5.5	4.3	4.1	1.0	1.2	0.2	18.2	27.9	4.9

Table 4-7C. Average Number of Years of Life Remaining at Selected Ages, by Sex: Nonwhite, 1900-1991

Age, race, and sex	Average number of years				Absolute change (in years)			Percent change		
	1991	1969-71	1939-41	1900-02	1971-91	1941-71	1902-41	1971-91	1941-71	1902-41
Nonwhite, total										
Birth	71.5	65.0	—	—	6.5	—	—	10.0	—	—
1 year	71.5	66.0	—	—	5.5	—	—	8.3	—	—
5 years	67.7	62.4	—	—	5.3	—	—	8.5	—	—
10 years	62.8	57.5	—	—	5.3	—	—	9.2	—	—
15 years	57.9	52.7	—	—	5.2	—	—	9.9	—	—
20 years	53.3	48.1	—	—	5.2	—	—	10.8	—	—
25 years	48.7	43.7	—	—	5.0	—	—	11.4	—	—
30 years	44.2	39.4	—	—	4.8	—	—	12.2	—	—
35 years	39.7	35.1	—	—	4.6	—	—	13.1	—	—
40 years	35.4	31.1	—	—	4.3	—	—	13.8	—	—
45 years	31.1	27.2	—	—	3.9	—	—	14.3	—	—
50 years	27.0	23.6	—	—	3.4	—	—	14.4	—	—
55 years	23.1	20.2	—	—	2.9	—	—	14.4	—	—
60 years	19.6	17.2	—	—	2.4	—	—	14.0	—	—
65 years	16.3	14.5	—	—	1.8	—	—	12.4	—	—
70 years	13.3	12.0	—	—	1.3	—	—	10.8	—	—
75 years	10.6	10.1	—	—	0.5	—	—	5.0	—	—
80 years	8.2	8.4	—	—	-0.2	—	—	-2.4	—	—
85 years	6.1	6.6	—	—	-0.5	—	—	-7.6	—	—
Nonwhite, male										
Birth	67.3	61.0	52.3	—	6.3	8.7	—	10.3	16.6	—
1 year	67.4	62.1	56.1	—	5.3	6.0	—	8.5	10.7	—
5 years	63.6	58.5	53.1	—	5.1	5.4	—	8.7	10.2	—
10 years	58.7	53.7	48.5	—	5.0	5.2	—	9.3	10.7	—
15 years	53.8	48.8	44.0	—	5.0	4.8	—	10.2	10.9	—
20 years	49.3	44.4	39.7	—	4.9	4.7	—	11.0	11.8	—
25 years	44.9	40.3	35.9	—	4.6	4.4	—	11.4	12.3	—
30 years	40.6	36.2	32.3	—	4.4	3.9	—	12.2	12.1	—
35 years	36.3	32.2	28.7	—	4.1	3.5	—	12.7	12.2	—
40 years	32.2	28.3	23.2	—	3.9	5.1	—	13.8	22.0	—
45 years	28.1	24.6	22.0	—	3.5	2.6	—	14.2	11.8	—
50 years	24.3	21.2	19.2	—	3.1	2.0	—	14.6	10.4	—
55 years	20.6	18.1	16.7	—	2.5	1.4	—	13.8	8.4	—
60 years	17.3	15.4	14.4	—	1.9	1.0	—	12.3	6.9	—
65 years	14.3	12.9	12.2	—	1.4	0.7	—	10.9	5.7	—
70 years	11.6	10.7	10.1	—	0.9	0.6	—	8.4	5.9	—
75 years	9.2	9.0	8.1	—	0.2	0.9	—	2.2	11.1	—
80 years	7.1	7.6	6.5	—	-0.5	1.1	—	-6.6	16.9	—
85 years	5.4	6.0	5.1	—	-0.6	0.9	—	-10.0	17.6	—
Nonwhite, female										
Birth	75.5	69.1	55.5	—	6.4	13.6	—	9.3	24.5	—
1 year	75.5	70.0	58.5	—	5.5	11.5	—	7.9	19.7	—
5 years	71.7	66.3	55.5	—	5.4	10.8	—	8.1	19.5	—
10 years	66.8	61.5	50.8	—	5.3	10.7	—	8.6	21.1	—
15 years	61.8	56.6	46.2	—	5.2	10.4	—	9.2	22.5	—
20 years	57.0	51.9	42.1	—	5.1	9.8	—	9.8	23.3	—
25 years	52.2	47.2	38.3	—	5.0	8.9	—	10.6	23.2	—
30 years	47.5	42.6	34.5	—	4.9	8.1	—	11.5	23.5	—
35 years	42.8	38.1	30.8	—	4.7	7.3	—	12.3	23.7	—
40 years	38.3	33.9	27.3	—	4.4	6.6	—	13.0	24.2	—
45 years	33.8	29.8	24.0	—	4.0	5.8	—	13.4	24.2	—
50 years	29.4	26.0	21.0	—	3.4	5.0	—	13.1	23.8	—
55 years	25.3	22.4	18.4	—	2.9	4.0	—	12.9	21.7	—
60 years	21.5	19.0	16.1	—	2.5	2.9	—	13.2	18.0	—
65 years	17.9	16.0	14.0	—	1.9	2.0	—	11.9	14.3	—
70 years	14.6	13.3	11.8	—	1.3	1.5	—	9.8	12.7	—
75 years	11.6	11.1	9.8	—	0.5	1.3	—	4.5	13.3	—
80 years	8.8	9.0	8.0	—	-0.2	1.0	—	-2.2	12.5	—
85 years	6.4	7.1	6.4	—	-0.7	0.7	—	-9.9	10.9	—

Table 4-7D. Average Number of Years of Life Remaining at Selected Ages, by Sex: Black, 1900-1991

Age, race, and sex	Average number of years				Absolute change (in years)			Percent change		
	1991	1969-71	1939-41	1900-02	1971-91	1941-71	1902-41	1971-91	1941-71	1902-41
Black, total										
Birth	69.3	64.1	53.9	—	5.2	10.2	—	8.1	18.9	—
1 year	69.5	65.3	57.2	—	4.2	8.1	—	6.4	14.2	—
5 years	65.7	61.6	54.1	—	4.1	7.5	—	6.7	13.9	—
10 years	60.8	56.8	49.5	—	4.0	7.3	—	7.0	14.7	—
15 years	55.9	51.9	44.9	—	4.0	7.0	—	7.7	15.6	—
20 years	51.3	47.3	40.7	—	4.0	6.6	—	8.5	16.2	—
25 years	46.8	43.0	36.9	—	3.8	6.1	—	8.8	16.5	—
30 years	42.3	38.7	33.2	—	3.6	5.5	—	9.3	16.6	—
35 years	38.0	34.5	29.5	—	3.5	5.0	—	10.1	16.9	—
40 years	33.8	30.5	26.1	—	3.3	4.4	—	10.8	16.9	—
45 years	29.7	26.7	22.8	—	3.0	3.9	—	11.2	17.1	—
50 years	25.7	23.1	19.9	—	2.6	3.2	—	11.3	16.1	—
55 years	22.0	19.8	17.4	—	2.2	2.4	—	11.1	13.8	—
60 years	18.6	16.8	15.2	—	1.8	1.6	—	10.7	10.5	—
65 years	15.5	14.2	13.0	—	1.3	1.2	—	9.2	9.2	—
70 years	12.7	11.8	10.9	—	0.9	0.9	—	7.6	8.3	—
75 years	10.2	9.9	9.0	—	0.3	0.9	—	3.0	10.0	—
80 years	7.9	8.2	7.3	—	-0.3	0.9	—	-3.7	12.3	—
85 years	5.9	6.5	5.9	—	-0.6	0.6	—	-9.2	10.2	—
Black, male										
Birth	64.6	60.0	52.3	32.5	4.6	7.7	19.8	7.7	14.7	60.9
1 year	64.9	61.2	55.9	42.5	3.7	5.3	13.4	6.0	9.5	31.5
5 years	61.1	57.6	53.0	45.1	3.5	4.6	7.9	6.1	8.7	17.5
10 years	56.2	52.8	48.3	41.9	3.4	4.5	6.4	6.4	9.3	15.3
15 years	51.3	48.0	43.7	38.3	3.3	4.3	5.4	6.9	9.8	14.1
20 years	46.9	43.5	39.5	35.1	3.4	4.0	4.4	7.8	10.1	12.5
25 years	42.6	39.5	35.7	32.2	3.1	3.8	3.5	7.8	10.6	10.9
30 years	38.4	35.4	32.1	29.3	3.0	3.3	2.8	8.5	10.3	9.6
35 years	34.3	31.4	28.5	26.2	2.9	2.9	2.3	9.2	10.2	8.8
40 years	30.3	27.6	25.1	23.1	2.7	2.5	2.0	9.8	10.0	8.7
45 years	26.4	24.0	21.9	20.1	2.4	2.1	1.8	10.0	9.6	9.0
50 years	22.7	20.7	19.1	17.3	2.0	1.6	1.8	9.7	8.4	10.4
55 years	19.3	17.7	16.6	14.7	1.6	1.1	1.9	9.0	6.6	12.9
60 years	16.2	14.9	14.4	12.6	1.3	0.5	1.8	8.7	3.5	14.3
65 years	13.4	12.5	12.2	10.4	0.9	0.3	1.8	7.2	2.5	17.3
70 years	10.9	10.4	10.1	8.3	0.5	0.3	1.8	4.8	3.0	21.7
75 years	8.7	8.8	8.2	6.6	-0.1	0.6	1.6	-1.1	7.3	24.2
80 years	6.7	7.4	6.6	5.1	-0.7	0.8	1.5	-9.5	12.1	29.4
85 years	5.1	5.9	5.3	4.0	-0.8	0.6	1.3	-13.6	11.3	32.5
Black, female										
Birth	73.8	68.3	55.6	35.0	5.5	12.7	20.6	8.1	22.8	58.9
1 year	73.9	69.4	58.5	43.5	4.5	10.9	15.0	6.5	18.6	34.5
5 years	70.1	65.7	55.4	46.0	4.4	10.3	9.4	6.7	18.6	20.4
10 years	65.2	60.9	50.8	43.0	4.3	10.1	7.8	7.1	19.9	18.1
15 years	60.3	56.0	46.1	39.8	4.3	9.9	6.3	7.7	21.5	15.8
20 years	55.4	51.2	42.0	36.9	4.2	9.2	5.1	8.2	21.9	13.8
25 years	50.7	46.6	38.2	33.9	4.1	8.4	4.3	8.8	22.0	12.7
30 years	46.0	42.0	34.4	30.7	4.0	7.6	3.7	9.5	22.1	12.1
35 years	41.4	37.6	30.8	27.5	3.8	6.8	3.3	10.1	22.1	12.0
40 years	36.9	33.3	27.2	24.7	3.6	6.1	2.5	10.8	22.4	10.1
45 years	32.5	29.3	23.9	21.4	3.2	5.4	2.5	10.9	22.6	11.7
50 years	28.3	25.5	21.0	18.7	2.8	4.5	2.3	11.0	21.4	12.3
55 years	24.3	22.0	18.4	15.9	2.3	3.6	2.5	10.5	19.6	15.7
60 years	20.6	18.7	16.1	13.6	1.9	2.6	2.5	10.2	16.1	18.4
65 years	17.2	15.7	14.0	11.4	1.5	1.7	2.6	9.6	12.1	22.8
70 years	14.1	13.0	11.8	9.6	1.1	1.2	2.2	8.5	10.2	22.9
75 years	11.2	10.9	9.8	7.9	0.3	1.1	1.9	2.8	11.2	24.1
80 years	8.6	8.9	8.0	6.5	-0.3	0.9	1.5	-3.4	11.3	23.1
85 years	6.3	7.0	6.4	5.1	-0.7	0.6	1.3	-10.0	9.4	25.5

Source: National Center for Health Statistics, "Vital Statistics of the United States: 1991, Volume II--Mortality Part A," National Center for Health Statistics, Hyattsville, MD, 1996, Table 6-4.

through 4-7D provide such information. If a white man (Table 4-7B) retired at age 65 in 1991, he could expect to live another 15.4 years. His black counterpart (Table 4-7D) could expect to live only 13.4 years, or two years less. If they had retired in the 1969-71 period at age 65, the gap between years of expected retirement for the black and white worker was only six months (12.5 versus 13.0 years of life after age 65, respectively).

Comparisons of life expectancy by race and sex between 1900-02 and 1991 (see the banks of columns titled "Absolute change (in years)" and "Relative change (in percent)" in Tables 4-7A through 4-7D) show twentieth-century U.S. mortality trends. The absolute change measured here is the number of years of life expectancy added to the person entering the age group between each historical period; the relative change measures the percentage increase in years of life expectancy between each period. Overall, the following trends are found:

1. The U.S. twentieth century mortality decline was not a process whereby each age group continuously benefitted from advances in life expectancy in each era. It was, rather, the sum of a variety of rapidly-diffusing medical advances (including new drugs, immunizations and surgical procedures) and public health efforts that vanquished specific diseases or ailments that often had very age-specific effects.

2. Early in this century, survival of the first year of life added greatly to life expectancy, but slower post-1941 declines in infant mortality have resulted in smaller gains in life expectancy at birth.

3. During the first four decades of this century the largest gains in life expectancy for men (Table 4-7A) resulted from control of death at younger ages (below 25 years). The 1941-71 period saw particular gains in life expectancy for the youngest and oldest men. From 1971-1991, male life expectancy gains have been concentrated among the middle-aged and especially the "young old" (those at ages 65-75 years).

4. Females of all ages showed some improvements in life expectancy in the 1902-41 period, especially those under age 5. Their annual rate of improvement in life expectancy sped up during the thirty years between 1941 and 1971; their gains at all ages over age 50 were particularly striking. During the two decades after 1971 their rate of improvement slackened somewhat, especially at the younger ages (here it resembles that of men during the 1971-91 period).

5. During 1902-41 and 1941-71, women's gains in longevity surpassed those of men, but in the most recent period men made slightly larger gains. Black women's gains surpassed those of black men in all three periods.

6. The comparative gains in life expectancy of the white versus black populations present a complex picture. During the 1902-41 period, black men and women gained more than whites; older blacks made particularly robust gains. (Of course, blacks were starting from a much lower level of life expectancy.) Younger black men (up to age 50 years) did better than younger whites during 1941-71, but among women, younger blacks (age 50 and under) and older whites (above age 50) gained more. In 1971-91, black men aged 25 years and above lagged behind the improvement in life expectancy shown by white males (especially at age 70 and above), and black females did better at age 55 years and below than did white females, and worse at older ages.

The two most recent periods (1941-71 and 1971-91) have not shown a uniform convergence of black on white life expectancy (that is, a higher percentage change for blacks than whites at every age group in each period). In the most recent period, the key racial gap in improvement of male life expectancy is not among teenagers and young adults, but among the middle-aged. We are not "losing a generation of young black men," at least in terms of aggregate mortality; we are losing middle-aged black men, who are failing to increase their longevity at the same rate as that of middle-aged white men.

7. In the 1900-02 and 1969-71 life tables, it appeared that life expectancy for blacks or nonwhites was lower than that for whites until about age seventy-five; thereafter, life expectancy was greater for black or nonwhite populations. By the 1991 life table, life expectancy was greater at all ages for white men or women than for their black or nonwhite counterparts. Current research suggests that the earlier finding of higher black or nonwhite than white longevity at age 75 and over (the black/white mortality crossover effect) may be an artifact of poor reporting of nonwhite or black deaths.

8. The sex differential persists at all ages. Although it declines in absolute size with advancing age, the relative differential (percentage difference) increases.

Life Expectancy at Birth in the 1990s

Between 1991 and the present, movement toward increasing life expectancy at birth has largely stalled for women but continues to increase moderately for men. The provisional life expectancy at birth estimates for 1995 (based on 90 percent of all death statistics) are 73.4 years for white men (versus 72.9 years in 1991), 79.6 years for white women (79.6 years in 1991), 65.4 years for black men (64.6 years in 1991), and 74.0 years for black women (73.8 years in 1991). The increase of almost a year in black male life expectancy at birth over the 1991-95 period is particularly striking given that this group's young adults were suffering from high mortality rates from HIV and homicide in the early 1990s. The lack of progress in increasing life expectancy among white women in the early 1990s is almost certainly not due to HIV infection, since this group has a low incidence of this disease (Table 7-8).

Table 4-8. Age-adjusted Death Rates[1] for 72 Selected Causes, by Race and Sex: 1991

Cause of death	All races			White		
	Total	Male	Female	Total	Male	Female
All causes	513.7	669.9	386.5	486.8	634.4	366.3
Shigellosis and amebiasis	...	...	...	...	...	...
Certain other intestinal infections	0.1	0.1	0.1	0.1	0.1	0.1
Tuberculosis	0.5	0.7	0.3	0.3	0.4	0.2
Tuberculosis of respiratory system	0.4	0.5	0.2	0.2	0.3	0.1
Other tuberculosis	0.1	0.1	0.1	0.1	0.1	0.1
Whooping cough	...	...	...	...	...	...
Streptoccocal sore throat, scarlatina, and erysipelas	...	...	...	...	...	...
Meningococcal infection	0.1	0.1	0.1	0.1	0.1	0.1
Septicemia	4.1	4.7	3.6	3.5	4.1	3.1
Acute poliomyelitis	...	...	...	...	...	...
Measles	...	...	...	...	...	...
Viral hepatitis	0.6	0.8	0.4	0.5	0.7	0.3
Syphilis	...	...	...	...	...	...
All other infectious and parasitic diseases	13.3	22.8	4.2	10.7	19.0	2.6
Malignant neoplasms, including neoplasms of lymphatic and hematopoietic tissues	134.5	165.0	112.6	131.3	159.5	111.2
Malignant neoplasms of lip, oral cavity, and pharynx	2.4	3.7	1.3	2.1	3.2	1.2
Malignant neoplasms of digestive organs and peritoneum	29.9	38.7	23.0	28.4	36.7	21.8
Malignant neoplasms of respiratory and intrathoracic organs	41.1	60.1	26.5	40.5	58.1	26.8
Malignant neoplasm of breast	12.4	0.1	22.7	12.2	0.1	22.5
Malignant neoplasms of genital organs	13.6	17.1	12.2	12.8	15.7	11.8
Malignant neoplasms of urinary organs	5.1	7.8	3.1	5.2	8.0	3.1
Malignant neoplasms of all other and unspecified sites	17.0	21.4	13.6	17.2	21.5	13.7
Leukemia	5.0	6.3	3.9	5.0	6.3	4.0
Other malignant neoplasms of lymphatic and hematopoietic tissues	7.9	9.8	6.4	7.9	9.8	6.4
Benign neoplasms, carcinoma in situ, and neoplasms of uncertain behavior and of unspecified nature	1.7	1.9	1.5	1.6	1.9	1.5
Diabetes mellitus	11.8	12.6	11.1	10.5	11.5	9.6
Nutritional deficiencies	0.5	0.5	0.4	0.4	0.4	0.4
Anemia	0.9	1.0	0.8	0.7	0.7	0.6
Meningitis	0.3	0.3	0.3	0.2	0.3	0.2
Major cardiovascular diseases	185.0	243.6	138.5	177.2	235.9	130.4
Diseases of the heart	148.2	201.0	106.3	143.1	196.1	100.7
Rheumatic fever and rheumatic heart disease	1.4	1.1	1.7	1.4	1.1	1.7
Hypertensive heart disease	4.7	5.5	4.1	3.5	4.1	3.0
Hypertensive heart and renal disease	0.5	0.5	0.4	0.3	0.4	0.3
Ischemic heart disease	99.1	138.7	68.0	98.8	139.7	66.4
Acute myocardial infarction	51.5	72.5	34.8	51.4	73.2	34.0
Other acute and subacute forms of ischemic heart disease	0.8	1.2	0.5	0.8	1.2	0.4
Angina pectoris	0.2	0.2	0.2	0.2	0.2	0.2
Old myocardial infarction and other forms of chronic ischemic heart disease	46.6	64.7	32.6	46.4	65.1	31.8
Other diseases of endocardium	2.5	3.0	2.2	2.5	3.0	2.2
All other forms of heart disease	39.9	52.2	29.9	36.5	47.9	27.1
Hypertension with or without renal disease	1.9	2.2	1.8	1.5	1.7	1.3
Cerebrovascular diseases	26.8	29.4	24.7	24.7	26.9	22.8
Intracerebral and other intracranial hemorrhage	5.1	5.8	4.5	4.3	4.9	3.9
Cerebral thrombosis and unspecified occlusion of cerebral arteries	2.9	3.3	2.6	2.8	3.1	2.5
Cerebral embolism	0.1	0.1	0.1	0.1	0.1	0.1
All other and late effects of cerebrovascular diseases	18.6	20.2	17.5	17.4	18.7	16.4
Atherosclerosis	2.6	3.0	2.2	2.6	3.0	2.2
Other diseases of arteries, arterioles, and capillaries	5.4	8.0	3.5	5.4	8.2	3.3
Acute bronchitis and bronchiolitis	0.1	0.2	0.1	0.1	0.1	0.1
Pneumonia and influenza	13.4	17.5	10.6	12.8	16.6	10.2
Pneumonia	13.2	17.3	10.4	12.5	16.4	10.0
Influenza	0.2	0.2	0.2	0.2	0.2	0.2

Table 4-8. Age-adjusted Death Rates[1] for 72 Selected Causes, by Race and Sex: 1991 (continued)

Cause of death	All races			White		
	Total	Male	Female	Total	Male	Female
Chronic obstructive pulmonary diseases and allied conditions	20.1	27.0	15.5	20.6	27.4	16.1
Bronchitis, chronic and unspecified	0.8	1.0	0.6	0.8	1.0	0.7
Emphysema	3.8	5.2	2.8	4.0	5.4	3.0
Asthma	1.5	1.3	1.6	1.2	1.0	1.4
Other chronic obstructive pulmonary diseases and allied conditions	14.1	19.4	10.5	14.5	19.9	11.1
Ulcer of stomach and duodenum	1.2	1.6	1.0	1.2	1.5	1.0
Appendicitis	0.1	0.1	0.1	0.1	0.1	0.1
Hernia of abdominal cavity and intestinal obstruction without mention of hernia	1.1	1.2	1.1	1.0	1.0	1.0
Chronic liver disease and cirrhosis	8.3	11.7	5.2	7.8	11.2	4.8
Cholelithiasis and other disorders of gallbladder	0.5	0.6	0.5	0.5	0.6	0.5
Nephritis, nephrotic syndrome, and nephrosis	4.3	5.4	3.5	3.7	4.7	3.0
Acute glomerulonephritis and nephrotic syndrome	0.1	0.1	...	...	0.1	...
Chronic glomerulonephritis, nephritis and nephropathy, not specified as acute or chronic, and renal sclerosis, unspecified	0.3	0.4	0.3	0.3	0.3	0.2
Renal failure, disorders resulting from impaired renal function, and small kidney of unknown cause	3.9	4.9	3.2	3.3	4.3	2.7
Infections of kidney	0.2	0.2	0.3	0.2	0.2	0.2
Hyperplasia of prostate	0.1	0.2	...	0.1	0.2	...
Complications of pregnancy, childbirth, and the puerperium	0.1	...	0.2	0.1	...	0.2
Pregnancy with abortive outcome	...	...	...	...	...	...
Other complications of pregnancy, childbirth, and the puerperium	0.1	...	0.2	0.1	...	0.2
Congenital anomalies	4.7	5.1	4.3	4.6	5.0	4.2
Certain conditions originating in the perinatal period	6.4	7.2	5.7	4.9	5.5	4.3
Birth trauma, intrauterine hypoxia, birth asphyxia, and respiratory distress syndrome	1.3	1.5	1.1	1.1	1.3	0.9
Other conditions originating in the perinatal period	5.1	5.6	4.6	3.8	4.2	3.4
Symptoms, signs, and ill-defined conditions	7.2	9.1	5.3	6.2	8.0	4.5
All other diseases (residual)	38.5	45.9	32.5	36.2	43.2	30.6
Accidents and adverse effects	31.0	45.3	17.2	30.3	43.9	17.0
Motor vehicle accidents	17.0	24.1	10.1	17.2	24.2	10.4
All other accidents and adverse effects	13.9	21.2	7.2	13.0	19.7	6.6
Suicide	11.4	18.8	4.3	12.1	19.9	4.8
Homicide and legal intervention	10.9	17.3	4.5	6.2	9.4	3.0
All other external causes	0.9	1.4	0.5	0.9	1.2	0.5

Age- and Cause-Specific Mortality Rates

Since death results from many different diseases or events, an understanding of mortality levels and trends requires a subdivision of the death rate into causes. With such cause-specific death rates (see Definitions Box), it is possible to disaggregate the crude death rate and the age-specific death rate into cause-of-death components. U.S. vital statistics of death are reported by cause-of-death categories according to the International Statistical Classification of Diseases, Injuries and Causes of Death. (This classification system is revised periodically, which affects comparability; the most recent revision was for 1979—see Technical Appendix 2-2). Table 4-8 is a report of the rate of death per 100,000 population in 1991 from each of seventy-two cause-of-death categories. The data for 1991 are reported not only for the total population but also by sex and race. Although the list of disease categories is lengthy, the rates for most of them are quite low.

Table 4-8 shows that the overall population is most at risk from two major forms of death: various forms of cancer, and cardiovascular disease, especially diseases of the heart. As can be seen from Figure 4-6, the rate of incidence of all of the major causes of death in 1991 had a curvilinear relationship with age (except for malignant neoplasms): the very young and the old were most at risk. For four major causes of death (diseases of the heart, malignant neoplasms, cerebrovascular diseases, and chronic obstructive pulmonary diseases) there was a striking increase in the incidence of the cause of death from late childhood (ages 5-14, usually the safest age) to the elderly years.

Since the U.S. population is aging rapidly, and since we all must eventually die of some cause ("old age" is not a cause of death), it is not surprising that causes of death found primarily among the elderly (cancer and cardiovascular disease) predominate. Yet it is a more difficult task to

Table 4-8. Age-adjusted Death Rates[1] for 72 Selected Causes, by Race and Sex: 1991 (continued)

Cause of death	All other					
	Total			Black		
	Total	Male	Female	Total	Male	Female
All causes	672.8	890.2	502.1	780.7	1,048.8	575.1
Shigellosis and amebiasis	...	...	...	...	...	...
Certain other intestinal infections	0.2	0.2	0.2	0.2	0.3	0.2
Tuberculosis	1.8	2.6	1.1	2.0	3.0	1.2
Tuberculosis of respiratory system	1.3	2.1	0.8	1.5	2.5	0.8
Other tuberculosis	0.4	0.5	0.4	0.5	0.5	0.4
Whooping cough	...	...	...	...	...	...
Streptoccocal sore throat, scarlatina, and erysipelas	...	...	...	...	...	...
Meningococcal infection	0.1	...	...	0.1	...	...
Septicemia	8.0	9.6	6.7	9.5	11.6	7.9
Acute poliomyelitis	...	...	...	...	...	...
Measles	...	...	...	...	...	...
Viral hepatitis	0.9	1.2	0.7	0.7	0.9	0.6
Syphilis	0.1	0.1	0.1	0.1	0.2	0.1
All other infectious and parasitic diseases	27.3	44.9	12.1	35.5	58.9	15.6
Malignant neoplasms, including neoplasms of lymphatic and hematopoietic tissues	156.7	207.4	121.2	179.3	242.4	136.3
Malignant neoplasms of lip, oral cavity, and pharynx	3.9	6.6	1.7	4.5	7.8	2.0
Malignant neoplasms of digestive organs and peritoneum	40.8	54.1	30.9	45.0	60.6	33.7
Malignant neoplasms of respiratory and intrathoracic organs	45.2	74.1	23.9	52.9	88.4	27.4
Malignant neoplasm of breast	13.5	0.2	23.8	15.8	0.3	27.6
Malignant neoplasms of genital organs	20.0	29.3	14.8	23.3	35.7	16.6
Malignant neoplasms of urinary organs	4.7	6.6	3.3	5.3	7.7	3.7
Malignant neoplasms of all other and unspecified sites	16.1	20.7	12.7	18.3	24.2	14.0
Leukemia	4.4	5.6	3.5	4.8	6.3	3.8
Other malignant neoplasms of lymphatic and hematopoietic tissues	8.1	10.1	6.6	9.2	11.6	7.5
Benign neoplasms, carcinoma in situ, and neoplasms of uncertain behavior and of unspecified nature	1.9	2.2	1.8	2.3	2.6	2.1
Diabetes mellitus	21.7	20.8	22.2	25.4	24.6	25.7
Nutritional deficiencies	0.7	1.0	0.6	0.8	1.1	0.6
Anemia	2.1	2.3	1.9	2.5	2.8	2.3
Meningitis	0.6	0.7	0.5	0.7	0.8	0.6
Major cardiovascular diseases	237.0	297.5	191.4	272.9	345.4	219.8
Diseases of the heart	182.2	234.0	143.1	210.9	272.7	165.5
Rheumatic fever and rheumatic heart disease	1.3	1.0	1.5	1.3	1.1	1.5
Hypertensive heart disease	13.8	16.1	11.8	16.9	20.3	14.2
Hypertensive heart and renal disease	1.6	1.7	1.5	1.9	2.2	1.8
Ischemic heart disease	99.0	127.6	77.6	112.0	144.5	88.3
Acute myocardial infarction	51.1	65.8	40.1	57.9	74.6	45.8
Other acute and subacute forms of ischemic heart disease	1.1	1.6	0.8	1.3	1.9	0.9
Angina pectoris	0.2	0.2	0.2	0.2	0.2	0.3
Old myocardial infarction and other forms of chronic ischemic heart disease	46.6	60.0	36.5	52.5	67.8	41.4
Other diseases of endocardium	2.1	2.5	1.7	2.4	2.8	2.0
All other forms of heart disease	64.5	85.0	49.0	76.4	101.9	57.7
Hypertension with or without renal disease	5.2	5.6	4.8	63.0	6.9	5.8
Cerebrovascular diseases	41.7	48.2	36.9	46.8	54.9	41.0
Intracerebral and other intracranial hemorrhage	9.6	11.8	7.9	10.5	13.0	8.6
Cerebral thrombosis and unspecified occlusion of cerebral arteries	4.2	5.1	3.5	4.8	5.8	4.0
Cerebral embolism	0.1	0.2	0.1	0.2	0.2	0.1
All other and late effects of cerebrovascular diseases	27.8	31.2	25.3	31.4	35.8	28.3
Atherosclerosis	2.5	3.0	2.3	2.9	3.5	2.5
Other diseases of arteries, arterioles, and capillaries	5.3	6.7	4.3	6.0	7.4	5.0
Acute bronchitis and bronchiolitis	0.1	0.2	0.1	0.1	0.2	0.1
Pneumonia and influenza	16.8	23.2	12.2	18.7	26.2	13.5
Pneumonia	16.7	23.1	12.1	18.5	26.0	13.4
Influenza	0.1	0.2	0.1	0.1	0.1	0.1

Table 4-8. Age-adjusted Death Rates[1] for 72 Selected Causes, by Race and Sex: 1991 (continued)

	All other					
	Total			Black		
Cause of death	Total	Male	Female	Total	Male	Female
Chronic obstructive pulmonary diseases and allied conditions	15.2	22.8	10.1	17.1	25.9	11.3
Bronchitis, chronic and unspecified	0.6	0.9	0.4	0.6	1.0	0.4
Emphysema	2.1	3.5	1.1	2.3	3.9	1.2
Asthma	3.0	3.0	3.0	3.5	3.5	3.5
Other chronic obstructive pulmonary diseases and allied conditions	9.5	15.4	5.6	10.6	17.5	6.2
Ulcer of stomach and duodenum	1.5	2.1	1.1	1.6	2.2	1.1
Appendicitis	0.1	0.2	0.1	0.2	0.3	0.1
Hernia of abdominal cavity and intestinal obstruction without mention of hernia	1.6	2.0	1.4	1.9	2.3	1.6
Chronic liver disease and cirrhosis	10.7	15.0	7.3	12.3	17.4	8.2
Cholelithiasis and other disorders of gallbladder	0.6	0.6	0.7	0.7	0.6	0.7
Nephritis, nephrotic syndrome, and nephrosis	8.8	10.6	7.4	10.3	12.8	8.6
Acute glomerulonephritis and nephrotic syndrome	0.1	0.1	0.1	0.2	0.2	0.2
Chronic glomerulonephritis, nephritis and nephropathy, not specified as acute or chronic, and renal sclerosis, unspecified	0.6	0.8	0.6	0.7	0.9	0.6
Renal failure, disorders resulting from impaired renal function, and small kidney of unknown cause	8.0	9.7	6.7	9.4	11.7	7.8
Infections of kidney	0.3	0.3	0.4	0.4	0.3	0.4
Hyperplasia of prostate	0.1	0.3	...	0.1	0.3	...
Complications of pregnancy, childbirth, and the puerperium	0.3	...	0.6	0.4	...	0.8
Pregnancy with abortive outcome	0.1	...	0.1	0.1	...	0.2
Other complications of pregnancy, childbirth, and the puerperium	0.3	...	0.5	0.3	...	0.6
Congenital anomalies	5.0	5.4	4.5	5.5	6.2	5.0
Certain conditions originating in the perinatal period	11.7	13.0	10.2	14.8	16.6	12.9
Birth trauma, intrauterine hypoxia, birth asphyxia, and respiratory distress syndrome	2.1	2.4	1.8	2.7	3.1	2.2
Other conditions originating in the perinatal period	9.6	10.6	8.5	12.1	13.6	10.7
Symptoms, signs, and ill-defined conditions	11.9	15.1	9.1	14.2	18.4	10.8
All other diseases (residual)	52.1	63.8	43.2	61.1	75.9	50.1
Accidents and adverse effects	35.3	54.3	18.7	38.9	61.0	19.9
Motor vehicle accidents	16.3	24.7	8.9	16.8	26.2	8.7
All other accidents and adverse effects	19.0	29.7	9.8	22.0	34.8	11.2
Suicide	6.9	12.1	2.3	6.9	12.5	1.9
Homicide and legal intervention	33.3	56.7	11.5	41.9	72.5	13.9
All other external causes	1.3	2.0	0.7	1.6	2.4	0.9

[1] Per 100,000 U.S. standard million population.

Source: National Center for Health Statistics, "Vital Statistics of the United States: 1991, Volume II--Mortality Part A," National Center for Health Statistics, Hyattsville, MD, 1996, Table 1-8.

show whether individuals are now at higher risk from these diseases than in the past. As other causes of death declined, perhaps more people do die from these diseases, but at much older ages. On the other hand, perhaps twentieth-century changes in nutrition, exercise, smoking or exposure to environmental carcinogens have led to increases in deaths from causes such as cancer or heart disease.

In order to standardize and summarize the risks from various diseases, mortality specialists who wish to compare the same population at two points in time (or populations with different age distributions) apply the age-specific risks of death to a standard population. In this way an estimate of the force of mortality from each cause of death can be obtained that is relatively uncontaminated by differences in age composition. In Table 4-8, such a standard population is used to take into account the different age distributions of the racial groups in the U.S. in 1993, and in Table 4-9, it is used to control for the differential age distribution of the U.S. population between 1950 and 1993.

Trends in Major Causes of Death

The age-adjusted death rates are presented in Table 4-9, and show that between 1950 and 1993, the risk of death for all races and both sexes has dropped from 840.5 to 513.3 (per 100,000 population per year), or 38.9 percent. These age-adjusted death rates (and the more specific

Figure 4-6. Profile of Selected Age-specific Causes of Death: 1991

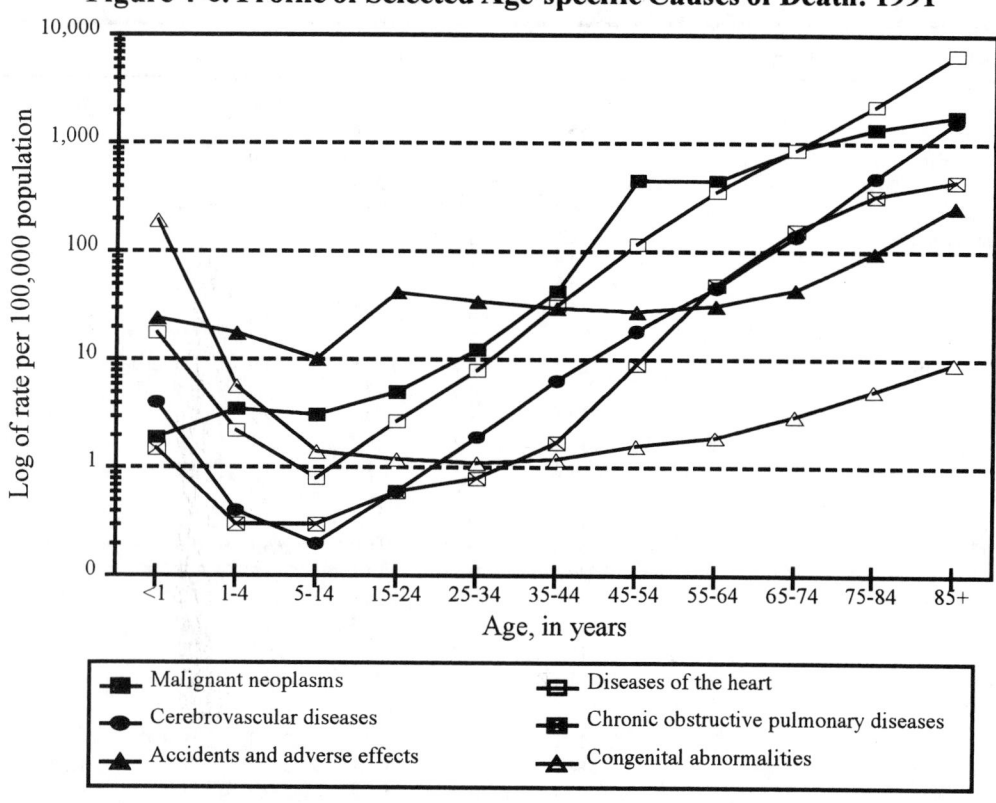

Source: 1991 National Center for Health Statistics data.

cause-of-death categories given in Table 4-8) can help us to examine the major trends in groups of causes of death over the past several decades:

Infectious and Parasitic Diseases: Many of these diseases have been reduced to very low levels of incidence, or else modern medicine has greatly reduced their ability to kill their victims. Such diseases as dysentery, measles, pertussis (whooping cough), typhoid, diphtheria, poliomyelitis, and meningitis, once major killers (especially of children), now account for less than 1 percent of all deaths. Immunization, antibiotics, improved sanitation and public health, and improved levels of nutrition and living standards have been responsible for the great decline in this category of disease. Overall, about 4 percent of all deaths are due to infectious and parasitic diseases, including all those listed in Table 4-8 through "all other infectious and parasitic diseases." Two of these diseases stand out: septicemia (4.1 deaths per 100,000) and tuberculosis (0.5). Septicemia can result from a number of sources, including food poisoning (such as from salmonella), from hospital wound infections (such as Staphylococcus aureus), or from streptococcal infections. Those with compromised immune systems or liver damage (often due to alcohol or drug abuse) are at risk for septicemia. Compared to the rate of death from septicemia among the

general population, the death rate is almost twice as high for black women and more than three times as high among black men.

Tuberculosis, particularly drug-resistant tuberculosis, staged a comeback in the United States between 1985 and 1992. This upsurge was linked to the growth of the population that was homeless (and frequently housed in large, crowded shelters) or in overcrowded prisons. The growth of the AIDS epidemic and an influx of immigrants and visitors from nations where tuberculosis is still common had an effect on this scourge of early industrialized nations. The tuberculosis death rate was six times as high among black men (3.0 per 100,00) as in the general population. Elevated rates of tuberculosis have also been found among those in health care occupations, funeral directors, and those whose occupation brings them into contact with silica.

Human Immunodeficiency Virus (HIV) Infection: Since the coding and classification of this cause of death only began in 1987, it is not listed among the usual 72 Selected Causes of Death (Table 4-8); however, its 1990 and 1993 mortality rates are given in Table 4-9. As will be shown in Chapter 7, its counterpart, Acquired Immunodeficiency Syndrome (AIDS), grew rapidly in the U.S. during the 1980s (Table 7-8) and is now well-established throughout the nation (Table 7-9), even in rural areas. Between

Table 4-9. Age-adjusted Death Rates[1] for Selected Causes of Death, by Sex and Race: 1950-1993

Sex, race, and cause of death	1993	1990	1985	1980	1970	1960[2]	1950[2]
All races, both sexes, all causes	513.3	520.2	548.9	585.8	714.3	760.9	840.5
Natural causes	459.7	465.1	493.0	519.7	636.9	695.2	766.6
Diseases of heart	145.3	152.0	181.4	202.0	253.6	286.2	307.2
Ischemic heart disease	94.9	102.6	126.1	149.8	—	—	—
Cerebrovascular diseases	26.5	27.7	32.5	40.8	66.3	79.7	88.6
Malignant neoplasms	132.6	135.0	134.4	132.8	129.8	125.8	125.3
Respiratory system	40.8	41.4	39.1	36.4	28.4	19.2	12.8
Colorectal	12.9	13.6	14.9	15.5	16.8	17.7	19.0
Prostate[3]	16.4	16.7	14.7	14.4	13.3	13.1	13.4
Breast[3]	21.5	23.1	23.3	22.7	23.1	22.3	22.2
Chronic obstructive pulmonary diseases	21.4	19.7	18.8	15.9	13.2	8.2	4.4
Pneumonia and influenza	13.5	14.0	13.5	12.9	22.1	28.0	26.2
Chronic liver disease and cirrhosis	7.9	8.6	9.7	12.2	14.7	10.5	8.5
Diabetes mellitus	12.4	11.7	9.7	10.1	14.1	13.6	14.3
Nephritis, nephrotic syndrome, and nephrosis	4.5	4.3	4.9	4.5	—	—	—
Septicemia	4.1	4.1	4.1	2.6	—	—	—
Human immunodeficiency virus infection	13.8	9.8	—	—	—	—	—
External causes	53.6	55.1	55.9	66.1	77.4	65.7	73.9
Unintentional injuries	30.3	32.5	34.8	42.3	53.7	49.9	57.5
Motor vehicle crashes	16.0	18.5	18.8	22.9	27.4	22.5	23.3
Suicide	11.3	11.5	11.5	11.4	11.8	10.6	11.0
Homicide and legal intervention	10.7	10.2	8.3	10.8	9.1	5.2	5.4
Drug-induced causes	4.8	3.6	3.5	3.0	—	—	—
Alcohol-induced causes	6.7	7.2	7.0	8.4	—	—	—
White male	627.5	644.3	693.3	745.3	893.4	917.7	963.1
Natural causes	554.3	567.6	613.4	651.2	788.6	825.8	860.1
Diseases of heart	190.3	202.0	246.2	277.5	347.6	375.4	381.1
Ischemic heart disease	133.0	145.3	182.1	218.0	—	—	—
Cerebrovascular diseases	26.8	27.7	33.0	41.9	68.8	80.3	87.0
Malignant neoplasms	156.4	160.3	160.4	160.5	154.3	141.6	130.9
Respiratory system	56.3	59.0	58.7	58.0	49.9	34.6	21.6
Colorectal	15.4	16.5	17.8	18.3	18.9	18.9	19.8
Prostate	14.9	15.3	13.4	13.2	12.3	12.4	13.1
Chronic obstructive pulmonary diseases	28.2	27.4	28.7	26.7	24.0	13.8	6.0
Pneumonia and influenza	16.6	17.5	17.5	16.2	26.0	31.0	27.1
Chronic liver disease and cirrhosis	10.8	11.5	12.7	15.7	18.8	14.4	11.6
Diabetes mellitus	12.2	11.3	9.2	9.5	12.7	11.6	11.3
Nephritis, nephrotic syndrome, and nephrosis	4.9	4.6	5.4	4.9	—	—	—
Septicemia	4.0	4.2	4.3	2.8	—	—	—
Human immunodeficiency virus infection	19.0	15.0	—	—	—	—	—
External causes	73.1	76.7	80.0	94.1	104.8	91.9	103.0
Unintentional injuries	42.9	46.4	50.5	62.3	76.2	70.5	80.9
Motor vehicle crashes	22.5	26.3	27.6	34.8	40.1	34.0	35.9
Suicide	19.7	20.1	19.9	18.9	18.2	17.5	18.1
Homicide and legal intervention	8.9	8.9	8.1	10.9	7.3	3.9	3.9
Drug-induced causes	6.2	4.2	4.0	3.2	—	—	—
Alcohol-induced causes	9.7	9.9	9.2	10.8	—	—	—
Black male	1,052.2	1,061.3	1,053.4	1,112.8	1,318.6	1,246.1	1,373.1
Natural causes	905.2	915.2	920.7	942.6	1,095.4	1,093.4	1,209.2
Diseases of heart	267.9	275.9	310.8	327.3	375.9	381.2	415.5
Ischemic heart disease	139.2	147.1	170.4	196.0	—	—	—
Cerebrovascular diseases	51.9	56.1	62.7	77.5	122.5	141.2	146.2
Malignant neoplasms	238.9	248.1	239.9	229.9	198.0	158.5	126.1
Respiratory system	86.0	91.0	87.7	82.0	60.8	36.6	16.9
Colorectal	20.7	21.6	20.2	19.2	17.3	15.0	13.8
Prostate	35.8	35.3	31.2	29.1	25.4	22.2	16.9
Chronic obstructive pulmonary diseases	28.6	26.5	14.8	20.9	—	—	—
Pneumonia and influenza	25.9	28.7	27.5	28.0	53.8	70.2	63.8
Chronic liver disease and cirrhosis	16.1	20.0	23.8	30.6	33.1	14.8	8.8
Diabetes mellitus	26.3	23.6	18.2	17.7	21.2	16.2	11.5
Nephritis, nephrotic syndrome, and nephrosis	12.4	12.9	14.5	14.2	—	—	—
Septicemia	11.0	11.6	12.2	8.0	—	—	—

Table 4-9. Age-adjusted Death Rates[1] for Selected Causes of Death, by Sex and Race: 1950-1993 (continued)

Sex, race, and cause of death	1993	1990	1985	1980	1970	1960[2]	1950[2]
Black male, continued							
Human immunodeficiency virus infection	70.0	44.2	—	—	—	—	—
External causes	147.1	146.0	132.6	170.2	223.2	152.7	163.9
Unintentional injuries	59.8	62.4	67.6	82.0	119.5	100.0	105.7
Motor vehicle crashes	25.3	28.9	28.0	32.9	50.1	38.2	39.8
Suicide	12.9	12.4	11.5	11.1	9.9	7.8	7.0
Homicide and legal intervention	70.7	68.7	50.2	71.9	82.1	44.9	51.1
Drug-induced causes	13.0	8.4	8.9	5.8	—	—	—
Alcohol-induced causes	21.3	26.6	27.7	32.4	—	—	—
White female	367.7	369.9	391.0	411.1	501.7	555.0	645.0
Natural causes	342.8	344.2	363.9	380.0	463.8	522.7	607.7
Diseases of heart	99.2	103.1	121.7	134.6	167.8	197.1	223.6
Ischemic heart disease	63.7	68.6	82.9	97.4	—	—	—
Cerebrovascular diseases	22.7	23.8	27.9	35.2	56.2	68.7	79.7
Malignant neoplasms	110.1	111.2	110.5	107.7	107.6	109.5	119.4
Respiratory system	27.6	26.5	22.7	18.2	10.1	5.1	4.6
Colorectal	10.5	10.9	12.3	13.3	15.3	17.0	19.0
Breast	21.2	22.9	23.4	22.8	23.4	22.4	22.5
Chronic obstructive pulmonary diseases	17.8	15.2	12.9	9.2	5.3	3.3	2.8
Pneumonia and influenza	10.4	10.6	9.9	9.4	15.0	19.0	18.9
Chronic liver disease and cirrhosis	4.6	4.8	5.6	7.0	8.7	6.6	5.8
Diabetes mellitus	10.0	9.5	8.1	8.7	12.8	13.7	16.4
Nephritis, nephrotic syndrome, and nephrosis	3.2	3.0	3.4	2.9	—	—	—
Septicemia	3.2	3.1	3.0	1.8	—	—	—
Human immunodeficiency virus infection	1.9	1.1	—	—	—	—	—
External causes	24.8	25.7	27.1	31.1	37.9	32.3	37.3
Unintentional injuries	16.6	17.6	18.4	21.4	27.2	25.5	30.6
Motor vehicle crashes	9.7	11.0	10.8	12.3	14.4	11.1	10.6
Suicide	4.6	4.8	5.3	5.7	7.2	5.3	5.3
Homicide and legal intervention	3.0	2.8	2.9	3.2	2.2	1.5	1.4
Drug-induced causes	2.8	2.5	2.5	2.6	—	—	—
Alcohol-induced causes	2.7	2.8	2.8	3.5	—	—	—
Black female	578.8	581.6	594.8	631.1	814.4	916.9	1,106.7
Natural causes	542.1	545.1	559.8	588.4	757.9	867.3	1,054.8
Diseases of heart	165.3	188.1	188.3	201.1	251.7	292.6	349.5
Ischemic heart disease	85.7	88.8	101.6	116.1	—	—	—
Cerebrovascular diseases	39.9	42.7	50.6	61.7	107.9	139.5	155.6
Malignant neoplasms	135.3	137.2	131.8	129.7	123.5	127.8	131.9
Respiratory system	27.3	27.5	22.8	19.5	10.9	5.5	4.1
Colorectal	15.2	15.5	16.2	15.3	16.1	15.4	15.0
Breast	27.1	27.5	25.5	23.3	21.5	21.3	19.3
Chronic obstructive pulmonary diseases	12.2	10.7	8.8	6.3	—	—	—
Pneumonia and influenza	13.5	13.7	12.5	12.7	29.2	43.9	50.4
Chronic liver disease and cirrhosis	6.6	8.7	10.2	14.4	17.8	8.9	5.7
Diabetes mellitus	26.9	25.4	21.3	22.1	30.9	27.3	22.7
Nephritis, nephrotic syndrome, and nephrosis	9.2	9.4	10.6	10.3	—	—	—
Septicemia	7.8	8.0	8.1	5.4	—	—	—
Human immunodeficiency virus infection	17.3	9.9	—	—	—	—	—
External causes	36.7	36.6	35.0	42.7	56.5	49.6	51.9
Unintentional injuries	20.1	20.4	20.9	25.1	35.3	35.9	38.5
Motor vehicle crashes	8.5	9.3	8.2	8.4	13.8	10.0	10.3
Suicide	2.1	2.4	2.1	2.4	2.9	1.9	1.7
Homicide and legal intervention	13.4	13.0	10.9	13.7	15.0	11.8	11.7
Drug-induced causes	4.4	3.4	3.3	2.7	—	—	—
Alcohol-induced causes	5.5	7.7	8.0	10.6	—	—	—

[1] Per 100,000 resident population.

[2] Includes deaths of persons who were not residents of the 50 states and the District of Columbia.

[3] Prostate rates are for males only; breast rates are for females only.

Source: National Center for Health Statistics, "Health United States 1995," Public Health Service, Hyattsville, MD, 1996, Table 30.

1987 and 1993, the overall death rate from HIV infection grew from 5.5 to 13.8 per 100,000 people (age-adjusted). The 25-44 year age group of males has particularly high annual death rates from HIV infection: 137.1 per 100,000 for blacks, 68.0 for Hispanics, 37.7 for non-Hispanic whites, 16.1 for Native American or Alaskan Natives, and 9.8 for Asian or Pacific Islanders. The rate of death among black (34.1) and Hispanic (12.3) females in this age group is also high.

HIV infection is now the second-leading cause of death among the population aged 25-44 years. Yet its effect is also spreading to other age categories. Among those aged 15-24, it now stands as the sixth most common cause of death, and has reached eighth place for those aged 45-64 years (Hispanic males in particular have a relatively older distribution of deaths from HIV infection). Due to the vertical transmission of AIDS from mother to infant, HIV infection is now the sixth most common cause of death among those aged 1-4 years (at a rate of 1.3 deaths per 100,000 in 1993). Deaths from HIV infection are actually almost twice as common among those under 1 year (a rate of 2.2) as among those aged 1-4 years, but deaths from this cause fail to make the list of top ten causes of infant death because these fragile beings run so many other risks of death.

Major Cardiovascular Diseases: Diseases of the heart have dropped by more than one-half, from 307.2 to 145.3 per 100,000, for the total population between 1950 and 1993. Since 1980, ischemic heart disease (a category that includes heart attacks) has declined by 36 percent, while the other forms of heart disease (including such forms as rheumatic heart disease, hypertensive heart disease and arteriosclerosis) have declined only about 6 percent. White males tend to die in larger proportions from ischemic heart disease: 70 percent of their deaths from heart disease are from this cause, compared to 64 percent among white females and about 52 percent among black males and females. Thus white males have benefitted to a greater degree than the other groups in the reduction of death from this cause. However, white male death rates are still almost twice as high as those found among white females; a similar sex differential prevails among blacks, whose mortality rates from heart disease are roughly half again as high as those of whites.

Cerebrovascular Disease: The death rate from cerebrovascular disease (stroke) decreased by more than two-thirds (from 88.6 to 26.5) between 1950 and 1993. In 1950, the rate of death from this cause was roughly equivalent between the sexes, although the black rate of death was far higher. Between 1950 and 1993, the decline in the death rate of black women from cerebrovascular disease (155.6 to 39.9 per 100,000) outpaced that of black men (who dropped from 146.2 to 51.9). The decline in this cause of

death among white females (79.7 to 22.7) was more similar to that of white males (87.0 to 26.8).

Malignant Neoplasms (Cancer): While death rates from malignant neoplasms have increased slightly (from 125.3 to 132.6 per 100,000 between 1950 and 1993), the distribution of the death rate from various forms of cancer has changed. Deaths from cancers of the respiratory system (primarily lung cancer) have more than tripled (12.8 to 40.8), colorectal cancer has declined slightly, and prostate and breast cancer mortality rates have changed little.

In 1993, white females had the lowest rate of death from cancer (at 110.1 per 100,000); the white male rate was 42 percent higher, the black female rate was 23 percent higher, and the black male rate was 117 percent higher. Since cancers tend to occur more at older ages (Figure 4-6), the relatively younger age distribution of the black population tends to mask how much higher black risks from cancer are when we examine only the race-specific numbers of cancer cases in any year.

Attempts to determine whether cancer rates have declined or increased over the past forty years are confounded by a number of factors. It was only in the early 1950s that a definition of cancer was agreed upon, including the requirement that the disease had to be confirmed from a tissue biopsy. Several decades ago, many Americans (especially black Americans) died without such a confirmed diagnosis of cancer before death or an autopsy after death. In addition, many people who had already developed cancer died of other causes before the cancer metastasized to such an extent that it proved fatal. Declines in competing risks of death may partially explain the increases in the death rate from breast cancer among black women and from prostate cancer among black men (white rates for these cancers have stayed roughly the same since 1950).

On the other hand, such problems of classification cannot explain away the huge increase in one form of malignant neoplasms between 1950 and 1993—those of the respiratory system, primarily lung cancer. Between these dates, this cancer increased its death rate by more than 2.6 times among white males, 5.1 times among black males, 6 times among white females, and 6.7 times among black females (see the Textbox, "Cigarette Smoking and Mortality").

Diseases of the Respiratory System (other than Neoplasms): The age-adjusted death rates also show that the death rates from influenza and pneumonia have been halved over the past four decades, with most of the decrease coming after 1970. Influenza deaths tend to fluctuate from year to year and become a significant cause of death only in infrequent years of epidemic outbreaks.

The death rate from chronic obstructive pulmonary disease (which includes bronchitis, emphysema, asthma, and other conditions) is now almost five times as high as in 1950. Until recently, the rate for males was much higher than for females, except for asthma, which has a higher rate for females. Emphysema is a particularly male-dominated disease, although the sex differential narrowed sharply between 1970 and 1991, probably in connection with changes in the smoking history of women, their entry into more polluted occupations, and environmental changes. The black population tended to have lower rates than the white for most of these diseases (especially pneumonia) in 1993; however, at the younger ages, the rate of asthma for blacks tends to be higher than for whites. With the aging of the black population, it will probably see higher death rates from bronchitis and influenza; however, whether it will suffer as much from emphysema and asthma among the elderly (blacks tend to have to live in areas with more air pollution but they now smoke less than whites) remains to be seen.

Causes Related to Pregnancy and Birth: Childbirth now presents few dangers to mothers and reduced risks to infants. Later sections on infant and maternal mortality deal with these topics in more detail.

Other Diseases and Disorders: Among the leading causes of death from disease not discussed previously are diabetes mellitus, cirrhosis of the liver, and nephritis. The death rate from diabetes is roughly the same for each sex, and the black death rate is about double the white rate. There has been a slight decline in the death rate from this disease among white women, stability among men, and an increase among blacks (small for women, large for men) over the past forty years. All groups showed a peak in deaths from chronic liver disease and cirrhosis between 1960 and 1980, but the death rate has declined in recent years. The black death rate is about 50 percent higher than the white rate for this cause, probably reflecting a higher rate of hepatitis B prevalence among the black population.

External Causes of Death (Nondisease): A very significant proportion of deaths (10.4 percent) result from one of four external causes: unintentional injuries (including motor vehicle crashes), suicide, homicide, or other nondisease causes. Unintentional injury ranks fifth, suicide ranks ninth, and homicide and legal intervention ranks tenth among the U.S. population's leading causes of death in 1993. Because of incomplete and possibly biased reporting, these external causes may be underreported or misreported more than causes based primarily on a physician's diagnosis.

Unintentional Injuries (including Motor Vehicle Crashes): From age 1 to age 44, unintentional injuries were the leading cause of death in 1993. Males are almost three times as likely to die from "accidents and adverse effects" (another term for unintentional injuries; see Table 4-8) than are females. Deaths from unintentional injuries are particularly common (they are the second-leading cause of death) among male American Indians and Alaskan Natives.

About one-half of all deaths from unintentional injuries are from motor vehicle crashes, and one-half from all other forms of accident. Males are more than twice as likely to die in motor vehicle crashes as females. Between 1970 and 1985 significant reductions in deaths from motor vehicle crashes were made, with less progress since then. Reduction in motor vehicle deaths has been attributed to lowering the legal speed limits (imposed as an energy conservation measure) and to stricter enforcement in many parts of the country of laws against drunken driving. Since 1970, black men have reduced their death rates from motor vehicle crashes and from other unintentional injuries by about half, and white men have done almost as well.

Suicide: Since 1950, there has been remarkable stability in the overall rate of this cause of death, but in reality this is due to a changing population composition canceling out the effects of changing rates of suicide . This is one of the few causes of death where white men and women lead other race and ethnic groups. During 1993, the age-adjusted suicide rate for white men (Table 4-9) was 19.7 per 100,000. The suicide rate for black men has risen (from 7.0 in 1950 to 12.9 in 1993), but it is still well below that of white males. The 1993 age-adjusted suicide rate of Hispanic males (obtained from other NCHS sources) was 12.6, of American Indian or Alaskan Native males 18.7, and of Asian and Pacific Islander males 9.2 per 100,000. The equivalent rates for females were: whites, 4.6; blacks, 2.1; Hispanics, 2.1; American Indian or Alaskan Natives, 5.5; and Asian and Pacific Islanders, 3.8 per 100,000.

Suicide rates also vary among race and ethnic groups by their pattern of age distribution as well as by their overall level of occurrence. There are two major age patterns found among U.S. race and ethnic groups in the early 1990s. Some groups have a pattern of increasing suicide rates (at least successful ones that become causes of death) with age; these include white non-Hispanic males, Hispanic males, and both male and female Asian and Pacific Islanders. Among this group, white males (including both non-Hispanics and some Hispanics) have by far the steepest rate of increase in suicide with age: their rate is 41.5 per 100,000 for age 65 and over, and 72.1 for age 85 and over. In the other age pattern, the suicide rate peaks between age 15 and 54 years (the peak age differs between groups) and then declines at older ages. This pattern is found among white women, black men and women, and Hispanic women. The version of this pattern found among Native American and Alaskan Native men and women is remarkable for a peak in suicides in the 15-

Cigarette Smoking and Mortality

The widespread use of cigarettes in the United States is very much a twentieth-century phenomenon. Per capita consumption in 1900 stood at only 54 cigarettes per year. It rose rapidly (particularly during major wars and economic boom times) to peak at 4,287 per year in 1966, at roughly the same time that the famous U.S. Surgeon General's report on the dangers of smoking was made public. Since then, it has fallen to 2,493 cigarettes consumed per capita in 1994. Due to the growth of the population, the total annual number of cigarettes consumed in the U.S. had a slightly different track, peaking at 650 billion cigarettes in 1981 and dropping to 480 billion in 1994.

At the height of cigarette popularity in 1965, 42.4 percent of all adults (50.1 million) reported that they were currently smokers, and another 13.6 percent (16.0 million) reported that they were former smokers. The prevalence of current smokers declined and that of former smokers increased over the next quarter-century; the decline in smoking in the 1980s was particularly sharp. Between 1965 and 1991, the proportion of current smokers fell by 39.4 percent, the proportion of former smokers rose by 77.2 percent, and the proportion of adults who had never smoked rose a modest 14.1 percent (from 44.0 to 50.2). During the early 1990s, however, evidence suggests that the rate of decline in smoking has slowed.

A sizable proportion of all smokers have been able to quit. In 1965, about a quarter (24.3 percent) of those in the U.S. population who had ever smoked were former smokers; by 1991, this proportion had risen to almost one-half (48.5 percent). Smoking cessation among men, the heaviest smokers, was particularly sharp; by 1991 51.6 percent were former smokers. Blacks lagged behind whites in smoking cessation; only a third (33.4 percent) of all black smokers had successfully quit smoking by 1991. The sharp decline in smoking among white males has undoubtedly made a major contribution to their increase in survivorship at ages 40-60 years, a trend noted elsewhere in this chapter.

There is considerable variability in smoking across different parts of the nation. The state-wide prevalence of smoking in 1995 ranged from 13.2 to 27.8 percent of all adults. In three states (California, Hawaii, and Utah) smokers made up less than 20 percent of all male adults; in Alabama, North Carolina, and Ohio they were more than 30 percent. Smokers were less than 18 percent of all adult women in five states (California, Georgia, Hawaii, New Jersey, and Utah) and

more than 26 percent of adult women in four states (Indiana, Kentucky, Nevada, and West Virginia).

Statisticians at the Centers for Disease Control and Prevention (CDC) have developed models for estimating the years of potential life lost that are attributable to cigarette smoking. Cigarette smoking leads to increased death rates from cancer and burns, from cardiovascular and respiratory disease, from deaths to infants whose mothers smoked, and to children and adults exposed to environmental tobacco smoke. About 20 percent of all deaths (418,690) were at-

tributed to smoking; twice as many occurred to men as to women. Somewhat surprisingly, more smoking-attributable deaths were due to cardiovascular disease (179,820) than to neoplasms (151,322); of the latter, lung cancer (119,920) was the major contributor. Almost 99,000 deaths from ischemic heart disease were attributable to smoking, as were 1,711 deaths to infants.

Smoking was a significant contributor to years of potential life lost both before and after age 65. The CDC model shows that in 1990, the YPLL before age 65 attributable to smoking was 1,919.1

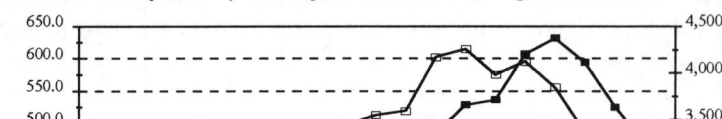

Total and Per-capita Yearly Consumption of Manufactured Cigarettes: 1900-1994[1]

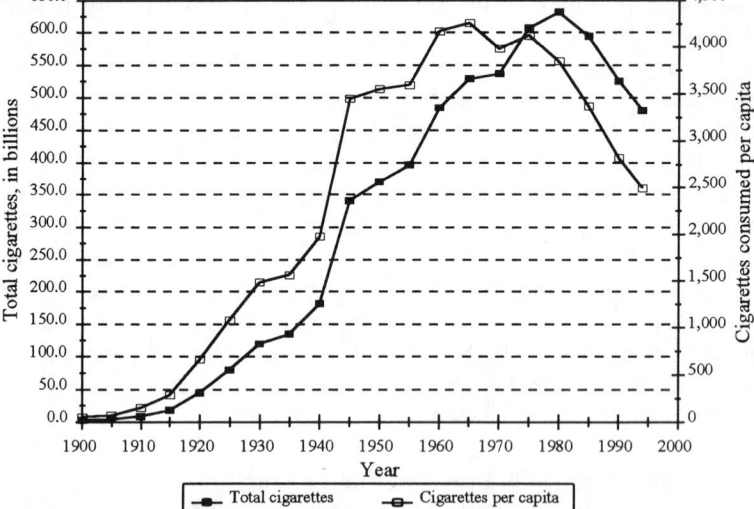

[1] 1994 data are estimated, based on projections for the entire year. U.S. military forces overseas are included in the total consumption for 1940 and in the per capita consumption for 1930-1994.
Source: 1900-1994 Centers for Disease Control data.

Estimated Smoking-attributable Years of Potential Life Lost[1] (YPLL), by Age and Sex: 1990

Age and sex category	Before age 65		At all ages	
	Number	Rate[2]	Number	Rate[2]
Total	1,152,635	1,325.8	5,048,740	4,541.3
Males, 35 years and over	732,389	1,919.1	3,124,208	6,233.7
Females, 35 years and over	308,801	764.6	1,797,024	3,070.7
Infants under 1 year	111,445	—	127,508	—

[1] YPLL estimates do not include about 3,000 deaths per year from passive smoking, nor do they include deaths from cigar smoking, pipe smoking, smokeless tobacco, or effects of confounders (such as the joint effects of alcohol and cigarettes).
[2] Per 100,000 persons age 35 years and over, adjusted to the 1980 U.S. population.

Source: Centers for Disease Control and Prevention, "Cigarette Smoking-attributable Mortality and Years of Potential Life Lost--United States, 1990," Morbidity and Mortality Weekly Report 42, 33, 1993: 645-49.

Percent of the Population Age 18 Years and Over Who were Current[1] or Former[2] Smokers or Who Never Smoked: 1965-1991

Smoking status	1991	1983	1974	1965	Percent change 1965-91
Total					
Current smoker	25.7	32.1	37.1	42.4	-39.4
Former smoker	24.1	21.8	19.5	13.6	77.2
Never smoked	50.2	46.1	43.4	44.0	14.1
Male					
Current smoker	28.1	35.1	43.1	51.9	-45.9
Former smoker	29.9	28.3	27.7	19.8	51.0
Never smoked	42.1	36.6	29.2	28.3	48.8
Female					
Current smoker	23.5	29.5	32.1	33.9	-30.7
Former smoker	19.0	15.9	12.7	8.0	137.5
Never smoked	57.6	54.6	55.2	58.1	-0.9

[1] Those who reported smoking 100 or more cigarettes and who currently smoke.

[2] Those who reported smoking 100 or more cigarettes and who do not currently smoke.

Source: Centers for Disease Control and Prevention, "Surveillance for Selected Tobacco-use Behaviors—United States, 1900-1994," Morbidity and Mortality Weekly Report, CDC Surveillance Summaries 43, SS-3, 1994: 8.

Percent of the Population Age 18 Years and Over Who Have Ever Smoked Who are Former[1] Smokers (Prevalence of Cessation), by Sex and Race-ethnicity: 1965-1991

Characteristic	1991	1983	1974	1965	Percent change 1965-91
Total	48.5	40.4	34.5	24.3	99.6
Sex					
Male	51.6	44.6	39.2	27.6	87.0
Female	44.7	35.1	28.3	19.1	134.0
Race-ethnicity					
White	50.2	41.8	36.1	25.2	99.2
Black	33.4	28.3	19.7	15.5	115.5
Hispanic	45.6	38.4	—	—	—

[1] Those who reported smoking 100 or more cigarettes and who do not currently smoke.

Source: Centers for Disease Control and Prevention, "Surveillance for Selected Tobacco-use Behaviors--United States. 1900-1994," Morbidity and Mortality Weekly Report, CDC Surveillance Summaries 43, SS-3, 1994: 20.

tervention for black males (YPLL of 2,287.7 in 1990), and come in second after all malignant neoplasms (to which, of course, it is a significant contributor) for white and black women (YPLL of 828.8 and 960.7 per 100,000, respectively). In 1996 the Council of State and Territorial Epidemiologists added **prevalence of cigarette smoking** to the list of conditions designated as reportable by states to CDC. "The addition of prevalence of cigarette smoking marks the first time a behavior, rather than a disease or illness, has been considered nationally reportable" (MMWR, June 28, 1996; Vol. 45, No. 25, p. 537).

It is hard to overemphasize the effect of this entirely preventable factor on American mortality. The decline in rates of cigarette smoking among adults may indicate that the public is slowly recognizing this fact. However, the 1995 Youth Risk Behavior Survey reported that 34.8 percent of all U.S. high school students had smoked on at least one of the 30 days preceding the survey, and 16.1 percent had smoked on 20 or more of the 30 days. In addition, 11.4 percent of all students had used smokeless tobacco (chewing tobacco or snuff) on at least one of the 30 days preceding the survey. If today's 68.74 million young people under the age of 18 have the same prevalence of smoking as persons aged 18-30 years, the CDC estimates that 16.62 million of them will become smokers and that 5.318 million will die prematurely from smoking-related illnesses. The CDC has linked the increases in the initiation of smoking among adolescents to increases in advertising and promotional expenditures by tobacco companies; between 1980 and 1989 their cigarette advertising expenditures doubled (in constant dollars) and their promotional expenditures quadrupled.

Sources

Centers for Disease Control and Prevention. "Cigarette smoking-attributable mortality and years of potential life lost--United States, 1990." Morbidity and Mortality Weekly Report 42, (August 27, 1993): 645-49.

————. "Youth risk behavior surveillance—United States, 1995." Morbidity and Mortality Weekly Report, Supplement, 45, SS-4(September 27, 1996).

————. "Projected smoking-related deaths among youth—United States." Morbidity and Mortality Weekly Report 45, (November 8, 1996): 971-74.

————. "State-specific prevalence of cigarette smoking—United States, 1995." Morbidity and Mortality Weekly Report 45, 44(November 8, 1996): 962-66.

Giovino, Gary A., et al. "Surveillance for Selected Tobacco-Use Behaviors—United States 1900-1994." In CDC Surveillance Summaries, Morbidity and Mortality Weekly Report 43 (November 18, 1994): 2-43.

Thun, M.J., Day-Lally, C.A., Calle, E.E., Flanders, W.D., and Heath, C.W. "Excess Mortality among Cigarette Smokers: Changes in a 20-Year Interval." American Journal of Public Health 85(1995): 1223-30.

U.S. Department of Health and Human Services. Preventing tobacco use among young people: a report of the Surgeon General. Atlanta, GA: Public Health Service, CDC, National Center for Chronic Disease Prevention and Health Promotion, Office on Smoking and Health. 1994.

per 100,000 for males and 764.6 per 100,000 for females. Because these smoking-related diseases also have a strong effect on the population over age 65, the YPLL at all ages in 1990 rises to 6,233.7 per 100,000 for men and to 3,070.7 per 100,000 for women. In total, the model estimates that the U.S. population lost over 5 million years of potential life to smoking (including 1.152 million years for those under age 65) in 1990.

If cigarette smoking had been considered as a separate cause of YPLL in 1990, it would have surpassed all other individual causes of death for white males, trailed only homicide and legal in-

24 year age group; white women, on the other hand, do not reach their peak rate of suicide until age 45-54 years. Both of these general age patterns appear to be of long standing; they reach back as far as 1950 for whites and blacks and to the 1970s and 1980s for the other groups (when such data began to be systematically collected).

Overall, in 1993 suicide is the third leading cause of death among the population aged 15-24 years, the fifth leading cause of death among those aged 25-44 years, and the ninth leading cause of death among those aged 45-64 years. Due to a doubling of suicide rates among white males and females aged 5-14 years during the 1980-85 period and the maintenance of this higher level of suicides since then, it is also the fifth leading cause of death for this age group. Suicide rates have risen among the elderly as well: between 1980 and 1992, they increased by 10.8 percent among those 75-79 years, by 35.2 percent among those 80-84 years, and by 15.3 percent among those 85 years and over. Both sex and marital status appear to have strong influences on suicide among the elderly: divorced or widowed men have a suicide rate that is 17 times higher than that of elderly married women.

Homicide and Legal Intervention: The rate of death from homicide in the United States is probably the highest in the developed world. The current level of deaths from state-sanctioned execution (legal intervention) is so low as to be almost statistically imperceptible. In 1993, the homicide rate stood at 10.7 per 100,000, but there were huge differences in the level of risk between the races and sexes. White women had the lowest rate of death by homicide, at 4.6, followed by white males at 8.9. Homicide rates stood at 13.4 for black females and at 70.7 for black males. The latter group had 24 times the chance of dying as a homicide victim as did white females.

Homicide is highly age-related. For ages 15-24, it is the second leading cause of death, and is in third place for those aged 5-14 years. What is less well-known is its effect on children and infants. A 1986-87 CDC study found homicide to be the fourth-leading cause of death among children aged 1-4, and the rate of death from homicide among infants (8.1) was more than three times that of children aged 1-4.

Homicide drops off quite sharply with age: for the 25-44 year age group, it is the sixth-leading cause of death, and after 45 years it no longer appears among the ten leading causes of death. As will be shown later, however, its frequency among the young gives it a strong effect on the years of potential life lost (YPLL) by the population.

Drug-induced and Alcohol-induced Causes: From 1980 on, the NCHS began to list deaths that were directly attributable to the effects of drugs and alcohol. While alcohol-related deaths have declined since then (particularly for black females, who cut their rate of death in half),

the rates of drug-induced mortality have almost doubled for white males and more than doubled for black males in little more than a decade. The increased drug-induced death rates are somewhat puzzling in light of the population's overall decline in many forms of illegal drug use since the mid-1980s (see Chapter 7).

Changes in Cause-Specific Mortality, 1950-93

When the age-adjusted death rates for sex and race groups between 1950 and 1993 are compared some of the major differentials in cause-specific health risks become clearer. The total black male age-adjusted death rate in 1993 still lags behind the white male death rate of 1950 (1,052.2 to 963.1). When the black and white male age-adjusted death rates for 1993 are compared, black men lead whites in almost every major category, often having twice or three times as many deaths from each of these causes. Deaths from HIV are more than three times as high among black as among white males in 1993 (70.7 versus 19.0 per 100,000), and deaths from external causes are more than twice as high (147.1 to 73.1).

The overall 1993 black female age-adjusted death rate (578.8 per 100,000) is roughly the same as the 1960 white female rate (555.0). Black women have higher death rates from diseases of the heart, cerebrovascular disease, and malignant neoplasms than do white women in 1993. The latter group surpasses the death rates of black women only for chronic obstructive pulmonary diseases (17.8 to 12.2) and suicide (4.6 to 2.1 per 100,000). The death rate from HIV among black women is more than nine times greater than among white women (17.3 to 1.9) in 1993.

What do these figures tell us about the changing patterns of death in the United States? It is clear that cancers of the respiratory system (mainly lung cancer) and chronic obstructive pulmonary disease have greatly increased during the twentieth century. Since few cases of lung cancer are cured even today (see Table 7-18), the death rate of this cancer is a good guide to its overall incidence. A large proportion of the increases in these causes of death is due to cigarette smoking, a largely twentieth-century phenomenon. The improvements in diagnosis and treatment of other major cancers (such as breast, colorectal and prostate cancers) and changes in their survival rates make it difficult to link their mortality rates to increases or decreases in their incidence.

The major decline since 1950 in the age-adjusted death rate from heart disease is probably due to several factors. While the occupational structure now has many more sedentary jobs, and the population is more overweight (Table 7-14), fewer Americans now have high levels of serum cholesterol in their bloodstream (Table 7-13) than in the early 1960s. Doctors and hospitals are now much better equipped to deal with patients with heart problems, and the population is much more aware of the importance of the early warning signs of heart disease. Of course, this has come at some cost: diseases of the heart are the most common diagnosis for entry into non-federal short-stay hospitals for men and the second most common diagnosis (after delivery) for women (see Tables 7-19A and 7-19B).

Infant and Maternal Mortality

The infant mortality rate (see Definitions Box) has declined remarkably in recent years to a low level previously thought to be almost medically impossible to attain. By 1991, of each 1,000 live-born babies, fewer than nine die during their first year of life. This is half the rate of only twenty years earlier and less than one-eleventh the rate of 1915-19. Table 4-10 and Figure 4-7 report the impressive conquest of infant death made in this century, which continues to the present.

Despite this progress, during the first year of life infants incur a risk of death greater than the combined risk of the next three or four decades of life. These risks are about 25 percent greater for male than for female infants (Table 4-11). Black infants suffer a grave disadvantage; their rate (1,757.1 per 100,000 live births in 1991) is almost twice as high as that of white infants (894.4). These differentials have persisted at approximately the same magnitudes since 1900, when data first became available. Thus, there has been a convergence of absolute differences in

mortality between the sexes and the black and white races, but a maintenance of substantial and inflexible relative differentials.

Age and Infant Mortality

Infant mortality is far from uniform throughout the first year of life. It is greatest during the twenty-four hours following birth and declines daily for the first week, weekly for the first month, and monthly for the first year. Table 4-11 reports rates by day, week, and month of age for 1991.

The sex differential in infant mortality continues a pattern formed soon after conception; the primary sex ratio (at conception) is thought to be between 130-200 males to every 100 females. A higher rate of male miscarriages results in a secondary sex ratio (at birth) of about 105 in many white and Asian populations and about 102 for many black African and black American populations. The 1991 data in Table 4-11 show that while the sex ratio of mortality is slightly higher among blacks than among whites for the first 27 days of life (sex ratios of 126.9 and 124.1, respectively), this racial pattern reverses itself during the next month (days 28 to 59 have sex ratios of 118.0 and 135.2, respectively). For the entire first year of life, a higher proportion of black than white male infants survive (sex ratios of mortality of 123.4 and 131.1, respectively).

Because more than 60 percent of infant mortality

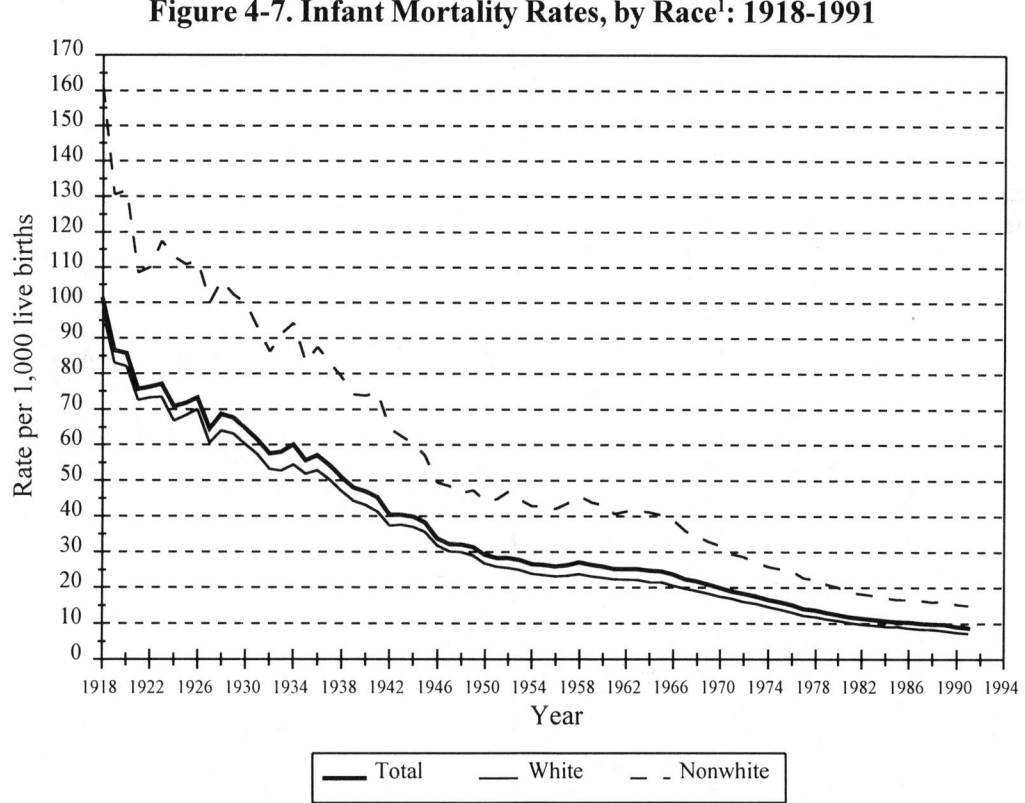

Figure 4-7. Infant Mortality Rates, by Race[1]: 1918-1991

[1] Deaths based on race of decedent; live births based on race of mother from 1970-1991 and on race of infant prior to 1970.
Source: 1918-1991 National Center for Health Statistics data.

Table 4-10. Infant Mortality Rates[1], by Race[2]: 1915-1991[3]

Year	Total	White	Nonwhite Total	Black
1991	8.9	7.3	15.1	17.6
1990	9.2	7.6	15.5	18.0
1989	9.8	8.1	16.3	18.6
1988	10.0	8.4	16.1	18.5
1987	10.1	8.5	16.5	18.8
1986	10.4	8.8	16.7	18.9
1985	10.6	9.2	16.8	19.0
1984	10.8	9.3	17.1	19.2
1983	11.2	9.6	17.8	20.0
1982	11.5	9.9	18.3	20.5
1981	11.9	10.3	18.8	20.8
1980	12.6	10.9	20.2	22.2
1979	13.1	11.3	20.9	22.6
1978	13.8	11.9	22.1	23.9
1977	14.1	12.2	22.7	24.4
1976	15.2	13.2	24.6	26.4
1975	16.1	14.0	25.3	27.0
1974	16.7	14.7	25.9	27.5
1973	17.7	15.6	27.1	28.8
1972	18.5	16.2	28.7	30.3
1971	19.1	17.0	29.4	30.9
1970	20.0	17.6	31.8	33.3
1969	20.9	18.4	32.9	34.8
1968	21.8	19.2	34.5	36.2
1967	22.4	19.7	35.9	37.5
1966	23.7	20.6	38.8	40.2
1965	24.7	21.5	40.3	41.7
1964	24.8	21.6	41.1	42.3
1963	25.2	22.2	41.5	42.8
1962	25.3	22.3	41.4	42.6
1961	25.3	22.4	40.7	41.8
1960	26.0	22.9	43.2	44.3
1959	26.4	23.2	44.0	44.8
1958	27.1	23.8	45.7	46.3
1957	26.3	23.3	43.7	44.2
1956	26.0	23.2	42.1	42.4
1955	26.4	23.6	42.8	43.1
1954	26.6	23.9	42.9	42.9
1953	27.8	25.0	44.7	44.5
1952	28.4	25.5	47.0	46.9
1951	28.4	25.8	44.8	44.3
1950	29.2	26.8	44.5	43.9
1949	31.3	28.9	47.3	46.8
1948	32.0	29.9	46.5	45.7
1947	32.2	30.1	48.5	47.7
1946	33.8	31.8	49.5	48.8
1945	38.3	35.6	57.0	56.2
1944	39.8	36.9	60.3	59.3

Table 4-10. Infant Mortality Rates[1], by Race[2]: 1915-1991[3] (continued)

Year	Total	White	Nonwhite Total	Black
1943	40.4	37.5	62.5	61.5
1942	40.4	37.3	64.6	64.2
1941	45.3	41.2	74.8	74.1
1940	47.0	43.2	73.8	72.9
1939	48.0	44.3	74.2	73.2
1938	51.0	47.1	79.1	77.9
1937	54.4	50.3	83.2	82.0
1936	57.1	52.9	87.6	86.1
1935	55.7	51.9	83.2	81.9
1934	60.1	54.5	94.4	91.0
1933	58.1	52.8	91.3	85.4
1932	57.6	53.3	86.2	84.1
1931	61.6	57.4	93.1	92.7
1930	64.6	60.1	99.9	99.5
1929	67.6	63.2	102.2	101.5
1928	68.7	64.0	106.2	105.9
1927	64.6	60.6	100.1	99.9
1926	73.3	70.0	111.8	112.1
1925	71.7	68.3	110.8	112.0
1924	70.8	66.8	112.9	114.1
1923	77.1	73.5	117.4	119.9
1922	76.2	73.2	110.0	111.6
1921	75.6	72.5	108.5	110.7
1920	85.8	82.1	131.7	135.6
1919	86.6	83.0	130.5	134.3
1918	100.9	97.4	161.2	162.5
1917	93.8	—	—	—
1916	101.0	99.0	184.9	184.3
1915	99.9	98.6	181.2	—

[1] Per 1,000 live births.

[2] Deaths based on race of decedent; live births based on race of mother from 1970-1991 and on race of infant prior to 1970.

[3] United States from 1933-1991 and birth-registration states prior to 1933.

Source: National Center for Health Statistics, "Vital Statistics of the United States: 1991, Volume II--Mortality Part A," National Center for Health Statistics, Hyattsville, MD, 1996, Table 2-2.

Table 4-11. Infant Mortality Rates[1] by Age, Sex, and Race[2]: 1991

Age	All races			White			Black		
	Total	Male	Female	Total	Male	Female	Total	Male	Female
Under 1 year	894.4	999.7	784.2	729.9	825.5	629.6	1,757.1	1,937.9	1,570.7
Under 28 days	559.0	617.4	497.9	453.5	501.0	403.6	1,124.7	1,255.9	989.4
Under 1 day	337.2	370.1	302.7	263.5	290.4	235.3	728.4	806.5	647.9
Under 1 hour	104.6	112.2	96.6	86.7	93.5	79.5	199.8	216.8	182.4
1 to 23 hours	232.6	257.9	206.1	176.8	196.9	155.8	528.6	589.7	465.6
1 day	41.8	47.3	36.0	33.7	37.8	29.5	85.7	99.9	71.1
2 days	30.0	35.0	24.7	26.2	29.8	22.3	50.4	62.9	37.5
3 days	19.7	22.0	17.2	18.2	21.1	15.2	28.3	28.6	28.0
4 days	12.6	13.9	11.1	11.7	12.5	10.9	18.3	22.5	14.0
5 days	10.4	11.5	9.3	9.3	10.2	8.5	16.1	17.9	14.3
6 days	8.6	9.6	7.6	7.7	8.7	6.7	13.2	14.7	11.6
7 to 13 days	47.1	52.9	41.0	39.4	43.8	34.8	87.8	101.6	73.5
14 to 20 days	30.1	32.7	27.3	25.7	27.5	23.8	54.6	60.9	48.2
21 to 27 days	21.7	22.4	21.0	17.9	19.0	16.7	41.9	40.4	43.4
28 to 59 days	84.0	94.3	73.2	69.2	79.5	58.5	160.4	173.5	147.0
2 months	67.7	78.8	56.0	57.3	69.6	44.4	122.3	130.8	113.6
3 months	53.4	63.4	42.8	44.4	55.8	32.4	99.3	105.4	93.1
4 months	35.4	40.4	30.3	28.4	32.4	24.3	69.3	78.5	59.8
5 months	24.6	26.9	22.1	19.2	21.8	16.4	50.1	51.4	48.8
6 months	19.1	22.2	15.9	16.0	18.6	13.1	33.7	38.1	29.2
7 months	14.4	16.5	12.2	11.6	13.0	10.2	26.8	33.2	20.2
8 months	11.6	13.4	9.8	9.8	11.7	7.9	20.8	23.1	18.4
9 months	9.1	9.7	8.6	7.2	7.8	6.6	18.3	19.1	17.6
10 months	7.9	8.5	7.2	6.5	7.2	5.8	15.4	15.9	14.9
11 months	8.3	8.2	8.4	6.8	7.2	6.4	16.0	13.3	18.7

[1] Per 100,000 live births.

[2] Deaths based on race of decedent; live births based on race of mother.

Source: National Center for Health Statistics, "Vital Statistics of the United States: 1991, Volume II--Mortality Part A," National Center for Health Statistics, Hyattsville, MD, 1996, Table 2-3.

occurs during the first month of life, and because medical and health experts have noted differentials in causes of death between the first month and the following eleven months, it has become customary to divide the infant mortality rate into two periods, the neonatal (during the first twenty-seven days) and the postneonatal (during days 28 to 365) periods (see Definitions Box). Table 4-12 analyzes differences in these two classes of rates for 1991 separately for the major racial and ethnic groups. Blacks have the highest rate of infant mortality, followed by the American Indian, Aleut and Eskimo group. The lowest rates of infant mortality are found among Chinese and Filipino infants; however, there is some question as to whether infant deaths to certain Asian groups are recorded correctly (they may be recorded as whites on some death certificates).

It is thought that physiological factors may be more important in determining the neonatal mortality rate, and environmental factors are more important in determining the postneonatal mortality rate. Table 4-13 shows the changes in these two components of the infant mortality rate for whites and nonwhites between 1915 and 1991. In 1916 (the first year race-specific data are available), the white neonatal mortality rate was 43.5, and the nonwhite rate was 55.5 per 1,000 live births. There was a much greater racial differential in the postneonatal mortality rate in that year: it stood at 55.5 per 1,000 live births for whites and 116.0 for nonwhites.

Between 1916 and 1970, the nonwhite neonatal mortality rate was roughly 50 percent higher than the white rate in each year even though each rate was declining. After 1970, a more rapid rate of decline in the white neonatal mortality rate widened this ratio to a two-to-one gap in white-to-nonwhite neonatal mortality. Trends in postneonatal mortality differentials between the races took a different tack. Until about 1950, nonwhite mortality was about

Table 4-12. Infant, Neonatal, and Postneonatal Mortality Rates[1] by Sex and Detailed Race[2] and Hispanic Origin: 1991

Race and sex	Mortality rates		
	Infant	Neonatal	Postneonatal
All races	8.9	5.6	3.4
Male	10.0	6.2	3.8
Female	7.8	5.0	2.9
White	7.3	4.5	2.8
Male	8.3	5.0	3.2
Female	6.3	4.0	2.3
Black	17.6	11.2	6.3
Male	19.4	12.6	6.8
Female	15.7	9.9	5.8
American Indian, Aleut, Eskimo	10.4	4.8	5.6
Male	10.2	4.4	5.8
Female	10.7	5.2	5.5
Chinese	3.6	1.7	1.9
Male	3.9	...	2.4
Female	3.1	1.8	...
Japanese	3.6	...	...
Male	...	...	...
Female	...	...	...
Hawaiian	8.8	5.3	3.6
Male	10.8	6.4	...
Female	...	...	...
Filipino	3.9	2.3	1.6
Male	4.0	2.4	1.6
Female	3.8	2.1	1.7
Other Asian/Pacific Islander	5.2	3.2	2.0
Male	5.6	3.3	2.2
Female	4.8	3.0	1.8
Hispanic	7.5	4.6	2.8

[1] Per 1,000 live births.

[2] Deaths based on race of decedent; live births based on race of mother.

Source: National Center for Health Statistics, "Vital Statistics of the United States: 1991, Volume II--Mortality Part A," National Center for Health Statistics, Hyattsville, MD, 1996, Tables 2-5 and 2-24.

twice as high as white mortality. The racial gap widened thereafter, reaching an almost three-to-one ratio of non-white-to-white postneonatal mortality in the late 1950s and early 1960s. After that point, the gap narrowed to the earlier two-to-one ratio by 1975, where it has remained until the present day.

In 1991, the ratio of the neonatal to postneonatal death rates for all infants in the United States was 1.64 (see Table 4-12). While both white male and female infants had lower neonatal to postneonatal death ratios than blacks (1.56 to 1.85 for males and 1.73 to 1.70 for females, respectively), the sexes differ by race with regard to which has the highest mortality ratio. The

very low neonatal to postneonatal mortality ratios of male and female American Indian, Aleut and Eskimo infants (0.75 and 0.95, respectively) indicate that post-neonatal mortality is a relatively more important problem among this group.

Since 1960, the rate of neonatal mortality has dropped by almost three-quarters for white infants and by about two-thirds for nonwhite infants (Table 4-14). Among both whites and non-whites, the ratio of the rate of male-to-female neonatal deaths has declined somewhat, indicating a relatively greater rate of improving survivorship for male infants in the first 28 days of life. The sex ratio of postneonatal survivorship has actually worsened for white

Table 4-13. Neonatal and Postneonatal Mortality Rates[1], by Race[2]: 1915-1991[3]

Year	Neonatal mortality rates				Postneonatal mortality rates			
	Total	White	Nonwhite		Total	White	Nonwhite	
			Total	Black			Total	Black
1991	5.6	4.5	9.5	11.2	3.4	2.8	5.6	6.3
1990	5.8	4.8	9.9	11.6	3.4	2.8	5.7	6.4
1989	6.2	5.1	10.3	11.9	3.6	2.9	6.0	6.7
1988	6.3	5.3	10.3	12.1	3.6	3.1	5.7	6.5
1987	6.5	5.4	10.7	12.3	3.6	3.1	5.8	6.4
1986	6.7	5.7	10.8	12.3	3.6	3.1	5.9	6.6
1985	7.0	6.0	11.0	12.6	3.7	3.2	5.8	6.4
1984	7.0	6.1	10.9	12.3	3.8	3.2	6.2	6.8
1983	7.3	6.3	11.4	12.9	3.9	3.3	6.4	7.0
1982	7.7	6.7	12.0	13.6	3.8	3.2	6.3	6.9
1981	8.0	7.0	12.5	14.0	3.9	3.4	6.3	6.8
1980	8.5	7.4	13.2	14.6	4.1	3.5	7.0	7.6
1979	8.9	7.8	13.6	14.8	4.2	3.5	7.3	7.7
1978	9.5	8.3	14.7	16.0	4.3	3.6	7.4	7.9
1977	9.9	8.7	15.4	16.6	4.2	3.6	7.3	7.8
1976	10.9	9.6	17.1	18.5	4.3	3.6	7.5	7.9
1975	11.6	10.3	17.5	18.9	4.5	3.8	7.8	8.1
1974	12.3	11.0	17.9	19.2	4.4	3.7	8.0	8.3
1973	13.0	11.7	18.5	19.8	4.8	3.9	8.6	9.0
1972	13.6	12.3	19.9	21.1	4.8	4.0	8.8	9.1
1971	14.2	12.9	20.2	21.4	4.9	4.0	9.2	9.5
1970	15.1	13.7	22.1	23.2	4.9	4.0	9.8	10.1
1969	15.6	14.2	22.5	23.9	5.3	4.2	10.4	10.8
1968	16.1	14.7	23.0	24.3	5.7	4.5	11.6	11.9
1967	16.5	15.0	23.8	25.0	5.9	4.7	12.1	12.5
1966	17.2	15.6	24.8	25.9	6.5	5.0	13.9	14.3
1965	17.7	16.1	25.4	26.5	7.0	5.4	14.9	15.2
1964	17.9	16.2	26.5	27.5	6.9	5.4	14.6	14.9
1963	18.2	16.7	26.1	27.0	7.0	5.5	15.4	15.8
1962	18.3	16.9	26.1	27.1	7.0	5.5	15.3	15.5
1961	18.4	16.9	26.2	27.1	6.9	5.5	14.5	14.7
1960	18.7	17.2	26.9	27.8	7.3	5.7	16.4	16.5
1959	19.0	17.5	27.7	28.4	7.4	5.7	16.4	16.4
1958	19.5	17.8	29.0	29.7	7.6	6.0	16.7	16.6
1957	19.1	17.5	27.8	28.5	7.3	5.8	15.9	15.7
1956	18.9	17.5	27.0	27.6	7.1	5.7	15.0	14.8
1955	19.1	17.7	27.2	27.8	7.3	5.9	15.6	15.3
1954	19.1	17.8	27.0	27.5	7.5	6.1	15.9	15.4
1953	19.6	18.3	27.4	27.8	8.2	6.7	17.3	16.7
1952	19.8	18.5	28.0	28.5	8.6	7.0	19.0	18.5
1951	20.0	18.9	27.3	27.6	8.4	7.0	17.5	16.7
1950	20.5	19.4	27.5	27.8	8.7	7.4	16.9	16.1
1949	21.4	20.3	28.6	28.8	9.9	8.5	18.8	18.1
1948	22.2	21.2	29.1	29.3	9.8	8.7	17.4	16.4
1947	22.8	21.7	31.0	31.1	9.4	8.4	17.5	16.6
1946	24.0	23.1	31.5	31.7	9.7	8.7	17.9	17.1
1945	24.3	23.3	32.0	32.2	13.9	12.3	25.0	24.0
1944	24.7	23.6	32.5	32.7	15.1	13.3	27.8	26.6

**Table 4-13. Neonatal and Postneonatal Mortality Rates[1], by Race[2]: 1915-1991[3]
(continued)**

Year	Neonatal mortality rates				Postneonatal mortality rates			
			Nonwhite				Nonwhite	
	Total	White	Total	Black	Total	White	Total	Black
1943	24.7	23.7	32.9	33.1	15.6	13.8	29.6	28.4
1942	25.7	24.5	34.6	34.9	14.7	12.8	30.0	29.3
1941	27.7	26.1	39.0	39.3	17.7	15.1	35.8	34.9
1940	28.8	27.2	39.7	39.9	18.3	16.0	34.1	33.0
1939	29.3	27.8	39.6	39.7	18.7	16.5	34.7	33.4
1938	29.6	28.3	39.1	39.2	21.4	18.8	40.0	38.7
1937	31.3	29.7	42.1	42.2	23.2	20.6	41.1	39.8
1936	32.6	31.0	43.9	43.8	24.6	21.9	43.7	42.2
1935	32.4	31.0	42.7	42.7	23.3	20.9	40.6	39.2
1934	34.1	32.3	45.3	46.0	26.0	22.3	49.2	45.0
1933	34.0	32.1	45.8	45.7	24.1	20.7	45.5	39.7
1932	33.5	32.0	43.7	44.4	24.1	21.3	42.5	39.8
1931	34.6	33.2	45.2	45.4	27.0	24.2	47.9	47.4
1930	35.7	34.2	47.4	47.6	28.9	25.9	52.6	51.9
1929	36.9	35.6	47.3	47.5	30.7	27.6	54.9	54.0
1928	37.2	35.7	48.8	49.1	31.5	28.3	57.4	56.8
1927	36.1	35.0	46.1	46.3	28.5	25.7	54.0	53.7
1926	37.9	37.1	48.0	48.3	35.4	32.9	63.9	63.7
1925	37.8	36.8	49.5	50.3	33.8	31.5	61.2	61.6
1924	38.6	37.4	51.2	51.8	32.2	29.4	61.7	62.3
1923	39.5	38.6	49.9	51.4	37.6	34.9	67.4	68.5
1922	39.7	38.8	49.9	50.7	36.4	34.3	60.2	60.9
1921	39.7	38.7	50.3	51.3	35.9	33.8	58.2	59.4
1920	41.5	40.4	55.0	56.5	44.3	41.7	76.7	79.0
1919	41.5	40.3	55.2	56.6	45.2	42.7	75.3	77.7
1918	44.2	43.3	60.5	60.9	56.7	54.2	100.7	101.5
1917	43.4	—	—	—	50.4	—	—	—
1916	44.1	43.5	68.9	68.9	56.9	55.5	116.0	115.5
1915	44.4	—	—	—	55.6	—	—	—

[1] Per 1,000 live births.

[2] Deaths based on race of decedent; live births based on race of mother from 1970-1991 and on race of infant
   prior to 1970.

[3] United States from 1933-1991 and birth-registration states prior to 1933.

Source: National Center for Health Statistics, "Vital Statistics of the United States: 1991, Volume II--
   Mortality Part A," National Center for Health Statistics, Hyattsville, MD, 1996, Table 2-2.

males compared to white females: in 1960 there was a mortality ratio of 1.25 (a postneonatal white male death rate of 8.1, and a female rate of 6.5), and by 1991 this had widened to 1.39. The sex ratio of postneonatal mortality of nonwhites was the same (1.20) in 1960 and 1991.

Causes of Infant Deaths

Infants have a unique cause-of-death pattern. They die from several causes from which adults are not at risk. Three general factors appear to be important in predicting levels of infant mortality, especially neonatal mortality: birth weight, gestational age (a measure of prematurity), and whether the infant is developmentally immature (intrauterine growth-retarded, IUGR). Infants who have low birth weights, early gestational ages and are interuterine growth-retarded are far more likely to die in infancy.

Among the 33,466 infant deaths in 1993, 7,129 (21.3 percent) were due to congenital abnormalities, 4,669 (14.0 percent) were due to sudden infant death syndrome, and 5,473 (16.5 percent) were due to various disorders related

Table 4-14. Neonatal and Postneonatal Mortality Rates[1], by Race[2] and Sex: 1960-1991

| | White | | | | Nonwhite | | | |
| | Neonatal | | Postneonatal | | Neonatal | | Postneonatal | |
Year	Male	Female	Male	Female	Male	Female	Male	Female
1991	5.0	4.0	3.2	2.3	10.8	8.9	6.1	5.1
1990	5.4	4.2	3.1	2.4	10.6	8.9	6.8	5.3
1985	6.9	5.3	3.7	2.7	11.3	9.1	6.3	5.2
1980	8.3	6.6	4.0	3.0	13.5	11.5	7.0	6.1
1975	11.7	9.0	4.2	3.3	18.5	15.4	8.2	6.9
1970	15.5	11.9	4.4	3.5	23.8	18.9	10.7	8.6
1960	19.7	14.7	8.1	6.5	30.0	23.6	17.8	14.8

[1] Per 1,000 live births.

[2] Deaths based on race of decedent; live births based on race of mother from 1990-1991 and on race of infant prior to 1990.

Source: National Center for Health Statistics, "Vital Statistics of the United States: Volume II--Mortality Part A," (1991, 1990, 1985, 1980, 1975, 1970, and 1960), Table 2-5 in 1991 and Table 2-4 in other years, National Center for Health Statistics, Hyattsville, MD, 1996, 1994, 1988, 1985, 1979, 1974, and 1963.

to short gestation, prematurity, complications of pregnancy or delivery and unspecified low birth weight, perinatal infection, respiratory distress syndrome, and so on.

Over 60 percent of all infant deaths occur in the neonatal period. Some forms of death, however, are more evenly distributed throughout the first year of life: of all infant deaths in 1993, 898 (2.7 percent) were due to unintentional injuries, and another 530 (1.6 percent) died of pneumonia and influenza. Homicide is a surprisingly common form of death in the postneonatal period; a 1986-87 CDC study found that it was the third leading cause of death for white infants and the leading cause of death for black infants (contributing 27 percent of all postneonatal deaths). A significant part of the decline in the postneonatal mortality rate since 1983 has been due to the decline in sudden infant death syndrome, or SIDS (see Textbox, "The Decline in Sudden Infant Deaths").

The race differentials in infant mortality are to a large extent mirrored in racial differences in early prenatal care (Table 7-1) and by differences in the rate of low or very low birth weight infants (3 percent of all black births and 1 percent of all white births in 1991; Table 7-5). In 1991, infants with a birth weight of 2,500 grams or more had an infant mortality rate of 3.6 per 1,000 live births, those with a birth weight of less than 2,500 grams (low birth weight) had an IMR of 74.3, and those with a weight of less than 1,500 grams (very low birth weight) had an IMR of 305.4. One recurring puzzle of infant mortality is why Mexican-American infants, whose families suffer from economic deprivation, have mortality rates that are very similar to those of more advantaged non-Hispanic whites.

Maternal Mortality

Death as a result of pregnancy, childbirth, or the puerperium (period at and immediately following childbirth) are now so low in the United States (as in other developed nations) as to present only minor risks, especially before age thirty-five. Table 4-15 presents maternal mortality rates by race for the United States from 1915-1991. In 1915-1919, the risk to a white woman bearing a child was more than 120 times as great as in 1991; for a nonwhite woman, the risk was 80 times as great.

The key decade in the decline in maternal mortality for whites was the 1940-50 period, when the maternal mortality rate dropped to less than one-fifth its previous level (from 319.8 to 61.1 maternal deaths per 10,000 live births). As late as 1925-29, black women suffered under an almost unimaginable maternal mortality rate of 1,217.3 per 100,000 live births; at that level of risk, a mother of five children had a one-in-twenty (4.77 percent) chance of dying during her childbearing years due to this cause of death alone. By 1940, black maternal mortality dropped to 781.7, and by 1950 it stood at 223.0 per 100,000 births.

Despite these accomplishments in lifesaving, attributable to both prenatal self-care and medical care (such as the large increase in the use of fetal monitoring and Caesarean section deliveries between 1970 and 1990; Figure 7-2), there still remains a major differential between the races. Black women's maternal mortality now lags about a quarter of a century behind the rate of white women.

Another point of concern is the lack of progress in reducing the maternal mortality rate over the past decade. This is the first decade in which there was no significant

Table 4-15. Maternal Mortality Rates[1], by Race: 1915-1991[2]

Year	Total	White	Nonwhite Total	Black
1991	7.9	5.8	15.6	18.3
1990	8.2	5.4	19.1	22.4
1989	7.9	5.6	16.5	18.4
1988	8.4	5.9	17.4	19.5
1987	6.6	5.1	12.0	14.2
1986	7.2	4.9	16.0	18.8
1985	7.8	5.2	18.1	20.4
1984	7.8	5.4	16.9	19.7
1983	8.0	5.9	16.3	18.3
1982	7.9	5.8	16.4	18.2
1981	8.5	6.3	17.3	20.4
1980	9.2	6.7	19.8	21.5
1979	9.6	6.4	22.7	25.1
1978	9.6	6.4	23.0	25.0
1977	11.2	7.7	26.0	29.2
1976	12.3	9.0	26.5	29.5
1975	12.8	9.1	29.0	31.3
1974	14.6	10.0	35.1	38.3
1973	15.2	10.7	34.6	38.4
1972	18.8	14.3	38.5	40.7
1971	18.8	13.0	45.3	48.3
1970	21.5	14.4	55.9	59.8
1969	22.2	15.5	55.7	59.5
1968	24.5	16.6	63.6	65.9
1967	28.0	19.5	69.5	72.6
1966	29.1	20.2	72.4	74.2
1965	31.6	21.0	83.7	88.3
1964	33.3	22.3	89.9	93.8
1963	35.8	24.0	96.9	101.1
1962	35.2	23.8	95.9	99.4
1961	36.9	24.9	101.3	105.4
1960	37.1	26.0	97.9	103.6
1959	37.4	25.8	102.1	105.0
1958	37.6	26.3	101.8	104.5
1957	41.0	27.5	118.3	121.6
1956	40.9	28.7	110.7	114.3
1955	47.0	32.8	130.3	134.3
1954	52.4	37.2	143.8	145.9
1953	61.1	44.1	166.1	168.3
1952	67.8	48.9	188.1	189.2
1951	75.0	54.9	201.3	204.2
1950	83.3	61.1	221.6	223.0
1949	90.3	68.1	234.8	237.6
1948	116.6	89.4	301.0	303.6
1947	134.5	108.6	334.6	336.2
1946	156.7	130.7	358.9	363.6
1945	207.2	172.1	454.8	456.7
1944	227.9	189.4	506.0	513.9

Table 4-15. Maternal Mortality Rates[1], by Race: 1915-1991[2] (continued)

Year	Total	White	Nonwhite Total	Black
1943	245.2	210.5	509.9	512.8
1942	258.7	221.8	544.0	549.1
1941	316.5	226.0	678.1	690.2
1940	376.0	319.8	773.5	781.7
1935-1939	493.9	439.9	875.5	884.1
1930-1934	636.0	575.4	1,080.7	1,047.4
1925-1929	668.6	615.0	1,163.7	1,217.3
1920-1924	689.5	649.2	1,134.3	—
1915-1919	727.9	700.3	1,253.5	—

[1] Per 100,000 live births.

[2] United States from 1933-1991 and birth-registration states prior to 1933.

Source: National Center for Health Statistics, "Vital Statistics of the United States: 1991, Volume II--Mortality Part A," National Center for Health Statistics, Hyattsville, MD, 1996, Table 1-16.

improvement in this rate (since 1930, the maternal death rate usually dropped by half during each decade). In 1982 and 1991 the white maternal deaths were the same (5.8), and the black rate actually rose (from 18.2 to 18.3 maternal deaths per 100,000 live births) between these dates.

Much of this recent lack of decline in the maternal death rate is probably due to the lack of prenatal care in the United States. As is shown in Chapter 7 (see Table 7-1), in 1992 only 80.8 percent of white and 63.9 percent of black mothers began prenatal care during the first trimester, and 5.2 percent of all mothers began their care during the final trimester or had no prenatal care at all. These are poor levels of prenatal care for an industrialized nation, and undoubtedly contribute to the lack of progress in maternal mortality over the last decade. While about 99 percent of all U.S. births have taken place in hospitals since 1970 (Table 7-2), lack of prenatal care can put mothers and their infants at risk even when sophisticated life-saving medical technology is available.

The higher maternal death rate among black women may also be due to a relatively larger proportion of births to older mothers (who may have more medical problems) and to very young mothers (who may have had inadequate prenatal care). In addition, CDC studies indicate that the largest race-specific maternal mortality differentials occurred in cases of ectopic pregnancy, induced or spontaneous abortion, or gestational trophoblastic disease.

The Decline in Sudden Infant Deaths

Parents have always had to accept the fact that they cannot completely protect their children from the risks of death. As the infectious diseases that affect infants and young children decreased, and as treatments were developed for congenital abnormalities, a few causes of infant death remained curiously resistant to treatment.

Sudden infant death syndrome (SIDS) remains one of these parental nightmares. It is, as CDC researchers point out, "a diagnosis of exclusion." If, after an autopsy and an examination of the death scene and clinical history, no explanation for the sudden death of an infant can be found, then the death is classified as due to SIDS.

This condition is no rare event; SIDS is the major cause of postneonatal mortality. It accounts for about one-third of all postneonatal deaths; almost 62,000 infants died of SIDS between 1983 and 1994. As late as 1990 it was the eighth leading cause of death in terms of years of potential life lost (YPLL) before age 65. This condition was leading to the death of 5,000-6,000 infants per year; the mortality rate peaked at 1.5 deaths per 1,000 live births in 1980. It was more common during the winter than the summer months. Male infants were (and still are) about 50 percent more likely to fall victim to SIDS than were female infants. About 90 percent of all SIDS deaths occur after the first and before the eighth month of life.

Between 1983 and 1994, there was a steady decline in the rate of SIDS among the U.S. population. Overall, the rate of SIDS fatalities per 100,000 live births dropped from 152.5 in 1980 to 103.0 in 1994, a decline of 32.5 percent. While the rate of SIDS has remained more than twice as common among black infants as among white ones, the rate of decline in the rate of SIDS is very similar for both racial groups (the black/white ratio of the SIDS death rate was 2.35 in 1980 and 2.28 in 1994). Contrary to usual patterns, the rate of decline increased during the 1990s; the National Institute of Child Health and Development announced that the national SIDS death rate declined by 30 percent between October 1993 and October 1995.

One puzzling aspect of SIDS is its regional distribution. It was more than twice as common in the Midwest (a rate of 195.2 per 100,000) as in the Northeast (80.7) in the 1983-89 period, and more common in the West (166.8) than in the South (135.5). With many diseases or conditions, public awareness leads to the worst areas "catching up" as political and public health authorities devote more resources to the problem. In the case of SIDS, while all regions benefitted from the decline, by 1990-94 the best region (the Northeast, at 65.7 per 100,000) had experienced a greater decline in the rate of SIDS (18.7 percent) than did the worst region, the Midwest (which had a decline of only 11.5 percent to 172.8 SIDS deaths per 100,000 live births in 1990-94).

Why did the rate of SIDS decline so much in recent years? When SIDS became of major concern (in the late 1970s and early 1980s), there were a number of hypotheses advanced to explain why apparently healthy infants suddenly stopped breathing, usually while sleeping. SIDS has been linked to a number of risk factors, including low birth weight, young maternal age, poor socioeconomic status, lack of breastfeeding, exposure to tobacco smoke, and overheating. By 1990, researchers in the United States (and earlier research in Europe) established a strong association between a prone sleeping position for infants and SIDS. In 1992, the American Academy of Pediatrics made a recommendation that parents place infants on their backs or sides during sleep.

A nationally publicized "Back to Sleep" campaign for infants in 1994 helped to make parents more aware of the risks of the prone sleeping position; surveys indicated that the prone infant sleeping position declined from 78 percent in 1992 to 43 percent in 1994. However, other changes in the population (such as the incidence of breastfeeding and smoking, and the effects of a concurrent campaign against the overheating of infants' sleeping rooms) make it difficult to ascribe all of the decline in SIDS to changes in infant sleeping position alone. In addition, it is unlikely that any past or present regional differences in infant sleeping position can explain the continuing (and widening) differences in regional SIDS rates.

Surprisingly, SIDS, the leading cause of postneonatal mortality, was not even mentioned in the U.S. Department of

Rates[1] and Change in Sudden Infant Death Syndrome (SIDS), by Region: 1983-89 and 1990-94.

Time period	Northeast	Midwest	South	West
1990-94	65.7	172.8	121.7	128.4
1983-89	80.7	195.2	135.5	166.8
Percent change				
1983-1994	-18.6	-11.5	-10.2	-23.0

[1] Per 100,000 live births.

Source: Centers for Disease Control and Prevention, "Sudden Infant Death Syndrome--United States, 1983-1994," Morbidity and Mortality Weekly Report 45, 40, 1996:861.

Health and Human Services' National Health Promotion and Disease Objectives (*Healthy People 2000*, published in 1990) or in its *Midcourse Review and 1995 Revisions* of these objectives. While the CDC was involved in epidemiologic studies of SIDS in the late 1980s and early 1990s, SIDS was, apparently, not a high priority topic for the federal health bureaucracy. On the other hand, in 1992 the U.S. Senate and U.S. House of Representatives recommended that the U.S. Department of Health and Human Services Interagency Panel on Sudden Infant Death Syndrome develop better methods of collecting information on SIDS by establishing a standard scene investigation protocol for sudden, unexplained infant deaths (SUIDs) for use by local authorities. The form of such a SUIDs protocol was discussed in a 1993 interagency workshop; the final version was published in the Morbidity and Mortality Weekly Review of June 21, 1996. As of 1996, only four states (California, Minnesota, Missouri, and New Mexico) have detailed, written protocols to guide those investigating the scenes of SUIDs.

Sources

CDC. "Sudden Infant Death Syndrome--United States, 1980-1988." Morbidity and Mortality Weekly Report 41, (July 17, 1992): 515-17.

____. "Guidelines for death scene investigation of sudden, unexplained infant deaths: Recommendations of the interagency panel on Sudden Infant Death Syndrome." Morbidity and Mortality Weekly Report Recommendations and Reports 45, RR-10 (June 21, 1996).

____. "Sudden Infant Death Syndrome--United States, 1983-1994." Morbidity and Mortality Weekly Report 45, (October 11, 1996): 859-63.

____. "Type of certifier and autopsy rates for Sudden Infant Death Syndrome--Washington, 1980-1994." Morbidity and Mortality Weekly Report 45, (October 11, 1996):863-66.

National Institute of Child Health and Development. "SIDS death rate declines by 30 percent." Press release, June 24, 1996.

Task Force on Infant Positioning and SIDS, American Academy of Pediatrics. "Positioning and SIDS." Pediatrics 89(1992): 1120-26.

Williger, M. "SIDS prevention." Pediatric Annals 24(1995): 358-64.

Number of Cases and Rate[1] of Sudden Infant Death Syndrome (SIDS), by Race[2]: 1980-1994

Year	Total		White		Black	
	Number	Rate	Number	Rate	Number	Rate
1994	4,073	103.0	2,655	85.1	1,235	194.1
1993	4,669	116.7	3,056	97.0	1,442	218.9
1992	4,891	120.3	3,239	101.2	1,471	218.4
1991	5,349	130.1	3,572	110.2	1,589	232.8
1990	5,417	130.3	3,643	110.7	1,578	230.6
1989	5,634	139.4	3,773	118.2	1,671	240.2
1988	5,476	140.1	3,771	121.6	1,520	238.0
1987	5,230	137.3	3,605	118.4	1,447	236.8
1986	5,278	140.5	3,654	121.0	1,451	244.7
1985	5,315	141.3	3,757	123.7	1,357	233.2
1984	5,245	142.9	3,656	123.2	1,439	253.3
1983	5,305	145.8	3,613	122.6	1,518	269.8
1980	5,510	152.5	3,448	119.0	1,651	280.0
Percent change						
1980-94	—	-32.5	—	-28.5	—	-30.7

[1] Per 100,000 live births.

[2] Race for infants who died from SIDS was determined by the race of the infant; race for all live-born infants was determined by the race of the mother.

Source: Centers for Disease Control and Prevention, "Sudden Infant Death Syndrome--United States, 1983-1994," Morbidity and Mortality Weekly Report 45, 40, 1996:860, and "Sudden Infant Death Syndrome--United States, 1980-1988," Morbidity and Mortality Weekly Report 41, 28, 1992:515.

Table 4-16. Years of Potential Life Lost Before Age 65[1] for Selected Causes of Death, by Sex and Race: 1970-1993

Sex, race, and cause of death	1993	1990	1985	1980	1970
All races, both sexes, all causes	5,477.6	5,623.0	5,660.2	6,416.0	8,595.9
Diseases of heart	632.6	632.2	752.6	841.3	1,108.9
Ischemic heart disease	336.2	350.0	448.4	544.3	—
Cerebrovascular diseases	109.0	110.7	119.6	140.8	241.1
Malignant neoplasms	827.2	848.6	875.3	907.5	1,013.0
Respiratory system	191.7	203.0	207.6	211.9	190.7
Colorectal	59.8	60.6	65.1	68.7	78.9
Prostate[2]	7.9	8.7	8.4	8.5	8.2
Breast[2]	102.2	109.4	107.1	105.5	115.6
Chronic obstructive pulmonary diseases	63.5	61.0	61.1	57.2	73.2
Pneumonia and influenza	77.5	81.2	81.1	97.5	392.1
Chronic liver disease and cirrhosis	98.6	103.1	113.7	145.3	187.8
Diabetes mellitus	71.2	67.0	54.8	56.2	80.6
Human immunodeficiency virus infection	423.8	303.4	—	—	—
Unintentional injuries	891.6	984.7	1,087.9	1,373.1	1,599.1
Motor vehicle crashes	514.7	615.5	660.8	840.8	889.4
Suicide	306.4	312.0	313.5	309.0	250.2
Homicide and legal intervention	386.2	374.3	291.7	373.6	271.8
White male, all causes	6,291.1	6,503.1	6,697.6	7,611.5	9,757.4
Diseases of heart	836.8	847.7	1,034.8	1,179.1	1,607.4
Ischemic heart disease	516.3	545.5	707.8	869.7	—
Cerebrovascular diseases	97.2	93.9	104.5	122.6	215.0
Malignant neoplasms	826.8	843.1	887.5	935.1	1,036.9
Respiratory system	234.2	251.6	266.8	286.0	287.8
Colorectal	65.4	66.1	71.2	73.5	81.2
Prostate[2]	14.2	16.2	15.0	15.2	14.4
Chronic obstructive pulmonary diseases	61.9	60.3	63.2	64.2	88.8
Pneumonia and influenza	75.0	76.3	77.6	88.7	353.2
Chronic liver disease and cirrhosis	134.1	132.5	136.8	166.9	209.8
Diabetes mellitus	70.1	65.7	53.9	52.5	75.3
Human immunodeficiency virus infection	576.3	451.2	—	—	—
Unintentional injuries	1,262.3	1,420.1	1,606.9	2,071.0	2,261.3
Motor vehicle crashes	726.2	886.8	985.2	1,301.7	1,296.5
Suicide	521.2	532.3	529.4	509.0	369.6
Homicide and legal intervention	308.1	313.3	275.0	365.4	201.9
Black male, all causes	14,344.0	14,365.8	12,675.5	14,381.9	20,283.5
Diseases of heart	1,394.1	1,387.8	1,561.7	1,661.4	2,022.2
Ischemic heart disease	548.6	552.5	684.9	800.9	—
Cerebrovascular diseases	261.3	279.9	295.8	349.3	595.6
Malignant neoplasms	1,079.1	1,131.9	1,141.3	1,175.8	1,216.0
Respiratory system	341.8	378.2	386.0	400.4	376.7
Colorectal	84.4	83.8	79.4	76.7	80.8
Prostate[2]	30.0	30.5	33.1	34.1	35.2
Chronic obstructive pulmonary diseases	120.6	121.9	114.6	110.8	146.8
Pneumonia and influenza	213.6	261.4	254.9	315.2	1,308.9
Chronic liver disease and cirrhosis	197.1	242.4	305.8	391.9	463.5
Diabetes mellitus	149.3	133.7	106.1	102.2	144.0
Human immunodeficiency virus infection	1,857.2	1,224.5	—	—	—
Unintentional injuries	1,714.9	1,807.4	1,891.1	2,308.9	3,500.6
Motor vehicle crashes	797.8	919.9	893.7	1,022.4	1,466.1
Suicide	407.6	376.3	336.9	323.8	237.5
Homicide and legal intervention	2,676.0	2,580.7	1,689.1	2,274.9	2,234.6

Table 4-16. Years of Potential Life Lost Before Age 65[1] for Selected Causes of Death, by Sex and Race: 1970-1993 (continued)

Sex, race, and cause of death	1993	1990	1985	1980	1970
White female, all causes	3,216.8	3,330.7	3,542.3	3,983.2	5,527.4
Diseases of heart	313.9	309.6	369.4	401.2	497.4
Ischemic heart disease	152.2	155.9	195.4	227.9	—
Cerebrovascular diseases	83.0	84.5	93.0	111.6	180.1
Malignant neoplasms	805.0	829.1	846.4	858.3	974.6
Respiratory system	147.1	150.2	144.9	132.6	89.8
Colorectal	51.6	52.2	57.9	64.0	77.0
Breast[2]	199.8	217.5	215.1	211.7	233.4
Chronic obstructive pulmonary diseases	55.3	52.7	51.8	43.0	46.5
Pneumonia and influenza	52.1	50.5	52.1	64.0	247.2
Chronic liver disease and cirrhosis	50.1	51.3	58.9	79.1	114.7
Diabetes mellitus	54.6	52.0	43.2	45.4	65.1
Human immunodeficiency virus infection	62.0	35.0	—	—	—
Unintentional injuries	452.0	494.2	532.4	647.8	755.6
Motor vehicle crashes	300.6	351.6	364.2	437.3	466.5
Suicide	122.2	126.3	137.7	154.4	157.2
Homicide and legal intervention	102.6	97.5	98.1	109.3	69.7
Black female, all causes	7,182.4	7,382.2	6,961.4	7,927.2	12,188.8
Diseases of heart	806.2	782.4	856.7	937.2	1,292.7
Ischemic heart disease	272.0	272.3	325.1	382.7	—
Cerebrovascular diseases	211.1	235.8	248.8	289.0	564.7
Malignant neoplasms	956.6	972.7	936.8	968.4	1,044.8
Respiratory system	143.6	149.0	137.6	132.8	89.3
Colorectal	67.4	72.9	74.7	70.3	81.4
Breast[2]	267.2	264.1	236.4	210.9	209.3
Chronic obstructive pulmonary diseases	93.9	80.6	74.5	62.5	93.3
Pneumonia and influenza	131.8	145.6	141.1	187.4	888.7
Chronic liver disease and cirrhosis	91.9	122.7	146.7	210.9	295.6
Diabetes mellitus	130.2	125.8	100.8	109.3	179.7
Human immunodeficiency virus infection	556.0	336.7	—	—	—
Unintentional injuries	621.9	614.4	616.8	718.5	1,169.9
Motor vehicle crashes	299.7	305.6	283.1	296.8	478.4
Suicide	62.2	69.8	59.1	70.3	81.9
Homicide and legal intervention	517.5	509.8	399.8	492.0	460.3

[1] Per 100,000 population under 65 years of age.

[2] Prostate rates are for males only; breast rates are for females only.

Source: National Center for Health Statistics, "Health United States 1995," Public Health Service, Hyattsville, MD, 1996, Table 31.

Years of Potential Life Lost, 1970-93

The distribution of the causes of premature death in the United States differs considerably from the overall distribution of cause of death. The years of potential life lost (YPLL) measure provides a way of measuring the effect of these causes of premature death by computing the number of years of life lost before age 65 to these causes of death for various groups in the population. The distribution of years of potential life lost for all causes and for specific causes for selected years between 1970 and 1993 for all races and black and white men and women are shown in Table 4-16 and Figure 4-8.

In 1970, the total U.S. population could expect to lose a total of 8,595.9 years of life per 100,000 population under age 65. By 1993, the YPLL had dropped to 5,477.6 per 100,000, a decline of about 36 percent. The 1970-93 period is remarkable for very different trends in increase and decrease among different causes of death.

In 1970, unintentional injuries (1,599.1 years lost before age 65 per 100,000 population) was the leading contributor to the overall YPLL, followed by heart disease and malignant neoplasms, both with slightly more than 1,000 years lost per 100,000 population. Pneumonia and influenza was a distant fourth (392.1 years lost per 100,000), followed by a cluster of diseases and causes of death with similar rates: homicide and legal intervention (271.8), suicide (250.2), cerebrovascular diseases (241.1), and chronic liver disease and cirrhosis (187.8). Diseases with much lower levels of YPLL included diabetes mellitus (80.6) and chronic obstructive pulmonary diseases (73.2 years lost before age 65 per 100,000 population).

Figure 4-8. Years of Potential Life Lost Before Age 65 for Major Causes of Death: 1970-1993

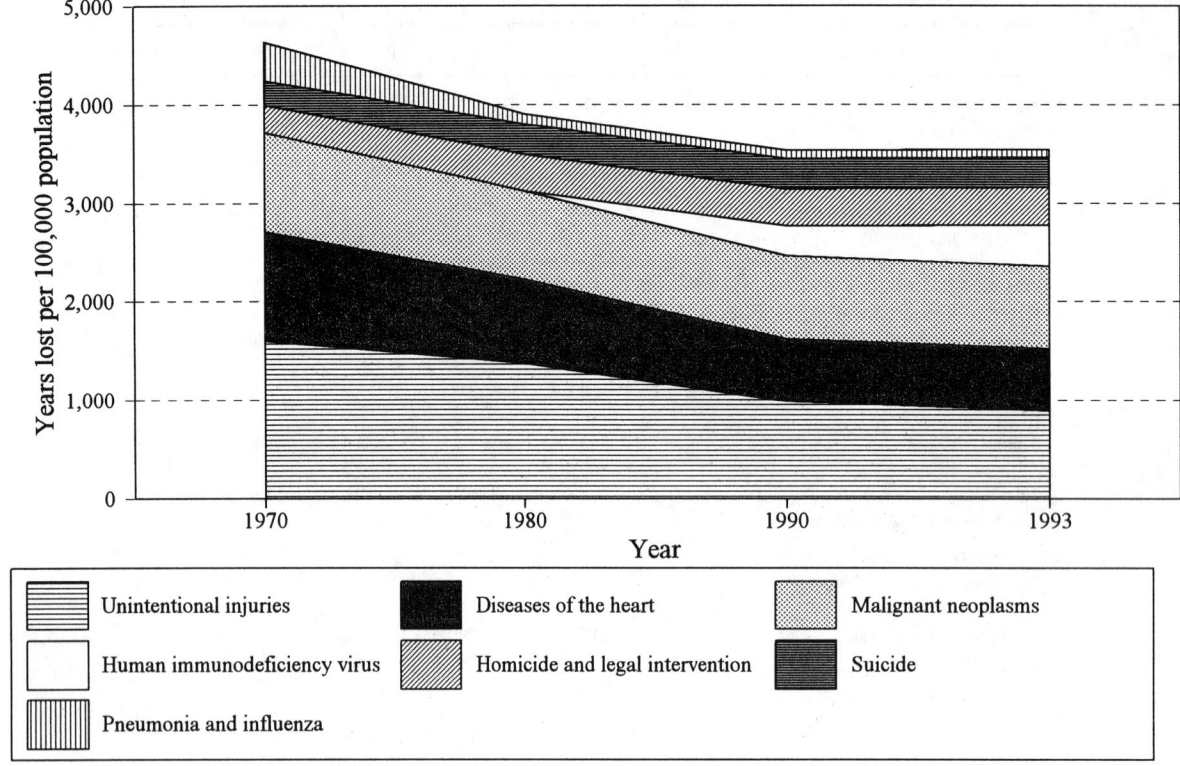

Source: 1970-1993 National Center for Health Statistics data.

By 1993, there was a different ordering of these diseases and causes of death in terms of their ranking. The YPLL of unintentional injuries had dropped 44 percent in these 22 years to 891.6 years lost before age 65 per 100,000 population, and barely led malignant neoplasms, which had dropped only 18 percent to 827.2 years per 100,000. Heart disease continued in third place, but had decreased by 43 percent to 632.6 years lost before age 65 per 100,000. A huge decrease (80 percent) in YPLL due to pneumonia and influenza (from 392.1 to 77.5 per 100,000) pushed this cause of YPLL from fourth to ninth place. A new and rapidly-increasing cause of YPLL, human immunodeficiency virus infection (HIV), had risen to fourth place (423.8 years lost before age 65 per 100,000 population under age 65) only seven years after its introduction as a cause of death.

Two other causes of YPLL had risen since 1970: homicide and legal intervention (a 42 percent rise to fifth place, at 386.2 years lost per 100,000) and suicide (a 22 percent rise to sixth place at 306.4 years lost per 100,000). These were followed by two diseases that exhibited large declines: cerebrovascular disease (which dropped 55 percent to 109.0 years lost per 100,000, now in seventh place) and chronic liver disease and cirrhosis (which declined by 47 percent to 98.6 years lost per 100,000, which put it in

eighth place). Two causes of death that experienced only minor declines in their YPLL between 1970 and 1992, diabetes mellitus and chronic obstructive pulmonary diseases, rounded out the expanded list of 11 major causes of YPLL in 1993.

Evaluating Cause-Specific Mortality by Different Measures

Does it matter whether we think of cause-specific mortality in terms of YPLL or in terms of leading causes of death? By only considering deaths before age 65, YPLL focuses more on avoidable mortality. For example, among the age-adjusted causes of death in 1993 (Table 4-9), diseases of the heart (145.3 per 100,000) and malignant neoplasms (132.6) were far higher than the third-ranking cause of death, unintentional injuries (30.3). Using YPLL, unintentional injuries now become the highest-ranking cause in 1993 (891.6 years of life lost per 100,000 people under age 65), followed by malignant neoplasms (827.2) and diseases of the heart (632.6), and the gap between these causes and the fourth-leading cause (HIV, at 423.6) is much smaller as well. While diseases of the heart and malignant neoplasms have an important effect on the death rate of those under age 65, they are nowhere near as important for this age group as for those age 65 and over.

The use of YPLL can also contribute to a better understanding of the differential risks of mortality by sex and race in the United States. For example, the ratio of the 1993 age-adjusted death rate (Table 4-9) of black females to white females is 1.57, and of white males to black males is 1.68. If we measure mortality risk by YPLL, however, these two ratios shift to 2.23 and 2.28, respectively. The ratio of the highest mortality group (black males) to the lowest mortality group (white females) is 2.86 using the age-adjusted mortality rate, but it jumps to 4.46 when their YPLL are compared. Using the YPLL shows how the race differentials in mortality place blacks (and especially black men) under age 65 years at a particular disadvantage. In addition, the lack of progress in the decline of the YPLL among black males since 1980 has increased the gap between this group and the others (see Figure 4-9).

Key Contributing Factors to Years of Potential Life Lost

As our knowledge about health and the potential to prevent unnecessary disease and disability has increased, the national perspective on health and disease has changed dramatically. A 1994 assessment by the Centers for Disease Control and Prevention (CDC) estimated that nearly 47 percent of premature deaths among Americans could have been avoided by changes in individual behaviors and another 17 percent by reducing environmental risks. In contrast an estimated 11 percent of premature deaths among Americans are deemed preventable through improvements in access to medical treatment.

Deaths from unintended injuries (especially motor vehicle crashes), HIV infection, homicide and suicide are all amenable to reduction; many nations have much lower rates of death from these causes than does the United States. The dramatic drops in the death rate from cerebrovascular disease and diseases of the heart over the past forty years (much of it a decline in death rates of those under age 65) have shown how screening programs, aggressive treatment and public education could change behavior toward less life-threatening paths.

What about life after age 65? In 1940, only seven people out of a hundred who reached age 65 would survive to age 90. By 1980, this proportion jumped to 25 out of 100, and by 2000 there will be a further small increase to 26 people. In 1991, the top five causes of death among the elderly (those 65 years or older) were heart disease (597,000 deaths), malignant neoplasms (355,000 deaths), cerebrovascular diseases (125,000), chronic obstructive pulmonary

Figure 4-9. Years of Potential Life Lost Before Age 65 for All Causes of Death, by Sex and Race: 1970-1993

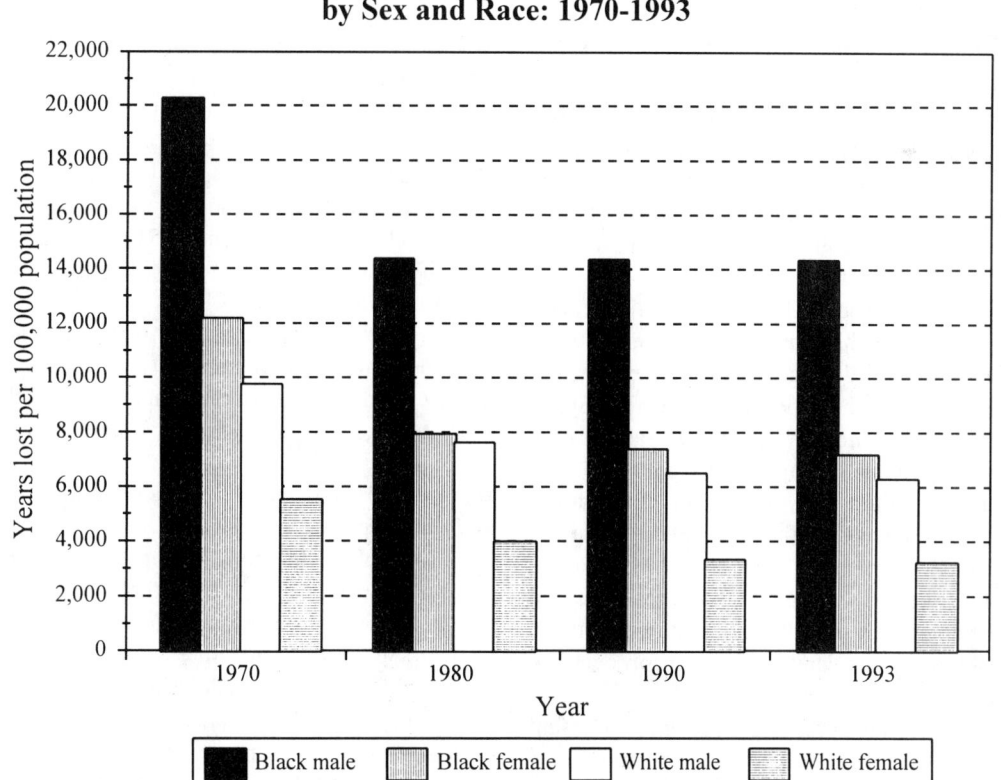

Source: 1970-1993 National Center for Health Statistics data.

diseases (76,000), and influenza and pneumonia (76,000). Compared to the number of elderly deaths in 1980 (when the elderly population was smaller), the number of deaths from cerebrovascular diseases actually declined (from 146,000), and the number of heart disease victims was almost exactly the same (597,000). Only the number of deaths from malignant neoplasms (258,000), pneumonia and influenza (46,000), and chronic obstructive pulmonary diseases (44,000) was considerably lower in 1980.

It appears that the good health of many elderly Americans is allowing them to live such extended lifespans that they eventually die of cancer rather than from other causes. Cancers can differ markedly with the speed with which they develop, and those who live a very long time may be eventually felled by a slow-growing malignancy. In addition, the growing importance of pneumonia, influenza and chronic obstructive pulmonary diseases may be due to increasing levels of frailty and breakdowns in the immune systems of the "old-old." The slow growth of cancers (most neoplasms increase their incidence with increasing age) and the increasing frailty of the older population may put some finite limits on how far life can be extended. On the other hand, NCHS calculations from U.S. Bureau of the Census life table projections (see below) report that by 2050, 42 out of the hypothetical people reaching age 65 will see age 90 (or six times as many as in 1940).

International Comparisons of Life Expectancy and the Infant Mortality Rate

In terms of life expectancy at birth, the United States ranked twenty-third for males and eighteenth for females among the world's states and territories with populations of one million or more (Table 4-17). Its life expectancies at age 65 years (15.4 years for men and 19.2 years for women) gave it higher ranks—tenth in the world for men and ninth in the world for women in 1992.

With regard to possible achievements in life expectancy, the United States has narrowed the gap between itself and the nation with the highest male life expectancy (Japan) during the 1987-1992 period. The United States increased its life expectancy at birth by 0.9 years for men during these five years, while Japan added only 0.4 years. Yet women in the United States added only 0.8 years of life expectancy while Japanese women increased their life expectancy by 0.9 years in the same era. Both men and women in the United States lag about four years behind their Japanese counterparts in life expectancy at birth, so there is probably still considerable room for improvement in U.S. longevity.

One of the key areas for improvement is in infant mortality. As Table 4-18 shows, the United States ranks twenty-second in the world in terms of its infant mortality rate in 1991. However, when the infant mortality rates of U.S. race/ethnic groups are compared to those of other world populations, the degree of differentiation between these groups becomes clearer.

If U.S. Asian/Pacific Islanders were a separate nation, their infant mortality rate would rank them sixth in the world. Both U.S. whites and U.S. Hispanics would rank after Australia (currently in seventeenth place), while U.S. American Indians and Alaskan Natives (Aleuts and Eskimos) would rank behind Cuba, now at twenty-seventh place. U.S. blacks would rank behind Bulgaria, at thirty-fifth place, but ahead of Romania. Obviously, the very poor rankings of these last two U.S. groups (particularly when compared to nations with far fewer resources to spend on health services) leave room for improvement.

Future Mortality Trends

As was pointed out earlier in this chapter, the history of mortality reduction in the U.S. has not been a story of incremental addition of years of life to people of every age. Instead, it has been a series of major declines for some age, sex and race groups for certain periods of time, interspersed with eras of relative stagnation in mortality decline. The emergence of HIV as a major cause of death and the continuing importance of homicide (especially for blacks) make us uncomfortably aware that there may be other surprises lurking in the future, waiting to entrap those who simply assume that death rates will decline by a certain proportion in the future.

As part of its ongoing program of population projections, the Bureau of the Census has recently released its latest projections of life expectancy from 1995 through 2050 (Table 4-19). In the "low assumption," there is a slight decline in life expectancy at birth for the three major groups (whites, blacks and Hispanics). The increasing proportions of minority populations, coupled with their lower life expectancies, results in a decline of overall male life expectancy at birth from 72.5 to 70.9 years and of female life expectancy from 79.3 to 78.8 years in the 55 years between 1995 and 2050.

In the "middle assumption," white and Hispanic male life expectancy rise dramatically (by 8.4 and 9.5 years, respectively) and the life expectancies of the other groups rise between 5.2 to 7.4 years. As a result, overall male life expectancy rises to 79.7 years in 2050 (7.2 years higher than in 1995), and overall female life expectancy rises to 84.3 years (5 years higher).

Only under the "high assumption" do several groups reach a life expectancy at birth that surpasses age 90 by the year 2050. In this projection, white males gain 13.2 years (to 86.8 years) and white females add 12.5 years (to 92.3 years); black males gain 16.4 years (to 81.2 years) and black females add 15.3 years to reach a life expectancy at birth of 89.8 years. Hispanics are predicted to make gains as well (although they make only slight gains over the "medium" model): the life expectancy at birth of males would rise from 74.9 to 85.5 years (an increase of 10.6

Table 4-17. Life Expectancy at Birth and at Age 65, by Sex: Selected Countries, 1987 and 1992

Country	At birth				At age 65			
	1992[1]		1987[2]		1992[1]		1987[2]	
	Male	Female	Male	Female	Male	Female	Male	Female
Australia	74.8	80.8	73.2	79.8	15.6	19.6	14.9	19.0
Austria	72.9	79.5	71.6	78.2	15.0	18.4	14.3	17.6
Belgium	72.3	79.1	71.4	78.2	14.0	18.4	13.6	17.8
Bulgaria	67.8	74.8	68.3	74.6	12.9	15.5	12.6	15.0
Canada	74.9	81.4	73.3	80.2	16.1	20.4	15.1	19.6
Chile	69.4	76.5	70.0	75.7	14.0	17.6	13.7	16.7
Costa Rica	73.3	77.8	72.1	76.9	15.2	17.6	14.0	16.8
Cuba	72.9	76.8	73.0	76.5	15.9	17.8	16.2	17.9
Czech Republic	68.5	76.3	67.9	75.2	12.2	16.0	11.7	15.1
Denmark	72.7	78.1	71.9	78.0	14.3	18.0	14.2	18.2
England and Wales	73.9	79.5	72.6	78.3	14.6	18.5	13.9	17.9
Finland	71.7	79.6	70.7	78.9	14.0	18.3	1.5	17.7
France	73.8	82.3	72.6	81.1	16.4	21.1	15.4	20.2
Germany	72.7	79.3	—	—	14.5	18.3	—	—
Greece	74.7	80.0	74.1	78.9	15.8	18.4	15.4	17.7
Hungary	64.5	73.8	65.7	73.9	11.9	15.5	12.1	15.4
Ireland	72.6	78.2	71.6	77.3	13.6	17.3	13.1	16.6
Israel	74.7	78.5	73.4	77.0	15.5	17.6	14.9	16.0
Italy	73.7	80.5	72.7	79.2	15.2	19.2	14.3	18.2
Japan	76.3	83.0	75.9	82.1	16.6	21.1	16.4	20.4
Netherlands	74.3	80.5	73.6	80.3	14.7	19.4	14.4	19.3
New Zealand	72.8	79.2	71.0	77.3	14.7	16.8	13.7	17.6
Northern Ireland	72.7	78.7	71.1	77.2	13.8	17.7	13.0	16.9
Norway	74.2	80.5	72.8	79.8	15.0	19.2	14.4	18.8
Poland	66.7	75.8	66.8	75.2	12.5	16.3	12.3	15.9
Portugal	70.7	78.2	70.6	77.5	14.3	17.7	14.3	17.6
Puerto Rico	69.6	78.9	70.7	78.9	16.3	19.4	16.3	19.2
Romania	66.0	73.3	67.1	72.7	12.7	15.0	12.8	14.7
Russian Federation[3]	62.0	73.7	65.0	74.6	11.9	15.8	—	—
Scotland	71.7	77.4	70.5	76.6	13.4	17.1	12.8	16.7
Singapore	73.2	78.9	71.3	76.5	15.0	18.5	13.5	16.6
Slovakia	69.7	77.7	68.3	76.5	13.3	17.3	13.0	16.6
Spain	73.4	80.7	73.1	79.7	15.5	19.3	15.0	18.4
Sweden	75.5	81.1	74.2	80.4	15.7	19.6	15.1	19.1
Switzerland	74.6	81.7	74.0	81.0	15.9	20.3	15.4	19.7
UNITED STATES	72.3	79.1	71.4	78.3	15.4	19.2	14.7	18.7

[1] Data for Belgium and Chile are for 1989; data for Cuba are for 1990; data for Costa Rica, Italy, Puerto Rico, and Spain are for 1991.

[2] Data for Romania are for 1984; data for Spain are for 1985; data for Puerto Rico are for 1985-87; data for Belgium, Greece, Israel, and Italy are for 1986; data for New Zealand are for 1986-88; data for Costa Rica and Czechoslovakia are for 1988.

[3] Data for 1987 are for the former USSR.

Source: National Center for Health Statistics, "Health United States 1995," Public Health Service, Hyattsville, MD, 1996, Table 28.

Table 4-18. Infant, Neonatal, and Postneonatal Mortality Rates[1]: Selected Countries in 1992 and U.S. Racial and Ethnic Groups[2] in 1991

Country/U.S. race-ethnic group[2]	Infant	Neonatal	Postneonatal
Japan	4.53	2.00	2.13
Singapore	4.90	2.94	2.94
Sweden	5.19	3.14	2.05
U.S. ASIAN/PACIFIC ISLANDER	5.80	3.60	2.20
Northern Ireland	5.98	4.06	1.92
Germany	6.17	3.39	2.78
Switzerland	6.41	3.94	2.47
England and Wales	6.58	4.28	2.30
France	6.82	3.31	3.51
Australia	6.91	4.46	2.45
U.S. WHITE	7.10	4.40	2.60
U.S. HISPANIC	7.10	4.50	2.60
New Zealand	7.31	3.70	3.61
Italy	8.19	6.28	1.91
U.S. TOTAL	8.52	5.38	3.14
Greece	8.56	5.79	2.77
Israel	9.43	5.88	3.55
Cuba	10.66	6.53	4.13
U.S. AMERICAN INDIAN	11.30	5.50	5.80
Belgium	12.38	8.51	3.87
Costa Rica	13.83	8.63	5.20
Poland	14.45	10.16	4.29
Bulgaria	15.93	8.83	7.10
U.S. BLACK	16.60	10.70	5.90
Romania	23.35	9.33	14.02

[1] Per 1,000 live births.
[2] Race-ethnicity of mother.

Source: National Center for Health Statistics, "Health United States 1995," Public Health Service, Hyattsville, MD, 1996, Tables 20 and 27.

years), and females would add 9.2 years, rising to a life expectancy of 91.4 years by 2050.

How plausible are these predictions? The history of life expectancy in the United States in the twentieth century would suggest that the kind of slow but steady rise in life expectancy within each group is unlikely; instead, we may see groups advance in fits and starts, and often not in any parallel fashion with other groups. The "low assumption" model is clearly a pessimistic one: it posits a minor decline in life expectancy among the race and ethnic groups, and a resulting more major decline in overall life expectancy as the white population shrinks as a proportion of the total.

The "middle assumption" would appear to be possible if prior U.S. demographic history continues and the current trends in high life expectancy nations like Japan and Sweden are applicable to the U.S. There does not seem to be any necessary limit to the age of human popu-

lations; or, if there is, much of the U.S. population is now dying well in advance of it. To attain this goal, the white population would have to surpass current Japanese life expectancy by six to seven years by the year 2050. The black population would have to attain roughly the 1991 level of white longevity by 2050, and the Hispanic population would have to surpass the longevity of the white population in 2050 by several years. This last assumption would probably be the hardest goal to achieve, since currently on several socioeconomic measures (notably income) Hispanics are actually declining relative to whites.

An optimistic prediction of further increases in mortality decline implicitly assumes four conditions. First, it assumes that there will be no outbreaks of "new" (at least in the United States) diseases like AIDS among our population. Given that ease of travel has placed the U.S. population in much closer touch with populations throughout the globe, there is much greater chance for the rapid trans-

Table 4-19. Projection of Life Expectancy at Birth and at Age 65, by Sex and Race-ethnicity: 1995-2050

Life expectancy at birth

Assumption and year	Total Male	Total Female	White Male	White Female	Black Male	Black Female	Hispanic Male	Hispanic Female
Low assumption								
1995	72.5	79.3	73.6	80.1	64.8	74.5	74.9	82.2
2000	72.1	79.2	73.2	80.0	64.1	74.2	74.2	82.0
2005	71.7	79.1	72.8	79.9	63.4	74.0	73.5	81.8
2010	71.2	78.9	72.5	79.8	62.7	73.7	72.9	81.6
2015	71.2	78.9	72.5	79.8	62.7	73.8	72.9	81.6
2020	71.2	78.9	72.5	79.8	62.8	73.8	72.9	81.6
2025	71.1	78.8	72.5	79.8	62.8	73.8	73.0	81.6
2030	71.1	78.8	72.5	79.8	62.8	73.9	73.0	81.6
2035	71.0	78.8	72.5	79.8	62.9	73.9	73.0	81.6
2040	71.0	78.8	72.5	79.8	62.9	73.9	73.0	81.6
2045	70.9	78.8	72.4	79.9	63.0	73.9	73.1	81.7
2050	70.9	78.8	72.4	79.9	63.0	74.0	73.1	81.7
Middle assumption								
1995	72.5	79.3	73.6	80.1	64.8	74.5	74.9	82.2
2000	73.0	79.7	74.2	80.5	64.6	74.7	75.2	82.8
2005	73.5	80.2	74.7	81.0	64.5	75.0	75.5	83.3
2010	74.1	80.6	75.5	81.6	65.1	75.5	76.4	84.0
2015	74.8	81.1	76.3	82.1	65.8	76.0	77.4	84.7
2020	75.5	81.5	77.1	82.6	66.5	76.5	78.3	85.4
2025	76.2	82.0	77.9	83.2	67.2	77.0	79.3	86.0
2030	76.9	82.4	78.7	83.7	67.9	77.6	80.3	86.7
2035	77.6	82.9	79.5	84.2	68.6	78.1	81.3	87.4
2040	78.3	83.3	80.3	84.8	69.3	78.6	82.3	88.1
2045	79.0	83.8	81.2	85.3	70.0	79.2	83.3	88.8
2050	79.7	84.3	82.0	85.9	70.8	79.7	84.4	89.6
High assumption								
1995	72.5	79.3	73.6	80.1	64.8	74.5	74.9	82.2
2000	73.7	80.4	74.7	81.1	66.2	75.8	75.8	83.0
2005	74.9	81.5	75.8	82.2	67.5	77.1	76.7	83.8
2010	76.1	82.7	77.0	83.3	68.9	78.4	77.6	84.6
2015	77.3	83.8	78.1	84.4	70.4	79.8	78.6	85.4
2020	78.5	85.0	79.3	85.5	71.8	81.1	79.5	86.3
2025	79.8	86.2	80.5	86.6	73.3	82.5	80.5	87.1
2030	81.1	87.4	81.8	87.8	74.8	83.9	81.5	87.9
2035	82.4	88.6	83.0	89.0	76.4	85.4	82.5	88.8
2040	83.7	89.8	84.3	90.1	77.9	86.8	83.5	89.6
2045	85.1	91.1	85.5	91.3	79.5	88.3	84.5	90.5
2050	86.4	92.3	86.8	92.6	81.2	89.8	85.5	91.4

Life expectancy at age 65

Assumption and year	Total Male	Total Female	White Male	White Female	Black Male	Black Female	Hispanic Male	Hispanic Female
Low assumption								
1995	15.5	19.2	15.7	19.4	13.6	17.6	18.5	21.8
2000	15.4	19.1	15.6	19.3	13.6	17.6	18.4	21.7
2005	15.4	19.1	15.6	19.3	13.6	17.6	18.3	21.7
2010	15.3	19.1	15.6	19.3	13.6	17.6	18.3	21.6
2015	15.3	19.1	15.6	19.4	13.6	17.6	18.3	21.6
2020	15.3	19.1	15.7	19.4	13.7	17.6	18.3	21.6
2025	15.3	19.1	15.7	19.4	13.7	17.7	18.3	21.7
2030	15.3	19.1	15.7	19.4	13.7	17.7	18.4	21.7
2035	15.3	19.1	15.7	19.5	13.7	17.7	18.4	21.7
2040	15.3	19.1	15.8	19.5	13.8	17.7	18.4	21.7
2045	15.3	19.1	15.8	19.5	13.8	17.7	18.4	21.7
2050	15.3	19.1	15.8	19.6	13.8	17.7	18.4	21.7
Middle assumption								
1995	15.5	19.2	15.7	19.4	13.6	17.6	18.5	21.8
2000	15.9	19.5	16.2	19.7	13.8	17.8	19.1	22.4
2005	16.4	19.7	16.8	20.0	14.0	18.0	19.8	23.0
2010	16.8	20.0	17.3	20.4	14.3	18.3	20.4	23.5
2015	17.2	20.3	17.8	20.8	14.6	18.5	21.0	24.0
2020	17.6	20.6	18.3	21.1	14.8	18.8	21.6	24.5
2025	18.0	20.9	18.8	21.5	15.1	19.0	22.2	25.0
2030	18.5	21.2	19.3	21.9	15.4	19.3	22.9	25.6
2035	18.9	21.5	19.9	22.3	15.7	19.5	23.5	26.1
2040	19.3	21.8	20.4	22.7	15.9	19.8	24.2	26.7
2045	19.8	22.1	21.0	23.1	16.2	20.1	24.9	27.3
2050	20.3	22.4	21.6	23.6	16.5	20.3	25.6	27.9
High assumption								
1995	15.5	19.2	15.7	19.4	13.6	17.6	18.5	21.8
2000	16.2	20.0	16.4	20.2	14.1	18.4	19.0	22.4
2005	16.9	20.8	17.2	21.0	14.8	19.1	19.7	23.0
2010	17.7	21.6	18.0	21.9	15.4	19.9	20.3	23.6
2015	18.5	22.5	18.8	22.8	16.1	20.7	20.9	24.3
2020	19.3	23.4	19.7	23.7	16.8	21.6	21.6	25.0
2025	20.2	24.4	20.7	24.7	17.5	22.5	22.3	25.6
2030	21.1	25.4	21.6	25.7	18.3	23.4	23.0	26.3
2035	22.1	26.5	22.6	26.8	19.0	24.4	23.7	27.1
2040	23.1	27.5	23.7	27.9	19.9	25.4	24.5	27.8
2045	24.1	28.7	24.8	29.0	20.7	26.5	25.3	28.6
2050	25.2	29.9	26.0	30.2	21.6	27.6	26.1	29.4

Source: U.S. Bureau of the Census, Current Population Reports, "Population Projections of the United States by Age, Sex, Race, and Hispanic Origin: 1995 to 2050," Series P25, Number 1130, U.S. Government Printing Office, Washington, D.C., 1996, Tables B-1 and B-2

mission of such diseases to our population centers. A similar risk now exists for the development and spread of drug-resistant forms of old diseases like tuberculosis and malaria; they may be spread from outside the United States, or they could develop among medically underserved populations within this nation.

Second, there is an implicit assumption that public health conditions will get no worse than they are now. While there has been some nationwide improvement in rates of immunization against childhood epidemic diseases in the early 1990s, rates of immunization coverage have dropped in some major cities. In Detroit and Chicago, for example, only about 60 percent of all children 19-36 months of age are fully immunized against all childhood diseases. In some neighborhoods of these cities a level of coverage may soon be reached where "herd immunity" no longer protects against outbreaks of these diseases (as happened in the urban outbreak of measles in 1989), and where both non-immunized children and adults are at risk of infection.

Third, it is unlikely that major progress in life expectancy can be made without a major decrease in two increasing causes of death: homicide and suicide. The number of young people (who are most prone to violence) will be increasing over the next decade or so, and the proportion of minority youth (who are often victims of homicide) is increasing. It appears that there will be no turnaround in the near future in the increasing proportion of young people being raised in poverty. All of these trends will put increased pressure on the institutions and individuals (schools, police, hospitals, and social service agencies) that can help families and individuals avoid these tragedies. The striking increases in suicide among elderly males over the past decade may also begin to have a significant demographic impact.

Fourth, this nation's success in lowering its mortality rates over the next few decades will be determined, in large measure, by whether it can attack the greatest threat to U.S. longevity: cigarette smoking. Since the age cohorts with the greatest rate of cigarette smoking (either past or present) are only now reaching the ages at which they are most likely to die from lung cancer, emphysema, heart disease and other ills, we may not yet have reached the high-water mark of deaths from this completely avoidable cause. The complex interplay of a large, regionally-based industry, American notions of freedom of choice in drug addiction, and the waning power of the federal health bureaucracy may yet mean that the battle against cigarettes will be lost. On the other hand, the people of the United States now appear far more likely to be able to make smoking a socially unacceptable habit than do their counterparts in Europe, Asia or other parts of the globe.

Conclusion

During the twentieth century the population of the United States moved from the end of the era of receding epidemics and pandemics, through the era of endemic diseases, and entered the age of the dominance of chronic and man-made diseases. By the 1990s, many of the deaths before age 65 were avoidable, either through changes in individual behavior or through changes in societal priorities. The striking declines in mortality from such major killers as heart and cerebrovascular disease and pneumonia and influenza over the past four decades show that much can be done to lower the mortality rates of the elderly as well.

This chapter's emphasis on the downward (and sometimes upward) movement of mortality over time has emphasized that it is not a continuous process, but rather moves in an irregular fashion. Different age, sex and social groups receive greater or lesser benefits from specific forms of progress against certain diseases or other forms of death. The invention and diffusion of antibiotics had a huge effect on white maternal mortality in the 1940s; lowering the motor vehicle speed limit to 55 miles per hour nationwide in the 1970s appears to have had a far greater benefit for black males than for white females. The introduction of 9-1-1 emergency service in the last third of the century helped men suffering heart attacks and choking children, but did little for women dying of cervical or breast cancer.

While there are many social improvements that benefit all (cleaner air and water, much more rapid response to food poisoning outbreaks, and so on), the death rate also declines as the product of many small, often difficult and frequently controversial (at least at the time) steps in public health and social improvement. Lower mortality in the next few decades may be as much a product of societal compliance with avoiding relatively obvious (wearing seat belts) or non-obvious (avoiding fatty foods) risks as it is a result of new scientific breakthroughs.

Bibliography

Antonovsky, A. "Social Class, Life Expectancy and Overall Mortality." Milbank Memorial Fund Quarterly 45(1967): 31-73.

Brooks, C.H. "Social, Economic, and Biological Correlates of Infant Mortality in City Neighborhoods." Journal of Health and Social Behavior 21(1980): 2-11.

Bunker, J., Gomby, D.,and Kehrer, B.(eds.). Pathways to Health: The Role of Social Factors. Menlo Park, CA: Henry J. Kaiser Family Foundation. 1989.

Chang, H.C., and Pendleton, B.F. "Demographic, Environmental, and Sex-Specific Correlates of Noninfant Mortality in the North Central Region." Sociology and Social Research 66 (1981): 52-68.

Coale, A.J., and Kisker, E.E. "Defects in Data on Old-Age Mortality in the United States." Asia and Pacific Population Forum 4(1990): 1-31.

Cooper, R. "Health Status of Blacks in the United States." Annual Review of Epidemiology 3(1993): 137-44.

Crimmins, E.M., Hayward, Mark D., and Saito, Yashuhiko. "Changing Mortality and Morbidity Rates and Life Expectancy of the Older Population." Demography 31(1994): 159-75.

Duleep, H. "Measuring Socioeconomic Mortality Differentials Over Time." Demography 26(1993): 345-51.

Feinleib, Manning, Fabsitz, Richard, and Sharrett, A. R. Mortality from Cardiovascular and Noncardiovascular Diseases for U.S. Cities 1949-50, 1959-61 and 1969-71 with Selected Environmental Descriptors. Washington, D.C.: U.S. Public Health Service. 1979.

Feinstein, J. "The Relationship between Socioeconomic Status and Health." The Milbank Memorial Fund Quarterly 71(1993): 279-322.

Feldman, J.J., Makuc, D.M., Kleinman, J.C., and Cornoni-Huntley, J. "National Trends in Educational Differentials in Mortality." American Journal of Epidemiology 129(1989): 919-33.

Fingerhut, L.A. "Changes in Mortality Among the Elderly: United States, 1940-78." Vital and Health Statistics (Series 3, No. 22). Hyattsville, MD: National Center for Health Statistics. 1982.

Frisbie, W. Parker, Forbes, Douglas, and Pullum, Starling G. "Compromised Birth Outcomes and Infant Mortality Among Racial and Ethnic Groups." Demography 33(1996): 469-82.

Garrett, Laurie. The Coming Plague: Newly Emerging Diseases in a World Out of Balance. New York: Farrar, Straus and Giroux. 1994.

Gibson, R. "The Age-by-Race Gap in Health and Mortality in the Older Population: A Social Science Research Agenda." The Gerontologist 34(1994): 454-62.

Haan, Mary, Kaplan, George, and Camacho, Terry. "Poverty and Health: Prospective Evidence from the Alameda County Study." American Journal of Epidemiology 125(1987): 989-98.

Himes, Christine L. "Age Patterns of Mortality and Cause of Death Structures in Sweden, Japan and the United States." Demography 31(1994): 633-50.

Hummer, Robert. "Black-White Differences in Health and Mortality: A Review and Conceptual Model." Sociological Quarterly 37(1996): 105-25.

Kitagawa, Evelyn M., and Hauser, Philip M. Differential Mortality in the United States: A Study in Socioeconomic Epidemiology. Cambridge, MA: Harvard University Press. 1973.

Klebba, A.I., Maurer, I.D., and Glass, E.I. "Mortality Trends: Age, Color, and Sex, United States, 1950-69." Vital and Health Statistics (Series 20, No. 15). Washington, D.C.: U.S. Government Printing Office. 1973.

_____. "Mortality Trends for Leading Causes of Death, United States, 1950-59." Vital and Health Statistics (Series 20, No. 16). Washington, D.C.: U.S. Government Printing Office. 1973.

Kochanek, K.D., Maurer, J.D., and Rosenberg, H.M. "Why Did Black Life Expectancy Decline from 1984 through 1989 in the United States?" American Journal of Public Health 84(1994): 938-44.

LaVeist, T.A. "Linking Residential Segregation and Infant Mortality in U.S. Cities." Social Science Research 73(1989):90-4.

Lillie-Blanton, Marsha, Parsons, P. Ellen, Gayle, Helen, and Anne Dievler. "Racial Differences in Health: Not Just Black and White, but Shades of Gray." Annual Review of Public Health 17(1996): 411-48.

Machenbach, J.P., Stronks, K., and Kunst, A. "The Contribution of Medical Care to Inequalities in Health: Differences between Socioeconomic Groups in Decline of Mortality from Conditions Amenable to Medical Intervention." Social Science Medicine 29(1989): 369-76.

Manton, K.G., Poss, S., and Wing, S. "The Black/White Mortality Crossover: Investigation from the Perspective of the Components of Aging." The Gerontologist 19(1979): 291-300.

Manton, K.G., and Soldo, Beth J. "Disability and Mortality among the Oldest Old: Implications for Current and Future Health and Long-term-care Service Needs." In Richard M. Suzman, David P. Willis, and Kenneth G. Manton (eds.). The Oldest Old. Oxford: Oxford University Press. 1992.

Manton, K.G., and Stallard, E. "Temporal Trends in U.S. Multiple Cause of Death Mortality Data: 1968 to 1977." Demography 19(1982): 527-47.

Manton, K.G., Patrick, C., and Johnson, K. "Health Differentials between Blacks and Whites: Recent Trends in Mortality and Morbidity." Milbank Memorial Fund Quarterly 65(supplement 1) (1987):129-99.

Mare, R.D. "Socioeconomic Effects on Child Mortality in the United States." American Journal of Public Health 72(1982): 539-47.

_____. "Socioeconomic careers and Differential Mortality among Older Men in the United States." In J. Vallin, S. D'Souza, and A. Palloni (eds.). Measurement and Analysis of Mortality—New Approaches. Oxford: Oxford University Press. 1990.

McCall, Patricia L., and Land, Kenneth C. "Trends in White Male Adolescent, Young-Adult, and Elderly Suicide: Are There Common Underlying Structural Factors?" Social Science Research 23(1994): 57-81.

McNeill, William H. Plagues and Peoples. New York: Anchor. 1976.

Morbidity and Mortality Weekly Report. "Surveillance of Postneonatal Mortality, United States, 1980-87." 40(SS-2)(1990): 43-55.

_____. "Differences in Maternal Mortality Among Black and White Women—United States, 1990." 44(1995): 6-14.

_____. "Proportionate Mortality from Pulmonary Tuberculosis Associated with Occupations—28 States, 1979-1990." 44(1995): 14-19.

_____. "Tuberculosis Morbidity—United States, 1994." 44(1995): 387-90.

_____. "Suicide among Older Persons—United States, 1980-1992." 45(1996): 3-6.

National Center for Health Statistics. Excess Deaths and Other Mortality Measures for the Black Population: 1979-81 and 1991. Hyattsville, MD: U.S. Department of Health and Human Services. 1994.

_____. Health, United States, 1995. Hyattsville, MD: Public Health Service. 1995.

Navarro, V. "Race or Class versus Race and Class: Mortality Differentials in the United States." Lancet 336(1990): 1238-40.

Olshansky, S. Jay, Carnes, Bruce A., and Cassel, Christine K. "The Aging of the Human Species." Scientific American 268(1993): 46-52.

Omran, Abdel R. "The Epidemiologic Transition: A Theory of the Epidemiology of Population Change (Part I)." Milbank Memorial Fund Quarterly 49(1971): 509-38.

Otten, M.C., Teutsch, S.M., Williamson D.F., and Marks, J.S. "The Effect of Known Risk Factors on the Excess Mortality of Black Adults in the United States." Journal of the American Medical Association 263(1990): 845-50.

Pappas, G., Queen, S., Hadden, W., and Fisher, G. "The Increasing Disparity in Mortality between Socioeconomic Groups in the United States, 1960 and 1986." New England Journal of Medicine 329(1993): 103-9.

Poldenak, A. Race and Ethnic Differences in Disease. New York: Oxford University Press. 1989.

Potter, Lloyd. "Socioeconomic Determinants of White and Black Life Expectancy Differentials." Demography 28(1991): 303-20.

Preston, Samuel H. Mortality Patterns in National Populations: With Special Reference to Recorded Causes of Death. New York: Academic Press. 1976.

Preston, Samuel H., Elo, Irma T., Rosenwaike, Ira, and Hill, Mark. "African-American Mortality at Older Ages: Results of a Matching Study." Demography 33(1996): 193-210.

Rogers, R.G. "Living and Dying in the United States: Socioeconomic Determinants of Death among Blacks and Whites." Demography 29(1992): 287-303.

Rogot, E. A Mortality Study of 1.3 Million Persons by Demographic, Social and Economic Factors: 1979-1985 Follow-up: U.S. National Longitudinal Mortality Study. Bethesda, MD: National Institute of Health, National Heart, Lung and Blood Institute. 1992.

Rosenwaike, Ira, and Dolinsky, Arthur. "The Changing Demographic Determinants of the Extreme Aged." The Gerontologist 27(1987): 275-80.

Ross, C.E., and Duff, R.S. "Medical Care, Living Conditions, and Children's Well-Being." Social Forces 61(1982): 456-74.

Ryan, Frank. The Forgotten Plague: How the Battle Against Tuberculosis was Won—and Lost. Boston: Little, Brown. 1993.

Sempros, C., Cooper, R., Kovar, M.G., and McMillen, M. "Divergence of the Recent Trends in Coronary Mortality for the Four Major Race-Sex Groups in the United States." American Journal of Public Health 78(1988): 1422-27.

Sheps, Mindel C. "Marriage and Mortality." American Journal of Public Health 59(1954): 1217-23.

Singer, R.B., and Levinson, L. Medical Risks: Patterns of Mortality Survival. Lexington, MA: Lexington Books. 1976.

Smith, K., and Waitzman, N. "Double Jeopardy: The Additive Interaction Effects of Marital and Poverty Status on the Risk of Mortality." Demography 31(1994): 487-508.

Snyder, Howard N., Sickmund, Melissa, and Poe-Yamagata, Eileen. Juvenile Offenders and Victims: 1996 Update on Violence. Washington, D.C.: Office of Juvenile Justice and Delinquency Prevention. 1996.

Sorlie, P.D., Backlund, E., Johnson, N.J., and Rogot, E. "Mortality by Hispanic Status in the United States." Journal of the American Medical Association 270(1993): 2464-68.

Sorlie, P.D., Rogot, E., and Johnson, N.J. "Validity of Demographic Characteristics on the Death Certificate." Epidemiology 3(1992): 181-84.

Stolnitz, George J. "A Century of International Mortality Trends: II." Population Studies 10(1976): 17-42.

Taeuber, Conrad, and Taeuber, Irene B. "Mortality." In The Changing Population of the United States. New York: John Wiley and Sons. 1958.

U.S. Bureau of the Census. Current Population Reports. 65+ in the United States. Special Studies, P23-190. Washington, D.C.: Government Printing Office. 1996.

U.S. Department of Health and Human Services, Public Health Service. Healthy People 2000: Midcourse Review and 1995 Revisions. Washington, D.C.: Government Printing Office. 1995.

Vaupel, James W., and Jeune, Bernard. The Emergence and Proliferation of Centenarians. Center for Health and Social Policy, Population Studies of Aging No. 12. Odense University. 1994.

Verbrugge, L.M. "Recent Trends in Sex Mortality Differentials in the United States." Women and Health 5(1981): 17-37.

Wagner, E., et al. "Assessment of Health Hazard/Health Risk Appraisal." American Journal of Public Health 72(1982): 337-39, 347-52.

Williams, David R. "Racism and Health: A Research Agenda." Ethnicity and Disease 6(1996): 1-6.

Williams, David R., and Collins, Chiquita. "U.S. Socioeconomic and Racial Differences in Health: Patterns and Explanations." Annual Review of Sociology 21(1995): 349-86.

Wise, P.H. "Confronting Racial Disparities in Infant Mortality: Reconciling Science and Politics." American Journal of Preventive Medicine 9(supplement)(1993): 7-16.

Wise, P.H., and Pursley, D.M. "Infant Mortality as a Social Mirror." New England Journal of Medicine 326(1992): 1558-60.

World Health Organization, and United Nations. Levels and Trends of Mortality Since 1950. New York: United Nations, Department of International Economic Social Affairs. 1982.

5

MARRIAGE AND MARITAL STATUS

Change in marital status certainly represents a common and major life cycle transition for the population of the United States. Four marital statuses are enumerated and reported by the U.S. Bureau of the Census: single, married, divorced, and widowed. Those married are further distinguished according to whether they are separated and by whether their spouse is present (see definitions box). For the great majority of the population, marriage (transition from singlehood to the married state) signals the formation of a family and likely anticipation of having children. Divorce or death of a spouse signals the dissolution of that particular family or a drastic change in its structure. Few events in the life cycle require more extensive changes and adjustments in activities, responsibilities, and living habits (or cause greater alterations in attitudes, rethinking of values, and alterations of outlook on life) than do marriage, divorce, and death of spouse. Marriage and divorce are considered so important that they are historically the occasion for specified social-legal ceremonies. These events are registered, tabulated, and reported as demographic "vital statistics" (see Chapter 2). Marriage registers were among the earliest civil records maintained. Socially and demographically, marriage is a validation of the privilege of childbearing with full social approval. To be sure, many people are now forming household unions in cohabitation without marriage (see Chapter 11). In addition, a significant and growing proportion of children are being born out of wedlock (see Chapter 6), and a much greater proportion are conceived out of wedlock. Nevertheless, the belief that children need and deserve to have both a father and a mother living together and cooperating in their upbringing is still largely endorsed, backed by the force of custom, tradition, and law, despite the growing exceptions. Consequently divorce (which has also become more com-

mon) has come to be viewed with concern for child welfare as well as for the welfare of the adults involved.

Marriage and divorce may be studied from two points of view: statically as a classification into marital status categories at points in time, and dynamically as rates at which the processes of marriage, divorce, and widowhood are occurring per unit of time. The first section of this chapter begins with a static approach to show the marital status composition of the population now and as it has been in the past. The second section will then take up the study of marriage as a dynamic process of family formation. Finally, the third section of this chapter will deal with divorce as a dynamic process of marriage dissolution, remarriage and redivorce, and the impacts of divorce on the children of these marriages. Sections two and three will reveal the forces at work that explain the prevalence of the particular marital statuses of "married" and "divorced." Chapter 4 discussed the mortality processes that determine the prevalence of the "widowed" status. Because the divorced and widowed statuses can be revoked by remarriage, the study of the dynamic processes can be confusing unless preceded by a comprehension of long-term trends in the marital status composition.

Marital Status

Information about the marital status of the population has been collected and reported for each decennial census since 1890. Annual estimates for years since 1947 are available from the Current Population Survey of the Census Bureau. The question "Is he now married, widowed, divorced, separated, or has he never been married?" evokes the response that the Bureau of the Census tabulates (see "marital status" in the Definition Box).

Chapter 5 Definitions
MARRIAGE AND MARITAL STATUS

Marital Status. All persons 15 years of age and over were asked whether they were now married, widowed, divorced, separated, or never married. Couples who live together (unmarried persons, persons in common-law marriages) were allowed to report the marital status they considered the most appropriate.

Never Married. Includes all persons who have never been married, including persons whose only marriage(s) was annulled.

Ever Married. Includes persons married at the time of enumuration (including those separated), widowed, or divorced.

Now Married, Except Separated. Includes persons whose current marriage has not ended through widowhood, divorce, or separation, regardless of previous marital history. The category may also include couples who live together or persons in common-law marriages if they consider this category the most appropriate. In certain tabulations, currently married persons are further classified as "spouse present," or "spouse absent."

Separated. Includes persons legally separated or otherwise absent from their spouse because of marital discord. Included are persons who have been deserted or who have parted because they no longer want to live together but who have not obtained a divorce.

Widowed. Includes widows and widowers who have not remarried.

Divorced. Includes persons who are legally divorced and who have not remarried.

Crude Marriage Rate (CMR). Number of marriages in a year per 1,000 population as of the midpoint of that year.

General Marriage Rate (GMR). Number of marriages in a year per 1,000 females aged fifteen and over as of the midpoint of that year.

General Nuptiality Rate (GNR). Number of marriages per 1,000 unmarried females aged 15 to 44 as of the midpoint of that year.

Age-specific Nuptiality Rate. Number of marriages for women of a given age per 1,000 unmarried females of the same age as of the midpoint of that year. This rate can also be calculated for males.

First Marriage Rate. Number of first marriages per 1,000 never-married women as of the midpoint of that year. This rate can also be calculated for males and may be computed on an age-specific basis.

Remarriage Rate. Number of marriages of previously married persons per 1,000 widowed or divorced population as of the midpoint of that year. This rate can also be computed on an age-specific basis.

Crude Divorce Rate (CDR). Number of divorces per 1,000 population as of the midpoint of that year.

General Divorce Rate (GDR). Number of divorces per 1,000 married women aged 15 and over as of the midpoint of that year.

Custody. The act or right of guarding, especially such a right granted by a court to a person(s) to act as a guardian of a child or children in the case of divorce.

Since marital status is self-reported (or reported for members of the household), it is possible that some mature or elderly never-married persons (especially those with children) may be misclassified as divorced or widowed and that some divorced or widowed persons may be misclassified as single. Demographers also frequently refer to the "ever married" population. This is the population that has been married at some time in its life. It is equal to the sum of the married, widowed, separated, and divorced, or to the total population minus the single (never married) population. Errors are perhaps more likely in such retrospective classifications of marital status but are not generally considered significant for population level analysis such as presented in this chapter.

Overview

Table 5-1 summarizes the census data since 1890 for marital status. The third and fourth columns of the table show that there was a steady decrease during the sixty-five years from 1890 to 1955 in the proportion of the population that was single, and a corresponding increase in the proportions married and ever married. In 1890, 44 percent of males and 34 percent of females fourteen years of age or older were single. This higher prevalence of bachelorhood was caused by delayed marriages and high proportions never marrying. During the half-century to 1940 there was a slow decline in the proportion of the single population, as marriage became more nearly universal and occurred at earlier ages.

For all recent censuses, men tend to be single (never married) in greater proportions than women. The reason for this is that women tend to marry about 2.5 years younger than men. Women also tend to be widowed or divorced in greater proportion than men. This is caused by their greater longevity and by the greater tendency for men with broken marriages to remarry.

Not as widely publicized as the "baby boom" of the 1940s to the 1960s was the "marriage boom" that accompanied it. Beginning suddenly in the early 1940s, marriage became tremendously popular at all ages, and the proportion of the population single shrank dramatically. This marriage boom was a sudden acceleration of the long-term downward trend in the proportion of single (never married) adults described above. It lasted until about 1957, at which time only about 24 percent of males and 18 percent of females were classed as single—far below the proportions of 1890. This was followed by a decade (1957-1967) of plateau, during which the single proportion of the population shrank.

By 1960 the proportion of single was clearly rising, reversing the marriage boom. Yet, the rise in singlehood has been relatively slow between 1960 and 1992. Most of the rise in singlehood was concentrated in the years of 1955 through 1975 with little change since. Despite this leveling in singlehood over nearly twenty years, many

Table 5-1. Marital Status of the Population and Estimated Median Age at First Marriage[1]: United States, 1890-1992

| Year | Median age at first marriage | | Percent distribution by marital status | | | | | | | |
| | | | Single | | Married | | Widowed | | Divorced | |
	Male	Female	Male	Female	Male	Female	Male	Female	Male	Female
1992	26.5	24.4	30.2	23.0	59.9	56.3	2.7	11.2	7.2	9.4
1990	26.1	23.9	29.9	22.8	60.7	56.8	2.5	11.5	6.8	8.9
1985	25.5	23.3	30.0	22.7	61.5	57.1	2.4	11.9	6.0	8.2
1980	24.7	22.0	29.3	22.4	63.4	59.0	2.5	11.9	4.8	6.6
1975	23.5	21.1	29.5	22.8	64.8	60.4	2.4	12.1	3.3	4.8
1970	23.2	20.8	28.1	22.1	66.9	61.7	2.9	12.5	2.2	3.5
1965	22.8	20.6	26.6	20.7	67.9	63.9	3.3	12.5	2.2	2.9
1960	22.8	20.3	25.3	19.0	69.1	65.6	3.7	12.8	1.9	2.6
1955	22.6	20.2	24.1	18.2	69.9	66.9	4.2	12.6	1.8	2.3
1950	22.8	20.3	26.1	19.6	68.2	66.1	4.0	12.1	1.6	2.2
1940	24.3	21.5	34.8	27.6	59.7	59.5	4.2	11.3	1.2	1.6
1930	24.3	21.3	35.8	28.4	58.4	59.5	4.5	10.8	1.1	1.3
1920	24.6	21.2	36.9	29.4	57.6	58.9	4.6	10.8	0.6	0.8
1910	25.1	21.6	40.4	31.8	54.2	57.1	4.4	10.3	0.5	0.6
1900	25.9	21.9	42.0	33.3	52.8	55.2	4.5	10.9	0.3	0.5
1890	26.1	22.0	43.6	34.1	52.1	54.8	3.8	10.6	0.2	0.4

[1] Figures before 1980 are for persons 14 years old and over. Figures since 1980 are for persons 15 years old and over.

Source: U.S. Bureau of the Census, "Marital Status and Living Arrangements," Current Population Reports, Series P-20, Nos. 468, 450, 410, 365, 287, 144, 62, and 35, U.S. Government Printing Office, Washington, D.C., 1992, 1990, 1985, 1981, 1975, 1965, 1955, and 1951, Table 1 in all sources.

persons today still view these recent changes with alarm, as if marriage and the family were losing their social and moral attractiveness and force. The fifth and sixth columns of Table 5-1 show that in 1990 and since, the institution of marriage was still more prevalent than in 1890 by a considerable margin. The peak percentage married among males and females was around 1955.

Meanwhile, the proportion of divorced persons has increased steadily and dramatically, especially since 1970. In 1890 divorced persons were practically nonexistent. By 1950 divorce had become the status for 1.6 percent of the male population and 2.2 percent of the female, having risen from less than 0.5 percent in 1900. By 1992 these proportions had more than quadrupled, to 7.2 percent for all males and 9.4 percent for all females fifteen years of age and over. These data are again for current marital status of divorced and not (yet) remarried. The percentage of ever-divorced persons is, of course, even greater.

Widowhood is a very common status for women. Because of their tendency to outlive their husbands, about one woman in nine is a widow who has not remarried. This proportion has changed comparatively little since 1890. There was a slight rise in female widowhood during the period of 1950 through 1960. Since then widowhood

has fallen fairly steadily to about the same level in 1992 as it was in 1940. Widowhood among men is much less prevalent and has diminished during the last half of this century. This decline is linked both to the dramatic increase in longevity of women. Both male and female widowhood have declined recently due, in part, to the increased propensity for elderly widowed men and women to remarry.

Another aspect of marital status worthy of particular notice is the category "separated." As defined in recent censuses and in recent sample surveys, this category measures roughly the number of marriages disrupted by marital discord that have not been terminated permanently by divorce. As of 1990, about 2.0 percent of all adult males and 2.6 percent of all adult females were separated. This represents a slight increase in male separation, from 1.9 percent, and a more substantial decrease in female separation, from 3.0 percent, since the last decennial census in 1980. Excluding those separated, the divorce statistics are quite incomplete as a measure of broken marriages. Also, in discussing married persons it is well to remember that nearly 1 percent of all married persons are not living with their spouses because of military service, work away from home, and other reasons not necessarily linked to marital discord.

Figure 5-1. Marital Status of the Population: 1990

Males

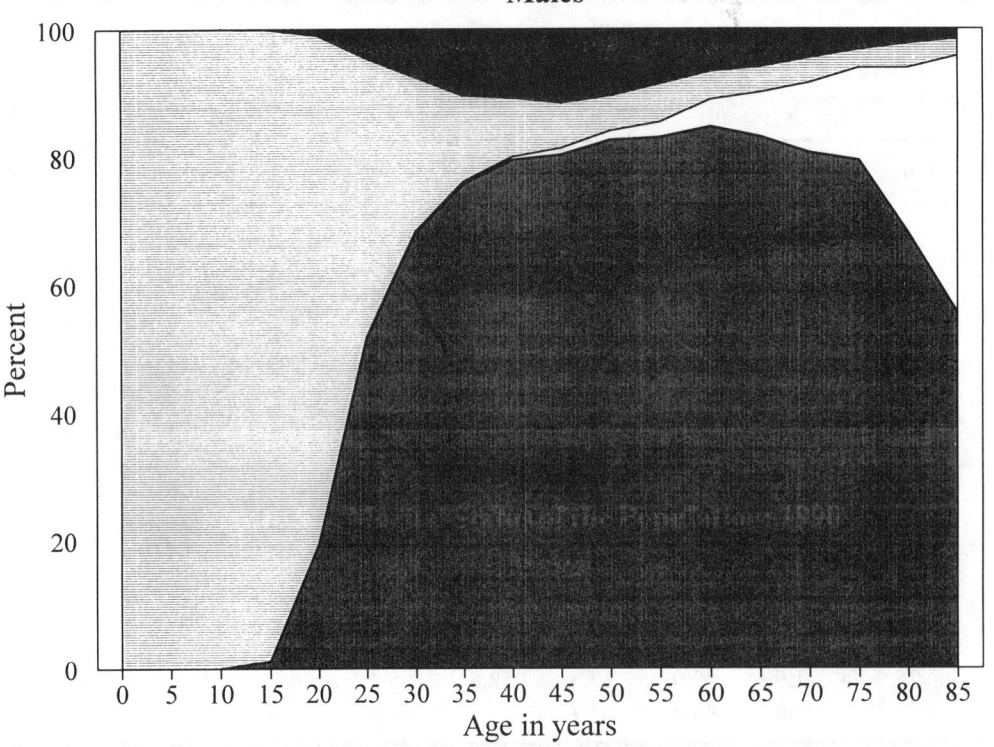

Females

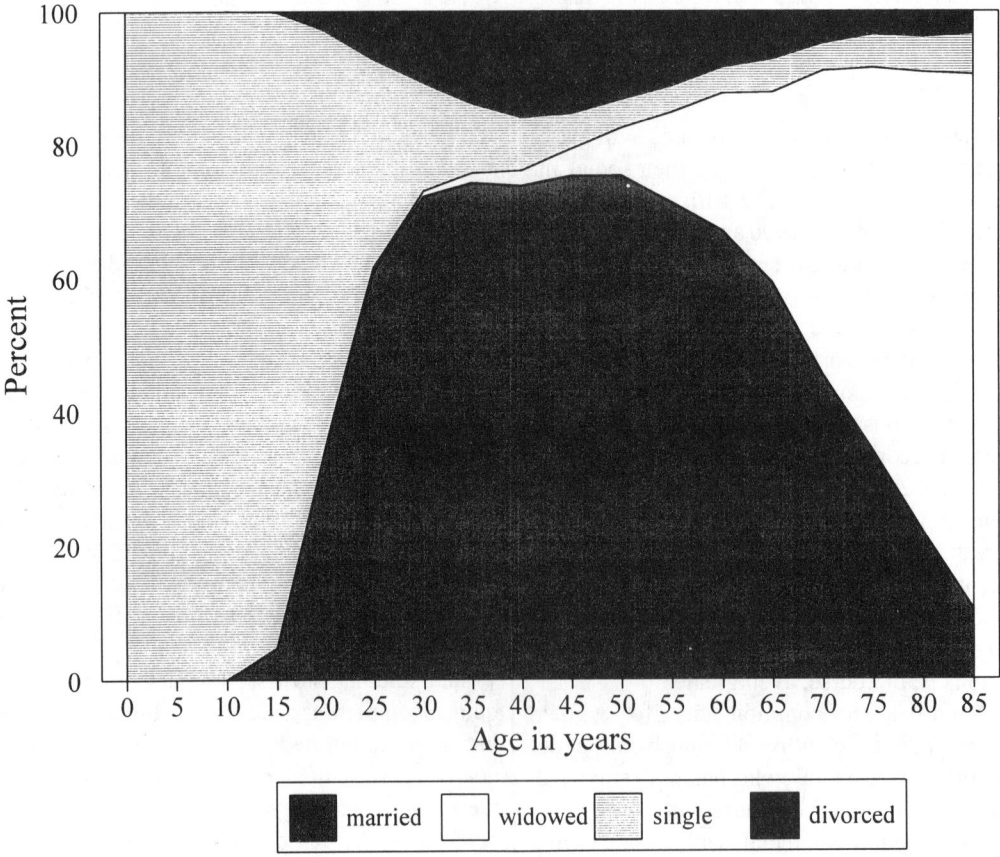

married   widowed   single   divorced

Source: 1990 unadjusted CPS data.

Table 5-2A. Percent of the Population¹ Classified as Single, by Age and Sex: 1890-1990

Marital status and age	1990²	1980	1970	1960	1950	1940	1930	1920	1910	1900	1890
Percent single male											
Total	28.9	29.7	28.6	24.9	26.4	34.8	35.8	36.9	40.4	42.0	43.6
14 years	—	—	98.8	99.4	99.1	99.9	99.9	99.7	99.9	99.9	100.0
15 to 19 years	98.7	97.2	95.9	96.1	96.7	98.3	98.0	97.7	98.3	98.8	99.4
20 to 24 years	79.6	68.2	55.5	53.0	59.1	72.2	70.0	70.7	74.9	77.6	80.7
25 to 29 years	43.6	32.1	19.6	20.8	23.8	36.0	36.7	39.4	42.8	45.8	46.0
30 to 34 years	24.0	14.9	10.7	11.9	13.2	20.7	21.2	24.1	26.0	27.6	26.5
35 to 39 years	13.4	8.7	8.2	8.8	10.1	15.3	15.4	[16.1	16.7	17.0	15.3]
40 to 44 years	9.2	6.7	7.5	7.3	9.0	12.6	13.1				
45 to 49 years	7.1	6.0	6.6	7.1	8.7	11.2	11.9	[12.0	11.1	10.3	9.1]
50 to 54 years	5.5	6.0	6.2	7.6	8.3	11.0	10.9				
55 to 59 years	6.0	5.6	6.4	8.2	8.3	10.8	10.3	[9.8	8.3	7.6	6.8]
60 to 64 years	4.4	5.2	6.6	7.6	8.6	10.5	9.9				
65 to 69 years	4.0	5.4	7.1	7.7	8.7	10.3	9.3				
70 to 74 years	3.9	5.5	7.3	7.8	8.3	9.9	8.6				
75 to 79 years	2.8	5.6	7.3	7.9	8.1	9.5		[7.3	6.2	5.7	5.6]
80 to 84 years	3.8	5.7	7.6	7.4	7.4	8.7	[7.0				
85 years and over	2.7	5.6	10.8	7.1	7.7	7.9					
Percent single female											
Total	22.8	22.9	22.6	19.0	20.0	27.6	28.4	29.4	31.8	33.3	34.1
14 years	—	—	98.6	98.9	99.3	99.7	99.6	99.4	99.6	99.4	99.8
15 to 19 years	95.1	91.2	88.1	83.9	82.9	88.1	86.8	87.0	87.9	88.7	90.3
20 to 24 years	62.9	51.2	36.3	28.4	32.3	47.2	46.0	45.6	48.3	51.6	51.8
25 to 29 years	31.3	21.6	12.2	10.5	13.3	22.8	21.7	23.0	24.9	27.5	25.4
30 to 34 years	16.3	10.6	7.4	6.9	9.3	14.7	13.2	14.9	16.1	16.6	15.2
35 to 39 years	10.5	6.7	5.9	6.1	8.4	11.2	10.4	[11.4	11.4	11.1	9.9]
40 to 44 years	8.0	5.3	5.4	6.1	8.3	9.5	9.5				
45 to 49 years	5.4	4.7	5.3	6.5	7.9	8.6	9.0	[9.6	8.5	7.8	7.1]
50 to 54 years	4.4	4.6	5.7	7.6	7.7	8.7	9.2				
55 to 59 years	4.0	4.7	6.5	8.2	7.7	8.7	9.0	[8.4	7.1	6.6	5.8]
60 to 64 years	3.9	5.2	7.2	7.7	8.2	9.3	8.9				
65 to 69 years	5.0	5.9	7.4	7.9	8.4	9.4	8.4				
70 to 74 years	4.1	6.6	7.8	8.4	9.0	9.5	8.4				
75 to 79 years	5.0	7.0	8.4	8.8	9.4	9.2		[7.1	6.3	6.0	5.6]
80 to 84 years	5.3	7.3	8.8	9.5	9.4	9.2	[7.3				
85 years and over	6.1	7.9	10.7	9.6	9.7	8.0					

¹ Prior to 1980, the total equals 14 years and over; after 1980 the total is for 15 years and over.

² Data from 1990 comes from CD-rom and may not match printed CPS document

Source: U.S. Bureau of the Census, "Annual Demographic Files" (CD-rom) Current Population Survey, March 1990, and "Detailed Population Characteristics: United States Summary," U.S. Government Printing Office, Washington, D.C., 1983, 1973, and 1965.

Table 5-2B. Percent of the Population[1] Classified as Married, by Age and Sex: 1890-1990

Marital status and age	1990[2]	1980	1970	1960	1950	1940	1930	1920	1910	1900	1890
Percent married male											
Total	62.0	62.5	65.7	69.6	67.5	59.7	58.4	57.6	54.2	52.8	52.1
14 years	—	—	1.0	0.6	0.6	0.1	0.1	0.3	0.1	0.1	...
15 to 19 years	1.2	2.7	3.9	3.8	3.1	1.7	1.7	2.1	1.1	1.0	0.5
20 to 24 years	19.4	29.5	42.9	45.9	39.9	27.4	28.1	28.3	24.0	21.6	18.9
25 to 29 years	51.7	61.1	77.1	77.2	74.2	62.7	61.3	58.7	55.5	52.6	52.7
30 to 34 years	68.2	76.3	85.7	85.7	84.3	77.2	76.0	73.2	71.4	69.8	71.3
35 to 39 years	75.8	82.4	87.9	88.3	86.8	81.6	81.0	79.8	79.2	78.8	80.9
40 to 44 years	79.5	84.7	87.9	89.1	87.1	83.2	82.1				
45 to 49 years	80.3	85.6	88.3	88.5	86.2	83.6	82.1	81.0	81.5	82.2	84.3
50 to 54 years	82.6	85.4	87.9	87.0	85.0	81.9	81.0				
55 to 59 years	83.0	85.8	86.6	84.8	83.1	79.9	79.5	77.9	79.0	79.7	82.3
60 to 64 years	84.7	85.3	84.5	82.9	79.3	76.7	76.2				
65 to 69 years	83.1	83.0	80.6	79.4	74.0	71.9	71.5				
70 to 74 years	80.6	79.6	75.8	73.1	67.5	64.9	64.7				
75 to 79 years	79.4	73.6	68.8	64.7	59.0	56.1		64.7	65.6	67.1	70.5
80 to 84 years	68.2	64.4	58.0	53.7	48.2	45.8	50.4				
85 years and over	55.6	48.4	43.4	38.7	33.6	33.0					
Percent married female											
Total	56.9	57.8	61.2	66.0	65.8	59.5	59.5	58.9	57.1	55.2	54.8
14 years	—	—	1.1	1.1	0.7	0.3	0.4	0.5	0.4	0.5	0.2
15 to 19 years	4.8	8.4	11.3	15.7	16.7	11.6	12.6	12.5	11.3	10.9	9.5
20 to 24 years	34.2	44.4	60.5	69.5	65.6	51.3	51.6	52.3	49.7	46.5	46.7
25 to 29 years	61.0	68.8	82.5	86.2	83.3	74.1	74.3	73.4	71.8	68.9	71.4
30 to 34 years	72.2	77.3	86.1	88.7	86.2	80.4	81.5	80.1	79.0	78.0	79.8
35 to 39 years	74.3	80.1	86.6	88.1	85.5	81.5	82.3	80.3	80.1	79.5	80.6
40 to 44 years	73.8	80.8	85.3	85.9	83.1	80.6	80.6				
45 to 49 years	75.3	80.2	83.2	82.5	79.8	78.3	77.6	74.0	74.8	73.9	73.9
50 to 54 years	75.4	77.7	78.7	77.0	75.0	73.3	72.3				
55 to 59 years	71.3	73.4	72.2	69.9	69.1	67.2	66.2	61.2	62.2	60.5	60.4
60 to 64 years	67.1	65.7	63.1	61.4	60.1	58.0	56.9				
65 to 69 years	59.3	54.8	52.0	51.6	48.9	46.5	46.6				
70 to 74 years	45.5	42.7	40.0	39.1	36.6	34.3	35.0				
75 to 79 years	34.1	29.5	27.9	27.4	24.7	23.0		33.9	35.0	34.2	35.4
80 to 84 years	22.0	17.7	17.2	16.2	14.2	13.5	18.2				
85 years and over	10.5	8.4	10.7	8.2	7.0	6.7					

[1] Prior to 1980, the total equals 14 years and over; after 1980 the total is for 15 years and over.

[2] Data from 1990 comes from CD-rom and may not match printed CPS document

Source: U.S. Bureau of the Census, "Annual Demographic Files" (CD-rom) Current Population Survey, March 1990, and "Detailed Population Characteristics: United States Summary," U.S. Government Printing Office, Washington, D.C., 1983, 1973, and 1965.

Table 5-2C. Percent of the Population[1] Classified as Widowed, by Age and Sex: 1890-1990

Marital status and age	1990[2]	1980	1970	1960	1950	1940	1930	1920	1910	1900	1890
Percent widowed male											
Total	2.4	2.5	3.0	3.4	4.1	4.2	4.5	4.6	4.4	4.5	3.8
14 years	—	—	0.1	...	0.2	...	...	...	...	...	...
15 to 19 years	...	...	0.1	...	0.1	...	...	...	...	...	...
20 to 24 years	...	0.1	0.2	0.1	0.2	0.1	0.3	0.5	0.4	0.4	0.2
25 to 29 years	0.1	0.1	0.3	0.2	0.3	0.4	0.8	1.1	1.1	1.2	1.0
30 to 34 years	0.2	0.2	0.3	0.3	0.4	0.7	1.3	1.8	1.8	2.0	1.8
35 to 39 years	0.3	0.3	0.5	0.5	0.7	1.3	2.0	3.0	3.2	3.6	3.3
40 to 44 years	0.5	0.5	0.8	0.8	1.2	2.1	3.0				
45 to 49 years	1.0	1.0	1.3	1.4	2.1	3.2	4.3	5.8	6.4	6.8	6.0
50 to 54 years	1.4	1.8	2.1	2.3	3.7	5.1	6.3				
55 to 59 years	2.4	2.8	3.2	3.8	5.9	7.4	8.4	11.2	11.7	11.9	10.2
60 to 64 years	4.2	4.6	5.2	6.5	9.6	11.1	12.4				
65 to 69 years	6.9	7.3	8.8	10.2	15.0	16.2	17.8				
70 to 74 years	10.9	11.2	13.8	16.7	22.2	23.8	25.4				
75 to 79 years	14.5	17.6	21.2	25.3	31.4	33.3		26.9	27.1	26.4	23.3
80 to 84 years	25.7	27.3	32.0	37.2	43.3	44.7	41.5				
85 years and over	40.1	43.8	43.4	52.8	57.9	58.5					
Percent widowed female											
Total	11.5	12.3	12.3	12.1	11.8	11.3	10.8	10.8	10.3	10.9	10.6
14 years	—	—	0.3	...	0.1	...	...	...	...	...	...
15 to 19 years	...	0.1	0.2	0.1	0.1	0.1	0.2	0.3	0.2	0.2	0.1
20 to 24 years	0.1	0.2	0.7	0.3	0.4	0.6	1.0	1.4	1.2	1.4	1.2
25 to 29 years	0.5	0.5	1.1	0.7	0.9	1.3	2.1	2.6	2.4	2.9	2.8
30 to 34 years	0.8	0.9	1.5	1.2	1.6	2.5	3.3	3.9	3.9	4.6	4.5
35 to 39 years	1.4	1.6	2.2	2.2	2.7	4.6	5.3	7.2	7.5	8.6	8.9
40 to 44 years	2.3	2.8	3.7	4.0	5.0	7.3	8.0				
45 to 49 years	4.0	5.0	5.9	6.7	8.6	10.7	11.6	15.3	15.7	17.6	18.4
50 to 54 years	7.0	8.7	10.0	11.1	13.9	15.9	16.9				
55 to 59 years	13.5	14.2	16.1	17.9	20.5	22.4	23.4	29.5	30.0	32.3	33.3
60 to 64 years	20.6	22.6	24.9	27.6	29.7	31.3	33.1				
65 to 69 years	28.5	33.8	36.5	37.9	41.1	43.1	44.1				
70 to 74 years	45.5	46.2	49.0	50.4	53.3	55.5	55.9				
75 to 79 years	57.4	60.0	61.1	62.2	65.1	67.3		58.4	58.1	59.3	58.6
80 to 84 years	68.8	72.3	71.9	73.1	75.9	77.1	73.9				
85 years and over	80.0	81.8	76.9	81.4	82.9	85.3					

[1] Prior to 1980, the total equals 14 years and over; in 1980 and after the total is for 15 years and over.

[2] Data from 1990 comes from CD-rom and may not match printed CPS documents.

Source: U.S. Bureau of the Census, "Annual Demographic Files" (CD-rom) Current Population Survey, March 1990, and "Detailed Population Characteristics: United States Summary," U.S. Government Printing Office, Washington, D.C., 1983, 1973, and 1965.

Table 5-2D. Percent of the Population[1] Classified as Divorced, by Age and Sex: 1890-1990

Marital status and age	1990[2]	1980	1970	1960	1950	1940	1930	1920	1910	1900	1890
Percent divorced male											
Total	6.6	5.3	2.7	2.1	2.0	1.2	1.1	0.6	0.5	0.3	0.2
14 years	—	—	0.1	...	0.1	...	...	...	...	...	...
15 to 19 years	...	0.1	0.1	0.1	0.1	...	...	...	...	...	...
20 to 24 years	1.1	2.2	1.4	1.0	0.9	0.3	0.4	0.2	0.1	0.1	...
25 to 29 years	4.7	6.7	3.0	1.8	1.7	0.9	1.0	0.5	0.4	0.2	0.2
30 to 34 years	7.6	8.7	3.3	2.2	2.1	1.4	1.4	0.7	0.5	0.4	0.2
35 to 39 years	10.5	8.6	3.4	2.5	2.4	1.8	1.5	[0.9	[0.7	[0.5	[0.3
40 to 44 years	10.8	8.0	3.8	2.7	2.7	2.0	1.6				
45 to 49 years	11.7	7.5	3.8	3.0	2.9	2.0	1.7	[1.0	[0.8	[0.6	[0.4
50 to 54 years	10.5	6.8	3.9	3.1	3.0	2.0	1.6				
55 to 59 years	8.6	5.8	3.9	3.1	2.7	1.9	1.6	[1.0	[0.8	[0.6	[0.5
60 to 64 years	6.7	5.0	3.6	3.0	2.5	1.7	1.5				
65 to 69 years	6.0	4.4	3.5	2.7	2.3	1.6	1.3				
70 to 74 years	4.7	3.7	3.1	2.4	1.9	1.3	1.1				
75 to 79 years	3.3	3.2	2.7	2.1	1.5	1.1	[	0.7	0.7	0.5	0.4
80 to 84 years	2.3	2.6	2.4	1.7	1.1	0.8	0.8				
85 years and over	1.6	2.1	2.4	1.4	0.8	0.6					
Percent divorced female											
Total	8.9	7.1	3.9	2.9	2.4	1.6	1.3	0.8	0.6	0.5	0.4
14 years	—	—	0.1	...	...	...	...	...	...	...	...
15 to 19 years	0.2	0.4	0.3	0.3	0.3	0.1	0.2	0.1	0.1	0.1	...
20 to 24 years	2.8	4.2	2.5	1.8	1.7	0.9	1.1	0.6	0.5	0.4	0.2
25 to 29 years	7.2	9.1	4.3	2.6	2.5	1.8	1.8	0.9	0.7	0.6	0.4
30 to 34 years	10.7	11.2	5.0	3.1	3.0	2.4	1.9	1.0	0.8	0.7	0.5
35 to 39 years	13.8	11.6	5.3	3.6	3.5	2.8	1.9	[1.1	[0.9	[0.7	[0.6
40 to 44 years	16.0	11.1	5.6	4.0	3.7	2.7	1.8				
45 to 49 years	15.3	10.1	5.5	4.3	3.6	2.4	1.7	[1.0	[0.8	[0.6	[0.5
50 to 54 years	13.2	9.0	5.5	4.2	3.3	2.0	1.5				
55 to 59 years	11.3	7.7	5.2	3.9	2.7	1.7	1.3	[0.8	[0.6	[0.5	[0.4
60 to 64 years	8.4	6.5	4.8	3.3	2.1	1.4	1.0				
65 to 69 years	7.2	5.5	4.1	2.7	1.5	1.0	0.8				
70 to 74 years	5.0	4.5	3.3	2.1	1.1	0.7	0.5				
75 to 79 years	3.4	3.6	2.7	1.5	0.7	0.4	[	0.4	0.4	0.3	0.3
80 to 84 years	4.0	2.7	2.1	1.1	0.5	0.3	0.3				
85 years and over	3.4	2.0	1.7	0.8	0.4	0.2					

[1] Prior to 1980, the total equals 14 years and over; after 1980 the total is for 15 years and over.

[2] Data from 1990 comes from CD-rom and may not match printed CPS document

Source: U.S. Bureau of the Census, "Annual Demographic Files" (CD-rom) Current Population Survey, March 1990, and "Detailed Population Characteristics: United States Summary," U.S. Government Printing Office, Washington, D.C., 1983, 1973, and 1965.

The Age Pattern of Marital Status

Each of the marital statuses has a characteristic age pattern. Figure 5-1 illustrates these patterns. Tables 5-2A through 5-2D present statistics of marital status by age from 1890 to 1990, by sex. This table has four parts; one part is devoted to each marital status. Until about age fifteen nearly all of the population is single. In the ten years between ages fifteen and twenty-five, the proportion married rises very swiftly and reaches a peak about age sixty for males and age 55 for females. From ages 30 through 60 the proportion of females married remains around three out of every four females. For males, around eight of ten are married between the ages of 40 through 80. Although the age pattern is similar for females, the transition from single to married begins at an earlier age and rises more quickly for women than for men (see Figure 5-1). The loss of marriage partners through death begins to be evident about age thirty, and at each year of age thereafter a larger proportion of the population is widowed. The proportion divorced in Table 5-2D also increases in size during the middle-age years and then tapers off at older ages. Finally, at age 75 for women the majority of the population is widowed (see Table 5-2C), a comparatively small part is single, and the balance is married. In 1980 a majority of the male population was widowed by age 85. However, by 1990 only 40 percent of the male population over 85 was widowed. Comparison among the four parts of Table 5-2 will show that for all ages a smaller proportion of the male population was single in 1990 than in 1890. The change was especially large at the younger ages (15 to 35 years of age).

From 1960 through 1990, however, the pattern of decreasing singlehood at these young ages has been dramatically reversed, and the proportion single at ages under 44 has risen while those at ages under 35 years of age are more likely to be single than at any census since 1920. The effect of fluctuations in the proportion single over the decades upon the proportion married at each of these ages may be observed from Table 5-2B. In 1940, for example, only 51.3 percent of women aged twenty to twenty-four were married, but in 1960, 69.5 percent of this age group were married. However, by 1990 only 34.2 percent, less than half as many as in 1960, of this age group were married.

Cohort Analysis of Marital Status

The data of Table 5-2 make it clear that the various generations have behaved unlike each other with respect to marriage. Some appear to have rushed into marriage at unusually early ages, while others delayed marriage. In interpreting such tables, it is useful to study the tables from a generational or "cohort analysis" perspective (see Chapter 10). Instead of simply comparing age groups across censuses (horizontal comparisons), it is useful to make such comparisons in terms of the behavior of generations. An age group of persons (such as persons aged 15-19 at one census) will be ten years older at the next census and twenty years older after two censuses. Therefore, by reading Table 5-2 diagonally and comparing how the groups differ from each other as they have proceeded through life, it is possible to gain a better perspective on differences in the life cycle behavior between various generations. This can be done for each marital status. Studying the tables in this fashion will show that:

1. The "marriage boom" of the 1940s and 1950s affected all age groups. A higher percentage of people who had delayed marriage until after age thirty-five became married than in previous generations.

2. The "marriage boom" had its greatest impact in the early marriage of persons under twenty-five. Table 5-1, which reports the estimated median age at first marriage, verifies this.

3. The "marriage market" behavior of the most recent entering generation of women has been to remain single in proportions not manifested since 1890 and may even surpass that level. Singlehood at older ages appears to be more likely than in any earlier cohort. For males the proportions are similar to the groups who became of marriageable age in the 1900s.

4. The age distribution of marital status in 1990 reflects the past behavior of at least four types of generations (ages are as of 1990):
   - Ages 15-35, the oncoming generation, which is tending to postpone or forgo marriage more frequently than in previous generations
   - Ages 35-65, the "marriage boom" cohorts, who married young and for whom marriage was apparently a very attractive status (more attractive than at any previous time in the last century)
   - Ages 65-80, persons who married in the 1920s and 1930s, when marriage was becoming economically difficult and declining in popularity
   - Ages 80 and older, persons who had delayed marriage in their youth, perhaps because of economic reasons and as a fertility control measure.

For most precise cohort analysis, it is preferable to deal with generations as persons in single-year rather than five-year age groups. Table 5-3 provides single-year age data for the percentage single for white and black women less than 30 years of age for the 1940-80 period. These data provide details of the marriage "boom" and "bust" of the late 1970s and the 1980s. The "marriage bust" was already underway for white women aged 17-25 and for black women of all ages in 1970. The marriage bust between 1970 and 1990 has been far more drastic among the black than among the white population. Figure 5-2 shows that the marriage bust has continued to increase in the most recent decade. This figure also demonstrates the more considerable decline in marriage among the black population.

The Never Married

A certain proportion of the population goes through its entire life without ever marrying. This tendency also has fluctuated with the generations. In general, those generations that tend to marry very early in life also tend to have higher proportions ever marrying, while those generations with later ages at marriage tend to have higher proportions never marrying. Demographers tend to take the proportion of persons aged 50-54 as an indicator of

tendency to remain single permanently. (For ages older than this, the data may be biased by misreporting of marital status and because of selective mortality.) This statistic is a crude indicator of the proportion of the men and women who do not significantly participate in childbearing. By examining the proportions of persons single at age 50-54 (from Table 5-2A), one can see that the proportion for males varies between 5 and 11 percent and that for females varies between 4 and 9 percent. Since permanent

Table 5-3. Percent of Women Single (Never Married) for Single Years of Age 15-29, by Race: 1940-1990

Age, by race	1990	1980	1970	1960	1950	1940
White women						
15 years	99.4	98.7	98.3	97.7	98.1	99.0
16 years	99.0	97.4	96.2	94.3	94.2	96.6
17 years	96.6	93.9	91.6	88.0	87.5	92.0
18 years	90.5	87.0	82.3	75.5	76.4	83.8
19 years	88.3	77.7	70.2	59.4	63.2	74.5
20 years	73.8	67.2	56.1	45.2	50.5	64.6
21 years	69.0	57.6	43.5	33.7	39.2	55.7
22 years	60.3	47.4	30.9	24.5	30.4	47.5
23 years	53.4	38.7	23.2	18.3	24.0	39.8
24 years	44.5	31.6	18.5	14.6	19.4	33.7
25 years	38.9	26.1	14.7	12.2	16.5	29.2
26 years	31.4	21.6	11.8	10.5	14.6	25.6
27 years	26.0	18.2	10.2	9.4	12.8	22.4
28 years	25.4	15.5	9.0	8.7	11.6	20.4
29 years	19.2	13.6	8.2	8.2	10.3	18.0
Black women[1]						
15 years	100.0	98.5	98.0	97.1	96.8	97.4
16 years	100.0	98.5	95.6	93.2	90.7	92.4
17 years	100.0	96.9	91.1	86.4	81.3	83.6
18 years	96.3	93.5	83.1	76.4	68.8	71.1
19 years	94.8	88.3	72.1	61.7	56.1	60.7
20 years	91.9	81.6	59.8	51.4	44.4	49.6
21 years	85.7	74.8	49.7	41.3	36.7	42.4
22 years	77.1	66.6	41.3	33.7	30.3	35.8
23 years	67.3	60.0	33.9	27.0	24.6	30.4
24 years	67.4	53.0	28.0	23.3	20.8	26.6
25 years	58.7	45.6	26.3	19.8	18.1	24.1
26 years	53.6	40.6	23.2	17.2	16.0	21.0
27 years	50.3	36.4	19.8	15.2	13.1	18.7
28 years	45.1	32.1	19.8	13.5	12.1	17.2
29 years	52.0	29.0	16.8	12.7	10.8	15.3

[1] Nonwhite for 1960 and preceding years.

Source: U.S. Bureau of the Census, "Annual Demographic Files" (CD-rom) Current Population Survey, March 1990, and "Detailed Population Characteristics: United States Summary," 1980, 1970, 1960, 1950, and 1940 Census of Population, U.S. Government Printing Office, Washington, D.C., 1983, 1973, 1964, 1952, and 1942.

Figure 5-2. Percent Single (Never Married) for Females Age 16-29, by Race: 1980 and 1990

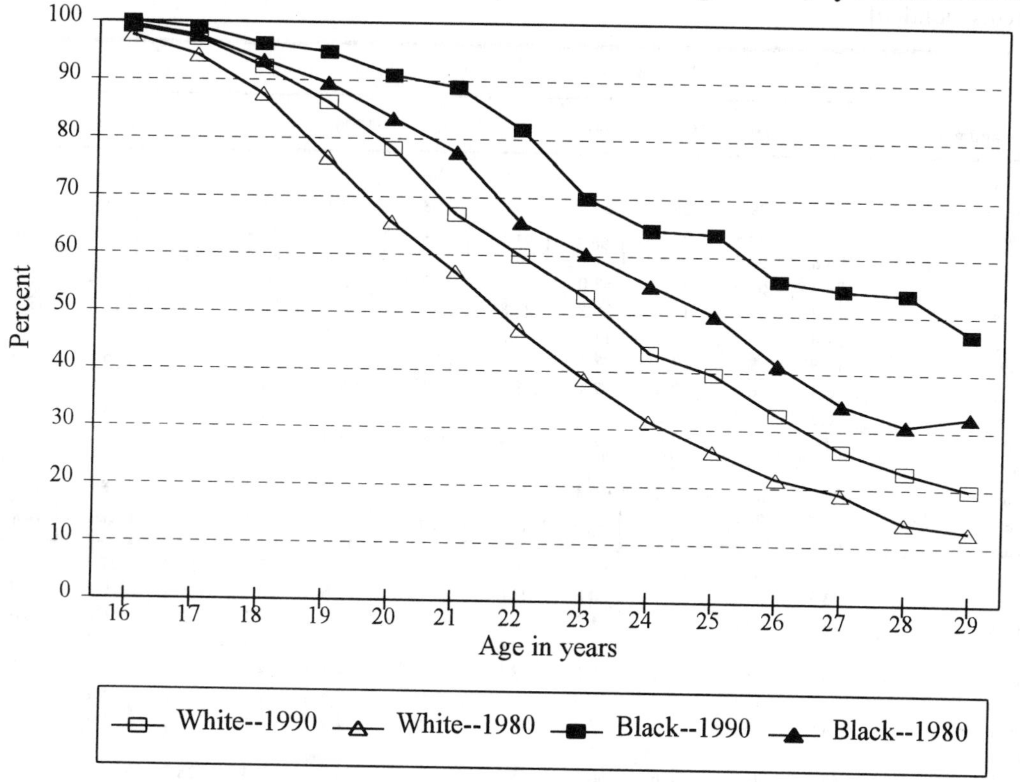

Source: 1990 and 1980 CPS data.

single status tends to be a generational phenomenon, one cannot take the percentage single at age 50-54 in 1990 as a tendency for permanent bachelorhood among persons younger than this in 1990.

Race-Ethnic Differentials in Marital Status

There are substantial differences in marital status among the major race-ethnic categories, even when sex and age are taken into consideration. Tables 5-3 and 5-4A through 5-4E report the percentage of each group in each marital status. (One table is devoted to each marital status, showing data for that status by age, sex, and three race-ethnicity groups.)

In Table 5-4A, Hispanic individuals tend to marry at younger ages than whites with a smaller proportion single at younger ages. Percent single is highest among the black population, especially at ages 35-64. Hispanics are more similar to the white population over these ages but have a somewhat higher proportion single.

Widowhood is considerably more prevalent among the black population than among the white or Hispanic population at all ages older than thirty-five. This is true for both sexes but is especially pronounced for females. It is about equal for the white and Hispanic populations across ages. However, because of the much older age composition of the white population, the prevalence for all ages combined is nearly twice as high among whites and blacks as among Hispanics.

Divorce is much more prevalent among the black population than among the white population at all ages beyond thirty for females and beyond thirty-five for males. Divorce among whites is notably higher than among blacks at ages younger than these for both males and females. For Hispanic males a smaller proportion are divorced at all but the very youngest ages than for whites. Hispanic females younger than forty-five also have a smaller proportion divorced than for the white population, but for specific age groups (45-54 and 65 or more years of age) this difference is dramatically reversed. In all race-ethnic groups, the proportion divorced is higher for women than for men.

For both the black and the Hispanic population, there is a very strong tendency for a substantial part of the population to be married but separated from their spouses. In fact, for the black population the prevalence of separation at most ages is higher than for divorce. (Separation is sometimes called "the poor person's divorce.") The white population, although it has a substantial percentage of separation, tends to have more divorce than separation. The status is at its maximum at ages 25-54 for women and 30-44 for men. In Table 5-4C the separated category does not include those separated from spouse because the spouse is in the armed forces or is just away from home because of work.

Table 5-4A. Marital Status of the Population, by Sex, Race-ethnicity, and Age: Single, 1940-1990
[percent distribution]

Race-ethnicity and age	Males						Females					
	1990	1980	1970	1960	1950	1940	1990	1980	1970	1960	1950	1940
All races, single												
15 years and over	29.9	29.3	28.2	24.9	26.4	34.8	22.8	22.4	22.1	19.0	20.0	27.6
15 to 17 years	99.8	99.4	99.3	[96.7	97.1	98.5]	98.5	97.0	97.3	[86.4	85.6	90.0]
18 to 19 years	96.8	94.2	92.5				90.3	82.8	75.5			
20 to 24 years	79.3	68.6	55.2	53.0	59.1	72.2	62.8	50.2	35.9	28.4	32.3	47.2
25 to 29 years	45.2	32.4	19.7	20.8	23.8	36.0	31.1	20.8	10.7	10.5	13.3	22.8
30 to 34 years	27.0	15.7	9.6	11.9	13.2	20.7	16.4	9.5	6.4	6.9	9.3	14.7
35 to 44 years	12.8	7.4	7.2	8.1	9.6	14.0	9.3	5.6	5.2	6.1	8.3	10.4
45 to 54 years	6.3	6.4	7.6	7.4	8.5	11.1	5.0	4.7	4.9	7.0	7.8	8.7
55 to 64 years	5.8	5.7	7.6	8.0	8.4	10.7	3.9	4.6	6.8	8.0	7.9	9.0
65 years and over	4.2	5.1	7.8	7.7	8.4	9.8	4.9	5.9	7.7	8.5	8.9	9.3
White, single												
15 years and over	28.0	28.0	27.1	24.3	26.1	34.7	20.6	20.9	21.3	18.6	19.9	27.7
15 to 17 years	99.7	99.4	99.3	[96.7	97.2	98.7]	98.2	96.7	97.2	[86.5	86.1	90.8]
18 to 19 years	96.5	93.6	92.0				89.1	81.5	75.5			
20 to 24 years	77.7	66.9	54.5	52.5	59.5	73.5	59.9	47.2	34.7	27.4	32.4	48.4
25 to 29 years	43.3	31.1	17.9	20.0	23.6	36.7	27.6	18.3	9.5	9.8	13.2	23.2
30 to 34 years	24.5	14.6	9.4	11.3	13.1	20.7	13.5	8.2	5.7	6.6	9.3	15.0
35 to 44 years	11.7	6.6	6.4	7.7	9.6	13.8	7.6	4.8	4.7	6.0	8.5	10.7
45 to 54 years	5.4	5.8	7.3	7.2	8.6	11.1	4.3	4.4	4.9	7.2	8.2	9.0
55 to 64 years	5.2	5.6	7.5	7.8	8.6	10.8	3.6	4.4	7.0	8.2	8.2	9.3
65 years and over	4.0	5.0	7.8	7.8	8.6	10.1	4.9	6.1	8.0	8.8	9.3	9.7
Black, single												
15 years and over	43.4	40.2	36.6	30.2	28.5	35.5	36.9	33.4	28.0	21.9	20.7	26.1
15 to 17 years	100.0	99.4	99.5	[96.7	96.3	97.3]	100.0	98.3	98.2	[86.2	82.3	84.1]
18 to 19 years	98.9	97.7	95.8				95.5	90.9	73.9			
20 to 24 years	86.7	79.0	59.4	56.8	54.7	60.4	77.5	68.7	43.3	35.2	31.2	37.2
25 to 29 years	55.4	42.7	32.0	27.4	25.2	30.5	52.1	37.2	19.0	15.7	14.1	19.4
30 to 34 years	44.8	26.7	9.5	17.1	14.4	21.3	35.4	19.0	10.8	9.6	8.9	12.6
35 to 44 years	21.8	14.7	13.6	11.2	9.8	15.5	21.0	10.6	9.5	7.1	6.4	7.9
45 to 54 years	15.5	12.3	10.3	8.7	7.7	10.8	10.0	7.6	4.5	6.0	4.6	5.2
55 to 64 years	11.3	7.0	7.5	9.3	6.2	8.7	6.8	5.7	4.7	6.0	4.1	4.5
65 years and over	5.7	5.8	5.6	6.5	5.5	7.0	5.3	4.5	4.1	4.4	4.4	4.1
Hispanic, single												
15 years and over	36.9	32.6	32.2	—	—	—	27.5	27.6	26.5	—	—	—
15 to 17 years	99.8	98.5	95.8	—	—	—	96.3	94.6	89.2	—	—	—
18 to 19 years	93.8	92.2	87.4	—	—	—	80.2	79.2	70.6	—	—	—
20 to 24 years	73.5	59.9	49.9	—	—	—	55.6	42.9	33.4	—	—	—
25 to 29 years	43.0	26.9	19.4	—	—	—	28.1	22.5	13.7	—	—	—
30 to 34 years	25.1	11.2	11.0	—	—	—	17.3	11.3	8.4	—	—	—
35 to 44 years	15.5	5.7	7.3	—	—	—	8.5	7.4	6.6	—	—	—
45 to 54 years	5.4	6.5	6.2	—	—	—	8.4	7.1	6.1	—	—	—
55 to 64 years	6.0	4.4	6.0	—	—	—	4.7	7.9	6.7	—	—	—
65 years and over	2.6	9.7	8.9	—	—	—	5.4	5.0	7.7	—	—	—

Source: U.S. Bureau of the Census, "Marital Status and Living Arrangements," Current Population Reports, Series P-20, nos. 450, 365, and 212, and "Persons of Spanish-origin in The United States," Series P-20, no. 290, U.S. Government Printing Office, Washington, D.C., 1990, 1981, 1971, and 1976. Data from 1940-1960 from "U.S. Summary," 1960 Census of Population, U.S. Government Printing Office, Washington, D.C., 1964.

Table 5-4B. Marital Status of the Population, by Sex, Race-ethnicity, and Age: Married (spouse present), 1940-1990 [percent distribution]

Race-ethnicity and age	Males						Females					
	1990	1980	1970	1960	1950	1940	1990	1980	1970	1960	1950	1940
All races, married												
15 years and over	57.9	60.8	64.1	69.6	67.5	59.7	53.3	55.4	58.4	66.0	65.8	59.5
15 to 17 years	0.1	0.2	0.2	[3.2	[2.7	[1.4	1.3	2.3	2.2	[13.2	[14.0	[9.8
18 to 19 years	2.8	5.1	6.8				8.2	14.7	20.8			
20 to 24 years	18.4	27.9	41.5	45.9	39.9	27.4	31.1	42.0	56.0	69.5	65.6	51.3
25 to 29 years	47.4	59.1	75.2	77.2	74.2	62.7	56.6	64.9	79.7	86.2	83.3	74.1
30 to 34 years	61.2	72.6	84.4	85.7	84.3	77.2	67.0	72.7	83.5	88.7	86.2	80.4
35 to 44 years	71.8	80.9	86.0	88.7	87.0	82.4	69.4	76.2	82.8	87.1	84.3	81.0
45 to 54 years	77.8	81.9	84.6	87.8	85.7	82.8	70.7	75.0	77.9	79.9	77.6	76.0
55 to 64 years	79.5	82.4	83.0	84.0	81.4	78.5	66.1	67.1	63.7	66.0	65.0	63.0
65 years and over	74.2	75.5	68.4	70.8	65.7	63.8	39.7	38.0	33.7	37.4	35.7	34.3
White, married												
15 years and over	60.4	63.0	66.0	70.3	67.9	59.9	56.4	58.1	60.2	66.7	66.2	59.8
15 to 17 years	0.2	0.3	0.2	[3.2	[2.6	[1.3	1.6	2.6	2.4	[13.2	[13.6	[9.0
18 to 19 years	3.1	5.7	7.4				9.3	15.9	20.9			
20 to 24 years	19.8	29.5	42.6	46.3	39.4	26.1	33.9	45.0	58.0	70.5	65.6	50.3
25 to 29 years	49.3	60.7	77.5	78.1	74.4	62.1	60.4	68.8	82.5	87.2	83.7	74.1
30 to 34 years	63.9	74.4	85.6	86.4	84.6	77.3	71.2	76.2	86.5	89.6	86.5	80.7
35 to 44 years	73.8	82.9	88.5	89.3	87.2	82.8	73.0	79.8	85.7	87.9	84.9	81.8
45 to 54 years	79.9	84.3	86.2	88.3	85.9	83.1	74.0	78.2	80.1	80.7	78.4	76.9
55 to 64 years	81.7	84.3	83.6	84.6	81.6	78.7	69.5	69.6	65.3	66.9	65.8	63.8
65 years and over	76.3	77.1	69.7	71.2	65.8	63.8	41.1	39.0	34.6	37.9	36.2	34.8
Black, married												
15 years and over	38.8	42.3	48.6	62.8	64.4	58.2	31.4	34.0	42.0	60.5	62.0	56.9
15 to 17 years	0.0	0.0	0.4	[3.2	[3.5	[2.6	0.0	0.8	1.1	[13.4	[17.3	[15.4
18 to 19 years	0.9	1.7	3.0				3.6	7.2	21.0			
20 to 24 years	11.6	17.2	35.3	42.4	43.9	38.7	16.4	23.5	42.6	62.3	65.7	59.6
25 to 29 years	35.7	46.7	57.7	70.4	72.4	67.6	33.1	38.5	59.7	78.8	80.2	74.3
30 to 34 years	39.0	54.8	75.3	79.3	82.2	75.6	38.7	45.1	61.3	82.2	83.1	77.0
35 to 44 years	54.2	60.7	64.4	83.3	85.1	79.1	42.9	49.2	58.3	80.3	80.0	74.3
45 to 54 years	57.5	60.1	67.3	83.1	83.3	79.6	45.4	48.5	56.9	72.1	69.2	65.5
55 to 64 years	60.2	61.2	76.6	77.5	78.4	76.0	40.0	42.9	46.3	56.9	54.3	52.5
65 years and over	54.2	60.9	54.6	66.7	64.4	63.7	25.3	27.7	21.5	32.1	29.0	27.4
Hispanic, married												
15 years and over	49.7	58.2	58.4	—	—	—	51.3	52.1	54.5	—	—	—
15 to 17 years	0.0	0.9	3.2	—	—	—	3.7	4.7	8.3	—	—	—
18 to 19 years	4.9	7.6	10.2	—	—	—	17.9	16.0	23.1	—	—	—
20 to 24 years	22.9	35.2	43.0	—	—	—	38.5	46.6	55.3	—	—	—
25 to 29 years	46.6	65.4	71.4	—	—	—	59.5	62.4	72.4	—	—	—
30 to 34 years	61.8	76.4	79.7	—	—	—	62.5	69.1	75.9	—	—	—
35 to 44 years	63.9	83.2	82.9	—	—	—	65.9	71.0	75.1	—	—	—
45 to 54 years	70.7	81.3	82.1	—	—	—	59.9	64.6	70.1	—	—	—
55 to 64 years	76.6	81.8	78.9	—	—	—	62.6	57.9	55.7	—	—	—
65 years and over	73.3	66.8	63.8	—	—	—	40.0	35.3	30.8	—	—	—

Source: U.S. Bureau of the Census, "Marital Status and Living Arrangements," Current Population Reports, Series P-20, nos. 450, 365, and 212, and "Persons of Spanish-origin in The United States," Series P-20, no. 290, U.S. Government Printing Office, Washington, D.C., 1990, 1981, 1971, and 1976. Data from 1940-1960 from "U.S. Summary," 1960 Census of Population, U.S. Government Printing Office, Washington, D.C., 1964.

Table 5-4C. Marital Status of the Population, by Sex, Race-ethnicity, and Age: Separated, 1940-1990
  [percent distribution]

Race-ethnicity and age	Males						Females					
	1990	1980	1970	1960	1950	1940	1990	1980	1970	1960	1950	1940
All races, separated												
15 years and over	2.0	1.8	1.3	—	—	—	2.9	2.8	2.2	—	—	—
15 to 17 years	...	—	—	—	—	—	0.1	0.2	0.1	—	—	—
18 to 19 years	0.2	0.1	0.2	—	—	—	0.6	0.9	1.0	—	—	—
20 to 24 years	0.9	1.1	1.0	—	—	—	2.6	3.0	2.5	—	—	—
25 to 29 years	1.9	2.1	1.5	—	—	—	3.9	4.3	3.5	—	—	—
30 to 34 years	2.9	2.8	1.3	—	—	—	4.5	4.7	3.3	—	—	—
35 to 44 years	2.8	2.6	2.0	—	—	—	4.0	4.3	2.9	—	—	—
45 to 54 years	2.3	2.6	1.7	—	—	—	3.8	3.3	3.0	—	—	—
55 to 64 years	2.3	2.1	1.6	—	—	—	2.3	2.0	2.5	—	—	—
65 years and over	1.5	1.2	1.5	—	—	—	1.0	0.9	0.9	—	—	—
White, separated												
15 years and over	1.6	1.4	0.9	—	—	—	2.2	1.9	1.3	—	—	—
15 to 17 years	...	—	—	—	—	—	0.1	0.1	0.1	—	—	—
18 to 19 years	0.2	0.1	0.2	—	—	—	0.6	0.9	0.8	—	—	—
20 to 24 years	1.0	1.0	0.9	—	—	—	2.5	2.7	1.8	—	—	—
25 to 29 years	1.6	1.8	1.1	—	—	—	3.3	2.9	2.2	—	—	—
30 to 34 years	2.3	2.3	1.0	—	—	—	3.4	3.2	1.7	—	—	—
35 to 44 years	2.3	2.1	1.1	—	—	—	3.1	2.6	1.4	—	—	—
45 to 54 years	1.8	1.6	0.9	—	—	—	2.7	2.0	1.8	—	—	—
55 to 64 years	1.7	1.4	1.3	—	—	—	1.4	1.4	1.6	—	—	—
65 years and over	1.0	0.7	1.3	—	—	—	0.6	0.6	0.6	—	—	—
Black, separated												
15 years and over	5.4	6.0	5.0	—	—	—	7.8	9.8	10.0	—	—	—
15 to 17 years	0.0	—	—	—	—	—	0.0	0.3	0.1	—	—	—
18 to 19 years	0.0	—	0.3	—	—	—	0.5	1.0	2.5	—	—	—
20 to 24 years	0.8	2.4	1.7	—	—	—	2.9	5.0	8.3	—	—	—
25 to 29 years	4.5	5.1	5.1	—	—	—	6.7	13.7	13.9	—	—	—
30 to 34 years	8.0	7.2	3.5	—	—	—	11.9	16.6	16.1	—	—	—
35 to 44 years	7.9	8.1	10.2	—	—	—	10.7	17.2	14.9	—	—	—
45 to 54 years	7.1	11.4	10.5	—	—	—	12.4	13.7	14.3	—	—	—
55 to 64 years	7.8	10.3	5.0	—	—	—	9.8	8.5	12.5	—	—	—
65 years and over	6.5	6.3	4.8	—	—	—	5.9	4.7	3.8	—	—	—
Hispanic, separated												
15 years and over	2.6	2.1	1.8	—	—	—	5.4	5.4	4.2	—	—	—
15 to 17 years	0.2	—	0.2	—	—	—	0.0	0.3	0.6	—	—	—
18 to 19 years	0.6	—	0.4	—	—	—	1.0	2.6	1.6	—	—	—
20 to 24 years	0.8	2.2	1.5	—	—	—	2.1	5.1	3.8	—	—	—
25 to 29 years	2.0	1.8	2.3	—	—	—	5.9	6.7	5.6	—	—	—
30 to 34 years	2.6	2.4	2.3	—	—	—	7.2	6.9	6.1	—	—	—
35 to 44 years	4.8	2.7	2.3	—	—	—	8.5	7.0	5.9	—	—	—
45 to 54 years	2.6	3.0	2.4	—	—	—	8.3	7.1	5.4	—	—	—
55 to 64 years	2.8	3.5	2.6	—	—	—	4.7	5.8	4.9	—	—	—
65 years and over	5.2	2.7	2.3	—	—	—	2.9	3.0	2.6	—	—	—

Source: U.S. Bureau of the Census, "Marital Status and Living Arrangements," Current Population Reports, Series P-20, nos. 450, 365, and
  212, and "Persons of Spanish-origin in The United States," Series P-20, no. 290, U.S. Government Printing Office, Washington, D.C., 1990,
  1981, 1971, and 1976. Data from 1940-1960 from "U.S. Summary," 1960 Census of Population, U.S. Government Printing Office,
  Washington, D.C., 1964.

Table 5-4D. Marital Status of the Population, by Sex, Race-ethnicity, and Age: Widowed, 1940-1990
[percent distribution]

Race-ethnicity and age	Males						Females					
	1990	1980	1970	1960	1950	1940	1990	1980	1970	1960	1950	1940
All races, widowed												
15 years and over	2.5	2.5	3.0	3.4	4.1	4.2	11.5	11.9	12.5	12.2	11.8	11.3
15 to 17 years	...	—	—	—	[0.1	—	...	—	...	[0.1	[0.1	[0.1
18 to 19 years	...	—	—	—		—	...	0.1	...			
20 to 24 years	...	—	...	0.1	0.2	0.1	0.1	0.2	0.3	0.3	0.4	0.6
25 to 29 years	0.1	0.1	0.1	0.2	0.3	0.4	0.4	0.4	0.3	0.7	0.9	1.3
30 to 34 years	0.2	0.1	0.1	0.3	0.4	0.7	0.8	1.2	0.8	1.2	1.6	2.5
35 to 44 years	0.4	0.4	0.6	0.7	0.9	1.7	1.8	2.2	2.5	3.0	3.8	5.9
45 to 54 years	1.2	1.6	1.6	1.8	2.8	4.1	5.3	7.0	8.1	8.8	11.1	13.1
55 to 64 years	3.3	4.0	3.9	5.0	7.6	9.0	17.2	18.9	21.3	22.3	24.7	26.4
65 years and over	14.2	13.6	18.1	19.1	24.1	25.1	48.6	51.0	54.6	52.1	54.3	55.6
White, widowed												
15 years and over	2.4	2.3	2.9	3.3	4.0	4.1	11.6	11.8	12.4	11.9	11.5	10.8
15 to 17 years	...	—	—	—	[0.1	—	...	—	...	[0.1	[0.1	[0.1
18 to 19 years	...	—	—	—		—	...	0.1	...			
20 to 24 years	...	—	—	0.1	0.1	0.1	0.1	0.2	0.3	0.3	0.3	0.4
25 to 29 years	0.1	0.1	0.1	0.1	0.2	0.3	0.4	0.3	0.3	0.5	0.7	0.9
30 to 34 years	0.1	0.1	0.1	0.2	0.3	0.6	0.8	1.1	0.6	0.9	1.3	1.9
35 to 44 years	0.4	0.3	0.4	0.5	0.7	1.5	1.5	1.8	1.9	2.6	3.1	4.8
45 to 54 years	1.2	1.2	1.4	1.5	2.5	3.8	4.6	6.1	7.4	8.0	9.9	11.8
55 to 64 years	3.0	3.6	3.7	4.5	7.1	8.7	15.5	17.7	20.6	21.3	23.6	25.4
65 years and over	13.3	13.1	17.0	18.7	23.7	24.8	48.1	50.3	53.6	51.3	53.4	54.7
Black, widowed												
15 years and over	3.4	3.9	4.3	4.6	5.2	5.3	11.6	13.0	13.5	13.9	14.6	15.4
15 to 17 years	...	—	—	[0.1	[0.1	—	...	—	—	[0.1	[0.2	[0.3
18 to 19 years	...	—	—			—	...	—	—			
20 to 24 years	...	—	0.2	0.2	0.5	0.5	0.1	0.4	0.4	0.7	1.1	2.0
25 to 29 years	...	—	—	0.4	0.7	1.1	0.5	0.8	0.3	1.8	2.3	4.2
30 to 34 years	0.7	0.8	0.6	0.8	1.1	1.9	1.0	2.4	2.0	3.3	4.1	7.7
35 to 44 years	1.1	1.4	2.3	1.8	2.4	3.8	3.9	5.4	7.3	7.0	9.5	15.2
45 to 54 years	1.3	5.3	4.3	4.4	6.2	7.9	10.1	14.5	15.4	16.3	22.8	27.3
55 to 64 years	6.2	8.9	4.9	9.8	12.9	14.0	28.7	30.9	28.5	33.2	39.4	41.7
65 years and over	23.4	19.6	31.9	24.3	28.6	28.3	53.7	57.5	67.3	61.5	65.6	67.9
Hispanic, widowed												
15 years and over	1.4	1.4	2.0	—	—	—	6.1	6.4	7.6	—	—	—
15 to 17 years	...	—	0.1	—	—	—	...	—	0.2	—	—	—
18 to 19 years	...	—	0.1	—	—	—	...	—	0.2	—	—	—
20 to 24 years	...	—	0.1	—	—	—	0.1	0.9	0.7	—	—	—
25 to 29 years	...	0.3	0.2	—	—	—	0.2	0.3	1.0	—	—	—
30 to 34 years	0.1	0.3	0.3	—	—	—	1.3	1.4	1.5	—	—	—
35 to 44 years	0.4	0.7	0.7	—	—	—	2.5	2.0	3.1	—	—	—
45 to 54 years	2.2	1.3	1.7	—	—	—	5.0	8.7	8.4	—	—	—
55 to 64 years	3.8	3.4	4.7	—	—	—	17.6	15.8	22.8	—	—	—
65 years and over	12.6	13.1	18.2	—	—	—	42.2	49.8	53.2	—	—	—

Source: U.S. Bureau of the Census, "Marital Status and Living Arrangements," Current Population Reports, Series P-20, nos. 450, 365, and 212, and "Persons of Spanish-origin in The United States," Series P-20, no. 290, U.S. Government Printing Office, Washington, D.C., 1990, 1981, 1971, and 1976. Data from 1940-1960 from "U.S. Summary," 1960 Census of Population, U.S. Government Printing Office, Washington, D.C., 1964.

Table 5-4E. Marital Status of the Population, by Sex, Race-ethnicity, and Age: Divorced, 1940-1990
[percent distribution]

Race-ethnicity and age	Males						Females					
	1990	1980	1970	1960	1950	1940	1990	1980	1970	1960	1950	1940
All races, divorced												
15 years and over	6.8	4.8	2.2	2.1	2.0	1.2	8.9	6.6	3.5	2.9	2.4	1.6
15 to 17 years	...	0.1	—	[0.1	[0.1	—	...	0.1	...	[0.3	[0.3	[0.1
18 to 19 years	...	0.2	...			—	0.4	0.6	0.4			
20 to 24 years	1.1	1.6	1.1	1.0	0.9	0.3	2.8	3.6	2.3	1.8	1.7	0.9
25 to 29 years	4.7	5.3	2.3	1.8	1.7	0.9	7.1	8.5	4.3	2.6	2.5	1.8
30 to 34 years	7.9	7.9	2.9	2.2	2.1	1.4	10.5	11.1	4.6	3.6	3.0	2.4
35 to 44 years	11.1	8.0	2.9	2.6	2.5	1.9	14.8	10.8	5.4	3.8	3.6	2.7
45 to 54 years	11.1	6.7	3.6	3.1	3.0	2.0	14.4	9.2	4.9	4.3	3.5	2.2
55 to 64 years	8.1	5.0	3.0	3.1	2.6	1.8	9.9	6.7	4.5	3.6	2.4	1.6
65 years and over	5.0	3.7	2.4	2.3	1.9	1.3	5.1	3.4	2.3	2.0	1.1	0.7
White, divorced												
15 years and over	6.8	4.7	2.2	2.1	2.0	1.3	8.6	6.4	3.4	2.8	2.4	1.6
15 to 17 years	0.1	—	—	[0.1	[0.1	—	...	0.1	...	[0.3	[0.3	[0.1
18 to 19 years	...	—	0.1			—	0.5	0.7	0.4			
20 to 24 years	1.1	1.7	1.0	1.0	0.9	0.3	3.1	3.9	2.4	1.8	1.6	0.9
25 to 29 years	4.9	5.5	2.4	1.8	1.8	0.9	7.4	8.7	4.1	2.5	2.4	1.7
30 to 34 years	8.3	7.8	2.7	2.1	2.1	1.4	10.5	10.7	4.6	2.9	2.9	2.4
35 to 44 years	11.0	7.5	2.5	2.5	2.5	1.9	14.2	10.3	5.1	3.6	3.5	2.7
45 to 54 years	10.6	6.3	3.4	3.0	3.0	2.0	13.7	8.6	4.7	4.1	3.5	2.2
55 to 64 years	7.6	4.6	2.9	3.0	2.7	1.8	9.5	6.2	4.5	3.6	2.4	1.6
65 years and over	4.7	3.5	2.5	2.3	1.9	1.3	4.7	3.2	2.3	2.0	1.1	0.7
Black, divorced												
15 years and over	8.1	6.4	2.9	2.4	1.9	1.0	11.2	8.7	4.3	3.6	2.7	1.7
15 to 17 years	...	0.4	—	[0.1	[0.1	—	...	0.2	—	[0.2	[0.2	[0.2
18 to 19 years	0.2	0.1	—			—	...	—	0.2			
20 to 24 years	1.0	0.9	1.5	0.7	0.9	0.4	1.9	2.1	1.5	1.7	1.9	1.2
25 to 29 years	3.8	4.0	1.9	1.7	1.7	0.8	5.8	8.0	5.6	3.6	3.4	2.1
30 to 34 years	6.8	9.7	4.6	2.9	2.4	1.2	11.5	15.9	5.4	4.8	3.9	2.7
35 to 44 years	13.6	13.9	5.5	3.7	2.8	1.6	20.4	15.7	8.1	5.7	4.2	2.6
45 to 54 years	16.9	9.5	5.9	3.9	2.8	1.7	21.2	14.3	7.1	5.5	3.4	2.0
55 to 64 years	13.0	9.7	3.4	3.4	2.5	1.4	13.8	11.3	5.5	3.9	2.2	1.3
65 years and over	8.3	5.4	1.8	2.4	1.5	1.0	9.3	4.9	2.5	2.0	1.0	0.6
Hispanic, divorced												
15 years and over	5.1	3.5	2.3	—	—	—	8.0	6.9	4.4	—	—	—
15 to 17 years	...	0.1	0.1	—	—	—	...	0.1	0.2	—	—	—
18 to 19 years	0.3	—	0.2	—	—	—	0.6	0.3	0.7	—	—	—
20 to 24 years	0.7	0.7	1.4	—	—	—	2.0	2.5	2.6	—	—	—
25 to 29 years	4.4	3.3	2.6	—	—	—	4.7	5.8	4.5	—	—	—
30 to 34 years	4.7	5.2	2.8	—	—	—	9.7	10.3	5.4	—	—	—
35 to 44 years	9.1	5.6	3.1	—	—	—	12.7	11.4	6.5	—	—	—
45 to 54 years	9.8	4.3	3.6	—	—	—	16.2	11.2	7.4	—	—	—
55 to 64 years	7.5	5.1	4.1	—	—	—	7.6	10.3	7.0	—	—	—
65 years and over	4.3	6.9	3.5	—	—	—	8.6	5.6	3.9	—	—	—

Source: U.S. Bureau of the Census, "Marital Status and Living Arrangements," Current Population Reports, Series P-20, nos. 450, 365, and 212, and "Persons of Spanish-origin in The United States," Series P-20, no. 290, U.S. Government Printing Office, Washington, D.C., 1990, 1981, 1971, and 1976. Data from 1940-1960 from "U.S. Summary," 1960 Census of Population, U.S. Government Printing Office, Washington, D.C., 1964.

Table 5-4B shows that the black population falls far below the other race-ethnic groups in the married with spouse present status. Because of the propensity not to marry at all and a greater propensity to suffer all of the forces of marital dissolution (widowhood, divorce, and separation) more acutely, less than one-half of the black women at prime childbearing ages (20-44) are married and living with their spouses. This percentage has dropped markedly even in just the past decade. Only 35 to 55 percent of black men are in this status during the same years of age. This has profound implications for the bearing of children out of wedlock (see Chapter 6). The white population has the highest prevalence of adults married and living with spouse during the prime childbearing and child rearing ages. The Hispanic population, although it has a much higher proportion than the black population, suffers greater attrition from separation, divorce, and widowhood at these ages. As a result, Hispanic women have a lower percentage married with spouse present than do whites at all ages over twenty-five.

Because of the great differences in their age composition and because the proportions of each marital status differ so radically by age, one can arrive at very erroneous conclusions by looking only at the marital status for all ages by race-ethnicity. Only by comparing the race-ethnic groups in terms of their age-specific patterns can a proper interpretation be made. Even such detailed analysis should be done on a cohort basis if trends are to be assessed.

Urban-Rural Residence and Marital Status

The patterns of marital status described above take significantly different forms in urban and rural areas. Table 5-5 provides percentage distributions by marital status according to several categories of residence. The data are provided for five major race-ethnicity groups by sex. In all categories the following generalizations apply with a few minor exceptions.

In general urban areas tend to be more "anti-nuptial" and rural areas to be more "pro-nuptial." In fact there is a continuum of this pattern, with anti-nuptiality highest in central cities and pro-nuptiality being highest in rural areas. This pattern is consistent for each category of the race-ethnic groups. Each group preserves the differences noted above, but the following differentials are quite uniformly patterned within each ethnic group:

1. In rural areas the proportion of persons who are single is lower than in urban areas. This difference is most marked for whites and Asian or Pacific Islanders. Persons who live in rural places either marry or selectively relocate into urban areas. Relocation is likely more than a minor influence upon these percentages single.

2. In rural areas the proportion of divorced females is considerably lower than in urban areas. This difference

is far less dramatic, although in the same direction, for males.

3. In rural areas the proportion of females separated is considerably lower than in urban areas. Again, this pattern is generally consistent but less dramatic for males. The one exception to lower rural percentages divorced is the Asian or Pacific Islander population.

4. In rural areas the proportion of persons classed as "married and living with spouse" is substantially higher than in urban areas for both sexes.

5. Central cities and those reaches outside metropolitan areas both tend to have a higher prevalence of widowhood among females. This is primarily an indirect effect of age composition.

Virtually all of these differentials are more significant for the white than for the other race-ethnic groups. Thus, Table 5-5 shows that the crest of the wave of the marriage bust that has swept the nation had its locus in central cities and its trough in rural areas. This is true for each sex and for all race-ethnic groups. Again, however, it is important to remember that mobility differs by age (see Chapter 8) and that relocation in search of either employment or marriage opportunities may influence these geographic comparisons. The comparisons are profoundly affected by the different age composition (see Chapters 1 and 10) across urban and rural areas.

Beyond the general trends noted, American Indians are unique in having a higher proportion divorced, both in urban and rural areas, than any other race-ethnic group. This population also has high proportions separated. Marital instability appears to be almost equally great among rural and urban Native Americans as among rural black families. In both rural and urban areas, American Indian marital disruption is higher than Hispanic marital disruption. In contrast the Asian and Pacific Islander groups have the lowest prevalence of divorce and separation of any other group, including the white.

Marital Disruption and Remarriage

The proportion of persons reported as divorced or widowed in a census or survey greatly understates the magnitude of marital disruption since many persons who have suffered a broken marriage have remarried. In order to measure the total impact of disruption, the 1990 Census asked a "marital history" question, wherein each ever-married woman was asked whether she had been married more than once, and if so, how the previous marriage ended. Table 5-6 reports the percent of ever-married persons aged 20-54 who have ever had a marital termination. The proportions are much higher than the sum of widowed and divorced at these ages as reported in Tables 5-2 and 5-4, and for all ages in Table 5-5. Over one-third of all ever-married white persons now aged 35 to 49 have suffered marital disruption. This proportion is higher for blacks,

Table 5-5. Marital Status, by Residence, Sex, and Race-ethnicity: 1990 [percent distribution]

Place of Residence: 1990	Males 15 years and over					Females 15 years and over				
	Single	Married[1]	Separated	Widowed	Divorced	Single	Married[1]	Separated	Widowed	Divorced
White										
United States	28.1	60.3	1.6	2.5	7.5	20.8	55.5	1.8	12.4	9.4
Inside metropolitan area	29.2	59.1	1.6	2.5	7.6	22.0	54.3	1.9	12.0	9.8
In central city	34.4	52.2	1.9	2.8	8.8	25.9	46.9	2.3	13.5	11.4
Not in central city	26.5	62.8	1.5	2.3	7.0	19.9	58.3	1.7	11.1	9.0
Outside metropolitan area	24.4	64.1	1.4	2.8	7.4	17.0	59.4	1.6	13.9	8.1
Urban	28.0	59.5	1.4	3.0	8.0	20.1	51.4	1.8	16.5	10.2
Rural	22.4	66.6	1.3	2.6	7.0	15.0	64.3	1.4	12.4	6.9
Black										
United States	44.4	38.5	5.5	3.3	8.3	38.3	30.9	7.5	11.9	11.4
Inside metropolitan area	44.5	38.2	5.5	3.1	8.6	38.7	30.5	7.6	11.2	12.0
In central city	45.9	35.5	6.0	3.5	9.0	40.0	27.6	8.1	12.1	12.2
Not in central city	41.7	43.7	4.5	2.3	7.7	35.9	37.2	6.4	9.1	11.4
Outside metropolitan area	43.6	39.9	5.3	4.2	7.0	35.7	33.2	6.9	15.7	8.5
Urban	45.2	37.6	5.3	4.2	7.6	37.6	28.8	7.6	15.8	10.1
Rural	42.4	41.6	5.2	4.3	6.5	34.0	36.9	6.3	15.6	7.2
American Indian, Eskimo, or Aleut										
United States	38.7	45.8	2.9	2.3	10.2	29.7	44.7	4.1	8.7	12.8
Inside metropolitan area	38.1	45.3	3.2	2.0	11.4	29.0	44.0	4.6	7.7	14.6
In central city	42.4	39.4	3.7	2.0	12.4	32.8	37.6	5.5	8.0	16.1
Not in central city	34.5	50.2	2.8	1.9	10.6	25.8	49.7	3.8	7.4	13.3
Outside metropolitan area	39.5	46.4	2.6	2.6	8.8	30.5	45.5	3.6	9.7	10.7
Urban	40.0	44.8	2.7	2.4	10.1	30.6	42.1	4.1	9.6	13.5
Rural	39.2	47.0	2.6	2.7	8.4	30.5	46.8	3.4	9.8	9.5
Asian or Pacific Islander										
United States	38.2	56.1	1.3	1.3	3.1	27.6	58.7	1.8	7.2	4.7
Inside metropolitan area	38.0	56.4	1.4	1.3	3.0	27.7	58.6	1.8	7.2	4.7
In central city	41.0	52.8	1.6	1.5	3.1	30.3	54.6	2.1	8.1	4.9
Not in central city	34.8	60.1	1.1	1.1	2.9	25.1	62.5	1.6	6.3	4.5
Outside metropolitan area	41.6	51.5	1.2	1.7	4.0	25.8	60.9	1.4	6.9	5.0
Urban	43.4	50.2	1.1	1.5	3.8	28.3	58.3	1.4	6.8	5.1
Rural	37.6	54.5	1.4	2.1	4.4	21.0	65.7	1.3	7.2	4.8
Hispanic										
United States	39.6	50.1	2.9	1.4	5.9	29.9	49.4	5.0	6.8	8.9
Inside metropolitan area	40.1	49.6	3.0	1.4	5.9	30.3	48.8	5.2	6.7	9.1
In central city	41.7	47.1	3.4	1.5	6.2	32.1	45.2	6.0	7.1	9.6
Not in central city	38.0	52.9	2.4	1.2	5.4	27.9	53.7	3.9	6.2	8.2
Outside metropolitan area	35.4	54.0	2.4	1.9	6.3	25.4	55.6	3.4	7.9	7.8
Urban	35.9	53.2	2.4	1.9	6.6	26.6	52.4	3.9	8.3	8.7
Rural	34.8	55.1	2.3	1.8	6.0	23.7	60.2	2.7	7.2	6.3

[1] Married excludes separated.

Source: U.S. Bureau of the Census, "General Population Characteristics," 1990 Census of Population, CP-1-1, U.S. Government Printing Office, Washington, D.C., 1992, Tables 42-46.

reaching nearly half of those aged 40 to 44. The proportion ever divorced after first marriage reaches a maximum of just under 30 percent, and is lowest, for Hispanic women.

The extent of remarriage is indicated by remarriage proportions for females, also shown in Table 5-6. A high percentage of persons who divorce eventually remarry. The proportion tends to rise with age because of the longer exposure time for remarriage following divorce. It is above 50 percent for the white population for all ages above twenty-five years. It reaches a maximum for the white population with nearly seven of ten remarrying among those now aged 40 to 44. Remarriage tends to be less for blacks than for whites or Hispanics. However, even among blacks the percentage remarried after divorce is over 50 percent in those now above age 35.

Remarriage is also changing over time. In the total population the percentage remarried after divorce has declined at all ages since 1975. These changes across time are most dramatic at younger ages indicating that remarriages which do occur may have longer intervals to remarriage. At ages of below thirty, and at ages 50-54, the percentage remarried has dropped by at least eight percent. The smallest decrease is a decline in those remarried after divorce now aged 35 to 39 of 1.5 percent.

Table 5-6. Marriage Experience for Women, by Age and Race-ethnicity: 1975-1990

Marriage type	Total				White				Black				Hispanic		
	1990	1985	1980	1975	1990	1985	1980	1975	1990	1985	1980	1975	1990	1985	1980
Percent ever married															
20 to 24 years	38.5	43.3	49.5	62.5	41.3	46.6	52.2	64.9	23.5	23.9	33.3	47.5	45.8	56.7	55.4
25 to 29 years	69.0	74.0	78.6	87.2	73.2	77.4	81.0	88.8	45.0	53.4	62.3	76.5	69.6	78.4	80.2
30 to 34 years	82.2	85.8	89.9	93.1	85.6	88.1	91.6	93.9	61.1	70.9	77.9	87.1	83.0	88.0	88.3
35 to 39 years	89.4	91.6	94.3	95.5	91.4	93.1	95.3	96.2	74.9	80.7	87.4	90.1	88.9	91.6	91.2
40 to 44 years	92.0	94.6	95.1	95.8	93.4	95.6	95.8	95.9	82.1	86.1	89.7	95.1	92.8	90.3	94.2
45 to 49 years	94.4	94.4	95.9	95.9	95.1	95.1	96.4	95.9	89.7	88.4	92.5	95.4	91.7	91.1	94.4
50 to 54 years	95.5	95.2	95.3	95.8	96.1	95.4	95.8	96.0	91.9	93.4	92.1	94.6	91.8	92.5	95.0
Percent divorced after first marriage															
20 to 24 years	12.5	13.9	14.2	11.2	12.8	14.4	14.7	11.3	9.6	11.0	10.5	10.6	6.8	11.0	9.4
25 to 29 years	19.2	21.0	20.7	17.1	19.8	21.5	21.0	17.7	17.8	18.2	20.2	15.3	13.5	14.8	13.9
30 to 34 years	28.1	29.3	26.2	19.8	28.6	29.0	25.8	20.0	26.6	34.4	31.4	20.5	19.9	19.2	21.1
35 to 39 years	34.1	32.0	27.2	21.5	34.6	32.0	26.7	21.2	35.8	34.6	32.9	22.7	29.7	26.3	21.9
40 to 44 years	35.8	32.1	26.1	20.5	35.2	32.0	25.5	19.7	45.1	36.9	33.7	27.4	26.6	22.8	19.7
45 to 49 years	35.2	29.0	23.1	21.0	35.5	28.4	22.7	20.3	39.8	36.0	29.0	26.9	24.6	24.3	23.9
50 to 54 years	29.5	25.7	21.8	18.0	28.5	24.6	21.0	16.8	39.2	33.7	29.0	29.7	22.9	21.8	22.5
Percent remarried after divorce															
20 to 24 years	38.1	44.3	45.5	47.9	39.3	46.0	47.0	50.1	—	—	—	—	—	—	—
25 to 29 years	51.8	55.3	53.4	60.2	52.8	58.3	56.4	62.0	44.4	25.4	27.9	43.1	49.5	50.5	—
30 to 34 years	59.6	61.4	60.9	64.4	61.4	64.3	63.3	67.5	42.0	41.1	42.0	41.8	45.9	44.9	58.3
35 to 39 years	65.0	63.0	64.9	69.5	66.5	64.9	66.9	70.9	54.0	44.8	50.6	52.6	51.2	57.1	45.2
40 to 44 years	67.1	64.7	67.4	69.7	69.5	67.5	68.6	71.9	50.3	45.4	58.4	57.1	53.9	50.6	—
45 to 49 years	65.9	67.9	69.2	69.6	67.2	69.6	70.4	70.7	55.0	54.6	62.7	61.7	51.0	78.9	—
50 to 54 years	63.0	68.2	72.0	73.5	65.4	68.4	72.6	73.4	50.2	64.3	72.7	73.7	62.2	—	—

Source: U.S. Bureau of the Census, Current Population Reports, "Marriage, Divorce, and Remarriage in the 1990's," Series P-23, No. 180, U.S. Government Printing Office, Washington, D.C., 1992, Table B.

Table 5-7. Marital Status, by Region, State, and Sex: 1990

Region, division, and state	Males 15 years and over						Females 15 years and over					
	Total	Never married	Married, spouse present	Separated	Widowed	Divorced	Total	Never married	Married, spouse present	Separated	Widowed	Divorced
United States, total	100.0	30.7	57.3	2.0	2.5	7.4	100.0	23.4	52.4	2.6	12.0	9.5
Northeast region	100.0	33.5	55.6	2.2	2.9	5.8	100.0	26.9	49.5	3.0	12.8	7.8
New England	100.0	33.3	55.9	1.5	2.7	6.5	100.0	26.9	50.4	2.1	11.9	8.6
Middle Atlantic	100.0	33.5	55.5	2.5	3.0	5.5	100.0	26.9	49.2	3.3	13.2	7.5
Midwest region	100.0	29.8	58.7	1.4	2.6	7.5	100.0	23.1	53.5	1.8	12.3	9.3
East North Central	100.0	30.4	57.8	1.5	2.6	7.6	100.0	23.8	52.5	1.9	12.1	9.6
West North Central	100.0	28.3	60.9	1.2	2.5	7.1	100.0	21.4	55.8	1.5	12.6	8.7
South region	100.0	28.6	58.8	2.4	2.5	7.7	100.0	21.6	53.2	3.0	12.5	9.7
South Atlantic	100.0	29.2	58.0	2.6	2.6	7.6	100.0	22.2	52.5	3.2	12.6	9.5
East South Central	100.0	27.3	60.3	1.8	2.7	7.9	100.0	20.7	53.6	2.4	13.6	9.7
West South Central	100.0	28.4	59.1	2.3	2.3	7.9	100.0	21.1	54.3	3.0	11.6	10.1
West region	100.0	32.4	55.1	2.0	2.1	8.4	100.0	23.4	52.9	2.6	9.8	11.2
Mountain	100.0	28.7	58.4	1.6	2.1	9.2	100.0	21.1	55.8	2.0	9.7	11.4
Pacific	100.0	33.6	54.1	2.1	2.1	8.1	100.0	24.2	52.0	2.8	9.9	11.1
New England												
Maine	100.0	27.3	60.7	1.2	2.6	8.1	100.0	21.0	55.4	1.5	12.1	10.0
New Hampshire	100.0	28.6	60.2	1.4	2.3	7.5	100.0	22.6	56.4	1.7	10.2	9.1
Vermont	100.0	31.0	57.5	1.5	2.4	7.6	100.0	24.3	53.6	1.8	11.0	9.3
Massachusetts	100.0	36.1	53.5	1.7	2.8	5.9	100.0	29.7	47.7	2.4	12.1	8.1
Rhode Island	100.0	33.2	55.8	1.4	3.1	6.5	100.0	26.5	49.3	2.0	13.3	8.9
Connecticut	100.0	32.5	56.8	1.4	2.7	6.6	100.0	25.8	51.6	2.0	11.8	8.8
Middle Atlantic												
New York	100.0	35.8	53.2	2.8	2.9	5.3	100.0	28.9	46.9	4.0	12.7	7.6
New Jersey	100.0	32.8	56.8	2.2	2.9	5.4	100.0	25.9	51.1	2.9	12.7	7.5
Pennsylvania	100.0	30.6	58.0	2.2	3.3	5.9	100.0	24.4	51.4	2.7	14.2	7.3
East North Central												
Ohio	100.0	28.7	59.1	1.4	2.7	8.0	100.0	22.6	53.0	1.8	12.4	10.1
Indiana	100.0	27.6	60.3	1.2	2.4	8.5	100.0	21.3	54.7	1.5	12.1	10.4
Illinois	100.0	32.6	56.1	1.7	2.7	7.0	100.0	25.4	50.8	2.3	12.5	9.1
Michigan	100.0	31.2	56.6	1.7	2.6	8.0	100.0	24.7	51.6	2.2	11.5	10.1
Wisconsin	100.0	30.5	58.9	1.2	2.6	6.8	100.0	23.8	54.7	1.5	11.9	8.1
West North Central												
Minnesota	100.0	30.8	59.2	1.1	2.2	6.6	100.0	24.1	55.4	1.3	11.1	8.1
Iowa	100.0	27.2	62.6	1.0	2.6	6.6	100.0	20.5	56.8	1.2	13.6	8.0
Missouri	100.0	27.2	60.4	1.7	2.7	7.9	100.0	20.9	54.0	2.2	13.3	9.7
North Dakota	100.0	30.7	60.7	0.7	2.3	5.6	100.0	21.2	58.8	0.9	12.7	6.4
South Dakota	100.0	28.5	61.4	0.9	2.6	6.5	100.0	20.5	57.8	1.0	13.4	7.2
Nebraska	100.0	27.9	61.8	1.0	2.6	6.7	100.0	21.0	56.8	1.2	12.8	8.1
Kansas	100.0	26.5	62.3	1.1	2.4	7.8	100.0	19.2	57.5	1.3	12.4	9.6

Table 5-7. Marital Status, by Region, State, and Sex: 1990 (continued)

Region, division, and state	Males 15 years and over						Females 15 years and over					
	Total	Never married	Married, spouse present	Separated	Widowed	Divorced	Total	Never married	Married, spouse present	Separated	Widowed	Divorced
South Atlantic												
Delaware	100.0	30.6	57.4	2.1	2.7	7.2	100.0	24.9	52.0	2.6	11.4	9.2
Maryland	100.0	32.4	55.4	3.3	2.4	6.4	100.0	26.1	50.3	4.1	10.9	8.6
District of Columbia	100.0	50.8	32.0	5.5	3.6	8.1	100.0	45.0	26.1	6.1	12.8	10.1
Virginia	100.0	30.7	57.8	2.8	2.2	6.5	100.0	23.6	53.6	3.4	11.1	8.3
West Virginia	100.0	25.8	62.4	1.2	3.1	7.5	100.0	18.9	55.6	1.5	15.3	8.7
North Carolina	100.0	28.7	59.3	3.1	2.4	6.5	100.0	21.9	53.5	3.8	12.8	8.1
South Carolina	100.0	29.8	58.1	3.0	2.5	6.6	100.0	23.2	52.2	4.0	12.8	7.8
Georgia	100.0	29.8	57.6	2.3	2.2	8.2	100.0	22.9	52.0	3.1	11.7	10.3
Florida	100.0	26.6	59.2	2.1	3.1	9.0	100.0	19.0	53.6	2.5	13.8	11.1
East South Central												
Kentucky	100.0	26.2	61.8	1.4	2.6	7.9	100.0	19.4	55.8	1.9	13.2	9.7
Tennessee	100.0	26.7	60.5	1.8	2.5	8.5	100.0	20.1	54.0	2.4	13.1	10.4
Alabama	100.0	27.3	60.4	1.8	2.7	7.8	100.0	20.8	53.3	2.5	14.1	9.4
Mississippi	100.0	30.1	57.3	2.5	3.0	7.1	100.0	23.6	50.1	3.3	14.4	8.6
West South Central												
Arkansas	100.0	24.2	63.2	1.7	2.9	8.1	100.0	17.5	56.5	2.1	14.4	9.4
Louisiana	100.0	30.9	56.3	3.0	2.8	7.0	100.0	24.4	50.0	3.9	12.9	8.9
Oklahoma	100.0	24.9	62.1	1.5	2.5	9.0	100.0	17.3	56.6	1.9	13.0	11.2
Texas	100.0	29.0	58.7	2.3	2.1	7.9	100.0	21.4	54.6	3.1	10.6	10.3
Mountain												
Montana	100.0	26.5	61.1	1.2	2.5	8.7	100.0	18.4	58.5	1.5	11.8	9.9
Idaho	100.0	24.9	63.5	1.2	2.0	8.5	100.0	17.7	60.9	1.4	10.2	9.7
Wyoming	100.0	25.6	61.9	1.0	2.1	9.4	100.0	17.8	60.6	1.2	10.0	10.4
Colorado	100.0	29.7	57.3	1.8	1.9	9.3	100.0	22.0	54.7	2.3	9.1	12.0
New Mexico	100.0	29.3	57.8	1.6	2.3	9.0	100.0	22.5	54.2	2.0	10.0	11.3
Arizona	100.0	29.6	57.3	1.8	2.3	9.0	100.0	21.7	54.1	2.2	10.4	11.6
Utah	100.0	28.6	62.0	1.1	1.6	6.7	100.0	22.6	59.2	1.4	8.1	8.7
Nevada	100.0	28.2	53.5	2.3	2.3	13.8	100.0	19.1	54.2	2.6	9.0	15.1
Pacific												
Washington	100.0	29.0	57.9	1.7	2.1	9.4	100.0	20.8	55.4	2.1	9.9	11.8
Oregon	100.0	27.0	59.3	1.7	2.3	9.7	100.0	19.4	55.5	2.1	11.2	11.8
California	100.0	35.0	52.9	2.2	2.1	7.8	100.0	25.2	50.8	3.1	9.9	11.0
Alaska	100.0	31.9	54.5	2.0	1.2	10.4	100.0	21.8	59.1	2.4	4.8	11.9
Hawaii	100.0	34.5	54.8	1.5	2.1	7.2	100.0	24.9	55.3	1.8	9.0	9.0

Source: U.S. Bureau of the Census, "General Population Characteristics: United States Summary," 1990 Census of Population, U.S. Government Printing Office, Washington, D.C., 1993, Table 263.

Table 5-8. Number and Rates of Marriages and Divorces: 1920-1990

		Marriages				Divorces		
			Rates				Rates	
Year	Number	Per 1,000 population (CMR)	Per 1,000 women 15+ years (CNR)	Per 1,000 unmarried women 15+ years (GMR)	Per 1,000 unmarried women 15-44 years (GNR)	Number	Per 1,000 population (CDR)	Per 1,000 married women 15+ years (GDR)
1990	2,448,000	9.8	24.2	56.9	93.3	1,175,000	4.7	20.7
1989	2,404,000	9.7	23.8	56.2	92.1	1,163,000	4.7	20.7
1988	2,395,926	9.7	23.9	54.6	91.0	1,167,000	4.8	20.8
1987	2,403,378	9.9	24.2	55.7	92.4	1,166,000	4.8	20.9
1986	2,407,099	10.0	24.5	56.2	93.9	1,178,000	4.9	21.4
1985	2,412,625	10.1	24.8	57.0	94.9	1,190,000	5.0	21.9
1984	2,477,192	10.5	25.8	59.5	99.0	1,169,000	5.0	21.6
1983	2,445,604	10.5	25.7	59.9	99.3	1,158,000	5.0	21.9
1982	2,456,278	10.6	26.1	61.4	101.9	1,170,000	5.1	21.9
1981	2,422,145	10.6	26.1	61.7	103.1	1,213,000	5.3	22.6
1980	2,390,252	10.6	26.1	61.4	102.6	1,189,000	5.2	22.6
1975	2,152,662	10.0	25.6	66.9	118.5	1,036,000	4.9	20.3
1970	2,158,802	10.6	28.4	76.5	140.2	708,000	3.5	14.9
1965	1,800,000	9.3	26.0	75.0	144.3	479,000	2.5	10.6
1960	1,523,000	8.5	24.0	73.5	148.0	393,000	2.2	9.2
1955	1,531,000	9.3	25.8	80.9	161.1	377,000	2.3	9.3
1950	1,667,231	11.1	29.8	90.2	166.4	385,144	2.6	10.3
1945	1,612,992	12.2	30.5	83.6	138.2	485,000	3.5	14.4
1940	1,595,879	12.1	32.3	82.8	122.4	264,000	2.0	8.8
1935[1]	1,327,000	10.4	28.8	74.0	111.0	218,000	1.7	7.8
1930	1,126,856	9.2	26.3	67.8	99.0	195,961	1.6	7.5
1925	1,188,334	10.3	30.5	78.1	112.6	175,449	1.5	7.2
1920	1,274,476	12.0	36.2	92.3	131.0	170,505	1.6	8.0

[1] Data for 1920-1935 estimated as from Bogue, The Population of the United States, New York: Free Press, 1985.

Source: National Center for Health Statistics, "Advance Report of Final Marriage Statistics, 1988," Monthly Vital Statistics Report, Volume 40, No. 4, Supplement, 1991, "Births, Marriages, Divorces, and Deaths for 1989," Monthly Vital Statistics Report, Volume 38, No. 12, 1990, and "Births, Marriages, Divorces, and Deaths for 1990," Monthly Vital Statistics Report, Volume 39, No. 12, 1991.

Regional and State Variation in Marital Status

Just as the population's marital status composition differs between town and country, there are substantial variations in composition across regions and states. Many of the differences in marital status composition at such a level of analysis are due to underlying differences in the age composition across areas. Table 5-7 provides the marital status for each region and state by sex for persons at least 15 years of age. The percentage of never married persons among either sex is highest in the Northeast and Pacific West. The percentage divorced is lowest in the Northeast. At the state level, the highest percentage of never married males and females is found in the District of Columbia, followed by the Commonwealth of Massachusetts. The highest percentage of males and females married with spouse present is found in Idaho. The greatest percentage of separated males and females is found in the District of Columbia followed by Maryland. Washington, D.C. has the highest proportion of widowers (3.7 percent), while West Virginia's proportion of widows (15.3 percent) places it first among all other states. Finally, those divorced are the highest percentage in Nevada for both males and females.

Marital Status a Variable in Subsequent Chapters

Because of its importance in marking life cycle transitions, marital status is treated as a variable by which most of the topics to be discussed in later chapters of this book are cross-classified. Fertility, educational attainment, mortality, migration, labor force participation, occupation, and income are examples. The reader who is interested in learning about the relationships between marital status and other population characteristics and events should consult the index, where the portions of the chapters dealing with marital status are identified.

Figure 5-3. General Marriage Rate and General Divorce Rate: 1920-1990

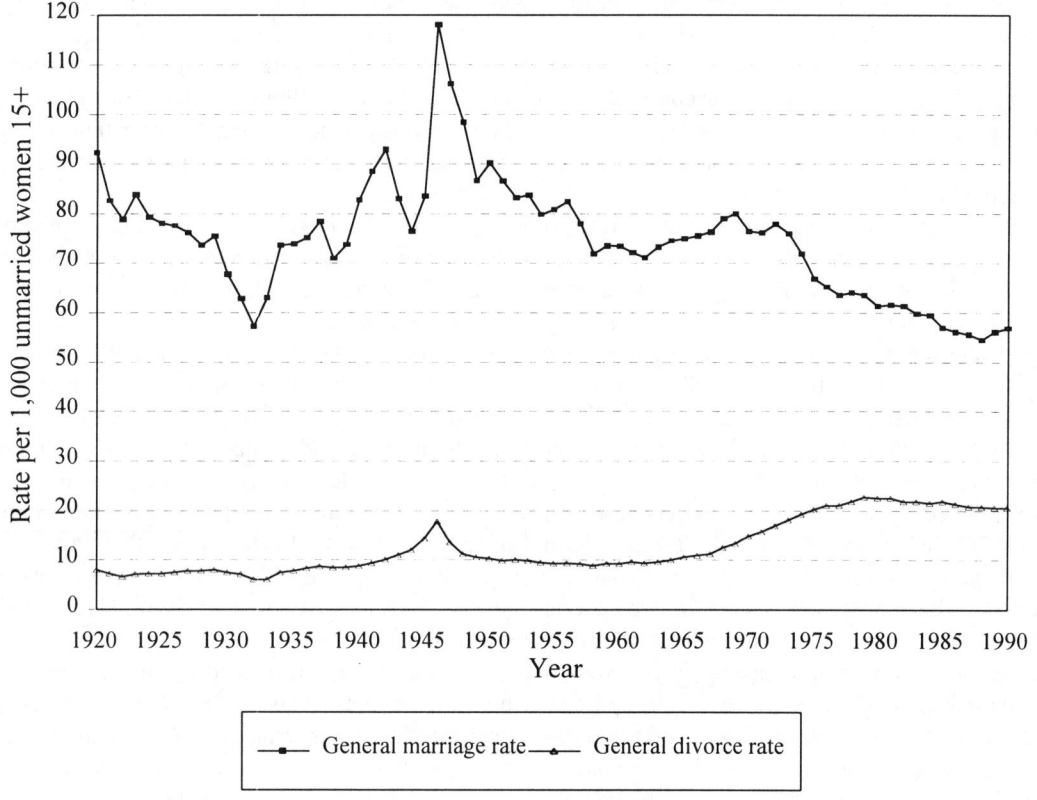

Source: National Center for Health Statistics data.

Marriage as a Demographic Event

The preceding discussion has treated marriage and divorce as statuses that persons occupy at the time of a census or other enumeration. In this section and the next they are studied as events. An official record is made of each marriage and divorce; hence they can be counted and tabulated. In 1990 about 2,450,000 marriages and 1,175,000 divorces occurred in the United States. The National Center for Health Statistics of the U.S. Public Health Service, which bears responsibility for assembling information on marriage and divorce from each of the states, publishes an annual summary that includes data concerning certain characteristics of the brides and grooms and of persons involved in divorce (see Chapter 2).

The appropriate statistics for measuring the incidence of the marriage and divorce events are rates--the number of events per 1,000 persons "exposed" to the occurrence of the event. Table 5-8 reports estimates of the number of marriages and divorces, with the rates, since 1920. Unfortunately, there is no obviously best denominator that specifies the "exposed" population. The National Center for Health Statistics provides four versions of marriage rates and two versions of divorce rates. The four marriage rates use increasingly refined estimates of the population exposed to risk of marriage. The crude

marriage rate (CMR) is the number of marriages times 1,000 divided by the total population. The crude nuptiality rate (CNR) divides the number of marriages times 1,000 by women aged 15 or greater. The general marriage rate (GMR) uses unmarried females aged 15 or greater and the general nuptiality rate (GNR) uses unmarried females aged 15 to 44 as a population denominator exposed to risk of marriage. Similarly, divorce is measured by the crude divorce rate (CDR) or the number of divorces times 1,000 divided by the total population and the general divorce rate (GDR) using married females of at least 15 years of age as a denominator. The general nuptiality rate and the general divorce rate have the most precisely defined denominators and hence should be regarded as the best measures of the force of the marriage and divorce processes upon the population. However, the general marriage rate and general divorce rate are often paired in presentation since they have the same denominator.

Marriage and Divorce as a Dynamic Process

The marriage boom of the 1940s and 1950s, followed by the marriage relapse of the 1970s through the late 1980s, is clearly evident from Figure 5-3, which graphically illustrates the trend of the general marriage rate (GMR) and the general divorce rate (GDR). Before 1920, when a small marriage boom was caused by the military demobilization of World War I, the historical trend of marriage was at a plateau. This was followed by a gradual decline during the 1920s until 1930, when a sharp decline coincided with the economic depression. However, in the late 1930s the rates began to climb despite the economic depression, and they climbed further during the war years. The rates peaked in 1946, at the same time as demobilization following World War II. Large numbers of postponed marriages were celebrated in that one year. Marriage rates remained high during the immediate postwar years. Although they declined gradually, they remained above the long-term level until 1957, at which time they began to decline rather precipitously. Not surprisingly, divorces also peaked as the marriage rate skyrocketed in 1945-47. The GDR was higher in 1946 than at any time until the mid-1970s.

In 1990 the GMR was only three-quarters of what it had been in 1970. Since 1988, the marriage rate has stopped declining and has turned up slightly. How significant this recent upturn may be remains to be seen. One explanation commonly given for the sudden downturn in the marriage rate is the increased economic independence of women caused by their increased levels of education and employment, and emphasis on women's rights and equal status. Changing sex codes, more permissive with regard to premarital and extramarital sex relations (combined with use of modern contraceptive methods), may also support many cohabiting couples' decisions not to get married, whereas in earlier years they may have done so out of moral beliefs or in response to social pressures. On the other hand, economic factors should not be overlooked. Since marriage usually entails the establishment of a new household with appropriate amenities, a substantial monetary outlay (either in credit or in savings) is required. The 1970s and early 1980s were years of significant unemployment, high inflation, and periodic economic recession. These adverse conditions had their greatest impact upon young persons leaving school and seeking to join the work force. Thus, an improving economy in the early 1990s may presage a resurgence of marriage behavior.

The rise in divorce, as indicated by the GDR, was also marked during the 1970s. This rise is amplified in significance because it accompanied a period of declining, rather than rising, marriage rates. The same causes which have been used to explain the fall in marriages during this time have been used to explain rising divorce rates. However, unlike the decline in marriage rates which continued into the 1980s, the GDR began to level off and decline in the 1980s.

It is commonly believed that, other factors held constant, marriage rates rise in times of economic prosperity and fall in periods of economic decline. The lowest nuptiality rates on record are those of 1932, a year of great financial and economic turmoil. Divorce rates were also low during these years. The low marriage rates of 1980-1982 occurred as the nation suffered a severe economic recession. Recent rising marriage rates accompany lower interest rates in the 1990s which provide greater access to home buying and new household formation. Divorce rates, however, have appeared more or less high and stable over recent years.

Wars also have affected the marriage and divorce rate markedly. Mobilization for defense has tended to cause a rise in marriages, followed by a drop when men are shipped to combat centers, and hence no longer available for marriage. As the men return and are demobilized, marriage rates rise sharply to compensate for marriages postponed by military duty. Yet, the dramatic rise in marriages also frequently produces an echoed rise in divorce rates. This kind of cycle for marriages occurred after World War I (1919-20), was most dramatic during the demobilization after World War II (1946-47), and though fewer persons were involved, reappeared at the time of the Korean War (1950). Only the divorce echo of World War II demobilization is notable.

Marriage is influenced by factors other than economic conditions and wars, however. The high or low priority placed upon marriage vis-a-vis alternative living arrangements is one such factor, and it seems to fluctuate somewhat after the behavior of fashion rather than follow a tradition. During the years 1923 to 1929, which witnessed a great rise in the nation's prosperity, the marriage rate declined—perhaps because the attitudinal climate of the "roaring twenties" made marriage less appealing. It should also be noted that the marriage rate reversed its downward trend and began an upward trend several years before the economic depression of the 1930s ended. Apparently, couples for whom marriage has a high priority in their life plan will postpone marriage only for a limited number of months or years because of economic hardship and then will marry despite unfavorable conditions.

Regional and State Variation in Marital Rates

Again, there are considerable variations among states in marriage rates. These variations arise from differences in population composition and demographic and economic regional histories. Table 5-9 provides the number and rate of marriages for regions, divisions and states of the country for 1980 and 1990. Dramatic differences can be seen in regional marriage patterns. Marriage rates are lowest in the Middle Atlantic states of the Northeast. They are far and away the highest in the Mountain states of the West. By the American tradition of traveling to Nevada to marry, this state has a marriage rate which is 13.5 times higher than the national marriage rate.

Table 5-9. Marriage Rates, by Region and State: 1980 and 1990

Region, division, and state	Number 1990	Number 1980	Rate 1990	Rate 1980
United States, total	2,443,489	2,390,252	9.8	10.6
Northeast region	406,900	400,313	8.0	8.1
New England	110,454	106,328	8.4	8.6
Middle Atlantic	296,446	293,965	7.9	8.0
Midwest region	522,415	569,237	8.7	9.7
East North Central	366,910	395,517	8.7	9.5
West North Central	155,505	173,720	8.8	10.1
South region	930,746	880,185	10.9	11.7
South Atlantic	457,214	413,113	10.5	11.2
East South Central	185,207	168,828	12.2	11.5
West South Central	288,325	296,244	10.8	12.6
West region	581,428	540,517	11.0	12.5
Mountain	248,414	241,704	18.1	21.3
Pacific	333,014	298,813	8.5	9.4
New England				
Maine	11,915	12,040	9.7	10.7
New Hampshire	10,535	9,251	9.5	10.0
Vermont	6,126	5,226	10.9	10.2
Massachusetts	47,696	46,273	7.9	8.1
Rhode Island	8,134	7,490	8.1	7.9
Connecticut	26,046	26,048	7.9	8.4
Middle Atlantic				
New York	154,774	144,518	8.6	8.2
New Jersey	58,747	55,794	7.6	7.6
Pennsylvania	84,925	93,673	7.1	7.9
East North Central				
Ohio	96,076	99,832	9.0	9.2
Indiana	53,169	57,853	9.6	10.5
Illinois	100,632	109,823	8.8	9.6
Michigan	76,099	86,896	8.2	9.4
Wisconsin	38,934	41,111	7.9	8.7
West North Central				
Minnesota	33,688	37,641	7.7	9.2
Iowa	24,931	27,474	9.0	9.4
Missouri	49,063	54,625	9.6	11.1
North Dakota	4,762	6,094	7.5	9.3
South Dakota	7,716	8,800	11.1	12.7
Nebraska	12,625	14,239	8.0	9.1
Kansas	22,720	24,847	9.2	10.5
South Atlantic				
Delaware	5,639	4,437	8.4	7.5
Maryland	46,316	46,278	9.7	11.0
District of Columbia	4,960	5,182	8.2	8.1
Virginia	71,043	60,210	11.4	11.3
West Virginia	13,003	17,391	7.2	8.9
North Carolina	51,923	46,718	7.8	7.9
South Carolina	55,754	53,915	15.9	17.3
Georgia	66,760	70,638	10.3	12.9
Florida	141,816	108,344	10.9	11.1
East South Central				
Kentucky	49,790	32,727	13.5	8.9
Tennessee	68,019	59,175	13.9	12.9
Alabama	43,050	49,018	10.6	12.6
Mississippi	24,348	27,908	9.4	11.1
West South Central				
Arkansas	38,020	26,513	15.3	11.6
Louisiana	40,443	43,460	9.6	10.3
Oklahoma	33,249	46,509	10.6	15.4
Texas	178,613	181,762	10.5	12.8

Table 5-9. Marriage Rates, by Region and State: 1980 and 1990 (continued)

Region, division, and state	Number 1990	Number 1980	Rate 1990	Rate 1980
Mountain				
Montana	6,924	8,336	8.6	10.6
Idaho	14,064	13,426	13.9	14.2
Wyoming	4,852	6,868	10.7	14.6
Colorado	32,632	34,917	9.8	12.1
New Mexico	13,324	16,641	8.8	12.8
Arizona	36,842	30,223	10.0	11.1
Utah	19,427	16,958	11.2	11.6
Nevada	120,619	114,333	99.0	142.8
Pacific				
Washington	46,554	47,728	9.5	11.6
Oregon	25,348	23,004	8.9	8.7
California	237,135	210,864	7.9	8.9
Alaska	5,671	5,361	10.2	13.3
Hawaii	18,306	11,856	16.4	12.3

Source: Natonal Center for Health Statistics, "Advance Report of Final Marriage Statistics, 1989 and 1990," Monthly Vital Statistics Report, Volume 43, No. 12, Supplement, 1995, Table 2.

First Marriages and Remarriages

Just above 60 percent of the marriages that occur are first marriages for either the bride or the groom. In all other cases one or both of the partners have been married previously. Figure 5-4 shows that remarriage rates peaked in the early seventies and have declined as first marriages have over the past two decades. The much higher marriage rates of the early 1970s happened at a time of a higher General Marriage Rate and a rising General Divorce Rate between 1970 and 1974 (see Figure 5-3). Although the population of those eligible for remarriage may have ultimately decreased as first marriages declined and may have risen as the divorce rate rose, remarriage trends seem to have been largely independent of trends in the population eligible for remarriage. Instead, the remarriage rate of the previously divorced and that of the widowed seems to have declined alongside all marriage rates regardless of prior marital status.

Remarriages to previously divorced males have the highest rate followed by previously divorced females at a much lower level. In the early 1970s the remarriage rate for divorced males was nearly double that of females. By 1990 this gap had narrowed considerably, but the remarriage rate of divorced males was still about one and one-half that of females. The lowest marriage rates are for previously widowed females who remarry at just about one-fifth the rate of widowed males. The remarriage rates of those widowed have also dropped dramatically in the past twenty years. The remarriage rates of widowed males

**Figure 5-4. Marriage Rates by Previous Marital Status:
Marriage-registration Area, 1970-1990**

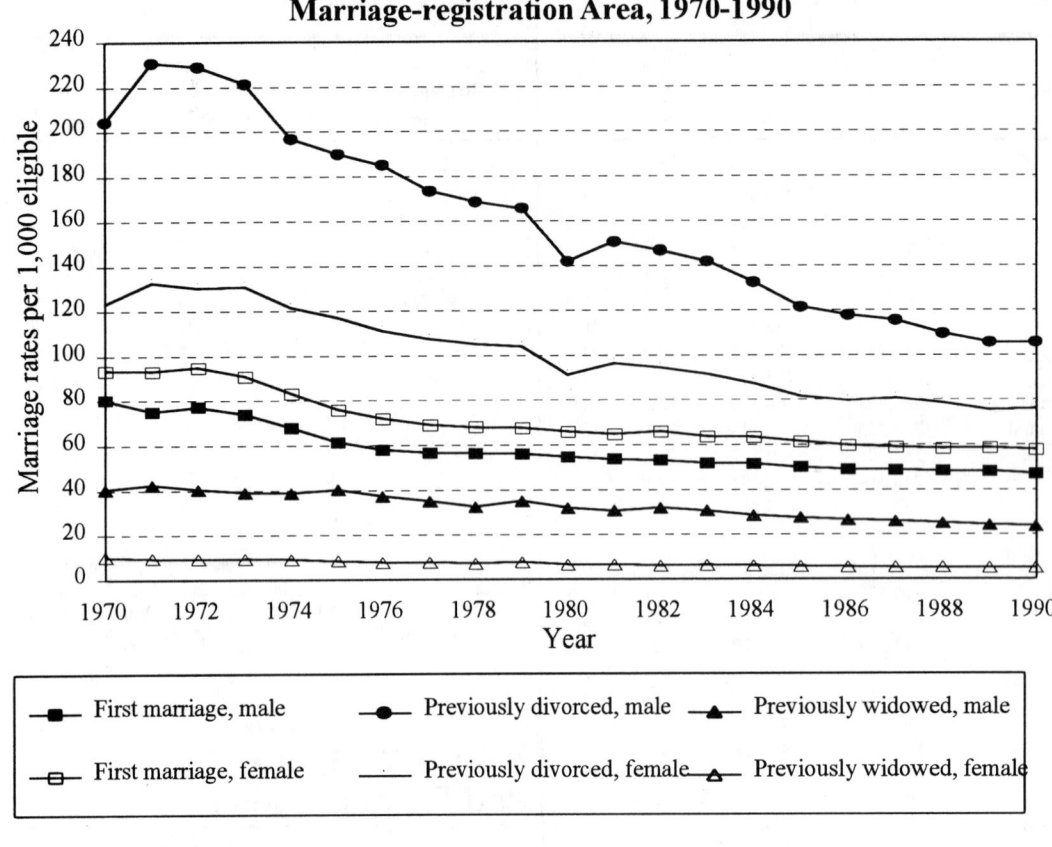

Source: 1970-1990 NCHS data.

Figure 5-5. Age Profile of Marriage Rates: 1990

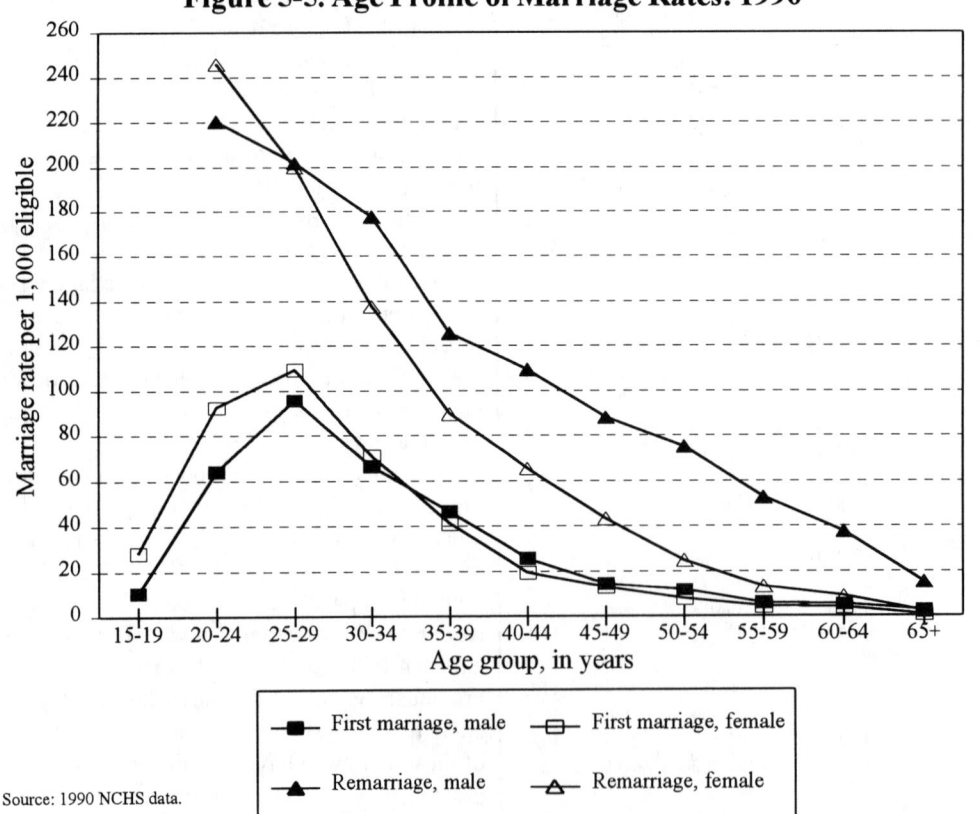

Source: 1990 NCHS data.

Same-Sex Marriage

by Janet Tonner-Wagner

The word "marriage" has been applied to both ceremonial events and to legal contracts and has varied in both nature and form throughout history. Although a number of religious institutions currently perform and recognize ceremonies celebrating same-sex unions, the United States does not legally recognize same-sex marriages. To date, full and equal legal marriage for same-sex couples is unavailable anywhere in the world. Domestic registration, which very closely approximates marriage, is available in Denmark, Greenland, Norway and Sweden. Other countries and cities and municipalities in the U.S. provide varying degrees of domestic partner benefits such as health care benefits and sick and/or bereavement leave, but none are as extensive as the rights and benefits conferred upon married heterosexual couples.

Same-sex marriage, while a contested issue for some time in the United States, came to the foreground in 1993 when a Hawaii Supreme Court ruled in *Baehr v. Lewin* that the denial of marriage licenses to same-gender couples appears to violate the state's equal protection guarantee. A final decision from the Hawaii Supreme Court is still pending. Nonetheless, seeing potential consequences, conservative activists have mobilized to enact state legislation blocking recognition of same-sex marriage in 15 states. Their attempts have been unsuccessful in 20 states and are pending in two states.

Statewide Laws Blocking Recognition of Same-sex Marriages: 1996

Law passed	Failed bill	Pending
Alaska	Alabama	New Jersey
Arizona	California	Pennsylvania
Delaware	Colorado	
Georgia	Florida	
Idaho	Hawaii	
Illinois	Iowa	
Kansas	Kentucky	
Michigan	Louisiana	
Missouri	Maine	
North Carolina	Maryland	
Oklahoma	Minnesota	
South Carolina	Mississippi	
South Dakota	New Mexico	
Tennessee	New York	
Utah	Rhode Island	
	Virginia	
	Washington	
	West Virginia	
	Wisconsin	
	Wyoming	

Source: American Civil Liberties Union, press release, September 4, 1996.

Politicians seeking to preempt same-sex marriages at the federal level introduced the Defense of Marriage Act (DOMA). This legislation was signed into law in 1996. The DOMA defines marriage in Federal law for the first time as a "union between one man and one woman," and maintains the right of states to ignore same-sex marriages performed in other states. Opponents of the DOMA contend it violates the U.S. Constitution's 'Full Faith and Credit' clause which requires that the court judgements of one state be honored by other states. Yet, this clause has not been consistently applied to the regulation of marriage by states. At this time it is unclear whether the DOMA will hold up to legal scrutiny.

The majority of empirical social science research on gay and lesbian relationships dates from the mid-1970's and has been largely descriptive. Few demographers, including those from the U.S. Bureau of the Census, General Social Survey (GSS) and the National Health and Social Life Survey (NHSLS), solicit explicit information regarding same-sex couples (see Chapter 11 for attempts to identify same sex householding). *The Social Organization of Sexuality*, the most comprehensive recent representative survey of sexual behavior in the general population, notes "Since same-gender marriage is not legally recognized in the United States, we assume that all the marriages are between men and women" (Laumann, Gagnon, Michael, Michaels 1994:302). Even when survey information is gathered, gay and lesbian couples are often wary of providing personal information for fear of discrimination. It is, of course, also difficult to identify unions 'equivalent' to marriage without civil ceremony regardless of sexual orientation. Thus, it is very difficult, if not impossible, to accurately identify the number of same-sex couples who consider themselves in a union which is in various ways equivalent to marriage.

Smaller, less representative studies have been conducted to explore the nature and duration of gay and lesbian relationships. In surveys of gay men, between 40% and 60% of the men questioned were currently involved in a steady relationship (Bell & Weinberg 1978; Harry 1983; Peplau & Cochran 1981). However, the percentages become smaller as additional criteria of cohabitation and length of relationship are introduced (Harry 1983). It is estimated that only about half of gay male couples actually live together (Harry 1983). In studies of lesbians, between 45% and 80% of women surveyed were currently in a steady relationship, although in most studies the proportion of lesbians in a couple relationship is 75% (Bell & Weinburg 1978; Peplau and Cochran 1990).

Sources

Bell, A. P., and M. S. Weinberg. *Homosexualities: A Study of Diversity Among Men and Women*. New York: Simon & Schuster, 1878.

Harry, J. "Gay Male and Lesbian Relationships." *Contemporary Families and Alternative Lifestyles: Handbook on Research and Theory*. Eds. E. Macklin and R. Rubin. Beverly Hills, California: Sage, 1983.

Laumann, E. O., and J. H. Gagnon, R. T. Michael, S. Michaels. *The Social Organization of Sexuality: Sexual Practices in the United States*. Chicago and London: The University of Chicago Press, 1994.

Peplau, L. A., and S. D. Cochran. "A Relational Perspective on Homosexuality." *Homosexuality/Heterosexuality: Concepts of Sexual Orientation*. Eds. P. McWhirter, S. Sanders, and J. Reinisch. Vol. 2 of the Kinsey Institute Series. New York and Oxford: Oxford University Press, 1990.

Table 5-10. Median Age of Bride and Groom, by Previous Marital Status: Marriage-registration Area, 1964-1990

| | All marriages | | First marriages | | Remarriages | | | | | |
| | | | | | All remarriages | | Previously divorced | | Previously widowed | |
Year	Bride	Groom	Bride	Groom	Bride	Groom	Bride	Groom	Bride	Groom
1990	26.7	28.7	24.0	25.9	35.0	38.3	34.2	37.4	54.0	63.1
1989	26.4	28.4	23.9	25.7	34.7	38.3	34.0	37.3	53.8	62.9
1988	26.1	28.1	23.7	25.5	34.5	38.0	33.6	37.0	53.9	63.0
1987	25.9	28.0	23.6	25.3	34.1	37.7	33.3	36.7	53.9	62.8
1986	25.7	27.8	23.3	25.1	33.9	37.5	33.1	36.6	54.3	62.9
1985	25.3	27.5	23.0	24.8	33.6	37.1	32.8	36.1	54.6	62.7
1984	25.0	27.2	22.8	24.6	33.3	36.8	32.5	35.9	54.2	62.4
1983	24.8	27.0	22.5	24.4	32.9	36.2	32.0	35.3	54.0	62.0
1982	24.4	26.7	22.3	24.1	32.5	35.7	31.6	34.9	54.1	61.7
1981	24.1	26.3	22.0	23.9	32.1	35.3	31.2	34.4	53.6	61.0
1980	23.7	25.9	21.8	23.6	32.0	35.2	31.0	34.0	53.6	61.2
1979	23.4	25.8	21.6	23.4	31.9	35.3	30.8	33.9	55.2	61.7
1978	23.2	25.5	21.4	23.2	31.5	35.1	30.5	33.6	52.6	59.7
1977	22.9	25.2	21.1	23.0	31.4	34.9	30.2	33.6	53.1	60.1
1976	22.7	25.0	21.0	22.9	31.7	35.1	30.1	33.7	53.0	60.0
1975	22.4	24.7	20.8	22.7	32.0	35.5	30.2	33.6	52.4	59.4
1974	22.0	24.2	20.6	22.5	32.1	35.7	30.0	33.6	51.9	59.2
1973	21.9	24.1	20.6	22.5	32.3	36.3	30.2	33.9	52.1	59.3
1972	21.7	23.8	20.5	22.4	32.8	36.5	30.3	34.0	51.4	59.1
1971	21.7	23.7	20.5	22.5	32.9	36.9	30.2	34.1	51.8	59.1
1970	21.7	23.6	20.6	22.5	33.3	37.5	30.1	34.5	51.2	58.7
1969	21.6	23.5	20.6	22.4	33.8	38.2	30.4	34.7	51.3	59.0
1968	21.5	23.6	20.6	22.4	33.8	38.3	30.7	35.1	50.6	57.9
1967	21.4	23.8	20.5	22.6	35.0	39.1	31.3	35.5	50.0	57.7
1966	21.5	23.8	20.3	22.6	35.2	39.2	31.4	35.8	50.2	57.9
1965	21.4	23.6	20.4	22.5	35.5	39.6	31.7	36.0	50.1	57.8
1964	21.4	23.6	20.4	22.4	35.6	39.7	31.7	36.4	50.3	58.0

Source: Natonal Center for Health Statistics, "Advance Report of Final Marriage Statistics, 1989 and 1990," Monthly Vital Statistics Report, Volume 43, No. 12, Supplement, 1995, Table 9.

and females have fallen to nearly half of what they were twenty years ago.

Age of First Marriage and Remarriages

The age patterns of remarriage are considerably different from those of first marriages. The pattern is, however, not what one might expect at first. Remarriage rates peak at a younger age group than do first marriage rates (see Figure 5-5). Many of those who are divorced or widowed at young ages apparently hasten to remarry without delay. However, as the ages of divorced or widowed persons increase their remarriage rate declines. And, this drop in remarriage rates is more precipitous among females compared to males. Women have a higher rate of remarriage than do men at ages less than 24 years. How-

ever, the rate of remarriage for females drops well below that of males at ages 30 and above. At ages 45 and above the remarriage rate for females falls to less than half that of males and by age 55 it is only a seventh of the remarriage rate for males. In contrast, first marriage rates rise to a peak between 25-29 years of age, then fall for both males and females as age increases. As with remarriage, the first marriage rate of females declines more quickly with age than does that of males. The gap in first marriage rates between males and females is, however, far less dramatic than for remarriage rates.

The median age of first marriages and remarriages has also followed very different trends over the recent past. Table 5-10 reports the median age for brides and grooms across the years since 1964 for all marriages, first marriages, all remarriages and for remarriages to the previ-

Table 5-11. Marriage Rates, by Previous Marital Status and Age: Marriage-registration Area: 1970-1990

	Grooms			Brides		
	1990	1980	1970	1990	1980	1970
All marriages	56.2	66.8	80.8	47.8	54.2	64.8
15 to 17 years[1]	1.5	3.0	4.0	10.8	20.2	26.3
18 to 19 years	22.3	39.2	74.4	53.8	90.9	156.7
20 to 24 years	67.2	100.4	205.7	100.0	130.8	234.2
25 to 29 years	107.1	131.2		127.4	126.3	
30 to 34 years	90.9	122.8		97.2	95.0	
35 to 39 years	79.4	102.0	164.0	69.3	62.3	111.3
40 to 44 years	69.7			50.0		
45 to 49 years	59.1			36.2		
50 to 54 years	53.2			21.4		
55 to 59 years	34.8	49.1	54.9	11.7	17.3	20.9
60 to 64 years	27.2			8.1		
65 years and over	12.5	15.2	15.6	1.9	2.2	2.4
First marriages	47.0	54.7	72.1	57.7	66.0	93.4
15 to 17 years[1]	1.5	2.9	3.9	10.7	19.8	25.6
18 to 19 years	22.1	38.4	73.0	52.5	87.3	151.4
20 to 24 years	64.0	94.5	195.7	92.6	119.8	220.1
25 to 29 years	95.7	109.9		109.4	101.6	
30 to 34 years	66.2	75.5		70.8	56.3	
35 to 39 years	46.3	37.2	119.6	41.1	27.1	82.5
40 to 44 years	25.7			19.5		
45 to 49 years	14.3			12.9		
50 to 54 years	11.7			7.8		
55 to 59 years	5.8	11.6	14.1	4.2	7.0	8.8
60 to 64 years	5.0			3.8		
65 years and over	2.5	2.9	3.4	0.7	0.9	1.1
Remarriages	84.5	108.3	116.5	35.8	38.3	36.6
15 to 19 years[1]	—	219.2	350.9	—	231.0	317.6
20 to 24 years	220.4			245.9		
25 to 29 years	201.8	225.2		200.0	178.6	
30 to 34 years	177.5	203.9		137.7	129.0	
35 to 39 years	125.7	162.0	298.0	89.6	78.5	142.3
40 to 44 years	109.5			65.2		
45 to 49 years	88.0			43.3		
50 to 54 years	75.0			24.8		
55 to 59 years	52.8	74.4	95.6	13.0	19.7	24.8
60 to 64 years	37.7			8.7		
65 years and over	15.0	19.0	19.9	20.0	2.3	2.5
Previously divorced	105.9	142.1	204.5	76.2	91.3	123.3
15 to 19 years[1]	—	217.6	204.2	—	236.4	413.4
20 to 24 years	225.0			252.3		
25 to 29 years	200.3	220.1		199.8	180.8	
30 to 34 years	173.7	201.8		137.5	131.8	
35 to 39 years	124.5	161.7	325.4	92.8	83.7	179.6
40 to 44 years	110.4			69.3		
45 to 49 years	86.6			47.3		
50 to 54 years	72.9			28.2		
55 to 59 years	51.4	79.1	108.7	17.1	30.3	42.6
60 to 64 years	35.3			11.5		
65 years and over	19.1	22.8	23.6	4.5	5.3	6.1
Previously widowed	23.8	32.2	40.6	5.2	6.7	10.2
15 to 44 years[1]	82.4	106.7	107.8	43.6	51.0	54.1
45 to 64 years	49.8	59.2	79.2	11.0	12.2	17.7
65 years and over	14.0	17.8	19.4	1.7	2.1	2.3

[1]Age group starts at 14 years in 1970.

Source: Natonal Center for Health Statistics, "Advance Report of Final Marriage Statistics, 1989 and 1990," Monthly Vital Statistics Report, Volume 43, No. 12, Supplement, Table 6, "Vital Statistics of the United States, Volume III—Marriages and Divorces:1980," Table 1-20, and ":1970," Table 1-20, National Center for Health Statistics, Hyattsville, MD, 1995, 1985, and 1974.

ously divorced and previously widowed. The median age of first marriages was relatively stable for both brides and grooms from 1964 to 1974 and has risen relatively steadily since. In contrast, the median age for remarriages of brides and grooms fell from 1964 to 1977 by roughly four and a half years of age and has risen slowly back to ages comparable to the late 1960s over the years since 1977. This U-shaped trend in median age over the past quarter century of remarriage is confined to remarriages of the previously divorced. The median age of remarriage among the previously widowed has shown a gradual unsteady rise of four to five years in age of brides and grooms over the same period.

Rates of First Marriage and Remarriage

Table 5-11 reports the nuptiality rates that prevailed between 1970 and 1990, in each of several age groups, for grooms and for brides. The rates for all marriages, first marriages, all remarriages and those for remarriage of divorced and widowed persons are all given separately. In computing these age-specific nuptiality rates, at each age the appropriate unmarried population has been used as the denominator. The rates of first marriage have been based on the single (never married) population, while the rates of remarriage have been based on the widowed and divorced population (see "Definitions"), subdivided into age groups. The data of Table 5-11 are not reported for all states (see Chapter 2). The rates reported are not exactly the same as complete national rates, but the age patterns are probably very near to the unknown national age-at-marriage patterns.

According to the estimates of Table 5-11, the rates for first marriage begin low (at ages 15-17), climb quickly to reach a peak at ages 25-29 for brides and for grooms, and then decline gradually with advancing age. The age at which first marriage peaks has advanced over the past two decades. At the time of the 1980 Census the peak age of first marriage for females was the 20-24 year age group as it was for males in the 1970 Census. Between the ages of fifteen and thirty-four, the probability that a single woman will marry within a year is greater than that for men. But at older ages, single women have nuptiality rates much lower than those for men, and the female rates decline more swiftly. In the years after age sixty-five the probability of a single woman marrying during a one-year period is less than one-third as great as that for men, but it is very low for both.

Rates of remarriage are not very trustworthy before age twenty-five, because the number of previously married persons is so small that the numbers are unstable. But, as noted above, the remarriage rates at these young ages is very high for both males and females. The rate of remarriage is higher for males than for females at all ages. Remarriage rates are higher than first marriage rates, more

Table 5-12. Percent of All Marriages That Are Remarriages, by Sex and Race: 1955-1990

Year	Brides			Grooms		
	Total	White	Black	Total	White	Black
1990	38.0	39.6	28.1	37.3	38.4	31.0
1989	37.1	38.7	26.5	36.4	37.5	28.8
1988	37.3	38.7	27.4	36.4	37.5	29.5
1987	37.1	38.7	26.6	36.7	38.0	29.2
1986	34.6	39.2	27.0	35.0	38.4	29.7
1985	34.3	38.0	27.0	34.9	38.0	29.6
1984	34.1	37.7	26.3	34.9	37.9	29.5
1983	34.1	37.5	26.7	35.2	38.0	29.7
1982	33.7	37.0	26.1	35.0	38.0	29.2
1981	33.6	37.0	26.4	35.2	38.0	30.1
1980	32.6	35.6	26.2	34.1	36.6	29.1
1979	32.4	35.2	25.8	34.2	36.0	29.2
1978	31.8	34.7	25.8	33.7	36.0	29.1
1977	31.7	34.5	25.7	33.5	35.8	28.7
1976	30.8	33.6	25.3	32.7	34.9	28.6
1975	30.0	32.4	25.1	31.3	33.3	27.5
1974	28.0	30.4	22.3	29.1	31.1	24.9
1973	26.8	29.1	20.7	27.6	29.6	22.9
1972	25.1	27.2	19.5	25.9	27.6	21.9
1971	24.4	26.1	18.3	25.1	26.1	20.8
1970	23.9	25.5	19.5	24.2	25.5	20.8
1969	23.1	24.6	19.3	23.2	24.3	21.5
1968	22.5	24.1	18.4	22.6	23.7	20.2
1967	22.7	24.3	18.5	22.8	24.0	20.4
1966	22.8	23.9	18.6	22.9	23.8	20.4
1965	22.6	22.7	18.9	22.8	22.7	20.6
1964	23.1	23.2	19.3	22.9	22.8	21.3
1963	23.2	23.3	20.1	22.6	22.3	22.0
1962	23.1	22.8	22.3	22.4	22.3	23.4
1961	23.0	22.7	20.5	22.7	22.3	21.6
1960	22.9	22.5	22.7	21.9	21.3	23.4
1955	23.3	23.3	23.8	22.2	21.9	24.6

Source: National Center for Health Statistics, "Advance Report of Final Marriage Statistics, 1989 and 1990," Monthly Vital Statistics Report, Volume 43, No. 12, Supplement, Table 10, "Advance Report of Final Marriage Statistics, 1988," Monthly Vital Statistics Report, Volume 40, No. 4, Supplement, Table 11, "Advance Report of Final Marriage Statistics, 1987," Monthly Vital Statistics Report, Volume 38, No. 12, Supplement, Table 10, and "Vital Statistics of the United States, Volume III--Marriages and Divorces: 1955, and 1960-86," National Center for Health Statistics, Hyattsville, MD, Table 1-15.

so for males than females. As a group, previously married men remarry at a rate more than twice as high as previously married women. This disparity has declined since 1980 when remarriage among men overall was more than three times as high as among women. Despite the fact that a very high proportion of remarriages occur after age thirty, the rate of remarriage is at its peak in the twenties and thirties and declines very sharply after age forty-five. As noted above (see Figure 5-5) this decline in remarriage rates with increasing age is more precipitous for females than for males. At every age the rate of remarriage is higher for both men and women than the rate of first marriage. Remarriage of divorced persons has a higher rate than for widowed persons, at every age. These data imply that once they have entered the married state, both sexes try to remain there. If their marriage is broken they tend to remarry rather promptly if they are younger than forty-five, and at a significant rate at older ages. However, remarriage rates have declined since 1970 for both males and females and at all ages. The reduction in remarriage over time has been particularly large at the younger ages.

Percentage of Remarriage Among Marriages

Table 5-12 shows that the percent of all marriages which are remarriages has increased considerably since 1955. This increase has been more substantial for whites than for blacks. For all remarriages the increase has been most substantial in more recent years. Despite similarly increasing trends in the percentage of marriages which are remarriages, this percentage remains sharply higher for white than it is for black brides and grooms. Overall, since 1970, the percentage of marriages which are remarriages has increased from roughly a quarter of all marriages to well over a third of all marriages.

The ratio of remarriages to all marriages also varies greatly with age, as is shown by Table 5-13. At ages below twenty years, about 98 percent of all marriages for women are first marriages. During the years 20-29, first marriages are predominant, but an increased proportion for each successively older age group consists of remarriage. By ages 30-34, among both women and men, the majority of marriages are remarriages. At ages older than forty-five, nearly 90 percent or more of all marriages are remarriages. Of the comparatively few marriages that occur after age sixty-five, 95 percent or more are remarriages.

The trend in the age composition of the percentage of marriages which are remarriages is also reported for all marriages in Table 5-13 for brides and grooms. Remarriages for brides have declined in the younger ages under thirty as a percentage of all marriages and have increased slightly as a percentage of all marriages in most older age groups. For grooms the remarriage rate has declined at all

Table 5-13. Percent of All Marriages That Are Remarriages, by Age and Sex: 1955-1990

Sex and age	1990	1985	1980	1975	1970	1965	1960	1955
Brides	34.9	33.6	32.6	30.0	32.9	22.6	22.6	23.3
Under 20 years	1.8	2.1	2.5	2.7	2.1	1.8	[5.8	2.0
20 to 24 years	9.6	10.9	13.1	14.1	11.1	9.9		10.5
25 to 29 years	27.5	32.7	41.3	48.1	43.2	40.2	38.7	36.7
30 to 34 years	53.3	31.2	69.9	72.4	66.3	63.9	58.5	59.8
35 to 44 years	78.3	82.1	84.7	84.8	80.4	77.2	75.6	73.7
45 to 54 years	90.6	90.5	[90.6	89.4	87.0	86.0	85.0	84.4
55 to 64 years	92.9	91.6		91.2	91.1	89.0	89.2	90.2
65 years and over	94.7	94.2	93.6	94.0	92.9	92.8	93.8	93.1
Grooms	34.5	34.2	34.1	31.3	24.3	22.8	21.6	22.1
Under 20 years	0.5	0.8	0.9	0.8	0.6	0.5	[3.2	0.4
20 to 24 years	5.0	5.6	6.6	7.3	5.3	4.2		3.9
25 to 29 years	17.5	20.9	27.9	32.3	26.3	21.2	16.4	16.8
30 to 34 years	41.5	49.1	58.8	61.7	52.3	46.1	41.1	39.7
35 to 44 years	71.0	77.0	80.8	79.4	71.8	67.2	62.7	62.0
45 to 54 years	89.9	89.5	[89.0	86.7	84.2	81.8	81.5	77.9
55 to 64 years	92.5	91.2		90.2	90.2	88.8	87.8	86.8
65 years and over	94.4	94.0	94.0	95.1	93.3	93.2	91.8	93.1

Source: National Center for Health Statistics, "Advance Report of Final Marriage Statistics, 1989 and 1990," Monthly Vital Statistics Report, Volume 43, No. 12, Supplement, Table 8, and "Vital Statistics of the United States, Volume III--Marriages and Divorces: 1955, 1960, 1965, 1970, 1975, 1980, and 1985," National Center for Health Statistics, Hyattsville, MD, Table 1-28.

Table 5-14. Marriages by Previous Marital Status of Bride by Previous Marital Status of Groom, by Race: 1960-1990

Marital status of bride and year	Marital status of white grooms of white brides				Marital status of black grooms of black brides			
	Total	Single	Widowed	Divorced	Total	Single	Widowed	Divorced
Single								
1990	100.0	82.9	0.5	16.7	100.0	81.7	1.0	17.3
1981[1]	100.0	82.7	0.5	16.8	100.0	83.4	1.2	15.4
1970	100.0	90.4	0.8	8.8	100.0	89.8	1.9	8.3
1960	100.0	92.5	1.2	6.3	100.0	89.6	2.2	8.2
Widowed								
1990	100.0	13.4	42.2	44.5	100.0	20.8	27.0	52.2
1981[1]	100.0	12.5	44.5	43.0	100.0	25.7	37.4	36.8
1970	100.0	15.2	47.1	37.8	100.0	26.8	43.2	30.0
1960	100.0	22.9	45.9	31.2	100.0	28.9	46.6	24.5
Divorced								
1990	100.0	31.7	3.0	64.5	100.0	41.2	4.7	54.1
1981[1]	100.0	29.9	4.1	66.0	100.0	39.5	5.9	54.6
1970	100.0	32.3	7.3	60.4	100.0	41.7	11.8	46.5
1960	100.0	38.3	9.0	52.7	100.0	42.5	15.8	41.7

[1] Data for 1980 were unavailable.

Source: National Center for Health Statistics, "Public Use Data File: Marriage Data, Detail, 1990," 1995, and "Vital Statistics of the United States, Volume III--Marriages and Divorces: 1981, 1970, and 1960," National Center for Health Statistics, Hyattsville, MD, 1986, 1974, and 1964, Table 1-43.

but ages above forty-five. Compared to 1955, the percent of all marriages which are remarriages has increased most dramatically for brides in the 25-34 and 45-54 year age groups and grooms in the 45-54 year age group.

Marriages by Previous Marital Status

It is important to realize that widows and divorcees have been much more prone to remarry since World War II than they were previously. Among those members of the population who remarry, divorced persons are far more common than widows, for both men and women. A major element in this differential is the fact that divorced persons are considerably younger on the average than widowed persons. There also appears to be a tendency for previously married persons to marry persons who have been married before. In fact, there seems to be a tendency for widowed persons to marry widowed persons, and for divorced persons to marry divorced persons.

Table 5-14 shows the marital status of grooms by bride's race and the previous marital status of brides from 1960 to 1990. For each previous marital status of bride (single, widowed, or divorced), the previous marital status of the groom is reported as a percent distribution. This

Table 5-15. Percent of Remarriages That Are Second and Higher Order Marriages: 1955-1990

	Number of this marriage			
	Brides		Grooms	
Year	Second	Higher order	Second	Higher order
1990	75.3	24.7	75.7	24.3
1985	77.7	22.3	77.6	22.4
1980	79.8	20.2	80.2	19.8
1975	81.6	18.4	82.7	17.3
1970	82.4	17.6	84.1	15.9
1965	82.1	17.9	83.8	16.2
1960	82.2	17.8	82.5	17.5
1955	86.3	13.7	86.6	13.4

Source: National Center for Health Statistics, "Public Use Data File: Marriage Data, Detail, 1990," 1995, and "Vital Statistics of the United States, Volume III--Marriages and Divorces: 1985, 1980, 1975, 1970, 1965, 1960 and 1955," National Center for Health Statistics, Hyattsville, MD, Table 1-34.

is shown for both white and black brides, and for a thirty-year period. The evidence is strong that single persons tend to marry single persons, widowed to marry widowed, and divorced to marry divorced. Age selectivity, perhaps more than marital status selectivity, is involved. The long-term trend has been toward an increased proportion of divorced grooms, irrespective of the marital status or race of the bride.

Number of Times Married

One might want to know what proportions, among the population that remarries, are marrying for the third or higher-order time. In 1990 the proportion was 24.7 percent for females and 24.3 for males. Table 5-15 shows the long-term trend toward a slow rise in the proportion of third or higher-order marriages among both brides and grooms who remarry. In the last forty-five years the proportion of brides and grooms with higher-order marriages has risen from less than 14 percent to nearly one quarter of all re-marriages. These proportions, of course, vary greatly with age.

Differences in Age of Brides and Grooms

The average age difference between brides and grooms is a very crude generalization. There is wide varia-tion among couples in the differences in age of partners. The pattern of age difference between the marriage part-ners varies according to the age group concerned and also according to whether the marriage is a first marriage or a remarriage. In Figure 5-6, the age of the groom is reported according to how many years older or younger he is than his bride. The highest degree of similarity be-tween the ages of bride and groom at first marriage is found among brides who marry at ages twenty-two and twenty-three. Over half of those brides at age twenty-three have a groom who is either the same age or within two years (plus or minus) of the bride's age. At ages younger than twenty the groom tends to be older than the bride, while at ages older than twenty-three there is an increasing (still small) proportion of brides who have a groom three or more years younger than they are. By age twenty-nine over a quarter of all brides have a groom who

Figure 5-6. Comparison of Age of Bride and Groom, by Age of Bride: 1990

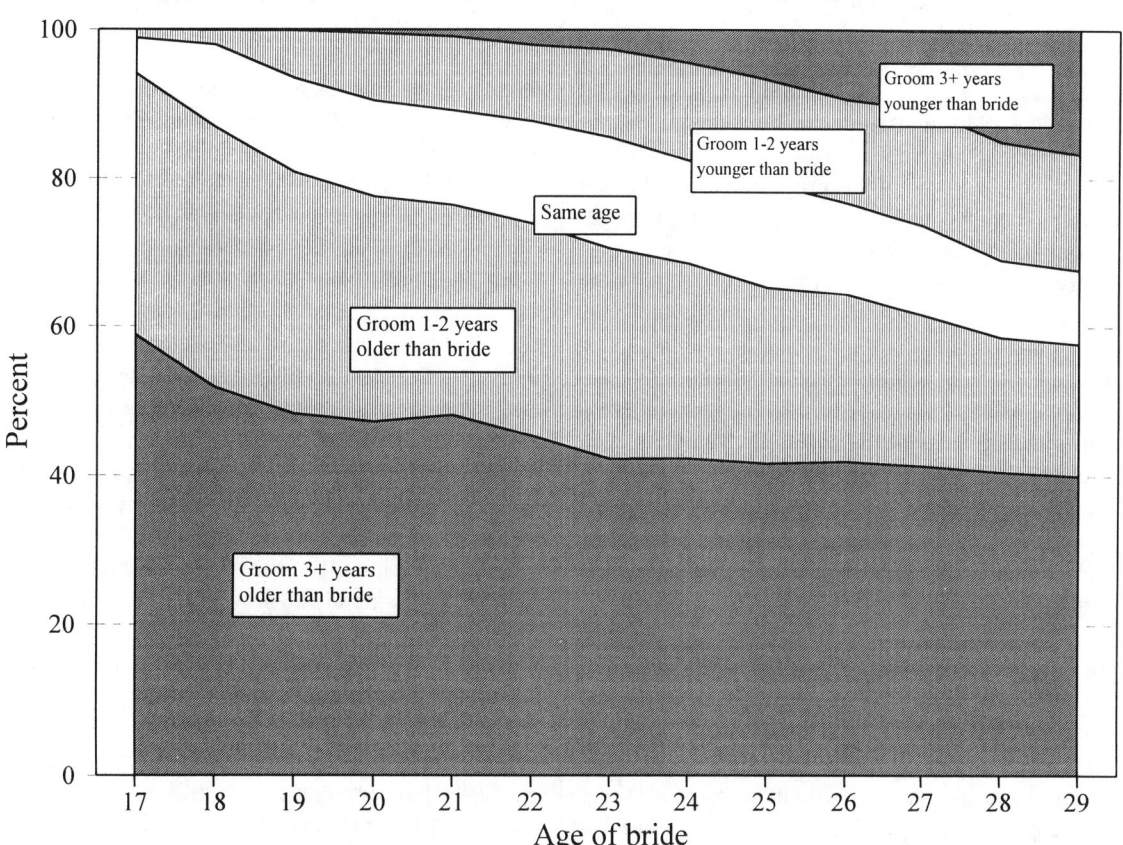

is at least one year younger than they are. However, even at these older ages roughly 40 percent of all brides have a groom at least three years older than they are.

Month and Season of Marriage

If couples were to consider no particular month of the year more appropriate than any other as a time to marry, roughly one-twelfth (8.3 percent) of all marriages would occur each month. Variations in the number of days in the month would affect these proportions slightly, and the monthly proportions would probably vary from year to year as a result of changes in the number of weekends in the respective months. Table 5-16 reports the percent of marriages occurring in each month, showing which months are preferred for marriages, and by how much. When they are ranked in descending order of preference, the months fall into the following order:

June, September, August, May, July, October, December, November and April (tied), March, February and January. The month of June is so popular that it attracts roughly half again as many more marriages than its number of days would suggest, while January is so unpopular that it has roughly a third fewer marriages than its proportionate share. This concentration of marriages in the summer and early autumn months also has a slight seasonal effect on the distribution of births.

Future Trend of Marriage Rates

Since the 1980s marriage rates have appeared to be at a crossroads (see Figure 5-3), with many experts asking themselves and each other what course they will follow in the future. Will they continue to decline, because younger generations will become even less supportive of marriage and family as a way of life? Will they stabilize at or near their present level, with marriages occurring at later ages but taking place eventually? Or will there be a resurgence of marriage popularity, with another marriage boom? Plausible arguments can be made for each of these alternatives. In assessing these possibilities, the following considerations should be kept in mind.

1. In many respects the present situation of delayed marriage is extreme only when viewed in the light of the marriage boom. In terms of long-term trends it is still within the realm of past history, hence "normal."

2. Many sociologists and psychologists of the family were extremely critical of the marriage boom phenomenon, the early age of marriage which accompanied it, and the impact of these early marriages on women's educational achievement or economic independence. In many respects the increasing ages at which marriage is taking place in the past two decades would tend to be defined as almost ideal by these experts.

3. Low and late marriage rates do not necessarily predestine low fertility rates. The United States had high fertility rates in the period between 1890 and 1920, when marriage postponement was popular.

4. Economic stagnation combined with inflation in the 1970s, followed by the acute economic recession of the early 1980s, may have caused substantial postponement of marriages, yet these lower marriage rates have persisted into the later 1980s. This phenomenon occurred in the late years of the Great Depression. The very slight recovery of the General Marriage Rate in 1989 and 1990 may presage an end, or perhaps even a turnaround, in the falling marriage rates of the past fifteen years.

5. Generational life-styles can fluctuate cyclically rather than follow a uniform pattern. Many moralists who saw marriage rates declining in the 1920s and the liberal political movement among young persons during the 1930s forecast a great de-emphasis of marriage and the family. As a consequence the marriage boom of the 1940s and 1950s was wholly unpredicted and ran counter to moralists' as well as theorists' expectations. Similar fluctuations could reappear, equally unexpected and equally contrary to predictions based on trends and current behavior.

6. The movement toward greater equality for women has forced many women to choose between marriage and the struggle for alternative self-realization. New living and work patterns could work to reduce this conflict, with the result that marriage in early adulthood could be a normal and consistent part of women's advancement. However, it is at least equally possible that the opportunities which modern life has opened up as alternative lifestyles for women will result in a more or less permanent depression of marriage rates into the future.

7. Living in a non-family situation carries a number of economic, personal, and even psychic or emotional risks for many of its practitioners. These include long-term economic and social insecurity for women, possible anxiety about stability and duration of intense personal relationships, and more uncertainty in developing a life plan. The problems of remaining single also appear to increase with age. Yet, alternative living arrangements are on the rise and the prevalence of civil marriage may be eroded by these alternative choices. Nonetheless, there may be limits to the proportion of the population that will choose this lifestyle for an entire lifetime.

Considering all of the above, it would appear that marriage rates since 1980 may represent a new somewhat lower plateau of marriage (with a new higher plateau of divorce) which will change only gradually into the year 2000. However, forecasting marriage and divorce behavior is clearly a difficult task beyond the near horizon. And, the lower marriage and higher divorce rates experienced since 1980 have brought clearly different patterns of marriage and have impacted the composition of marriages. Given today's high divorce rates (see next section) and the propensity for divorced persons to remarry, it is now

Table 5-16. Month of Marriage, by Marriage Order and Race: Brides, 1950-1990
[percent ofmarriage occurring in each month]

Marriage order and race	January	February	March	April	May	June	July	August	September	October	November	December
All marriages												
1990	4.4	5.8	6.7	7.3	9.5	12.4	9.0	10.3	10.9	8.6	7.3	7.8
1985	4.5	5.5	6.6	7.3	9.5	13.0	8.8	11.5	9.5	8.5	7.8	7.5
1980	4.9	6.0	6.7	7.2	10.2	12.1	8.8	12.1	8.7	8.4	7.8	7.1
1975	5.4	6.0	6.8	7.2	9.6	12.2	8.8	12.1	8.1	7.9	8.0	7.9
1970	6.3	6.3	6.3	7.1	8.4	12.8	8.8	11.6	8.6	8.1	7.5	8.2
1965	6.3	6.6	5.7	6.8	8.5	12.0	10.1	10.9	9.0	8.5	7.7	7.9
1960	6.3	6.9	5.1	7.5	8.1	12.2	9.8	9.9	9.6	8.7	7.7	8.2
1955	6.5	6.5	5.6	8.0	8.0	11.9	9.3	9.1	9.5	8.9	7.9	8.7
1950	5.8	6.2	5.2	7.8	7.5	11.5	9.2	9.9	11.3	8.8	8.1	8.7
First marriages, white												
1990	4.0	5.3	6.5	7.3	10.0	13.4	8.5	10.3	11.3	8.9	7.1	7.4
1985	4.0	5.1	6.5	7.5	10.2	14.4	8.3	11.7	10.0	8.6	7.3	6.4
1980	4.4	5.4	6.5	7.2	10.8	13.1	8.6	12.5	8.9	8.5	7.6	6.4
1975	5.1	5.6	6.4	7.0	10.0	13.5	8.8	12.8	8.3	7.8	7.6	7.1
1970	6.4	5.9	6.0	6.9	8.6	14.7	8.5	12.3	8.4	7.7	7.1	7.7
1965	6.1	6.5	5.2	6.5	9.0	13.9	10.5	11.8	9.1	7.8	6.9	6.7
1960	5.9	6.9	4.5	7.5	8.0	12.9	10.1	10.2	10.2	8.5	7.4	7.8
First marriages, black												
1990	5.0	6.3	7.5	7.5	8.7	11.4	10.0	11.2	9.4	6.8	7.2	9.1
1985	5.6	6.3	7.2	7.4	8.3	12.2	10.1	11.8	8.0	6.7	7.6	8.7
1980	6.0	6.7	7.2	7.3	7.9	11.7	10.1	11.6	7.8	6.9	7.9	8.9
1975	6.8	6.5	7.7	7.3	7.7	12.3	9.8	11.1	7.6	6.6	7.4	9.3
1970	7.2	6.9	7.6	7.8	8.2	12.4	8.5	10.7	7.8	7.1	7.1	8.7
1965	7.3	7.3	7.5	7.3	7.8	10.3	9.9	10.5	8.0	7.6	7.3	9.2
1960	7.9	6.5	6.6	7.2	7.3	11.2	9.2	10.2	8.5	8.5	8.1	8.7
All remarriages												
1990	5.1	6.8	7.3	7.7	9.0	11.2	9.3	9.4	9.3	8.1	7.9	9.0
1985												
1980	6.0	7.3	7.4	7.2	9.5	10.4	8.6	10.5	7.6	8.3	8.6	8.8
1975	5.9	6.7	7.3	7.4	9.3	10.1	8.6	10.4	7.4	7.8	9.0	10.0
1970	6.5	6.9	7.0	7.4	8.7	9.9	9.1	9.5	8.2	8.7	8.4	9.8
1965	6.8	6.8	6.7	7.6	8.4	9.5	9.8	9.1	8.0	8.8	8.8	9.7
1960	6.8	6.9	6.4	7.7	8.2	10.1	9.1	8.9	8.5	9.3	8.7	9.3
Remarriages, white												
1990	5.2	7.0	7.4	7.8	9.0	11.1	8.9	9.2	9.2	8.1	8.1	9.0
1985	5.2	6.5	7.3	7.6	9.0	11.2	8.8	10.2	7.9	8.0	8.7	9.5
1980	6.1	7.3	7.4	7.3	9.5	10.2	8.5	10.0	7.6	8.3	8.8	8.8
1975	6.1	6.8	7.4	7.4	9.4	9.8	8.7	10.2	7.3	8.1	9.0	10.0
1970	6.7	6.9	7.1	7.5	9.0	10.0	9.1	9.4	8.1	8.4	8.3	9.4
1965	6.9	6.8	6.8	8.0	8.5	9.6	10.2	9.1	7.9	8.8	8.1	9.3
1960	7.1	6.6	6.5	7.5	8.4	10.2	9.4	9.4	8.4	8.9	8.3	9.3
Remarriages, black												
1990	6.4	6.8	7.7	8.1	7.8	10.0	10.1	9.9	9.0	7.2	7.2	9.7
1985	6.4	5.8	8.0	8.3	7.5	11.3	9.0	11.2	8.2	7.6	8.0	8.8
1980	6.8	6.6	7.5	7.9	8.5	10.5	9.3	11.0	7.7	7.4	8.0	8.8
1975	6.7	6.6	8.2	7.4	8.1	10.3	8.9	10.0	8.2	6.9	8.9	9.6
1970	7.1	7.5	7.7	7.7	8.9	11.2	8.4	8.4	7.8	8.6	6.9	9.6
1965	7.7	5.7	8.4	8.1	8.4	9.2	9.0	10.1	7.9	8.2	7.7	9.6
1960	5.6	9.1	4.5	8.9	5.5	9.3	7.5	7.5	7.7	11.0	11.3	12.1

Source: National Center for Health Statistics, "Public Use Data File: Marriage Data, Detail, 1990," 1995, and "Vital Statistics of the United States,
   Volume III—Marriages and Divorces: 1985, 1980, 1975, 1970, 1965, 1960, 1955 and 1950," National Center for Health Statistics, Hyattsville, MD,
   Table 1-16.

Table 5-17. Trends in Basic Divorce Measures: 1940-1990

Year	Number (in thousands)	Rates		Median duration of marriage	Median age at time of decree		Median age at time of marriage	
		Per 1,000 population	Per 1,000 married women 15+		Husband	Wife	Husband	Wife
1990	1,182	4.7	20.9	7.2	35.6	33.2	24.9	22.6
1989	1,157	4.7	20.4	7.2	35.4	32.9	24.8	22.5
1988	1,167	4.8	20.7	7.1	35.1	32.6	24.6	22.3
1987	1,166	4.8	20.8	7.0	34.9	32.5	24.5	22.2
1986	1,178	4.9	21.2	6.9	34.6	32.1	24.3	22.0
1985	1,190	5.0	21.7	6.8	34.4	31.9	24.1	21.8
1984	1,169	5.0	21.5	6.9	34.3	31.7	24.0	21.7
1983	1,158	5.0	21.3	7.0	34.0	31.5	23.8	21.5
1982	1,170	5.1	21.7	7.0	33.6	31.1	23.7	21.3
1981	1,213	5.3	22.6	7.0	33.1	30.6	23.4	21.1
1980	1,189	5.2	22.6	6.8	32.7	30.3	23.3	20.9
1979	1,181	5.3	22.8	6.8	32.5	30.1	23.2	20.9
1978	1,130	5.1	21.9	6.6	32.0	29.7	23.0	20.7
1977	1,091	5.0	21.1	6.6	32.4	29.9	23.1	20.7
1976	1,083	5.0	21.1	6.5	32.3	29.7	23.1	20.7
1975	1,036	4.8	20.3	6.5	32.2	29.5	23.0	20.6
1974	977	4.6	19.3	6.5	32.2	29.5	23.0	20.6
1973	915	4.3	18.2	6.6	32.4	29.7	22.9	20.5
1972	845	4.0	17.0	6.7	32.6	29.8	23.0	20.5
1971	773	3.7	15.8	6.7	32.9	29.8	23.0	20.5
1970	708	3.5	14.9	6.7	32.9	29.8	23.0	20.4
1969	639	3.2	13.4	6.9	33.5	30.1	23.6	20.7
1968	584	2.9	12.5	7.0	33.9	30.5	23.7	20.7
1967	523	2.6	11.2	7.1	33.6	30.1	23.5	20.3
1966	499	2.5	10.9	7.1	33.8	30.4	23.5	22.8
1965	479	2.5	10.6	7.2	34.1	30.5	23.7	20.4
1964	450	2.4	10.0	7.4	34.0	30.6	23.7	20.4
1963	428	2.3	9.6	7.5	34.8	31.3	23.9	20.6
1962	413	2.2	9.4	7.3	34.5	31.0	24.0	20.7
1961	414	2.3	9.6	7.1	34.0	30.8	23.8	20.6
1960	393	2.2	9.2	—	34.1	30.9	24.2	20.9
1959	395	2.2	9.3	7.0	—	—	—	—
1958	368	2.1	8.9	6.4	—	—	—	—
1957	381	2.2	9.2	6.7	—	—	—	—
1956	382	2.3	9.4	6.5	—	—	—	—
1955	377	2.3	9.3	6.4	—	—	—	—
1954	379	2.4	9.5	—	—	—	—	—
1953	390	2.5	9.9	—	—	—	—	—
1952	392	2.5	10.1	—	—	—	—	—
1951	381	2.5	9.9	—	—	—	—	—
1950	385	2.6	10.3	—	—	—	—	—
1949	397	2.7	10.6	—	—	—	—	—
1948	408	2.8	11.2	—	—	—	—	—
1947	483	3.4	13.6	—	—	—	—	—
1946	610	4.3	17.9	—	—	—	—	—
1945	485	3.5	14.4	—	—	—	—	—
1944	400	2.9	12.0	—	—	—	—	—
1943	359	2.6	11.0	—	—	—	—	—
1942	321	2.4	10.1	—	—	—	—	—
1941	293	2.2	9.4	—	—	—	—	—
1940	264	2.0	8.8	—	—	—	—	—

Source: National Center for Health Statistics, "Advance Report of Final Divorce Statistics, 1989 and 1990," Monthly Vital Statistics Report, Volume 43, No. 9, Supplement, 1995, Tables 1, 7, 9, and 10, and "Vital Statistics of the United States," annual volumes from 1940-1985, National Center for Health Statistics, Hyattsville, MD.

Figure 5-7. Crude Divorce Rate (CDR) and General Divorce Rate (GDR): 1920-1990

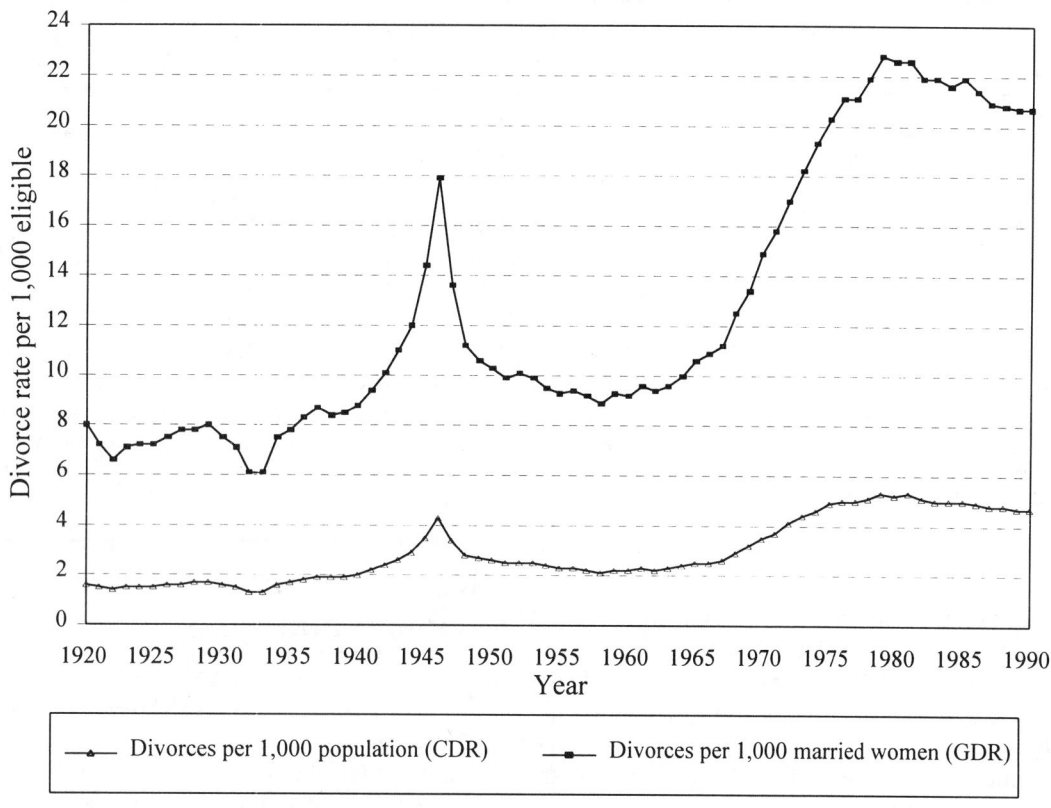

Source: 1920-1990 NCHS data.

more common for marriages to be remarriages and for remarriages to be higher-order marriages. If these behaviors persist, it will be even more common in future years for individuals to have three or more marriages over their life course.

Divorce as a Demographic Event

The population exposed to divorce is currently married couples. Hence, the appropriate rate is the general divorce rate (GDR), defined in the opening of the last section. Although a crude divorce rate, based on total population, is published, it can be misleading because of the marked change in age composition that the American population has undergone.

The phenomenal increase in divorce that has taken place since 1940, and especially since 1970, is reported by the statistics of Table 5-17 and illustrated in Figure 5-7. The number of divorces in 1990 was three times greater than in 1960, and the general divorce rate more than doubled over these three decades. Thus population growth does not account for the increase in the number of divorces. It is this development that has caused media commentators to speak of the "epidemic" of divorce, which has swept the nation since World War II and especially, if one discounts the spike in divorce immediately following the war, since 1960.

Because the reporting of divorce statistics is more incomplete than marriage data, and fewer characteristics are tabulated, far less is known about divorce as a demographic event than is desirable to know. The following tables synthesize what has been assembled by the National Center for Health Statistics as a result of decades of intensive efforts to develop better reporting. When interpreting these tables it should be remembered that this data has been subject to changing coverage over the past.

Duration of Marriage Prior to Divorce

Only a small proportion of divorces results from immediate negative reaction to marriage. The median duration of marriage is almost six years. Summary data are presented in Table 5-17. The median duration of marriage has recently increased to nearly the same length it was in the early 1960s when divorce rates were relatively low. The shortest durations of marriage reported in the table were during 1955 and again during the early 1970s while divorce was on the rise. The median throughout the period included in the table gives credence to the stereotypical "seven-year itch" in that median durations have ranged from approximately 6.5 to 7.5 years of marriage prior to divorce since 1955.

Table 5-18. Duration of Marriage: 1950-1990 [percent distribution]

Year	Total	Less than 1 year	1 to 4 years	5 to 9 years	10 to 14 years	15 to 19 years	20 to 24 years	25 years and over
1990	100.0	3.3	31.7	28.3	15.0	9.2	6.2	6.2
1985	100.0	4.0	33.9	26.2	14.8	9.3	5.7	6.1
1980	100.0	4.4	33.7	27.7	14.8	8.3	5.3	5.7
1975	100.0	4.5	35.0	27.2	13.6	8.0	5.6	6.2
1970	100.0	4.8	34.1	25.2	13.8	9.0	7.0	5.9
1965	100.0	5.3	32.8	23.6	13.7	11.2	6.5	6.7
1960	100.0	6.2	31.4	24.5	17.0	8.9	12.0	
1955	100.0	6.3	35.6	26.9	12.8	7.8	4.7	5.9
1950	100.0	6.4	40.0	22.6	12.2	7.3	5.2	6.1

Source: Natonal Center for Health Statistics, "Advance Report of Final Divorce Statistics, 1989 and 1990," Monthly Vital Statistics Report, Volume 43, No. 9, Supplement, 1995, Table 2, and "Vital Statistics of the United States," 1950-1985, Table 2-10, National Center for Health Statistics, Hyattsville, MD.

Table 5-18 presents the duration of marriage in detailed categories rather than simply the median age of divorce. The percentage of divorces from marriages of less than one year duration and those of 1 to 4 years duration has actually declined (if unsteadily) since 1950. The percentage of marriages lasting 5 to 9 and those lasting 10 to 14 years before divorce has, conversely, increased. Actually, the duration pattern has not changed much during the recent "epidemic." The great majority of couples have apparently made an earnest effort at succeeding in marriage, and termination comes only after some years of marriage.

Divorce by Race of Husband and Wife

The vast majority of marriages and divorces in this country are to white husbands and wives. The next greatest percentage are to black husbands and wives (see Table 5-19). Each racial category accounts for approximately the same percent of divorces among husbands and wives. And, ignoring persons who do not state a race category, mixed marriages between husbands and wives of differing race (i.e. using only white, black and other categories) account for less than three percent of all divorces in the United States.

Table 5-19. Divorces by Race of Husband and Wife: 1990

Race of husband	Race of Wife				
	All races	White	Black	Other	Not stated
Number of divorces					
All races	464,736	383,240	51,080	9,311	21,105
White	383,021	376,346	1,689	3,499	1,487
Black	52,566	2,990	48,962	342	272
Other	8,374	2,625	262	5,414	73
Not stated	20,775	1,279	167	56	19,273
Percent of total divorce					
All races	100.0	82.5	11.0	2.0	4.5
White	82.4	81.0	0.4	0.8	0.3
Black	11.3	0.6	10.5	0.1	0.1
Other	1.8	0.6	0.1	1.2	...
Not stated	4.5	0.3	...	...	4.1

Source: National Center for Health Statistics, "Advance Report of Final Divorce Statistics, 1989 and 1990," Monthly Vital Statistics Report, Volume 43, No. 9, Supplement, 1995, Table 12.

Table 5-20. Divorce Rates, by Region and State: 1980 and 1990

Region, division, and state	Number		Rate	
	1990	1980	1990	1980
United States, total	1,168,872	1,188,654	4.7	5.2
Northeast region	169,406	173,739	3.3	3.5
New England	44,039	49,049	3.3	4.0
Middle Atlantic	125,367	124,690	3.3	3.4
Midwest region	273,603	292,030	4.6	5.0
East North Central	197,347	212,405	4.7	5.1
West North Central	76,256	79,625	4.3	4.6
South region	466,554	448,897	5.5	6.0
South Atlantic	227,039	206,344	5.2	5.6
East South Central	91,508	87,528	6.0	6.0
West South Central	148,007	155,025	—	6.5
West region	259,309	273,988	5.1	6.3
Mountain	79,425	86,088	6.5	7.6
Pacific	179,884	187,900	4.6	5.9
New England				
Maine	5,176	6,205	4.2	5.5
New Hampshire	4,933	5,254	4.5	5.7
Vermont	2,491	2,623	4.4	5.1
Massachusetts	16,258	17,873	2.7	3.1
Rhode Island	3,754	3,606	3.7	3.8
Connecticut	11,427	13,488	3.5	4.3
Middle Atlantic				
New York	58,283	61,972	3.2	3.5
New Jersey	27,113	27,796	3.5	3.8
Pennsylvania	39,971	34,922	3.4	2.9
East North Central				
Ohio	53,504	58,809	4.9	5.4
Indiana	39,571	40,006	7.1	7.3
Illinois	45,977	50,997	4.0	4.5
Michigan	40,568	45,047	4.4	4.9
Wisconsin	17,727	17,546	3.6	3.7
West North Central				
Minnesota	15,595	15,371	3.6	3.8
Iowa	10,913	11,854	3.9	4.1
Missouri	25,701	27,595	5.0	5.6
North Dakota	2,320	2,142	3.6	3.3
South Dakota	2,651	2,811	3.8	4.1
Nebraska	6,496	6,442	4.1	4.1
Kansas	12,580	13,410	5.1	5.7
South Atlantic				
Delaware	2,986	2,313	4.5	3.9
Maryland	16,607	17,494	3.5	4.1
District of Columbia	2,291	4,682	3.8	7.3
Virginia	27,307	23,615	4.4	4.4
West Virginia	9,775	10,273	5.4	5.3
North Carolina	34,039	28,050	5.1	4.8
South Carolina	16,182	13,595	4.6	4.4
Georgia	36,857	34,743	5.7	6.4
Florida	80,995	71,579	6.2	7.3
East South Central				
Kentucky	20,897	16,731	5.7	4.6
Tennessee	32,198	30,206	6.6	6.6
Alabama	25,678	26,745	6.3	6.9
Mississippi	12,735	13,846	4.9	5.5
West South Central				
Arkansas	16,655	15,882	7.1	6.9
Louisiana	12,525	18,108	—	4.3
Oklahoma	24,977	24,226	7.9	8.0
Texas	93,850	96,809	5.5	6.8

Table 5-20. Divorce Rates, by Region and State: 1980 and 1990 (continued)

Region, division, and state	Number		Rate	
	1990	1980	1990	1980
Mountain				
Montana	4,049	4,940	5.1	6.3
Idaho	6,446	6,596	6.4	7.0
Wyoming	3,132	4,003	6.9	8.5
Colorado	18,665	18,571	5.6	6.4
New Mexico	9,327	10,426	6.1	8.0
Arizona	25,088	19,908	6.8	7.3
Utah	8,950	7,802	5.2	5.3
Nevada	13,095	13,842	10.8	17.3
Pacific				
Washington	28,757	28,642	5.9	6.9
Oregon	15,734	17,762	5.5	6.7
California	127,044	133,541	4.3	5.6
Alaska	3,170	3,517	5.7	8.8
Hawaii	5,179	4,438	4.6	4.6

Source: Natonal Center for Health Statistics, "Advance Report of Final Divorce Statistics, 1989 and 1990," Monthly Vital Statistics Report, Volume 43, No. 9, Supplement, 1995, Table 2.

Divorce Rates by Region and State

Just as there are substantial regional differences in nuptiality, divorce rates vary across different states. Table 5-20 shows the number and rate of divorces for regions and individual states in 1980 and 1990. The divorce rate has fallen within most regions of the country. The highest divorce rate in both 1980 and 1990 was in the Mountain West region of the country. The lowest divorce rate in 1980 was in the Middle Atlantic states, which are tied with New England for the lowest divorce rate in 1990. As is the case with nuptiality rates, the high rate of the Mountain West is artificially boosted by the popularity of Nevada as a state in which to gain a divorce. Nevada's divorce history extends well back prior to the availability of standardized divorce statistics. However, even discounting Nevada, many states of the Mountain West have high divorce rates which may be attributed to their relatively young populations. High divorce rates are also evident for Oklahoma, Indiana, Arkansas, Tennessee, Alabama and Florida. Notably low divorce rates are apparent in Massachusetts and New York.

Age Patterns of Divorce

Age-Specific Divorce Rates

Table 5-21 is an estimated set of age-specific divorce rates for husbands and wives of each age in 1970, 1980 and 1990. Rates are superior to the percentage distribution of divorced persons by age, because they measure

Table 5-21. Age-specific Divorce Rates: 1970-1990 [rates per 1,000
married persons of age group]

Age at time of decree	Husband			Wife		
	1990	1980	1970	1990	1980	1970
All ages	19.2	19.8	14.2	18.7	19.5	14.0
15 to 19 years	32.8	29.3	15.1	48.6	42.4	26.9
20 to 24 years	50.2	46.9	33.6	46.0	47.2	33.3
25 to 29 years	39.3	41.4	30.0	36.6	37.8	25.7
30 to 34 years	31.9	33.8	22.3	27.9	29.2	18.9
35 to 39 years	25.9	26.8	17.9	23.1	23.3	14.8
40 to 44 years	21.9	21.0	13.8	19.3	16.7	11.9
45 to 49 years	17.3	14.5	10.7	13.8	10.8	8.5
50 to 54 years	12.0	9.5	7.6	8.2	6.6	5.6
55 to 59 years	7.8	5.8	5.1	4.8	3.9	3.5
60 to 64 years	4.7	3.7	3.4	2.9	2.7	2.3
65 years and over	2.1	1.9	1.9	1.4	1.4	1.3

Source: National Center for Health Statistics, "Advance Report of Final Divorce Statistics, 1989
and 1990," Monthly Vital Statistics Report, Volume 43, No. 9, Supplement, 1995, Table 5.

Figure 5-8. Percent of Women Redivorced after Remarriage, by Age: 1980 and 1990

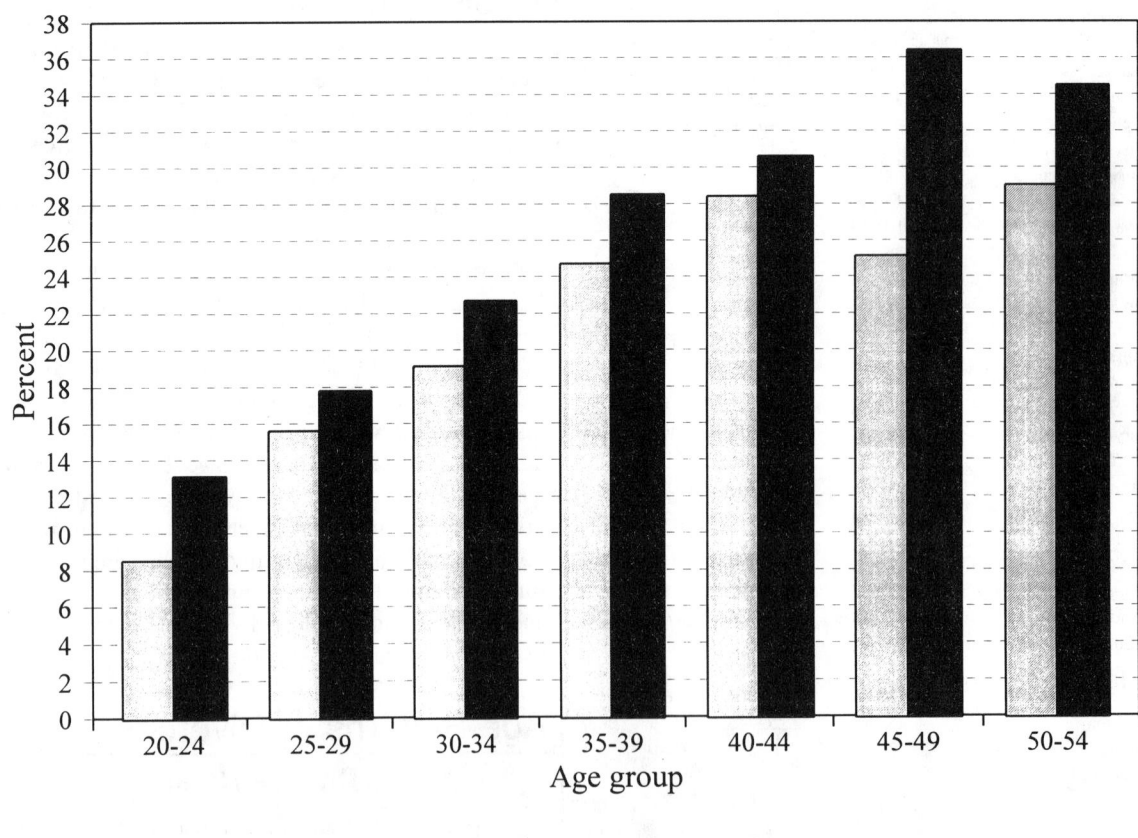

Source: 1980 and 1990 CPS data.

Table 5-22. Percent of Women Whose Marriage Ended in Divorce and May Eventually End in Divorce: June 1990

Age and type of marriage	Ended in divorce by June 1990	May end in divorce if their future experience is similar to older cohorts during:		
		1985 to 1990	1980 to 1985	1975 to 1980
First marriage				
20 to 24 years	12.5	37.6	—	49.2
25 to 29 years	19.2	39.0	—	46.4
30 to 34 years	28.1	40.8	—	46.2
35 to 39 years	34.1	42.0	—	44.8
40 to 44 years	35.8	39.9	—	41.9
45 to 49 years	35.2	36.2	—	38.7
50 to 54 years	29.5	30.2	—	32.0
Remarriage				
20 to 24 years	13.1	46.8	62.1	—
25 to 29 years	17.8	42.4	57.1	—
30 to 34 years	22.7	42.8	57.6	—
35 to 39 years	28.5	40.1	55.6	—
40 to 44 years	30.6	38.5	49.4	—
45 to 49 years	36.4	40.9	49.8	—
50 to 54 years	34.5	38.3	45.7	—
55 to 59 years	31.1	31.1	38.3	—
60 to 65 years	27.0	—	—	—

Source: U.S. Bureau of the Census, Current Population Reports, "Marriage, Divorce, and Remarriage in the 1990's," Series P-23, No. 180, U.S. Government Printing Office, Washington, D.C., 1992, Tables C and D.

the strength of the attrition force on each age group of remaining married individuals. They show that married persons 20 to 24 years of age are subject to very high rates and that the divorce rate declines sharply in the oldest ages. Since 1970 the divorce rate at the youngest ages has increased dramatically, more than doubling for husbands under 19 years of age and nearly doubling for wives under 19 years of age. The divorce rates for males and females have increased since 1970 across all ages. One result of this shift in divorce is that divorce rates are less narrowly concentrated in the younger ages than they were in 1970. In 1990 the rate of divorce among married males and females aged 45-49 years of age is nearly that of husbands and wives ten years younger, i.e. 35-39 years of age, in 1970. Over these two decades divorce was increasing across all ages. But, the proportionate increase in divorce was greatest in the youngest couples and later middle ages.

Age at Redivorce

The significant and increasing number of multiple divorces/remarriages suggests that the age of redivorce among those remarried is also important in considering age patterns of nuptiality. Figure 5-8 illustrates the change

over the last decade in the percentage of women at each age who are redivorced after remarriage. The percentage is higher at each age in 1990 than it was in 1980. Over a third of remarried women over forty-five have redivorced in 1990. This increase is the most dramatic difference from 1980 where just over a quarter of such women were redivorced. Redivorce has also increased among the remarrieds less than 20-24 years of age which might indicate rising rates of redivorce among those with short intervals between marriages prevalent in those remarried before age twenty-four.

Eventual Cohort Divorce

Since they have not yet lived out their lives, tabulations by age understate the overall likelihood of divorce among individuals of a given age during their life span. Table 5-22 presents the percent of first and remarriages at each age which have ended in divorce alongside the percentage which may end in divorce if the future experience of these individuals is similar to the older cohorts during 1975-1990. The percentage of first marriages eventually ending in divorce will be much lower if their divorce rates are similar to older cohorts of 1985-1990 than if their experience is similar to the older cohorts of 1975-1980. Similarly, the percentage of remarriages eventually ending in divorce will be much lower if rates are similar to the older cohorts of 1985-1990 than to those of five years earlier, i.e. 1980-1985. These tabulations suggest that the increasing patterns of divorce at older ages may not necessarily indicate rising life-long divorce probabilities over time. First, married women who are 35-39 years of age would likely end up having the highest percentage eventually divorced if rates are similar to the older cohorts of 1985-1990. Among remarried women, those aged 20-34 are likely to have considerably higher lifetime percentages divorced if they follow the experience of older cohorts of 1985-1990. Yet, these percentages of eventual divorce will all be lower than if the experience of older cohorts of a decade earlier were to be in effect over the remainder of these women's lifetimes.

Age at Marriage of Divorced Persons

The percentage distribution of divorces by the age of individuals at the time of their marriage is reported in Table 5-23 for divorces in 1970, 1980 and 1990. The data of this table suggest that marriages contracted before age twenty-four are subject to very high attrition from divorce. This pattern of most divorces being from among those married younger is of long standing since most marriages are also early in the life course. However, there have been some changes in the age composition of divorces since 1970. In the past two decades the percentage of divorces to those married under 20 years of age has declined; the percentage of divorces to those married in the 20-24 year age group has increased for females and declined for males; and, the percentage of divorces occurring to those

Table 5-23. Percent Distribution of Divorces by Age at Time of This Marriage: 1970-1990

Age at time of this marriage	Husband			Wife		
	1990	1980	1970	1990	1980	1970
All ages	100.0	100.0	100.0	100.0	100.0	100.0
Under 20 years	11.7	18.0	19.3	27.6	39.9	46.1
20 to 24 years	38.8	44.0	43.8	36.6	35.5	30.3
25 to 29 years	22.3	18.4	16.4	16.4	11.4	9.5
30 to 34 years	11.6	8.1	7.6	8.5	5.6	4.8
35 to 39 years	6.5	4.5	4.6	5.1	3.1	3.4
40 to 44 years	3.9	2.8	3.2	2.7	1.9	2.3
45 years and over	5.2	4.2	5.2	3.0	2.6	3.5

Source: Natonal Center for Health Statistics, "Advance Report of Final Divorce Statistics, 1989 and 1990," Monthly Vital Statistics Report, Volume 43, No. 9, Supplement, 1995, Table 8.

Table 5-24. Number and Percent Distribution of Children Involved in Divorces: 1950-1990

Year	Estimated number (in thousands)	Percent distribution of children under 18 years involved					
		Total	None	One	Two	Three	Four or more
1990	1,075	100.0	47.0	25.1	20.0	6.1	1.8
1985	1,091	100.0	46.6	25.7	19.6	6.3	1.8
1980	1,174	100.0	44.4	25.9	20.1	6.9	2.7
1975	1,123	100.0	42.9	25.5	18.9	8.0	4.6
1970	870	100.0	40.1	24.6	18.7	9.5	7.1
1965	630	100.0	40.2	23.2	18.0	10.2	8.3
1960	463	100.0	43.3	23.0	17.4	9.7	6.6
1955	347	100.0	51.9	22.8	14.5	6.8	4.0
1950	299	100.0	56.0	23.8	12.2	5.0	3.1

Source: National Center for Health Statistics, "Advance Report of Final Divorce Statistics, 1989 and 1990," Monthly Vital Statistics Report, Volume 43, No. 9, Supplement, 1995, Tables 3 and 4, and "Vital Statistics of the United States," annual volumes for 1950-1985, National Center for Health Statistics, Hyattsville, MD, Table 2-13.

Figure 5-9. Estimated Number of Children Involved in Divorce: 1950-1990

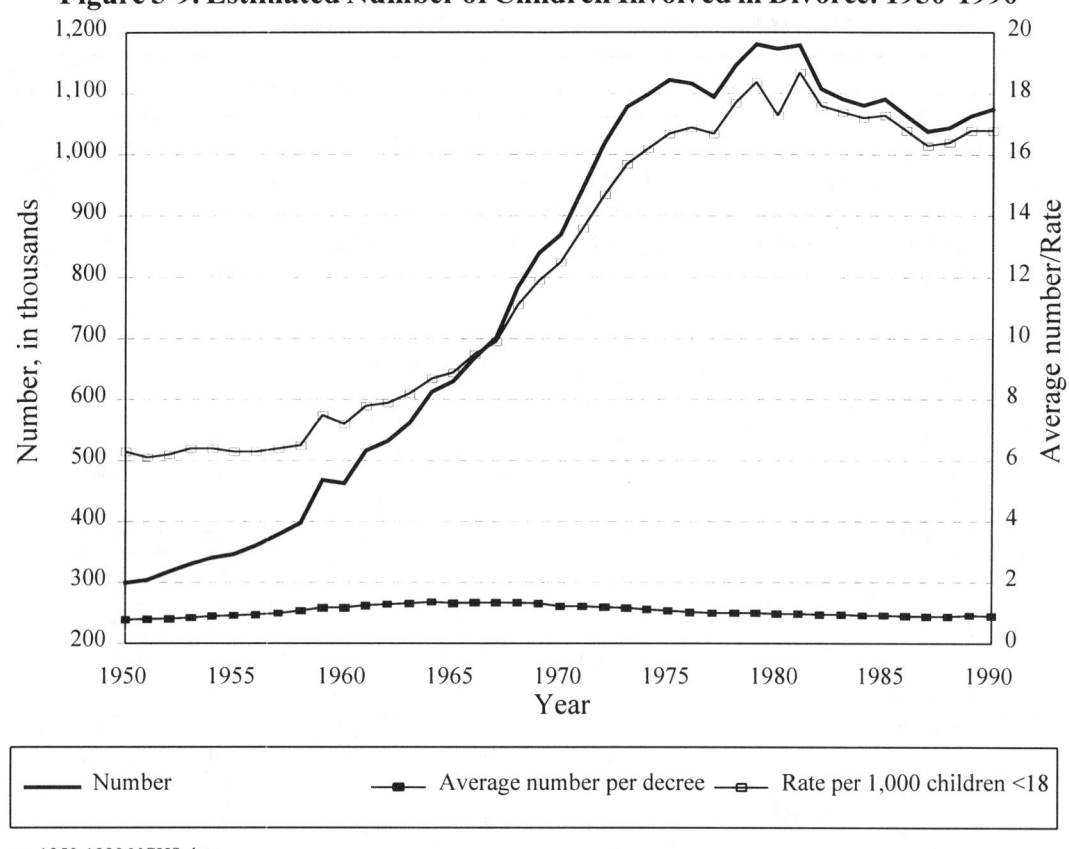

Source: 1950-1990 NCHS data.

Children Involved in Divorce

Each year since the early 1970s, over one million children under eighteen years of age have been involved in divorce. As Figure 5-9 shows, both the estimated number of children involved in divorce and the rate per 1,000 children under eighteen rose steadily from the late 1950s through the mid-1970s. Since 1980 there has been a slight decline, or at least a leveling, in both the number and rate of children involved in divorce. Less apparent in Figure 5-9 is a slight rise in the average number of children involved per decree (or divorce) around the mid-sixties and following the peak of the baby boom years. Among marriages which fueled the baby boom and higher fertility during the mid-1950s and early 1960s it is not surprising to find more children per decree at the time of divorce in the mid- to late 1960s. Table 5-24 shows the percentage distribution of the number of children under 18 years of age involved in decrees for each five years between 1950 to 1990. The greatest changes over this time were the higher percentages of divorce involving three or more children during 1960 to 1975. A less dramatic, but very steady, trend appears in the corresponding decline during 1960 to 1975 in divorces which involved no children. The temporary bulge in divorces involving three or more children and the corresponding temporary (i.e. U-shaped) decline in divorces involving no children may be attributed to the baby boom (see Chapter 6). The table shows a more or less steady rise in the percentage of divorces involving one or two children across the four decades. Adjusting for the temporary effects of the baby boom on children involved in divorce it would seem fair to say that the general trend over the recent past has been for a rising proportion of divorces to involve small families as fertility has declined and divorce has risen.

Custody Awards

As noted above, not all states report detailed divorce statistics. In Table 5-25 the number and percentage distribution of children by the person to whom custody was awarded is reported for nineteen states which report this information. The most frequent custody award arrangement is that of a custody award to the wife. A smaller percentage of awards are for joint custody, followed by awards to the husband. Only a very small fraction of

Table 5-25. Number and Percent Distribution of Children Under 18 Years for Whom Custody was Reported, by Person(s) Awarded Custody: 1990

Area	Custody awarded to:				
	Total	Husband	Wife	Joint	Other person
Total, 19 reporting states	221,883	22,906	160,946	34,820	3,211
Alabama	14,400	1,540	11,550	1,245	65
Alaska	1,677	238	1,058	327	54
Connecticut	7,708	406	4,476	2,808	18
Idaho	5,964	622	3,300	1,980	62
Illinois	18,680	1,720	14,090	2,820	50
Kansas	11,544	780	5,444	5,034	286
Michigan	33,280	3,720	24,580	4,740	240
Missouri	23,135	2,540	16,910	3,430	255
Montana	3,854	325	1,788	1,694	47
Nebraska	7,220	882	5,872	298	168
New Hampshire	4,567	502	3,674	326	65
Oregon	13,290	1,675	9,525	1,855	235
Pennsylvania	32,560	3,260	24,980	3,300	1,020
Rhode Island	1,840	100	1,145	584	11
Tennessee	22,210	2,500	17,530	1,910	270
Utah	7,414	718	6,016	664	16
Vermont	961	102	686	164	9
Virginia	8,500	985	6,030	1,175	310
Wyoming	3,079	291	2,292	466	30
Percent, 19 reporting states	100.0	10.3	72.5	15.7	1.4
Alabama	100.0	10.7	80.2	8.6	0.5
Alaska	100.0	14.2	63.1	19.5	3.2
Connecticut	100.0	5.3	58.1	36.4	0.2
Idaho	100.0	10.4	55.3	33.2	1.0
Illinois	100.0	9.2	75.4	15.1	0.3
Kansas	100.0	6.8	47.2	43.6	2.5
Michigan	100.0	11.2	73.9	14.2	0.7
Missouri	100.0	11.0	73.1	14.8	1.1
Montana	100.0	8.4	46.4	44.0	1.2
Nebraska	100.0	12.2	81.3	4.1	2.3
New Hampshire	100.0	11.0	80.4	7.1	1.4
Oregon	100.0	12.6	71.7	14.0	1.8
Pennsylvania	100.0	10.0	76.7	10.1	3.1
Rhode Island	100.0	5.4	62.2	31.7	0.6
Tennessee	100.0	11.3	78.9	8.6	1.2
Utah	100.0	9.7	81.1	9.0	0.2
Vermont	100.0	10.6	71.4	17.1	0.9
Virginia	100.0	11.6	70.9	13.8	3.6
Wyoming	100.0	9.5	74.4	15.1	1.0

Source: National Center for Health Statistics, "Advance Report of Final Divorce Statistics, 1989 and 1990," Monthly Vital Statistics Report, Volume 43, No. 9, Supplement, 1995, Table 18.

custody awards are to persons other than the husband or wife of the divorce.

Variability in custody awards across states are also notable. The percentage of custody awards to the husband vary from only just over 5 percent in Connecticut and Rhode Island, to a high of over 14 percent in Alaska and over 12 percent in Oregon and Nebraska. Awards of child custody to the wife vary from just over 46 percent in Montana and Kansas to over 80 percent in Nebraska, New Hampshire and Alaska. Some of this variation from state to state seems to clearly reflect state dispositions toward certain custody arrangements. Rhode Island, with one of the lowest percentage awards to husbands, appears to favor awards of joint custody. Similarly, Montana and Kansas, with the lowest percentage awards to wives, again appear to favor awards of joint custody and are the two states with the highest percentage of such awards.

Without more adequate reporting and detailed data it is difficult to determine whether the different distribution of custody awards across states reflects simple judicial predispositions or the different characteristics of divorce cases across the states. Clearly, however, the substantial differences from state to state in custody awards is a subject that will garner more attention as higher levels of divorce persist.

The Future Trend of Divorce Rates

Rising divorce rates, like many demographic trends, are often given simplistic explanations grounded in public stereotypes. Frequently, for example, rising divorce is approached as a problem among the young. However, in interpreting today's high divorce rates, and attempting to envision the future course of divorce in the United States, one should remember that the recent rise in divorce rates has not been created by an epidemic of divorce among the younger generation. In contrast, divorce rates have risen across ages and divorce at both younger and older ages has become more common over the past two decades.

Recent divorce rates appear for the present to be stabilizing at a higher level or plateau than in the past. Higher divorce rates may well be a more permanent feature of the population as it becomes a more accepted social behavior and background, as women have become less dependent upon marriage for economic security, and as other pronuptial norms have changed in response to changing cultural sentiments about such topics as spouse abuse, single parenthood, etc. While it is difficult to always envision the termination of a marriage which was entered into with brighter hopes as a positive event, it is equally important to recognize the fact that the rise in divorce rates accompanied a period of social liberalization in the United States. For many women, and men, the rising divorce rates reflect a newfound ability to escape un-

happiness without the social constraints and stigma of past generations.

However, it is also important to remember that a component of divorce remains preventable. Although divorce has become a more acceptable social behavior, it is still true that high divorce rates are linked to correlates such as early marriage, low education, and poverty. Some divorces represent both losses to individual lives and society which are attributable to social conditions under which few marriages can survive. The recent slight downward trend in divorce might well reflect an easing of such life conditions among more recent post-baby boom cohorts. And, as younger generations delay marriage and become better educated and at least as economically secure as young persons in the past, we might well witness a decline or stabilization in divorce rates. On the basis of these considerations, a reasonable prediction is that divorce rates will level and even continue a slight decline into the early 2000s. However, like many demographic behaviors, social and economic trends yet to unfold may sharply change the expected course of divorce trends.

Bibliography

Amato, Paul R., and Booth, Alan. "Changes in Gender Role Attitudes and Perceived Marital Quality." American Sociological Review 60(1995): 58-66.

Beale, Calvin L. "Increased Divorce Rates Among Separated Persons as a Factor in Divorce Since 1940." Social Forces 19(1950): 72-74.

Becker, G., Landes, E., and Michael, R. "An Economic Analysis of Marital Instability." Journal of Political Economy 85(1977): 1141-87.

Bennett, Neil G., Bloom, David E., and Miller, Cynthia K. "The Influence of Nonmarital Childbearing on the Formation of First Marriages." Demography 32(1995): 47-62.

Bernardo, D.H. "Divorce and Remarriage at Middle Age and Beyond." American Academy of Political and Social Science Annals 464(1982): 132-39.

Bogue, Donald J. "Marriage and Marital Dissolution." In Principles of Demography. New York: John Wiley & Sons. 1969.

Bumpass, Larry L., and Sweet, James A. "Differentials in Marital Instability: 1970." American Sociological Review 37(1972): 754-66.

Bumpass, Larry L., Sweet, James A., and Cherlin, Andrew. The Role of Cohabitation in Declining Rates of Marriage. Journal of Marriage and the Family 53(1991): 913-27.

Cherlin, Andrew S. Marriage, Divorce, Remarriage. Cambridge, MA: Harvard University Press. 1992.

Cherlin, Andrew, Kiernan, Kathleen E., and Chase-Lansdale, P. Lindsay. "Parental Divorce in Childhood and Demographic Outcomes in Young Adulthood." Demography 32(1995): 299-318.

Cooney, Teresa M., and Hogan, Dennis P. "Marriage in an Institutionalized Life Course: First Marriage Among American Men in the Twentieth Century." Journal of Marriage and the Family 53(1991): 178-90.

Davis, Kingsley. "Statistical Perspective on Marriage and Divorce." Annals of the American Academy of Political and Social Science 272(1950): 12-15.

DeMaris, Alfred, and Rao, K. V. "Premarital Cohabitation and Subsequent Marital Stability in the United States: A Reassessment." Journal of Marriage and the Family 54(1992): 178-90.

Frieden, A. "The United States Marriage Market." Journal of Political Economy 82(1974): 534-53.

Frisbie, W. "Recent Changes in Marital Stability Among Mexican Americans: Convergence with Black and Anglo Trends." Social Forces 58(1980): 1205-20.

Frisbie, W., Bean, Frank D., and Eberstein, Isaac W. "Patterns of Marital Instability Among Mexican Americans, Blacks, and Anglos." In The Demography of Racial and Ethnic Groups. Frank D. Bean and W. Parker Frisbie (eds.). New York: Academic Press. 1978.

Furstenberg, Frank K., Hoffman, Saul D., and Shrestha, Laura. "The Effect of Divorce on Intergenerational Transfers: New Evidence." Demography 32(1995): 319-34.

Glenn, Norval D. "The Recent Trend in Marital Success in the United States." Journal of Marriage and the Family 53(1991): 261-70.

Glick, Paul C. American Families. New York: John Wiley & Sons. 1957.

Glick, Paul C., and Norton, A.J. "Marrying, Divorcing, and Living Together in the U.S. Today." Population Bulletin 32(1977): 3-39.

Goldscheider, Frances K., and Waite, Linda J. "Nest-leaving Patterns and the Transition to Marriage for Young Men and Women." Journal of Marriage and the Family 49(1987): 507-16.

Hajnal, John. "The Marriage Boom." Population Index 19(1953): 80.

Jacobson, Paul H. American Marriage and Divorce. New York: Rinehart. 1959.

Johnson, Robert A. Religious Assortative Marriage in the United States. New York: Academic Press. 1980.

Kitagawa, E.M. "New Life Styles: Marriage Patterns, Living Arrangements, and Fertility Outside of Marriage." American Academy of Political and Social Science Annual 453(1981): 1-27.

Lichter, Daniel T., McLaughlin, Diane K., Kephart, George, and Landry, David J. "Race and the Retreat from Marriage: A Shortage of Marriageable Men?" American Sociological Review 57(1992): 781-99.

Lillard, Lee A., and Waite, Linda J. "A Joint Model of Marital Childbearing and Marital Disruption." Demography 30(1993): 653-82.

Manning, Wendy D., and Smock, Pamela. "Why Marry? Race and the Transition to Marriage Among Cohabitators." Demography 32(1995): 509-20.

Marini, M.M. "Transition to Adulthood: Sex Differences in Educational Attainment and Age at Marriage." American Sociological Review 43(1978): 483-507.

McCarthy, J. "A Comparison of the Probability of the Dissolution of First and Second Marriages." Demography 15(1978): 345-60.

Menken, J., Trussell, J., Stempel, D., and Babakol, O. "Proportional Hazards Life Table Models: An Illustrative Analysis of Socio-Demographic Influences on Marital Dissolution in the United States." Demography 18(1981): 181-200.

Monahan, Thomas P. "When Married Couples Part: Statistical Trends and Relationships in Divorce." American Sociological Review 27(1962): 625-33.

Mott, F., and Moore, S. "The Causes of Marital Disruption Among Young American Women: An Interdisciplinary Perspective." Journal of Marriage and the Family 41(1979): 355-65.

_____. "Tempo of Remarriages Among Young American Women." Journal of Marriage and the Family 45(1983): 427-36.

Mueller, C., and Pope, H. "Marital Instability: A Study of Its Transmission Between Generations." Journal of Marriage and the Family 39(1977): 83-93.

National Center for Health Statistics. Vital Statistics of the United States, Volume III--Marriages and Divorces. Hyattsville, MD: National Center for Health Statistics. Annual volumes for 1940 through 1986.

_____. Advance Report of Final Marriage Statistics, 1987. Monthly Vital Statistics Report 38(12, Supplement)(1990).

_____. Births, Marriages, Divorces, and Deaths for 1989. Monthly Vital Statistics Report 38(12)(1990).

_____. Advance Report of Final Marriage Statistics, 1988. Monthly Vital Statistics Report 40(4, Supplement)(1991).

_____. Births, Marriages, Divorces, and Deaths for 1990. Monthly Vital Statistics Report 39(12)(1991).

_____. Advance Report of Final Divorce Statistics, 1989 and 1990. Monthly Vital Statistics Report 43(9, Supplement)(1995).

_____. Advance Report of Final Marriage Statistics, 1989 and 1990. Monthly Vital Statistics Report 43(12, Supplement)(1995).

_____. Public Use Data File: Marriage Data, Detail, 1990. CD-rom. Hyattsville, MD: National Center for Health Statistics. 1995.

Peters, H. Elizabeth, Argys, Laura M., Maccoby, Eleanor E., and Mnookin, Robert H. "Enforcing Divorce Settlements: Evidence from Child Support Compliance and Award Modifications." Demography 30(1993): 719-36.

Plateris, Alexander A. "Divorce by Marriage Cohort." Vital and Health Statistics (Series 21, no. 34). Washington, D.C.: U.S. Government Printing Office. 1979.

_____. "Duration of Marriage Before Divorce: United States." Vital and Health Statistics (Series 21, no. 38). Washington, D.C.: U.S. Government Printing Office. 1981.

_____. "100 Years of Marriage and Divorce Statistics: 1867-1967." Vital and Health Statistics (Series 21, no. 24). Washington, D.C.: U.S. Government Printing Office. 1981.

Preston, S., and McDonald, J. "The Incidence of Divorce Within Cohorts of American Marriages Contracted Since the Civil War." Demography 16(1979): 1-25.

Qian, Zhenchao, and Preston, Samuel. "Changes in American Marriage, 1972 to 1987: Availability and Forces of Attraction by Age and Education." American Sociological Review 58(1993): 482-95.

Rawlings, Steve W. "Perspectives on American Husbands and Wives." Current Population Reports (Series P-23, no. 77). Washington, D.C.: U.S. Government Printing Office. 1978.

Rele, J.R. "Some Correlates of the Age at Marriage in the United States." Eugenics Quarterly 12(1965): 1-6.

Sander, William. "Catholicism and Marriage in the United States." Demography 30(1993): 373-84.

Schoen, Robert. "First Unions and the Stability of First Marriages." Journal of Marriage and the Family 54(1992): 281-84.

Schoen, Robert, and Weinick, Robin M. "The Slowing Metabolism of Marriage: Figures from 1988 U.S. Marital Status Life Tables." Demography 30(1993): 737-46.

Smock, Pamela. "The Economic Costs of Marital Disruption for Young Women Over the Past Two Decades." Demography 30(1993): 353-72.

South, Scott, and Lloyd, Kim M. "Marriage Markets and Nonmarital Fertility in the United States." Demography 29(1992): 247-64.

_____. "Spousal Alternatives and Marital Dissolution." American Sociological Review 60(1995): 21-35.

Spanier, G.B., and Glick, P.C. "The Life Cycle of American Families: An Expanded Analysis." Journal of Family History 5(1980): 97-111.

Stouffer, S.A., and Spencer, L.M. "Recent Increases in Marriage and Divorce." American Journal of Sociology 44(1939): 551-54.

Sweet, J. Differentials in Remarriage Probabilities. Madison, WI: University of Wisconsin, Center for Demography and Ecology. 1973.

Taeuber, Irene B., and Taeuber, Conrad. "Marital Status." In People of the United States in the 20th Century. Washington, D.C.: U.S. Bureau of the Census. 1971.

Teachman, Jay D. "Historical and Subgroup Variations in the Association between Marriage and First Childbirth: A Life-Course Perspective." Journal of Family History 10(1985): 379-401.

Thornton, A. "Decomposing the Remarriage Process." Population Studies 31(1977): 383-92.

_____. "Cohabitation and Marriage in the 1980s." Demography 25(1988): 497-505.

Treas, Judith. "Money in the Bank: Transaction Costs and the Economic Organization of Marriage." American Sociological Review 58(1993): 723-34.

U.S. Bureau of the Census. Detailed Population Characteristics: United States Summary. 1940 Census of Population. Washington, D.C.: U.S. Government Printing Office. 1942.

_____. Marital Status and Living Arrangements. Current Population Reports, Series P-20, Number 35. Washington, D.C.: U.S. Government Printing Office. 1951.

_____. Detailed Population Characteristics: United States Summary. 1950 Census of Population. Washington, D.C.: U.S. Government Printing Office. 1952.

_____. Marital Status and Living Arrangements. Current Population Reports, Series P-20, Number 62. Washington, D.C.: U.S. Government Printing Office. 1955.

_____. Detailed Population Characteristics: United States Summary. 1960 Census of Population. Washington, D.C.: U.S. Government Printing Office. 1964.

_____. Marital Status and Living Arrangements. Current Population Reports, Series P-20, Number 144. Washington, D.C.: U.S. Government Printing Office. 1965.

_____. Subject Reports: Age at First Marriage, Data on Duration of Marriage, Times Married, Difference in Age Between Husband and Wife. 1960 Census of Population. Washington, D.C.: U.S. Government Printing Office. 1966.

_____. Social and Economic Variations in Marriage, Divorce and Remarriage: 1967. Current Population Reports, Series P-20, Number 223. Washington, D.C.: U.S. Government Printing Office. 1971.

_____. Marital Status and Living Arrangements. Current Population Reports, Series P-20, Number 212. Washington, D.C.: U.S. Government Printing Office. 1971.

_____. Subject Reports: Marital Status. 1970 Census of Population. Washington, D.C.: U.S. Government Printing Office. 1972.

_____. Detailed Population Characteristics: United States Summary. 1970 Census of Population. Washington, D.C.: U.S. Government Printing Office. 1973.

_____. Marital Status and Living Arrangements. Current Population Reports, Series P-20, Number 287. Washington, D.C.: U.S. Government Printing Office. 1975.

_____. Marriage, Divorce, Widowhood, and Remarriage by Family Characteristics. Current Population Reports, Series P-20, Number 312. Washington, D.C.: U.S. Government Printing Office. 1975.

_____. Number, Timing and Duration of Marriages and Divorces in the United States: June, 1975. Current Population Reports, Series P-20, Number 297. Washington, D.C.: U.S. Government Printing Office. 1976.

_____. Persons of Spanish Origin in the United States. Current Population Reports, Series P-20, Number 290. Washington, D.C.: U.S. Government Printing Office. 1976.

_____. Household and Family Characteristics: March 1977. Current Population Reports, Series P-20, Number 326. Washington, D.C.: U.S. Government Printing Office. 1978.

_____. Marital Status and Living Arrangements (March 1977, 1979, and 1981). Current Population Reports, Series P-20, Numbers 323, 349, and 372. Washington, D.C.: U.S. Government Printing Office. 1978, 1980, and 1982.

_____. Households and Families by Type: March 1980 (Advance Report). Current Population Reports, Series P-20, Number 57. Washington, D.C.: U.S. Government Printing Office. 1980.

_____. Marital Status and Living Arrangements. Current Population Reports, Series P-20, Number 365. Washington, D.C.: U.S. Government Printing Office. 1981.

_____. Household, Families, Marital Status and Living Arrangements. Current Population Reports, Series P-20, Number 382. Washington, D.C.: U.S. Government Printing Office. 1983.

_____. Detailed Population Characteristics: United States Summary. 1980 Census of Population. Washington, D.C.: U.S. Government Printing Office. 1983.

_____. Marital Status and Living Arrangements. Current Population Reports, Series P-20, Number 410. Washington, D.C.: U.S. Government Printing Office. 1985.

_____. Annual Demographic Files (CD-rom). Current Population Survey. March 1990.

_____. Marital Status and Living Arrangements. Current Population Reports, Series P-20, Number 450. Washington, D.C.: U.S. Government Printing Office. 1990.

_____. Marital Status and Living Arrangements. Current Population Reports, Series P-20, Number 468. Washington, D.C.: U.S. Government Printing Office. 1992.

_____. Marriage, Divorce, and Remarriage in the 1990's. Current Population Reports, Series P-23, Number 180. Washington, D.C.: U.S. Government Printing Office. 1992.

_____. General Population Characteristics. 1990 Census of Population. Washington, D.C.: U.S. Government Printing Office. 1993.

_____. U.S. National Center for Health Statistics. Advance Report of Final Marriage Statistics (Annual). Monthly Vital Statisitcs Report, Report for 1980, Volume 32, Number 5, Supplement. Washington, D.C.: U.S. Government Printing Office. 1983.

_____. Weed, James. National Estimates of Marriage Dissolution and Survivorship: United States. Vital and Health Statistics, Series 3, Number 19. Washington, D.C.: U.S. Government Printing Office. 1980.

_____. Remarriage of Women 15-44 Years of Age Whose First Marriage Ended in Divorce: United States 1976, Advance Data Number 58. Washington, D.C.: U.S. Government Printing Office. 1980.

Waite, Linda. "Does Marriage Matter?" Demography 32(1995): 483-508.

Waite, L., and Spitze, G. "Young Women's Transition to Marriage." Demography 18(1980): 681-94.

Webster, Pamela S., Orbuch, Terri L., and House, James S. "Effects of Childhood Family Background on Adult Marital Quality and Perceived Stability." American Journal of Sociology 101(1995): 404-32.

Weishaus, Sylvia, and Field, Dorothy. "A Half Century of Marriage: Continuity or Change?" Journal of Marriage and the Family 50(1988): 763-74.

Weitzman, L.J. The Marriage Contract. New York: Free Press. 1981.

White, L.K. "Note on Racial Differences in the Effect of Female Economic Opportunity on Marriage Rates." Demography 18(1981): 349-54.

Wilson, Barbara F., and Hume, Elaine. "First Marriages: United States, 1968-1976." Vital and Health Statistics, Series 21, Number 35. Washington, D.C.: U.S. Government Printing Office. 1979.

Wolfe, W., and MacDonald, M. "The Earnings of Men and Remarriage." Demography 16(1979): 389-99.

CHAPTER

6

FERTILITY AND REPRODUCTION

I n order for the human race to perpetuate itself, people who die must be replaced by births. If births outnumber deaths, the population grows. When births and deaths are exactly equal, a condition of zero growth occurs. If zero growth continues for a sustained time, demographers characterize the population as at the "replacement level." Fertility is sufficient to neutralize the effects of mortality, but insufficient for growth. If births remain at a nearly fixed level for a considerable time, mortality remains unchanged, and immigration is proportionately insignificant, then the population will have a nearly fixed age composition and is referred to as "stationary." However, even slight growth, or rising fertility, can profoundly affect the age structure of a population. The population of the United States is not stationary due to the remarkable cohort fluctuations in fertility over recent generations, e.g. the baby boom. Yet, the population appears to have fertility levels which are now hovering around the replacement level.

Although there are differentials in fertility levels among the various races, socioeconomic groups, and regional sectors of the population, with only a few exceptions these differentials are minor variations on the dominant theme of replacement-level fertility. Nonetheless, these differentials and changing patterns of fertility behavior are profound in their impact upon personal lives and public policy needs. Many of the topics covered in the present chapter have minor impact upon overall growth trends but are highly significant to understanding trends in the changing life course of the United States population.

Bearing and rearing children has been a major personal ambition and social expectation throughout the nation's history. Pronatalism is still stronger in the United States than in the northwestern European nations of its colonial origin. Having replacement-level fertility does not necessarily signify that a population is repudiating childrearing and abandoning cultural expectations about population replacement. But, the declining fertility in the United States has implied significant changes in ideal family size,

the age composition of the population, and almost every other topic on which this book focuses. This chapter describes the fertility trends which have shaped recent cohorts of the population and the changing values which have shaped fertility trends themselves.

The core material of this chapter focuses upon fertility behavior and trends viewed from a variety of demographic perspectives emphasizing such issues as overall fertility levels, age and cohort patterns of fertility, birth timing and family-building strategies, marital and out-of-wedlock fertility, etc. The second portion of this chapter focuses upon more recently available data regarding Hispanic fertility and upon major socioeconomic differentials in fertility. The third section addresses major behaviors related to fertility outcome including contraceptive behaviors of the United States population, teenage pregnancy, induced abortion, childlessness, etc. Finally, the implications of these findings for overall net reproduction of the population and plausible fertility forecasts into the coming century are discussed in the concluding sections of the chapter.

Sources of Fertility Data

As noted in Chapter 2, the principal source of statistical information about births is the annual volume Vital Statistics of the United States: Volume I-Natality, published by the National Center for Health Statistics of the U.S. Department of Health and Human Services. The book presents a tabulation of actual births as documented on birth certificates. In addition, the U.S. Bureau of the Census periodically publishes fertility-related reports in Current Population Reports (Series P-20). The National Institute of Health and Human Development also sponsors periodic national fertility surveys. These are supplemented by other surveys taken by private survey organizations, sometimes with subsidies from the federal government. This chapter will present the highlights of the findings from these sources.

Chapter 6 Definitions
FERTILITY AND REPRODUCTION

Crude Birth Rate (CBR). Number of births in a year per 1,000 total midyear population residing in an area.

General Fertility Rate (or Fertility Rate)(GFR). Number of births in a year per 1,000 women aged 15-44 residing in an area as of midyear. (In some cases different age limits are used, e.g. 15-49, where fertility beyond age 44 is appreciable.)

Age-Specific Fertility Rate (ASFR). The number of live births in a year to women of a specified age (or grouping of ages) per 1,000 women in the same age or age grouping residing in an area at midyear. In the United States it is customary to declare age fifteen as the lower age limit for fertility statistics and to include the comparatively small number of births to females under fifteen in this group. Similarly age forty-four is defined as the oldest age in the reproductive span, and the few births occurring to women age forty-five and over are included in this group. The United Nations defines forty-nine as the upper limit for reproduction and sometimes has birth rates for an age group under fifteen years of age.

Total Fertility Rate (TFR). The sums of age-specific birth rates across the entire reproductive span. If ASFRs are reported in five-year age groups, their sum is multiplied by five. This rate specifies how many children 1,000 women would bear if they experienced the age-specific fertility rates for a given year throughout their reproductive lives. When divided by 1,000, TFR reports the average number of children each woman in the population would bear under these assumptions.

Cumulative Fertility Rate. Number of live births ever born per 1,000 women in a cohort (hypothetical or real) from the onset of their potential childbearing years (age fifteen) to a specified age. This statistic is derived by summing age-specific fertility rates.

Completed Fertility Rate. The cumulative fertility rate of a cohort of women who have passed their forty-fifth birthday. For hypothetical, or synthetic, cohorts it is equal to TFR.

Cohort Fertility Rate. Fertility of real cohorts of women, obtained by tracing them longitudinally from year to year. Cohort rates may be age-specific or cumulative. For completed cohorts (which have passed their forty-fifth birthday) it is possible to compute GFR, TFR, and other summary measures.

Birth Order. The ordinal order of a birth to a particular woman (first, second, and so on).

Order-Specific Fertility Rate. Number of live births of a given birth order in a year (1, 2, 3, and so on) per 1,000 women aged 15-44 years.

Nuptial Fertility Rate (NFR). The number of live births in a year to married women aged 15-44. This rate may be made specific for age, race, and birth order.

Parity. The number of children a woman has ever borne. This is a fertility characteristic of women. (Zero parity represents childlessness, parity 1 represents having borne one child, and so on.)

Nonmarital (Illegitimacy or Out-of-Wedlock) Birth Rate. Number of live births to unmarried women per 1,000 unmarried women aged 15-44. This rate may be made specific for age, race, and birth order.

Nonmarital Birth Ratio. The ratio of out-of-wedlock births in a year per 1,000 total live births during the same year. This ratio may be made specific for age, race, and birth order.

Children Ever Born. The cumulative number of children women have borne at the time they are interviewed in a census or survey. This measure is a form of cumulative fertility that may be reported on an age-specific basis or on a cumulative basis.

Birth Probabilities. The probability that a woman will have a live birth within a specified year of age.

Parity-Specific Fertility Rate or Parity-Specific Birth Probability. Annual number of live births of a given order per 1,000 women of a parity one child lower than the birth order (for example, first births to zero parity women). Such measures may be computed either as rates or as probabilities.

Sex Ratio at Birth. Number of male live-born infants per 100 or per 1,000 female live-born infants in a given year. Proportion female for births is the proportion of all births that were female in a specified year.

Pregnancies. Pregnancies are medically recognized conceptions, often defined as beginning at implantation or nidation (roughly a week after fertilization).

Induced Abortion. Abortion or termination of pregnancy following a deliberate intervention.

Fetal Loss. Fetal loss includes stillbirths, miscarriages and spontaneous abortions. Fetal loss excludes induced abortions and does not generally include the termination of life at early stages before recognition of pregnancy (i.e. embryonic mortality).

Net Reproduction Rate (NRR). The sum of age-specific birth rates by five-year age groups of mothers multiplied by five and the probability (as determined from the life table for the year) of women surviving to a specified age group and by the proportion of births that were female. These rates represent the average number of daughters that a hypothetical cohort of women would bear if they experienced a given set of age-specific mortality and fertility rates until attaining age forty-five.

Fertility as a Demographic Process

In addition to the crude birth rate (CBR) (introduced in Chapter 1), three widely used measures of fertility are the general fertility rate (GFR), the age-specific fertility rates (ASFR), and the total fertility rate (TFR). These rates are defined in the Definition Box. The crude birth rate is strongly affected by age and sex composition. The GFR and TFR, which are based on women of childbearing age, are preferred summary measures of fertility. They are highly correlated and usually lead to almost identical conclusions. (For most years, the TFR is roughly thirty times the GFR, because GFR represents the rate of childbearing in one year and TFR estimates the results of such childbearing if it were to continue unchanged for the thirty years of the reproductive span of ages fifteen to forty-four.) Many demographers prefer to use TFR because of its clear implications for average family size.

Table 6-1 provides statistics on the number of births and the crude birth rate for each year since 1909. Data are provided separately for the white and black populations. (Before 1959 birth data for the black population were pooled with births to the "other nonwhite" populations—American Indian, Chinese-American, Japanese-American, and so on. Before the mid-1960s, the black population was 95

Table 6-1. Live Births and Crude Birth Rates, by Race[1]: 1909-1992
[rates per 1,000 population]

Year[2]	Number (in thousands)		All other		Crude birth rate[3]		All other	
	All races	White	Total	Black	All races	White	Total	Black
1992	4,065	3,202	863	674	15.9	15.0	20.5	21.3
1991	4,111	3,241	870	683	16.3	15.4	21.1	21.9
1990	4,158	3,290	868	684	16.7	15.8	21.7	22.4
1989	4,041	3,192	849	673	16.4	15.4	21.6	22.3
1988	3,910	3,102	807	639	16.0	15.0	21.0	21.5
1987	3,809	3,044	766	611	15.7	14.9	20.4	20.8
1986	3,757	3,019	737	593	15.6	14.8	20.1	20.5
1985	3,761	3,038	723	582	15.8	15.0	20.1	20.4
1984	3,669	2,967	702	568	15.6	14.8	20.0	20.1
1983	3,639	2,956	692	563	15.6	14.8	20.1	20.2
1982	3,681	2,985	696	569	15.9	15.1	20.7	20.7
1981	3,629	2,948	682	565	15.8	15.0	20.8	20.8
1980	3,612	2,936	676	568	15.9	15.1	21.3	21.3
1979	3,494	2,808	686	578	15.6	14.5	22.2	22.0
1978	3,333	2,681	652	552	15.0	14.0	21.6	21.3
1977	3,327	2,691	636	544	15.1	14.1	21.6	21.4
1976	3,168	2,568	600	514	14.6	13.6	20.8	20.5
1975	3,144	2,552	592	512	14.6	13.6	21.0	20.7
1974	3,160	2,576	584	507	14.8	13.9	21.2	20.8
1973	3,137	2,551	586	513	14.8	13.8	21.7	21.4
1972	3,258	2,656	603	531	15.6	14.5	22.8	22.5
1971	3,556	2,920	636	565	17.2	16.1	24.6	24.4
1970	3,731	3,091	640	572	18.4	17.4	25.1	25.3
1969	3,600	2,994	607	543	17.9	16.9	24.5	24.4
1968	3,502	2,912	589	531	17.6	16.6	24.2	24.2
1967	3,521	2,923	598	544	17.8	16.8	25.0	25.1
1966	3,606	2,993	613	558	18.4	17.4	26.1	26.2
1965	3,760	3,124	636	581	19.4	18.3	27.6	27.7
1964	4,027	3,369	658	608	21.1	20.0	29.2	29.5
1963	4,098	3,326	639	581	21.7	20.7	29.7	—
1962	4,167	3,394	642	585	22.4	21.4	30.5	—
1961	4,268	3,601	667	611	23.3	22.2	31.6	—
1960	4,258	3,601	657	602	23.7	22.7	32.1	31.9
1959	4,245	3,597	647	606	24.0	22.9	32.9	—
1958	4,246	3,595	651	—	24.5	23.3	34.0	—
1957	4,300	3,646	654	—	25.3	24.0	35.0	—
1956	4,210	3,570	640	—	25.2	24.0	35.1	—
1955	4,097	3,485	613	—	25.0	23.8	34.5	—
1954	4,071	3,472	599	—	25.3	24.2	34.7	—
1953	3,959	3,387	572	—	25.1	24.0	33.9	—
1952	3,909	3,356	553	—	25.1	24.1	33.4	—
1951	3,820	3,275	545	—	24.9	23.9	33.7	—
1950	3,632	3,108	524	—	24.1	23.0	33.3	—
1949	3,649	3,136	513	—	24.5	23.6	33.0	—
1948	3,637	3,141	495	—	24.9	24.0	32.4	—
1947	3,817	3,347	469	—	26.6	26.1	31.2	—
1946	3,441	2,990	420	—	24.1	23.6	28.4	—

Table 6-1. Live Births and Crude Birth Rates, by Race[1]: 1909-1992
[rates per 1,000 population] (continued)

Year[2]	Number (in thousands)				Crude birth rate[3]			
	All races	White	All other		All races	White	All other	
			Total	Black			Total	Black
1945	2,858	2,471	388	—	20.4	19.7	26.5	—
1944	2,939	2,545	394	—	21.2	20.5	27.4	—
1943	3,104	2,704	400	—	22.7	22.1	28.3	—
1942	2,989	2,605	384	—	22.2	21.5	27.7	—
1941	2,703	2,330	374	—	20.3	19.5	27.3	—
1940	2,559	2,199	360	—	19.4	18.6	26.7	—
1939	2,466	2,117	349	—	18.8	18.0	26.1	—
1938	2,496	2,148	348	—	19.2	18.4	26.3	—
1937	2,413	2,071	342	—	18.7	17.9	26.0	—
1936	2,355	2,027	328	—	18.4	17.6	25.1	—
1935	2,377	2,042	334	—	18.7	17.9	25.8	—
1934	2,396	2,058	338	—	19.0	18.1	26.3	—
1933	2,307	1,982	325	—	18.4	17.6	25.5	—
1932	2,440	2,099	341	—	19.5	18.7	26.9	—
1931	2,506	2,170	335	—	20.2	19.5	26.6	—
1930	2,618	2,274	344	—	21.3	20.6	27.5	—
1929	2,582	2,244	339	—	21.2	20.5	27.3	—
1928	2,674	2,325	349	—	22.2	21.5	28.5	—
1927	2,802	2,425	377	—	23.5	22.7	31.1	—
1926	2,839	2,441	398	—	24.2	23.1	33.4	—
1925	2,909	2,506	403	—	25.1	24.1	34.2	—
1924	2,979	2,577	401	—	26.1	25.1	34.6	—
1923	2,910	2,531	380	—	26.0	25.2	33.2	—
1922	2,882	2,507	375	—	26.2	25.4	33.2	—
1921	3,055	2,657	398	—	28.1	27.3	35.8	—
1920	2,950	2,566	383	—	27.7	26.9	35.0	—
1919	2,740	2,387	353	—	26.1	25.3	32.4	—
1918	2,948	2,588	360	—	28.2	27.6	33.0	—
1917	2,944	2,587	357	—	28.5	27.9	32.9	—
1916	2,964	2,599	—	—	29.1	28.5	—	—
1915	2,965	2,594	—	—	29.5	28.9	—	—
1914	2,966	2,588	—	—	29.9	29.3	—	—
1913	2,869	2,497	—	—	29.5	28.8	—	—
1912	2,840	2,467	—	—	29.8	29.0	—	—
1911	2,809	2,435	—	—	29.9	29.1	—	—
1910	2,777	2,401	—	—	30.1	29.2	—	—
1909	2,718	2,344	—	—	30.0	29.2	—	—

[1] From 1980-1992, the racial classification was based on the race of the mother. Prior to that it was based
on the race of the child.

[2] Births prior to 1959 have been adjusted for underregistration.

[3] For 1917-1919 and 1941-1946, rates are based on the population including armed forces abroad.

Source: National Center for Health Statistics, "Vital Statistics of the United States, Volume I--Natality:
1992," National Center for Health Statistics, Hyattsville, MD, 1995, Table 1-1.

percent or more of that remaining population after the white population was subtracted from the total population; hence the "all other" total and the black categories yield almost identical rates and trends.) Table 6-2 reports the general fertility rate and the total fertility rate for the same years, by race. Figure 6-1 graphs the trend of the total number of births, Figure 6-2 graphs the crude birth rates, and Figure 6-3 graphs the trend of the general fertility rate for the white, non-white and the black population.

In this century fertility has passed through four phases:

1. Gradual decline from high to replacement-level fertility, from 1900 to 1933, with a small upsurge following World War I.
2. The "baby boom," from 1940 to 1957, with a rising rate and number of births.
3. The "baby bust," from 1957 to 1976, with a declining rate and number of births.
4. A low-level plateau ("baby boom echo"), from 1976 to 1992, with a level rate and a rising number of births.

It has already been shown (in Chapter 1) how these fluctuations have created cohort "bulges" in the population age distribution. Starting about 1977, an "echo" began to be created in the number of births, even though fertility rates were low, because the women born during the "baby boom" were passing through the prime childbearing years. Because the number of women of childbearing age increased, the number of births each year rose.

A total fertility rate of 2,100 (2.1 births per woman) roughly represents replacement fertility. At this rate adults are able to replace themselves, with a small margin for infants and children who die before reaching reproductive age. A general fertility rate of 70 also approximately represents replacement, which corresponds roughly to a crude birth rate of 15.5 or 16.0 births per 1,000 total population per year. A basic demographic rule of thumb for contemporary populations is that any population with a crude death rate of 15.0 is either very close to or slightly below replacement level, and a population with a crude birth rate of 17.0 or more is above replacement. Thus, it can be seen from Table 6-2 that about 1973 fertility in the United States sank below the replacement fertility level and has generally remained there. Since its low point in 1976, the crude birth rate has risen slowly. Yet, these recent fertility trends must still be considered minor in comparison to the dramatic fertility changes of the past century. Despite replacement levels of fertility, the number of births has continued to be higher than the number of deaths because of the young age composition of the population left over from the baby boom. Between 1969 and 1971 there was a significant rise in fertility rates, leading to speculation that a new baby boom was developing, but in 1972-76 there was a relapse to lower levels. A low point in fertility (CBR of 14.6, GFR of 65.0, and TFR of 1,738) occurred in 1976; after 1976 there was a slight rise to

a point closer to but still below replacement level by 1980. Following the recovery between 1976 and 1980, the birth rate wandered along on a plateau for two years with no apparent trend. In 1983 it took another dip, perhaps in reaction to the severe recession of 1982 and 1983, then remained at this lower level through 1987. The birth rate has slowly risen back to replacement levels between 1988 and 1992. There are many possible explanations of the slight recent rise in fertility which are explored in this chapter.

A decade ago, demographers were hesitant about predicting what course the birth rate would take for the remainder of the century. Because of economic recovery some predicted a small rise, while others predicted further declines because of the trends toward later marriage and rising divorce rates (described in Chapter 5). With another decade of experience with the population at a near replacement level, fertility trends into the early 2000s seem less uncertain. Few demographers would forecast either a resurgence of fertility equivalent to the baby boom of 1940-1957 or a dramatic fall in fertility to below the replacement level in the near future. Instead, the likely prospect seems to be small ripples in a plateau hovering either just below or at the replacement level. Advance survey data for 1994 indicate that births in this year fell below the 4 million mark for the first time since 1988, suggesting the short-term rise in official statistics through 1992 has already receded. Given the explanations for recent fertility trends explored in this chapter it is likely that the slight recent rise in fertility does not represent a long-term trend rising substantially above replacement levels. Nonetheless, the recovering economy of the mid-1990s and perhaps some millennial fertility behavior may sustain these slight rising trends into the turn of the century.

Differentials in Fertility Between the Black and White Population

In 1992 the TFR for black women was 2,442, which is 16 percent above the replacement level of 2,100. This difference represents a considerable rise above replacement for black women. As recently as 1985 black women were roughly at replacement-level fertility. In contrast, the TFR of white women in 1992 was 1,993.5, which is 5 percent below replacement level. If the current differential were to persist, black females would bear an average of nearly one half, i.e. 0.4485, more children than would white females, a total fertility rate 1.22 times that of the white population (see Tables 6-2 and 6-3). With respect to replacement fertility, this differential has shifted since the 1980s in that it is now due more to the rising (and above replacement) level of fertility of the black population than it is to the below replacement level of fertility of the white population.

One of the impressive facts about fertility trends in the United States has been the tendency for black and

Table 6-2. General Fertility Rate and Total Fertility Rate, by Race[1]: 1909-1992

Year[2]	General fertility rate		All other		Total fertility rate		All other	
	All races	White	Total	Black	All races	White	Total	Black
1992	68.9	66.5	79.5	83.2	2,065.0	1,993.5	2,343.0	2,442.0
1991	69.6	67.0	81.5	85.2	2,073.0	1,995.5	2,383.0	2,480.0
1990	70.9	68.3	83.2	86.8	2,081.0	2,003.0	2,398.0	2,480.0
1989	69.2	66.4	82.7	86.2	2,014.0	1,931.0	2,360.5	2,432.5
1988	67.3	64.5	80.3	82.6	1,934.0	1,856.5	2,264.5	2,298.0
1987	65.8	63.3	77.8	80.1	1,872.0	1,804.5	2,168.5	2,198.0
1986	65.4	63.1	76.8	78.9	1,837.5	1,776.0	2,114.5	2,135.5
1985	66.3	64.1	77.3	78.8	1,844.0	1,787.0	2,106.5	2,109.0
1984	65.5	63.2	77.0	78.2	1,806.5	1,748.5	2,078.5	2,070.5
1983	65.7	63.4	77.9	78.7	1,799.0	1,740.5	2,084.0	2,066.0
1982	67.3	64.8	80.3	80.9	1,827.5	1,767.0	2,132.0	2,106.5
1981	67.3	64.8	81.1	82.0	1,812.0	1,748.0	2,133.5	2,117.5
1980	68.4	65.6	83.9	84.7	1,839.5	1,773.0	2,199.0	2,176.5
1979	67.2	63.4	88.5	88.3	1,808.0	1,715.5	2,309.5	2,263.2
1978	65.5	61.7	87.0	86.7	1,760.0	1,667.5	2,264.5	2,218.0
1977	66.8	63.2	87.7	88.1	1,789.5	1,703.0	2,278.5	2,251.0
1976	65.0	61.5	85.8	85.8	1,738.0	1,652.0	2,222.5	2,187.0
1975	66.0	62.5	87.7	87.9	1,774.0	1,686.0	2,276.0	2,243.0
1974	67.8	64.2	89.8	89.7	1,835.0	1,748.5	2,338.5	2,298.5
1973	68.8	64.9	93.4	93.6	1,879.0	1,783.0	2,443.0	2,411.0
1972	73.1	68.9	99.5	99.9	2,010.0	1,906.5	2,627.5	2,601.0
1971	81.6	77.3	109.1	109.7	2,266.5	2,160.5	2,919.5	2,902.0
1970	87.9	84.1	113.0	115.4	2,480.0	2,385.0	3,066.7	3,099.5
1969	86.1	82.2	111.6	112.1	2,455.5	2,360.3	3,061.2	3,042.8
1968	85.2	81.3	111.9	112.7	2,464.2	2,365.6	3,108.4	3,099.8
1967	87.2	82.8	117.1	118.5	2,557.7	2,446.9	3,299.2	3,311.8
1966	90.8	86.2	123.5	124.7	2,721.4	2,602.9	3,531.5	3,545.3
1965	96.3	91.3	131.9	133.2	2,912.6	2,783.4	3,807.9	3,828.5
1964	104.7	99.8	140.0	142.6	3,190.5	3,065.0	4,070.2	4,138.6
1963	108.3	103.6	143.7	—	3,318.8	3,193.5	4,203.0	—
1962	112.0	107.5	147.8	—	3,461.3	3,341.3	4,340.1	—
1961	117.1	112.3	153.0	—	3,620.3	3,496.9	4,496.8	—
1960	118.0	113.2	153.6	153.5	3,653.6	3,532.9	4,522.1	4,541.8
1959	118.8	113.9	156.0	—	3,670.0	3,544.0	4,595.0	—
1958	120.0	114.8	159.1	—	3,701.0	3,560.0	4,727.0	—
1957	122.7	117.6	161.7	—	3,767.0	3,625.0	4,798.0	—
1956	121.0	115.9	159.7	—	3,689.0	3,546.0	4,723.0	—
1955	118.3	113.7	154.3	—	3,580.0	3,446.0	4,550.0	—
1954	117.9	113.5	152.2	—	3,543.0	3,415.0	4,474.0	—
1953	115.0	110.9	146.4	—	3,424.0	3,306.0	4,283.0	—
1952	113.8	110.0	142.7	—	3,358.0	3,250.0	4,147.0	—
1951	111.4	107.7	141.7	—	3,269.0	3,157.0	4,091.0	—
1950	106.2	102.3	137.3	—	3,091.0	2,977.0	3,928.0	—
1949	107.1	103.6	135.1	—	3,110.0	3,009.0	3,855.0	—
1948	107.3	104.3	131.6	—	3,109.0	3,022.0	3,742.0	—
1947	113.3	111.8	125.9	—	3,274.0	3,230.0	3,575.0	—
1946	101.9	100.4	113.9	—	2,943.0	2,901.0	3,238.0	—

Table 6-2. General Fertility Rate and Total Fertility Rate, by Race[1]: 1909-1992
(continued)

Year[2]	General fertility rate				Total fertility rate			
	All races	White	All other		All races	White	All other	
			Total	Black			Total	Black
1945	85.9	83.4	106.0	—	2,491.0	2,421.0	3,017.0	—
1944	88.8	86.3	108.5	—	2,568.0	2,501.0	3,075.0	—
1943	94.3	92.3	111.0	—	2,718.0	2,664.0	3,128.0	—
1942	91.5	89.5	107.6	—	2,628.0	2,577.0	3,022.0	—
1941	83.4	80.7	105.4	—	2,399.0	2,328.0	2,956.0	—
1940	79.9	77.1	102.4	—	2,301.0	2,229.0	2,870.0	—
1939	77.6	74.8	100.1	—	—	—	—	—
1938	79.1	76.5	100.5	—	—	—	—	—
1937	77.1	74.4	99.4	—	—	—	—	—
1936	75.8	73.3	95.9	—	—	—	—	—
1935	77.2	74.5	98.4	—	—	—	—	—
1934	78.5	75.8	100.4	—	—	—	—	—
1933	76.3	73.7	97.3	—	—	—	—	—
1932	81.7	79.0	103.0	—	—	—	—	—
1931	84.6	82.4	102.1	—	—	—	—	—
1930	89.2	87.1	105.9	—	—	—	—	—
1929	89.3	87.3	106.1	—	—	—	—	—
1928	93.8	91.7	111.0	—	—	—	—	—
1927	99.8	97.1	121.7	—	—	—	—	—
1926	102.6	99.2	130.3	—	—	—	—	—
1925	106.6	103.3	134.0	—	—	—	—	—
1924	110.9	107.8	135.6	—	—	—	—	—
1923	110.5	108.0	130.5	—	—	—	—	—
1922	111.2	108.8	130.8	—	—	—	—	—
1921	119.8	117.2	140.8	—	—	—	—	—
1920	117.9	115.4	137.5	—	—	—	—	—
1919	111.2	—	—	—	—	—	—	—
1918	119.8	—	—	—	—	—	—	—
1917	121.0	—	—	—	—	—	—	—
1916	123.4	121.8	—	—	—	—	—	—
1915	125.0	123.2	—	—	—	—	—	—
1914	126.6	124.6	—	—	—	—	—	—
1913	124.7	122.4	—	—	—	—	—	—
1912	125.8	123.3	—	—	—	—	—	—
1911	126.3	123.6	—	—	—	—	—	—
1910	126.8	123.8	—	—	—	—	—	—
1909	126.8	123.6	—	—	—	—	—	—

[1] From 1980-1992, the racial classification was based on the race of the mother. Prior to that it was based on
   the race of the child.
[2] Births prior to 1959 have been adjusted for underregistration.

Source: National Center for Health Statistics, "Vital Statistics of the United States, Volume I--Natality: 1992,"
   National Center for Health Statistics, Hyattsville, MD, 1995, Tables 1-1 and 1-9. Data on total fertility
   rates prior to 1960 from U.S. Bureau of the Census, "Historical Statistics of the United States: Colonial
   Times to 1970," U.S. Government Printing Office, Washington, D.C., 1975, Table B 11-19.

Table 6-3. Differences Between the Black and White Fertility Rates: 1960-1992

| | General fertility rate | | Total fertility rate | | | |
| | | | | | Deviation from replacement[1] | |
Year	Difference	Ratio	Difference	Ratio	White[2]	Black[2]
1992	16.7	1.25	448.5	1.22	-106.5	342.0
1991	18.2	1.27	484.5	1.24	-104.5	380.0
1990	18.5	1.27	477.0	1.24	-97.0	380.0
1989	19.8	1.30	501.5	1.26	-169.0	332.5
1988	18.1	1.28	441.5	1.24	-243.5	198.0
1987	16.8	1.27	393.5	1.22	-295.5	98.0
1986	15.8	1.25	359.5	1.20	-324.0	35.5
1985	14.7	1.23	322.0	1.18	-313.0	9.0
1984	15.0	1.24	322.0	1.18	-351.5	-29.5
1983	15.3	1.24	325.5	1.19	-359.5	-34.0
1982	16.1	1.25	339.5	1.19	-333.0	6.5
1981	17.2	1.27	369.5	1.21	-352.0	17.5
1980	19.1	1.29	403.5	1.23	-327.0	76.5
1979	24.9	1.39	547.7	1.32	-384.5	163.2
1978	25.0	1.41	550.5	1.33	-432.5	118.0
1977	24.9	1.39	548.0	1.32	-397.0	151.0
1976	24.3	1.40	535.0	1.32	-448.0	87.0
1975	25.4	1.41	557.0	1.33	-414.0	143.0
1974	25.5	1.40	550.0	1.31	-351.5	198.5
1973	28.7	1.44	628.0	1.35	-317.0	311.0
1972	31.0	1.45	694.5	1.36	-193.5	501.0
1971	32.4	1.42	741.5	1.34	60.5	802.0
1970	31.3	1.37	714.5	1.30	285.0	999.5
1969	29.9	1.36	682.5	1.29	260.3	942.8
1968	31.4	1.39	734.2	1.31	265.6	999.8
1967	35.7	1.43	864.9	1.35	346.9	1,211.8
1966	38.5	1.45	942.4	1.36	502.9	1,445.3
1965	41.9	1.46	1,045.1	1.38	683.4	1,728.5
1964	42.8	1.43	1,073.6	1.35	965.0	2,038.6
1963	—	—	—	—	1,093.5	—
1962	—	—	—	—	1,241.3	—
1961	—	—	—	—	1,396.9	—
1960	40.3	1.36	1,008.9	1.29	1,432.9	2,441.8

[1] Replacement is approximately 2,100.

[2] From 1980-1992, the racial classification was based on the race of the mother. Prior to that it was based on the race of the child.

Source: National Center for Health Statistics, "Vital Statistics of the United States, Volume I--Natality: 1992," National Center for Health Statistics, Hyattsville, MD, 1995, Tables 1-1 and 1-9.

Figure 6-1. Trends in Total Births, by Race: 1909-1992

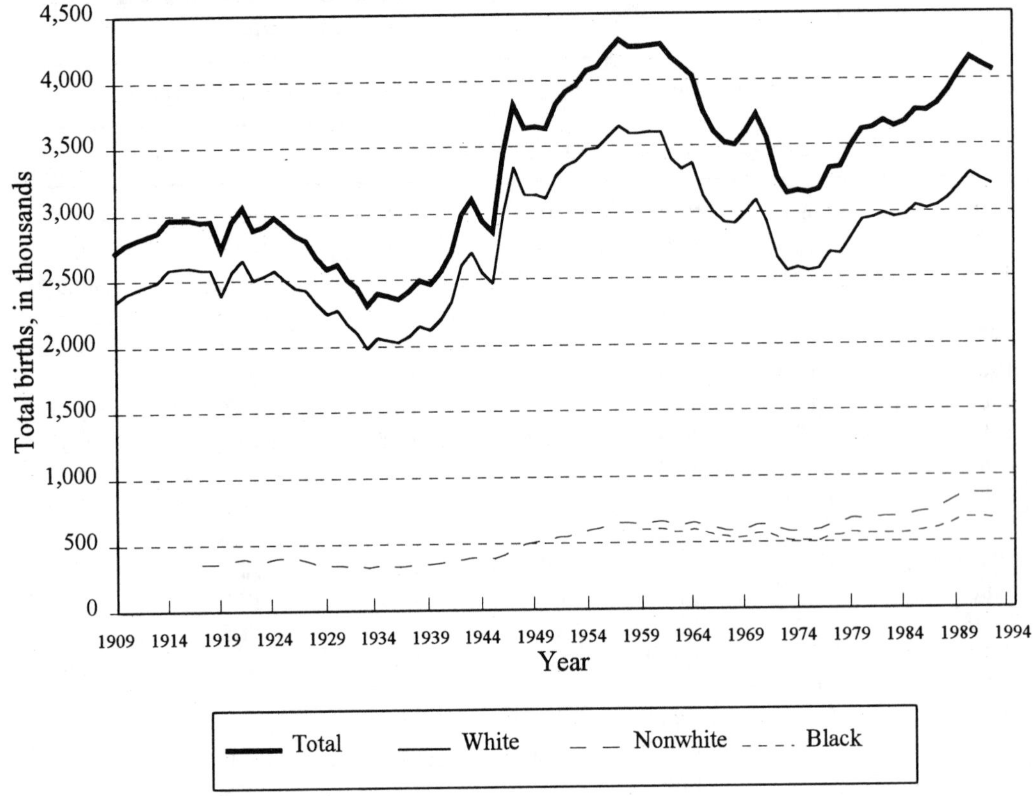

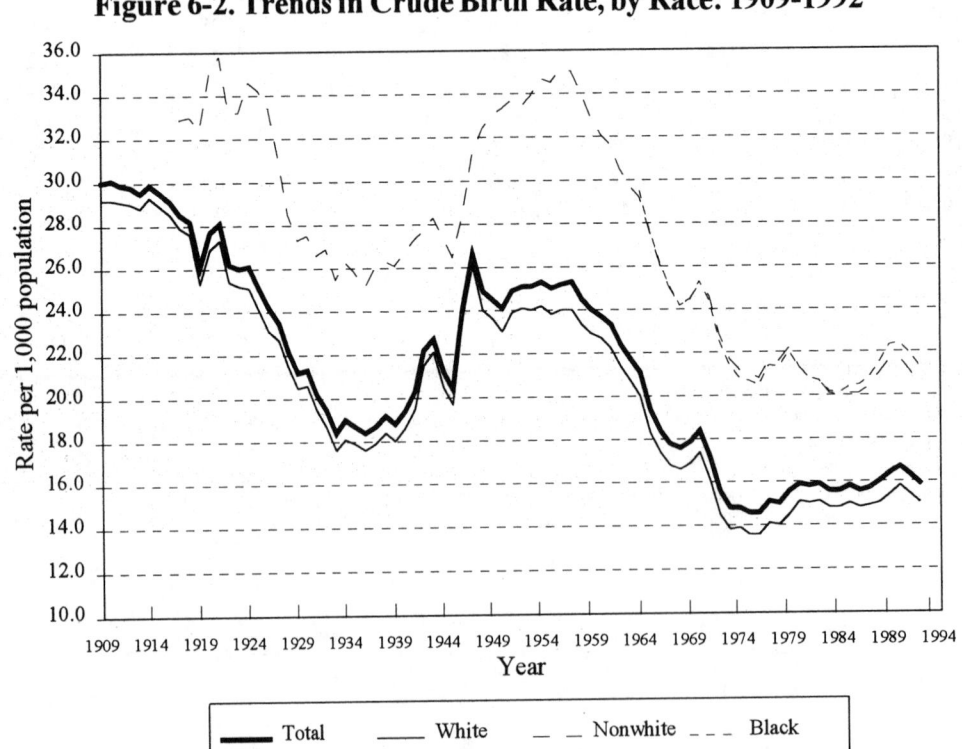

Source: 1909-1992 NCHS data.

Figure 6-2. Trends in Crude Birth Rate, by Race: 1909-1992

Source: 1909-1992 NCHS data.

white birth rates to follow parallel paths, fluctuating upward and downward almost simultaneously. Figures 6-2 and 6-3 illustrate this propensity. However, the trends are not wholly parallel, and the differentials by race have changed over time. Table 6-3 and Figure 6-4 examine these differentials in more detail. The differentials are expressed in three ways:

1. Absolute difference in GFR and TFR (black fertility minus white fertility).
2. Relative ratio for GFR and TFR (black fertility divided by white fertility).
3. Deviation from replacement (TFR minus 2,100).

Although these three series of data emphasize the similarity of the trends, with both racial groups tending toward replacement, certain significant points need to be mentioned.

At the onset of the "baby boom" the absolute differentials tended to widen. Although the fertility of both black and white populations rose, the fertility of the black population rose by a larger amount while the ratio of black-to-white fertility remained almost unchanged. After the onset of the "baby bust" in 1958 there was a steady narrowing of the absolute differentials while the relative differential remained about the same up through 1985. This meant that the birth rate of the black population was declining by a greater amount than the white population, causing the rates to converge, but the ratio was constant. From 1985 to 1989 the difference rose sharply along with the ratio as black fertility once again diverged from that of

whites. Some of this divergence is related to rising black non-marital fertility at younger ages. However, black fertility rose across all ages during this period. Since 1989 black-white fertility differences and ratios have once again begun to converge.

Age-Specific Fertility Rates

Fertility has a very distinctive age pattern in modern societies. It begins at nearly zero for ages under fifteen, is low for ages 15-17, considerably higher for ages 18-19, and peaks in the 20-24 and 25-29 age groups. At ages thirty and above, the rate declines swiftly to be again nearly zero at ages 40-44 (see Figure 6-5). This age pattern is strongly influenced by the pattern of age at first marriage and by the gradual decline in ability to conceive as the age of menopause is approached. However, exposure to the risk of pregnancy and physiological factors pertaining to conception only establish broad limits. Within these limits the level of fertility can and does vary greatly, depending upon the prevalence and effectiveness of fertility regulation practiced. Table 6-4 shows the age-specific fertility rates for the U.S. population, by race, for each year since 1940. This table has four parts. Table 6-4A is for all races; Table 6-4B is for the white population; Table 6-4C is for the nonwhite (i.e. black and other) population; and Table 6-4D is for the black population.

Fluctuations in fertility have tended to occur at all ages; the curve for one date is stacked neatly below or

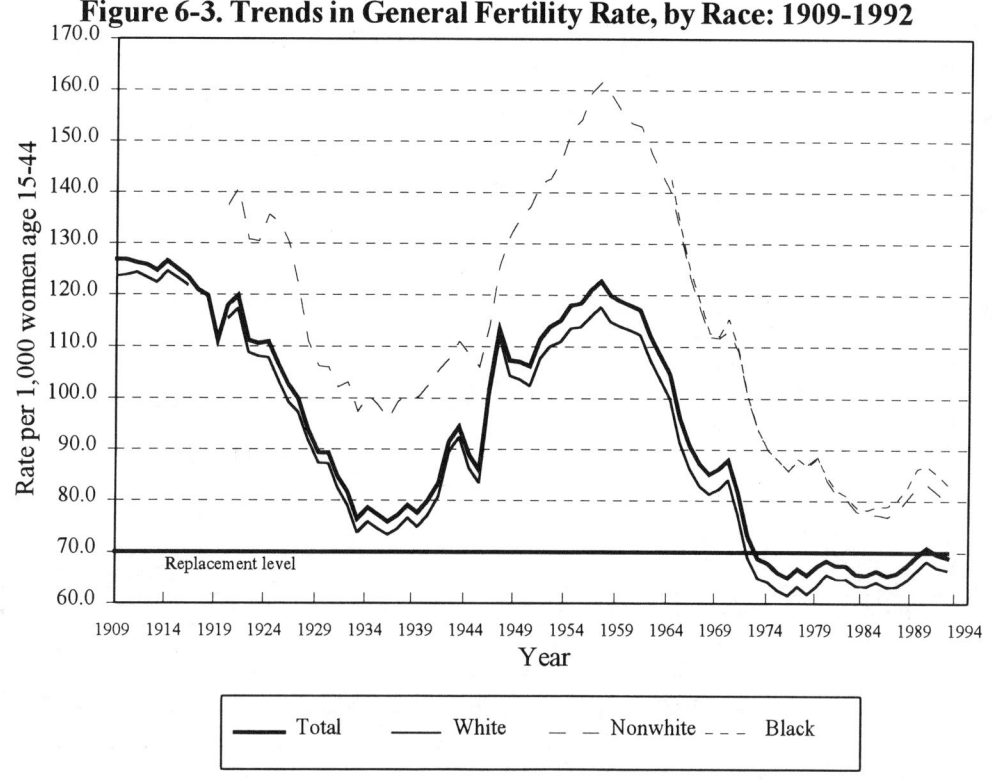

Figure 6-3. Trends in General Fertility Rate, by Race: 1909-1992

Source: 1909-1992 NCHS data.

Figure 6-4. Differences Between the Black and White Total Fertility Rates: 1964-1992

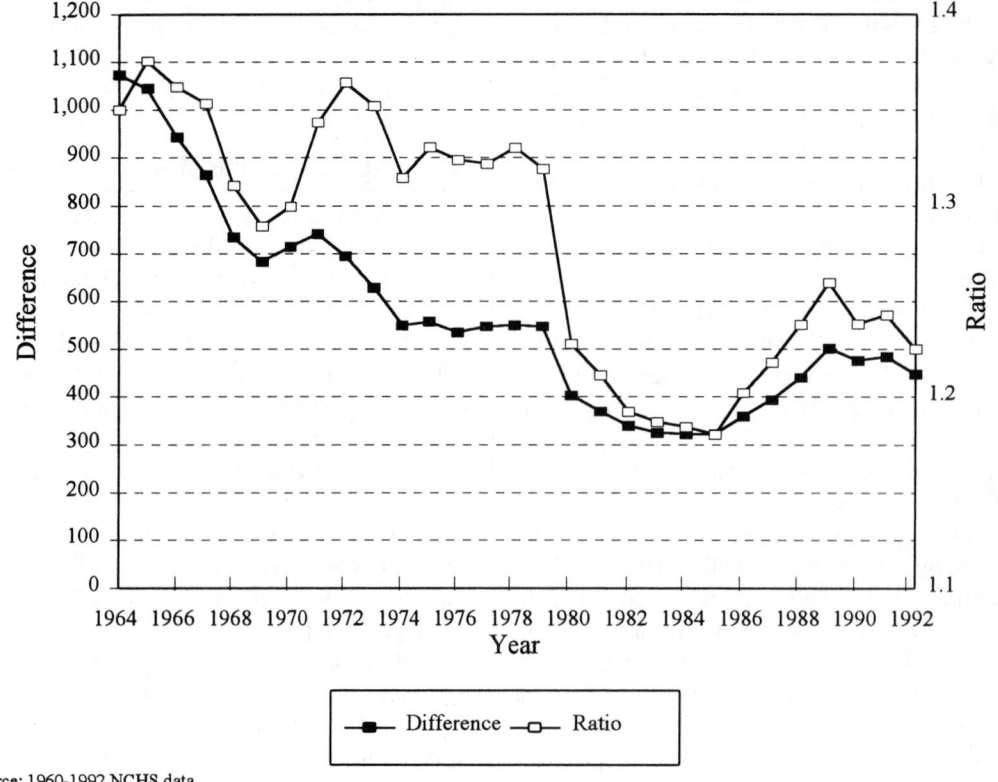

Source: 1960-1992 NCHS data.

Figure 6-5. Age-specific Fertility Rates of the Population, by Race: 1960 and 1990

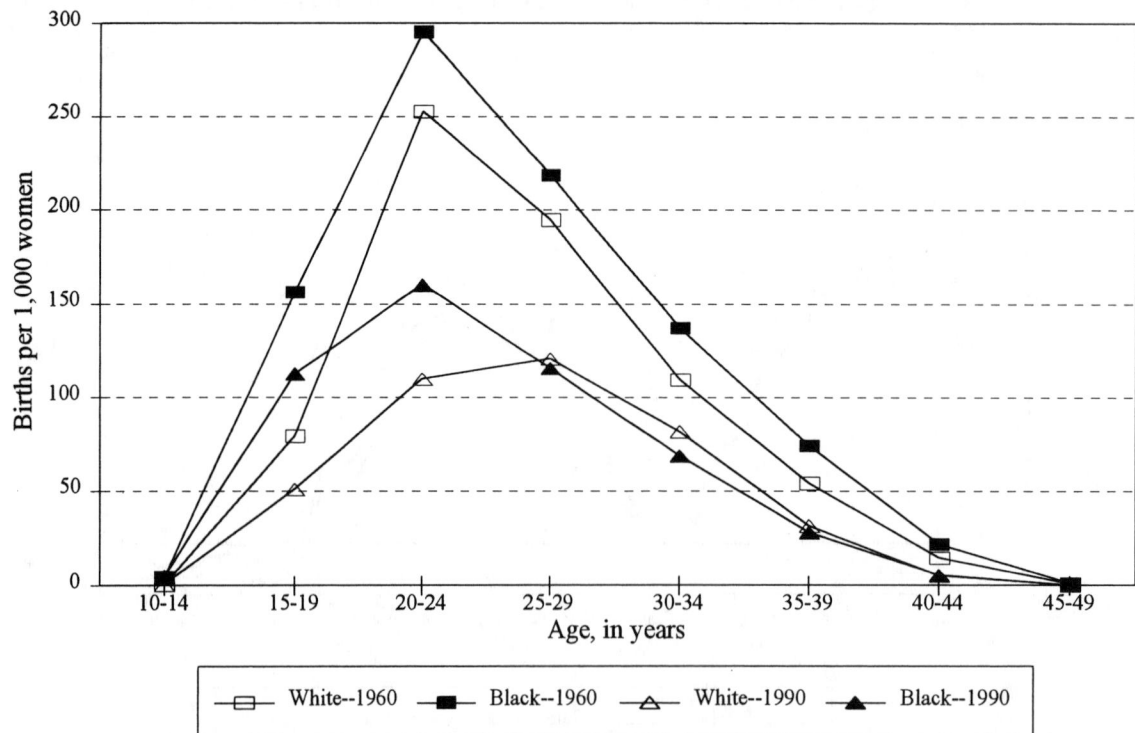

Source: 1960 and 1990 NCHS data.

above the curve for another. However, a detailed examination of the age-specific fertility rates for two recent points of time is instructive (1) near the peak of the baby boom (1960), and (2) at a subsequent lower point of fertility in 1990. These are graphed for the white and black population in Figure 6-5. Birth rates only thirty years apart can be seen to fluctuate widely. This comparison shows that:

1. The declines from the peak to the trough encompass all ages. Absolute declines are greatest at ages 20-24 and 25-29, while the greatest relative decline occurs at ages thirty-five and over.

2. Teenage pregnancy (ages 15-19) declines less, both absolutely and relatively, than pregnancy in any of the other age groups lower than thirty-five years of age.

3. Declines in age-specific fertility since 1960 have been greater at younger ages among whites and greater at older ages among blacks resulting in higher age-specific fertility for blacks at younger ages and higher age-specific fertility for whites at older ages in 1990.

The trend of change in each of the six age-specific fertility rates for the total population is charted in Figure 6-6. That all age groups between twenty and forty-five and over have shared a common trend over time is made evident by this figure. Also the upturn in fertility following 1975 was most heavily concentrated in the age group 30-34. The more recent rise in fertility since 1987 can be seen to have had a substantial component in the 15-19 age group but cuts across all groups less than 40 years old.

Race differentials in fertility can also better be understood in terms of age-specific components. Figure 6-7 graphs the trend of fertility rates for the white, nonwhite and black population by age between 1940 and 1992. Table 6-5 shows the absolute and relative measures of differential fertility between the races for each age group. Data are presented for three points in time: (1) the peak of the baby boom, 1956; (2) the trough of the baby bust, 1976; and (3) 1990.

Among teenage women aged 15-19, fertility for the black population is more than double that for the white population. At ages 20-24 the fertility of black women is about one-third higher than that of the white population. At ages 25-29, the race differential almost disappears—the rates are practically the same for both groups. At ages thirty-five and over, although the rates are low for both races, nonwhite fertility tends to be 30 percent or more greater than white fertility. Thus the race differential is of greatest magnitude at the youngest ages. The race differential is of greatest relative magnitude at both the youngest and oldest ages of the childbearing span. More than 80 percent of the difference between races is generated by fertility among those under twenty-five years of age. (Ages

Figure 6-6. Trends in the Age-specific Fertility Rate, All Races: 1940-1992

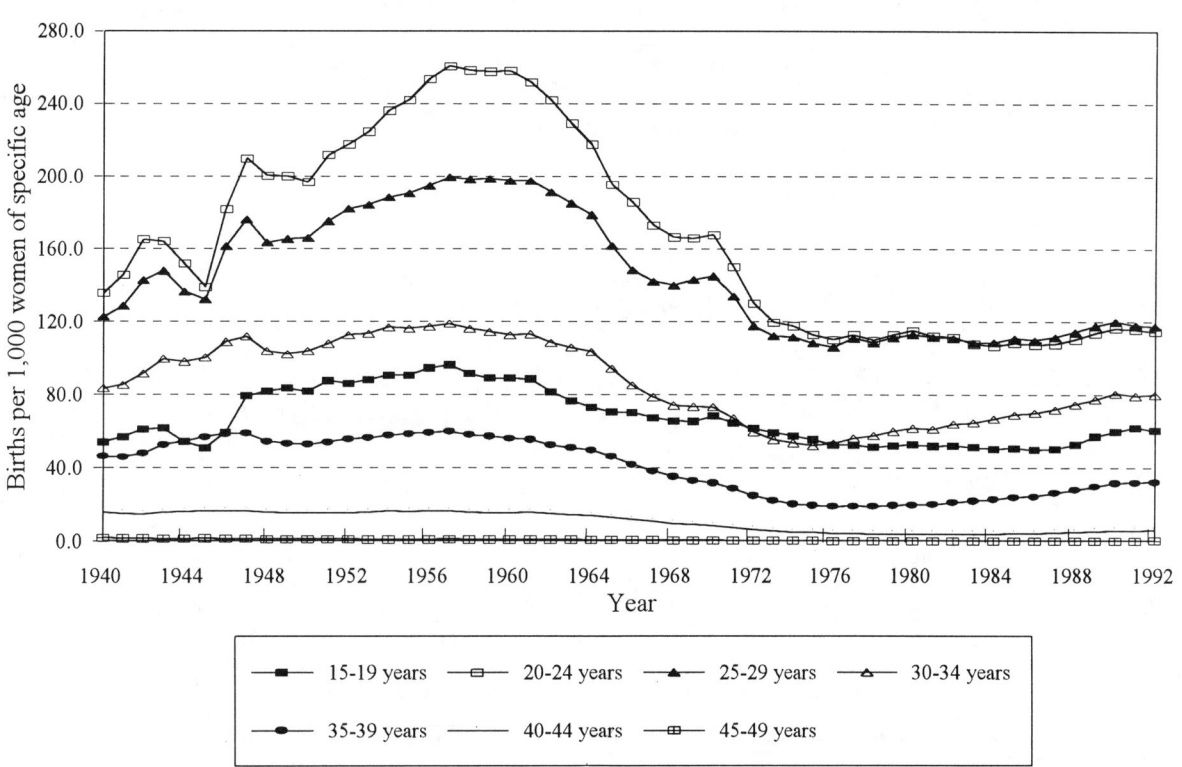

Source: 1940-1959 U.S. Census data, 1960-1992 NCHS data.

Figure 6-7. Fertility Rates of Women for Specified Ages, by Race[1]: 1940-1992

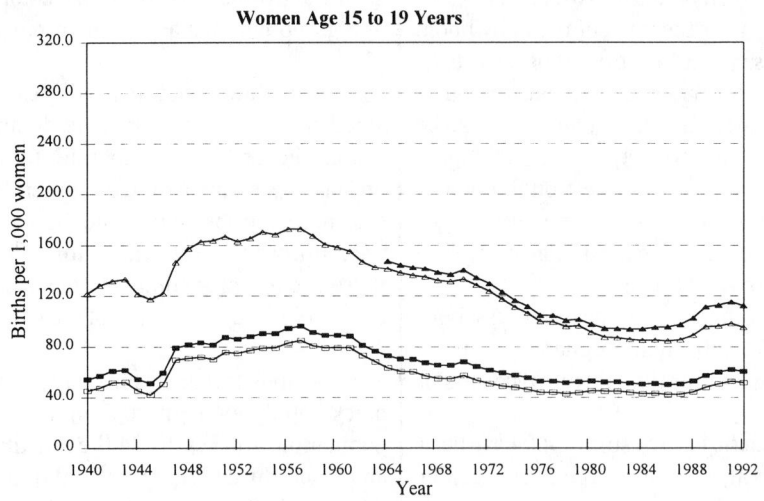

Women Age 15 to 19 Years

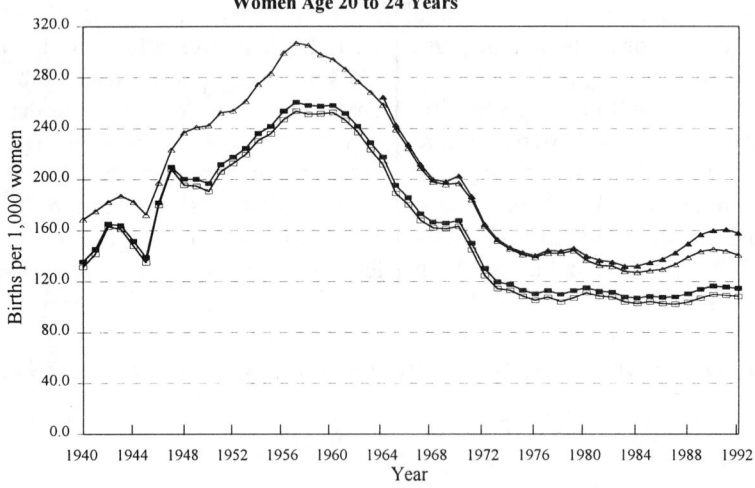

Women Age 20 to 24 Years

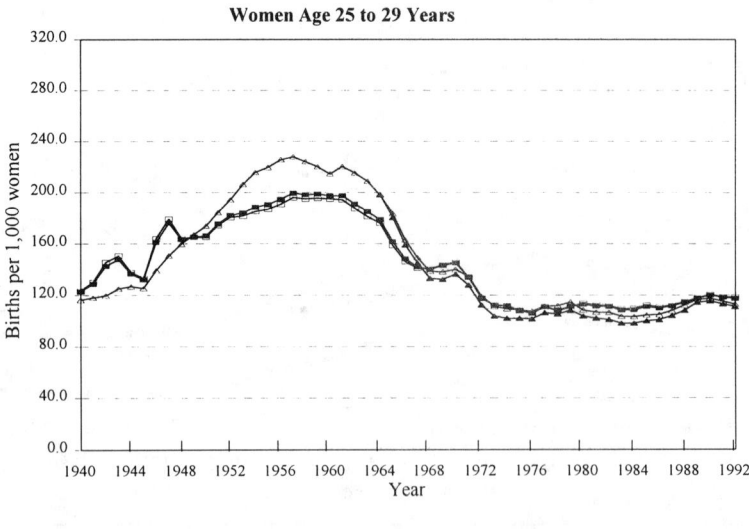

Women Age 25 to 29 Years

■— Total   □— White   △— Nonwhite   ▲— Black

[1] From 1980-1992, the racial classification was based on the race of the mother. Prior to that it was based on the
  race of the child.
Source: 1940-1959 U.S. Census data, 1960-1992 NCHS data.

Figure 6-7. Fertility Rates of Women for Specified Ages, by Race[1]: 1940-1992 (continued)

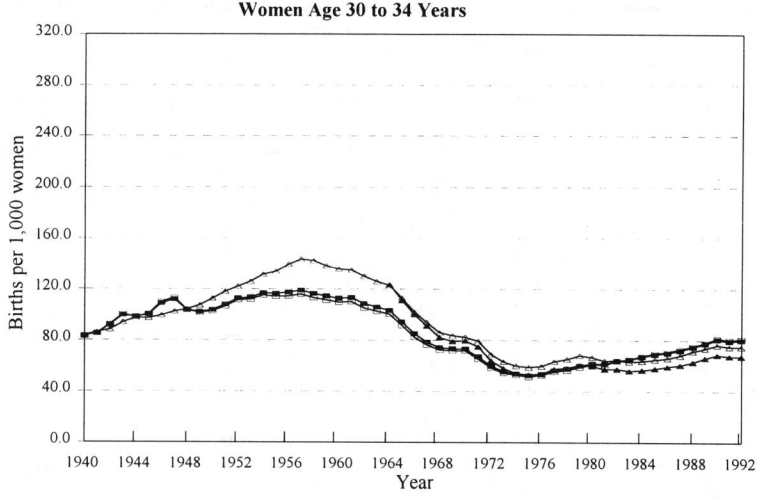

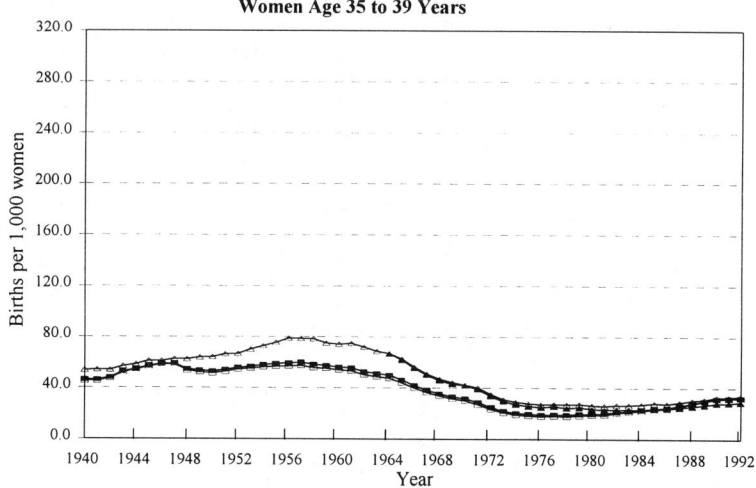

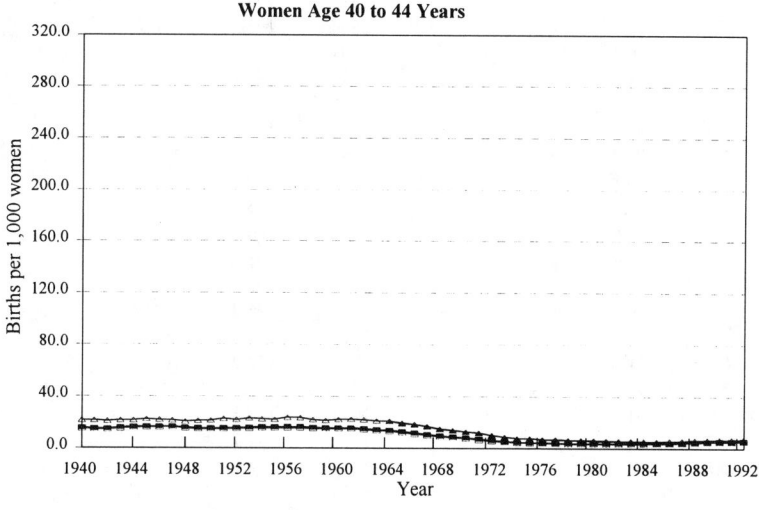

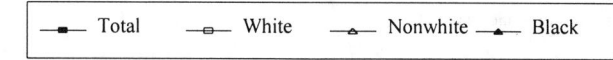

[1] From 1980-1992, the racial classification was based on the race of the mother. Prior to that it was based on the race of the child.
Source: 1940-1959 U.S. Census data, 1960-1992 NCHS data.

Table 6-4A. Age-specific Fertility Rates, All Races[1]: 1940-1992

			Age of mother								
			15 to 19 years								
Year[2]	Total fertility rate	10 to 14 years	Total	15 to 17 years	18 to 19 years	20 to 24 years	25 to 29 years	30 to 34 years	35 to 39 years	40 to 44 years	45 to 49 years
1992	2,065.0	1.4	60.7	37.8	94.5	114.6	117.4	80.2	32.5	5.9	0.3
1991	2,073.0	1.4	62.1	38.7	94.4	115.7	118.2	79.5	32.0	5.5	0.2
1990	2,081.0	1.4	59.9	37.5	88.6	116.5	120.2	80.8	31.7	5.5	0.2
1989	2,014.0	1.4	57.3	36.4	84.2	113.8	117.6	77.4	29.9	5.2	0.2
1988	1,934.0	1.3	53.0	33.6	79.9	110.2	114.4	74.8	28.1	4.8	0.2
1987	1,872.0	1.3	50.6	31.7	78.5	107.9	111.6	72.1	26.3	4.4	0.2
1986	1,837.5	1.3	50.2	30.5	79.6	107.4	109.8	70.1	24.4	4.1	0.2
1985	1,844.0	1.2	51.0	31.0	79.6	108.3	111.0	69.1	24.0	4.0	0.2
1984	1,806.5	1.2	50.6	31.0	77.4	106.8	108.7	67.0	22.9	3.9	0.2
1983	1,799.0	1.1	51.4	31.8	77.4	107.8	108.5	64.9	22.0	3.9	0.2
1982	1,827.5	1.1	52.4	32.3	79.4	111.6	111.0	64.1	21.2	3.9	0.2
1981	1,812.0	1.1	52.2	32.0	80.0	112.2	111.5	61.4	20.0	3.8	0.2
1980	1,839.5	1.1	53.0	32.5	82.1	115.1	112.9	61.9	19.8	3.9	0.2
1979	1,808.0	1.2	52.3	32.3	81.3	112.8	111.4	60.3	19.5	3.9	0.2
1978	1,760.0	1.2	51.5	32.2	79.8	109.9	108.5	57.8	19.0	3.9	0.2
1977	1,789.5	1.2	52.8	33.9	80.9	112.9	111.0	56.4	19.2	4.2	0.2
1976	1,738.0	1.2	52.8	34.1	80.5	110.3	106.2	53.6	19.0	4.3	0.2
1975	1,774.0	1.3	55.6	36.1	85.0	113.0	108.2	52.3	19.5	4.6	0.3
1974	1,835.0	1.2	57.5	37.3	88.7	117.7	111.5	53.8	20.2	4.8	0.3
1973	1,879.0	1.2	59.3	38.5	91.2	119.7	112.2	55.6	22.1	5.4	0.3
1972	2,010.0	1.2	61.7	39.0	96.9	130.2	117.7	59.8	24.8	6.2	0.4
1971	2,266.5	1.1	64.5	38.2	105.3	150.1	134.1	67.3	28.7	7.1	0.4
1970	2,480.0	1.2	68.3	38.8	114.7	167.8	145.1	73.3	31.7	8.1	0.5
1969	2,455.5	1.0	65.5	35.7	112.4	165.7	143.0	73.5	33.1	8.8	0.5
1968	2,464.2	1.0	65.6	35.1	113.5	166.5	140.0	74.2	35.4	9.6	0.6
1967	2,557.7	0.9	67.5	35.3	116.7	172.9	142.1	78.7	38.3	10.6	0.7
1966	2,721.4	0.8	70.3	35.7	120.3	185.6	148.2	85.1	41.9	11.7	0.7
1965	2,912.6	0.8	70.5	36.6	124.5	195.3	161.6	94.4	46.2	12.8	0.8
1964	3,190.5	0.9	73.1	37.2	142.8	217.5	178.7	103.4	49.9	13.8	0.8
1963	3,318.8	0.9	76.7	36.9	147.6	229.1	185.1	105.8	51.2	14.2	0.9
1962	3,461.3	0.8	81.4	38.1	150.8	241.9	191.1	108.6	52.6	14.9	0.9
1961	3,620.3	0.9	88.6	43.8	155.2	251.9	197.5	113.2	55.6	15.6	0.9
1960	3,653.6	0.8	89.1	43.9	166.7	258.1	197.4	112.7	56.2	15.5	0.9
1959	3,670.0	0.9	89.1	—	—	257.5	198.6	114.4	57.3	15.3	0.9
1958	3,701.0	0.9	91.4	—	—	258.2	198.3	116.2	58.3	15.7	0.9
1957	3,767.0	1.0	96.3	—	—	260.6	199.4	118.9	59.9	16.3	1.1
1956	3,689.0	1.0	94.6	—	—	253.7	194.7	117.3	59.3	16.3	1.0
1955	3,580.0	0.9	90.5	—	—	242.0	190.5	116.2	58.7	16.1	1.0
1954	3,543.0	0.9	90.6	—	—	236.2	188.4	116.9	57.9	16.2	1.0
1953	3,424.0	1.0	88.2	—	—	224.6	184.1	113.4	56.6	15.8	1.0
1952	3,358.0	0.9	86.1	—	—	217.6	182.0	112.6	55.8	15.5	1.3
1951	3,269.0	0.9	87.6	—	—	211.6	175.3	107.9	54.1	15.4	1.1
1950	3,091.0	1.0	81.6	—	—	196.6	166.1	103.7	52.9	15.1	1.2
1949	3,110.0	1.0	83.4	—	—	200.1	165.4	102.1	53.5	15.3	1.3
1948	3,109.0	1.0	81.8	—	—	200.3	163.4	103.7	54.5	15.7	1.3
1947	3,274.0	0.9	79.3	—	—	209.7	176.0	111.9	58.9	16.6	1.4
1946	2,943.0	0.7	59.3	—	—	181.8	161.2	108.9	58.7	16.5	1.5
1945	2,491.0	0.8	51.1	—	—	138.9	132.2	100.2	56.9	16.6	1.6
1944	2,568.0	0.8	54.3	—	—	151.8	136.5	98.1	54.6	16.1	1.4
1943	2,718.0	0.8	61.7	—	—	164.0	147.8	99.5	52.8	15.7	1.5
1942	2,628.0	0.7	61.1	—	—	165.1	142.7	91.8	47.9	14.7	1.6
1941	2,399.0	0.7	56.9	—	—	145.4	128.7	85.3	46.1	15.0	1.7
1940	2,301.0	0.7	54.1	—	—	135.6	122.8	83.4	46.3	15.6	1.9

[1] From 1980-1992, the racial classification was based on the race of the mother. Prior to that it was based on the race of the child.
[2] Births prior to 1959 have been adjusted for underregistration.

Source: National Center for Health Statistics, "Vital Statistics of the United States, Volume I--Natality: 1992," National Center for Health Statistics, Hyattsville, MD, 1995, Table 1-9. Data prior to 1960 is from U.S. Bureau of the Census, "Historical Statistics of the United States: Colonial Times to 1970," U.S. Government Printing Office, Washington, D.C., 1975, Table B 11-19.

Table 6-4B. Age-specific Fertility Rates, White[1]: 1940-1992

			Age of mother								
				15 to 19 years							
Year[2]	Total fertility rate	10 to 14 years	Total	15 to 17 years	18 to 19 years	20 to 24 years	25 to 29 years	30 to 34 years	35 to 39 years	40 to 44 years	45 to 49 years
1992	1,993.5	0.8	51.8	30.1	83.8	108.2	118.4	81.4	32.2	5.7	0.2
1991	1,995.5	0.8	52.8	30.7	83.5	109.0	118.8	80.5	31.8	5.2	0.2
1990	2,003.0	0.7	50.8	29.5	78.0	109.8	120.7	81.7	31.5	5.2	0.2
1989	1,931.0	0.7	47.9	28.1	72.9	106.9	117.8	78.1	29.7	4.9	0.2
1988	1,856.5	0.6	44.4	26.0	69.6	103.7	114.8	75.4	27.7	4.5	0.2
1987	1,804.5	0.6	42.5	24.6	68.9	102.3	112.3	73.0	25.9	4.1	0.2
1986	1,776.0	0.6	42.3	23.8	70.1	102.7	110.8	70.9	23.9	3.8	0.2
1985	1,787.0	0.6	43.3	24.4	70.4	104.1	112.3	69.9	23.3	3.7	0.2
1984	1,748.5	0.6	42.9	24.3	68.4	102.7	109.8	67.7	22.2	3.6	0.2
1983	1,740.5	0.6	43.9	25.0	68.8	103.8	109.4	65.3	21.3	3.6	0.2
1982	1,767.0	0.6	45.0	25.5	70.8	107.7	111.9	64.0	20.4	3.6	0.2
1981	1,748.0	0.5	44.9	25.4	71.5	108.3	112.3	61.0	19.0	3.4	0.2
1980	1,773.0	0.6	45.4	25.5	73.2	111.1	113.8	61.2	18.8	3.5	0.2
1979	1,715.5	0.6	43.7	24.7	71.0	107.0	110.8	59.0	18.3	3.5	0.2
1978	1,667.5	0.6	42.9	24.9	69.4	104.1	107.9	56.6	17.7	3.5	0.2
1977	1,703.0	0.6	44.1	26.1	70.5	107.7	110.9	55.3	18.0	3.8	0.2
1976	1,652.0	0.6	44.1	26.3	70.2	105.3	105.9	52.6	17.8	3.9	0.2
1975	1,686.0	0.6	46.4	28.0	74.0	108.2	108.1	51.3	18.2	4.2	0.2
1974	1,748.5	0.6	47.9	28.7	77.3	113.0	111.8	52.9	18.9	4.4	0.2
1973	1,783.0	0.6	49.0	29.2	79.3	114.4	112.3	54.4	20.7	4.9	0.3
1972	1,906.5	0.5	51.0	29.3	84.3	124.8	117.4	58.4	23.3	5.6	0.3
1971	2,160.5	0.5	53.6	28.5	92.3	144.9	134.0	65.4	26.9	6.4	0.4
1970	2,385.0	0.5	57.4	29.2	101.5	163.4	145.9	71.9	30.0	7.5	0.4
1969	2,360.3	0.4	54.7	26.4	99.2	161.3	143.7	71.9	31.5	8.1	0.5
1968	2,365.6	0.4	54.9	25.6	100.5	162.1	140.3	72.4	33.7	8.9	0.5
1967	2,446.9	0.3	56.9	25.7	104.0	167.9	141.0	76.4	36.5	9.8	0.6
1966	2,602.9	0.3	60.4	26.6	108.2	180.0	146.0	82.5	39.9	10.8	0.7
1965	2,783.4	0.3	60.6	27.8	111.9	189.0	158.4	91.6	44.0	12.0	0.7
1964	3,065.0	0.3	63.4	29.1	129.7	211.6	175.9	100.5	47.6	13.0	0.7
1963	3,193.5	0.3	68.2	28.4	133.2	223.5	181.1	102.6	48.8	13.4	0.8
1962	3,341.3	0.4	73.2	29.5	136.7	237.0	187.4	105.2	50.1	14.2	0.8
1961	3,496.9	0.4	79.2	35.3	143.8	246.7	194.2	110.1	53.1	14.8	0.9
1960	3,532.9	0.4	79.4	35.5	154.6	252.8	194.9	109.6	54.0	14.7	0.8
1959	3,544.0	0.4	79.2	—	—	251.7	195.5	111.3	55.1	14.7	0.9
1958	3,560.0	0.5	81.0	—	—	251.4	194.8	113.0	55.8	14.8	0.8
1957	3,625.0	0.5	85.2	—	—	253.8	195.8	115.9	57.4	15.4	0.8
1956	3,546.0	0.3	83.2	—	—	247.1	190.6	114.4	57.0	15.4	0.8
1955	3,446.0	0.3	79.2	—	—	236.0	186.8	114.1	56.7	15.4	0.9
1954	3,415.0	0.4	79.0	—	—	230.7	185.0	115.1	56.2	15.4	0.9
1953	3,306.0	0.4	77.2	—	—	219.6	181.5	111.9	55.1	15.0	0.9
1952	3,250.0	0.4	75.0	—	—	212.5	180.5	111.4	54.4	14.8	0.9
1951	3,157.0	0.4	75.9	—	—	206.0	174.2	106.5	52.6	14.6	1.0
1950	2,977.0	0.4	70.0	—	—	190.4	165.1	102.6	51.4	14.5	1.0
1949	3,009.0	0.4	72.1	—	—	194.6	165.2	101.5	52.2	14.6	1.1
1948	3,022.0	0.4	71.1	—	—	195.5	163.9	103.6	53.5	15.2	1.1
1947	3,230.0	0.4	69.8	—	—	207.9	179.1	113.0	58.4	16.1	1.2
1946	2,901.0	0.3	50.6	—	—	179.8	164.0	110.0	58.4	15.9	1.3
1945	2,421.0	0.3	42.1	—	—	134.7	133.1	100.5	56.3	16.0	1.4
1944	2,501.0	0.3	45.3	—	—	147.9	137.7	98.2	54.1	15.5	1.2
1943	2,664.0	0.3	52.1	—	—	161.1	150.7	100.2	52.2	15.0	1.3
1942	2,577.0	0.3	51.8	—	—	162.9	145.6	92.3	47.2	14.1	1.3
1941	2,328.0	0.2	47.6	—	—	141.6	130.1	85.2	45.1	14.3	1.4
1940	2,229.0	0.2	45.3	—	—	131.4	123.6	83.4	45.3	15.0	1.6

[1] From 1980-1992, the racial classification was based on the race of the mother. Prior to that it was based on the race of the child.
[2] Births prior to 1959 have been adjusted for underregistration.

Source: National Center for Health Statistics, "Vital Statistics of the United States, Volume I--Natality: 1992," National Center for Health Statistics, Hyattsville, MD, 1995, Table 1-9. Data prior to 1960 is from U.S. Bureau of the Census, "Historical Statistics of the United States: Colonial Times to 1970," U.S. Government Printing Office, Washington, D.C., 1975, Table B 11-19.

Table 6-4C. Age-specific Fertility Rates, Nonwhite[1]: 1940-1992

Year[2]	Total fertility rate	10 to 14 years	15 to 19 years Total	15 to 17 years	18 to 19 years	20 to 24 years	25 to 29 years	30 to 34 years	35 to 39 years	40 to 44 years	45 to 49 years
1992	2,343.0	3.8	95.4	67.9	135.7	140.8	113.1	74.8	33.4	6.9	0.4
1991	2,383.0	3.9	98.4	70.3	137.2	144.1	115.2	75.0	32.8	6.8	0.4
1990	2,398.0	4.0	96.3	69.1	132.4	145.4	117.7	76.3	32.8	6.7	0.4
1989	2,360.5	4.2	95.9	69.2	132.5	143.6	116.6	73.7	31.1	6.6	0.4
1988	2,264.5	4.1	89.2	64.7	125.2	138.9	112.3	71.5	30.2	6.3	0.4
1987	2,168.5	4.0	85.5	62.1	120.6	133.4	108.0	68.0	28.6	5.8	0.4
1986	2,114.5	3.9	84.8	60.4	121.6	129.5	105.0	66.1	27.5	5.7	0.4
1985	2,106.5	3.8	85.4	60.8	120.6	128.6	104.7	65.1	27.9	5.4	0.4
1984	2,078.5	3.7	85.1	61.4	118.0	127.1	103.4	63.7	26.8	5.5	0.4
1983	2,084.0	3.5	85.9	62.6	117.8	128.0	103.7	63.2	26.4	5.7	0.4
1982	2,132.0	3.5	87.1	63.1	120.8	132.0	106.7	64.4	26.4	5.8	0.5
1981	2,133.5	3.5	87.5	63.1	122.7	132.6	106.9	64.0	25.8	6.0	0.4
1980	2,199.0	3.8	91.4	66.7	127.7	136.5	108.5	66.7	26.3	6.2	0.4
1979	2,309.5	4.1	96.5	70.5	134.9	144.3	114.6	68.3	27.3	6.4	0.4
1978	2,264.5	4.0	96.0	70.4	134.4	142.1	111.9	65.2	26.9	6.4	0.4
1977	2,278.5	4.3	99.5	74.8	136.8	142.3	111.5	63.4	27.3	6.9	0.5
1976	2,222.5	4.3	99.9	75.5	137.2	138.9	107.6	59.5	26.9	6.9	0.5
1975	2,276.0	4.7	106.4	80.5	146.1	141.0	108.7	58.8	27.6	7.5	0.5
1974	2,338.5	4.6	111.3	84.9	153.1	145.5	109.5	59.9	28.8	7.6	0.5
1973	2,443.0	5.0	117.5	90.5	160.9	151.6	111.2	63.2	30.9	8.6	0.6
1972	2,627.5	4.7	123.8	93.8	173.3	163.4	119.3	68.9	34.8	9.9	0.7
1971	2,919.5	4.7	128.5	94.0	185.6	184.0	134.6	79.3	40.2	11.7	0.9
1970	3,066.7	4.8	133.4	95.2	195.4	196.8	140.1	82.5	42.2	12.6	0.9
1969	3,061.2	4.5	131.3	91.8	195.1	195.9	138.2	83.6	44.1	13.7	1.0
1968	3,108.4	4.3	132.3	92.8	197.5	197.7	138.6	85.9	46.9	14.8	1.2
1967	3,299.2	4.1	135.0	93.8	203.6	208.7	149.2	93.9	50.9	16.7	1.2
1966	3,531.5	4.0	136.4	92.7	210.9	224.7	163.0	102.1	56.3	18.4	1.4
1965	3,807.9	4.0	138.4	93.9	218.5	239.2	183.5	113.0	62.7	19.3	1.5
1964	4,070.2	4.0	141.5	93.7	233.8	258.6	198.0	122.7	66.8	20.9	1.6
1963	4,203.0	4.0	142.6	91.6	224.5	268.4	208.7	125.7	68.7	21.1	1.5
1962	4,340.1	3.9	147.1	92.9	230.2	276.9	215.2	130.0	71.8	21.8	1.5
1961	4,496.8	4.0	155.2	101.7	241.6	286.6	220.4	134.7	74.9	22.3	1.4
1960	4,522.1	4.0	158.2	103.1	251.8	294.2	214.6	135.6	74.2	22.0	1.7
1959	4,595.0	4.2	160.5	—	—	297.9	220.2	138.1	75.0	21.2	1.8
1958	4,727.0	4.3	167.3	—	—	305.2	224.2	142.3	78.4	21.8	1.9
1957	4,798.0	5.6	172.8	—	—	307.0	228.1	143.5	78.7	23.5	2.0
1956	4,723.0	4.7	172.5	—	—	299.1	225.9	139.4	78.8	23.6	2.0
1955	4,550.0	4.8	168.3	—	—	283.4	219.6	133.5	75.4	22.1	2.1
1954	4,474.0	4.9	170.3	—	—	274.7	215.7	131.3	72.9	22.5	2.1
1953	4,283.0	5.1	165.4	—	—	261.4	206.4	125.7	70.0	23.0	2.2
1952	4,147.0	5.2	162.9	—	—	254.0	194.2	122.0	66.6	21.9	2.2
1951	4,091.0	5.4	166.7	—	—	252.5	184.2	117.9	66.5	22.6	2.2
1950	3,928.0	5.1	163.5	—	—	242.6	173.8	112.6	64.3	21.2	2.6
1949	3,855.0	5.1	162.8	—	—	241.3	167.0	107.3	63.9	21.1	2.5
1948	3,742.0	4.9	157.3	—	—	237.0	159.6	104.1	62.5	20.4	2.8
1947	3,575.0	4.6	146.6	—	—	223.7	150.6	102.4	62.7	21.4	3.1
1946	3,238.0	3.7	121.9	—	—	197.3	139.2	99.3	61.0	21.8	3.5
1945	3,017.0	3.9	117.5	—	—	172.1	125.4	97.1	61.3	22.3	3.7
1944	3,075.0	3.9	121.5	—	—	182.4	126.8	97.3	58.4	21.5	3.2
1943	3,128.0	4.0	133.4	—	—	187.2	125.1	93.9	56.9	21.5	3.7
1942	3,022.0	3.9	131.8	—	—	182.3	119.6	88.1	54.0	20.8	4.0
1941	2,956.0	4.0	128.3	—	—	175.0	118.1	86.2	54.1	21.5	4.1
1940	2,870.0	3.7	121.7	—	—	168.5	116.3	83.5	53.7	21.5	5.2

[1] From 1980-1992, the racial classification was based on the race of the mother. Prior to that it was based on the race of the child.
[2] Births prior to 1959 have been adjusted for underregistration.

Source: National Center for Health Statistics, "Vital Statistics of the United States, Volume I--Natality: 1992," National Center for Health Statistics, Hyattsville, MD, 1995, Table 1-9. Data prior to 1960 is from U.S. Bureau of the Census, "Historical Statistics of the United States: Colonial Times to 1970," U.S. Government Printing Office, Washington, D.C., 1975, Table B 11-19.

Table 6-4D. Age-specific Fertility Rates, Black[1]: 1960-1992

Year	Total fertility rate	10 to 14 years	15 to 19 years Total	15 to 17 years	18 to 19 years	20 to 24 years	25 to 29 years	30 to 34 years	35 to 39 years	40 to 44 years	45 to 49 years
1992	2,442.0	4.7	112.4	81.3	157.9	158.0	111.2	67.5	28.8	5.6	0.2
1991	2,480.0	4.8	115.5	84.1	158.6	160.9	113.1	67.7	28.3	5.5	0.2
1990	2,480.0	4.9	112.8	82.3	152.9	160.2	115.5	68.7	28.1	5.5	0.3
1989	2,432.5	5.1	111.5	81.9	151.9	156.8	114.4	66.3	26.7	5.4	0.3
1988	2,298.0	4.9	102.7	75.7	142.7	149.7	108.2	63.1	25.6	5.1	0.3
1987	2,198.0	4.8	97.6	72.1	135.8	142.7	104.3	60.6	24.6	4.8	0.2
1986	2,135.5	4.7	95.8	69.3	135.1	137.3	101.1	59.3	23.8	4.8	0.3
1985	2,109.0	4.5	95.4	69.3	132.4	135.0	100.2	57.9	23.9	4.6	0.3
1984	2,070.5	4.4	94.1	69.2	128.1	132.2	98.4	56.7	23.3	4.8	0.2
1983	2,066.0	4.1	93.9	69.6	127.1	131.9	98.4	56.2	23.3	5.1	0.3
1982	2,106.5	4.0	94.3	69.7	128.9	135.4	101.3	57.5	23.3	5.1	0.4
1981	2,117.5	4.0	94.5	69.3	131.0	136.5	102.3	57.4	23.1	5.4	0.3
1980	2,176.5	4.3	97.8	72.5	135.1	140.0	103.9	59.9	23.5	5.6	0.3
1979	2,263.2	4.6	101.7	75.7	140.4	146.3	108.2	60.7	24.7	6.1	0.4
1978	2,218.0	4.4	100.9	75.0	139.7	143.8	105.4	58.3	24.3	6.1	0.4
1977	2,251.0	4.7	104.7	79.6	142.9	144.4	106.4	57.5	25.4	6.6	0.5
1976	2,187.0	4.7	104.9	80.3	142.5	140.5	101.6	53.6	24.8	6.8	0.5
1975	2,243.0	5.1	111.8	85.6	152.4	142.8	102.2	53.1	25.6	7.5	0.5
1974	2,298.5	5.0	116.5	90.0	158.7	146.7	102.2	54.1	27.0	7.6	0.6
1973	2,411.0	5.4	123.1	96.0	166.6	153.1	103.9	58.1	29.4	8.6	0.6
1972	2,601.0	5.1	129.8	99.5	179.5	165.0	112.4	64.0	33.4	9.8	0.7
1971	2,902.0	5.1	134.5	99.4	192.6	186.6	128.0	74.8	38.9	11.6	0.9
1970	3,099.5	5.2	140.7	101.4	204.9	202.7	136.3	79.6	41.9	12.5	1.0
1969	3,042.8	4.8	137.0	96.9	202.5	198.0	132.3	79.1	42.9	13.5	1.0
1968	3,099.8	4.7	138.7	98.2	206.1	199.8	133.1	82.2	45.8	14.5	1.2
1967	3,311.8	4.4	141.8	99.5	213.4	211.9	145.3	91.1	50.1	16.6	1.2
1966	3,545.3	4.2	142.7	97.9	219.2	227.9	159.0	100.3	55.4	18.2	1.4
1965	3,828.5	4.3	144.6	99.3	227.6	243.1	180.4	111.3	61.9	18.7	1.4
1964	4,138.6	4.3	147.6	98.7	242.4	264.7	198.5	123.5	66.8	20.8	1.5
1963	—	—	—	—	—	—	—	—	—	—	—
1962	—	—	—	—	—	—	—	—	—	—	—
1961	—	—	—	—	—	—	—	—	—	—	—
1960	4,541.8	4.3	156.1	—	—	295.4	218.6	137.1	73.9	21.9	1.1

[1] From 1980-1992, the racial classification was based on the race of the mother. Prior to that it was based on the race of the child.

Source: National Center for Health Statistics, "Vital Statistics of the United States, Volume I--Natality: 1992," National Center for Health Statistics, Hyattsville, MD, 1995, Table 1-9.

under twenty have a significant component of nonmarital fertility, a topic discussed in a later section of this chapter.)

Since 1940 the greatest fertility differentials across all ages appear to have been during the rise and fall of the baby boom. More recently there has been a divergence of nonwhite (including black) and black fertility as the two populations diverge further in composition. Also of note is the fact that the temporary rise in fertility prior to 1991 appears to have cut across all age and race groups.

Did the various age groups of the black and white populations behave differently during the transition from the peak baby boom in 1956 to the trough of the baby bust in 1976 and since then? The answer to this question, supplied in Table 6-5, reveals that in absolute terms the decline from 1956 to 1976 was greater at all age groups among the black than among the white population. However, in relative terms (percent decline) the performances of the two race groups was nearly identical-both declined roughly by the same percentage at each age. The main exception was in the 15-19 year age group. Despite the fact that this group for the black population had a much larger absolute decline in teenage fertility than did the same ages for the white population, the relative size of the decline was smaller, perhaps because of the very high initial rate. To a lesser degree, the same phenomenon characterized the 20-24 year age group. Since 1976 the rise in fertility has been greater in percentage terms for the white population in all but the 20-24 year old group. Past age 40 black fertility has continued to decline. White fertility has increased most dramatically at younger and older ages, whereas black fertility has risen most sharply in the prime childbearing ages of 20-34 years.

Table 6-5. Age-specific Fertility Rates, at Baby Boom Peak (1956), Baby Bust (1976), and Baby Boom Echo (1990)

Age	White 1956	White 1976	White 1990	Black 1956[1]	Black 1976	Black 1990	Percent change 1956 to 1976 White	Percent change 1956 to 1976 Black	Percent change 1976 to 1990 White	Percent change 1976 to 1990 Black
Total fertility rate	3,546.0	1,652.0	2,003.0	4,723.0	2,187.0	2,480.0	-53.4	-53.7	21.2	13.4
10 to 14 years	0.3	0.6	0.7	4.7	4.7	4.9	100.0	0.0	16.7	4.3
15 to 19 years	83.2	44.1	50.8	172.5	104.9	112.8	-47.0	-39.2	15.2	7.5
15 to 17 years	—	26.3	29.5	—	80.3	82.3	—	—	12.2	2.5
18 to 19 years	—	70.2	78.0	—	142.5	152.9	—	—	11.1	7.3
20 to 24 years	247.1	105.3	109.8	299.1	140.5	160.2	-57.4	-53.0	4.3	14.0
25 to 29 years	190.6	105.9	120.7	225.9	101.6	115.5	-44.4	-55.0	14.0	13.7
30 to 34 years	114.4	52.6	81.7	139.4	53.6	68.7	-54.0	-61.5	55.3	28.2
35 to 39 years	57.0	17.8	31.5	78.8	24.8	28.1	-68.8	-68.5	77.0	13.3
40 to 44 years	15.4	3.9	5.2	23.6	6.8	5.5	-74.7	-71.2	33.3	-19.1
45 to 49 years	0.8	0.2	0.2	2.0	0.5	0.3	-75.0	-75.0	0.0	-40.0

[1] Figures for 1956 are for nonwhite instead of blac

Source: National Center for Health Statistics, "Vital Statistics of the United States, Volume I--Natality: 1992," National Center for Health Statistics, Hyattsville, MD, 1995, Table 1-9. Data prior to 1960 is from U.S. Bureau of the Census, "Historical Statistics of the United States: Colonial Times to 1970," U.S. Government Printing Office, Washington, D.C., 1975, Table B 11-19.

Birth Order

With fertility rates below replacement level, it is not surprising to find that more than 40 percent of all births are first births, over 32 percent are second births and only 4.35 percent of all births are fifth and higher-order children. Table 6-6 presents data on the fertility rates by birth order (see "Parity-specific fertility rates" in the Definition Box). These rates, in effect, subdivide the GFR into components, showing the part of the general fertility rate due to births of each order. Figure 6-8 illustrates the trend in the order-specific rates, by race. By tracing the trend in the order-specific components over time, one can gain insight into the impact of the baby boom and the baby bust.

In 1940, before the onset of the baby boom, the order-specific rates were quite similar to those of 1981 for the first three birth orders. The baby boom changed that dramatically. There was a substantial increase in first births, followed a few years later by an increase in second births. There was a progressive increase in all birth orders, but the absolute increase was substantial only for the first four birth orders. This means that, despite the baby boom, there was no important tendency toward a return to the really large family of five children or more.

As the baby bust developed, the process was reversed. The rates for fourth and higher-order births declined sharply to levels below those of 1940. In 1975 the rate for third and higher-order births dropped to a point below that of 1940. The slight recovery of the fertility rate since 1975 is due to increases in the birth rates for the second, third and fourth parities. The rates for first births have remained relatively stable or decreasing, the rates for fifth births have remained stable and the rates for higher-order births have continued to decrease substantially. The rise to replacement-level fertility since the mid-seventies then appears to represent a rise in the number of those moving to have more than one child yet still maintaining relatively small family sizes.

For the nonwhite population (Table 6-6C) the order-specific pattern for 1992 is a radical change from 1940 and the intervening years. Between 1940 and 1965 the rates for higher-order births rose substantially. Beginning in 1965 and until 1986 the rates for third and higher-order births declined sharply to very low levels. This pattern is true for the black population included in these nonwhite birth rates (Table 6-6D). After 1985 the nonwhite birth rates increased at a faster pace than the slight increase in white births. Figure 6-8 illustrates the more marked fertility recovery among nonwhites and blacks. However, the recent trend overall, and in the past few years especially, has been toward a convergence of white, nonwhite and black order-specific rates.

Table 6-6 emphasizes that the United States population (both white and black) has not progressively abandoned childbearing. It has simply forgone bearing large numbers of children, especially of fourth and higher-order parities, and perhaps is postponing the bearing of those fewer children to the late twenties and early thirties instead of rushing into childbearing at ages 20-24.

Table 6-6A. Birth Rates for All Races[1], by Live-birth Order: 1940-1992

Year[2]	Total	\-\- Live-birth order \-\- 1	2	3	4	5	6 and 7	8 and over
1992	68.9	27.8	22.3	11.3	4.4	1.7	1.0	0.3
1991	69.6	28.3	22.4	11.4	4.5	1.7	1.0	0.3
1990	70.9	29.0	22.8	11.7	4.5	1.7	1.0	0.3
1989	69.2	28.4	22.4	11.3	4.3	1.6	0.9	0.3
1988	67.3	27.6	22.0	10.9	4.1	1.5	0.9	0.3
1987	65.8	27.2	21.6	10.5	3.9	1.4	0.8	0.3
1986	65.4	27.2	21.6	10.3	3.8	1.4	0.8	0.3
1985	66.3	27.6	22.0	10.4	3.8	1.4	0.8	0.3
1984	65.5	27.4	21.7	10.1	3.7	1.4	0.9	0.3
1983	65.7	27.8	21.5	10.1	3.7	1.4	0.9	0.3
1982	67.3	28.6	22.0	10.2	3.8	1.4	0.9	0.3
1981	67.3	29.0	21.6	10.1	3.8	1.5	0.9	0.4
1980	68.4	29.5	21.8	10.3	3.9	1.5	1.0	0.4
1979	67.2	28.6	21.6	10.1	3.8	1.5	1.0	0.4
1978	65.5	27.8	21.1	9.8	3.8	1.5	1.0	0.4
1977	66.8	28.2	21.6	10.0	3.8	1.6	1.1	0.5
1976	65.0	27.5	20.8	9.5	3.8	1.6	1.2	0.6
1975	66.0	28.1	20.9	9.4	3.9	1.7	1.3	0.7
1974	67.8	28.7	21.4	9.5	4.1	1.9	1.5	0.8
1973	68.8	28.6	21.0	9.8	4.5	2.2	1.8	0.9
1972	73.1	29.8	21.4	10.6	5.3	2.6	2.2	1.2
1971	81.6	32.0	23.1	12.5	6.4	3.3	2.8	1.5
1970	87.9	34.2	24.2	13.6	7.2	3.8	3.2	1.8
1969	86.1	32.6	23.3	13.4	7.3	4.0	3.5	2.0
1968	85.2	31.9	22.4	13.1	7.5	4.2	3.9	2.3
1967	87.2	30.7	22.5	13.9	8.3	4.8	4.5	2.7
1966	90.8	30.9	22.4	14.7	9.1	5.4	5.2	3.1
1965	96.3	29.7	23.3	16.6	10.7	6.4	6.0	3.7
1964	104.7	30.3	25.1	18.7	12.2	7.3	6.9	4.1
1963	108.3	29.9	26.1	19.9	13.1	7.8	7.3	4.3
1962	112.0	29.9	26.9	21.0	13.8	8.2	7.6	4.5
1961	117.1	30.9	28.3	22.4	14.6	8.5	7.9	4.5
1960	118.0	31.1	29.2	22.8	14.6	8.3	7.6	4.3
1959	118.8	31.5	29.9	23.0	14.5	8.2	7.4	4.2
1958	120.2	32.2	30.6	23.3	14.4	8.1	7.3	4.2
1957	122.9	33.7	31.7	23.9	14.4	7.9	7.1	4.2
1956	121.2	33.5	31.9	23.6	13.9	7.6	6.8	4.0
1955	118.5	32.9	31.9	23.1	13.3	7.2	6.4	3.8
1954	118.1	33.6	32.4	22.7	12.8	6.8	6.0	3.8
1953	115.2	33.4	32.5	21.9	12.0	6.3	5.5	3.6
1952	113.9	34.0	32.7	21.3	11.3	5.8	5.2	3.6
1951	111.5	34.9	32.6	20.0	10.2	5.3	5.0	3.6
1950	106.2	33.3	32.1	18.4	9.2	4.8	4.7	3.6
1949	107.1	36.2	32.1	17.1	8.6	4.7	4.7	3.7
1948	107.3	39.6	30.9	16.1	8.0	4.5	4.6	3.6
1947	113.3	46.7	30.3	15.6	7.9	4.5	4.6	3.7
1946	101.9	38.5	27.9	14.5	7.8	4.5	4.7	3.8
1945	85.9	28.9	22.9	13.4	7.5	4.5	4.8	4.0
1944	88.8	30.2	23.8	13.8	7.6	4.5	4.9	4.0
1943	94.3	34.7	25.5	13.5	7.4	4.4	4.8	4.0
1942	91.5	37.5	22.9	11.9	6.6	4.1	4.6	3.9
1941	83.4	32.2	20.7	11.2	6.4	4.1	4.7	4.1
1940	79.9	29.3	20.0	10.9	6.4	4.1	4.8	4.3

[1] From 1980-1992, the racial classification was based on the race of the mother. Prior to that it was based on the race of the child.

[2] Births prior to 1960 are adjusted for underregistration.

Source: National Center for Health Statistics, "Vital Statistics of the United States, Volume I--Natality: 1992," National Center for Health Statistics, Hyattsville, MD, 1995, Table 1-11. Data prior to 1960 are from U.S. Bureau of the Census, "Historical Statistics of the United States: Colonial Times to 1970," U.S. Government Printing Office, Washington, D.C., 1975, Table B 11-20.

Table 6-6B. Birth Rates for Whites[1], by Live-birth Order: 1940-1992

Year[2]	Total	Live-birth order						
		1	2	3	4	5	6 and 7	8 and over
1992	66.5	27.3	22.0	10.8	4.0	1.4	0.8	0.2
1991	67.0	27.8	22.0	10.8	4.0	1.4	0.8	0.2
1990	68.3	28.4	22.4	11.1	4.0	1.4	0.8	0.2
1989	66.4	27.6	21.9	10.7	3.8	1.3	0.7	0.2
1988	64.5	26.8	21.6	10.4	3.6	1.2	0.7	0.2
1987	63.3	26.5	21.3	10.0	3.5	1.2	0.7	0.2
1986	63.1	26.6	21.3	9.8	3.4	1.2	0.7	0.2
1985	64.1	27.0	21.8	9.9	3.4	1.2	0.7	0.2
1984	63.2	26.8	21.4	9.6	3.3	1.2	0.7	0.2
1983	63.4	27.2	21.2	9.5	3.3	1.2	0.7	0.2
1982	64.8	28.0	21.6	9.6	3.4	1.2	0.7	0.3
1981	64.8	28.4	21.1	9.5	3.4	1.2	0.8	0.3
1980	65.6	28.8	21.3	9.6	3.4	1.3	0.8	0.3
1979	63.4	27.4	20.8	9.4	3.4	1.3	0.8	0.3
1978	61.7	26.6	20.2	9.2	3.3	1.3	0.8	0.3
1977	63.2	26.9	20.9	9.4	3.4	1.4	0.9	0.4
1976	61.5	26.3	20.2	8.9	3.4	1.4	1.0	0.4
1975	62.5	26.7	20.3	8.8	3.5	1.5	1.1	0.5
1974	64.2	27.2	20.8	9.0	3.8	1.7	1.2	0.6
1973	64.9	27.0	20.4	9.2	4.1	1.9	1.5	0.7
1972	68.9	28.1	20.9	10.1	4.9	2.3	1.8	0.8
1971	77.3	30.5	22.5	12.0	6.0	3.0	2.3	1.0
1970	84.1	32.9	23.7	13.3	6.8	3.4	2.7	1.2
1969	82.2	31.4	22.9	13.1	7.0	3.6	2.9	1.4
1968	81.3	30.8	22.0	12.8	7.1	3.8	3.2	1.6
1967	82.8	29.6	22.1	13.5	7.8	4.3	3.7	1.8
1966	86.2	30.0	21.9	14.3	8.6	4.9	4.3	2.1
1965	91.3	28.9	22.9	16.2	10.1	5.8	5.0	2.4
1964	99.8	29.8	24.8	18.4	11.7	6.7	5.7	2.7
1963	103.6	29.4	25.9	19.6	12.6	7.1	6.1	2.9
1962	107.5	29.6	26.8	20.8	13.3	7.5	6.3	3.0
1961	112.3	30.6	28.3	22.2	14.0	7.7	6.4	3.0
1960	113.2	30.8	29.2	22.7	14.1	7.5	6.1	2.8
1959	113.9	31.2	29.9	22.9	13.9	7.3	5.9	2.8
1958	114.9	31.9	30.6	23.1	13.8	7.2	5.7	2.7
1957	117.7	33.4	31.7	23.7	13.7	7.0	5.6	2.7
1956	116.0	33.2	31.9	23.4	13.1	6.6	5.2	2.6
1955	113.8	32.6	32.0	22.9	12.6	6.2	4.9	2.5
1954	113.6	33.3	32.8	22.6	12.0	5.9	4.6	2.5
1953	111.0	33.3	32.9	21.6	11.1	5.4	4.3	2.5
1952	110.0	34.1	33.1	21.0	10.4	5.0	4.0	2.5
1951	107.7	35.0	32.9	19.5	9.4	4.5	3.9	2.5
1950	102.3	33.3	32.3	17.9	8.4	4.1	3.7	2.5
1949	103.6	36.3	32.2	16.6	7.9	4.0	3.8	2.7
1948	104.3	39.9	31.1	15.7	7.4	3.9	3.7	2.6
1947	111.8	47.8	30.8	15.3	7.4	4.0	3.8	2.7
1946	100.4	39.5	28.5	14.4	7.3	4.0	3.9	2.8
1945	83.4	29.0	23.3	13.2	7.0	3.9	4.0	3.0
1944	86.3	30.4	24.2	13.6	7.1	4.0	4.1	3.1
1943	92.3	35.2	25.9	13.2	6.9	3.9	4.0	3.1
1942	89.5	38.3	23.1	11.5	6.1	3.6	3.8	3.1
1941	80.7	32.5	20.7	10.7	5.9	3.6	3.9	3.2
1940	77.1	29.4	20.0	10.5	5.9	3.6	4.1	3.5

[1] From 1980-1992, the racial classification was based on the race of the mother. Prior to that it was based on the race of the child.

[2] Births prior to 1960 are adjusted for underregistration.

Source: National Center for Health Statistics, "Vital Statistics of the United States, Volume I--Natality: 1992," National Center for Health Statistics, Hyattsville, MD, 1995, Table 1-11. Data prior to 1960 are from U.S. Bureau of the Census, "Historical Statistics of the United States: Colonial Times to 1970," U.S. Government Printing Office, Washington, D.C., 1975, Table B 11-20.

Table 6-6C. Birth Rates for Nonwhites[1], by Live-birth Order: 1940-1992

Year[2]	Total	Live-birth order							
		1	2	3	4	5	6 and 7	8 and over
1992	79.5	30.1	23.6	13.7	6.5	3.0	2.0	0.7
1991	81.5	30.9	24.2	14.1	6.7	3.0	2.0	0.7
1990	83.2	31.7	24.7	14.4	6.7	3.0	2.0	0.7
1989	82.7	32.0	24.6	14.2	6.5	2.9	1.9	0.6
1988	80.3	31.3	24.1	13.6	6.2	2.7	1.8	0.6
1987	77.8	30.6	23.3	13.1	5.9	2.6	1.7	0.6
1986	76.8	30.3	23.0	12.8	5.8	2.5	1.7	0.6
1985	77.3	30.5	23.2	12.9	5.9	2.6	1.7	0.6
1984	77.0	30.5	23.0	12.8	5.8	2.5	1.7	0.6
1983	77.9	30.9	23.2	12.9	5.9	2.6	1.8	0.6
1982	80.3	31.5	24.0	13.4	6.1	2.7	1.8	0.7
1981	81.1	32.0	24.2	13.4	6.1	2.7	1.9	0.8
1980	83.9	33.5	24.8	13.7	6.3	2.8	2.0	0.9
1979	88.5	35.7	26.2	14.2	6.4	2.9	2.1	1.0
1978	87.0	35.0	25.8	13.8	6.3	2.9	2.2	1.1
1977	87.7	35.6	25.7	13.5	6.2	3.0	2.4	1.3
1976	85.8	35.2	24.7	12.8	6.0	3.0	2.5	1.5
1975	87.7	36.7	24.6	12.6	6.1	3.1	2.8	1.8
1974	89.8	37.7	24.7	12.5	6.3	3.3	3.1	2.1
1973	93.4	38.8	24.4	13.0	6.9	3.9	3.7	2.6
1972	99.5	40.6	25.0	13.7	7.7	4.6	4.6	3.4
1971	109.1	41.6	26.8	15.5	9.0	5.6	5.9	4.6
1970	113.0	42.4	26.9	15.9	9.7	6.1	6.7	5.3
1969	111.6	41.0	25.6	15.4	9.8	6.5	7.2	6.1
1968	111.9	39.5	24.6	15.3	10.1	6.8	8.3	7.2
1967	117.1	37.6	25.3	16.5	11.2	7.9	9.9	8.8
1966	123.5	36.6	25.5	17.7	12.6	9.2	11.4	10.5
1965	131.9	35.3	26.2	19.3	14.4	10.7	13.6	12.4
1964	140.0	34.4	27.1	20.9	15.8	12.0	15.6	14.3
1963	143.7	33.5	27.4	21.6	16.8	13.0	16.4	15.0
1962	147.8	32.9	27.8	22.7	17.7	13.6	17.5	15.6
1961	153.0	33.5	28.7	23.6	18.7	14.0	18.4	16.0
1960	153.6	33.6	29.3	24.0	18.6	14.1	18.4	15.6
1959	156.0	33.9	29.8	24.4	19.1	14.5	18.7	15.6
1958	160.5	34.7	31.0	25.4	19.5	14.9	19.1	15.9
1957	163.0	36.1	31.6	25.7	19.8	15.3	19.0	15.6
1956	160.9	35.9	31.7	25.2	19.7	15.0	18.7	15.0
1955	155.3	35.0	30.7	24.4	19.1	14.6	17.4	14.1
1954	153.2	35.6	29.7	24.4	19.1	14.2	16.5	13.5
1953	147.2	34.1	29.5	23.8	18.4	13.3	15.4	12.8
1952	143.3	33.1	29.2	24.0	18.1	12.4	14.2	12.4
1951	142.1	34.1	29.9	23.9	16.9	11.2	13.5	12.2
1950	137.3	33.8	30.3	22.9	15.3	10.4	12.6	12.0
1949	135.1	35.4	30.8	21.2	14.0	9.8	12.2	11.8
1948	131.6	37.3	29.5	19.4	12.9	9.2	11.7	11.6
1947	125.9	38.4	26.2	17.3	12.1	8.8	11.4	11.6
1946	113.9	31.1	23.4	16.0	11.8	8.7	11.3	11.7
1945	106.0	27.9	20.1	14.7	11.3	8.7	11.3	11.9
1944	108.5	28.7	21.1	15.6	11.7	8.6	11.3	11.6
1943	111.0	31.0	22.2	15.5	11.4	8.4	11.0	11.6
1942	107.6	31.0	21.1	14.9	10.8	8.1	10.5	11.1
1941	105.4	29.8	20.6	14.5	10.6	8.0	10.6	11.3
1940	102.4	28.6	19.6	14.1	10.5	7.8	10.4	11.3

[1] From 1980-1992, the racial classification was based on the race of the mother. Prior to that it was based on the race of the child.

[2] Births prior to 1960 are adjusted for underregistration.

Source: National Center for Health Statistics, "Vital Statistics of the United States, Volume I--Natality: 1992," National Center for Health Statistics, Hyattsville, MD, 1995, Table 1-11. Data prior to 1960 are from U.S. Bureau of the Census, "Historical Statistics of the United States: Colonial Times to 1970," U.S. Government Printing Office, Washington, D.C., 1975, Table B 11-20.

Table 6-6D. Birth Rates for Blacks[1], by Live-birth Order: 1960-1992

| Year | Total | Live-birth order | | | | | | |
		1	2	3	4	5	6 and 7	8 and over
1992	83.2	30.6	24.3	15.0	7.2	3.3	2.2	0.6
1991	85.2	31.5	25.0	15.4	7.4	3.3	2.1	0.6
1990	86.8	32.4	25.6	15.6	7.4	3.2	2.0	0.6
1989	86.2	32.9	25.4	15.3	7.1	3.0	1.9	0.6
1988	82.6	31.8	24.6	14.4	6.6	2.8	1.8	0.5
1987	80.1	31.2	23.8	13.9	6.3	2.7	1.7	0.5
1986	78.9	31.0	23.4	13.5	6.1	2.6	1.7	0.5
1985	78.8	31.0	23.4	13.4	6.1	2.6	1.7	0.5
1984	78.1	30.9	23.0	13.2	6.0	2.6	1.7	0.6
1983	78.7	31.1	23.1	13.2	6.1	2.7	1.8	0.6
1982	80.9	31.7	23.9	13.8	6.3	2.7	1.8	0.7
1981	82.0	32.3	24.2	13.7	6.3	2.8	1.9	0.8
1980	84.9	33.7	24.7	14.0	6.5	2.9	2.1	0.9
1979	88.3	35.3	25.8	14.4	6.6	3.0	2.2	1.0
1978	86.7	34.6	25.4	13.9	6.5	3.0	2.3	1.1
1977	88.1	35.6	25.5	13.6	6.4	3.1	2.4	1.4
1976	85.8	35.2	24.4	12.9	6.2	3.1	2.6	1.5
1975	87.9	36.9	24.2	12.6	6.3	3.2	2.9	1.9
1974	89.7	37.7	24.2	12.6	6.5	3.4	3.3	2.2
1973	93.6	38.9	24.0	13.0	7.0	4.0	3.9	2.8
1972	99.9	40.7	24.6	13.7	7.9	4.7	4.8	3.6
1971	109.7	41.7	26.6	15.5	9.2	5.7	6.2	4.8
1970	115.4	43.3	27.1	16.1	10.0	6.4	7.0	5.6
1969	112.1	41.2	25.4	15.4	9.9	6.6	7.4	6.3
1968	112.7	39.8	24.4	15.3	10.2	7.0	8.5	7.5
1967	118.5	38.0	25.3	16.5	11.4	8.1	10.1	9.1
1966	124.7	36.9	25.5	17.7	12.7	9.4	11.7	10.8
1965	133.2	35.6	26.1	19.3	14.5	10.9	14.0	12.7
1964	142.6	35.0	27.3	21.1	16.1	12.3	16.1	14.7
1963	—	—	—	—	—	—	—	—
1962	—	—	—	—	—	—	—	—
1961	—	—	—	—	—	—	—	—
1960	153.5	33.6	29.3	24.0	18.6	14.1	18.4	15.6

[1] From 1980-1992, the racial classification was based on the race of the mother. Prior to that it was based on the race of the child.

Source: National Center for Health Statistics, "Vital Statistics of the United States, Volume I--Natality: 1992," National Center for Health Statistics, Hyattsville, MD, 1995, Table 1-11.

Median Age of Mother at Birth of Children

The typical birth mother in the United States is over twenty-six years old at the time of child-bearing (see Table 6-7). Despite the fact that the median age at marriage has fluctuated over a range of more than three years since 1940 and the level of fertility has risen and fallen sharply, the overall median age at childbearing has been only moderately affected. The median age at motherhood does not necessarily rise when the birth rate falls, because lower fertility means fewer higher-order births at older ages. At the height of the baby boom it declined by slightly more than one year; it continued to decline into the 1980s but has risen back to levels near the 1940s in the late 1990s. The decline during the 1980s was caused by cessation of childbearing at later ages rather than the earlier onset of childbearing. The more recent rise is accounted for by a slight rise in childbearing at higher parities and slightly increasing ages of childbearing at the first through third birth order. In fact, as Table 6-7 shows, the age of childbearing at birth orders beyond four has actually decreased.

The median age at childbearing becomes progressively older with increasing birth order. For example, the median age of mothers at the birth of their first child was 24.1 years (for whites) and 22.3 years (for nonwhites) in 1992. For the second birth the median age was about three years later, and for the third and fourth children it was less than one and a half years later than the preceding birth. The median age at first birth is more sensitive to age at marriage than are higher order births.

In all cases the median age of bearing children of a given order is higher for the white than for the other populations. These differentials have been steadily shrinking,

Table 6-7. Median Age of Women at Childbirth, by Race[1] and Birth Order: 1940-1992

Year and race	Total	\multicolumn{7}{c}{Birth order}
		1	2	3	4	5	6 and 7	8 and over
All races								
1992	26.3	23.8	26.9	28.4	29.6	30.8	32.5	36.4
1990	26.3	23.8	26.9	28.4	29.7	31.1	32.8	36.4
1985	26.1	23.5	26.6	28.3	30.0	31.5	33.5	37.1
1980	25.7	23.0	26.1	28.1	30.0	32.0	34.1	37.7
1975	25.3	22.3	25.5	27.8	29.9	32.0	34.2	37.3
1970	25.4	22.1	24.7	27.5	29.4	31.2	32.9	36.0
1965	25.8	21.9	24.2	27.0	28.8	30.3	32.0	35.1
1960	25.4	21.8	24.0	26.6	28.5	29.8	31.6	35.0
1950	25.9	22.5	25.3	27.6	29.2	30.7	32.6	36.7
1940	26.6	23.2	25.6	27.4	29.0	30.9	33.1	37.7
White								
1992	26.6	24.1	27.2	28.9	30.3	31.6	33.5	37.0
1990	26.6	24.1	27.2	28.9	30.3	31.7	33.5	37.0
1985	26.4	23.9	26.9	28.7	30.5	32.1	34.1	37.5
1980	25.9	23.3	26.3	28.4	30.5	32.4	34.6	37.5
1975	25.6	22.7	25.8	28.2	30.5	32.5	34.5	37.5
1970	25.6	22.3	25.0	27.7	29.8	31.7	33.4	36.4
1965	25.9	22.2	24.4	27.3	29.2	31.0	32.7	35.9
1960	25.5	22.0	24.2	26.9	28.8	30.5	32.4	35.8
1950	26.1	22.8	25.7	28.1	29.9	31.6	33.3	37.2
1940	26.9	23.6	26.1	28.0	29.6	31.5	33.7	37.7
Nonwhite								
1992	24.9	22.3	25.2	26.6	27.7	29.0	30.9	34.6
1990	24.9	22.3	25.1	26.7	27.8	29.3	31.3	35.0
1985	24.8	21.9	25.1	27.0	28.5	30.1	32.3	36.3
1980	24.6	21.4	24.7	26.8	28.4	30.3	32.8	37.1
1975	24.1	20.4	23.9	26.1	28.1	30.0	32.8	36.8
1970	24.3	20.4	23.2	25.2	27.4	28.9	31.2	35.4
1965	25.0	20.1	22.7	24.4	26.4	27.9	29.8	34.3
1960	24.9	19.9	22.5	24.1	25.9	27.6	29.6	34.2
1950	24.6	19.8	22.5	24.1	26.2	28.1	30.5	35.6
1940	24.8	19.4	22.2	23.9	26.2	28.4	31.0	36.4
Black								
1992	24.1	21.3	24.3	25.9	27.4	28.6	30.4	33.7
1990	24.1	21.3	24.3	26.2	27.5	28.9	30.9	34.4
1985	24.2	21.1	24.4	26.6	28.3	29.8	32.2	35.6
1980	24.2	20.8	24.2	26.5	28.2	30.1	32.7	36.7
1975	23.8	19.8	23.5	25.7	27.8	29.8	32.7	36.6
1970	24.1	20.0	22.9	24.8	27.1	28.8	31.1	35.3
1965	24.8	19.8	22.5	24.2	26.2	27.8	29.7	34.2
1960	24.8	19.6	22.3	24.0	25.9	27.7	29.6	32.9

[1] From 1980-1992, the racial classification was based on the race of the mother. Prior to that it was based on the race of the child.

Source: National Center for Health Statistics, "Vital Statistics of the United States, Volume I--Natality: 1992," National Center for Health Statistics, Hyattsville, MD, 1995, Table 1-55.

Figure 6-8. Trends in Order-specific Birth Rates, by Race[1]: 1940-1992

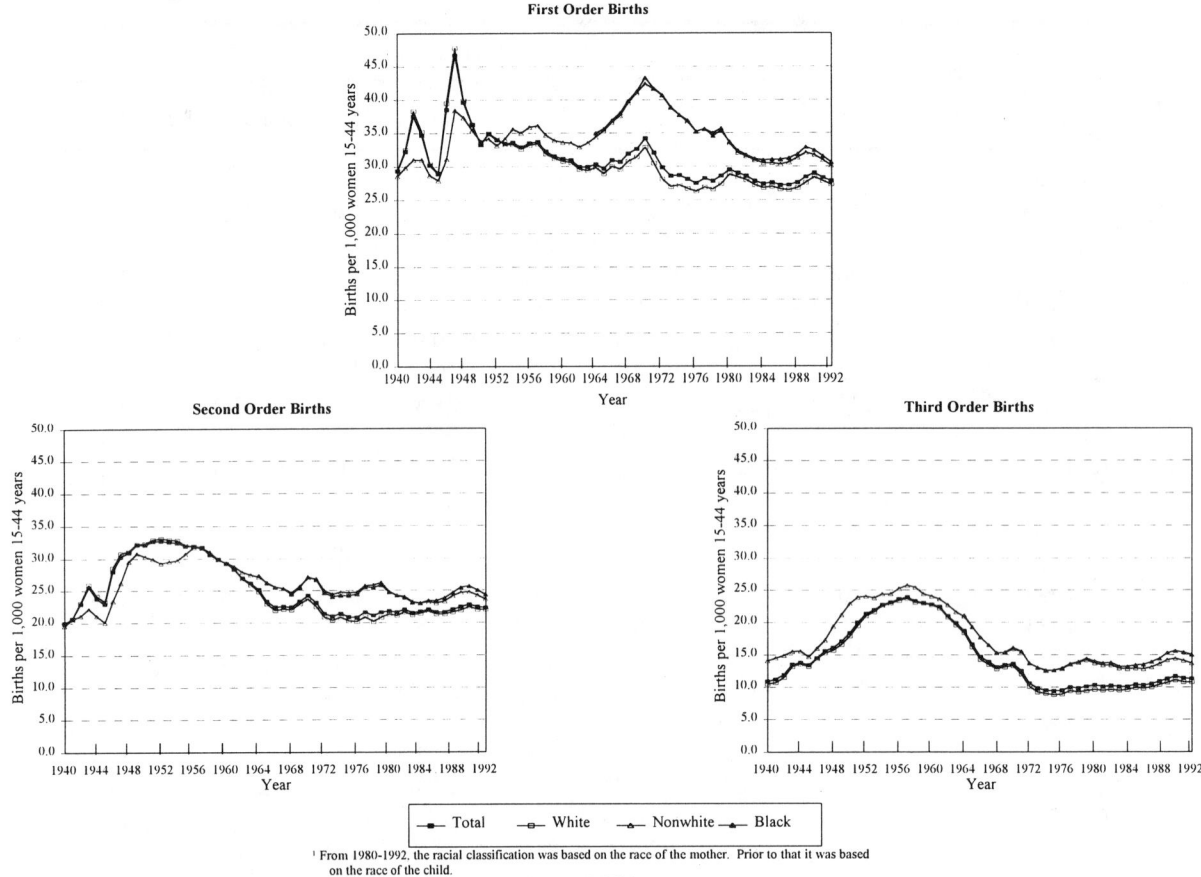

[1] From 1980-1992, the racial classification was based on the race of the mother. Prior to that it was based
on the race of the child.
Source: 1940-1959 U.S. Census data. and 1960-1992 NCHS data.

however. Differentials in white and nonwhite median age at birth have converged most clearly at lower parities. The median age at bearing second children and children of each higher order rose from 1960 through 1980. However, since 1985, the median age at bearing third and higher order children has fallen.

With the onset of the baby boom the median age at the birth of a first, second, third, and fourth child declined in comparison with 1940. With the beginning of the baby bust the process was reversed, and the median age at childbearing at each order became practically identical with what existed in 1940. Median age of mothers at each order has risen substantially since 1960 as fertility declined, especially for second and third births. This implies both a later age at the start of childbearing (with consequent later age at bearing the second child or additional children) and greater spacing between births. The more recent declines in age at birth of higher parities implies some shrinkage in interbirth intervals among the smaller group of women going on to have much larger families. This is likely a selection effect in that women having larger families at younger ages, whether planned or unplanned, are increasingly represented in the population of large families as women who delay childbirth longer at younger parities become less likely to proceed to such high parities.

Overall, as fertility declines and most women bear only one or two children, the ages at which those births occur are drifting slowly upward. However, the rarity of third and higher-order births means that a high percentage of all childbearing is being compressed into ages 25-29 with some spillover into ages 30-34.

Sex Ratio at Birth

Among newborn infants about 51.28 percent are male and 48.72 percent are female. This tendency for male infants to outnumber female infants is observed among almost all human populations. Demographers express this differential as the sex ratio at birth—number of males per 100 or per 1,000 females. Table 6-8 reports the sex ratio for selected years from 1940 to 1992. Sex ratios are also shown separately for the white and black populations. In 1992 the sex ratio of the white population is 105.3 male births for each 100 female births. The corresponding figure for the black population is 103.6. There is little evidence of a trend in the white sex ratio. However, there is a trend toward a rising sex ratio in black births. There is some evidence which suggests that trends in the sex ratio may be related to trends in age at birth. Convergence of white and black sex ratios may then be related to convergence in

Figure 6-8. Trends in Order-specific Birth Rates, by Race[1]: 1940-1992 (continued)

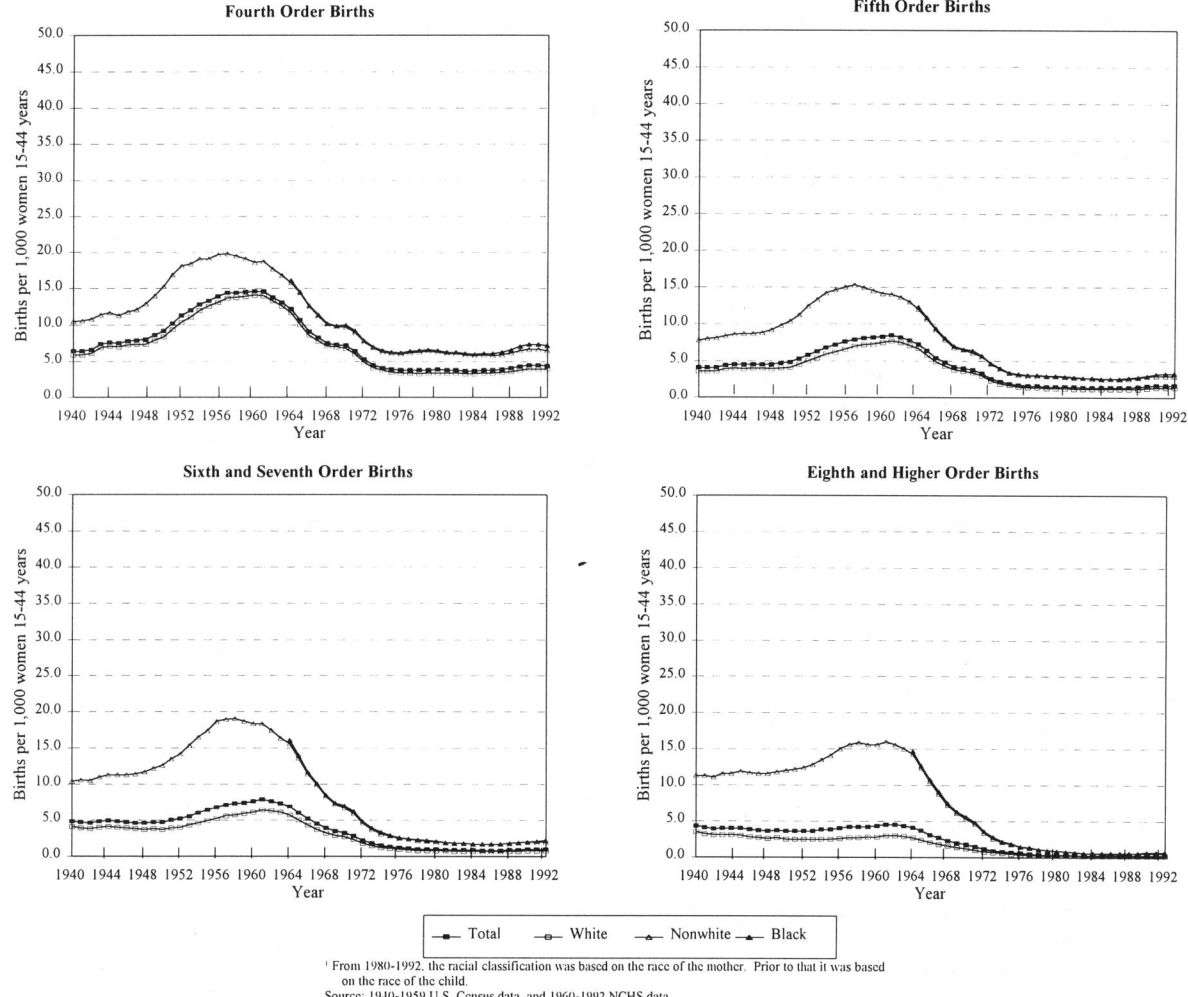

[1] From 1980-1992, the racial classification was based on the race of the mother. Prior to that it was based on the race of the child.
Source: 1940-1959 U.S. Census data, and 1960-1992 NCHS data.

these groups' age-specific fertility rates (Figure 6-8). However, the causes for the race difference in sex ratio at birth and these trends are not fully known. Another theory cites the poor health status and higher rate of pregnancy loss among the nonwhite population as leading to a lower sex ratio. If this were the case, one would have expected a rather dramatic rise in the sex ratio at birth among the black population as prenatal and postnatal care improved. Such a development, if it has taken place, is erratic and negligible in size. And, given the completeness of birth registration, differences in reporting are not a plausible explanation. The fact that the sex ratio of infants, as enumerated at the census, contains this same race differential suggests that it is a genuine difference with a social or physiological explanation not yet fully elaborated.

Nonmarital Fertility or 'Out-of-Wedlock' Births

Until relatively recently it was presumed by many that "normal childbearing" in America (as in Europe and most cultures in less developed countries) should take place within the context of a family in which the father and mother live together and jointly care for their offspring. Sociologists and anthropologists have frequently interpreted this arrangement as a near-universal human adaptation developed in response to the dependent status of women during pregnancy and childbearing and the double task of gaining a livelihood while caring for and shaping the social behavior of helpless infants and dependent children. These social scientists have, for more than half a century, noted the gradual diminution (though not total loss) of other functions formerly performed by the family: production of food and clothing, education, religion, security, recreation and leisure activities, mutual aid in time of crisis, and others. But few of them anticipated or predicted that the family would also lose its tight monopoly of two of its most basic functions: the bearing of children and sex relations. Chapter 11 documents the dramatic increase in premarital and extramarital conjugal living arrangements that have emerged in recent years. This has been paralleled by an unprecedented propensity to bear children out of marriage. Demographers, sociologists, and social welfare experts now discuss changing arrangements for bearing and rearing children in terms of a revolution in family life.

As of 1992, 3 out of every 10 children in the United States were born out of wedlock. For the white population the ratio was nearly 2.3 of every 10, and for the black population it was more than 6.8 of every ten children. This ratio of nonmarital to marital births has increased nearly threefold in the past two decades. And, although the ratio of nonmarital births is much higher among the black population, the increase in this ratio is much higher for whites over the past two decades. The nonmarital ratio for whites in 1992 is nearly fourfold what it was in 1970 and nearly thirteen times greater than what it was in 1950.

Nonmarital childbearing may be measured from two perspectives: from the perspective of the children and from that of the unmarried women who bear them. When viewed from the perspective of children, the appropriate measure is the "out-of-wedlock birth ratio." When viewed from the perspective of women, the appropriate statistic is a birth rate for unmarried women or "nonmarital birth rate," which relates the births to the number of unmarried women (see Definition Box). Figure 6-9 graphs the out-of-wedlock birth ratio for years since 1940. The dramatic rise in the ratios of all race groups is self-evident. This rise in nonmarital fertility represents a stark new phenomenon for the United States population which may prove compa-

Table 6-8. Male: Female Sex Ratio at Birth, by Race[1]: 1940-1992

Year	Total	White	Black
1992	105.0	105.3	103.6
1990	105.0	105.4	102.9
1985	105.2	105.6	102.9
1980	105.3	105.8	102.8
1975	105.4	105.9	103.0
1970	105.5	105.9	103.1
1965	105.1	105.6	102.6
1960	104.9	105.5	101.6
1955	105.1	105.6	102.0
1950	105.4	105.8	102.4
1945	105.5	106.1	102.0
1940	105.5	106.0	102.6

[1] From 1980-1992, the racial classification was based on the race of the mother. Prior to that it was based on the race of the child.

Source: National Center for Health Statistics, "Vital Statistics of the United States, Volume I--Natality: 1992," National Center for Health Statistics, Hyattsville, MD, 1995, Table 1-32.

Table 6-9. Estimated Number of Births to Unmarried Women[1] and Ratio to all Births, by Race[2]: 1940-1992

Year	Number of births				Ratio per 1,000 births			
	Total	White	Nonwhite	Black	Total	White	Nonwhite	Black
1992	1,224,876	721,986	502,890	458,969	301.3	225.5	582.5	681.3
1990	1,165,384	669,698	495,686	455,304	280.3	203.5	571.1	665.3
1985	828,174	445,595	382,579	356,205	220.2	146.7	529.4	612.2
1980	665,747	328,984	336,763	318,799	184.3	112.0	498.2	561.2
1975	447,900	186,400	261,600	249,600	142.5	73.0	441.7	487.9
1970	398,700	175,100	223,600	215,100	106.9	56.6	349.3	375.8
1965	291,200	123,700	167,500	—	77.4	39.5	263.2	—
1960	224,300	82,500	141,800	—	52.7	22.9	215.8	—
1955	183,300	64,200	119,200	—	45.3	18.6	202.4	—
1950	141,600	53,500	88,100	—	39.8	17.5	179.6	—
1945	117,400	56,400	60,900	—	42.9	23.6	179.3	—
1940	89,500	40,300	49,200	—	37.9	19.5	168.3	—

[1] Data on marital status for 1980-1992 were either reported on the birth certificate or inferred from other items on the birth certificate. Prior to 1980, births to unmarried women were estimated for the U.S. from data for registration areas in which the marital status of the mother was reported.

[2] From 1980-1992, the racial classification was based on the race of the mother. Prior to that it was based on the race of the child.

Source: National Center for Health Statistics, "Vital Statistics of the United States, Volume I--Natality: 1992," National Center for Health Statistics, Hyattsville, MD, 1995, Table 1-76.

Figure 6-9. Percent of Births Born out of Wedlock[1], by Race[2]: 1940-1992

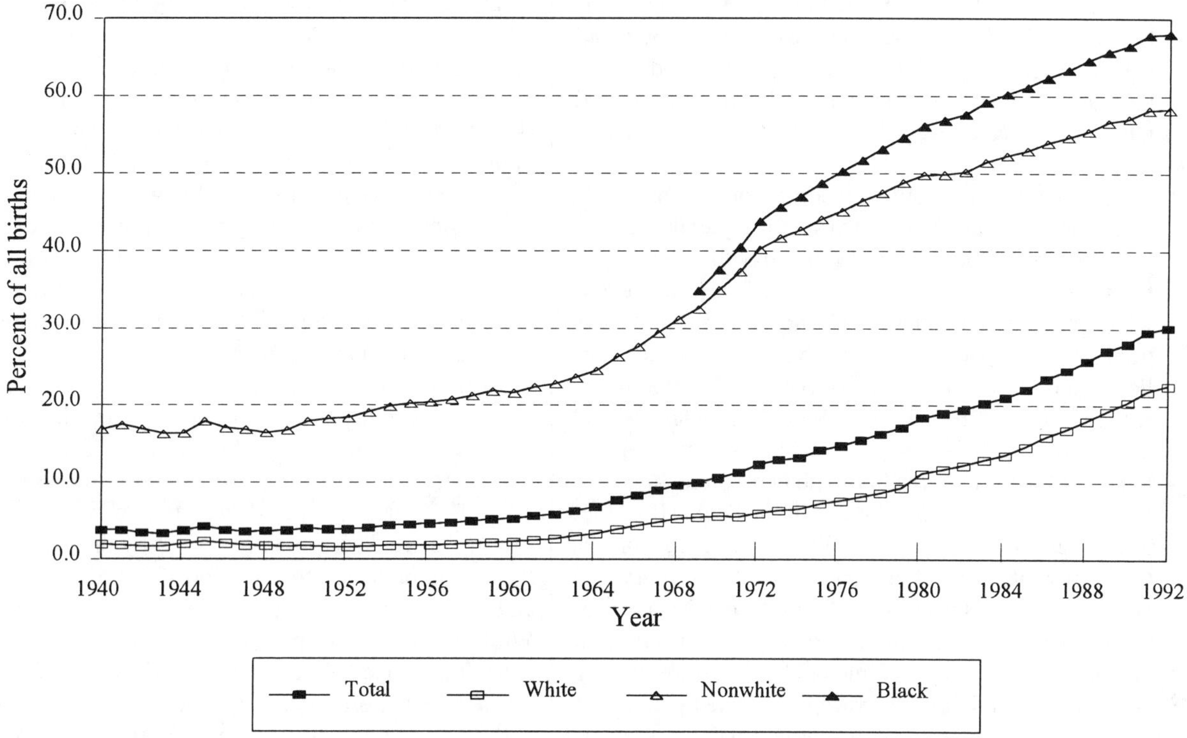

[1] Data on marital status were reported/inferred for 1980-1992 and estimated prior to 1980.
[2] From 1980-1992, the racial classification was based on the race of the mother. Prior to that it was based on the race of the child.
Source: 1940-1992 NCHS data.

Table 6-10. Births to Unmarried Women by Age and Age-specific Nonmarital Birth Ratios, by Race of Mother: 1992

Age of mother	Percent distribution				Ratio per 1,000 live births			
	Total	White	Black	Hispanic	Total	White	Black	Hispanic
All ages	100.0	100.0	100.0	100.0	301.3	225.5	681.3	391.3
Under 15 years	0.9	0.6	1.4	0.9	913.3	848.3	976.4	818.4
15 to 19 years	28.9	28.6	29.6	26.4	700.2	603.5	926.4	618.6
15 years	2.1	1.8	2.6	2.1	869.9	793.2	970.0	762.0
16 years	4.0	3.8	4.4	4.0	815.2	733.4	961.3	712.1
17 years	6.0	6.1	6.1	5.6	755.0	669.0	945.4	652.5
18 years	7.8	8.0	7.7	7.0	692.4	600.0	923.4	605.8
19 years	8.9	9.1	8.8	7.7	609.8	511.0	888.5	543.8
20 to 24 years	35.6	35.8	35.4	34.3	407.0	317.1	752.4	423.1
25 to 29 years	19.1	19.1	18.9	21.4	198.0	142.7	549.8	308.4
30 to 34 years	10.4	10.5	10.2	11.3	143.0	101.5	467.0	272.3
35 to 39 years	4.3	4.5	3.8	4.7	152.2	114.0	447.0	284.7
40 to 49 years	0.8	0.9	0.6	1.0	177.0	146.0	421.2	308.8

Source: National Center for Health Statistics, "Vital Statistics of the United States, Volume I--Natality: 1992," National Center
for Health Statistics, Hyattsville, MD, 1995, Tables 1-46 and 1-79.

rable to the contraceptive revolution or baby boom in its impact on future generations. Although great caution must be exercised in condemnation of new demographic behaviors, the current social fabric does not provide adequate support for single parents and their children (see Chapter 15) and the rise in nonmarital fertility must inevitably be viewed as tragic and with a very real sense of alarm.

It appears that out-of-wedlock births among the nonwhite population have always been higher than among the white population, but in 1940 and before the proportions were a comparative minority of all births to the nonwhite population. In other words, nonwhites followed the traditional two-parent prescription in five out of six families, and only one family in six was an exception to this pattern. Since 1976 the norm for childbearing in the black population has become one of nonmarital fertility; the number of black children born into two-parent families is fewer than the number born out of wedlock. If present trends persist, nonmarital fertility will also become the norm for white populations in the early 21st century.

Nonmarital births, by age of mother and by race, are reported in Table 6-10 as percent distributions and nonmarital birth ratios. Table 6-11 reports age-specific nonmarital fertility rates by race for selected years. Out-of-wedlock childbearing has two principal forms: premarital childbearing by single (never married) women and childbearing by separated, divorced, and widowed women at generally older ages. Table 6-10 makes it clear that teenagers account for a large part (nearly 29 percent) but by no means a majority of the out-of-wedlock childbearing. Over half (roughly 55 percent) of nonmarital fertility occurs between the ages of 20 and 29. A decade earlier, in 1980, teenagers accounted for nearly 40 percent of out-of-wedlock births.

The right-hand panel of Table 6-10 shows that the ratio of out-of-wedlock births to all births is nearly 93 out of every 100 live births to black females under nineteen years of age and is more than 75 percent of live births for those 20-24 years of age. The ratios for white (roughly 85 percent) and Hispanic (nearly 82 percent) women aged 15-19 are nearly as high. The out-of-wedlock ratio declines rapidly for white females after age nineteen and plateaus at about 12 percent after age twenty-five. For black and Hispanic women the ratio of out-of-wedlock births to all births declines more slowly across older ages. Among older black women the nonmarital birth ratio never drops below 42 percent. Among older Hispanic women the nonmarital birth ratio drops to a low point of roughly 27 percent between 30 and 34 years of age.

The rate of bearing children out of wedlock (Table 6-11) has risen significantly since 1975 after nearly fifteen years of relatively stable levels near 25 births per 1,000 unmarried women. For the nonwhite and black populations there have been significant absolute declines in the out-of-wedlock birth rate, especially for ages under twenty-

five. For the white population the rates have risen rapidly for all ages. Thus, in terms of exposure to the bearing of an illegitimate child, the young black unmarried female population appears to be decreasing its exposure to the risk of bearing an out-of-wedlock child, probably by the more prevalent and more effective practice of contraception (which can only still be low). The young unmarried white population is increasing its exposure to risk as a result of premarital sexual activity, possibly with only moderately prevalent use of contraception, and as a matter of choice for some.

As discussed in Chapter 4, there is a possibility that the rates of marital dissolution will stabilize in future years and that postponement of marriage will plateau. If this happens and if the rates of out-of-wedlock childbearing stabilize or decline, there could well be a leveling off in the number of out-of-wedlock births in the late 1990s and thereafter.

The increasing prevalence of out-of-wedlock childbearing is creating a situation whereby the state and the local community are forced to provide economic and social necessities formerly provided by two-parent families. While out-of-wedlock parenthood can no longer be viewed as a minor and temporary aberration, it is still the case that single parents, often female, have not been socially enabled to provide equivalent economic support for children. In fact, given political retrenchment or reduction in social services, the net support available to single-parent children and out-of-wedlock children has likely decreased over the same years as the rising rates of such births. Nonetheless, out-of-wedlock birth has now become an established and widespread situation along with single parents as a family type (see Chapter 11). The prospects for a radical reversal of these new behaviors is not imminent. Thus, new social means for bearing, financing, and rearing children should gain additional moral, economic, and political par with the passage of time along with other necessary cultural adjustments.

Nuptial Fertility

Nuptial fertility is the ratio of "legitimate" births to married women of childbearing age. Because it deals with a universe of women who are highly exposed to childbearing, the rates are much higher than rates based on total women. Table 6-12 reports age-specific nuptial fertility rates for the population, by race. For very young women the rates are extremely high because many are pregnant at the time of marriage or make immediate efforts to become pregnant without delay. As a consequence in a given year about 60 percent of all married girls aged 15-17 bear a child. The rate drops sharply for the successive age groups.

Despite the high rates of out-of-wedlock births for the black population and the rising rates for the white, nuptial fertility rates are far higher at each age for married than for unmarried women (Figure 6-10). Thus, a promi-

Table 6-11. Birth Rates for Unmarried Women[1], by Age of Mother and Race[2]: 1940-1992

| Year and race | 15 to 44 years | 15 to 19 years | | | 20 to 24 years | 25 to 29 years | 30 to 34 years | 35 to 39 years | 40 to 44 years |
		Total	15 to 17 years	18 to 19 years					
All races									
1992	45.2	44.6	30.4	67.3	68.5	56.5	37.9	18.8	4.1
1990	43.8	42.5	29.6	60.7	65.1	56.0	37.6	17.3	3.6
1985	32.8	31.4	22.4	45.9	46.5	39.9	25.2	11.6	2.5
1980	29.4	27.6	20.6	39.0	40.9	34.0	21.1	9.7	2.6
1975	24.5	23.9	19.3	32.5	31.2	27.5	17.9	9.1	2.6
1970	26.4	22.4	17.1	32.9	38.4	37.0	27.1	13.6	3.5
1965	23.4	16.7	—	—	39.6	49.1	37.2	17.4	4.5
1960	21.6	15.3	—	—	39.7	45.1	27.8	14.1	3.6
1950	14.1	12.6	—	—	21.3	19.9	13.3	7.2	2.0
1940	7.1	7.4	—	—	9.5	7.2	5.1	3.4	1.2
White									
1992	35.2	33.0	21.6	51.5	52.7	45.4	31.5	16.2	3.6
1990	32.9	30.6	20.4	44.9	48.2	43.0	29.9	14.5	3.2
1985	22.5	20.8	14.5	31.2	31.7	28.5	18.4	9.0	2.0
1980	18.1	16.5	12.0	24.1	25.1	21.5	14.1	7.1	1.8
1975	12.4	12.0	9.6	16.5	15.5	14.8	9.8	5.4	1.5
1970	13.9	10.9	7.5	17.6	22.5	21.1	14.2	7.6	
1965	11.6	7.9	—	—	22.0	24.3	16.6	4.9	
1960	9.2	6.6	—	—	18.2	18.2	10.8	3.9	
1950	6.1	5.1	—	—	10.0	8.7	5.9	2.0	
1940	3.6	3.3	—	—	5.7	4.0	2.5	1.2	
Nonwhite									
1992	76.1	87.9	64.2	123.9	121.2	86.9	53.6	25.4	5.7
1990	79.7	88.3	65.0	120.6	124.3	94.3	57.8	24.6	5.2
1985	70.1	76.6	57.6	104.7	101.0	74.4	46.4	20.0	4.4
1980	75.2	80.2	62.1	109.3	103.5	76.4	45.2	18.5	5.4
1975	79.0	86.3	70.7	114.3	102.1	73.2	47.9	20.0	6.9
1970	89.9	90.8	73.3	126.5	121.0	93.8	69.8	32.0	10.7
1965	97.4	77.1	—	—	147.8	161.0	131.9	38.7	
1960	98.3	76.5	—	—	166.5	171.8	104.0	35.6	
1950	71.2	68.5	—	—	105.4	94.2	63.5	20.0	
1940	35.6	42.5	—	—	46.1	32.5	23.4	9.3	
Black									
1992	86.5	105.9	78.0	147.8	144.3	98.2	57.7	25.8	5.4
1990	90.5	106.0	78.8	143.7	144.8	105.3	61.5	25.5	5.1
1985	77.0	87.6	66.8	117.9	113.1	79.3	47.5	20.4	4.3
1980	81.1	87.9	68.8	118.2	112.3	81.4	46.7	19.0	5.5
1975	84.2	93.5	76.8	123.8	108.0	75.7	50.0	20.5	7.2
1970	95.5	96.9	77.9	136.4	131.5	100.9	71.8	32.9	10.4

[1] Data on marital status for 1980-1992 were either reported on the birth certificate or inferred from other items on the birth certificate. Prior to 1980, births to unmarried women were estimated for the U.S. from data for registration areas in which marital status was reported.
[2] From 1980-1992, the racial classification was based on the race of the mother. Prior to that it was based on the race of the child.

Source: National Center for Health Statistics, "Vital Statistics of the United States, Volume I--Natality: 1992," National Center for Health Statistics, Hyattsville, MD, 1995, Table 1-77.

Table 6-12. Birth Rates for Married Women[1], by Age of Mother and Race[2]: 1950-1992

Year and race	15 to 44 years	15 to 19 years Total	15 to 17 years	18 to 19 years	20 to 24 years	25 to 29 years	30 to 34 years	35 to 39 years	40 to 44 years
All races									
1992	89.0	397.8	579.9	358.8	212.9	160.0	98.5	37.3	6.8
1990	93.2	420.2	610.9	385.1	216.7	161.8	97.7	36.4	6.2
1985	93.3	357.4	483.7	327.5	206.2	149.6	84.9	27.7	4.6
1980	97.0	349.5	486.1	318.0	202.4	145.2	72.5	22.0	4.4
1975	92.1	313.1	482.1	270.6	178.5	129.7	58.6	21.3	5.3
1970	121.1	443.7	720.3	386.3	246.6	164.3	79.2	34.2	9.5
1965	130.2	462.7	—	—	273.6	178.6	100.4	49.9	14.8
1960	156.6	530.6	—	—	353.6	221.0	123.9	61.8	18.3
1950	141.0	410.4	—	—	282.6	191.8	115.7	59.0	18.3
White									
1992	89.6	389.2	—	—	211.8	161.6	99.1	37.0	6.6
1990	94.1	414.4	—	—	216.3	164.4	98.9	36.1	6.0
1985	94.1	348.5	—	—	204.9	151.3	86.1	27.1	4.3
1980	97.5	352.7	—	—	201.9	147.1	71.9	21.0	4.0
1975	91.5	309.4	—	—	177.0	130.1	58.2	20.1	4.9
1970	119.6	431.8	—	—	244.0	164.9	78.2	32.7	8.8
1965	127.5	443.2	—	—	270.9	177.3	98.9	30.8	
1960	153.6	513.0	—	—	352.5	220.5	121.6	39.7	
1950	139.3	398.5	—	—	281.2	193.1	115.9	39.3	
Nonwhite									
1992	84.8	492.6	—	—	221.6	149.5	94.9	39.5	8.0
1990	87.4	507.9	—	—	220.3	145.7	90.4	37.9	8.0
1985	87.4	484.2	—	—	217.3	137.7	77.1	32.4	6.5
1980	93.5	320.0	—	—	207.2	131.3	76.2	29.6	7.0
1975	96.2	342.5	—	—	189.1	126.8	62.1	30.4	8.3
1970	132.8	522.4	—	—	267.6	159.3	86.7	46.1	14.5
1965	150.9	602.4	—	—	293.3	188.6	110.3	42.9	
1960	180.9	659.3	—	—	361.8	225.0	142.1	53.5	
1950	155.8	475.2	—	—	292.4	180.2	113.9	46.9	
Black									
1992	76.8	511.0	—	—	222.3	132.8	79.2	31.8	6.0
1990	79.7	486.8	—	—	225.2	130.6	75.4	30.1	6.1
1985	81.8	556.5	—	—	212.8	127.9	66.4	26.5	5.2
1980	89.2	340.4	—	—	205.7	122.3	67.0	25.7	6.1
1975	91.8	318.8	—	—	188.7	117.3	54.3	27.6	8.3
1970	130.3	533.3	—	—	263.2	148.3	81.0	44.6	14.2

[1] Data on marital status for 1980-1992 were either reported on the birth certificate or inferred from other items on the birth certificate. Prior to 1980, births to unmarried women were estimated for the U.S. from data for registration areas in which marital status was reported.

[2] From 1980-1992, the racial classification was based on the race of the mother. Prior to that it was based on the race of the child.

Source: National Center for Health Statistics, "Vital Statistics of the United States, Volume I--Natality: 1992," National Center for Health Statistics, Hyattsville, MD, 1995, Table 1-78.

Figure 6-10. Age-specific Nuptial and Nonmarital Fertility Rates, by Race of Mother: 1992

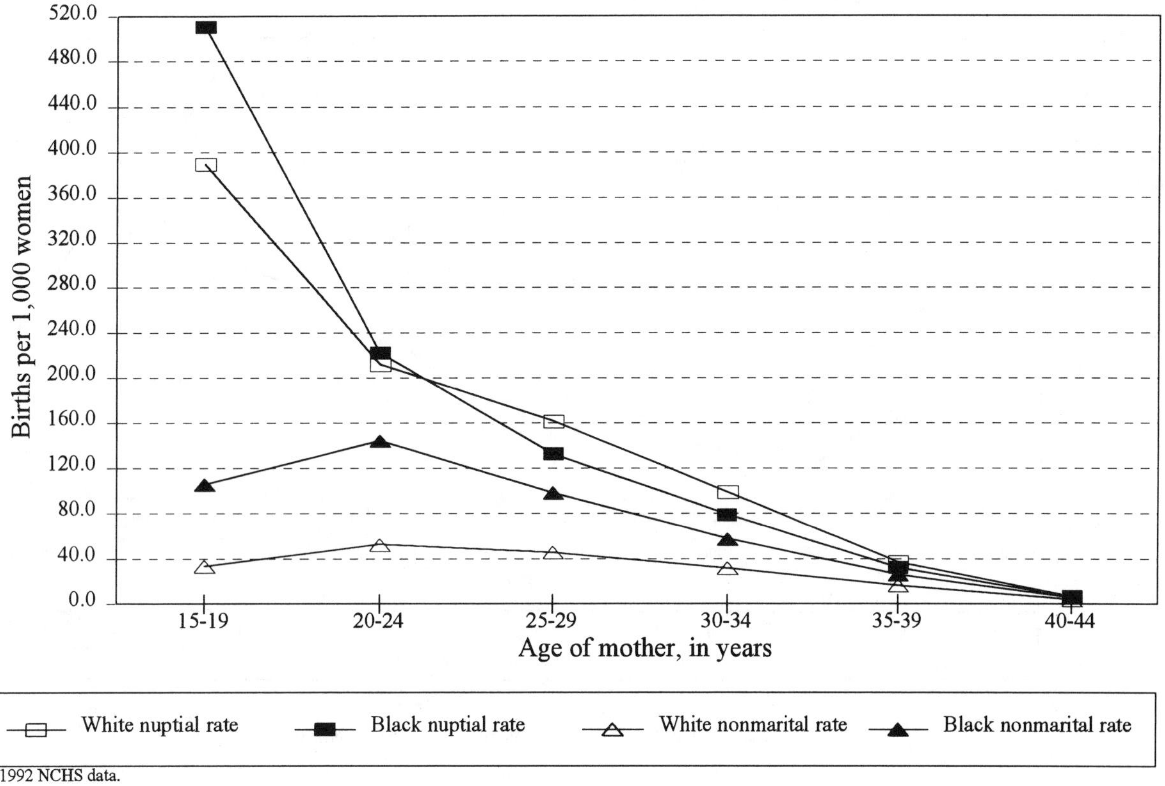

Source: 1992 NCHS data.

nent indirect cause for fertility decline has been postponement of marriage, even though that postponement meant more out-of-wedlock childbearing. The race differential in fertility is also much lower among the married than among the unmarried population. In fact, past age twenty-four (including peak childbearing years), black nuptial fertility is lower than that of whites. For younger ages there is substantially higher black than white fertility within marriage. The main source of the race differential in nuptial fertility has been in the greater childbearing of black wives under twenty-five years of age.

For the age group 20-24 the race differential has been quite modest—even during the baby boom. The decline in fertility since 1960—the baby bust—is a joint contribution of both black and white married couples of all ages. The fertility decline has been greater on an absolute basis (change in fertility rate) and a relative basis (percentage change in fertility rate) for the black than for the white married couples.

Cohort Fertility

The measures of fertility discussed thus far are all cross-sectional or static, because they refer to the rate of childbearing in a particular year. In order to develop summary measures suggesting fertility across the life course, such as the total fertility rate, it has been necessary to imagine a hypothetical situation where a group of women go through life exposed to the conditions of fertility that happen to be in effect in that single year. This hypothetical experience is sometimes called a 'synthetic' cohort. An alternative approach is to study real cohorts of women, tracing them from year to year and observing their birth rates as they change in response to increasing age, number of children already born, and changing social and economic conditions. Real cohorts may differ from each other. One cohort may be exposed to a set of social and economic conditions greatly different from that faced by another, with the result that its fertility may be stimulated or retarded. Changing attitudes and values with respect to marriage, family life, childbearing, and women's status may cause one cohort to behave very differently than another with respect to fertility.

Completed Real Cohort Fertility

If the births that occur to a cohort of women, such as those born between 1941 and 1945, are cumulated statistically, by 1990 those women all passed their forty-fifth birthday and the children they have borne per 1,000 women can be considered their completed cohort fertility. The cohort of women born between 1931 and 1935, a decade

**Figure 6-11. Cumulative Cohort Fertility of Birth Cohorts
Reaching Age 45-49 Between 1940 and 1990**

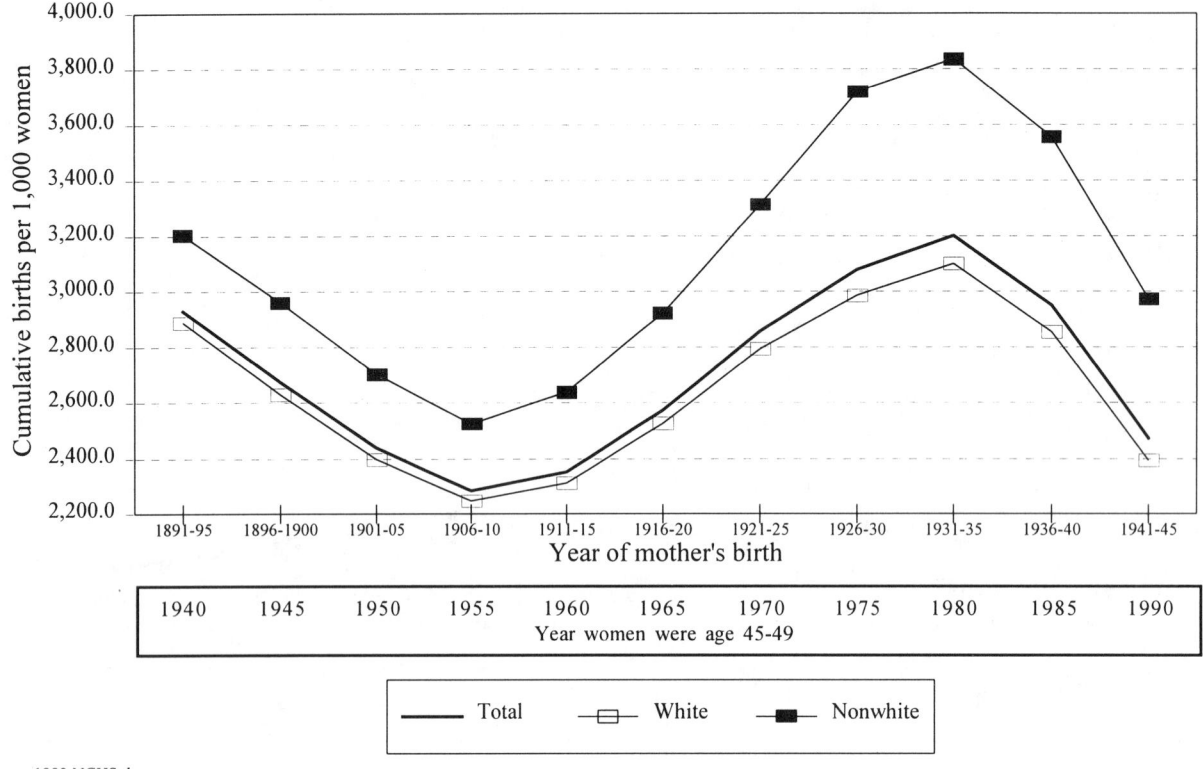

Source: 1992 NCHS data.

earlier, completed their childbearing by 1980. This earlier cohort happens to be one that produced much of the peak fertility of the baby boom. They married early (see Chapter 5) and were at prime childbearing age (22 to 27) when the baby boom reached its pinnacle in 1957. They continued to bear children at a time when birth rates were declining moderately. When the "baby bust" period began in earnest (1970) these women had already reached ages 35-40 and hence were not greatly affected by it. As a consequence the completed cohort fertility for this group of women is quite high—3.2 live births per woman. In contrast, the most recent cohort to complete fertility, i.e. those born from 1941 to 1945, married at somewhat older ages and were at prime childbearing age toward the tail end of the baby boom (see Figure 6-11).

The lowest completed cohort fertility on record thus far is for women born in 1906-10. They married between 1926 and 1930 and reached prime childbearing age just in time to suffer the full impact of the Great Depression. When economic prosperity finally began to return in the 1940s, they were already past thirty-five years of age and too near menopause to participate much in the rising fertility. As a consequence the completed cohort fertility for this group is very low—only 2.3 births per woman, or nearly one child less than the "baby boom" cohort. Table 6-13 summarizes the completed cohort fertility of eleven five-

year cohorts of women and by race. These data report not only the cumulative fertility per 1,000 women when they had reached age forty-five or beyond, but also the distribution of these births by order—how many were first births, second births, and so on.

Figure 6-11 charts the completed fertility of these women. The completed fertility of the real cohort that participated most in the baby boom was attained in 1980 at the height of a "baby bust." The women who created the baby boom had a larger average number of children upon completing fertility than any generation of women born since 1891.

The cohort fertility of the black population follows the same historical trend as that of the white, but with an important difference: The baby boom boosted the completed fertility of black women born in 1931-35 to a peak far higher than that of any generation of black women on record—3.8 births per woman. The disparity between the two races narrowed during the years of declining fertility but widened dramatically during the years of the baby boom generation. As fertility has declined in the baby bust to levels near those after the turn of the last century, these differentials have again begun to decrease.

The cohort approach emphasizes that the fertility behavior of women is influenced not only by their age but also by the number of children they have already borne

Table 6-13. Cumulative Fertility Rate and Live Birth Order, by Race for Cohorts of Women Age 45-49 Years and Born Between 1891 and 1945

Race and cohort	As of January 1	Total	Live-birth order							
			1	2	3	4	5	6	7	8 and over
Total										
1941-1945	1990	2,471.5	884.7	749.4	438.6	212.5	96.9	45.8	21.8	21.8
1936-1940	1985	2,949.4	910.4	803.3	557.6	321.5	168.9	88.9	46.5	52.3
1931-1935	1980	3,201.2	912.8	816.5	597.7	373.6	213.7	122.3	69.8	94.8
1926-1930	1975	3,078.7	894.5	780.8	554.3	344.6	201.2	119.2	71.7	112.4
1921-1925	1970	2,856.1	891.4	739.4	490.6	293.6	170.1	102.1	62.6	106.3
1916-1920	1965	2,572.9	851.0	672.0	420.2	245.6	142.8	87.0	55.0	99.3
1911-1915	1960	2,352.7	809.8	601.2	363.1	213.2	128.0	81.8	53.0	102.6
1906-1910	1955	2,284.4	784.4	559.2	340.5	209.0	131.5	87.1	57.9	114.8
1901-1905	1950	2,439.6	798.0	570.4	364.2	234.8	154.5	105.9	71.2	140.6
1896-1900	1945	2,673.5	805.4	604.7	409.4	272.8	184.9	131.4	89.9	175.0
1891-1895	1940	2,929.6	807.2	635.3	458.0	318.7	220.8	159.3	110.9	219.4
White										
1941-1945	1990	2,394.1	882.6	747.5	424.6	193.5	81.1	34.9	15.4	14.5
1936-1940	1985	2,854.7	913.7	806.6	549.0	301.9	147.0	70.5	33.3	32.7
1931-1935	1980	3,101.0	921.5	824.7	593.6	357.1	191.2	100.7	52.5	59.7
1926-1930	1975	2,985.8	905.9	791.7	551.6	329.3	180.5	99.3	54.8	72.7
1921-1925	1970	2,793.1	905.8	755.1	490.6	281.8	153.8	85.9	49.1	71.0
1916-1920	1965	2,525.9	865.4	689.5	420.8	235.6	129.1	73.8	43.5	68.2
1911-1915	1960	2,312.2	822.6	617.6	363.5	204.5	116.5	70.5	43.1	73.9
1906-1910	1955	2,247.4	792.1	574.0	340.8	201.9	122.3	77.7	49.7	88.9
1901-1905	1950	2,397.5	802.0	582.5	364.2	228.4	146.1	96.7	63.1	114.5
1896-1900	1945	2,629.1	806.8	614.7	408.8	267.3	178.3	123.1	82.0	148.1
1891-1895	1940	2,888.0	808.2	640.7	456.1	314.7	216.7	152.4	104.6	194.6
Nonwhite										
1941-1945	1990	2,972.0	897.6	761.1	531.0	338.0	199.6	115.6	62.3	66.8
1936-1940	1985	3,555.3	888.2	780.5	612.3	446.7	309.6	208.2	131.3	178.5
1931-1935	1980	3,835.5	854.9	761.5	620.7	480.2	358.5	260.2	181.8	317.7
1926-1930	1975	3,717.9	812.6	701.7	571.6	450.5	344.2	258.4	189.1	389.8
1921-1925	1970	3,314.1	782.2	618.8	487.0	378.8	289.7	221.0	164.7	371.9
1916-1920	1965	2,921.6	733.7	531.7	410.8	319.6	247.0	189.3	144.4	345.1
1911-1915	1960	2,638.0	703.8	471.5	355.1	276.8	212.5	166.5	127.5	324.3
1906-1910	1955	2,525.5	712.5	445.8	331.2	258.0	197.9	154.3	118.7	307.1
1901-1905	1950	2,702.5	749.5	473.6	355.8	274.8	212.4	169.3	130.2	336.9
1896-1900	1945	2,960.9	772.4	517.5	403.2	305.7	231.4	192.4	149.8	388.5
1891-1895	1940	3,204.3	777.5	570.9	458.4	343.8	251.1	210.7	162.1	429.8

Source: National Center for Health Statistics, "Vital Statistics of the United States, Volume I--Natality: 1992," National Center for Health Statistics, Hyattsville, MD, 1995, Table 1-16.

and how many more they wish to have. Therefore, one of the most sensitive ways of studying birth trends is to examine the changes that take place in birth probabilities (see Definition Box), made specific for both parities. Table 6-13 also presents cumulative fertility rates by live birth order. These data reflect the fertility trends discussed earlier in this chapter.

Those in prime childbearing years during the emergence from the Great Depression in 1940 were born roughly between 1906 and 1920. The earlier they were born the more likely they were older at the time of the emergence and hence at higher orders of childbearing during that event. Those in the 1910 cohort had the lowest cumulative fertility rates at birth orders under four, indicating the impact of the Depression on early childbearing. By the 1911 cohort, cumulative fertility at smaller, earlier, parities had begun to increase once again. In the nonwhite population this increase in fertility after the Depression was

Table 6-14. Percent Distribution of Live Births, by Interval Since last Live Birth, and Age and Race of Mother: 1992

Race and interval since last live birth	Total, second or higher order births	Age of mother									
		Under 15 years	15 to 19 years			20 to 24 years	25 to 29 years	30 to 34 years	35 to 39 years	40 to 44 years	45 to 49 years
			Total	15 to 17 years	18 to 19 years						
All races	100.0	100.0	100.0	100.0	100.0	100.0	100.0	100.0	100.0	100.0	100.0
0 months (plural deliveries)	2.0	15.2	2.7	3.9	2.4	1.8	1.9	2.0	2.1	1.7	2.2
1 to 11 months	1.8	12.0	6.8	8.7	6.3	3.0	1.3	0.8	0.6	0.5	—
12 to 17 months	11.5	44.9	32.0	39.0	30.0	17.8	9.7	6.8	5.5	4.1	2.2
18 to 23 months	14.0	18.4	25.0	26.0	24.7	18.6	13.3	11.1	9.0	6.8	4.7
24 to 35 months	23.8	8.0	23.9	18.6	25.4	27.4	24.5	22.8	18.4	14.7	9.7
36 to 47 months	15.3	—	7.2	3.1	8.3	15.6	16.3	16.4	13.8	11.1	8.3
48 to 59 months	9.5	—	1.9	0.5	2.3	8.4	10.7	10.5	9.9	8.5	7.3
60 to 71 months	6.2	—	0.4	0.1	0.5	4.2	7.5	7.2	7.4	6.7	7.7
72 months and over	16.0	—	0.1	—	0.1	3.3	14.8	22.4	33.3	46.0	57.4
White	100.0	100.0	100.0	100.0	100.0	100.0	100.0	100.0	100.0	100.0	100.0
0 months (plural deliveries)	1.9	19.0	2.8	4.4	2.4	1.7	1.8	2.0	2.2	1.8	2.9
1 to 11 months	1.4	—	6.3	8.7	5.7	2.4	1.1	0.7	0.5	0.5	—
12 to 17 months	10.3	43.8	31.5	39.9	29.6	16.7	9.1	6.3	5.2	3.9	—
18 to 23 months	13.9	15.3	25.6	26.2	25.5	18.8	13.6	11.3	9.2	7.0	3.8
24 to 35 months	24.8	—	24.8	17.7	26.4	28.5	25.7	24.0	19.3	15.4	9.6
36 to 47 months	16.0	—	7.0	2.6	8.0	16.0	16.9	17.1	14.5	11.5	8.3
48 to 59 months	9.8	—	1.7	0.4	2.0	8.5	10.8	10.7	10.2	8.7	7.3
60 to 71 months	6.3	—	0.3	—	0.4	4.2	7.4	7.1	7.5	6.8	7.6
72 months and over	15.5	—	0.1	—	0.1	3.1	13.7	20.7	31.5	44.5	58.8
Black	100.0	100.0	100.0	100.0	100.0	100.0	100.0	100.0	100.0	100.0	100.0
0 months (plural deliveries)	2.2	13.4	2.7	3.3	2.4	2.1	2.1	2.2	2.2	1.5	—
1 to 11 months	3.5	10.6	7.6	8.6	7.2	4.5	2.6	1.7	1.1	0.7	—
12 to 17 months	16.1	44.9	32.4	37.8	30.3	20.3	12.1	8.7	6.8	4.5	—
18 to 23 months	14.1	21.3	24.1	26.0	23.4	17.6	11.3	8.9	7.3	5.0	—
24 to 35 months	19.8	9.3	22.9	19.8	24.1	24.5	18.2	15.2	13.0	10.3	—
36 to 47 months	12.2	—	7.5	3.8	9.0	14.4	13.3	11.3	9.4	7.6	—
48 to 59 months	8.2	—	2.2	0.5	2.8	8.1	10.6	9.0	7.7	6.7	—
60 to 71 months	5.8	—	0.5	—	0.7	4.4	8.4	7.5	6.3	6.2	—
72 months and over	18.2	—	0.1	—	0.2	4.1	21.5	35.5	46.2	57.4	61.7

Source: National Center for Health Statistics, "Vital Statistics of the United States, Volume I--Natality: 1992," National Center for Health Statistics, Hyattsville, MD, 1995, Table 1-63.

more significant and shows an impact across all parities. By the 1921 cohort cumulative fertility for the total population increased across all parities. Similarly, the peak fertility at the time of the 1955 peak of the baby boom would have been for those in the 1931 to 1935 cohort, which displays the highest cumulative fertility across all but the very highest, i.e. greater than seven, parities for both the white and nonwhite population. And, the most recent cohort with completed fertility, that born in 1941-1945, shows a decrease of cumulative fertility at all parities leading into the 1976 baby bust. Again, the decrease in fertility is evident in both the white and nonwhite population.

Birth Intervals

Instead of measuring fertility in terms of fertility rates, demographers often study it in terms of the intervals between live births. Some couples appear to be more fecund (conceive more readily) than others. As a result, the inter-

val between one birth and the next is very short, unless the couple does something to postpone conception. Some deliberately have births at a rapid pace and then stop childbearing, while others space them farther apart or postpone them until particular objectives have been attained. Hence the study of the changing length between intervals reveals changes in the timing and spacing of births. In turn, the study of birth spacing reveals much about the family building patterns and intentions of the population which may reflect either current circumstances or changing norms of behavior.

Table 6-14 provides statistics that reveal the basic pattern of birth spacing in the population by race and age of mother. Nearly one-quarter of all births have an interval of 24-35 months (2-3 years) from the preceding live birth, with a wide dispersion between 12-17 months on one side and over 72 months (six years) on the other. The percentage of births that occur after extremely long intervals of seven years or more has increased substantially over the

Table 6-15. Mean Interval Since Last Live Birth, by Live-Birth Order and Age and Race of Mother: 1992 [in months]

Live-birth order and race of mother	Total	Under 15 years	15 to 19 years	20 to 24 years	25 to 29 years	30 to 34 years	35 to 39 years	40 to 44 years	45 to 49 years
All races, mean interval -- all births of second and higher order	45.5	46.6	22.0	31.5	43.5	52.6	67.0	88.5	113.0
Interval between first and second births	45.8	16.3	22.7	34.3	46.8	54.8	69.8	91.9	121.4
Interval between second and third births	47.5	18.8	19.6	28.5	43.1	55.5	73.9	106.8	157.0
Interval between third and fourth births	43.2	—	17.7	24.0	35.5	47.5	64.3	93.0	129.8
Interval between fourth and fifth births	40.4	—	16.6	21.5	30.2	41.5	56.7	80.0	118.0
Interval between fifth and sixth births	36.9	—	17.0	19.5	26.1	35.2	47.7	67.8	92.0
Interval between sixth and seventh births	35.2	—	—	18.7	23.5	30.7	42.7	59.4	81.5
Interval since last child and eighth and higher births	32.6	—	—	23.8	22.7	27.3	32.9	45.2	59.4
White, mean interval -- all births of second and higher order	45.3	16.8	22.0	31.8	42.9	51.1	64.8	86.2	116.2
Interval between first and second births	44.9	16.1	22.5	33.8	45.2	52.2	65.9	87.3	118.1
Interval between second and third births	47.9	—	19.9	28.8	42.6	54.0	71.7	104.6	158.2
Interval between third and fourth births	44.2	—	18.2	24.6	35.6	46.7	62.6	91.0	132.4
Interval between fourth and fifth births	42.0	—	17.0	22.2	30.8	41.3	55.8	77.2	117.1
Interval between fifth and sixth births	38.8	—	—	20.6	26.8	35.3	48.0	66.3	93.7
Interval between sixth and seventh births	37.2	—	—	20.0	24.5	31.1	42.7	57.6	89.8
Interval since last child and eighth and higher births	34.7	—	—	26.9	25.2	28.5	33.1	45.9	64.9
Black, mean interval -- all births of second and higher order	46.2	16.6	22.1	31.3	48.4	65.3	83.8	108.0	121.6
Interval between first and second births	51.3	16.6	23.2	36.7	60.8	83.1	109.1	141.8	135.0
Interval between second and third births	45.8	—	19.3	28.1	46.1	67.0	92.8	126.6	159.4
Interval between third and fourth births	39.8	—	17.4	23.2	35.8	51.6	73.8	106.8	120.3
Interval between fourth and fifth births	36.4	—	16.4	21.0	29.4	42.5	60.5	91.8	—
Interval between fifth and sixth births	32.9	—	17.1	19.0	25.3	35.6	47.4	75.2	—
Interval between sixth and seventh births	31.3	—	—	18.2	22.7	30.2	43.4	65.3	—
Interval since last child and eighth and higher births	29.1	—	—	20.7	20.9	26.2	33.4	46.8	61.5

Source: National Center for Health Statistics, "Vital Statistics of the United States, Volume I--Natality: 1992," National Center for Health Statistics, Hyattsville, MD, 1995, Table 1-65.

Table 6-16. Percent Distribution of Live Births, by Interval Since Last Live Birth, Live-birth Order, and Age of Mother: 1992

Interval since last birth and live-birth order	Number	Total	Percent distribution by age of mother						
			15 to 19 years	20 to 24 years	25 to 29 years	30 to 34 years	35 to 39 years	40 to 44 years	45 to 49 years
Second births since birth of first child	1,311,397	100.0	7.8	27.2	31.5	24.3	8.2	1.1	...
0 months (plural deliveries)	16,561	100.0	13.1	23.5	28.7	23.9	9.2	1.2	0.1
1 to 11 months	17,229	100.0	33.5	38.5	17.2	8.1	2.2	0.3	...
12 to 17 months	124,062	100.0	23.1	38.0	22.6	12.3	3.5	0.3	...
18 to 23 months	169,467	100.0	14.3	33.8	27.9	18.4	5.0	0.5	...
24 to 35 months	310,566	100.0	7.9	30.4	31.3	23.5	6.2	0.6	...
36 to 47 months	203,728	100.0	3.8	29.2	32.4	26.2	7.5	0.8	...
48 to 59 months	121,702	100.0	1.7	28.2	34.8	25.8	8.4	1.0	...
60 to 71 months	77,496	100.0	0.6	23.9	39.5	25.8	9.1	1.2	...
72 months and over	192,797	100.0	0.1	7.8	36.3	35.9	17.0	2.9	0.1
Third births since birth of first child	665,150	100.0	3.3	22.2	31.4	29.4	12.0	1.7	...
0 months (plural deliveries)	14,568	100.0	5.7	22.6	30.7	28.9	10.8	1.2	0.1
1 to 11 months	11,544	100.0	16.7	45.5	23.5	10.9	3.1	0.3	...
12 to 17 months	71,056	100.0	11.6	40.6	26.9	15.8	4.5	0.5	...
18 to 23 months	83,663	100.0	6.2	34.9	30.6	21.4	6.3	0.6	...
24 to 35 months	138,173	100.0	2.8	28.6	33.2	26.4	8.2	0.8	...
36 to 47 months	92,411	100.0	0.9	20.9	35.9	31.2	10.2	0.9	...
48 to 59 months	61,969	100.0	0.3	14.4	38.4	33.8	12.0	1.2	...
60 to 71 months	42,600	100.0	0.1	8.8	39.1	36.4	14.1	1.5	...
72 months and over	114,895	100.0	...	2.1	23.6	42.4	26.4	5.3	0.2
Fourth births since birth of first child	260,751	100.0	1.5	18.1	30.2	31.5	15.8	2.8	0.1
0 months (plural deliveries)	7,589	100.0	2.7	19.3	30.1	32.2	14.0	1.6	...
1 to 11 months	6,181	100.0	7.5	43.6	29.1	15.1	4.4	0.4	...
12 to 17 months	35,617	100.0	4.6	37.2	31.6	19.6	6.4	0.6	...
18 to 23 months	37,080	100.0	2.0	27.3	33.8	26.4	9.4	1.0	...
24 to 35 months	55,141	100.0	0.7	19.4	34.6	31.3	12.4	1.5	...
36 to 47 months	32,371	100.0	0.3	12.3	34.1	36.0	15.0	2.2	...
48 to 59 months	20,754	100.0	0.1	7.1	32.9	39.1	18.2	2.5	0.1
60 to 71 months	14,094	100.0	0.1	3.7	29.4	42.1	21.5	3.2	0.1
72 months and over	37,126	100.0	...	1.0	14.6	39.0	35.1	9.8	0.4

Source: National Center for Health Statistics, "Vital Statistics of the United States, Volume I–Natality: 1992," National Center for Health Statistics, Hyattsville, MD, 1995, Table 1-66.

past decade as older women have increased their fertility. If an interval of at least two years is accepted as minimally desirable for the health of both the mother and child, then more than one-quarter of all births in the United States are too closely spaced. Close spacing is somewhat more prevalent among the black than among the white population, but the black population also has higher proportions with extremely long spacing. Spacing is likely to be short for women under twenty-five who bear children, and very short for teenage mothers. For women aged thirty and above, the percentage with extremely long intervals tends to increase sharply with age. A high proportion of such births occur to women who bore their last child in their twenties and then have another in their late thirties. Long spacing is particularly prevalent among older black women.

Unfortunately, data which would allow one to follow cohorts of women through their life history of birth spacing within completed fertility groups is not routinely available. Table 6-15, however, does present birth intervals by age and parity. The current pattern of birth spacing is that of longer intervals in the first few parities and decreasing birth intervals with increasing parity. Since only those with relatively shorter birth intervals will likely progress to higher parities within their fecund years, this pattern is typical. The black population, however, has much longer intervals between the first and second, as well as second and third births, then has shorter birth intervals at higher parities. These racial differences reflect the higher rates of adolescent pregnancy with longer delays before continued childbearing among the black population coupled with higher fertility at older ages among the white population (see Figure 6-5). These same racial differences persist in the prime childbearing years when age is controlled for.

As women get older, the length of birth intervals increases at all parities. However, the greatest absolute increase in birth intervals with age is for those women at the lowest parities (see Figure 6-12). To some extent this represents an increasing proportion of subfecund women, contraceptive failures and birth spacing, and women at older ages and low parities who nonetheless end up progressing to the next parity. Racial differences in birth intervals across parities, with longer intervals at earlier parities for blacks and longer intervals at later parities for whites, persist across all ages. The racial gap in birth intervals generally widens in absolute terms as women advance in age.

Table 6-16 looks at birth intervals in a different fashion. This table shows the percent distribution of women across age who have birth intervals of a given duration at parities two through four. This table more clearly shows that those at longer intervals are predominantly older women. Among second births, those with intervals from 1 to 23 months have a median age of 20 to 24 years. Those with second birth intervals over 24 months have a median age of 25 to 29 years. At third births the median age of

Table 6-17. Percent Distribution of Live Births, by Interval Since Last Live Birth and Race of Mother: Baby Boom Tail (1969), Baby Bust (1976), and Baby Boom Echo (1990)

Race and interval since last live birth	Baby boom echo (1990)	Baby bust (1976)	Baby boom tail (1969[1])
All races	100.0	100.0	100.0
0 months (plural deliveries)	1.8	1.4	⎡ 3.5
1 to 11 months	1.7	1.7	⎣
12 to 17 months	11.6	10.5	14.3
18 to 23 months	13.9	12.7	14.3
24 to 35 months	23.1	22.9	24.0
36 to 47 months	15.1	16.4	15.2
48 to 59 months	9.8	11.2	9.9
60 to 71 months	6.5	8.0	6.4
72 months and over	16.4	15.2	12.3
White	100.0	100.0	100.0
0 months (plural deliveries)	1.8	1.4	⎡ 3.1
1 to 11 months	1.3	1.5	⎣
12 to 17 months	10.4	9.8	13.4
18 to 23 months	13.9	12.7	14.1
24 to 35 months	24.2	23.7	24.5
36 to 47 months	15.9	16.9	15.6
48 to 59 months	10.1	11.3	10.1
60 to 71 months	6.6	8.0	6.6
72 months and over	15.8	14.9	12.6
Black	100.0	100.0	100.0
0 months (plural deliveries)	2.1	1.5	⎡ 6.1
1 to 11 months	3.4	2.9	⎣
12 to 17 months	16.4	13.2	20.3
18 to 23 months	13.8	12.5	15.7
24 to 35 months	18.4	19.2	20.7
36 to 47 months	11.9	14.3	12.5
48 to 59 months	8.4	10.7	8.4
60 to 71 months	6.1	8.2	5.4
72 months and over	19.6	17.5	11.0

[1] 1969 was the earliest year for which these data were available

Source: National Center for Health Statistics, "Vital Statistics of the United States, Volume I--Natality: 1990,"Table 1-64, "--Natality: 1976," Table 1-22, and "--Natality: 1969," Table 1-22, National Center for Health Statistics, Hyattsville, MD, 1994, 1980, and 1974.

those with intervals of 72 months or longer is 30-34 years, and for fourth births the median age of those with intervals of over 36 months is 30-34 years. Aging, parity progression and longer birth intervals are all interconnected in describing the typical childbearing patterns within the population.

Over the recent past birth intervals changed only a modest amount when the birth rate fluctuated widely. This may be verified from Table 6-17, which provides distributions of birth intervals by race for years representing the tail of the baby boom (1969), the baby bust (1976) and the baby boom echo (1990). Earlier data during the peak of the baby boom were not available. Over these three periods the median birth interval for all races remained at 24-

Figure 6-12. Mean Interval Between Live Births, by Parity and Age of Mother: 1992

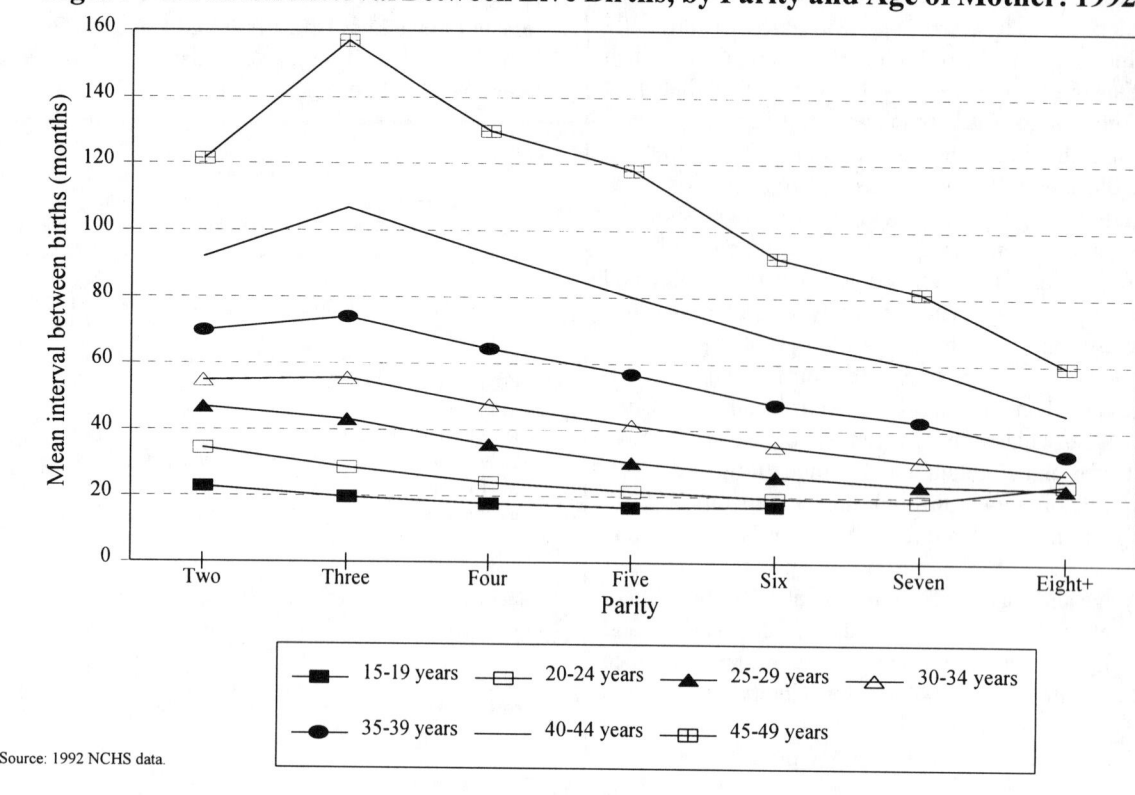

Source: 1992 NCHS data.

Figure 6-13. Mean Interval Since Birth of Previous Child: 1969-1992

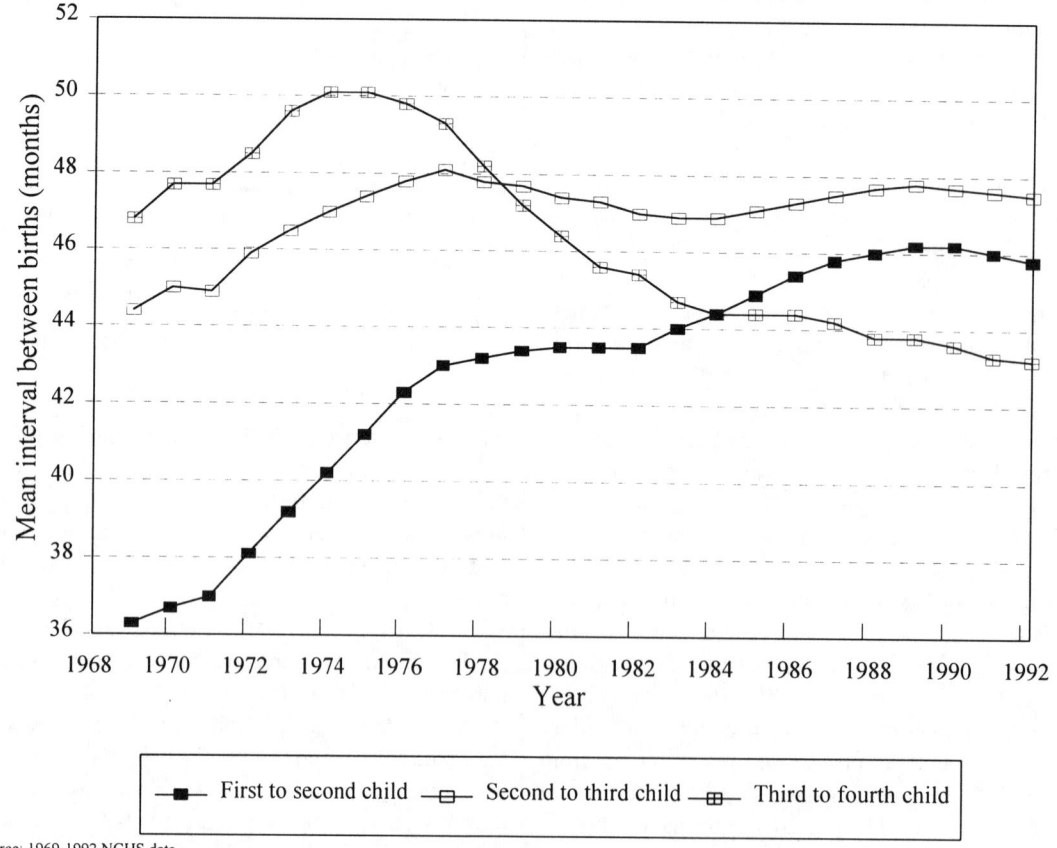

Source: 1969-1992 NCHS data.

Impaired Fecundity and Infertility

by Pamela R. Davidson

The National Survey of Family Growth classifies women who report that it is impossible, difficult or dangerous for them to become pregnant or carry a baby to term as having impaired fecundity. In 1982, 4.5 million women 15-44 years of age reported impaired fecundity. In 1988, the number had increased to 4.9 million. Despite this increase in the absolute number of women reporting impaired fecundity, the percent with impaired fecundity did not change significantly since 1982. As in 1982, the percent of women with impaired fecundity in 1988 was 8.4 percent or one in 12 women. The increase in the absolute number of women with impaired fecundity can be explained by delayed childbearing among the Baby Boom generation (born 1946-64) who entered into the age range of 25 to 44 years in the 1980s. In 1995, the number of women with impaired fecundity increased to 5.1 million women. It is projected that this number will decrease to 4.7 million in 2015. The number of women with impaired fecundity should then rise to 5.9 million in 2020.

Impaired fecundity is more prevalent among childless couples than couples who already have at least one child. In 1988, 20.5 percent of all childless couples with wives 18-44 years of age and 8.4 percent of couples with at least one child reported a fecundity impairment. For childless couples, the percent with impaired fecundity has remained relatively stable since 1976 when 21.4 percent reported impaired fecundity. In contrast, the proportion of wives with children with a fecundity impairment was almost twice as high in 1976 (14.3 percent) as in 1988. The percent with impaired fecundity is not only higher, but it also increases more rapidly with age among childless couples. In 1988, 8.4 percent of all childless married couples

with wives 15-24 years of age and 36.4 percent of wives 35-44 years of age had impaired fecundity. For couples with children the percent with impaired fecundity ranges between 7 and 9 percent. Within the age categories, the percent with impaired fecundity has decreased since 1976. The greatest decrease was for childless couples with wives 35-44 years of age. For wives within this age category, the percent with impaired fecundity decreased from 53.9 percent in 1976 to 36.4 percent in 1988. By 1988, impaired fecundity was not more prevalent in any one racial category.

Available since 1965, data on infertility have a longer time trend than data on impaired fecundity. Using this measure of difficulty in having a baby reveals results comparable to those using data on impaired fecundity. Infertility is defined as the inability of wives to conceive after at least one year of unprotected intercourse. Unlike data on impaired fecundity, data on infertility are limited to married couples only. In 1988, approximately 2.3 million married couples with wives 15-44 years of age were infertile. This constitutes 8 percent of all married couples, about the same proportion as in 1982. This represents a decrease in the proportion of married couples who were infertile from 11 percent in 1965.

Medical innovations since the 1970s have decreased many of the risks associated with delayed childbearing and maternal mortality rates for older women have decreased. As infertility technologies became more common, the proportion of women using infertility services increased. This increase took place even as infertility rates remained constant. In 1988, it was estimated that a total of 2.3 million women had ever received infertility services. This represents only 4% of the total

Percent of Women Age 15 to 44 Reporting Infertility and Impaired Fecundity, by Age, Parity, and Marital Status: Selected Years, 1965-1988

| Parity and age | Currently married women | | | | | | All women | |
| | Infertility | | | Impaired fecundity | | | Impaired fecundity | |
	1988	1982	1965	1988	1982	1976	1988	1982
All parities, total	7.9	8.5	11.2	10.7	10.8	15.7	8.4	8.4
15 to 24 years	—	—	—	7.6	8.8	10.8	4.8	4.3
25 to 34 years	—	—	—	10.9	9.7	15.5	9.6	10.0
35 to 44 years	—	—	—	11.4	13.1	19.1	10.6	12.1
Parity 0, total	18.5	19.6	14.5	20.5	21.7	21.4	8.8	8.4
15 to 24 years	—	—	—	8.4	11.1	10.6	4.1	4.1
25 to 34 years	—	—	—	20.0	21.1	27.3	13.4	14.7
35 to 44 years	—	—	—	36.4	47.8	53.9	21.4	25.7
Parity 1 or more	5.4	6.0	10.8	8.4	8.4	14.3	8.1	8.5
15 to 24 years	—	—	—	7.1	7.2	11.1	7.7	5.2
25 to 34 years	—	—	—	8.3	7.3	13.2	7.8	8.1
35 to 44 years	—	—	—	8.8	10.0	16.8	8.5	10.1

Source: U.S. Bureau of the Census, "Fecundity and Infertility in the United States, 1965-1988," Advance Data from Vital and Health Statistics, Number, 192, 1990, Tables 1, 2, and 3.

population of women 15-44 years of age in 1988 or less than half (43 percent) of all women reporting impaired fecundity. Services usually entail giving couples advice on how to become pregnant (25 percent) and fertility-related tests for women and their partners (20 percent). The most common specialized infertility treatment included drugs to induce ovulation (20 percent). The least common treatment was in-vitro fertilization (2 percent). The characteristics most typically associated with the use of infertility services are sociodemographic. Women over thirty are more likely to seek infertility services than younger women, although the likelihood decreases again for women over forty. Approximately half of all women 30-39 years of age with impaired fecundity obtained fertility services compared with between 20 and 30 percent of women under 30 years of age. Highly educated women and women in higher income categories are significantly more likely to seek infertility services (60 and 52 percent respectively). Non-Hispanic white women are more likely to have obtained infertility services than black women (47 and 30 percent respectively).

One consequence of the increasing success of infertility treatments is the rise in the numbers of multiple births. The U.S. IVF-ET registry reported that close to half (48.4 percent) of the total 12,327 live births in registered clinics between 1990 and 1991 were from multiple gestations. Between 1972 through 1974 and 1985 through 1989 there was a 113 percent increase in the rate of higher-order multiple births among whites compared to a 22 percent increase among blacks. The increase in multiple births is attributable to delayed childbearing and the use of infertility drugs and assisted reproductive technologies.

Sources

Kiely, John L., Kleinman, Joel C., and Kiely, Michele. "Triplets and Higher-Order Multiple Births." American Journal of Disorders in Children 146(1992): 862-68.

Mosher, William D., and Pratt, William F. Fecundity and Infertility in the United States, 1965-1988. DHHS publication no. (PHS)91-1250. Hyattsville, Maryland: National Center for Health Statistics: Advance Data no. 192, 1990.

Stephen, E. H. "Projections of Impaired Fecundity Among Women in the United States: 1995 to 2020." Fertility and Sterility 66(1996): 205.

Wilcox, Lynne S., Kiely, John L., Melvin, Cathy L., and Martin, Mary C. "Assisted Reproductive Technologies: Estimates of Their Contribution to Multiple Births and Newborn Hospital Days in the United States." Fertility and Sterility 65(1996):361-66.

Wilcox, Lynne S., and Mosher, William D. "Use of Infertility Services in the United States." Obstetrics and Gynecology 82(1993):122-27.

Percent of Women Age 15 to 44 with Impaired Fecundity Utilizing Any Infertility Services: 1988

Characteristic	Percent
Total	42.9
Age	
15 to 19 years	20.3
20 to 24 years	29.7
25 to 29 years	39.3
30 to 34 years	49.2
35 to 39 years	53.1
40 to 44 years	42.0
Race-ethnicity	
White, non-Hispanic	47.3
Black, non-Hispanic	30.3
Hispanic	30.6
Educational attainment	
Less than high school	32.4
High school diploma	40.4
Some college	41.9
College degree or higher	60.3
Percentage below poverty level	
0 to 149	23.9
150 to 399	43.3
400 or higher	51.6
Age/parity	
15 to 29/0	38.9
15 to 29/1 or more	29.0
30 to 44/0	57.8
30 to 44/1 or more	42.4

Source: Wilcox, L.S., and W.D. Mosher, "Use of Infertility Services," Obstetrics and Gynecology 82(1993): 122-27, Table 2.

35 months. However, the distribution of birth intervals did change. During the baby boom a significantly smaller percentage of women of all races had the median interval. During the baby bust a greater percentage of women had intervals above the median birth interval. However, by 1990, the distribution of women above the median had returned to nearly the same percentages as in the baby boom tail of 1969. Part of the explanation for the apparent paradox that birth intervals did not change more radically in these years lies in the phenomenon of open intervals. The data above refer only to intervals between births. In contemporary developed countries much of their lower fertility is caused by termination of childbearing, bearing a first or second child and then never having another. This creates a very long open interval following the last birth in which no other birth has occurred at the time the woman is interviewed or a census taken. Also by post-

ponement of marriage or of exposure to childbearing, a longer open interval is created between the menarche and the birth of the first child, which can also reduce fertility. For this reason, closed birth interval statistics provide less information about fertility trends as those trends are caused by reliance upon termination, rather than spacing, of childbearing.

Family Building Patterns

Nonetheless, birth intervals do vary across time and provide insight into the family building patterns prevalent in the population and changes in these patterns over time. Figure 6-13 shows the change in birth intervals among the three most prevalent parity progressions, i.e. from first to second, second to third, and third to fourth births. Leading into the mid-1970s there was a substantial increase in the mean interval between all three of these parities. For earlier periods only median birth intervals are available. Those median intervals suggest that the rise in birth intervals at these three parities began in the early 1960s after birth intervals had remained steady or had fallen since the post-war period. By the mid 1970s, and persisting since, there has been a steady decline in the interval between third and fourth births at the same time that the rate of fourth births first decreased and then increased (see Table 6-6A). Since that time third birth intervals have changed little while there has been some rise in second birth intervals as the fertility rate at third and second parities has changed little. The recent drop in all three birth intervals, although slight, may be connected with the slight declines in fertility rates at these parities between 1990 and 1992.

One highly significant corollary of Figure 6-13 is that even with today's delayed marriage and wider spacing of births, there is plenty of time within the reproductive span for women to bear five children or more should they wish. Only rigorous control of the open interval, e.g. stopping through contraception, will prevent it.

The reader may be puzzled at the long average interval between births (three to four years), even when birth rates are high. Several factors account for this. One is that there is always a period of "postpartum amenorrhea" after the birth of a child (temporary infertility when ovulation had not resumed following childbirth.) This averages at least three months in the United States. Another factor is that, when couples decide to have another child, they do not always succeed the first month they begin trying to get pregnant. Means are also affected disproportionately by the significant proportion of couples who are "subfecund" and must wait long periods of time (often undergoing medical treatment—see Textbox) before conception takes place. In addition, once conceived, it takes nine months before the child is delivered. If to this is added a year or eighteen months of planned contraception to permit the previously born child to mature and the mother to prepare for another pregnancy, three years have elapsed. Thus, about one-half of a three-year average birth interval seems to be caused by physiological factors and one-half by planned intervention. Contraception, surgical sterilization, and infertility together account for almost all of the long "open interval" that terminates childbearing. The changing length of birth intervals in Figure 6-13 shows, in short, how modern contraceptive methods and family planning have become accepted and are now heavily employed in managing the family life course to achieve changing personal objectives across cohorts and circumstances.

Hispanic Fertility

Several of the tables presented above include information on Hispanic fertility. However, for many tables, and nearly all those involving historical data, detail on Hispanic fertility is not available. This ethnic group was not separately identified in fertility data until 1978, when births to Hispanic parents began to be identified in seventeen states with large Hispanic populations; by 1980 the number of states reporting this information had expanded to twenty-two accounting for nearly 90 percent of all Hispanic births in the United States. By 1992 forty-nine states and the District of Columbia reported this information. Thus a special section emphasizing the detail available in this more recent Hispanic fertility data is warranted.

The recent fertility data available are not only for the Hispanic population as a whole but for the mother's primary place-of-origin group within that population. Table 6-18 (first panel) probes birth, fertility, total fertility and age-specific fertility rates for the Hispanic population by origin subgroups as of 1992. There is a great diversity among the origin subgroups. Those of Mexican origin have a TFR of 3.2 children per woman, while Puerto Ricans have roughly 2.6 children per woman and Cubans are reported to have extremely low fertility of 1.5 children per woman, far below replacement fertility levels. Despite their lower fertility, women of Puerto Rican origin have even higher fertility than those of Mexican origin at ages under 24 and yet remarkably lower fertility at ages over 30 years. Other Hispanics whose origin was not specified have fertility of 3.0 births per woman. Thus, the so-called high fertility of Hispanics is due almost exclusively to the Mexican and the 'other' (which includes Central or South American) origin groups. The higher Mexican fertility occurs at every age.

An interesting facet of Table 6-18 is the fertility rates for the white non-Hispanic population. Earlier in this chapter the TFR for the white population in 1992 was reported to be 1,994 births per 1,000 women. Because Hispanics are predominantly classified as white, their fertility helps to inflate the TFR for the white population. When they are removed, the non-Hispanic white TFR sinks to 1,811 births per 1,000 women or a decrease of nearly 9.2 percent. Without the contribution of white Hispanic fertility, the white population is even farther below replacement than previously indicated.

Birth Order of Hispanic Births

The percentage of births of each order (second panel) are also provided in Table 6-18 for Hispanic origin groups. As would be expected from knowledge of the total fertility and general fertility rates, the percentage of Mexican births which are fourth births or higher is greater than for any of the other Hispanic groups. The percentage of Cuban births which are first or second children is, conversely, substantially lower than all other Hispanic groups. This shows that higher Mexican fertility is largely due to women having larger family sizes, rather than simply more women having children, and that family sizes among Cubans are very small. And, once again, removal of Hispanics from

Table 6-18. Birth Rates and Fertility Indicators for the Hispanic Population: 1992

| | | Origin of mother | | | | | | | | |
| | | Hispanic | | | | | | Non-Hispanic | | |
Fertility indicator	All origins	Total	Mexican	Puerto Rican	Cuban	Central or South American	Other Hispanic	Total	White	Black
Birth rate	15.9	26.5	27.8	23.2	10.1	—	27.9	14.8	13.5	21.9
Fertility rate	68.9	108.6	116.0	89.9	50.3	—	107.0	64.4	60.2	85.5
Total fertility rate	2,065.0	3,043.0	3,196.5	2,644.5	1,485.5	—	3,076.0	1,941.0	1,810.5	2,514.0
Birth rates by age of mother										
10 to 14 years	1.4	2.6	2.5	3.5	1.0	—	2.5	1.2	0.5	4.8
15 to 19 years	60.7	107.1	108.8	110.4	26.3	—	112.1	54.4	41.7	116.0
15 to 17 years	37.8	71.4	—	—	—	—	—	33.2	22.7	83.9
18 to 19 years	94.5	159.7	—	—	—	—	—	85.5	69.8	162.9
20 to 24 years	114.6	190.6	202.3	204.9	51.6	—	172.9	104.7	93.9	163.0
25 to 29 years	117.4	154.4	166.3	106.6	98.4	—	157.8	112.7	111.5	114.6
30 to 34 years	80.2	96.8	99.1	66.7	86.2	—	106.6	78.4	78.7	69.1
35 to 39 years	32.5	45.6	47.7	30.0	28.9	—	50.3	31.2	30.5	29.4
40 to 44 years	5.9	10.9	11.8	6.5	4.7	—	12.5	5.4	5.1	5.7
45 to 49 years	0.3	0.6	0.8	0.3	—	—	0.5	0.2	0.2	0.2
Distribution of births by live-birth order										
Total	100.0	100.0	100.0	100.0	100.0	100.0	100.0	100.0	100.0	100.0
First child	40.2	37.6	37.0	38.3	42.5	38.3	39.5	40.7	41.7	36.6
Second child	32.2	29.0	28.2	29.4	35.4	30.6	30.7	32.9	34.0	29.1
Third child	16.4	17.8	18.0	17.5	15.2	18.0	17.0	16.1	15.8	17.9
Fourth child	6.4	8.5	9.1	7.7	4.4	7.5	7.3	6.0	5.3	8.6
Fifth child	2.4	3.6	4.0	3.1	1.3	2.9	2.7	2.2	1.7	3.9
Sixth child	1.0	1.6	1.8	1.3	0.5	1.2	1.2	0.9	0.6	1.8
Seventh child	0.5	0.7	0.8	0.5	0.2	0.5	0.5	0.4	0.3	0.8
Eighth child and over	0.5	0.7	0.8	0.5	0.1	0.4	0.4	0.4	0.3	0.8
Not stated	0.5	0.4	0.2	1.6	0.3	0.7	0.7	0.4	0.4	0.5
Births to unmarried women per 1,000 total births										
All ages	301.8	391.3	362.9	575.4	202.5	439.3	375.6	284.9	185.5	683.5
Under 15 years	913.3	818.4	776.3	942.9	909.1	909.5	844.1	940.8	880.6	977.6
15 to 19 years	700.0	618.6	569.5	827.0	579.7	715.9	656.1	721.9	597.2	927.7
20 to 24 years	407.2	423.1	383.2	619.8	291.5	514.0	423.6	403.3	283.0	754.3
25 to 29 years	198.4	308.4	285.0	445.1	138.8	383.9	249.4	178.8	107.2	551.0
30 to 34 years	143.3	272.3	251.1	387.8	132.4	347.5	198.3	125.8	74.6	467.1
35 to 39 years	152.5	284.7	260.9	394.8	175.7	359.0	210.3	133.9	85.4	447.3
40 to 49 years	177.2	308.8	277.3	445.9	242.4	392.3	237.6	154.7	111.3	420.4

Source: National Center for Health Statistics, "Vital Statistics of the United States, Volume I--Natality: 1992," National Center for Health Statistics, Hyattsville, MD, 1995, Tables 1-13, 1-44, and 1-46.

the white population amplifies the low fertility of the white non-Hispanic population.

Out-of-Wedlock Births to Hispanic Mothers

Both Puerto Rican and Central or South American women are much more likely to bear children out of wedlock than are the other Hispanic or white non-Hispanic women. This difference cuts across all age groups. Table 6-18 also shows Cuban women are much less inclined to bear children out of wedlock than the general population. Only the white non-Hispanic population has lower nonmarital birth ratios than the Cuban Hispanic population. Again, the nonmarital birth ratios are substantially inflated by the inclusion of higher fertility Hispanic origin

groups in computing white nonmarital birth ratios. Out-of-wedlock births to white non-Hispanic origin women are also more highly confined to the teenage years than are those to all white women.

Socioeconomic Differentials

Birth certificates contain comparatively little information about the social and economic characteristics of the mothers and fathers of children. Hence, to study socioeconomic differentials in fertility, it is necessary to turn either to sample surveys or to census sources. Information on births within the past year from the Current Population Survey (see Chapter 2) has been cross-classified by age of mother and selected socioeconomic characteristics of the mother in Table 6-19.

Table 6-19. Births Within the Last Year per 1,000 Women by Selected Characteristics, Age of Mother, and Birth Order of Child: 1994

Characteristics	Total, 15 to 44 years			15 to 29 years			30 to 44 years		
	Number of women (thousands)	Total births per 1,000	First births per 1,000	Number of women (thousands)	Total births per 1,000	First births per 1,000	Number of women (thousands)	Total births per 1,000	First births per 1,000
Total, women 15 to 44 years	60,088	64.7	27.4	27,893	85.6	46.3	32,195	46.6	11.0
Marital Status									
Currently married	31,659	91.1	35.1	8,917	174.3	88.9	22,742	58.4	14.0
Spouse present	29,218	94.0	36.5	8,053	182.3	94.4	21,165	60.5	14.5
Spouse absent	2,441	55.4	17.9	864	100.4	38.4	1,576	30.8	6.7
Widowed or divorced	5,697	20.1	4.3	948	59.8	21.1	4,749	12.2	1.0
Never married	22,733	39.2	22.5	18,028	43.1	26.6	4,705	24.3	6.8
Educational attainment									
Less than high school	12,369	67.3	28.3	8,732	76.4	38.0	3,637	45.5	5.2
High school, 4 years	18,543	70.3	28.1	7,426	116.7	60.0	11,117	39.3	6.9
College: 1 or more years	29,176	60.1	26.6	11,735	72.9	44.0	17,441	51.5	14.9
No degree	12,672	53.6	23.3	6,448	68.6	39.3	6,224	38.0	6.7
Associate degree	4,756	63.4	29.1	1,536	112.2	73.6	3,221	40.2	7.9
Bachelor's degree	8,850	70.3	31.4	3,292	65.6	40.8	5,559	73.1	25.8
Graduate or professional degree	2,897	52.2	22.1	459	53.4	32.1	2,438	52.0	20.2
Labor force status									
In labor force	42,996	48.1	22.6	18,889	64.0	38.4	24,106	35.6	10.2
Employed	39,644	46.3	21.8	16,690	60.4	37.1	22,954	36.0	10.7
Unemployed	3,352	69.2	31.9	2,199	91.0	48.4	1,153	27.4	0.3
Not in labor force	17,092	106.7	39.6	9,003	131.0	63.0	8,089	79.5	13.5
Occupation									
Managerial and professional	10,880	51.0	23.9	3,190	66.1	42.0	7,690	44.7	16.4
Technical, sales, admin. support	16,903	42.9	21.4	7,781	55.0	36.3	9,122	32.7	8.7
Service occupations	7,544	47.5	21.2	4,042	60.1	33.3	3,502	33.0	7.1
Farming, forestry, fishing	469	37.2	25.4	215	53.0	53.0	255	23.8	2.2
Precision production, craft, repair	831	55.5	30.2	261	106.2	71.9	570	32.2	11.1
Operators, fabricators, laborers	3,016	44.0	14.9	1,202	73.5	30.9	1,815	24.4	4.4
Family income									
Under $10,000	7,555	89.0	34.9	4,282	123.3	57.4	3,273	44.2	5.5
$10,000 to $19,999	8,956	73.7	28.7	4,897	98.8	48.9	4,059	43.4	4.3
$20,000 to $24,999	4,758	76.8	34.6	2,394	111.2	55.6	2,364	41.9	13.3
$25,000 to $29,999	4,593	62.6	28.8	2,310	90.1	52.4	2,283	34.7	4.9
$30,000 to $34,999	4,341	62.2	23.0	1,963	77.6	43.9	2,378	49.4	5.8
$35,000 to $49,999	10,239	58.0	26.9	4,324	78.5	47.9	5,915	43.0	11.6
$50,000 to $74,999	9,571	54.4	24.8	3,715	58.2	40.1	5,856	52.0	15.1
$75,000 and over	6,494	48.8	17.9	2,468	29.2	14.5	4,026	60.8	20.0
Income not reported	3,582	56.8	28.0	1,540	79.5	48.9	2,042	39.6	12.2
Region of residence									
Northeast	11,756	59.3	24.5	5,324	69.7	37.1	6,432	50.6	14.1
Midwest	14,296	65.5	28.8	6,682	91.3	51.4	7,614	42.9	8.9
South	20,920	62.8	26.2	9,812	83.0	43.3	11,109	45.0	11.0
West	13,116	71.8	30.5	6,075	97.6	53.7	7,040	49.5	10.6

Source: U.S. Bureau of the Census, Current Population Reports, "Fertility of American Women: June 1994," Series P-20, Number 482, U.S. Government Printing Office, Washington, D.C., 1995, Table A.

Marital Status

Not surprisingly, births for all women are heavily concentrated among the currently married and most prevalent among those with spouse present. Again, as would be expected, births to these women are heavily concentrated below thirty years of age. Births among the widowed or divorced are surprisingly high among those aged 15 to 29 years of age and decline dramatically in older women. Given the much higher occurrence of births to the never married in this age group and the lower prevalence of widowhood at younger ages this pattern primarily reflects out-of-wedlock fertility among the divorced. It is also the case that first births to such women are much less common and relatively rare (1 per 1,000 women) for those over 30 years of age. First births, of course, generally decline with age for all nuptiality groups.

Educational Attainment

The relationship between the amount of education women have and their fertility has become more complex over the past several decades as educational attainment has risen overall, the resources required for advanced education have increased, and abilities to plan the timing of fertility have improved. Overall, fertility generally declines as women achieve higher levels of education. However, lower levels of educational attainment are, of course, correlated with age and the higher fertility of younger women coupled with a rise in nonmarital fertility contribute to the high fertility of women with a high school diploma or less in Table 6-19. The effect of age on this association is clear in the much higher fertility of women with a high school diploma under thirty years of age (the highest of all attainment groups) and the much lower fertility at older ages (next to the lowest of all attainment groups). Fertility declines for women with some college but with less than a baccalaureate degree. Many of these women are, of course, still in college and delaying childbearing. The highest fertility group are those women with a baccalaureate degree. This relationship is most dramatic in the group of women over thirty years of age where schooling of this level is more likely completed for at least a majority of women. Finally, however, fertility declines again for women with a graduate or professional degree. There are several factors contributing to this highly educated group's lower fertility, including lower probabilities of marriage, diversion of personal resources to education, alternative consumption and lifestyle possibilities, etc.

Labor Force Participation

One of the most dramatic changes in the past two decades has been the tremendous rise in the percentage of women having children while participating in the labor force (see Figure 6-14). Nonetheless, both total births and first births are highest among those women not in the labor force and second highest among those who are unemployed. Despite a rising consciousness of the necessity for family leaves to accommodate pregnancy and child rearing, a substantial component of this association is still due to the decision or necessity of withdrawing from the labor force during family building. This association cannot be interpreted, by itself, as solely due to higher fertility due to nonparticipation in the labor force or its socioeconomic correlates (see Chapter 13). The dramatic decline in first births to unemployed women past age thirty, while first births remain most common among those not in the labor force, is suggestive. Fertility among unemployed women over thirty is lower overall than for any group. Unemployment thus seems to have a clear negative impact on continued fertility not evident at younger ages, while those wishing to bear children at these older ages instead completely withdraw from labor force participa-

tion. Of course, more detailed fertility studies provide much greater insight into these complex causal relationships and their differences among various social groups than do general population profiles such as those in Table 6-19. One of the most important aspects of these data is the significant increase in fertility among those who are in the labor force. This trend has created a need to accommodate fertility within the workplace and social demands for the assistance required to combine employment and child rearing.

Occupation of Women

As with education and labor force participation, the effects of occupation upon fertility of women have become more complex in recent times. Generally, women who hold high-prestige white-collar positions (managers, professional workers, technicians, and administrative workers) have tended to have lower fertility than women with blue-collar and service occupations. A part of this could be an indirect reflection of the amount of education the woman has received. However, Table 6-19 reveals some contradiction to these typical expectations. The highest fertility is indeed among production, craft and repair professions and fertility is also high among service occupations. However, fertility is also very high among managerial and professional women. This higher than anticipated fertility may well reflect the rise in older-aged births (see Table 6-4) as women who have achieved substantial career aspirations decide to have children. This argument receives some support from the fact that women of this group have a higher rate of first births at older ages than other occupation groups. In addition, fertility is unexpectedly low among operators, fabricators and laborers. These lower fertility rates may reflect the economic difficulties and declining wages over the past several decades within many manufacturing and industrial enterprises (Chapters 14 and 15).

Income

Overall fertility declines with increasing family income, as seen in Table 6-19. This relationship also holds with relatively minor exceptions across major race and ethnicity groups (see Figure 6-15). The fertility of low-income Hispanics is considerably above that of low-income whites and blacks, as it is for most income categories. The decline in fertility by income is less pronounced among whites than blacks and less pronounced among blacks than Hispanics. Fertility among white women does not appear as responsive to income levels as these other groups. There are also fluctuations in the association of fertility across income groups in Table 6-19 and Figure 6-15 with higher fertility among some middle-income groups, depending upon age and race or ethnicity. Both blacks and Hispanics display a higher fertility among a middle or upper-middle-income group ($25-29,000 for Hispanics and

Figure 6-14. Women[1] Who Have Had a Child in the Last Year, by Labor Force Status: 1976-1994

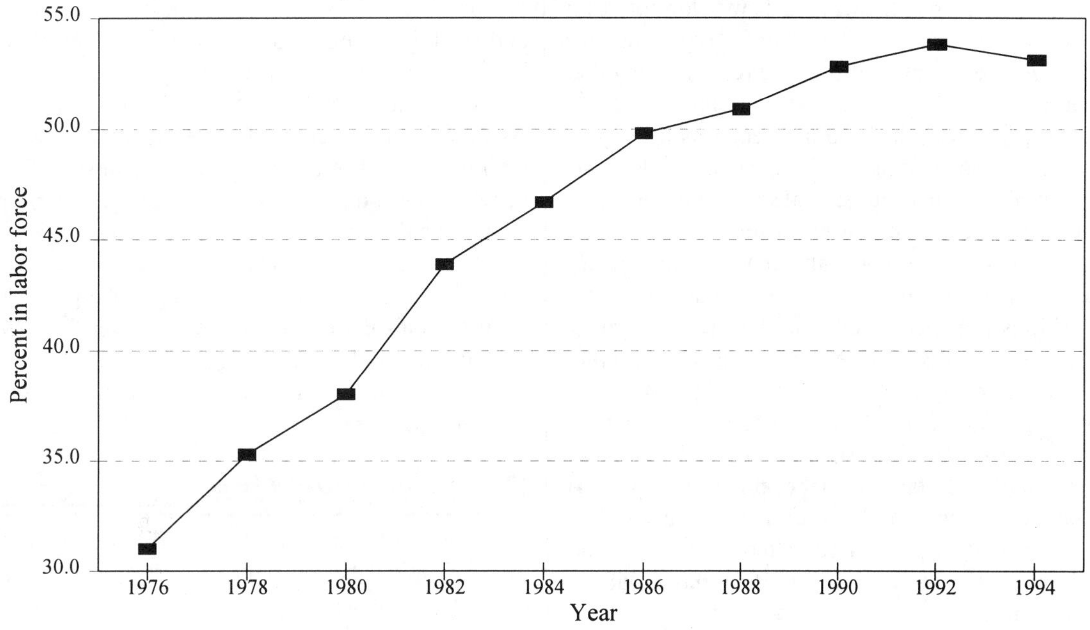

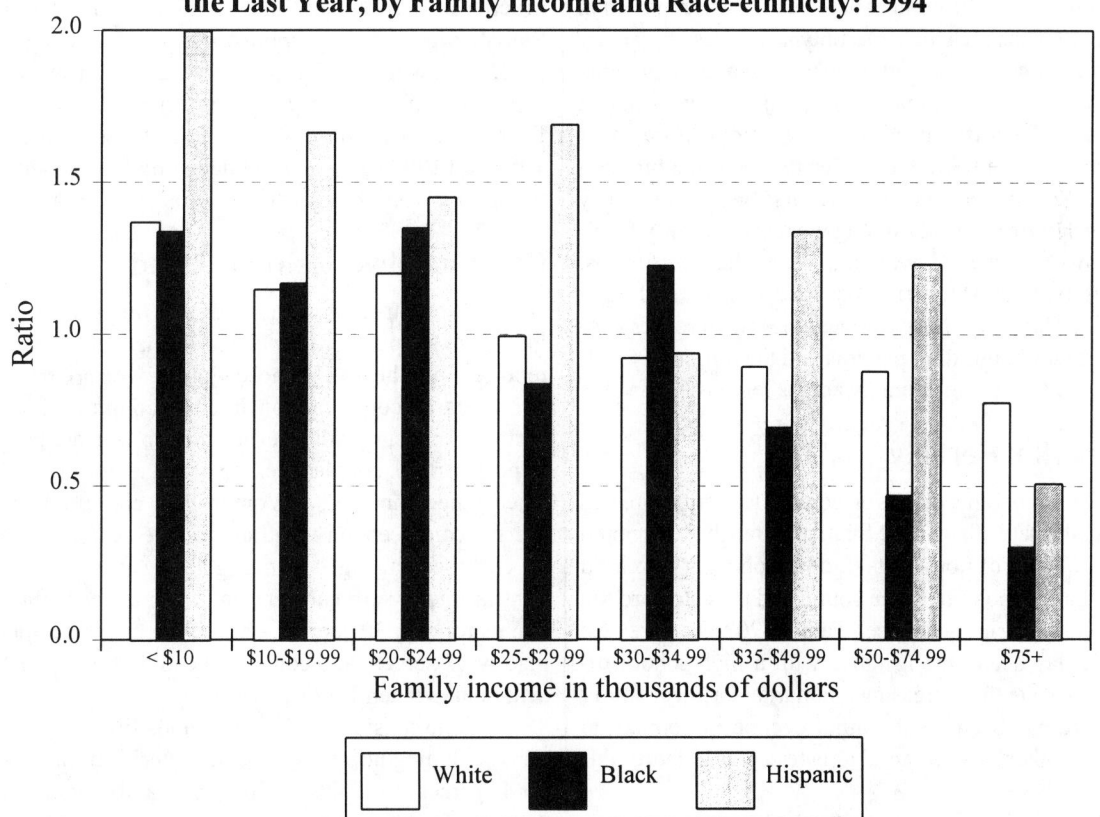

[1] Age 15 to 44 in 1990-1994; age 18 to 44 prior to 1990.
Source: 1976-1994 CPS data.

Figure 6-15. Differentials[1] of Fertility Among Women Who Have Had a Child in the Last Year, by Family Income and Race-ethnicity: 1994

[1] Ratio of births per 1,000 women in each race/ethnic and family income category to the total for all races/all incomes.
Source: 1994 CPS data.

$30-$49,000 for blacks) which is not clearly apparent for white women.

The association of higher income with lower fertility is well known and has many correlates. Higher incomes may require investment of efforts in directions other than childbearing and may also provide alternative lifestyle choices or pressures which do not center as heavily on having children and raising families. Income is also associated with education, occupational status, etc., which are frequently associated with lower fertility. However, this relationship is also profoundly altered when looking only at older women. For those over thirty years of age the relationship is J-shaped with higher fertility at lower incomes, lowest fertility in lower middle incomes and then much higher fertility at the very highest income levels. The very highest first birth levels among older women are also at the very highest income groups (as they were with higher occupational status and labor force participation). The changing association between income and fertility across age again suggests these patterns reflect the fact that older successful women are entering into childbearing at older ages.

Geographic Differentials

Most socioeconomic differentials in fertility are now quite small in the United States and have been converging for several decades. The same is true for geographic differentials. The differences between regions reported in Table 6-19 with much higher fertility in the West are largely a product of age composition. This becomes somewhat more evident in the comparison of fertility for women of a given age. The differences in fertility among those under thirty are notable for the lower fertility and first births in the Northeast where fertility and first births over thirty years of age are highest. Among women over thirty fertility is lowest in the Midwest and West where fertility is, conversely, highest under thirty years of age. Although fertility differentials have declined these differences suggest that family building patterns and the timing of fertility may still vary considerably across regions.

Nonmarital Fertility

Socioeconomic effects on nonmarital fertility are less historically stable than those for marital fertility. As noted earlier, the rate of nonmarital motherhood has increased dramatically among both the young and those toward the end of childbearing years (see Table 6-20). The greatest increase has been among those with a high school diploma. Despite the increasing nonmarital fertility at older ages there has been a substantial decline in nonmarital births to mothers with a baccalaureate degree or more education.

One finding of Table 6-20 which is not surprising but runs counter to many stereotypes is that the increase in nonmarital fertility has been heavily concentrated in those in the labor force. This finding again suggests the profound need for social accommodation of childbearing and rearing among employed women. Out-of-wedlock births to working women imply a special parental burden, and a profound social obligation to assist in child rearing. As one might anticipate from educational associations with nonmarital fertility, the increase in such fertility is heavily concentrated outside the managerial and professional occupations.

Again, differences in nonmarital fertility by region are not as great as they have been in the past. The increase in out-of-wedlock births, however, has been disproportionately higher in regions other than the South, which have risen to similar levels of nonmarital fertility in more recent years.

Contraceptive Use

One of the most profound historical demographic transformations has been the revolution in contraceptive methods which has spread throughout much of the world over the past half century. The contraceptive revolution has, of course, affected some social groups more than others. It has, nonetheless, spread throughout most of the United States population and has left few demographic behaviors or trends unaltered. Census and vital registration data do not provide direct insight into contraceptive practices. Fortunately, the National Center for Health Statistics periodically sponsors a "National Survey of Family Growth" in order to collect data on fertility, contraceptive practices, and aspects of maternal and child health. Data from these surveys, especially those of the 1973, 1982 and 1990 surveys, provide the bulk of the information in this section regarding contraceptive practices.

Contraceptive Methods Used

The contraceptive methods that the American public uses to keep its fertility at near-replacement levels are reported in Table 6-21. Those women who are presumed non-users of contraception include couples where one partner is nonsurgically sterile, women who are pregnant or post-partum, couples seeking pregnancy and self-identified other non-users. Women thus classified as non-users of contraception constitute 35.5 percent of all women of childbearing age. Among those presumed to be contraceptors, surgical sterilization (male or female) accounts for over 30 percent, oral pills account for approximately 17 percent and condoms account for over 10 percent of all women 15-44 years of age

If one considers only the composition of contraceptors, excluding non-users, surgical sterilization accounts for 47 percent, oral pills for 26 percent and condoms for 16 percent of presumed contracepting women aged 15 to 44 years. The IUD and the diaphragm protect roughly an

Table 6-20. Fertility Indicators for Never-married Women 15 to 44 Years Old by Selected Characteristics: 1994 and Percent Change 1990 to 1994

Characteristics	1994				Percent change 1990-94	
	Total (thousands)	Number of mothers (thousands)	Mothers as percent of total	Children ever born per 1,000 women	Mothers as percent of total	Children ever born per 1,000 women
Total	22,733	4,603	20.2	378	11.6	17.0
Age						
15 to 19 years	8,405	544	6.5	81	16.1	19.1
20 to 24 years	6,121	1,237	20.2	315	4.7	1.0
25 to 29 years	3,502	1,052	30.0	603	2.0	8.6
30 to 34 years	2,233	861	38.6	842	17.0	26.0
35 to 39 years	1,509	605	40.1	853	12.0	15.1
40 to 44 years	963	304	31.6	729	5.3	13.2
Educational attainment						
Less than high school	7,833	1,458	18.6	398	1.6	7.3
High school, 4 years	5,203	1,876	36.1	668	36.2	49.8
College: 1 or more years	9,697	1,268	13.1	206	15.9	13.8
No degree	5,118	819	16.0	251	14.3	9.6
Associate degree	1,101	240	21.8	361	—	—
Bachelor's degree and above	3,478	209	6.0	92	-14.3	-14.8
Labor force status						
In labor force	15,780	2,718	17.2	301	15.4	27.5
Not in labor force	6,953	1,885	27.1	553	6.3	5.3
Occupation						
Managerial and professional	2,840	243	8.6	136	-3.4	0.7
Other	11,037	1,959	17.7	306	19.6	32.5
Region of residence						
Northeast	5,105	987	19.3	361	16.3	26.7
Midwest	5,487	1,180	21.5	392	20.8	20.6
South	7,464	1,565	21.0	403	2.9	7.8
West	4,676	871	18.6	339	12.0	18.9

Source: U.S. Bureau of the Census, Current Population Reports, "Fertility of American Women: June 1994," Series P-20, Number 482, U.S. Government Printing Office, Washington, D.C., 1995, Table J.

additional 4 percent of the contracepting population. Only about 7 percent of the contracepting population uses methods known to give only moderate or poor protection. Thus, it is quite accurate to say that fertility is highly controlled in the American culture. When women say they expect to have only one or two children, they are prepared to effect the desired outcome.

Age and Contraception

The patterns of changing contraception are more clearly seen by examining different age groups by changing type of contraception. Table 6-22 shows the percentage of all women of prime childbearing ages, i.e. aged 25 to 34, who use oral contraceptives and condoms has increased significantly since 1982. The percentage of those using condoms has increased dramatically for those under 35 years of age and especially for those under 25 years of age. Thus, oral contraceptives are, in fact, being used later into the life course for many women while condoms are becoming a more preferred method at younger ages.

Other trends in age-specific contraception are somewhat surprising for those of middle age. Sterilization is a contraceptive method which clearly advances in use with age. However, Table 6-22 shows that sterilization is actually declining slightly in use among those less than 35 years of age. This age group also has a surprising increase in those not seeking pregnancy but using no con-

Table 6-21. Number of Women 15 to 44 Years Old and Percent Distribution by Current Contraceptive Status and Method, by Race-ethnicity: 1982 and 1990

Contraceptive status and method	Total		White, non-Hispanic		Black, non-Hispanic		Hispanic Hispanic	
	1990	1982	1990	1982	1990	1982	1990	1982
All women	58,381	54,099	42,968	41,279	7,510	6,825	5,500	4,393
Total percent	100.0	100.0	100.0	100.0	100.0	100.0	100.0	100.0
Pill	16.9	15.6	17.3	15.1	16.7	19.5	16.4	15.3
IUD	0.8	4.0	0.8	3.3	0.8	4.8	1.0	9.7
Diaphragm	1.7	4.5	1.8	5.3	1.0	1.7	0.8	2.4
Condom	10.5	6.7	10.3	7.5	11.4	3.3	8.9	3.5
Periodic abstinence	1.6	2.1	1.6	2.2	0.7	1.6	1.9	2.0
Withdrawal	0.6	1.1	0.6	1.2	0.4	0.7	0.4	1.3
Other methods	2.3	2.7	2.2	2.6	2.8	3.8	2.3	2.5
Sterile	32.1	27.1	32.9	28.4	34.0	23.9	27.5	20.5
Surgically sterile	30.2	25.6	31.2	26.9	31.4	22.3	23.9	18.4
Female	22.7	19.2	21.9	19.1	30.5	21.5	20.5	16.1
Male	7.5	6.4	9.3	7.8	0.9	0.8	3.4	2.3
Nonsurgically sterile	1.9	1.5	1.7	1.5	2.6	1.6	3.6	2.1
Pregnant or postpartum	5.4	5.0	5.2	4.6	5.5	5.6	7.7	7.3
Seeking pregnancy	4.0	4.2	3.7	3.8	4.7	5.5	5.1	6.4
Other nonusers	24.2	26.9	23.6	25.9	22.1	29.8	28.3	29.2
Never had intercourse	9.4	13.6	8.7	13.8	7.0	10.4	16.4	14.7
No intercourse in last month	7.0	8.3	7.2	8.2	7.5	8.7	5.1	7.7
Had intercourse in last month	7.8	5.0	7.7	3.9	7.6	10.7	6.8	6.8

Source: National Center for Health Statistics, "Contraceptive Use in the United States: 1982-1990," Advance Data from Vital and Health Statistics, Number 260, 1995, Table 1.

traception. This increase may reflect an increasing proportion of single women within the age group (see Chapter 5).

The only significant group of reproductive age whose fertility is not being tightly regulated are generally the premaritally or extramaritally sexually active. This group is also evident in the data of Table 6-22 showing use of contraception by age. For those under 25 years of age over half are presumed nonusers of contraception. Among contraceptors this group has a lower use of higher efficacy sterilization and a greater use of condoms and oral contraceptives.

Marital Contraception

A large-scale shift from use of the pill to the use of sterilization has occurred for currently married women, which as Figure 6-16 indicates occurred between 1973 and 1990. This represents a transition from a reversible to a permanent method, a step taken by couples who have decided they have all the children they wish and who do not want to risk accidental pregnancy. Concern about the long-term effects of the oral pills on health has also stimulated a shift to sterilization and other methods. The per-

centage of currently married women aged 15-44 using oral contraceptives dropped from 25 percent to less than 15 percent of all currently married women over the past two decades. Note, however, that the use of oral contraceptives overall (i.e. not limited to currently married women) has increased slightly according to Table 6-21. The use of IUDs among currently married women of childbearing age has also declined dramatically since 1973. Early aversion to the IUD might be related to tragic consequences of particular products (e.g. the Dalkon Shield). However, more recent shifts are likely due to changing preferences among methods. In contrast to the decline in married women's use of oral contraceptives, the percentage using condoms has risen slightly. This shift may be related to the efficacy of condoms as a barrier method and prevention of viral transmissions including AIDS/HIV. Rising condom use by married couples may also reflect rising fertility among some older women and the greater flexibility of condoms as an occasional or temporary contraceptive method.

Nonmarital Contraception

Concerns over adolescent or teen pregnancy generate considerable public concerns over the early use of

Table 6-22. Number of Women 15 to 44 Years Old and Percent Distribution by Current Contraceptive Status and Method, by Age: 1982 and 1990

Contraceptive status and method	15 to 24 years		25 to 34 years		35 to 44 years	
	1990	1982	1990	1982	1990	1982
All women	17,637	20,150	21,728	19,644	19,016	14,305
Total percent	100.0	100.0	100.0	100.0	100.0	100.0
Pill	23.9	23.5	22.0	17.1	4.7	2.3
IUD	0.2	1.4	0.4	6.5	1.8	4.2
Diaphragm	0.2	3.7	2.3	6.8	2.4	2.4
Condom	13.9	5.5	11.0	7.6	6.7	7.0
Periodic abstinence	1.0	1.2	2.0	2.8	1.6	2.6
Withdrawal	0.6	1.2	0.6	1.2	0.5	0.8
Other methods	1.4	1.9	3.0	3.2	2.4	3.2
Sterile	3.8	3.3	26.4	27.9	64.6	60.0
Surgically sterile	3.1	2.6	24.8	26.4	61.1	57.2
Female	2.6	1.5	18.9	19.4	45.4	44.2
Male	0.5	1.1	5.9	7.0	15.7	13.0
Nonsurgically sterile	0.7	0.7	1.6	1.5	3.5	2.8
Pregnant or postpartum	7.0	6.3	7.9	6.5	1.2	1.0
Seeking pregnancy	1.8	3.5	7.6	6.2	2.0	2.5
Other nonusers	46.4	48.6	17.1	14.3	12.0	13.8
Never had intercourse	26.4	32.5	2.8	2.7	1.3	2.0
No intercourse in last month	7.7	10.6	7.1	7.1	6.4	6.7
Had intercourse in last month	12.3	5.5	7.2	4.5	4.3	5.1

Source: National Center for Health Statistics, "Contraceptive Use in the United States: 1982-1990," Advance Data from Vital and Health Statistics, Number 260, 1995, Table 2.

contraception, especially by those not yet married. However, with a growing population of unmarried women, adolescents are only one age group contributing to nonmarital fertility. Figure 6-17 provides data on the contraceptive methods among all unmarried women aged 14 to 44 according to the 1982 and 1990 National Surveys of Family Growth. The single largest group among unmarried women are the presumed non-users of contraception. Non-users have, however, declined over the past decade as those who are contraceptively sterile, using oral contraceptives and using condoms have increased. The use of intrauterine devices and diaphragms has dropped to a negligible fraction of the non-married population. Among those methods with increasing use, condoms have increased in usage most significantly. Again, this increase may be most highly related to their efficacy as a barrier method in 'safe sex' practices averting viral transmission.

Teenage Pregnancy and Contraception at First Premarital Intercourse

The National Survey of Family Growth advance data for 1995 includes information on the number of women who had first premarital intercourse at 15 to 19 years of age during the periods of 1980-1982 and 1988-1990. These data suggest that the percentage of teenagers using any contraceptive method at the time of first intercourse has increased dramatically, from 52.9 percent in the earlier period to 71.2 percent in the more recent period. In addition, the dramatic rise in condom use is also evident for this age group, increasing from 28 percent in 1980-1982 to 55 percent by 1988-1990. Contraceptive use by teenagers at time of first intercourse in the 1988-1990 period was highest among the white non-Hispanic population (75.7 percent) and lower among the black non-Hispanic (63.8 percent) and Hispanic (67.3) populations. Given social concerns over adolescent pregnancy and the spread of AIDS/HIV, these data are encouraging in the trend toward greater contraceptive use and greater use of barrier methods, but remain disappointing in the substantial numbers of contraceptive non-users at the time of first intercourse. Three of every ten adolescent women still use no method at the time of first premarital intercourse. Only slightly over half, 5.5 of every 10, use a barrier method with efficacy for avoidance of AIDS/HIV transmission at time of first premarital intercourse.

**Figure 6-16. Contraceptive Use Among Currently Married Women
Age 15 to 44: 1973 and 1990**

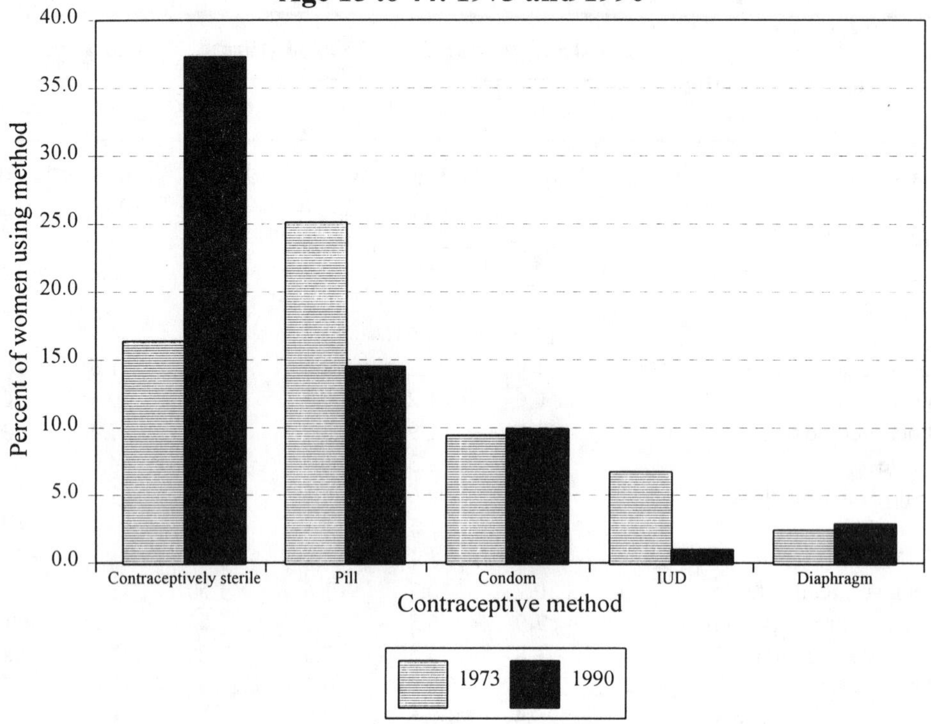

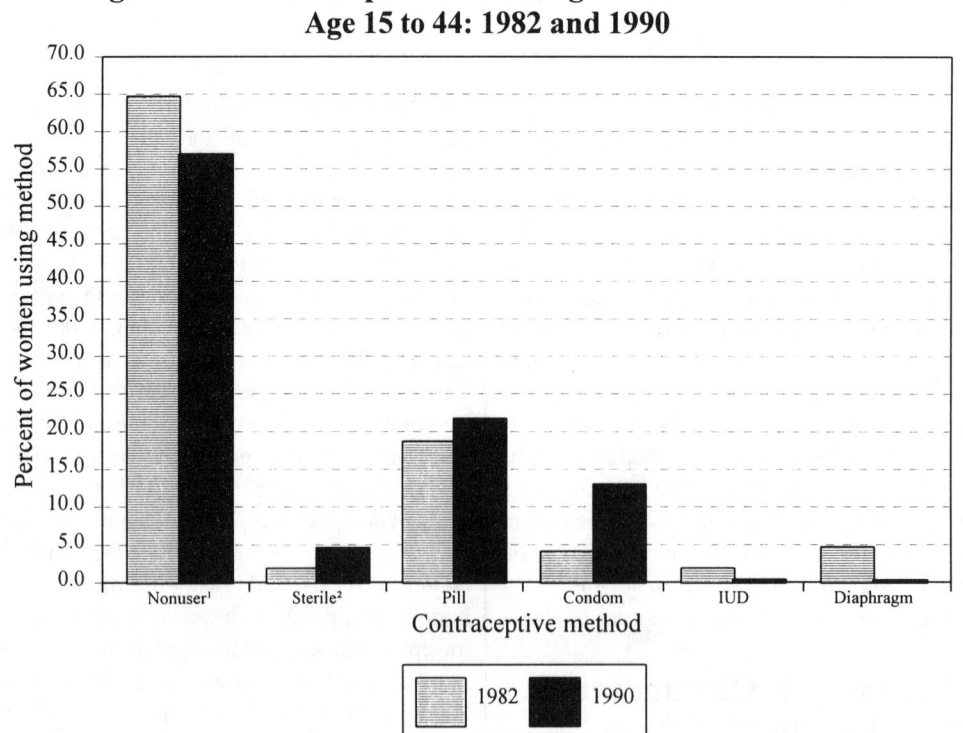

Source: Data from the 1973 and 1990 National Surveys of Family Growth.

**Figure 6-17. Contraceptive Use Among Never Married Women
Age 15 to 44: 1982 and 1990**

[1] Includes those who are noncontraceptively sterile, nonsurgically sterile, pregnant or post partum, seeking pregnancy, and other nonusers.
[2] Contraceptively sterile through surgical means.
Source: Data from the 1982 and 1990 National Surveys of Family Growth.

Figure 6-18. Contraceptive Use Among Women Age 15 to 44, by Fertility Intentions: 1990

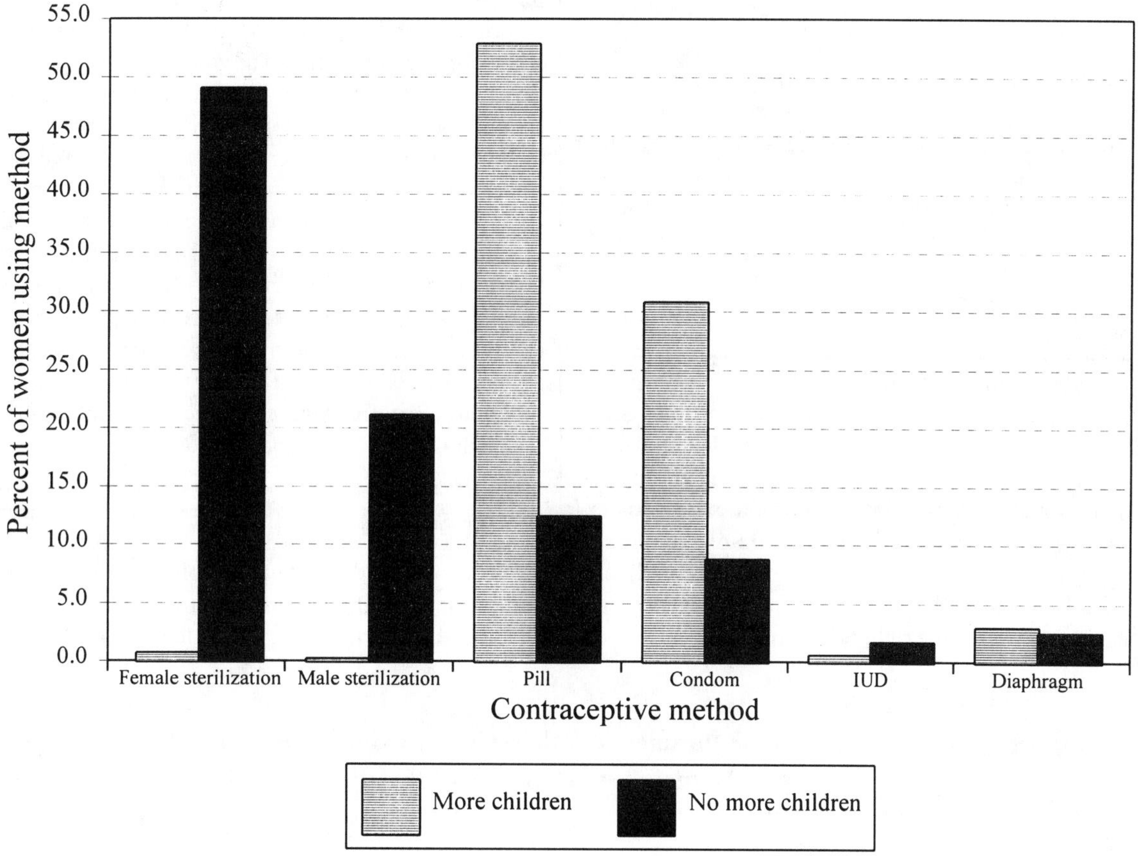

Source: Data from the 1990 National Survey of Family Growth.

Table 6-23. Pregnancies, by Outcome, Age of Woman, and Race-ethnicity: 1991

Rate per 1,000 women	Total	Under 15 years	15 to 19 years	20 to 24 years	25 to 29 years	30 to 34 years	35 to 39 years	40 years and over
White, non-Hispanic								
Pregnancies	91.8	1.3	84.7	151.4	154.7	107.6	47.3	8.6
Live births	61.0	0.5	43.4	95.7	112.7	77.9	30.2	4.8
Induced abortions	17.9	0.7	28.4	39.6	22.0	12.9	7.4	2.2
Fetal losses	12.9	0.2	13.0	16.0	20.0	16.8	9.7	1.6
Black, non-Hispanic								
Pregnancies	174.8	11.0	216.7	337.2	232.3	142.7	63.9	14.4
Live births	87.6	4.9	118.9	166.1	116.3	69.3	28.9	5.7
Induced abortions	65.9	5.1	80.5	136.4	86.3	47.1	23.0	6.2
Fetal losses	21.3	0.9	17.2	34.7	29.7	26.3	12.1	2.4
Hispanic								
Pregnancies	167.4	4.8	180.2	285.6	224.3	143.9	74.8	19.8
Live births	108.1	2.4	106.7	186.3	152.8	96.1	44.9	11.1
Induced abortions	36.2	1.4	40.4	68.1	44.4	27.1	15.5	5.2
Fetal losses	23.2	1.0	33.1	31.2	27.1	20.7	14.4	3.6

Source: National Center for Health Statistics, "Monthly Vital Statistics Report," Volume 43, Number 12, 1995.

Fertility Intentions and Contraception

Contraceptive methods used are, of course, clearly related to future fertility intentions. As Figure 6-18 shows, only a few unfortunate couples have selected sterilization as a method and yet want more children. In contrast, the vast majority of women using oral contraceptives or condoms do desire to have more children. This selection of methods shows the efficacy with which women in the United States can select specific methods to terminate childbearing and others to delay or space pregnancies to more desirable times in their life course.

Abortion

Another fundamental explanation of how birth rates in the United States are kept low is by abortion. Since 1973 abortion has been available as a normal medical procedure in all states of the nation. Before 1967 all states in the nation had laws prohibiting abortion except for extreme situations, usually to save the life of the mother. Between 1967 and 1973 some states passed more liberal abortion laws, but the Supreme Court decided in 1973 that state laws restricting the right of a woman to choose abortion rather than childbirth during the first three months of pregnancy were unconstitutional. The trough of the baby bust coincides with the widespread availability of this additional choice for dealing with unwanted pregnancies when contraceptives failed or were not used. In 1996 the Federal Drug Administration gave approval for the dissemination of RU-486 which may provide greater access to abortion services and provides a greater range of abortion method choices. This additional family planning choice, availability of the 'morning after pill,' and the morning after use of higher dosage oral contraceptives to avert births after intercourse may also blur many of the sharp public distinctions between abortion and other contraceptive methods. However, it is incorrect to view abortion as "just another method of family planning;" its ability to function retroactively gives all methods of abortion a dimension that contraception lacks.

Abortion and Fertility

A rough indicator of the role abortion has played and continues to play in influencing U.S. fertility may be developed by considering the outcome of all medically

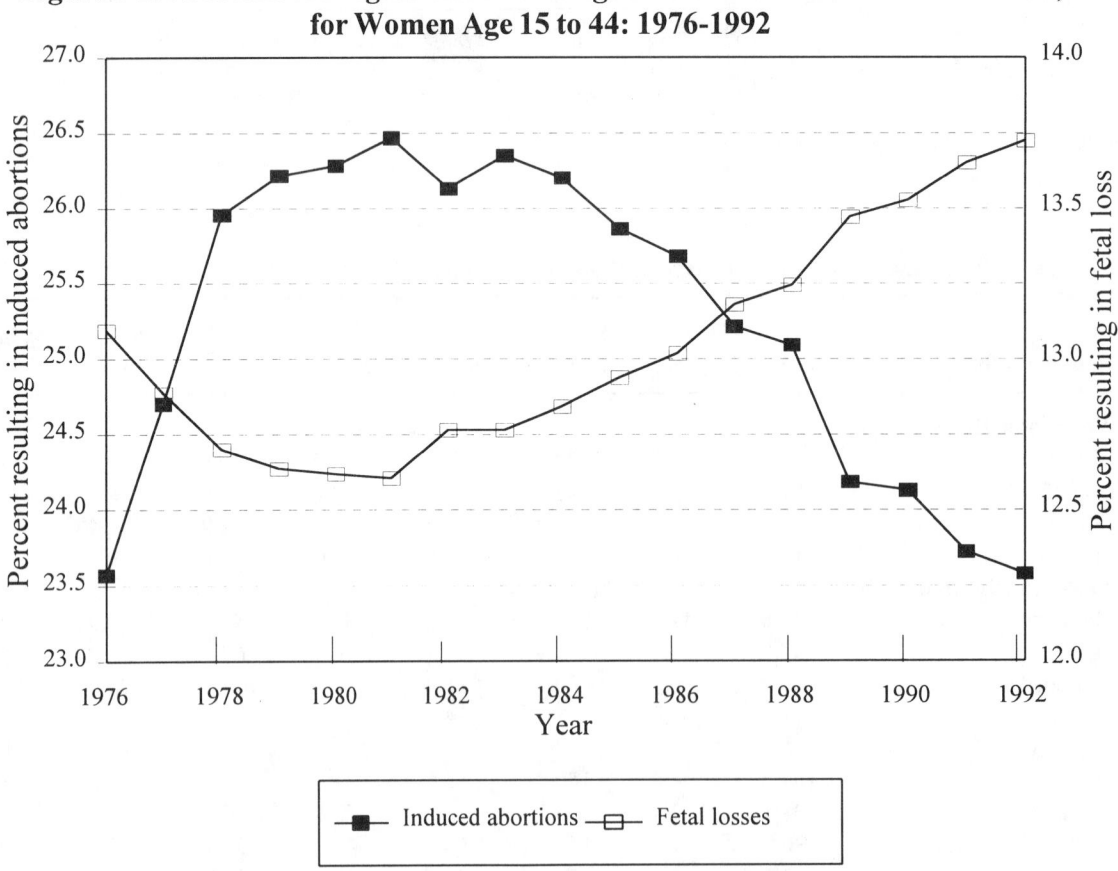

Figure 6-19. Percent of Pregnancies Resulting in Induced Abortion or Fetal Loss, for Women Age 15 to 44: 1976-1992

Source: Pregnancy data from annual NCHS reports, data on induced abortions from reports from the Alan Guttmacher Institute, and data on fetal losses from the National Survey of Family Growth.

Table 6-24. Abortion Opinion Results from the General Social Survey: 1978-1991

Reason	Percent saying yes to the question: "Please tell me whether or not you think it should be possible for a pregnant woman to obtain a legal abortion."							
	1991	1990	1989	1987	1984	1982	1980	1978
If the woman's health is seriously endangered	92	92	94	89	90	92	90	90
If she became pregnant as a result of rape	86	85	89	81	80	86	83	84
If there is a strong chance of serious defect in the baby	83	81	81	79	80	84	83	86
If the family has a low income and cannot afford any more children	48	48	46	45	46	52	52	47
If she is not married and does not want to marry the man	45	45	44	42	44	49	48	41
If she is married and does not want any more children	45	45	40	42	43	48	47	40

Sources: National Opinion Research Center, General Social Surveys, 1978-1991, survey results reported in Public Opinion, May/June 37 (1989), and Craig and O'Brien 1993, 252-254.

recognized pregnancies. Table 6-23 presents the rate of pregnancy and of various pregnancy outcomes by age and race-ethnicity for 1991. The rate of pregnancy is 91.8 per 1,000 non-Hispanic white women. It is considerably higher for non-Hispanic blacks (174.8) and Hispanics (167.4). The pregnancy rate reaches a peak for women 25 to 29 years of age and is again considerably higher for non-Hispanic blacks and Hispanics in this age group. The live birth rate for non-Hispanic white women is 61.0, indicating that two-thirds (66.8 percent) of all pregnancies result in a live birth for these women. A slightly higher percentage of pregnancies result in live births (64.6 percent) for Hispanic women. Only 50 percent of pregnancies result in a live birth among non-Hispanic black women.

Induced abortions as a percentage of all pregnancies are highest for non-Hispanic black women (37.7 percent), followed by Hispanic women (21.6 percent) and non-Hispanic white women (19.5 percent). Induced abortions are also highest at a younger age than are live births, peaking in the 20 to 24 year old age group. Among those women in this age group the percentage of all pregnancies resulting in induced abortion are considerably lower for Hispanic women (23.8 percent) and non-Hispanic white women (26.2 percent) than for non-Hispanic black women (40.5 percent). Despite variations by race-ethnicity and age, it is clear that induced abortion has a major impact upon fertility. Roughly 1 in 5 pregnancies results in an induced abortion among Hispanics and non-Hispanic whites while just over 1 in 3 pregnancies result in induced abortion among non-Hispanic blacks.

Some pregnancies result in fetal loss prior to live birth or induced abortion. The rate of fetal loss is highest for non-Hispanic white women (14.1 percent of all pregnancies), followed by Hispanic women (13.9 percent of all pregnancies), and is lowest for non-Hispanic black women (12.2 percent of all pregnancies). The higher rate of fetal loss among non-Hispanic white women is largely related to a shift to older ages of childbearing in this group (see Figure 6-5). Fetal loss may also be related to trends in the prevalence of induced abortion. Some percentage of pregnancies which are not terminated will result in fetal loss. And, if it is assumed that induced abortion is more frequently employed in higher-risk pregnancies, then a decrease in induced abortion might lead to a rise in fetal loss. Figure 6-19 suggests just such a relationship between the trends in the percentage of pregnancies resulting in induced abortion or fetal loss between 1976 and 1992. As the percentage of induced abortions rose in the period from 1976 to 1981, fetal loss declined. And, with the falling percentages of induced abortion since the early 1980s the percentage of fetal losses has risen. In the period of rising induced abortion fetal losses declined by roughly a ratio of 1 fetal loss averted per 6 induced abortions. As induced abortions declined fetal losses rose by roughly a ratio of over 1 fetal loss per 3 induced abortions averted. The greater trade-off between fetal loss and abortion in more recent years may be related to older ages of childbearing or a decline in induced abortion to levels affecting a greater percentage of high-risk births.

The high proportions of abortions among pregnancies have two other important fertility implications. First, the picture presented earlier of fertility under tight control through contraception is only partially accurate. Second, with such high abortion proportions combined with such a high prevalence of contraception, fewer babies that are truly unwanted are allowed to be born. The incidence of unwanted babies can only have diminished during the 1970s.

Adoption

by Alison Kadlec Donta

Adoption has historically been a way to build families instead of or in addition to childbearing. Over half of all children are adopted as healthy infants, and the rest are considered children with special needs. The latter category includes older children, those who are members of a sibling group, or those who have physical, emotional, or behavioral problems. Children can be adopted by a stepparent or other relative, or by a non-relative. Although the latter situation is that which receives the most media and popular attention, it has been estimated that in 1992 adoptions by stepparents made up an average of 42% of all adoptions. Adoption by any relative, including stepparents, represented as much as 63% of all adoptions in some reporting states.

In 1990, the Current Population Survey reported that 15.9% of all children of householders under age 18 lived with one biological parent and one stepparent. This percent has increased from 14.9% in 1985 and 12.8% in 1980. In those same years, 2.1%, 1.9%, and 2.9% of these same children lived with adoptive mothers and fathers. Taken together, this indicates that 18% of all children of householders under age 18 lived with at least one non-biological parent in 1990.

Despite recent interest in the topic of adoption, there is no central, national database for adoption statistics. The recently established federal Adoption and Foster Care Data Analysis and Reporting System (AFCARS) requires social service agencies to report information on all adoptions conducted by public agencies. The regulations of the AFCARS also encourage states to report data on adoptions made through private means, but these data are by no means consistent or complete. In 1992, thirty-six states indicated the proportions of adoptions carried out through public agencies. This proportion ranged from 6% to 30% with a median of 15%. It is evident that reporting of adoptions carried out by individuals or private agencies is highly variable. Privately arranged adoptions are often adoptions by relatives, and thus most of the reliable information on adoptions concerns unrelated adoptions.

According to state-reported data, the number of adoptions has remained fairly constant from 1987 to 1992. In 1992 there were 126,951 adoptions. This compares with the 118,138 adoptions in 1990 and 118,449 that occurred in 1987. In contrast, the figure below illustrates the fluctuations in unrelated domestic adoptions during the period 1951-1992. There were 51,157 such adoptions in 1951, a peak of 89,200 in 1970, and approximately 63 thousand unrelated domestic adoptions in 1992. These fluctuations reflect different data collection techniques and changing regulations regarding adoption rights as well as actual changes in the absolute number of adoptions.

The National Council for Adoption reports that foreign adoptions have been increasing during the past decade from 5,707 in 1982 to 8,327 in 1984, to a peak of 10,097 in 1987. The same agency estimates 6,500 foreign adoptions in 1992. In the late 1970's and early 1980's, the majority of foreign adoptees were from Asia and a direct result of refugee situations in various war-torn countries. Since the mid-1980's, however, there has been a steady decrease in the number of children adopted from Asia and an increase in adoptions from Europe. In 1991, these European adoptions were primarily from Romania but by 1993 the greatest proportion of European adoptees were coming from former republics of the Soviet Union. Again, this reflects the political situations in the countries affected and media attention in the United States devoted to the plight of different groups of foreign adoptees. Media attention within this country has also called attention to the increasing number of children with special needs waiting for adoption, especially those affected by substance abuse and/or infected with HIV, since the 1980's.

Percentage of Women Age 15 to 44 Who Have Ever Sought to Adopt, by Race and Selected Characteristics: 1988

Characteristic	Nonblack	Black
All women	3.5	3.5
Age		
15 to 24 years	0.5	0.5
25 to 29 years	1.5	1.9
30 to 34 years	4.4	6.0
35 to 39 years	5.8	6.9
40 to 44 years	8.4	6.3
Marital status		
Currently married	5.2	5.0
Previously married	4.5	6.1
Never married	0.5	1.7
Educational attainment		
Less than high school	2.0	1.3
High school graduate	3.6	3.2
Some college	3.7	5.3
College graduate	5.0	6.4
Desired number of children		
None	1.9	5.3
One	2.6	1.6
Two	3.1	3.3
Three or more	4.4	4.2
Fecundity status		
Contraceptively sterile	4.9	4.9
Noncontraceptively sterile	10.3	8.2
Nonsurgically sterile	24.4	4.0
Subfecund	10.6	7.8
Long interval	15.3	3.4
Fecund	1.2	2.2
Miscarriages or stillbirths		
None	2.7	2.8
One	4.9	5.0
Two or more	10.0	6.7
Children ever born		
None	2.9	2.6
One or more	4.0	3.9
Ever sought infertility services?		
Yes	17.1	15.4
No	1.6	2.3

Source: Bachrach, C.A., K.A. London, and P.L. Maza, "On the Path to Adoption: Adoption Seeking in the United States, 1988," Journal of Marriage and the Family 53 (1991):705-18, Table 2.

Adoption is sought by parents for a variety of different reasons including infertility, subfecundity, or desire to welcome a needy child into their home. The 1988 National Survey of Family Growth asked women aged 15 to 44 detailed questions relating to fertility, family planning, and other reproductive issues. In that year, 2,031,000 women sought to adopt (3.5% of all women aged 15 to 44) and 30.5% of those had adopted at least one child. The accompanying table illustrates some of the characteristics of women seeking adoption. Women with higher educational status and those in higher age groups are more likely to have sought to adopt than are those in the lower age or educational categories. Most likely to have sought adoption are nonblack women who are nonsurgically sterile (24.4%). Desire to adopt is more associated with sterility and/or subfecundity among nonblack women than among black women. However, the odds of having sought adoption are nearly five times higher for both black and nonblack women who have ever sought infertility services.

Sources

Bachrach, Christine A., London, Kathryn A., and Maza, Penelope L. " On the Path to Adoption: Adoption-Seeking in the United States, 1988." Journal of Marriage and the Family 53(1991):705-18.

Flango, Victor E., and Flango, Carol R. How Many Children were Adopted in 1992? Child Welfare 74(1995):1018-32.

Groze, Victor. Successful Adoption Families: A Longitudinal Study of Special Needs Adoption. Westport, CT: Praeger Publishers. 1996.

National Center for Health Statistics. Adoption in the 1980's. Advance Data from Vital and Health Statistics, Number 181, 1990.

National Council for Adoption. NCFA's Factsheet on Adoption. Http://www.ncfa-usa.org/factsht.htm, 1996.

United States Bureau of the Census. Marriage, Divorce, and Remarriage in the 1980's. Current Population Reports, Series P-23, Number 180, 1992.

Number of Unrelated Domestic Adoptions: 1951-1992

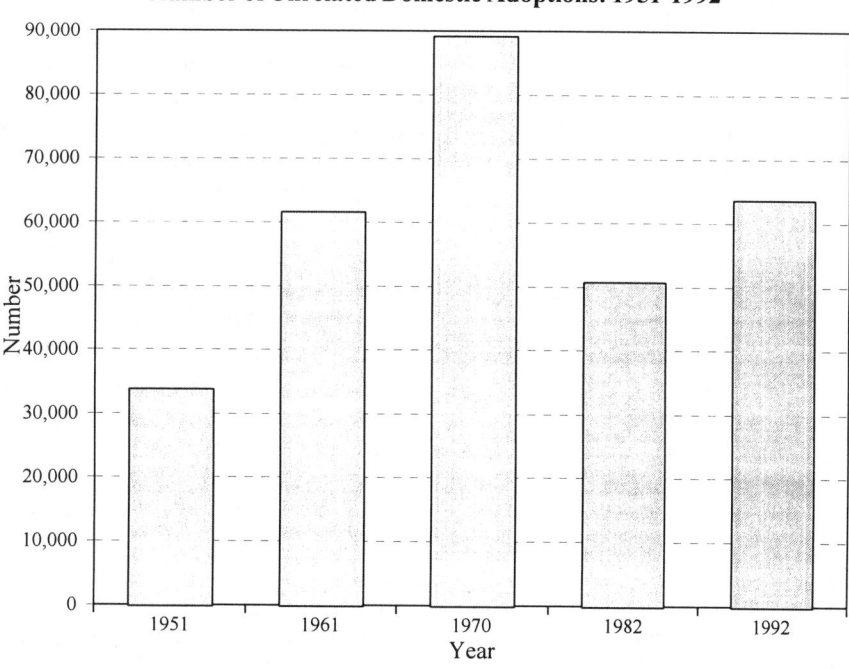

Source: 1951-1982 National Council for Adoption data and estimated 1992 number from 1992 National Center for State Courts, Adoption Technical Assistance Project data.

Abortion Opinions and Policies

Induced abortion is only the latest method of fertility control which has been socially and politically controversial. However, attitudes and opinions do affect policies which may in turn limit fertility control choices. Table 6-24, taken from the General Social Surveys from 1978 to 1991, shows a remarkable constancy in public attitudes toward abortion over these years with somewhat of a temporary decline in approval of abortion across all circumstances in the mid to later 1980s. A large majority of the population favors abortion in the cases of endangered health, rape and possible birth defects. Nearly half the population favors abortion as a choice in less severe circumstances. Various survey methods, and the treatment of non-responses, can affect these percentages to some extent. Yet, the constancy of these opinions and the substantial portion of the population favoring these fertility choices are consistent across scientifically conducted surveys.

Public opinion can, in turn, profoundly affect political policies, and policies can limit or restrict fertility choices. Table 6-25 lists individual states ordered by the number of various restrictions on abortion they impose alongside the ratio of abortions to every 1,000 births. The correlation coefficient at the bottom of this table suggests a modest negative correlation between policies and abortion ratios is evident. The greater the number of policy restrictions the less the abortion ratio. The causality of this relationship may, however, run both directions, with those states where abortion is less condoned and practiced hav-

Table 6-25. Abortion Policy Restrictions in 1988 and Abortion Ratios in 1992, by State

State	Number of restrictions	Abortions to 1,000 births
Missouri	18	175
North Dakota	17	149
Pennsylvania	17	302
Illinois	16	361
Kentucky	15	191
Louisiana	15	195
Utah	14	104
Massachusetts	12	472
Minnesota	12	251
Idaho	11	97
Nevada	11	591
South Dakota	11	92
Tennessee	11	243
Nebraska	10	246
Rhode Island	10	461
Florida	9	438
Georgia	9	350
Montana	9	298
Oklahoma	9	193
Arizona	8	295
Indiana	8	185
Wyoming	7	74
Arkansas	6	213
Delaware	6	502
Maine	6	282
California	5	519
New Mexico	5	228
New York	5	694
Ohio	5	294
South Carolina	5	229
Virginia	5	373
Wisconsin	5	223
Iowa	4	185
Maryland	4	454
Mississippi	4	176
New Jersey	4	460
Texas	4	297
Alabama	3	277
Michigan	3	393
North Carolina	3	357
Washington	3	447
West Virginia	3	134
Alaska	2	222
Colorado	2	362
Hawaii	2	617
Kansas	2	353
New Hampshire	2	269
Connecticut	1	444
Oregon	1	372
Vermont	1	393
Correlation Coefficient		-0.312

Source: Wetstein, M.E., "Abortion Rates in the United States: The Influence of Opinion and Policy," Albany, NY, State University of New York Press, 1996, Tables 23 and 31.

ing more restrictive policies as a result. In either case, abortion is one of the most heavily restricted fertility choices in the United States and future trends will depend both upon public opinion and public policies.

Childlessness

In all societies a significant proportion of women remain childless throughout their lifetime. This may be caused by inability to conceive due to either male or female sterility or by a combination of lifetime abstinence or contraception. Because of a rising age at marriage and postponement of childbearing, the proportion of young women who are still childless by the time they reach thirty is rising. This has caused some demographers to predict that lifetime childlessness may reach very high proportions, as much as 30 percent. Figure 6-20 provides the estimated percent of ever-married women who remain childless at ages 40 to 44, by race, between 1940 and 1990. As can be seen from the figure, until the onset of the baby boom, childlessness was a state for a high percentage of women who arrived at their fortieth birthday. The Great Depression, with its delayed marriage, low fertility rates, and high proportions of women never marrying, created the situation where about one-fifth of all women arrived at menopause without having had a child. This proportion declined steadily from 1950 to 1980; as a result of the "marriage boom" described in Chapter 5 and the baby boom described earlier in this chapter, a much higher proportion of women than ever before were exposed to the likelihood of pregnancy. Throughout this time childlessness was substantially higher among the black than among the white population. Physiologists estimate that roughly 5 percent of all women are unable to bear children because either they or their husbands are sterile. Thus in 1980 the proportion childless was not far from the estimated biological minimum. Even these biological limitations are being challenged by many couples seeking fertility assistance when confronting subfecundity (see Textbox). Clearly, there had been a great deal more childlessness, through choice or necessity, in the preceding years.

Starting in 1982 the proportion of childlessness began to rise again for the white and the black populations. The Current Population Survey found that 10.1 percent of all women aged 40-44 were childless in 1983, and 11.3 percent of all such women were childless in 1990. Whether or not childlessness among ever married women will return to its former very high levels, however, is questionable.

Table 6-26 reports the proportion childless in 1994 among women aged 35-44 having selected characteristics. A fairly consistent pattern emerges. Childlessness is highest among women who have the following characteristics when they reach later life stages and menopause: living in the Northeast and West, having a college or post-graduate degree, living in a central city, and employed as

Figure 6-20. Percent Childlessness Among Ever-married Women Age 40 to 44: 1940-1990

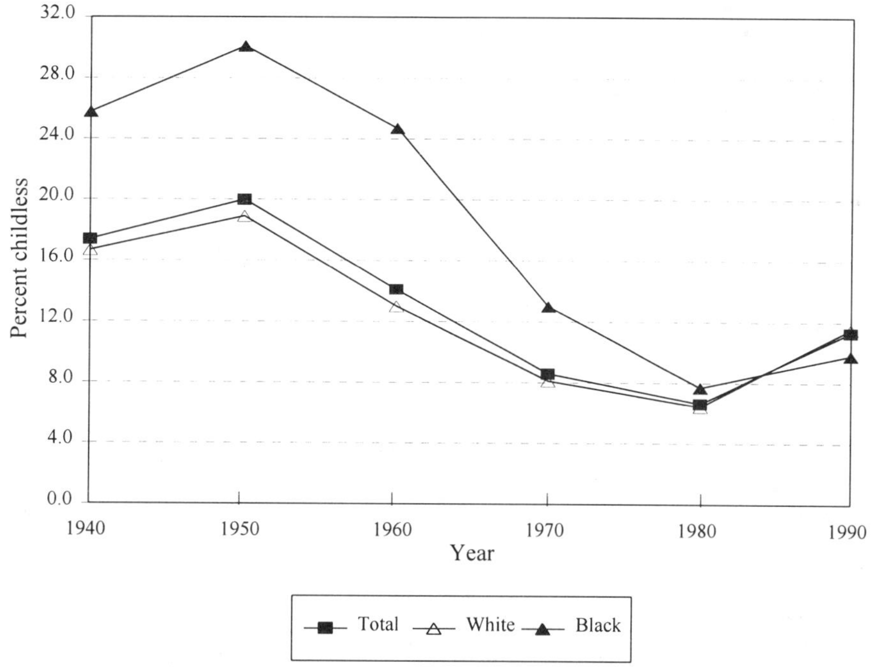

Source: 1940-1970 U.S. Census data, 1980 and 1990 CPS data.

a white-collar worker. In none of these groups except Hispanic women with college degrees does childlessness reach one in four women. Childlessness is generally higher among white women but rises more rapidly with education among Hispanic women.

Net Reproduction Rates

Population growth can be measured in a more precise way than simply looking at fertility and mortality rates. Temporary effects of age composition need to be controlled, and fertility and mortality need to be measured in age-specific terms rather than as crude rates. Demographers have developed the net reproduction rate (NRR— see Definition Box) to reveal what the long-term growth trends in the population would be if the age-specific birth and death rates were applied to the population's future age distribution. Table 6-27 reports the NRR by race for each year since 1940. This rate measures the extent to which the population is replacing itself on a long-term basis, given its present birth and death rates. Using an age distribution that would result if the population were exactly replacing itself (stationary population) at current fertility and mortality, the net reproduction rate states how many daughters 1,000 women bear each year if they follow the fixed prevailing age-specific pattern of fertility and mortality (1,000 represents exact replacement). As of 1992, the white population was 935/1,000 or 6.5 percent below replacement compared to 16.7 percent below re-

placement in 1980. The nonwhite population is 1,211/1,000 or about 21.1 percent above replacement compared to 10.6 percent above replacement in 1980. Thus the nonwhite population replaces itself at 1,211/935, or 1.295 times the rate (29.5 percent greater) of the white population in 1990. This differential has declined from 1106/833, or 1.328 (32.8 percent greater) in 1980.

Conclusion: Future Trend of Fertility

Despite the great amount of information available about fertility and the insights into trends and causes that intensive research and rich data sources provide, it is impossible to predict with any high degree of confidence whether fertility rates will rise, fall, or stay the same in the coming century. It is quite unlikely that they will change radically over the near term from their present levels. When making its long-term projections of population, the U.S. Bureau of the Census made three assumptions about the possible future course of the TFR (see Table 6-28): These merit attention as a possible set of boundaries to use in "bracketing" the range of future trends. Considering these assumptions it seems plausible to conclude that for the remainder of this century and far into the next the white population will continue to reproduce at below replacement level, that the black population will continue to rise in fertility but at a very slow level and that the Hispanic populations will experience little fertility change. Given

Table 6-26. Percent Childlessness Among Ever-married Women Age 35 to 44, by
        Selected Characteristics and Race-ethnicity: 1994

Characteristics	Total	White	Black	Hispanic
Total	12.7	13.2	8.6	9.2
Region of residence				
Northeast	14.2	14.7	8.0	16.5
Midwest	11.1	11.1	10.2	12.6
South	11.7	12.7	7.1	9.9
West	14.7	14.9	16.5	6.2
Educational attainment				
Not a high school graduate	5.8	5.5	6.6	3.6
High school, 4 years	10.1	10.7	6.5	6.5
College: 1 or more years	15.8	16.1	10.7	18.6
No degree	10.9	11.1	7.2	14.5
Associate degree	12.8	13.2	9.6	5.9
Bachelor's degree	19.6	20.1	17.1	29.5
Graduate or professional degree	22.4	22.7	13.3	—
Metropolitan residence				
Metropolitan	13.5	14.1	8.8	9.5
In central cities	14.9	16.4	8.6	10.5
Outside central cities	12.8	13.1	9.0	8.6
Nonmetropolitan	9.8	10.1	7.5	5.4
Labor force status				
In labor force	14.3	14.9	8.7	10.8
Employed	14.4	15.0	8.7	10.3
Unemployed	12.8	13.0	8.4	15.8
Not in labor force	7.8	8.0	8.3	6.8
Occupation				
Managerial and professional	19.0	19.4	13.4	15.5
Technical, sales, administrative support	13.8	14.4	7.0	12.5
Service occupations	9.9	10.0	7.3	6.4
Farming, forestry, fishing	10.0	11.2	—	—
Precision production, craft, repair	6.6	6.2	—	—
Operators, fabricators, laborers	8.7	9.5	5.8	4.3

Source: U.S. Bureau of the Census, Current Population Reports, "Fertility of American Women: June 1994,"
        Series P-20, Number 482, U.S. Government Printing Office, Washington, D.C., 1995, Table 2.

data reviewed in this chapter, however, it is still quite plausible to presume a reasonable scenario of fertility change which lies somewhere between the middle and low assumptions of Table 6-28. That is, the white and black populations may fluctuate around fertility levels consistent with replacement while Hispanic fertility declines slowly toward these levels. In such long-range projections a great deal of uncertainty is inherent. Long-term fertility trends do, however, suggest that only exceptional circumstances would produce substantial rising fertility into the first half of the coming century.

Bibliography

Anderson, Douglas K. "Adolescent Mothers Drop Out." American Sociological Review 58(1993): 735-38.

Bean, Frank D., and Swicegood, Gray. "Generation, Female Education and Mexican American Fertility." Social Science Quarterly 63(1982):131-44.

Bennett, Neil G., Bloom, David E., and Miller, Cynthia K. "The Influence of Nonmarital Childbearing on the Formation of First Marriages." Demography 32(1995): 47-62.

Blake, Judith. "Is Zero Preferred? American Attitudes Toward Childlessness in the 1970s." Journal of Marriage and the Family 41(1979):245-57.

Bloom, David E., and Pebley, Anne R. "Voluntary Childlessness: A Review of the Evidence and Implications." Population Research and Policy Review 1(1982):203-24.

Bouvier, Leon F. "America's Baby Boom Generation: The Fateful Bulge." Population Bulletin 35 (1980):1-35.

Table 6-27. Net Reproductive Rates, by Race of Child: 1940-1992

Year[1]	Total	White	Nonwhite
1992	990	935	1,211
1991	995	939	1,229
1990	997	941	1,233
1989	964	907	1,207
1988	925	873	1,155
1987	896	849	1,106
1986	879	836	1,075
1985	881	841	1,072
1984	864	823	1,055
1983	859	819	1,058
1982	873	832	1,079
1981	864	823	1,078
1980	876	833	1,106
1979	861	817	1,099
1978	837	793	1,076
1977	851	809	1,082
1976	825	785	1,053
1975	841	800	1,076
1974	869	828	1,103
1973	889	844	1,152
1972	950	902	1,238
1971	1,071	1,022	1,369
1970	1,168	1,125	1,433
1969	1,161	1,113	1,473
1968	1,166	1,116	1,495
1967	1,213	1,158	1,582
1966	1,288	1,231	1,678
1965	1,376	1,314	1,802
1964	1,507	1,447	1,923
1963	1,564	1,506	1,973
1962	1,633	1,577	2,033
1961	1,704	1,648	2,100
1960	1,715	1,662	2,093
1959	1,722	1,667	2,118
1958	1,736	1,675	2,178
1957	1,765	1,701	2,206
1956	1,729	1,665	2,184
1955	1,676	1,617	2,101
1954	1,657	1,601	2,062
1953	1,597	1,546	1,959
1952	1,563	1,516	1,897
1951	1,521	1,472	1,865
1950	1,435	1,387	1,780
1949	1,439	1,397	1,743
1948	1,430	1,400	1,679
1947	1,505	1,492	1,594
1946	1,344	1,331	1,435
1945	1,132	1,106	1,323
1944	1,163	1,139	1,334
1943	1,228	1,211	1,348
1942	1,185	1,171	1,293
1941	1,075	1,052	1,242
1940	1,027	1,002	1,209

[1] Births prior to 1959 have been adjusted for underregistration.

Source: National Center for Health Statistics, "Vital Statistics of the United States, Volume I--Natality: 1992," National Center for Health Statistics, Hyattsville, MD, 1995, Table 1-5.

Table 6-28. Total Fertility Projections, by Race-ethnicity: 1995-2050

Year and race-ethnicity	Fertility assumption		
	Low	Middle	High
Total			
1995	2,055.3	2,055.3	2,055.3
2000	1,937.5	2,071.6	2,194.3
2005	1,860.7	2,086.9	2,303.3
2010	1,791.4	2,107.5	2,423.7
2020	1,822.8	2,144.0	2,465.2
2030	1,855.0	2,180.4	2,505.8
2040	1,881.3	2,211.4	2,541.6
2050	1,909.6	2,244.7	2,580.2
White			
1995	1,983.8	1,983.8	1,983.8
2000	1,874.0	2,003.7	2,122.4
2005	1,802.7	2,021.8	2,231.4
2010	1,738.9	2,045.8	2,352.7
2020	1,779.8	2,092.5	2,405.2
2030	1,822.0	2,139.4	2,456.7
2040	1,859.8	2,183.1	2,506.4
2050	1,901.0	2,229.8	2,558.9
Black			
1995	2,426.7	2,426.7	2,426.7
2000	2,273.4	2,430.8	2,574.8
2005	2,170.8	2,434.7	2,687.2
2010	2,172.4	2,438.1	2,803.8
2020	2,078.9	2,445.6	2,812.4
2030	2,085.6	2,452.7	2,819.8
2040	2,092.3	2,459.6	2,826.9
2050	2,099.2	2,466.7	2,834.0
Hispanic			
1995	2,976.9	2,976.9	2,976.9
2000	2,783.5	2,976.9	3,152.5
2005	2,653.0	2,976.9	3,284.0
2010	2,529.0	2,976.9	3,421.6
2020	2,529.0	2,976.9	3,421.6
2030	2,529.0	2,976.9	3,421.6
2040	2,529.0	2,976.9	3,421.6
2050	2,529.0	2,976.9	3,421.6

Source: U.S. Bureau of the Census, Current Population Reports, "Population Projections of the United States, by Age, Sex, Race, and Hispanic Origin: 1995 to 2050," Series P-25, Number 1130, U.S. Government Printing Office, Washington, D.C., 1996, Tables A-1, A-2, A-3, and A-6.

Caldwell, John C. The Theory of Fertility Decline. New York: Academic Press. 1982.

Carlson, E. "Dispersion of Childbearing Outside Marriage." Sociology and Social Research 66 (1982):335-47.

Casterline, John, and Trussell, James. "Age at First Birth." Comparative Studies 15(1980).

Chen, Renbao, and Morgan, S. Philip. "Recent Trends in Timing of First Birth in the United States." Demography 28(1991): 513-34.

Cochrane, Susan H. "Effects of Education and Urbanization on Fertility." In Determinants of Fertility in Developing Countries. Rodolfo Bulatao and Ronald D. Lee (eds.). New York: Academic Press. 1983.

Coombs, L.C., and Fernandez, D. "Husband-Wife Agreement about Reproductive Goals." Demography 15(1978):57-73.

Cummings, M., and Cummings, S. "Family Planning Among the Urban Poor: Sexual Politics and Social Policy." Family Relations 32(1983):47-58.

Dryfoos, John. "Contraceptive Use, Pregnancy Intentions and Pregnancy Outcomes Among U.S. Women." Family Planning Perspectives 14(1982):81-93.

Duncan, Greg J., and Hoffman, Saul D. "Welfare Benefits, Economic Opportunities, and Out-of-Wedlock Births Among Black Teenage Girls." Demography 27(1990): 519-36.

Easterlin, Richard A. Birth and Fortune: The Impact of Numbers on Personal Welfare. New York: Basic Books. 1980.

Easterlin, Richard A., and Crimmins, Eileen M. The Fertility Revolution: A Supply-Demand Analysis. Chicago: University of Chicago Press. 1985.

Ewbank, Douglas C. "Estimating Birth Stopping and Spacing Behavior." Demography 26(1989): 473-84.

Feeney, G. "Population Dynamics Based on Birth Intervals and Parity Progression." Population Studies 35(1982): 65-78.

Huber, J. "Will U.S. Fertility Decline Toward Zero?" Sociological Quarterly 21(1980):481-92.

Jain, A.K. "Effect of Female Education on Fertility: A Simple Explanation," Demography 18 (1981):577-95.

James, W.H. "Causes of the Decline in Fecundability with Age." Social Biology 26(1979):330-34.

Joyce, Theodore, and Kaestner, Robert. "The Effect of Expansions in Medicaid Income Eligibility on Abortion." Demography 33(1996): 181-92.

Kahn, Joan R. "Intergenerational Patterns of Teenage Fertility." Demography 29(1992): 39-58.

Kahn, Joan R., Rindfuss, Ronald R., and Guilkey, David K. "Adolescent Contraceptive Method Choices." Demography 27(1990): 323-36.

Keyfitz, N. "On the Momentum of Population Growth." Demography 7(1971):71-80.

Kitagawa, Evelyn M. "New Life-Styles: Marriage Patterns, Living Arrangements, and Fertility Outside of Marriage." American Academy of Political and Social Science Annals 453 (1981):1-27.

Kraft, Joan Marie, and Coverdill, James E. "Employment and the Use of Birth Control by Sexually Active Single Hispanic, Black, and White Women." Demography 31(1994): 593-602.

Lee, Ronald D. "Demographic Forecasting and the Easterlin Hypothesis." Population and Development Review 2(1976):459-68.

Lopez, D.E., and Sabagh, G. "Untangling Structural and Normative Aspects of the Minority Status-Fertility Hypothesis." American Journal of Sociology 83(1978):1491-97.

Macunovich, Diane J., Easterlin, Richard A., Crimmins, Eileen M., and Schaeffer, Christine M. "Echoes of the Baby Boom and Bust." Demography 32(1995): 17-28.

Marini, M.M. "Effects of the Number and Spacing of Children on Marital and Parental Satisfaction ." Demography 17(1980): 225-42.

_____. "Effects of the Timing of Marriage and First Birth on Fertility." Journal of Marriage and the Family 43(1981):27-46.

Mason, Karen Oppenheim, and Kuhlthau, Karen. "The Perceived Impact of Child Care Costs on Women's Labor Supply and Fertility." Demography 29(1992): 523-44.

McCann, Carole R. Birth Control Politics in the United States, 1916-1945. Ithaca, NY: Cornell University Press. 1994.

Meier, Kenneth J., Haider-Markel, Donald P., Stanislawski, Anthony J., and McFarlane, Deborah R. "The Impact of State-Level Restrictions on Abortion." Demography 33(1996): 307-12.

Mineau, G.P., and Trussel, T.J. "A Specification of Marital Fertility by Parent's Age, Age at Marriage, and Marital Duration." Demography 19(1982):335-49.

Modell, Judith S. Kinship with Strangers: Adoption and Interpretations of Kinship in American Culture. Berkeley: University of California Press. 1994.

Mosher, William D., Williams, Linda B., and Johnson, David P. "Religion and Fertility in the United States: New Patterns." Demography 29(1992): 199-214.

Nathanson, Constance A., and Kim, Young J. "Components of Change in Adolescent Fertility, 1971-1979." Demography 26(1989): 85-98.

National Center for Health Statistics. Vital Statistics of the United States, Volume I—Natality. Hyattsville, MD: National Center for Health Statistics, annual volumes 1969-1991.

_____. Contraceptive Use in the United States: 1973-1988. Advance Data from Vital and Health Statistics, Number 182, 1990.

_____. Monthly Vital Statistics Reports, Volume 41, Number 6, Supplement, 1993.

_____. Contraceptive Use in the United States: 1982-1990. Advance Data from Vital and Health Statistics, Number 260, 1995.

_____. Monthly Vital Statistics Reports, Volume 43, Number 12, 1995.

_____. Vital Statistics of the United States, Volume I—Natality: 1992. Hyattsville, MD: National Center for Health Statistics. 1995.

National Institutes of Child Health and Human Development. "Fertility Change after the Baby Boom: The Role of Economic Stress, Female Employment, and Education." Population and Environment 3(1980).

National Opinion Research Center. General Social Surveys, 1978-1991. Public Opinion 37(1989):252-54.

O'Connell, Martin. "Comparative Estimates of Teenage Illegitimacy in the United States, 1940-44 to 1970-74." Demography 17(1980):13-23.

Pampel, Fred C. "Relative Cohort Size and Fertility: The Socio-Political Context of the Easterlin Effect." American Sociological Review 58(1993): 496-514.

Pebley, A. "Changing Attitudes Toward the Timing of First Births." Family Planning Perspectives 13(1981):171-75.

Pfeffer, Naomi. The Stork and the Syringe: A Political History of Reproductive Medicine. Cambridge, MA: Polity Press. 1993.

Plotnick, Robert D. "The Effects of Attitudes on Teenage Premarital Pregnancy and Its Resolution." American Sociological Review 57(1992): 800-11.

Population Reference Bureau. "Fertility." Population Bulletin 37(1982):7-11.

Presser, Harriet B. "Can We Make Time for Children? The Economy, Work Schedules, and Child Care." Demography 26(1989): 523-44.

Preston, S.H. The Effects of Infant and Child Mortality on Fertility. New York: Academic Press. 1978.

RagonJ, Helena. Surrogate Motherhood: Conception in the Heart. Boulder, CO: Westview. 1994.

Rindfuss, Ronald R. "The Young Adult Years: Diversity, Structural Change, and Fertility." Demography 28(1991): 493-512.

Rindfuss, Ronald R., and Bumpass, Larry. "How Old Is Too Old? Age and the Sociology of Fertility." Family Planning Perspectives 8(1976):43-55.

Rindfuss, Ronald R., and Sweet, James. Postwar Fertility Trends and Differentials in the United States. New York: Academic Press. 1977.

Rindfuss, Ronald R., Morgan, S. Philip, and Offutt, Kate. "Education and the Changing Age Pattern of American Fertility: 1963-1989." Demography 33(1996): 277-90.

Schultz, T. Paul. Economics of Population. Reading, MA: Addison-Wesley. 1981.

Sheps, M.C., and Menken, J.A. Mathematical Models of Conception and Birth. Chicago: University of Chicago Press. 1973.

Smith, Herbert L., Morgan, S. Philip, and Koropeckyj-Cox, Tanya. "A Decomposition of Trends in the Nonmarital Fertility Ratios of Blacks and Whites in the United States, 1960-1992." Demography 33(1996): 141-52.

St. John, Craig. "Race Differences in Age at First Birth and the Pace of Subsequent Fertility: Implications for the Minority Group Status Hypothesis." Demography 19(1982):301-14.

Suchindran, C.M., and Koo, Helen P. "Age at Last Birth and Its Components." Demography 29(1992): 227-46.

Thompson, Warren S., and Whelpton, P.K. Population Trends in the United States. New York: McGraw-Hill. 1933.

Thomson, Elizabeth, and Brandreth, Yvonne. "Measuring Fertility Demand." Demography 32(1995): 81-96.

Tilly, C. (ed.). Historical Studies of Changing Fertility. Princeton, NJ: Princeton University Press. 1978.

Trussell, James, Menken, Jane, and Coale, Ansley J. "A General Model for Analyzing the Effect of Nuptiality on Fertility." In Nuptiality and Fertility: Proceedings of a Conference. L. Ruzicka (ed.). Liege, Belgium: Ordina Editions. 1982.

United States Bureau of the Census. "Historical Statistics of the United States: Colonial Times to 1970." Washington, D.C.: U.S. Government Printing Office. 1975.

_____. Fertility of American Women: June 1980. Current Population Reports, Series P-20, Number 375. Washington, D.C.: U.S. Government Printing Office. 1982.

_____. Fertility of American Women: June 1990. Current Population Reports, Series P-20, Number 454. Washington, D.C.: U.S. Government Printing Office. 1991.

_____. Fertility of American Women: June 1994. Current Population Reports, Series P-20, Number 482. Washington, D.C.: U.S. Government Printing Office. 1995.

_____. Population Projections of the United States, by Age, Sex, Race, and Hispanic Origin: 1995 to 2050. Current Population Reports, Series P-25, Number 1130. Washington, D.C.: U.S. Government Printing Office. 1996.

Upchurch, Dawn M., McCarthy, James, and Ferguson, Linda R. "Childbearing and Schooling: Disentangling Temporal and Causal Mechanisms." American Sociological Review 58(1993): 738-40.

Wachter, Kenneth W., and Lee, Ronald D. "U.S. Births and Limit Cycle Models." Demography 26(1989): 99-116.

Westoff, Charles F., and Ryder, Norman B. The Contraceptive Revolution. Princeton, NJ: Princeton University Press. 1977.

Wetstein, Matthew E. Abortion Rates in the United States: The Influence of Opinion and Policy. Albany, NY: State University of New York Press. 1996.

Wu, Lawrence L. "Effects of Family Instability, Income, and Income Instability on the Risk of a Premarital Birth." American Sociological Review 61(1996): 386-406.

Wu, Lawrence L., and Martinson, Brian C. "Family Structure and the Risk of a Premarital Birth." American Sociological Review 58(1993): 210-32.

Zelnik, Melvin, and Kantner, John. "Sexuality, Contraception and Pregnancy Among Young Unwed Females in the U.S." In Demographic and Social Aspects of Population Growth (Vol. I, Commission on Population Growth and the American Future, Research Reports). Charles Westoff and Robert Parks, Jr. (eds.). Washington, DC: U.S. Government Printing Office. 1972.

HEALTH AND DISABILITY

Several conflicting trends are affecting the health and disability of the United States population. The aging of the population is one of the most important influences on prevalent disabilities. As more of the population is found at older ages, different forms of disability are more common. An increasing proportion of disability in the population is not purely physical, but now involves mental illness or drug and alcohol dependence. Another major influence on disability and health care delivery systems is the increasing incidence of various conditions, such as asthma and autoimmune deficiency syndrome, which can have debilitating effects over a substantial portion of life.

Paradoxically, even modern medicine's ability to save accident victims and premature infants has also now frequently resulted in survivors with severe life-long disabilities. Changing lifestyles and behavior have also influenced the population's health. Disability is affected by high and increasing rates of obesity in the population. Although smoking and related diseases have begun to decline for some segments of the population, these hazardous behaviors have increased for others. Some evidence supports concern over resurgent socioeconomic differentials in the health of the population. Violent crime and homicide, trends now in slight decline, present a threatening urban environment which is increasingly concentrated in the disadvantaged segments of society. The complex factors affecting the health of the population mean that policy considerations and the needs for health data are constantly evolving.

Nonetheless, most demographers have exhibited curiously little interest in the health and disability of the population, even though these factors can affect such demographic variables as fertility, mortality and family composition. Health and disability can obviously also have a profound effect on the quality of life and on labor force participation. The inclusion of new questions on disability on the 1990 Census and the increasing availability of survey data on various aspects of these topics during the 1980's and 1990's also allow us to provide more detail concerning health and disability.

Public health specialists, on the other hand, tend to emphasize the incidence of new cases for different diseases and conditions rather than their prevalence and long-term trends. While the publication of a set of national goals in *Healthy People 2000* in 1991 gave renewed attention to some of the shortcomings of our national health system, it emphasized bureaucratic targets for incidence rates and failed to provide a systematic analysis of health. The goals also frequently failed to emphasize subgroups of the population (often minority groups) who had far higher than average rates of incidence or prevalence of some conditions. Many of these subgroups sometimes occupy socioeconomic positions in American society which could make any cure or convergence on majority rates of disease more difficult than might otherwise be assumed.

This chapter will consider the diseases, disabilities and conditions to which each age is particularly prone and those which present major problems to specific segments of the population. Fatal conditions are reserved for the mortality chapter. Here we are concerned with the origins of disabilities, the successes and shortcomings of the medical system, and the new and largely unpredicted threats to health (ranging from AIDS to repetitive motion injuries) that have emerged in the last decade. While some diseases, conditions and injuries affect people at different ages, they will usually be examined in relation to the age group on which they have the greatest effect.

Three other aspects of health will also be considered here. The self-evaluation of health and disability is an area where national survey and census data are just beginning to become available, and some of these findings will be presented. We are also becoming increasingly aware that the United States' health resources are

Chapter 7 Definitions
HEALTH AND DISABILITY

The following definitions of health and disability terms are primarily drawn from Health, United States 1994 and other sources. Specific definitions used by the substantial variety of data sources referenced in this chapter may differ slightly.

Health. A complete state of mental, physical, and emotional well-being.

Disability. A reduction in a person's activity, either short- or long-term, as a result of any acute or chronic condition.

Incidence. The number of new cases of a disease during a specified time period. It is often expressed as an incidence rate per population group (e.g. per 100,000 population).

Prevalence. The number of existing cases of a disease in a population at a specific point in time (point prevalence) or over a specified time period (period prevalence). It is often expressed as a prevalence rate per population group (e.g. per 100,000 population).

Acute Condition. A departure from a state of physical or mental well-being that has lasted less than three months. Most injuries (e.g. fractures and sprains) are initially classified as acute conditions although they may eventually have chronic manifestations.

Chronic Condition. A departure from a state of physical and/or mental well-being that has lasted three months or more. In addition, some conditions, such as diabetes, arthritis, and emphysema, are considered chronic regardless of their time of onset.

Restricted-activity Days. Any day on which, due to an injury or an illness, a person reduces his or her usual activities by more than one-half day. Such days are often used to indicate partially restricted mobility or productivity.

Bed-disability Days. Any day on which, due to a specific injury or illness, a person stays in bed for more than one-half of his or her normal waking hours. Such days are frequently used to indicate more seriously restricted mobility.

Work Disability. A reduction in a person's activity, either short- or long-term, as a result of any acute or chronic condition related to a person's work or working conditions.

Mobility or Self-care Limitations. Reduction in a person's ability to conduct individual personal care and/or mobility due to a specific injury or illness. Limitations are frequently linked to the injury or illness responsible.

Inpatient Care. The provision of medical care in a hospital setting requiring patient residence in that hospital for the duration of that care.

Outpatient Care. The provision of medical care in either a hospital, clinic, or physician's office not requiring patient residence in the facility. Outpatient visits generally last less than a few hours. Routine visits to the emergency room are typically classified as outpatient care.

Prenatal Care. Preventive medical care given to pregnant women designed to in-

crease the probability of delivering a healthy, full-term infant. Ideally, prenatal care should begin as soon as possible in the first trimester of pregnancy.

Fetal Care. Medical care, especially monitoring, given to a fetus usually immediately before birth designed to prevent and minimize fetal distress.

Discharge. The completion of any continuous stay in a hospital as an inpatient. Alternatively, it can be considered as the formal release of an inpatient by a hospital due to death, or transfer to another facility or place of residence. Discharge data do not generally include releases of healthy newborn infants. Discharge data are frequently presented as an alternative indicator of admissions.

Cancer Survival. Usually quantified as the number of years a person lives after being diagnosed with cancer, whether or not the cancer has been cured, cancer survival is often measured by the percentage of the population of cases surviving past a given number (e.g. 5 or 10) of years after initial diagnosis.

Quality of Life. Usually a self-reported measure of overall satisfaction of health status and ability to maintain personal activities. Often measured with respect to ability to carry out various activities required for independent daily living.

Ergonomic Hazards. Hazards to workers resulting from the design of workplace equipment or from the ways in which such equipment is commonly used.

---

not unlimited. Data on the changing nature of institutionalization for various mental conditions and the sharp decline in the average length of stay in hospitals for different causes, two other major trends in health, will be presented.

The Health of Infants

While there have been some recent declines in infant mortality in the United States (see the mortality chapter), the United States ranks below a number of other industrialized nations in its infant mortality rate (in 1990 it ranked twenty-fourth in its infant mortality rate and eighteenth in its feto-infant mortality rate; Health, United States 1993:88). This is particularly surprising since it ranks first among these countries in terms of proportion of Gross Domestic Product (13.2 percent) devoted to total health expenditure (Health, United States 1993:220).

One major reason for this poor performance in infant health and mortality is the low proportion of mothers who begin prenatal care in their first trimester of preg-

nancy. As Table 7-1 shows, only about three out of every four mothers begin their prenatal care and education in the first trimester, and this proportion has not risen appreciably since 1980. For minority groups the record is even worse; just over six in ten black, American Indian or Hispanic origin mothers began prenatal care in the first trimester in 1992. The percent of all mothers receiving only third trimester or no prenatal care actually increased (from 5.1 to 5.2 percent) during the 1980-90 period, with black (9.9 percent) and American Indian, Eskimo and Aleut (11.0 percent) mothers having the highest proportions receiving very late or no prenatal care in 1992.

While early prenatal care is lacking for one out of every four births, the overwhelming majority of births continue to take place in hospitals. In 1970, about 0.6 percent of all births took place outside of hospitals (Table 7-2); this figure grew to 1.1 percent in 1991, due to a quadrupling of non-hospital births among whites. The percentage of births attended by midwives has increased steadily since 1975 to 4.4 percent in 1991, but this in-

Table 7-1. Prenatal Care for Live Births, by Race-ethnicity of Mother: 1970-1992

Prenatal care and race-ethnicity of mother	Percent of all live births[1]					
	1970	1975	1980	1985	1990	1992
Prenatal care begun during 1st trimester						
Total	68.0	72.4	76.3	76.2	75.8	77.7
White	72.3	75.8	79.2	79.3	79.2	80.8
Black	44.2	55.5	62.4	61.5	60.6	63.9
American Indian, Eskimo, Aleut	38.2	45.4	55.8	57.5	57.9	62.1
Asian or Pacific Islander	—	—	73.7	74.1	75.1	76.6
Hispanic[2]	—	—	60.2	61.2	60.2	64.2
Prenatal care begun during 3rd trimester or no prenatal care						
Total	7.9	6.0	5.1	5.7	6.1	5.2
White	6.3	5.0	4.3	4.8	4.9	4.2
Black	16.6	10.5	8.9	10.2	11.3	9.9
American Indian, Eskimo, Aleut	28.9	22.4	15.2	12.9	12.9	11.0
Asian or Pacific Islander	—	—	6.5	6.5	5.8	4.9
Hispanic[2]	—	—	12.0	12.4	12.0	9.5

[1] Excludes live births for whom data on beginning of prenatal care is unknown.

[2] Trend data for Hispanics are affected by expansion of the reporting area for an Hispanic-origin item on the birth certificate and by immigration. The number of states in the reporting area increased from 22 in 1980 to 23 and the District of Columbia in 1983-87, to 48 and DC in 1990, and to 49 and DC in 1991-92.

Source: National Center for Health Statistics, "Health United States: 1994," Public Health Service, Hyattsville, MD, 1995, Table 9.

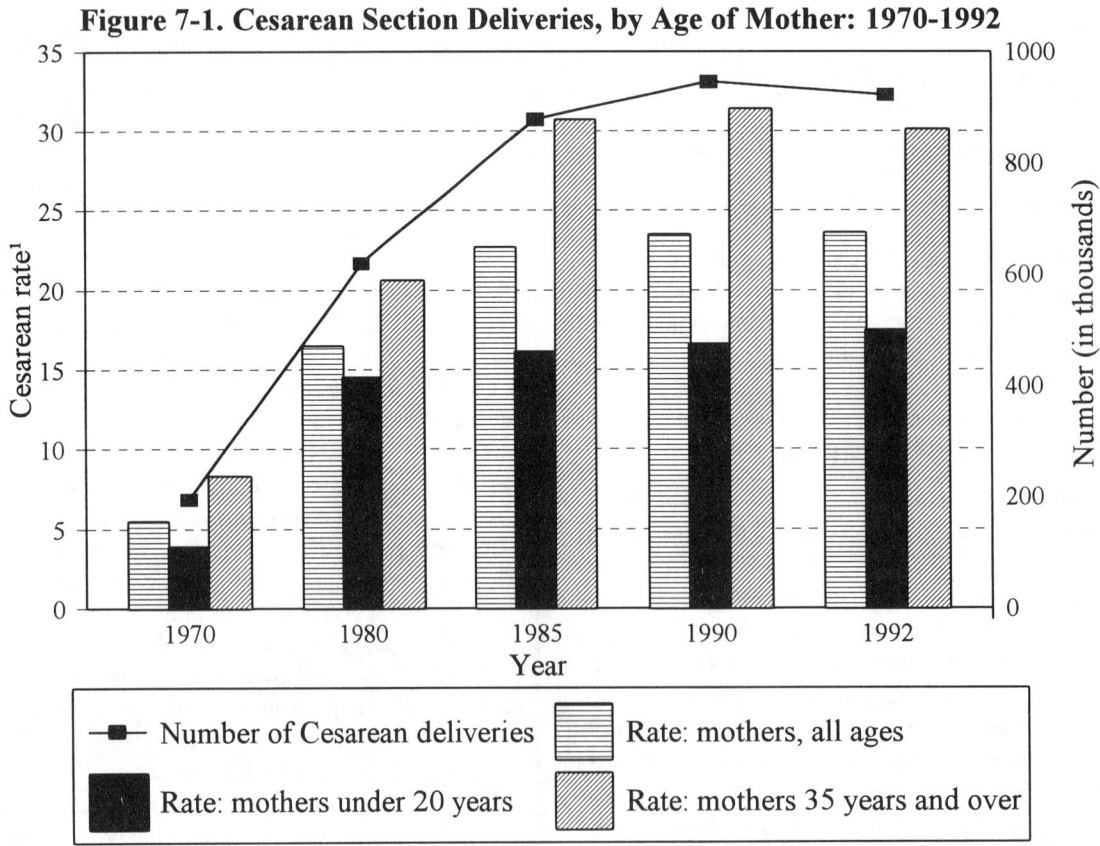

Figure 7-1. Cesarean Section Deliveries, by Age of Mother: 1970-1992

Legend:
- Number of Cesarean deliveries
- Rate: mothers under 20 years
- Rate: mothers, all ages
- Rate: mothers 35 years and over

[1] Rate is the number of Cesarean deliveries per 100 total deliveries.
Source: U.S. National Center for Health Statistics data.

Table 7-2. Live Births by Place of Delivery, Attendant, and Race of Child: 1970-1991

| Year and race | Total births | Percent of live births | | | | | |
| | | In hospital[1] | | | Not in hospital | | |
		Total	Physician	Midwife	Total	Physician	Midwife
All races							
1991	4,110,907	98.9	94.5	3.9	1.1	0.3	0.5
1990	4,158,212	98.8	95.0	3.4	1.2	0.4	0.5
1985	3,760,561	99.0	96.4	2.3	1.0	0.3	0.4
1980[2]	3,612,258	99.0	97.1	1.4	1.0	0.3	0.3
1975[2]	3,144,198	99.1	98.4	0.6	0.9	0.4	0.3
1970[3]	3,731,386	99.4	—	—	0.6	0.1	0.4
White							
1991	3,174,030	98.8	94.8	3.6	1.2	0.3	0.6
1990	3,225,343	98.8	95.3	3.1	1.2	0.3	0.6
1985	2,991,373	98.9	96.6	2.0	1.1	0.3	0.5
1980[2]	2,898,732	99.0	97.3	1.2	1.0	0.3	0.3
1975[2]	2,551,996	99.3	98.8	0.4	0.7	0.3	0.2
1970[3]	3,091,264	99.7	—	—	0.3	0.1	0.1
Black							
1991	725,163	99.1	93.7	4.8	0.9	0.4	0.1
1990	724,576	99.1	94.0	4.4	0.9	0.4	0.1
1985	608,193	99.4	95.9	3.1	0.6	0.3	0.1
1980[2]	589,616	99.3	96.5	2.4	0.7	0.4	0.2
1975[2]	511,581	98.3	96.6	1.5	1.7	0.6	0.9
1970[3]	572,362	97.6	—	—	2.4	0.2	2.0

[1] Includes births occurring en route to or on arrival at hospital. Before 1975 includes all births in hospitals or institutions
   and births in clinics only if attended by physicians. Beginning in 1975 includes all births in clinics regardless of attendant.
[2] Based on 100 percent of births in selected states and on a 50 percent sample of births in all other states .
[3] Based on a 50 percent sample of births.

Source: U.S. National Center for Health Statistics, "Vital Statistics of the United States: Volume I," 1991, Tables 87 and 88,
   and 1975, Table 35, Public Health Service, Washington, D.C., 1995 and 1975.

crease has been almost entirely in midwife-attended deliveries within hospitals.

One factor compensating for the nation's shortcomings in prenatal care and education was a revolution in
late term fetal care. Advances in the monitoring of fetal
distress and maternal health led to a great increase in
Cesarean section deliveries. In 1970, there were 195,000
Cesarean deliveries in the U.S., or 5.5 percent of all deliveries (Figure 7-1). By 1992, the total of Cesarean deliveries had risen to 921,000, or 23.6 percent of all births.
Older mothers are more likely to have Cesarean deliveries, and the shift in the 1980's towards a larger proportion of births contributed by older mothers also influenced
this trend towards a larger proportion of births by Cesarean section.

Another key indicator of prenatal health is birth
weight. How have the changes in medical practice and
technology and the profound changes in ages of mothers

and marital behavior affected the weight of infants at birth?
The median birth weight of white babies rose from 7 lb.-
5 oz. in 1970 to 7 lb.-9 oz. in 1985-88, then dropped an
ounce during 1989-91 (Table 7-3). Black infants followed
a similar pattern of rise and decline, but their median
weight rose only one ounce (to 6 lb.-15 oz.) between 1970
and 1991.

While median birth weight is of interest, more concern is usually directed at the proportion of all births that
are of low (since 1975 defined as births of less than 2,500
grams, or less than 5 lb.-8 oz.) or very low (below 1,500
grams or 3 lb. 4 oz.) birth weight. Between 1970 and
1991, the proportion of all births with low birth weight
declined from 7.9 to 7.1 percent of all births (Table 7-4).
However, the more rapid decline of the proportion of white
compared to black low birth rate babies resulted in an
increasing racial gap. In 1970, black low birth weight
babies were 104 percent more common than white ones;

Table 7-3. Median Birth Weight, by Race of Mother and Weeks of Gestation: 1970-1991

Race and weeks of gestation[1]	1970*		1975**		1980**		1985		1990		1991	
	lbs	oz	lbs	oz	lbs	oz	lbs	oz	lbs	oz	lbs	oz
All races	7	4	7	5	7	7	7	7	7	7	7	7
20 to 27 weeks	2	6	2	1	2	1	2	2	1	13	1	13
28 to 31 weeks	4	3	4	0	4	0	4	2	4	0	3	15
32 to 35 weeks	5	13	5	13	5	14	5	15	5	14	5	13
36 weeks	6	6	6	7	6	7	6	7	6	7	6	7
37 to 39 weeks	7	1	7	2	7	4	7	4	7	4	7	4
40 weeks	7	7	7	9	7	10	7	11	7	11	7	11
41 weeks[2]	7	11	7	12	7	14	7	14	7	14	7	14
42 weeks and over[3]	7	10	7	11	7	13	7	13	7	13	7	12
White	7	5	7	7	7	8	7	9	7	8	7	8
20 to 27 weeks	2	3	2	0	2	0	2	1	1	13	1	13
28 to 31 weeks	4	0	3	15	3	14	4	0	3	14	3	13
32 to 35 weeks	5	12	5	13	5	13	5	14	5	14	5	13
36 weeks	6	6	6	7	6	8	6	8	6	8	6	7
37 to 39 weeks	7	2	7	3	7	5	7	5	7	6	7	6
40 weeks	7	8	7	9	7	11	7	13	7	13	7	13
41 weeks[2]	7	12	7	13	7	15	7	15	8	0	8	0
42 weeks and over[3]	7	11	7	12	7	15	7	14	7	14	7	14
Black	6	14	6	15	7	0	7	0	7	0	6	15
20 to 27 weeks	2	10	2	3	2	2	2	2	1	14	1	14
28 to 31 weeks	4	9	4	4	4	4	4	6	4	3	4	2
32 to 35 weeks	6	0	5	15	5	15	6	0	5	14	5	13
36 weeks	6	6	6	6	6	6	6	6	6	5	6	5
37 to 39 weeks	6	13	6	14	6	15	7	0	7	0	6	15
40 weeks	7	3	7	3	7	5	7	5	7	5	7	5
41 weeks[2]	7	4	7	5	7	6	7	7	7	7	7	7
42 weeks and over[3]	7	3	7	4	7	5	7	5	7	5	7	5

[1] Births with periods of gestation of less than 20 weeks and not stated are included in the totals but not shown separately.
[2] 41 to 42 weeks in 1975 and earlier.
[3] 43 weeks and over in 1975 and earlier.
* Based on a 50 percent sample of births.
** Based on 100 percent of births in selected states and on a 50 percent sample of births in all other states.   .

Source: U.S. National Center for Health Statistics, "Vital Statistics of the United States: Volume I," Table 111 in 1991 and 1990, Table 42 in 1985 and 1980, and Table 40 in 1975 and 1970, Public Health Service, Washington, D.C., 1995, 1994, 1988, 1984, 1978, and 1975.

by 1991, this difference had risen to 134 percent. In addition, the incidence of very low birth weight babies was 1.0 percent among whites and 3.0 percent among blacks in 1991. Since the incidence of neonatal and post-neonatal death and disability are more common among low birth weight (and especially very low birth weight) infants, this widening racial gap shows one more area where the life chances of black Americans are diminished, in this case from the moment of birth on.

The Health of Children and Adolescents

One key factor influencing the long- and short-term disability of children and adolescents is the incidence of epidemic and endemic diseases. Effective vaccinations for such major childhood diseases as diphtheria, pertussis and tetanus (the DPT vaccination); polio; and measles, mumps and rubella (the MMR or measles-containing vaccine) have existed since the 1960's. Vaccines for hemophilus B (HIB) and hepatitis B (HBV) have been available since the 1980's. Trends in levels of immunization for infants and children from 1965 to 1991 are presented in Table 7-5.

Around 1965, almost three out of every four children aged 1-4 years were immunized against DPT and polio. Yet these levels of immunization peaked in 1965 to 1970 and then declined until 1985. By 1985 about two-thirds of all children and less than half of all nonwhite children aged 1-4 were immunized against DTP,

Table 7-4. Percent of Live Births with Low Birthweight and Very Low Birthweight, by Race of Mother: 1970-1991.

Year	Total number of live births			Percent low birthweight[1]			Percent very low birthweight[2]		
	Total	White	Black	Total	White	Black	Total	White	Black
1991	4,110,907	3,174,030	725,163	7.1	5.8	13.6	1.3	1.0	3.0
1990	4,158,212	3,225,343	724,576	7.0	5.7	13.3	1.3	1.0	2.9
1985	3,760,561	2,991,373	608,193	6.8	5.6	12.4	1.2	1.0	2.6
1980[3]	3,612,258	2,898,732	589,616	6.8	5.7	12.5	1.1	0.9	2.4
1975[3]	3,144,198	2,551,996	511,581	7.4	6.3	13.1	1.1	0.9	2.3
1970*	3,731,386	3,091,264	572,362	7.9	6.8	13.9	1.1	0.9	2.4

[1] Less than 2,500 grams (5lbs 8oz).

[2] Less than 1,500 grams (3lbs 4oz).

[3] Based on 100 percent of births in selected states and on a 50 percent sample of births in all other states.

* Based on a 50 percent sample of births.

Source: U.S. National Center for Health Statistics, "Vital Statistics of the United States: Volume I," Table 111 in 1991 and 1990, Table 42 in 1985 and 1980, and Table 40 in 1975 and 1970, Public Health Service, Washington, D.C., 1995, 1994, 1988, 1984, 1978, and 1975.

Table 7-5. Percent of Children Age 1-4 Years Vaccinated for Selected Diseases, by Race: 1965-1991

Year	DTP[1] (three doses or more)			Polio (three doses or more)			Measles-containing[2]		
	Total	White	Other races	Total	White	Other races	Total	White	Other races
1991	65.8	68.6	54.6	50.6	52.7	42.1	77.6	77.9	76.4
1985	64.9	68.7	48.7	55.3	58.9	40.1	60.8	63.6	48.8
1979	65.4	69.0	49.2	59.1	63.6	38.9	63.5	66.2	51.2
1976	71.4	75.3	53.2	61.6	66.2	39.9	65.9	68.3	54.8
1970	76.1	79.7	58.8	65.9	69.2	50.1	57.2	60.4	41.9
1965	73.9	77.8	53.3	73.9	76.6	59.6	—	—	—

[1] Diphtheria-tetanus-pertussis.

[2] Measles in 1965-1985 and MMR (measles-mumps-rubella) in 1991.

Source: U.S. National Center for Health Statistics, "Health United States," Table 51 in 1992, Table 25 in 1982, and Tables 47 and 48 in 1975, Public Health Service, Hyattsville, MD, 1993, 1982, and 1975 (based on data from the United States Immunization Survey).

Table 7-6. Percent of Children Age 19-35 Months Vaccinated for Selected Diseases, by Race, Poverty Status, and Residence: 1992

| Vaccination and type of respondent | Race | | | Poverty status[1] | | Location of residence | | |
| | | | | | | Inside MSA | | |
	Total	White	Black	Below poverty	At or above poverty	Central city	Remaining areas	Outside MSA
All respondents								
DTP[2] (three or more doses)	83.0	84.8	74.7	79.7	84.6	82.5	84.4	80.7
Polio (three or more doses)	72.4	74.1	62.7	66.6	74.7	74.1	72.6	69.0
Measles-containing[3]	82.5	83.6	77.9	80.2	84.3	84.5	83.3	77.2
HIB*	66.6	69.2	54.9	58.1	70.5	65.3	67.9	65.8
Respondents consulting vaccination records or reporting no vaccinations**								
DTP[2] (three or more doses)	86.8	87.8	84.6	79.5	89.9	86.1	86.8	87.9
Polio (three or more doses)	74.1	75.0	66.4	70.3	76.3	77.6	72.7	71.6
Measles-containing[3]	84.5	85.0	85.8	83.9	85.7	85.0	84.9	82.7
HIB*	81.7	82.0	82.8	77.0	84.0	81.1	83.5	79.0

[1] Poverty status is based on family income and family size using Bureau of the Census poverty thresholds.
[2] Diphtheria-tetanus-pertussis.
[3] Respondents were asked about measles-containing or MMR (measles-mumps-rubella) vaccines.
* Haemophilus influenza, type B.
** Refusals and unknowns were omitted (15-17 percent for DTP, polio, or MMR vaccines, 9 percent for HIB).

Source: U.S. National Center for Health Statistics, "Health United States:1993," Public Health Service, Hyattsville, MD, 1994, Table 59 (based on data from the National Health Interview Survey).

polio or measles. After a measles outbreak in 1989-90, a renewed emphasis on childhood immunization led to increased rates of vaccination for DTP and measles. Rates for polio immunization have continued to decline in the white population, and overall. The 1992 Health Interview Survey (conducted after the campaign for increased vaccination, and using a different survey methodology from the U.S. Immunization Survey) showed that there are still significant differentials in immunization coverage by race, poverty status, location of residence and type of vaccine (Table 7-6). The DTP (diphtheria-tetanus-pertussis) and measles-containing (measles-mumps-rubella) vaccines had the highest rates of coverage; over 82 percent of all children aged 19 to 35 months had been immunized against these diseases. The rate of DTP immunization was about ten percent lower among black than among white children, and children in households at below the poverty level lagged about five percent below those children above the poverty line. Children outside an MSA had lower vaccination rates than those in central cities, and children in the "remaining areas" of an MSA (i.e. suburban areas) had the highest rates of coverage. The other three major vaccinations showed very similar trends of racial, poverty-status and location of residence differ-

entials; their major difference with the DTP vaccination was lower rates of coverage. The HIB (hemophilus B) vaccine had the worst coverage (protecting only 66.6 percent of all children aged 19 to 35 months), and had particularly poor coverage among black children, children in families below the poverty level and those living in central cities.

How effective have the programs for immunization and other public health programs been in controlling epidemic and endemic diseases? Table 7-7 shows the number of cases of major notifiable diseases per 100,000 in the United States since 1950. Some diseases show remarkable declines: poliomyelitis dropped from a rate of 22.02 to 1.77 per 100,000 between 1950 and 1960 (due to the Salk vaccine), and dropped further to 0.02 in 1970 (due to the added influence of the Sabin vaccine). Measles declined from 245.42 per 100,000 in 1960 to 23.23 per 100,000 in 1970 and to 5.96 per 100,000 in 1980 because of the introduction of the measles vaccine, and mumps showed a similar pattern of decline.

One problem with evaluating the overall trends in protection against certain diseases and their incidence in the population (especially among children) is that these rates measure only cases reported to a physician and cor-

Table 7-7. Selected Notifiable Disease Rates, by Disease: 1950-1992

Disease	Cases per 100,000 population					
	1950	1960	1970	1980	1990	1992
Diphtheria	3.83	0.51	0.21	...	...	...
Hepatitis A	—	—	27.87	12.84	12.64	9.06
Hepatitis B	—	—	4.08	8.39	8.48	6.32
Mumps	—	—	55.55	3.86	2.17	1.03
Pertussis (whooping cough)	79.82	8.23	2.08	0.76	1.84	1.60
Poliomyelitis, total	22.02	1.77	0.02	...	...	...
Paralytic[1]	—	1.40	0.02	...	...	...
Rubella (German measles)	—	—	27.75	1.72	0.45	0.06
Rubeola (measles)	211.01	245.42	23.23	5.96	11.17	0.88
Salmonellosis, excluding typhoid fever	—	3.85	10.84	14.88	19.54	16.04
Shigellosis	15.45	6.94	6.79	8.41	10.89	9.38
Tuberculosis[2]	80.45	30.83	18.28	12.25	10.33	10.46
Varicella (chickenpox)	—	—	—	96.69	120.06	176.54
Sexually transmitted diseases[3]						
Syphilis*	146.02	68.78	45.26	30.51	53.80	45.30
Primary and secondary	16.73	9.06	10.89	12.06	20.10	13.70
Early latent	39.71	10.11	8.08	9.00	22.10	20.10
Late and late latent	70.22	45.91	24.94	9.30	10.30	10.00
Congenital**	8.97	2.48	0.97	0.12	1.30	1.60
Gonorrhea	192.45	145.33	297.22	444.99	276.60	201.30
Chancroid	3.34	0.94	0.70	0.35	1.70	0.80
Granuloma inguinale	1.19	0.17	0.06	0.02	...	...
Lymphogranuloma venereum	0.95	0.47	0.30	0.09	0.10	0.10

[1] Data beginning in 1986 may be updated due to late reports.

[2] Data after 1974 are not comparable to prior years because of changes in reporting criteria effective in 1975.

[3] Newly reported civilian cases prior to 1991; includes military cases beginning in 1991.

* Includes stage of syphilis not stated.

** Data reported for 1989 and later years reflect changes in case definition introduced in 1988.

Source: U.S. National Center for Health Statistics, "Health United States:1993," Public Health Service, Hyattsville, MD, 1994, Table 60.

rectly diagnosed. For example, many cases of childhood hepatitis A or B are asymptomatic (and very mild) and are either never reported or are incorrectly diagnosed.

Another problem with evaluating current and future trends in diseases of children and adolescents is that many children who have not been immunized are clustered in poor, immigrant and minority neighborhoods. But there has been little research into what the current community-wide levels of vaccination are in such neighborhoods. Biostatisticians have developed models of the probable levels of immunization needed to prevent the outbreak and rapid spread of various childhood diseases. This collective immunity level can vary according to the characteristics of the disease itself and the efficacy of the vaccine. A reasonably high level of national vaccine coverage does not necessarily ensure against sporadic outbreaks of childhood diseases in areas where vaccine coverage is low.

The Health of Working-Age Adults

Any consideration of the health of adults under the age of 50 in the 1990's has to begin with the acquired immunodeficiency syndrome (AIDS). While the impact of AIDS has also been examined in the mortality chapter, the long-term effects of the disease prior to death also have had profound effects on public health and social organization in this country (see Table 7-8).

Auto-Immune Deficiency Syndrome

Government statistics demonstrate that there have been surges in the number of newly-diagnosed AIDS cases in 1988, 1990, and particularly in 1993. For the twelve months ending on September 30, 1993, the rate of AIDS cases was 37 per 100,000, putting this deadly disease ahead of all other notifiable diseases in 1992 except gonorrhea, varicella (chickenpox), and syphilis. However, a

Table 7-8. Acquired Immunodeficiency Syndrome (AIDS) Cases, by Sex, Age at Diagnosis, and Race-ethnicity: 1985-1993

Age, Sex, and Race-ethnicity	All years[1]		1985	1988	1990	January-September 1993	12 months ending September 30, 1993 cases per 100,000 population[2]
	Percent	Number					
Total	—	328,392	8,189	30,648	41,558	83,814	37.0
Males							
Total, 13 years and over	100.0	285,063	7,538	27,049	36,300	70,396	80.2
Race-ethnicity:							
White, non-Hispanic	56.4	160,861	4,787	16,008	20,903	36,336	54.3
Black, non-Hispanic	28.8	82,110	1,704	7,153	10,268	23,047	244.3
Hispanic	13.7	38,914	987	3,647	4,731	10,125	125.3
American Indian, Eskimo, Aleut	0.2	614	7	34	72	223	36.9
Asian or Pacific Islander	0.7	1,992	48	163	255	540	20.0
Age:							
13 to 19 years	0.3	934	31	84	102	299	—
20 to 29 years	18.2	51,945	1,468	5,449	6,814	12,052	—
30 to 39 years	46.3	131,858	3,610	12,581	16,802	32,116	—
40 to 49 years	24.8	70,729	1,657	6,105	8,908	18,935	—
50 to 59 years	7.6	21,657	605	1,990	2,651	5,289	—
60 years and over	2.8	7,940	167	840	1,023	1,705	—
Females							
Total, 13 years and over	100.0	38,684	522	3,034	4,540	12,789	13.4
Race-ethnicity:							
White, non-Hispanic	26.6	10,288	141	854	1,225	3,379	4.6
Black, non-Hispanic	56.1	21,707	285	1,650	2,539	7,171	64.3
Hispanic	16.2	6,285	92	497	736	2,091	27.0
American Indian, Eskimo, Aleut	0.3	103	3	6	10	43	6.5
Asian or Pacific Islander	0.6	228	1	22	19	86	3.1
Age:							
13 to 19 years	1.1	418	4	23	63	157	—
20 to 29 years	24.3	9,418	173	768	1,104	2,962	—
30 to 39 years	47.1	18,224	236	1,503	2,091	6,131	—
40 to 49 years	17.9	6,919	44	411	788	2,523	—
50 to 59 years	5.6	2,148	26	151	275	681	—
60 years and over	4.0	1,557	39	178	219	335	—
Children							
Total, under 13 years	100.0	4,645	129	565	718	629	1.7
Race-ethnicity:							
White, non-Hispanic	21.1	979	27	149	159	110	0.4
Black, non-Hispanic	57.7	2,680	83	300	384	380	6.9
Hispanic	20.2	937	19	112	168	128	2.6
American Indian, Eskimo, Aleut	0.3	14	...	...	3	2	0.4
Asian or Pacific Islander	0.5	22	...	4	4	4	0.2
Age:							
Under 1 year	39.2	1,820	54	190	284	224	—
1 to 12 years	60.8	2,825	75	375	434	405	—

[1] Includes cases prior to 1985.

[2] Resident population estimates for 1992 based on extrapolation from 1990 census counts from the U.S. Bureau of the Census.

Source: U.S. National Center for Health Statistics, "Health United States:1993," Public Health Service, Hyattsville, MD, 1994, Table 61.

Figure 7-2. Use of Selected Substances by Young People Age 12 to 17, by Sex: 1974-1992

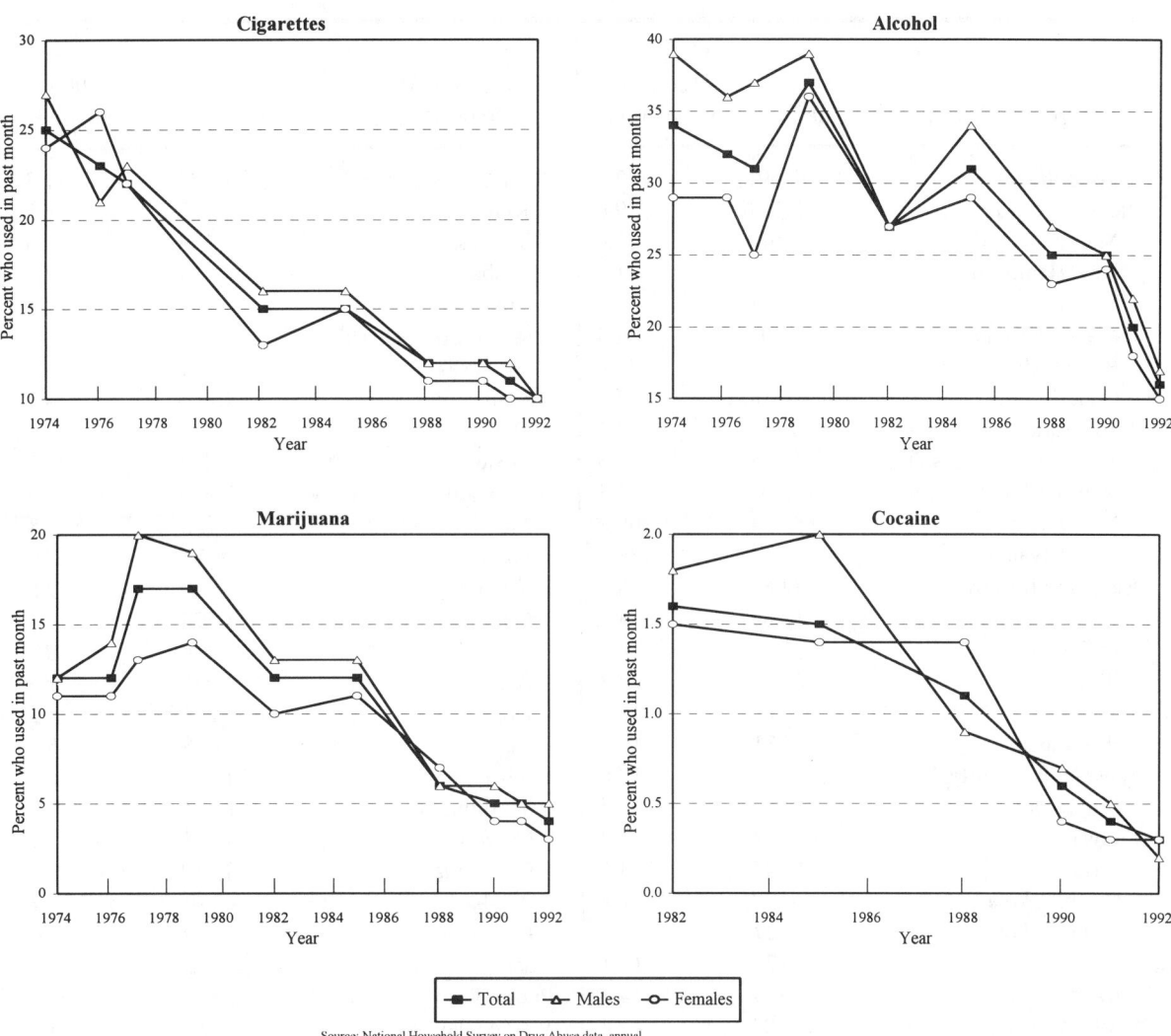

Source: National Household Survey on Drug Abuse data, annual.

significant proportion of the increase in AIDS cases was due to a broader definition of the disease used by reporting agencies as of Jan. 1, 1993. CDC data show that after a very rapid rise in reported cases under the new definition early in 1993, the number of reported cases fell back to a higher plateau of about 6,000 reported cases per month during most of 1993 and 1994.

AIDS is very differentially distributed among population groups. Over 80 percent of those diagnosed with the disease in the twelve months ending September 30, 1993 were males aged 13 years and over, over 13 percent were females aged 13 years and over, and only 1.7 percent were children of either sex. Among males aged 13 years and over, only 0.3 percent of those diagnosed during this period were age 13-19 years; almost four out of five cases were age 30-59 years, and only 2.8 percent of cases were age 60 years and over. While women diag-

nosed with AIDS tended to be slightly younger, only 1.1 percent of females aged 13 years and over were in the 13-19 year age group. The proportion of children under age 13 diagnosed with AIDS as a proportion of all newly-diagnosed cases appears to be dropping, declining from a peak of 1.7 percent of all cases in 1990 to 0.7 percent of all cases in the January-September 1993 period.

AIDS has shown a very rapid increase in the black and Hispanic populations in the late 1980's and early 1990's. For the twelve months ending September 30, 1993, the number of cases per 100,000 population was 54.3 for non-Hispanic white males, 244.3 for non-Hispanic black males, and 125.3 for Hispanic males. American Indian and Asian or Pacific Islander males had rates below those of non-Hispanic whites. For females, the equivalent rates were 4.6 per 100,000 for non-Hispanic whites, 64.3 for non-Hispanic blacks, 27.0 for Hispanics,

Table 7-9. Distribution of Acquired Immunodeficiency Syndrome (AIDS) Cases, by Region and State: 1993

Region and state	Number	Cases per 100,000 population	Region and state (continued)	Number	Cases per 100,000 population
United States[1]	103,691	40.2	**East South Central**	2,720	17.3
New England	5,158	39.0	Kentucky	323	8.5
Maine	149	12.0	Tennessee	1,203	23.6
New Hampshire	124	11.0	Alabama	733	17.5
Vermont	74	12.8	Mississippi	461	17.4
Massachusetts	2,703	45.0	**West South Central**	10,136	36.2
Rhode Island	348	34.8	Arkansas	404	16.7
Connecticut	1,758	53.6	Louisiana	1,464	34.1
Mid Atlantic	26,115	68.5	Oklahoma	725	22.4
New York (excl. NYC)	3,565	32.6	Texas	7,543	41.8
New York City	13,902	191.1	**Mountain**	3,913	26.5
New Jersey	5,434	69.0	Montana	32	3.8
Pennsylvania	3,214	26.7	Idaho	77	7.0
East North Central	8,069	18.8	Wyoming	46	9.8
Ohio	1,585	14.3	Colorado	1,324	37.1
Indiana	954	16.7	New Mexico	294	18.2
Illinois	2,959	25.3	Arizona	1,238	31.5
Michigan	1,840	19.4	Utah	264	14.2
Wisconsin	731	14.5	Nevada	638	45.9
West North Central	3,181	17.6	**Pacific**	21,460	52.0
Minnesota	659	14.6	Washington	1,564	29.8
Iowa	202	7.2	Oregon	778	25.7
Missouri	1,745	33.3	California	18,689	59.9
North Dakota	11	1.7	Alaska	70	11.7
South Dakota	29	4.1	Hawaii	359	30.6
Nebraska	179	11.1	Guam	2	1.5
Kansas	356	14.1	Puerto Rico	3,199	90.8
South Atlantic	22,783	49.8	Virgin Islands	57	55.9
Delaware	375	53.6	North Mariana Islands	...	...
Maryland	2,528	50.9	American Samoa	...	...
District of Columbia	1,585	274.2			
Virginia	1,625	25.0			
West Virginia	106	5.8			
North Carolina	1,368	19.7			
South Carolina	1,476	40.5			
Georgia	2,789	40.3			
Florida	10,931	79.9			

[1] Total reported through December 31, 1993. Total includes 158 cases with unknown state of residence.

Source: Centers for Disease Control and Prevention, "Summary of Notifiable Diseases: United States, 1993," Morbidity and Mortality Weekly Report, Volume 42 (53):4, U.S. Public Health Service, Atlanta, GA, October 21, 1994.

6.5 for American Indians, and 3.1 for Asian and Pacific Islanders. Although new cases for males are far more frequent and more than doubled in the first nine months of 1993 compared to all of 1990, the cases for females nearly tripled. While the disease was initially concentrated in large urban areas, it has now become more common in non-urban areas, especially in the Southeast (see Table 7-9).

Without a medical breakthrough, a very large proportion of those diagnosed with AIDS will die over the next decade. In the meantime, the medical and social problems of AIDS are having a significant impact on those with the disease and on their families, partners, and communities. Without an effective immunization against AIDS (and no such immunization appears to be on the horizon), it is difficult to engage in any optimistic speculation that the AIDS epidemic will begin to spread less rapidly in the near future.

It is also difficult to predict the direction of the AIDS epidemic because there are no representative national data on the prevalence of the human immunodeficiency virus (HIV), the precursor to AIDS. A much larger proportion of the population tests positive for HIV than shows clinical symptoms of AIDS. For a variety of social and political reasons, it has not been possible to conduct regular national representative surveys to collect the blood samples needed to ascertain trends in prevalence of HIV in the population. Recent national surveys on drug use and sexual practices (the two major routes of HIV infection in the U.S.) have helped to better specify some of the parameters of how the HIV infection may spread. Yet the inability to measure the prevalence of HIV and changes in prevalence over time remains a significant weakness in modeling how the disease spreads, and in developing plans for the battle against this disease.

Cigarette Smoking and Other Addictive Substances

There is some reason for optimism with regard to cigarette smoking, the major cause of lung cancer and a major cause of a number of other diseases (such as emphysema and heart disease) that can disable people for a long period of time before they actually kill. Between 1965 and 1992, the age-adjusted percent of people who were current cigarette smokers declined from 42.3 to 26.4 percent. In this area of health improvement men did far better than women, and black men (especially young black men) did better than white men (see Table 7-10). For example, the proportion of black men aged 18-24 years who were current smokers dropped from 62.8 percent in 1965 to 16.2 percent in 1992. This decrease in smoking is all the more remarkable when it is remembered that it took place during an era when many young black men were shifting from farm occupations (where smoking was

discouraged because of its danger) to manufacturing or service jobs, and when their rising incomes would have allowed them to spend more on consumption habits like cigarettes.

Overall, smoking dropped by more than 20 percent among black and white men, but by less than 10 percent among black and white women. Since men were far more likely to be smokers in 1965, this means that by 1992, there are still more smokers among men than among women. However, the rapid decline of smoking among men should show substantial benefits in terms of better health in the years to come. While gains from smoking cessation will not be as pronounced for women, there should be, nonetheless, significant future improvements in women's health as well.

The decline in cigarette smoking can also be seen among the next generation of potential smokers. Since 1974, national surveys have measured cigarette use in the last month, and these surveys show striking declines among youth aged 12-17 years (Figure 7-2). In 1974, 27 percent of all boys and 24 percent of all girls in this age group reported smoking cigarettes in the past month. By 1985, these proportions had declined by about 10 percent for each sex, with a further 5 percent decline by 1992. Yet since 1985, the percentage of recent cigarette smokers remains much higher for white, non-Hispanic youth aged 12-17 than for black non-Hispanic or Hispanic youth (see Figure 7-3).

Alcohol use has also declined markedly for youth, to a lesser extent for young adults, and only marginally for those 35 years and over (Table 7-11 and Figure 7-2). In 1974, 34 percent of young people aged 12 to 17 years had used alcohol in the past month, but by 1992, this figure had dropped to 16 percent. However, alcohol use in the past month declined only 10 percent (from 69 to 59 percent) for 18- to 25-year-olds during this time period, and there was only a three percent reduction in alcohol use (from 49 to 46 percent) for those 35 years of age and older between 1974 and 1992. Whether today's young people can retain their relatively low rates of cigarette and alcohol use in the face of the usual increases in use of these substances which come with increasing age will have a key impact on their future health as adults.

The use of illegal drugs among the population has also registered significant declines since the mid-1970's. In 1974, eight percent of the population aged 12 years and over had used marijuana in the past month (Table 7-11). This proportion peaked at 13 percent in 1979; by 1992 only four percent of the population reported such recent drug use. Almost all sub-groups of the population showed a similar pattern of rise and decline in marijuana use over the 1974-92 period. By 1992, only the 18 to 25 year age group had more than one in 10 of its members (11 percent) engaging in recent marijuana use. For most legal and illegal substance use, males outnumber females,

Table 7-10. Percent of Persons 18 Years and Over Who Currently Smoke Cigarettes, by Age, Sex, and Race: 1965-1992

Age and race	1965 Males	1965 Females	1974 Males	1974 Females	1979 Males	1979 Females	1985 Males	1985 Females	1990 Males	1990 Females	1992[1] Males	1992[1] Females
All races												
Total, age adjusted	51.6	34.0	42.9	32.5	37.2	30.3	32.1	28.2	28.0	23.1	28.2	24.8
Total, crude	51.9	33.9	43.1	32.1	37.5	29.9	32.6	27.9	28.4	22.8	28.6	24.6
18 to 24 years	54.1	38.1	42.1	34.1	35.0	33.8	28.0	30.4	26.6	22.5	28.0	24.9
25 to 34 years	60.7	43.7	50.5	38.8	43.9	33.7	38.2	32.0	31.6	28.2	32.8	30.1
35 to 44 years	58.2	43.7	51.0	39.8	41.8	37.0	37.6	31.5	34.5	24.8	32.9	27.3
45 to 64 years	51.9	32.0	42.6	33.4	39.3	30.7	33.4	29.9	29.3	24.8	28.6	26.1
65 years and over	28.5	9.6	24.8	12.0	20.9	13.2	19.6	13.5	14.6	11.5	16.1	12.4
White												
Total, age adjusted	50.8	34.3	41.7	32.3	36.5	30.6	31.3	28.3	27.6	23.9	28.0	25.7
Total, crude	51.1	34.0	41.9	31.7	36.8	30.1	31.7	27.7	28.0	23.4	28.2	25.1
18 to 24 years	53.0	38.4	40.8	34.0	34.3	34.5	28.4	31.8	27.4	25.4	30.0	28.5
25 to 34 years	60.1	43.4	49.5	38.6	43.6	34.1	37.3	32.0	31.6	28.5	33.5	31.5
35 to 44 years	57.3	43.9	50.1	39.3	41.3	37.2	36.6	31.0	33.5	25.0	30.9	27.6
45 to 64 years	51.3	32.7	41.2	33.0	38.3	30.6	32.1	29.7	28.7	25.4	28.1	25.8
65 years and over	27.7	9.8	24.3	12.3	20.5	13.8	18.9	13.3	13.7	11.5	14.9	12.6
Black												
Total, age adjusted	59.2	32.1	54.0	35.9	44.1	30.8	39.9	30.7	32.2	20.4	32.0	23.9
Total, crude	60.4	33.7	54.3	36.4	44.1	31.1	39.9	31.0	32.5	21.2	32.2	24.2
18 to 24 years	62.8	37.1	54.9	35.6	40.2	31.8	27.2	23.7	21.3	10.0	16.2	10.3
25 to 34 years	68.4	47.8	58.5	42.2	47.5	35.2	45.6	36.2	33.8	29.1	29.5	26.9
35 to 44 years	67.3	42.8	61.5	46.4	48.6	37.7	45.0	40.2	42.0	25.5	47.5	32.4
45 to 64 years	57.9	25.7	57.8	38.9	50.0	34.2	46.1	33.4	36.7	22.6	35.4	30.9
65 years and over	36.4	7.1	29.7	8.9	26.2	8.5	27.7	14.5	21.5	11.1	28.3	11.1

[1] Data for 1992 are not strictly comparable to prior years because beginning in 1992, the definition of "current smoker" was modified to specifically include persons who smoked only on "some days."

Source: U.S. National Center for Health Statistics, "Health United States:1993," Public Health Service, Hyattsville, MD, 1994, Table 72 (based on data from the National Health Interview Survey).

Figure 7-3. Use of Selected Substances by Young People Age 12 to 17, by Race-ethnicity: 1985-1992

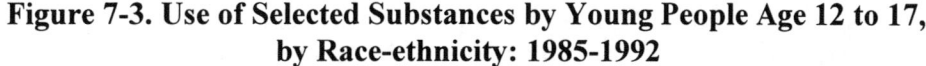

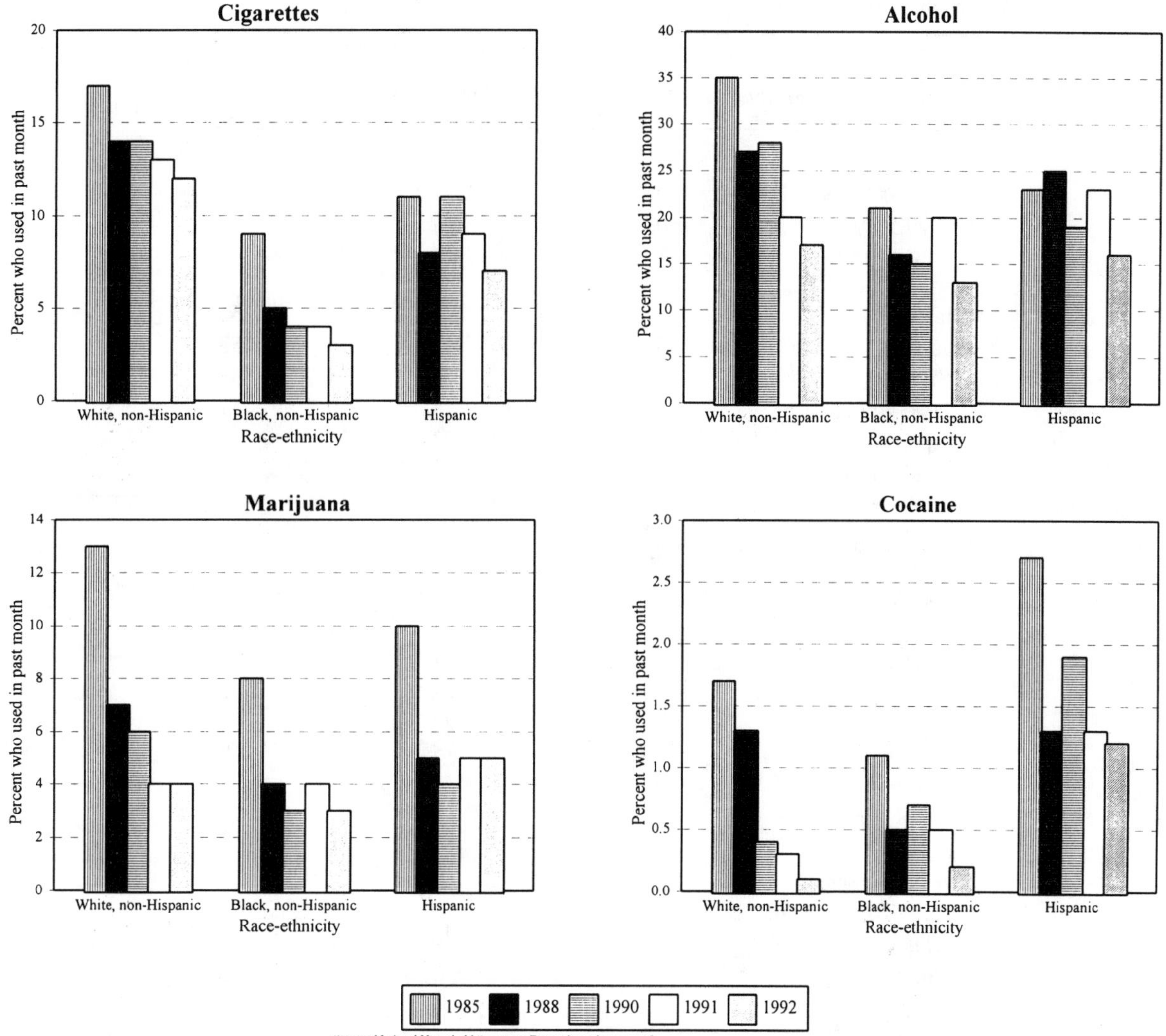

Cigarettes

Alcohol

Marijuana

Cocaine

| 1985 | 1988 | 1990 | 1991 | 1992 |

Source: National Household Survey on Drug Abuse data, annual.

but for this age group, the differential is particularly high: 15 percent of males aged 18 to 25 years report recent marijuana use, compared to only eight percent of females in this age group.

Cocaine use appears to have had an even more rapid peak and decline in terms of its prevalence in the U.S. population over the past two decades. Racial and ethnic disparities in cocaine use persist, with the highest percentage of recent use among Hispanics aged 12-17 (see Figure 7-3). By 1985, 2.9 percent of the population reported cocaine use in the last month, but by 1992, this proportion fell to 0.6 percent. As with marijuana, the 18 to 25 year age group was most vulnerable, with the peak and decline figures at 7.6 and 1.8 percent, respectively. However, since 1990, males and whites in the 18 to 25 year age group have actually shown an increase in re-

ported cocaine use, which may presage a new surge in cocaine use in the general population, or may be due to sampling variability. Contrary to much popular belief, among the 18-25 year age group in 1992, recent cigarette, alcohol, marijuana and cocaine use were all more common among whites than among blacks.

Hypertension, Serum Cholesterol Levels and Obesity

Hypertension has been linked to a number of fatal diseases and conditions. The most prominent of these is cerebrovascular disease, a leading cause of death in the United States (see Chapter 4). Data from the 1960-62 to 1988-91 periods (Table 7-12) show marked differences in the prevalence of hypertension between various seg-

Table 7-11. Percent of Persons 18 Years and Over Who Used Alcohol, Marijuana, or Cocaine in the Past Month, by Age, Sex, and Race-ethnicity: 1974-1992

Substance, age, sex, and race-ethnicity	1974	1979	1985	1990	1992
Alcohol[1]					
18 to 25 years	69	76	71	63	59
26 to 34 years	68	70	70	63	61
35 years and over	49	58	57	49	46
Persons 18 to 25 years					
Males	—	84	78	74	66
Females	—	68	65	53	53
White, non-Hispanic	—	—	76	66	63
Black, non-Hispanic	—	—	58	59	51
Hispanic	—	—	58	57	53
Marijuana					
18 to 25 years	25	35	22	13	11
26 to 34 years	8	17	17	9	8
35 years and over	—[2]	2	2	2	2
Persons 18 to 25 years					
Males	—	45	27	17	15
Females	—	26	17	9	8
White, non-Hispanic	—	—	22	14	12
Black, non-Hispanic	—	—	24	13	11
Hispanic	—	—	15	8	8
Cocaine					
18 to 25 years	3.1	9.3	7.6	2.2	1.8
26 to 34 years	—	—	6.1	1.7	1.4
35 years and over	—	—	0.5	0.2	0.2
Persons 18 to 25 years					
Males	—	—	9.0	2.8	2.9
Females	—	—	6.2	1.6	0.8
White, non-Hispanic	—	—	8.0	1.9	2.0
Black, non-Hispanic	—	—	6.5	3.6	1.4
Hispanic	—	—	6.4	3.1	1.8

[1] In surveys conducted from 1979 on, private answer sheets were used for alcohol questions; prior to 1979, respondents answered questions aloud.

[2] Relative standard error greater than 50 percent.

Source: U.S. National Center for Health Statistics, "Health United States:1993," Public Health Service, Hyattsville, MD, 1994, Table 72 (based on data from the National Household Survey on Drug Abuse).

ments of the population. Overall, 36.9 percent of the population (age-adjusted) had hypertension in 1960-62; this proportion rose to 39.0 by 1976-80, then declined to 23.4 percent in 1988-91.

Throughout this period, the sex difference in the hypertension rate has remained the same: the prevalence of hypertension among males is about six to ten percent higher than among females. There have been clear improvements in minority health, however. Black females, a majority of whom (50.8 percent) suffered from hyper-

tension in 1960-62, had a hypertension prevalence of 31.3 percent in 1988-91. Black males improved their health only by about half as much, cutting their hypertension prevalence rate from 48.1 to 37.4 percent in the same period. Mexican-American females had a hypertension prevalence rate of 20.8 percent in 1988-91, compared to a white non-Hispanic female rate of 18.9 percent, and Mexican-American males' rate was 26.9 percent (compared to male non-Hispanic whites' rate of 25.4 percent in 1988-91).

Table 7-12. Percent of Population 20 Years and Over with Hypertension[1], by Age, Sex, and Race-ethnicity: 1960-1991

Age, sex, and race-ethnicity	1960-1962	1971-1974	1976-1980[2]	1988-1991
20 to 74 years, age-adjusted				
All races	36.9	38.3	39.0	23.4
Male	40.0	42.4	44.0	26.3
Female[3]	33.7	34.3	34.0	20.3
White				
Male	39.3	41.7	43.5	25.1
Female[3]	31.7	32.4	32.3	19.0
Black				
Male	48.1	51.8	48.7	37.4
Female[3]	50.8	50.3	47.5	31.3
Mexican-American				
Male	—	—	25.0	26.9
Female[3]	—	—	21.8	20.8
Male				
20 to 34 years	22.8	24.8	28.9	9.2
35 to 44 years	37.7	39.1	40.5	20.0
45 to 54 years	47.6	55.0	53.6	35.7
55 to 64 years	60.3	62.5	61.8	46.7
65 to 74 years	68.8	67.2	67.1	59.0
75 years and over	—	—	—	63.7
Female[3]				
20 to 34 years	9.3	11.2	11.1	3.0
35 to 44 years	24.0	28.2	28.8	12.3
45 to 54 years	43.4	43.6	47.1	23.2
55 to 64 years	66.4	62.5	61.1	46.5
65 to 74 years	81.5	78.3	71.8	57.8
75 years and over	—	—	—	75.2

[1] Hypertension is defined as either having elevated blood pressure (systolic pressure of at least 140 mmHg or diastolic pressure of at least 90 mmHg) or taking antihypertensive medication.

[2] Data for Mexican-Americans are for 1982-1984.

[3] Excludes pregnant women.

Source: U.S. National Center for Health Statistics, "Health United States:1993," Public Health Service, Hyattsville, MD, 1994, Table 78 (based on data from the National Health Examination Survey).

The prevalence of hypertension in the population is determined by a complex set of factors: diet, levels of stress, proportion of those taking anti-hypertensive medication, and so on. Since 1976-80, there have been major strides in controlling the incidence of hypertension among the white and black female populations; black males and Mexican-Americans have not benefited as much.

While there is some debate among medical authorities on the precise relationship between levels of serum cholesterol and propensity for heart attack, most public health specialists are concerned about the large proportion of the population with high levels of serum cholesterol. Table 7-13 shows that, as with hypertension, there has been a significant decline in the proportion of the population with high serum cholesterol between 1960-62 and 1988-91. In 1960-62, black men and women had smaller proportions of their populations with high serum cholesterol. By 1988-91, the proportions of women of both races with this condition were virtually the same, and the difference between white and black men had shrunk slightly. Mexican-American males and females (for whom we have national survey data only from 1976-80 on) appear to be very similar to whites in terms of their proportion of the population with high serum cholesterol. Insofar as heart attacks (one of the major killers and also a leading cause of disability in the United States) are closely linked with high levels of serum cholesterol, a decline of about one-third in the proportion of the popu-

Table 7-13. Percent of Population 20 Years and Over with High Serum Cholesterol[1], by Age, Sex, and Race-ethnicity: 1960-1991

Age, sex, and race-ethnicity	1960-1962	1971-1974	1976-1980[2]	1988-1991
20 to 74 years, age-adjusted				
All races	31.8	27.2	26.3	19.7
Male	28.7	25.8	24.6	19.0
Female	34.5	28.2	27.6	20.2
White				
Male	29.4	25.9	24.6	19.3
Female	35.1	28.1	28.0	20.3
Black				
Male	24.5	25.1	24.1	16.5
Female	30.7	29.2	24.9	20.7
Mexican-American				
Male	—	—	18.8	20.3
Female	—	—	20.0	19.4
Male				
20 to 34 years	15.1	12.4	11.9	9.3
35 to 44 years	33.9	31.8	27.9	19.3
45 to 54 years	39.2	37.4	36.9	26.1
55 to 64 years	41.6	36.2	36.8	31.4
65 to 74 years	38.0	34.7	31.7	27.7
75 years and over	—	—	—	19.9
Female				
20 to 34 years	12.4	10.9	9.8	8.3
35 to 44 years	23.1	19.3	20.7	11.7
45 to 54 years	46.9	38.7	40.5	25.2
55 to 64 years	70.1	53.1	52.9	40.4
65 to 74 years	68.5	57.7	51.6	43.2
75 years and over	—	—	—	39.2

[1] High serum cholesterol is defined as greater than or equal to 240 mg/dL (6.20 mmol/L).

[2] Data for Mexican-Americans are for 1982-1984.

Source: U.S. National Center for Health Statistics, "Health United States:1993," Public Health Service, Hyattsville, MD, 1994, Table 79 (based on data from the National Health Examination Survey).

lation with this condition between 1960-62 and 1988-91 could mean that the population will live longer and have a smaller proportion of disabled individuals in the future. In addition, the decline in cigarette smoking (often a factor in heart attacks) may also lead to a further reduction of death and disability from heart attacks.

Obesity is one area where the health of the U.S. population has declined significantly. In 1960-62, 24.4 percent of the population (age-adjusted) was overweight (Table 7-14). This held fairly constant until 1976-80, but between then and 1988-91 the overweight proportion of the population ballooned from 25.4 to 33.3 percent. A larger proportion of all females than males at age 20 years and over were obese in 1960-62, and until 1988-91 women have maintained their 3 percent edge in overweight indi-

viduals. Yet most of the sex difference is not due to non-Hispanic whites (who have a 1.5 percent difference in proportion overweight between the sexes), but rather to minority groups. In 1988-91, 49.6 percent of all black women were overweight, compared to 31.5 percent of all black men, and 47.9 percent of Mexican-American women were overweight, compared to 39.5 percent of Mexican American men (data on other Hispanic origin groups was unavailable).

Until 1976-80, as men aged, their proportion overweight peaked at about 45-54 years, and then declined at later ages. Yet in 1988-91, the 65-74 year age group of men had the largest proportion of overweight members (42.9 percent). The effects of increasing proportions of overweight men at ages when they are also increasingly

Table 7-14. Percent of Population 20 Years and Over Who are Overweight[1], by Age, Sex, and Race-ethnicity: 1960-1991

Age, sex, and race-ethnicity	1960-1962	1971-1974	1976-1980[2]	1988-1991
20 to 74 years, age-adjusted				
All races	24.4	24.9	25.4	33.3
Male	22.9	23.6	24.0	31.6
Female[3]	25.6	25.9	26.5	35.0
White				
Male	23.1	23.8	24.2	32.0
Female[3]	23.5	24.0	24.4	33.5
Black				
Male	22.2	24.3	25.7	31.5
Female[3]	41.7	42.9	44.3	49.6
Mexican-American				
Male	—	—	31.0	39.5
Female[3]	—	—	41.4	47.9
Male				
20 to 34 years	19.6	19.2	17.3	22.2
35 to 44 years	22.8	29.4	28.9	35.3
45 to 54 years	28.1	27.6	31.0	35.6
55 to 64 years	26.9	24.8	28.1	40.1
65 to 74 years	21.8	23.0	25.2	42.9
75 years and over	—	—	—	26.4
Female[3]				
20 to 34 years	13.2	14.8	16.8	25.1
35 to 44 years	24.1	27.3	27.0	36.9
45 to 54 years	30.7	32.3	32.5	41.6
55 to 64 years	43.2	38.5	37.0	48.5
65 to 74 years	42.9	38.0	38.4	39.8
75 years and over	—	—	—	30.9

[1] Overweight is defined for men as a body mass index greater than or equal to 27.8 kg/m², and for women as a body mass index greater than or equal to 27.3 kg/m².
[2] Data for Mexican-Americans are for 1982-1984.
[3] Excludes pregnant women.

Source: U.S. National Center for Health Statistics, "Health United States:1993," Public Health Service, Hyattsville, MD, 1994, Table 80 (based on data from the National Health Examination Survey).

at risk from other diseases or conditions associated with overweight (heart disease, hypertension, high serum cholesterol, and so on) may mean new challenges in the care of late middle-aged and elderly men. Women show a slightly different pattern; they have high proportions overweight by age 55-64 years, but have no decline at age 65-74 years. In 1988-91 even at age 20-34 years, a quarter of all women were overweight, and almost one-half (48.5 percent) of all women were overweight at age 55-64 years. The apparent decline in the proportion overweight at the oldest ages (39.8 percent at age 65-74 years and 30.9 percent at age 75 years and over) may reflect the movement of slimmer prior cohorts into these older ages and may change for the worse in future decades.

Injuries and Acute Conditions

Data from the National Health Interview Survey show that almost sixty million people in the United States in 1991 had injuries that required medical attention or led to restricted activity (Table 7-15). Although males 5 to 17 years of age had the highest rate of injury (36.3 per 100 per year in 1991), males aged 18 to 44 years had by far the highest number of injuries (15.4 million). Women had remarkably similar rates of injury in each age group, but men age 45 and over had a lower rate of injury than that of younger age groups.

The National Health Interview Survey also provides data on the mean number of restricted-activity days and

Table 7-15. Persons Injured, by Type of Injury, Age, Sex, and Race-ethnicity:1991

Age and type of injury	Number of injuries (in thousands)					Rate per 100 population				
	All races			White	Black	All races			White	Black
	Total	Male	Female			Total	Male	Female		
Total	59,717	32,218	27,499	51,583	6,660	24.0	26.7	21.5	24.8	21.6
Under 5 years	4,490	2,132	2,358			23.2	21.5	24.9		
5 to 17 years	13,663	8,571	5,092	15,384	2,372	29.6	36.3	22.6	29.3	23.0
18 to 44 years	27,090	15,419	11,671	23,094	3,187	25.6	29.7	21.7	26.3	24.2
45 years and over	14,473	6,095	8,378	13,105	1,101	18.7	17.3	19.9	19.3	14.8
Type of injury										
Fractures and dislocations	7,505	3,936	3,569	6,768	544	3.0	3.3	2.8	3.3	1.8
Sprains and strains	13,470	7,451	6,019	11,196	1,840	5.4	6.2	4.7	5.4	6.0
Open wounds and lacerations	11,799	7,653	4,146	10,350	1,277	4.7	6.3	3.2	5.0	4.1
Contusions and superficial injuries	11,717	5,824	5,893	10,350	1,002	4.7	4.8	4.6	5.0	3.2
Other injuries	15,225	7,353	7,872	12,920	1,998	6.2	6.1	6.2	6.2	6.5

Source: National Center for Health Statistics, "Vital and Health Statistics," Series 10, Number 184, Public Health Service, Hyattsville, MD, 1992, Tables 2, 3, 7, and 8.

Table 7-16. Disability Days Associated with Acute Conditions, by Age: 1983-1992

Age and type of disability days	Number per person					
	1983	1985	1987	1989	1990	1992
Restricted-activity day						
Total[1]	7.2	6.8	6.8	7.5	7.0	7.2
Under 15 years	8.2	6.9	7.5	8.4	7.6	7.1
Under 5 years	9.5	7.5	9.4	9.6	9.5	8.7
5 to 14 years	7.5	6.7	6.6	7.8	6.5	6.3
15 to 44 years	6.6	6.5	6.5	7.3	6.9	6.9
45 to 64 years	6.3	6.0	6.1	5.9	5.8	6.4
65 years and over	9.2	9.6	8.0	9.1	8.7	10.8
65 to 74 years	8.7	8.9	8.2	8.2	7.6	10.0
75 years and over	10.1	10.9	7.7	10.4	10.3	12.0
Bed-disability days[2]						
Total[1]	3.4	3.1	3.0	3.5	3.1	3.0
Under 15 years	4.0	3.4	3.4	4.2	3.5	3.2
Under 5 years	4.7	3.5	4.4	4.5	4.5	3.9
5 to 14 years	3.6	3.3	2.8	4.0	3.0	2.9
15 to 44 years	3.0	2.8	2.8	3.2	3.0	2.8
45 to 64 years	2.8	2.7	2.6	2.8	2.7	2.6
65 years and over	4.5	3.9	3.4	4.2	3.2	4.5
65 to 74 years	4.4	2.8	3.7	3.6	2.6	4.2
75 years and over	4.7	5.7	3.0	5.0	4.0	4.9

[1] Age-adjusted.

[2] A subset of restricted-activity days.

Source: U.S. National Center for Health Statistics, "Health United States:1993," Public Health Service, Hyattsville, MD, 1994, Table 70 (based on data from the National Health Interview Survey).

bed-disability days among the population. Such disabilities can be due to either illness or injury. These data are shown for selected years between 1983 and 1992 in Table 7-16. Overall, the mean number of restricted-activity days have been remarkably stable over the past decade, and the mean annual number of bed-disability days has declined from 3.4 days in 1983 to 3.0 days in 1992. This overall decline in bed-disability days is due to a large decline at age 14 years and under, and a small decline between ages 15 and 74 years. While it would be comforting to think that children are now healthier than in 1983, it is equally plausible that more working parents are now dispatching children with colds or mild fevers off to school or day care rather than staying home to take care of them.

The 1990 Census shows the distribution of those who said they had a work disability inside and outside of the labor force. Figures 7-4A and 7-4B divide all persons 16 through 64 years by sex, and each diagram shows the distribution of labor force participation and work disability status. In 1990 there were 80.65 million women aged 16-64 years (Figure 7-4B), of whom 68.08 percent

(54.91 million) were in the labor force. Of those in the labor force, 1.96 million claimed a work disability, or about 3.5 percent of all women in the labor force (and 2.43% of all women in this age group). Of the 25.74 million women not in the labor force, 21.58 million claimed no work disability, 3.44 million said they were prevented from working by a work disability, and 0.73 million said they had a work disability but were not prevented from working. The sum of the three groups with a work disability totals 6.12 million women, or 7.59 percent of all women aged 16 to 64 years. Of this group of women with a work disability, almost one-third (1.96 of 6.12 million) are in the labor force.

Men aged 16-64 years (Figure 7-4A) show even higher rates of work disability, and have a more pronounced tendency to continue working even with a work disability. Of the 76.67 million men in this age group, 64.79 million (or 85.5 percent) were in the labor force in 1990. Almost five percent (3.08 million) of males in the labor force had a work disability. Among the 11.88 million men not in the labor force, 3.16 million said they were prevented from being in the labor force by a work

Figure 7-4A. Work Disability Status of Males Age 16 to 64 Years, by Labor Force Status: 1990

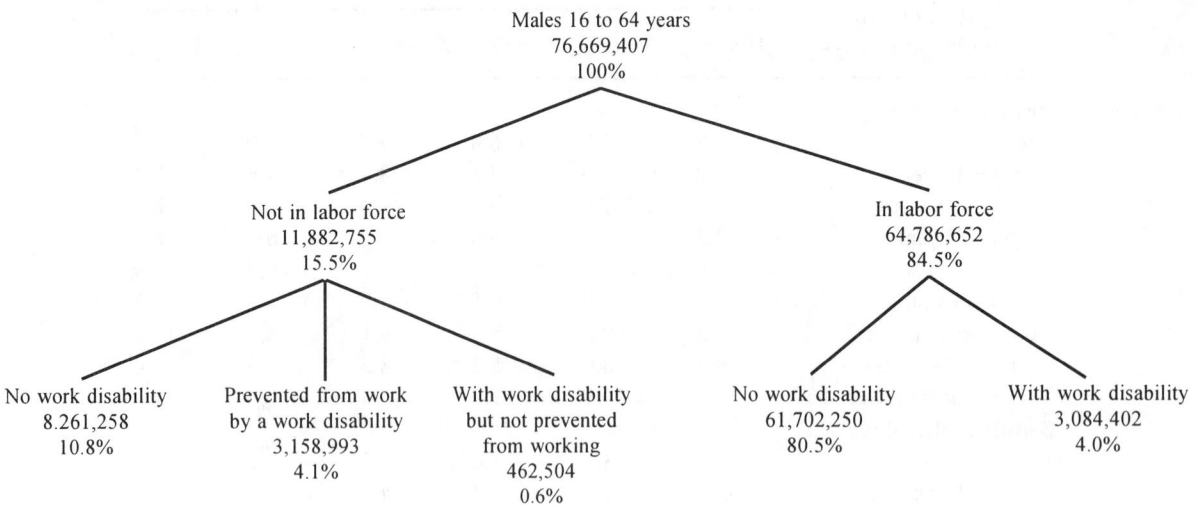

Source: 1990 U.S. Census data.

Figure 7-4B. Work Disability Status of Females Age 16 to 64 Years, by Labor Force Status: 1990

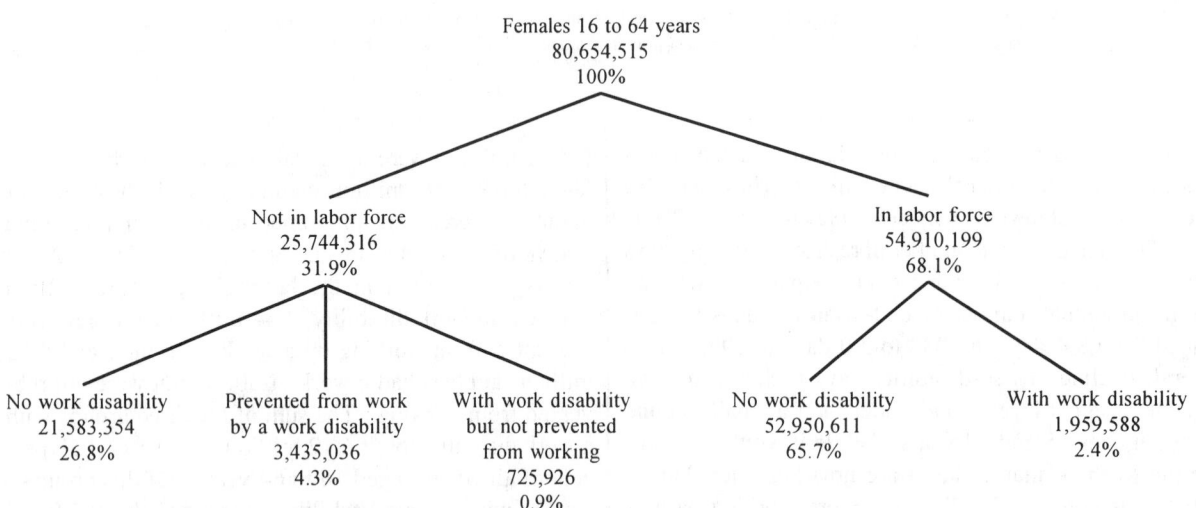

Source: 1990 U.S. Census data.

Repetitive Motion Injuries

Repetitive motion injuries (also known as cumulative trauma disorders, CTD's) are a class of injuries that are associated with mass production, and which have been recognized by medical authorities for over sixty years. They are the result of repetitive movements or exertions of the body, usually of the upper extremities. While they were often found among individuals who serve repetitive machinery, their more recent manifestations have included carpal tunnel syndrome associated with long-term use of computer keyboards and other service industry disorders. As the Women's Bureau of the Department of Labor has pointed out, many of the industries with high rates of repetitive motion injuries are also industries with high proportions of women workers. Groups of women workers with elevated rates of repetitive motion injuries include garment workers, dental hygienists, musicians, and assembly workers.

In addition to private industry, employees in the federal work force have also been found to be at risk. The introduction of mail sorting equipment and computerized mail forwarding systems require postal clerks to sit or stand in the same position for long periods of time, or to perform rapid repetitive movements. The new work requirements have led to cases of carpal tunnel syndrome, tendonitis, the development of ganglion cysts, back and neck pain, visual disorders, increased stress and other problems.

"The Occupational Safety and Health Administration has stated that finding solutions to the problems posed by ergonomic hazards may be the most significant workplace safety and health issue of the 1990's" (Women's Bureau, Department of Labor, 1994:181). For many workers, these repetitive motion injuries may be a relatively minor annoyance, resulting in a small amount of pain; but in the industries listed above and in some specific jobs in other industries, the poor design of the job can destroy a worker's career. Since many of these industries employ large proportions of women, minorities, and immigrants, this issue is of interest to health studies and policy initiatives which focus upon differences in health across occupational and social strata.

The 20 Industries with the Highest Illness Rates of Disorders Associated with Repeated Trauma in the Private Sector: 1989

Industry (SIC Code)	Incidence rate[1]
Meatpacking plants (2,011)	799.1
Poultry slaughtering and processing (2,015)	527.7
Motor vehicles and car bodies (3,711)	453.2
Household laundry equipment (3,633)	348.9
Household refrigerators and freezers (3,632)	273.9
Men's and boys' work clothing (2,326)	258.5
Sausages and other prepared meats (2,013)	252.4
Frozen specialties, n.e.c. (2,038)	248.5
Men's footwear, except athletic (3,143)	244.4
Shipbuilding and repairing (3,731)	241.8
Automotive and apparel trimmings (2,396)	241.8
Men's and boys' trousers and slacks (2,325)	227.3
Frozen bakery products, except bread (2,053)	218.8
Nonferrous wire drawing and insulating (3,357)	217.6
Hardwood dimension and flooring mills (2,426)	213.9
Pens and mechanical pencils (3,951)	206.4
Knit underwear mills (2,254)	200.4
Automotive stampings (3,465)	200.2
Metal office furniture (2,522)	194.8
Motor vehicle parts and accessories (3,714)	192.0

[1] Number of disorders associated with repeated trauma per 10,000 full-time workers.

Source: U.S. Department of Labor, Women's Bureau, "1993 Handbook on Women Workers: Trends and Issues," Department of Labor, Washington, D.C., 1993, page 180, Table 1.

disability, and another 462,000 said they had a work disability but were not in the labor force for some other reason. If these three groups of men with work disabilities are summed, they total 8.74 percent of all men aged 16 to 64 years. Thus about 46 percent of all men aged 16 to 64 years with a work disability remain in the labor force.

Because the 1990 Census also asked other questions about the health status of this 16-64 year age group, other aspects of disability can also be ascertained. For example, 412,000 men and 378,000 women in the labor force report a mobility disability. Among the age group 16-64 years, 2.637 million men and 2.746 million women report a self-care limitation. While in many cases mobility and self-care disabilities may also overlap with reports of work disability, it is clear that even this age group, upon whom the young and the old rely for succor, has significant problems of its own.

The Health of Older Americans

The aging and declining fertility of the United States' population have raised general concern over the potential burdens of an older population on social pro-

grams and services, economic productivity and families. Health among the elderly, and how health care services are provided, may profoundly affect the extent of these possible burdens as we move beyond the year 2000.

Prevalence of Selected Chronic Conditions

While many diseases of older Americans affect younger ones as well, there are a number of diseases and health conditions that increase sharply with age. Table 7-17 shows the major chronic conditions (i.e. conditions for which at least one age-sex category had more than 100 cases per 1,000 persons) afflicting the U.S. population in 1991. All of the leading four chronic conditions, i.e. sinusitis, deformities/orthopedic impairments, high blood pressure and arthritis, increase in prevalence sharply after age 45. Whereas sinusitis then declines past age 64, high blood pressure and arthritis continue to increase rapidly into older ages. While the prevalence of high blood pressure peaks in the 65 to 74 year age group for both sexes, arthritis continues to increase into the oldest ages. Hearing impairments, which affected almost 23 million

Lyme Disease

by Alison Kadlec Donta

A growing concern for the health of the United States population is the increase in Lyme disease incidence over the past decade. Lyme disease is infection with the *Borrelia burgdorferi* bacterium and is now the most common vector-borne disease in the United States. It can manifest itself in both early and chronic, persistent forms. Early signs of infection include the presence of an erythema migrans rash, headache, fatigue, arthritis and arthralgia, and general malaise. Although Lyme disease can be identified serologically, diagnosis is often difficult, and many cases of Lyme disease go unidentified for years. Symptoms can persist for years, greatly affect quality of life, and sometimes lead to premature death. Researchers have estimated the rate of chronic Lyme disease as somewhere between 10-70% of all cases, depending on factors such as patient demographics, treatment time, treatment duration, serologic profile, and initial presenting symptoms.

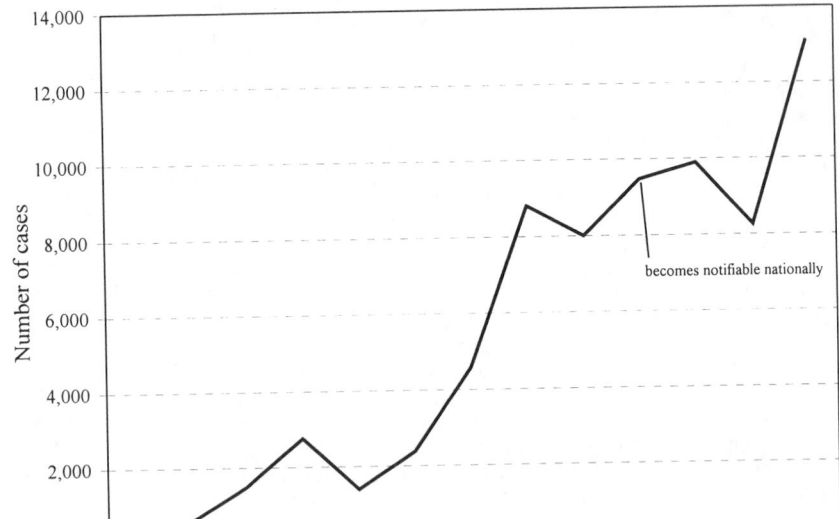

Number of Cases of Lyme Disease Reported Annually: 1982-1994

becomes notifiable nationally

Source: U.S. Centers for Disease Control and Prevention data.

In 1982, the Centers for Disease Control and Prevention (CDC) initiated surveillance for Lyme disease, and it became a nationally notifiable disease in 1991. The figure below indicates the steady increase in number of cases of Lyme disease over this collection period. In 1982, there were only 497 cases reported to the CDC and in 1994 there were 13,083 cases reported. This represents an increase of 2532.4% over the past twelve years. Although some of this increase can be explained by the addition of more states to the surveillance system over time, the number of cases has continued to increase since 1991 when the disease became reportable nationally. In 1991, there were 9,465 cases reported, and there has been an average an-

nual increase of 8.4% although there was a drop in the number of reported cases in 1993. Because the CDC relies on passive surveillance and strict reporting criteria to ascertain Lyme disease incidence, there is a strong possibility of underreporting of cases.

The national rate of Lyme disease per 100,000 population was 5.03 in 1994. As can be seen in the table, the disease rate varies greatly by region of the United States. The divisions most affected by Lyme disease in 1994 were New England and the Middle Atlantic. In fact, the Northeast region of the country accounted for 84.1% of the total Lyme cases reported. Other states with high rates of incidence include Wisconsin (with an incidence rate of 8.05 per 100,000 population), and Maryland (7.95 per 100,000 population). For the nation as a whole, the sex ratio of incidence was nearly equal, although among those age 10 to 19 years, males were more likely to be affected (55%), and females age 30 to 39 years were more likely to be affected (56%) than males of that age group.

A study of 503 patients by the Lyme Foundation found that 40.0% of the patients surveyed reported permanent physical damage (primarily arthritic and neurologic) as a result of the disease. In addition, 19.1% believe that the disease led to the loss of a job, and another 19.1% lost school time. Mental anguish was reported by 72.2% of this sample, and two deaths were attributed to Lyme disease. Given the current number of Lyme Disease patients, the possibility of underreporting, and the trend of increase in disease incidence, Lyme Disease will continue to play a large role in disability of the population and will also place a great monetary burden on the country's medical system and patients suffering from the disease.

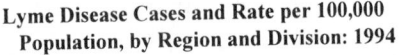

Lyme Disease Cases and Rate per 100,000 Population, by Region and Division: 1994

Region and division	Number of cases	Rate per 100,000 population
United States, total	13,083	5.03
Northeast	10,998	21.40
New England	2,827	21.30
Middle Atlantic	8,171	21.43
Midwest	870	1.42
East North Central	525	1.22
West North Central	345	1.89
South	1,101	1.21
South Atlantic	911	1.96
East South Central	43	0.27
West South Central	147	0.52
West	114	0.20
Mountain	18	0.12
Pacific	96	0.23

Source: U.S. Centers for Disease Control and Prevention, "Morbidity and Mortality Weekly Report," Volume 44, Number 24, U.S. Public Health Service, Atlanta, GA, 1995, page 460.

Additional Sources:

Centers for Disease Control and Prevention. "Lyme Disease--United States, 1994." *Morbidity and Mortality Weekly Report* 44(24):459-462, 1995.

Shadick, Nancy A., et al. "The Long-term Clinical Outcomes of Lyme Disease: A Population-based Retrospective Cohort Study." *Annals of Internal Medicine* 121(8):560-567, 1994.

Varderhoof, Irwin T., and Vanderhoof-Forschner, Karen M.B. "Lyme Disease: The Cost to Society." *Contingencies* January/February:42-48, 1993.

Vogt, Richard L. "National Survey of State Epidemiologists to Determine the Status of Lyme Disease Surveillance." *Public Health Reports* 107(6):644-646, 1992.

Table 7-17. Prevalence of Selected Chronic Conditions, by Age and Sex: 1991

		Conditions per 1,000 population							
		Male				Female			
Chronic condition	Number (in thousands)	Under 45 years	45 to 64 years	65 to 74 years	75 years and over	Under 45 years	45 to 64 years	65 to 74 years	75 years and over
Chronic sinusitis	32,168	99.1	148.0	119.5	96.0	132.9	192.5	186.2	124.3
Deformities/orthopedic impairments	28,725	94.0	159.6	168.5	166.7	93.7	149.5	166.0	209.1
High blood pressure (hypertension)	27,800	30.7	242.4	319.4	281.0	27.9	245.4	422.8	415.6
Arthritis	27,200	24.8	193.2	335.5	481.3	34.9	284.7	498.4	630.9
Hay fever/allergic rhinitis without asthma	24,248	95.8	98.0	81.3	66.7	102.6	115.5	78.0	60.6
Hearing impairments	22,680	44.0	178.5	330.6	436.6	29.7	107.0	214.1	383.9
Heart conditions	20,537	24.3	152.7	290.4	324.2	37.3	116.9	229.1	372.2
Visual impairments	7,989	27.0	63.5	72.6	133.8	12.2	32.7	44.0	101.2
Varicose veins of lower extremities	7,939	5.1	26.1	48.0	17.2	27.1	88.7	124.7	89.9
Diabetes	7,222	7.6	57.9	97.3	95.1	10.0	57.0	109.0	91.1
Cataracts	6,587	1.6	16.1	105.0	202.1	3.1	23.9	146.0	266.3
Tinnitus	6,490	9.8	57.5	118.9	63.3	9.2	43.4	76.3	62.2

Source: National Center for Health Statistics, "Vital and Health Statistics," Series 10, Number 184, Public Health Service, Hyattsville, MD, 1992, Tables 58 and 63.

Table 7-18. Estimated New Cases of Cancer in 1993 and Five-year Survival Rates: 1974-1976 to 1983-1989

| Site | Estimated new cases[1], 1993 (in thousands) | | | 5-year relative survival rates (percent) | | | | | | | |
| | Total | Male | Female | White | | | | Black | | | |
				1974-76	1977-79	1980-82	1983-89	1974-76	1977-79	1980-82	1983-89
All sites[2]	1,170	600	570	50.2	50.7	51.5	54.5	38.7	38.8	39.1	39.4
Lung	170	100	70	11.0	12.0	12.0	13.4	11.3	11.0	12.1	11.2
Breast[3]	183	1	182	74.8	75.1	76.7	80.5	62.9	62.5	65.6	64.1
Colon	109	53	56	50.2	52.7	55.3	59.3	45.5	47.6	48.7	48.7
Prostate	165	165	—	67.6	71.7	74.0	79.4	57.7	61.9	63.9	64.4
Bladder	52	39	13	73.6	75.6	78.6	79.9	47.8	54.8	57.5	60.9
Rectum	43	24	19	48.6	50.4	52.7	57.5	41.6	37.7	37.7	45.2
Corpus uteri	31	—	31	88.6	86.1	82.5	84.6	60.4	57.8	53.6	55.5
Non-Hodgkin's lymphoma*	43	24	19	47.5	48.1	51.4	52.3	47.8	49.6	50.0	43.8
Oral cavity and pharynx	30	20	10	54.8	54.1	54.9	54.4	35.7	36.0	30.4	32.6
Leukemia*	29	17	13	34.5	37.2	37.5	38.7	31.1	30.1	31.5	30.4
Melanoma of skin	32	17	15	79.8	81.5	81.9	84.2	68.5	51.7	59.5	72.3
Pancreas	28	14	14	2.7	2.2	2.8	3.0	2.2	3.8	4.8	4.9
Kidney	27	17	10	51.5	50.6	50.7	55.7	48.6	52.4	55.1	51.1
Stomach	24	15	9	14.4	16.1	16.1	17.1	16.4	15.3	19.1	17.8
Ovary	22	—	22	36.2	37.5	38.6	40.2	40.7	39.5	37.3	40.2
Cervix uteri**	14	—	14	69.2	68.8	67.3	69.1	63.2	61.8	60.1	57.0

[1] Estimates provided by American Cancer Society are based on rates from the National Cancer Institute's SEER program.
[2] Includes other sites not shown separately.
[3] Survival rates for females only.
* All types combined.
** Invasive cancer only.

Source: U.S. Bureau of the Census, "Statistical Abstract of the United States: 1994," U.S. Government Printing Office, Washington, D.C., 1994, Table 213.

people, were the next most common conditions at the oldest ages, and while they increased rapidly with age, they affected men at an earlier age than women. Heart conditions (affecting 20.5 million) showed a similar pattern of earlier onset for men and a rapid increase with age for both sexes.

The first and fifth most common conditions, chronic sinusitis (32.2 million persons) and hay fever and allergic rhinitis without asthma (24.2 million persons), showed little or no increase with age, and actually decline in prevalence past age 65. After these seven major conditions come five less common conditions, none of which affect more than 8 million people. Visual impairments are heavily concentrated among those 75 years and over, and are more common among men. Tinnitus (ringing in the ear) also shows a slow increase with age. Diabetes has a rapid increase until the 65 to 74 year age category, then levels off. Varicose veins of the lower extremities increase with age, and are much more common among women than men. Cataracts, which affect 6.6 million persons, also increase rapidly with age, especially among the oldest women. If we consider only the oldest women (age 75 years and over), a representative group of ten such women would include six who suffered from arthritis, two or more with cataracts and another with some other form of visual impairment, about four with hearing impairment and one with tinnitus, two with deformities or orthopedic impairments, one with diabetes, almost four with heart conditions and four with high blood pressure, and one each with varicose veins, hay fever and chronic sinusitis. Since almost all of these chronic conditions require some form of diagnosis and treatment, and since women age 75 years and above are among the fastest growing groups in U.S. society, the source of some of the escalating cost of medical care can be more readily identified.

Cancer

In 1993 there were about 1.17 million new cancer cases diagnosed, the majority of them among older persons (see Table 7-18). While cancer mortality rates were discussed in the mortality chapter, changes in survival rates are also of interest. One of the most commonly-used measures is the 5-year relative survival rate, which estimates the proportion of all persons diagnosed with this cancer who will live out the next five years (controlling for the effects of other competing risks of death).

Whites had a 5-year relative survival rate of 50.2 percent in 1974-76 and a survival rate of 54.5 percent in 1983-89. This moderate rate of increase in survival was the product of considerable progress in treatment and patient survival for some cancers and little progress in the treatment of others. Black Americans, on the other hand, saw a much smaller increase in survivorship: 38.7 percent of all black cancer patients survived for five years in 1974-76, and 39.4 percent survived in 1983-89.

A brief survey of the major cancers can show where the most progress has been made. Lung cancer survival increased from 11.0 percent to 13.4 percent for whites over this time period, and actually decreased slightly (from 11.3 to 11.2 percent) for blacks. The low level of survivorship for those with lung cancer and the lack of progress in fighting this form of cancer attest to the importance of continuing the decline in cigarette smoking, which appears to have stalled for the 18-34-year-old age group during the 1990-92 period (see Table 7-10). Breast cancer, the most common form of cancer in the United States, saw a rise in survivorship from 74.8 percent to 80.5 percent for white women, but the racial gap in survivorship grew as black women increased their survivorship only from 62.9 to 64.1 percent between 1974-76 and 1983-89. Colon cancer, a cancer more evenly divided among the sexes, also saw a considerable improvement in white survivorship and a small improvement in black survivorship, leading to another growing racial gap. Prostate cancer, a cancer limited to men, recorded the largest improvement in 5-year relative survival rates (from 67.6 to 79.4 percent for whites and from 57.7 to 64.4 percent for blacks), but here again, the increase in survivorship was twice as great for whites as for blacks. Cancer diagnosis and treatment have improved since 1974, but the racial gap in survivorship for many cancers is increasing.

Heart Disease, Cerebrovascular Disease, and Other Diseases and Conditions

Heart disease and cerebrovascular disease are the two major killers of Americans today (cancer is third), but blacks and whites of both sexes have shown significant declines in mortality from these two causes of death in the past two decades. As Table 7-19A shows, however, heart disease is by far the most common reason for hospital admission for males. And, as Table 7-19B shows, it is the second most common reason for hospital admission for women (delivery is first). These tables report the discharge statistics for non-federal short-stay hospitals, and the first-listed diagnosis given in these discharge statistics are a rough measure of the prevalence of, and admissions for, each of these health conditions. Between 1980 and 1992, the rate of hospital discharge per thousand for heart disease decreased for men aged 15-64 years and for women aged 45-64; however, older age groups had increased discharges for heart disease. Increased recognition and early diagnosis of heart disease, and changes in lifestyles, may account for decreased disability within the younger population from this cause, and for an increased survivorship.

For those age 45 and over, cerebrovascular disease remains a major health problem. Between 1980 and 1992, for males aged 45-64 and 65-74 years, cerebrovascular

Table 7-19A. Rates of Discharge in Non-Federal Short-stay Hospitals for Males, by Age and Selected First-listed Diagnoses: 1980-1992

Age and first-listed diagnosis	Number of discharges per 1,000 population		
	1980	1985	1992
All ages[1] [2]	140.1	123.5	98.9
Diseases of the heart	15.9	16.8	16.5
Malignant neoplasms	8.2	7.8	6.0
Pneumonia, all forms	4.1	3.9	4.4
Fracture, all sites	5.2	4.7	3.6
Psychoses	2.1	2.6	3.1
Inguinal hernia	4.3	3.0	0.8
Under 15 years[2]	78.7	63.8	49.4
Acute respiratory infection	5.9	5.2	4.5
Bronchitis, emphysema, and asthma	4.0	4.1	4.6
Pneumonia, all forms	5.2	4.3	4.2
Congenital abnormalities	4.0	3.8	2.7
Fracture, all sites	3.7	3.2	2.1
Otitis media and eustachian tube disorders	4.5	2.2	1.4
Chronic disease of tonsils and adenoids	5.4	3.5	0.9
15 to 44 years[2]	91.5	75.4	54.4
Psychoses	3.0	3.7	4.1
Fracture, all sites	6.3	5.3	3.8
Diseases of the heart	2.9	3.0	2.7
Intervertebral disc disorders	2.3	2.9	2.1
Alcohol dependence syndrome	3.5	3.5	2.3
Lacerations and open wounds	3.4	2.6	1.6
45 to 64 years[2]	195.4	176.2	134.7
Diseases of the heart	33.7	36.6	32.6
Malignant neoplasms	14.4	13.1	9.8
Cerebrovascular diseases	4.7	5.0	4.1
Psychoses	2.6	3.2	3.8
Pneumonia, all forms	3.2	3.4	3.5
Alcohol dependence syndrome	6.4	4.5	2.1
Inguinal hernia	6.9	5.1	1.0
65 to 74 years[2]	347.4	319.9	292.9
Diseases of the heart	64.3	68.7	74.9
Malignant neoplasms	41.4	38.2	32.2
Cerebrovascular diseases	17.7	18.2	16.1
Pneumonia, all forms	10.2	10.6	11.2
Hyperplasia of the prostate	16.8	13.3	10.8
Eye diseases and conditions	11.7	5.1	2.2
75 years and over[2]	534.0	527.9	470.0
Diseases of the heart	105.4	108.3	111.0
Malignant neoplasms	55.3	56.0	36.9
Pneumonia, all forms	24.2	29.6	35.1
Cerebrovascular diseases	37.3	37.8	27.3
Hyperplasia of the prostate	20.6	19.7	17.3

[1] Age-adjusted.

[2] Includes discharges with first-listed diagnoses not shown separately.

Source: U.S. National Center for Health Statistics, "Health United States:1993," Public Health Service, Hyattsville, MD, 1994, Table 96 (based on data from the National Hospital Discharge Survey).

Table 7-19B. Rates of Discharge in Non-Federal Short-stay Hospitals for Females, by Age and Selected First-listed Diagnoses: 1980-1992

Age and first-listed diagnosis	Number of discharges per 1,000 population		
	1980	1985	1992
All ages[1] [2]	178.1	152.7	124.9
Delivery	29.0	27.7	27.1
Diseases of the heart	10.7	11.0	10.9
Malignant neoplasms	7.3	7.3	5.3
Pneumonia, all forms	3.0	3.2	3.5
Fracture, all sites	4.4	4.0	3.4
Pregnancy with abortive outcome	4.1	2.8	1.2
Under 15 years[2]	64.2	50.2	40.8
Pneumonia, all forms	3.6	3.6	3.3
Acute respiratory infection	4.6	3.6	3.2
Bronchitis, emphysema, and asthma	2.5	2.6	2.6
Congenital abnormalities	3.2	1.9	2.2
Noninfectious enteritis and colitis	3.7	2.3	1.8
Chronic disease of tonsils and adenoids	6.4	3.7	0.9
15 to 44 years[2]	206.9	173.4	137.1
Delivery	70.7	67.8	66.2
Psychoses	2.4	3.4	4.1
Pregnancy with abortive outcome	9.9	6.7	3.0
Benign neoplasms	4.8	3.4	2.9
Cholelithiasis	2.6	2.4	2.4
Inflammatory disease of female pelvic organs	5.1	3.7	1.7
Disorders of menstruation	6.6	2.6	1.0
45 to 64 years[2]	194.3	163.4	127.6
Diseases of the heart	17.8	17.9	17.1
Malignant neoplasms	16.6	15.6	10.8
Cholelithiasis	4.7	4.4	4.2
Psychoses	3.1	4.1	4.7
Benign neoplasms	6.7	5.1	4.4
Diabetes	6.3	3.8	3.4
65 to 74 years[2]	291.7	275.2	242.2
Diseases of the heart	47.2	49.3	50.2
Malignant neoplasms	26.9	29.5	21.5
Cerebrovascular diseases	13.6	15.0	11.6
Arthropathies and related disorders	7.4	7.0	10.6
Pneumonia, all forms	6.0	6.8	8.3
Diabetes	10.6	6.7	5.0
Eye diseases and conditions	12.6	5.7	2.2
75 years and over[2]	464.3	448.6	412.0
Diseases of the heart	88.9	92.0	91.4
Fracture, all sites	31.7	32.1	28.8
Cerebrovascular diseases	32.5	33.9	26.7
Pneumonia, all forms	14.8	18.2	23.1
Malignant neoplasms	30.6	26.4	21.0
Eye diseases and conditions	21.5	11.4	3.9

[1] Age-adjusted.

[2] Includes discharges with first-listed diagnoses not shown separately.

Source: U.S. National Center for Health Statistics, "Health United States:1993," Public Health Service, Hyattsville, MD, 1994, Table 96 (based on data from the National Hospital Discharge Survey).

diseases were the third most common first-listed diagnosis. For males aged 75 years and over, cerebrovascular diseases were the third most common first-listed diagnosis in 1980 (at 37.3 per 1,000 population), but they dropped to fourth place (at 27.3 per 1,000 and surpassed by pneumonia) in 1992. The decrease in the rate of hypertension among blacks and whites over the past few decades appears to have led to a decrease in cerebrovascular disease in the future, but an influx of Asian migrants (who are particularly prone to this disease) may prevent the overall rate of cerebrovascular disease from declining dramatically in the near future.

Self-Assessment of Health and Disability

Another way of assessing health in the United States is to ask people to evaluate their own health status. The National Health Interview Survey has asked such a question over the past few years. Table 7-20 presents the proportion of people answering that they had only fair to poor health in the years between 1987 and 1992. Overall, a little less than one out of every ten people gave these responses to the survey between 1987 and 1992. There seems to be no clear temporal trend in the proportion with fair or poor health. Those 65 years and older are slightly more pleased with their health between 1987 and 1992, and those at younger ages are slightly less satisfied. On the other hand, respondent assessment of health is heavily affected by age. Less than 3 percent of those under age 15 years saw themselves with fair or poor health, whereas more than one out of every four persons age 65 years and over fell in this category. Blacks, those with low family incomes, those in the South and those living outside of Metropolitan Statistical Areas all seemed much less satisfied with their current condition of health.

In 1993, the Centers for Disease Control began to use its Behavioral Risk Factor Surveillance System (BRFSS) to measure health-related quality of life (HRQOL) through a large-scale telephone survey. Respondents were asked (in all states except Wyoming) to rate their health in terms of overall quality and mean days of good health per month. Table 7-21 shows the state-level responses to these two questions. Not too surprisingly, those in the Southern and North Central states rated their health less positively than those in the upper Midwest, Washington, New England (excluding Maine), New Jersey, and Washington, D.C. To a large extent, these subjective self-evaluations of health mirror a number of other state-level findings about the prevalence of different diseases and chronic conditions, as well as state differences in income and the distribution of medical personnel. While the field of comparative self-evaluation of health is a relatively new one, these initial results indicate that subjective measures of health can be an important new area of research and concern.

Table 7-20. Respondent-assessed Health Status, by Selected Characteristics: 1987-1992

Characteristic	Percent with fair or poor health[1]			
	1987	1989	1990	1992
Total[2]	9.5	9.1	8.9	9.7
Age				
Under 15 years	2.4	2.4	2.4	2.8
Under 5 years	2.6	2.6	2.9	2.9
5 to 14 years	2.3	2.3	2.2	2.8
15 to 44 years	5.4	5.6	5.4	6.4
45 to 64 years	17.4	16.1	16.0	17.2
65 years and over	30.8	28.5	27.7	28.7
65 to 74 years	28.2	26.3	25.1	25.7
75 years and over	34.9	32.0	31.7	33.2
Age and sex				
Male[2]	9.0	8.6	8.4	9.4
Under 15 years	2.5	2.6	2.6	2.9
15 to 44 years	4.5	4.6	4.5	5.7
45 to 64 years	16.6	15.4	15.5	16.5
65 to 74 years	28.9	27.2	25.0	26.8
75 years and over	36.0	33.0	31.7	33.5
Female[2]	9.9	9.5	9.3	10.1
Under 15 years	2.3	2.3	2.2	2.7
15 to 44 years	6.3	6.6	6.3	7.2
45 to 64 years	18.1	16.8	16.5	17.8
65 to 74 years	27.7	25.6	25.1	24.7
75 years and over	34.2	31.5	31.6	33.0
Age and race				
White[2]	8.5	8.2	8.1	8.9
Under 15 years	2.0	2.0	1.9	2.5
15 to 44 years	4.6	4.9	4.8	5.7
45 to 64 years	15.6	14.5	14.6	15.5
65 to 74 years	26.8	24.5	23.9	24.1
75 years and over	33.2	30.8	30.7	31.9
Black[2]	16.7	15.9	15.1	16.3
Under 15 years	4.1	4.4	4.8	4.4
15 to 44 years	10.5	10.2	9.9	10.7
45 to 64 years	32.9	29.6	28.3	30.9
65 to 74 years	42.9	44.7	38.4	42.1
75 years and over	52.4	45.2	42.9	48.4
Family income[2][3]				
Less than $14,000	20.5	19.4	18.6	20.7
$14,000 to $24,999	14.1	10.1	10.8	11.6
$25,000 to $34,999	11.0	6.9	7.5	8.1
$35,000 to $49,999	7.1	5.1	5.3	6.0
$50,000 or more	4.7	3.7	4.0	3.8
Geographic region[2]				
Northeast	7.9	7.2	7.2	8.0
Midwest	8.8	8.3	7.9	8.6
South	11.7	11.2	11.2	11.8
West	8.2	8.5	8.1	9.5
Location of residence[2]				
Within MSA	9.0	8.6	8.5	9.3
Outside MSA	10.8	10.8	10.4	11.3

[1] Percent with fair or poor as opposed to good, very good, or excellent health.
[2] Age-adjusted.
[3] Family income categories for 1989-1992. Income categories for 1987 are: less than $10,000; $10,000-$14,999; $15,000-$19,999; $20,000-$34,999; and $35,000 or more.

Source: U.S. National Center for Health Statistics, "Health United States: 1993," Public Health Service, Hyattsville, MD, 1994, Table 71 (based on data from the National Health Interview Survey).

Table 7-21. Percent of Survey Respondents Who Reported Good to Excellent Health and Mean Number of Good Health Days per Month, by State[1]: 1993

State	Percent reporting good or excellent health	Mean number of good health days per month	State (continued)	Percent reporting good or excellent health	Mean number of good health days per month
United States	86.6	24.8	Missouri	83.8	24.5
Alabama	85.3	26.2	Montana	86.5	24.0
Alaska	91.6	25.3	Nebraska	88.0	25.1
Arizona	87.5	25.0	Nevada	87.0	23.2
Arkansas	80.3	24.5	New Hampshire	90.8	25.0
California	87.0	24.1	New Jersey	90.8	25.5
Colorado	88.9	24.1	New Mexico	87.4	25.3
Connecticut	90.0	25.8	New York	87.6	24.4
Delaware	87.2	24.1	North Carolina	82.8	25.0
District of Columbia	89.9	27.3	North Dakota	86.4	24.4
Florida	84.6	24.4	Ohio	86.3	25.0
Georgia	86.3	25.3	Oklahoma	82.9	24.8
Hawaii	86.2	26.1	Oregon	88.0	24.5
Idaho	88.1	24.1	Pennsylvania	87.2	24.7
Illinois	87.4	25.6	Rhode Island	85.2	24.0
Indiana	85.3	24.2	South Carolina	82.7	24.9
Iowa	90.7	26.0	South Dakota	89.4	26.1
Kansas	88.0	25.8	Tennessee	81.5	25.1
Kentucky	79.9	24.5	Texas	86.0	24.9
Louisiana	83.9	25.2	Utah	88.4	24.7
Maine	87.4	25.7	Vermont	89.5	25.0
Maryland	89.2	25.2	Virginia	89.0	25.1
Massachusetts	89.6	24.3	Washington	90.5	24.8
Michigan	87.0	24.4	West Virginia	76.6	24.0
Minnesota	89.6	24.5	Wisconsin	89.0	24.8
Mississippi	78.4	24.5			

[1] Excludes Wyoming.

Source: Centers for Disease Control and Prevention, "Morbidity and Mortality Weekly Report, Volume 44, Number 11," U.S. Public Health Service, Atlanta, GA, March 24, 1995 (based on Behavior Risk Factor Surveillance System data).

Mobility and Self-Care Limitations

The 1990 Census included questions on work disability and also asked respondents about whether household members had mobility or self-care limitations in their daily lives. The mobility question asked whether the person had a health condition lasting at least six months that caused him or her difficulty in going "outside the home alone, for example, to shop or visit a doctor's office." The self-care question asked whether the person had a similar condition that limited taking care of personal needs "such as bathing, dressing or getting around inside the home."

Younger adults (aged 16-64; see Table 7-22) were more likely to report work disabilities than mobility or self-care disabilities. About 8.8 percent of males in this age group reported a work disability, compared to 4.5 percent reporting a mobility or self-care limitation. Women in this age group were less likely to report a work disability (7.6 percent) and more likely to report a mobility or self-care limitation (4.7 percent); this may be due to lower levels of labor force participation by women (see Figures 7-3 and 7-4). Black males aged 16-64 were almost three times more likely than their white counterparts to report a mobility or self-care limitation (9.6 compared to 3.6 percent), but the black-white ratio of work disability is less than twice as high (11.6 compared to 8.8 percent). Overall, American Indians, Aleuts and Eskimos had the highest proportions of those with work dis-

Table 7-22. Percent of the Civilian Noninstitutionalized Population with Work and Mobility/Self-care Disabilities, by Age, Sex, and Race-ethnicity: 1990

Age and Sex	Total	White	Black	American Indian, Eskimo, Aleut	Asian or Pacific Islander	Other races	Hispanic
Male							
16 to 64 years	76,669,407	62,558,308	8,043,162	596,490	2,345,354	3,126,093	6,884,794
Work disabilities	8.8	8.6	11.6	14.5	4.2	6.8	7.0
Mobility or self-care disabilities	4.5	3.6	9.6	7.5	6.0	6.6	6.5
65 to 74 years	7,871,539	7,030,646	595,410	32,295	129,251	83,937	286,026
Mobility or self-care disabilities	11.8	10.8	22.0	21.1	15.2	18.0	16.4
75 years and over	4,215,939	3,783,747	312,633	15,082	65,182	39,295	138,377
Mobility or self-care disabilities	24.2	23.2	34.2	33.3	27.9	32.8	31.1
Female							
16 to 64 years	80,654,515	64,591,783	9,916,909	639,701	2,557,858	2,948,264	6,755,403
Work disabilities	7.6	7.2	10.6	12.8	4.2	6.9	6.7
Mobility or self-care disabilities	4.7	3.7	9.9	7.9	6.1	6.9	6.6
65 to 74 years	10,062,013	8,862,482	881,761	40,569	163,946	113,255	377,840
Mobility or self-care disabilities	14.6	13.3	25.7	22.9	17.8	23.7	21.2
75 years and over	7,414,020	6,656,961	596,112	25,106	75,767	60,074	225,543
Mobility or self-care disabilities	34.1	33.1	43.9	40.6	36.1	45.0	42.7

Source: U.S. Bureau of the Census, "Social and Economic Characteristics," 1990 Census of Population, 1990 CP-2-1, U.S. Government Printing Office, Washington, D.C., 1993, Table 40.

Table 7-23. Additions to Mental Health Organizations and Rate per 100,000 Civilian Population, by Type of Service and Organization:1983-1990

Service and organization	Additions (in thousands)				Rate per 100,000 civilian population			
	1983	1986	1988	1990	1983	1986	1988	1990
Inpatient and residential treatment								
All organizations	1,633	1,817	1,999	2,036	701.4	759.9	819.1	833.5
State and county mental hospitals	339	330	304	276	146.0	139.1	124.5	113.2
Private psychiatric hospitals	165	235	381	407	70.9	98.0	156.2	166.5
Non-Federal general hospital psychiatric services	786	849	877	960	336.8	354.8	359.4	393.2
Department of Veterans Affairs psychiatric services[1]	149	180	246	198	64.3	75.1	100.7	81.2
Residential treatment centers for emotionally disturbed children	17	25	23	42	7.1	10.2	9.6	17.0
All other[2][3]	177	198	168	153	76.3	82.7	68.7	62.4
Outpatient treatment								
All organizations	2,665	2,765	2,988	3,005	1147.5	1155.7	1223.8	1230.9
State and county mental hospitals	84	62	94	43	36.3	26.0	38.5	17.5
Private psychiatric hospitals	78	123	125	121	33.4	51.5	51.2	49.7
Non-Federal general hospital psychiatric services	469	494	466	605	202.1	206.3	190.8	247.8
Department of Veterans Affairs psychiatric services[1]	103	125	214	164	44.5	52.3	87.7	67.2
Residential treatment centers for emotionally disturbed children	33	62	56	86	14.1	25.8	22.8	35.3
Freestanding psychiatric outpatient clinics[3]	538	391	554	462	231.7	163.2	226.8	189.3
All other[2][3]	1,360	1,508	1,479	1,524	585.4	630.6	606.0	624.1
Partial care treatment								
All organizations	177	189	276	293	76.3	78.9	113.1	120.2
State and county mental hospitals	4	6	6	5	1.6	2.4	2.3	2.2
Private psychiatric hospitals	6	9	39	42	2.4	3.7	16.1	17.2
Non-Federal general hospital psychiatric services	46	39	39	54	19.8	16.4	16.1	21.9
Department of Veterans Affairs psychiatric services[1]	10	7	16	19	4.4	3.1	6.5	8.0
Residential treatment centers for emotionally disturbed children	3	5	9	13	1.5	2.3	3.5	5.5
Freestanding psychiatric outpatient clinics[3] *	5	—	—	—	2.3	—	—	—
All other[2][3] **	103	123	167	160	44.3	51.0	68.6	65.4

[1] Includes Department of Veterans Affairs neuropsychiatric hospitals, general hospital psychiatric services, and psychiatric outpatient clinics.

[2] Includes other multiservice mental health organizations with inpatient and residential treatment services that are not elsewhere classified.

[3] Beginning in 1983, a definitional change sharply increased the number of multiservice mental health organizations while decreasing the number of freestanding psychiatric outpatient clinics.

* Beginning in 1986, outpatient psychiatric clinics providing partial care are counted as multiservice mental health organizations in the "all other" category.

** Includes freestanding psychiatric partial care organizations.

Source: National Center for Health Statistics, "Health United States, 1993," U.S. Public Health Service, Hyattsville, MD 1994, Table 103.

abilities among both men and women in the working ages, but working-age black men and women reported the highest proportions with mobility and self-care limitations.

At ages 65-74 years, black and American Indian, Aleut and Eskimo males had levels of mobility and self-care limitation that were almost double those of white males; among women, this ratio was slightly lower. The proportion of those with mobility and self-care limitations among Asian and Pacific Islanders, those of other races and all Hispanics aged 65 to 74 years stood between black and white levels. By age 75 years and above, one out of every four white or Asian and Pacific Islander males and one out of every three white females, black, American Indian, Aleut and Eskimo, Other Race or Hispanic males, or Asian and Pacific Islanders of either sex had a mobility or self-care limitation. For this oldest age group, 43.9 percent of all black women, 40.6 percent of American Indian, Aleut and Eskimo women, 45.0 percent of women of Other Races and 42.7 percent of all Hispanic women had similar limitations. The higher female level of mobility and self-care limitations in this oldest age group is not the result of some male superiority in aging, but rather is because the women in this age group are considerably older, on average, than the men, and hence have more time to develop various degenerative problems (see Table 7-17).

The high rates of reported mobility and self-care limitations pose major problems to many American social institutions as the population ages. Children in their seventies must now help parents in their nineties. Grandchildren in their fifties, some of whom suffer from disabilities, must now help both. The growth of the elderly population has also had significant effects on the kind of care that must be provided. Between 1977 and 1985, the proportion of all residents of nursing homes who could dress independently dropped from 30.6 percent to 24.6 percent; the proportion who could walk independently declined from 33.9 to 29.3 percent; and the proportion who could eat independently slid from 67.4 to 60.7 percent. Ironically, during the same period, both the vision and hearing of nursing home residents (as measured by the proportion with unimpaired senses) improved by about 9 percent (Health, United States 1993:194). Thus while a rapidly aging population requires more intensive care, they are often more aware of their surroundings than prior cohorts.

Population Utilization of Health Resources

Almost all discussions of the population's health include questions about the effective use of existing health care resources and possible burdens placed upon resources by an aging population in the future. Current trends in use of specific health care resources (e.g. shorter length of hospital stays) give some reason for optimism. Another oft-voiced concern is that trends in decreased utilization reflect a growing lack of access to quality health care resources. In many cases changing policies, programs and measurement confound any attempt to determine whether declining utilization reflects improvements in the population's health, decreased access to quality care, or simply improved treatment regimens.

The system of medical care in the United States has also undergone major changes since 1980. There have been continual changes in the proportion of the population covered by health insurance, in the nature of such coverage, in the relation of patients and doctors (such as the emergence of health maintenance organizations and paid provider organizations), and so on. Only the broadest outlines of these trends can be captured in the summary statistics available.

Mental Health: Changing Patterns of Care for the Population

Mental health is an area where contradictory social and institutional trends in health care utilization make it difficult to assess (or even measure) possible improvements or declines in health. Since the late 1960's, there has been a great decline in the number of patients in mental institutions, and an increased emphasis on outpatient and community care. This reflects changes in governmental policies, health care paradigms and possibly even diagnostic changes in determining the need for institutional treatment.

However, recent trends in annual additions to mental health organizations during the 1983-90 period (Table 7-23) are more complex than any simple trend might suggest. The additions in inpatient and residential treatment increased from 1.633 million in 1983 to 2.036 million in 1990, with a particular surge in admissions to private psychiatric hospitals. Outpatient treatment additions showed a similar increase (from 2.665 to 3.005 million) in the same period. Some of this increase in mental health treatment was due to an increasing population, but for both inpatient and outpatient treatment the rates per hundred thousand population show sizeable increases between 1983 and 1990. Yet, even with these increases in inpatient and residential additions, the number of inpatient days stayed virtually the same between 1983 and 1990 (at about 82 million days; Health, United States 1993:196), with a resulting shorter stay per patient in later years.

Residential facilities for the mentally retarded underwent a significant change between 1970 and 1991 (see Table 7-24). There was a major decline in the state's role in the operation of such facilities. Between 1970 and 1991, the number of mentally retarded persons living in state-operated facilities declined from 186,743 to 88,132, while the number of such persons in private facilities grew

Table 7-24. Characteristics of Residential Facilities for Persons with Mental Retardation: 1970-1991

Year and type of facility	Number of facilities[1]	End of year population	Rate per 100,000 population
State-operated			
1991	1,477	88,132	35.2
1990	1,321	91,640	34.7
1985	881	112,183	47.5
1980	394	140,230	62.2
1970	190	186,743	92.5
Private			
1991	45,309	201,238	79.8
1990	41,588	188,902	76.0
1982	14,605	115,032	50.0
1977	10,219	89,120	40.9

[1] Beginning in 1985, reflects the development of a large number of community based state-operated facilities which were developed in the early 1980's.

Source: U.S. Bureau of the Census, "Statistical Abstract of the United States: 1994," 1004.U.S. Government Printing Office, Washington, D.C., 1994, Table No. 196.

from 89,120 to 201,238 between 1977 and 1991. While the total number of persons in such residential facilities grew from about 243,000 in 1977 (an extrapolated estimate) to 289,370 in 1991, the rate of growth only barely kept up with overall population growth. In 1977, there were about 112 persons per 100,000 in state-operated or private residential facilities for the mentally retarded; by 1991, this rate had increased to 115 per 100,000.

Interval Since Last Physician Contact

While there are a number of possible measures of availability and utilization of medical care, one frequently-used indicator is the proportion of the population that has seen a physician in the last year (see Figure 7-5). This measure is useful because it shows the extent to which some part of the population (for whatever reason) is being rationed or is rationing medical care to itself at below an optimal level in terms of acute and preventive care.

Males aged 15 to 44 years are the least likely group to see a doctor; only 63 percent of them saw a physician in 1992, the lowest increase at all ages since 1987. Those under 5 years and over 75 years (not shown in the figure) were most likely to have seen a doctor in the last year; their rate of annual physician contact exceeded ninety percent. In general, women, the young and the old, those within MSAs and in the Northeast were more likely to make regular visits to a physician. It is interesting to note that blacks are only slightly less likely to see physicians

Table 7-25. Days of Care in Short-stay Hospitals, by Selected Patient Characteristics: 1964, 1987, and 1992

Patient characteristic	Days of care per 1,000 population		
	1964	1987	1992
Total[1]	970.9	649.7	567.1
Age			
Under 15 years	405.7	263.9	227.7
Under 5 years	731.1	489.2	422.8
5 to 14 years	229.1	143.8	123.5
15 to 44 years	760.7	407.0	340.5
45 to 64 years	1559.3	987.9	801.5
65 years and over	2292.7	2111.1	2045.2
65 to 74 years	2150.4	1862.8	1630.3
75 years and over	2560.4	2507.8	2667.2
Sex[1]			
Male	1010.2	702.9	637.6
Female	933.4	605.7	509.0
Race[1]			
White	961.4	621.5	547.2
Black[2]	1062.9	942.8	736.0
Family income[1] [3]			
Less than $14,000	1051.2	1086.0	988.8
$14,000 to $24,999	1213.9	956.9	616.3
$25,000 to $34,999	939.8	701.1	534.7
$35,000 to $49,999	882.6	573.1	399.8
$50,000 or more	918.9	475.5	305.8
Geographic region[1]			
Northeast	993.8	620.5	632.2
Midwest	944.9	657.5	554.8
South	968.0	768.9	614.8
West	985.9	471.5	435.9
Residence[1]			
Within MSA	1015.4	656.3	545.5
Outside MSA	871.9	634.0	635.6

[1] Age-adjusted.
[2] 1964 data include all other races.
[3] Family income categories for 1992. Income categories in 1964 are: less than $2,000, $2,000-$3,999, $4,000-$6,999, $7,000-$9,999, and $10,000 or more; and in 1987 are: less than $10,000, $10,000-$14,999, $15,000-$19,999, $20,000-$34,999, and $35,000 or more.

Source: National Center for Health Statistics, "Health United States, 1993," U.S. Public Health Service, Hyattsville, MD, 1994, Table 93.

Figure 7-5. Percent of Population with a Less than One Year Interval Since Last Physician Visit, by Age, Sex, Race, and Family Income: 1964, 1987, and 1992

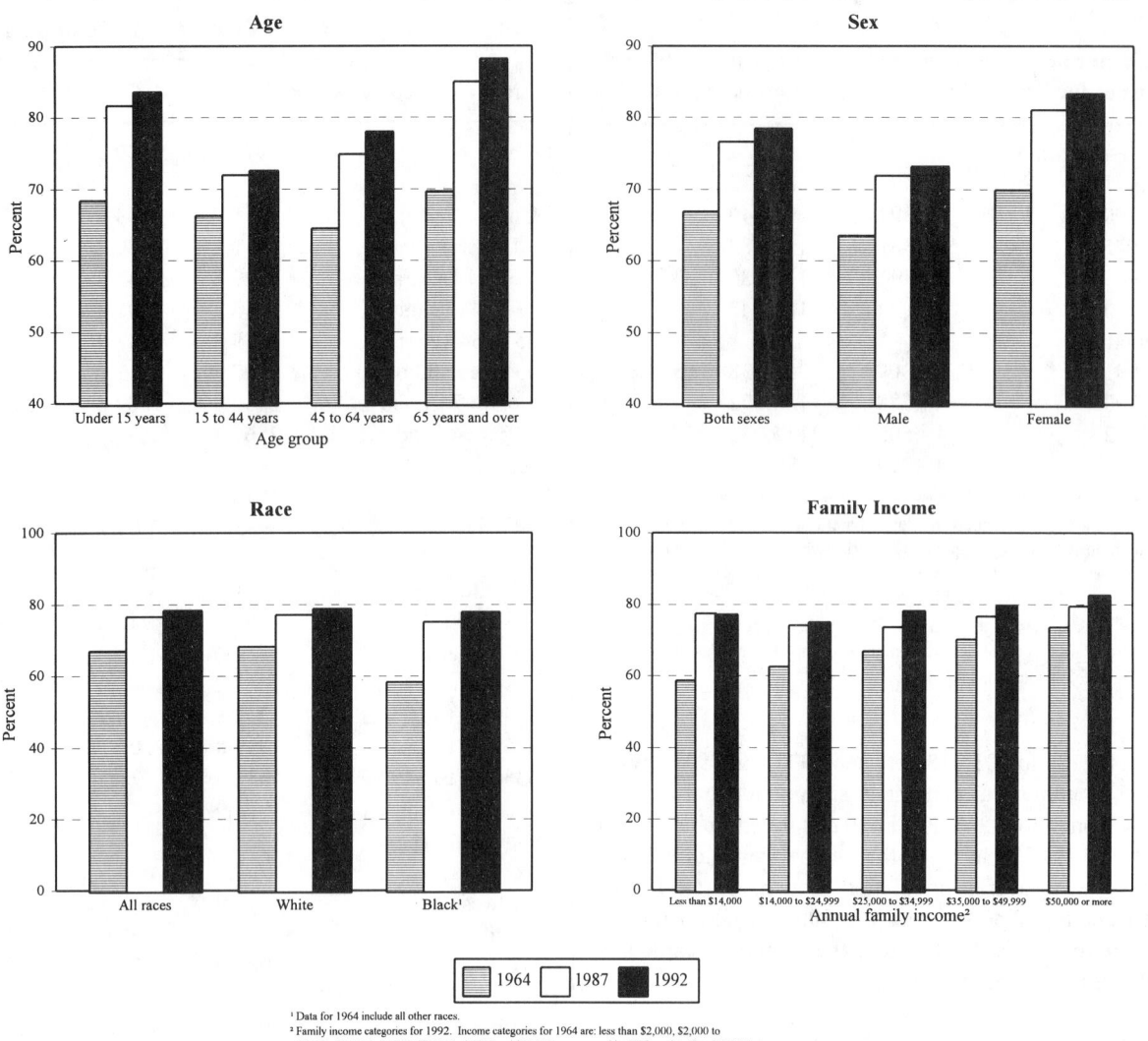

¹ Data for 1964 include all other races.
² Family income categories for 1992. Income categories for 1964 are: less than $2,000, $2,000 to
   $3,999, $4,000 to $6,999, $7,000 to $9,999 and $10,000 or more; and in 1987 are: less than $10,000,
   $10,000 to $14,999, $15,000 to $19,999, $20,000 to $34,999, and $35,000 or more.
Source: National Health Interview Survey data.

regularly than whites (and at some ages black rates exceed those of whites), and it is the working class (those making between $14,000 and $24,999 in 1992) rather than the poorest group that has the least regular contact with physicians. All socio-demographic groups have increased their annual frequency of contact with physicians between 1964 and 1992, some by as much as twenty percent.

Days of Hospital Care for the Population

While the population's number of annual contacts with physicians has risen sharply since 1964, the number of days of hospital care per 100,000 persons has dropped precipitously for some age groups (see Table 7-25). In 1964, each 100,000 persons in the United States received 970.9 days of hospital care; by 1992, they received 567.1 days. While the rate of hospital days per 100,000 actu-

ally increased for those 75 years and over (from 2,560.4 to 2,667.2), the rate of hospital care declined a great deal for those aged 74 and under. Interestingly enough, the greatest declines in number of hospital days per 100,000 persons since 1964 were found among those with high incomes, whites, those inside MSAs and those in the West of the United States. This pattern of decline in hospital days suggests that along with changes in medical practice and efforts by hospitals to move patients out of beds as soon as possible, the healthiest segments of the population are successfully avoiding hospitals.

Nursing Home Residents

Complex changes in the nation's age distribution, family structure and perception of the government's role in health care financing have led to a great increase in the

Figure 7-6. Nursing Home and Personal Care Home Residents 65 Years of Age and Over, by Sex and Race: 1963, 1974, 1977, 1985, and Projections for 1995[1]

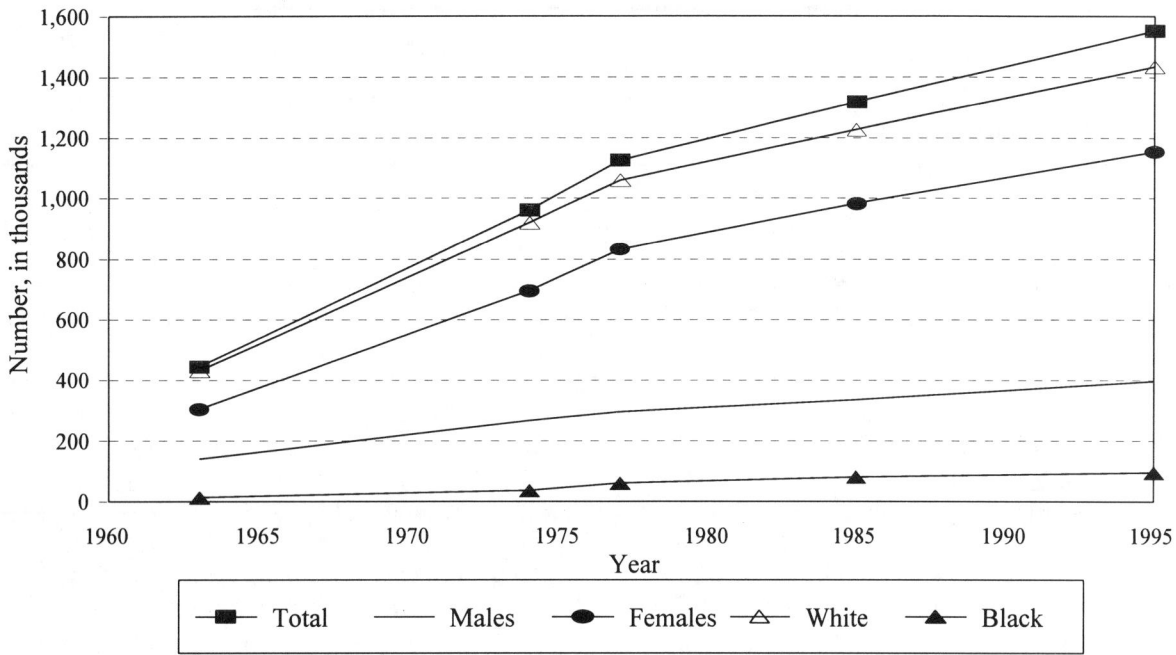

[1] 1995 projections were calculated using the average annual rate of change in nursing home residence rate for 1977-1985 and U.S. Census population projections (middle series) for 1995.

Source: 1995 U.S. Census population projections and National Center for Health Statistics data.

number of nursing home residents, from 1.49 residents of nursing homes per 1,000 population in 1970 to 7.12 per 1,000 population by 1990 (see Chapter 11, Textbox - Trends in Institutionalized Populations). Detailed age-specific rates of nursing home residence among the oldest of these residents are available only to 1985 (Health, United States 1993:193). Between 1963 and 1985, the number of nursing home residents age 65 years and over nearly tripled, and the rate of nursing home residents per 1,000 persons aged 65 years and over rose from 25.4 to 46.2. By 1985, 220.3 out of every 1,000 persons aged 85 years and over lived in a nursing home. Women and whites are more likely to inhabit nursing homes, and while the proportion of blacks in nursing homes has been rising faster than that of whites since 1963, the sex ratio of residents of nursing homes continues to favor women by a large margin. Moving into a nursing home is often precipitated by an elderly person's disability and a lack of someone to care for them. Since women frequently outlive their spouses, they are more likely to move to nursing homes.

So far, nursing homes have not yet seen the effects of age cohorts where large numbers of people have no one in the home to care for them, such as divorced women now in their fifties, or the large number of younger people—particularly black males—who may never marry. When these groups reach retirement age, there may be an increased proportion of the population residing in nursing homes unless alternative modes of living can be found. Assuming no change in incidence, applying the 1985 rates of nursing home residence to the 1990 population distribution still results in substantial increases in the nursing home population (Table 7-26 and Figure 7-6). On the other hand, if rates of disability decline and self-assessed health status continues to improve as it has since 1970, many elderly persons may not require nursing home residence until much later in life.

Conclusion

The United States continues to have a poor record in prenatal health care and in low birth weight among black infants. While there have been increases in the proportions of children immunized against common epidemic diseases in the early 1990's, the concentration of children in poverty and expected overall cutbacks in social and medical programs suggest that we may have already seen the peak of the effort in this direction.

For young adults, HIV and AIDS are the key health problem, and the rates of infection are rapidly increasing for blacks and Hispanics. The disease has now spread throughout the United States, and is truly a national problem. Cigarettes, alcohol and illegal drug use, on the other hand, show significant declines, particularly among black

Table 7-26. Nursing Home and Personal Care Home Residents 65 Years of Age and Over, and Rate per 1,000 Population, by Age, Sex, and Race: 1963, 1973-1974, 1977, 1985, and 1990

Age, sex, and race	Residents					Rate per 1,000 population	
	1963	1973-1974[1]	1977[2]	1985	1990	1963	1985
Age							
Total	445,600	961,500	1,126,000	1,318,300	1,443,373	25.4	46.2
65 to 74 years	89,600	163,100	211,400	212,100	226,332	7.9	12.5
75 to 84 years	207,200	384,900	464,700	509,000	580,180	39.6	57.7
85 years and over	148,700	413,600	449,900	597,300	678,560	148.4	220.3
Sex							
Male	141,000	265,700	294,000	334,400	364,390	18.1	29.0
65 to 74 years	35,100	65,100	80,200	80,600	85,769	6.8	10.8
75 to 84 years	65,200	102,300	122,100	141,300	161,932	29.1	43.0
85 years and over	40,700	98,300	91,700	112,600	124,967	105.6	145.7
Female	304,500	695,800	832,000	983,900	1,081,378	31.1	57.9
65 to 74 years	54,500	98,000	131,200	131,500	140,276	8.8	13.8
75 to 84 years	142,000	282,600	342,600	367,700	417,606	47.5	66.4
85 years and over	108,000	315,300	358,200	484,700	555,839	175.1	250.1
Race[3]							
White	431,700	920,600	1,059,900	1,227,400	1,328,539	26.6	47.7
65 to 74 years	84,400	150,100	187,500	187,800	197,122	8.1	12.3
75 to 84 years	202,000	369,700	443,200	473,600	534,129	41.7	59.1
85 years and over	145,400	400,800	429,100	566,000	637,627	157.7	228.7
Black	13,800	37,700	60,800	82,000	87,799	10.3	35.0
65 to 74 years	5,200	12,200	22,000	22,500	23,153	5.9	15.4
75 to 84 years	5,300	13,400	19,700	30,600	35,103	13.8	45.3
85 years and over	3,300	12,100	19,100	29,000	32,571	41.8	141.5

[1]Excludes residents in personal care or domiciliary care homes.
[2]Includes residents in domiciliary care homes.
[3]In 1973-1974 and 1977, all Hispanics were included in the white category. In 1963, black includes all other races.

Source: National Center for Health Statistics, "Health United States, 1993," U.S. Public Health Service, Hyattsville, MD, 1994, Table 101.

hand, show significant declines, particularly among black youth.

Hypertension and high serum cholesterol levels in the population have generally dropped, but obesity, especially among minority Americans, has increased over the last two decades. Injuries and disability days remain relatively stable. A significant part of the female and male workforce report work disabilities, and a sizable part of those not in the workforce report that they cannot work because of work-related disabilities.

The rapid increase in the number of older Americans has led to an increasing number of chronic conditions among the population, especially such diseases of aging as arthritis, high blood pressure, hearing impairments and heart conditions. Cancer is still common, and five-year survival rates have improved only marginally between 1974-76 and 1983-89 for many cancers. These

survival rates have improved more for whites than for blacks, resulting in a widening racial gap in cancer survivorship. While the death rates from heart and cerebrovascular disease have declined markedly over the past several decades, there has been a price: hospital admissions for heart disease are up, and those for cerebrovascular disease have declined only slightly.

Since the data on self-assessment of health and disability are relatively new, it is difficult to establish historical trends in this area. In general, about one out of every ten persons reported only fair or poor health, and minorities and older individuals were far more likely to report work, mobility, or self-care disabilities. There was considerable variation between states in terms of their populations' self-evaluation of health.

The population's access to, and utilization of, health resources present a mixed picture. While the number of persons getting inpatient or outpatient treatment for mental health disorders increased from 1983 to 1990, there was a shorter average stay for inpatients. Similarly, the number of the mentally retarded in residential treatment increased between 1977 and 1991, but only at the same rate of growth of the total population. Americans increased the rate at which they saw physicians on an annual (or more frequent) basis between 1964 and 1992, but the average number of days of hospital care for those under age 75 dropped markedly between these dates. Both the number and proportion of those aged 65 years and above in nursing homes increased greatly between 1963 and 1985, and these residents now require more care than ever before.

The possibilities and prospects for health care reform in the United States are closely linked to the changing demographic composition of the population. Clearly, by the year 2000 and well beyond, the aging of the United States population will have a major impact on the health of the population. But many demographic differences in health, such as racial differences in low birth weight, AIDS, hypertension and cancer incidence, and respondent assessed health status, have also proven to be persistent concerns that are surprisingly resilient to measures designed to spread health care in an equitable fashion across the population.

Bibliography

American Hospital Association. Hospital Statistics, 1993-94 Edition: Data from the American Hospital Association 1992 Annual Survey. Amer. Hospital Assoc., Chicago, 1993.

Atkinson, Thomas, Liem, Ramsey, and Liem, Joan H. "The Social Costs of Unemployment: Implications for Social Support." Journal of Health and Social Behavior 27(1986): 317-331.

Buck, Jeffrey A., and Klemm, John. "Recent Trends in Medicaid Expenditures." Health Care Financing Review Annual Supplement (1992): 271-284.

Carlton, Thomas O., and Poole, Dennis L. "Trends in Maternal and Child Health Care: Implications for Research and Issues for Social Work Practice." Social Work in Health Care 15(1990): 45-62.

Cassel, Christine K., and Neugarten, Bernice L. "A Forecast of Women's Health and Longevity: Implications for an Aging America." Western Journal of Medicine 149(1988): 712-717.

Castillo, Patricia A., and Pousada, Lidia. "Emergency Services Use by Elderly Individuals." Clinics in Geriatric Medicine 9(1993): 491-546.

Cates, Willard. "Acquired Immunodeficiency Syndrome, Sexually Transmitted Diseases, and Epidemiology: Past Lessons, Present Knowledge, and Future Opportunities." American Journal of Epidemiology 131(1990): 749-758.

Centers for Disease Control and Prevention. "Summary of Notifiable Diseases, United States, 1993." Morbidity and Mortality Weekly Report, Washington, D.C.: U.S. Department of Health and Human Services, Public Health Service, 42(1994).

Coburn, David, and Pope, Clyde R. "Socioeconomic Status and Preventive Health Behavior." Journal of Health and Social Behavior 15(1974): 67-78.

Cohen, Mark. Health and the Rise of Civilization. New Haven, CT: Yale University Press 1989.

Cramer, James C. "Racial and Ethnic Differences in Birthweight: The Role of Income and Financial Assistance." Demography 32(1995): 231-247.

Crimmins, Eileen M., Haywood, Mark D., and Saito, Yasuhiko. "Changing Mortality and Morbidity Rates and the Health Status and Life Expectancy of the Older Population." Demography 31(1994): 159-175.

Ezzati, T. M., Massey, J. T., and Waksberg, J. "Plan and Operation of the Third National Health and Nutrition Examination Survey, 1988-94." National Center for Health Statistics, Vital Health Statistics 1(1994).

Health Systems Review. "Trends in Psychiatric Outpatient Care: Providers Look Closely at Follow-up and 'Continuum of Care' and Other Outpatient Strategies to Hold Down Treatment Costs." 24(1991): 28-30.

House, James S., Landis, Karl R., and Umberson, Debra. "Social Relationships and Health." Science 241(1988): 40-45.

Garber, Alan M., and MaCurdy, Thomas E. "Nursing Home Discharges and Exhaustion of Medicare Benefits." Journal of the American Statistical Association 88(1993): 727-736.

Judkins, D. R., Mosher, W. D., and Botman, S. "National Survey of Family Growth: Design, estimation and inference." National Center for Health Statistics, Vital Health Statistics 2(1991).

Kallan, Jeffrey E. "Race, Intervening Variables, and Two Forms of Low Birth Weight." Demography 30(1993): 489-506.

Karon, John M., and Dondero, Timothy J. "HIV Prevalence Estimates and AIDS Case Projections for the United States: Report Based on Workshop." Morbidity and Mortality Weekly Report, Washington, D.C.: U.S. Department of Health and Human Services, Public Health Service, 39(1990).

Kent, Vicky, and Hanley, Barbara. "Home Health Care: Policy Evolution, Cost-effectiveness, and Trends." Nursing and Health Care: Official Publication of National League for Nursing 11(1990): 234-241.

Kestenbaum, Bert. "A Description of the Extreme Aged Population Based on Improved Medicare Enrollment Data." Demography 29(1992): 565-580.

Kinter, Hallie J. "Demographic Change in a Corporate Health Benefits Population, 1983-87." American Journal of Public Health 79(1989): 1655-1656.

Kovar, M. G. "Data Systems of the National Center for Health Statistics." National Center for Health Statistics, Vital Health Statistics 1(1989).

Levit, Katharine R., Freeland, Mark S., and Waldo, Daniel R. "National Health Care Spending Trends: 1988." Health Affairs 9(1990): 171-184.

Makuc, Diane M. "National Trends in the Use of Preventive Health Care by Women." American Journal of Public Health 79(1989): 21-26.

Manderscheid, R. W., and Sonnenschein, M. A. (eds.) Mental Health, United States 1992. Center for Mental Health Services. Washington, D.C.: U.S. Department of Health and Human Services, 1992.

Manton, Kenneth G. "Epidemiological, Demographic, and Social Correlates of Disability Among the Elderly." Milbank Quarterly 67(suppl. 2, 1989): 13-58.

Midanik, Lorraine T., Klatsky, Arthur L., and Armstrong, Mary A. "Changes in Drinking Behavior: Demographic, Psychosocial and Biomedical Factors," International Journal of the Addictions 25(1990): 599-619.

Mollica, Richard F., Milic, Mladen, and Bollini, Paola. "Trends in Mental Health Care: Categorical Treatment and the Concept of 'Positionality'." International Journal of Mental Health 18(1989-90): 31-47.

Morris, J. N. "Inequalities in Health: Ten Years and Little Further On." Lancet 336(1990): 491-493.

Mossey, Joan M., and Shapiro, Evelyn. "Self-Rated Health: A Predictor of Mortality Among the Elderly." American Journal of Public Health 72(1982): 800-808.

National Cancer Institute, Cancer Statistics Review, 1973-90. Bethesda, MD: National Institute of Health, Public Health Service, 1993.

National Center for Health Statistics. Health, United States, 1993. Hyattsville, MD: Public Health Service, 1994.

_____. Health, United States, 1994. Hyattsville, MD: Public Health Service, 1995.

Power, C., Fox, A., and Fogelman, K. "Health in Childhood and Social Inequalities in Health in Young Adults." Journal of the Royal Statistical Society 153(1990): 17-28.

Public Health Service. Healthy people 2000: National health promotion and disease prevention objectives- full report, with commentary. Washington, D.C.: U.S. Department of Health and Human Services, Public Health Service, 1991.

Reilly, Thomas W., Clauser, Steven B., and Baugh, David K. "Trends in Medicaid Payments and Utilization, 1975-89." Health Care Financing Review Annual Supplement (1990): 15-88.

Riley, James C. "The Risk of Being Sick: Morbidity Trends in Four Countries." Population and Development Review 16(1990): 403-432.

Ross, Catherine E., and We, Chia-ling. "The Links Between Education and Health." American Sociological Review 60(1995): 719-745.

Schwenk, Nancy E. "Health Care Trends." Family Economics Review 5(1992): 18-24.

Tu, Xin Ming, Meng, Xiao-Li, and Pagano, Marcello. "The AIDS Epidemic: Estimating Survival after AIDS Diagnosis from Surveillance Data." Journal of the American Statistical Association 88(1993): 26-36.

U.S. Bureau of the Census. Statistical Abstract of the United States: 1994. Washington, D.C.: U.S. Government Printing Office, 1994.

U.S. Department of Labor, Bureau of Labor Statistics. "Occupational Injuries and Illnesses: Counts, Rates and Characteristics, 1992." Bulletin 2455. Washington, D.C.: U.S. Government Printing Office, 1995.

Winkleby, M. A., Jatulis, D. E., Frank, E., and Fortmann, S. P. "Socioeconomic Status and Health: How Education, Income, and Occupation Contribute to Risk Factors for Cardiovascular Disease." American Journal of Public Health 82(1992): 816-820.

Women's Bureau, Department of Labor. 1993 Handbook on Women Workers: Trends and Issues. Washington, D.C.: U.S. Department of Labor, 1994.

8

SPATIAL MOVEMENT AND REGIONAL GEOGRAPHIES

People moving, or changing their place of residence, is a major source of change in an area's population. Residential changes are usually classified into three types: local movement, internal migration, and immigration from abroad. This chapter considers all of these changes, plus immobility. It is as important to understand why persons do not move as to understand why they do.

Persons who depart from a place diminish the population count and change the population composition of the place of departure according to the pattern of their personal characteristics. When those persons arrive at their new residence, they increase the population count and similarly change the population composition at their destination. People who arrive in the place from which others leave tend to replenish the population count, but usually do not exactly replicate the characteristics of those who left.

The absolute impact (the number of persons gained or lost) through mobility is a product of the population size of the sending or receiving territory and the mobility rate—the probability of moving (mobile persons per 100 residents). A mobility rate measures the average propensity to move, and is analogous to birth and death rates. Numbers of arriving and departing persons are analogous to the number of births and deaths which occur in a population. In-migration can be a substitute for births and out-migration a substitute for deaths in stimulating population growth or decline. A very large population can have a big mobility impact on its smaller neighbors, even if its rate of moving to their locale is relatively low. This chapter gives close attention both to absolute sizes of mobility streams and to mobility rates which generate those streams, both at sending and receiving localities. Furthermore, it attempts to assess the relative impact of mobility on the size and composition of population at sending and receiving places. Residential mobility also has economic, social, political, and even psychological causes

and effects—which this chapter can only summarize.

As in all nations, residential mobility in the U.S. (especially immigration from abroad) is closely linked to public policy and subject to administrative regulation. Consequently it often is the object of opposing and strongly held opinions and recommendations. This has especially been the case during the 1980's and 1990's. Past mobility trends and patterns appear to be undergoing important modification or even reversal, and new developments, not yet fully understood, have emerged. Research and debate are voluminous, reflecting deep concern. This chapter describes these policy concerns, but makes few judgements about them. Instead, it aims to present an integrated factual picture of what has happened in the recent past and both prospects and options for the future.

The population of the United States is very prone to move internally within its own borders (has high mobility rates applied to its large population). Each year during the decade 1982-92 about 38-42 million persons (17-18 percent) moved from one house or apartment to another elsewhere in the country. Compare this with the nation's concurrent annual average of 4.1 million births and 2.1 million deaths. Only Canada and Australia are more mobile than this. Obviously, spatial mobility is an important component of U.S. population dynamics. In addition, each year the nation is legally admitting about 750,000 immigrants from abroad, plus an estimated 250,000 illegal ("undocumented") persons from other nations. This annual net increment of about 1 million immigrants is roughly equal to one-half of the country's vital increase (excess of births over deaths). In other words, one-third of the nation's overall current growth is due to immigration from abroad. Because internal migration and external immigration are closely interrelated and interact with each other, this chapter discusses the unique aspects of each but integrates them into a total mobility picture, and considers their impact upon each other.

Chapter 8 Definitions
SPATIAL MOVEMENT AND REGIONAL GEOGRAPHIES

Residence X Years Ago. Most data for residential mobility is obtained from an inquiry about the place of residence of each person at some specified date in the past. The inquiry for the 1990 census is prototypical. Two questionnaire items were asked: (a) "Did this person live in this house or apartment 5 years ago (on April 1, 1985)?" For those for whom the response was negative, the question was then asked: (b) "Where did this person live 5 years ago?". Four categories of area were provided for reporting residence 5 years ago:

• Same house / Different house
• State (or foreign country)
• County (for those living in the U.S.)
• City or town (for those living in the U.S.)

To improve the quality of response to the last category, a supplementary probing question "Did this person live inside (or outside) the city or town limits?" was asked.

These questions were not asked for children under 5 years of age. Where no information on residence in 1985 was reported for a person, information for other family members, if available, was used to assign a location. Cases for which previous residence could not be assigned in this manner were allocated the previous residence of another person with similar characteristics who provided complete information.

The category "Same house" includes all persons 5 years old and over who did not move during the 5 years as well as those who have moved but by 1990 had returned to their 1985 residence. Persons reporting "Different house" were then further subdivided according to two different mobility status systems [each defined separately below]:

(a) General (county-level) mobility status
(b) Detailed (metropolitan-level) mobility status

Mobility Interval. The time elapsed between the date specified for previous residence and the date of enumeration, usually one year or five years. The censuses of 1940, 1960, 1970, 1980, and 1990 specify five years, while the census of 1950 specifies 1 year. The Current Population Surveys have specified intervals of one, two, three, four, and five years.

Mobility Stream. The number of mobile persons who move from one specified type of place of origin (residence at beginning of mobility period) to a different specified type of place of destination (residence at end of mobility period).

General (County-Level) Mobility Status. A classification based on a comparison of the place of residence of each individual at the date of a census enumeration or survey (destination) and the place of residence as of some specified earlier date (origin). National, state and county boundaries are used to categorize the type of movement. Mobility status falls into four main categories:

Stayers (nonmobile persons). Persons classified as living in the same house at the time of the census as at the date of origin. Movers (mobile persons, persons living in a different house) are further classified as to where they were living at the earlier date.

Local Movers. Mobile persons living in the same county at census time as at the date of origin.

Internal Migrants. Mobile persons who were living in a different county at census time from the county of residence at the date of origin. Migrants may be subclassified further:

  a. *Intrastate migrants.* Persons living in a different county but within the same state.

  b. *Interstate migrants.* Persons living in a different state.

  c. *Interregional migrants.* Persons living in a different geographic region.

International migrants. Persons living abroad (outside the U.S. at the date of origin. This includes those living in Puerto Rico) and in U.S. outlying areas.

Detailed (Metropolitan-Level) Mobility Status. A system of subdividing mobile persons into categories according to their place of residence with respect to metropolitan statistical areas at the beginning and end of the mobility interval. Information on city or town of residence in addition to county boundaries are employed. Residence at prior date is reported as follows:

Unlike fertility and mortality, spatial mobility is reversible and repeatable. Under typical peacetime conditions, it is a volitional mechanism by which individuals or households adjust to changing socioeconomic events and conditions in their lives. A change of residence results from a decision. There are many specific reasons why people may wish to change residence. Although economic reasons are predominant, there are also many noneconomic factors including cultural, communal-environmental, familial, medical, psychological, political, religious, and racial reasons for mobility. Often these reasons are dichotomized into "pushes" (negative aspects of the present place of residence) and "pulls" (positive aspects of alternative places of residence). This is an oversimplification; spatial mobility is typically a net resultant of several positive and negative factors simultaneously impelling individuals to stay and to move. Stayers are more attracted to their present residence than alternatives, while movers are more attracted to other places than to their present location. Where the combinations of attraction or repulsion are both about equally strong, a situation of "residential stress" develops and a decision must be made on some other basis.

Clearly, spatial mobility may be considered from both the social-psychological (individual) level and the ecological (group) level. These correspond to the adaptive view of mobility as a decision making process and the redistributive aspects of mobility with concomitant aggregate causes and consequences in the population.

• *Individual—Social-psychological*: Mobile persons (movers) are compared with nonmobile persons (stayers). Understanding the personal motives and decisions which underlie the calculus of moving or staying in particular types of places is a key concern.

• *Group—Ecological:* The aggregate of newly arriving residents is compared with the aggregate of departing residents and with the stock of residents who do not move. Comparative environmental and socioeconomic conditions in the sending and receiving areas are hypothesized to be both causes, and impacted by the consequences, of mobility.

Same house (as above)
Different house
    Central City this MSA/PMSA
    Metropolitan Ring (remainder) this
    MSA/PMSA ("suburb")
    Different MSA/PMSA
      (a) Central city;
      (b) Metropolitan ring
    Not in an MSA/PMSA (nonmetro-
    politan).
Abroad

Tabulations of these data for the central cities and metropolitan rings of particular metropolitan areas permits the following mobility flows to be specified:

Same house
    Central City; Metropolitan Ring
Intrametropolitan movement
    Movement within Central Cities;
    Movement within Metropolitan
    Rings; Movement from Central
    Cities to Metropolitan Rings;
    Movement from Metropolitan
    Rings to Central Cities
Intermetropolitan in-migration
    To Central Cities from other Cen-
    tral Cities; To Central Cities
    from other Metropolitan Rings;
    To Metropolitan Ring from other
    Central Cities; To Metropolitan
    Ring from other Metropolitan
    Rings
Nonmetropolitan out-migration to Met-
    ropolitan Areas
    To Central Cities; To Metropolitan
    Rings
Nonmetropolitan in-migration from
    Metropolitan Areas
    From Central Cities; From Metro-
    politan Rings
Immigration from Abroad
    To Central Cities; To Metropolitan
    Rings

Tabulation of these data for a non-metropolitan area (nation, state, region, county) permits the following mobility flows to be specified:

Same house
Between Nonmetropolitan areas
From Metropolitan to Nonmetropolitan
    Areas
From abroad

Most published census tabulations do not permit advantage to be taken of all of these possibilities specified above. However, sample surveys can and do provide this detail. Special post-census mobility tabulations provide much of this detail for individual places.

Mobility Rates. The number of persons in a specified mobility status per 100 or per 1,000 population of the area in which they resided as of the end of the mobility interval. Such rates may refer to any of the categories of nonmobile or mobile persons specified above. Mobility rates may be specific for age, race, sex, or other trait. The denominator may also be the estimated population as of the origin date or as of the midpoint of the migration interval.

In-migration. Internal migrants arriving at a particular place of destination, with no reference to the place of origin.

Out-migration. Internal migrants departing from a particular place of origin, with no reference to the place of their destination.

Immigration. Migrants who have arrived in a country from a residence abroad.

Emigration. Migrants who have departed from the country to reside abroad

from a former residence inside the country.

Net Migration. The balance of arrivals and departures from an area, obtained by subtracting out-migration from the sum of in-migration and immigration. [In some tabulations, this calculation is confined to internal migration.] The resulting numbers may be either positive or negative. Negative numbers indicate net loss through migration; positive numbers represent net gain through migration.

Place of Birth. Respondents are asked to report the U.S. state, commonwealth or territory, or the foreign country where they were born. Persons born outside the United States are asked to report their place of birth as of current international boundaries. Some persons born abroad may report their place of birth in terms of boundaries that existed at the time of their birth or emigration, or in accordance with their national preference. From these data measures of "lifetime mobility" are obtainable:

Native Born (born as citizens within the
    United States)
    Living in state of birth
    Living in different state (specify
    state or region)

Foreign Born (immigrants born as citi-
    zens of a country other than the
    United States)

Persons not reporting their place of birth were assigned the birthplace of another family member or were allocated the response of another person with similar characteristics. Persons allocated as foreign born were not assigned a specific country.

Recent research demonstrates that these two views are not incompatible, but complementary. This chapter considers both the individual and the ecological perspectives, but gives stronger emphasis to the ecological. As a consequence, it concentrates on exploring the causes and effects of residential mobility for regions, metropolitan/nonmetropolitan areas, states, counties, and even smaller units of area.

Mobility decisions are being formulated daily not only by American citizens, but also by hundreds of millions of people residing elsewhere in the world considering migration to other nations. The worldwide network of mass communication continuously informs the entire planet about living conditions elsewhere. And, almost since its founding, the United States has been considered one of the most desirable places to live. When population density in the U.S. was low, public resistance to immigration from abroad also was comparatively low. Today, with practically no territorial frontiers and much higher densities, there is increasingly strong and prevalent resistance. Because more than two-thirds of the

world's population lives in developing nations under circumstances far less agreeable than those of the U.S., the pressure to enter the U.S. by any means, legal or illegal, is high and may be expected to continue. A similar situation is faced by the developed nations of Europe, Japan, Australia, New Zealand, etc. Even the sovereign right of a richer nation to limit access to residence within its national boundaries by enterprising residents of poorer nations is progressively being challenged. The physical capability and political will of developed nations to enforce their immigration laws is being severely tested. The U.S. is a prime focal point of this immigration pressure and is apparently destined to remain so for most if not all of the next century.

Definitions of Mobility and Systems of Classification

In all mobility definitions (see Definitions Box), mobility is inferred by comparing the place of residence at some earlier date with the place of residence of the respondent at time of enumeration. A mobile person is one who is found living at an address which is different from the address of residence at some specified earlier time. (See 'General Mobility Status' in the Definitions Box.) There are two major sources of official mobility data for the U.S., the decennial censuses and the Current Population Survey. Many other sample surveys also include mobility questions. The definition is determined by two elements: (a) the time span and (b) the type of move. With respect to time span (mobility interval), it is customary to collect data with respect to address change within a single year or during the five years preceding the enumeration. A one-year time span is statistically ideal, but may not be representative of longer trends (especially for a decennial census). Mobility data for the census of 1990 are based on the question, "Where were you living on April 1, 1985?" A similar 5-year time span was used for the censuses of 1940, 1960, 1970 and 1980. For the census of 1960, a 1-year time span was employed. The Current Population Survey (taken annually) usually measures mobility over a 1-year time period, with a 5-year interval for the mid-census year (1985, 1995, etc.). An additional measure of residential mobility, with an indeterminate time span, is place of birth. Persons enumerated at a place different from that in which they were born (country, state, county) obviously have been mobile.

With respect to type of move, classification is based on the type of political boundary crossed in the act of moving. Two systems of classification are currently in use: (a) General Mobility Status and (b) Detailed 'Metropolitan' Mobility Status (see Definitions Box). The first is useful in examining broad geographic patterns involving regions, states, and counties. The second recognizes that a very important share of residential movement is between particular metropolitan or nonmetropolitan areas, either as places of origin or of destination, and their constituent parts (central cities and the remainder of the metropolitan area here termed 'metropolitan rings'). This chapter makes use of both systems, but places strong emphasis on the second, because metropolitan areas are involved in some of the most noteworthy population changes. Each metropolitan area represents a unique major component of the national economic and social structure: a labor market, a housing market, and an interdependent commercial-industrial-financial network. Hence, the more than 300 census-delimited Metropolitan Statistical Areas (MSA's) are much more specific units of origin and destination for residential change than are the 50 states, nine geographic divisions, or four regions.

One-Year Mobility Rates

Measuring mobility status in terms of one-year intervals (place of residence a year ago) conforms to procedures used in the study of birth, death, and marriage. It enables computation of annual rates comparable to those of the vital processes. Such rates can be interpreted as annual probabilities of making specified types of residential change. The characteristics of mobile persons, and socioeconomic environmental conditions at time of movement, can be measured or inferred more accurately with one-year rates.

Table 8-1 reports rates for each general mobility status of the population for selected years from 1950 to 1992. The overall impression is one of near-uniformity for all categories of mobility. Over the 42-year period, the overall mobility rate has declined from 21 percent to 17 percent, with a temporary upsurge around 1984-85. It is desirable to subdivide mobility into its sub-types, and study each individually.

Nearly two-thirds of all change of residence is local as indicated by those living in a different house but in the same county as a year ago. During 1991-92, 10.7 percent of the population was locally mobile. Persons routinely make local housing switches in response to frequently occurring life cycle events such as marriage-divorce-widowhood, birth of children, choice of public schools, youth leaving home, change of jobs, becoming a homeowner, upward or downward socioeconomic mobility, change in characteristics of neighborhood, retirement, etc. Except for a temporary upsurge in 1984-85, local mobility has showed no evidence of either upward or downward trend since 1970. However, local mobility is unmistakably lower in the two most recent decades than during the 1950-70 period. Its apparent constancy at a national level is deceptive. The important impact which this very large volume of short-distance movement can have in causing particular neighborhoods to undergo comparatively rapid and significant change, either positive or negative, is often overlooked and under-researched.

The annual rate of internal migration (moving from one county to another) has fluctuated around a nearly constant level of 6-7 percent per year since 1950. Because of the greater average distance involved, internal migration tends to be associated with major career or life-course changes (which may also include combinations of the events cited for local mobility). Because migration has remained at the same level while local mobility has declined, the ratio of migration to local moving has increased in recent years. Slightly less than one-half of each year's 15 million internal migrants change the state of their residence, an indication of generally longer-distance movement. This 50-50 split between shorter-distance and longer-distance migration has persisted over the decades. To better identify the truly long-distance movers, a subset of migrants who change geographic region of residence is specified in Table 8-1. About 1/12 of all migrants are inter-regionally mobile.

Movers from abroad contribute an annual increase

Table 8-1. One-Year General Mobility Rates[1], by Type of Movement: Selected One-year Periods 1950-1992

| Mobility period | Total movers | Same county | Internal mobility: different house in the U.S. | | | | External mobility: movers from abroad |
			Total	Same state	Different state	Different region	
1991-92	17.3	10.7	6.0	3.2	2.9	1.3	0.5
1990-91	17.0	10.3	6.1	3.2	2.9	1.4	0.6
1989-90	17.9	10.6	6.6	3.3	3.3	1.6	0.6
1988-89	17.8	10.9	6.3	3.3	3.0	1.4	0.6
1987-88	17.8	11.0	6.2	3.3	3.0	1.3	0.5
1986-87	18.6	11.6	6.5	3.7	2.8	1.5	0.5
1985-86	18.6	11.3	6.7	3.7	3.0	1.6	0.5
1984-85	20.2	13.1	6.5	3.5	3.0	1.6	0.6
1983-84	17.3	10.4	6.4	3.6	2.8	1.6	0.5
1982-83	16.6	10.1	6.0	3.3	2.7	1.4	0.4
1981-82	17.0	10.3	6.2	3.3	3.0	1.6	0.5
1980-81	17.2	10.4	6.2	3.4	2.8	1.5	0.6
1975-76	17.7	10.8	6.4	3.4	3.0	1.6	0.6
1970-71	18.7	11.4	6.5	3.1	3.4	2.0	0.8
1965-66	19.8	12.7	6.6	3.3	3.3	1.8	0.5
1960-61	20.6	13.7	6.3	3.1	3.2	1.7	0.6
1955-56	21.1	13.7	6.8	3.6	3.1	—	0.6
1950-51	21.2	13.9	7.1	3.6	3.5	—	0.2

[1] Mobile persons per 100 residents 1+ years old.

Source: U.S. Bureau of the Census, Current Population Reports, "Current Geographical Mobility: March 1991 to March 1992," Series P-20, Number 473, Table A, U.S. Government Printing Office, Washington, D.C., 1993.

of 0.5 to 0.6 percent to the population. Although this includes some members of the Armed Forces returning from duty abroad, almost all of these individuals are legal or illegal immigrants. A high percentage of these immigrants remain and become permanent residents. And, cumulated over a decade, this annual addition amounts to a major component of national population growth. Immigration from abroad has especially strong impacts upon particular areas which are points of entry including New York, Los Angeles, Chicago, Miami, and cities in the Southwest along the border with Mexico. Although there are small annual fluctuations, Table 8-1 indicates that the rate of immigration has remained nearly constant since 1955. However, the number of immigrants has increased at about the same pace as the increasing size of the U.S. population.

Demographic Mobility Differentials

Averages covering the entire national population conceal the important fact that mobility status varies greatly according to a few key demographic characteris-

tics. Some categories of the population are very mobile while others have quite low mobility. Knowing the current situation of basic demographic mobility differentials, which tend to be deep-seated and surprisingly consistent in both time and space, is a prerequisite to understanding the details of most migration flows. In this section differences by age, sex, and race-ethnicity are discussed in some detail. Table 8-2 provides data which sketch out the principal differentials. Mobility differences are dichotomized into local mobility (different house, same county) and migration (different county). A later section summarizes these mobility differentials for a few additional key socio-economic characteristics which are correlated with unusually high or unusually low mobility.

Age Mobility Differentials

Mobility of adults is closely linked to the major life-cycle transitions, particularly from youth to adulthood. Beginning with age 15-19, the mobility rate ascends very quickly. Persons age 20-24 are twice as mobile (35.3 percent per year) as the national average, and the rate for

Table 8-2. Average One-year Mobility Rates¹ by Age, Sex, and Race-ethnicity: 1990-1992

| Age, sex, and race-ethnicity | Total movers | Internal mobility: different house in the U.S. | | | | | External mobility: Movers from abroad |
| | | Same county | Different county | | | | |
			Total	Same state	Different state	Different region	
All persons	16.9	10.5	6.1	3.2	2.9	1.4	0.5
Age							
1-4 years	22.4	14.8	7.2	3.6	3.7	1.9	0.4
5-9 years	17.6	11.4	5.9	3.2	2.7	1.3	0.5
10-14 years	14.6	9.6	4.7	2.5	2.3	1.1	0.4
15-19 years	17.3	10.9	6.0	3.1	2.9	1.3	0.7
20-24 years	35.3	21.8	12.8	7.1	5.7	2.7	1.4
25-29 years	32.3	20.2	11.6	6.6	5.0	2.4	1.0
30-34 years	21.8	13.9	7.6	4.1	3.5	1.7	0.7
35-39 years	16.3	10.0	6.0	3.0	3.0	1.4	0.5
40-44 years	13.0	7.9	4.9	2.5	2.4	1.1	0.4
45-49 years	10.9	6.3	4.5	2.1	2.4	1.0	0.3
50-54 years	9.5	5.6	3.7	1.9	1.8	0.8	0.3
55-59 years	8.0	4.5	3.3	1.5	1.8	0.8	0.4
60-64 years	6.5	3.6	2.8	1.2	1.6	0.6	0.2
65-69 years	5.6	3.2	2.3	1.3	1.1	0.4	0.2
70-74 years	4.6	2.3	2.3	0.9	1.3	0.6	0.1
75-79 years	4.6	2.6	1.9	1.1	0.9	0.5	0.2
80-84 years	5.4	3.3	2.1	1.0	1.1	0.5	0.2
85 + years	5.4	2.8	2.6	1.0	1.6	0.6	0.0
Sex							
Male	17.0	10.7	6.3	3.3	3.0	1.4	0.6
Female	16.2	10.4	5.9	3.1	2.8	1.3	0.5
M:F sex ratio	0.99	0.97	1.03	1.02	1.03	1.04	1.21
Race-ethnicity							
White	16.2	10.0	6.1	3.3	2.9	1.4	0.4
Black	18.8	13.3	5.5	2.6	2.9	1.2	0.4
Hispanic	21.5	16.6	4.9	2.9	1.9	1.0	1.9
White, non-Hispanic	15.8	9.4	6.2	3.3	2.9	1.4	0.4

¹ Mobile persons per 100 residents of each group.

Source: U. S. Bureau of the Census, Current Population Reports, "Current Geographical Mobility: March 1991 to March 1992," Table B, and "March 1990 to March 1991," Table B, Series P-20, Numbers 473 and 463, U.S. Government Printing Office, Washington, D.C, 1993 and 1992.

persons age 25-29 is almost as high. Even adults in their early thirties are much more mobile than the general population. After reaching its peak, with further advancing age the mobility rate decreases progressively, until at ages above 65 it is only one-third or less the national average. But Americans never get too old to change residence; even at the more advanced ages the rate plateaus at about 5.4 percent per year, about one-half of which is migration and not simply local movement. Figure 8-1 portrays the migration age curve. To compare age profiles without regard to level, this figure expresses age-specific mobil-

ity rates as a ratio to the average mobility rate across ages for each particular type of mobility. For most countries, when mobility data for both sexes combined are examined, an age-specific curve with the general shape depicted in Figure 8-1 emerges.

The age pattern of mobility is understandable in view of the fact that eighteen years is the modal age for graduating from high school, which often signals departure from the parental home. A change of residence normally is involved in either going to college or seeking work. Furthermore, the median age of marriage for

Figure 8-1. Age Pattern of Mobility: 1990-1992

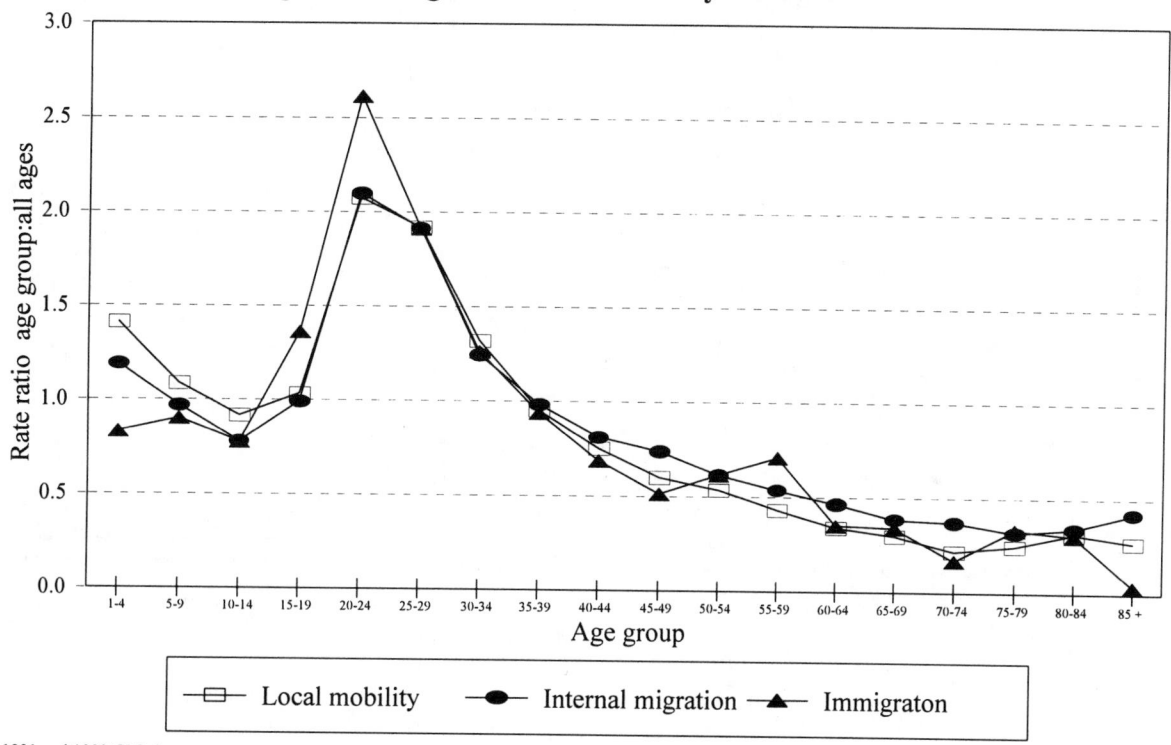

Source: 1991 and 1992 CPS data.

women and men alike falls in the 20-29 age interval; marriage usually involves a change of residence for bride or groom, if not both. The arrival of a first, second, or third child may require parents to make further changes in residence. As savings are accumulated, transitions from modest to more comfortable living quarters and from the status of renter to that of homeowner are made by a great many families while the householder is between the ages of 25 and 55.

Mobility rates for young children, especially those less than ten years old, are surprisingly high. As dependents of their young adult parents, children appear to be less of a deterrent to mobility than one might imagine. However, age 10-14 is a time of comparatively lower mobility for children. Parents of children this age have passed through the ages of peak mobility of young adulthood and have entered the phase of declining mobility rates with advancing maturity.

Local mobility and migration have very similar, but not identical, age patterns. The child population tends to exhibit relatively higher rates of local mobility than of migration. Immigration involves fewer children, with an extraordinarily high concentration of young persons. Immigration rates for the elderly are also elevated. This is possibly caused by use of family reunification provisions of U. S. immigration laws to get U.S. public medical benefits for elderly parents. Among the elderly popu-

lation there appears to be a slight upturn in mobility at the most advanced ages which may be partially caused by movement to living arrangements which combine housing and health care for those with disabilities. At ages above 65 the rate of migration is almost identical to the rate of local moving (both in the range of 2-3 percent annually).

Sex Mobility Differentials

Difference in mobility rates between the sexes is quite small (Table 8-2). Men appear to be slightly more mobile with respect to residence than women. This difference exists for both local mobility and for all categories of migration. It is due in part to mobility of armed forces personnel, which are predominantly male. Yet, small sex mobility differentials do not necessarily imply sex-equality either of opportunity or choice in residential movement. Because spouses tend to have similar characteristics, women who migrate as dependents or subordinates of men can only replicate male mobility patterns.

There are significant sex differences in age patterns of mobility as illustrated in Figure 8-2. Beginning with age 10-14 and continuing through age 20-24, women tend to be both locally mobile and more migratory than males. However, males catch up with and surpass females in mobility around age 25 and maintain higher rates until

Figure 8-2. Mobility Rates, by Sex: 1992

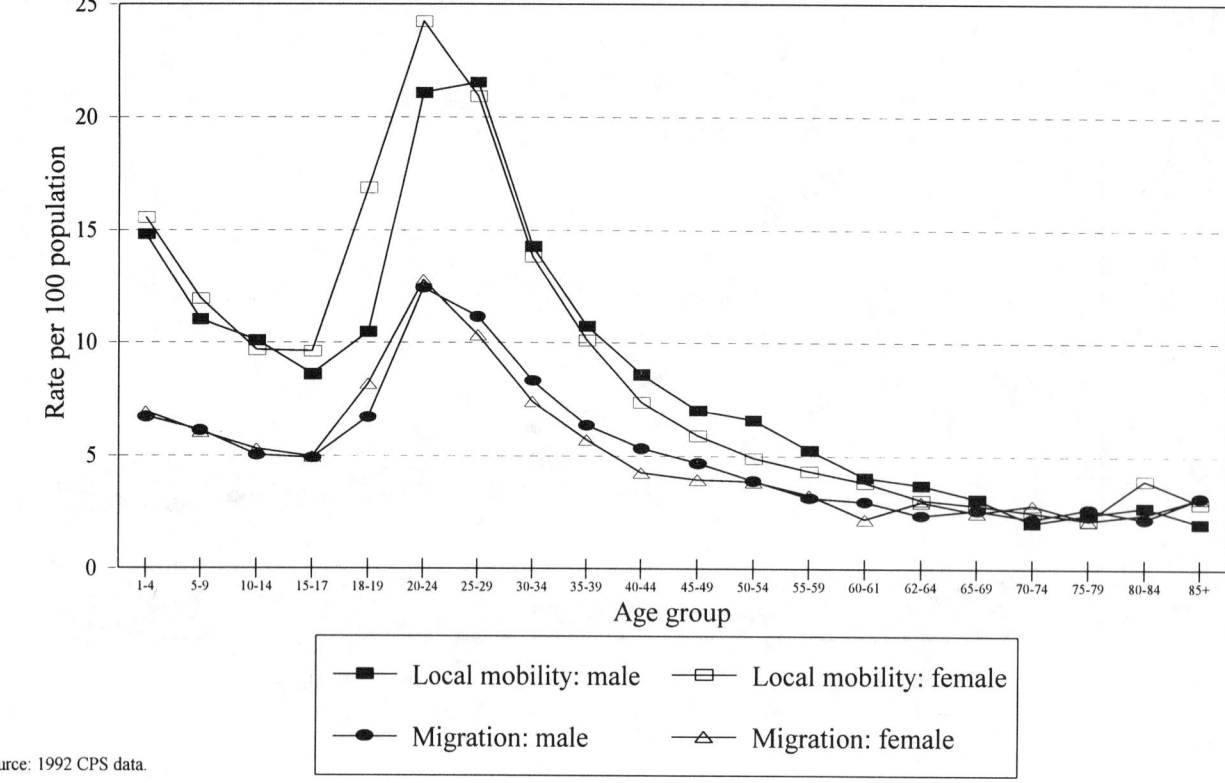

Source: 1992 CPS data.

they reach age 45. From ages 45 to 65 the sex differences become negligible, as the rates for both decline to small numbers. At the most advanced ages females again tend to be somewhat more mobile than males, perhaps because of widowhood.

Race-Ethnicity Mobility Differentials

The probability of moving locally, migrating, or of having moved from abroad varies among the major race-ethnic groups (Table 8-2). In 1990-92, total residential mobility for the black population was higher (18.8 percent) than for the white population (16.2 percent) However, this difference is an average of two opposite patterns. The black population manifests considerably more local mobility than the white population. On the other hand, the white population is slightly more migratory than the black population. When the black-white comparison is made with the Hispanic component removed (white non-Hispanic), the differences are even greater. During 1990-92, blacks were 4 percentage points more locally mobile than white non-Hispanic, but the white non-Hispanic were 0.7 percentage points more migratory than blacks.

Hispanic populations are more mobile than either the white or the black population. Because of steady im-

migration a high percentage (1.9 percent vs. 0.4 percent for other groups) are classed as movers from abroad. In addition, Hispanics have considerably higher rates of local mobility than other race-ethnic groups, and a rate of internal migration only slightly lower than that of the black population. As discussed below, a number of policy factors not easy to predict will influence the future rate of Hispanic immigration from abroad. However, once inside the national boundaries, the Hispanic population displays strong propensities for internal movement, yet will likely converge toward national patterns with increasing length of stay.

Five-Year Mobility Rates

Although one-year mobility data are superior for computing precise probabilities of residential change, and for comparing characteristics of mobile and non-mobile persons, the one-year interval immediately preceding a census may be atypical of what has been the pattern for the preceding decade. And much mobility is caused by repeat-movers, who may make a quick return to the previous place of residence or rove on to a new destination. Because five-year mobility rates use a broader span of time (and encompass a larger volume of movement) it may reveal long-term trends and changes better than data

Table 8-3. Five-Year General Mobility Rates[1], by Race-ethnicity: 1970, 1980, and 1990

Year and race-ethnicity	Non-mobile	Mobile	Mobility status: residence 5 years ago						Percent of internal migration interstate	Percent of migration from abroad
			Local mobility	Internal Migration			Immigration from abroad			
				Total	Intrastate	Interstate				
1990										
All races	53.3	46.7	25.5	19.0	9.7	9.4	2.2		49.2	10.4
White	54.5	45.5	24.2	19.9	10.2	9.8	1.3		49.0	6.3
Black	52.5	47.5	31.0	14.7	7.0	7.8	1.7		52.6	10.5
American Indian, Eskimo, Aleut	47.3	52.7	29.6	22.1	11.7	10.5	1.0		47.3	4.4
Asian, Pacific Islander	39.0	61.0	25.0	17.6	8.5	9.1	18.3		51.8	51.0
Hispanic	43.8	56.2	32.4	14.1	7.9	6.3	9.6		44.2	40.5
White, non-Hispanic	55.0	45.0	23.8	20.3	10.3	10.0	0.9		49.1	4.3
1980										
All races	53.6	46.4	25.1	19.5	9.8	9.7	1.9		49.7	8.8
White	53.9	46.1	24.3	20.6	10.4	10.1	1.3		49.3	5.7
Black	56.8	43.2	29.4	12.7	5.7	7.0	1.2		55.4	8.4
American Indian, Eskimo, Aleut	47.1	52.9	28.8	23.0	11.6	11.4	1.1		49.5	4.5
Asian, Pacific Islander	34.9	65.1	21.6	17.3	7.8	9.4	26.2		54.7	60.3
Hispanic	44.8	55.2	32.2	14.3	7.7	6.6	8.8		46.1	38.0
White, non-Hispanic	54.2	45.8	24.0	20.8	10.5	10.3	1.0		49.3	4.5
1970										
All races	53.0	47.0	23.3	17.1	8.4	8.6	1.4		50.7	7.8
White	53.3	46.7	22.5	18.0	9.0	9.1	1.4		50.3	7.1
Black	51.4	48.6	29.8	9.5	4.2	5.3	0.9		55.8	8.9
Hispanic	42.5	57.5	30.4	14.7	7.7	7.0	7.1		47.8	32.6
White, non-Hispanic	53.5	46.5	22.3	18.1	9.0	9.1	1.2		50.3	6.4

[1] Persons per 100 residents of group.

Source: U.S. Bureau of the Census, "Social and Economic Characteriatics: United States Summary," 1990 Census of Population, Table 80, and "General Social and Economic Characteristics: United States Summary," 1980 Census of Population, Table 259, and 1970 Census of Population, Table 87, U.S. Government Printing Office, Washington, D.C, 1993, 1983, and 1973.

for a single-year interval. Table 8-3 reports 5-year mobility rates, by race-ethnicity, for the censuses of 1970, 1980, and 1990.

Over the five-year interval, nearly one-half of the population is mobile. Almost one-fifth (19.0 percent) are internal migrants. When the five-year mobility interval is used, the mobility rates are not five times as large as those for a single year because persons who move more than once within the 5-year interval are counted only once. Multiplying the rates of Tables 7-1 and 7-2 by 5 and comparing them with the rates of Table 8-3 demonstrate that 5-year rates understate the annual probability of local moving by almost 50 percent, and the annual probability of migrating by about 40 percent. The implied annual rates for immigration from abroad also are understated by 5-year data. (This implies a return of immigrants to the country of origin or census under-enumeration of immigration, or a combination of both.)

The five-year data concur with the 1-year data that there was very little overall change in mobility levels between 1970 and 1990, with slightly higher rates for local mobility in 1985-90 in comparison with 1965-70. The race-ethnic differentials noted for 5-year rates are similar to those for 1-year rates. The black and Hispanic groups are much more locally mobile, but considerably less internally migratory, than the white. The 5-year data indicate a slightly higher level of immigration for both Hispanic and black populations for the 1985-90 than for the 1975-80 period. The census is also able to report mobility data for American Indian-Eskimo-Aleut and Asia-Pacific Islander populations, both too small to estimate with

CPS sample surveys. The Indian group has above average internal mobility, while the Asia-Pacific Island group has below average internal mobility, at both censuses. The rates of immigration are, as would be expected, very low for American Indians. However, since the Korean War the Asia-Pacific Island group has had a very high level of immigration, increasing more than 20 percent every five years. The unusually high immigration rates for Asians is due in part to the large influx of political asylum-seekers and war refugees added to a previously comparatively small resident Asian population. Its high annual numerical volume is likely to increase further, causing it eventually to become a sizable and even more influential minority ethnic category, perhaps destined to be as large as black and Hispanic groups.

Regional-Level Mobility

Internal migration has two components, in-migration, which brings people to a community from other places, and out-migration, which takes them away from a community to live in other places (see Mobility Stream in the Definition Box). Their effect is indicated by net migration, which is in-migration minus out-migration. Since Colonial days, the nation has experienced very strong migratory moves among its regions. Large net gains of residents from other regions and abroad have been the principal reasons for the rapid population growth of some states and stagnation or population decline in others. There have been three great interregional migration flows, each of which has persisted for many decades:

Table 8-4. Average Annual In-migration, Out-migration, Net Migration and Movers from Abroad, by Region: 1990-1992[1] [numbers in thousands]

Type of mobility	Northeast	Midwest	South	West
Numbers				
Population	50,052	59,256	84,282	52,542
In-migrants	378	799	1,363	795
Out-migrants	817	838	1,034	647
Net internal migration	-439	-39	329	148
Immigrants from abroad	232	192	367	530
Net migration, including abroad	-207	153	696	678
Rate per 100 residents				
In-migrants	0.8	1.3	1.6	1.5
Out-migrants	1.6	1.4	1.2	1.2
Net internal migration	-0.9	-0.1	0.4	0.3
Immigrants from abroad	0.5	0.3	0.4	1.0
Net migration, including abroad	-0.4	0.3	0.8	1.3

[1]Average of 1991 and 1992 CPS surveys.

Source: U. S. Bureau of the Census, Current Population Reports, "Current Geographical Mobility: March 1991 to March 1992," Table C, and "March 1990 to March 1991," Table C, Series P-20, Numbers 473 and 463, U.S. Government Printing Office, Washington, D.C, 1993 and 1992.

(a) the westward movement, especially from the Northeast and subsequently from the Midwest and South regions; (b) southward movement from 'Frostbelt' to the 'Sunbelt' states, and especially the coastal segments of the Sunbelt; and (c) the flow to urban (particularly metropolitan) areas from rural and small-town communities throughout the nation.

The situation in 1991-92 is reported in Table 8-4, which averages the in-, out- and net-migration for the years 1991 and 1992. This table indicates that together the South and West combined are gaining almost 500,000 persons per year, largely at the expense of the Northeast (which has experienced a dramatic loss of population through migration). During these years the West was receiving only a net of 148,000 migrants per year, at an annual in-migration rate of 0.28 percent. At the heyday of the go-West movement during the 19th and first half of the present century, annual rates 10 times this were common. The 1990-92 levels are roughly consistent with recent decades. Table 8-5 presents estimates of in-migration, out-migration, and net migration for five-year

intervals between 1965 and 1980, plus data for 1990-92, to summarize recent trends in the direction and amounts of regional population flows. (Average annual net migration data for 1990-92 should be multiplied by 5 to be very roughly comparable to the earlier quinquennia.) In evaluating these quantities, keep in mind that as of 1990-92 the natural increase of the national population (excess of births over deaths) was 2.1 million persons per year. Thus, regional migration can have the effect of suspending growth completely in some places and directing a large share of the national growth to other places.

Northeast and Midwest: Net Migration Loss

For the past three decades, both the Northeast and the North Center have suffered net migration loss, while both the South and West have been net migration gainers. As Figure 8-3 shows, during the 1990's the Westward movement and the Sunbelt movement are continuing to dominate the interregional migration picture. The original industrial-commercial states of the Northeast and Midwest, which formerly were magnetic poles for more than a century, have lost their attractive powers and instead turned into a vast "counter-urbanization" territory losing population through massive out-migration. During the two years 1991-92, the Northeast region lost an average of 439,000 persons per year, for an annual rate of -0.88 percent. The rate of out-migration was more than double the rate of in-migration. The amount of in-migration to the Northeast was smaller and the amount of out-migration was greater than for any other region. Meanwhile, the Midwest suffered a similar, but much smaller, net loss from migration. In fact, this region very nearly had a zero-migration balance: a rate of only -0.06 percent per year. The next census may indicate that the Midwest region has reached a more or less stable equilibrium, or even acquired some small net attractive power, with respect to the other regions. Predicting for how many decades into the next century the exodus from the Northeast will continue, and how large the annual drain will be, are major topics for ongoing research. There is some evidence that particular metropolitan areas of the Northeast may be approaching the end of the process, and soon may even enjoy some "regentrification" migration benefits.

Table 8-5. Interregional Migration: Annual Average 1990-1992[1] and Selected Five-year Periods 1965-1980 [numbers in thousands]

Period and type of migration	Northeast	Midwest[2]	South	West
1990-1992				
In-migrants	378	799	1363	795
Out-migrants	817	838	1034	647
Net migration	-439	-39	329	148
1975-1980				
In-migrants	1106	1993	4204	2838
Out-migrants	2592	3166	2440	1945
Net migration	-1486	-1173	1764	893
1970-1975				
In-migrants	1057	1731	4082	2347
Out-migrants	2399	2926	2253	1639
Net migration	-1342	-1195	1829	708
1965-1970				
In-migrants	1273	2024	3142	2309
Out-migrants	1988	2661	2486	1613
Net migration	-715	-637	656	696

[1] The data for 1990-1992 represent an average of 1991 and 1992 CPS data. The data for the other time periods represent a change in current residence compared to residence five years earlier. Thus, the data for 1990-1992 are not strictly comparable to those from the other time periods.

[2] North Central in 1980 and earlier.

Source: U.S. Bureau of the Census, Current Population Reports, "Geographical Mobility: March 1991 to March 1992," Table C, "March 1990 to March 1991," Table C, and March 1975 to March 1980," Table A, Series P-20, Numbers 473, 463, and 368, U.S. Government Printing Office, Washington, D.C., 1993, 1992, and 1984.

Figure 8-3. Mobility and Net Migration for the Sunbelt, the Remainder of the South and West, and the Non-Sunbelt U.S.: 1987-1988 and 1991-1992

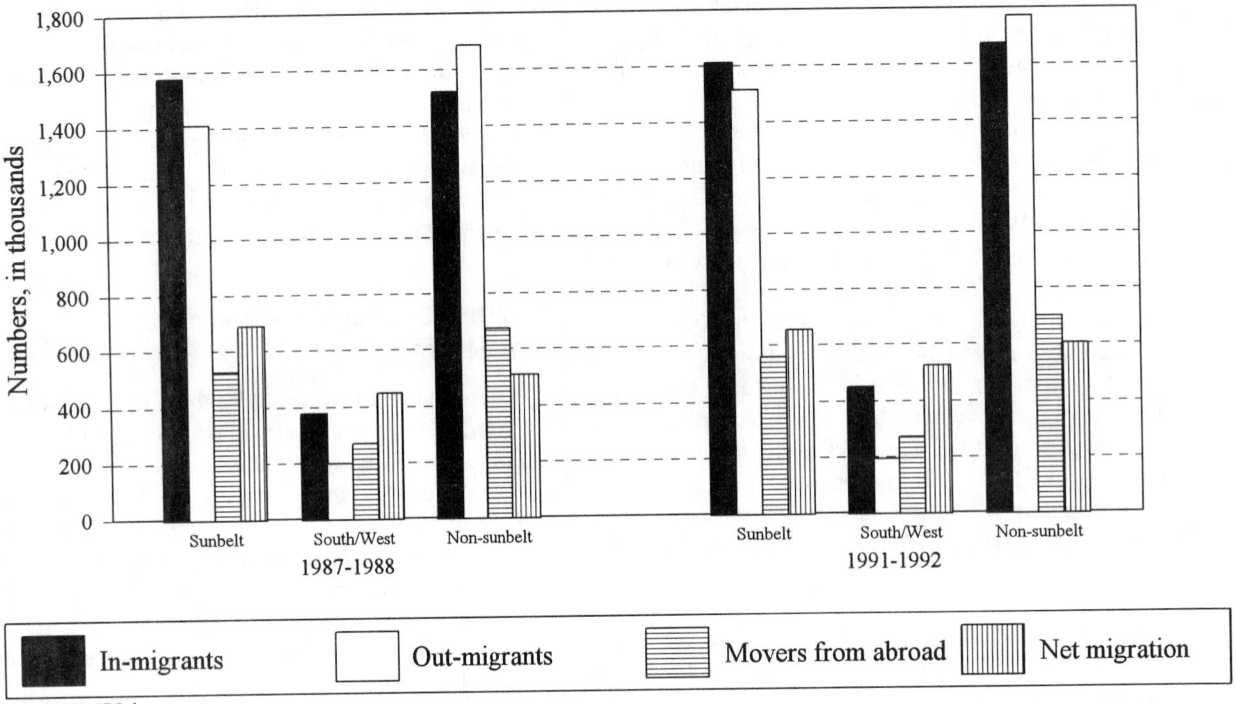

Source: 1988 and 1992 CPS data.

North-South Movement

During 1990-92 the South region enjoyed a substantial net inflow of migrants. It captured 2.5 times as much net migration as the West, and had a net migration rate of 0.39 percent per year. This is a reversal of an historic trend of population loss (except in Florida and the Gulf Coast) that persisted right up until 1980. Between the close of the Civil War and 1950, the South region (the inland and northern sections and particularly Appalachia) lost population heavily, and a very large share of it was absorbed by expanding industrial-commercial centers in the Northeast, Midwest and West regions. The great industrial and commercial expansion that took place in the Northeast region and in the metropolitan areas on the Great Lakes attracted many millions of persons from the (then) economically depressed rural South. Both white and black migrants flowed in great numbers along this channel . (Texas, Florida, Maryland, and Delaware were exceptions to the general loss through migration.) The northward flow peaked during and immediately following World War II. Between 1970 and 1980 the net northward flow of movement completely dried up and disappeared. During the 1980's the flow resumed, but in the opposite direction. Since 1980, the South not only has demonstrated great capability to retain its natural population increase, but also to be a net gainer in interregional migration exchange. The entire Gulf Coast—from the mouth of the Rio Grande in Texas, past Corpus Christi and Houston, across the coastal portions of lower Louisiana, Mississippi, and Alabama, and on to include all of Florida—has undergone a rapid and intensive economic development. This movement was already under way in 1870 and has continued without interruption since. It accelerated greatly during the 1950-60 and 1960-70 decades, has became the leading focal point of population redistribution in 1970-90, and is expected to continue at a very strong pace well into the next century. Instead of being confined simply to coastal areas and Texas, during the 1980's and since it has expanded to include all of the South. Recession induced by falling petroleum prices gave setbacks, probably temporary, for some localities. Since 1970 the volume of net movement to Florida has exceeded that of movement to California. Interior states like Kentucky, Tennessee, and Arkansas, which all had suffered net migration losses since 1870, gained by net migration in the 1970-80 decade and since. As pointed out above, the South gains migrants from every other region, but the gains from the Midwest and the West are comparatively small; most of its tremendous gains currently are coming from the Northeast.

Movement to the West

During 1990-92, the annual flow into the West region has continued at about the same level as during the 1980's. Unlike earlier decades, this flow is not directed primarily toward California and Hawaii, but to other states in the region. High density, pollution, unemployment, congestion, overburdening of the fresh water supply, and other problems comparable to those in the Northeast appear to have hit California. The renowned climatic and scenic amenity assets of the entire region continue to make it attractive, and appear to be diverting the westward flow to less congested sites. However, the big interregional migration gainer has been and continues to be the South. Since 1970 the South's net gains have consistently been more than double those of the West.

Table 8-4 reveals some very important additional pieces of information that should not be overlooked: The net migration loss of the Northeast through internal migration is cut in half by arrivals from abroad. Including immigration doubles the migration gains of the South, triples those of the West, and overwhelmingly cancels the interregional migration loss of the Midwest. Therefore, in order to understand the population change within any area in the United States, it now is necessary to know how great are its powers to retain its residents and to attract migrants from places elsewhere in the nation, and how many immigrants it is receiving from abroad.

Interregional Migration Streams

Table 8-6 subdivides inter-regional migration during 1990-92 into specific streams, to reveal the sources of net migratory loss or gain of each region with respect to every other region. Although the Northeast region loses population with respect to every other region, more than one-half of its loss goes to the South. The Midwest gains migrants in exchange with the Northeast, but loses even

Table 8-6. Average Annual Interregional Flows of Migration, by Race-ethnicity: 1990-1992[1] [numbers in thousands]

Residence in later year (In-migration)	Total	Residence in earlier year (out-migration)				Net migration			
		Northeast	Midwest	South	West	Northeast	Midwest	South	West
All races									
Total	3,339	816	838	1,034	652	-434	-39	330	143
Northeast	383	—	89	225	69	—	63	272	99
Midwest	799	151	—	448	201	-63	—	37	65
South	1,363	497	484	—	382	-272	-37	—	-21
West	795	168	266	361	—	-99	-65	21	—
White									
Total	2,820	655	723	882	561	-330	-17	243	105
Northeast	325	—	69	197	59	—	64	186	81
Midwest	706	133	—	385	189	-64	—	44	37
South	1,125	383	429	—	314	-186	-44	—	-14
West	665	140	226	300	—	-81	-37	14	—
Black									
Total	379	124	83	115	58	-83	-12	80	15
Northeast	41	—	16	22	3	—	-5	79	9
Midwest	72	12	—	53	8	5	—	-6	13
South	194	100	47	—	47	-79	6	—	-7
West	73	12	20	41	—	-9	-13	7	—
Hispanic									
Total	212	60	33	75	44	-44	-3	28	19
Northeast	16	—	4	8	5	—	-1	36	9
Midwest	31	3	—	24	4	1	—	1	1
South	103	44	24	—	35	-36	-1	—	9
West	63	14	5	44	—	-9	-1	-9	—

[1] Average of 1991 and 1992 CPS surveys.

Source: U. S. Bureau of the Census, Current Population Reports, "Current Geographical Mobility: March 1991 to March 1992," and "March 1990 to March 1991," Series P-20, Numbers 473 and 463, U.S. Government Printing Office, Washington, D.C, 1993 and 1992, Table 20.

more to the West, and a modest amount to the South. The gains of the West come entirely from the Northeast and Midwest; it suffers a small migration loss in exchange with the South.

Inter-regional migratory flows are strongly influenced by race-ethnicity. The lower panels of Table 8-6 subdivide each inter-regional stream into its race-ethnic components. Limitations of sampling error make it necessary to treat these numbers only as general indicators of magnitude. However, they suggest that all race-ethnic groups generally follow the overall patterns described above, with some interesting exceptions and facets. The black and Hispanic groups share strongly in the heavy loss of the Northeast region to the South, but their net positive flow to the West are comparatively smaller. For black citizens, the Midwest shows very little net regional migration attractiveness. The South makes almost zero net migration gains of black and Hispanic residents of the Midwest, and appears to have a negative balance of Hispanic internal migration with respect to the West. The West attracts black migrants from the Midwest and North-east, and Hispanics from the Northeast and South.

The summary in Table 8-7 for the inter-regional movement of the black population, matching that for the total population (Table 8-5), documents the continuation of the very dramatic reversal of direction in the inter-regional flow of the black population during the 1970s and since. Instead of attracting black population from the South (as they did for decades before 1970), both the Northeast and the Midwest regions have suffered net migratory losses of black population, which instead has flowed primarily back to the South and to the West.

The net migration 1990-92 (multiplied by 5) indicates that the "black flight" from the Northeast may even have accelerated, and that the net movement of black persons from the Midwest continues toward the West, but not the South. As yet there is no consensus about the meaning and durability of these trends. Does it imply that employment and other livelihood necessities are now more attractive for black citizens in the South and West regions than in the North? Some researchers consider it to have a very large 'return migration' component of black persons (and their descendants) who left the South during the great trek North before 1960.

Interstate Migration: Components of Growth

Mobility phenomena in each of the individual states is similar to, but not identical with, their regional situation described above. Moreover, the preceding discussion has not reported the relative influence of natural increase, internal migration, and immigration in determining the rate of population growth in these geographic areas. This information, for 1990-92, is supplied by Table 8-8. Since the 1990 census, every state east of the Mississippi River except two (Indiana and Wisconsin) are estimated to have continued to lose population through net internal migration. However, the overall population growth rate is negative for only Massachusetts and Connecticut. Comparatively small excesses of births over deaths, combined with expanded immigration, is enabling the others to show a small growth. In New York, New Jersey, and Illinois immigration has been a major factor counteracting substantial net losses from internal migration .

In the North Central region, the least metropolitanized states made small net migration gains, except for North Dakota and Kansas. The big losers through net internal migration exodus were the most metropolitanized states of Illinois, Michigan, and Ohio. Meanwhile, states which have not had a reputation for attracting

Table 8-7. Interregional Migration of Blacks: Annual Average 1990-1992[1] and Selected Five-year Periods 1965-1980 [numbers in thousands]

Period and type of migration	Northeast	Midwest[2]	South	West
1990-1992				
In-migrants	41	72	194	73
Out-migrants	124	83	115	58
Net migration	-83	-11	79	15
1975-1980				
In-migrants	99	170	415	193
Out-migrants	274	221	220	163
Net migration	-175	-51	195	30
1970-1975				
In-migrants	118	150	302	153
Out-migrants	182	202	288	51
Net migration	-64	-52	14	102
1965-1970				
In-migrants	146	203	162	150
Out-migrants	110	111	378	61
Net migration	36	92	-216	89

[1] The data for 1990-1992 represent an average of 1991 and 1992 CPS data. The data for the other time periods represent a change in current residence compared to residence five years earlier. Thus, the data for 1990-1992 are not strictly comparable to those from the other time periods.

[2] North Central in 1980 and earlier.

Source: U.S. Bureau of the Census, Current Population Reports, "Geographical Mobility: March 1991 to March 1992," Table C, "March 1990 to March 1991," Table C, and "March 1975 to March 1980," Table B, Series P-20, Numbers 473, 463, and 368, U.S. Government Printing Office, Washington, D.C., 1993, 1992, and 1984.

Table 8-8. Migration and Other Components of Population Change, by Regions, Divisions, and States: 1990-1992[1] [numbers in thousands]

Area	Population 1990	Change 1990-92	Percent change	Natural increase	Net immigration	Net internal migration[2]	Return U.S. citizens
United States	248,710	6,372	2.6	4,446	1,736	0	190
Northeast	50,809	309	0.6	704	423	-837	20
New England	13,207	-7	...	192	61	-266	6
Middle Atlantic	37,602	316	0.8	512	361	-571	14
Midwest	59,669	1,044	1.8	895	225	-101	25
East North Central	42,009	744	1.8	660	181	-112	15
West North Central	17,660	301	1.7	237	44	10	10
South	85,446	2,697	3.2	1,445	371	791	90
South Atlantic	43,567	1,494	3.4	673	185	578	58
East South Central	15,176	352	2.3	198	20	123	10
West South Central	26,703	851	3.2	573	166	90	22
West	52,786	2,322	4.4	1,401	717	148	56
Mountain	13,659	723	5.3	323	57	330	12
Pacific	39,127	1,599	4.1	1,079	659	-183	44
States, by division							
New England							
Maine	1,228	7	0.6	13	1	-8	1
New Hampshire	1,109	2	0.1	18	1	-19	...
Vermont	563	7	1.2	8	1	-2	...
Massachusetts	6,016	-18	-0.3	89	35	-144	2
Rhode Island	1,003	2	0.2	12	7	-18	1
Connecticut	3,287	-6	-0.2	51	16	-75	2
Middle Atlantic							
New York	17,990	129	0.7	288	266	-432	7
New Jersey	7,730	59	0.8	117	64	-125	3
Pennsylvania	11,882	128	1.1	107	31	-14	4
East North Central							
Ohio	10,847	169	1.6	149	24	-8	4
Indiana	5,544	118	2.1	81	10	26	2
Illinois	11,431	201	1.8	202	105	-112	5
Michigan	9,295	141	1.5	160	31	-54	3
Wisconsin	4,892	115	2.3	66	11	36	1
West North Central							
Minnesota	4,375	105	2.4	73	15	16	1
Iowa	2,777	36	1.3	27	7	2	1
Missouri	5,117	76	1.5	62	10	1	3
North Dakota	639	-3	-0.4	7	1	-12	1
South Dakota	696	15	2.2	10	1	4	1
Nebraska	1,578	27	1.7	21	4	1	1
Kansas	2,478	45	1.8	36	8	-1	3

Table 8-8. Migration and Other Components of Population Change, by Regions, Divisions, and States: 1990-1992[1] [numbers in thousands] (continued)

Area	Population 1990	Change 1990-92	Percent change	Natural increase	Net immigration	Net internal migration[2]	Return U.S. citizens
South Atlantic							
Delaware	666	23	3.5	12	1	9	1
Maryland	4,781	127	2.7	97	27	-1	5
District of Columbia	607	-18	-3.0	9	9	-37	1
Virginia	6,187	190	3.1	115	28	30	16
West Virginia	1,793	19	1.0	7	2	10	...
North Carolina	6,629	214	3.2	101	9	93	11
South Carolina	3,487	117	3.3	63	5	43	6
Georgia	6,478	273	4.2	132	13	121	7
Florida	12,938	550	4.2	137	90	310	11
East South Central							
Kentucky	3,685	69	1.9	42	5	19	3
Tennessee	4,877	147	3.0	64	7	73	3
Alabama	4,041	95	2.4	52	6	34	3
Mississippi	2,573	41	1.6	41	3	-4	2
West South Central							
Arkansasa	2,351	48	2.0	25	3	19	1
Louisiana	4,220	67	1.6	78	14	-28	3
Oklahoma	3,146	67	2.1	40	11	13	3
Texas	16,987	669	3.9	431	138	87	14
Mountain							
Montana	799	25	3.1	10	1	13	1
Idaho	1,007	61	6.0	21	3	36	1
Wyoming	454	13	2.8	8	1	3	...
Colorado	3,294	176	5.3	71	16	85	4
New Mexico	1,515	66	4.4	37	7	20	2
Arizona	3,665	167	4.6	88	16	61	3
Utah	1,723	90	5.2	60	7	22	1
Nevada	1,202	126	10.4	28	7	90	1
Pacific							
Washington	4,867	269	5.5	96	28	139	6
Oregon	2,842	135	4.7	40	14	81	1
California	29,760	1,107	3.7	892	593	-408	30
Alaska	550	37	6.7	21	2	11	2
Hawaii	1,108	51	4.6	30	23	-6	5

[1] Time interval in April 1, 1990 to July 1, 1992.

[2] "Net internal migration" is a residual, and includes the net balance of errors of estimates for the other components, assumed to be zero.

Source: U.S. Bureau of the Census, Current Population Reports, "Estimates of the Population of States: 1980-92," Series P-25, Number 1106, U.S. Government Printing Office, Washington, D.C., 1993, Table 1.

immigrants (Minnesota, Iowa, Missouri, Kansas) made moderate gains from this source.

Every state of the South except Louisiana, Mississippi, and Maryland had significant gains from net internal migration. But to this was added significant gains from immigration for Maryland, Virginia, Florida, Texas, Georgia, Louisiana, and Oklahoma. The South's recent migration gain of 1 million persons in two years through migration was 2/3 net internal migration and 1/3 immigration from abroad. In North Carolina, Georgia, Florida, and Tennessee the combined migration components were of larger size than natural increase.

In the West, internal migration is a powerful force for growth in every state except California, Hawaii, and Wyoming. California suffered a net loss of 408,000 through internal migration, but more than replaced it with 593,000 immigrants. Hawaii also had a smallish net internal migration loss, but had net immigration equal to more than three times this loss. Colorado, Arizona, Washington, Oregon, Mexico, Nevada, and Utah all had substantial infusions of immigration to add to their hefty gains from internal migration.

The migration patterns reported in Table 8-6 are those most likely to dominate the few remaining years of this century.

Metropolitan-Level Mobility

Simultaneous with the broad local, inter-county, inter-state and inter-regional flows of movement described above has been a two-century long flow of people from rural areas to urban centers, resulting in the creation of large metropolitan agglomerations and many smaller urban places. A refinement of the regional perspective, presented in the preceding section, is to study mobility in terms of the type of community of residence. For more than half a century, the older and larger central cities (the high-density cores of metropolitan agglomerations) have been undergoing extensive mobility losses of population (deconcentration) as their residents moved to the 'urban fringe' or 'metropolitan rings,' the broad band of numerous and heterogeneous communities that have developed surrounding the central city or central cities. These metropolitan rings still are officially called 'suburbs' as a vestige from earlier days when they were indeed little more than half-urban/half-rural dormitory settlements immediately adjoining the central cities. Emergence in the metropolitan ring of clusters of manufacturing, professional, technical, financial, commercial, governmental, and other public and private service activities has caused the metropolitan rings to take on a complex economic life of their own, semi-independently of or even in competition with the central cities. Their numerous and large-scale shopping malls compete successfully with downtown retail establishments. Major educational, medi-

cal-health, and other institutions have selected ring rather than central city locations. Meanwhile, some of the larger or older metropolitan areas (rings and central cities combined) have suffered substantial population declines, while other rapidly-growing medium-size cities have developed suburban rings and only more recently attained metropolitan status. Because residential mobility has been and continues to be the primary mechanism for these trends, this chapter re-examines them in these terms. The Bureau of Census provides such data using detailed metro-level mobility-status definitions (see Definitions Box).

Using these definitions, six distinct topics may be addressed including (a) immobility: the propensity not to change residence, (b) mobility flows between metropolitan and nonmetropolitan areas, (c) mobility flows within the same metropolitan area, (c) mobility flows between different metropolitan areas, (d) mobility flows within nonmetropolitan areas, and (e) immigration from abroad to metropolitan and nonmetropolitan areas. Each of these will be explored in a separate subsection, using the Current Population Surveys of mobility taken since 1990. In order to reduce sampling error, two Current Population Surveys (March 1991 and March 1992) are combined and averaged. Each survey measured mobility over the preceding one year. Unless otherwise noted, the following data refer to average annual measures for movement between March 1990 and March 1992.

As reported above, of the 247,380,000 persons residing in the U.S. in 1992, 204,590,000 (80 percent) were immobile or did not change residence. The 43,790,000 residentially mobile persons were distributed as follows by the detailed classification:

Mobility of the 1992 United States Resident Population

Type of mobility	Number [in thousands]	Percent	Percent of mobile
Resident mobility	247,380	100.00	—
Non-mobile	204,590	82.7	—
Mobile	42,790	17.3	100.0
Flows within same metro areas	24,424	9.9	57.1
Flows between metro areas	7,256	2.9	17.0
Flows between metro and non-metro areas	3,503	1.4	8.2
Flows within non-metro areas	6,352	2.6	14.8
Immigration from abroad	1,255	0.5	2.9

Curiously, the greatest popular and scientific attention is currently being given to the two smallest streams in the above classification: nonmetropolitan metropolitan exchange and immigration. The complaint is not that they receive too much attention, but that the others receive too little. Almost six of every ten residential switches involve moving within the same metropolitan area. This reemphasizes, in a meaningful way, the preponderant

**Table 8-9. Metropolitan-level Migration, by Region and
Race-ethnicity: 1990-1992 [numbers in thousands]**

Area, type of migration, and race-ethnicity	United States	Regions			
		Northeast	Midwest	South	West
All races					
Inside MSA's					
In-migrants	1,805	145	462	846	353
Out-migrants	1,710	212	460	663	376
Net migration	95	-67	3	183	-23
Central cities of MSA's					
In-migrants	3373	331	747	1292	1003
From rings of MSA's	2634	291	541	962	842
From outside MSA's	738	40	206	331	162
Out-migrants	5808	695	1136	2338	1641
To rings of MSA's	5092	644	905	2080	1465
To outside MSA's	717	52	231	258	176
Net migration	-2,436	-364	-390	-1,046	-637
Rings of MSA's					
In-migrants	6159	748	1161	2595	1656
From central cities	5092	644	905	2080	1465
From outside MSA's	1067	106	256	515	191
Out-migrants	3628	452	769	1366	1042
To central cities	2634	291	541	962	842
To outside MSA's	994	161	228	405	200
Net migration	2531	297	392	1229	614
Outside MSA's					
In-migrants	1710	212	460	663	376
Out-migrants	1805	145	462	846	353
Net migration	-95	67	-3	-183	23
White					
Inside MSA's					
In-migrants	1593	136	436	706	315
Out-migrants	1582	204	443	579	357
Net migration	12	-68	-7	128	-42
Central cities of MSA's					
In-migrants	2824	277	621	1041	886
From rings of MSA's	2203	243	428	785	748
From outside MSA's	622	35	194	256	138
Out-migrants	4770	566	982	1817	1406
To rings of MSA's	4138	522	765	1610	1243
To outside MSA's	633	45	218	208	163
Net migration	-1,947	-289	-362	-776	-520
Rings of MSA's					
In-migrants	5110	623	1008	2060	1420
From central cities	4138	522	765	1610	1243
From outside MSA's	972	102	243	450	177
Out-migrants	3152	402	653	1156	942
To central cities	2203	243	428	785	748
To outside MSA's	950	159	225	371	195
Net migration	1958	222	355	904	478
Outside MSA's					
In-migrants	1582	204	443	579	357
Out-migrants	1593	136	436	706	315
Net migration	-12	68	7	-128	42

Table 8-9. Metropolitan-level Migration, by Region and Race-ethnicity: 1990-1992 [numbers in thousands] (continued)

Area, type of migration, and race-ethnicity	United States	Regions			
		Northeast	Midwest	South	West
Black					
Inside MSA's					
In-migrants	164	9	14	126	15
Out-migrants	95	7	7	75	7
Net migration	69	2	8	52	8
Central cities of MSA's					
In-migrants	443	49	16	225	63
From rings of MSA's	346	44	95	154	53
From outside MSA's	97	6	11	72	10
Out-migrants	736	88	104	426	118
To rings of MSA's	672	81	98	377	115
To outside MSA's	65	7	7	49	3
Net migration	-294	-39	2	-201	-56
Rings of MSA's					
In-migrants	738	84	11	432	120
From central cities	672	81	98	377	115
From outside MSA's	67	4	3	55	5
Out-migrants	376	44	95	180	57
To central cities	346	44	95	154	53
To outside MSA's	30	...	...	26	4
Net migration	363	41	6	253	64
Outside MSA's					
In-migrants	95	7	7	75	7
Out-migrants	164	9	14	126	15
Net migration	-69	-2	-8	-52	-8
Hispanic					
Inside MSA's					
In-migrants	87	2	9	46	32
Out-migrants	89	6	18	35	31
Net migration	-2	-4	-9	11	...
Central cities of MSA's					
In-migrants	331	14	29	122	167
From rings of MSA's	272	12	24	87	150
From outside MSA's	6	2	5	35	17
Out-migrants	666	32	37	292	307
To rings of MSA's	620	29	27	265	30
To outside MSA's	46	3	9	27	7
Net migration	-335	-18	-8	-170	-141
Rings of MSA's					
In-migrants	647	29	31	274	314
From central cities	620	29	27	265	30
From outside MSA's	28	...	4	10	14
Out-migrants	314	15	32	94	173
To central cities	272	12	24	87	15
To outside MSA's	43	3	9	7	24
Net migration	334	14	-1	181	141
Outside MSA's					
In-migrants	89	6	18	35	31
Out-migrants	87	2	9	46	32
Net migration	2	4	9	-11	...

[1] Average of CPS mobility surveys of 1991 and 1992.

Source: U.S. Bureau of the Census, Current Population Reports, "Geographical Mobility: March 1991 to March 1992," and "March 1990 to March 1991," Series P-20, Numbers 473 and 463, U.S. Government Printing Office, Washington, D.C, 1993 and 1992, Table 23.

short-distance local flow of persons within the same general labor market-housing market-commercial area. The flow of persons from one metropolitan area to another is the second-largest category (17 percent). Almost as large is the residential change within nonmetropolitan areas. Less than 1/12 of all movement involves the flow of persons between metropolitan and nonmetropolitan areas.

Table 8-9 provides summary measures of metro-level mobility, cross-classified by regions. This table provides a transition from the preceding regional analysis to the detailed mobility analysis to follow, and provides numbers to supplement the mobility rates which will be the major unit of analysis below. In lower panels of Table 8-9, data for the total population is subdivided by race-ethnicity.

Taken as wholes, metropolitan areas receive 1.8 million new arrivals which is almost completely canceled by the exodus of 1.7 residents each year. The 'efficiency quotient' given as net migration divided by gross migration (i.e. the sum of in- and out- migration without regard to sign) is practically zero. The migration efficiency quotient is a rough measure of the degree of population change which a particular type of movement engenders, but has no connection to the size of the population at origin or destination, and hence is not a rate. In the Northeast and West regions, metropolitan areas lost population through net migration. In the Midwest region the small positive balance is not significantly different from zero. Only in the South were metropolitan areas able to grow significantly at the expense of nonmetropolitan areas. The white and Hispanic populations shared this overall pattern; the nonmetropolitan black populations in all regions continued to move toward metropolitan areas. In the South, one-third of all net migration metropolitan growth was contributed by black migrants.

Central cities continue to suffer heavy net migration losses (2.4 million persons per year). This is taking place in all regions, particularly the South and West, although particular MSA's may be exceptions. This migration out of the most dense areas occurred for all races and in all regions (except for the black population of the Midwest, where such movement was nil). All but a small fraction of this loss is due to net movement to rings rather than to nonmetropolitan areas. Rings of

MSA's are gaining the equivalent of all of the net mobility losses of central cities plus a small increment of in-movement from nonmetropolitan areas directly to rings rather than to central cities.

Although the movement to metropolitan rings is overwhelmingly one of white population, the long-predicted suburbanization of the black population is underway on a comparatively small scale in all regions except the Midwest. Meanwhile, Hispanics are swarming into metropolitan rings in both the South and West, their areas of greatest concentration—far in excess of the suburbanization of the black population of those regions. Perhaps because of employment possibilities in agriculture and other rural and small-town industries, Hispanics are less inclined to leave nonmetropolitan areas for residence within a metropolitan area than are black residents of the same regions. Thus a tiny portion of the metropolitan turnaround phenomenon is being contributed by Hispanics, though there is as yet little evidence that once inside the metropolis they return to nonmetropolitan residences, as do substantial numbers of whites.

Table 8-10. Average Annual Rates of Non-mobility[1] in the United States by Age, Sex, and Race-ethnicity: 1990-1992[2]

			SMA's		
			Central	Metro	
Characteristic	United States	MSA's	cities	rings	Outside MSA's
Total	82.9	82.2	79.5	84.0	85.0
Male	82.4	81.8	78.7	83.7	84.6
Female	83.3	82.7	80.2	84.3	85.4
Race-ethnicity					
White, non-Hispanic	79.1	78.0	80.4	79.1	84.8
Black	76.6	76.7	76.5	76.9	75.0
Hispanic	83.8	83.3	79.9	84.9	85.2
Sex and age					
Male					
Under 20 years	82.2	82.0	79.0	84.0	83.0
20 to 34 years	69.8	69.3	65.3	72.2	72.2
35 to 49 years	85.3	84.6	82.3	86.0	87.6
50 to 64 years	91.3	90.9	89.2	91.9	92.5
65 years and over	95.0	95.0	94.5	95.4	95.1
Female					
Under 20 years	80.8	80.5	79.4	82.1	82.1
20 to 34 years	70.1	69.4	66.3	72.7	73.1
35 to 49 years	86.2	85.7	84.9	87.4	88.0
50 to 64 years	92.1	91.5	90.9	92.5	93.9
65 years and over	94.9	94.7	94.7	94.4	95.3

[1] Non-mobile persons per 100 resident population.
[2] An average of 1991 and 1992 CPS data.

Source: U.S. Bureau of the Census, Current Population Reports, "Geographical Mobility, March 1991 to March 1992," and "March 1990 to March 1991," Series P-20. Numbers 473 and 463, U.S. Government Printing Office, Washington, D.C., 1993 and 1992, Table 26

Metro-level Immobility

It is worthwhile to note that each year an overwhelming proportion of the population passes the year without changing residence. These immobile people are presumed to be 'residentially adjusted.' Although they may be tempted to live in some other place(s), a weighing of the pros and cons for moving and those for staying causes them to stay. Table 8-10 provides non-mobility rates by sex, race-ethnicity, and age for each of the major metropolitan-level categories. The most important finding is that (on an annual basis) all age and sex categories are preponderantly immobile. However, there are significant differences.

Persons living in metropolitan rings are considerably more immobile (84.0 compared to 79.5 percent) than those living in central cities. Persons living in nonmetropolitan areas are slightly more immobile than those living in metropolitan rings. Females are slightly more immobile than males. White non-Hispanic persons are more immobile than all other race-ethnic groups. Hispanics are least immobile, with blacks occupying an intermediate position of immobility. All of these differences in immobility hold for each age group individually, except for the elderly; persons 65 and over have practically the same non-mobility rate (95 percent per year). Even among the most mobile of ages (20-34 years), between 66 and 73 percent of the population remains non-mobile. Highest immobility is reported for males living in metropolitan rings; lowest immobility is reported for females living in central cities. A minor part of the race-ethnic differences noted above are due to the older age composition of the white and younger age composition of black and Hispanic populations, not controlled in Table 8-10.

Movement Between Metropolitan and Nonmetropolitan Areas

About 1965 the historic net outflow of people from nonmetropolitan to metropolitan areas not only came to a surprising halt, but was reversed. Instead, nonmetropolitan areas made considerable net migration gains (metropolitan areas lost) in the metropolitan-nonmetropolitan migration exchange. Under an expanded set of areas defined as metropolitan, this reversal appears to have ended about 1982, beginning to flow again in favor of metropolitan areas. Since 1990 the drift to metropolitan areas has continued, but apparently with diminishing velocity. The course of this much-publicized "nonmetropolitan turnaround" trend is estimated in Table 8-11.

The rather modest net loss from metropolitan areas due to internal migration between 1965 and 1970 was greatly increased during both five-year periods of the 1970s. Some of the movement from metropolitan to nonmetropolitan areas was to rapidly growing nonmetropolitan counties, later to be redefined as metropolitan. (Periodic expansion of the list of counties classed as metropolitan causes a bias in favor of metropolitan areas.) Between 1985 and 1990, using a further expanded definition of metropolitan areas, the net migration balance favored metropolitan areas. By 1991-92 the reported annual positive balance for metropolitan areas was 73,000 (implying a 5-year amount of about 365,000—nearly one-half the amount of the 1985-90 period).

Table 8-12 explores the 1990-92 movement between nonmetropolitan and metropolitan areas in terms both of amounts and rates. The major point of this table is that out-migration rates for nonmetropolitan to metropolitan are double those of the reverse out-migration rate

Table 8-11. Metropolitan and Non-metropolitan Migration: 1991-1992, 1985-1986, and Selected Five-year Periods 1965-1980 [numbers in thousands]

Area and type of migration	One-year periods		Five-year periods		
	1991-1992	1985-1986	1975-1980	1970-1975	1965-1970
Metropolitan					
In-migration	1,793	2,034	5,993	5,127	5,457
Out-migration	1,720	1,731	7,337	6,721	5,809
Net migration	73	303	-1,344	-1,594	-352
Non-metropolitan					
In-migration	1,720	1,731	7,337	6,721	5,809
Out-migration	1,793	2,034	5,993	5,127	5,457
Net migration	-73	-303	1,344	1,594	352

Source: U.S. Bureau of the Census, Current Population Reports, "Geographical Mobility: March 1991 to March 1992," Table 23, "March 1987 to March 1990," Table C, and "March 1975 to March 1980," Table C, Series P-20, Numbers 473, 456, and 368, U.S. Government Printing Office, Washington, D.C., 1993, 1991, and 1984.

Table 8-12. Average Annual Mobility Between Metropolitan and Non-metropolitan Areas, by Age, Sex, and Race-ethnicity: 1990-1992[1] [numbers in thousands]

Characteristic	Movers from non-metro to metro			Movers from metro to non-metro			Net migration ("to metro" minus "from metro")		
	Total to metro	To central cities	To metro rings	Total from metro	From central cities	From metro rings	Total metro	Central cities	Metro rings
Number of persons									
Total	1,805	738	1,067	1,710	717	994	95	22	73
Male	918	371	548	878	368	511	40	3	37
Female	888	368	520	833	349	483	55	19	37
Race-ethnicity									
White, non-Hispanic	1,545	565	956	1,512	586	902	33	-21	54
Black	164	97	67	95	64	31	69	33	36
Hispanic	87	60	27	89	46	43	-2	14	-16
Rates of mobility[2]									
Total	3.30	1.35	1.95	0.89	0.97	0.85	2.41	0.38	1.10
Male	3.44	1.39	2.05	0.94	1.03	0.89	2.50	0.36	1.16
Female	3.16	1.31	1.85	0.85	0.90	0.81	2.32	0.41	1.04
Race-ethnicity									
White, non-Hispanic	3.24	1.18	2.00	1.04	1.28	0.93	2.20	-0.09	1.08
Black	3.31	1.96	1.35	0.37	0.37	0.36	2.94	1.59	0.99
Hispanic	5.88	4.04	1.83	0.45	0.41	0.49	5.43	3.63	1.35
Age and sex									
Male									
Under 20 years	3.48	1.25	2.22	0.99	0.97	1.00	2.49	0.28	1.22
20 to 34 years	6.97	3.08	3.89	1.35	1.45	1.28	5.62	1.63	2.62
35 to 49 years	2.77	1.09	1.68	0.73	0.93	0.63	2.03	0.15	1.05
50 to 64 years	1.43	0.67	0.74	0.66	0.54	0.72	0.77	0.12	0.02
65 years and over	1.11	0.45	0.63	0.48	0.55	0.44	0.63	-0.10	0.19
Female									
Under 20 years	3.31	1.31	1.98	0.95	0.98	0.93	2.36	0.32	1.06
20 to 34 years	6.48	2.93	3.57	1.35	1.50	1.23	5.13	1.42	2.35
35 to 49 years	2.49	0.89	1.58	0.67	0.66	0.68	1.82	0.24	0.91
50 to 64 years	1.20	0.48	0.73	0.46	0.32	0.54	0.74	0.16	0.20
65 years and over	1.18	0.59	0.60	0.36	0.38	0.33	0.82	0.21	0.27

[1] An average of 1991 and 1992 CPS data.

[2] Per 100 origin population.

Source: U.S. Bureau of the Census, Current Population Reports, "Geographical Mobility, March 1991 to March 1992," and "March 1990 to March 1991," Series P-20, Numbers 473 and 463, U.S. Government Printing Office, Washington, D.C., 1993 and 1992, Table 26.

from metropolitan to nonmetropolitan areas. In other words, the propensity of nonmetropolitan residents to move to metropolitan sites is twice that of the propensity of metropolitan residents to move to nonmetropolitan sites. The apparent migration equilibrium between metropolitan and nonmetropolitan areas is due entirely to the differential size of their populations (nonmetropolitan population is only one-third as large as metro), not to an equality of their rates. However, the propensity for metropolitan residents to seek a nonmetropolitan haven is not negligible (1.27 percent for whites, much lower for blacks and Hispanics). Overall, this rate is as high as the general death rate. If it enjoys even a small increase, the flows between metropolitan and nonmetropolitan areas could cancel each other or again favor nonmetropolitan areas (holding areas constant).

All race-ethnic groups in nonmetropolitan areas show a strong propensity to move to metropolitan areas. Hispanics and blacks are more prone to move to central cities than to suburbs; white non-Hispanics are prone to avoid moving to the central city and instead settle directly in metropolitan rings. Table 8-12 implies that roughly 70 percent of the net loss of nonmetropolitan to metropolitan areas is due to the black population continuing its historic retreat from nonmetropolitan to metropolitan areas (primarily in the South). Hispanics redistributed between metropolitan and nonmetropolitan areas in practically equal numbers, leaving a small positive balance in central cities which was almost exactly offset by a net negative balance for metropolitan rings. The white non-Hispanic population living in central cities showed a small net loss in its exchange with nonmetropolitan areas. Thus, for the white non-Hispanic group, the "metropolitan turnaround" still is trickling central city population into nonmetropolitan sites.

Young adults are quite amenable to move to central cities. Mature adults, and especially those with children, coming from nonmetropolitan areas prefer to locate in the metropolitan rings. Age data of Table 8-12 suggest that the overall change in the age composition of exchange between nonmetropolitan and metropolitan areas is to 'rejuvenate' slightly central city populations, due to nonmetropolitan areas exporting young adults to the central cities, and to contribute to the middle-age population of nonmetropolitan areas, because those who forsake metropolitan for nonmetropolitan areas tend to be middle-age or older adults with or without dependent children.

What is the redistributive power of these differentials? The above comparison of rates does not take into account the sizes of the populations to which the rates apply. Because the nonmetropolitan population is now only about 1/5 (22 percent in 1992) of the national total, and the smaller but not negligible rate of moving from metropolitan to nonmetropolitan areas applies to 4/5 of the population, internal migration from nonmetropolitan

areas is unlikely to be an important future source for further net growth for most metropolitan areas. Despite higher out-mobility rates for nonmetropolitan areas, inequality in size has created a quasi-equilibrium between metropolitan and nonmetropolitan areas which shows little signs of making a major shift in favor of either. The population which metropolitan areas gain from young high school and college graduates from the hinterland seeking their fortune in the central city and more staid nonmetropolitan families moving to metropolitan rings will be largely offset by mature and elderly adults (both from central cities and metropolitan rings) moving beyond the boundaries of the metropolis, seeking a less congested environment in which to earn a livelihood, rear their family, and retire.

Meanwhile, within nonmetropolitan areas, movement from rural and small-town places to cities with nearly 50,000 inhabitants can boost those cities into the metropolitan category through reclassification, thereby creating the illusion of significant growth in pre-existing metropolitan areas.

Mobility Within Same MSA: Decentralization

Slow growth in central cities (frequently actual population loss), with concomitant rapid growth of metropolitan rings, has been the dominant pattern of population change in metropolitan areas since 1950. Although a small part of this difference is due to higher birth and lower death rates in the metropolitan rings than in central cities, residential mobility (cumulated over several decades) is the primary cause. Persons changing residence have preferred to choose metropolitan rings, rather than central cities, as the site of their new home. There are four ways in which residential mobility can enable metropolitan rings to gain population at the expense of the central city: (a) movement from the central city to the ring of the same metropolitan area; (b) movement from the central city of one MSA to the ring of a different MSA, instead of going to the central city; (c) movement from nonmetropolitan areas to a metropolitan ring instead of to the central city; and (d) immigrants from abroad moving directly to a metropolitan ring instead of to the central city. All four of these processes are at work, and it is desirable to study each one separately before making broad statements about the "decentralization" of metropolitan areas. This section takes up the first of these four components.

Table 8-13 provides data on mobility within the same MSA. As already noted, this category constitutes almost 60 percent of all mobility. Two forms of 'circular' mobility and two forms of 'redistributive' mobility can occur. First, in circular intra-metropolitan mobility, residents of central cities can move to a different house in

Table 8-13. Average Annual Movement Within Same Metropolitan Area, by Age, Sex, and Race-ethnicity: 1990-1992[1] [numbers in thousands]

Characteristic		Movers within same MSA					Net to ring
	Total	Within central city	Between central cities	Within metro rings	Central city to ring	Ring to central city	
Number of persons							
Total	23,608	8,950	366	9,513	3,240	1,540	1,700
Male	11,689	4,380	204	4,702	1,618	787	832
Female	11,918	4,570	163	4,811	1,622	754	868
Race-ethnicity							
White, non-Hispanic	16,119	4,821	226	7,603	2,320	1,150	1,170
Black	3,868	2,380	70	784	437	198	240
Hispanic	3,491	1,733	66	1,039	476	179	298
M:F sex ratio							
Total	0.98	0.96	1.25	0.98	1.00	1.04	—
White, non-Hispanic	1.00	1.00	1.41	0.98	1.02	1.02	—
Black	0.86	0.85	0.82	0.81	0.92	1.05	—
Hispanic	1.08	1.07	1.30	1.07	1.01	1.23	—
Age composition, by sex							
Male	100.0	100.0	100.0	100.0	100.0	100.0	—
Under 20 years	30.0	32.2	23.9	29.5	28.1	26.0	—
20 to 34 years	43.6	43.9	48.3	42.0	44.2	48.9	—
35 to 49 years	18.0	15.6	19.5	19.4	19.8	19.0	—
50 to 64 years	6.1	6.0	6.2	6.8	5.4	4.2	—
65 years and over	2.3	2.3	2.2	2.3	2.5	1.9	—
Female							
Under 20 years	100.0	100.0	100.0	100.0	100.0	100.0	—
20 to 34 years	29.6	28.8	32.3	29.6	29.8	26.5	—
35 to 49 years	44.3	46.8	45.9	42.3	42.7	46.6	—
50 to 64 years	16.6	14.8	17.9	18.2	17.5	16.7	—
65 years and over	5.7	5.6	3.1	5.9	6.1	6.7	—
65-over	3.8	3.9	1.1	4.0	3.9	3.7	—
Rate of mobility[2]							
Total	12.33	12.06	0.49	8.12	4.37	1.31	3.05
Male	12.55	12.29	0.57	8.18	4.54	1.37	3.17
Female	12.12	11.85	0.42	8.06	4.20	1.26	2.94
Race-ethnicity							
White, non-Hispanic	11.07	10.51	0.49	7.62	5.06	1.15	3.91
Black	15.11	13.93	0.41	9.22	2.56	2.32	0.24
Hispanic	17.67	15.68	0.59	11.94	4.31	2.05	2.26
Age and sex							
Male							
Under 20 years	13.18	13.85	0.47	8.41	4.35	1.25	3.09
20 to 34 years	21.17	19.48	0.94	13.87	7.06	2.74	4.32
35 to 49 years	10.46	9.53	0.57	7.02	4.35	1.16	3.19
50 to 64 years	6.16	6.51	0.36	4.19	2.08	0.44	1.63
65 years and over	3.04	3.03	0.13	1.91	1.20	0.27	0.93
Female							
Under 20 years							
20 to 34 years	13.81	10.88	1.12	8.45	5.57	1.47	4.10
35 to 49 years	21.67	17.37	1.56	13.22	7.85	2.82	5.02
50 to 64 years	9.40	7.34	0.81	6.03	4.30	1.07	3.23
65 years and over	5.37	4.55	0.23	3.25	2.45	0.72	1.73
65-over	3.50	2.72	0.07	2.38	1.36	0.42	0.93

[1] An average of 1991 and 1992 CPS data.

[2] Per 100 origin population.

Source: U.S. Bureau of the Census, Current Population Reports, "Geographical Mobility, March 1991 to March 1992," and "March 1990 to March 1991," Series P-20, Numbers 473 and 463, U.S. Government Printing Office, Washington, D.C., 1993 and 1992, Table 26.

the same city, to a different house in the same metropolitan ring, or to a different central city within the same MSA (e.g. twin city areas). Also, if an MSA has two or more counties, persons can 'migrate' from one county to another while remaining within the same MSA. Second, in redistributive intra-metropolitan mobility, residents of a central city can move to the metropolitan ring of the same metropolitan area, or residents of a metropolitan ring can move to the central city of that metropolitan area. Data for all of these streams of movement, by demographic characteristics of the movers, are reported in Table 8-13.

With respect to intra-metropolitan circulation, central city residents are much more likely to circulate within the city (12.06 %) than suburban residents are to circulate within the suburbs (8.12%). Together these two circulatory kinds of moves account for nearly one-half of the nation's annual residential change. They can and do have major impacts on the individual neighborhoods of both central cities and suburbs. Hispanic populations have highest rates of intra-metropolitan circulation, followed by blacks, and then white non-Hispanics. There is a disproportionately large share of young persons in this movement, and within central cities children are circulated at high rates.

In intra-metropolitan redistribution, each year 3.24 million persons exchange their central city home for a dwelling in the ring of the same MSA, and 1.54 million persons make the reverse move from a metropolitan ring to the same central city. The net balance is 1.7 million annual population gain for the metropolitan ring. The rate of out-migration from the central city to its ring (4.37 %) is three times that of out-migration from the ring to its central city (1.31 %). This deconcentration is equal in size, rate, and selectivity to the interregional migration described in the preceding section. These data emphasize that exodus from the central city to its own periphery is far from over. The net rate of departure from the central city is especially heavy for the white non-Hispanic (3.91 percent) and the Hispanic (2.26 percent), but is practically nil for the black population (0.24 percent). However, these data also reveal that the movement is not all one way; the rate and numbers of persons returning to central cities are sizable. Despite an unfavorable balance in the rates for the black population, numerically there is a strong black ring-ward movement. The explanation for this apparently discrepant situation is one of differences in population sizes. The rate of out-migration for the black population is reasonably high (2.56 percent), but the rate of the reverse flow from ring to central city is very nearly as high (2.32 percent). Because these rates apply to the very large black population in central cities and the comparatively small black population in suburbs, the net numerical effect is the annual transfer of nearly a quarter million black residents to suburbs. Decades of laws mandating equal opportunity in housing markets appears to

be enabling the black population to join the exodus to metropolitan rings in a significant way, even though there is a strong reverse flow (perhaps temporary) back to the city of the smallish black population already living in metropolitan rings. Meanwhile, special note should be taken of the vigorous Hispanic suburban redistribution. Despite the smaller size of the Hispanic population, the volume of annual Hispanic net movement to the suburbs (298,000) is considerably larger than for the black population.

All age groups participate in moves from central city to suburbs. Although young adults (and accompanying children) constitute the largest component, the rates for mature, middle-age, and elderly adults are moderately high in comparison with the average rates for those ages. There is no hint that elderly residents of metropolitan rings tend to move back into the central city in unusual numbers or proportions.

Migration Between Metropolitan Areas

Inter-metropolitan circulation results in an annual flow of 7.34 million persons from one metropolitan area to another (Table 8-14). As metropolitan economies compete with each other and with economies overseas, their respective labor markets reflect their successes and failures and the labor force reacts. Consequently the local metropolitan labor force and housing markets of MSAs compete with one another. The results may have impacts on which MSAs gain and lose population. Table 8-14 shows that this form of mobility is equally strong for black, Hispanic, and white non-Hispanic populations. Males have slightly higher rates of inter-metropolitan mobility than females. Although young persons and children are major participants, rates for persons of mature and older age are relatively higher, in comparison with the average rate, than intra-metropolitan mobility. Most of it is movement from one central city to another (2.58 percent) or from one ring to another (2.14 percent).

There is also considerable inter-metropolitan redistribution. For large segments of the population making a move between two metropolises, choice of residence in central city or ring is discretionary. In exercising this choice, there is a strong additional transfer (especially of white non-Hispanic persons) from central city to metropolitan rings. From Table 8-14 note that the rate of movement from a central city to the ring of a different MSA (2.50 percent) is very nearly as high as any of the rates of inter-metropolitan circulation. For the white non-Hispanic population, an out-rate of 3.11 percent is combined with an in-rate of only 0.85 percent; of the 757,000 population metropolitan rings gain annually from this source, 573,000 (75%) consists of white non-Hispanics. For the black population the rates of inter-metropolitan moves appear to benefit the central cities, but because of unequal popu-

Table 8-14. Average Annual Movement Between Metropolitan Areas, by Age, Sex, and Race-ethnicity: 1990-1992[1] [numbers in thousands]

		Movers between MSA's				
Characteristic	Total	Between central cities	Between metro rings	Central city to ring	Ring to central city	Net to ring
Number of persons						
Total	7,374	1,918	2,509	1,852	1,095	757
Male	3,735	961	1,272	941	560	381
Female	3,640	958	1,236	911	535	376
Race-ethnicity						
White, non-Hispanic	5,629	1,258	2,096	1,426	853	573
Black	980	392	205	235	149	86
Hispanic	648	254	156	145	94	51
M:F sex ratio						
Total	1.03	1.00	1.03	1.03	1.05	—
White, non-Hispanic	1.05	1.03	1.02	1.09	1.06	—
Black	0.93	0.95	1.06	0.81	0.94	—
Hispanic	1.05	1.00	1.17	1.02	1.03	—
Age composition, by sex						
Male	100.0	100.0	100.0	100.0	100.0	—
Under 20 years	24.3	22.0	26.3	25.6	21.3	—
20 to 34 years	44.9	47.8	39.3	46.0	50.3	—
35 to 49 years	20.4	20.9	21.7	18.9	19.1	—
50 to 64 years	6.9	5.6	8.2	6.3	7.4	—
65 years and over	3.4	3.3	4.4	3.0	1.6	—
Female	100.0	100.0	100.0	100.0	100.0	—
Under 20 years	25.4	25.7	27.1	28.2	23.6	—
20 to 34 years	42.4	45.3	37.7	42.4	44.0	—
35 to 49 years	19.2	17.5	20.8	17.3	20.1	—
50 to 64 years	7.4	6.9	8.2	7.1	7.1	—
65 years and over	5.6	4.7	6.3	4.8	5.0	—
Rates of mobility[2]						
Total	3.85	2.58	2.14	2.50	0.93	1.56
Male	4.01	2.70	2.21	2.64	0.97	1.67
Female	3.70	2.48	2.07	2.36	0.90	1.47
Race-ethnicity						
White, non-Hispanic	3.86	2.74	2.10	3.11	0.85	2.25
Black	3.83	2.29	2.41	1.37	1.75	-0.37
Hispanic	3.28	2.30	1.79	1.31	1.07	0.23
Age and Sex						
Male						
Under 20 years	3.26	1.96	1.98	2.19	0.71	1.47
20 to 34 years	6.68	4.38	3.43	4.05	1.96	2.09
35 to 49 years	3.63	2.63	2.07	2.30	0.81	1.48
50 to 64 years	2.13	1.24	1.34	1.35	0.54	0.81
65 years and over	1.36	0.91	0.98	0.80	0.16	0.64
Female						
Under 20 years	3.07	2.34	2.07	2.40	0.80	1.60
20 to 34 years	5.37	4.05	3.16	3.55	1.64	1.92
35 to 49 years	2.83	2.09	1.84	1.94	0.79	1.15
50 to 64 years	1.81	1.34	1.22	1.29	0.47	0.82
65 years and over	1.35	0.79	0.99	0.76	0.35	0.40

[1] An average of 1991 and 1992 CPS data.

[2] Per 100 origin population.

Source: U.S. Bureau of the Census, Current Population Reports, "Geographical Mobility, March 1991 to March 1992," and "March 1990 to March 1991," Series P-20, Numbers 473 and 463, U.S. Government Printing Office, Washington, D.C., 1993 and 1992, Table 26.

Table 8-15. Average Annual Movement within Non-metropolitan Areas, by Age, Sex, and Race-ethnicity: 1990-1992[1] [numbers in thousands]

| Characteristic | Movers within non-metropolitan areas | | | Difference |
	Total	Within same county	To different county	
Number of persons				
Total	6,354	4,695	1,649	3,046
Male	3,142	2,310	833	1,477
Female	3,212	2,386	817	1,569
Race-ethnicity				
White, non-Hispanic	638	515	123	392
Black	254	200	54	147
Hispanic	5,408	3,939	1,468	2,471
M:F sex ratio				
Total	0.98	0.97	1.02	—
White, non-Hispanic	0.85	0.81	1.07	—
Black	1.11	1.05	1.43	—
Hispanic	0.99	0.99	1.00	—
Age composition, by sex				
Male	100.0	100.0	100.0	—
Under 20 years	33.8	34.1	32.8	—
20 to 34 years	38.7	39.4	36.9	—
35 to 49 years	17.2	17.0	17.3	—
50 to 64 years	6.5	5.5	9.1	—
65 years and over	3.8	3.9	3.7	—
Female	100.0	100.0	100.0	—
Under 20 years	34.5	36.4	29.3	—
20 to 34 years	38.2	38.5	37.6	—
35 to 49 years	16.3	15.6	18.2	—
50 to 64 years	6.1	5.0	9.0	—
65 years and over	5.0	4.5	6.2	—
Rates of mobility[2]				
Total	11.61	8.58	3.01	5.57
Male	11.78	8.66	3.12	5.54
Female	11.45	8.51	2.91	5.60
Race-ethnicity				
White, non-Hispanic	12.90	10.42	2.49	7.93
Black	17.22	13.59	3.63	9.95
Hispanic	11.33	8.25	3.08	5.18
Age and Sex				
Male				
Under 20 years	13.38	9.93	3.45	6.47
20 to 34 years	21.32	15.94	5.40	10.54
35 to 49 years	9.43	6.88	2.53	4.35
50 to 64 years	5.38	3.36	2.00	1.36
65 years and over	3.49	2.59	0.88	1.72
Female				
Under 20 years	14.35	11.24	3.13	8.12
20 to 34 years	20.68	15.46	5.22	10.24
35 to 49 years	9.23	6.59	2.65	3.94
50 to 64 years	4.60	2.83	1.75	1.08
65 years and over	3.59	2.43	1.16	1.27

[1] An average of 1991 and 1992 CPS data.

[2] Per 100 resident population.

Source: U.S. Bureau of the Census, Current Population Reports, "Geographical Mobility, March 1991 to March 1992," and "March 1990 to March 1991," Series P-20, Numbers 473 and 463, U.S. Government Printing Office, Washington, D.C., 1993 and 1992, Table 26.

lation sizes, the net effect is an additional annual contribution of 86,000 black residents to metropolitan rings. For Hispanics, the redistributive effect is a moderately small gain for metropolitan rings.

Mobility Within Nonmetropolitan Areas

As Table 8-15 shows, the lower rates of residential mobility for nonmetropolitan areas are due almost entirely to low rate of local mobility within the same county (8.58 %). Rates of nonmetropolitan migration (to a different nonmetropolitan county) are 3.01%, which are nearly identical to the migration rates for the nation. Moreover, this low local mobility is strongest among the white non-Hispanic population. Black and Hispanic nonmetropolitan residents are much more locally mobile and even somewhat more migratory. Local mobility has a more or less average age-rate pattern, but migration rates of the nonmetropolitan elderly, relative to migration of the metropolitan elderly, are lower. Social and economic conditions within nonmetropolitan areas seem to change less or else require fewer same-community residential adjustments. However, the propensity of youth and working adults to take advantage of inter-community differences in nonmetropolitan opportunities appear to be about as strong as in metropolitan areas.

Mobility Variation Among Metropolitan Areas

The above analysis aggregates all metropolitan areas into a single category. The findings are averages. Because each metropolitan area is a unique entity, with a particular geographic location, economic base, labor market, housing market, environmental amenities and disamenities, and race/ethnic composition, one must expect there to be considerable variation among MSA's. Limitations of space and data prevent detailed description of this variation. Table 8-16 provides data for 1992 for the ten largest MSA's. Four consolidated metropolitan areas, New York, Los Angeles, Chicago, and San Francisco are experiencing very heavy migration loss. One older metropolitan area, Philadelphia, appears to have passed through this phase. These larger and older (except for Houston) MSAs tend to be major 'ports of entry' for immigrants. They are not typical of the hundreds of smaller MSA's. However, they demonstrate that among themselves there are variations, and verify that they do not fully conform to the general averages presented above.

Immigration from Abroad

The destinations of the average annual influx of 1,320,000 arrivals from abroad reported in the Current Population Survey for 1992 and 1993 are distributed as shown in Table 8-17. About 90 percent of all immigrants go directly to metropolitan areas. Immigration increases the growth of metropolitan areas almost three times as much as it stimulates growth in nonmetropolitan areas (see Table 8-18). This is just as true of Hispanic as of other ethnic origin groups. (For these data, the average time interval since entry is six months; it is presumed that the residence at survey date was the type of residence of their port-of-entry.) Although 128,000 migrants annually enter nonmetropolitan areas, presumably to work in agriculture-related industries, this now is a minor part of immigration from abroad; the stereotype of Hispanic immigrants being predominantly farm workers is at least a quarter-century out of date.

Table 8-16. Net Migration for Selected Large Metropolitan Statistical Areas (MSA's), by Race-ethnicity: 1991-1992

MSA's	Total	White	Black	Hispanic
Total net migration for MSA's below	-615	-545	-89	-127
New York-New Jersey-Long Island, NY-NJ-CT CMSA	-254	-202	-33	-44
Los Angeles-Anaheim-Riverside, CA CMSA	-181	-170	-9	-43
Chicago-Gary-Lake County, IL-IN-WI CMSA	-137	-87	-61	-12
San Fransisco-Oakland-San Jose, CA CMSA	-111	-117	...	3
Philadelphia-Wilmington-Trenton, PA-NJ-DE-MD CMSA	6	4	1	-1
Detroit-Ann Arbor, MI CMSA	-23	-32	-2	...
Boston-Lawrence-Salem, MA-NH CMSA	-17	6	-16	-4
Dallas-Forth Worth, TX CMSA	19	6	7	-14
Houston-Galveston-Brazoria, TX CMSA	101	84	9	...
Washington, DC-MD-VA CMSA	-18	-37	15	-12

Source: U.S. Bureau of the Census, Current Population Reports, "Geographical Mobility, March 1991 to March 1992," Series
   P-20, Number 473, U.S. Government Printing Office, Washington, D.C., 1993, Table 42.

Table 8-17. Average Annual Immigration from Abroad, by Age, Sex, and Race-ethnicity: 1990-1992[1]
[numbers in thousands]

Characteristic	Movers from abroad					Net to metro	Net to metro rings
	To U.S. total	To MSA's total	To central cities	To metro rings	To non-metro areas		
Number of persons							
Total	1,320	1,193	615	578	128	1,065	-37
Male	722	645	334	312	77	568	-22
Female	598	548	281	267	51	497	-15
Race-ethnicity							
White, non-Hispanic	718	645	333	312	74	571	-21
Black	127	109	61	48	17	92	-13
Hispanic	406	381	213	168	25	356	-45
M:F sex ratio							
Total	1.21	1.18	1.19	1.17	1.51	—	—
White, non-Hispanic	1.23	1.18	1.18	1.19	1.68	—	—
Black	1.61	1.68	1.42	2.10	1.20	—	—
Hispanic	1.25	1.24	1.36	1.10	1.50	—	—
Age composition, by sex							
Male	100.0	100.0	100.0	100.0	100.0	—	—
Under 20 years	24.2	24.0	25.0	22.9	25.8	—	—
20 to 34 years	48.5	48.9	51.7	45.6	45.6	—	—
35 to 49 years	18.0	17.7	16.3	19.2	21.2	—	—
50 to 64 years	6.4	6.8	4.7	9.2	2.8	—	—
65 years and over	2.6	2.5	2.1	2.9	3.8	—	—
Female	100.0	100.0	100.0	100.0	100.0	—	—
Under 20 years	30.3	30.3	26.1	35.0	30.2	—	—
20 to 34 years	42.4	42.0	43.8	39.9	48.0	—	—
35 to 49 years	15.3	15.4	14.8	16.1	14.3	—	—
50 to 64 years	8.2	8.6	11.0	5.9	4.9	—	—
65 years and over	3.7	4.5	5.3	3.6	...	—	—
Rates of mobility[2]							
Total	0.54	0.62	0.83	0.49	0.23	0.39	-0.34
Male	0.60	0.69	0.94	0.54	0.29	0.40	-0.39
Female	0.47	0.56	0.73	0.45	0.18	0.38	-0.28
Race-ethnicity							
White, non-Hispanic	0.37	0.44	0.73	0.31	0.15	0.29	-0.41
Black	0.41	0.42	0.35	0.56	0.33	0.09	0.21
Hispanic	1.91	1.93	1.92	1.93	1.70	0.23	0.01
Age and Sex							
Male							
Under 20 years	0.48	0.55	0.78	0.40	0.23	0.32	-0.38
20 to 34 years	1.11	1.24	1.67	0.92	0.57	0.67	-0.75
35 to 49 years	0.48	0.54	0.73	0.43	0.26	0.27	-0.30
50 to 64 years	0.29	0.36	0.37	0.35	0.05	0.30	-0.02
65 years and over	0.14	0.17	0.20	0.15	0.08	0.09	-0.05
Female							
Under 20 years	0.49	0.58	0.67	0.53	0.18	0.41	-0.15
20 to 34 years	0.76	0.85	1.11	0.66	0.37	0.48	-0.45
35 to 49 years	0.31	0.36	0.50	0.28	0.12	0.25	-0.22
50 to 64 years	0.26	0.33	0.61	0.17	0.05	0.28	-0.43
65 years and over	0.12	0.17	0.26	0.11	...	0.17	-0.14

[1] An average of 1991 and 1992 CPS data.
[2] Per 100 destination population.

Source: U.S. Bureau of the Census, Current Population Reports, "Geographical Mobility, March 1991 to March 1992," and March 1990 to March 1991," Series P-20, Numbers 473 and 463, U.S. Government Printing Office, Washington, D.C., 1993 and 1992, Table 26.

Table 8-18. Destinations of Immigration from Abroad: 1990-1992 [numbers in thousands]

| Destination | Average of 1991 and 1992 CPS surveys | | | | 1990 Census (5-years) |
	Total	White, non-Hispanic	Black	Hispanic	
Number of immigrants					
Total	1,320	718	127	406	5,109
To MSA's	1,193	645	109	381	4,765
Central cities	615	333	61	213	2,521
Metro rings	578	312	48	168	2,244
To non-metro areas	128	74	17	25	343
Percent distribution					
Total	100.0	100.0	100.0	100.0	100.0
To MSA's	90.4	89.8	85.8	93.8	93.3
Central cities	46.6	46.4	48.0	52.5	49.4
Metro rings	43.8	43.5	37.8	41.4	43.9
To non-metro areas	9.7	10.3	13.4	6.2	6.7

Source: U.S. Bureau of the Census, Current Population Reports, "Geographical Mobility, March 1991 to March 1992,"
Table 26, and "March 1990 to March 1991," Table 26, Series P-20, Numbers 473 and 462, and "Social and Economic
Characteristics," 1990 Census of Population, Table 32, U.S. Government Printing Office, Washington, D.C., 1993,
1992, and 1993.

**Table 8-19. The Net Mobility Components of Metropolitan Growth,
Race-ethnicity: 1990-1992[1] [numbers in thousands]**

Destination	Total	White, non-Hispanic	Black	Hispanic
Metro areas, total	1,288	678	178	379
Metro-non-metro	95	33	69	-2
Within same MSA	...	...	...	...
Between MSA's	...	...	...	...
Immigration from abroad	1,193	645	109	381
Central cities	-1,820	-1,431	-232	-122
Metro-non-metro	22	-21	33	14
Within same MSA	-1,700	-1,170	-240	-298
Between MSA's	-757	-573	-86	-51
Immigration from abroad	615	333	61	213
Metro rings	3,108	2,109	710	501
Metro-non-metro	73	54	336	-16
Within same MSA	1,700	1,170	240	298
Between MSA's	757	573	86	51
Immigration from abroad	578	312	48	168

[1] An average of 1991 and 1992 CPS data.

Source: U.S. Bureau of the Census, Current Population Reports, "Geographical Mobility, March 1991 to
March 1992," and "March 1990 to March 1991," Series P-20, Numbers 473 and 463, U.S. Government
Printing Office, Washington, D.C., 1993 and 1992, Table 26.

Of the masses of immigrants to metropolitan areas, a little more than one-half go to central cities and a little less than one-half to metropolitan rings. Today, direct arrival in metropolitan rings is very common for immigrants, even for Hispanic and black immigrants. White non-Hispanic immigrants are already even more ready to prefer metropolitan rings and nonmetropolitan destinations. Table 8-19 summarizes the net sources of metropolitan growth (total MSA, central cities, and rings) and reveals the importance of immigration in all, while providing race-ethnic detail. The lower panel of Table 8-17 reports in-migration rates for the respective destinations. Preceding tables in this series reported out-migration rates. Such rates are a measure of how immigration contributes to population growth at the destination, not of the probability of leaving a place abroad to reside in the U.S. Hispanics have rates nearly four times the national average. It is noteworthy that the rate (but not the number) of black immigrants (from Africa, Haiti, and the Caribbean) is now equal to or higher than that of white non-Hispanic immigrants. However, these rates apply to populations of smaller size. Consequently, the number and percent composition by race/ethnic make-up of immigrants in 1990-92 was estimated to be:

Immigrants to Metropolitan Areas,
  by Race-ethnicity: 1990-1992

Race-ethnicity	Number (in thousands)	Percent
Total	1,330	100.0
White, non-Hispanic	718	54.0
Black	406	30.5
Hispanic	127	9.5
Other	79	5.9

Despite the dramatic increase in immigration from Asia, Africa, and Latin America, a bare majority of immigrants to the United States still are white non-Hispanic.

Socioeconomic Differentials in Mobility

The significant differentials among the rates of each type of mobility according to demographic traits such as age and race-ethnicity were described above. In addition, there are significant differentials according to social and economic traits.

Educational Attainment

Table 8-20 presents detailed mobility rates by educational attainment. Although central cities are exporting citizens of all educational levels to their own rings, the rate of local mobility (within the same metropolitan

area or same nonmetropolitan county) is lowest (though nevertheless substantial) at the two extremes of the educational scale: the least educated and the most educated residents. This holds true both for central cities and rings, and for movement in both directions between the central city and ring of the same MSA. Persons with 1-4 years of college are most inclined to move from central cities to the ring, and have low inclination to make the reverse move. The intra-metropolitan exchanges clearly are tending to restrain the very lowest educational group from moving to the suburbs.

Movement between MSAs is even more selective on educational attainment; the more education, the greater the tendency to make an inter-metropolitan shift. This holds true both for central cities and rings and for movement in both directions between central cities and rings of different MSAs, with the better educated preferring a ring rather than a central city destination. Because the rate for central city to ring movement is more than twice that of the reverse flow, inter-metropolitan shifts are having the effect of further depleting the upper educational levels of central cities and additionally enhancing the educational level of metropolitan rings. Migration from nonmetropolitan to metropolitan areas is highest for the better educated and lowest for the least educated. This flow strengthens the education qualifications of both central cities and rings, with somewhat more benefit to rings than central cities.

Rates of immigration from abroad (based on resident U.S. population) have a pronounced "U" shape, with highest rates for both the least educated and the most educated segments. Governments of developing countries have complained for decades about the 'brain drain' of their best educated citizens to the U.S. On the other hand, some U.S. migration experts have feared the proletarianization effect of the arrival of large numbers of today's immigrants (particularly from Mexico and elsewhere in Latin America) with low education and poor labor force qualifications. The evidence supports both points of view. However, neither the brain drain nor the proletarianization effect is tied to one specific country or region of the world; each is more complicated than that. Meanwhile, it is true that a large segment of immigrants from all continents has less education than the high-technology economy of the U.S. seems to need, and appears to be adding to the surplus of under-qualified natives already here. Some observers say the proletarian newcomers mostly take jobs which members of the native underclass disdain; others think they take lower-paying jobs from the natives and depress wages in those sectors. Perhaps because many unsuccessful immigrants return to their country of origin, the average long-term work career trajectory of immigrants is equal to or more steeply upward than that of natives of the same educational attainment. To what extent this is achieved at the expense of native-

Table 8-20. Detailed Mobility Rates[1] of the Population 25 years of Age and Over, by Level of Educational Attainment: 1991-1992

Type of mobility	Total	Elementary	9-12 years high school	High school graduate	Some college or associate's degree	Bachelor's degree	Graduate or professional degree
Within same MSA	10.89	9.60	12.13	10.43	11.67	11.78	8.69
Within central city	10.61	9.67	12.46	10.56	10.95	11.02	7.57
Between central cities	0.50	0.51	0.37	0.36	0.69	0.71	0.36
Within metro rings	7.04	6.48	7.31	6.65	7.42	7.96	5.94
Central city to ring	4.04	1.58	3.79	4.23	5.03	4.65	3.37
Ring to central city	1.20	0.97	1.08	1.16	1.42	1.21	1.08
Balance[2] to metro ring	2.84	0.61	2.71	3.07	3.61	3.43	2.30
Between SMA's	3.42	1.82	2.55	2.81	3.64	4.77	5.67
Between central cities	2.22	1.34	1.85	1.90	2.35	2.77	3.94
Between metro rings	1.92	1.24	1.23	1.55	2.13	2.75	2.68
Central city to ring	2.15	0.74	1.65	1.84	2.08	3.46	3.89
Ring to central city	0.91	0.33	0.53	0.74	1.06	1.20	1.62
Balance[2] to metro ring	1.24	0.41	1.12	1.10	1.02	2.26	2.27
Non-metro to metro	2.53	0.77	1.35	2.40	3.42	4.29	4.67
To central cities	1.09	0.40	0.35	1.05	1.39	2.04	2.30
To metro rings	1.45	0.38	1.00	1.35	2.03	2.25	2.37
Metro to non-metro	0.79	0.61	0.79	0.77	0.89	0.85	0.74
From central cities	0.82	0.63	0.79	0.73	0.89	1.03	0.90
From metro rings	0.78	0.60	0.78	0.79	0.89	0.75	0.64
Balance[2] to metro	1.74	0.16	0.56	1.63	2.53	3.44	3.93
Balance[2] to central cities	0.27	-0.23	-0.44	0.32	0.51	1.01	1.40
Balance[2] to metro rings	0.67	-0.23	0.22	0.56	1.14	1.50	1.73
Non-metro to non-metro	9.09	6.66	10.41	9.08	10.32	8.98	6.98
Within same county	6.49	4.79	7.62	6.50	7.28	6.17	4.99
To different county	2.60	1.85	2.77	2.59	3.05	2.81	1.92
Immigration from abroad	0.45	0.76	0.23	0.27	0.44	0.68	0.88
To MSA's	0.51	0.76	0.30	0.32	0.48	0.75	0.96
To central cities	0.59	0.59	0.54	0.44	0.47	0.89	1.08
To metro rings	0.46	0.93	0.10	0.26	0.48	0.67	0.88
To non-metro areas	0.17	0.11	0.02	0.10	0.32	0.31	0.45
Balance[2] to MSA's	0.34	0.65	0.28	0.22	0.15	0.44	0.51
Balance[2] to metro rings	-0.13	0.34	-0.44	-0.18	0.01	-0.22	-0.20

[1] Per 100 persons in place of origin. Per 100 persons in place of destination for immigrants from abroad.
[2] "Balance" represents the rate difference.

Source: U.S. Bureau of the Census, Current Population Reports, "Geographical Mobility: March 1991 to March 1992," Series P-20, Number 473, U.S. Government Printing Office, Washington, D.C., 1993, Table 41.

born citizens at all educational levels, remains a key topic for research. Unfortunately, practicable research models which are wholly unbiased on this point are very difficult to construct.

Income

In general, the mobility patterns for income groups are similar to those for education: low at the extremes and higher in the middle. In Table 8-21 mobility data are presented for individuals and their personal income as well as for householders and household income. Low income persons and households are more locally mobile than higher income groups, but higher income groups are more migratory than lower income groups. Having a personal or household annual income of $40,000 per year is a strong deterrent to circulatory local mobility within the same MSA. The one exception is for movement from

Table 8-21. Detailed Mobility Rates[1] of the Population Age 25 Years and Over, by Individual and Household Income and Housing Tenure: 1990-92[2]

Type of mobility	Individual income					Household income						Housing tenure	
	Total	<$10,000	$10,000-$19,999	$20,000-$39,999	$40,000 and over	Total	<$10,000	$10,000-$19,999	$20,000-$39,999	$40,000-$59,999	$60,000 and over	Owner	Renter
Within same MSA	12.06	12.14	14.24	12.07	7.68	12.41	16.13	15.85	13.73	9.91	7.27	5.31	23.72
Within central city	11.57	12.47	13.41	10.46	6.20	11.82	15.76	14.80	11.85	8.53	6.12	4.07	19.15
Between central cities	0.51	0.45	0.52	0.68	0.38	0.51	0.42	0.54	0.57	0.54	0.43	0.22	0.78
Within metro rings	7.94	7.75	9.14	8.42	5.61	8.12	9.82	10.09	9.66	6.93	5.28	3.95	18.00
Central city to ring	4.34	3.56	5.06	5.00	3.98	4.16	2.73	4.48	4.66	4.66	4.00	3.01	5.25
Ring to central city	1.36	1.35	1.88	1.33	0.78	1.48	2.71	2.14	1.73	1.08	0.57	0.42	4.00
Balance[3] to metro ring	2.98	2.21	3.18	3.67	3.20	2.68	0.02	2.35	2.93	3.59	3.43	2.59	1.26
Between SMA's	3.92	3.96	4.16	3.81	3.67	3.71	3.88	3.96	3.92	3.51	3.27	1.90	6.59
Between central cities	2.68	2.86	2.64	2.62	2.31	2.55	2.58	2.85	2.58	2.58	1.99	1.14	3.88
Between metro rings	2.13	2.08	2.18	2.14	2.21	2.01	2.22	2.07	2.01	1.92	1.96	1.21	3.90
Central city to ring	2.49	2.33	2.69	2.57	2.69	2.12	1.50	1.68	2.39	2.56	2.46	1.47	2.73
Ring to central city	1.00	1.02	1.19	0.88	0.85	1.05	1.37	1.38	1.17	0.77	0.79	0.35	2.69
Balance[3] to metro ring	1.49	1.30	1.50	1.69	1.84	1.07	0.14	0.30	1.23	1.79	1.68	1.12	0.04
Non-metro to metro	3.36	3.57	3.26	3.12	3.44	2.97	3.11	3.26	2.70	2.73	3.32	0.98	8.39
To central cities	1.41	1.60	1.40	1.30	0.95	1.41	1.94	1.77	1.22	1.01	0.84	0.28	4.49
To metro rings	1.95	1.96	1.86	1.81	2.47	1.56	1.17	1.50	1.50	1.71	2.41	0.70	3.92
Metro to non-metro	0.86	1.04	1.00	0.72	0.44	0.78	1.06	1.04	0.85	0.66	0.39	0.50	1.24
From central cities	0.95	1.23	1.03	0.71	0.50	0.81	1.05	0.91	0.87	0.60	0.43	0.51	1.10
From metro rings	0.81	0.91	0.98	0.74	0.40	0.77	1.08	1.15	0.83	0.69	0.36	0.49	1.42
Balance[3] to metro	2.50	2.53	2.25	2.40	3.00	2.19	2.05	2.22	1.85	2.07	2.93	0.48	7.15
Balance[3] to central cities	0.46	0.37	0.37	0.59	0.44	0.60	0.89	0.86	0.34	0.41	0.41	-0.23	3.39
Balance[3] to metro rings	1.14	1.05	0.87	1.07	2.07	0.79	0.10	0.35	0.67	1.02	2.05	0.21	2.49
Non-metro to non-metro	10.99	11.73	11.64	9.24	6.66	10.76	14.54	12.94	10.24	7.19	5.73	5.10	26.17
Within same county	7.99	8.44	8.63	6.78	4.75	8.01	10.95	9.71	7.56	5.35	4.11	3.77	19.53
To different county	3.00	3.30	3.02	2.45	1.93	2.76	3.60	3.23	2.69	1.84	1.67	1.33	6.63
Immigration from abroad	0.56	0.59	0.44	0.31	0.24	0.38	0.69	0.45	0.38	0.25	0.21	0.11	0.88
To MSA's	0.65	0.70	0.52	0.33	0.25	0.43	0.79	0.56	0.42	0.28	0.23	0.12	0.93
To central cities	0.90	0.98	0.63	0.41	0.40	0.57	1.00	0.62	0.51	0.37	0.30	0.08	1.04
To metro rings	0.50	0.51	0.44	0.29	0.18	0.33	0.50	0.51	0.36	0.23	0.21	0.14	0.79
To non-metro areas	0.24	0.25	0.19	0.19	0.14	0.22	0.42	0.16	0.24	0.12	0.13	0.08	0.62
Balance[3] to MSA's	0.41	0.45	0.32	0.14	0.12	0.21	0.37	0.41	0.18	0.16	0.10	0.04	0.30
Balance[3] to metro rings	-0.40	-0.47	-0.20	-0.13	-0.22	-0.24	-0.50	-0.11	-0.14	-0.13	-0.09	0.06	-0.24

[1] Per 100 persons in place of origin. Per 100 persons in place of destination for immigrants from abroad.
[2] An average of 1991 and 1992 CPS data
[3] "Balance" represents the rate difference

Source: U.S. Bureau of the Census, Current Population Reports, "Geographical Mobility, March 1991 to March 1992," Table 41, and "March 1990 to March 1991," Table 39, Series P-20, Numbers 473 and 463, U.S. Government Printing Office, Washington, D.C., 1993 and 1992.

Residential Segregation

by Karla L. Egan

Many American cities are effectively divided into separate race-ethnic enclaves. Even with the enactment of fair housing and anti-discrimination laws, segregation continues to be a problem in American cities. In order to understand the depth and complexity of residential patterns, at least five dimensions of segregation are generally considered including spatial eveness, exposure, centralization, concentration, and clustering.

Eveness can be interpreted as the proportion of minority members that would have to change tracts in order to achieve an evenly distributed population. This is measured by the index of dissimilarity which varies between 0 and 1.0 where a score of 1.0 reflects maximum unevenness or need for redistribution to achieve an evenly distributed minority population.

Exposure refers to the probability that members of the minority group will come in contact with members of the majority group. The index of exposure varies between 0 and 1.0 where higher scores signify a greater chance of interaction between the minority and majority group.

Centralization measures the extent to which a minority group is located near the central business district of a city (last identified in the 1982 economic census for all MSA's presented here except Nassau/Suffolk). This index varies between -1.0 and +1.0 where positive values indicate a tendency for members of the minority group to locate around the CBD. A score of 0 means that the minority group is evenly distributed throughout the city with respect to the CBD.

Concentration refers to the amount of physical space that a minority group occupies. This is measured by the relative density concentration index which measures the difference in the average amount of area residentially occupied by the majority and minority groups relative to that difference if the minority group were minimally concentrated and the majority group were maximally concentrated. A score of 1 means the minority group is maximally concentrated while a score of -1 means the converse. A score of 0 signifies that the groups are evenly concentrated.

Finally, clustering refers to the fact that minority groups reside in areas that are often near or adjoining each other. The spatial proximity index measures the degree of residential and industrial clustering found in each MSA. A score of 1 means that neither minority nor majority groups are clustered together. A score greater than 1 means minority communities are generally closer to each other than to other communities while a score that is less than one means the converse.

The five indices were computed using non-Hispanic blacks as a minority group and non-Hispanic whites as the majority group. The first table for this textbox presents the segregation indices (based on census tract level data) for non-Hispanic blacks in the 25 largest MSA's. Cleveland and Detroit appear to be the most segregated relative to the other cities. When each of the indices are ranked from scores that indicate most to least segregated, these cities rank among the top 10 on all dimensions.

Segregation Indices[1] for Blacks in the Twenty-five Largest MSA's

MSA's in descending order	Dissimilarity index	Exposure index	Centralization index	Relative density concentration index	Spatial proximity index
Los Angeles	0.72	0.17	0.69	0.16	2.05
New York	0.77	0.13	0.73	0.38	2.00
Chicago	0.89	0.13	0.82	0.32	2.11
Philadelphia	0.76	0.25	0.81	0.23	2.11
Detroit	0.88	0.17	0.85	0.29	2.17
Washington, DC	0.66	0.30	0.82	0.24	2.11
Houston	0.67	0.27	0.43	0.13	2.03
Boston	0.66	0.37	0.86	0.16	2.15
Atlanta	0.68	0.32	0.11	0.24	2.09
Nassau/Suffolk	0.73	0.38	—	0.04	2.05
San Bernardino/Riverside	0.38	0.52	0.88	0.00	2.12
Dallas	0.62	0.34	0.70	0.15	2.06
San Diego	0.48	0.41	0.87	0.06	2.09
Minneapolis	0.59	0.62	0.95	0.08	2.17
St. Louis	0.77	0.29	0.91	0.22	2.17
Anaheim	0.33	0.58	0.51	0.01	2.01
Baltimore	0.72	0.28	0.85	0.30	2.09
Phoenix	0.41	0.55	0.92	0.02	2.05
Oakland	0.65	0.28	0.78	0.17	2.09
Tampa	0.70	0.43	0.62	0.07	2.06
Pittsburgh	0.72	0.46	0.74	0.14	2.14
Seattle	0.52	0.58	0.91	0.05	2.12
Miami	0.87	0.17	0.84	0.27	1.99
Cleveland	0.86	0.18	0.89	0.27	2.16
Newark	0.81	0.18	0.90	0.37	2.11

[1] See text for definitions of these indices.

Source: U.S. Bureau of the Census, "Census of Population and Housing, 1990: Summary Tape File 3A," tract-level data, U.S. Bureau of the Census, Washington, D.C., 1991 [machine-readable data files].

Segregation Indices[1] for Hispanic Whites in the Twenty-five Largest MSA's

MSA's in descending order	Dissimilarity index	Exposure index	Centralization index	Relative density concentration index	Spatial proximity index
Los Angeles	0.53	0.23	0.72	0.52	2.00
New York	0.55	0.26	0.77	0.35	2.02
Chicago	0.66	0.42	0.79	0.17	2.09
Philadelphia	0.55	0.44	0.73	0.06	2.07
Detroit	0.44	0.75	0.68	0.03	2.00
Washington, DC	0.37	0.58	0.76	0.09	2.08
Houston	0.47	0.42	0.40	0.20	2.03
Boston	0.48	0.60	0.78	0.12	2.09
Atlanta	0.33	0.70	0.17	0.07	2.05
Nassau/Suffolk	0.36	0.68	—	0.05	2.02
San Bernardino/Riverside	0.34	0.51	0.81	0.19	1.99
Dallas	0.46	0.50	0.75	0.11	2.04
San Diego	0.40	0.48	0.84	0.06	2.00
Minneapolis	0.37	0.83	0.87	0.05	2.08
St. Louis	0.31	0.85	0.68	0.03	1.99
Anaheim	0.49	0.44	0.62	0.23	2.03
Baltimore	0.34	0.75	0.61	0.02	1.95
Phoenix	0.45	0.55	0.90	-0.07	2.02
Oakland	0.32	0.51	0.61	0.08	1.99
Tampa	0.44	0.71	0.53	-0.00	2.07
Pittsburgh	0.42	0.88	0.54	0.02	2.04
Seattle	0.21	0.82	0.82	0.02	2.01
Miami	0.51	0.23	0.80	0.48	1.99
Cleveland	0.57	0.75	0.83	0.06	2.09
Newark	0.61	0.41	0.83	0.18	2.04

[1] See text for definitions of these indices.

Source: U.S. Bureau of the Census, "Census of Population and Housing, 1990: Summary Tape File 3A," tract-level data, U.S. Bureau of the Census, Washington, D.C., 1991 [machine-readable data files].

Detroit ranks among the top five most segregated MSA's on all dimensions except centralization. Cleveland ranks in the top five on evenness and clustering.

The indices were also computed using Hispanics as the minority group and non-Hispanic whites as the majority group. The second table presents the segregation indices for Hispanics in the 25 largest MSA's. Newark along with Chicago are among the most segregated cities for Hispanics. These cities rank among the top 10 most segregated cities on all dimensions of segregation. Chicago ranks among the top five on all dimensions except centralization and concentration. Newark ranks in the top five on all dimensions except clustering and concentration.

central city to ring. The greater the income, the greater is the tendency to move outward, and the less the tendency to move from the ring to the central city. Although rings are making net gains of all income groups, the greatest relative gains are being made at the upper income levels.

Overall circulatory movement between different metropolitan areas tends to affect all income groups equally, but in the process it enhances the income composition of metropolitan rings and reduces the income level of the central cities. The rate of mobility from metropolitan to nonmetropolitan areas tends to be greater for lower and middle income groups than for the highest. Within nonmetropolitan areas, circulatory mobility is strongly concentrated in the lower income groups.

Much has been written about the immobility of the poor, and their incapacity to use residential mobility as a tool for improving their condition. Although it has a factual basis, it can be exaggerated. Even for the lowest income levels, the annual mobility rates for moving between metropolitan areas, from nonmetropolitan to metropolitan areas or the reverse, or from central cities to their own suburbs, are impressively high; about 1/10 of the poor make a potentially status-improving move each year. Although this is considerably less than that of the middle-income groups, the reality is far from zero. On the other hand, perhaps too little is made of the mobility-suppressing effects of wealth. Wealthy people presumably are better adjusted both employment-wise and housing-wise than other groups; they also tend to fall in the older (lower-mobility) age groups; they tend to have low-mobility occupations and they tend to be home-owners (see below). For this combination of reasons they manifest a weaker than average propensity to move.

Occupation

The mobility rates for occupational groups do not have the neat patterns reported above for education and income. These data report occupation after changing residence; it is necessary to make the unsatisfactory assumption that occupation before movement was in the same general category. To the extent that there are differences, they appear to be only reflections of education and income—and not something inherent in the occupations themselves. Consequently no detailed data are provided. Among men (less among women), the two highest prestige occupational groups, managers and professionals, are considerably less locally mobile than other occupation groups and are older and better educated. At the other extreme, lowest-skilled occupations have below-average mobility. For both sexes, the exchange between central cities and metropolitan rings tends to favor the outward flow of all occupations except for men in lower status occupations. Thus, intermediate level technical, skilled, clerical, semi-skilled and service workers of varied occupations are contributing to the growth of the metropoli-

tan rings. Even more diffuse and without clear patterns are the rates of occupational mobility associated with movement between metropolitan areas, movement between metropolitan and nonmetropolitan areas and movement within nonmetropolitan areas. Managers and skilled industrial workers are less inclined to move from nonmetropolitan to metropolitan areas than are those in professional, technical, sales and service occupations.

Housing Tenure Status

Among the sharpest and most consistent mobility differentials yet discovered by researchers is that renters are far more mobile than home owners. The two right-hand columns of Table 8-21 present rates by housing tenure status. For all forms of mobility, renters are three to six times more mobile than owners. These are difficult statistics to interpret, because home ownership is a net resultant of all of the variables and differentials discussed above including age, race-ethnicity, education, income, and occupation, in addition to consumer housing preferences. Home ownership is perhaps more an effect of the mobility process (successful social and economic adaptation) than an 'anchor' discouraging further mobility. An important pending research problem is to disentangle the effect on mobility of home ownership from the other variables with which it is so highly correlated.

Numbers and National Origins of Immigrants

Data on total immigration have been included in preceding tables without detail on numbers from each country of origin. Table 8-22 provides detail for legally admitted persons for the two decades 1971-80 and 1981-90, and for each of the 5 years between 1989 and 1993. The 904,292 legal immigrants of 1993 came from more than 100 nations; almost every nation in the world with 1 million inhabitants or more is represented in the table.

During the 1980's, the annual volume of immigration almost doubled, and has risen precipitously since. During the 1990's the U.S. is annually legally admitting more persons per year than at any time since 1905-14, the period of great exodus from Italy, Russia, and other nations of Southern and Eastern Europe. For many nations there are extraordinary peaks and for most nations considerable fluctuation in number of arrivals. This reflects unstable or unusually unfavorable political, economic, and social conditions in the country of origin, as well as the state of the U.S. economy. These statistics are partly fictitious, reflecting the ex post facto 'amnesty' legalization of illegal immigrants during 1989-91.

Although numerically the largest, Mexico contributes a little more than 1/8 of the total legal new residents. Several other Latin American countries less seldom mentioned (Dominican Republic, Haiti, El Salvador, Guate-

Table 8-22. Migrants by Country of Birth: Decades 1971-1980 and 1981-1990, and Years 1989-1993[1]

Country of birth	Thousands of persons		Persons				
	1971-1980	1981-1990	1989	1990	1991	1992	1993
All countries	4,493	7,338	1,090,924	1,536,483	1,827,167	973,977	904,292
Europe	801	706	82,891	112,401	135,234	145,392	158,254
Albania	—	—	71	78	142	682	1,400
Austria	—	—	501	675	589	701	549
Belgium	—	—	548	682	525	780	657
Bulgaria	—	—	265	428	623	1,049	1,029
Czechoslovakia	—	—	992	1,412	1,156	1,181	1,000
Denmark	—	—	593	666	601	764	735
Finland	—	—	325	369	333	525	544
France	18	23	2,598	2,849	2,450	3,288	2,864
Germany	66	70	6,708	7,388	6,509	9,888	7,312
Greece	94	29	2,491	2,742	2,079	1,858	1,884
Hungary	—	—	1,193	1,655	1,534	1,304	1,091
Ireland	14	33	6,961	10,333	4,767	12,226	13,590
Italy	130	33	2,910	3,287	2,619	2,592	2,487
Latvia	—	—	57	45	86	419	668
Lithuania	—	—	63	67	157	353	529
Netherlands	—	—	1,193	1,424	1,283	1,586	1,430
Norway	—	—	482	524	486	665	608
Poland	44	97	15,101	20,537	19,199	25,504	27,846
Portugal	105	40	3,758	4,035	4,524	2,748	2,081
Romania	18	39	4,573	4,647	8,096	6,500	5,601
Soviet Union, former	43	84	11,128	25,524	56,980	43,614	58,571
Armenia	—	—	—	—	—	6,145	6,287
Azerbaijan	—	—	—	—	—	1,640	2,943
Belarus	—	—	—	—	—	3,233	4,702
Moldova	—	—	—	—	—	1,705	2,646
Russia	—	—	—	—	—	8,857	12,079
Ukraine	—	—	—	—	—	14,383	18,316
Uzbekistan	—	—	—	—	—	1,712	2,664
Other republics	—	—	—	—	—	1,286	1,565
Unknown republics	—	—	—	—	—	4,653	7,369
Spain	30	16	1,550	1,886	1,849	1,631	1,388
Sweden	—	—	1,078	1,196	1,080	1,463	1,393
Switzerland	—	—	788	845	696	1,023	972
United Kingdom	124	142	14,090	15,928	13,903	19,973	18,783
Yugoslavia	42	19	2,496	2,828	2,713	2,604	2,809
Other Europe	—	—	378	351	255	471	433
Asia	1,634	2,817	312,149	338,581	358,533	356,955	358,047
Afghanistan	2	27	3,232	3,187	2,879	2,685	2,964
Bangladesh	—	—	2,180	4,252	10,676	3,740	3,291
Burma	—	—	1,170	1,120	946	816	849
Cambodia	8	117	6,076	5,179	3,251	2,573	1,639
China	203	389	46,246	46,966	46,299	55,251	79,907
Mainland	203	389	32,272	31,815	33,025	38,907	65,578
Taiwan	—	—	13,974	15,151	13,274	16,344	14,329
Hong Kong	48	63	9,740	9,393	10,427	10,452	9,161
India	177	262	31,175	30,667	45,064	36,755	40,121
Indonesia	—	—	1,513	3,498	2,223	2,916	1,767

Table 8-22. Migrants by Country of Birth: Decades 1971-1980 and 1981-1990, and Years 1989-1993[1] (continued)

Country of birth	Thousands of persons		Persons				
	1971-1980	1981-1990	1989	1990	1991	1992	1993
Iran	46	155	21,243	24,977	19,569	13,233	14,841
Iraq	23	20	1,516	1,756	1,494	4,111	4,072
Israel	27	36	4,244	4,664	4,181	5,104	4,494
Japan	48	43	4,849	5,734	5,049	11,028	6,908
Jordan	30	33	3,921	4,449	4,259	4,036	4,741
Korea	272	339	34,222	32,301	26,518	19,359	18,026
Kuwait	—	—	710	691	861	989	1,129
Laos	23	146	12,524	10,446	9,950	8,696	7,285
Lebanon	34	42	5,716	5,634	6,009	5,838	5,465
Macau	—	—	246	301	267	320	334
Malaysia	—	—	1,506	1,867	1,860	2,235	2,026
Pakistan	31	61	8,000	9,729	20,355	10,214	8,927
Philippines	360	495	57,034	63,756	63,596	61,022	63,457
Saudi Arabia	—	—	381	518	552	584	616
Singapore	—	—	566	620	535	774	798
Sri Lanka	—	—	757	976	1,377	1,081	1,109
Syria	13	21	2,675	2,972	2,837	2,940	2,933
Thailand	44	64	9,332	8,914	7,397	7,090	6,654
Turkey	19	21	2,007	2,468	2,528	2,488	2,204
Vietnam	180	401	37,739	48,792	55,307	77,735	59,614
Yemen	—	—	966	1,945	1,547	2,056	1,793
Other Asia	—	—	663	809	720	834	922
North America	1,645	3,125	607,398	957,558	1,210,981	384,047	301,380
Canada	115	119	12,151	16,812	13,504	15,205	17,156
Mexico	637	1,653	405,172	679,068	946,167	213,802	126,561
Caribbean	760	893	88,932	115,351	140,139	97,413	99,438
Antigua-Barbados	—	—	979	1,319	944	619	554
Bahamas	—	—	861	1,378	1,062	641	686
Barbados	21	17	1,616	1,745	1,460	1,091	1,184
Cuba	277	159	10,046	10,645	10,349	11,791	13,666
Dominica	—	—	748	963	982	809	683
Dominican Republic	148	252	26,723	42,195	41,405	41,969	45,420
Grenada	—	—	1,046	1,294	979	848	827
Haiti	59	140	13,658	20,324	47,527	11,002	10,094
Jamaica	142	214	24,523	25,013	23,828	18,915	17,241
St. Kitts and Nevis	—	—	795	896	830	626	544
St. Lucia	—	—	709	833	766	654	634
St. Vincent	—	—	892	973	808	687	657
Trinidad and Tobago	62	40	5,394	6,740	8,407	7,008	6,577
Other Caribbean	—	—	942	1,033	792	753	1,769
Central America	132	459	101,034	146,202	111,093	57,558	58,162
Belize	—	—	2,217	3,867	2,377	1,020	1,035
Costa Rica	—	—	1,985	2,840	2,341	1,480	1,368
El Salvador	34	215	57,878	80,173	47,351	26,191	26,818
Guatamala	26	88	19,049	32,303	25,527	10,521	11,870
Honduras	17	50	7,593	12,024	11,451	6,552	7,306
Nicaragua	13	44	8,830	11,562	17,842	8,949	7,086
Panama	23	29	3,482	3,433	4,204	2,845	2,679

Table 8-22. Migrants by Country of Birth: Decades 1971-1980 and 1981-1990, and Years 1989-1993[1] (continued)

Country of birth	Thousands of persons		Persons				
	1971-1980	1981-1990	1989	1990	1991	1992	1993
Other North America	—	—	109	125	78	69	63
South America	284	456	58,926	85,819	79,934	55,308	53,921
Argentina	25	26	3,301	5,437	3,889	3,877	2,824
Bolivia	—	—	1,805	2,843	3,006	1,510	1,545
Brazil	14	24	3,332	4,191	8,133	4,755	4,604
Chile	18	23	3,037	4,049	2,842	1,937	1,778
Colombia	78	124	15,214	24,189	19,702	13,201	12,819
Ecuador	50	56	7,532	12,476	9,958	7,286	7,324
Guyana	48	95	10,789	11,362	11,666	9,064	8,384
Paraguay	—	—	529	704	538	514	668
Peru	29	64	10,175	15,726	16,237	9,868	10,447
Uruguay	—	—	948	1,457	1,161	716	568
Venezuela	—	—	2,099	3,142	2,622	2,340	2,743
Other South America	—	—	165	243	180	240	217
Africa	92	192	25,166	35,893	36,179	27,086	27,783
Algeria	—	—	230	302	269	407	360
Cameroon	—	—	187	380	452	236	262
Cape Verde	—	—	1,118	907	973	757	936
Egypt	26	31	3,717	4,117	5,602	3,576	3,556
Ethiopia	—	27	3,389	4,336	5,127	4,602	5,276
Ghana	—	—	2,045	4,466	3,330	1,867	1,604
Kenya	—	—	910	1,297	1,185	953	1,065
Liberia	—	—	1,175	2,004	1,292	999	1,050
Libya	—	—	210	268	314	286	343
Morocco	—	—	984	1,200	1,601	1,316	1,176
Nigeria	9	35	5,213	8,843	7,912	4,551	4,448
Senegal	—	—	141	537	869	337	178
Sierra Leone	—	—	939	1,290	951	693	690
Somalia	—	—	228	277	458	500	1,088
South Africa	—	—	1,899	1,990	1,854	2,516	2,197
Sudan	—	—	272	306	679	675	714
Tanzania	—	—	507	635	500	352	426
Uganda	—	—	393	674	538	437	415
Zimbabwe	—	—	230	272	261	296	308
Other Africa	—	—	1,379	1,792	2,012	1,730	1,691
Other countries	37	42	4,360	6,182	6,236	5,169	4,902
Australia	14	14	1,546	1,754	1,678	2,238	2,320
Fiji	—	—	968	1,353	1,349	807	854
New Zealand	—	—	789	829	793	967	1,052
Tonga	—	—	646	1,375	1,685	703	348
Other Oceania	—	—	411	871	731	454	328
Not reported	—	—	34	49	70	18	5

[1] Data refer to fiscal years, October 1 to September 30.

Source: U.S. Immigration and Naturalization Serivce, "Statistical Yearbook of the Immigration and Naturalization Service, 1994 and 1993," U.S. Government Printing Office, Washington, D.C., 1995 and 1994, Tables 2, 7, and 8.

Table 8-23. Immigration, by World Region of Last Residence: Decades 1821-1991

Decade	All countries	Europe	Asia	Canada	Mexico	Caribbean	Central America	South America	Africa	Oceania	Not specified
Number of persons											
1821 to 1830	143,439	98,797	30	2,277	4,817	3,834	105	531	16	2	33,030
1831 to 1840	599,125	495,681	55	13,624	6,599	12,301	44	856	54	9	69,902
1841 to 1850	1,713,251	1,597,442	141	41,723	3,271	13,528	368	3,579	55	29	53,115
1851 to 1860	2,598,214	2,452,577	41,538	59,309	3,078	10,660	449	1,224	210	158	29,011
1861 to 1870	2,314,824	2,065,141	64,759	153,878	2,191	9,046	95	1,397	312	214	17,791
1871 to 1880	2,812,191	2,271,925	124,160	383,640	5,162	13,957	157	1,128	358	10,914	790
1881 to 1890	5,246,613	4,735,484	69,942	393,304	1,913	29,042	404	2,304	857	12,574	789
1891 to 1900	3,687,564	3,555,352	74,862	3,311	971	33,066	549	1,075	350	3,965	14,063
1901 to 1910	8,795,386	8,056,040	323,543	179,226	49,642	107,548	8,192	17,280	7,368	13,024	33,523
1911 to 1920	5,735,811	4,321,887	247,236	742,185	219,004	123,424	17,159	41,899	8,443	13,427	1,147
1921 to 1930	4,107,209	2,463,194	112,059	924,515	459,287	74,899	15,769	42,215	6,286	8,726	228
1931 to 1940	528,431	347,566	16,595	108,527	22,319	15,502	5,861	7,803	1,750	2,483	25
1941 to 1950	1,035,039	621,147	37,028	171,718	60,589	49,725	21,665	21,831	7,367	14,551	142
1951 to 1960	2,515,479	1,325,727	153,249	377,952	299,811	123,091	44,751	91,628	14,092	12,976	12,491
1961 to 1970	3,321,677	1,123,492	427,642	413,310	453,937	470,213	101,330	257,940	28,954	25,122	93
1971 to 1980	4,493,314	800,368	1,588,178	169,939	640,294	741,126	134,640	295,741	80,779	41,242	12
1981 to 1990	7,338,062	761,550	2,738,157	156,938	1,655,843	872,051	468,088	461,847	176,893	45,205	1,032
Percent distribution											
1821 to 1830	100.0	68.9	...	1.6	3.4	2.7	0.1	0.4	...	...	23.0
1831 to 1840	100.0	82.7	...	2.3	1.1	2.1	...	0.1	...	...	11.7
1841 to 1850	100.0	93.2	...	2.4	0.2	0.8	...	0.2	...	...	3.1
1851 to 1860	100.0	94.4	1.6	2.3	0.1	0.4	...	...	...	...	1.1
1861 to 1870	100.0	89.2	2.8	6.6	0.1	0.4	...	0.1	...	0.4	0.8
1871 to 1880	100.0	80.8	4.4	13.6	0.2	0.5	...	...	...	0.4	...
1881 to 1890	100.0	90.3	1.3	7.5	...	0.6	...	...	...	0.2	...
1891 to 1900	100.0	96.4	2.0	0.1	...	0.9	...	...	...	0.1	0.4
1901 to 1910	100.0	91.6	3.7	2.0	0.6	1.2	0.1	0.2	0.1	0.1	0.4
1911 to 1920	100.0	75.3	4.3	12.9	3.8	2.2	0.3	0.7	0.1	0.2	...
1921 to 1930	100.0	60.0	2.7	22.5	11.2	1.8	0.4	1.0	0.2	0.2	...
1931 to 1940	100.0	65.8	3.1	20.5	4.2	2.9	1.1	1.5	0.3	0.5	...
1941 to 1950	100.0	60.0	3.6	16.6	5.9	4.8	2.1	2.1	0.7	1.4	...
1951 to 1960	100.0	52.7	6.1	15.0	11.9	4.9	1.8	3.6	0.6	0.5	0.5
1961 to 1970	100.0	33.8	12.9	12.4	13.7	14.2	3.1	7.8	0.9	0.8	...
1971 to 1980	100.0	17.8	35.3	3.8	14.2	16.5	3.0	6.6	1.8	0.9	...
1981 to 1990	100.0	10.4	37.3	2.1	22.6	11.9	6.4	6.3	2.4	0.6	...

Source: U.S. Immigration and Naturalization Serivce, "Statistical Yearbook of the Immigration and Naturalization Service, 1993," U.S. Government Printing Office, Washington, D.C., 1994, Table 4.

mala, Colombia, Peru, Honduras, Nicaragua) combine to contribute Spanish-speaking immigrants equal to legal arrivals from Mexico. Asia contributes the largest number, and most U.S. migration experts predict long-term and sustained political, economic, and forced-entry pressures for immigration from India, China, Philippines, Indonesia, Bangladesh, Pakistan, Vietnam, Laos and others with dense and rapidly growing populations. And migration from all of the populous nations of Europe still is substantial, especially from nations which formerly were a part of the Soviet Union or the Eastern Europe nations which it dominated. Expanding international trade may stimulate the flow of Europeans and Americans with special qualifications to and from the U.S. Finally, immigration from selected nations in sub-Sahara Africa (Ethiopia, Nigeria, South Africa, Ghana, Kenya, Liberia, Somalia) and from Arab North Africa and Middle East nations (Iran, Iraq, Israel, Jordan, Syria, Lebanon, Egypt, Turkey, Morocco) is sizable, and may increase in future years, once the phase of "colonization" and routinization of flow has been institutionalized for each of these populous and very rapidly growing nationalities.

In addition to these legally admitted entrants, there is a large volume of undocumented (illegal) immigration, for which there are differing estimates. By no means is illegal entry limited to Mexico—it is multi-national; it is driven by intense motivation, and aided and guided by organized skill and creativity in circumventing immigration control agencies. Table 8-23 provides a historical summary backdrop against which to contrast recent and current developments. For each decade since 1821 it reports the volume of legal immigration from major world regions, and from adjoining nations. The accompanying percent distributions reveal how the nationality/ethnic composition of the U.S. population is evolving from European dominance toward being more representative of the entire planet.

Major changes to U.S. laws regulating migration were made in 1965, 1978, 1986, and 1990. The objectives of these laws were to replace an old quota system, which practically excluded nationalities not already residing in the country, with a more equitable system, while regulating the formerly little-restricted in-flow of persons from other nations of the Western Hemisphere. Unforeseen and undesired consequences of each of the first three of these laws have necessitated revisions. The 1986 law, expanded in 1989, granted amnesty and residence rights to almost three million accumulated resident aliens, while authorizing fines and other punishment (with limited enforcement mechanism) for employers who knowingly hire undocumented aliens. It placed emphasis on employability skills and reunification of families. The 1990 law attempts to limit what appears to be excessive use of the family-reunification provisions and strengthen employment skills provisions. Periodically Congress has passed

emergency laws providing humanitarian asylum or temporary haven for political refugees and special emergencies such as fugitives from wars completed in Korea, Vietnam, and El Salvador; invasions of boat-people from Vietnam, Cuba and Haiti; suppression of democracy activists in China, Guatemala, Nicaragua; and others. Each had the effect of temporarily swelling immigration numbers for particular countries in particular years. Similar future actions should be expected, as well as compromises of immigration controls as terms of future treaties and pacts aimed at establishing expanded common markets and promoting freer worldwide trade.

By the end of 1991, the authorized ex post facto adjustments and major temporary asylum actions were largely completed. Hence, the data for 1992 and 1993 reflect what may be a typical 'mix' of nationalities and total number of legal entrants in the near future, pending new laws and the strength of efforts to enforce them. Since the volume of attempted illegal immigration tends to vary inversely with the ease of legal immigration, many anticipate that the total volume of immigration will not level off at legally imposed levels, but continue to rise. With the estimated average 'success ratio' of a planned attempted illegal entry standing at two successful entries for every apprehension (0.67), those willing to make a second effort if the first one does not succeed have a 9-out-of-10 chance of crossing a border successfully. Once here, the chances of finding employment or public dependency support better than in the country of origin seem to be of about the same magnitude. Even after the amnesties and new more punitive legislation, an estimated 4.0 to 5.0 million undocumented persons resided in the United States in 1995, fueled in part by chronic economic crises and political upheaval in Mexico and elsewhere. Together these changes and trends indicate that during the 1990's immigration policy and immigration numbers are in a state of flux. Recent changes have been, and future trends will be, shaped by migration laws, the success of their enforcement, and the cooperation of other nations.

Effects of Immigration

For more than a century, the implicit or explicit argument for immigration restriction has been to reserve jobs for citizens. Both theory and empirical research between 1940 and 1980 concluded that the groups which suffer from immigration are low income native Americans; it suspends or slows progress toward less unequal distribution of income. More recent research tends to find that immigrants have been absorbed into the American labor market with little adverse effect on natives, while acknowledging short-run adverse effects for low income groups and areas of entry. Much of it claims that in the long run the total economy benefits sufficiently to offset this temporary suffering. Labor unions and representatives of low income minority groups long have been most vociferous in opposing increasing immigration. Immigration, both legal and illegal, is a major issue in national, state, and local politics and elections, with views strongly held on all sides—especially in the metropolises and border areas which are leading 'ports of entry.'

Bibliography

Acevedo, Dolores, and Espenshade, Thomas J. "Implications of a North American Free Trade Agreement for Mexican Migration into the United States." Population and Development Review 18 (1992): 729-44.

Alperovich, Gershon, Bergsman, Joel, and Ehemann, Christian. "An Econometric Model of Migration between U. S. Metropolitan Areas." Urban Studies 14 (1977): 135-45.

Bartel, Ann P. "Where Do the New U.S. Immigrants Live?" Journal of Labor Economics (1989): 371-91.

Beale, Calvin L., and Fugitt, Glenn V. "The New Pattern of Nonmetropolitan Change." In Social Demography. Karl E. Taeuber, Larry Bumpass, and James A. Sweet (eds.). New York: Academic Press, 1978.

Belanger, Alain, and Rogers, Andrei. "The Internal Migration and Spatial Redistribution of the Foreign-Born Population in the United States: 1965-70 and 1975-80." International Migration Review 26 (1992): 1342-69.

Biafora, Frank A., and Longino, Jr., Charles F. "Elderly Hispanic Migration in the United States." Journal of Gerontology 45 (1990): 212-19.

Biggar, J.C. The Graying of the Sunbelt: A Look at the Impact of the U.S. Elderly Migration. Washington, D.C.: Population Reference Bureau, 1984.

Bogue, Donald J. "A Migrant's Eye View of the Costs and Benefits of Migration to a Metropolis." In Internal Migration: A Comparative Perspective. Alan A. Brown and Egon Neuberger (eds.). New York: Academic Press, 1977.

Bogue, Donald J. (ed.). "Spatial Mobility and Migration Research." Ch. 14 in Readings in Population Research Methodology. Donald J. Bogue, Eduardo E. Arriaga, and Douglas L. Anderton (eds.). Chicago: Social Development Center, 1993.

Bohland, J. R., and Rowles, G. D. "The Significance of Elderly Migration to Changes in Elderly Population Concentration in the United States: 1960-1980." Journal of Gerontology: Social Sciences 43 (1988): 145-52.

Borjas, George J., Bronars, Stephen G., and Trejo, Stephen . "Self-Selection and Internal Migration in the United States." Journal of Urban Economics 32 (1992): 159-85.

Borjas, George J., and Freeman, Richard. Immigration and the Work Force. Chicago: University of Chicago Press, 1992.

Bowles, Gladys K., Beale, Calvin L., and Lee, Everett S. Net Migration of the Population, 1969-70, by Age, Sex, and Color. Washington, D.C.: U.S. Government Printing Office, 1975.

Burr, Jeffrey A., Potter, Lloyd B., Galle, Omer R. ,and Fossett, Mark A. "Migration and Metropolitan Opportunity Structures: A Demographic Response to Racial Inequality." Social Science Research 21 (1992): 380-405.

Buttrick, John. "Migration Between Canada and the United States, 1970-85: Some New Estimates." International Migration Review 26(4) (Winter 1992): 1448-56.

Cadwallader, Martin. Migration and Residential Mobility: Macro and Micro Approaches. Madison: University of Wisconsin Press, 1992.

Chiswick, Barry R. "Is the New Immigration Less Skilled than the Old?" Journal of Labor Economics 4 (1986): 168-92.

Clark, W.A.V. Human Migration. Beverly Hills, CA: Sage Publications, 1986.

Courgeau, Daniel. "From the Group to the Individual: What Can be Learned from Migratory Behavior." Population 49 (1994): 7-25.

Cromartie, John, and Stack, Carol B. "Reinterpretation of Black Return and Non-return Migration to the South, 1975-1980." The Geographical Review 79 (1989): 297-310.

Cushing, Brian J. "The Effect of the Social Welfare System on Metropolitan Migration in the U.S. by Income Group, Gender and Family Structure." Urban Studies 30 (1993): 325-37.

DeJong, Gordon F., and Gardner, Robert W. (eds.). Migration Decision Making. New York: Pergamon Press, 1981.

Espenshade, Thomas J. "Does the Threat of Border Apprehension Deter Undocumented U.S. Immigration?" Population and Development Review 20 (1994): 871-92, 922-25.

Filer, Randall K. "The Effect of Immigrant Arrivals on Migratory Patterns of Native Workers." In Immigration and the Work Force. George J. Borjas and Richard B. Freeman (eds.). Chicago: University of Chicago Press, 1992.

Frey, William H. "Interstate Migration and Immigration for Whites and Minorities, 1985-90: The Emergence of Multi-Ethnic States." Population Studies Center Research Report 93-297, October 1993.

_____. "Minority Suburbanization and Continued 'White Flight' in U.S. Metropolitan Areas: Assessing Findings from the 1990 Census." Research on Community Sociology 4 (1994): 15-42.

_____. "Immigration and Internal Migration 'Flight': A California Case Study." Population and Environment 16 (1995): 353-75.

Frey, William H., and Speare, Jr., Alden. "Components of Metropolitan Growth and Decline," Ch. 3 in their Regional and Metropolitan Growth and Decline in the United States. New York: Russell Sage Foundation, 1988.

Fix, Michael, and Passel, Jeffrey. Immigration and Immigrants: Setting the Record Straight. Washington, DC: The Urban Institute, 1994.

Freeman, Richard B. "Immigration from Poor to Wealthy Countries: Experience of the United States." European Economic Review 37 (1993): 443-51.

Frisbie, William P., and Poston, Jr., Dudley L. Migration in Nonmetropolitan America. Iowa City: University of Iowa Press, 1978.

Fuguitt, Glenn V. "The Nonmetropolitan Population Turnaround." Annual Review of Sociology 11 (1985): 259-290.

Galle, Omer R., and Taeuber, Karl E. "Metropolitan Migration Efficiency." Demography 9 (1972): 655-64.

Greenwood, Michael J. Migration and Economic Growth in the United States: National, Regional and Metropolitan Perspectives. New York: Academic Press, 1981.

_____. "Migration: A Review." Regional Studies 27 (1993): 295-383.

Hamilton, C. Horace. "The Negro Leaves the South." Demography 1 (1964): 275-95.

Herzog, Henry W., Schlottmann, Alan M., and Boehm, Thomas P. "Migration as Spatial Job-Search: A Survey of Empirical Findings." Regional Studies 27 (1993): 347-340.

Hing, Bill O. Asian America. Stanford, CA: Stanford University Press, 1994.

Hinze, Kenneth E. Causal Factors in the Net Migration Flow to Metropolitan Areas of the United States, 1960-70. Chicago: Community and Family Study Center, University of Chicago, 1977.

Huddle, Donald L. "Dirty Work: Are Immigrants Only Taking Jobs That the Native Underclass Does Not Want?" Population and Environment 14 (1993): 515-38.

Jasso, Guillermina, and Rosenzweig, Mark R. The New Chosen People: Immigrants in the United States. New York: Russell Sage Foundation, 1990.

Jensen, Leif. The New Immigration: Implications for Poverty and Public Assistance Utilization. New York: Greenwood Press, 1989.

Jobes, Patrick C, Stinner, William F., and Wardwell, John M. (eds.). Community, Society, and Migration: Noneconomic Migration in America. Lanham, MD: University Press of America, Inc., 1992.

Johnson, Daniel M., and Campbell, Rex. Black Migration in America: A Social Demographic History. Durham, NC: Duke University Press, 1981.

Kallan, Jeffrey E. "A Multilevel Analysis of Elderly Migration." Social Science Quarterly 74 (1993): 403-16.

Krieg, Randall G. "Black-White Regional Migration and the Impact of Education: A Multinomial Logit Analysis." Annals of Regional Science 27 (1993): 211-22.

Lee, Barrett A., Oropesa, R. S., and Kanan, James W. "Neighborhood Context and Residential Mobility." Demography 31 (1994): 249-70.

Lewis, Staughton Y. "Impacts of Immigrants on U.S. Natives' Employment and Earnings: A Summary of the Evidence." Ch. 4 in A Stone's Throw from Ellis Island: Economic Implications of Immigration to New Jersey. Thomas J. Espenshade (ed.). Lanham, MD: University Press of America, 1994.

Long, Larry. Migration and Residential Mobility in the United States. New York: Russell Sage Foundation, 1988.

Longino, Charles F., and Haas, William H. "Migration and the Rural Elderly." In Aging in Rural America. Neil Bull (ed.). California: Sage Publications, 1993.

Martin, Philip L. "The Missing Bridge: How Immigrant Networks Keep Americans out of Dirty Jobs." Population and Environment 14 (1993): 539-65.

Massey, Douglas S., and Singer, Audrey . "New Estimates of Undocumented Mexican Migration and the Probability of Apprehension." Demography 32 (1995): 203-213.

McHugh, Kevin E. "Black Migration Reversal in the United States." Geographical Review 77 (1987): 171-87.

_____. "Hispanic Migration and Population Redistribution in the United States." Professional Geographer 41 (1989): 429-39.

Miller, Ann R. "Interstate Migrants in the United States: Some Social-Economic Differences by Type of Move." Demography 14 (1977): 1-17.

_____. "Net Intercensal Migration to Large Urban Areas of the United States, 1930-40, 1940-50, 1950-60." Analytical and Technical Reports VIII. Philadelphia: Population Studies Center, University of Pennsylvania Press, 1964.

Morris, Earl W., Crull, Sue R., and Winter, Mary . "Housing Norms, Housing Satisfaction, and the Propensity to Move." Journal of Marriage and the Family 38 (1976): 309-21.

Mueller, Charles F. The Economics of Labor Migration--A Behavioral Analysis. New York: Academic Press, 1982.

Passel, Jeffrey S., and Woodrow, Karen A. "Change in the Undocumented Alien Population in the United States, 1970-1983." International Migration Review 21 (1987): 1304-23.

_____. "Change in the Undocumented Alien Population in the United States, 1979-83." International Migration Review 21 (1987): 1404-23.

Plane, David A. "Demographic Influences on Migration." Regional Studies 27 (1993): 375-83.

Porell, F. W. "Intermetropolitan Migration and Quality of Life." Journal of Regional Science 22 (1982): 137-58.

Portes, Alejandro and Rumbaut, Ruben . Immigrant America: A Portrait. Berkeley: University of California Press, 1990.

Reder, Melvin W. "The Economic Consequences of Increased Immigration." The Review of Economics and Statistics 45 (1963): 221-30.

Rogers, Andrei, Frey, William H., Rees, Philip, Speare, Alden, and Warnes, Anthony. Elderly Migration and Population Redistribution: A Comparative Study. London: Belhaven Press, 1992.

Rogers, Andrei, and Woodward, Jennifer. "The Sources of Regional Elderly Population Growth: Migration and Aging-in-Place." The Professional Geographer 40 (1988): 450-59.

Rossi, Peter H., and Schlay, A. B. "Residential Mobility and Public Policy Issues: Why Families Move Revisited." Journal of Social Issues 38 (1982): 31-54.

Rothman, Eric S., and Espenshade, Thomas J. "Fiscal Impacts of Immigration to the United States." Population Index 58 (1992): 381-415.

Russell, Sharon S., and Teitelbaum, Michael S. "International Migration and International Trade." World Bank Discussion Paper 160, 1992.

Sandefur, Gary D., and Jeon, Jiwon. "Migration, Race, and Ethnicity, 1960-1980." International Migration Review 25 (1991): 392-407.

Schachter, J., and Althaus, P. G. "Neighborhood Quality and Climate as Factors in U.S. Net Migration Patterns, 1974-76." American Journal of Economics and Sociology 41 (1981): 590-98.

Schlottmann, A. M., and Herzog, H. W. "Employment Status and the Decision to Migrate." Review of Economics and Statistics 63 (1981): 590-98.

Schnore, Leo F. "Components of Population Change in Large Metropolitan Suburbs." American Sociological Review 23 (1958): 590-98.

Serow, William J. "Determinants of Interstate Migration: Differences Between Elderly and Non-Elderly Movers." Journal of Gerontology 42 (1987): 95-100.

_____. "Unanswered Questions and New Directions in Research on Elderly Migration: Economic and Demographic Perspectives." Journal of Aging and Social Policy 4 (1992): 73-89.

Shelley, Mack C., and Koven, Steven G. "Interstate Migration: A Test of Competing Interpretations." Public Policy Journal 21 (1993): 243-61.

Shryock, Henry S., Jr. Population Mobility within the United States. Chicago: Community and Family Study Center, University of Chicago, 1964.

Sly, David F., and Tayman, Jeffrey M. "The Ecological Approach to Human Migration Re-examined." American Sociological Review 42 (1977): 783-95.

Speare, Alden Jr., Goldstein, Sidney, and Frey, William. Residential Mobility, Migration and Metropolitan Change. Cambridge, MA: Ballinger, 1975.

Spengler, J. J. "Issues and Interests in American Immigration Policy." Annals of the American Academy of Political and Social Science CCCXIV (1958): 48-50.

Stanback, Jr., Thomas M. The New Suburbanization: Challenge to the Central City. Boulder, Colorado: Westview Press, 1991.

Taeuber, Karl E., and Taeuber, Alma F. "The Changing Character of Negro Migration." American Journal of Sociology 60 (1965): 429-41.

Termote, Marc. "Causes and Economic Consequences of International Migration." International Studies 24 (1993): 51-61.

Thomas, Dorothy S. "Age and Economic Differentials in Interstate Migration." Population Index 24, 4 (1958): 313-25.

Treyz, George I., Rickman, Dan S., Hunt, Gary L., and Greenwood, Michael J. "The Dynamics of U.S. Internal Migration." Review of Economics and Statistics 75 (1993): 209-14.

Watkins, John F. "Gender and Race Differentials in Elderly Migration." Research on Aging 11 (1989): 33-52.

Wertheimer, Richard F. The Monetary Rewards of Migration within the U.S. Washington, DC: Urban Institute, 1970.

White, Michael J., and Imai, Yoshie. "The Impact of U.S. Immigration Upon Internal Migration." Population and Environment 15 (1994): 189-209.

White, Michael J., and Mueser, Peter R. "Changes in the Determinants of U. S. Population Mobility: 1940-1980." Review of Regional Studies 24 (1994): 245-64.

White, Michael J., Biddlecom, Ann E., and Guo, Shenyang. "Immigration, Naturalization, and Residential Assimilation Among Asian Americans in 1980." Social Forces 72 (1993): 93-117.

Woodrow, Karen A. "Undocumented Immigrants Living in the United States." American Statistical Association (1990): 77-82.

9

RACE, ETHNICITY AND ANCESTRY

The population of the United States is becoming increasingly diverse. The black population, our country's second largest group of citizens, constituted nearly 13 percent of the nation's population in 1994. Meanwhile, the growth rates of the Hispanic and the Asian or Pacific Islander populations are the highest among major racial and ethnic groups in the United States. Racial and ethnic diversity, however, varies considerably across selected regions of the country. Asian and Pacific Islanders, for example, are disproportionately concentrated in the western United States where they constitute 8 percent of the population. One half of the American Indian, Eskimo and Aleut population lives in the West. And, California's Hispanic population is projected to double between 1993 and the year 2000. Increasing racial and ethnic diversity in the United States is closely tied to an increasing geographic diversity of the population.

Because the increasing diversity of the United States population is both a basic population feature and important in many social respects, other chapters address many trends in racial composition and the full range of demographic behaviors within racial or ethnic groups. The present chapter does not repeat these emphases. Instead, this chapter focuses upon further detail concerning the composition of the population and additional information on the diversity of the population with respect to ethnicity and ancestry. While this chapter presents further detail on the diversity of the United States population it is important to remember that the categories provided for self- identification of race, ethnicity and ancestry by the census are themselves groupings of populations with considerable further diversity. Race, ethnicity and ancestry groups all span different mixes of national origin, cultures, socioeconomic strata, etc. Intermarriage, multiple ancestry and simple differences in self-identification all con-

found the identification of such groups. One important additional dimension of diversity, however, is ascertainable using census data. The geographic dispersion of various populations throughout the United States has created locally unique population diversity. This chapter also emphasizes the distribution of various population groups throughout the country and geographic patterns of population diversity which result from these residential patterns.

An Historical Overview of Population Diversity

Only a small proportion of the population of the United States is comprised of indigenous peoples and their ancestors. Native populations were rapidly displaced and decimated by the European invasion of the North American continent. Throughout the subsequent history of this nation the population has been largely comprised of European immigrants and their descendants. Approximately 80.9% of the 1990 United States population identified themselves as white (see Table 1-4). That percentage is nearly the same as over two hundred years earlier in 1790 when 80.7% of the population was classified as white. The composition of this white population has, however, changed considerably over the country's history and is one subject of the present chapter.

Because most of the early colonies were initially founded as slave holding societies, the percentage of the United States population which is black, or African-American, has also been substantial throughout the country's history and remains so (see Figure 9-1). When the nation was founded, and for its first half-century, almost one resident in five was black (preponderantly slaves). When the importation of slaves was forbidden and as the floodgates of immigration from Europe were opened further,

Chapter 9 Definitions
RACE, ETHNICITY AND ANCESTRY

Race. Data on race were derived from answers to questionnaire item 4. The concept of race as used by the Census Bureau reflects self-identification; it does not denote any clear-cut scientific definition of biological stock. The data for race represent self-classification by people according to the race with which they most closely identify. Furthermore, it is recognized that the categories of the race item include both racial and national origin or sociocultural groups. If a person could not provide a single response to the race question, he or she was asked to select, based on self-identification, the group which best described his or her racial identity. If a person could not provide a single race response, the race of the person's mother was used. If a single race could not be provided for the person's mother, the first race reported by the person was used. The racial categories used in the 1990 census data products are provided below:

White. Includes persons who indicated their race as white or reported entries such as Canadian, German, Italian, Lebanese, Near Easterner, Arab, or Polish.

Black. Includes persons who indicated their race as black or Negro or reported entries such as African American, Afro-American, Black Puerto Rican, Jamaican, Nigerian, West Indian, or Haitian.

American Indian, Eskimo, or Aleut. Includes persons who classified themselves as such in one of the following specific race categories:

American Indian. Includes persons who indicated their race as American Indian, entered the name of an Indian tribe, or reported such entries as Canadian Indian, French-American Indian, or Spanish-American Indian.

Eskimo. Includes persons who indicated their race as Eskimo or reported entries such as Arctic Slope, Inupiat, and Yupik.

Aleut. Includes persons who indicated their race as Aleut or reported entries such as Alutiiq, Egegik, and Pribilovian.

Asian or Pacific Islander. Includes persons who reported in one of the Asian or Pacific Islander groups listed on the questionnaire or who provided write-in responses such as Thai, Nepali, or Tongan.

Asian. Includes persons who identified themselves in one of the following categories listed on the questionnaire or provided write-in responses such as Cambodian, Hmong, Laotian, or Thai. In some tables, Other Asian may not be shown separately but is included in the total Asian population.

Chinese. Includes persons who indicated their race as Chinese or who identified themselves as Cantonese, Tibetan, or Chinese American. In standard census reports, persons who reported as Taiwanese or Formosan are included here with Chinese. In special reports on the Asian or Pacific Islander population, information on persons who identified themselves as Taiwanese are shown separately.

Filipino. Includes persons who indicated their race as Filipino or reported entries such as Philipino, Philipine, or Filipino American.

Japanese. Includes persons who indicated their race as Japanese, Nipponese, or Japanese American.

Asian Indian. Includes persons who indicated their race as Asian Indian or who identified themselves as Bengalese, Bharat, Dravidian, East Indian, or Goanese.

Korean. Includes persons who indicated their race as Korean or Korean American.

Vietnamese. Includes persons who indicated their race as Vietnamese or Vietnamese American.

Pacific Islander. Includes persons who indicated their race as Pacific Islander by classifying themselves into one of the following groups or identifying themselves as one of the Pacific Islander cultural groups of Polynesia, Micronesia, or Melanesia.

Hawaiian. Includes persons who indicated their race as Hawaiian, Part Hawaiian, or Native Hawaiian.

Samoan. Includes persons who indicated their race as Samoan, American Samoan, or Western Samoan.

Guamanian. Includes persons who indicated their race as Guamarian, Chamorro, or Guam.

Other Race. Includes all other persons not included in the White, Black, American Indian, Eskimo, or Aleut, and the Asian or Pacific Islander race categories described above. Persons reporting in the Other Race category and providing write-in entries such as multiracial, multiethnic, mixed, interracial, Wesort, or a Spanish/Hispanic origin group are included here.

Hispanic Origin. Data on Hispanic origin are derived from answers to questionnaire item 7. Persons of Hispanic origin are those who classified themselves in one of the specific Hispanic origin categories listed on the questionnaire (Mexican, Puerto Rican, or Cuban) as well as those who indicated that they were of other Spanish/Hispanic origin. The latter refers to persons whose origins are from Spain, the Spanish-speaking countries of Central or South America, or the Dominican Republic, or they are persons of Hispanic origin identifying themselves generally as Spanish, Spanish-American, Hispanic, Hispano, Latino, and so on.

Origin can be viewed as the ancestry, nationality group, lineage, or country of birth of the person or the person's parents or ancestors before their arrival in the United States. Persons of Hispanic origin may be of any race. If a person could not provide a single origin response, he or she was asked to select, based on self-identification, the group which best described his or her origin or descent. If a person could not provide a single group, the origin of the person's mother was used. If a single group could not be provided for the person's mother, the first origin reported by the person was used.

The 1990 data on Hispanic origin are generally comparable with those for the 1980 census. The 1990 and 1980 census data on the Hispanic population are not directly comparable with the 1970 Spanish origin data because of overall improvements in the 1990 and 1980 censuses, better coverage of the population, improved questionnaire designs, and an effective public relations campaign by the Census Bureau.

Ancestry. Derived from answers to questionnaire item 13, the data on ancestry represent self-classification by people according to the ancestry group(s) with which they most closely identify. Ancestry refers to a person's ethnic origin or descent, "roots," heritage, or the place of birth of the person or the person's parents or ancestors before their arrival in the United States. The ancestry question allowed respondents to report one or more ancestry groups. While a large number of respondents listed a single ancestry, the majority of answers included more than one ethnic entry. Generally, only the first two responses reported were coded in 1990.

Nativity. Classification as native or foreign born, according to place of birth. The "native" category comprises persons born in the United States, Puerto Rico, or an outlying area of the United States, as well as the small number of persons born at sea or in a foreign country with at least one American parent. Persons not classifiable as "native" are classified as "foreign born."

Place of Birth. Data on place of birth were derived from answers to questionnaire item 8 in which respondents were asked to report the U.S. state, commonwealth or territory, or the foreign country where they were born. Persons born outside the United States were asked to report their place of birth according to current international boundaries. Since numerous changes in boundaries of foreign countries have occurred in the last century, some persons may have reported their place of birth in terms of countries that existed at the time of their birth or emigration, or in accordance with their own national preference.

Citizenship. Data on citizenship were derived from answers to questionnaire item 9 which identified persons as belonging to one of two categories: citizens and non-citizens. "Citizens" includes native-born persons as well as foreign-born persons who indicated that they have become naturalized.

Year of Entry. Derived from answers to questionnaire item 10. This question, "When did this person come to the United States to stay?" was asked of persons who indicated on the question on citizenship that they were not born in the United States. All persons who were born and resided outside the United States before becoming residents of the United States have a date of entry. Some of these persons are U.S. citizens by birth. To avoid any possible confusion concerning the date of entry of persons who are U.S. citizens by birth, the term "year of entry" is used instead of the term "year of immigration."

Language Spoken at Home. Data on language spoken at home were derived from the answers to questionnaire items 15a and 15b which were asked of a sample of persons born before April 1, 1985. Respondents indicated whether or not they sometimes or always spoke a language other than English at home, and if so they were asked to print the name of the non-English language in question 15b. These languages were coded into more than 380 detailed language categories which were further classified into groups.

Ability to Speak English. Persons 5 years old and over who reported that they spoke a language other than English in question 15a were also asked in question 15c to indicate their ability to speak English. The data on ability to speak English represent the person's own perception about his or her own ability or, because census questionnaires are usually completed by one household member, the responses may represent the perception of another household member.

this proportion declined by almost half. Its lowest point was reached in 1930. During the most recent half-century, higher black than white fertility, along with reduced immigration from abroad, has caused the proportion of blacks to climb back to about the proportion it was in 1790. Were it not for the continuing inflow of white immigrants from Latin America and other nations the proportion would climb more quickly.

While other minorities have been historically important to the United States, their percentage representation in the population has become demographically significant only with the dramatic rise in these groups over the past two decades. All of the racial groups tabulated by the census since 1900, other than the white and black population, have increased as a percentage of the population over the course of the twentieth century. Those classified in the American Indian, Chinese, Filipino and Other races have increased most dramatically in the past two decades.

American Indians appeared to be almost an endangered group at the close of the Civil War (1870), with only 26,000 reported in the census. The enumeration of this group at the various censuses has been erratic and, until 1960, incomplete. In recent censuses the group has increased to a more substantial size, showing phenomenal growth. The change to a self-identification method of enumerating race in 1980, when almost a doubling of the American Indian population within a decade was recorded, may have contributed to this rise. By the census of 1990 there were nearly two million persons, still less than one percent of the population, who identified themselves as American Indians.

The Chinese population entered the United States in large numbers from 1870 to 1900. Japanese immigration, with temporary interruption during World War II, was greatest from the turn of the century into the 1950s. Both Chinese and Japanese groups have increased in size at a rapid rate since World War II. The Filipino population, which began entering the nation in large numbers in the 1920s, has grown especially rapidly since 1950. And, substantial immigration of Koreans and Vietnamese has occurred primarily since 1960. In the 1990 Census there were approximately 7.3 million individuals, about 3 percent of the population, who identified themselves as Asian or Pacific Islanders.

Finally, beyond these major race and ethnicity categories, those identifying themselves as in "other" races have had the most explosive recent growth (see Figure 9-1). This growth among other groups largely reflects the increasing diversity of immigrants to the United States. Many populations have experienced substantial increases in immigration associated with recent changes throughout the world, political refugees, and the continuing desirability of the United States as a migration destination for many.

Trends toward increasing racial diversity overlap with a recent rise in ethnic population groups. The largest and most visibly increasing ethnic subgroup in the United States is the Hispanic population. Despite some change in the way the Census Bureau has identified Hispanics (see Definition Box), the number of those identified as Hispanic has more than doubled in the past two decades. Hispanics are designated as an ethnic group in the census since individuals of many different racial categories identify themselves as Hispanic. While those of Hispanic origin are tabulated by the Census Bureau as an ethnic group, many cultural groups and different national origins are represented within the Hispanic population. Table 9-1 presents the number, percentage change, percent of the United States population and sex ratios for the total Hispanic population and several major national origin groups among Hispanics. The total Hispanic population has risen from 4.5 percent of the United States population in 1970 to 9.0 percent in 1990. As Table 9-1 indicates, those of Mexican origin are the fastest increasing of the Hispanic subgroups and now constitute over half of the United States Hispanic population. As Hispanic migration from island and Central American countries has increased over the past decade, those of other Hispanic (not Mexican, Puerto Rican or Cuban) origin have increased most rapidly among the Hispanic subgroups.

Figure 9-1. Percent Composition of the United States Population: 1900 to 1990

Total Population

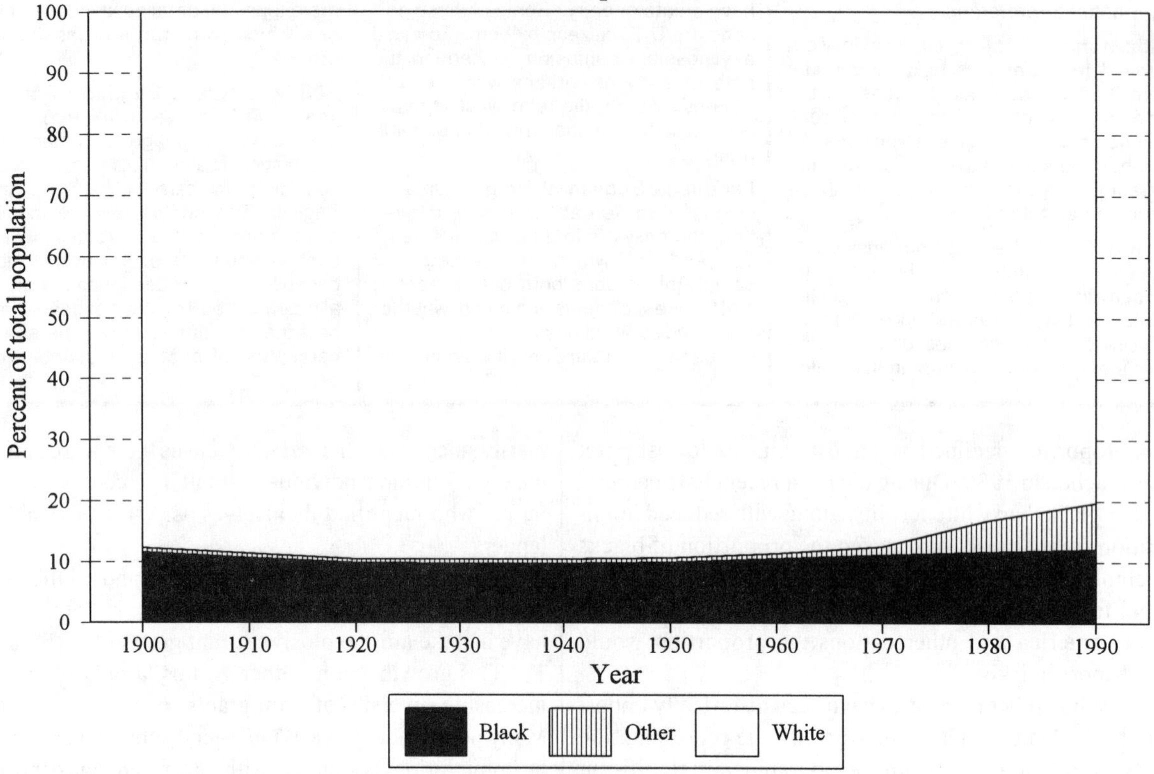

Other Races in Detail

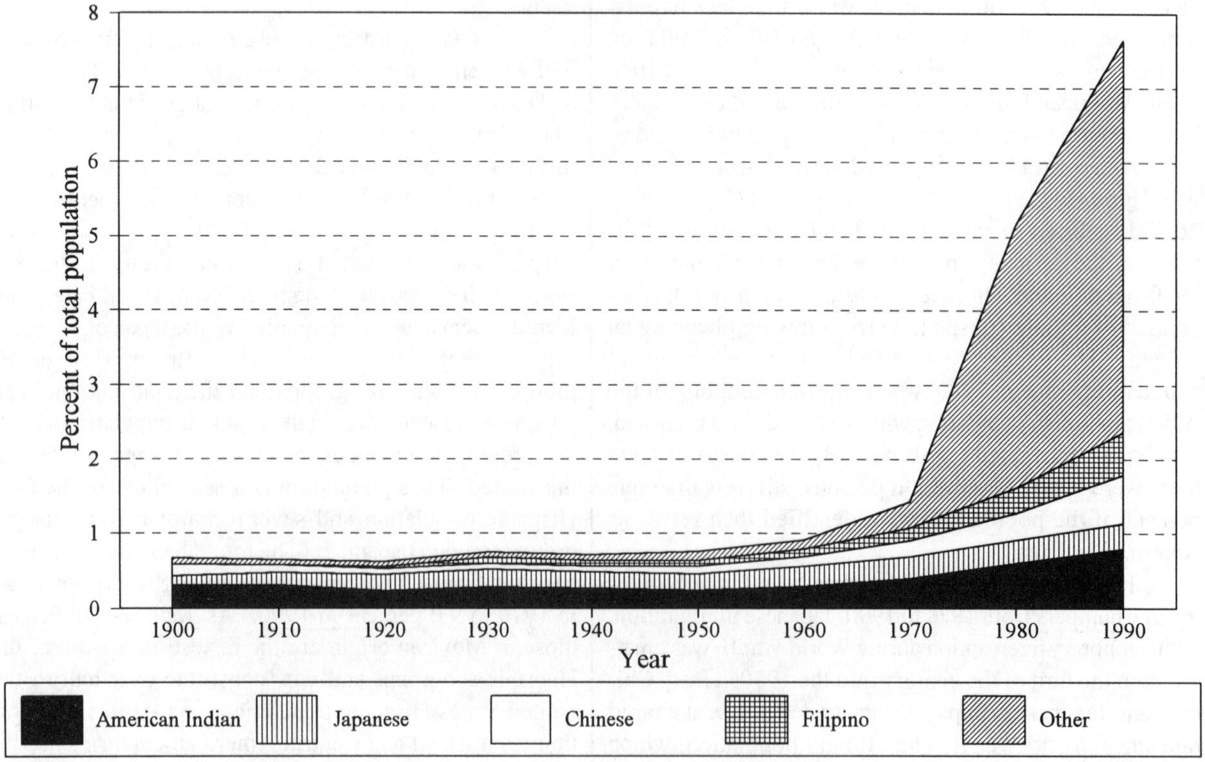

Source: 1900 to 1990 U.S. Census data.

Table 9-1. Hispanic Population, by National Origin: 1970 to 1990

Population characteristics	Total Hispanic	National origin			
		Mexican	Puerto Rican	Cuban	Other
Number, in thousands					
1990	22,354	13,496	2,728	1,044	5,086
1980	14,609	8,740	2,014	803	3,051
1970	9,073	4,532	1,429	545	2,566
Percent change					
1980-1990	53.0	54.4	35.5	30.0	66.7
1970-1980	61.0	92.9	40.9	47.3	18.9
Percent of U.S. population					
1990	9.0	5.4	1.1	0.4	2.0
1980	6.4	3.9	0.9	0.4	1.3
1970	4.5	2.2	0.7	0.3	1.3
M:F sex ratio					
1990	1.03	1.08	0.95	0.97	0.98
1980	0.99	1.03	0.95	0.91	0.93
1970	0.96	0.98	0.97	0.90	0.94

Source: U.S. Bureau of the Census, "General Population Characteristics: U.S. Summary," 1990 Census of Population, Table 24, 1980 Census of Population, Table 39, and "Special Reports, Spanish-Origin Population," 1970 Census of Population, Table 1, U.S. Government Printing Office, Washington, D.C., 1993, 1983, and 1973.

The dramatic recent growth in racial and ethnic diversity has predictably generated alarm among some elements of society. However, it is worth remembering that diversity among the white population itself has been no less the subject of similar alarmist and racist concerns in the recent past of the United States. Diversity is as clearly grounds for celebration as it may be for concern. And, despite the recent, and predictable future, growth in racial and ethnic diversity, the United States population will remain predominantly white and non-Hispanic well into the immediate future (see Chapter 1 for racial composition forecasts). Nonetheless, the political, economic and cultural consequences of increasing racial diversity will present both significant opportunities and challenges over the coming century (see Chapter 3 for a detailed discussion).

Racial and Ethnic Self-Identification

In the 1990 Census all persons were asked to classify themselves as belonging to one racial group. The resulting data therefore show how the respondents identified themselves by race, as they interpreted the census question. The fifteen different race categories used by the census (see the Definition Box for detail) are obviously not a scientific classification of distinctive, genetically determined biological stocks. They are, rather, a set of categories deemed to be important for social, economic, and administrative purposes in one or more of the fifty states. Because the 1990 Census was again primarily one of self-enumeration, and because public ideas of what constitutes categories of race probably are subject to great variation, the data may have substantial response errors. For example, many respondents who should have classified themselves as white (especially non-black Spanish-speaking) apparently regarded it as a nationality question, and when they did not find their nation of origin mentioned, simply marked "other." Similarly, some respondents appear to have interpreted the question as one of nebulous ideological affiliation in identifying themselves as "American Indian." Questions regarding ethnicity and ancestry are plagued by similar self- identification difficulties. A disproportionate number of blacks and socioeconomically disadvantaged individuals, for example, appear to have identified themselves as having American or United States ancestry.

Composition and Demographic Trends of Racial and Ethnic Groups

The basic racial composition of the United States is presented in the first chapter of this volume (see Table 1-7). The detailed age and sex composition for selected racial and ethnic groups are presented in the graphical form of population pyramids in Figure 9-2. The unique histories and sub-cultures of major racial and ethnic

Ethnic Identity in the American Indian, Eskimo, and Aleut Population

by Alison Kadlec Donta

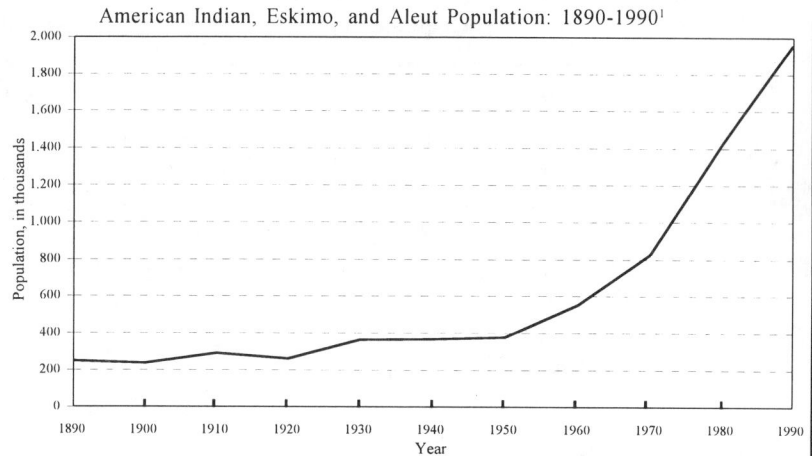

American Indian, Eskimo, and Aleut Population: 1890-1990[1]

[1] Data for 1920 are partially estimated and in 1940 the Eskimo and Aleut populations are based on 1939 counts.
Source: 1890-1990 U.S. Census data.

The American Indian, Eskimo, and Aleut population represented 0.8% of the total United States population in 1990. Of the 1,959,234 persons who identified themselves in this racial category, 95.9% were American Indian, 2.9% were Eskimo, and 1.2% self-identified as Aleut. As illustrated in the accompanying figure, the number of American Indians, Eskimos, and Aleuts has been increasing since 1890, the first census for which a complete census of this group was obtained. Between 1980 and 1990, there was a 38.0% increase in the American Indian, Eskimo, and Aleut population. The most dramatic intercensal increase was between 1970 and 1980 when there was a 71.7% increase in this segment of the population.

This increase in the American Indian, Eskimo, and Aleut population, especially since 1960, cannot be attributed only to natural increase. Other factors such as improvements in the Census Bureau enumeration procedure, greater propensity for individuals to report themselves as American Indian, and improved outreach programs and promotion campaigns by the Census Bureau have contributed to this increase. In 1960, the Census Bureau moved from a system where enumerators assigned each person a race to a system which allowed persons to self-identify according to race. This switch to self-identification is believed to have contributed significantly to the 46.4% increase in American Indian, Eskimo, and Aleut population between 1950 and 1960. After 1960, however, census racial classification procedures continued to rely on self-identification and were no longer a major explanation for the growth in this segment of the population. Instead, new expressions of identity and an ongoing process of ethnic renewal can account for some increase in the population since 1960.

Between 1960 and 1990, the American Indian, Eskimo, and Aleut population has increased by a factor of 2.5. Population growth and changing enumeration techniques alone cannot begin to account for this change. Instead, much of this growth comes as a result of "ethnic switching," where persons who previously identified themselves as non-Indian changed their race to American Indian, Eskimo, or Aleut in later censuses. This new self-identification may be explained by an ethnic renewal, either racial or symbolic, brought about by

changes in American ethnic politics since the 1960's, historical changes in federal Indian policies, and increasing American Indian political activism. The change in self-identification especially affected persons of mixed Indian heritage who may have originally been classified as non-Indian by their parents.

The changing distribution of the American Indian, Eskimo, and Aleut population also reflects this increasing propensity for previously categorized non-Indians to self-identify as Indian in later censuses. In 1930, 77% of the American Indian, Eskimo, and Aleut population lived in nine states plus the territory of Alaska. These states are considered the "old" Indian region. Since 1930, there has been a decrease in the percentage of the American Indian, Eskimo, and Aleut population which resides in this old region. In 1990, only 49.5% of that population lived in the old region. Conversely, there has been a dramatic increase in the proportion of American Indians, Eskimos, and Aleuts living in "new" Indian regions, especially in the East. There has been some out-migration from the old regions to the new regions, especially to urban centers. Again, this alone cannot explain the change; a resurgence in Indian ethnic

identity can account for much of this population redistribution over the past few decades.

The table below indicates the ten states with the largest number of American Indians, Eskimos, and Aleuts in 1990. North Carolina, New York, and Michigan are the only states east of the Mississippi. Similarly, all ten of the largest reservations are located in the West. The Navajo reservation, with 143,405 residents, is the largest reservation in the country. In 1990, 22.3% of the American Indian, Eskimo, and Aleut population lived on reservations and trust lands. Another 10.2% lived in tribal jurisdiction statistical areas, 2.7% lived in tribal designated statistical areas, 2.45% lived in Alaska Native Village statistical areas, and 62.3% of this population lived in the remainder of the United States. There are 500 recognized American Indian tribes in the United States, although not every person identifying as American Indian, Eskimo, or Aleut listed tribal affiliation. Among those who did, approximately 16% identified themselves as Cherokee. The Navajo, Chippewa, and Sioux were the next most commonly listed tribes. Most tribes had populations of less than 10,000 in 1990.

Population of the Ten Largest American Indian Tribes and Reservations and Ten States with the Largest Number of American Indians, Eskimos, and Aleuts: 1990 [numbers in thousands]

Tribe	Population	Reservation	Population	State	Population
Cherokee	308	Navajo, AZ-NM-UT[3]	143	Oklahoma	252
Navajo	219	Pine Ridge, NE-SD[3]	11	California	242
Chippewa	104	Fort Apache, AZ	10	Arizona	204
Sioux[1]	103	Gila Rive, AZ	9	New Mexico	134
Choctaw	82	Papapgo, AZ	8	Alaska	86
Pueblo	53	Rosebud, SD[3]	8	Washington	81
Apache	50	San Carlos, AZ	7	North Carolina	80
Iroquois[2]	49	Zuni Pueblo, AZ-NM	7	Texas	66
Lumbee	48	Hopi, AZ[3]	7	New York	63
Creek	44	Blackfeet, MT	7	Michigan	56

[1] Any entry with the spelling "Siouan" was miscoded to Sioux in North Carolina.
[2] Reporting and/or processing problems have affected the data for this tribe.
[3] Includes trust lands.

Source: U.S. Bureau of the Census, "We, the First Americans," U.S. Government Printing Office, Washington, D.C., 1993, Figures 2, 3, and 12.

Additional Sources

Eschbach, Karl. "Changing Identification among American Indians and Alaskan Natives." Demography 30(1993): 635-52.

Nagel, Joane. "American Indian Ethnic Renewal: Politics and the Resurgence of Identity." American Sociological Review 60(1995):947-65.

Snipp, C. Matthew. American Indians: The First of This Land. New York: Russell Sage Foundation, 1989.

Figure 9-2. Distribution of the U.S. Population, by Age, Sex, and Race-ethnicity: 1990

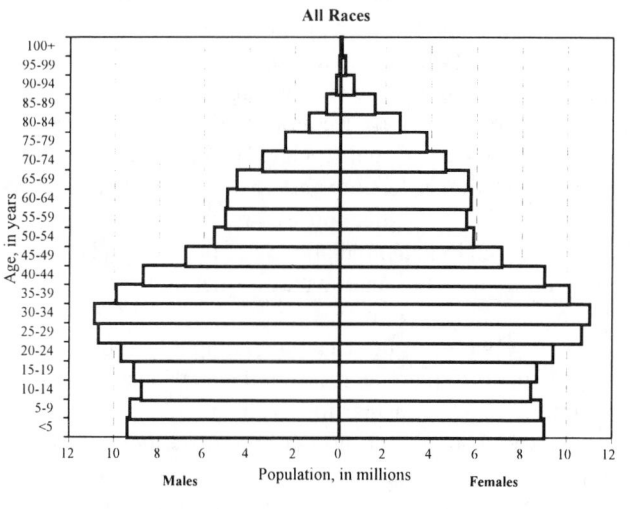

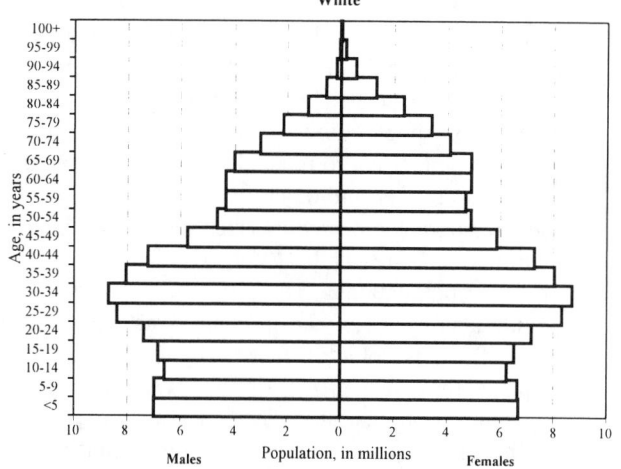

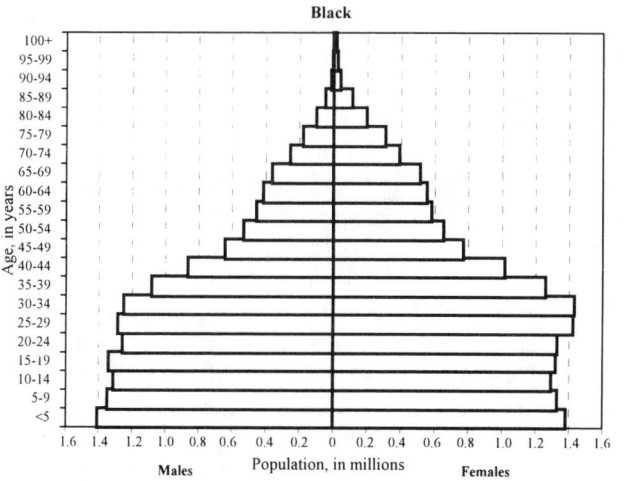

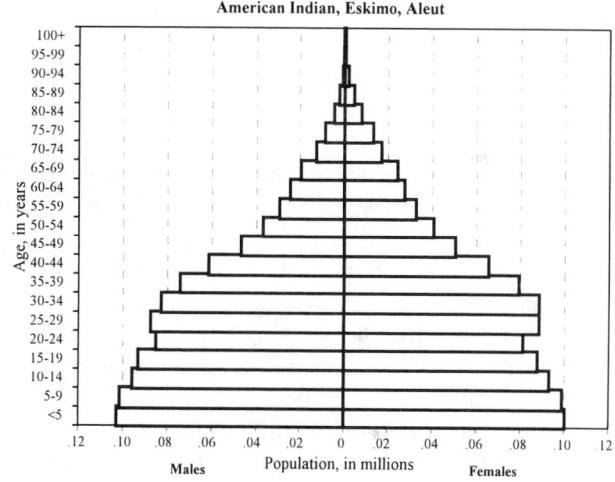

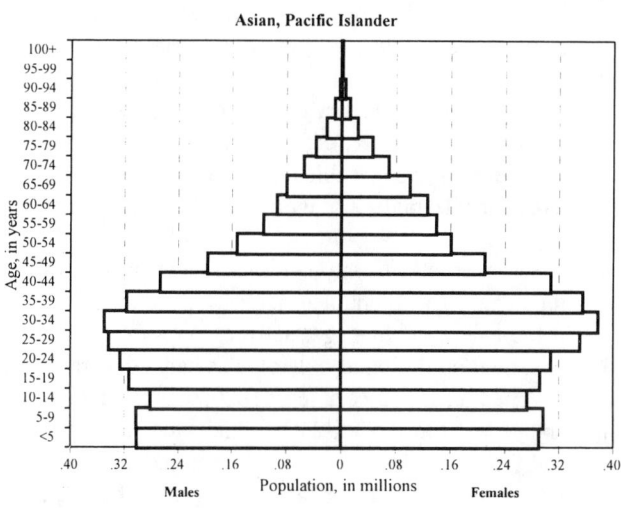

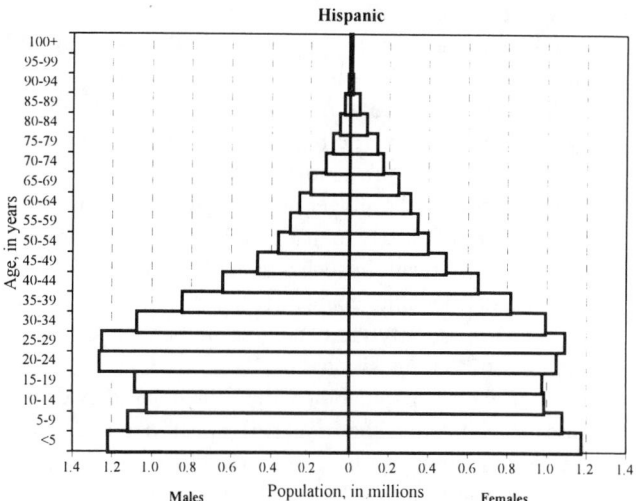

Source: 1990 U.S. Census data.

groups in the population are reflected in frequently different demographic histories and, hence, current population characteristics. These population pyramids emphasize both differences in population composition and those in recent demographic histories. Significant demographic differences, especially in age composition, clearly exist across these populations.

It is important to remember such demographic diversity (and other additional dimensions of diversity in sociodemographic behavior) when discussing the policy concerns, social research, characterizations, etc., of racial or ethnic populations. The different histories of these populations have resulted in many overlapping dimensions of demographic diversity. Higher fertility, for example, among some groups results in their having generally younger populations. The concerns of such a population (e.g. pre-schooling, school funding, child care, etc.) will likely differ from those of a population which is substantially more aged (e.g. Medicare, retirement, long term health care, etc.). And, the casual use of statistics which do not control for these differences in composition (e.g. crude unemployment rates, cross-sectional nuptiality typologies, etc.) to compare racial and ethnic groups may be misleading.

Both the white and the Asian/Pacific Islander populations show evidence of a substantial boom in the larger cohorts now entering middle ages and a clear constriction of growth in the smaller cohorts at younger age groups. However, not all groups share this population profile. This population composition is characteristic of declining fertility following the baby boom, declining mortality across cohorts, and either small levels of immigration or immigration of individuals with a composition similar to that of the population as a whole. A different population history will result in a different population composition. The age pattern observed in the population pyramids for whites and Asian or Pacific Islanders is often characterized as a population in transition from higher fertility to a more stable lower fertility population characteristic of more 'developed' countries. Such a population is also referred to as an 'aging' population due to the increasing proportion of older individuals over time.

The Asian/Pacific Islander population itself, however, has a more substantial continuing immigration at working ages and younger as is suggested by the lower percentages of elderly in that population. Higher mortality could also result in such a pattern and we must resort to the data from other chapters (see especially Chapters 4, 6 and 8) to identify the demographic behaviors responsible for this composition.

The black population of the United States evidences less of a population boom, yet still reflects declining fertility as indicated by the leveling of that population in younger age groups. The earlier boom and subsequent fertility decline, however, are less pronounced for blacks than among the white and the Asian/Pacific Islander populations. The higher mortality of blacks, and especially that of younger black males, is not so readily apparent in a simple visual comparison of population composition.

Hispanics (which, again, may belong to any of the race groups) have a somewhat younger or more recent population boom and have a continuing higher fertility as evidenced in the larger percentages of the population in infancy. Such higher fertility patterns, also characteristic of many less developed countries, are most pronounced in the American Indian population. Again, the social concerns within such a population may be markedly different from those in an aging population.

Less obvious in the changing composition of race groups is the different sex ratios among various population groups. As the proportion of the population which has survived to the older ages (where male mortality is higher) increases, the sex ratio of a population group will generally tend to decline. Conversely, higher fertility or mortality increases the proportion of the population at younger ages (where biological sex ratios favoring males predominate) and the sex ratio will tend to increase. However, the most profound effects upon sex ratio among subgroups of the United States population have been due to sex selective immigration and mortality effects.

Table 9-2 shows the historical sex ratios among racial groups. Among whites, the long unsteady decline in sex ratios this century mirrors the extension of the population's life span and declining fertility. Blacks have experienced a similar decline in this century but have had a lower sex ratio throughout the decade. A higher selective mortality of males is at least a partial explanation for this lower sex ratio among blacks. American Indians have experienced a less steady decline in sex ratios over this century and have a slightly higher sex ratio at present. Lower gains in extending life spans and higher fertility again provide some explanation. The lowest sex ratios in Table 9-2 are those for two of the Asian/Pacific Islander groups, the Japanese and Filipino. Yet these groups, and the Chinese, historically had the very highest sex ratios in the recent past due to selective migration of males into the United States labor force. During the end of the nineteenth century there were more than 25 men to every Chinese woman in the population. All three of the Asian/Pacific Islander groups in Table 9-2 have had times when there were nearly 10 males for every female in the population.

Differences in age composition across racial or ethnic groups can also be characterized by general differences in average or median ages across groups. As Table 9-3 shows, the population as a whole has had a generally increasing median age since at least 1820, with the exception of the years from 1950 to 1970 which were impacted by the baby boom. However, the white population has, with some variability, aged more dramatically than the black population over this period. The black population was actually somewhat older in 1820 and is now considerably

Table 9-2. M:F Sex Ratio of the U.S. Population, by Race: 1790 to 1990

Year	Total	White	Black	American Indian	Japanese	Chinese	Filipino	Other
1990	0.95	0.95	0.90	0.98	0.85	1.00	0.86	1.05
1980	0.95	0.95	0.90	0.98	0.85	1.02	0.93	1.03
1970	0.95	0.95	0.91	0.96	0.85	1.11	1.23	1.03
1960	0.97	0.97	0.93	1.01	0.94	1.33	1.75	1.11
1950	0.99	0.99	0.94	1.09	1.09	1.68	2.71	1.09
1940	1.01	1.01	0.95	1.06	1.19	2.25	4.57	1.09
1930	1.03	1.03	0.97	1.05	1.29	2.96	7.06	1.15
1920	1.04	1.04	0.99	1.05	1.60	4.66	4.85	1.17
1910	1.06	1.07	0.99	1.04	3.49	9.26	9.44	1.29
1900	1.05	1.05	0.99	1.02	4.87	13.85	—	1.07
1890	1.05	1.05	1.00	1.03	6.87	26.79	—	—
1880	1.04	1.04	0.98	1.05	9.57	21.07	—	—
1870	1.02	1.03	0.96	0.95	5.88	12.84	—	—
1860	1.05	1.05	1.00	1.19	—	18.58	—	—
1850	1.04	1.05	0.99	—	—	—	—	—
1840	1.04	1.05	0.99	—	—	—	—	—
1830	1.03	1.04	1.00	—	—	—	—	—
1820	1.03	1.03	1.03	—	—	—	—	—
1810	—	1.04	—	—	—	—	—	—
1800	—	1.04	—	—	—	—	—	—
1790	—	1.04	—	—	—	—	—	—

Source: U.S. Bureau of the Census, "General Population Characteristics," 1990 Census of Population, Tables 16 and 23, 1980 Census of Population, Table 40, and "Historical Statistics of the United States," Series A 91-104, U.S. Government Printing Office, Washington, D.C., 1992, 1983, and 1975.

Figure 9-3. Median Age of the U.S. Population, by Race-ethnicity: 1800-1990

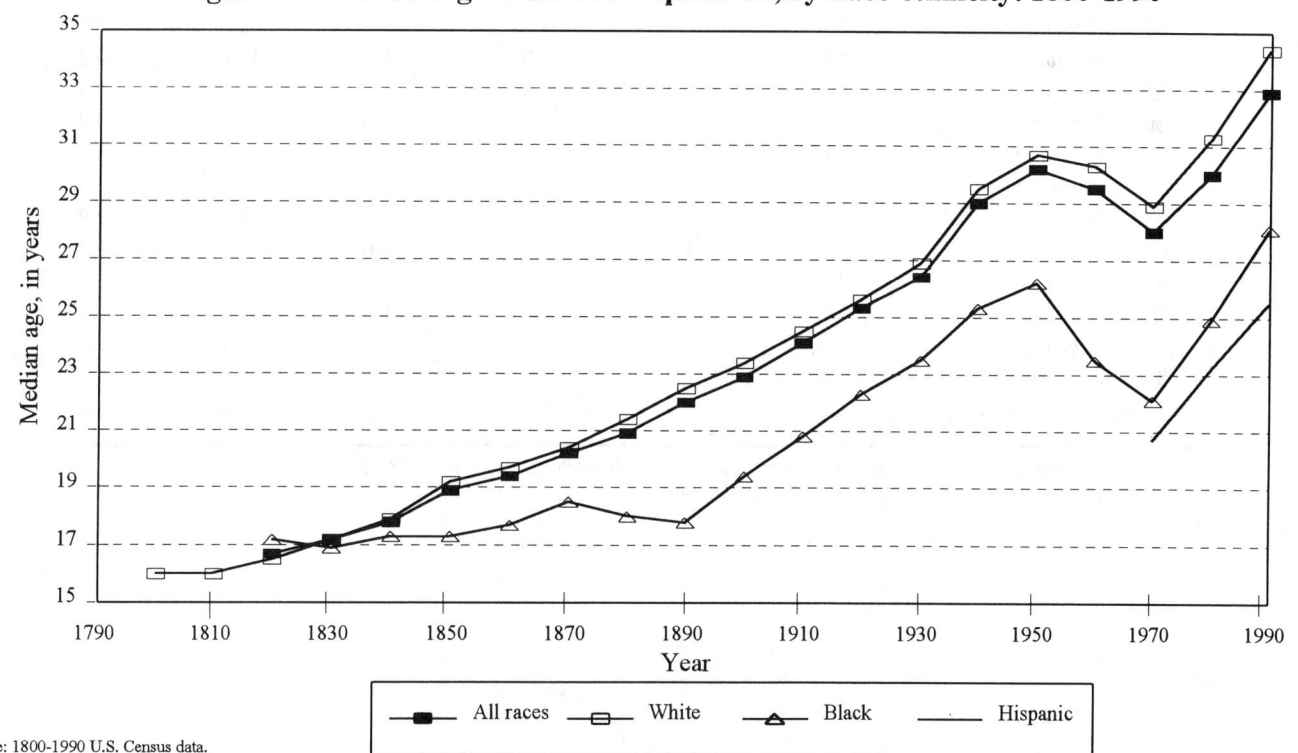

Source: 1800-1990 U.S. Census data.

Table 9-4. Age Composition of the U.S. Population, by Race-ethnicity: 1990

Age	Total	White	Black	American Indian, Eskimo, Aleut	Asian, Pacific Islander	Hispanic
Total population	248,709,873	199,686,070	29,986,060	1,959,234	7,273,662	22,354,059
Under 5 years	18,354,443	13,649,490	2,785,902	201,950	589,845	2,387,524
5 to 9 years	18,099,179	13,616,268	2,671,109	199,446	596,133	2,193,852
10 to 14 years	17,114,249	12,853,558	2,601,590	188,000	551,552	2,001,617
15 to 19 years	17,754,015	13,342,703	2,658,493	180,516	603,761	2,053,957
20 to 24 years	19,020,312	14,523,912	2,578,953	165,549	632,258	2,304,441
25 to 29 years	21,313,045	16,638,544	2,707,765	175,577	691,069	2,341,239
30 to 34 years	21,862,887	17,351,513	2,681,724	170,668	726,183	2,062,303
35 to 39 years	19,963,117	16,081,606	2,336,766	150,182	669,818	1,660,726
40 to 44 years	17,615,786	14,506,390	1,876,062	126,154	572,194	1,284,268
45 to 49 years	13,872,573	11,585,703	1,405,766	96,817	405,590	953,910
50 to 54 years	11,350,513	9,504,871	1,179,011	76,714	311,651	755,989
55 to 59 years	10,531,756	8,968,416	1,032,749	61,819	250,633	639,308
60 to 64 years	10,616,167	9,211,123	961,619	51,389	218,517	553,642
65 to 69 years	10,111,735	8,899,637	863,045	42,710	178,497	436,257
70 to 74 years	7,994,823	7,126,564	640,415	29,270	122,234	286,772
75 to 79 years	6,121,369	5,485,025	481,270	21,152	80,139	213,265
80 to 84 years	3,933,739	3,552,695	293,638	12,116	43,850	130,425
85 years and over	3,080,165	2,788,052	230,183	9,205	29,738	94,564
Percent distribution	100.0	100.0	100.0	100.0	100.0	100.0
Under 5 years	7.4	6.8	9.3	10.3	8.1	10.7
5 to 9 years	7.3	6.8	8.9	10.2	8.2	9.8
10 to 14 years	6.9	6.4	8.7	9.6	7.6	9.0
15 to 19 years	7.1	6.7	8.9	9.2	8.3	9.2
20 to 24 years	7.6	7.3	8.6	8.4	8.7	10.3
25 to 29 years	8.6	8.3	9.0	9.0	9.5	10.5
30 to 34 years	8.8	8.7	8.9	8.7	10.0	9.2
35 to 39 years	8.0	8.1	7.8	7.7	9.2	7.4
40 to 44 years	7.1	7.3	6.3	6.4	7.9	5.7
45 to 49 years	5.6	5.8	4.7	4.9	5.6	4.3
50 to 54 years	4.6	4.8	3.9	3.9	4.3	3.4
55 to 59 years	4.2	4.5	3.4	3.2	3.4	2.9
60 to 64 years	4.3	4.6	3.2	2.6	3.0	2.5
65 to 69 years	4.1	4.5	2.9	2.2	2.5	2.0
70 to 74 years	3.2	3.6	2.1	1.5	1.7	1.3
75 to 79 years	2.5	2.7	1.6	1.1	1.1	1.0
80 to 84 years	1.6	1.8	1.0	0.6	0.6	0.6
85 years and over	1.2	1.4	0.8	0.5	0.4	0.4

Source: U.S. Bureau of the Census, "General Population Characteristics: United States Summary," 1990 Census of Population, U.S. Government Printing Office, Washington, D.C., 1993, Table 16.

Table 9-5. Intercensal Percent Change in Age Groups, by Race-ethnicity: 1970-1980 and 1980-1990

	All races		White		Black		American Indian, Eskimo, Aleut[1]		Asian, Pacific Islander[2]		Hispanic	
	1980-90	1970-80	1980-90	1970-80	1980-90	1970-80	1980-90	1970-80	1980-90	1970-80	1980-90	1970-80
Total population	9.8	11.5	6.0	6.0	13.2	17.3	37.9	86.8	107.8	129.3	53.0	57.2
Under 5 years	12.3	-4.7	8.0	-12.4	14.4	0.1	35.3	63.2	101.0	119.6	43.6	42.8
5 to 9 years	8.4	-16.3	4.5	-22.9	7.2	-9.3	36.0	44.5	97.3	113.9	42.7	23.6
10 to 14 years	-6.2	-12.3	-11.1	-18.2	-2.7	-4.9	20.5	59.1	97.1	98.1	35.7	27.8
15 to 19 years	-16.1	11.0	-21.3	3.6	-10.9	23.2	6.1	105.2	109.3	114.6	27.9	64.4
20 to 24 years	-10.8	30.2	-16.0	21.1	-5.4	50.2	11.0	128.3	97.5	133.2	45.3	94.0
25 to 29 years	9.2	44.8	4.1	35.3	16.6	62.5	40.5	141.2	87.2	193.4	70.2	97.6
30 to 34 years	24.5	53.6	18.5	46.9	42.0	50.7	59.2	131.3	95.5	213.5	82.7	86.4
35 to 39 years	42.9	25.7	36.7	21.0	60.3	21.9	78.4	115.6	142.0	138.8	94.4	53.1
40 to 44 years	51.0	-2.6	47.6	-7.4	50.0	4.4	81.9	92.5	159.2	98.0	80.3	38.1
45 to 49 years	25.1	-8.5	22.5	-12.8	23.0	1.8	66.7	84.0	123.9	92.5	53.5	45.8
50 to 54 years	-3.1	5.5	-6.4	1.6	4.4	14.1	48.7	84.5	97.9	130.4	34.0	86.3
55 to 59 years	-9.3	16.5	-12.4	13.7	-0.4	18.7	37.7	81.4	92.9	130.3	40.7	81.8
60 to 64 years	5.2	17.1	2.6	15.0	10.4	18.7	51.5	68.1	123.5	107.1	72.5	59.7
65 to 69 years	15.1	25.6	13.9	24.0	11.1	23.9	50.9	63.2	123.9	106.9	65.4	65.2
70 to 74 years	17.6	24.9	16.9	22.3	13.6	35.5	47.1	79.8	110.6	106.8	48.2	95.8
75 to 79 years	27.7	25.0	27.3	21.3	24.2	52.2	53.7	85.1	105.0	137.3	56.4	118.0
80 to 84 years	34.0	28.5	32.3	26.7	46.8	38.8	71.0	73.4	108.4	105.3	96.1	88.3
85 years and over	37.5	48.3	36.3	48.5	44.8	35.4	56.8	58.2	114.7	84.5	93.6	88.3

[1] "Indian" in 1970.

[2] For 1970, this category represents those listed as Japanese, Chinese, Filipino, Korean, or Hawaiian with the exception of Koreans and Hawaiians residing in Alaska who were included in the "All Other Races" category.

Source: U.S. Bureau of the Census, "General Population Characteristics: United States Summary," 1990 Census of Population, Table 16, 1980 Census of Population, Table 43, 1970 Census of Population, Table 52, and "Detailed Population Characteristics: United States Summary," 1970 Census of Population, Table 190, U.S. Government Printing Office, Washington, D.C., 1993, 1983, and 1973.

younger with a median age of six years less than that of the white population for the past four decades. Much of this difference between the white and black population was established before the turn of the century, as Figure 9-3 shows. From the turn of the century until the baby boom, differences actually narrowed slightly. Through the baby boom the differences between median ages of blacks and whites again increased. And, for the few decades in which data is available, median age of Hispanics has paralleled other groups in aging but remains even lower than that of the black population. These differences in median age dramatically illustrate historical differences in a typical age member of these population groups.

Although historical data concerning demographic composition is less available for groups other than the white and black population, Table 9-4 provides the detailed 1990 age distribution for the total population in each major racial and ethnic group corresponding to Figure 9-2. These patterns are what one would expect from the recent fertility, mortality and migration histories of these groups. Fairly recent historical changes are presented in Table 9-5, which shows the intercensal percentage change in the population of each group at each age over the past two decades. Changes in the total population for whites and for blacks are dominated by the decreasing percentages in the 5-14 year old population during the 1970s and then in the 10-24 year old population during the 1980s as a result of declining fertility. As the baby boom cohorts

aged both the white and black populations also evidenced their greatest absolute increase in numbers among those of early middle age, and then middle age, across the two decades. Finally, both blacks and whites experienced a substantial increase in the populations at the oldest ages, beyond 75 years of age, with blacks experiencing greater change a decade after the comparable white population increase in these older ages.

Other racial and ethnic groups in Table 9-5 experienced no decrease in the population of any age group. Asian and Pacific Islanders are again the most rapidly increasing group with the population aged 25-34 years more than doubling during the 1970s. The increase in this population at these prime ages of childbearing has in turn influenced the size of younger cohorts composed of births to these individuals. As noted elsewhere in this text, increases in American Indian populations are more difficult to analyze since these data likely reflect changes in self-identification across the decades. The dramatic increase in this population group is concentrated between the 1970 and 1980 censuses and increases are more heavily concentrated in ages from 15 to 54 years of age. No American Indian age group's percentage increase between the 1980 to 1990 census is as great as those reported for the prior decade. Finally, although the Hispanic population increased across all age groups, the changes are, similar to the total population, concentrated most heavily near baby boom cohorts and, even more dramatically, at older ages. Despite persistently higher fertility and a generally young

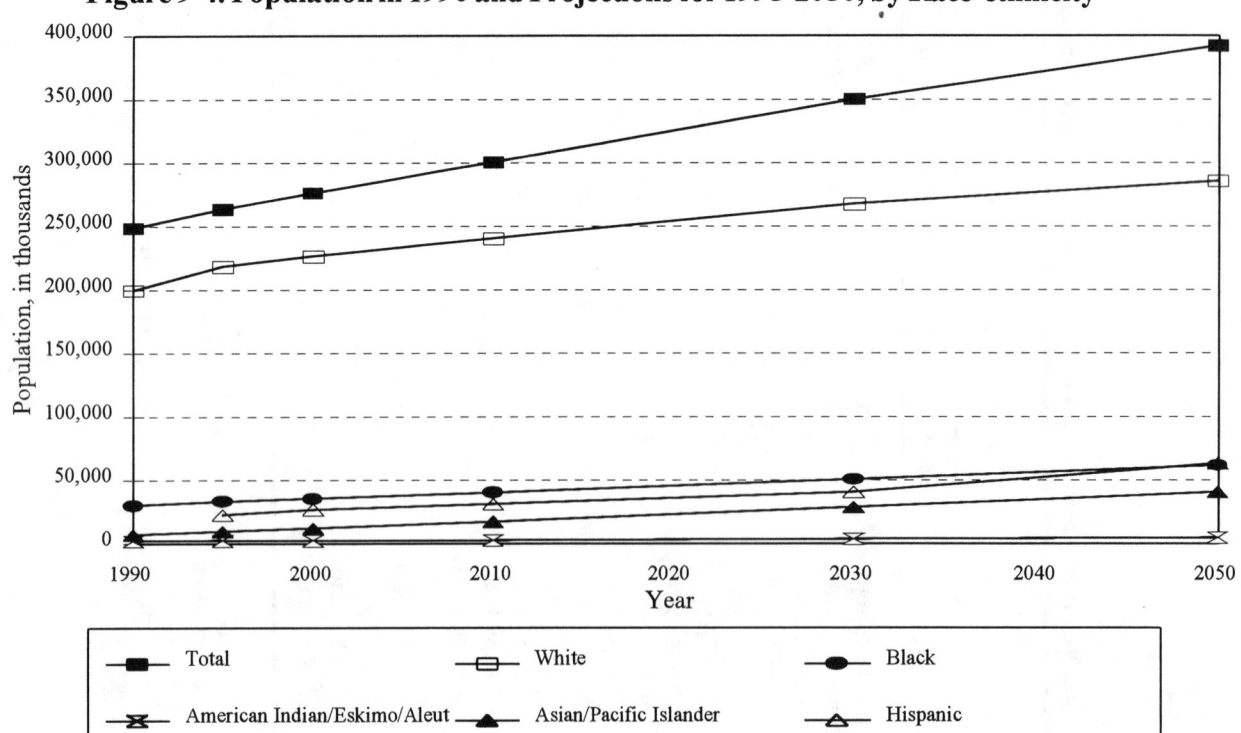

Figure 9-4. Population in 1990 and Projections for 1995-2050, by Race-ethnicity

Source: 1990 U.S. Census data and 1993 CPS projections.

age composition, absolute increases illustrate the significant growth in the adult Hispanic population.

The growth in diversity which arises from the population trends noted is a major topic dealt with in Chapters 1 and 3 of this text. Figure 9-4 summarizes the projected population for the major race and ethnic groups to the year 2050. As noted in earlier chapters, the growing diversity of the population is expected to continue well into the near future. Black, Asian/Pacific Islander, and Hispanic segments of the population will certainly increase substantially beyond their present numbers, and their proportionate representation, in the United States population by the year 2050. Yet, despite the increasing diversity of the population it will remain a substantially white population in the near term. The prevalent historical origins of the United States population in European immigration are still reflected in the racial and ethnic composition. Growth

of the white population is forecast to level somewhat by the year 2030 while Hispanics and Asian/Pacific Islander populations are forecast to experience an increase in growth rates at that time. Since a large portion of Hispanic immigrants are classified as white, this immigration stream has slowed the declining proportion of the population which is identified as white. Yet, the diversity of the United States white population is itself substantially increasing through this immigration.

Regional and City Distribution of Racial and Ethnic Groups

Racial and ethnic subgroups have been historically distributed quite differently across different regions and cities of the United States. Many of these differences reflect the original immigration avenues of various groups

Table 9-6. Racial and Ethnic Composition of the U.S. Population, By Region and Division: 1990

Region and division	All races	White	Black	American Indian, Eskimo, Aleut	Asian, Pacific Islander	Hispanic
Total population	248,709,873	199,686,070	29,986,060	1,959,234	7,273,662	22,354,059
Northeast region	50,809,229	42,068,904	5,613,222	125,148	1,335,375	3,754,389
New England	13,206,943	12,032,983	627,547	32,794	231,656	568,240
Middle Atlantic	37,602,286	30,035,921	4,985,675	92,354	1,103,719	3,186,149
Midwest region	59,668,632	52,017,957	5,715,940	337,899	768,069	1,726,509
East North Central	42,008,942	35,764,043	4,817,436	149,939	572,673	1,437,720
West North Central	17,659,690	16,253,914	898,504	187,960	195,396	288,789
South region	85,445,930	65,582,199	15,828,888	562,731	1,122,248	6,767,021
South Atlantic	43,566,853	33,390,885	8,923,558	172,281	631,133	2,132,751
East South Central	15,176,284	12,049,158	2,976,704	40,839	84,464	95,285
West South Central	26,702,793	20,142,156	3,928,626	349,611	406,651	4,538,985
West region	52,786,082	40,017,010	2,828,010	933,456	4,047,970	10,106,140
Mountain	13,658,776	11,761,851	373,584	480,516	217,120	1,991,732
Pacific	39,127,306	28,255,159	2,454,426	452,940	3,830,850	8,114,408
Percent distribution	100.0	80.3	12.1	0.8	2.9	9.0
Northeast region	100.0	82.8	11.0	0.2	2.6	7.4
New England	100.0	91.1	4.8	0.2	1.8	4.3
Middle Atlantic	100.0	79.9	13.3	0.2	2.9	8.5
Midwest region	100.0	87.2	9.6	0.6	1.3	2.9
East North Central	100.0	85.1	11.5	0.4	1.4	3.4
West North Central	100.0	92.0	5.1	1.1	1.1	1.6
South region	100.0	76.8	18.5	0.7	1.3	7.9
South Atlantic	100.0	76.6	20.5	0.4	1.4	4.9
East South Central	100.0	79.4	19.6	0.3	0.6	0.6
West South Central	100.0	75.4	14.7	1.3	1.5	17.0
West region	100.0	75.8	5.4	1.8	7.7	19.1
Mountain	100.0	86.1	2.7	3.5	1.6	14.6
Pacific	100.0	72.2	6.3	1.2	9.8	20.7

Source: U.S. Bureau of the Census, "General Population Characteristics: United States Summary," 1990 Census of Population, U.S. Government Printing Office, Washington, D.C., 1993, Table 253.

into the country. The American southern border states, for example, are among the primary immigration destinations for many Latin American Hispanics due to the closeness of these states to Mexico and ports of entry. Similarly, the original exodus of Cubans to nearby Florida created a remarkable population concentration of Cubans in one area of the country. In other cases these differences reflect the subsequent attractions of climate, pre-existing communities, labor opportunities, etc., to specific racial and ethnic groups. Black migrations were heavily influenced by the rise of urban industry during the peak periods of movement northward. And, Cubans are now, for example, more likely to migrate to Florida because of the cultural familiarity and social support which Little Havana provides. Finally, as in many countries some population subgroups in the United States have been subjected to forced relocations as in the case of the Native American reservation system and the Japanese internments of World War II.

Broad differences in racial composition exist both between and within regions of the country. Table 9-6 presents the distribution of racial and ethnic groups in different regions and population divisions of the United States

as of the 1990 Census. Divisions with the greatest percentage of white residents are New England and the West North Central. Still reflecting the history of slavery, the South Atlantic and the East South Central have the greatest percentage of black residents. Similarly, the forced relocation of many American Indians to reservations of the western United States is apparent in their heavy concentration within the Mountain division. The impact of migration to specific destinations on geographic diversity is clearly shown by the concentration of both Asian/Pacific Islander and Hispanic populations in the Pacific division and of Hispanics in the West South Central and Mountain regions of the country. These broad differences in composition lend both unique social and political character, as well as different racial or ethnic perceptions, to regional populations throughout the country.

Most racial and ethnic subgroups of the United States population are more heavily concentrated in the country's large cities and urban areas. Table 9-7 presents the 1990 racial and ethnic composition of the ten largest incorporated places in the United States. Although the composition of these cities clearly reflects corresponding regional differences, the diversity across major cities is

Table 9-7. Racial and Ethnic Composition of the Ten Largest Incorporated Places: 1990

Incorporated place	All races	White	Black	American Indian, Eskimo, Aleut	Asian, Pacific Islander	Hispanic
Population						
New York city, NY	7,322,564	3,827,088	2,102,512	27,531	512,719	1,783,511
Los Angeles city, CA	3,485,398	1,841,182	487,674	16,379	341,807	1,391,411
Chicago city, IL	2,783,726	1,263,524	1,087,711	7,064	104,118	545,852
Houston city, TX	1,630,553	859,069	457,990	4,126	67,113	450,483
Philadelphia city, PA	1,585,577	848,586	631,936	3,454	43,522	89,193
San Diego city, CA	1,110,549	745,406	104,261	6,800	130,945	229,519
Detroit city, MI	1,027,974	222,316	777,916	3,655	8,461	28,473
Dallas city, TX	1,006,877	556,760	296,994	4,792	21,952	210,240
Phoenix city, AZ	983,403	803,332	51,053	18,225	16,303	197,103
San Antonio city, TX	935,933	676,082	65,884	3,303	10,703	520,282
Percent distribution						
New York city, NY	100.0	52.3	28.7	0.4	7.0	24.4
Los Angeles city, CA	100.0	52.8	14.0	0.5	9.8	39.9
Chicago city, IL	100.0	45.4	39.1	0.3	3.7	19.6
Houston city, TX	100.0	52.7	28.1	0.3	4.1	27.6
Philadelphia city, PA	100.0	53.5	39.9	0.2	2.7	5.6
San Diego city, CA	100.0	67.1	9.4	0.6	11.8	20.7
Detroit city, MI	100.0	21.6	75.7	0.4	0.8	2.8
Dallas city, TX	100.0	55.3	29.5	0.5	2.2	20.9
Phoenix city, AZ	100.0	81.7	5.2	1.9	1.7	20.0
San Antonio city, TX	100.0	72.2	7.0	0.4	1.1	55.6

Source: U.S. Bureau of the Census, "General Population Characteristics: United States Summary," 1990 Census of Population, U.S. Government Printing Office, Washington, D.C., 1993, Table 276.

Inequity in Housing and Environmental Risks

by John Michael Oakes

Housing, residential location, and related environmental risks are important aspects of quality of life and social welfare. Since the early works of William Petty and John Grant in the 1650's, health research has linked health risks to housing and residential environment. In the United States today, ambient and toxic pollutants are concentrated in urban areas. Rates of homicide (and mortality in general) are higher in urban centers. Residential crowding increases the risk of certain illnesses and many older homes throughout the nation contain lead-based paint or asbestos. Immigrants, the poor, and minorities have historically been forced to live in substandard housing or less desirable residential areas and bear the burdens of related risks.

It is possible to document the relationship between housing characteristics associated with environmental risks and racial/ethnic groups. More white households are single-family dwellings while black and Hispanic households are more likely to reside in multiple-family dwellings. National-level statistics show that 68.3% of white households, 52.6% of black households, and 51.3% of Hispanic households are single-family dwellings. The median number of persons in a housing unit is 2.24 for whites, 2.52 for blacks and 3.29 for Hispanics. For white households, the median number of rooms is 5.4 but is only 4.8 and 4.2 for black and Hispanic households, respectively. These figures show that Hispanic households are, in general, more densely crowded than black households which are, in turn, more densely crowded than white households.

Minorities are also concentrated in the urban centers of the United States which themselves tend to be the more residentially crowded areas of the country. Approximately 28.1% of white households, 59.9% of black households, and 53.9% of Hispanic households are located in central places. Compared to whites, blacks and Hispanics are more likely to live in urban areas and to be exposed to the associated environmental risks.

Inequities extend beyond residential density and urban locations to the condition of housing. If a housing unit lacks either hot or cold piped water, a shower or bath, or a flush toilet, it is designated by the Census Bureau as lacking complete plumbing facilities. The percentage of black and Hispanic households lacking complete plumbing is roughly three times greater than it is for white households. Property ownership alone does not explain these relationships.

An examination of the distribution of households occupying older occupied housing structures (those built prior to 1960) also reveals differences in the condition of housing by race/ethnicity. Three quarters of U.S. housing built prior to 1978 contains some lead paint, and older housing is most likely to contain it. In fact, some 57 million homes may contain some lead paint. About half of black households reside in housing structures built prior to 1960, and thus are at greater risks for the adverse health outcomes related to lead paint exposure.

Data collected in the U.S. Census of Population and Housing are not sufficiently detailed to assess quality of life or specific environmental risks related to housing and residential location. These data do, however, suggest that historical inequities and concerns persist.

Occupancy and Structural Characteristics of Housing Units, by Race-ethnicity of Householder: 1990

Characteristics of housing units	White	Black	Hispanic	White, non-Hispanic
Total housing units	76,880,105	9,976,161	6,001,718	73,633,749
Percent single family dwelling	68.3	52.6	51.3	68.8
Median persons in unit	2.24	2.52	3.29	2.21
Percent in central place	28.1	59.9	53.9	27.1
Percent single family dwelling	55.8	47.0	41.9	56.6
Median persons in unit	2.03	2.42	3.20	1.99
Percent in rural areas	26.4	11.4	7.8	27.1
Percent single family dwelling	77.2	68.2	66.7	77.4
Median persons in unit	2.40	2.79	3.43	2.40
Total occupied housing units	76,959,531	9,919,313	5,822,000	73,811,344
Percent lacking plumbing facilities	0.6	1.8	1.6	0.5
Percent built before 1960	41.3	48.0	43.6	41.3
Percent owner occupied	68.2	43.4	42.2	69.0
Percent lacking plumbing facilities	0.5	1.5	1.2	0.5
Percent built before 1960	42.1	51.9	42.8	42.1
Percent renter occupied	31.8	56.6	57.8	31.0
Percent lacking plumbing facilities	0.7	2.0	1.9	0.6
Percent built before 1960	39.4	45.1	44.2	39.3

Source: U.S. Bureau of the Census, "Detailed Housing Characteristics," Tables 41 and 44, and "General Housing Characteristics," Tables 6, 7, 10, and 11, 1990 Census of Housing, U.S. Government Printing Office, Washington, D.C., 1993 and 1992.

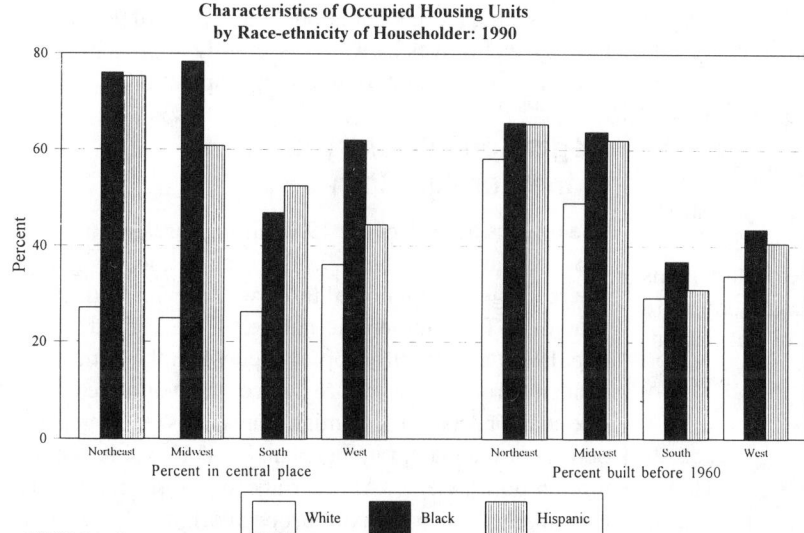

Characteristics of Occupied Housing Units by Race-ethnicity of Householder: 1990

Percent in central place / Percent built before 1960

□ White ■ Black ▨ Hispanic

Source: 1990 U.S. Census data.

Additional Sources:

Agency for Toxic Substances and Disease Registry (ATSDR). The Nature and Extent of Lead Poisoning in Children in the United States: A Report to Congress. Atlanta, GA: Centers for Disease Control. 1988.

Edwards, John N., Fuller, Theodore D., Vorakitphokatorn, Sirudee, and Sermsri, Santhat. Household Crowding and Its Consequences. Boulder, CO: Westview Press. 1994.

Smith, David M. Industrial Location. New York: John Wiley and Sons. 1971.

Wilner, Daniel M., Walkley, Rosabelle Price, Pinkerton, Thomas C, and Tayback, Matthew. The Housing Environment and Family Life: A Longitudinal Study of the Effects of Housing on Morbidity and Mental Health. Baltimore, MD: Johns Hopkins Press. 1962.

even more pronounced than that across geographic divisions. In addition, there are clearly major cities which are more or less unique in their composition. The high percentage of white residents in Phoenix, San Antonio and San Diego reflect very small percentages of black residents. At the same time, Phoenix has the highest percentage of American Indian residents, San Antonio has the highest percentage of Hispanics, and San Diego has the highest percentage of Asian/Pacific Islanders among these ten largest incorporated places. Detroit, meanwhile, is unique among these ten cities precisely because of the very high concentration of black residents. Most eastern and southern cities have more substantial black populations than do those incorporated places in the western and southwestern United States.

Further Indicators of Ethnic Diversity in Census Data

It is true that most citizens of the United States are descendants of immigrants from other continents. But, much of the migration of their forbears occurred a century or more ago and has been followed by intermarriage and substantial assimilation into a national entity. Despite clear limits to the notion of the United States as an assimilative "melting pot," much of the public at large has, at best, only incomplete knowledge of its ethnic roots. Even if a complicated genealogical question were to be included in the census, most persons would lack the information requested. And, if a complete accurate genealogy were provided for every person in the United States it is not at all clear what meaningful taxonomies of the population would be discernible or worthwhile from such data. The statistics collected on this subject must be comparatively simple, hence incomplete. Nonetheless, much of the unique national character of the United States is a product of its historical diversity. Many groups of different nationality and ancestry have played, and play, important and distinctive historical roles in our social and cultural history. Understanding of, or appreciation for, the diversity of the population extends beyond the divisions apparent in crude racial and ethnic categorizations.

The census approached this task by identifying four population characteristics (see the Definition Box for more details): Nativity—whether native born or foreign born; Country of birth—asked of the foreign born; Ancestry—a self-identification of ethnicity; and Language Spoken at Home and ability to speak English. Supplementary items of information, particularly about the foreign born, were asked (year of immigration and whether or not respondents have become naturalized citizens).

The Foreign Born

The 19.8 million foreign-born residents of the United States in 1990 exceeded the number of such residents counted by all previous censuses. Table 9-8 provides data on numbers and proportions of foreign born since 1850. The large number in 1990, an increase of nearly 5.7 million people over 1980, is the cumulative result of the increased flow of immigrants, both refugee and under quotas, since World War II and especially since the Vietnam War. However, because the population is now so much larger than before, foreign-born persons comprise only 7.9 percent of the total, whereas in 1910, at the height of the influx from Southern and Eastern Europe, foreign-born persons accounted for 14.7 percent of the total population.

The slackening of immigration during the Depression of the 1930s and the aging and dying off of some larger contingents of migrants (i.e. predominantly adult male Chinese laborers who did not marry and reproduce) from the late nineteenth century caused the proportion of foreign born to decline to only 5.4 percent by 1970. Increasing immigration since the 1970s has caused a reversal or suspension of this trend.

A significant new development, resulting from new immigration policies, is the renewal of black immigration. As Table 9-8 shows, before World War II almost all immigration was white; immigration of black population was negligible. Not since the end of the slave trade had large numbers of black persons immigrated to the United States. After World War II black immigrants from the Caribbean began to alter this pattern. Opening up the quotas to immigrants from Africa in the 1970s and to special populations of islanders in the 1980s helped to cause a rise in the percentage of all foreign born who are black from 2.6 in 1970 to 5.8 in 1980 and to 7.3 in 1990.

More than two-thirds (69.5 percent) of the Chinese and more than one-third (35.8 percent) of the Hispanic residents were foreign born in 1990. The two groups have been prominent in immigration since World War II and especially during the 1970s and 1980s. The number of Chinese foreign born increased over five and one-half (5.6) times over these two decades while the number of Hispanic foreign born increased nearly that much (5.3 times). The Hispanic foreign born population, most of whom also classify themselves as white, is rapidly approaching the total size of the white foreign-born population.

Region and Country of Birth of the Foreign Born

The regions of birth of the 19.7 million foreign-born persons are shown in Table 9-9. For each nationality group, a percentage distribution of those who are now citizens is provided. The multiethnic nature of the United States population can be fully appreciated when the number of residents from the various regions of the world are noted. The changing nature of immigration across recent generations is also apparent in the changing composition of the foreign born by age. At older ages the foreign born are most likely to have been of European origin. However, in

Table 9-8. Foreign-born Population, by Race-ethnicity: 1850-1980 [numbers in thousands]

Year	Foreign-born population							Percent foreign-born						
	Total	White	Black	American Indian	Japanese	Chinese	Hispanic	Total	White	Black	American Indian	Japanese	Chinese	Hispanic
1990	19,767	10,023	1,455	47[1]	281	1,143	7,842	7.9	5.0	4.9	2.4	33.1	69.5	35.8
1980	14,080	9,324	816	37	203	514	4,173	6.2	4.9	3.1	2.7	29.0	63.8	28.6
1970	9,619	8,734	253	14	123	204	1,454	4.7	4.9	1.1	1.8	20.8	46.9	15.6
1960	9,738	9,294	125	—	102	93	—	5.4	5.9	0.7	...	22.0	39.2	—
1950	10,347	10,095		252[2]				6.8	7.5	—	—	—	—	—
1940	11,595	11,419	84	4	47	37	—	8.8	9.6	0.7	1.2	16.5	34.9	—
1930	14,204	13,983	99	4	70	44	—	11.5	12.7	0.8	1.2	25.1	43.1	—
1920	13,921	13,713	74	6	81	43	—	13.1	14.4	0.7	2.5	36.7	50.6	—
1910	13,516	13,346	40	3	68	57	—	14.7	16.3	0.4	1.1	44.4	60.6	—
1900	10,341	10,214	20	2	24	81	—	13.6	15.3	0.2	0.8	27.9	68.1	—
1890	9,250	9,122	20	1	2	105	—	14.7	16.6	0.3	0.4	100.0	98.1	—
1880	6,680	6,560	14	2	...	104	—	13.3	15.1	0.2	3.0	—	98.1	—
1870	5,567	5,494	10	1	...	63	—	14.4	16.4	0.2	3.8	—	98.4	—
1860	—	4,096	7[3]	—	—	—	—	—	15.2	—	—	—	—	—
1850	—	2,240	4[3]	—	—	—	—	—	11.5	—	—	—	—	—

[1] Includes Eskimos and Aleuts.
[2] Data in 1950 are for Negro and other races.
[3] Free Negroes only. Data on nativity were not collected for slaves.

Source: U.S. Bureau of the Census, "Social and Economic Characteristics: U.S. Summary," 1990 Census of Population, Tables 43 and 107, "General Social and Economic Characteristics: U.S. Summary," 1980 Census of Population, Tables 122 and 161, 1970 Census of Population, Table 86, "Detailed Population Characteristics," 1970 Census of Population, Table 190, U.S. Summary," 1980 Census of Population, Tables 122 and 161, 1970 Census of Population, Table 86, "Detailed Population Characteristics," 1970 Census of Population, Table 190, and "Historical Statistics of the United States," Series A105-118, U.S. Government Printing Office, Washington, D.C., 1993, 1983, 1973, and 1975.

Table 9-9. Foreign-born Persons, by Nativity, Citizenship, and Age: 1990

Age group	Total number foreign-born	Percent distribution by region of birth[1]							Percent who are citizens							
		Europe	Soviet Union	Asia	North & Central America	South America	Africa	Oceania	Total	Europe	Soviet Union	Asia	North & Central America	South America	Africa	Oceania
Total	19,767,316	20.3	1.7	25.2	41.1	5.2	1.8	0.5	40.5	64.7	58.9	40.8	29.3	30.8	34.1	34.0
Under 5 years	261,078	6.8	2.3	22.7	54.6	4.8	1.7	0.6	14.4	15.7	5.2	14.2	12.9	13.2	17.0	7.5
5 to 9 years	486,854	7.0	2.2	28.7	49.4	5.8	1.9	0.6	11.9	14.0	5.0	11.5	11.3	10.3	8.6	14.0
10 to 14 years	736,234	6.8	1.7	31.8	48.1	5.9	1.7	0.5	16.6	18.3	21.0	18.2	14.8	13.1	18.0	19.5
15 to 19 years	1,161,997	6.7	1.4	30.2	50.9	4.7	1.5	0.5	20.8	23.5	37.0	28.6	15.4	17.4	25.3	20.3
20 to 24 years	1,797,420	8.1	0.7	25.0	54.0	5.1	1.6	0.5	23.6	30.9	47.2	34.8	17.3	21.2	24.1	26.7
25 to 34 years	4,521,666	10.9	0.8	26.8	47.2	6.3	2.8	0.6	28.9	38.3	34.8	34.2	24.6	25.2	23.4	25.7
35 to 44 years	3,753,307	17.2	1.1	29.9	38.9	6.0	2.5	0.6	41.6	55.0	43.5	49.3	31.9	34.3	38.2	30.0
45 to 54 years	2,552,359	26.1	1.3	26.2	35.1	5.9	1.5	0.5	50.4	62.8	66.0	56.3	37.8	43.1	56.8	36.9
55 to 64 years	1,800,803	34.6	1.7	21.6	32.7	4.7	1.0	0.5	57.4	74.5	63.5	52.1	44.5	46.8	63.6	52.6
65 to 74 years	1,308,199	39.9	3.3	16.9	32.1	3.0	0.7	0.7	64.9	83.0	69.8	42.8	55.6	44.9	64.5	69.2
75 to 84 years	936,530	49.8	6.0	11.1	26.3	1.6	0.5	0.2	74.7	88.0	83.4	48.1	60.3	43.9	69.6	70.9
85 years and over	450,869	60.7	8.0	6.6	17.2	0.9	0.2	0.2	83.3	91.2	91.4	54.3	63.8	53.1	76.6	80.9

[1] Categories are not exhaustive and percentages may not total 100.0.

Source: U.S. Bureau of the Census, "The Foreign-born Population of the United States," 1990 Census of Population, U.S. Government Printing Office, Washington, D.C., 1993, Table 1.

Table 9-10. Year of Immigration and Citizenship Status of the Foreign-born, for Selected Countries of Birth: 1990

Country of birth	Total foreign-born	Percent immigrated					Percent citizens
		1987 to 1990	1985 or 1986	1982 to 1984	1980 or 1981	Before 1980	
Total[1]	19,767,316	15.9	8.8	9.2	9.9	56.2	40.5
Europe[1]	4,016,678	7.6	3.4	3.8	3.2	82.1	64.7
France	119,233	15.6	4.9	5.4	3.5	70.6	52.6
Germany	711,929	5.5	2.0	2.2	1.6	88.8	71.9
Greece	177,398	4.7	2.3	2.8	3.0	87.2	71.2
Hungary	110,337	5.7	2.1	2.5	1.6	88.1	82.1
Ireland	169,827	9.4	4.8	3.1	2.0	80.6	67.8
Italy	580,592	2.4	1.2	1.4	1.3	93.6	75.8
Poland	388,328	11.8	5.8	7.0	5.4	70.0	62.4
Portugal	210,122	6.3	4.9	4.4	6.0	78.4	44.0
United Kingdom	640,145	9.5	4.2	5.5	4.9	75.9	49.6
Yugoslavia	141,516	6.3	3.7	3.2	2.7	84.2	68.5
Soviet Union	333,725	27.9	1.7	2.1	7.7	60.6	58.9
Asia[1]	4,979,037	19.5	11.0	13.5	12.2	43.9	40.8
Cambodia	118,833	10.0	16.8	30.4	28.7	14.2	20.1
China	529,837	20.8	11.1	12.7	9.0	46.5	44.1
Hong Kong	147,131	17.2	7.7	12.2	7.1	55.7	54.5
India	450,406	19.6	12.2	14.1	9.8	44.3	34.9
Iran	210,941	18.1	12.9	11.3	7.2	50.4	27.2
Japan	290,128	35.4	8.4	5.5	3.4	47.3	28.2
Korea	568,397	19.3	11.0	14.8	11.0	43.9	40.6
Laos	171,577	20.4	10.2	10.0	35.8	23.6	17.0
Philippines	912,674	15.5	10.8	13.0	9.6	51.0	53.9
Taiwan	244,102	20.5	13.1	21.2	10.7	34.6	38.7
Thailand	106,919	21.5	10.4	11.8	12.0	44.3	25.4
Vietnam	543,262	15.6	8.9	14.3	23.0	38.2	42.7
North America[1]	8,124,257	16.4	9.9	9.1	11.6	53.0	29.3
Canada	744,830	7.3	3.1	3.5	2.7	83.4	54.1
Mexico	4,298,014	18.7	11.0	8.9	11.3	50.1	22.6
Caribbean[1]	1,938,348	11.2	7.5	8.6	13.2	59.6	39.7
Cuba	736,971	4.5	2.3	2.9	15.8	74.5	51.0
Dominican Republic	347,858	18.4	11.8	13.1	9.8	46.9	27.6
Haiti	225,393	13.0	13.6	14.3	17.9	41.1	27.4
Jamaica	334,140	13.5	9.8	11.7	11.4	53.7	38.4
Trinidad/Tabago	115,710	17.4	7.2	7.6	7.9	59.9	32.1
Central America[1]	1,133,978	22.9	14.0	14.4	16.1	32.6	20.7
El Salvador	465,433	21.2	14.2	16.8	23.0	24.8	15.4
Guatemala	225,739	24.3	15.6	13.8	14.6	31.7	16.9
Honduras	108,923	24.3	14.9	14.7	11.6	34.4	26.1
Nicaragua	168,659	32.9	17.6	14.2	9.3	26.0	15.1
Panama	85,737	15.9	6.1	7.1	7.9	63.0	51.3
South America[1]	1,037,497	18.3	11.4	11.4	11.1	47.9	30.8
Columbia	286,124	15.0	12.7	10.7	12.8	48.8	29.0
Ecuador	143,314	14.4	9.8	9.4	9.8	56.7	26.3
Guyana	120,698	16.3	12.8	17.6	13.6	39.7	39.9
Peru	144,199	22.2	13.2	14.1	11.2	39.2	26.8
Africa	363,819	20.5	11.5	14.3	12.9	40.7	34.1
Oceania	104,145	21.4	8.4	9.1	7.3	53.9	34.0

[1] Includes countries not listed separately.

Source: U.S. Bureau of the Census, "The Foreign-born Population of the United States," 1990 Census of Population, U.S. Government Printing Office, Washington, D.C., 1993, Table 1.

younger age groups with more recent immigrants the foreign born are most likely to have been born in North and Central America.

Citizenship is generally higher at older ages. However, most of the elderly (i.e. 65-84 years of age) foreign born Asian and South American populations are less likely to be citizens. Across ages the highest levels of naturalization are among those born in Europe and the Soviet Union, followed by Asia. The lowest levels of naturalization are among the foreign born from North and Central America or South America. These low levels of naturalization partially reflect the greater recent arrival of immigrants from these countries. However, there may be some additional explanation for low levels of naturalization among this population in the circular migration noted between the United States and countries south of its border. Many of these immigrants return to their countries of origin either permanently or occasionally and are not anxious to surrender their native citizenship. And, many do not feel the need to establish United States citizenship to obtain employment and social benefits which often motivate their migration.

Table 9-10 presents the specific countries of birth for the foreign born population along with the timing of their immigration and the percentage which are naturalized citizens. All continents and all major nations of all continents (except for the Middle East and Africa) are well represented. Countries with over 500,000 immigrants living in the United States include: Germany, Italy, the United Kingdom, China, Korea, the Philippines, Vietnam, Canada and Cuba. Several additional countries including Poland, the Soviet Union, India, the Dominican Republic, Jamaica, El Salvador and Columbia all have between 250,000 and 500,000 immigrants living in the United States.

Place of Residence of the Foreign Born

The foreign born population is not evenly distributed throughout the United States. Particular nationality groups, like racial and ethnic groups, tend to be concentrated in particular geographic regions and cities. Table 9-11 presents these patterns in broad outline. The distribution of each foreign born group by country of birth is shown for regions, by residence in metropolitan and non-metropolitan areas, and by urban-rural residence. The table shows:

1. Groups from Northwest Europe are more evenly distributed throughout the regions and are more inclined to live in suburbs and non-metropolitan areas and in rural areas than other foreign born groups.

2. Immigrants from Asia are highly concentrated in the West region and in central cities of other regions.

3. Immigrants from Italy, Poland, and other nations of Eastern and Southern Europe are most inclined to live in the Northeast and North Central regions, in central cit-

ies, or in metropolitan rings, but not in non-metropolitan areas.

4. Immigrants from Mexico and Latin America are inclined to concentrate in the South and West and in central cities of all regions.

Many of these points have already been described in Chapter 1 in discussing the United States population's racial and ethnic composition. Table 9-11 provides nation-of-origin detail. Several of these detailed country of birth groups are very highly concentrated in specific regions. Dominicans, for example, are nearly exclusively (88.7%) concentrated in the Northeast and in central cities (82.9%). Those born in Guyana, Portugal, Ecuador, Trinidad and Jamaica are nearly as concentrated in the Northeast and somewhat less concentrated in central cities. The most concentrated group in the Midwest are those born in Yugoslavia (41.4%) and Poland (31.8%). Persons born in Cuba (72.1%), Nicaragua (54.3%), Honduras (40.7%) and Haiti (40.0%) are the most concentrated in the South. And, there are a large number of groups of which over half live in the West. Those born in the Philippines (67.0%), Mexico (66.2%), El Salvador (62.5%), Guatemala (62.1%), Iran (59.6%), Vietnam (58.4%), Cambodia (58.3%) and countries of Oceania (65.1%) are the most concentrated among these persons.

Social Characteristics of the Foreign Born, by Region of Birth

Selected social characteristics for the foreign born population across principal regions of origin or birth are provided in Table 9-12. The sex ratio of migrants from Africa indicates a preponderance of male immigrants while that of Europe and the former Soviet Union suggests a greater number of female immigrants. Notably, the sex ratios for the foreign born in North and Central America do not indicate the high sex ratio which might be expected if labor opportunities had selectively attracted male immigration from Central America. Unique events, such as significant war mortality among the former Soviet Union states, account to some extent for these sex ratio differences. Most, however, such as the dominant male migration from Africa are explained better by selective labor force incentives and behaviors.

The percentage of those married with spouse present varies less across regions of origin or birth than does the percent never married and of those separated, widowed or divorced. The percentages of those never married vary from over 28% among those born in North and Central America or Africa to less than half that percentage among those born in Europe or the former Soviet Union. Conversely, nearly a quarter, or even more, of the foreign born from Europe and the former Soviet Union are separated, widowed or divorced while less than one in ten of those from Asia falls in that category. Many of these differences are accounted for by age of the respective immigrant population.

Table 9-11. Place of Residence of the Foreign-born Population, for Selected Countries of Birth: 1990
[numbers in thousands]

Country of birth	Region					Urban/rural residence				
	Total	Northeast	Midwest	South	West	Total	Central place	Urban fringe	Other urban	Rural
Total foreign-born	19,767	5,231	2,131	4,582	7,823	19,767	9,831	7,624	1,049	1,263
Percent foreign-born	7.9	10.6	3.7	5.5	15.2	7.9	12.5	9.6	3.6	2.0
Percent distribution										
Total[1]	100.0	26.5	10.8	23.2	39.6	100.0	49.7	38.6	5.3	6.4
Europe[1]	100.0	41.6	18.9	18.0	21.5	100.0	39.8	44.4	5.4	10.3
France	100.0	31.2	11.3	27.8	29.6	100.0	43.2	40.2	5.9	10.6
Germany	100.0	28.1	20.4	26.5	25.0	100.0	32.6	43.5	7.8	16.0
Greece	100.0	49.5	21.9	15.9	12.8	100.0	47.7	45.5	3.1	3.8
Hungary	100.0	40.0	21.0	16.2	22.8	100.0	41.0	45.4	4.5	9.1
Ireland	100.0	61.4	12.7	11.2	14.7	100.0	44.8	44.3	3.7	7.2
Italy	100.0	65.7	14.2	9.4	10.6	100.0	41.0	49.5	3.7	5.8
Poland	100.0	45.9	31.8	11.9	10.4	100.0	52.1	40.1	2.8	5.0
Portugal	100.0	77.0	0.7	3.9	18.5	100.0	49.4	39.1	4.6	7.0
United Kingdom	100.0	28.8	14.3	26.3	30.6	100.0	32.3	46.5	7.1	14.0
Yugoslavia	100.0	33.7	41.4	7.8	17.1	100.0	43.3	46.7	3.3	6.6
Soviet Union	100.0	47.6	14.5	10.4	27.4	100.0	59.6	34.9	2.0	3.5
Asia[1]	100.0	21.3	12.0	17.6	49.1	100.0	49.2	43.3	4.1	3.4
Cambodia	100.0	19.1	8.4	14.2	58.3	100.0	72.1	23.5	2.8	1.6
China	100.0	34.2	8.2	10.9	46.8	100.0	63.2	32.2	2.7	1.9
Hong Kong	100.0	31.3	7.1	10.3	51.3	100.0	56.3	39.6	2.2	1.9
India	100.0	35.4	18.9	24.0	21.7	100.0	37.3	53.5	4.6	4.6
Iran	100.0	12.9	7.5	20.0	59.6	100.0	43.2	51.7	2.9	2.2
Japan	100.0	19.6	12.8	17.1	50.6	100.0	38.9	47.8	7.1	6.3
Korea	100.0	22.6	11.7	19.7	46.0	100.0	44.7	48.0	3.9	3.4
Laos	100.0	8.1	25.6	15.2	51.1	100.0	66.9	21.2	8.0	3.9
Philippines	100.0	12.0	9.0	12.0	67.0	100.0	47.4	43.0	5.4	4.3
Taiwan	100.0	22.0	10.0	19.2	48.9	100.0	37.2	56.8	3.2	2.8
Thailand	100.0	12.7	16.0	21.8	49.5	100.0	53.0	35.9	5.8	5.3
Vietnam	100.0	10.0	7.4	24.2	58.4	100.0	52.9	42.3	2.7	2.1
North America[1]	100.0	17.7	6.9	28.9	46.4	100.0	53.4	33.1	6.6	6.9
Canada	100.0	27.6	16.3	20.4	35.7	100.0	30.8	43.1	9.4	16.6
Mexico	100.0	1.6	8.2	24.0	66.2	100.0	51.4	30.1	9.6	8.8
Caribbean[1]	100.0	49.6	2.4	43.1	4.9	100.0	61.5	35.4	1.4	1.8
Cuba	100.0	17.3	2.6	72.1	7.9	100.0	49.7	46.9	1.4	2.0
Dominican Republic	100.0	88.7	0.8	9.0	1.4	100.0	82.9	15.5	0.6	1.0
Haiti	100.0	56.8	1.8	40.0	1.4	100.0	63.4	34.2	1.7	0.7
Jamaica	100.0	60.4	3.8	31.8	4.0	100.0	57.1	38.9	1.8	2.2
Trinidad/Tabago	100.0	66.8	2.4	24.9	6.0	100.0	68.0	27.9	1.8	2.3
Central America[1]	100.0	17.6	3.5	28.9	50.1	100.0	61.7	34.2	2.1	2.0
El Salvador	100.0	13.0	1.5	23.4	62.1	100.0	63.6	33.4	1.7	1.4
Guatemala	100.0	15.5	6.5	15.5	62.5	100.0	64.3	31.7	2.0	2.0
Honduras	100.0	29.3	4.0	40.7	25.9	100.0	63.3	31.2	3.1	2.5
Nicaragua	100.0	8.1	1.5	54.3	36.2	100.0	54.2	43.3	1.5	1.0
Panama	100.0	40.0	5.8	34.3	19.9	100.0	58.9	31.7	4.4	5.0
South America[1]	100.0	49.4	5.0	27.3	18.3	100.0	54.1	41.3	2.0	2.6
Columbia	100.0	50.3	4.1	33.3	12.3	100.0	51.0	44.5	1.8	2.8
Ecuador	100.0	66.7	5.3	13.5	14.5	100.0	66.7	30.9	1.0	1.3
Guyana	100.0	78.2	2.9	14.8	4.1	100.0	75.9	21.8	1.1	1.2
Peru	100.0	38.0	4.5	28.1	29.4	100.0	48.7	47.5	1.8	2.0
Africa	100.0	34.0	11.4	31.8	22.8	100.0	54.6	38.4	3.3	3.6
Oceania	100.0	11.7	7.8	15.5	65.1	100.0	39.2	44.7	8.2	7.9

[1] Includes countries not listed separately.

Source: U.S. Bureau of the Census, "Social and Economic Characteristics: United States Summary," 1990 Census of Population, U.S. Government Printing Office, 1993, Tables 14 and 144.

Table 9-12. Selected Social Characteristics of the Foreign-born Population, by Region[1] of Birth: 1990

Social Characteristics	Total foreign-born	Europe	Soviet Union	Asia	North & Central America	South America	Africa	Oceania
Number of persons	19,767,316	4,016,678	333,725	4,979,037	8,124,257	1,037,497	363,819	104,145
M:F sex ratio	0.96	0.78	0.82	0.96	1.04	0.93	1.46	0.83
Marital status, persons 15+ (percent)								
Never married	24.1	11.9	13.1	26.5	28.3	26.1	28.1	22.1
Married, spouse present	60.0	64.3	58.2	63.7	56.9	58.1	58.9	63.8
Separated/widowed/divorced	16.0	23.8	28.7	9.8	14.8	15.8	12.9	14.1
Children ever born per 1,000:								
Women age 15 to 24 years	385	237	198	187	539	261	200	270
Women age 25 to 34 years	1,466	1,131	1,365	1,135	1,814	1,139	1,295	1,352
Women age 35 to 44 years	2,254	1,865	1,690	1,997	2,718	1,931	2,202	2,187
Educational attainment, persons 25+ (percent)								
Less than high school diploma	41.2	36.5	36.0	24.0	58.4	28.7	12.1	23.0
High school diploma	19.6	25.4	20.5	16.6	16.9	25.6	14.6	24.4
Some college	18.8	20.1	16.4	20.4	15.6	25.7	26.2	28.4
Bachelor's degree	11.5	9.0	12.6	22.6	5.4	11.6	24.8	13.2
Graduate/professional degree	8.8	9.0	14.5	16.3	3.7	8.4	22.3	11.0
Ability to speak English, persons 5+ (percent)								
Speak another language than English	79.1	59.5	81.1	91.6	81.6	82.8	74.9	46.1
Do not speak English "very well"	47.0	26.1	52.1	49.9	56.8	48.1	23.4	17.5

[1] Categories are not exhaustive.

Source: U.S. Bureau of the Census, "The Foreign-born Population of the United States," 1990 Census of Population, U.S. Government Printing Office, Washington, D.C., 1993, Tables 1 and 3.

Fertility, as indicated by children ever born per 1,000 persons, varies dramatically among the foreign born by region of birth. The foreign born from North and Central America have the greatest number of children ever born per 1,000 persons across all ages. Lower fertility in some groups where one might expect high fertility, e.g. those born in Africa, may be influenced by selective migration pressures. The lowest number of children ever born among those less than twenty-five years of age is among women born in Asia. The lowest number of children ever born to women thirty-five years of age or older is among those born in the countries of the former Soviet Union.

Educational attainment also varies dramatically among the foreign born population twenty- five years of age or older. Well over half of the foreign born from North and Central America, and over a third of those from Europe and countries of the former Soviet Union, have less than a high school diploma. In contrast, nearly half of the foreign born from Africa, and over forty percent of those born in Asia, have a college degree. English language abilities are best in those countries with either regular language contact or generally higher levels of education among the foreign born. Those with the greatest English language abilities are those from Europe, Oceania and Africa. Roughly half of the foreign born from all other regions in Table 9-12 do not speak English "very well."

Economic Characteristics of the Foreign Born, by Region of Birth

Selected economic characteristics for the foreign born population are provided by regions of origin or birth in Table 9-13. Labor force participation of the foreign born of both sexes is lowest among those born in Europe and countries of the former Soviet Union. However, lower labor force participation is affected by the relative age composition of the populations compared within Table 9-13. Despite lower labor force participation, unemployment is not high among those born in Europe who are in the labor force. Yet, the foreign born from former countries of the Soviet Union have low labor force participation coupled with the highest unemployment for both sexes followed by those born in North and Central America. Female unemployment is also higher among those from South America and Africa. Not surprisingly, income and poverty data reflect these differences in employment. The lowest median family incomes, lowest per capita incomes, and highest poverty levels are among foreign born families and persons from countries of the former Soviet Union and those from North and Central America.

Population Projections of the Foreign Born

The data in Table 9-14 and 9-15 provide decennial projections of the foreign born population to the year 2010.

These projections are not those of the Census Bureau but those of independent researchers and reflect assumptions providing reasonable estimates (see source article in references to this chapter for detail). According to the projections of Table 9-14 the total foreign born population will increase from 7.9% to 10.4% of the population between 1900 and 2010. This is an increase of 57.1% in the foreign born. The most distinctive projected trend in the foreign born is the nearly level numbers of the foreign born from Europe and countries of the former Soviet Union. Table 9-15 provides age-specific projections for the total foreign born population. Under the assumptions employed in these projections the foreign born population will age significantly over the period between 1990 and 2010.

Ancestry

Before 1980 the Bureau of the Census attempted to use objective definitions to determine the ancestry of the population. This was done through the concepts of "parentage" and "foreign stock." As the population became heavily mixed by intermarriage this approach was abandoned in favor of a subjective approach in which people were simply asked to report their ethnic origins in broad categories, as they perceived themselves. This was done by using ancestry questions (see Definition Box). The responses to ancestry questions face problems similar to those discussed above for self-identification of race and ethnicity.

When asked to specify ancestry in 1990, 89.5 percent of the population complied (up from 83 percent in 1980). Only 59.8 percent reported a single ancestry (up from 52 percent in 1980), and 29.7 percent indicated multiple ancestry—intermarriage of nationality groups. Table 9-16 shows the frequency of various ancestry groups within the population and within regions of the United States. Excluding the overall "Other" ancestry category, the most common ancestries in the population are, in order, German, Irish, English, Italian, French and Polish. This composition reflects the largely European origins of early immigrants to the United States. The sizable categories of "Other" and "United States or American" caution against ruling out the significance of categories other than those tabulated and the possibly selective use of those categories by some populations. The small number reporting Subsaharan African ancestry, for example, may be due to a greater use of other categories among blacks.

Ancestry groups are, like racial and ethnic groups, unevenly distributed across the regions of the United States. The Northeast has a greater diversity and lower concentration of those of European ancestry than the population as a whole. Yet, the same region has greater concentration of those of Italian ancestry. The Midwest, in contrast, has a marked concentration of those of German ancestry reflecting the historical patterns of settlement in the region. The South and West have greater

Table 9-13. Selected Economic Characteristics of the Foreign-born Population, by Region[1] of Birth: 1990

Economic Characteristics	Total foreign-born	Europe	Soviet Union	Asia	North & Central America	South America	Africa	Oceania
Percent in the labor force, persons 16 and over	64.3	53.4	39.7	66.4	68.5	73.7	75.1	66.6
Males	76.9	66.8	50.3	76.2	82.1	85.0	84.0	81.7
Females	52.3	43.0	31.1	57.1	54.2	63.2	61.7	54.3
Percent unemployed, civilians 16 and over	7.8	4.8	13.3	5.6	10.1	7.5	6.8	5.5
Males	7.1	4.5	12.9	5.2	9.0	6.2	6.0	5.3
Females	8.6	5.2	13.7	6.1	11.8	9.1	8.5	5.7
Median income per family, in dollars	31,785	40,428	28,799	39,395	24,963	32,750	36,783	39,775
Mean income per family, in dollars	42,350	52,022	41,100	50,541	32,288	41,327	50,102	51,889
Per capita income, in dollars	15,033	20,904	15,012	16,661	11,225	14,955	20,117	19,200
Percent families below poverty level	14.9	5.1	18.5	13.1	21.5	11.7	11.7	11.6
Percent persons below poverty level	18.2	8.3	25.0	16.2	24.1	14.1	15.7	13.7

[1] Categories are not exhaustive.

Source: U.S. Bureau of the Census, "The Foreign-born Population of the United States," 1990 Census of Population, U.S. Government Printing Office, Washington, D.C., 1993, Tables 4 and 5.

Table 9-14. Foreign-born Population by Country of Birth: 1990 and Series B[1] Projections for 2000 and 2010

Country of Birth	Population, in thousands			Percent distribution		
	1990	2000	2010	1990	2000	2010
Total population	249,424	275,833	299,152	100.0	100.0	100.0
Total native-born	229,596	250,132	268,003	92.1	90.7	89.6
Total forgeign-born	19,828	25,701	31,149	7.9	9.3	10.4
Mexico	4,482	5,855	7,188	1.8	2.1	2.4
Central America	1,187	1,809	2,413	0.5	0.7	0.8
Other Americas	3,116	4,308	5,324	1.2	1.6	1.8
Philippines	963	1,366	1,709	0.4	0.5	0.6
Other Asia/Pacific Islands	3,686	5,371	6,873	1.5	1.9	2.3
English-speaking	1,679	1,721	1,799	0.7	0.6	0.6
Europe/former USSR	3,679	3,784	3,992	1.5	1.4	1.3
Middle East/North Africa	753	1,005	1,213	0.3	0.4	0.4
Subsaharan Africa	282	474	637	0.1	0.2	0.2

[1] Series B is the higher projection series as defined by the authors.

Source: John R. Pitkin and Patrick A Simmons, "The Foreign-born Population to 2010: A Prospective Analysis by Country of Birth, Age, and Duration of U.S. Residence," Journal of Housing Research, Volume 7, Issue 1, 1996, Table C.1.

Table 9-15. Foreign-born Population by Age: 1990 and Series B[1] Projections for 2000 and 2010

Country of Birth	Population, in thousands			Percent distribution		
	1990	2000	2010	1990	2000	2010
Total population	249,424	275,833	299,152	100.0	100.0	100.0
Total native-born	229,596	250,132	268,003	92.1	90.7	89.6
Total foreign-born	19,828	25,701	31,149	7.9	9.3	10.4
Under 5 years	260	286	375	0.1	0.1	0.1
5 to 9 years	491	564	677	0.2	0.2	0.2
10 to 14 years	739	850	887	0.3	0.3	0.3
15 to 19 years	1,150	1,273	1,402	0.5	0.5	0.5
20 to 24 years	1,788	1,902	2,221	0.7	0.7	0.7
25 to 29 years	2,238	2,333	2,503	0.9	0.8	0.8
30 to 34 years	2,289	2,819	2,775	0.9	1.0	0.9
35 to 39 years	2,023	3,040	2,982	0.8	1.1	1.0
40 to 44 years	1,776	2,789	3,220	0.7	1.0	1.1
45 to 49 years	1,385	2,248	3,155	0.6	0.8	1.1
50 to 54 years	1,179	1,856	2,757	0.5	0.7	0.9
55 to 59 years	947	1,442	2,229	0.4	0.5	0.7
60 to 64 years	867	1,187	1,798	0.3	0.4	0.6
65 to 69 years	789	931	1,368	0.3	0.3	0.5
70 to 74 years	529	769	1,040	0.2	0.3	0.3
75 to 79 years	506	622	749	0.2	0.2	0.3
80 to 84 years	419	357	527	0.2	0.1	0.2
85 years and over	454	433	485	0.2	0.2	0.2

[1] Series B is the higher projection series as defined by the authors.

Source: John R. Pitkin and Patrick A Simmons, "The Foreign-born Population to 2010: A Prospective Analysis by Country of Birth, Age, and Duration of U.S. Residence," Journal of Housing Research, Volume 7, Issue 1, 1996, Table C.2.

Table 9-16. Ancestry of the United States Population, by Region: 1990

Ancestry	United States	Northeast	Midwest	South	West
All persons	248,709,873	50,809,229	59,668,632	85,445,930	52,786,082
All persons (percent)	100.0	100.0	100.0	100.0	100.0
Ancestry specified	89.5	91.9	90.7	86.1	91.3
Single ancestry	59.8	59.7	54.7	63.3	60.1
Multiple ancestry	29.7	32.2	36.0	22.9	31.1
Ancestry unclassified/not reported	10.5	8.1	9.3	13.9	8.7
Total ancestries reported	497,419,746	101,618,458	119,337,264	170,891,860	105,572,164
Total ancestries reported (percent)	100.0	100.0	100.0	100.0	100.0
Acadian	0.1	0.0	0.0	0.4	0.0
Arab	0.2	0.3	0.2	0.1	0.2
Armenian	0.1	0.1	0.0	0.0	0.2
Austrian	0.2	0.3	0.2	0.1	0.2
Belgian	0.1	0.0	0.2	0.0	0.1
British	0.2	0.2	0.2	0.3	0.3
Canadian	0.1	0.2	0.1	0.1	0.1
Croatian	0.1	0.1	0.2	0.1	0.1
Czech	0.3	0.1	0.6	0.2	0.2
Czechoslovakian	0.1	0.1	0.1	0.0	0.1
Danish	0.3	0.1	0.5	0.1	0.7
Dutch	1.3	1.0	1.8	1.0	1.2
English	6.6	5.8	6.1	6.7	7.7
European	0.1	0.1	0.1	0.1	0.2
Finnish	0.1	0.1	0.3	0.0	0.2
French (except Basque)	2.1	2.6	2.2	1.7	2.0
French Canadian	0.4	1.0	0.4	0.2	0.3
German	11.7	9.8	18.8	8.6	10.3
Greek	0.2	0.4	0.2	0.1	0.2
Hungarian	0.3	0.6	0.4	0.2	0.2
Irish	7.8	9.3	8.1	7.6	6.4
Italian	3.0	7.4	2.0	1.5	2.2
Lithuanian	0.2	0.3	0.2	0.1	0.1
Norwegian	0.8	0.2	1.7	0.2	1.2
Pennsylvanian German	0.1	0.2	0.1	0.0	0.0
Polish	1.9	3.4	2.9	0.8	1.0
Portuguese	0.2	0.6	0.0	0.1	0.4
Romanian	0.1	0.1	0.1	0.0	0.1
Russian	0.6	1.3	0.4	0.3	0.6
Scandinavian	0.1	0.1	0.2	0.1	0.3
Scotch-Irish	1.1	0.8	0.9	1.5	1.1
Scottish	1.1	1.1	1.0	1.0	1.3
Slovak	0.4	0.7	0.5	0.2	0.2
Subsaharan African	0.1	0.2	0.1	0.1	0.1
Swedish	0.9	0.7	1.6	0.4	1.4
Swiss	0.2	0.2	0.3	0.1	0.3
Ukrainian	0.1	0.4	0.1	0.1	0.1
United States of American	2.6	1.4	1.9	4.6	1.4
Welsh	0.4	0.4	0.4	0.3	0.5
West Indian (excluding Hispanic)	0.2	0.6	0.0	0.2	0.1
Yugoslavian	0.1	0.1	0.1	0.0	0.1
Other ancestries	13.1	10.0	8.4	15.3	18.1

Source: U.S. Bureau of the Census, "Social and Economic Characteristics: United States Summary," 1990 Census of Population, U.S. Government Printing Office, Washington, D.C., 1993, Table 13.

Table 9-17. Selected Social Characteristics of the Population, by Selected Ancestry: 1990

Social Characteristics	Total	English	French (ex. Basque)	German	Irish	Italian	Polish	Scotch-Irish	Scottish	Swedish	U.S./American
Number of persons	248,710	22,704	6,204	45,584	22,721	11,287	6,543	4,334	3,315	2,882	13,040
Percent foreign-born	7.9	2.8	2.7	1.8	1.2	5.7	6.2	0.7	4.6	2.0	0.1
M:F sex ratio	0.95	0.92	0.85	0.99	0.89	0.98	0.95	0.88	1.12	0.91	0.92
Marital status, persons 15+ (percent)											
Never married	26.5	20.1	23.0	24.3	24.2	27.2	25.6	18.7	20.4	21.9	23.0
Married, spouse present	55.5	61.6	58.7	59.9	58.0	57.2	58.0	60.6	62.8	61.5	57.8
Separated/widowed/divorced	18.0	18.3	18.2	15.8	17.8	15.6	16.5	20.7	16.9	16.7	19.2
Children ever born per 1,000:											
Women age 15 to 24 years	305	194	265	222	238	174	172	159	161	186	395
Women age 25 to 34 years	1,330	1,201	1,302	1,251	1,216	1,024	1,059	1,080	1,065	1,206	1,551
Women age 35 to 44 years	1,960	1,814	1,927	1,875	1,890	1,718	1,709	1,727	1,706	1,843	2,050
Educational attainment, persons 25+ (percent)											
Less than high school diploma	24.8	15.8	21.0	17.3	20.4	22.7	21.5	14.7	11.4	12.7	37.3
High school diploma	30.0	27.8	33.1	33.4	31.7	32.4	31.4	28.0	24.9	29.4	35.5
Some college	24.9	28.0	27.6	27.3	26.6	23.9	24.0	29.1	30.1	30.5	18.0
Bachelor's degree	13.1	18.1	12.2	14.7	14.0	13.5	14.1	18.1	21.5	18.4	6.3
Graduate/professional degree	7.2	10.3	6.1	7.3	7.2	7.4	9.0	10.1	12.2	9.1	2.9
Ability to speak English, persons 5+ (percent)											
Speak another language than English	13.8	2.0	7.2	4.0	2.2	12.5	12.8	1.9	2.4	4.0	3.0
Do not speak English "very well"	6.1	0.5	1.9	1.0	0.5	4.2	4.6	0.5	0.5	0.8	0.9

Source: U.S. Bureau of the Census, "Ancestry of the Population of the United States," 1990 Census of Population, U.S. Government Printing Office, Washington, D.C., 1993, Tables 1 and 3.

Table 9-18. Selected Economic Characteristics of the Population, by Selected Ancestry: 1990

Economic Characteristics	Total	English	French (ex. Basque)	German	Irish	Italian	Polish	Scotch-Irish	Scottish	Swedish	U.S./American
Percent in the labor force, persons 16 and over	65.3	62.5	66.1	69.2	66.9	66.2	66.0	59.8	66.1	66.3	60.5
Males	74.4	73.0	76.2	78.0	75.8	75.8	74.8	69.4	75.3	75.2	71.6
Females	56.8	53.1	57.8	60.7	57.9	58.4	57.9	51.6	55.7	58.5	50.8
Percent unemployed, civilians 16 and over	6.3	4.3	5.9	4.5	4.9	5.2	4.8	4.4	4.0	4.2	6.9
Males	6.4	4.5	6.2	4.6	5.1	5.4	5.1	4.7	4.1	4.4	6.8
Females	6.2	4.2	5.5	4.3	4.8	4.9	4.5	4.1	3.9	4.0	6.9
Median income per family, in dollars	35,225	40,875	36,237	38,216	38,101	42,242	41,700	39,816	43,293	40,459	27,198
Mean income per family, in dollars	43,803	51,507	43,846	46,229	46,686	51,442	51,539	49,592	54,519	49,443	33,567
Per capita income, in dollars	14,420	18,594	14,850	15,896	15,957	17,384	17,722	18,700	21,403	17,720	10,623
Percent families below poverty level	10.0	4.5	7.2	5.5	6.5	4.9	4.3	3.9	3.5	4.5	13.4
Percent persons below poverty level	13.1	6.8	9.3	7.7	8.7	6.9	6.6	6.1	5.8	6.7	15.8

Source: U.S. Bureau of the Census, "Ancestry of the Population of the United States," 1990 Census of Population, U.S. Government Printing Office, Washington, D.C., 1993, Tables 4 and 5.

concentrations in the "Other" category, likely reflecting the greater use of this category by Hispanic and Asian populations in those regions.

Social Characteristics of Ancestry Groups

It is to be expected that those ancestry groups that have been most diluted by intermarriage and most assimilated through long-time residence in the United States would come closest to the national average composition for the various population characteristics, while those least diluted and assimilated would be more likely to show distinctively different traits. Tables 9-17 and 9-18, presenting selected social and economic characteristics for the main ancestry groups, confirm this expectation.

The percent of the population which is foreign born is greatest among those with Polish, Italian and Scottish ancestry. But all of the major ancestry groups identified in Table 9-17 have a lower percentage of foreign birth than the total population. Sex ratios are relatively low for the French (excluding Basque), Irish and the Scotch-Irish while they are relatively high for the Scottish. Given the largely native character of all the selected ancestry groups no immediate explanation is available for these variations other than, perhaps, sex biases in self-reporting of ancestry. The percentage never married is notably high for those of Italian and Polish ancestry while it is lower for the Scotch-Irish. And, the percentage separated, widowed or divorced is somewhat lower for those reporting German, Italian, Polish, Scottish and Swedish ancestry. Again, differences in nuptiality may reflect reporting biases. They may also reflect age differences among ancestry groups. However, in the case of marriage timing and propensity it is clearly plausible that cultural influences among ancestry groups might also be reflected in these differences.

Variations in fertility do not directly parallel those of nuptiality as one might suspect if assimilation of these ancestry groups were more or less homogeneous. The Scotch-Irish, for example, have the lowest percentage never married but also have the fewest children ever born per 1,000 women under age 25. The highest reporting of children ever born is among those reporting United States or American ancestry. Again, this may be due to the inclusion of some higher fertility minority groups within this ancestry category.

Educational and language abilities differ markedly across these groups, indicating the cultural robustness of even those immigrant groups thought to be heavily exposed to assimilative influences. Those with the greatest proportion of the population without a high school degree, and the only selected group with more of such individuals than the population as a whole, are those claiming United States or American ancestry. Again, this reflects the greater proportion of socially disadvantaged and minority groups reporting such ancestry. The next highest percentages without a high school diploma are among those reporting Italian, Polish, French and Irish ancestry. All of these groups, however, are below the percentage without a high school degree reported for the total population.

All of the selected ancestry groups have a smaller percentage of the population that do not speak English very well, and a lower percentage that speak another language other than English, than do those in the total population. The ability to speak a language other than English is a plausible indicator for the strength of cultural ancestry ties since the most likely language is that associated with the ancestry group. The ability to speak another language other than English is much higher among those reporting Italian and Polish ancestry, and higher among those reporting French ancestry, than among other selected ancestry groups. And, all three of these groups have a somewhat lower percentage that speak English very well. Again, however, even among these groups the percentage able to speak another language other than English is lower than the total population.

Economic Characteristics of Ancestry Groups

Among the selected ancestry groups in Table 9-18 only the Scotch-Irish have a notably low labor force participation rate among both males and females. This lower labor force participation may reflect the more aged nature of those claiming this ancestry. Scotch-Irish ancestry in the United States population was largely a result of immigration from the historically bounded settlement of Ulster and Northern Ireland. More recent immigrants may be more likely to identify themselves as Irish or Scottish. Thus this group may have a more definite decline in those identifying with the ancestry than is true of the other selected ancestry groups. The lowest labor force participation of women among the selected groups is among those reporting United States or American ancestry. Once again, this is probably the result of the likelihood that some disadvantaged groups, including minorities, are more liable to report this ancestry. The greater representation of the disadvantaged in the United States or American ancestry group is also reflected in the fact that this group has the lowest labor force participation among all persons 16 years of age and older and yet the highest unemployment rates among both males and females. The next highest rates of unemployment are among those claiming French ancestry. All groups other than those claiming United States or American ancestry have, however, lower rates of unemployment than in the total population for both males and females.

The same bias arising from the composition of those claiming United States or American ancestry is apparent in other indicators of Table 9-18. This group has the lowest median and mean family income, the lowest per capita income, and the highest percent of families and persons

Table 9-19. Persons Five Years and Over Speaking Various Languages at Home: 1990

Language spoken at home	Number	Percent
Total persons	230,445,777	100.0
Speak only English	198,600,798	86.2
Spanish	17,345,064	7.5
French	1,930,404	0.8
Italian	1,308,648	0.6
Portuguese	430,610	0.2
German	1,547,987	0.7
Yiddish	213,064	0.1
Other West Germanic	232,461	0.1
Scandinavian	198,904	0.1
Polish	723,483	0.3
Russian	241,798	0.1
South Slavic	170,449	0.1
Other Slavic	270,863	0.1
Greek	388,260	0.2
Indic	555,126	0.2
Other Indo-European languages	578,076	0.3
Chinese	1,319,462	0.6
Japanese	427,657	0.2
Mon-Khmer	127,441	0.1
Korean	626,478	0.3
Tagalog	843,251	0.4
Vietnamese	507,069	0.2
Arabic	355,150	0.2
Hungarian	147,902	0.1
Native North American languages	331,758	0.1
Other languages	1,023,614	0.4
Ability to speak English		
Spanish	17,345,064	100.0
Speak English "very well" or "well"	12,841,031	74.0
Speak English "not well" or "not at all"	4,504,033	26.0
Other Indo-European languages	8,790,133	100.0
Speak English "very well" or "well"	7,803,098	88.8
Speak English "not well" or "not at all"	987,035	11.2
Asian and Pacific Island languages	4,471,621	100.0
Speak English "very well" or "well"	3,407,273	76.2
Speak English "not well" or "not at all"	1,064,348	23.8
All other languages	1,238,161	100.0
Speak English "very well" or "well"	1,121,376	90.6
Speak English "not well" or "not at all"	116,785	9.4

Source: U.S. Bureau of the Census, "Social and Economic Characteristics: United States Summary," 1990 Census of Population, U.S. Government Printing Office, Washington, D.C., 1993, Table 13.

below the poverty level. All other selected ancestry groups have a higher median and mean income than the total population. The highest mean and median family incomes are among those claiming Scottish, Italian, English and Polish ancestry. The lowest median and mean income per family are those of persons claiming French ancestry. Those of French ancestry also have the highest percentage of both families and persons below the poverty level followed by those reporting Irish, and then German, ancestry.

Language Spoken at Home

In Table 9-19 the languages commonly spoken at home are reported for the United States population as a whole. English is, not surprisingly, the most commonly spoken language with 86.2 percent of the population speaking only English at home. Spanish is the second most commonly spoken language at home with 7.5 percent of the population speaking this language. All other languages reported are spoken by less than one percent of the population at home. Four of these languages, French, Italian, Portuguese and Chinese, are spoken by more than one-half of one percent of the population at home.

Among those who speak Spanish, nearly three-quarters (74.0 percent) also report the ability to speak English either "very well" or "well." Almost nine out of ten (88.8 percent) of those who speak other Indo-European languages report the ability to speak English well. And, over three-quarters (76.2 percent) of those speaking an Asian or Pacific Island language report their ability to speak English well. Of all persons who speak some other language, over nine out of ten (90.6 percent) report the ability to speak English very well. English is clearly the most universal language among the population of the United States. Yet, communication in other languages is required to effectively communicate with nearly one-quarter of those who speak either Spanish or one of the Asian and Pacific Island languages. Although Spanish is the second most widely spoken language in the United States population it is clear that a variety of languages are required to speak effectively to the full variety of citizens in the nation.

Bibliography

Alba, R.D., and Chamlin, M.B. "Preliminary Examination of Ethnic Identification Among Whites." American Sociological Review 48 (1983): 240-47.

Alba, R.D., and Moore, G. "Ethnicity in the American Elite." American Sociological Review 47 (1982): 373-83.

Anderton, D.L., Anderson, A.B., Rossi, P.H., Oakes, J.M., Fraser, M.R., Weber, E.W., and Calabrese, E.J. 1994a. "Hazardous Waste Facilities: Environmental Equity Issues in Metropolitan Areas." Evaluation Review 18(1994): 123-40.

Barringer, Herbert R., Gardner, Robert W., and Levin, Michael J. Asians and Pacific Islanders in the United States. New York: Russell Sage Foundation. 1993.

Bean, Frank D., and Tienda, Marta. The Hispanic Population of the United States. New York: Russell Sage Foundation. 1987.

Chiswick, Barry R., and Sullivan, Teresa A. "The New Immigrants." In State of the Union: America in the 1990s, Volume Two: Social Trends. Reynolds Farley (ed.). New York: Russell Sage Press. 1995.

Denton, N.A., and Massey, D.S. "Patterns of neighborhood transition in a multiethnic world: U.S. metropolitan areas, 1970-1980." Demography 28(1991): 41-63.

Duncan, Otis D., and Lieberson, Stanley. "Ethnic Segregation and Assimilation." American Journal of Sociology 64(1959): 364-74.

Farley, Reynolds. "Residental Segregation of Social and Economic Groups Among Blacks, 1970-1980." In The Urban Underclass. Christopher Jencks and Paul E. Peterson (eds.). Washington, D.C.: The Brookings Institution. 1991.

Farley, Reynolds, and Frey, William H. "Changes in the Segregation of Whites from Blacks During the 1980s: Small Steps Toward a More Integrated Society." American Sociological Review 59(1994): 23-45.

Frey, William H. "Minority Suburbanization and Continued 'White Flight' in U.S. Metropolitan Areas: Assessing Findings from the 1990 Census." Research Reports No. 92-247. Ann Arbor: Population Studies Center, University of Michigan. 1992.

_____. "Minority Suburbanization and Continued 'White Flight' in U.S. Metropolitan Areas: Assessing Findings from the 1990 Census." Research on Community Sociology 4(1994): 15-42.

Frey, William H., and Farley, Reynolds. "Latino, Asian and Black Segregation in U.S. Metropolitan Areas: Are Multiethnic Metros Different?" Demography 33(1996): 35-50.

Garcia, P. "Trends in the Relative Income Position of Mexican-Origin Workers in the U.S.: The Early Seventies." Sociology and Social Research 66(1982): 467-83.

Gardner, Robert W., Robey, Bryant, and Smith, Peter C. "Asian Americans: Growth, Change, and Diversity." Population Bulletin 40(October 1985): 1-44.

Glazer, Nathan. "Ethnic Groups in America." In Freedom and Control in Modern Society. Morroe Berger, Theodore Abel, and Charles Page (eds.). New York: Van Nostrand. 1954.

Glazer, Nathan, and Moynihan, Daniel P. (eds.). Ethnicity: Theory and Experience. Cambridge, MA: Harvard University Press. 1975.

Greeley, Andrew M. Why Can't They Be Like Us? America's White Ethnic Groups. New York: E.P. Dutton. 1971.

Handlin, Oscar. The American People in the Twentieth Century. Cambridge, MA: Harvard University Press. 1954.

Hardley, J. Nixon. "Demography of the American Indians." In American Indians and American Life. George E. Simpson and J. Milton Yinger (eds.). Annals of the American Academy of Political and Social Science 311(May 1957): 1-165.

Harrison, Roderick J., and Bennett, Claudette E. "Racial and Ethnic Diversity." In State of the Union: America in the 1990s, Volume Two: Social Trends. Reynolds Farley (ed.). New York: Russell Sage Press. 1995.

Jasso, Guillermina, and Rosenzweig, Mark R. The New Chosen People: Immigrants in the United States. New York: Russell Sage Foundation. 1990.

Kasarda, J. "Structural factors affecting the location and timing of urban underclass growth." Urban Geography 11(1990): 234-64.

Krivo, Lauren J. "Immigrant Characteristics and Hispanic Anglo Housing Inequality." Demography 32(1995): 599-615.

Kritz, Mary M., and Nogel, June Marie. "Nativity Concentration and Internal Migration among the Foreign-Born." Demography 31(1994): 509-24.

Logan, John R., and Alba, Richard D. "Locational returns to human capital: Minority access to suburban community resources." Demography 30(1993): 243-67.

Logan, John R., and Schneider, Mark. "Racial Segregation and Racial Change in American Suburbs, 1970-80." American Journal of Sociology 89(1984): 874-88.

Lieberson, Stanley. Ethnic Patterns in American Cities. New York: Free Press. 1963.

Massey, D.S. "Research Notes on Residential Succession: The Hispanic Case." Social Forces 61(1983): 825-33.

Massey, D.S., and Denton, N. A.. "The dimensions of residential segregation." Social Forces 67(1988): 281-315.

_____. "Hypersegregation in U.S. metropolitan areas: black and Hispanic segregation along five dimensions." Demography 26(1989): 373-91.

_____. American Apartheid: Segregation and the Making of the Underclass. Cambridge, MA: Harvard University Press. 1993.

McHugh, Kevin E. "Hispanic Migration and Population Redistribution in the United States." Professional Geographer 41(1989): 429-39.

McKinney, S. "Change in Metropolitan Area Residence Integration, 1970-1980." Population Research and Policy Review 8(1989): 143-64.

Montero, D. "Japanese Americans: Changing Patterns of Assimilation over Three Generations." American Sociological Review 46(1981): 829-39.

Park, R.E., and Burgess, E.W. The City. Chicago: University of Chicago Press. 1967.

Passel, Jeffrey S., and Woodrow, Karen A. "Geographic Distribution of Undocumented Immigrants: Estimates of Undocumented Aliens Counted in the 1980 Census by State." International Migration Review 18(1984): 642-71.

Peach, Ceri, Robinson, Vaughan, and Smitt, Susan. Ethnic Segregation in Cities. Athens, GA: University of Georgia Press. 1981.

Pitkin, John R., and Simmons, Patrick A. "The Foreign-born Population to 2010: A Prospective Analysis by Country of Birth, Age, and Duration of U.S. Residence." Journal of Housing Research 7(1996): 1-31.

Portes, Alejandro, and Rumbaut, Ruben. Immigrant America: A Portrait. Berkeley: University of California Press. 1990.

Roof, W.C., and Spain, D. "Research Notes on City-Suburban Socioeconomic Differences Among American Blacks." Social Forces 56(1977): 15-20.

Sandefur, Gary D. "American Indian Migration and Economic Opportunities." International Migration Review 20(1986): 55-68.

Sandefur, Gary D., and Jeon, Jiwon. "Migration, Race and Ethnicity, 1960-1980." International Migration Review 25(1991): 392-407.

Schneider, M., and Phelan, T. "Black suburbanization in the 1980s." Demography 30(1993): 269-79.

Tienda, Marta. "Familism and Structural Assimilation of Mexican Immigrants in the U.S." International Migration Review 14(1980): 383-408.

United Church of Christ (UCC). "Toxic Wastes and Race in the United States: A National Report on the Racial and Socioeconomic Characteristics of Communities with Hazardous Waste Sites." United Church of Christ: New York. 1987.

U.S. Bureau of the Census. Detailed Population Characteristics: United States Summary. 1970 Census of Population. Washington, D.C.: U.S. Government Printing Office. 1973.

_____. General Population Characteristics: United States Summary. 1970 Census of Population. Washington, D.C.: U.S. Government Printing Office. 1973.

_____. General Social and Economic Characteristics: United States Summary. 1970 Census of Population. Washington, D.C.: U.S. Government Printing Office. 1973.

_____. Special Reports, Spanish-Origin Population. 1970 Census of Population. Washington, D.C.: U.S. Government Printing Office. 1973.

_____. Historical Statistics of the United States. Washington, D.C.: U.S. Government Printing Office. 1975.

_____. Statistical Abstract of the United States: 1982-1983. Washington, D.C.: U.S. Government Printing Office. 1982.

_____. General Population Characteristics: United States Summary. 1980 Census of Population. Washington, D.C.: U.S. Government Printing Office. 1983.

_____. General Social and Economic Characteristics: United States Summary. 1980 Census of Population. Washington, D.C.: U.S. Government Printing Office. 1983.

_____. General Population Characteristics: United States Summary. 1990 Census of Population. Washington, D.C.: U.S. Government Printing Office. 1992.

_____. Ancestry of the Population of the United States. 1990 Census of Population. Washington, D.C.: U.S. Government Printing Office. 1993.

_____. The Foreign-Born Population of the United States. 1990 Census of Population. Washington, D.C.: U.S. Government Printing Office. 1993.

_____. Population Projections of the United States, by Age, Sex, Race, and Hispanic Origin: 1993 to 2050. Current Population Reports, Series P-25, Number 1104. Washington, D.C.: U.S. Government Printing Office. 1993.

_____. Social and Economic Characteristics: American Indian and Alaska Native Areas. 1990 Census of Population. Washington, D.C.: U.S. Government Printing Office. 1993.

_____. Social and Economic Characteristics: United States Summary. 1990 Census of Population. Washington, D.C.: U.S. Government Printing Office. 1993.

_____. We, the American Asians. Washington. D.C.: U.S. Government Printing Office. 1993.

_____. We, the American Blacks. Washington. D.C.: U.S. Government Printing Office. 1993.

_____. We, the American Hispanics. Washington. D.C.: U.S. Government Printing Office. 1993.

_____. We, the American Pacific Islanders. Washington. D.C.: U.S. Government Printing Office. 1993.

_____. We, the First Americans. Washington. D.C.: U.S. Government Printing Office. 1993.

White, Michael J. American Neighborhoods and Residential Differentiation. New York: Russell Sage Foundation. 1987.

Wilson, William J. The Truly Disadvantaged: The Inner City, the Underclass, and Public Policy. Chicago: University of Chicago Press. 1987.

CHAPTER

10

AGING AND GENDER: COMPOSITION, THE LIFE CYCLE AND COHORTS

Age and sex are two fundamental biological dimensions of a population's composition, and hence, both its present state and future progress. For this reason, the basic age and sex composition of the United States was introduced in the first chapter of this text alongside other fundamental elaborations of the population's composition and historical trends. However, age and sex are also among the primary dimensions of social stratification. Age and sex groupings, along with the events typically experienced by these groups, largely define the stages of the typical life cycle (see Definition Box) within a population. In turn, a person's age and sex at the time of significant events can color their encounter with the sociocultural experiences which influence cohorts of individuals throughout their lives. Finally, age and sex can be determinants or correlates of many other behaviors within a population.

Some behaviors are formally restricted to certain age and sex groups. Education, military service, driving of automobiles, voting, consumption of regulated goods such as tobacco and liquor, etc., are examples of the many institutionalized age limits to certain behaviors. Some constraints upon military service still exist according to sex and even such behaviors as voting have been limited by sex in the country's recent past. Many more constraints on behavior are embodied in the expectations we hold for acceptable behavior according to age and sex. Our notions of proper styles of dress, occupations, leisure activities, personal mannerisms, courting and sexual behavior, and what sometimes seems to include nearly everything else in human behavior, are influenced heavily by the age and sex of the individuals involved. In addition to the force of normative expectations alone, blatant discrimination by both age and sex tend to reinforce these expectations. Comparable worth, workplace child-care, mandatory retirement, age and sex discrimination in hiring, paternity leave, and innumerable important policy

issues arise from attempts to combat the inequities arising from age and sex-graded behavioral expectations.

The present chapter both expands upon the description of age and sex composition within segments of the population and devotes somewhat more detail to these behavioral aspects of the age and sex composition of the United States population. The concerns of the present chapter begin again with the age and sex composition of the population. Differences in population composition are examined for some of the significant social subgroups or strata within the United States. The remainder of the chapter attempts to go beyond the biological composition of the population to address some of the prevalent social implications of age and sex and their changing distributions in the U. S. population. These social aspects of age and sex composition are considered, first, for several major life cycle events and transitions (e.g. employment, marriage, home ownership, etc.). Next, the age and sex distribution is examined for a variety of social behaviors which co-vary along these biosocial dimensions (e.g. voting, religion, consumption, sexual behavior, crime, etc.). The range of behaviors which can be reasonably considered is, unfortunately, limited. However, many specific age and sex issues of great policy concern are further elaborated in following chapters on education, employment, occupation, income and poverty, etc.

A major focus of this chapter is on the social construction and the demographic implications of aging and gender. To emphasize this focus, the chapter examines a wider range of population behaviors than are typical in demographic profiles. Some of these behaviors such as householding, educational transitions, labor force participation, etc., are indeed discussed in context and considerably more detail elsewhere in this text. Analysis of several other age and sex-related behaviors such as voting, religion, sexual behavior, etc., is limited to that given in this wide-reaching chapter. This chapter brings together

Chapter 10 Definitions
AGING AND GENDER:
COMPOSITION, THE LIFE CYCLE AND COHORTS

Because this chapter surveys a variety of demographic, and demographically related, behaviors, most terms relied upon in this chapter are defined elsewhere in the text. Definitions are limited here to the important concepts emphasized in the present chapter.

Age-Sex Composition. The composition of a population is simply a description (e.g., frequency or percentages) of relevant subgroups within the population. For demographic, and many cultural phenomena, basic composition distinctions are biological ones. This chapter focuses upon the self reported biological age and sex composition of the population. Race or ethnicity, discussed in detail in the preceding chapter, is sometimes included in the underlying biological dimensions of composition despite their more culturally grounded meaning in many cases. Information on the age, sex and race composition of the population is included in this chapter and throughout the text.

Sex and Sexual Behavior. In this chapter it is useful to distinguish between biological divisions which are used to define or identify population composition and the behavioral differences among these population groups (see Udry, 1994). By sex, we mean to identify the biologically referential division of the population's composition. In accordance with conventional usage this term may also refer to sexual intercourse. Where possible we distinguish intercourse and other behavior with erotic implication through use of the phrase sexual behavior. This distinction is one of convenience and is not meant to limit or constrain the definition of sexual behavior as exclusively referring to sexual intercourse and reproductive activity.

Gender and Gendered Behavior. By gender, we mean to identify the description of behaviors which largely reflect cultural norms and conceptions of the 'sexes.' In describing gender related, or gendered, behavior reference is most frequently still made to the sex of individual respondents. Thus males' and females' behaviors, or men's and women's behaviors, are described as illustrating the gender differences in society reflected in tabulation by sex.

Age, Age Effects and Aging. Age refers directly to the chronological age of individual population members. This age can be measured and summarized for a population in many different ways. Typically age is referred to through age groups of individuals with the same completed years of age. Age effects refer to the behavioral influences which age alone is responsible for independently of other (e.g., period, cohort) effects.

We use aging to distinguish the behavioral changes and underlying cultural norms which accompany advancing age in the population. Although many behaviors, e.g., retirement, marriage, etc., are often tied to the typical ages at which they occur, the behaviors are not determined by the biological aging process. Thus, many behavioral implications of aging should be remembered to reflect distinctly culturally determined associations with age.

Period and Period Effects. A period refers to a specific point in time or a time interval. Period effects then refer to the effects on behavior of being at a specific point in time. A period of high inflation, war, pestilence, prosperity, etc., may have unique and immediate effects on behavior which are independent of other (e.g., age, cohort) effects.

Cohort and Cohort Effects. A cohort is simply a group of individuals identified as having experienced a similar significant effect in a specific time period. The most frequent use of cohorts is for longitudinal observation of successive periods following the cohort of individuals through subsequent (or prior) life-cycle experiences. The most typical cohort reference is to birth cohorts of individuals born in the same period. This usage is so common that the unqualified term cohort may generally be assumed to refer to birth cohorts. Marriage cohorts refer to individuals married, usually first-married, within a given period. Unique cohorts, such as individuals who first entered full time employment in a given period, are used to follow the experiences of these individuals through subsequent life histories and are frequently correlated with birth cohorts.

Substantively, cohort effects refer to the effects on behavior which are due to the cohort membership and are independent of other (e.g., age, period) effects. It is difficult to statistically disentangle age, period and cohort effects in an empirical analysis. Nonetheless, it is substantively convincing that a particular cohort, (e.g., the depression cohort, the baby boomers) at times has a unique history of events at certain periods and ages that results in unique cohort histories with independent causal influence on subsequent cohort behaviors. Indeed, many of the tabulations in the second section of the present chapter are intended to illustrate such unique cohort histories and potential cohort effects.

Generation. The term generation is used in reference to birth cohorts, a group of individuals born at the same general period of time. A definition of a particular generation often takes on a cultural meaning of individuals facing a common circumstance and not as clearly defined in years of birth as a birth cohort. Generation labels such as 'Depression Era Workers,' 'Generation X' or 'Baby Boomer' for example have been used with differing date boundaries by different writers who are more concerned with the circumstances these birth cohorts encountered.

Baby Boom. The phrase 'baby boom' refers to the rising trend in births which characterized many countries in the post World War II period and peaking in the 1960's. Thus a reference to 'baby boomers' refers to the generation born during this period. The phrase 'baby bust,' 'birth dearth' and 'Generation X' have been used to refer to the relatively smaller birth cohorts following the baby boom.

Easterlin Hypothesis. The size, or relative numbers, of a birth cohort has a significant negative effect on its economic well being and relative income. Since fertility of a generation is positively influenced by its relative income this may lead to generational cycles in age distributions, fertility and births (see Easterlin, 1980). On occasion, reference to the Easterlin hypothesis is used to refer to the more general age structure phenomena including many other cases where a preceding larger cohort may diminish the opportunity structure of a following cohort or a smaller preceding cohort may result in vacancies in the opportunity structure. Such inter-cohort age structure effects can, however, be considerably more complex.

Life Cycle. The life cycle is conceptualized as a sequence of stages through which individuals, families or households may pass. The individual life cycle begins with birth and ends with death. The life cycle may be described by the typical timing, i.e. age, of major life cycle events and stages; the duration spent in these various stages of the life cycle, i.e. widowed, or through the frequency of individuals in various life cycle stages at any given time or age. Family or household life cycles begin with formation and end with dissolution. Any life cycle description makes reference to life cycle stages. These stages are defined by major events over the life cycle which may be either typical events (e.g. marriage, childbearing, widowhood) or may be atypical departures from the normal pattern designed to highlight differences from prevalent behaviors.

these diverse behaviors as significant illustrations of the many behaviors related to aging and gender. They are, at the same time, selected but important elements of population composition in their own right. Our presentation of these data emphasizes the importance of changing social differences in behavior through stressing the changing nature of these behaviors over time for those of a given age or gender. In many instances these differences are presented graphically through the changing distribution of population characteristics across historical cohorts.

Changing Age and Sex Composition

The social nature of aging and gender often mirror simple changes in the age and sex composition of the population. For example, the aging of the sizable 'baby boom' cohort has affected social norms and behaviors across several decades. This cohort's influence is reflected in everything from the products we see advertised to the social programs receiving greatest attention and support. Similarly, a sizable group of the United States population carries with them the common history of having experienced the Great Depression or World War II. A much larger group shares the experience of having parents who lived through those events. Such common historical experiences have had a profound influence upon a wide range of attitudes and behaviors among affected cohorts. These everyday examples indicate how the composition of the population can affect social experiences and how those experiences can create differences in the composition of the population, respectively.

Our first task in this chapter is simply to provide a more detailed look at the age and sex composition of the United States population. Table 10-1 provides the detailed breakdown of the United States population by single years of age. The general population structure and major characteristics of the age and sex of the population have already been discussed in Chapter 1. Single year figures provide somewhat more detail and insight into the year-to-year population fluctuations in age groups. The age distribution of the United States population is being profoundly affected by the aging baby boom cohorts through the early middle ages. The baby boom cohorts have entered into ages of higher mortality and the size of the 'baby bulge' will be mediated somewhat as mortality takes its toll. Nonetheless, this group will severely impact programs for the elderly and social priorities as they continue to move into older ages in the near future. In 1990 the largest single year of age population groups were those between 26 and 35 years of age. The largest single year age group were those 30 years old. At this young age the effects of higher male mortality have not yet taken their toll and males still outnumber females.

The year-to-year divergence in the sex composition also highlights the dramatic relative decline in males,

due primarily to mortality. In the five years following age 62 the sex composition among one's peers changes on a yearly basis for both surviving males and females. At 62 years of age there are 1.14 females for every male. By age 77 there are approximately one and a half females for every male and by age 83 there are nearly two surviving females for every male.

The current age and sex composition is, of course, a highly transitory product of dramatic behavioral changes over the recent past. Single year of age comparisons are suggestive of specific historical events and more general trends over time. Figure 10-1 shows the population pyramids for the United States population in 1940 and 1990. These pyramids show the transition of the population from the pyramidal shape characteristic of a high fertility population to a much more rectangular shape characteristic of a lower fertility population. The boom of individuals aged 20 to 45 is clearly evident. And, the larger relative proportion of the population living over age 75 is also evident as is the greater surplus of women at these ages.

Racial and Ethnic Differences in Composition

As the preceding chapter has made clear, different race and ethnic groups in the United States have had their own unique demographic histories of fertility, immigration and mortality. Accordingly, many social groups have different age and sex distributions from one another. Table 10-2 presents the age distributions and sex ratios for selected race and ethnic groups. The white population, largely because of lower fertility, has clearly smaller percentages of young men and women than do other groups. Whites have somewhat lower mortality at various life stages, also contributing to the greater numbers of elderly among that group. Hispanics and American Indian populations have much younger populations in accord with both higher fertility and mortality. Among Hispanics and Asian or Pacific Islanders the population composition is also likely influenced by immigration of individuals in the young adult ages of 15-34. Both groups have disproportionately large cohorts at these ages. The Asian or Pacific Islander population, however, has a less young population than the Hispanic and the American Indian, Eskimo, or Aleut population groups. Blacks have an age composition which is nearly midway between whites and other population groups with some evidence of immigration and intermediary levels of fertility.

The sex ratio of various groups at different ages reflects both the sex ratio at birth and the cumulative migration or mortality experiences of individuals at those age groups. Not surprisingly, in the youngest age groups, many groups have similar sex ratios. However, greater infant mortality and differences in cause-specific child mortality among the black population contribute to a notably lower sex ratio for this group. This difference be-

Table 10-1. Single Years of Age by Sex: 1990

Age	Both sexes		Males		Females	
	Number	Percent	Number	Percent	Number	Percent
Total	248,709,873	100.0	121,239,418	100.0	127,470,455	100.0
Under 1 year	3,217,312	1.3	1,644,801	1.4	1,572,511	1.2
1 year	3,949,107	1.6	2,022,292	1.7	1,926,815	1.5
2 years	3,815,040	1.5	1,952,242	1.6	1,862,798	1.5
3 years	3,683,177	1.5	1,884,023	1.6	1,799,154	1.4
4 years	3,689,807	1.5	1,889,051	1.6	1,800,756	1.4
5 years	3,689,533	1.5	1,889,177	1.6	1,800,356	1.4
6 years	3,577,632	1.4	1,829,832	1.5	1,747,800	1.4
7 years	3,645,761	1.5	1,865,700	1.5	1,780,061	1.4
8 years	3,508,668	1.4	1,794,355	1.5	1,714,313	1.3
9 years	3,677,585	1.5	1,883,463	1.6	1,794,122	1.4
10 years	3,653,177	1.5	1,874,172	1.5	1,779,005	1.4
11 years	3,455,515	1.4	1,771,334	1.5	1,684,181	1.3
12 years	3,423,450	1.4	1,752,999	1.4	1,670,451	1.3
13 years	3,339,000	1.3	1,706,417	1.4	1,632,583	1.3
14 years	3,243,107	1.3	1,662,245	1.4	1,580,862	1.2
15 years	3,321,609	1.3	1,705,780	1.4	1,615,829	1.3
16 years	3,304,890	1.3	1,697,995	1.4	1,606,895	1.3
17 years	3,410,062	1.4	1,758,400	1.5	1,651,662	1.3
18 years	3,641,238	1.5	1,862,377	1.5	1,778,861	1.4
19 years	4,076,216	1.6	2,078,146	1.7	1,998,070	1.6
20 years	4,009,414	1.6	2,044,082	1.7	1,965,332	1.5
21 years	3,817,220	1.5	1,947,811	1.6	1,869,409	1.5
22 years	3,655,792	1.5	1,865,082	1.5	1,790,710	1.4
23 years	3,742,903	1.5	1,900,305	1.6	1,842,598	1.4
24 years	3,794,983	1.5	1,918,316	1.6	1,876,667	1.5
25 years	4,212,100	1.7	2,128,319	1.8	2,083,781	1.6
26 years	4,168,508	1.7	2,089,771	1.7	2,078,737	1.6
27 years	4,256,124	1.7	2,135,488	1.8	2,120,636	1.7
28 years	4,253,634	1.7	2,133,374	1.8	2,120,260	1.7
29 years	4,422,679	1.8	2,208,984	1.8	2,213,695	1.7
30 years	4,734,587	1.9	2,370,937	2.0	2,363,650	1.9
31 years	4,151,337	1.7	2,060,115	1.7	2,091,222	1.6
32 years	4,448,958	1.8	2,214,154	1.8	2,234,804	1.8
33 years	4,307,844	1.7	2,138,926	1.8	2,168,918	1.7
34 years	4,220,161	1.7	2,092,801	1.7	2,127,360	1.7
35 years	4,381,379	1.8	2,190,853	1.8	2,190,526	1.7
36 years	4,039,788	1.6	1,994,887	1.6	2,044,901	1.6
37 years	3,960,965	1.6	1,962,032	1.6	1,998,933	1.6
38 years	3,784,903	1.5	1,872,696	1.5	1,912,207	1.5
39 years	3,796,082	1.5	1,881,775	1.6	1,914,307	1.5
40 years	3,956,970	1.6	1,960,986	1.6	1,995,984	1.6
41 years	3,430,115	1.4	1,683,874	1.4	1,746,241	1.4
42 years	3,792,198	1.5	1,874,883	1.5	1,917,315	1.5
43 years	3,686,510	1.5	1,820,999	1.5	1,865,511	1.5
44 years	2,749,993	1.1	1,351,242	1.1	1,398,751	1.1
45 years	3,033,291	1.2	1,500,522	1.2	1,532,769	1.2
46 years	2,843,408	1.1	1,391,830	1.1	1,451,578	1.1
47 years	2,940,252	1.	·45,216	1.2	1,495,036	1.2

Table 10-1. Single Years of Age by Sex: 1990 (continued)

Age	Both sexes		Males		Females	
	Number	Percent	Number	Percent	Number	Percent
48 years	2,546,830	1.0	1,242,348	1.0	1,304,482	1.0
49 years	2,508,792	1.0	1,230,681	1.0	1,278,111	1.0
50 years	2,537,983	1.0	1,240,132	1.0	1,297,851	1.0
51 years	2,191,015	0.9	1,064,572	0.9	1,126,443	0.9
52 years	2,294,122	0.9	1,117,210	0.9	1,176,912	0.9
53 years	2,170,359	0.9	1,051,596	0.9	1,118,763	0.9
54 years	2,157,034	0.9	1,041,228	0.9	1,115,806	0.9
55 years	2,205,152	0.9	1,061,296	0.9	1,143,856	0.9
56 years	2,024,012	0.8	970,951	0.8	1,053,061	0.8
57 years	2,089,901	0.8	998,969	0.8	1,090,932	0.9
58 years	2,043,408	0.8	969,949	0.8	1,073,459	0.8
59 years	2,169,283	0.9	1,033,205	0.9	1,136,078	0.9
60 years	2,209,589	0.9	1,039,557	0.9	1,170,032	0.9
61 years	2,018,714	0.8	948,483	0.8	1,070,231	0.8
62 years	2,209,518	0.9	1,031,185	0.9	1,178,333	0.9
63 years	2,093,966	0.8	970,712	0.8	1,123,254	0.9
64 years	2,084,380	0.8	957,110	0.8	1,127,270	0.9
65 years	2,201,718	0.9	996,570	0.8	1,205,148	0.9
66 years	1,999,363	0.8	901,946	0.7	1,097,417	0.9
67 years	2,010,737	0.8	904,098	0.7	1,106,639	0.9
68 years	1,985,205	0.8	882,016	0.7	1,103,189	0.9
69 years	1,914,712	0.8	847,677	0.7	1,067,035	0.8
70 years	1,817,009	0.7	787,423	0.6	1,029,586	0.8
71 years	1,611,869	0.6	697,537	0.6	914,332	0.7
72 years	1,622,781	0.7	693,843	0.6	928,938	0.7
73 years	1,506,979	0.6	632,968	0.5	874,011	0.7
74 years	1,436,185	0.6	597,535	0.5	838,650	0.7
75 years	1,420,300	0.6	576,084	0.5	844,216	0.7
76 years	1,288,590	0.5	515,320	0.4	773,270	0.6
77 years	1,214,654	0.5	475,918	0.4	738,736	0.6
78 years	1,134,677	0.5	434,529	0.4	700,148	0.5
79 years	1,063,148	0.4	397,917	0.3	665,231	0.5
80 years	977,849	0.4	353,349	0.3	624,500	0.5
81 years	829,584	0.3	296,518	0.2	533,066	0.4
82 years	800,448	0.3	277,509	0.2	522,939	0.4
83 years	704,073	0.3	236,260	0.2	467,813	0.4
84 years	621,785	0.3	202,458	0.2	419,327	0.3
85 years	560,545	0.2	175,581	0.1	384,964	0.3
86 years	469,208	0.2	143,684	0.1	325,524	0.3
87 years	398,712	0.2	117,746	0.1	280,966	0.2
88 years	325,721	0.1	93,513	0.1	232,208	0.2
89 years	306,061	0.1	83,512	0.1	222,549	0.2
90 to 94 years	769,481	0.3	190,089	0.2	579,392	0.5
95 to 99 years	213,131	0.1	45,672	...	167,459	0.1
100 to 104 years	30,947	...	5,944	...	25,003	...
105 years and over	6,359	...	1,957	...	4,402	...

Source: U.S. Bureau of the Census, "General Population Characteristics," 1990 Census of Population, CP-1-1, U.S.
    Government Printing Office, Washington, D.C., 1992, Table 13.

Figure 10-1. Comparative Population Distributions of the United States in 1940 and 1990, by Age and Sex

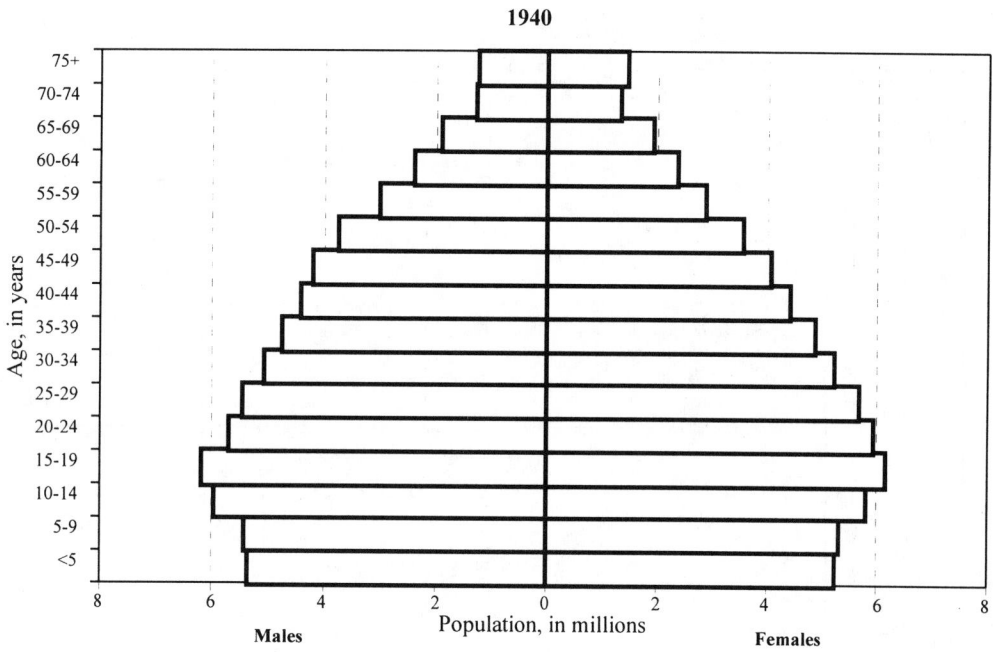

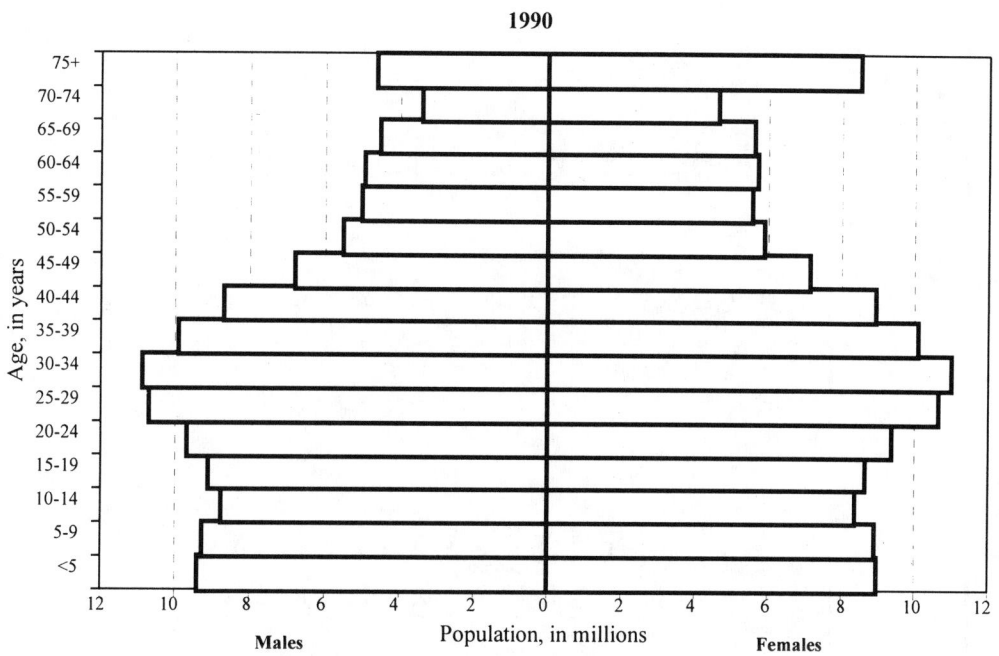

Source: 1940 and 1990 U.S. Census data

Table 10-2. Age by Sex, by Race-ethnicity: 1990

Age	All races Total	All races Age distribution	All races M:F sex ratio	White Total	White Age distribution	White M:F sex ratio	Black Total	Black Age distribution	Black M:F sex ratio
Total	248,709,873	100.0	0.95	199,686,070	100.0	0.95	29,986,060	100.0	0.90
Under 5 years	18,354,443	7.4	1.05	13,649,490	6.8	1.05	2,785,902	9.3	1.02
5 to 9 years	18,099,179	7.3	1.05	13,616,268	6.8	1.06	2,671,109	8.9	1.02
10 to 14 years	17,114,249	6.9	1.05	12,853,558	6.4	1.06	2,601,590	8.7	1.02
15 to 19 years	17,754,015	7.1	1.05	13,342,703	6.7	1.05	2,658,493	8.9	1.02
20 to 24 years	19,020,312	7.6	1.04	14,523,912	7.3	1.04	2,578,953	8.6	0.95
25 to 29 years	21,313,045	8.6	1.01	16,638,544	8.3	1.02	2,707,765	9.0	0.90
30 to 34 years	21,862,887	8.8	0.99	17,351,513	8.7	1.01	2,681,724	8.9	0.87
35 to 39 years	19,963,117	8.0	0.98	16,081,606	8.1	1.00	2,336,766	7.8	0.86
40 to 44 years	17,615,786	7.1	0.97	14,506,390	7.3	0.99	1,876,062	6.3	0.86
45 to 49 years	13,872,573	5.6	0.96	11,585,703	5.8	0.98	1,405,766	4.7	0.84
50 to 54 years	11,350,513	4.6	0.94	9,504,871	4.8	0.96	1,179,011	3.9	0.82
55 to 59 years	10,531,756	4.2	0.92	8,968,416	4.5	0.93	1,032,749	3.4	0.79
60 to 64 years	10,616,167	4.3	0.87	9,211,123	4.6	0.89	961,619	3.2	0.76
65 to 69 years	10,111,735	4.1	0.81	8,899,637	4.5	0.82	863,045	2.9	0.73
70 to 74 years	7,994,823	3.2	0.74	7,126,564	3.6	0.75	640,415	2.1	0.66
75 to 79 years	6,121,369	2.5	0.64	5,485,025	2.7	0.65	481,270	1.6	0.59
80 to 84 years	3,933,739	1.6	0.53	3,552,695	1.8	0.53	293,638	1.0	0.52
85 to 89 years	2,060,247	0.8	0.42	1,864,553	0.9	0.42	152,974	0.5	0.46
90 to 94 years	769,481	0.3	0.33	702,256	0.4	0.32	53,391	0.2	0.38
95 to 99 years	213,131	0.1	0.27	191,138	0.1	0.26	17,944	0.1	0.33
100 to 104 years	30,947	...	0.24	25,881	...	0.22	4,208	...	0.32
105 years and over	6,359	...	0.44	4,224	...	0.39	1,666	...	0.51

Table 10-2. Age by Sex, by Race-ethnicity: 1990 (continued)

Age	American Indian, Eskimo, or Aleut			Asian or Pacific Islander			Hispanic		
	Total	Age distribution	M:F sex ratio	Total	Age distribution	M:F sex ratio	Total	Age distribution	M:F sex ratio
Total	1,959,234	100.0	0.97	7,273,662	100.0	0.96	22,354,059	100.0	1.04
Under 5 years	201,950	10.3	1.03	589,845	8.1	1.04	2,387,524	10.7	1.04
5 to 9 years	199,446	10.2	1.03	596,133	8.2	1.03	2,193,852	9.8	1.04
10 to 14 years	188,000	9.6	1.04	551,552	7.6	1.04	2,001,617	9.0	1.05
15 to 19 years	180,516	9.2	1.06	603,761	8.3	1.07	2,053,957	9.2	1.12
20 to 24 years	165,549	8.4	1.06	632,258	8.7	1.06	2,304,441	10.3	1.21
25 to 29 years	175,577	9.0	0.99	691,069	9.5	0.98	2,341,239	10.5	1.15
30 to 34 years	170,668	8.7	0.94	726,183	10.0	0.93	2,062,303	9.2	1.09
35 to 39 years	152,754	7.8	0.94	669,818	9.2	0.90	1,660,726	7.4	1.04
40 to 44 years	126,154	6.4	0.94	572,194	7.9	0.87	1,284,268	5.7	0.99
45 to 49 years	96,817	4.9	0.94	405,590	5.6	0.93	953,910	4.3	0.96
50 to 54 years	76,714	3.9	0.93	311,651	4.3	0.95	755,989	3.4	0.93
55 to 59 years	61,819	3.2	0.90	250,633	3.4	0.83	639,308	2.9	0.90
60 to 64 years	51,389	2.6	0.89	218,517	3.0	0.76	553,642	2.5	0.85
65 to 69 years	42,710	2.2	0.82	178,497	2.5	0.80	436,257	2.0	0.81
70 to 74 years	29,270	1.5	0.75	122,234	1.7	0.80	286,772	1.3	0.72
75 to 79 years	21,152	1.1	0.67	80,139	1.1	0.85	213,265	1.0	0.64
80 to 84 years	12,116	0.6	0.60	43,850	0.6	0.96	130,425	0.6	0.61
85 to 89 years	6,243	0.3	0.56	20,449	0.3	0.82	66,623	0.3	0.57
90 to 94 years	2,039	0.1	0.56	6,944	0.1	0.57	20,383	0.1	0.50
95 to 99 years	659	...	0.48	1,853	...	0.36	5,916	...	0.45
100 to 104 years	180	...	0.61	357	...	0.52	1,051	...	0.43
105 years and over	84	...	0.58	135	...	0.65	591	...	0.81

Source: U.S. Bureau of the Census, "General Population Characteristics," 1990 Census of Population, CP-1-1, U.S. Government Printing Office, Washington, D.C., 1992, Table 13.

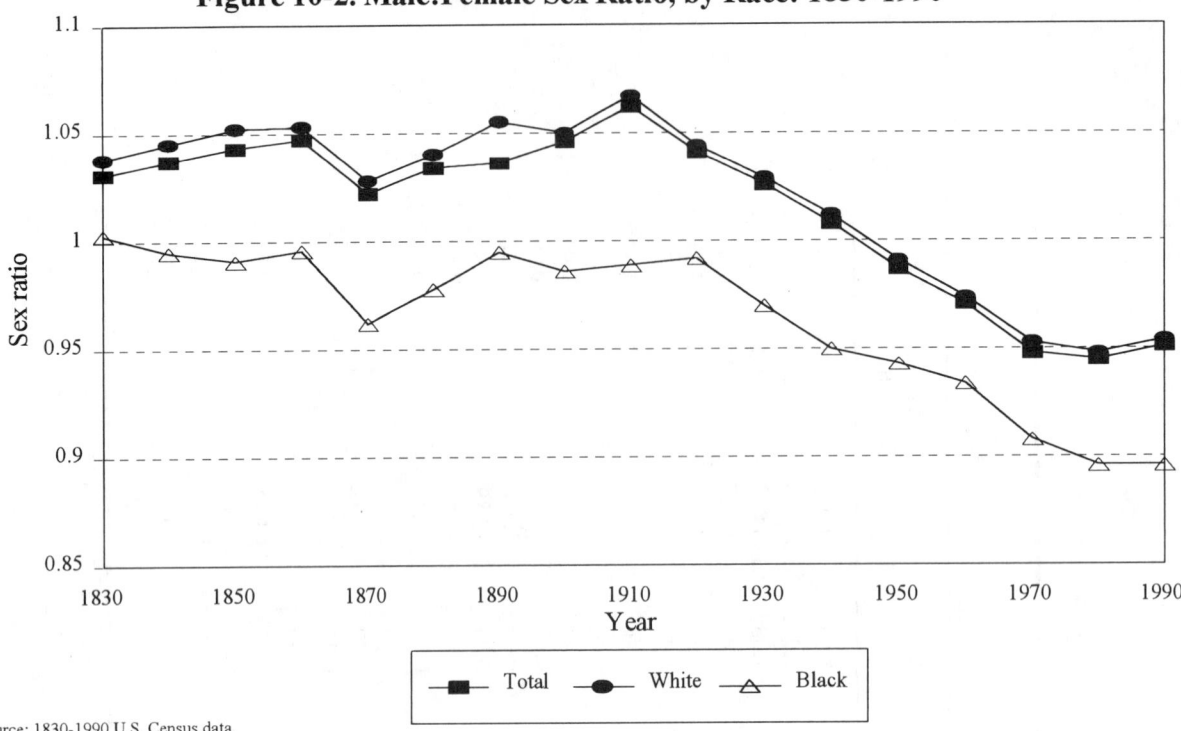

Figure 10-2. Male:Female Sex Ratio, by Race: 1830-1990

Source: 1830-1990 U.S. Census data.

tween the black population and other groups increases dramatically during the ages of 20-34 in which young adult black males have experienced disproportionate mortality. The persistence of a lower sex ratio among blacks through retirement ages suggests that these differences are not limited to recent cohorts. In fact, Figure 10-2 shows that the sex ratio for blacks has moved parallel to that of the total population but has always remained at a lower level since at least 1830. The greater mortality faced by black males is the predominant lasting social inequality underlying this difference in population composition. Overall, sex ratios for the entire population declined from 1910 to 1970 as both the population aged and life expectancy was extended. As a result there were greater proportions of surviving females in the aging population. Declining sex ratios were temporarily suspended by the effects of the baby boom and appear to have remained nearly level from 1970 to 1990. However, as the baby boom ages one can only anticipate a further decline in the sex ratio due to differential survival by sex at older ages.

Males of all race and ethnic groups face higher mortality levels at most ages. Figure 10-3 shows the overall decline in sex ratios across the life cycle which results from greater male mortality across the life cycle. There are two exceptions to the predominant decline in sex ratios with advancing age. The first largely reflects the migration of younger, working-age Hispanic males raising the sex ratio for Hispanics between ages 20 and 29.

The second is again largely due to male-dominated migration, now in older cohorts of 70 to 89 years of age, in the Asian and Pacific Islander population. Also of interest is that the sex ratio for all other groups is higher among the oldest ages, e.g. over 80 years of age, than it is for the white population. Greater survival among older white females, and perhaps some disproportionate mortality experience of elderly white males, appears to predominate at these older ages. Other groups have much higher sex ratios among the oldest old.

Regional Differences in Composition

Unique regional histories have also contributed to the more localized variety of age and sex distributions in different areas of the United States. Table 10-3 presents the age distributions and sex ratios for regions of the United States in both 1940 and 1990. The changes in age composition over the past half century have been dramatic in all regions of the country. However, the decrease in younger aged populations has been greatest in the South which entered the 1940s with a significantly younger population than other regions. Regional differences also reflect a fairly recent rise in fertility among the Northeast and Western regions, as evidenced by the increasing proportion of the population under five and under nine years of age, respectively, in these regions.

The most dramatic percentage change in the age composition of regional populations over the past half

Figure 10-3. Male:Female Sex Ratio, by Age and Race-ethnicity: 1990

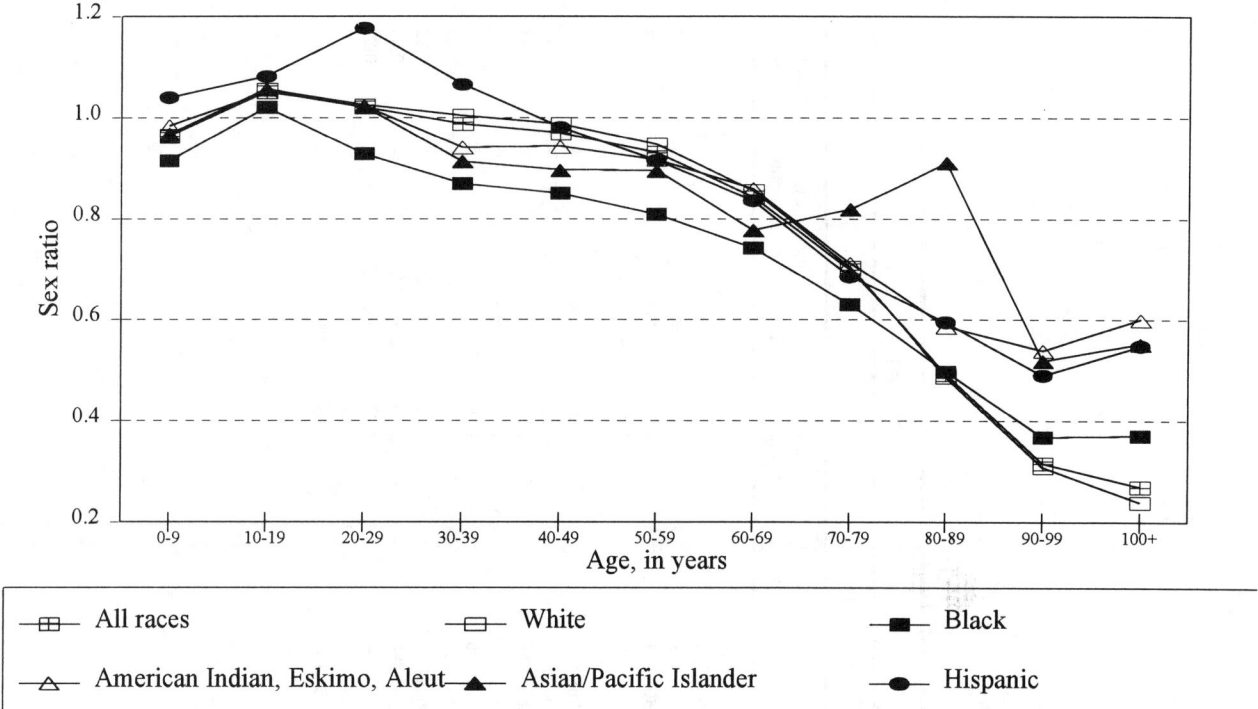

Source: 1990 U.S. Census data.

century has been the rise of elderly across all regions. The aging of the population is somewhat less in the West, which has the smallest percentages of population in age groups beyond 45 years of age. This younger population composition reflects both fertility and immigration differences. The increase in elderly has again been most dramatic in the South, which began the 1940s with a younger population than other regions. The greatest percentages of population over 75 years of age, however, are found in the Northeast and Midwest. These older populations reflect lower fertility and net out-migration of working-age adults and families.

Differences in sex ratios between 1940 and 1990 again clearly reflect declines in adult male mortality over the period. All regions had an increase of sex ratios among those in their twenties. Among the elderly the sex ratio has dropped dramatically in all regions reflecting an increasing survival rate of elderly women. For age groups in the years of initial employment and household formation, the notably higher sex ratios in the West are likely impacted by a disproportionate migration of young males into that region.

Urban and Rural Differences in Composition

With the dramatic shift in the population from rural to urban areas over the past half century it is not surprising that there have also been changes in the age and sex composition of the urban and rural populations. These changes reflect both the selective nature of migration and the higher fertility in areas where young adults establish families and raise their children. In the 1940s a majority of the country's population still resided in rural areas. Rural populations at this time had a significantly younger age composition than urban areas with more of the population in every age group under 19 years of age (see Table 10-4). Some trace of this same difference was still apparent in 1990. Yet, the greater percentages of the 1990 rural population in age groups from 5-19 years of age are less dramatic than those of 1940. In addition, the urban population of 1990 actually had a greater percentage of persons under five years of age.

Both urban and rural populations have increased percentages of the elderly by 1990. Any differences in percentages at these older age groups are slight. Half a century ago there was a slightly higher percentage of the rural population which was over 75 years of age. By the census of 1990 there were slightly more of these older individuals in urban areas. As an aging population confronts the declining access to rural health care, trends may encourage urban residence by the elderly.

Differences in sex ratios have been pronounced between urban and rural areas. The sex ratios in Table 10-4, however, may be profoundly affected by effects of

Table 10-3. Age by Sex, by Region: 1940 and 1990

Age	Northeast 1940 Total	1940 Age distribution	1940 M:F sex ratio	Northeast 1990 Total	1990 Age distribution	1990 M:F sex ratio	Midwest 1940 Total	1940 Age distribution	1940 M:F sex ratio	Midwest 1990 Total	1990 Age distribution	1990 M:F sex ratio
Total	35,976,777	100.0	0.99	50,809,229	100.0	0.93	40,143,332	100.0	1.02	59,668,632	100.0	0.94
Under 5 years	2,390,840	6.6	1.04	3,504,805	6.9	1.05	3,087,134	7.7	1.04	4,404,822	7.4	1.05
5 to 9 years	2,251,305	7.1	1.03	3,321,058	6.5	1.05	3,054,478	7.6	1.04	4,478,004	7.5	1.05
10 to 14 years	2,995,165	8.3	1.03	3,172,486	6.2	1.05	3,402,844	8.5	1.03	4,268,868	7.2	1.05
15 to 19 years	3,229,577	9.0	1.01	3,452,039	6.8	1.04	3,623,156	9.0	1.01	4,375,708	7.3	1.02
20 to 24 years	3,151,861	8.8	0.95	3,901,432	7.7	1.00	3,419,962	8.5	0.97	4,398,543	7.4	1.00
25 to 29 years	3,046,187	8.5	0.94	4,326,910	8.5	0.99	3,268,599	8.1	0.97	4,904,652	8.2	0.98
30 to 34 years	2,879,382	8.0	0.95	4,448,567	8.8	0.98	3,063,929	7.6	0.99	5,139,811	8.6	0.98
35 to 39 years	2,725,967	7.6	0.97	4,048,823	8.0	0.97	2,895,959	7.2	1.00	4,718,207	7.9	0.98
40 to 44 years	2,628,893	7.3	0.99	3,662,866	7.2	0.95	2,745,101	6.8	1.03	4,119,269	6.9	0.97
45 to 49 years	2,478,853	6.9	1.02	2,920,773	5.7	0.94	2,660,376	6.6	1.06	3,272,049	5.5	0.96
50 to 54 years	2,176,138	6.0	1.05	2,396,918	4.7	0.92	2,365,947	5.9	1.09	2,736,508	4.6	0.95
55 to 59 years	1,743,742	4.8	1.06	2,284,175	4.5	0.90	1,924,457	4.8	1.08	2,555,778	4.3	0.92
60 to 64 years	1,404,873	3.9	0.97	2,373,221	4.7	0.86	1,549,898	3.9	1.05	2,597,283	4.4	0.89
65 to 69 years	1,093,745	3.0	0.92	2,237,172	4.4	0.79	1,239,884	3.1	1.02	2,433,583	4.1	0.82
70 to 74 years	752,123	2.1	0.88	1,793,197	3.5	0.71	885,420	2.2	1.01	1,952,687	3.3	0.73
75 years and over	748,126	2.1	0.77	2,964,787	5.8	0.51	956,188	2.4	0.93	3,362,860	5.6	0.53

Table 10-3. Age by Sex, by Region: 1940 and 1990 (continued)

Age	South 1940			South 1990			West 1940			West 1990		
	Total	Age distribution	M:F sex ratio	Total	Age distribution	M:F sex ratio	Total	Age distribution	M:F sex ratio	Total	Age distribution	M:F sex ratio
Total	41,665,901	100.0	1.00	85,445,930	100.0	0.94	13,883,265	100.0	1.06	52,786,082	100.0	1.00
Under 5 years	4,006,966	9.6	1.02	6,233,070	7.3	1.05	1,056,584	7.6	1.04	4,211,746	8.0	1.05
5 to 9 years	4,068,691	9.8	1.02	6,231,362	7.3	1.05	1,010,148	7.3	1.03	4,068,755	7.7	1.05
10 to 14 years	4,267,442	10.2	1.02	5,980,309	7.0	1.05	1,080,484	7.8	1.03	3,692,586	7.0	1.05
15 to 19 years	4,299,018	10.3	0.99	6,302,317	7.4	1.05	1,181,772	8.5	1.02	3,673,951	7.0	1.08
20 to 24 years	3,832,313	9.2	0.95	6,545,151	7.7	1.02	1,183,699	8.5	1.03	4,175,186	7.9	1.12
25 to 29 years	3,584,683	8.6	0.95	7,307,025	8.6	1.00	1,197,169	8.6	1.04	4,774,458	9.0	1.07
30 to 34 years	3,189,326	7.7	0.97	7,391,615	8.7	0.98	1,109,751	8.0	1.07	4,882,894	9.3	1.04
35 to 39 years	2,887,720	6.9	0.96	6,737,460	7.9	0.97	1,035,731	7.5	1.07	4,458,627	8.4	1.02
40 to 44 years	2,451,621	5.9	0.99	6,001,335	7.0	0.97	962,228	6.9	1.07	3,832,316	7.3	1.01
45 to 49 years	2,198,387	5.3	1.02	4,773,205	5.6	0.96	917,609	6.6	1.09	2,906,546	5.5	1.00
50 to 54 years	1,872,235	4.5	1.04	3,925,396	4.6	0.93	842,526	6.1	1.14	2,291,691	4.3	0.98
55 to 59 years	1,497,249	3.6	1.04	3,648,508	4.3	0.90	698,417	5.0	1.15	2,043,295	3.9	0.95
60 to 64 years	1,209,878	2.9	1.03	3,644,995	4.3	0.85	563,691	4.1	1.10	2,000,668	3.8	0.89
65 to 69 years	1,042,041	2.5	1.03	3,509,129	4.1	0.80	430,987	3.1	1.02	1,931,851	3.7	0.84
70 to 74 years	632,300	1.5	1.04	2,754,348	3.2	0.74	299,689	2.2	1.03	1,494,591	2.8	0.80
75 years and over	626,031	1.5	0.91	4,460,705	5.2	0.55	312,780	2.3	0.96	2,346,921	4.4	0.60

Source: U.S. Bureau of the Census, "General Population Characteristics," 1990 Census of the Population, Tables 66, 116, 166, and 216, and "Characteristics of the Population," 1940 Census of Population, Table 26, U.S. Government Printing Office, Washington, D.C., 1992 and 1943.

Table 10-4. Age by Sex, by Urban/Rural Residence: 1940 and 1990

Age	Urban 1940 Total	Urban 1940 Age distribution	Urban 1940 M:F sex ratio	Urban 1990 Total	Urban 1990 Age distribution	Urban 1990 M:F sex ratio	Rural 1940 Total	Rural 1940 Age distribution	Rural 1940 M:F sex ratio	Rural 1990 Total	Rural 1990 Age distribution	Rural 1990 M:F sex ratio
Total	74,423,702	100.0	0.96	187,053,487	100.0	0.94	57,245,573	100.0	1.08	61,656,386	100.0	1.00
Under 5 years	5,007,137	6.7	1.03	13,989,160	7.5	1.05	5,534,387	9.7	1.03	4,365,283	7.1	1.05
5 to 9 years	5,083,240	6.8	1.02	13,288,047	7.1	1.04	5,601,382	9.8	1.04	4,811,132	7.8	1.06
10 to 14 years	5,854,770	7.9	1.01	12,273,417	6.6	1.04	5,891,165	10.3	1.05	4,840,832	7.9	1.07
15 to 19 years	6,493,936	8.7	0.95	13,188,758	7.1	1.03	5,839,587	10.2	1.07	4,565,257	7.4	1.11
20 to 24 years	6,755,377	9.1	0.88	15,371,060	8.2	1.02	4,832,458	8.4	1.09	3,649,252	5.9	1.09
25 to 29 years	6,725,909	9.0	0.91	16,898,657	9.0	1.01	4,370,729	7.6	1.06	4,414,388	7.2	1.01
30 to 34 years	6,286,218	8.4	0.93	16,779,795	9.0	0.99	3,956,170	6.9	1.06	5,083,092	8.2	1.00
35 to 39 years	5,906,293	7.9	0.95	14,944,849	8.0	0.97	3,639,084	6.4	1.05	5,018,268	8.1	1.02
40 to 44 years	5,490,678	7.4	0.98	13,013,170	7.0	0.96	3,297,165	5.8	1.07	4,602,616	7.5	1.03
45 to 49 years	5,107,716	6.9	1.01	10,070,112	5.4	0.94	3,147,964	5.5	1.10	3,802,461	6.2	1.03
50 to 54 years	4,419,140	5.9	1.03	8,208,772	4.4	0.92	2,837,706	5.0	1.14	3,141,741	5.1	1.02
55 to 59 years	3,462,821	4.7	1.00	7,657,284	4.1	0.89	2,381,044	4.2	1.16	2,874,472	4.7	0.98
60 to 64 years	2,758,293	3.7	0.94	7,801,852	4.2	0.84	1,970,047	3.4	1.17	2,814,315	4.6	0.97
65 to 69 years	2,152,883	2.9	0.86	7,520,892	4.0	0.78	1,653,774	2.9	1.19	2,590,843	4.2	0.91
70 to 74 years	1,455,824	2.0	0.84	5,981,647	3.2	0.71	1,113,708	1.9	1.20	2,013,176	3.3	0.85
75 year and over	1,463,922	2.0	0.75	10,066,015	5.4	0.51	1,179,203	2.1	1.08	3,069,258	5.0	0.66

Source: U.S. Bureau of the Census, "General Population Characteristics," 1990 Census of Population, Table 14, and "Characteristics of the Population," 1940 Census of Population, Table 14, U.S. Government Printing Office, Washington, D.C., 1992 and 1943.

the Great Depression. It is unlikely that the European and Asian unrest which would lead to World War I had yet impacted these data. The most pronounced difference is a much lower ratio of males to females in working-age adults of urban areas (i.e. 15-44 years of age). In rural areas there were, uncharacteristically, more males than females at every age in 1940. In urban areas of 1940 there were more males at youngest ages, under 14 years of age, and at older working ages, 45-59 years of age. Even in 1990 the sex ratio of rural areas remains uncharacteristically high and there are more males than females in every age group under 55 years of age. In contrast, the sex ratios of the 1990 urban population indicates there are more males than females only under 29 years of age. Another notable change, as we have seen in earlier chapters, is the dramatic decline in sex ratios among the elderly for both urban and rural areas as improvements in female survivorship in the older ages outpaced those of males. In both the 1940 and 1990 census there was an even lower sex ratio among the elderly in urban areas.

As these data by race-ethnicity, region and urban-rural residence indicate, unique social groups in the United States population may have very different demographic histories and hence different age and sex composition. Differences in composition may be even more dramatic when one considers more unique social groups with greater historical sources of variation in demographic processes (e.g. particular recently arrived immigrant groups, war-impacted cohorts). While empirical comparisons suggest these differences in composition reflect past histories, it is equally important to remember these differences will impact future sociodemographic trajectories of the populations concerned.

Gender, Aging and Major Life Cycle Events

The tumultuous history of the 20th century and the relatively dramatic changes in age structure over the past half century give reason to suspect that the social and demographic experiences of successive birth cohorts must have been very different from each other. Many historical events and trends have contributed to differences among cohorts and age groups. One aspect of the changing history experienced by successive cohorts of individuals is the different demographic behaviors and expectations of different generations. Many of the social and demographic differences between recent U.S. cohorts are as substantial as those found in cross-national or cross-cultural comparisons to entirely different populations. Yet, generations which have experienced very different lives are often less aware of these intergenerational differences in culture than they are of the more apparent cross-sectional differences across geographic regions. Intergenerational diversity is, nonetheless, an important

feature and dimension of stratification within a population.

The cultural norms and expectations we attach to gender roles are perhaps nowhere as clearly revealed as when comparing the changes in men's and women's life cycles across generations. In the twentieth century gender roles have been largely redefined and they remain in a continual process of evolution. Full-time labor force participation, professional education and occupations, suffrage and office-seeking, single motherhood, etc., are just a few of the widely accepted behaviors for women in 1990 which were nearly scandalous a century ago. Social security and pensions, early retirement or retraining, lower family sizes, service occupations, dual career couples, etc., are examples of the changes across this century's generations of males and females. Major demographic trends in fertility, mortality, migration, labor force participation, income, health, etc., have all impacted the sexes, most often differently, and have affected gender roles over the past century. As roles are redefined across generations they impact the expectations and aspirations of younger generations. And, these changing roles clearly color the many differences which exist between individuals of different ages in the population.

Identifying the complex reciprocal relationships between the changing demographic composition of the United States population and sociocultural phenomena is a difficult, if not impossible, task. Short of any comprehensive analyses, it is, nonetheless, important to recognize the extent to which any given population is a product of many diverse individual histories and cohort experiences. The remainder of this chapter focuses upon differences in the population which reflect the unique sociodemographic experiences of different age and sex groups, or successive cohorts, in the United States population. These differences in turn reflect upon the changing social construction of aging and gender over the past century.

For some clarity, and by recent convention, we refer to biological attributes of the population as age and sex while referring to behavioral differences as reflecting social characterizations of aging and gender (see Definition Box) across these groups. Many of the behaviors we consider here as a means of discussing aging and gender differences in the population are considered in context and in more detail in other chapters. Our emphasis here is on presenting selected examples from these chapters and a survey of additional behaviors, with a focus upon birth cohorts of individuals to illustrate the heterogeneous experiences shaping the lives of individuals represented in the current population.

Life Cycle Stages

Responding to fertility, mortality and migration trends, the age composition of the population has, in re-

Figure 10-4. Age Composition of the U.S. Population in Terms of Life Cycle: 1880-1990

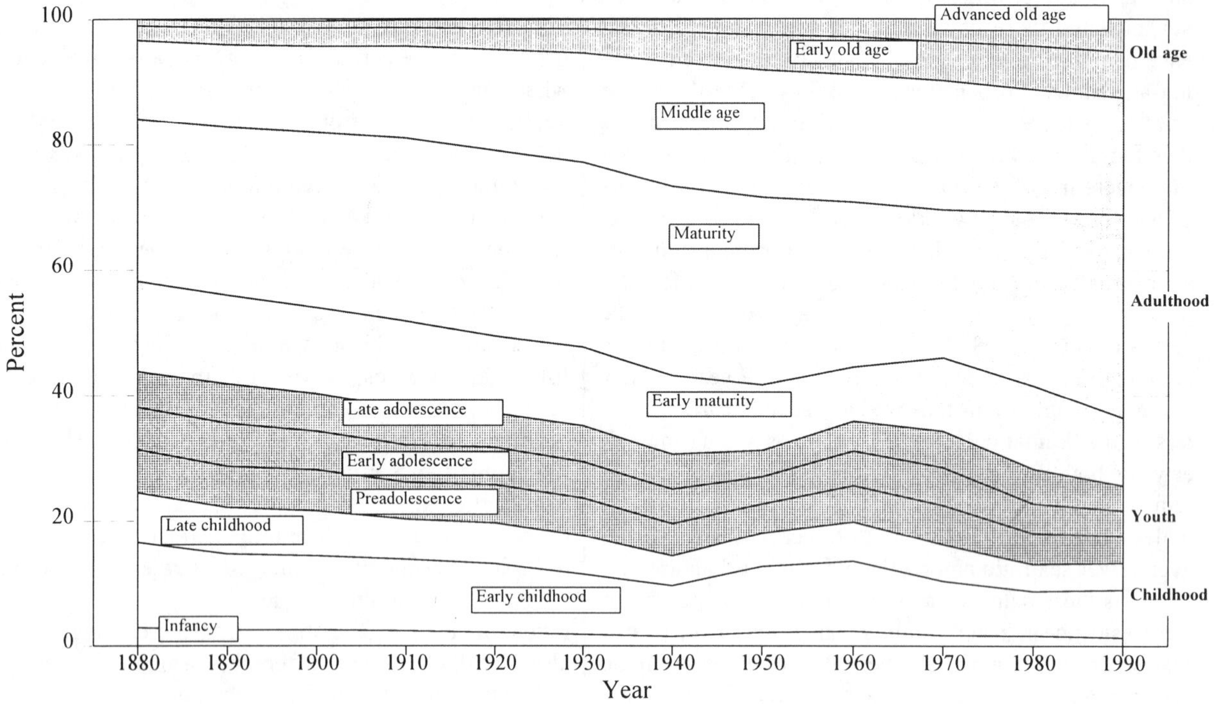

Source: U.S. Census data.

cent times, changed significantly from one generation to the next. And, in turn, the proportion of the population in various stages of the life cycle changes has been different across time. Figure 10-4 shows the proportion of the population in different life cycle stages as defined by age over the past century. Infancy is defined as under 1 year of age; childhood as 1-5 (early childhood) and 6-8 (late childhood) years of age; adolescence as 9-11 (preadolescence), 12-14 (early adolescence) and 15-17 (late adolescence) years of age; maturity as 18-24 (early maturity), 25-44 (maturity), and 45-64 (middle age); and old age as 65-74 (early old age) and 75 or more (advanced old age) years of age. Life cycle stages can also be defined through events (e.g. first full-time employment, marriage, parenthood, surviving widow or widower, etc.) and this approach is reflected in the tabulations which follow later in this chapter. Meanwhile, to characterize the entire population, regardless of whether they have experienced specific life cycle events, this figure illustrates the changing percentage of the population in each of a series of life cycle ages between 1880 and 1990. The proportion of population in old age life stages, and especially advanced old age, have increased dramatically since 1880. While still a small proportion of the population, the aging of the population will mean an even greater increase in the proportion of the population in these life stages over the coming years. Similarly, the proportion of the population in adulthood has increased overall. However, those in early maturity or young adulthood have declined while those

in middle age and maturity have increased as a proportion of the population.

All younger life stages have seen a decline in their representation in the U.S. population over the past century. Adolescence and childhood have declined from approximately 42 percent to approximately 33 percent of the population. And, the sum of those from infancy through early maturity has declined from approximately 59 percent of the population to about 37 percent of the population. In short, since the 1930s the U.S. population has been characterized by a growing majority of those who are either mature adults or older.

The profile of life cycle stages since 1880 again reveals the impact of the baby boom on the composition of the population. From 1940 through 1960 the proportion of the population in youth and childhood increased. Between 1950 and 1970 these individuals entered early maturity with the rise most pronounced in the 1960s. Then, as these individuals entered mature adulthood there was a dramatic expansion of the population of mature adults between 1970 and 1990. Eventually, the impact of these baby boomers on the later life cycle stages, e.g. advanced old age, will bring further changes in the life cycle composition of the population and a corresponding array of social policy issues to be addressed. Again, it is important to note that the culture experienced by individuals in each life cycle stage depends heavily upon the composition of the population as a whole. For example, even those in the youngest life cycle stages will soon encounter a culture focused upon the issues of aging and quite different from the experiences of those growing up in the 'cult of youth' following the baby boom.

Education

Much of the early life cycle experience of recent generations has been dominated by the national experiment in compulsory public primary and secondary education. So successful has that experiment been that much of the current population takes this social program for granted as both a common history and a given feature of the social landscape into the foreseeable future. As Table 10-5 indicates, the percentage graduating from high school is over eighty percent for age groups up to 49 years of age, or across birth cohorts since a half century ago. In older cohorts this percentage drops dramatically as one might expect. Among the elderly population over 75 years of age less than half of the surviving population graduated from high school. There are fairly limited differences between the percentage of each age group graduating from high school by sex. Overall, women are slightly more likely to have graduated from high school in most age groups. Different experiences in compulsory education clearly reflect greater differences in aging across recent cohorts than gender differences. This reflects the relatively egalitarian nature of compulsory education.

The situation is quite different for post-secondary volitional education as reflected in college graduation with a bachelor's degree (see Table 10-5). Over a fifth, and for some ages a fourth, of those under 50 years of age have a bachelor's degree. In the youngest age groups it is almost certain that these percentages will continue to rise as more of these individuals complete further college education. The percentage with a bachelor's degree again drops more or less steadily with age to under one tenth of the population at the oldest ages. Again, there are clear differences in education across cohorts and the typical experience of college education in the course of aging. Unlike the case of compulsory secondary education, there are also clearly substantial gender differences across cohorts in the experience of college education. In the most recent, youngest cohort there are more female baccalaureates awarded than there are for males. But, as one turns to older groups the college education gap between males and females favors males. For those now at ages 40-44 years, there are a third more males with bachelor's degrees than there are females with similar degrees. Among those now approaching and entering retirement (60-69 years of age) there are eighty to ninety percent more male than female baccalaureates. These gender differences moderate slightly at the very oldest ages representing cohorts where such degrees were less common overall. These differences in male and female baccalaureates by

Table 10-5. Indicators of Educational Attainment, by Age and Sex: 1990

Age	Percent high school graduates			Percent bachelor's degree and higher		
	Both sexes	Male	Female	Both sexes	Male	Female
Total, 25 years and over	75.2	75.7	74.8	20.3	23.3	17.6
25 to 29 years	83.5	81.9	85.1	22.1	21.7	22.4
30 to 34 years	84.7	83.5	85.8	23.4	24.0	22.8
35 to 39 years	86.0	85.4	86.5	26.4	28.0	24.8
40 to 44 years	85.2	85.2	85.1	27.7	31.7	23.8
45 to 49 years	80.4	80.4	80.4	23.5	27.8	19.5
50 to 54 years	75.3	75.5	75.1	19.4	23.7	15.4
55 to 59 years	70.4	70.8	70.1	17.2	22.2	12.6
60 to 64 years	64.8	63.9	65.7	14.9	19.4	10.9
65 to 69 years	61.8	61.1	62.3	12.5	16.9	8.9
70 to 74 years	56.0	56.0	56.1	10.6	13.5	8.4
75 to 79 years	48.4	47.6	49.0	9.7	11.9	8.4
80 to 84 years	44.1	42.0	45.2	10.0	12.0	9.0
85 years and over	38.4	34.8	39.8	8.5	10.6	7.7

Source: U.S. Bureau of the Census, "Education in the United States: 1990," 1990 CP-3-4, U.S. Government Printing Office, Washington, D.C., 1994, Table 1.

age clearly reflect changing acceptability and standards of higher education for women across successive recent cohorts. It is also possible that these differences are slightly inflated at the oldest ages by a greater survivorship of females with college degrees.

We might reasonably suspect the changes in compulsory education across cohorts would be related to many other differences in behaviors and normative preferences across cohorts. We might equally suspect that the common experience of compulsory education across gender could account for some cultural homogeny within cohorts. However, the interaction of gender differences and aging are pronounced for college education across cohorts of the population. It is equally legitimate to conclude that the greatest heterogeneity in educational experiences has been lodged within the reaches of higher education throughout the century. There are indeed few social phenomena which can be comprehensively addressed without considering the impact of these basic differences and commonalities in the educational experiences of successive cohorts.

Labor Force Participation

Differences in labor force participation have been heavily influenced by gender over the history of the cohorts represented in the currently surviving population. Males have consistently participated in the labor force with a relatively predictable age pattern across past cohorts. As Figure 10-5A illustrates, the biggest change in patterns of male labor force participation across cohorts defined by first entry into the labor force has been the decline in the labor force participation of males at older ages. The reasons for, and details of, these patterns are discussed in later chapters devoted to the labor force. Again, however, the rise of social security, pensions, insurance and the ability to retire at relatively early ages has created substantial differences between the culture of current generations and that of individuals growing up and entering the labor force prior to the Great Depression. Despite recent policy concerns for pension security in the face of an aging population, it is likely that in the coming generations the experience of pension and retirement security will become a more uniform population experience than at any time in the prior history of the United States.

Dramatically increasing female labor force participation is one of the major social changes reflected in the generational experiences of the United States population. Figure 10-5B shows, with minor exceptions, that the labor force participation of females at each age increased across recent successive cohorts of women entering the labor force. This figure also demonstrates that the cohorts of women which first entered the labor force in 1930 through 1950 had limited, but generally higher, labor force participation in the mid-life years (i.e. 35-54 years of age).

These women frequently entered the labor force after the ages at which the heaviest burdens of child rearing were over. However, they were also among those drawn into the labor force during the years of World War II. The cohort entering the labor force in the 1950s participated at younger ages (i.e. 16-24 years of age) and at ages beyond thirty-five. This pattern is consistent with evidence that downward career mobility occurred for some women among these cohorts due to the interruption of careers for a return to childbearing and rearing. Among cohorts of those entering the labor force since 1960 the participation rate for females has increased steadily to levels near eighty percent of the labor force participation rate for males in similar cohorts and ages. For these same cohorts labor force participation has also increased steadily with aging. The decline of fertility is clearly at least one demographic trend influencing a decline in gender differences of labor force participation across ages among the most recent cohorts to enter the labor force. At the same time, labor force opportunities and commitments have likely influenced declines in fertility among these cohorts. And, what happens to these cohorts of women at older ages remains to be seen. Of considerable future interest is whether these, and successive, cohorts of women simply tend to converge toward male labor force participation rates or whether they develop unique patterns. Given the longer life expectancy of women it is quite possible that they may eventually demonstrate a higher age at retirement or unique post-retirement alternatives for income and part-time employment. Alternatively, these women may evidence a persistence of gender-specific influences by retiring at earlier ages consistent with the timing of retirement for a (generally older) spouse.

Again, with respect to labor force participation, there is ample evidence of important cohort differences associated with aging and gender which may explain further similarities and differences among the current population's age and sex groups. And, importantly, these differences again involve the interaction of aging and gender, not merely differences according to age and sex.

Occupations

Major occupational shifts and historically driven economic restructuring have occurred in the United States at the same time that the labor force participation of women has been rising, the baby boom cohorts have moved through their early careers, and the working elderly have increased as a percentage of the labor force. Other chapters address the changing aspects of the United States labor force in great detail. Attention here is limited to basic changes in the sex and age composition of various occupations over the recent past for both men and women. Figure 10-6 shows the sex ratio by age for major occupational categories. As one might expect, the

Figure 10-5A. Labor Force Participation of Males Age 16 and Over by Birth Cohort: 1896-1965, Observed Through 1990

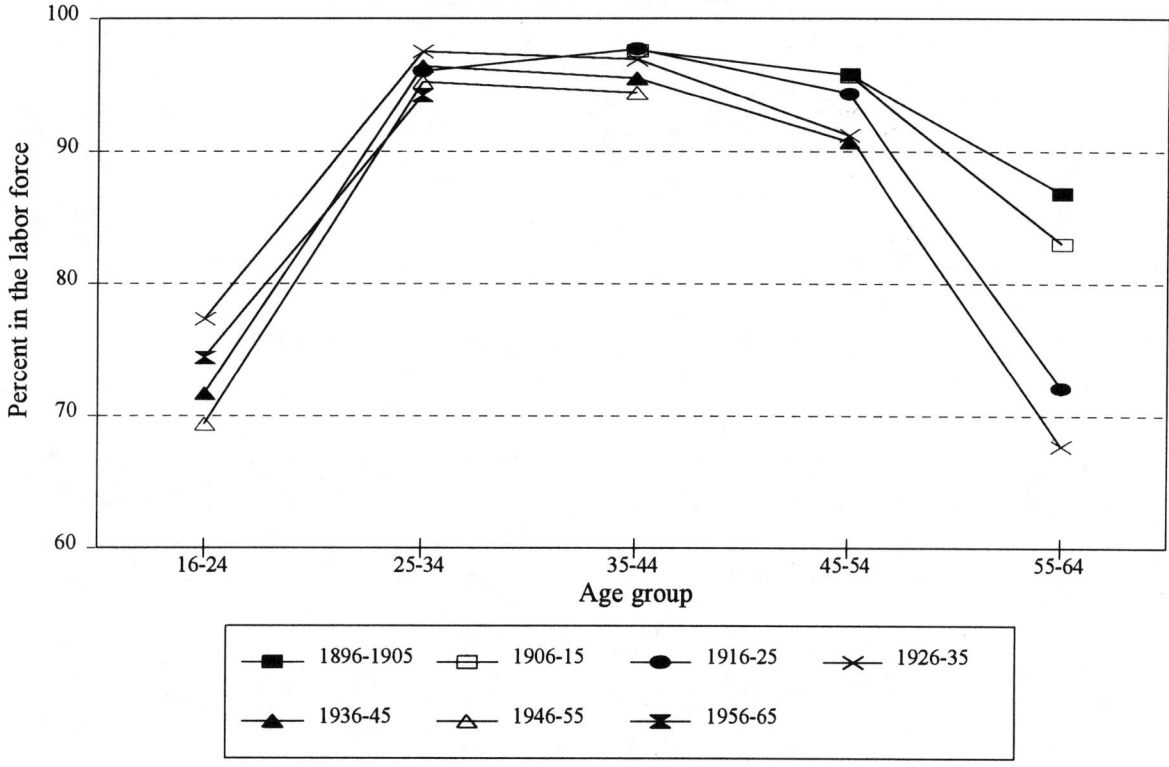

Source: 1950-1990 Bureau of Labor Statistics data.

Figure 10-5B. Labor Force Participation of Females Age 16 and Over by Birth Cohort: 1896-1965, Observed Through 1990

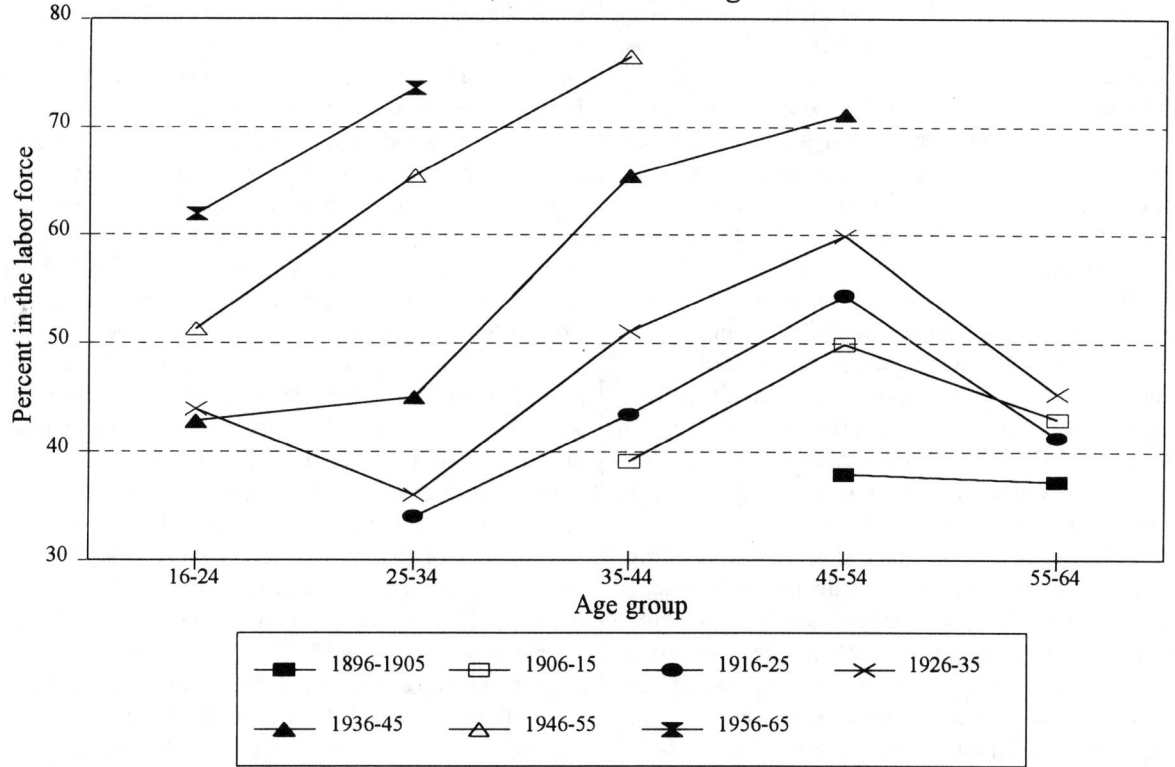

Source: 1950-1990 Bureau of Labor Statistics data.

Figure 10-6. Male:Female Sex Ratio of the Employed Labor Force, by Occupation and Age: 1990

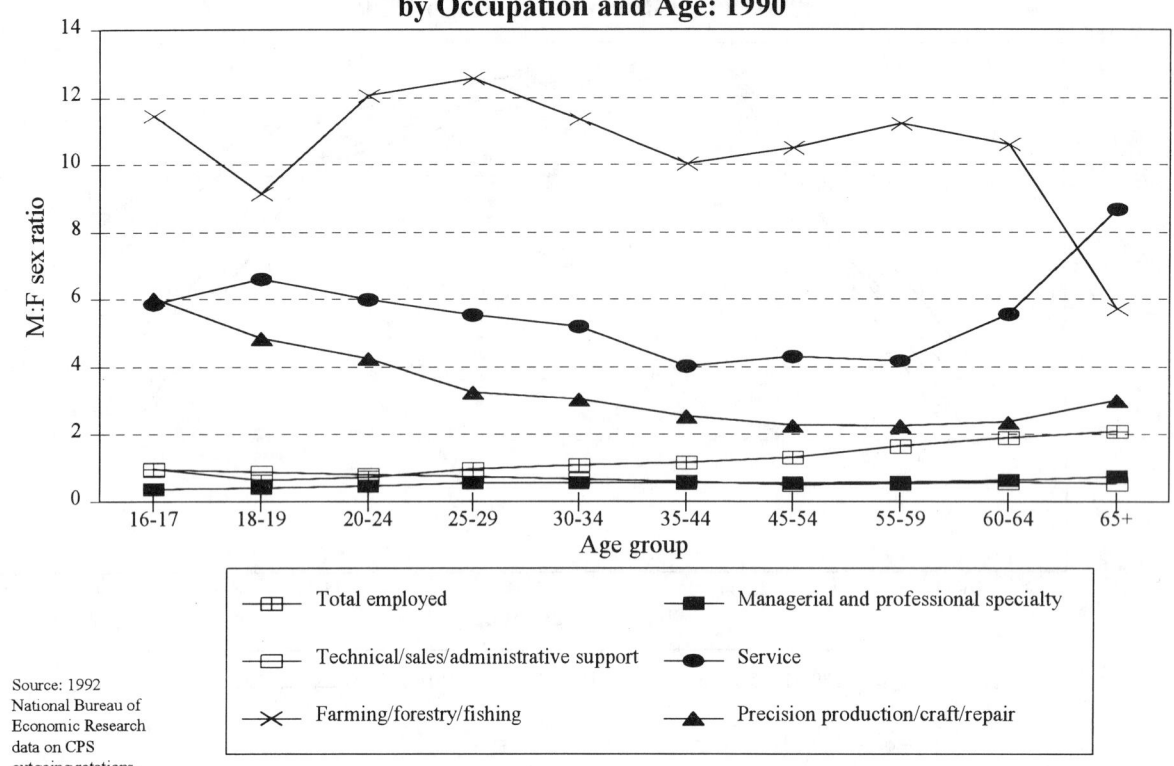

Source: 1992
National Bureau of
Economic Research
data on CPS
outgoing rotations.

farming, forestry and fishing occupations have the highest sex ratio with more than 10:1 males to females in most age groups. The next highest sex ratio is for the service occupations, which have between 9:1 and 4:1 males per females in each age group. This high sex ratio is at odds with frequent reference to the service occupations as dominated by women's labor. In line with traditional conceptions of male-dominated occupations, precision production, craft, and repair occupations have the third highest sex ratio with between 6:1 and 2:1 males per females in each age group.

There are considerable age variations in occupational sex ratios. Interestingly, the sex ratio in the agricultural occupations appears to decline radically in retirement ages. This is presumably an effect of both widowhood in family enterprises and retirement of males in commercial enterprises. The sex ratio for service occupations rises at older ages largely reflecting the recent entry of older males into these occupations in record numbers. And, the sex ratio of precision production, craft, and repair occupations is considerably higher in younger ages. This higher sex ratio may indicate the earlier entry of young males into these occupations. However, overall, the sex ratio of the total employed increases at ages beyond 18 years reflecting the greater tendency for younger women of more recent cohorts to be employed outside the home.

Changes in occupational age composition reflect recent changes in population composition overall and in employment opportunities over the recent past. Table 10-6A shows the age composition of the employed male labor force by occupation in 1990 and percentage change from five years earlier in 1985. Table 10-6B presents similar information for women. The occupation with the greatest percent in 18 to 24 years of age for males is that of handlers, equipment cleaners, helpers and laborers. A greater percent of 18 to 24 year old women is found in sales occupations. The occupation with the greatest percent of those over 45 years of age for males is that of executive, administrative and managerial occupations. A greater percent of women over 45 years of age are employed as machine operators, assemblers and inspectors. Women over 45 years of age are also employed in nearly the same percentage in the transportation and material moving occupations. Clearly men and women of a given age have very real and different occupational prospects.

Not surprisingly, both tables show a slight but increasing concentration of nearly all occupational groups in the middle years of life. This change is apparent in the second panel of Tables 10-6A and 10-6B which present the percentage change in the age group composition of occupations between 1985 and 1990. The uniform concentration in middle ages is again a reflection of the aging baby boom cohorts. This concentration in middle

Table 10-6A. Age Composition of the Employed Male Labor Force, by Occupation: 1990 and Percent Change 1985-1990

Occupation	Total	16 and 17	18 and 19	20 to 24	25 to 29	30 to 34	35 to 44	45 to 54	55 to 59	60 to 64	65 and over
1990											
Total employed, 16 years and over	100.0	1.9	3.2	10.3	14.0	15.0	25.7	16.7	6.0	4.1	3.1
Managerial and professional specialty occupations	100.0	0.2	0.4	4.4	11.4	14.9	31.5	21.2	7.3	5.2	3.7
Executive, administrative, and managerial occupations	100.0	0.1	0.3	4.1	10.1	14.3	31.7	22.5	7.7	5.5	3.7
Professional specialty occupations	100.0	0.2	0.5	4.7	12.8	15.6	31.3	19.7	6.9	4.7	3.6
Technical, sales, and administrative support occupations	100.0	1.6	3.4	11.8	14.6	14.6	24.9	15.8	5.4	4.2	3.7
Technicians and related support occupations	100.0	0.1	1.3	11.6	17.4	20.3	27.1	14.2	4.4	2.7	0.9
Sales occupations	100.0	2.1	3.3	10.1	13.6	13.5	25.5	16.9	5.8	4.7	4.5
Administrative support occupations, including clerical	100.0	1.4	4.6	15.1	15.0	13.8	22.9	14.5	5.3	3.9	3.5
Service occupations	100.0	6.8	7.9	15.2	14.3	12.7	19.1	11.8	5.0	3.8	3.4
Private household occupations	100.0	15.6	5.6	6.0	11.0	14.0	9.9	16.1	2.1	7.4	12.2
Protective service occupations	100.0	0.6	2.3	10.3	15.5	16.6	27.4	15.5	5.4	3.0	3.6
Other service occupations	100.0	9.0	9.9	17.0	13.9	11.3	16.1	10.4	4.9	4.1	3.3
Farming, forestry, and fishing occupations	100.0	4.4	5.1	11.4	12.8	12.4	19.1	13.0	6.3	6.0	9.5
Precision production, craft, and repair occupations	100.0	0.4	1.8	9.9	15.4	17.1	26.9	17.6	5.9	3.5	1.5
Operators, fabricators, and laborers	100.0	2.8	5.0	14.2	15.4	15.4	22.6	14.3	5.3	3.3	1.8
Machine operators, assemblers, and inspectors	100.0	0.6	3.0	13.2	16.4	16.5	24.5	16.0	5.6	3.1	1.2
Transportation and material moving occupations	100.0	0.5	2.2	9.9	13.7	16.3	26.3	17.7	6.4	4.4	2.6
Handlers, equipment cleaners, helpers, and laborers	100.0	7.8	10.5	20.2	16.0	13.0	16.2	8.5	3.8	2.3	1.7
Percent change 1985-1990											
Total employed, 16 years and over	7.7	-7.0	0.8	-9.6	0.9	12.2	19.9	14.5	-5.0	-0.1	19.2
Managerial and professional specialty occupations	12.8	52.4	-8.5	-8.0	2.1	7.5	17.6	25.6	2.6	12.2	22.1
Executive, administrative, and managerial occupations	13.5	277.1	-6.8	-7.1	3.0	11.6	18.2	23.2	0.4	9.9	23.0
Professional specialty occupations	12.1	14.3	-9.8	-8.9	1.2	3.5	16.9	28.8	5.7	15.3	21.2
Technical, sales, and administrative support occupations	10.5	2.5	20.4	-0.0	3.3	10.3	23.9	13.4	-7.7	2.0	27.5
Technicians and related support occupations	14.2	-59.4	-6.2	-6.3	-10.0	29.2	34.9	20.4	14.6	55.6	-11.0
Sales occupations	9.9	-0.4	18.8	-0.0	5.7	5.4	20.8	16.4	-8.9	2.2	19.5
Administrative support occupations, including clerical	10.0	20.8	27.7	2.6	8.6	7.6	24.3	4.3	-12.6	-9.6	62.8
Service occupations	11.1	-1.2	5.9	-4.7	14.8	31.1	25.7	14.2	4.0	-0.4	-1.4
Private household occupations	-18.8	-52.4	-65.2	-76.4	39.5	170.8	62.8	46.4	-74.6	271.0	48.5
Protective service occupations	13.8	47.8	40.3	10.3	17.3	16.6	16.5	20.6	-0.3	-11.4	-11.4
Other service occupations	10.3	-0.9	4.5	-6.9	13.7	39.8	32.0	10.8	6.6	2.2	2.4
Farming, forestry, and fishing occupations	-2.4	-29.3	-13.7	-16.4	11.8	12.9	17.7	-12.8	-21.0	-15.2	17.1
Precision production, craft, and repair occupations	1.9	-34.2	-8.4	-19.2	-5.5	6.5	17.3	11.0	-13.0	-10.6	-0.4
Operators, fabricators, and laborers	5.4	-5.9	-5.3	-11.3	-2.9	20.1	21.3	8.7	-3.7	-4.7	42.7
Machine operators, assemblers, and inspectors	2.7	-19.5	-11.5	-13.0	-4.9	9.5	17.1	14.9	-6.3	-22.5	13.5
Transportation and material moving occupations	5.7	-38.2	0.3	-15.6	-9.0	18.0	19.3	8.3	-7.3	6.9	57.6
Handlers, equipment cleaners, helpers, and laborers	8.7	-0.6	-4.2	-7.3	6.6	45.3	33.9	-2.5	9.2	12.4	51.0

Source: National Bureau of Economic Research, CPS Outgoing Rotation Groups CD-rom, 1992.

Table 10-6B. Age Composition of the Employed Female Labor Force, by Occupation: 1990 and Percent Change 1985-1990

Occupation	Total	16 and 17	18 and 19	20 to 24	25 to 29	30 to 34	35 to 44	45 to 54	55 to 59	60 to 64	65 and over
1990											
Total employed, 16 years and over	100.0	2.1	3.6	11.2	13.8	14.4	26.1	16.8	5.5	3.7	2.7
Managerial and professional specialty occupations	100.0	0.2	0.7	7.2	14.0	16.2	32.0	19.1	5.3	3.2	2.1
Executive, administrative, and managerial occupations	100.0	0.2	0.7	7.8	14.2	16.6	30.5	19.3	5.3	3.3	2.0
Professional specialty occupations	100.0	0.3	0.7	6.7	13.9	15.9	33.1	18.9	5.3	3.1	2.1
Technical, sales, and administrative support occupations	100.0	2.3	4.5	13.5	14.1	14.0	24.6	15.7	5.1	3.6	2.6
Technicians and related support occupations	100.0	0.1	1.3	10.6	18.7	19.6	29.3	13.6	3.8	2.0	0.9
Sales occupations	100.0	5.9	8.4	15.3	12.9	11.8	19.9	14.1	4.9	3.6	3.2
Administrative support occupations, including clerical	100.0	0.9	3.0	13.0	14.1	14.3	26.2	16.7	5.4	3.7	2.6
Service occupations	100.0	4.8	6.0	12.4	12.8	12.6	21.2	15.5	6.2	4.4	4.3
Private household occupations	100.0	8.3	6.1	10.8	7.8	8.3	15.3	15.5	7.1	8.4	12.4
Protective service occupations	100.0	4.4	4.7	9.6	15.5	17.4	25.8	13.8	5.1	0.9	2.8
Other service occupations	100.0	4.4	6.0	12.6	13.1	12.8	21.5	15.5	6.1	4.2	3.6
Farming, forestry, and fishing occupations	100.0	3.9	3.9	9.8	11.8	12.2	24.2	15.4	7.7	5.5	5.6
Precision production, craft, and repair occupations	100.0	0.4	2.1	8.8	13.2	16.3	29.0	18.1	5.7	3.5	2.8
Operators, fabricators, and laborers	100.0	1.3	3.0	9.7	13.8	14.8	26.1	18.4	6.9	4.1	1.8
Machine operators, assemblers, and inspectors	100.0	0.5	2.2	9.3	13.7	14.7	26.2	19.5	7.7	4.5	1.7
Transportation and material moving occupations	100.0	0.5	1.7	5.8	13.4	16.6	30.0	22.9	5.0	2.7	1.3
Handlers, equipment cleaners, helpers, and laborers	100.0	5.0	6.6	13.4	14.4	14.0	24.0	12.4	4.8	3.2	2.3
Percent change 1985-1990											
Total employed, 16 years and over	13.5	-4.3	0.1	-9.6	4.8	16.7	28.5	27.1	4.3	4.9	31.5
Managerial and professional specialty occupations	27.2	26.3	20.1	1.5	6.0	18.8	41.8	50.6	20.3	18.9	34.2
Executive, administrative, and managerial occupations	36.2	130.6	23.7	7.4	15.2	45.0	50.3	55.7	14.4	11.2	45.1
Professional specialty occupations	21.5	3.9	17.6	-3.1	0.0	4.5	36.7	47.0	25.1	25.7	27.7
Technical, sales, and administrative support occupations	10.9	4.2	0.8	-7.8	2.4	15.1	25.6	21.2	0.8	4.9	39.0
Technicians and related support occupations	24.5	1,462.2	17.8	-12.3	2.0	23.7	52.1	52.9	61.2	9.4	57.1
Sales occupations	15.3	15.8	15.2	1.4	12.3	22.2	25.0	22.2	2.7	13.6	17.1
Administrative support occupations, including clerical	7.5	-20.9	-14.0	-11.9	-1.3	11.3	22.7	18.3	-3.2	1.1	54.8
Service occupations	8.6	-15.6	0.3	-16.9	10.5	19.9	23.1	25.1	1.4	-1.8	27.9
Private household occupations	-21.8	-49.6	-1.5	-22.7	-16.4	-13.5	-12.6	-22.8	-31.6	-32.1	3.1
Protective service occupations	19.8	29.4	-22.3	-38.2	23.6	20.9	69.0	93.7	21.0	-74.5	85.4
Other service occupations	12.1	-6.3	1.2	-15.7	11.9	22.5	24.9	30.9	6.2	8.9	36.7
Farming, forestry, and fishing occupations	-2.6	-9.6	-8.7	-21.4	35.6	8.1	5.1	-22.1	-2.3	6.8	-3.6
Precision production, craft, and repair occupations	1.8	-13.9	-21.6	-22.4	-7.1	12.2	13.4	12.4	-23.1	-8.8	40.0
Operators, fabricators, and laborers	6.0	11.6	-10.0	-17.6	4.7	14.8	17.0	10.3	-0.3	-4.8	6.2
Machine operators, assemblers, and inspectors	2.3	-35.2	-17.0	-22.3	2.8	10.8	10.6	9.6	-0.7	-3.4	-10.3
Transportation and material moving occupations	12.6	-31.3	-48.6	-37.1	-0.7	24.3	36.3	28.8	8.0	-11.8	9.8
Handlers, equipment cleaners, helpers, and laborers	18.4	56.9	12.3	6.0	15.3	27.0	36.5	1.1	-2.4	-8.7	112.2

Source: National Bureau of Economic Research, CPS Outgoing Rotation Groups CD-rom, 1992.

The Changing Face of Retirement

by Alison Kadlec Donta

In 1990, 12.5% of the United States population was age 65 and over, and 1.2% of the population was age 85 and over. A dramatic jump in the proportion of the population aged 65 and over will begin in 2011 when the Baby Boom generation begins to reach age 65, and by 2050, it is estimated that 20.6% of the population will be aged 65 and over and those aged 85 and over will represent 4.6% of the total U.S. population. In addition, the life expectancy at birth was 68.2 years in 1950 and had increased to 75.4 years by 1990. For persons reaching 65 years, their life expectancy was 17.2 additonal years in 1990. This marked increase in the older population and life expectancy has great implications for the retirement age population.

Today, people can expect to live ten to thirty years after retirement, if not longer. In addition, there is a trend toward earlier retirement among men. As can be seen in the figure below, the proportion of the older male population in the labor force has steadily decreased since 1950. In 1950, 86.9% of the male population aged 55 to 64 was in the labor force compared to 67.7% in 1990. Similarly, the proportion of the male population aged 65 and over in the labor force decreased from 45.8% in 1950 to 26.8% in 1970 and to only 16.4% in 1990. This decrease is also expected to continue in the future.

For older women, there is an opposite trend toward an older age at retirement. While the proportion of women aged 65 and over in the labor force has remained relatively steady since 1950, there has been an increase in labor force participation rates among women aged 55 to 64. In 1950, only 27.0% of those women were in the labor force, but that had increased to 43.0% by 1970 and further increased to the 45.3% seen in 1990. More and more women have long-term experience in the work force, and women are increasingly entering retirement with pensions and other retirement income of their own. Yet, the increasingly early age of retirement for men, increased life expectancy, and increased proportion of the population who are elderly results in Social Security, savings, and pensions which are spread out over a longer period than ever before for many retirees.

At the same time, many younger retirees are now faced with the care of older relatives, especially parents. Never before has the four-generation family been more common. The table below illustrates this increasing burden of the oldest segment of the population on the youngest retirees. In 1950, there were only 12 persons aged 85 and over for every 100 persons aged 65 to

69. By 1990, that ratio had increased to 30 per 100 and is expected to further increase to 93 per 100 by the year 2050. This increase is expected to occur among all races and ethnic groups. For the first time, many of the recently retired are having to deal with the expense, concern, and sometimes physical care of frail older relatives. Much of this burden falls on daughters or daughters-in-law. These women provide up to 80 to 90 percent of personal care, transportation, shopping, and help with household tasks for the elderly. Some women are even forced to leave the work force to care for elderly relatives.

Some retirees, again often women, are now also assuming responsibility for the care of their grandchildren because many more mothers are now working outside the home. In 1991, 6.6% percent of all children with employed mothers were cared for by grandparents. This proportion increases for younger children and for children of single mothers. A full 15.8% of children aged 5 and under were cared for by grandparents either in the child's home or in another home. Among grade school-aged children, 10.2% of those with single mothers were cared for by grandparents compared to 3.8% of children with married mothers. This trend may continue with grandparents (and great-grandparents) living longer and more mothers with young children working outside the home.

The retirement years in the 1990s are considerably different than those in the past. For the oldest old, nearly half of their life could be spent in retirement. Those years are not always years of relaxation and leisure. Increasing numbers of retirees, especially the recently retired, are assuming the responsibility for the care of grandchildren and frail elderly relatives. Retirement assets are being distributed over a longer period, and more people are choosing to re-enter the workforce after retirement, usually on a part-time basis, perhaps in response to increasing demands upon the post-retirement population.

Two-elderly-generation Support Ratios[1], by Race-ethnicity: 1950 to 2050

Race-ethnicity	1950	1960	1970	1980	1990	2010	2030	2050
All races	12	14	22	26	30	47	42	93
White	12	14	22	26	31	49	44	97
Black	11	13	19	20	26	36	31	77
Other races	13	14	26	19	17	34	46	78
Hispanic	—	—	16	19	21	35	32	72

[1] The ratio of persons aged 85 years and over to 100 persons aged 65 to 69.

Source: U.S. Bureau of the Census, Current Population Reports, "Sixty-five Plus in America," Special Studies P23-178RV, Table 2-3, "General Population Characteristics," 1990 Census of Populaton, Table 16, 1980 Census of Population, Table 43, 1970 Census of Population, Table 52, "Detailed Population Characteristics," 1970 Census of Population, Table 190, and 1960 Census of Population, Table 158, U.S. Government Printing Office, Washington, D.C., 1993, 1992, 1983, 1973, 1973, and 1961.

Additional Sources:

Brody, Elaine M. Parent Care as a Normative Family Stress. Gerontologist, February 1985:19-29.

National Center for Health Statistics. Health, United States, 1993: Tables 26, 27, 32, and 69. Hyattsville, MD: Public Health Service, 1994.

Taeuber, Cynthia. Sixty-Five Plus in America. Current Population Reports, Series P23-178RV. Washington, D.C.: U.S. Government Printing Office, 1993.

U.S. Bureau of the Census. Who's Minding the Kids? Child Care Arrangements: Fall 1991. Current Population Reports, Series P-70 No. 36. Washington, D.C.: U.S. Government Printing Office, 1994.

U.S. Bureau of Labor Statistics. Handbook of Labor Statistics: Table 5. Washington, D.C.: U.S. Government Printing Office, 1989.

_____. Employment and Earnings, January 1991: Table 3. Washington, D.C.: U.S. Government Printing Office, 1991.

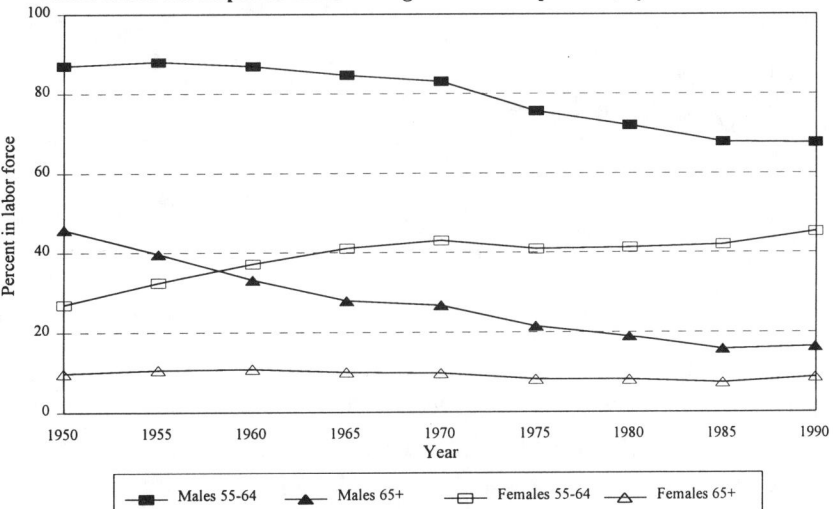

Labor Force Participation Rates Among the Older Population, by Sex: 1950-1990

Percent in labor force

Year

■ Males 55-64   ▲ Males 65+   ☐ Females 55-64   △ Females 65+

Source: 1950-1990 Bureau of Labor Statistics data.

ages is greater among males as one would expect of a population with greater labor force participation among those now in older age groups. Males who are in managerial and professional occupations are more likely than those in other occupations to be in their middle to later life cycle, e.g. 35-54. The percentage of these managers and professionals who are over 55 years old has declined in recent years as has the percentage of these positions held by those under 35 years of age. The increasing concentration of occupational populations in the middle years is seen, for males, most dramatically in the technical, sales and administrative support occupations.

While the similarity of age distributions across most occupations is pronounced, there have been some major changes in the age composition within occupations which clearly reflect the significant occupational restructuring in the United States economy. During this five year period, for example, there has been a dramatic decline in the percentage of younger males and females in service, and especially private household, occupations. The increase in the percentage of older males and females in service occupations indicates this shift is due to the entry of older individuals into the service occupations and not simply the aging of those already employed, or a decline in younger entries, in the service occupations. While this shift in age composition among the service occupations reflects changes in alternative occupational prospects, it may also presage a rise in the status of service occupations as they become more similar in age composition to other occupations.

The dramatic increase of the retirement age population in private household occupations and in farming, forestry and fishing occupations is merely one indication that individuals who would once have been considered of retirement age are increasingly represented in those employed across most occupations. It remains to be seen whether the increasing concentration of the baby boomers in administrative and managerial professions along with the rising percentage of the elderly in many occupations results in barriers to opportunity and advancement among those newly entering the labor force. At the least, the increasing percentage of baby boomers and working elderly across occupations has influenced, for example, the typical age of most occupational workers and generated a sense among some of barriers to entry for a younger generation.

Poverty

One of the major sociodemographic trends over the past quarter century has been the increasing concentration of children and female headed households in poverty. The concentration of poverty at younger ages followed the dramatic reductions in poverty among the elderly prior to the mid 1970s and is not simply a compositional result of that decline.

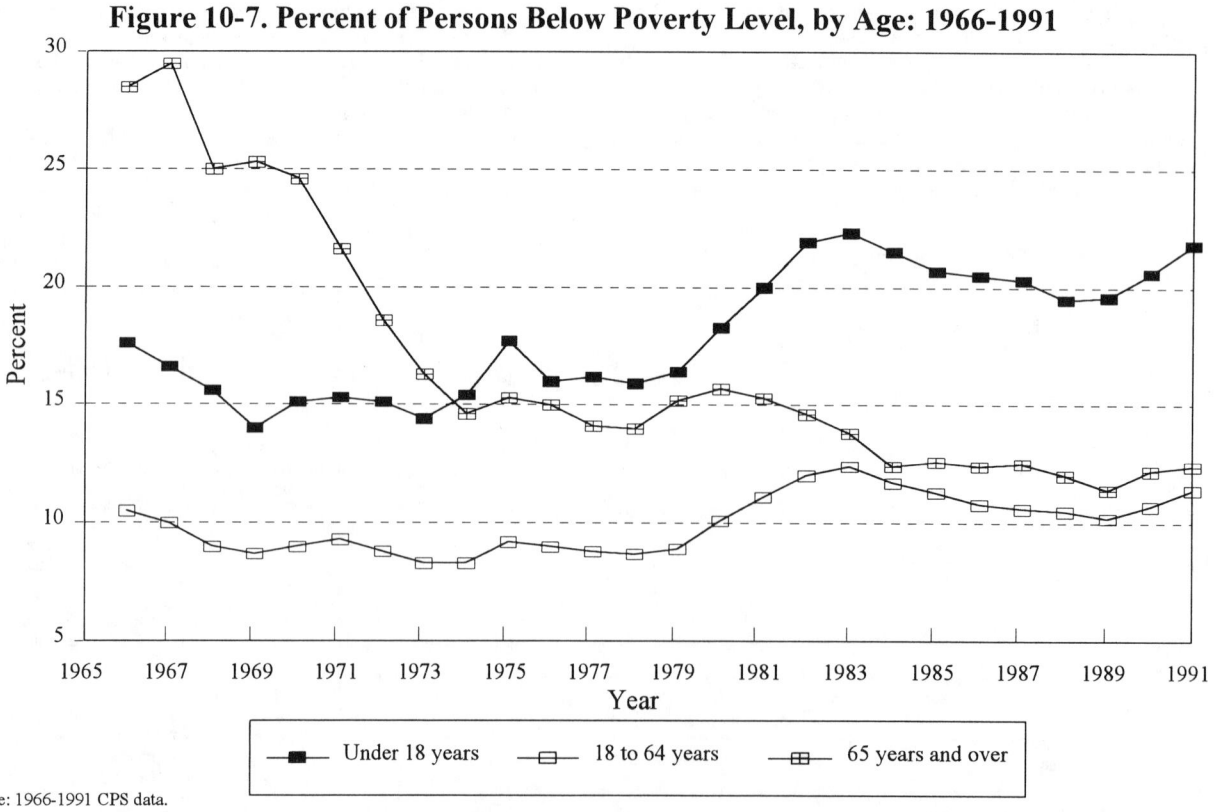

Figure 10-7. Percent of Persons Below Poverty Level, by Age: 1966-1991

Under 18 years   18 to 64 years   65 years and over

Source: 1966-1991 CPS data.

Figure 10-7 shows the rising percentage of those under 18 years of age in poverty and the dramatic decline in the percentage of the elderly below the poverty level. Successes in combating poverty among the elderly may, in the longer run, be overshadowed by the tragedy of raising a rising percentage of future generations in poverty. A good deal of the rising poverty among those under 18 years of age and those aged 18 to 64 years old occurred during the period from 1978 through 1983 and may reflect inflation adjustments as well as changing numbers of the impoverished. However, the influences behind the increasing exposure of children to poverty are complex, ranging from an intergenerational shift in wealth holding as life expectancy rises to an increasing percentage of children in female headed households with a typically higher rate of poverty. These families are also the most likely to be hurt by, and the least likely to have benefited from, the rising value of real estate assets, high interest rates, and general price inflation during these years.

The compositional aspects of the rise in poverty associated with female headed households are evident in Figure 10-8. The poverty rate among female headed households has actually declined somewhat since the early 1960s and remained relatively constant since the mid 1960s. Yet, as the percentage of female headed households has risen, the percentage of all poor families which are female headed households has risen dramatically. The frequently discussed feminization of poverty is in large part a persistence of poverty among women coupled with a feminization of householding. Effective social policies and programs to address the persistent aspects of poverty and its impact upon women and children are, sadly, still lacking and without immediate promise. The resulting prospects for a generation raised in relative poverty may well prove over the long run to be among the most socially and culturally significant of the compositional differences discussed in this chapter.

Marriage and Householding

The most dramatic changes in marriage behavior across surviving individuals are those in the most recent cohorts and have yet to play out across the entire life cycle. As Figures 10-9A and 10-9B demonstrate, cohort differences in the age-specific percentage of males and females who are married with spouse present are also not as dramatic as one might suspect from popular media accounts. With the exception of an apparent delay in young marriages during the Great Depression years and higher disruption of elderly marriages from mortality during the early part of this century, changes in age-specific marriage were relatively minor from the turn of the century until the 1960s. There is evidence of a decline in the percent married in middle age during the 1960s as divorce became more legitimate and prevalent. And, perhaps as this transition further increased an acceptance of

Figure 10-8. Indicators of Poverty in Families with Female Householders: 1959-1991

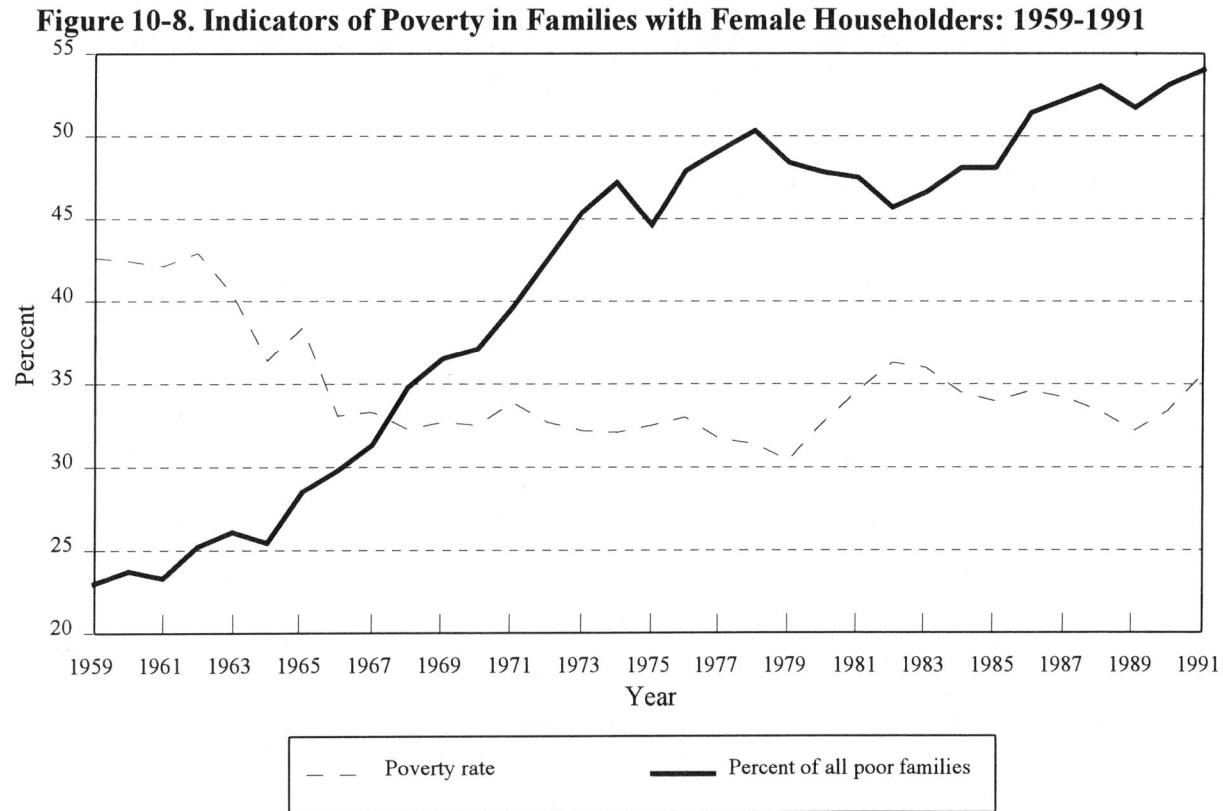

Source: 1959-1991 CPS data.

Figure 10-9A. Percent of Males Married, Spouse Present, by Birth Cohort: 1876-1965, Observed Through 1990

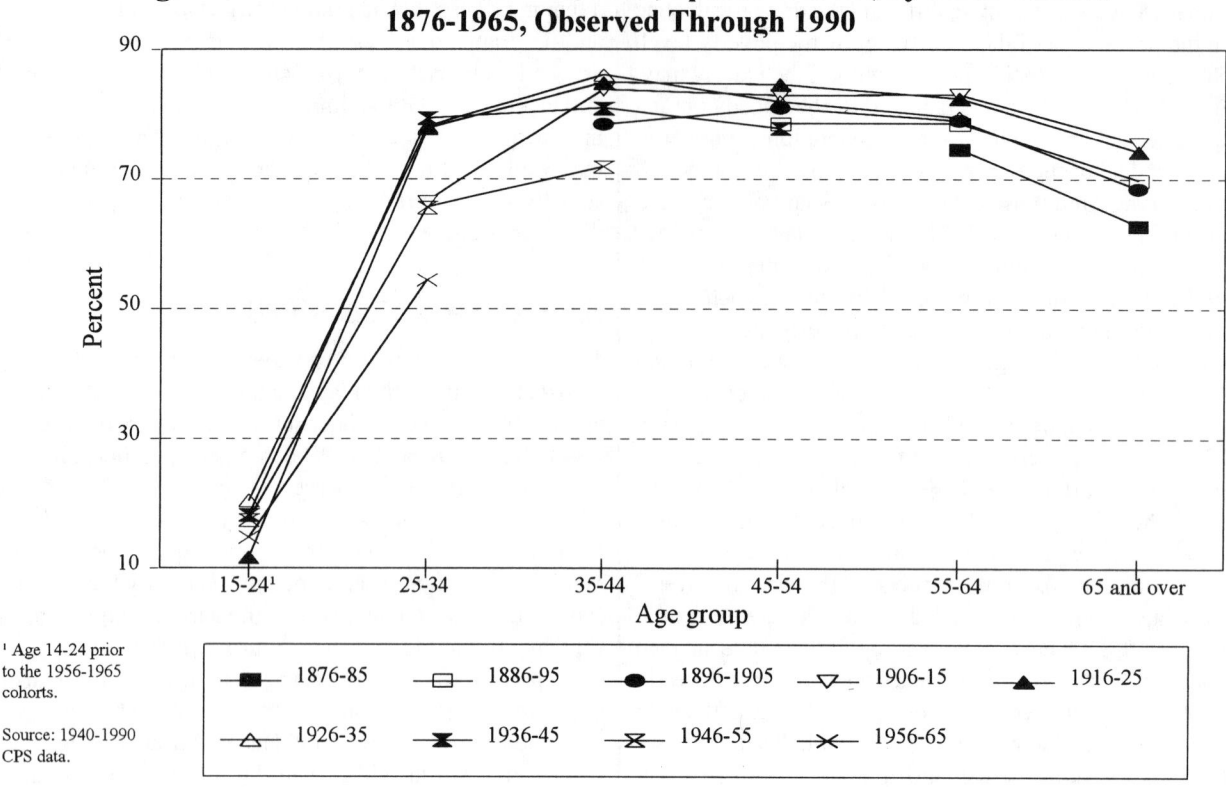

¹ Age 14-24 prior
to the 1956-1965
cohorts.

Source: 1940-1990
CPS data.

Figure 10-9B. Percent of Females Married, Spouse Present, by Birth Cohort: 1876-1965, Observed Through 1990

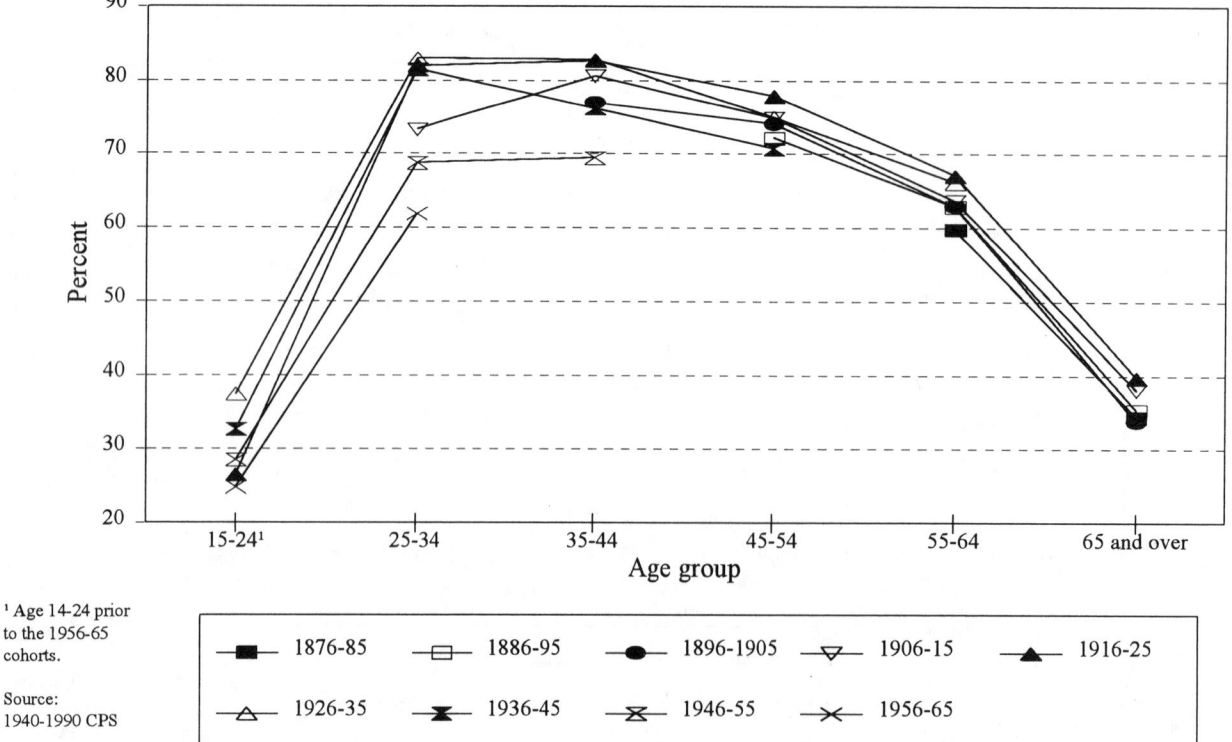

¹ Age 14-24 prior
to the 1956-65
cohorts.

Source:
1940-1990 CPS

Figure 10-10. Married-couple Households as Percent of All Households, by Age of Householder and Birth Cohort: 1876-1965, Observed Through 1990

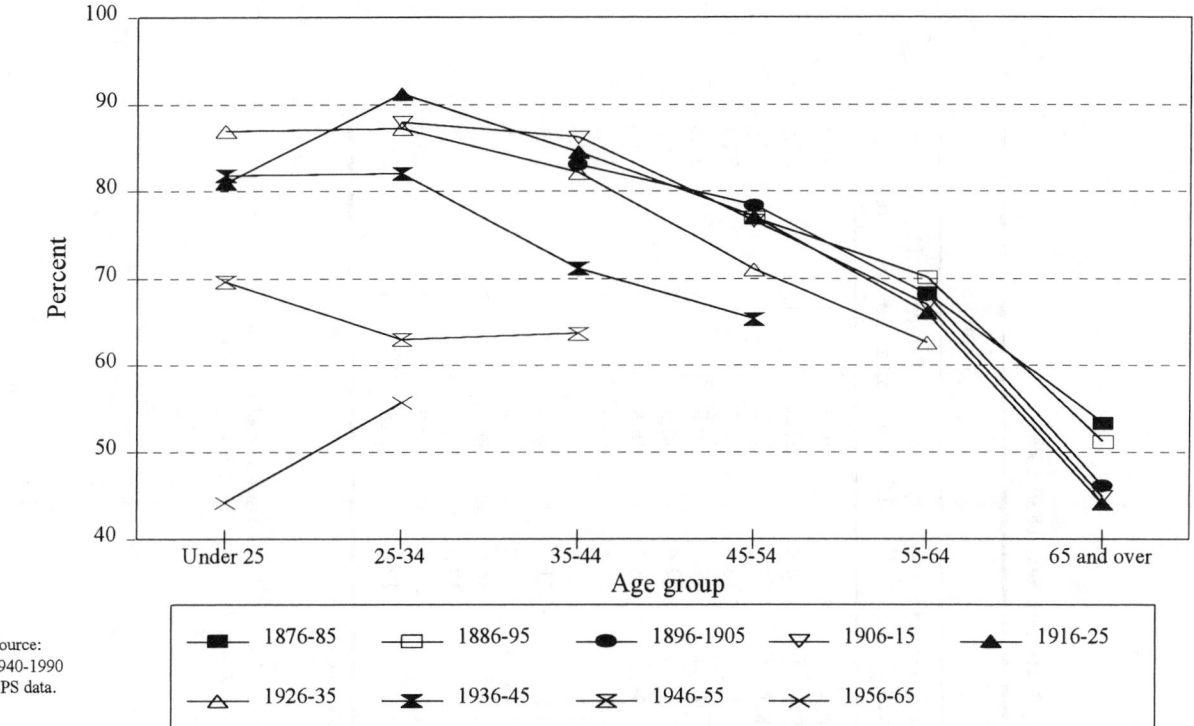

Source:
1940-1990
CPS data.

living out of wedlock, the most recent cohorts have seen an unparalleled decline in the percentage living as married couples at early ages among both males and females. It remains to be seen how these cohorts behave throughout older ages and whether the trend towards an even greater percentage living out of marriage continues into future cohorts. These individuals may represent a new delay of marriage and may ultimately marry in older ages. Or, these individuals may be permanently taking advantage of the increasing acceptance of a single lifestyle and economic opportunities for women. It is unlikely, however, that the options for living out of marriage which were once both normatively and economically more constrained will ever be as restrictive as in past cohorts.

Differences in the percentage of all households which consist of married couples are even more dramatic among recent cohorts. Figure 10-10 shows the drop in married-couple households began in the 1950s birth cohort and the prevalence of such households has continued to decline since. The decline in early marriages among these cohorts combined with substantially rising costs of establishing new households and other economic uncertainties amplify these differences. In the most recent period, i.e. the oldest age groups among these recent cohorts, the percent of married-couple households provides some evidence of a rise. The recent rise may, in turn,

reflect a drop in the price of household formation due to a relative stabilization of real estate costs or perhaps even lower costs of householding investment in the face of declining interest rates. This rise might also simply reflect the fact that marriage, and married-couple householding, has been delayed to older ages by these cohorts but is still an eventually desired outcome. In either case, the distinctive experiences of these recent cohorts and the decline or, at the least, delay in both marriage and married householding signify a substantial departure from the common experience of earlier cohorts. And, we have yet to learn what the eventual nuptiality and householding history of these most recent cohorts will be.

Dependency and Children

As a population, few changes have had as dramatic an impact upon composition of successive generations as has the striking decline in fertility and family size during this century. One ready indication of these changes is the decline in youth and old age dependency over past generations. Table 10-7 shows the decline in the percentage of the population under 15 years of age and the rising percentage of the population over 65 years of age since 1850. Despite increases during the baby boom years, the

Table 10-7. Percent of Population in Youth or Old Age and Dependency Ratio, by Sex: 1850-1990

Year	Both sexes Percent <15 years	Both sexes Percent 65 and over	Both sexes Dependency ratio	Males Percent <15 years	Males Percent 65 and over	Males Dependency ratio[1]	Females Percent <15 years	Females Percent 65 and over	Females Dependency ratio[1]
1990	21.7	12.6	51.7	22.6	10.4	24.4	20.5	14.7	27.3
1980	22.6	11.3	51.3	23.8	9.4	24.4	21.5	13.1	26.9
1970	28.5	9.9	62.3	29.8	8.5	30.3	27.2	11.2	32.0
1960	31.1	9.2	67.5	32.1	8.5	33.5	30.1	10.0	34.1
1950	26.9	8.1	53.8	27.5	7.7	29.2	36.0	8.5	37.3
1940	25.0	6.8	46.6	25.3	6.7	24.6	30.3	7.0	28.5
1930	29.4	5.4	53.4	29.4	5.4	26.4	26.8	5.5	24.0
1920	31.8	4.7	57.5	31.5	4.6	29.5	34.4	4.7	30.7
1910	32.1	4.3	57.3	31.5	4.2	28.9	32.7	4.4	28.3
1900	34.5	4.1	62.7	34.0	4.0	31.5	34.8	4.1	30.9
1890	35.6	3.9	65.2	35.2	3.8	33.0	35.8	3.9	32.0
1880	38.1	3.4	70.9	38.0	3.4	36.0	38.2	3.5	35.0
1870	39.2	3.0	73.0	39.3	3.0	37.0	39.1	3.0	36.0
1860	40.6	4.3[2]	81.4	40.2	4.2	41.1	40.9	4.4	40.0
1850	41.5	4.1[2]	84.1	41.2	4.1	42.6	41.8	4.2	41.5

[1] Males or females age <15 years and >65 years supported by population of both sexes age 15 to 64 years.
[2] 60 years and over.

Source: U.S. Bureau of the Census, "General Population Characteristics," 1990 Census of Population, Table 16, 1980 Census of Population, Table 44, and "Historical Statistics of the United States, Part I," (Series A 119-134), U.S. Government Printing Office, Washington, D.C., 1992, 1983, and 1975.

Figure 10-11. Families With Own Children Under 18 as Percent of All Families, by Age of Householder and Birth Cohort: 1896-1965, Observed Through 1990

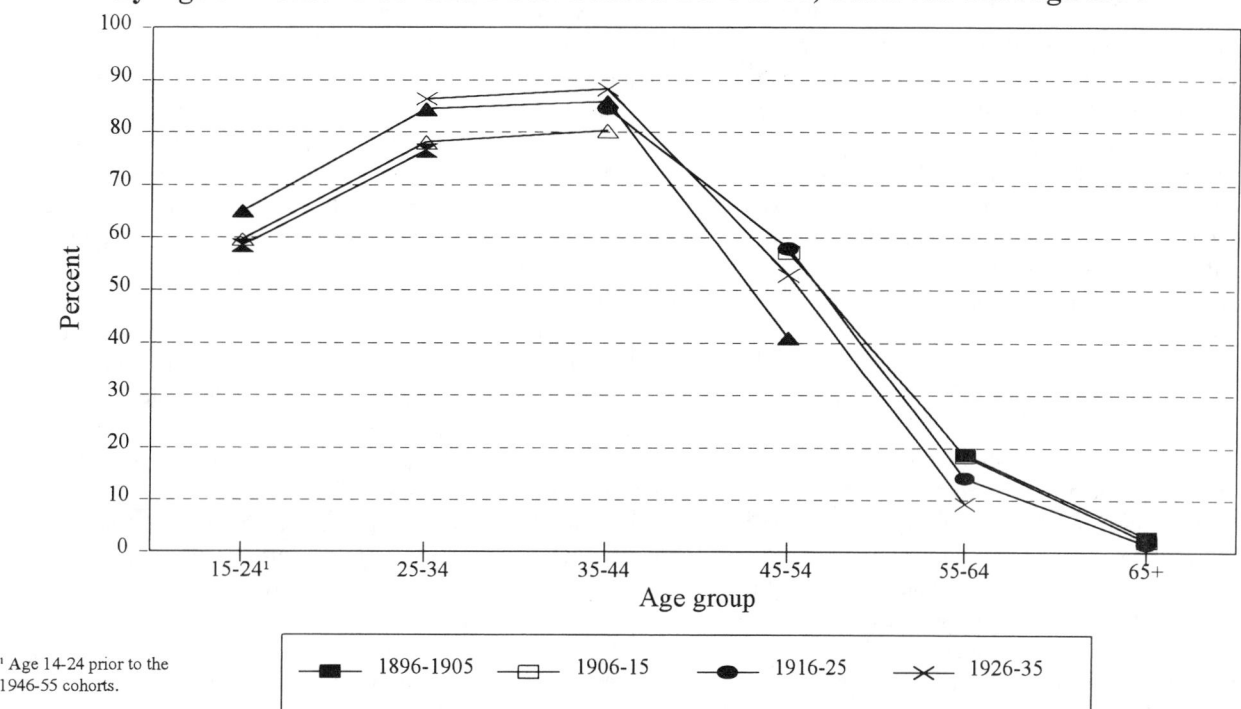

¹ Age 14-24 prior to the 1946-55 cohorts.

Source: 1960-1990 CPS data.

■ 1896-1905	□ 1906-15	● 1916-25	✕ 1926-35
▲ 1936-45	△ 1946-55	✕ 1956-65	

percentage of males and females under 15 years of age has fallen by nearly half of what it was in the middle of the last century. At the same time, increased longevity has shifted the so-called dependency burden of society more toward care for the aged, as children have declined as a percentage of the population and the elderly have increased. The increase in elderly is most heavily concentrated in the past fifty years. The overall dependency ratio of the young and elderly to working-age adults declined dramatically between 1850 and 1940. Dependency then rose during the baby boom years and has only recently declined again to levels near those half a century ago. The unsteady decline of dependency over the past generations will continue in the near future as the baby boom cohorts age out of the working years and into elderly ages. However, caution is merited concerning these dependency ratios. The extension of secondary and post-secondary education, child labor laws, etc., since 1850 suggests that the years spent as a dependent have substantially increased and may more than offset the decline in the percentage of youth as a social dependency burden. The percentage of young dependents would, for example, increase substantially over this same period if years spent in dependency increased by ten years of age since 1850. In the same fashion, it is arguable that the increased years spent in elderly dependency might be understated as both longevity increases and men leave the labor force at younger ages.

One remarkable aspect of generational experiences over the fertility decline is the similarity of these generations regarding their experiences in families raising children. Figure 10-11 shows the surprisingly consistent age patterns of families with own children in them across the life cycle of cohorts spanning the fertility decline. Despite the apparent consistency, there are of course significant differences also evidenced. There is clearly evidence that the 'empty nest' is confronted at younger ages in recent cohorts as fewer families with children are found among all families with householders over 45 years of age. And, there is a substantial overall decline in families with own children under 18 in the initial experiences of the most recent cohorts. These most recent declines may represent a variety of complex effects discussed in other chapters including delay of householding, delay of childbearing, further life-long reductions in fertility and rising alternative household possibilities for child rearing.

Gender, Aging and Selected Behaviors

There are numerous other behaviors which vary in likelihood according to an individual's gender and age but are only demographic behaviors in the sense of their apparent relationships to population composition and changing cohort experiences over time. And, there are other behaviors, such as sexual ones, which are distinctly demographic yet vary across compositional categories in a fashion which appears more culturally determined than demographically dependent. These behaviors are far too numerous to catalogue in a profile of the United States population. Yet, it is important to recognize the extent of demographic variation in the wider variety of social behavior and the different cultures represented in compositional subgroups of the population. Several major examples of behavioral and cultural variability along demographic dimensions are presented below and are at least sufficient to illustrate the importance of the interrelationships between population composition, culture and social behavior.

Home Ownership and Assets

The middle of this century witnessed dramatic changes in the prospects for individual home ownership. More recent householding behavior is also responsive to the economic possibilities for home ownership. Table 10-8 presents the number of households and the percentage of married- couple households which are owner-occupied over the past three decennial censuses. The number of households increased for all groups except younger married-couple households between 1970 and 1990. Married-couple households with householders under 25 years of age fell precipitously over this period from rising ages at marriage and declining household formation in these younger ages. Married-couple householders between 25 and 29 years of age first rose and then fell slightly during the same period. Despite the fall in younger married-couple households, the number of all households under 35 years of age increased significantly across these years with the greatest increase concentrated in the years between 1970 and 1980.

At the same time as households with household heads under 35 years of age continued to increase, this table shows that these households increased only slightly from 1980 to 1990 and the percentage of owner-occupied households among these younger adults fell dramatically in the same period after substantial increases in the preceding decade. A similar decline is evidenced for those 35 to 64 years of age. This decline is clearly too large to be accounted for by the aging of the population and the steady rise of households 65 years of age and older. Dramatically rising real estate prices, declining purchasing power and high interest rates, which characterized many of the years during this period, have had clear impacts upon the home owning possibilities and experiences of the recent generations.

The inflation of real estate values and changes in ownership possibilities by cohort are also evidenced in the adjusted mean house value by cohorts shown in Figure 10-12. Earlier (i.e. now older) birth cohorts which have been in the homes they own for longer periods of time are in households which have lower mean house value. This partially reflects the lack of reappraisal and inflation associated with resale of housing and also reflects the declining tendency to move upward in the housing market at older ages and, especially, with fixed income. In contrast, the younger cohorts which entered the housing market more recently during inflationary markets and those who participated in these markets through trying to upgrade housing investments have clearly higher

Table 10-8. Percent of All Households and Married-couple Households that are Owner Households, by Age or Householder: 1970-1990

Type of household and age of householder	Number of households			Percent owner-occupied		
	1990	1980	1970	1990	1980	1970
All households	93,347	79,108	63,445	64.1	68.0	62.9
Under 35 years	25,593	24,298	16,290	38.5	47.5	41.2
35 to 64 years	47,600	38,662	34,788	73.1	78.4	71.3
65 years and over	20,156	16,149	12,367	75.5	74.1	67.5
Married-couple households	52,317	48,179	43,217	77.9	80.1	70.7
Under 25 years	1,636	2,831	3,068	25.7	38.3	26.0
25 to 29 years	4,846	5,249	4,633	51.1	60.6	48.3
30 to 34 years	6,539	6,008	4,439	66.4	76.7	65.8
35 to 44 years	13,083	9,881	9,184	79.2	84.5	76.7
45 to 64 years	17,316	16,961	16,226	88.4	89.3	80.8
65 years and over	8,898	7,249	5,667	88.5	86.2	78.4

Source: U.S. Bureau of the Census, Current Population Characteristics, "Household and Family Characteristics: March 1990 and 1989," Series P-20, No. 447, Table 16, and "March 1980," Series P-20, No. 366, Table 24, and "Housing Characteristics by Household Composition," 1970 Census of Housing, Table A-5, U.S. Government Printing Office, Washington, D.C., 1990, 1981, and 1973.

Figure 10-12. Trajectories of Mean House Value[1] by Birth Cohorts: 1881-1965, Observed Through 1990

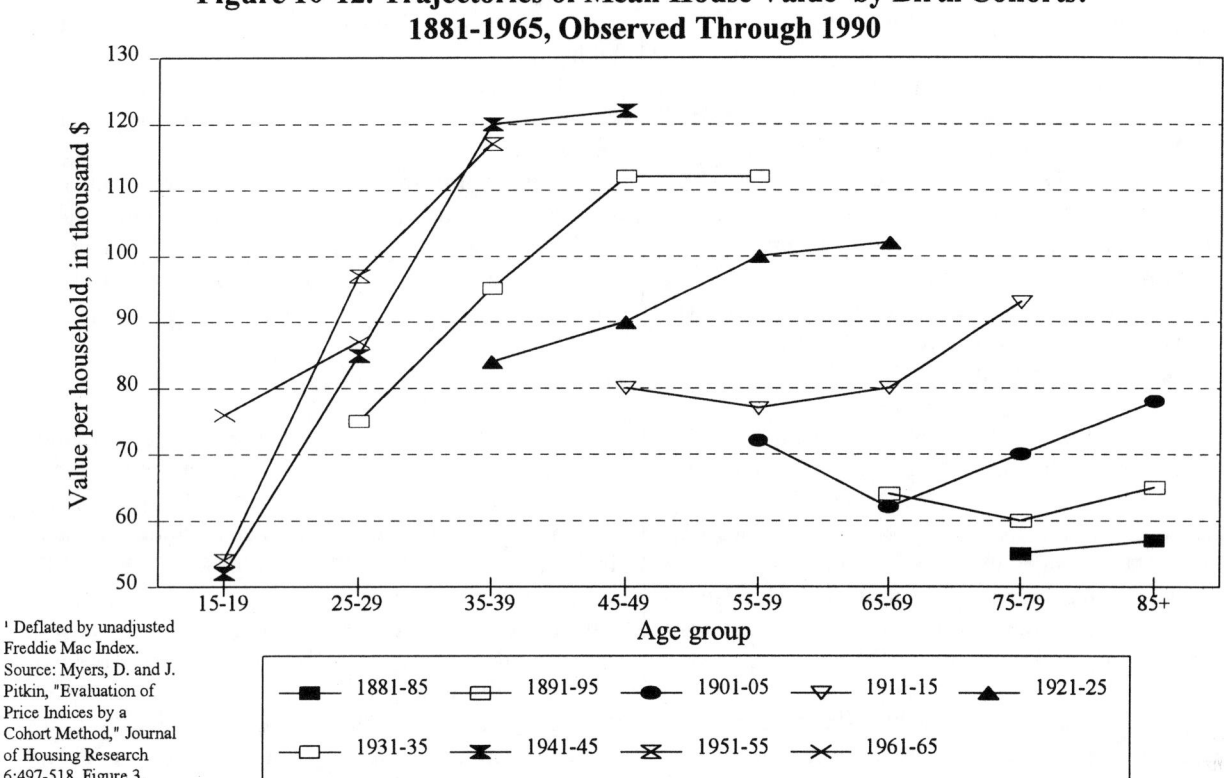

[1] Deflated by unadjusted Freddie Mac Index.
Source: Myers, D. and J. Pitkin, "Evaluation of Price Indices by a Cohort Method," Journal of Housing Research 6:497-518, Figure 3.

Table 10-9. Distribution of Measured Net Worth by Age of Householder and Asset Type: 1993

Asset type	Total	Under 35 years	35 to 44 years	45 to 54 years	55 to 64 years	65 years and over
Median measured net worth	$37,587	$5,786	$29,202	$57,755	$91,481	$86,324
Assets	$38,790	$6,631	$30,750	$59,545	$94,042	$86,756
Interest-earning assets	$5,788	$752	$3,037	$5,949	$12,533	$19,682
Real estate	$20,936	$3,136	$17,258	$33,498	$51,595	$45,234
Vehicles	$2,406	$1,053	$2,570	$3,754	$4,483	$3,194
Business or profession	$2,406	$613	$2,774	$5,198	$5,580	$2,072
Other assets[1]	$7,254	$1,076	$5,110	$11,147	$19,851	$16,574
Unsecured liabilities	-$1,203	-$845	-$1,548	-$1,790	-$2,561	-$432
Total percent net worth	100.0	100.0	100.0	100.0	100.0	100.0
Assets	103.2	114.6	105.3	103.1	102.8	100.5
Interest-earning assets	15.4	13.0	10.4	10.3	13.7	22.8
Real estate	55.7	54.2	59.1	58.0	56.4	52.4
Vehicles	6.4	18.2	8.8	6.5	4.9	3.7
Business or profession	6.4	10.6	9.5	9.0	6.1	2.4
Other assets[1]	19.3	18.6	17.5	19.3	21.7	19.2
Unsecured liabilities	-3.2	-14.6	-5.3	-3.1	-2.8	-0.5

[1] Includes other savings, stocks, bonds, IRA and Keogh accounts, mortgages held from sale of real estate or business, and other financial investments.
Source: U.S. Bureau of the Census, Current Population Reports, "Asset Ownership of Households: 1993," Series P-70, Number 47, U.S. Government Printing Office, Washington, D.C., 1995, Tables D and E.

mean value of housing. The result is a remarkable stratification of the current population by age and value of housing.

As Table 10-9 shows, real estate assets are, in fact, the highest percentage of total net worth for those of all ages. Real estate assets are greater, but in lower proportion to total net worth, for those aged 45 and over. Other fixed durable investments such as vehicles and business or professional assets also decline as a percentage of total worth across increasing ages. Between ages 35 and 64 there are significant increases in other assets, primarily financial investments, which are turned into interest earning assets after retirement, i.e. at ages of 65 years and older.

Real estate assets, vehicles, etc., generate the major liabilities for most householders in the form of mortgages, car loans and other secured debt. Under 35 years of age indebtedness in the form of unsecured liabilities (e.g. credit card debt, signature loans without collateral) is a substantial burden. Unsecured liabilities for those under 35 are nearly 15 percent of total net worth. This unsecured debt drops dramatically in older age groups. Most of this decline in unsecured debt is due to life cycle changes in accumulation of wealth. However, some of the age pattern may reflect different generational psychologies of debt. Future cohort patterns of indebtedness among those becoming accustomed to the convenience of credit card and unsecured debt will be of considerable import in shaping life cycle patterns of wealth holding.

Cohort changes in home ownership and investment will also have a significant potential to impact these overall age patterns of asset holding in the near future. However, some improvements in the housing market, interest rates, and economic prospects for younger adults since the 1990 census may significantly alter any attempted forecasting of such trends in cohort financial prospects or behaviors.

Consumer Expenditures

Throughout the life cycle the need for various products and services changes. In youth many basic needs are taken care of by parents and expenditures are more often devoted to luxury or peripheral items. However, upon reaching early adulthood the basic life necessities (e.g. food, housing and transportation) require major expenditures. As Figure 10-13 shows, young adults under twenty-five years of age still tend to spend more on apparel, entertainment and related other goods than do those at other ages. Transportation also constitutes a larger proportion of expenditures for these young adults. As the population ages into early maturity (e.g. 25-34 years of age), expenditures

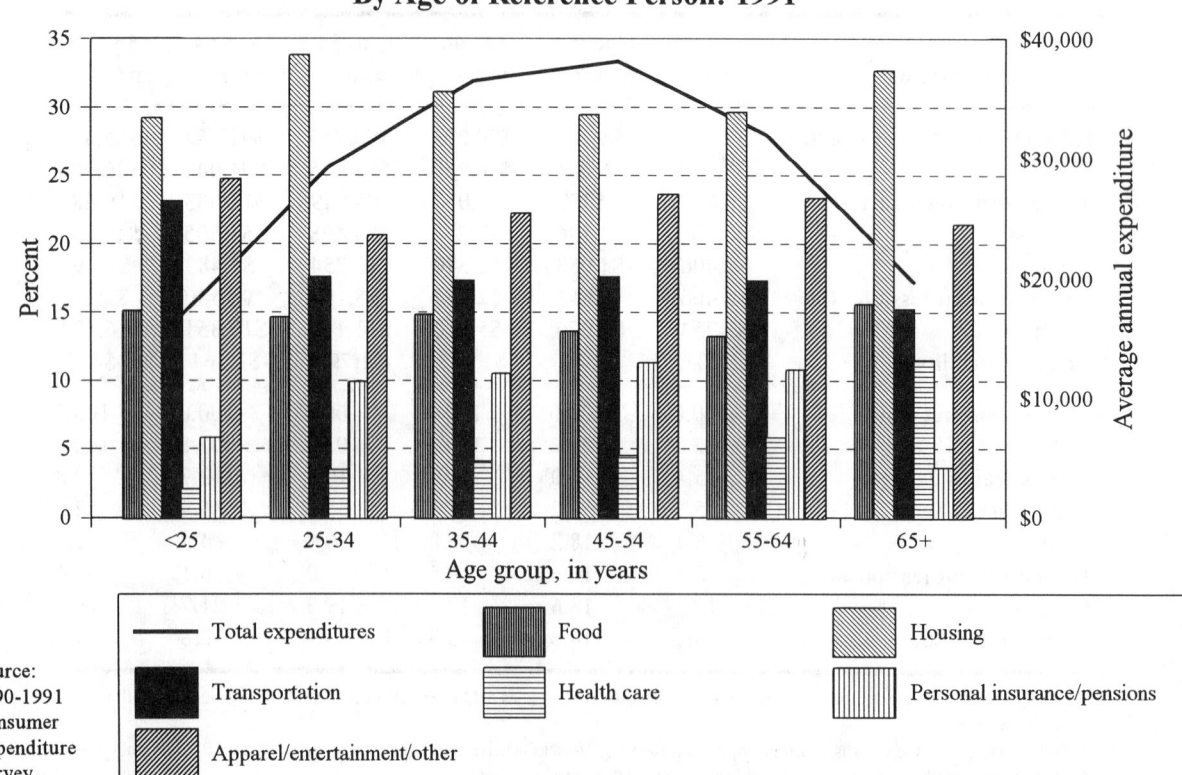

Figure 10-13. Percent Distribution of Total Consumer Expenditures, By Age of Reference Person: 1991

Source: 1990-1991 Consumer Expenditure Survey

rise and housing costs become more dominant among all expenditures.

The rise of housing expenditures is in line with the life cycle patterns of asset holding noted above. Over the entire life course total expenditures rise until middle ages, partially reflecting the course of rising and declining mortgages, provision for dependents, accumulation of assets and durable goods, etc., all of which are characteristic of providing for a household and raising children. As total expenditures rise though adulthood the proportion spent on basic housing declines. From middle age through pre-retirement years the only appreciable change in consumer expenditures are rising proportions of income spent on personal insurance or pensions and on health care.

After retirement there is a substantial rise in the proportion of income spent on housing as total expenditures fall rapidly. The proportion spent on health care climbs rapidly to largely absorb the declining proportion of expenditures on personal insurance or pensions. Remarkably, the proportion of expenditures on apparel, entertainment and related other expenses is relatively stable in older ages and the proportion of expenditures on transportation experiences only a slight decline as a percentage of all consumer expenditures.

Political Participation and Voting

Even casual observations often suggest that political participation and behavior vary in distinctive ways among different generations and ages and by gender. Political campaigns are even frequently directed toward specific targeted age groups through emphasis on age-related issues. And, it is not infrequent to hear references to a "gender gap" in campaigns of various sorts or with respect to major social issues and opinions.

Table 10-10 presents voting and registration percentages by age and sex for the presidential elections between 1964 and 1992. Several trends are notable in those reported registered. Male voter registration has declined overall, if unsteadily, with the most notable declines somewhat surprisingly concentrated in those 25 to 44 years of age. Decline in female voter registration is not so notable and registration among women over 65 years of age has actually increased over the period. Among those who reportedly voted, elections in the 1960s and 1970s had a greater percentage of males voting, while those in the 1980s and 1990s had a greater percentage of females voting. Voting by both men and women has declined (with a slight upswing in 1992) across the period. However, voting behavior by men has declined more rapidly than it has for women.

Political party affiliation of the voting age population is presented by sex in Figure 10-14. There are more Democrats, including weak or independent Democrats, than there are Republicans overall. And, women are more

likely to be among these strong Democrats or weak/independent Democrats than are men. Men are more likely to be strong Republicans, weak/independent Republicans or independents than are women. Differences in the percentages of men and women in those who are independent or apolitical are, however, very slight.

Party affiliation by age is given in Figure 10-15. The percentage of weak or independent affiliation with either the Democratic or Republican parties declines with older age while strong affiliations with either party increase with increasing age. Independents and those reporting themselves apolitical are similarly more frequent among the younger ages. Whether these age-graded differences represent a decline in traditional party affiliation across generations or an increase in political and ideological commitments with age is an intriguing question plagued by the traditional difficulties of disentangling age, period and cohort effects. As the population ages in coming years will the commitment to party affiliations experience a dramatic resurgence or stark decline? If aging influences political attitudes or if generations carry ideological commitments formed in cohort experiences, the association of political behaviors and affiliations with age suggest any long-term understanding of political trends must recognize the likely effects of demographic composition on political directions of our society.

Sexual Behavior

It has been noted that those who study population often manage to do so circuitously without discussing sexual behavior. In addition to the historical discomfort and political liabilities of frankly discussing sexual behavior, reliable information on sexual behavior can be extremely difficult to obtain. In the past, demographers instead largely contented themselves with discussing fertility outcomes of heterosexual behavior and biological aspects of fecundity. In a contraceptive and diverse society and a post-fertility transition era the linkage of sexual behavior to fertility is far less direct than in more traditional and non-contracepting populations. Sexual behavior is of as great an interest in modern society for its relationship to sexually transmitted diseases and mortality as it is for its link to fertility. And, interest in sexual behavior as one culturally influenced aspect of life and society has come of age as a major social science subject in its own right.

Data on sexual behavior are almost always difficult to obtain, are highly reactive measurements, and are of somewhat questionable reliability. The landmark National Health and Social Life Survey (see Michael et al. in this chapter's bibliography) has provided the most reliable recent information concerning sexual behaviors. In Table 10-11 the frequency of sex in the past 12 months according to this survey are summarized by age and sex. Overall the greatest percentage of those in all age groups

Table 10-10. Voting and Registration in the November Presidential Elections 1964-1992, by Age and Sex

	Reported registered				Reported voted			
	Number, in thousands		Percent		Number, in thousands		Percent	
	Male	Female	Male	Female	Male	Female	Male	Female
November 1992	59,254	67,324	66.9	69.3	53,312	60,554	60.2	62.3
18 to 20 years	2,274	2,421	46.6	49.9	1,786	1,962	36.6	40.5
21 to 24 years	3,797	4,294	53.0	57.4	3,086	3,607	43.1	48.2
25 to 44 years	25,022	27,704	62.6	67.0	22,319	25,069	55.8	60.6
45 to 64 years	17,681	19,335	74.9	75.7	16,490	17,909	69.8	70.2
65 years and over	10,481	13,568	81.1	75.7	9,631	12,006	74.5	67.0
November 1988	55,139	63,450	65.2	67.8	47,704	54,519	56.4	58.3
18 to 20 years	2,232	2,590	42.1	47.6	1,652	1,918	31.2	35.2
21 to 24 years	3,444	4,054	47.9	53.1	2,610	3,075	36.3	40.3
25 to 44 years	23,112	25,954	60.6	65.4	19,757	22,260	51.8	56.1
45 to 64 years	16,601	18,020	75.7	75.3	14,923	16,211	68.1	67.7
65 years and over	9,748	12,832	81.6	76.1	8,763	11,055	73.3	65.6
November 1984	54,032	62,074	67.3	69.3	47,354	54,524	59.0	60.8
18 to 20 years	2,492	2,793	45.0	49.0	1,892	2,239	34.1	39.2
21 to 24 years	4,309	4,768	52.7	55.7	3,417	3,859	41.8	45.1
25 to 44 years	22,405	24,893	64.5	68.6	19,540	21,953	56.3	60.5
45 to 64 years	16,103	17,836	76.6	76.6	14,681	16,243	69.8	69.8
65 years and over	8,722	11,785	80.2	74.7	7,824	10,230	71.9	64.8
November 1980	49,344	55,691	66.6	67.1	43,753	49,312	59.1	59.4
18 to 20 years	2,633	2,852	43.8	45.5	2,082	2,305	34.6	36.8
21 to 24 years	3,921	4,446	51.3	54.1	3,178	3,660	41.6	44.5
25 to 44 years	19,066	21,120	64.3	66.8	16,955	19,002	57.1	60.1
45 to 64 years	15,903	17,126	76.3	75.3	14,554	15,651	69.8	68.9
65 years and over	7,821	10,147	78.8	71.6	6,984	8,694	70.4	61.3
November 1976	46,260	51,501	67.1	66.4	41,079	45,620	59.6	58.8
18 to 20 years	2,687	3,011	46.0	48.1	2,121	2,478	36.3	39.6
21 to 24 years	3,929	4,209	54.7	54.9	3,210	3,559	44.7	46.4
25 to 44 years	16,997	18,545	64.8	66.1	15,187	16,696	57.9	59.5
45 to 64 years	15,718	16,949	76.1	74.9	14,390	15,374	69.7	67.9
65 years and over	6,930	8,787	76.6	67.8	6,172	7,513	68.3	58.0
November 1972	46,682	51,798	73.1	71.6	40,908	44,858	64.1	62.0
18 to 20 years	3,066	3,338	57.9	58.3	2,524	2,794	47.7	48.8
21 to 24 years	3,771	4,315	58.6	60.3	3,197	3,699	49.7	51.7
25 to 44 years	16,854	18,206	71.2	71.4	14,788	16,030	62.5	62.9
45 to 64 years	16,156	17,601	80.4	79.1	14,499	15,491	72.2	69.6
65 years and over	6,835	8,337	81.9	71.1	5,898	6,844	70.7	58.4
November 1968	41,379	45,196	76.0	72.8	38,014	40,951	69.8	66.0
18 to 20 years[1]	91	102	44.0	45.3	74	71	35.7	31.6
21 to 24 years	2,837	3,466	56.6	56.3	2,552	3,155	50.9	51.3
25 to 44 years	16,106	17,289	73.0	71.9	14,835	15,890	67.2	66.1
45 to 64 years	15,863	16,850	82.4	79.8	14,748	15,490	76.6	73.3
65 years and over	6,482	7,489	81.7	71.1	5,805	6,345	73.1	60.3
November 1964	—	—	—	—	37,480	39,191	71.9	67.0
18 to 20 years[1]	—	—	—	—	61	55	46.2	33.5
21 to 24 years	—	—	—	—	2,275	2,661	51.7	51.0
25 to 44 years	—	—	—	—	15,117	16,119	70.0	68.0
45 to 64 years	—	—	—	—	14,417	145,518	78.5	73.5
65 years and over	—	—	—	—	5,609	5,837	73.7	60.4

[1] Includes persons 18 to 20 years old in Georgia and Kentucky, 19 and 20 in Alaska, and 20 in Hawaii.

Source: U.S. Bureau of the Census, Current Population Reports, "Voting and Registration in the Election of November 1992," Series P-20, No. 466, Table 2 and Appendix A, U.S. Government Printing Office, Washington, D.C., 1993.

Figure 10-14. Political Party Affiliation of the Voting-age Population, by Sex: 1992

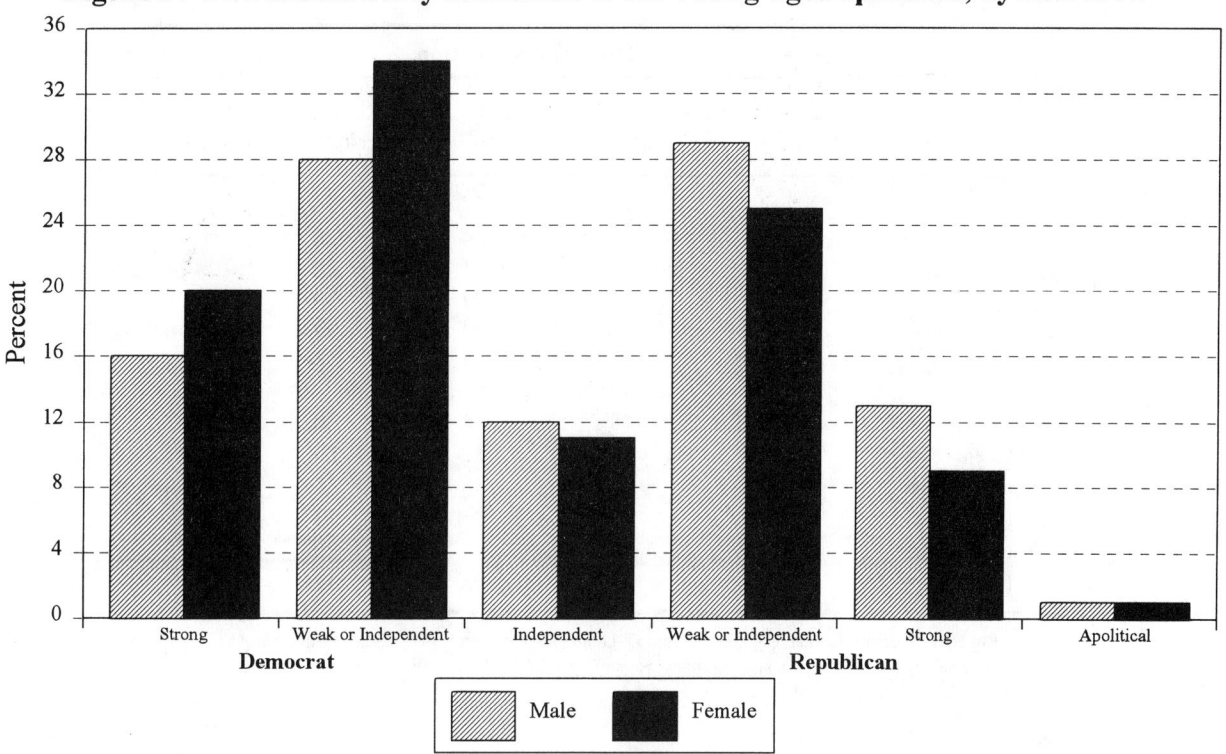

Source: University of Michigan Center for Political Studies data, based on the National Election Studies.

Figure 10-15. Political Party Affiliation of the Voting-Age Population, by Age: 1992

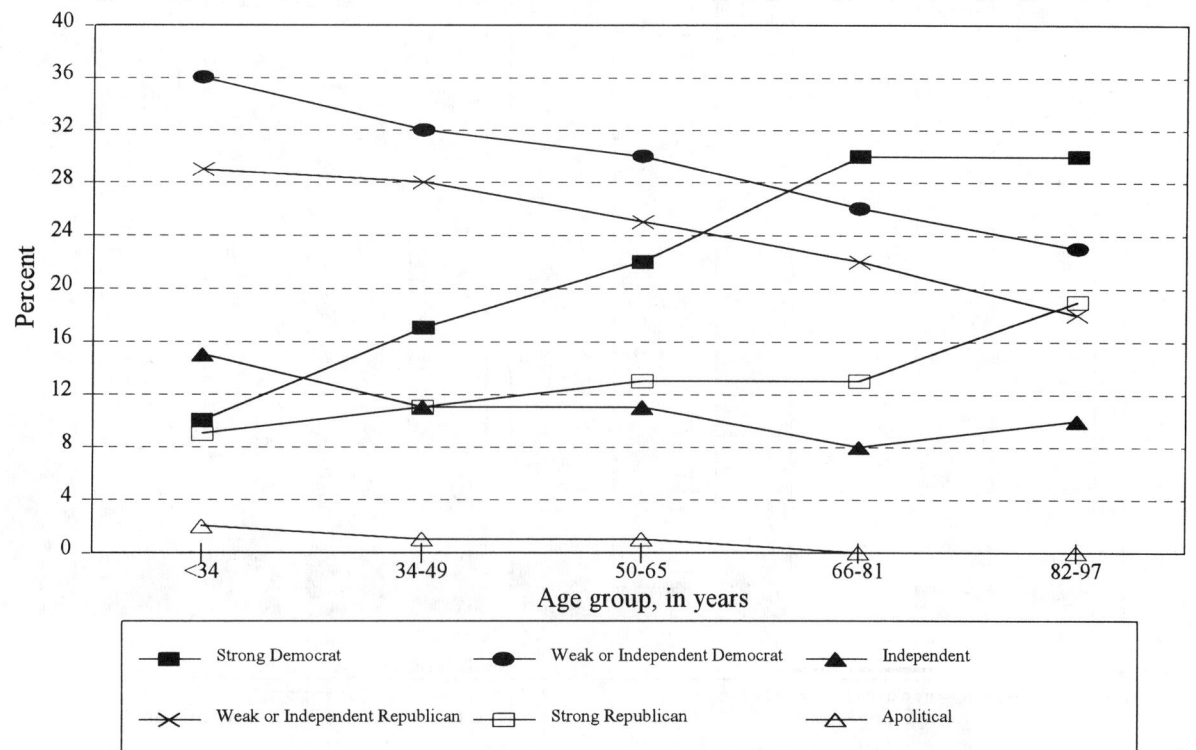

Source: University of Michigan Center for Political Studies data, based on the National Election Studies.

Table 10-11. Frequency of Sex in the Past Twelve Months, by Age and Sex: 1992

Age and sex	Percent distribution				
	Not at all	A few times per year	A few times per month	2 or 3 times a week	4 or more times a week
Male	14	16	37	26	8
18 to 24 years	15	21	24	28	12
25 to 29 years	7	15	31	36	11
30 to 39 years	8	15	37	33	6
40 to 49 years	9	18	40	27	6
50 to 59 years	11	22	43	20	3
Female	10	18	36	30	7
18 to 24 years	11	16	32	29	12
25 to 29 years	5	10	38	37	10
30 to 39 years	9	16	36	33	6
40 to 49 years	15	16	44	20	5
50 to 59 years	30	22	35	12	2

Source: Robert T. Michael, John H. Gagnon, Edward O. Laumann, and Gina Kolata, "Sex in America: A
Definitive Survey," Little, Brown and Company, Boston, MA, 1994, Table 8 (based on 1992 National
Health and Social Life Survey data).

Figure 10-16. Number of Sex Partners in the Past Twelve Months, by Age and Sex: 1992

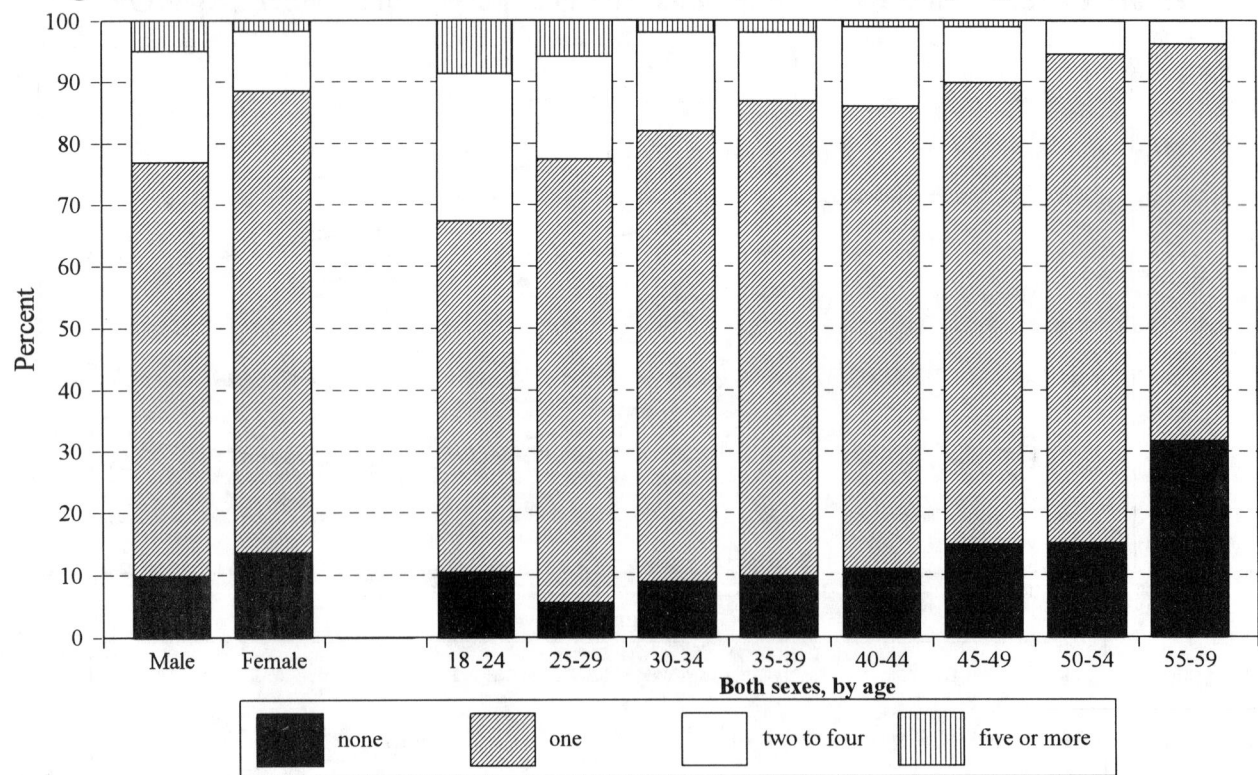

Source: 1992 National Health and Social Life Survey data.

Sports and Leisure Activities

by Alison Kadlec Donta

In 1992, Americans spent a total of 283.7 million dollars (constant 1987 dollars) on recreation expenditures. This number represents 8.5% of total personal consumption for that year and is higher than it has been for two decades. The percent of total personal consumption used for recreation expenditures was only 5.0% in 1970. The largest proportion of recreation expenditures in 1992 was the 70.3 million dollars Americans spent on video and audio products, computer equipment, and musical instruments. This was followed by nondurable toys and sport supplies (30.5 million) and wheel goods, sports and photographic equipment (29.2 million).

The table below illustrates the ten most popular sports activities of the U.S. population aged 7 and over in 1992. Exercise walking was the most popular sport, with 29.5% of the population participating in this activity. As was the case with most of the top ten sports activities, exercise walking was differentially distributed by sex, with females representing 65.8% of the participants. Aerobic exercise was an activity also dominated by women. For that sport, 81.8% of the participants were women. Conversely, golf, basketball, and fresh-water fishing had a higher proportion of male participants. Swimming was the most popular sport for men while exercise walking was the most popular among women.

Sports participation also varied by age. For the youngest persons surveyed, bicycle riding was the most popular sport, with swimming the most popular among those aged 12 to 17 and 18 to 24. Exercise walking was the sport most practiced by the population aged 25 and over. One of the reasons for the popularity of exercise walking among young adults and the middle-aged population is that it offers all the benefits of aerobic exercise and jogging without the drawback of high impact and stress on the joints.

More variation in sports participation preference is seen in the second most popular sport per age group. That sport was swimming for those aged 7 to 11, bicycle riding for persons aged 12 to 17, and bowling for persons aged 18 to 24. Swimming was reported to be the second most popular sport for those aged 25 to 34 and 65 and over, while fresh-water fishing was favored for those aged 45 to 64. Sports participation overall decreased with age with the exception of exercise walking which reached its peak participation rate in the 55 to 64 year age group. Both swimming and exercise walking offer opportunities for older persons to exercise with less stress on the body than many of the other sports categories listed.

As with sports activities, participation in leisure activities tends to decrease with age, as can be seen in the accompanying figure. Attendance at movies and amusement parks, in particular, shows a significant drop with age. Of those aged 18 to 24, 82% attended movies at least once a year. That percentage is cut in half by ages 55 to 64, with 40% of that population reporting movie attendance, and only 19% of those aged 75 to 96 attended movies. Similarly, 68% of those aged 18 to 24 had visited amusement parks in the prior twelve months, while only 14% of those aged 75 to 96 had done so. Attendance and participation in sporting events and participation in outdoor activities such as camping, hiking, and canoeing also showed a dramatic decline with age. As with the decline in sports participation with age, this decline could be a function of increasing lack of functional mobility among the older segments of the population. Among those aged 65 and over, the most popular leisure

activity was reading literature. For those aged 18 to 44, the most popular leisure activity was attending a movie, and for the 45 to 64 age group an exercise program was the most common activity reported. Unlike most of the leisure activities examined, home improvement and repair peaked among those aged 35 to 64, a time when many Americans are homeowners and are improving their homes. Before this age, people are less likely to own homes and older people may be unable to perform the necessary home improvements themselves.

The most popular leisure activity among men was an exercise program while women were more likely to read literature. The second most popular activity for both sexes was attendance at a movie, and an exercise program tied for the second most popular activity among females. The activity with the largest sex bias was reading literature. While 60% of women reported reading literature in the last 12 months, only 47% of men did so. Men, in contrast, were more likely to have participated in sports (50%) than women (29%) over the past year and to have attended sporting events.

Additional Sources:

National Demographics and Lifestyles. The Lifestyle Market Analyst. Des Plaines, IL: SRDS, 1995.

National Sporting Goods Association. Sports Participation in 1992: Series I. Mt Prospect, IL: National Sporting Goods Association, 1992.

Simmons Market Research Bureau. Study of Media and Markets: Sports and Leisure: P9. New York: Simmons Market Research Bureau, Inc., 1994.

U.S. Bureau of the Census. Statistical Abstract of the United States: 1994, Chapter 7. Washington, D.C.: U.S. Government Printing Office, 1994.

U.S. Bureau of Economic Analysis. The National Income and Product Accounts of the United States: Volume 2, 1959-1988. Washington, D.C.: U.S. Government Printing Office, 1992.

_____. Survey of Current Business, August 1993.

U.S. National Endowment for the Arts. Arts Participation in America: 1982 to 1992. Washington, D.C.: U.S. Government Printing Office, 1994.

Participation in the Ten Most Popular Sports Activities[1], by Age and Sex: 1992

| Sports activity | Overall rank | Sex | | | Age | | | | | | | |
		Both sexes	Male	Female	7-11 years	12-17 years	18-24 years	25-34 years	35-44 years	45-54 years	55-64 years	65+ years
Exercise walking[2]	1	29.5	19.0	37.7	10.1	13.9	24.1	32.5	35.4	38.5	40.3	29.1
Swimming[2]	2	27.5	26.8	28.1	59.2	50.5	29.4	29.4	27.5	16.7	13.3	8.6
Bicycle riding[2]	3	23.8	25.1	22.5	67.4	46.1	21.2	23.4	20.9	12.8	6.8	
Camping[3]	4	20.6	22.8	18.3	31.2	28.0	20.3	27.0	24.8	16.3	12.2	5.5
Bowling	5	18.5	19.5	17.5	26.9	27.4	26.9	25.6	18.7	11.4	7.2	4.9
Fishing--fresh water	6	18.1	25.3	11.4	22.7	22.0	16.4	23.0	20.8	18.0	13.8	7.7
Exercising with equipment[2]	7	17.1	17.1	17.1	3.4	16.9	26.4	25.6	19.9	17.0	10.8	7.2
Basketball	8	12.3	18.4	6.4	29.6	38.9	18.7	13.0	7.9	2.6	0.6	0.2
Aerobic exercising[2]	9	12.1	4.6	19.2	5.6	12.4	22.1	19.7	12.4	9.6	5.5	3.7
Golf	10	10.4	16.6	4.7	5.0	9.0	11.7	14.3	11.6	10.9	8.9	7.4

[1] Except as indicated, a participant plays a sport more than once in the past year.
[2] Participant engaged in activity at least six times a year.
[3] Vacation/overnight.

Source: U.S. Bureau of the Census, "Statistical Abstract of the United States: 1994." U.S. Government Printing Office, Washington, D. 1994, Table No. 406 (based on National Sporting Goods Association data).

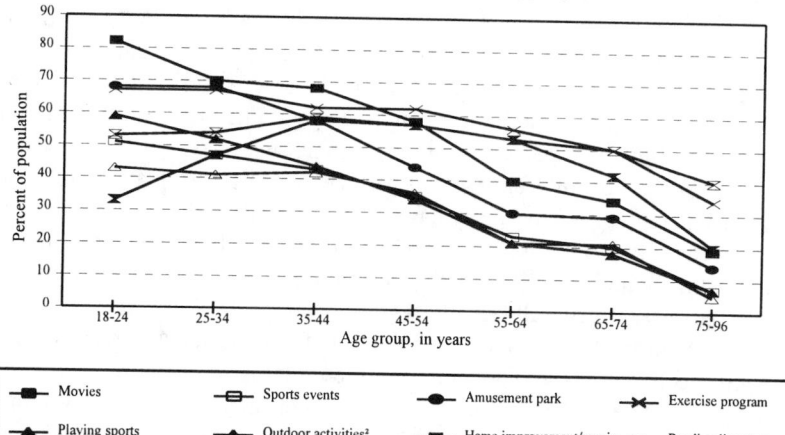

Participation in Various Leisure Activities[1], by Age: 1992

Legend: Movies | Sports events | Amusement park | Exercise program | Playing sports | Outdoor activities[2] | Home improvement/repair | Reading literature

[1] Covers activities engaged in at least once in the prior 12 months.
[2] Camping, hiking, and canoeing.
Source: 1992 U.S. National Endowment for the Arts data.

Figure 10-17. Adult Church Attendance in Previous Week: 1939-1994

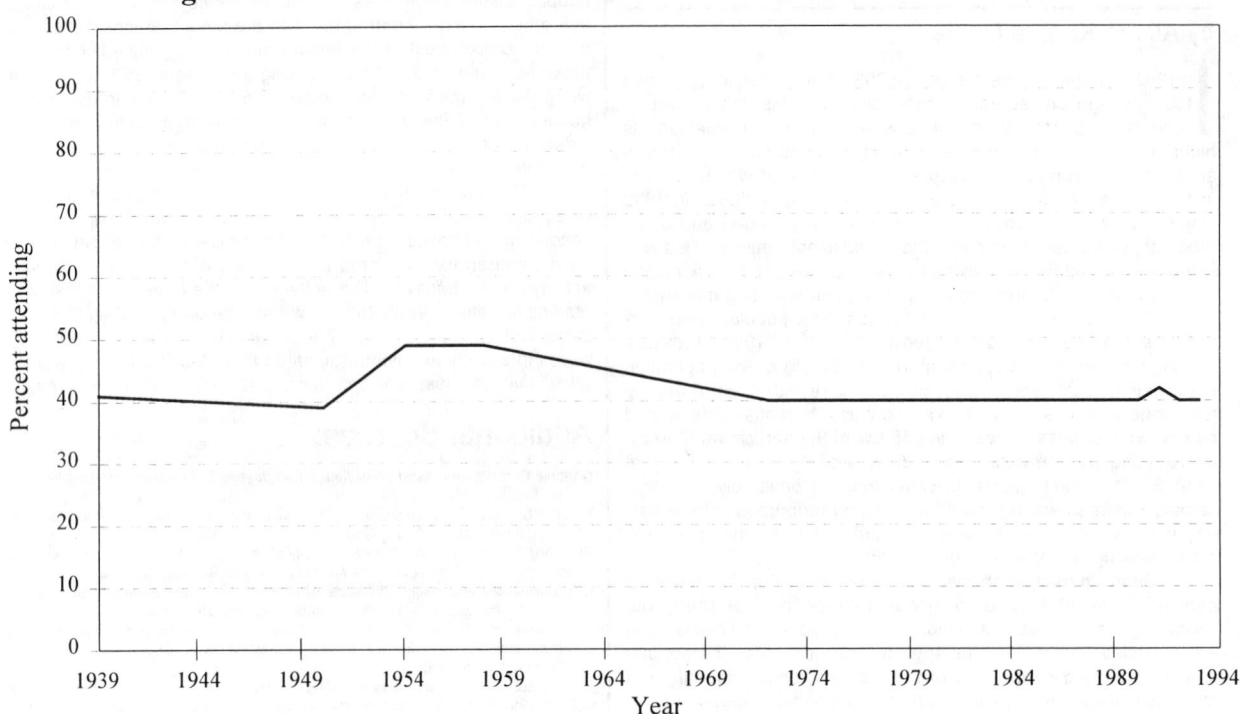

Source: Princeton Religious Research Center data.

and both sexes were those who had sex either a few times per month or two to three times per week.

The percentage of those who had no sex in the past year was greatest among the younger and older population. Perhaps surprisingly, the percentage of those having no sex in the past year was greater among men than women overall. And, abstinence was also greater among men 18 to 24 years of age than among men of all other ages. Abstinence among young women was greater than among those 25 to 39 years of age. However, the youngest groups of men and women (i.e. those aged 18 to 29 years of age) also had the greatest percentage of those reporting the most frequent sexual behavior (i.e. four or more times per week).

In Figure 10-16 data from the same survey are presented on the number of sex partners over the past twelve months. Among the more surprising findings of this survey is the very high percentage of all ages and sexes having either no, or only one, sexual partner over the past year. There are greater percentages of those with multiple partners among younger ages and for males. However, the frequency of those with five or more partners in the past year is generally small across all ages.

As more data becomes available, and frank discussion becomes more common, future editions of this book, and other demography texts, may well have chapters on sexual behavior alongside the other key demographic subjects discussed. It is, at the least, clear that without such information it will be difficult to have the broad so-cial and demographic dialogue which current public health concerns demand. For the present we must simply refer the reader in search of more extensive data to the survey citation noted above.

Religious Participation

Affiliation with a religious denomination and attendance at religious services are more of the many behaviors which are often suggested to vary across age and gender groups. Recent press coverage has suggested baby boomers are returning to religious observances as their children begin to reach appropriate ages for attendance. When baby boomers were adolescents concern over declining religious attendance was popular. Indeed, as Table 10-12 demonstrates, the differences by age and gender are substantial in the percentage attending either a church or synagogue. Females are considerably more likely to attend religious services on a regular basis. And, likelihood of regular participation increases as does age such that the highest participation in services is among those sixty- five years of age and over. Those never or seldom attending such services are somewhat higher among males and considerably higher among those under fifty years of age.

Whether data on religious attendance indicate changing cohort, or simply represent life cycle, behavioral patterns is less clear than are the differences across age and gender. Despite considerable recent populariza-

Table 10-12. Percent Attending Church or Synagogue, by Age and Sex: 1993

Age and sex	Attended last week	Frequency of attendance				
		Weekly	Almost weekly	Monthly	Seldom	Never
Both sexes	40	34	10	14	27	14
Male	34	29	9	14	30	16
Female	46	37	11	14	25	12
Age						
18 to 29 years	30	24	9	18	34	14
30 to 49 years	38	29	11	14	29	16
50 to 64 years	45	41	9	14	24	11
65 years and over	54	48	10	10	18	12

Source: Princeton Religious Research Center, "Emerging Trends," Volume 15, No. 13, 1993, page 4.

tion of the notion that generations of baby boomers are returning to the religious folds as they begin to rear children of their own, Figure 10-17 shows the remarkably level percentage of those attending church in the previous week between 1939 and 1994. Since approximately 1970 there has been virtually no change in the percentage of adult church attendance. Given declining family sizes, even among religious groups more resistant to fertility decline, this would suggest an overall decline in children attending church with their parents. In short, if there are generational or aging effects on adult church attendance they appear to have a negligible net impact over the past several decades.

Crime and Criminal Behavior

The percent of the population which is incarcerated has more than doubled over the past decade (see Chapter 11 Textbox on institutionalized populations). And, the strong relationships of both violent and property crimes to aging, gender and the socially disadvantaged are well-established. More than any other group, young minority males are being disproportionately incarcerated in ever increasing numbers. There are many reasons for the association of crimes with younger age groups. Youth are often in tumultuous periods of social readjustment to adult life, able to act as adults for the first time, in need of independent means of livelihood, facing difficult life prospects, subjected to peer pressure and bravado, etc. The ranks of crime are thinned across age through incarceration, socialization, homicide and mortality, and alternative adult answers to the problems confronted at earlier ages.

In Figure 10-18 the peak in violent crimes at ages 15-24 and the peak in property crimes at ages 15-19 are clearly evident. It is also important to note, however, that these relationships are not inviolate as the population's composition has changed. For both types of crime the increase in percentages at older ages is clear as the population has aged. This shift is due to both more individuals at older ages and the decline in the rate of arrests at younger ages. This shift has been most pronounced since 1980. If these trends continue, a higher percentage of criminal activity might well be spread into even older age groups. It should, of course, also be borne in mind that more complex factors such as a growing incarcerated population could generate shifts in criminal activity to older ages even if the probability of recidivism were held constant.

Criminal behavior and victimization, of course, also vary dramatically according to an individual's sex. According to FBI Uniform Crime Reports, the percent of total arrests in 1990 which were male was 81.6. And, male arrests were 88.7 percent of those for violent crimes while only 74.7 percent of those for property crimes. Data on victimization are less easily and reliably obtained. However, according to the National Crime Victimization Survey for 1992, the total victimization rate per 1,000 persons aged 12 or older was 101.4 for males and 81.8 for females. Among major crime categories only rape has a higher victimization rate for females (0.8) compared to males (0.6). The victimization rate is highest (171-177) for those 12 to 24 years of age and lowest for those 65 years of age or older (21.1). Victimization rates for minorities are much higher and the handgun crime victimization rate for black females is even higher than that for white males.

Criminal behavior and victimization are subject to a large variety of influences. Nonetheless, clear age and gender associations, the reflection of changing population composition in such behaviors and incidents, and the impact of incarceration or victimization on demographic phenomena (e.g. house holding, employment, fertility, mortality) indicate the importance of population trends

Figure 10-18. Distribution of Total Arrests by Age: 1970-1990

Violent crime[1]

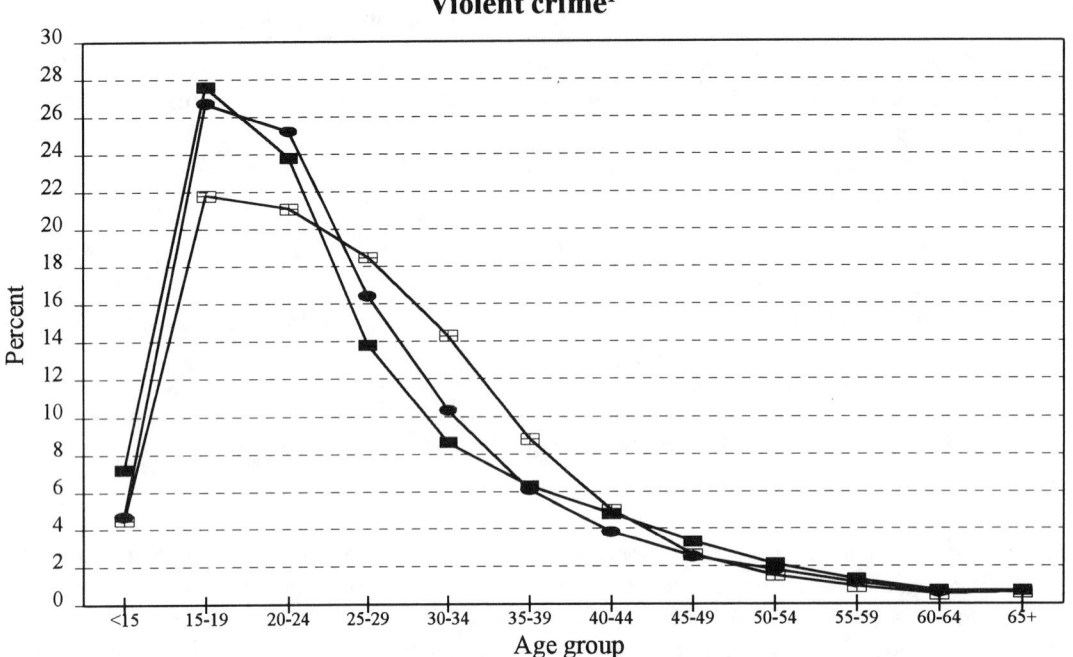

Property crime[1]

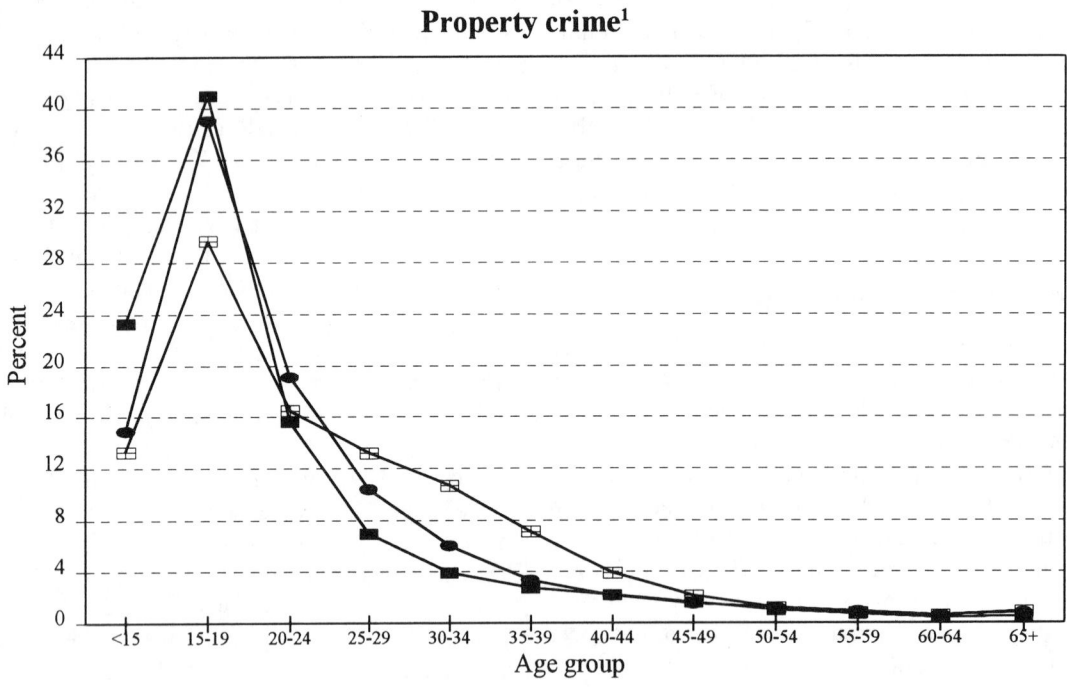

[1] Violent crime is offenses of murder, forcible rape, robbery, and aggravated assault.
[2] Property crime is offenses of burglary, larceny, and auto theft.
Source: 1970-1990 U.S. Federal Bureau of Investigation data.

and demographic studies in gaining a better understanding of these social trends.

Conclusion

This chapter has addressed only a limited number of illustrative, but significant, behaviors which vary across the age and sex groups of the United States population. It is clear that most social behavior varies across age, sex or both. The purpose in this chapter has not been to exhaustively catalogue such compositional differences in behavior. Instead, these examples have been selected to address major life cycle events and behaviors which are frequently mentioned with regard to age and sex composition as topics of recent popular discussion.

It is perhaps most notable that many discussions of age and sex-related behaviors are unclear as to whether such compositional differences reflect changing generations (cohorts), different concurrent social experiences (period effects) or a general aging process (maturation). These causal questions are notoriously difficult to resolve and attributions to one causal effect or another are frequently made without substantiation in any case. In many examples within this chapter one or another such explanation seems highly likely as a matter of common sense. The impact of recent periods of inflation and high interest rates in real estate markets on home ownership, for example, seem very probably predominant. Yet, in most cases these issues are not so readily apparent. This chapter does not resolve such difficult questions so much as to point out the relevance of population composition to an analysis of most social behaviors and the concomitant need to raise fundamental questions regarding the source of such differences in understanding behavioral trends.

Many of the demographic behaviors summarized in this chapter are explored in context and in greater detail elsewhere in the text. For some other social behaviors, this chapter's brief mention is their only allotted treatment. Such decisions are clearly not reflective of the social import of these topics (e.g. expenditures, religion, crime) but rather of their traditionally regarded centrality to demographic behavior and trends. Boundaries must, unfortunately, be drawn in all explorations of demographically correlated behaviors given the sheer range of such behaviors. Nonetheless, this brief excursion into the association of demographic composition with a broader range of social behavior demonstrates the importance of the more focused demographic material of the text for a wide range of issues.

The way in which people behave is highly influenced by the circumstances in which they find themselves and the expectations for their behavior which they, and others, hold. Aging and gender are highly correlated with individual circumstances. They are also among the predominant influences on both cultural and individual behavioral expectations. Biologically grounded differences associated with maturation and an individual's sex also constrain and influence social behaviors. Given such obvious relationships it is not surprising that many behaviors are correlated with aging and gender. Nor should it prove surprising that such behaviors both shape, and are shaped by, the changing composition of the United States population.

Bibliography

Amato, Paul R., and Booth, Alan. "Changes in Gender Role Attitudes and Perceived Marital Quality." American Sociological Review 60 (1995):58-66.

Bernhardt, Annette, Morris, Martina, and Handcock, Mark S. "Women's Gains or Men's Losses? A Closer Look at the Shrinking Gender Gap in Earnings." American Journal of Sociology 101 (1995):302-28.

Berger, Mark C. "Demographic Cycles, Cohort Size, and Earnings." Demography 26 (1989):311-21.

Beutel, Ann M., and Marini, Margaret Mooney. "Gender and Values." American Sociological Review 60 (1995):436-48.

Blau, Francine D., and Kahn, Lawrence. "Rising Wage Inequality and the U.S. Gender Gap." American Economic Review (Papers and Proceedings) 84 (1994):23-28.

Bumpass, Larry L. "What's Happening to the Family? Interactions between Demographic and Institutional Change." Demography 27 (1990):483-98.

Casper, Lynne M., McLanahan, Sara S., and Garfinkel, Irwin. "The Gender-Poverty Gap: What We Can Learn from Other Countries." American Sociological Review 59 (1994):594-605.

Clausen, John S. "Adolescent Competence and the Shaping of the Life Course." American Journal of Sociology 96 (1991):805-42.

DiPrete, Thomas A., and Grusky, David B. "Structure and Trend in the Process of Stratification for American Men and Women." American Journal of Sociology 96 (1990):107-43.

Easterlin, Richard. Birth and Fortune: The Impact of Numbers on Personal Welfare, 2nd ed. Chicago: University of Chicago Press, 1987.

Hayward, Mark D., Grady, William R., and McLaughlin, Steven D. "Recent Changes in Mortality and Labor Force Behavior among Older Americans: Consequences for Nonworking Life Expectancy." Journal of Gerontology: Social Sciences 43 (1988):S196.

Hogan, Dennis P., Eggebeen, David J., and Clogg, Clifford C. "The Structure of Intergenerational Exchanges in American Families." American Journal of Sociology 98 (1993):1428-58.

Hout, Michael. "More Universalism, Less Structural Mobility: The American Occupational Structure in the 1980s." American Journal of Sociology 93 (1988):1358-1400.

Huber, Joan. "Macro-Micro Links in Gender Stratification." American Sociological Review 55 (1990):1-10.

Hurd, Michael D. "Research on the Elderly: Economic Status, Retirement, and Consumption and Saving." Journal of Economic Literature 28 (1990):589-606.

Kilbourne, Barbara S., England, Paula, Farkas, George, Beron, Kurt, and Weir, Dorothea. "Returns to Skill, Compensating Differentials and Gender Bias: Effects of Occupational Characteristics on the Wages of White Women and Men." American Sociological Review 100 (1994):689-719.

Lancaster, Jane B., Altmann, J., Rossi, Alice S., and Sherrod, Lonnie R. (eds.). Parenting Across the Life Span. New York: Aldine de Gruyter, 1987.

Land, Kenneth C., McCall, Patricia L., and Cohen, Lawrence E. "Structural Covariates of Homicide Rates: Are There Any Invariances across Time and Social Space?" American Journal of Sociology 95 (1990):922-63.

Logan, John R., and Spitze, Glenna D. "Self-Interest and Altruism in Intergenerational Relations." Demography 32 (1995):353-64.

Mare, Robert D., and Tzeng, Meei-Shenn. "Father's Ages and the Social Stratification of Sons." American Journal of Sociology 95 (1989):108-31.

McLanahan, Sara S., Sørensen, Annemette, and Watson, Dorothy. "Sex Differences in Poverty, 1950-1980." Signs 15 (1989):102-22.

Michael, Robert T., Gannon, John H., Laumann, Edward O., and Kolata, Gina. Sex in America: A Definitive Survey. Boston: Little, Brown and Company, 1994.

Moore, Gwen. "Structural Determinants of Men's and Women's Personal Networks." American Sociological Review 55 (1990):726-35.

Myers, D., and Pitkin, J. "Evaluation of Price Indices by a Cohort Method." Journal of Housing Research 6 (1995):497-518.

Myers, George C. "Demography of Aging." In Handbook of Aging and the Social Sciences. L. Binstock and George L. Van Nostrand (eds.). New York, 1990.

National Bureau of Economic Research. CPS Outgoing Rotation Groups. CD-Rom Data Files, 1992.

Oppenheimer, Valerie Kincade. "A Theory of Marriage Timing." American Journal of Sociology 94 (1988):563-91.

Pampel, Fred C. "Population Aging, Class Context, and Age Inequality in Public Spending." American Journal of Sociology 100 (1994):153-95.

Petersen, Trond, and Morgan, Laurie A. "Separate and Unequal: Occupation-Establishment Sex Segregation and the Gender Wage Gap." American Journal of Sociology 101 (1995):329-65.

Preston, Samuel H., Himes, Christine, and Eggers, Mitchell. "Demographic Conditions Responsible for Population Aging." Demography 26 (1989):691-704.

Princeton Religious Research Center. Emerging Trends 15(1993):4.

Riley, Matilda White (ed.). Social Structures and Human Lives, Social Change and the Life Course, Volume 1. Newbury Park, CA: Sage Press, 1988.

Rindfuss, Ronald R. "The Young Adult Years: Diversity, Structural Change, and Fertility." Demography 28 (1991):493-512.

Rossi, Alice S. (ed.). Sexuality across the Life Course. Chicago: University of Chicago Press, 1994.

Sampson, Robert J., and Laub, John H. "Crime and Deviance over the Life Course: The Salience of Adult Social Bonds." American Sociological Review 55 (1990):609-27.

Smith, Scott J., and Trent, Katherine. "Sex Ratios and Women's Roles: A Cross-National Analysis." American Journal of Sociology 93 (1988):1096-15.

Stolzenberg, Ross M., Blair-Loy, Mary, and Waite, Linda J. "Religious Participation in Early Adulthood: Age and Family Life Cycle Effects on Church Membership." American Sociological Review 60 (1995):84-103.

Torrey, Barbara B., Kinsella, Kevin, and Taeuber, Cynthia M. An Aging World. U.S. Bureau of the Census International Population Reports, P-95 No. 78. Washington, D.C.: U.S. Government Printing Office, 1987.

Udry, J. Richard. "The Nature of Gender." Demography 31 (1994):561-73.

Umberson, Debra, and Chen, Meichu D. "Effects of a Parent's Death on Adult Children: Relationship Salience and Reaction to Loss." American Sociological Review 59 (1994):152-68.

U.S. Bureau of the Census. Asset Ownership of Households: 1993. Current Population Reports, Series P-70 No. 47. Washington D.C.: U.S. Government Printing Office, 1995.

_____. Characteristics of the Population, 1940 Census of Population. Washington D.C.: U.S. Government Printing Office, 1943.

_____. Education in the United States: 1990. Washington D.C.: U.S. Government Printing Office, 1994.

_____. General Population Characteristics, 1940 Census of Population. Washington D.C.: U.S. Government Printing Office, 1943.

_____. General Population Characteristics, 1970 Census of Population. Washington D.C.: U.S. Government Printing Office, 1973.

_____. General Population Characteristics, 1990 Census of Population. Washington D.C.: U.S. Government Printing Office, 1992.

_____. Historical Statistics of the United States, Part I, (Series A 119-134). Washington D.C.: U.S. Government Printing Office, 1975.

_____. Household and Family Characteristics: March 1960. Current Population Reports, Series P-20 No. 106. Washington D.C.: U.S. Government Printing Office, 1961.

_____. Household and Family Characteristics: March 1970. Current Population Reports, Series P-20 No. 218. Washington D.C.: U.S. Government Printing Office, 1971.

_____. Household and Family Characteristics: March 1980. Current Population Reports, Series P-20 No. 366. Washington D.C.: U.S. Government Printing Office, 1981.

_____. Household and Family Characteristics: March 1990 and 1989. Current Population Reports, Series P-20 No. 447. U.S. Washington D.C.: U.S. Government Printing Office, 1990.

_____. Housing Characteristics by Household Composition, 1970 Census of Housing. Washington D.C.: U.S. Government Printing Office, 1973.

_____. Marital Status and Housing Characteristics: March 1950. Current Population Characteristics, Series P-20 No 33. Washington, D.C.: U.S. Government Printing Office, 1951.

_____. Marital Status and Family Status: March 1960. Current Population Characteristics, Series P-20 No 105. Washington, D.C.: U.S. Government Printing Office, 1961.

_____. Marital Status and Family Status: March 1970. Current Population Characteristics, Series P-20 No 212. Washington, D.C.: U.S. Government Printing Office, 1971.

_____. Marital Status and Living Arrangements: March 1980. Current Population Characteristics, Series P-20 No 365. Washington, D.C.: U.S. Government Printing Office, 1981.

_____. Marital Status and Living Arrangements: March 1990. Current Population Characteristics, Series P-20 No 450. Washington, D.C.: U.S. Government Printing Office, 1991.

_____. Population Projections of the United States, by Age, Race, and Hispanic Origin: 1993 to 2050. Current Population Reports, Series P-25 No. 1104. Washington, D.C.: U.S. Government Printing Office, 1993.

_____. Poverty in the United States: 1991. Current Population Reports, Series P-60 No. 181. Washington, D.C.: U.S. Government Printing Office, 1992.

_____. Statistical Abstract of the United States: 1994. Washington D.C.: U.S. Government Printing Office, 1994.

_____. Voting and Registration in the Election of November 1992. Current Population Reports, Series P-20 No. 466. Washington D.C.: U.S. Government Printing Office, 1993.

U.S. Bureau of Labor Statistics. Consumer Expenditure Survey, 1990-1991, Bulletin No. 2425. Washington, D.C.: U.S. Government Printing Office, 1993.

_____. Employment and Earnings, January 1991. Washington, D.C.: U.S. Government Printing Office, 1991.

_____. Employment and Earnings, January 1991. Washington, D.C.: U.S. Government Printing Office, 1989.

U.S. Federal Bureau of Investigation. Crime in the United States: 1970. Uniform Crime Reports. Washington, D.C.: U.S. Government Printing Office, 1971.

_____. Crime in the U.nited States: 1980. Uniform Crime Reports. Washington, D.C.: U.S. Government Printing Office, 1981.

_____. Crime in the United States: 1990. Uniform Crime Reports. Washington, D.C.: U.S. Government Printing Office, 1991.

Verbrugge, Lois M. "A Health Profile of Older Women with Comparisons to Older Men." Research on Aging 6 (1984):292-311.

White, Lynn, and Edwards, John N. "Emptying the Nest and Parental Well-Being: An Analysis of National Panel Data." American Sociological Review 55 (1990):235-42.

HOUSEHOLD AND FAMILY

Most members of a population have a regular dwelling place and an identifiable set of living arrangements. The arrangements under which the members of a population live are of considerable importance to those who are concerned with research or administration in areas related to family relationships, housing problems, marketing, or city planning. Possible living arrangements are, of course, affected by the demographic characteristics and behavior of the population discussed in earlier chapters (e.g. fertility, mortality and migration). Establishing or maintaining a household is also generally costly and, as a result, economic circumstances also affect prevalent living arrangements. However, historical differences in an individual's choice of various living arrangements are not solely explained by demographic possibilities or economic constraints. It is difficult to determine the precise extent to which demographic possibilities, economic constraints and normative tastes have influenced any specific change in living arrangements. Nonetheless, it is clear that all these determinants of living arrangements have changed considerably in the recent past and have led to increasingly diverse living arrangements in the United States.

With respect to most items of census information, the members of a population are enumerated as individuals and the demographic characteristics for which statistics are tabulated involve such personal traits as age, sex, or educational attainment. However, information is also tabulated about certain groups of persons. The number of persons in the group, its type, and other characteristics (including any changes in its size or other characteristics) are the objects of investigation. When individuals are considered in an analysis of groups, it is to ascertain his or her status in the group, relationship to the group, the role the person plays in the group or the possible effects of the group as a context for personal behavior. Two of the most important groups about which the census collects information (and about which there is also widespread general interest) are households and families, that is, residential groups, clusters of people who occupy a residency jointly. In census terminology, each separate dwelling place is termed a "housing unit" (in earlier censuses it was called a "dwelling unit"), and the group of persons inhabiting it constitutes a "household." (See the Definition Box.)

The household is important as a unit of study for several reasons. Sociologists and anthropologists have a direct interest in living arrangements, in the composition of households, and in the relationships between members of a household. Economists, market analysts, public utility companies, and persons concerned with the subject of housing are especially interested in household statistics, because the household (rather than the person) is often the principal unit with which they deal. Telephone service, gas, water, and electricity are distributed to household units. Many products, such as television sets, washing machines, and home furnishings, are manufactured to satisfy the needs of household units. Information about the size, composition, and characteristics of households is very important to architects, contractors, and real estate firms as they design and sell houses and apartments. Social agencies that are concerned with crowded housing conditions and the general quality of living arrangements also strive to gather as much information as they can about the nation's households.

Because children are a product of families and are wholly dependent on families for both material needs and socialization, those who are interested in children and their welfare are concerned about the families where children reside. The living arrangements of elderly persons are of interest to those who study the problems of the aged. Since children and the elderly are both potentially dependent upon relatives or cohabitants for support, both the families and households of these individuals are of special interest to researchers and policy makers. There is also a considerable interest in the changing importance of the family in the flow of wealth among individuals across generations. Recent interests in the changing nature of the family have, at times, reflected contentious ideological and policy perspectives. The growing diversity of families in the United States is of considerable interest to all.

According to the 1990 Census, almost all (97.3 percent) of the population lives in housing units as defined by the census. The remaining 2.7 percent live in what the census defines as "group quarters." Of this small minority, 49.8 percent are institutionalized (e.g. correctional institutions, nursing homes, other institutions) and the rest are residents of dormitories, temporary shelters, group homes, boarding houses, army barracks, convents and monasteries, and similar mass residence units. The 1990 Census made a special effort in "Shelter-and-Streetnight" to survey selected elements of the homeless population.

While likely an incomplete count, 178,638 persons (0.07 percent of the total population, 2.67 percent of those in group quarters) were identified as residing in emergency shelters for the homeless, and an additional 49,734 persons (0.02 percent of the total population) were identified as visible in street locations.

This chapter deals primarily with residents of households. Since there are many social policy questions of importance that involve those not living in households, there is also a brief discussion of the characteristics of persons living in other circumstances toward the end of the chapter. Although the institutionalized, homeless, and others living in group quarters may represent significant social concerns, it is important to recognize this final section details characteristics of less than three percent of the population, according to the 1990 Census, and that these populations include groups considered difficult to

Table 11-1. Number of Households and Average Household Size: 1790-1992

Year	Number of households (in thousands)					Persons per household				
	Total	White	Black	Other	Hispanic	Total	White	Black	Other	Hispanic
1992	95,669	81,675	11,083	2,911	6,379	2.62	2.58	2.81	3.16	3.45
1991	94,312	80,968	10,671	2,673	6,220	2.63	2.58	2.87	3.27	3.44
1990	93,347	80,163	10,486	2,698	5,933	2.63	2.58	2.88	3.13	3.47
1985	86,789	75,328	9,480	1,981	4,883	2.69	2.64	2.96	3.27	3.44
1980	79,108	69,454	8,405	1,249	3,730	2.75	2.71	3.01	3.35	3.46
1975	71,120	62,945	7,262	913	—	2.94	2.89	3.27	3.44	—
1970	62,874	56,248	6,053	573	—	3.17	3.11	3.68	3.68	—
1965	57,251	51,441	5,808	—[1]	—	3.31	3.25	3.85	—[1]	—
1960	52,610	47,503	5,107	—[1]	—	3.35	3.28	3.95	—[1]	—
1955	47,788	43,380	4,408	—[1]	—	3.34	—	—	—[1]	—
1950	43,554	—	—	—	—	3.37	—	—	—	—
1940	34,949	31,680	3,142	127	—	3.67	—	—	—	—
1930	29,905	26,983	2,804	118	—	4.11	—	—	—	—
1920	24,352	21,826	2,431	95	—	4.34	—	—	—	—
1910	20,256	—	2,173	—	—	4.54	—	—	—	—
1900	15,964	14,064	1,834	66	—	4.76	—	—	—	—
1890	12,690	11,255	1,411	24	—	4.93	—	—	—	—
1880	9,946	—	—	—	—	5.04	—	—	—	—
1870	7,579	—	—	—	—	5.09	—	—	—	—
1860	5,211	—	—	—	—	5.28	—	—	—	—
1850	3,598	—	—	—	—	5.55	—	—	—	—
1790	558	—	—	—	—	5.79	—	—	—	—

[1] Other included as part of black.

Source: U.S. Bureau of the Census, "Household and Family Characteristics," Current Population Reports, Series P-20, nos. 467, 458, 447, 388, 381, 371, 366, 340, 291, 218, 153, 106, and 67, U.S. Government Printing Office, Washington, D.C., 1992, 1991, 1990 and 1989, 1981, 1979, 1976, 1971, 1966, 1961, and 1956. Data for 1790-1950 from the U.S. Bureau of the Census, Historical Statistics of the United States: Colonial Times to 1970, U.S. Government Printing Office, Washington, D.C., 1975.

Chapter 11 Definitions
Household, Family and Living Arrangements

Household. A household consists of all the persons who occupy a housing unit. A house, an apartment or other group of rooms, or a single room is regarded as a housing unit when it is occupied or intended for occupancy as separate living quarters; that is, when the occupants do not live and eat with any other persons in the structures and there is direct access from the outside or through a common hall. A household includes the related family members and all the unrelated persons, if any, such as lodgers, foster children, wards, or employees who share the housing unit. A person living alone in a housing unit, or a group of unrelated persons sharing a housing unit as partners, is also counted as a household. The count of households excludes group quarters (see definition below). The 1990 definition of a household is the same as that used in the 1980 Census.

Householder. A householder refers to the person (or one of the persons) in whose name the housing unit is owned or rented (maintained). If there is no such person in the household, any adult household member 15 years old and over could be designated as the householder, excluding roomers, boarders, or paid employees. If the house is owned or rented jointly by a married couple, the householder may be either the husband or the wife. The person designated as the householder is the "reference person" to whom the relationship of all other household members, if any, is recorded.

Two types of householders are distinguished by the Census, "family householders" and "non-family householders." A family householder is a householder living with one or more persons related to him or her by birth, marriage or adoption. A nonfamily householder is a householder living alone or with nonrelatives only. Prior to 1980, the husband was always considered the householder in married couple households. The term "household head" was used instead of "householder" prior to 1980.

Head versus Householder. Beginning with the 1980 Current Population Survey, the Bureau of the Census discontinued the use of the terms "head of household" and "head of family." Instead, the terms "householder" and "family householder" are used. Recent social changes have resulted in greater sharing of household responsibilities among the adult members and, therefore, have made the term "head" increasingly inappropriate in the analysis of household and family data. Specifically, the Bureau has discontinued classifying the husband as the reference person (head) when he and his wife are living together.

The term "householder" is used in the presentation of data that had previously been presented with the designation "head." The householder is the first adult household member listed on the questionnaire. The instructions call for listing first the person (or one of the persons) in whose name the home is owned or rented. If a home is owned jointly by a married couple, either the husband or the wife may be listed first, thereby becoming the reference person, or householder, to whom the relationship of other household members is to be recorded.

Family. A family is a group of two or more persons (one of whom is the householder) related by birth, marriage, or adoption who reside together. All such persons (including related subfamily members) are considered members of one family. Beginning with the 1980 Current Population Survey, unrelated subfamilies (referred to in the past as secondary families) are no longer included in the count of families, nor are the members of unrelated subfamilies included in the count of family members.

Family Household. A family household is a household maintained by a family (as defined above), and may include among the household members any unrelated persons (unrelated subfamily members and/or unrelated individuals) who may be residing there. The number of family households is equal to the number of families. The count of family household members differs from the count of family members, however, in that the family household members include all persons living in the household, whereas family members include only the householder and his or her relatives.

Stepfamily. A stepfamily is a married-couple family household with at least one child under age 18 years who is a stepchild (i.e., a son or daughter through marriage but not by birth) of the householder.

Related Subfamily. A related subfamily is a married couple with or without children, or one parent with one or more own single (never married) children under 18 years old, living in a household and related to, but not including, the person or couple who maintains the household. The most common example of a related subfamily is a young married couple sharing the home of the husband's or wife's parents. The number of related subfamilies is not included in the count of families.

Unrelated Subfamily. An unrelated subfamily (formerly called "secondary family") is a group of two or more persons who are related to each other by birth, marriage, or adoption, but who are not related to the householder. The unrelated subfamily may include persons such as guests, roomers, boarders, or resident employees and their relatives living in a household. The number of unrelated subfamily members is included in the number of household members but is not included in the count of family members.

Beginning in 1989, any person(s) who is not related to the householder and who is not the husband, wife, parent or child in an unrelated subfamily is counted as an unrelated individual.

Family Group. A family group is any two or more persons (not necessarily including a householder) residing together, and related by birth, marriage, or adoption. A household may be composed of one such group, more than one, or none at all. The count of family groups includes family households, related subfamilies, and unrelated subfamilies.

Married Couple. The Census defines a married couple as a husband and wife enumerated as members of the same household. The married couple may or may not have children living with them. The expression "husband-wife" or "married-couple" before the term "household," "family," or "subfamily" indicates that the household, family, or subfamily is maintained by a husband and wife. The number of married couples equals the count of married-couple families plus related and unrelated married-couple subfamilies.

Unmarried-Partner Households. An unmarried-partner household is a household other than a married-couple household that includes a householder and an "unmarried partner." An "unmarried partner" can be of the same sex or the opposite sex of the householder. An "unmarried partner" in such a household is an adult who is unrelated to the householder, but shares living quarters and has a close personal relationship with the householder.

Unmarried-Couple Households. An unmarried-couple household is comprised of two unrelated adults of the opposite sex (one of whom is the householder) who share a housing unit with or without the presence of children under 15 years old.

Unrelated Individuals. Unrelated individuals are persons of any age (other than inmates of institutions) who are not members of families or subfamilies.

Non-family Householder. A non-family householder is a person maintaining a household while living alone or exclusively with a person to whom they are not related (formerly called a primary individual).

Secondary Individual. A secondary individual is a person who resides in a household, but is not related to the householder (except unrelated subfamily members). Persons who reside in group quarters are also secondary individuals. Examples of a secondary individual include a partner, guest, roommate or resident employee, a foster child, or a person residing in a rooming house, halfway house, staff quarters at a hospital, or other types of group quarters.

Size of Household, Family, or Subfamily. The term "size of household" includes all persons occupying a housing unit. "Size of family" includes the family householder and all other persons in the living quarters who are related to the householder by birth, marriage, or adoption. "Size of related subfamily" includes the husband and wife or the lone parent and their never-married sons and daughters under 18 years of age. "Size of unrelated subfamily" includes the reference person and all other members related to the reference person. If a family has a related subfamily among its members, the size of the family includes the members of the related subfamily.

Related Persons and Family Members. In the classification of households by number of related persons, the person or couple who maintains the household or housing unit and all persons in the household related to them are included. In the classification of families by number of family members, all persons in the family are included. The number of family members is the same as the size of the family.

Related Children. Related children in a family include own children and all other children in the household who are related to the householder by birth, marriage, or adoption. For each type of family unit identified in the CPS, the count of own children under 18 years old is limited to single (never married) children; however, "own children under 25" and "own children of any age" include all children regardless of marital status. The totals include never-married children living away from home in college dormitories.

The count of related children in families was formerly restricted to never-married children. However, beginning with data for 1968 the Bureau of the Census includes ever-married children under the category of related children. The change added approximately 20,000 children to the category of related children in March, 1968.

Persons per Household. A measure calculated by dividing the number of persons in households by the number of households. In cases where persons in households are cross-classified by race or Hispanic origin, persons in the household are classified by the race or Hispanic origin of the household rather than the race or Hispanic origin of each individual.

Relationship to Householder. The data on relationship to householder were derived from answers to the 1990 Census questionnaire item 2 which was asked of all persons in housing units. One person in each household is designated as the householder (see definition of "householder" above). If there is no such person in the household, any adult household member 15 years old and over could be designated as the householder. When relationship was not reported for an individual, it was allocated according to the

responses for age and marital status for that person while maintaining consistency with responses for other individuals in the household.

Spouse—A person married to and living with a householder. This category includes persons in formal marriages as well as persons in common-law marriages.

Child—A son, daughter, stepchild, or adopted child of the householder regardless of the child's age or marital status. The category excludes sons-in-law, daughters-in-law and foster children. *Natural-Born or Adopted Son/Daughter.* A son or daughter of the householder by birth, regardless of the age of the child. This category also includes sons or daughters of the householder by legal adoption. If the stepson/stepdaughter of the household has been legally adopted by the householder, the child is still classified as a stepchild. *Stepson/Stepdaughter.* A son or daughter of the householder through marriage but not by birth, regardless of the age of the child. If the stepson/stepdaughter of the householder has been legally adopted by the householder, the child is still classified as a stepchild. *Own child.* A never-married child under 18 years who is a son or daughter by birth, a stepchild, or an adopted child of the householder. Own children of the householder living with two parents are by definition found only in married-couple families. In a subfamily, an "own child" is a never-married child under 18 years of age who is a son, daughter, stepchild, or an adopted child of a mother in a mother-child subfamily, a father in a father-child subfamily or either spouse in a married-couple family.

Other Relative—Any person related to the householder by birth, marriage, or adoption, who is not shown separately in the particular table (e.g., "uncle," "niece," or "cousin").

Nonrelative—Any person in the household not related to the householder by birth, marriage, or adoption. Roomers, boarders, partners, roommates, paid employees, wards, and foster children are included in this category.

Group Quarters. As of 1983, group quarters were defined in the Current Population Survey (CPS) as noninstitutional living arrangements for groups not living in conventional housing units containing ten or more unrelated persons or nine or more persons unrelated to the person in charge. Prior to 1983, group quarters included housing units containing five or more persons unrelated to the person in charge. Beginning in 1972, inmates of institutions have not been included in the CPS.

All persons not living in households are classified by the Census Bureau as living in group quarters. Two general categories of persons in group quarters are recognized: (1) institutionalized persons and (2) other persons in group quarters (also re-

ferred to as "noninstitutional group quarters").

Institutionalized Persons-Includes persons under formally authorized, supervised care or custody in institutions at the time of enumeration. Such persons are classified as "patients or inmates" of an institution regardless of the availability of nursing or medical care, the length of stay, or the number of persons in the institution. Generally, institutionalized persons are restricted to the institutional buildings and grounds (or must have passes or escorts to leave) and thus have limited interaction with the surrounding community. Also, they are generally under the care of trained staff who have responsibility for their safekeeping and supervision. Types of institutions include correctional institutions, nursing homes, mental hospitals, homes for the chronically ill, schools, hospitals or wards for the mentally retarded, schools, hospitals, or wards for the physically handicapped, hospitals and wards for drug/alcohol abuse, wards in general and military hospitals for patients who have no usual home elsewhere, and juvenile institutions.

Noninstitutionalized Persons-Includes all persons who live in group quarters other than institutions. Persons who live in the following living quarters are classified as *"other persons in group quarters"* when there are 10 or more unrelated persons living in the unit; otherwise these living quarters are classified as housing units: rooming houses, group homes, religious group quarters, and college quarters off campus. Persons residing in certain other types of living arrangements are classified as living in *"noninstitutional group quarters"* regardless of the number of people sharing the unit. These include: college dormitories, military quarters, agricultural workers' dormitories, other workers' dormitories, emergency shelters for homeless persons and visible in street locations, dormitories for nurses and interns in general and military hospitals, crews of maritime vessels, staff residents of institutions, other nonhousehold living situations, and living quarters for victims of natural disasters.

1990 Census and 1980 Census Comparability Summary. The 1990 definition of a household is the same as that used in 1980. The 1980 relationship category "Son/Daughter" has been replaced with two categories, "Natural-born or adopted son/daughter" and "Stepson/Stepdaughter." "Grandchild" has been added as a separate category. The 1980 nonrelative categories "Roomer, boarder" and "Partner, roommate" have been replaced by the categories "Roomer, boarder and foster child," "Housemate, roommate" and "Unmarried partner." The 1980 nonrelative category "Paid employee" has been dropped. New categories noted above have been added and other changes in more general definitions (e.g. race-ethnicity categories) are noted elsewhere in this text.

accurately survey. Only limited tabulations are presented for these groups and caution is given with respect to their accuracy.

The Bureau of the Census routinely collects data about households and families as a part of its Current Population Survey, and publishes a report, "Household and Family Characteristics," as a part of its Current Population Reports (Series P-20). Changes occur in definitions over time and major changes were made in 1980 for the census and the Current Population Surveys. Less dramatic changes were made in 1990 for the census. The reader who is not familiar with these changes should read all of the Definition Box carefully.

Growth in Households: Decline in Size

The number of households enumerated at each census since 1790, with data by race for censuses since 1890 and for survey data in recent intervening years, is pro-

vided in Table 11-1. In 1992 there were 95.7 million households housing 250.7 million persons, or 2.62 persons per household. During the decades since 1790 there has been a rather steady decline in the average size of the household. Today's household contains only 45 percent as many persons as the average household of 1790, which had 5.8 members. This decline has been due to lower fertility rates, a tendency for unmarried persons to live in housing units rather than as roomers or boarders in group quarters or with a family, a tendency for young unmarried adults to live apart from their parents instead of remaining at home until marriage, and an increased longevity that creates a great many households occupied by elderly couples or individuals. Since 1960, when the data are first available, household size of blacks and whites have declined and black households have become more similar in size to white households. In 1992 black households contained an average of 2.88 members, whereas white households were about 9 percent smaller (2.62 members). Since 1980 the household size of Hispanics

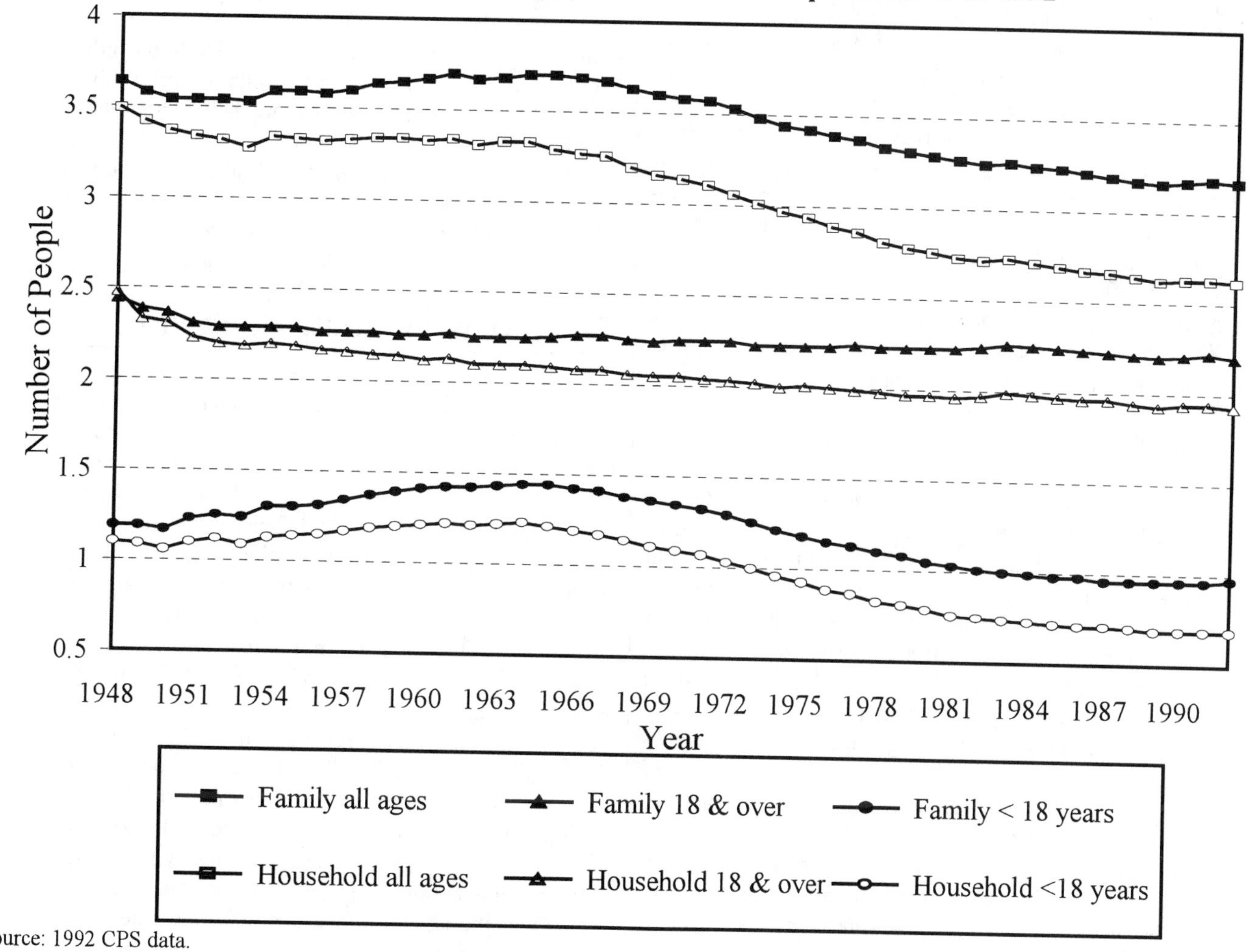

Figure 11-1. Average Family and Household Population: 1948-1992

does not appear to have declined appreciably and remained 33 percent larger (3.45 members) than the average white household in 1992.

Because households have declined in size, the number of households has increased at a faster rate than the population. As a result there has been a rather steady growth in the number of households, despite recent fertility declines. However, this trend may be changing somewhat. The average household and family sizes, especially for those under 18 years of age, appear to have declined at a far slower pace from 1980 to 1992 than in the preceding two decades (See Figure 11-1). The slowing in the decline of family sizes may reflect the leveling off of fertility decline and changing patterns of nuptiality. If the decline in household size abates in the near future, along with either continuing fertility decline or stabilization of fertility rates, the rate of household formation should noticeably decline in response.

Since the turn of the century, the number of households has risen approximately twenty-one percent each decade. The decades of the greatest growth in number of households were the 1900's, 1910's, 1940's and 1970's (26, 24 and 25 percent increases, respectively). In contrast, the 1980's and the early 1990's have seen the lowest growth rate in the number of households since the 1930's, a decade encompassing the Great Depression (16 percent). During the 1980's the number of households grew by only seventeen percent with the growth in households concentrated more heavily in the first five years of the decade. This sharp decline in the formation of new households came at a time when demographers were predicting a continuation of the trends of the 1980's, because the supply of persons born during the "baby boom" who were at prime ages for household formation was still large. Inflation in housing prices and a significant economic slowdown increased the costs of establishing new households during these years. In turn, economic conditions contributed to the slower decline in household size over the 1980's as older children remained in their parents' households until older ages.

While the growth in new households remains historically low, the small increase in 1991-2 (1.4 percent compared to 1.0 percent in 1990-1) may reflect an initial easing of the obstacles facing new household formation with an improved housing market and declining interest rates during these years. If so, household size may decline even further in the future when older children have a similar opportunity to take advantage of more favorable circumstances for forming a household. Nonetheless, the percentage increase in new households was lower in the first half of the twentieth century than the last half of the nineteenth century and has been lower since the 1950's than the prior century. Overlaying the short-term fluctuations in formation of households is an apparent decline in the rate of household formation paralleling long-term demographic trends.

Household Types and Diversity

Every household is presumed to have a leader, which in earlier censuses was called "household head" and, since the 1980 Census, has been referred to through the euphemistic term "householder." The Definition Box provides details of these changes.

Types of Households

The census divides all households into two categories: **Family households** are housing units occupied by a group of persons who are related to the householder by birth, marriage, or adoption. **Non-family households** are housing units occupied by a single person living alone or a householder living with one or more persons, none of whom are related to the householder by birth, marriage, or adoption.

Types of Family Households

Housing units occupied by a family are considered either "married-couple families" or "other family" depending on the sex of the householder and the presence of other relatives, such as children, in the household: **Married-couple families** are family households where the householder and his or her spouse are enumerated as members of the same household. **Female householder families**, also termed "female householder, no husband present" in some Census tables, are family households with a female householder and no spouse or other householder present. **Male householder families**, also termed "male householder, no wife present" in some Census tables, are family households with a male householder and no spouse or other householder present.

Types of Non-family Households

Non-family households are classified according to sex of the householder and whether or not the householder lives alone or with other non-relatives, i.e. female householder, living alone; female householder, living with others; male householder, living alone; and male householder, living with others. In the 1990 Census, the Bureau further identified household relationships among non-family householders living with others to more accurately describe contemporary living arrangements. The introduction of the **unmarried-partner household** reflects the recent growth in the number of couples who cohabit as well as recognizing same-sex partnerships. An unmarried partner is an adult unrelated to the householder, but sharing the housing unit and having a close personal relationship with the householder. The **unmarried-couple household** category includes households with two unrelated adults of the opposite sex who share living quarters with or without children 15 years old or younger.

Over the last three decades there have been substantial changes in the composition of American house-

Figure 11-2. Composition of American Households: 1960-1990

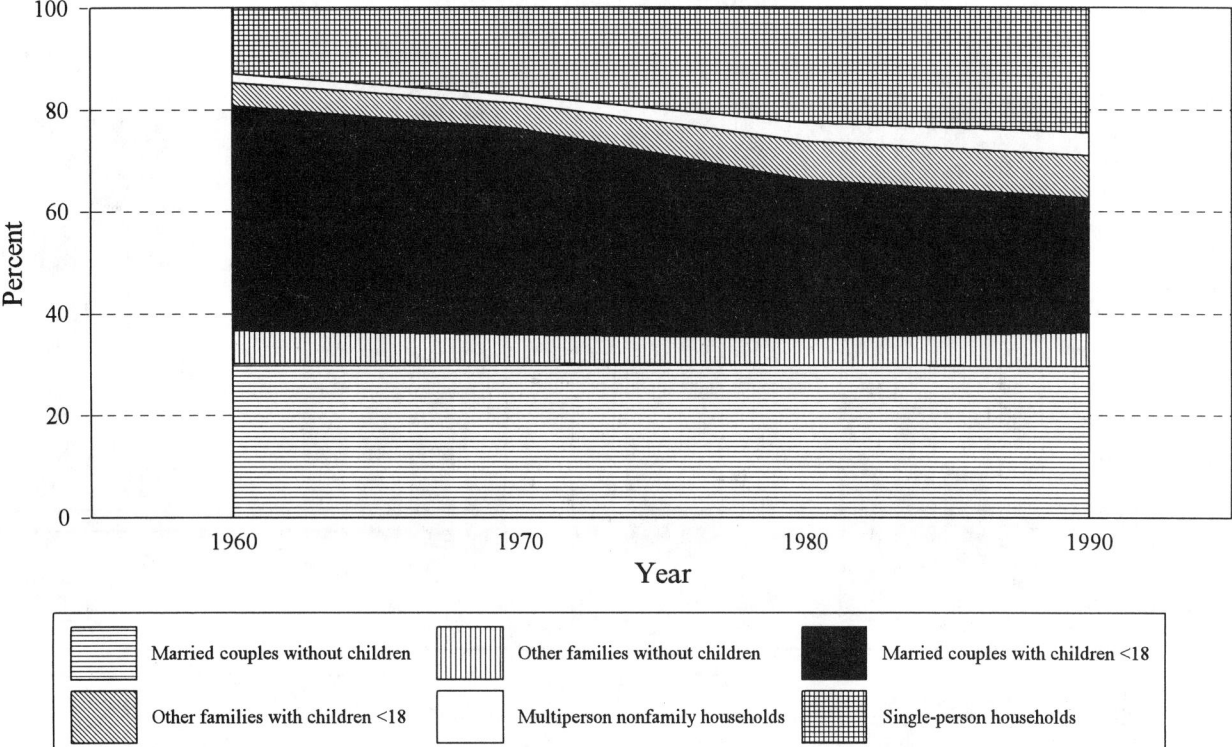

Source: 1960, 1970, 1980, and 1990 Census data.

holds. The single greatest change has been the decline in traditional households consisting of married couples with dependent children. As Figure 11-2 illustrates, these traditional households were over 2 of every 5 households in 1960 and yet had declined to just over 1 of every 5 households by the early 1990's. Some of this change may be accounted for by the increase in children living in other family arrangements. However, the percent of all family households with children has declined as fertility has continued to decline. A far greater proportion of the decline in traditional households over these years is accounted for by the increase in single person households and other multi-person non-family households. Single person households are now nearly as numerous as married-couple family households with children. Of course, single person households are small by definition and considerably more people still reside in married-couple families with and without children than in all other family types.

The proportion (prevalence) within the population of each of the major household types described above is reported in Table 11-2 for the year 1992, for each of the major race-ethnic groups. Overall, approximately 7 of every 10 households are occupied by families of one sort or another, while approximately 3 out of 10 are occupied as non-family households by persons either living alone or living with other unrelated persons. Hispanic households, and also 'other race' households, are more likely to consist of families than are either white or black households.

Family Households

For all except black households, the married-couple family is by far the dominant type of family household. About 55 percent of all households and 78 percent of all family households are of this conventional type. However, a significant proportion of the households (from 15 percent overall to approximately 37 percent for black and 26 percent for Hispanic households) consist of "no-spouse" families, either a male or female living with children or other relatives, but without a spouse. In only a small share of cases (3.2 percent of all households) is this a male. The prevalence of female no-spouse families is nearly four times higher.

The phenomenon of female no-spouse family households is twice as prevalent among the Spanish-ori-

Figure 11-3. One-Parent Family Groups by Marital Status of Reference Person: 1970, 1980, 1990, and 1992

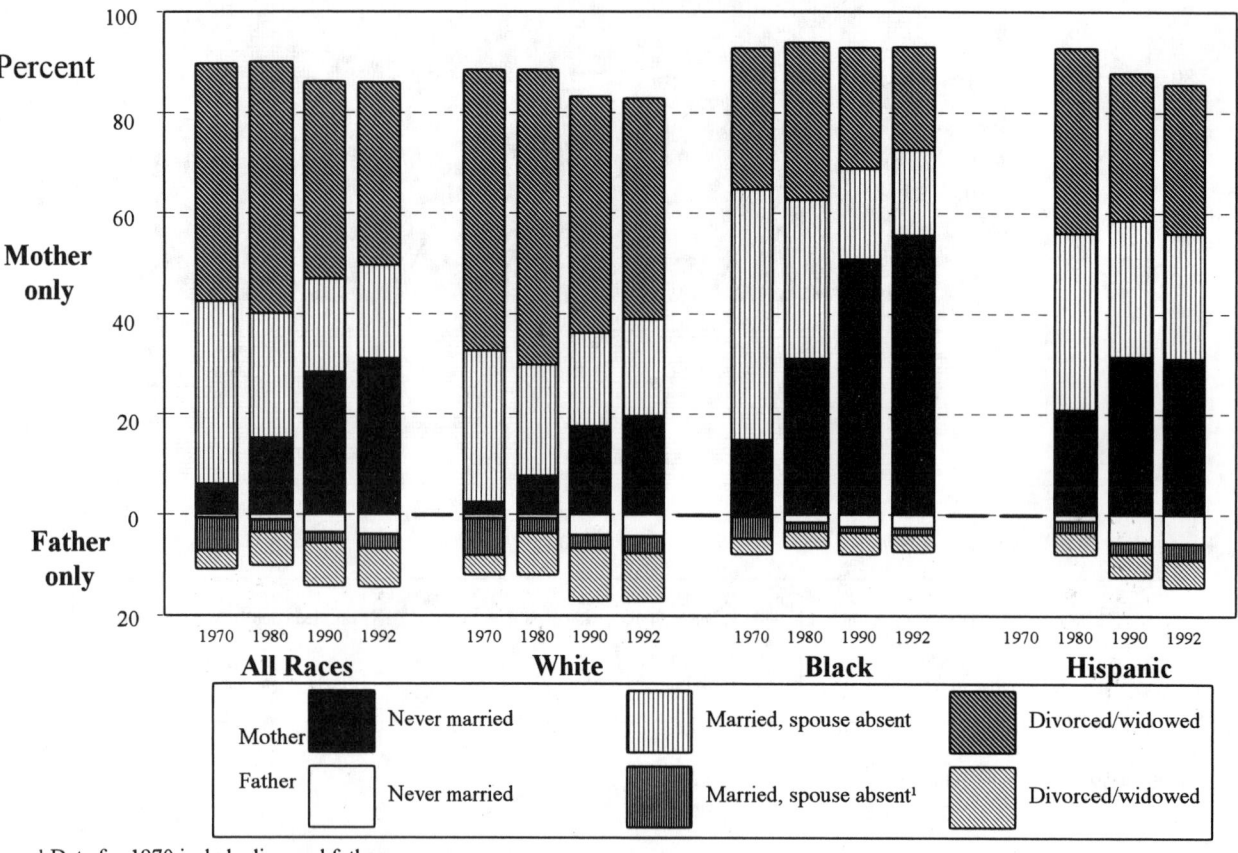

¹ Data for 1970 include divorced fathers.
Source: 1970, 1980, and 1990 Census data and March 1992 unadjusted CPS data.

gin population as among the white. Among the black population, it is almost a dominant trait: 32.3 percent of all black households (46.4 percent of all black family households) are comprised of women living with their children, but without a husband.

The proportion of father-only households increased between 1980 and 1990 for all major racial and ethnic groups in Figure 11-3. The most substantial increases in father-only households were in fathers never married and those divorced or widowed. The proportion of mother-only households correspondingly declined for all groups. However, all groups saw a continual dramatic increase in the percentage of mother-only households which consist of never-married women and their children. As these never-married women increased as a percentage of mother-only households there was a decrease in households consisting of married women who either had a spouse absent from the household and those who were divorced or separated from their husband. It is important to remember that the increasing percentage of one-parent families that are headed by never-married women, while a serious social concern, is partly rising at the expense of

other mother-only family types. From a policy standpoint, such as a general concern with children's welfare, those mother-only families that are declining (e.g. from divorce or marital separation) may have social costs equal to, or even greater than, those mother-only families which are increasing over this same period.

Non-family Households

In 1940 the ratio was 9 family households to each non-family household. By 1992 that ratio had declined to 2.3 family households to each non-family household. As Figure 11-2 shows, the greatest increase in household types between 1960 and 1990 was in single person households. This increase in single person and non-family households was most dramatic between 1970 and 1980. The rate of increase decelerated somewhat in the 1980's yet non-family households have continued to increase into the 1990's.

The great majority of non-family households (84 percent) consists of persons living alone. Among one-person households, women outnumber men. Thus, the

Table 11-2. Types of Households and Families, by Race-ethnicity: 1992 [numbers in thousands]

Type of household	Percent distribution (vertical)					Number of households	Percent distribution (horizontal)			
	Total	White	Black	Other	Hispanic		White	Black	Other	Hispanic
All households	100.0	100.0	100.0	100.0	100.0	95,669	85.4	11.6	3.0	6.7
Family households	70.2	70.1	69.6	76.7	81.2	67,173	85.2	11.5	3.3	7.7
Married couple family	54.8	57.7	32.8	58.5	55.4	52,457	89.8	6.9	3.3	6.7
Other: male householder	3.2	2.9	4.5	5.0	6.0	3,025	78.5	16.7	4.8	12.7
Other: female householder	12.2	9.5	32.3	13.2	19.8	11,692	66.1	30.6	3.3	10.8
Nonfamily households	29.8	29.9	30.4	23.3	18.8	28,496	85.8	11.8	2.4	4.2
Householders living alone	25.1	25.1	26.3	18.6	13.9	23,974	85.6	12.2	2.2	3.7
Male householder	10.0	9.8	11.9	9.1	7.0	9,613	83.5	13.7	2.8	4.6
Female householder	15.0	15.3	14.4	9.4	6.9	14,361	87.0	11.1	1.9	3.1
Householders living with others	4.7	4.8	4.1	4.7	4.9	4,522	87.0	10.0	3.0	7.0
Male householder	2.9	3.0	2.5	3.2	3.4	2,815	86.9	9.8	3.3	7.7
Female householder	1.8	1.8	1.6	1.5	1.6	1,707	87.0	10.4	2.6	5.8
Number of households	95,669	81,675	11,083	2,911	6,379	—	—	—	—	—

Source: U.S. Bureau of the Census, "Household and Family Characteristics," Current Population Reports, Series P-20, no. 467, U.S. Government Printing Office, Washington, D.C., 1993, Table 16.

long-term decrease in the proportion of family households is caused not so much by persons seeking alterative forms of group living as simply by persons (primarily women) choosing or forced by circumstances to live alone. Table 11-2 presents a separate column for each major race-ethnicity group. Living alone is slightly more prevalent among the black than among the white population. It is far less prevalent among the Hispanic population than either of the other major race-ethnic groups. Differences in the prevalence of specific non-family households within sex and race-ethnic groups are affected by group differences in age, mortality, and access to alternative forms of group living (e.g. relatives, affordable institutionalized care).

Changing Household Structure

The decline in family households has been largely due to a steady decline in the proportion of married-couple families. Table 11-3 gives longitudinal trends in household types from 1950 to 1992 for the total population and each major race-ethnicity group. The proportion of no-spouse family households (particularly those headed by females) has increased steadily. The most dramatic increase of no-spouse family households occurred during the 1980's at the same time as a general decrease in family households. The increased prevalence of divorce and the increased tendency to bear children out of wedlock (or, equivalently, not to necessarily marry when having a child) discussed in earlier chapters are among the leading causes of this increase in spouseless families. However, these long-term trends also seem to have leveled off more recently.

Between 1980 and 1992 the increase in family households headed by females without a spouse has increased less rapidly than during the preceding decade. This reversal of trends was most dramatic for the black population. Between 1970 and 1980 the percentage of black family households which were headed by women with no spouse present increased by 7 percent, yet from 1980 to 1990 these households increased by only 2.3 percent. From 1990 to 1992 there has been no discernable trend of continuing increase in black female headed family households. Female headed family households actually increased most rapidly, by 2.9 percent, among Hispanics between 1980 and 1990. Unlike blacks, the increase of such households continued for Hispanics, and whites, into the years since the 1990 Census.

It is worthy to note that male headed family households appeared to decrease until 1970 and have steadily increased since that time. These households increased for all three major race-ethnicity groups between 1980 and 1990.

As family households, and especially married-couple families, have declined, non-family households have also increased for all race-ethnicity groups in Table 11-3. Overall, male householders of non-family households have more than doubled (up 6.7% from 6.3% to 13.0%) in the years between 1980 and 1992. This increase has been most dramatic among white males and least among Hispanic men. During the same period female non-family householders increased less rapidly (up 4.4% from 12.4% to 16.8%) but remain a larger percentage of all households overall. Looking at race-ethnicity groups, however, females are a smaller percentage of non-family householders than males among Hispanics. With some minor reversals over time, the percentage of those living alone has increased for both genders and all race-ethnic groups.

Unmarried Couples and Partners

Not immediately apparent in these data is the increasing number of individuals who choose to live in alternative family types identified by the census. Reporting accuracy is of some question for alternative family types which may not be labeled consistent with the manner in which individuals identify as own family structure. Nonetheless, looking at unmarried couples of opposite sex within households, such households have increased dramatically over the past years. According to the Current Population Survey, there were 3.3 million unmarried-couple households in 1992. Two-thirds of these households (2.2 million) had no children under 15 years old present. The rate of unmarried couples per 1,000 households has increased from 8.3 in 1970 to 34.6 in 1992. Over the same period it has increased from 12.8 to 136.0 per 1,000 households among those aged less than twenty-five. The householder rate of unmarried couples has increased among all ages other than those sixty-five years of age and older over the period of 1970-1992.

In 1990, the Bureau of the Census introduced a new household category, the unmarried-partner household (see Definition Box). It is difficult to provide evidence for longitudinal trends in unmarried same-sex partners from data available. It is, in fact, difficult to provide estimates of the prevalence of such households which are not contested. Family structure identifications which are not necessarily marked by civil ceremony, legal certification, or specific residential arrangements, instead rely upon how individuals in the household regard their relationship. Data for such arrangements are highly influenced by social acceptability, self-identification, and other influences not necessarily reflecting the true prevalence of such arrangements. From the data which is available, of the 3,187,772 unmarried-partner households enumerated in the 1990 Census, 145,130 (4.6%) were same-sex unmarried-partner households. Of these unmarried-partner same-sex households 81,343 (56%) were male and 63,787 (44%) were female.

Table 11-3. Prevalence of Household and Family Types, by Race-ethnicity: 1950-1992

Type of household	Percent distribution of households						
	1992	1991	1990	1980	1970	1960	1950
All race households	100.0	100.0	100.0	100.0	100.0	100.0	100.0
Family households	70.2	70.3	70.8	73.9	81.3	85.0	89.2
Married couple family	54.8	55.3	56.0	60.9	70.6	74.3	78.2
Male householder	3.2	3.1	3.1	2.2	1.9	2.3	2.7
Female householder	12.2	11.9	11.7	10.8	8.7	8.4	8.3
Nonfamily households	29.8	29.7	29.2	26.1	18.7	15.0	10.8
Male householder	13.0	12.9	12.4	10.9	6.3	—	—
Living alone	10.0	10.0	9.7	8.6	—	—	—
Living with others	2.9	2.9	2.7	2.3	—	—	—
Female householder	16.8	16.8	16.8	15.3	12.4	—	—
Living alone	15.0	15.0	14.9	13.9	—	—	—
Living with others	1.8	1.8	1.8	1.4	—	—	—
White households	100.0	100.0	100.0	100.0	100.0	—	—
Family households	70.1	70.2	70.6	74.0	81.7	—	—
Married couple family	57.7	58.1	58.6	63.4	72.5	—	—
Male householder	2.9	2.8	2.9	2.0	1.8	—	—
Female householder	9.5	9.3	9.1	8.6	7.3	—	—
Nonfamily households	29.9	29.8	29.4	26.0	18.3	—	—
Male householder	12.8	12.7	12.4	10.5	5.9	—	—
Living alone	9.8	9.8	9.6	8.3	—	—	—
Living with others	3.0	2.9	2.8	2.2	—	—	—
Female householder	17.1	17.1	17.0	15.5	12.4	—	—
Living alone	15.3	15.3	15.2	14.1	—	—	—
Living with others	1.8	1.8	1.8	1.4	—	—	—
Black households	100.0	100.0	100.0	100.0	100.0	—	—
Family households	69.6	70.0	71.2	71.9	78.4	—	—
Married couple family	32.8	33.4	35.8	39.9	53.6	—	—
Male householder	4.5	4.4	4.3	3.1	2.9	—	—
Female householder	32.3	32.1	31.2	28.9	21.9	—	—
Nonfamily households	30.4	30.0	28.8	28.1	21.6	—	—
Male householder	14.4	14.3	12.5	13.6	8.9	—	—
Living alone	11.9	11.9	10.3	11.2	—	—	—
Living with others	2.5	2.5	2.2	2.4	—	—	—
Female householder	16.0	15.6	16.2	14.5	12.7	—	—
Living alone	14.4	14.2	14.5	13.0	—	—	—
Living with others	1.6	1.5	1.7	1.5	—	—	—
Hispanic households	100.0	100.0	100.0	100.0	—	—	—
Family households	81.2	80.1	81.6	83.1	—	—	—
Married couple family	55.4	55.5	57.2	63.6	—	—	—
Male householder	6.0	5.5	5.5	3.6	—	—	—
Female householder	19.8	19.1	18.8	15.9	—	—	—
Nonfamily households	18.8	19.9	18.4	16.9	—	—	—
Male householder	10.3	10.8	9.9	9.4	—	—	—
Living alone	7.0	7.3	7.0	—	—	—	—
Living with others	3.4	3.4	2.9	—	—	—	—
Female householder	8.5	9.1	8.5	7.5	—	—	—
Living alone	6.9	7.5	7.4	—	—	—	—
Living with others	1.6	1.6	1.1	—	—	—	—

Source: U.S. Bureau of the Census, "Household and Family Characteristics," Current Population Reports, Series P-20, nos. 467, 458, 447, 366, 218, U.S. Government Printing Office, Washington, D.C., 1992, 1991, 1989 and 1990, 1981, and 1971. Data for 1950-1960 from the U.S. Bureau of the Census, Historical Statistics of the United States: Colonial Times to 1970 (Part 1), U.S. Government Printing Office, Washington, D.C., 1975.

Differentials in Size of Households

The average size of American households as reported above (2.62 persons in 1992) is quite small. This is caused in part by the large component of non-family households, which have the very small average size of 1.23 persons. However, family households are also comparatively small with an average of only 3.22 per family. In the modal case, it is a husband, wife, and one child. Table 11-4 reports the average size of households according to household type and race-ethnic group for selected years since 1970.

Household size and trends in household size vary by type of household. Married couples tend to have the largest households, while women living in non-family households tend to have the smallest. Family households where a male or female householder is living without a spouse are very nearly, but not quite, as large as married-couple households.

Black households tend to be nearly 10 percent larger than white households of the same type. Black family households headed by a black female householder living with children or other relatives but without a husband are nearly 15 percent larger than the same type of households in the white population. However, the household size of black women living in a family without a spouse has declined (from 3.7 to 3.4) between 1980 and 1992 while the family size of similar white women has increased slightly (from 2.93 to 2.96), bringing the household size of these two groups closer together.

Hispanic households tend to be the largest of all households. The greatest disparity is in the Hispanic married-couple households, which are 16 percent larger than black and 27 percent larger than white married-couple households. Hispanic family households of either males or females without a spouse present are larger than similar households for either whites or blacks. Both types of households increased in size over the period from 1980 to 1990 faster than for other race-ethnicity groups. While black female headed family households decreased in size by 9 percent between 1980 and 1992, similar Hispanic households increased in size by over 5 percent during the same period.

The size of male headed family households with no spouse present has increased for all race-ethnicity groups since 1980. Since overall family sizes have declined over the same period this increase may reflect changes in the likelihood of men retaining custody or supervision of children in their own independent household following divorce or widowhood.

The differences between racial groups tend to be concentrated among the family households; differences among the non-family households, naturally, tend to be minor. Many of these households consist of single individuals living alone. Again, however, Hispanic non-family households are slightly larger for both males and females than any other race-ethnicity group. Between 1990 and 1992, the size of female non-family households has increased substantially for Hispanics, slightly for whites, and displays no trend for black women. The size of male non-family households has decreased for blacks and Hispanics, with some fluctuation over the years, yet remains larger than similar households in 1980.

Number of Persons Per Family

Whereas Table 11-4 provides data only for average family size, Table 11-5 provides data on the distribution of numbers of persons in family households. By definition, a family must contain at least two persons, and for all family types for all race-ethnicity groups except Hispanics, this is the modal size group. The four-person family is more common among Hispanic married-couple families than any other size. Almost 85 percent of husband-wife (married-couple) families contain two, three, or four members, and only just over five percent have six or more persons.

Dramatic differences between race-ethnic groups are evident in how many married couples are living with very small and very large families. Couple-only households are twice as likely among whites as they are among Hispanics. Over 4 of every 10 white married couples are living by themselves. Less than 3 of every 10 black and 2 of 10 Hispanic married couples live as couples without any children, parents, or other family members. In contrast, more than 3 of every 10 Hispanic married couples has five or more family members compared to just over 2 of every 10 black, and about 1.5 of every 10 white, married couples.

Female and male no-spouse families naturally tend to be even more concentrated in two or three person households than are married-couple families. This tendency is more pronounced for the male than for the female no-spouse family. The male-headed family of this type consists of two persons in almost two-thirds of the cases.

By providing data from 1970 to 1992 Table 11-5 offers insight into how the number of persons in families has changed in the recent past. In all types of households the trend has been toward a lower proportion of households with five or more persons and a larger number of households with two or three persons. The number of households with 7 or more members has declined by over 70 percent among white and black married couples since 1970.

Age of Householders

Very few householders are under age twenty-five, because at these ages comparatively few males are married and comparatively few unmarried persons have the financial resources to maintain a housing unit in their own name. Few households are maintained by persons seventy-five and over, because mortality has reduced the

Table 11-4. Average Household Size: Persons per Household, by Type and Race-ethnicity: 1970-1992

Type of household and race-ethnicity	Year				
	1992	1991	1990	1980	1970
All households	2.62	2.63	2.63	2.75	3.17
Family households	3.22	3.23	3.22	3.30	3.64
Married couple households	3.25	3.26	3.25	3.34	3.69
Male householder, no spouse	3.08	3.11	3.04	2.91	3.06
Female householder, no spouse	3.11	3.12	3.10	3.15	3.35
Nonfamily households	1.23	1.22	1.22	1.19	1.13
Male householder	1.32	1.32	1.33	1.29	1.19
Female householder	1.15	1.15	1.14	1.12	1.09
White households	2.58	2.58	2.58	2.71	3.11
Family households	3.16	3.16	3.16	3.24	—
Married couple households	3.20	3.21	3.20	3.30	—
Male householder, no spouse	3.01	3.05	2.98	2.86	—
Female householder, no spouse	2.96	2.92	2.92	2.93	—
Nonfamily households	1.23	1.22	1.21	1.19	—
Male householder	1.33	1.32	1.32	1.30	—
Female householder	1.15	1.14	1.13	1.11	—
Black households	2.81	2.87	2.88	3.01	3.68
Family households	3.51	3.58	3.53	3.72	—
Married couple households	3.64	3.68	3.60	3.78	—
Male householder, no spouse	3.28	3.27	3.27	3.14	—
Female householder, no spouse	3.40	3.52	3.49	3.70	—
Nonfamily households	1.20	1.22	1.24	1.21	—
Male householder	1.25	1.28	1.32	1.25	—
Female householder	1.17	1.17	1.18	1.17	—
Hispanic households	3.45	3.44	3.47	3.46	—
Family households	3.92	3.95	3.94	3.89	—
Married couple households	4.07	4.10	4.09	4.05	—
Male householder, no spouse	3.68	3.82	3.72	3.30	—
Female householder, no spouse	3.58	3.53	3.55	3.40	—
Nonfamily households	1.45	1.40	1.41	1.35	—
Male householder	1.57	1.53	1.62	1.51	—
Female householder	1.29	1.24	1.16	1.14	—

Source: U.S. Bureau of the Census, "Household and Family Characteristics," Current Population Reports, Series P-20, nos.467, 458, 447, 291, and 218, U.S. Government Printing Office, Washington, D.C., 1992, 1991, 1989 and 1990, 1981, and 1971.

number of such persons available to occupy households. Between these extremes, the age composition of householders largely reflects the age composition of the population during a particular decade and the relative costs of maintaining households. During the years between 1980 and 1992 many of the babies born during the baby boom had aged into the 35-44 age brackets. Accordingly, one would expect much growth in the number of household-

ers in this age group during the period. This is, in fact, the case, as the central panel of Table 11-6 details. The lower panel of the table shows that the greatest growth in households during the 1970-80 decade was also due to the baby boomers who were then aged 25-34. The tremendous growth in non-family households under age 35 during the 1970's has virtually disappeared. The nearest rates of growth in non-family households were only about half

Table 11-5. Percent Distribution and Average Persons per Family, by Type of Family and Race-ethnicity: 1970-1992

Number of persons	Married couple families				Female householder families				Male householder families			
	Total	White	Black	Hispanic	Total	White	Black	Hispanic	Total	White	Black	Hispanic
1992 total	100.0	100.0	100	100.0	100.0	100.0	100.0	100.0	100.0	100.0	100.0	100.0
2 persons	39.7	41.1	28.3	19.7	47.3	51.5	38.1	31.3	60.7	62.6	57.7	45.7
3 persons	21.9	21.8	24.5	20.5	28.8	29.6	27.7	29.8	23.9	23.7	25.0	27.9
4 persons	23.3	23.0	24.4	26.2	14.2	12.2	18.1	20.5	9.5	9.1	9.3	13.8
5 persons	10.0	9.7	13.4	17.4	5.8	4.4	9.0	9.3	3.2	2.2	5.8	5.5
6 persons	3.3	3.0	6.0	8.9	2.0	1.4	3.2	4.8	1.6	1.5	1.4	3.4
7 or more persons	1.8	1.5	3.5	7.2	2.0	1.0	3.9	4.4	1.2	0.9	1.0	3.7
Average per family	3.23	3.18	3.62	4.02	2.98	2.82	3.30	3.42	2.77	2.68	2.98	3.17
1990 total	100.0	100.0	100.0	100.0	100.0	100.0	100.0	100.0	100.0	100.0	100.0	100.0
2 persons	39.5	40.7	30.0	20.9	47.8	53.1	36.3	33.4	60.7	61.9	58.3	44.4
3 persons	22.0	21.9	24.1	20.6	28.7	28.7	28.7	28.6	24.4	24.2	23.8	28.6
4 persons	23.4	23.3	23.2	26.0	13.8	12.0	17.5	19.8	8.9	9.2	7.6	13.4
5 persons	10.0	9.7	13.5	16.9	5.3	3.7	8.8	10.3	3.5	3.0	5.6	7.6
6 persons	3.2	2.9	5.5	8.6	2.5	1.5	4.7	4.0	1.1	0.7	2.0	2.7
7 or more persons	1.8	1.5	3.6	7.0	1.9	1.0	4.0	3.9	1.3	1.0	2.7	3.3
Average per family	3.23	3.18	3.58	4.02	2.99	2.80	3.39	3.40	2.75	2.68	2.99	3.26
1980 total	100.0	100.0	100.0	100.0	100.0	100.0	100.0	100.0	100.0	100.0	100.0	100.0
2 persons	37.4	38.4	28.2	20.1	44.7	49.8	32.1	33.7	62.2	63.0	61.0	54.1
3 persons	21.9	21.8	23.5	21.8	28.2	29.1	26.0	30.6	21.9	22.7	15.2	19.1
4 persons	22.3	22.3	22.3	24.1	14.7	13.1	18.9	18.8	9.6	8.6	14.3	11.4
5 persons	10.9	10.7	11.8	16.4	6.8	5.4	10.0	9.8	3.4	3.4	3.5	7.0
6 persons	4.5	4.2	7.1	8.9	2.8	1.7	5.8	4.2	2.0	1.7	4.1	6.2
7 or more persons	3.0	2.5	7.1	8.6	2.8	0.9	7.2	3.0	0.9	0.6	1.8	2.1
Average per family	3.33	3.29	3.76	4.03	3.08	2.86	3.62	3.33	2.73	2.67	2.95	3.09
1970 total	100.0	100.0	100.0	100.0	100.0	100.0	100.0	100.0	100.0	100.0	100.0	100.0
2 persons	32.4	32.9	27.3	—	45.3	50.2	30.2	—	59.2	62.2	42.1	—
3 persons	20.5	20.5	19.5	—	23.9	25.1	20.2	—	20.8	20.1	25.2	—
4 persons	20.2	20.6	16.4	—	13.7	13.0	15.8	—	11.0	11.0	11.7	—
5 persons	13.4	13.5	11.7	—	7.9	6.4	12.6	—	3.8	3.7	4.0	—
6 persons	7.2	6.9	10.1	—	4.5	3.1	8.7	—	1.8	1.3	4.5	—
7 or more persons	6.3	5.6	14.9	—	4.7	2.2	12.5	—	3.3	1.6	12.6	—
Average per family	3.68	3.62	4.37	—	3.29	2.98	4.22	—	2.95	2.77	3.94	—

Table 11-6. Age Composition of Householders, by Type of Household: 1992 and Percent Change 1970-1992 and 1980-1992

Age of householder	All households	Family households				Nonfamily households		
		Total	Married couple	Single householder, no spouse present		Total	Householder	
				Male	Female		Male	Female
Total, 1992	100.0	100.0	100.0	100.0	100.0	100.0	100.0	100.0
Under 25 years	5.1	3.9	2.8	8.6	7.8	7.8	9.9	6.1
25-29 years	9.2	8.7	8.0	12.2	11.0	10.4	14.4	7.3
30-34 years	11.7	12.7	12.4	11.7	14.4	9.4	13.6	6.2
35-44 years	22.8	26.1	25.8	25.9	27.6	14.9	21.2	10.0
45-54 years	16.3	18.1	18.7	17.3	15.7	11.8	13.2	10.7
55-64 years	13.1	13.8	14.8	11.0	10.3	11.5	10.1	12.5
65-74 years	12.6	10.9	12.0	7.9	7.0	16.5	9.5	22.0
75 years and over	9.3	5.7	5.6	5.3	6.2	17.8	8.1	25.3
Median age	45.7	44.4	45.5	41.8	40.9	51.2	40.3	63.1
Percent change, 1980-92								
Under 25 years	-24.1	-29.1	-48.0	43.4	27.7	-17.0	-19.0	-14.3
25-29 years	-1.3	-8.7	-19.9	148.6	25.9	17.7	16.5	19.6
30-34 years	24.8	16.3	8.0	147.6	43.1	62.2	55.9	74.1
35-44 years	56.6	44.2	36.8	121.8	67.8	143.0	130.4	167.2
45-54 years	23.6	13.8	10.1	68.7	25.1	79.5	78.2	80.8
55-64 years	3.1	-0.0	-3.4	25.6	20.3	13.3	42.1	0.4
65-74 years	21.2	21.8	21.7	29.9	20.1	20.3	44.4	14.0
75 years and over	42.9	37.2	39.1	34.2	30.5	47.5	44.5	48.3
Percent change, 1970-80								
Under 25 years	48.6	7.8	-5.5	171.6	81.6	214.0	259.6	168.9
25-29 years	46.3	18.3	6.9	108.5	129.4	270.9	290.1	244.2
30-34 years	61.6	42.2	29.1	180.4	162.1	312.5	329.4	283.8
35-44 years	19.0	11.8	3.0	67.3	80.1	114.6	138.0	80.7
45-54 years	2.8	-1.0	-5.4	12.7	32.6	32.0	62.8	11.5
55-64 years	13.4	11.9	11.9	23.7	9.2	18.5	32.2	13.4
65-74 years	31.7	28.2	30.7	26.0	12.5	37.7	29.3	40.0
75 years and over	31.9	16.6	23.3	-30.6	9.9	47.6	24.8	54.8

Source: U.S. Bureau of the Census, "Household and Family Characteristics," Current Population Reports, Series P-20, nos. 467, 366, and 218, U.S. Government Printing Office, Washnigton, D.C., 1992, 1981 and 1971, Tables 16, 19, and 21.

those of the 1970's, seen only among the baby boomers aged 35-44.

Householders have very different age patterns depending on sex and family type. Families with no spouse are more likely to be among the younger age categories, less than 25 years of age, in comparison with married-couple households. Nearly three quarters (72%) of male non-family householders are younger than age 55, largely reflecting volitional behavior or choice. Well over half (58%) of female non-family householders are above the same age, largely reflecting different mortality rates by sex above this age.

Tables 11-7 and 11-8 report the age composition data of Table 11-6 broken down by white, black, and Hispanic households for family and non-family householders respectively. The data are for 1980 and 1992, which permits analysis of recent trends. White householders tend to be slightly older in married-couple and female headed households. Black male householders tend to be older than either white or Hispanic male headed family and non-family households. The greatest decline in prevalence over time has been among black married-couple householders under 20 years of age. The greatest increases have generally been in Hispanic householders of all types, male headed family households, and all non-family households. This increase is particularly dramatic among Hispanic males and the single greatest increase has been in Hispanic male headed family householders 40 to 44 years old.

Tables 11-6, 11-7 and 11-8 are unable to answer every important question that needs to be answered in order to interpret the implications of recent age trends in household growth: How great are differentials in the propensity to be a householder at a particular age? In order to measure this and thereby control the effects of changing age composition, "household rates" are reported in Table 11-9. To compute these rates, the number of householders of a given age are expressed as a rate per 1,000 of the "exposed" population of the same age. This is performed separately for each sex. The first page of Table 11-9 presents these rates for males by race-ethnicity while the second continuation page presents comparable data

for females. Males are most likely to be declared as householder in married-couple families in all but the very young stages. Black males are more likely than other males to live alone in non-family households, especially over 35 years of age. White males are next most likely to live alone in non-family households. Hispanic males are least likely to live alone at all ages. White female heads of household are most likely to be living alone, whereas black and Hispanic female headed households are more likely to be women with a family but without a spouse present. Between the ages of 35 and 54 white females are also more likely to be in family households without a spouse than to live alone. Female headed families are most common among black women at all ages. Figure 11-4 graphs householder rates for female race-ethnic groups by age. All groups of women have similar age patterns of living alone, with Hispanics less likely to live alone at all ages. The rate of householding without a spouse is much higher for black women at all ages but the percentage difference from other racial groups is most pronounced in childbearing ages between 20 and 45.

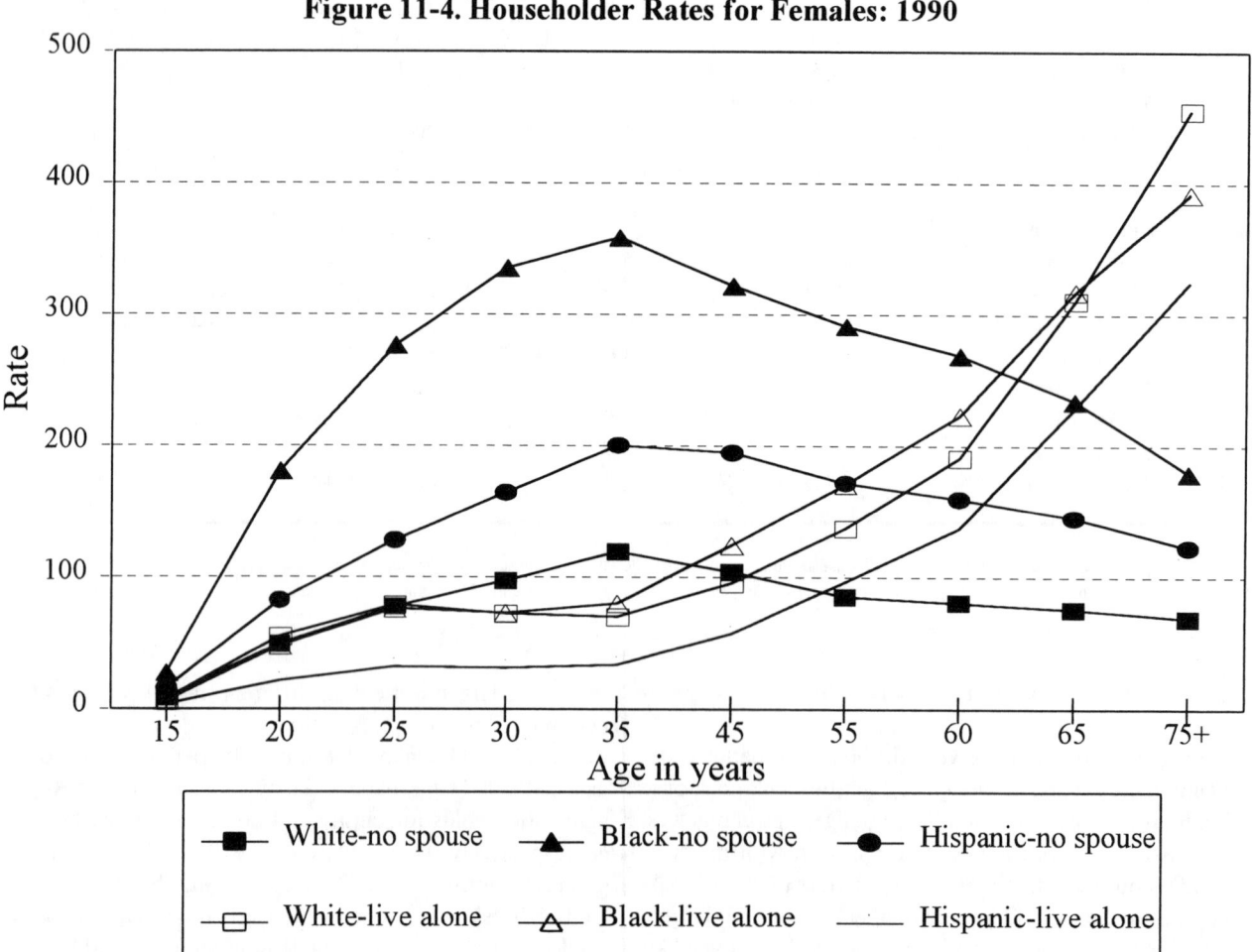

Figure 11-4. Householder Rates for Females: 1990

Source: 1990 Census data.

Marital Status of Householders

In recent years, a divergence of householding from marital arrangements has generated increasing interest in alternative householding arrangements. Married-couple families are classified as married with spouse present. Other categories of householders can, however, have any marital status except this. Table 11-10 provides information on "no spouse present family" households and "non-family" households. Of course, these labels do not reflect the full variety of what individuals may, themselves, consider their family arrangements to be. The table reports the marital status for all householders and for each of three principal race-ethnic groups. Using data for 1980 and 1992, along with a measure of percentage change across these years, highlights the forces that appear to be stimulating rapid increases in the less conventional types of households. Four forces appear to be working simultaneously to promote alternatives to the married-couple household type: widowhood, marital disruption (divorce and separation), the tendency for never-married persons to form non-family households, and the tendency to be a family householder though never married (bearing children out of wedlock).

In families with no spouse (either male or female householder) divorced is the most frequent marital status among whites, but separated, widowed, and single (never married) all are important marital statuses as well. Single or never-married women are very common for both blacks and Hispanics among those who head family households with no spouse present. Single female family householders are much less common among whites. Female no-spouse family households are also the fastest growing of all female headed households. Single female households increased by 103.5 percent among whites, 129.2 percent among blacks and 172.2 percent among Hispanics between 1980 and 1992.

Although male no-spouse family households comprise a small fraction of all households, they are unique in that for all race-ethnic groups, singlehood is a dominant marital status for the head of a no-spouse family. Nearly a third of white, just over a third of black, and nearly half of Hispanic no spouse present male headed families are single men. The extent to which this reflects unmarried sons or other single men maintaining a home for a parent or other relative and how much it represents fathers taking care of their children without having a spouse present is difficult to determine. Among male no-spouse families the fastest increase among whites and Hispanics has been in the divorced, while among blacks the single or never married have increased most rapidly. Starting from a much lower level of males living without a spouse in 1980, Hispanics have seen the greatest percentage increase in such households over the past twelve years.

Among female non-family householders, nearly half of white women, and roughly a third of black or Hispanic women, are widowed. Only among Hispanics is there a greater percentage of these women who are single rather than widowed. Male non-family householders are predominantly single (never married) for each of the major race/ethnic groups. However, for both sexes a substantial proportion of the non-family householders have suffered separation or divorce.

Between 1980 and 1992, divorced continued to become a more prevalent marital status for white and black householders, while the single and married with spouse absent became more common among Hispanics. The most rapidly increasing household type between 1980 and 1992 was, in fact, never-married Hispanic family households.

Children in Families

Less than one-half of all married-couple families contained a child under eighteen years of age in 1992 (Table 11-11). Lower fertility, baby boom cohorts aging out of the life course stage where children still reside at home, and longevity all combine to produce this result. By postponing childbearing or remaining childless, many couples of reproductive age reside in childless households. By surviving to an advanced age where all children have reached their eighteenth birthday and/or have left home, many older couples have "empty nest" families.

Families headed by a female without a spouse are much more likely to contain children. As has just been shown, many of these families are headed by women who had children out of marriage or have been divorced or separated, and a high percentage are still in the reproductive years. In a high proportion of cases such households constitute a family precisely because children are present. Families headed by a male without a spouse are still much less likely to contain children than those headed by females.

Where households do contain children, a large proportion contain only one or two children. Only ten percent of married-couple families contained three or more children in 1992. As would be expected from fertility patterns, female no-spouse families and Hispanic married couples are much more likely to contain children. Hispanic married couples are more than twice as likely as whites to contain three or more children. The likelihood that black married couples have children falls midway between that of whites and Hispanics. However, among female household families blacks are almost as likely as Hispanics to have children.

Families with a male head but no spouse present are a little more likely to contain children if the householder is white, and least likely if the householder is black. Where children are present in male family households with no spouse there tend to be fewer children; three or more children in such families is extremely rare.

Table 11-7. Age Composition of Family Householders, by Type of Family and Race-ethnicity: 1980 and 1992, and Percent Change 1980-1992 [percent distribution]

Age of householder	Married couple households				Female householder families				Male householder families			
	Total	White	Black	Hispanic	Total	White	Black	Hispanic	Total	White	Black	Hispanic
Total, 1992	100.0	100.0	100.0	100.0	100.0	100.0	100.0	100.0	100.0	100.0	100.0	100.0
Under 20 years	0.1	0.1	0.1	0.7	1.0	0.9	1.4	1.0	1.1	1.1	1.2	1.8
20-24 years	2.7	2.7	2.6	5.6	6.8	5.9	8.9	7.9	7.5	7.8	3.8	13.1
25-29 years	8.0	8.0	9.5	12.5	11.0	9.9	13.6	11.6	12.2	11.5	13.9	15.1
30-34 years	12.4	12.3	12.4	17.3	14.4	13.7	16.2	16.7	11.7	12.0	10.1	15.9
35-39 years	13.0	12.9	13.1	14.2	14.5	14.0	15.2	15.5	12.8	13.0	13.5	13.1
40-44 years	12.8	12.5	15.4	13.7	13.1	13.7	11.6	12.2	13.1	13.5	11.7	9.7
45-54 years	18.7	18.7	17.7	15.8	15.7	16.5	13.9	17.0	17.3	18.0	13.9	15.9
55-64 years	14.8	14.9	14.3	11.8	10.3	10.5	9.7	10.0	11.1	10.4	14.9	9.1
65-74 years	12.0	12.2	11.0	6.0	7.0	7.8	5.7	5.0	7.9	7.7	9.9	3.9
75 years and over	5.6	5.8	3.8	2.4	6.2	7.3	4.0	3.1	5.3	5.1	6.9	2.3
Median age	45.5	45.8	44	39.9	40.9	42.1	38.3	39.1	41.8	41.7	43.2	36.6
Total, 1980	100.0	100.0	100.0	100.0	100.0	100.0	100.0	100.0	100.0	100.0	100.0	100.0
Under 20 years	0.4	0.4	0.3	0.7	1.1	1.0	1.5	2.7	1.1	1.2	0.0	0.8
20-24 years	5.5	5.5	5.5	8.6	7.2	6.0	10.3	10.8	9.6	9.0	12.1	15.0
25-29 years	10.9	10.8	12.3	15.6	12.0	10.4	15.7	16.2	8.7	8.3	8.9	16.5
30-34 years	12.5	12.3	12.5	16.1	13.7	13.0	15.8	15.2	8.4	8.7	7.8	11.3
35-39 years	11.2	11.1	11.4	12.6	12.3	12.1	12.8	11.8	9.8	9.8	10.5	9.8
40-44 years	9.4	9.3	9.7	12.2	10.2	10.2	10.4	13.8	10.8	11.3	8.6	6.8
45-54 years	18.5	18.5	18.6	17.4	17.2	17.9	15.0	16.3	18.2	18.1	18.3	19.5
55-64 years	16.7	16.9	14.5	9.7	11.7	12.8	8.9	9.1	15.6	15.9	15.6	6.8
65-74 years	10.7	10.7	11.5	5.0	8.0	8.9	6.0	2.9	10.8	10.4	13.6	6.8
75 years and over	4.4	4.4	3.6	2.1	6.5	7.8	3.6	1.3	7.0	7.4	5.4	6.8
Percent Change 1980-1992												
Under 20 years	-61.5	-62.5	-81.8	50.0	26.6	19.3	36.1	-18.8	78.9	52.9	...	600.0
20-24 years	-47.1	-47.7	-48.4	-2.9	27.8	26.6	26.7	56.3	39.3	46.5	-38.7	150.0
25-29 years	-19.9	-20.8	-16.5	19.1	25.9	23.3	27.8	52.1	148.6	130.5	204.3	163.6
30-34 years	8.0	6.5	7.6	60.1	43.1	36.3	51.4	134.4	147.6	131.7	155.0	306.7
35-39 years	26.8	24.3	24.1	67.0	61.4	50.6	75.5	178.6	129.8	121.6	151.9	284.6
40-44 years	48.7	43.6	70.9	67.8	75.4	73.8	64.7	87.8	114.6	100.6	168.2	311.1
45-54 years	10.1	8.1	3.4	34.9	25.0	19.0	36.5	121.6	68.7	66.8	48.9	134.6
55-64 years	-3.4	-5.8	7.0	80.5	20.3	6.0	59.4	133.3	25.9	9.3	87.5	288.9
65-74 years	21.7	22.0	3.9	80.5	20.1	13.2	39.0	270.6	29.9	23.0	42.9	66.7
75 years and over	39.1	39.6	14.9	66.7	30.5	21.8	62.5	387.5	34.2	15.2	150.0	0.0

Source: U.S. Bureau of the Census, "Household and Family Characteristics," Current Population Reports, Series P-20, nos. 467 and 366, U.S. Government Printing Office, Washington, D.C., 1992 and 1981, Tables 17 and 22.

Table 11-8. Age Composition of Nonfamily Householders, by Sex and Race-ethnicity: 1980 and 1992, and Percent Change 1980-92 [percent distribution]

Age	Male householder				Female householder			
	Total	White	Black	Hispanic	Total	White	Black	Hispanic
Total 1992	100.0	100.0	100.0	100.0	100.0	100.0	100.0	100.0
Under 20 years	0.8	0.7	1.0	0.9	0.7	0.7	0.7	1.1
20-24 years	9.1	9.5	5.0	15.3	5.5	5.4	5.9	9.6
25-29 years	14.4	14.8	11.4	12.7	7.3	7.4	6.8	10.3
30-34 years	13.6	13.3	14.4	16.5	6.2	5.7	8.2	8.1
35-39 years	11.6	11.9	9.8	12.7	5.1	4.9	6.5	7.6
40-44 years	9.6	9.7	9.2	10.6	4.9	4.7	5.5	4.2
45-54 years	13.2	13.2	14.9	13.2	10.7	10.1	15.1	10.9
55-64 years	10.1	9.6	13.0	10.2	12.5	12.1	15.1	15.3
65-75 years	9.5	8.8	14.4	4.5	22.0	22.3	20.5	17.7
75 years and over	8.1	8.5	6.8	3.2	25.3	26.8	15.6	15.3
Median age	40.3	39.9	44.6	36.8	63.1	64.4	55.9	52.9
Total 1980	100.0	100.0	100.0	100.0	100.0	100.0	100.0	100.0
Under 20 years	2.2	2.5	0.7	6.3	1.4	1.4	1.1	2.9
20-24 years	15.5	16.3	10.1	16.5	8.1	8.0	9.2	9.0
25-29 years	17.8	18.2	15.5	18.8	8.1	8.0	7.9	10.4
30-34 years	12.6	12.4	13.6	11.7	4.7	4.6	4.4	7.2
35-39 years	8.0	8.0	8.1	8.8	2.7	2.5	3.8	4.7
40-44 years	5.3	5.1	6.6	5.1	2.3	2.1	3.7	4.7
45-54 years	10.7	10.1	15.0	12.8	7.9	7.0	14.2	15.1
55-64 years	10.2	9.6	14.4	7.7	16.6	16.3	19.7	17.9
65-75 years	9.5	9.5	9.6	8.8	25.7	26.2	21.7	21.1
75 years and over	8.1	8.4	6.3	3.7	22.7	23.8	14.3	7.9
Percent Change 1980-1992								
Under 20 years	-49.7	-58.3	100.0	-72.7	-37.3	-40.3	-7.1	-25.0
20-24 years	-14.6	-16.9	-30.4	74.1	-10.4	-12.1	-7.1	108.0
25-29 years	16.5	16.3	2.3	27.3	19.6	19.4	26.0	93.1
30-34 years	55.9	52.9	47.4	165.9	74.1	61.0	168.5	120.0
35-39 years	110.3	113.9	67.7	171.0	154.2	152.4	150.0	215.4
40-44 years	160.5	168.4	96.0	288.9	183.3	194.2	117.8	76.9
45-54 years	78.2	87.4	38.4	93.3	80.7	85.6	54.9	40.5
55-64 years	43.1	43.7	26.1	148.1	0.3	-3.5	11.7	66.0
65-75 years	44.4	33.1	108.2	-3.2	14.0	10.5	37.0	62.7
75 years and over	44.5	45.3	51.4	61.5	48.3	46.8	59.2	277.3

Source: U.S. Bureau of the Census, "Household and Family Characteristics," Current Population Reports, Series P-20, nos. 467 and 366, U.S. Government Printing Office, Washington, D.C., 1992 and 1981, Tables 17 and 22.

Table 11-9. Householder Rates[1] by Type of Household, Sex, Age, and Race-ethnicity of Householder: 1990

Age, sex, and race-ethnicity	Total number of householders	Family households		Nonfamily households	
		Married couple	No spouse	Live alone	Multiperson
White males					
Total	53,761,843	424.1	23.3	78.7	25.4
15 to 19 years	1,188,493	8.6	3.6	6.7	8.7
20 to 24 years	2,262,048	145.0	22.0	67.7	71.4
25 to 29 years	5,232,406	406.9	30.7	118.7	67.7
30 to 34 years	6,611,410	565.5	31.8	118.5	44.2
35 to 44 years	12,776,488	661.9	37.9	106.9	29.4
45 to 54 years	9,137,008	724.9	38.9	93.6	21.7
55 to 59 years	3,873,654	754.0	30.4	93.4	16.5
60 to 64 years	3,897,423	754.9	27.9	102.2	14.2
65 to 74 years	6,356,824	740.9	26.0	120.8	11.5
75 years and over	3,426,089	592.7	31.7	191.3	10.7
Black males					
Total	4,899,584	209.4	37.0	80.5	18.8
15 to 19 years	23,066	2.8	5.6	5.1	3.6
20 to 24 years	226,780	64.1	31.5	52.7	31.8
25 to 29 years	496,688	197.9	47.8	102.6	37.9
30 to 34 years	632,624	301.3	54.1	118.3	32.0
35 to 44 years	1,224,578	405.3	65.3	129.4	28.3
45 to 54 years	858,345	484.8	71.7	146.7	27.9
55 to 59 years	353,976	516.6	69.6	161.5	26.9
60 to 64 years	326,158	505.6	72.0	183.9	26.2
65 to 74 years	497,590	497.1	75.1	208.6	24.3
75 years and over	259,779	401.0	82.5	242.3	20.6
Hispanic males					
Total	4,132,072	266.6	37.7	39.1	19.4
15 to 19 years	30,700	8.3	9.0	4.4	6.7
20 to 24 years	303,050	123.8	49.2	29.7	37.4
25 to 29 years	599,722	322.4	63.7	52.6	41.1
30 to 34 years	662,600	460.3	62.8	60.2	33.6
35 to 44 years	1,058,946	555.0	65.3	65.0	27.3
45 to 54 years	644,855	613.4	66.2	71.8	23.7
55 to 59 years	244,210	646.0	58.0	83.5	21.2
60 to 64 years	208,548	645.3	54.7	98.6	19.2
65 to 74 years	257,502	625.0	52.4	123.3	16.8
75 years and over	121,939	492.0	60.8	166.0	15.8

Table 11-9. Householder Rates¹ by Type of Household, Sex, Age, and Race-ethnicity of Householder: 1990 (continued)

Age, sex, and race-ethnicity	Total number of householders	Family households		Nonfamily households	
		Married couple	No spouse	Live alone	Multiperson
White females					
Total	23,118,262	424.1	23.3	78.7	25.4
15 to 19 years	186,075	3.1	8.2	7.1	10.2
20 to 24 years	1,322,202	25.4	48.8	54.5	56.6
25 to 29 years	2,003,677	48.9	77.5	78.6	37.8
30 to 34 years	2,109,232	52.9	97.1	72.0	21.8
35 to 44 years	3,874,027	48.7	119.0	69.8	15.6
45 to 54 years	2,757,411	44.1	103.9	95.2	14.6
55 to 59 years	1,270,697	40.0	85.1	137.1	11.7
60 to 64 years	1,548,675	36.3	80.4	190.4	10.5
65 to 74 years	3,828,613	31.3	75.6	311.0	9.6
75 years and over	4,217,653	15.2	68.8	455.5	9.7
Black females					
Total	5,076,577	28.0	192.9	88.2	11.8
15 to 19 years	51,025	1.7	27.2	5.7	4.2
20 to 24 years	359,732	20.6	180.3	47.7	23.9
25 to 29 years	590,521	42.1	276.8	76.0	20.4
30 to 34 years	675,911	50.7	335.1	72.3	14.2
35 to 44 years	1,138,933	52.0	358.5	79.6	13.0
45 to 54 years	723,155	51.3	321.6	123.8	16.1
55 to 59 years	301,668	46.1	291.3	170.4	15.9
60 to 64 years	301,016	41.2	268.8	223.0	17.4
65 to 74 years	536,104	34.4	233.9	317.7	19.1
75 years and over	398,512	17.5	179.1	391.6	18.4
Hispanic females					
Total	1,869,646	23.9	96.9	40.4	9.4
15 to 19 years	27,601	4.7	15.5	3.5	4.8
20 to 24 years	158,679	27.9	82.0	21.1	21.2
25 to 29 years	240,827	43.8	127.6	31.5	17.8
30 to 34 years	251,809	47.0	164.3	31.0	12.6
35 to 44 years	421,232	45.3	199.9	32.8	10.8
45 to 54 years	267,213	40.5	194.6	56.7	12.5
55 to 59 years	105,490	32.8	171.6	95.9	12.6
60 to 64 years	100,961	28.5	159.5	137.1	12.5
65 to 74 years	167,209	23.1	144.9	228.7	13.2
75 years and over	128,625	11.8	122.4	324.4	14.3

¹ Rates were calculated by dividing the number of age, race, and sex-specific householders of each type by the total age, race, and sex-specific population. Rates are expressed per 1,000 population.

Source: U.S. Bureau of the Census, "General Population Characteristics," CP-1-1, U.S. Government Printing Office, Washington, D.C., 1992, Tables 28, 29, and 32. Statistical Abstract of the United States, U.S. Government Printing Office, Washington, D.C., 1992, Table 18.

Table 11-10. Marital Status of Householders, by Type of Household and Race-ethnicity: 1980 and 1992, and Percent Change 1980-1992 [percent distribution]

| Year and marital status | All households | No spouse families | | Nonfamily households | |
| | | Householder | | Householder | |
		Male	Female	Male	Female
All householders					
Total 1992	100.0	100.0	100.0	100.0	100.0
Married, spouse present	54.8	—	—	—	—
Married, spouse absent	4.8	15.1	17.5	9.9	5.2
Separated	3.8	11.2	15.0	7.2	3.9
Other reasons	1.0	3.9	2.5	2.8	1.2
Widowed	12.4	15.9	21.0	12.5	46.1
Divorced	12.8	34.8	36.6	28.5	21.2
Single (never married)	15.1	34.2	24.8	49.1	27.6
Total 1980	100.0	100.0	100.0	100.0	100.0
Married, spouse present	60.9	—	—	—	—
Married, spouse absent	4.7	15.6	20.3	12.0	5.4
Separated	3.7	12.3	17.5	9.0	3.8
Other reasons	0.9	3.3	2.8	2.9	1.6
Widowed	13.2	24.0	29.5	13.3	52.9
Divorced	9.4	28.0	34.7	25.1	15.1
Single (never married)	11.8	32.4	15.6	49.6	26.6
Percent Change 1980-92					
Married, spouse present	8.9	—	—	—	—
Married, spouse absent	24.0	72.2	18.2	19.9	26.0
Separated	23.0	62.2	17.6	14.4	36.9
Other reasons	27.9	107.0	21.8	37.2	0.0
Widowed	13.7	17.1	-2.4	36.1	15.8
Divorced	65.6	120.1	44.7	64.1	86.9
Single (never married)	54.5	87.5	118.4	43.0	37.8
White householders					
Total 1992	100.0	100.0	100.0	100.0	100.0
Married, spouse present	57.7	—	—	—	—
Married, spouse absent	3.8	13.6	17.0	8.4	4.2
Separated	2.9	10.2	14.5	5.9	3.1
Other reasons	0.9	3.5	2.5	2.5	1.2
Widowed	12.4	15.1	23.0	12.4	47.9
Divorced	12.6	39.0	43.2	29.3	21.0
Single (never married)	13.5	32.2	16.7	49.9	26.8
Total 1980	100.0	100.0	100.0	100.0	100.0
Married, spouse present	63.4	—	—	—	—
Married, spouse absent	3.5	14.5	16.9	10.0	4.4
Separated	2.6	11.0	13.9	7.3	2.8
Other reasons	1.7	7.1	6.0	5.4	3.2
Widowed	13.1	23.6	32.5	13.5	54.3
Divorced	9.0	29.3	39.9	25.7	14.9
Single (never married)	11.0	32.6	10.7	50.7	26.5
Percent Change 1980-92					
Married, spouse present	7.1	—	—	—	—
Married, spouse absent	28.5	57.3	30.5	19.6	25.5
Separated	32.3	54.5	35.4	14.9	43.1
Other reasons	-41.4	-17.0	-46.1	-33.9	-52.6
Widowed	11.4	6.9	-8.4	31.6	14.7
Divorced	63.7	123.4	40.3	62.8	84.3
Single (never married)	44.2	65.4	103.5	40.8	31.9

Table 11-10. Marital Status of Householders, by Type of Household and Race-ethnicity: 1980 and 1992, and Percent Change 1980-1992 [percent distribution] (continued)

Year and marital status	All households	No spouse families		Nonfamily households	
		Householder		Householder	
		Male	Female	Male	Female
Black householders					
Total 1992	100.0	100.0	100.0	100.0	100.0
Married, spouse present	32.8	—	—	—	—
Married, spouse absent	11.5	20.4	18.8	17.8	12.1
Separated	10.3	17.5	17.1	15.5	10.8
Other reasons	1.2	3.0	1.7	2.4	1.2
Widowed	13.8	20.6	16.3	14.1	34.6
Divorced	15.5	20.2	22.6	26.5	21.8
Single (never married)	26.4	38.9	42.3	41.5	31.5
Total 1980	100.0	100.0	100.0	100.0	100.0
Married, spouse present	39.9	—	—	—	—
Married, spouse absent	14.2	21.8	28.7	23.4	14.3
Separated	13.0	19.8	26.8	20.3	13.0
Other reasons	2.4	3.9	3.7	6.3	2.4
Widowed	15.1	26.8	22.2	12.1	43.1
Divorced	12.4	22.2	21.9	21.9	16.7
Single (never married)	18.3	29.6	27.2	42.6	25.9
Percent Change 1980-92					
Married, spouse present	8.2	—	—	—	—
Married, spouse absent	6.6	83.9	-3.4	6.0	23.0
Separated	4.0	72.5	-6.1	6.5	20.8
Other reasons	-33.0	50.0	-33.3	-47.2	-24.1
Widowed	20.1	50.7	8.5	62.3	16.5
Divorced	64.8	78.9	51.8	69.2	89.7
Single (never married)	90.3	157.9	129.2	35.9	76.6
Hispanic householders					
Total 1992	100.0	100.0	100.0	100.0	100.0
Married, spouse present	55.4	—	—	—	—
Married, spouse absent	9.0	21.4	25.8	17.4	9.6
Separated	6.6	9.4	21.7	9.7	8.1
Other reasons	2.4	12.0	4.0	7.7	1.5
Widowed	7.0	10.4	15.5	4.8	32.5
Divorced	11.1	23.8	30.0	20.8	19.2
Single (never married)	17.5	44.4	28.7	57.0	38.7
Total 1980	100.0	100.0	100.0	100.0	100.0
Married, spouse present	63.6	—	—	—	—
Married, spouse absent	8.7	24.8	32.5	21.1	9.3
Separated	6.7	13.5	28.8	12.3	6.8
Other reasons	4.0	24.1	7.4	17.7	4.3
Widowed	6.1	14.3	15.0	6.6	34.4
Divorced	8.9	15.0	30.1	21.1	21.5
Single (never married)	12.7	45.9	22.4	51.6	34.8
Percent Change 1980-92					
Married, spouse present	48.8	—	—	—	—
Married, spouse absent	76.9	148.5	68.4	55.4	100.0
Separated	66.5	100.0	60.2	48.8	131.6
Other reasons	4.7	43.8	15.9	-17.7	-33.3
Widowed	95.6	110.5	120.2	39.1	83.3
Divorced	114.2	355.0	111.2	85.1	73.3
Single (never married)	136.9	178.7	172.2	107.7	116.5

Source: U. S. Bureau of the Census, "Household and Family Characteristics," Current Population Reports, Series P-20, nos. 467 and 366, U.S. Government Printing Office, Washington, D.C., 1992 and 1981, Tables 16 and 21.

Table 11-11. Number of Own Children Under 18 Years of Age, by Type of Family and Race-ethnicity: 1992 and Percent Change 1980-1992 [percent distribution]

Number of own children under 18	Married couple families				Male household families				Female household families			
	Total	White	Black	Hispanic	Total	White	Black	Hispanic	Total	White	Black	Hispanic
1992												
Total	100.0	100.0	100.0	100.0	100.0	100.0	100.0	100.0	100.0	100.0	100.0	100.0
No own children under 18	53.4	54.3	47.0	34.3	57.6	56.2	63.5	58.7	39.8	41.9	34.8	32.4
With own children under 18	46.6	45.7	53.0	65.7	42.4	43.8	36.5	41.5	60.2	58.1	65.2	67.6
1 own child under 18	18.1	17.7	21.3	21.3	25.4	26.2	22.6	20.4	28.5	28.8	27.6	26.0
2 own children under 18	18.5	18.4	18.9	23.1	12.9	13.6	10.3	14.9	19.2	19.2	19.3	21.0
3 own children under 18	7.2	7.0	9.1	13.6	3.3	3.2	2.6	4.4	8.4	7.2	11.0	12.4
4 own children under 18	2.0	1.9	2.6	5.1	0.6	0.5	1.0	1.0	2.8	2.0	4.8	4.7
5 own children under 18	0.5	0.5	0.9	1.8	0.2	0.2	0.2	0.8	0.8	0.6	1.2	2.3
6+ own children under 18	0.2	0.2	0.4	0.7	...	...	...	...	0.6	0.4	1.1	1.2
Percent change 1980-1992												
No own children under 18	18.7	17.2	15.9	67.6	59.7	44.5	106.5	129.6	45.3	32.2	82.3	177.6
With own children under 18	-0.6	-2.9	2.2	40.6	110.7	110.5	80.4	341.7	31.9	27.7	33.8	91.3
1 own child under 18	0.1	-2.9	8.7	45.8	107.0	110.5	62.9	387.5	41.3	32.6	54.7	95.2
2 own children under 18	4.2	1.7	9.4	42.6	141.4	143.6	136.4	533.3	25.9	24.8	22.5	96.3
3 own children under 18	-2.1	-3.1	-1.2	51.7	59.7	43.4	44.4	112.5	36.5	25.1	47.9	73.3
4 own children under 18	-19.3	-19.7	-30.7	27.5	80.0	33.3	—	300.0	1.6	-4.4	8.2	59.5
5 own children under 18	-36.1	-37.7	-31.3	-1.5	-100.0	150.0	—	50.0	-11.3	27.8	-35.3	123.1
6+ own children under 18	-40.0	-43.0	-50.0	-34.3	-100.0	-100.0	—	—	20.0	163.6	-10.9	400.0

Source: U.S. Bureau of the Census, "Household and Family Characteristics," Current Population Reports, Series P-20, nos. 467 and 366, U.S. Government Printing Office, Washington, D.C., 1992 and 1981, Table 2.

Table 11-12. Living Arrangements of Children under 18 Years of Age[1], by Race-ethnicity: 1970, 1980, and 1992 [numbers in thousands]

Living arrangements	Number of children			Percent distribution		
	1992	1980	1970	1992	1980	1970
All Races						
Total	65,965	63,427	69,162	100.0	100.0	100.0
Living with:						
Two parents	46,638	48,624	58,939	70.7	76.7	85.2
One parent	17,578	12,466	8,199	26.6	19.7	11.9
Mother only	15,396	11,406	7,452	23.3	18.0	10.8
Father only	2,182	1,060	748	3.3	1.7	1.1
Other relatives	1,334	1,949	1,547	2.0	3.1	2.2
Nonrelatives only	415	388	477	0.6	0.6	0.7
White						
Total	52,493	52,242	58,790	100.0	100.0	100.0
Living with:						
Two parents	40,635	43,200	52,624	77.4	82.7	89.5
One parent	10,971	7,901	5,109	20.9	15.1	8.7
Mother only	9,250	7,059	4,581	17.6	13.5	7.8
Father only	1,721	842	528	3.3	1.6	0.9
Other relatives	643	887	696	1.2	1.7	1.2
Nonrelatives only	243	254	362	0.5	0.5	0.6
Black						
Total	10,427	9,375	9,422	100.0	100.0	100.0
Living with:						
Two parents	3,714	3,956	5,508	35.6	42.2	58.5
One parent	5,934	4,297	2,996	56.9	45.8	31.8
Mother only	5,607	4,117	2,783	53.8	43.9	29.5
Father only	327	180	213	3.1	1.9	2.3
Other relatives	625	999	820	6.0	10.7	8.7
Nonrelatives only	154	123	97	1.5	1.3	1.0
Hispanic						
Total	7,619	5,459	4,006[2]	100.0	100.0	100.0
Living with:						
Two parents	4,935	4,116	3,111	64.8	75.4	77.7
One parent	2,447	1,152	—	32.1	21.1	—
Mother only	2,168	1,069	—	28.5	19.6	—
Father only	279	83	—	3.7	1.5	—
Other relatives	196	183	—	2.6	3.4	—
Nonrelatives only	41	8	—	0.5	0.1	—

[1] Excludes persons under 18 years old who were maintaining household or family groups.
[2] All persons under 18 years.

Source: U.S. Bureau of the Census, "Marital Status and Living Arrangements," Current Population Reports, Series P-20, no. 468, U.S. Government Printing Office, Washington, D.C., 1992. Source of Hispanic data for 1970: 1970 Census of Population, PC(2)-1C, U.S. Government Printing Office, Washington, D.C, 1970.

The trend since 1980 is toward an increase in child-less families and a reduction in large numbers of children present in families. However, there has been a high rate of increase in the number of one-parent families because of higher divorce and separation rates. Among these families the most dramatic percentage increase is in male households with children present; children living in male households has become somewhat less uncommon over the past decade. And, starting from a low base in 1980, the most rapid increases in male family households without a spouse present have been, over the past twelve years, among Hispanic men.

Living Arrangements of Children

Because of declining fertility, there was an absolute decline between 1970 and 1980 in number of children under eighteen living in households. However, between 1980 and 1992 the children of the baby boom had their own children. With higher fertility among blacks and Hispanics this led to a slight resurgence, or at the least a leveling, in the absolute number of children under eighteen living in households.

Table 11-12 provides summary information about the living arrangements of children. The increase in children living with parents has been entirely among those living with one parent as those living with two parents have continued to decline in absolute number. Only Hispanics have seen an increase in the number of children living with two parents between 1980 and 1992. Even among this group the percentage of children living with two parents declined over the same twelve years. For all groups, increasing childbearing out of marriage and divorce have led to a rise in the proportions of children living with one parent, primarily the mother. However, as mentioned above, the greatest proportionate increase (nearly doubling from 1.7 percent to 3.3 percent) has been in children living only with fathers.

Detailed information about the living arrangements of children, by race-ethnicity, for 1992 and 1980 are provided in Table 11-13. Less than one-half of black children live with both parents and over half of black children live with their mother only. Overall, younger chil-

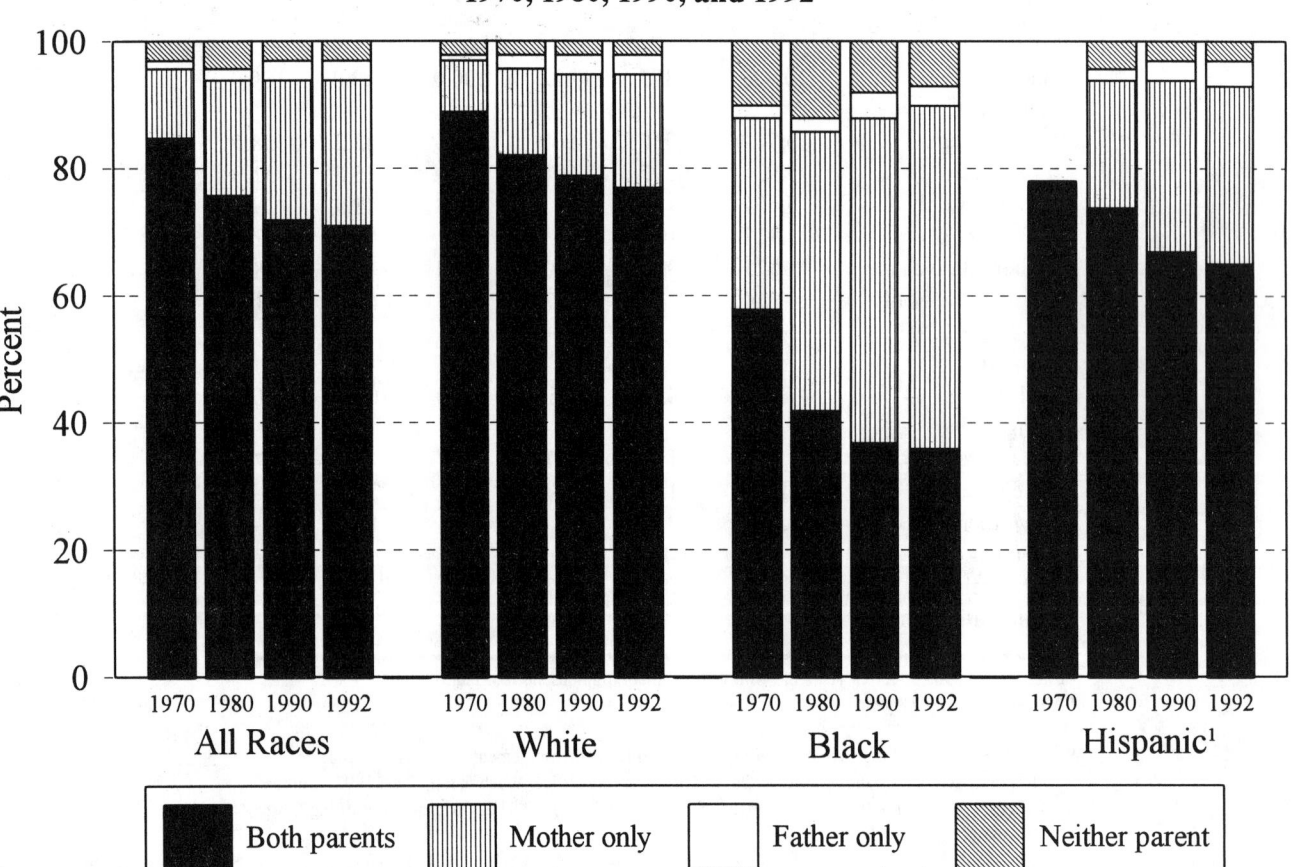

Figure 11-5. Children Under 18 Years of Age, by Presence of Parents: 1970, 1980, 1990, and 1992

¹ Hispanic data not available for 1970.

Source: 1970, 1980, and 1990 Census data and March 1992 unadjusted CPS data.

Table 11-13. Living Arrangements of Children under 18 Years of Age[1], by Age and Race-ethnicity: 1980 and 1992 [percent distribution]

Living arrangements	Total under 18 years	Under 3 years	3 to 5 years	6 to 9 years	10 to 14 years	15 to 17 years
All Races 1992	100.0	100.0	100.0	100.0	100.0	100.0
Living with:						
Two parents	70.7	71.5	71.6	71.1	70.7	68.1
One parent	26.6	27.1	26.5	26.6	26.6	26.5
Mother only	23.3	23.6	23.4	23.8	23.1	22.7
Father only	3.3	3.5	3.1	2.8	3.5	3.7
Neither parent	2.6	1.4	1.9	2.3	2.7	5.4
All Races 1980	100.0	100.0	100.0	100.0	100.0	100.0
Living with:						
Two parents	76.6	80.2	77.2	76.7	76.0	73.8
One parent	19.7	14.5	18.8	20.4	21.1	21.8
Mother only	18.0	13.4	17.7	19.3	19.1	19.1
Father only	1.7	1.1	1.1	1.1	2.0	2.7
Neither parent	3.7	5.3	4.0	2.9	2.9	4.4
White 1992	100.0	100.0	100.0	100.0	100.0	100.0
Living with:						
Two parents	77.4	79.2	79.0	77.5	77.0	74.0
One parent	20.9	20.1	19.9	21.2	21.2	22.1
Mother only	17.6	16.4	17.2	18.3	17.7	18.3
Father only	3.3	3.6	2.7	2.8	3.5	3.7
Neither parent	1.7	0.7	1.1	1.4	1.8	3.9
White 1980	100.0	100.0	100.0	100.0	100.0	100.0
Living with:						
Two parents	82.7	87.3	83.9	82.8	81.7	79.6
One parent	15.1	10.2	13.9	15.6	16.5	17.1
Mother only	13.5	9.2	13.0	14.5	14.6	14.4
Father only	1.6	1.0	0.9	1.1	1.9	2.7
Neither parent	2.2	2.4	2.2	1.6	1.7	3.3

dren are more likely to live with both parents as one might expect from the fact that risks of separation and mortality would cumulate with the aging of a couple's children. However, for blacks the very youngest children are slightly less likely to live in two-parent families. It is possible that this difference is an artifact of increasing single parenthood in more recent black cohorts or higher rates of childbearing out of marriage followed later by marriage at an older age. Figure 11-5 illustrates these differences and changes over time. In all groups the proportion of children under 18 years of age living with a mother only has significantly increased since 1970. This increase over time was greatest among blacks who also had the highest, but a decreasing, percentage of children living with neither parent.

Information about living arrangements of children who live with one parent only is provided in Table 11-14, by race-ethnicity and age of child, and marital status/parent, with comparable data for 1980 to show change. The very great increase in the proportion of children living in a one-parent household where the parent has never married is extraordinary, not only for the black population but for Hispanics and whites as well. By 1992, over half of the white children under three years of age and living with only one parent were living with a mother or father who had never married. This had doubled from the percentage of young white children living with never-married parents in 1980. Over half of Hispanic and three-fourths of black children under three and living with only one parent lived with a never-married mother or father.

Table 11-13. Living Arrangements of Children under 18 Years of Age[1], by Age and Race-ethnicity: 1980 and 1992 [percent distribution] (continued)

Living arrangements	Total under 18 years	Under 3 years	3 to 5 years	6 to 9 years	10 to 14 years	15 to 17 years
Black 1992	100.0	100.0	100.0	100.0	100.0	100.0
Living with:						
Two parents	35.6	31.4	32.3	37.2	38.4	37.5
One parent	56.9	63.7	61.6	55.2	53.9	51.0
Mother only	53.8	60.8	57.2	52.8	50.9	47.7
Father only	3.1	2.9	4.3	2.5	3.0	3.3
Neither parent	7.5	4.9	6.2	7.6	7.8	11.5
Black 1980	100.0	100.0	100.0	100.0	100.0	100.0
Living with:						
Two parents	42.2	41.1	41.3	43.0	43.8	40.2
One parent	45.8	37.9	44.8	47.1	47.2	49.7
Mother only	43.8	36.1	42.8	46.3	44.9	46.8
Father only	2.0	1.8	2.0	0.8	2.3	2.9
Neither parent	12.1	21.0	14.0	9.9	8.9	10.1
Hispanic 1992	100.0	100.0	100.0	100.0	100.0	100.0
Living with:						
Two parents	64.8	66.5	66.7	66.1	64.7	57.7
One parent	32.1	31.9	31.4	31.5	31.8	35.0
Mother only	28.5	27.5	28.1	28.3	28.1	31.1
Father only	3.7	4.3	3.3	3.2	3.7	3.9
Neither parent	3.1	1.7	1.9	2.4	3.4	7.3
Hispanic 1980	100.0	100.0	100.0	100.0	100.0	100.0
Living with:						
Two parents	76.1	78.5	78.0	78.8	74.5	69.5
One parent	20.5	17.4	19.4	19.1	23.0	23.4
Mother only	19.0	16.6	18.3	18.6	20.6	20.9
Father only	1.5	0.8	1.1	0.5	2.4	2.5
Neither parent	3.4	4.1	2.6	2.2	2.5	7.0

[1] Excludes persons under 18 years who were maintaining household or family groups.

Source: U.S. Bureau of the Census, "Marital Status and Living Arrangements," Current Population Reports, Series P-20, nos. 468 and 365, U.S. Government Printing Office, Washington, D.C., 1992 and 1981, Table 4.

Table 11-14. Presence and Marital Status of Parent for Persons under 18 Years of Age Living with Only One Parent, by Age and Race-ethnicity: 1980 and 1992 [percent distribution]

Marital Status	Total under 18 years[1]	Under 3 years	3 to 5 years	6 to 9 years	10 to 14 years	15 to 17 years
All races 1992	100.0	100.0	100.0	100.0	100.0	100.0
Living with mother only	87.6	87.0	88.4	89.5	86.9	85.9
Single (never married)	30.8	54.1	38.7	30.3	19.5	14.1
Married, spouse absent	21.6	18.2	23.8	22.5	22.6	19.9
Widowed/divorced	35.2	14.7	26.0	36.7	44.8	52.0
Living with father only	12.4	13.1	11.6	10.5	13.1	14.1
Single (never married)	3.4	8.4	5.2	2.0	1.6	0.5
Married, spouse absent	2.8	1.7	1.8	3.3	3.5	3.4
Widowed/divorced	6.2	3.0	4.6	5.3	8.1	10.2
All races 1980	100.0	100.0	100.0	100.0	100.0	100.0
Living with mother only	91.5	92.2	94.3	94.7	90.4	87.6
Single (never married)	14.2	33.6	22.9	114.7	9.4	3.9
Married, spouse absent	28.9	34.5	31.2	29.9	27.8	25
Widowed/divorced	48.5	24.0	8.4	10.3	15.5	21.5
Living with father only	8.5	7.8	5.7	5.3	9.6	12.4
Single (never married)	0.6	3.2	1.1	0.1	0.2	0.1
Married, spouse absent	2.3	2.3	1.5	1.4	3.1	2.6
Widowed/divorced	5.5	2.3	3.1	3.8	6.3	9.7
White 1992	100.0	100.0	100.0	100.0	100.0	100.0
Living with mother only	84.3	81.9	86.2	86.6	83.5	83.1
Single (never married)	18.4	40.9	24.2	17.1	9.0	6.2
Married, spouse absent	22.5	22.4	26.3	23.5	21.9	18.1
Widowed/divorced	43.5	18.6	35.7	46.1	52.6	58.9
Living with father only	15.7	18.1	13.8	13.4	16.5	16.9
Single (never married)	3.9	11.2	5.7	2.3	1.5	0.7
Married, spouse absent	3.4	2.3	2.6	4.0	4.2	3.1
Widowed/divorced	8.4	4.5	5.5	7.1	10.8	13.1
White 1980	100.0	100.0	100.0	100.0	100.0	100.0
Living with mother only	89.3	90.3	93.5	92.9	88.3	84.3
Single (never married)	6.5	22.3	9.7	6.4	3.4	1.5
Married, spouse absent	25.5	36.9	31.7	26.2	24.2	17.5
Widowed/divorced	14.7	8.1	9.1	10.1	16.5	23.1
Living with father only	10.7	9.7	6.5	7.1	11.7	15.7
Single (never married)	0.6	3.4	0.8	0.2	0.2	...
Married, spouse absent	2.8	3.5	2.1	1.7	3.6	2.8
Widowed/divorced	7.3	2.8	3.7	5.1	7.9	12.9

Table 11-14. Presence and Marital Status of Parent for Persons under 18 Years of Age Living with Only One Parent, by Age and Race-ethnicity: 1980 and 1992 [percent distribution] (continued)

Marital Status	Total under 18 years[1]	Under 3 years	3 to 5 years	6 to 9 years	10 to 14 years	15 to 17 years
Black 1992	100.0	100.0	100.0	100.0	100.0	100.0
Living with mother only	94.5	95.4	93.0	95.6	94.5	93.6
Single (never married)	53.8	74.6	61.3	56.3	40.4	32.6
Married, spouse absent	20.5	12.4	20.6	21.5	24.6	23.7
Widowed/divorced	20.2	8.4	11.0	17.8	29.4	37.3
Living with father only	5.5	4.6	7.0	4.4	5.6	6.4
Single (never married)	2.1	3.3	3.9	1.3	1.3	0.1
Married, spouse absent	1.2	0.7	0.4	1.3	1.6	2.3
Widowed/divorced	2.3	0.6	2.8	1.8	2.7	4.0
Black 1980	100.0	100.0	100.0	100.0	100.0	100.0
Living with mother only	95.7	95.1	95.6	98.3	95.1	94.2
Single (never married)	28.1	50.1	44.4	29.9	21.5	8.8
Married, spouse absent	35.2	31.0	30.3	36.9	35.1	39.6
Widowed/divorced	11.0	3.9	7.0	10.2	12.4	17.4
Living with father only	4.3	4.9	4.4	1.7	4.9	5.8
Single (never married)	0.7	3.1	1.8	...	0.2	...
Married, spouse absent	1.4	0.3	0.6	0.8	2.2	2.4
Widowed/divorced	2.1	1.5	2.0	0.9	2.7	3.5
Hispanic 1992	100.0	100.0	100.0	100.0	100.0	100.0
Living with mother only	88.6	86.4	89.8	89.8	88.3	88.8
Single (never married)	30.9	45.0	38.3	31.9	22.4	17.6
Married, spouse absent	27.5	26.7	26.7	27.4	26.2	31.6
Widowed/divorced	30.1	14.9	24.8	30.4	39.8	39.6
Living with father only	11.4	13.6	10.4	10.2	11.7	11.2
Single (never married)	4.7	10.7	7.1	3.1	2.4	0.5
Married, spouse absent	2.7	0.6	1.9	3.1	3.0	5.1
Widowed/divorced	4.0	2.3	1.4	4.1	6.4	5.6
Hispanic 1980	100.0	100.0	100.0	100.0	100.0	100.0
Living with mother only	92.8	95.6	94.1	97.6	89.4	89.1
Single (never married)	18.9	35.4	27.0	15.9	12.6	9.1
Married, spouse absent	38.9	41.5	42.1	43.0	36.7	31.9
Widowed/divorced	11.5	9.7	8.7	9.0	11.7	19.4
Living with father only	7.2	4.4	5.9	2.4	10.6	10.9
Single (never married)	1.1	3.0	0.9	0.8	0.9	...
Married, spouse absent	1.9	1.0	1.8	0.2	3.1	2.8
Widowed/divorced	4.2	0.4	3.2	1.4	6.6	8.1

[1] Excludes persons under 18 years who are husbands or wives and other persons maintaining households or related and unrelated subfamilies.

Source: U.S. Bureau of the Census, "Marital Status and Living Arrangements," Current Population Reports, Series P-20, nos. 468 and 365, U.S. Government Printing Office, Washington, D.C., 1992 and 1981, Table 5.

Table 11-15. Households with Two Unrelated Adults: 1992 [numbers in thousands]

Partner	Households with two unrelated adults	Age of householder			Marital status of householder	
		Under 25 years	25-64 years	65 years and over	Never married	Divorced
Total	4,872	22.0	73.1	4.9	60.6	27.8
Partner of opposite sex	3,308	20.0	75.6	4.4	55.0	33.4
Age of partner:						
Under 25 years	868	74.7	25.1	0.2	78.2	16.1
25-64 years	2,334	7.8	89.0	3.2	48.0	40.7
65 years and over	106	...	34.9	65.1	17.0	14.2
Marital status of partner:						
Never married	1,951	29.9	68.6	1.5	71.1	21.4
Divorced	1,054	4.6	89.3	6.1	30.3	57.2
Partner of same sex	1,564	26.3	67.8	5.9	72.6	15.7
Age of partner:						
Under 25 years	453	66.9	32.0	1.1	85.0	7.5
25-64 years	1,054	10.3	85.0	4.7	69.4	19.4
65 years and over	57	...	33.3	66.7	31.6	12.3
Marital status of partner:						
Never married	1,225	30.8	65.6	3.5	80.1	12.2
Divorced	213	7.0	82.2	10.8	50.7	37.1

Source: U.S. Bureau of the Census, "Marital Status and Living Arrangements," Current Population Reports, Series P-20, no. 468, U.S. Government Printing Office, Washington, D.C., 1992, Table 8.

Unrelated Adult Householders

In 1992 it was estimated that there were 4,872,000 households composed of two unrelated adults with 3,308,000 couples of opposite sex, and 1,564,000 couples of the same sex, sharing a housing unit while not married. Table 11-15 provides statistics about the age of such couples. It is widely assumed that many of these unrelated adult households are cohabiting couples. A high percentage of them have never married. The percentage divorced is highest among opposite-sex couples of middle age. The percentage never married is highest among young same-sex couples.

Some further details of the gender, age, marital status, and presence of children for these couples are reported in Table 11-16. The comparative scarcity of children in these households is evident. While both males and females have partners near the same age, female householders in such couples tend to be a little older and to have older partners than male householders in such couples. Since the tables include opposite-sex couples, age differences are likely due to traditional age differences in opposite-sex couples. Among males a higher percentage of those without children have never-married partners (61.1% compared to 51.8% of those with children) while among females a higher percentage of those with children have never-married partners (63.0% compared to 58.3% without children).

Subfamilies

About four percent of all family households contain a "family within the family," or subfamily. Most common is a never-married daughter with one or more children living in the home of her parents. A second common situation is that of a young married couple (with or without children) living in the home of the parents of either the husband or the wife. Subfamilies can also consist of an elderly couple living in the home of one of their children. In 1992 there were about 2,559,000 such families, with the composition shown in Table 11-17.

There had been a long-term decline in the share of married-couple subfamilies and a steady rise in the prevalence of mother-child households into the middle of the 1980's. There was an unprecedented fluctuation upward

Table 11-16. Presence of Children in Households of Two Unrelated Opposite Sex Adults, by Sex, Age, and Marital Status of Householder: 1992

Presence of children, age and marital status of partner	Households with two opposite sex unrelated adults	Age of householder (years)					Marital status of householder				
		Under 25	25 to 34	35 to 44	45 to 64	65 and over	Single	Married spouse absent — Separated	Other	Widowed	Divorced
Male Householders	100.0	100.0	100.0	100.0	100.0	100.0	100.0	100.0	100.0	100.0	100.0
No children in household	68.6	72.8	61.0	66.0	82.8	100.0	71.0	49.6	63.6	95.7	65.7
Age of partner:											
Under 25 years	29.4	84.3	32.6	5.3	...	...	40.5	10.5	28.6	...	13.0
25 to 34 years	36.9	15.7	58.7	44.1	11.1	3.0	41.6	19.3	42.9	13.3	32.7
35 to 44 years	16.4	...	7.6	37.2	32.7	9.1	11.0	40.4	28.6	15.6	23.8
45 to 64 years	14.7	...	1.2	11.7	51.8	56.1	4.8	29.8	...	46.7	28.6
65 years and over	2.7	...	...	1.6	4.4	31.8	2.2	...	...	24.4	1.8
Marital status of partner:											
Single (never married)	61.1	93.6	76.6	41.7	27.4	10.6	78.0	36.8	57.1	11.1	36.3
Married, spouse absent	4.5	3.4	3.1	4.0	9.7	1.5	4.6	15.8	42.9	...	2.8
Separated	3.9	3.4	2.5	4.0	7.5	1.5	4.1	15.8	...	...	2.3
Widowed	4.3	...	0.4	1.2	9.3	43.9	2.4	...	...	48.9	3.8
Divorced	30.2	2.6	20.0	53.0	53.5	43.9	15.2	47.4	...	40.0	57.5
With children in household	31.4	27.6	38.9	34.0	17.2	...	29.0	51.3	36.4	4.3	34.1
Age of partner:											
Under 25 years	29.8	68.5	30.7	5.5	14.9	...	40.2	11.9	75.0	100.0	16.7
25 to 34 years	56.3	30.3	64.4	59.1	38.3	...	52.3	79.7	25.0	...	56.7
35 to 44 years	12.5	...	4.9	33.1	36.2	...	6.5	6.8	...	...	24.1
45 to 64 years	1.4	...	0.3	2.4	8.5	...	0.6	...	...	...	2.5
65 years and over	...	...	...	...	...	...	...	...	...	...	...
Marital status of partner:											
Single (never married)	51.8	67.4	58.4	27.6	42.6	...	67.2	37.3	25.0	100.0	31.5
Married, spouse absent	12.0	10.1	9.7	22.0	4.3	...	7.4	40.7	75.0	...	9.9
Separated	11.5	9.0	9.7	19.7	4.3	...	7.1	40.7	25.0	...	9.9
Widowed	2.0	...	0.6	3.9	8.5	...	...	3.4	...	...	4.9
Divorced	34.2	22.5	31.3	46.5	42.6	...	25.4	18.6	...	...	54.2

Table 11-16. Presence of Children in Households of Two Unrelated Opposite Sex Adults, by Sex, Age, and Marital Status of Householder: 1992 (continued)

Presence of children, age and marital status of partner	Households with two opposite sex unrelated adults	Age of householder (years)					Marital status of householder				
		Under 25	25 to 34	35 to 44	45 to 64	65 and over	Single	Married spouse absent — Separated	Married spouse absent — Other	Widowed	Divorced
Female Householders	100.0	100.0	100.0	100.0	100.0	100.0	100.0	100.0	100.0	100.0	100.0
No children in household	62.9	62.7	50.5	55.1	91.1	100.0	66.3	39.5	66.7	91.4	54.4
Age of partner:											
Under 25 years	20.2	67.0	10.8	0.7	3.3	2.5	34.0	20.0	100.0	1.7	3.2
25 to 34 years	33.3	28.3	64.2	30.0	7.6	3.7	42.7	23.3	...	9.4	...
35 to 44 years	17.7	4.7	17.6	43.6	17.4	9.9	15.6	13.3	...	6.0	...
45 to 64 years	20.8	...	7.5	25.7	59.8	24.7	7.3	40.0	...	30.8	...
65 years and over	7.9	...	...	...	12.5	59.3	0.4	...	...	52.1	...
Marital status of partner:											
Single (never married)	58.3	89.6	76.0	40.7	21.7	28.4	81.4	50.0	100.0	23.1	...
Married, spouse absent	3.7	0.9	2.9	5.7	7.1	2.5	3.0	3.3	...	4.3	...
Separated	3.2	0.9	2.9	5.0	6.0	2.5	3.0	3.3	...	4.3	...
Widowed	4.6	...	1.1	...	8.7	27.2	0.6	...	...	28.2	...
Divorced	33.4	9.4	20.1	53.6	62.5	43.2	15.0	43.3	...	44.4	...
With children in household	37.1	37.3	49.5	44.9	8.4	...	33.7	61.8	33.3	8.6	...
Age of partner:											
Under 25 years	25.1	61.9	14.7	11.4	11.8	...	29.4	34.0	...	18.2	...
25 to 34 years	45.8	34.1	57.9	33.3	17.6	...	48.7	38.3	50.0	63.6	...
35 to 44 years	23.0	4.0	26.0	39.5	11.8	...	19.7	21.3	50.0	9.1	...
45 to 64 years	6.2	...	1.5	15.8	64.7	...	2.1	6.4	...	9.1	...
65 years and over	...	...	...	...	...	...	...	...	...	...	...
Marital status of partner:											
Single (never married)	63.0	90.5	61.5	41.2	35.3	...	72.7	78.7	50.0	63.6	...
Married, spouse absent	6.2	7.1	6.2	5.3	...	...	7.1	6.4	50.0	...	...
Separated	5.3	5.6	5.5	5.3	...	...	5.9	6.4	...	...	...
Widowed	0.2	...	0.4	...	...	...	...	...	...	9.1	...
Divorced	30.6	2.4	31.9	53.5	70.6	...	20.2	12.8	50.0	27.3	...

Source: U. S. Bureau of the Census, "Marital Status and Living Arrangemnts," Current Population Reports, Series P-20, no. 468, U.S Government Printing Office, 1992, Table 8.

Table 11-17. Subfamilies Related to Family Householder: 1940-1992

Year	Number of related subfamilies (in thousands)	Percent composition			Ratio of related subfamilies to families (per 100)
		Married couple	Father-child	Mother-child	
1992	2,559	37.6	5.2	57.1	3.8
1991	2,546	38.7	5.6	55.7	3.8
1990	2,403	36.2	6.4	57.3	3.6
1985	2,228	32.3	5.2	62.5	3.6
1980	1,150	50.6	4.7	44.5	1.9
1975	1,349	52.3	5.1	52.3	2.4
1970	1,150	53.7	4.2	42.1	2.2
1965	1,293	56.4	5.6	38.1	2.7
1960	1,514	57.5	7.6	34.9	3.4
1955	1,973	59.7	3.5	36.8	4.7
1950	2,402	68.7	4.7	26.6	6.2
1940	2,062	75.0	2.5	22.5	6.5

Source: U.S. Bureau of the Census, "Household and Family Characteristics," Current
Population Reports, Series P-20, no.467, U.S. Government Printing Office, Washington,
D.C., 1993, Table A-2.

with the number of subfamilies nearly doubling between 1981 and 1985, and most of this was in mother-child subfamilies which rose to constitute nearly two of every three subfamilies. In the years from 1980 to 1992 married-couple subfamilies have fallen from over 50 percent to around 38 percent of all subfamilies and mother-child subfamilies have increased from just under 45 percent to around 57 percent. Trends in the last three years of Table 11-17, from 1990 to 1992, have seen relatively little change in subfamilies.

Table 11-18 shows selected characteristics of subfamilies. Subfamilies occur much more frequently among black and Hispanic populations than among white, as shown by the percent of total family households comprised of subfamilies, for each race-ethnic group. In 1992, subfamiles occurred in 3.4 percent of all households, 1.9 percent of white households, 6.8 percent of black households and 3.7 percent of Hispanic households.

Mother-child subfamilies are 85.3 percent of all black, 55.7 percent of white and 47.5 percent of Hispanic subfamilies. Almost half of Hispanic subfamilies, and over a third of white subfamilies, are married-couple subfamilies, in sharp contrast to both black subfamilies. Mother-child black subfamilies are more likely to be young with 46.7 percent of such subfamilies being that of a woman less than twenty-five years old (compared to 36.1 percent for whites and 36.7 percent for Hispanics).

As Table 11-18 shows, subfamilies are not large. They usually consist of a husband and wife only or a parent and child.

In the era immediately following World War II, the subfamily was a convenient startup arrangement for young couples newly married and as a residential arrangement for an elderly dependent parent in the home of a son or daughter. In recent times, the subfamily is rapidly becoming a refuge for the one-parent family, especially for divorced and never-married women with a child. During times of economic difficulty, however, the subfamily continues to serve as a temporary arrangement for many young couples.

The rapid rise in subfamilies during the early 1980's, described above, may be due to economic trends, changing norms regarding marriage, or changes in social legislation that curtailed benefits to one-parent families. In the early 1980's curtailed benefits to one-parent families may indeed have forced low-income families to move in with a relative and become a subfamily. Later in the decade, economic recession coupled with a dramatic surge in real estate values and mortgage interests substantially reduced the ability of young families to purchase a home and establish an independent household. It is still premature to determine whether the leveling off seen in the rate of increase in subfamilies over the past few years reflects a leveling off of real estate inflation or lower interest rates in the early 1990's, both of which would increase the affordability of maintaining independent households. It is even more difficult to determine whether the surge in subfamilies during the early 1980's reflected a normative change in acceptable forms of householding which has leveled off in more recent years.

Households Containing Elderly Members

As the population ages, an increasing proportion of households are headed by elderly persons sixty-five and over. Just over 12.5 percent of the U.S. population was sixty-five and over in 1990. Of the roughly 12.1 million men over 65 years of age in 1990, 94.2 percent were either householders (89.4 percent) or were married to a woman identified as the householder (4.8 percent). Of the roughly 17.4 million women over 65 years of age, there were 52.7 percent identified as householders and 36.6 percent who identified themselves as the spouse of the householder.

The percentage of the elderly in independent households (i.e. who are householders or married to the householder) is lowest for the Hispanic elderly (78.4), significantly higher for the black elderly (86.2) and highest among the white elderly (92.5). However, elderly male householders are somewhat more common among Hispanics than among blacks.

Living Arrangements of the Elderly

Of those aged sixty-five and over living in households in 1992, two-thirds were living in families and one-third were living outside families. All but a small fraction of this latter group live alone. Table 11-19 provides comparative statistical data for years since 1970. As survivorship among the elderly has increased and elderly services have expanded, the percentage living alone has substantially increased. The greatest increase in the elderly living alone, however, appears to have been in the decade of the 1970's with only a very modest increase between 1980 and 1992. At the same time, the number of persons involved certainly has grown over the past decade as the population has aged.

The percentage widowed among the elderly has dropped slightly from 39.1 percent in 1970 to 34.4 percent in 1992. Also, the tendency for widowed persons living outside of a family context to live alone has increased substantially (from 51.3 in 1970 to 66.9 in 1980 and again to 69.5 in 1992).

Households and Place of Residence

The proportion of the U.S. population that resides within urban and metropolitan areas has nearly doubled over the past half century. As Table 11-20 shows, metropolitan households are most common in the Northeast and West (88.2 and 84.5 percent of all households respectively) and are less common in the Midwest and South (71.5 and 71.2 respectively). Black, Hispanic and Asian households are the most likely to be in metropolitan ar-

Table 11-18. Subfamilies, by Selected Characteristics and Race-ethnicity of Subfamily Reference Person: 1992

Characteristics of reference person	Subfamilies			
	Total[1]	Married couple	Father-child	Mother-child
All races				
Number (in thousands)	3,228	1,055	189	1,984
Percent	100.0	29.5	5.6	63.1
Marital status	100.0	100.0	100.0	100.0
Married, spouse present	32.7	100.0	...	...
Married, spouse absent	11.6	...	27.0	16.3
Widowed/divorced	19.0	...	42.9	26.7
Single (never married)	36.7	...	30.2	56.9
Age	100.0	100.0	100.0	100.0
Under 25 years	32.8	21.3	25.9	39.5
25-64 years	63.0	65.9	74.1	60.4
65 years and over	4.2	12.8	...	0.1
Average number of persons per subfamily	2.51	2.68	2.34	2.43
Average number of own children under 18 per subfamily	1.18	0.68	1.34	1.43
White				
Number (in thousands)	1,511	548	91	841
Percent	100.0	36.3	6.0	55.7
Marital status	100.0	100.0	100.0	100.0
Married, spouse present	37.7	100.0	...	...
Married, spouse absent	13.0	...	32.9	19.4
Widowed/divorced	22.9	...	45.9	35.8
Single (never married)	26.4	...	20.5	44.9
Age	100.0	100.0	100.0	100.0
Under 25 years	30.4	23.4	21.2	36.1
25-64 years	65.9	66.6	78.8	63.9
65 years and over	3.8	10.0	...	...
Average number of persons per subfamily	2.49	2.71	2.34	2.36
Average number of own children under 18 per subfamily	1.12	0.71	1.34	1.36

Table 11-18. Subfamilies, by Selected Characteristics and Race-ethnicity of Subfamily Reference Person: 1992 (continued)

Characteristics of reference person	Subfamilies			
	Total[1]	Married couple	Father-child	Mother-child
Black				
Number (in thousands)	751	54	38	660
Percent	100.0	8.6	5.1	85.3
Marital status	100.0	100.0	100.0	100.0
Married, spouse present	0.6	100.0	...	...
Married, spouse absent	10.0	...	5.3	11.1
Widowed/divorced	10.1	...	31.6	9.7
Single (never married)	72.7	...	63.2	79.1
Age	100.0	100.0	100.0	100.0
Under 25 years	44.8	22.2	40.5	46.7
25-64 years	54.1	66.7	59.5	53.0
65 years and over	1.1	11.1	...	0.3
Average number of persons per subfamily	2.54	—[2]	—[2]	2.54
Average number of own children under 18 per subfamily	1.47	—[2]	—[2]	1.54
Hispanic				
Number (in thousands)	238	107	12	113
Percent	100.0	45.0	5.0	47.5
Marital status	100.0	100.0	100.0	100.0
Married, spouse present	49.7	100.0	...	...
Married, spouse absent	11.1	...	18.5	22.4
Widowed/divorced	12.3	...	33.3	23.5
Single (never married)	26.9	...	48.1	53.7
Age	100.0	100.0	100.0	100.0
Under 25 years	31.7	27.6	29.6	36.7
25-64 years	61.5	59.0	70.4	63.3
65 years and over	6.8	13.4	...	...
Average number of persons per subfamily	2.63	2.82	—[2]	2.46
Average number of own children under 18 per subfamily	1.14	0.82	—[2]	1.46

[1] Total includes all married couple subfamilies, father-child and mother-child subfamilies, as well as other subfamilies not listed.

[2] Sample is too small to derive any meaningful measures.

Source: U.S. Bureau of the Census, "Household and Family Characteristics," Current Population Reports, Series P-20, no.467, U.S. Government Printing Office, Washington, D.C., 1993, Table 12.

eas, although this is less so for blacks in the South. The concentration of these groups in metropolitan areas is most pronounced in the Northeast. Black, Hispanic and Asian households of the Northeast are 98.9, 98.5 and 97.7 percent, respectively, located within metropolitan areas. The greater concentration of minorities in metropolitan areas, especially those areas with lower income housing and less desirable features of urban life, has led to recent concerns over environmental equity.

As might be expected from the historic migration of blacks from the South to cities in other regions of the country, the proportion of black households in metropolitan areas is higher than all other groups in all regions of the country other than the South. An even higher percentage of Hispanic households than of black households are found in metropolitan areas of the South, and nearly the same percentage are found in the metropolitan Northeast. The least likely groups to maintain households in metropolitan areas are, not surprisingly, indigenous peoples (i.e. American Indian, Eskimo and Aleut) in all regions other than the Northeast.

The types of households within metropolitan areas differ from those outside metropolitan areas and also differ across regions of the United States. Metropolitan households are somewhat less likely to be married couples with children in all regions except the Midwest. Metropolitan black household heads are less likely to have households consisting of married couples with children and significantly more likely to be female headed households with children than are non-metropolitan households in all regions except the South. In all regions other than the Northeast, the elderly among all major racial and ethnic groups are more likely to live outside metropolitan areas. This is most pronounced among the Asian households of the West, where elderly householders are 22.5 percent

Table 11-19. Number and Percent Distribution of Family Status and Living Alone for Persons 65 Years of Age and Older: 1970-1992 [numbers in thousands]

Subject	Total		In families		Not in families		Living alone	
	Number	Percent	Number	Percent	Number	Percent	Number	Percent
1992								
Persons 65 years and over	30,590	100.0	20,340	66.5	10,250	33.5	9,523	31.1
Not widowed	20,070	100.0	17,498	87.2	2,572	12.8	2,212	11.0
Total widowed	10,520	100.0	2,842	27.0	7,678	73.0	7,311	69.5
Women	17,789	100.0	10,001	56.2	7,788	43.8	7,437	41.8
Men	12,799	100.0	10,339	80.8	2,460	19.2	2,086	16.3
1980								
Persons 65 years and over	23,743	100.0	16,077	67.7	7,666	32.3	7,140	30.1
Not widowed	15,289	100.0	13,533	88.5	1,756	11.5	1,488	9.7
Total widowed	8,454	100.0	2,544	30.1	5,910	69.9	5,652	66.9
Women	13,960	100.0	7,961	57.0	5,999	43.0	5,703	40.9
Men	9,783	100.0	8,116	83.0	1,667	17.0	1,437	14.7
1970								
Persons 65 years and over	19,713	100.0	13,276	67.3	6,437	32.7	4,958	25.2
Not widowed	12,007	100.0	10,321	86.0	1,686	14.0	1,007	8.4
Total widowed	7,706	100.0	2,955	38.3	4,751	61.7	3,951	51.3
Women	11,349	100.0	6,641	58.5	4,708	41.5	3,829	33.7
Men	8,364	100.0	6,635	79.3	1,729	20.7	1,129	13.5

Source: U.S. Bureau of the Census, "Marital Status and Living Arrangements," Current Population Reports, Series P-20, nos. 468 and 365, 1992 and 1981, Tables 7 and 6, and "Marital Status and Family Status," Series P-20, no. 212, Table 6, U.S. Government Printing Office, Washington, D.C., 1971.

of households outside metropolitan areas compared to 12.7 percent of metropolitan households.

Family and Household

Every member of a family is classified according to his or her relationship to the householder (these relationships are explained in the Definition Box). Data on relationship can illuminate the structure of the family.

Family Relationships of Children and Young Adults

Table 11-21 provides information on the relationship of the child to the householder in order to show the significant differences that occur with age and that exist between race-ethnic groups. The status of being some child-relative other than a child of the householder (e.g. a grandchild, nephew or niece, etc.) is much more prevalent among black than among other children. Such child-relatives are also moderately prevalent among Hispanic children, especially when the child is under five years of

age, and less common among white children of all ages. For all groups, being a child-relative such as a grandchild is more prevalent among very young than among older children. And, through adolescence, a very high proportion of all children remain in the households of their parents.

Figure 11-6 illustrates changes in the living arrangements of young adults and their transition into their own households over the past three decades. Males and females aged 18-34 years old have become less likely to be householders themselves as they remain a 'child' in a parent's household, enter a non-family household, or seek alternative living arrangements. This is most pronounced among those aged 18-24 and likely reflects a number of trends in this age group including greater participation in post-secondary education, rising ages at marriage, and rising expenses of establishing a new household. Unmarried college students living in dormitories are classified as children of householders. Among those over 25 years of age there is almost no change in the percentage of females remaining as children in their parents' household, while the percentage of males doing so has increased

Figure 11-6. Living Arrangements of Young Adults: 1960, 1970, 1980, and 1990

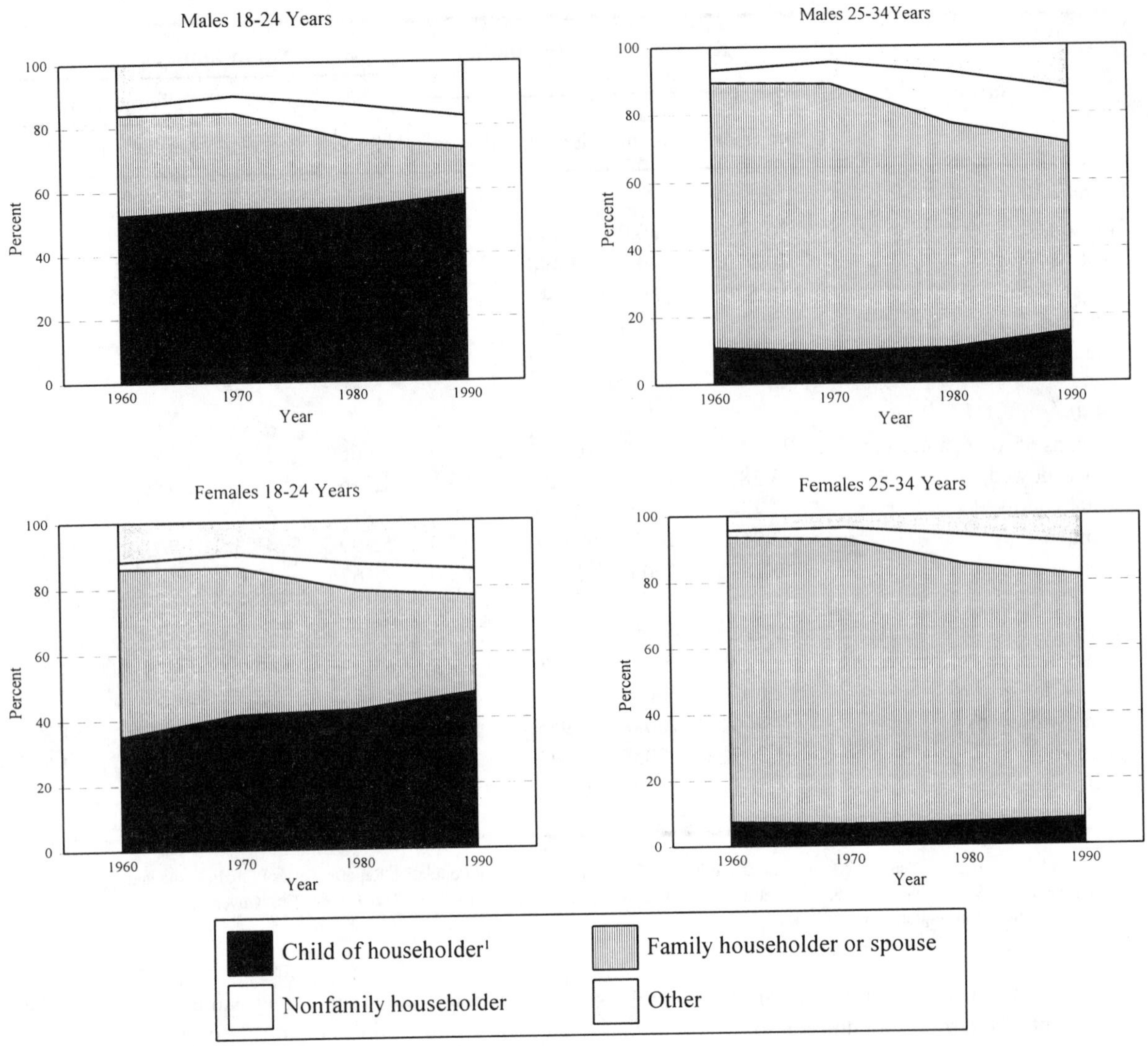

Males 18-24 Years

Males 25-34 Years

Females 18-24 Years

Females 25-34 Years

Child of householder[1]

Family householder or spouse

Nonfamily householder

Other

[1] Child of householder includes unmarried college students living in dormitories.
Source: 1960, 1970, 1980, and 1990 Census data.

slightly. For both sexes, however, the greatest increase in living arrangements for those over 25 years of age has been in non-family and other alternative household arrangements. The greatest percentage increase across both sexes and at all ages has been in non-family households.

Family and Household Relationships of the Elderly

As persons approach retirement, their family situation experiences a number of changes. Children have generally departed from home, their spouse could have died, ill health might have set in, or financial security may be lost. The adjustment to these transitions and tragedies is reflected in the family and household relationships of the elderly. Table 11-22 reports such information by sex and race for advanced ages.

As white, black or Hispanic men pass their seventy-fifth birthday, the proportion which continue to be primary householders declines substantially. By the time they approach their eighty-fifth birthday, less than half of all men remain as primary householders. This decline in primary householding is least among black males, roughly a third of whom are not in family groups prior to age sixty-five and throughout older years. The decline in householding is greatest among white males as is the rise in the percentage not in family groups, from 15.0 percent between ages 65-74, to over double that (34.5 percent) among those over 85 years of age. The percentage of males in related subfamilies or other family groups is most

Table 11-20. Selected Household Characteristics Inside and Outside Metropolitan Area, by Region and Race-ethnicity: 1990

Region and race-ethnicity	Number of households	Percent of households in metropolitan area	Inside metropolitan area (percent of households)			Outside metropolitan area (percent of households)		
			Married couples with own children <18 years	Female householder with own children <18 years	Householder 65 years and over	Married couples with own children <18 years	Female householder with own children <18 years	Householder 65 years and over
Northeast								
Total	18,872,713	88.2	23.5	6.4	23.2	26.9	5.3	24.8
White	16,123,125	86.4	24.0	4.2	25.2	26.9	5.2	25.1
Black	1,864,479	98.9	15.5	18.6	16.2	23.9	14.5	14.9
American Indian/ Eskimo/Aleut	41,978	83.4	22.2	13.7	13.7	27.7	13.0	13.7
Asian/Pacific Islander	374,245	97.7	41.6	3.8	6.9	37.3	5.1	4.6
Hispanic	1,108,546	98.5	25.2	18.7	10.7	31.6	12.8	12.1
Midwest								
Total	22,316,975	71.5	25.6	7.0	20.5	23.8	6.6	28.6
White	19,858,420	68.8	26.6	4.9	21.5	28.2	4.7	27.7
Black	1,938,405	96.2	14.9	22.1	16.4	20.5	17.4	19.8
American Indian/ Eskimo/Aleut	101,859	53.8	24.7	16.7	9.8	27.1	18.1	13.8
Asian/Pacific Islander	207,117	91.5	43.5	4.4	5.8	39.5	5.7	4.9
Hispanic	458,637	88.2	37.0	11.4	9.0	38.8	9.9	12.4
South								
Total	31,822,254	71.2	25.3	7.0	20.0	26.7	6.6	26.1
White	25,502,553	70.4	25.7	4.5	21.5	27.7	4.3	26.8
Black	5,209,880	73.0	19.3	18.7	15.8	19.9	18.3	24.2
American Indian/ Eskimo/Aleut	183,485	53.3	28.9	9.2	12.3	31.0	10.2	18.8
Asian/Pacific Islander	307,418	92.7	43.5	4.6	4.4	41.3	5.4	5.2
Hispanic	1,911,556	87.1	36.8	9.0	13.1	41.5	8.2	16.0
West								
Total	18,935,468	84.5	25.7	6.5	18.4	28.0	6.1	23.1
White	15,396,007	83.1	23.9	5.2	20.4	27.1	5.4	24.1
Black	963,397	97.8	18.7	16.6	13.4	28.5	12.0	15.9
American Indian/ Eskimo/Aleut	264,050	51.5	24.7	13.9	10.0	32.5	14.8	14.1
Asian/Pacific Islander	1,124,955	93.9	37.0	5.2	12.7	31.8	5.8	22.5
Hispanic	2,522,979	89.8	38.3	10.7	9.6	38.1	10.2	14.4

Source: U.S. Bureau of the Census, "General Population Characteristics," 1990 Census of Population, CP-1-1, U.S. Government Printing Office, Washington, D.C., 1992, Tables 52-61, 29-96, 102-111, 142-146, 152-161, 192-196, 202-211, and 242-246.

substantial for Hispanic males, especially those of advanced ages.

In contrast, white and Hispanic women are most likely to spend the years immediately after their sixty-fifth birthday as the spouse of a householder. Of women aged 65-74 only black women have a majority living as either primary householders or otherwise not in family groups. In fact, among the elderly only 10.0 percent of white, and 16.7 percent of Hispanic, women are primary householders while nearly one in four elderly black women, 24.7 percent, are primary householders. Hispanic women, like Hispanic men, are the least likely of all groups to live outside family groups. It is likely that many of those living outside family groups at advanced ages, over 85 years of age, are living in some formal support or caregiving environment. White women over 85 years of age are nearly twice as likely (62.4 percent) to live outside family groups as are black (39.9 percent) or Hispanic (30.2 percent) women of those ages. These differences, at least in part, reflect differences in affordability and accessibility to alternative householding arrangements among the elderly.

Table 11-21. Relationship to Householder of Population Under 15 Years of Age, by Sex and Race-ethnicity: 1992 [percent distribution]

Age and race-ethnicity	Child of householder	Other relative of householder	In unrelated subfamilies	Not in family groups
White males	93.4	5.0	1.4	0.3
Under 5 years	91.6	6.7	1.3	0.3
6 to 11 years	94.3	4.0	1.5	0.1
12 to 14 years	95.4	3.0	1.2	0.4
Black males	83.0	14.3	1.6	1.1
Under 5 years	79.3	17.1	2.1	1.5
6 to 11 years	86.8	11.3	1.2	0.6
12 to 14 years	83.5	14.1	1.2	1.3
Hispanic males	88.6	9.6	1.5	0.3
Under 5 years	85.8	12.7	1.2	0.3
6 to 11 years	90.2	7.2	2.2	0.4
12 to 14 years	92.3	6.7	1.0	...
White females	93.6	4.7	1.4	0.3
Under 5 years	91.7	6.5	1.6	0.2
6 to 11 years	94.8	3.4	1.4	0.3
12 to 14 years	94.9	3.4	1.2	0.4
Black females	80.3	16.7	1.2	1.8
Under 5 years	76.3	20.5	1.1	2.1
6 to 11 years	82.1	15.2	1.2	1.5
12 to 14 years	85.2	11.8	1.4	1.6
Hispanic females	87.5	9.9	2.1	0.6
Under 5 years	84.0	13.5	2.1	0.4
6 to 11 years	89.9	7.2	2.2	0.7
12 to 14 years	90.8	6.7	1.8	0.7

Source: U.S. Bureau of the Census, "Marital Status and Living Arrangements," Current Population Reports, Series P-20, no. 468, U.S. Government Printing Office, Washington, D.C., 1992, Table 3.

Persons in Group Quarters

Earlier this chapter noted that a small fraction of the population does not live in households but in "group quarters." This population possesses economic, social, political, and welfare significance much greater than its proportion. There have also been dramatic changes in the institutionalized population over the past several decades (see Textbox 11-A).

Table 11-23 presents percentage distributions of persons (rather than households or families) in group quarters by race-ethnicity and sex. Over two of every three males in group quarters are white as are over four of every five females. Yet, for some institutionalized populations the race-ethnicity and sex distributions provide evidence of profoundly troubling social patterns. Of those men in correctional institutions, for example, there are roughly the same percent of whites and blacks and under half as many Hispanics. However, that amounts to a gross over-representation of blacks and Hispanics among the correctional population. Only 18.1 percent of white males in group quarters are among the correctional population while 51.3 percent of black males, 46.4 percent of Hispanic males and 32.1 percent of those of other race in group quarters are in correctional institutions. These same patterns are even more dramatic for females despite the lower overall percentage of females in correctional institutions.

In contrast, some institutional settings seem highly influenced by privileged access. Roughly ninety percent

Table 11-22. Relationship to Householder of Persons 65 Years of Age and Older, by Sex and Race-ethnicity: 1992 [percent distribution]

Age and race-ethnicity	Householder	Spouse of householder	In related subfamilies	Other family	Not in family groups
White males	73.2	4.5	0.7	3.7	17.9
65 to 74 years old	77.4	3.8	0.6	3.2	15.0
75 to 84 years old	69.6	5.7	0.8	3.1	20.7
85 years and older	47.2	5.7	1.1	11.5	34.5
Black males	55.5	6.0	0.6	3.6	34.3
65 to 74 years old	56.9	6.5	0.8	2.6	33.2
75 to 84 years old	54.7	4.1	...	3.7	37.4
85 years and older	44.7	7.9	...	13.2	34.2
Hispanic males	66.9	3.7	8.0	8.4	13.1
65 to 74 years old	70.0	4.2	7.1	6.5	12.3
75 to 84 years old	64.6	2.4	10.2	8.7	14.2
85 years and older	42.9	3.6	7.1	28.6	17.9
White females	10.0	38.3	0.4	7.0	44.3
65 to 74 years old	9.7	50.0	0.6	4.3	35.4
75 to 84 years old	10.6	27.1	0.2	7.9	54.1
85 years and older	8.9	8.5	0.3	19.9	62.4
Black females	24.7	22.2	0.5	10.7	42.0
65 to 74 years old	25.1	28.5	0.5	5.7	40.2
75 to 84 years old	21.1	16.0	0.4	16.2	46.3
85 years and older	33.8	2.7	...	23.6	39.9
Hispanic females	16.7	30.4	3.7	21.3	27.9
65 to 74 years old	17.5	38.2	4.5	15.2	24.6
75 to 84 years old	14.2	20.8	2.8	28.3	34.0
85 years and older	20.9	2.3	...	46.5	30.2

Source: U.S. Bureau of the Census, "Marital Status and Living Arrangements," Current Population Reports, Series P-20, no.468, U.S. Government Printing Office, Washington, D.C., 1992, Table 2.

of those in nursing homes are white and over eighty percent of those in college dormitories are white. Black males in group quarters are nearly twice as likely, and black women are seven times more likely, to be in emergency shelters for the homeless than are whites living in group quarters.

Table 11-24 gives the race-ethnicity, age and sex distribution of the population in group quarters by those institutionalized and in other group quarters. Among all males and females the largest institutionalized group are those eighty-five years of age and older. Presumably these are largely individuals in nursing homes and other institutional care settings. However, among the black population there are larger percentages from age 15 to age 54 in the institutionalized population representing their greater likelihood of being in correctional institutions. The same age patterns are less pronounced among Hispanic populations and barely noticeable among the white population. The noninstitutionalized populations in group quarters are largest at ages 18 to 24 among all three groups, reflecting college dormitories and military quarters at these ages. However, the percentage of Hispanics in other quarters at these ages is under half that of whites and nearly half that of blacks.

Much can be learned from the institutional population. Perhaps no population better illustrates the deep social divides and daunting future prospects of the country than do those living in group quarters.

Table 11-23. Percent Distribution of Residents in Group Quarters: 1990

Percent Distribution (vertical)

Type of group quarters	Male					Female				
	Total	White	Black	Other race	Hispanic	Total	White	Black	Other race	Hispanic
Total persons in group quarters	100.0	100.0	100.0	100.0	100.0	100.0	100.0	100.0	100.0	100.0
Institutionalized persons	47.5	42.2	64.7	40.9	55.3	52.7	55.6	43.9	21.9	34.9
Correctional institutions	27.2	18.1	51.3	32.1	46.4	2.9	1.6	11.1	5.5	10.9
Nursing homes	13.0	16.7	5.7	3.5	3.4	43.9	48.5	24.0	10.9	16.0
Other institutions	7.3	7.4	7.6	5.3	5.6	5.8	5.4	8.8	5.6	7.9
Noninstitutionalized persons	52.5	57.8	35.3	59.1	44.7	47.3	44.4	56.1	78.1	65.1
College dormitories	24.9	30.4	9.9	23.8	8.9	34.7	33.9	33.7	52.1	29.8
Military quarters	14.1	14.8	12.1	13.8	10.0	2.0	1.4	5.4	3.2	3.4
Emergency shelters for homeless	3.3	2.4	5.3	3.9	4.7	1.9	1.0	7.0	4.6	7.3
Visible in street locations	1.0	0.7	1.7	1.6	3.5	0.4	0.2	1.3	1.1	2.2
Shelters for abused women	0.1	0.1	0.1	0.1	0.1	0.3	0.2	0.5	0.9	1.1
Group homes for drug/alcohol abuse	1.1	1.0	1.3	1.1	1.0	0.4	0.3	1.1	0.6	0.7
Other noninstitutional quarters	8.0	8.4	4.9	14.7	16.5	7.7	7.4	6.9	15.6	20.5
Percent distribution (horizontal)										
Total persons in group quarters	100.0	68.1	24.1	7.7	10.5	100.0	83.6	12.0	4.4	4.1
Institutionalized persons	100.0	60.5	32.8	6.6	12.2	100.0	88.2	10.0	1.8	2.7
Correctional institutions	100.0	45.3	45.6	9.1	17.9	100.0	46.3	45.5	8.2	15.4
Nursing homes	100.0	87.4	10.6	2.0	2.7	100.0	92.4	6.5	1.1	1.5
Other institutions	100.0	69.2	25.1	5.6	8.0	100.0	77.6	18.2	4.2	5.6
Noninstitutionalized persons	100.0	75.0	16.3	8.7	8.9	100.0	78.6	14.2	7.2	5.7
College dormitories	100.0	83.1	9.6	7.4	3.7	100.0	81.8	11.7	6.6	3.5
Military quarters	100.0	71.6	20.8	7.6	7.4	100.0	59.8	33.1	7.2	7.2
Emergency shelters for homeless	100.0	51.0	39.6	9.4	15.3	100.0	45.1	44.4	10.6	15.8
Visible in street locations	100.0	49.1	38.8	12.1	35.7	100.0	44.8	42.2	13.0	25.4
Shelters for abused women	100.0	54.2	32.6	13.2	17.9	100.0	59.3	17.8	12.1	14.3
Group homes for drug/alcohol abuse	100.0	62.5	29.5	8.0	9.8	100.0	60.4	33.0	6.6	7.4
Other noninstitutional quarters	100.0	71.0	14.8	14.2	21.5	100.0	80.4	10.7	8.8	10.9

Source: U. S. Bureau of the Census, "General Population Characteristics," 1990 Census of Population, CP-1-1, U.S. Government Printing Office, Washington, D.C., 1992, Table 35.

Trends in Institutionalized Populations

by Alison Kadlec Donta

In 1990, 1.3% of the U.S. population was institutionalized. Of these persons, 53.3% lived in nursing homes, 3.9% were in mental hospitals, 33.4% were in correctional institutions, and 9.5% resided in other institutions. These numbers represent a change in percent and distribution of institutionalized persons from the previous two decades. Only 0.6% of the U.S. population lived in an institutional setting in 1970 while the 1.1% of the 1980 population that was institutionalized was similar to the percent for 1990. The distribution of these persons, however, has changed. In 1970, for example, only 27% of the institutionalized population was found in nursing homes while mental hospitals accounted for 21.2% of this population. By 1980, in contrast, 57.2% of the institutionalized population resided in nursing homes, only 19.8% were found in mental hospitals, and 18.7% were inmates in a correctional institution.

This is further illustrated in the table below which presents the rates of institutionalization per 1,000 U.S. population for the years 1970, 1980, and 1990. In 1970, only 1.49 per 1,000 people in the U.S. lived in nursing homes but by 1980 that rate was up to 6.30 and further increased to 7.12 per 1,000 by 1990. The increase in rates of nursing home institutionalization can be explained, in part, by an increase in the elderly population most likely to be served by nursing homes. At the same time, this increase in nursing home rates may also represent the changing pattern of family organization with respect to the elderly. For many elderly people, living in a family means living with a spouse and with the death of that spouse, many of them are not incorporated into other families (such as those of their children or siblings), but instead live alone and/or in nursing homes. This trend has increased from 1970 to 1990. A third explanation for the rise in nursing home rates can be found in the decrease in rates of mental

hospital institutionalization over the same time period.

In 1970, there were 1.17 persons institutionalized in mental hospitals per 1,000 U.S. population. This rate was reduced slightly to 1.08 by 1980 and was then reduced by more than 50% to 0.52 by 1990. This great reduction in rate over the past decades is largely due to the burgeoning practice of deinstitutionalization. Many of the chronic mentally ill began to be deinstitutionalized beginning in the mid 1950's although it was not until the 1970's that large-scale population movements began to occur. Many of the mentally ill were moved from mental hospitals to nursing homes beginning in the late 1960's and 1970's following a decision in 1965 that now made nursing homes eligible to collect Medicaid payments.

A third major institutionalized population is that of correctional institutions. In the 1990 Census, there were 1,115,111 people residing in correctional institutions. The rate of this institutionalization has also changed over the past few decades. In 1980 the rate of institutionalization in correctional facilities in the U.S. was 2.06 per 1,000 population and this rate more than doubled to 4.48 in 1990. The U.S. has one of the highest prisoner-to-population ratios and one of the highest reported absolute number of prisoners in the world. Between 1980 and 1990, the number of persons under jurisdiction of state and federal prison authority rose 134% to reach a record 771,243 inmates at year end 1990. Prisons nationwide were operating between 18% and 29% in excess of their capacities in 1990. As of January 1, 1992, prisons in forty states, the District of Columbia, and over 500 jails were found by the courts to be characterized by overcrowding and related conditions in violation of federal or state constitutions.

The second table describes some of the demographic characteristics of this population. Since 1980, the rate of correctional institutionalization has increased for all major race-ethnic groups, but has increased proportion-

ally more for blacks and Hispanics. In 1980, 48.9% of the correctional population was white, 42.6% was black, and 10.0% was of Hispanic origin. By 1990, however, those percentages had changed to 45.4% white, 45.6% black, and 17.7% Hispanic. The increase in the percentage of the general population that was black (from 11.8% in 1980 to 12.3% in 1990) and Hispanic (from 6.5% to 9.0%) was not as great as the increase in the proportion of inmates who were of these groups. Although the sex ratio has decreased from 1980 to 1990, the number

Persons in Correctional Institutions per 1,000 Population, by Race-ethnicity, and Sex Ratio: 1980 and 1990

Characteristics	1990	1980
Total persons	4.48	2.06
White	2.42	1.17
Black	16.59	7.42
American Indian/Alaskan Native	8.57	5.94
Asian/Pacific Islander	0.99	0.59
Hispanic	8.75	3.14
Male: female ratio	12.1	16.2

Source: U.S. Bureau of the Census, 1990 Census of Population, "General Population Characteristics," Table 35, and 1980 Census of Population, "Detailed Population Characteristics," Table 266, U.S. Government Printing Office, Washington, D.C., 1992, 1983.

of males still greatly outweighs the number of females in correctional populations. The age distribution of new prison admissions has changed slightly. In 1985, 39.4% of new court commitments in 35 states were aged 18-24 and by 1990 this proportion was only 34.0%. In contrast, 1990 saw an increase in the proportion of new commitments aged 30-34 (from 15.3% to 18.3%) and those aged 35-44 (from 13.9% to 17.0%).

Future trends in institutionalization may include a continued increase in the numbers of people living in nursing homes due to an increasingly aging U.S. population as a whole. At the same time, the rates of institutionalization in correctional facilities also threaten to rise. The fate of mental hospitalization, however, remains unclear. Deinstitutionalization may not have been as effective as was originally envisioned and many people released from mental institutions have ended up untreated and/or homeless. States may begin to reconsider their policies of deinstitutionalization.

Additional Sources:

Bureau of Justice Statistics. *Sourcebook of Criminal Justice Statistics, 1990 and 1992.* Washington, D.C.: U.S. Government Printing Office, 1991 and 1993.

Bureau of Justice Statistics. *Prisons and Prisoners in the United States.* Washington, D.C.: U.S. Government Printing Office, 1992. NCJ-137002.

Institutionalized Persons per 1,000 Population: 1970-1990

Type of institution	1990	1980	1970
Nursing homes[1]	7.12	6.30	1.49
Mental hospitals	0.52	1.08	1.17
Correctional institutions	4.48	2.06	2.87
Other institutions	1.28	1.56	

[1] "Home for the aged" in 1970 and 1980.

Source: U.S. Bureau of the Census, 1990 Census of Population," General Population Characteristics," Table 35, 1980 Census of Population, "Detailed Population Characteristics," Table 266, and 1970 Census of Population, "Detailed Population Characteristics," Table 205, U.S. Government Printing Office, Washington, D.C., 1992, 1983, and 1973.

Table 11-24. Percent Persons in Group Quarters, by Age, Sex, and Race-ethnicity: 1990

Age (years)	Males in group quarters		Females in group quarters	
	Institutionalized	Other	Institutionalized	Other
White	1.1	1.5	1.3	1.1
Under 6	...	0.1	...	0.1
6 to 14	0.2	0.1	0.1	0.1
15 to 17	0.9	0.4	0.4	0.3
18 to 19	1.0	15.6	0.2	16.2
20 to 24	1.4	8.2	0.2	5.5
25 to 29	1.5	1.4	0.2	0.4
30 to34	1.3	0.8	0.2	0.2
35 to 44	0.9	0.6	0.2	0.2
45 to 54	0.7	0.4	0.3	0.2
55 to 59	0.7	0.4	0.4	0.2
60 to 64	0.8	0.4	0.6	0.3
65 to 74	1.4	0.3	1.6	0.3
75 to 84	4.7	0.3	7.5	0.4
85 and over	16.9	0.4	28.7	0.7
Black	4.2	2.3	1.0	1.2
Under 6	0.1	0.3	...	0.3
6 to 14	0.4	0.3	0.2	0.2
15 to 17	3.4	0.9	0.6	0.7
18 to 19	5.0	12.1	0.4	12.3
20 to 24	8.3	8.9	0.7	5.3
25 to 29	9.3	2.9	1.0	1.0
30 to34	8.3	2.3	0.9	0.6
35 to 44	5.6	1.8	0.6	0.4
45 to 54	2.5	1.1	0.5	0.2
55 to 59	1.9	0.8	0.6	0.2
60 to 64	2.1	0.7	0.9	0.2
65 to 74	2.8	0.4	2.0	0.2
75 to 84	5.9	0.3	6.2	0.2
85 and over	13.1	0.4	18.2	0.4
Hispanic	1.9	1.6	0.4	0.7
Under 6	...	0.3	...	0.3
6 to 14	0.2	0.3	0.1	0.2
15 to 17	1.7	0.8	0.3	0.5
18 to 19	2.3	6.5	0.2	5.4
20 to 24	3.3	4.5	0.3	2.2
25 to 29	3.7	1.9	0.4	0.6
30 to34	3.5	1.5	0.4	0.4
35 to 44	2.7	1.3	0.3	0.3
45 to 54	1.5	1.1	0.2	0.3
55 to 59	1.0	0.9	0.2	0.2
60 to 64	1.0	0.8	0.4	0.2
65 to 74	1.3	0.5	0.9	0.2
75 to 84	3.2	0.3	3.3	0.3
85 and over	9.1	0.4	12.0	0.6

Source: U.S. Bureau of the Census, "General Population Characteristics," 1990 Census of Population, CP-1-1, U.S. Government Printing Office, Washington, D.C., 1992, Table 26.

Conclusion

Household living arrangements are both more stable and more fluid than once believed. The general predominance of traditional living arrangements is likely to remain into the considerable future. However, even among these traditional households there are changing age patterns of entry into householding, increasing small fractions of the population seeking alternative arrangements, decreased family size within these households, and increased child-bearing out of wedlock, among other changes. Continued metropolitanization, entry of women into the labor force, decreased fertility, and an aging population are among the long-run social changes driving family structures. In the more recent past, economic recession (which saw real incomes decline, housing costs and interest rates rise, and the proportion of persons living in poverty rise) and a government policy of austerity and cutback in social programs have likely affected the family formation practices of youth and their living arrangements. Young persons who formerly could afford a residence of their own (either as a single or married person) have returned to their parents' homes, delayed household formation, or started sharing living space with others. The elderly are increasingly living alone into older ages. And the incarcerated population has increased dramatically even as those in some other institutional settings have been forced by social policies to seek out alternative living arrangements.

How long the trends documented in this chapter might continue remains to be seen. In any case, it appears to be very unlikely that family life and the household and family statistics will ever again resemble those of the 1950's, which may have represented an all-time high in familism in this country. It is also very unlikely that familism will diminish in popularity as an ideal. But the size, composition, and life cycle characteristics of the family will almost certainly undergo further modifications as the population searches for a better life.

As families and householding behaviors change, children are often those most clearly impacted as their living arrangements change without their choice and often without their consent or welfare in mind. At the same time, living arrangements for children which were once considered undesirable are now recognized as enduring features in our changing society. Nearly a quarter of all families with children are now single-parent families and many married-couple families contain stepchildren from prior marriages or children born out of wedlock. Single parent households are unlikely to disappear or even to dramatically diminish in the near future. If recent trends are any indication, children living with a single parent will be a growing percentage of all families and, although a small fraction of those will be headed by mothers, more single parent families will be headed by fathers.

There are also many other living arrangements, such as singlehood, cohabitation and same-sex partners, that have been considered undesirable or deviant in the past and which are now becoming more common and acceptable.

The composition and trends in the institutionalized population are also certain to be of growing social, economic, political and compassionate concern. The U.S. has one of the highest incarceration rates in the developed world. Many recent initiatives in the criminal justice system attempt to control, rather than accommodate, further growth in the correctional population through other release and residential arrangements. It is clearly troubling to many that the composition of the correctional population and of others living in group quarters reflect substantial social inequities.

Of all the demographic features of the U.S. population, the way in which we choose to live is perhaps most clearly reflected in the types of families and households in which we live. It is not surprising that our social trends, problems, and changing behaviors are reflected in our living arrangements. Nor is it thus surprising that some of these living arrangements themselves merit our concern and attention, as well as our celebration, in the near future.

Bibliography

Ahlburg, Dennis A., and De Vita, Carol J. "New Realities of the American Family." Population Bulletin Vol. 47 No. 2 (August 1992). Population Reference Bureau.

Aquilino, William S. "Family Structure and Home-leaving: A Further Specification of the Relationship." Journal of Marriage and the Family 53 (1991): 999-1010.

Beck, Rubye W., and Beck, Scott. "The Incidence of Extended Households Among Middle-Aged Black and White Women Estimates from a 15-year Panel Study." Journal of Family Issues 10 (1989): 147-68.

Becker, G.S. "A Theory of Marriage: The Economics of the Family." In The Economic Approach to Human Behavior. G.S. Becker (ed.). Chicago: University of Chicago Press, 1981.

_____ A Treatise on the Family. Cambridge: Harvard University Press, 1981.

Bianchi, Suzanne M. "America's Children: Mixed Prospects." Population Bulletin Vol. 45 No. 1 (1990). Population Reference Bureau.

_____ "Changing Concepts of Household and Family in the Census and CPS." In American Statistical Association, 1982 proceedings of the Social Statistics Section (1982):13-22. American Statistical Association, Washington, D.C.

Bianchi, S.M., and Farley, R. "Racial Differences in Family Living Arrangements and Economic Well-Being: An Analysis of Recent Trends." Journal of Marriage and the Family 41 (1979): 537-51.

Billingsley, Andrew. Black Families in White America. Englewood Cliffs, NJ: Prentice-Hall, 1968.

Bumpass, L., and Rindfuss, R.R. "Children's Experience of Marital Disruption." American Journal of Sociology 85 (1979): 49-65.

Burch, Thomas K. "Household and Family Demography: A Bibliographic Essay." Population Index 45 (1979): 173-95.

Burr, Jeffrey A., and Mutchler, Jan E. "The Living Arrangement of Unmarried Elderly Hispanic Females." Demography 29 (1992): 93-112.

Chadwick, Bruce A., and Heaton, Tim B. Statistical Handbook on the American Family. Statistical Handbook Series No. 4, 1992.

Cherlin, A. Marriage, Divorce, Remarriage. Cambridge: Harvard University Press, 1981.

_____ "Remarriage as an Incomplete Institution." American Journal of Sociology 84 (1978): 634-50.

Cherlin, Andrew, and McCarthy, James. "Remarried Couple Households: Data from the June 1980 Current Population Survey." Journal of Marriage and the Family 47 (1985): 23-30.

Cooney, R.S., and Min, K. "Demographic Characteristics Affecting Living Arrangements Among Young Currently Unmarried Puerto Rican, Non-Spanish Black, and Non-Spanish White Mothers." Ethnicity 8 (1981): 107-20.

Crouter, A.C. "Children of Working Parents." Human Ecology Forum 12 (1982): 22-6.

Danziger, S., et al. "Work and Welfare as Determinants of Female Poverty and Household Headship." Quarterly Journal of Economy 97 (1982): 519-34.

Darity, William A., and Myers, Samuel L. "Does Welfare Dependency Cause Female Headship? The Case of the Black Family." Journal of Marriage and the Family 46 (1984): 765-79.

Dawson, Deborah A. "Family Structure and Children's Health: United States, 1988." Vital and Health Statistics, Series 10. Data from the National Health Survey No. 178, 1991.

Espenshade, T.J., and Braun, R.E. "Life Course Analysis and Multistate Demography: An Application to Marriage, Divorce, and Remarriage." Journal of Marriage and the Family 44 (1982): 1025-36.

Ferris, Abott L. Indicators of Change in the American Family. New York: The Russell Sage Foundation, 1970.

Frey, William H., and Kobrin, Frances E. "Changing Families and Changing Mobility: Their Impact on the Central City." Demography 19 (1982): 261-77.

Frisbie, W. Parker, Bean, Frank D., and Poston, Dudley L. "Household and Family Demography of Hispanics, Blacks and Anglos." University of Texas-Austin, Texas Population Research Center, Vol. 284. January 1985.

Garfinkel, Irwin, and McLanahan, Sara S. Single Mothers and Their Children: A New American Dilemma. Washington, D.C.: Urban Institute Press, 1986.

Glick, Paul C. "American Families: As they are and were." Social Science Research 74 (1990): 139-45.

_____ "The Future Marital Status and Living Arrangements of the Elderly." The Gerontologist 19 (1979): 301-09.

Glick, P., and Spanier, G. "Married and Unmarried Cohabitation in the United States." Journal of Marriage and the Family 32 (1980): 19-30.

Goldscheider, Frances K., and DaVanzo, Julie. "Living Arrangements and the Transition to Adulthood." Demography 22 (1985): 545-63.

Goldscheider, Frances K., and Goldscheider, Calvin (eds.). Ethnicity and the New Family Economy: Living Arrangements and Intergenerational Financial Flows. Boulder, CO/London, England:Westview Press, 1989.

Goldscheider, Frances, Thornton, Arland, and Young-DeMarco, Linda. "A Portrait of the Nestleaving Process in Early Adulthood." Demography 30 (1993): 683-99.

Goldscheider, Frances K., and Waite, Linda J. New Families, No Families? The Transformation of the American Home. Berkeley:University of California Press, 1991.

Gyourko, J., and Linneman, P. "The Affordability of the American Dream: An Examination of the Last 30 Years." Journal of Housing Research 4 (1993): 39-72.

Grossbard-Shechtman, A. "Gary Becker's Theory of the Family: Some Interdisciplinary Considerations." Sociology and Social Research 66 (1981): 1-11.

Heller, P.L. et al. "Familism in Rural and Urban America: Critique and Reconceptualization of a Construct." Rural Sociology 46 (1981): 446-64.

Hernandez, Donald J. "Studies in Household and Family Formation: When Households Continue, Discontinue, and Form." Current Population Reports, Series P-23 No. 179, U.S. Bureau of the Census. Washington D.C.:U.S. Government Printing Office, 1992.

Himes, Christine L. "Social Demography of Contemporary Families and Aging." Generations 17 (1992): 13-6.

Hofferth, Sandra L. "Recent Trends in the Living Arrangements of Children: A Cohort Life Table Analysis." In Family Demography: Methods and Their Application. John Bongaarts, Thomas K. Burch, and Kenneth W. Wachter (eds.). International Studies in Demography, Oxford: Oxford University Press, 1987.

Johnson, B.L., and Waldman, E. "Marital and Family Patterns of the Labor Force." Monthly Labor Review 104 (1981): 36-8.

Keeley, M. "The Economics of Family Formation." Economic Inquiry 15 (1977): 238-50.

Kent, M.O. "Remarriage: A Family Systems Perspective." Social Casework 61 (1980): 146-53.

Kenyatta, M.L. "In Defense of the Black Family: The Impact of Racism on the Family as a Support System." Monthly Review 34 (1983): 12-21.

Kitagawa, E.M. "New Life-Styles: Marriage Patterns, Living Arrangements, and Fertility Outside of Marriage." American Academy of Political and Social Science Annual 453 (1981): 1-27.

Kobrin, F.E. "The Fall in Household Size and the Rise of the Primary Individual in the United States." Demography 13 (1976): 127-38.

_____ "The Primary Individual and the Family: Changes in Living Arrangements in the U.S. Since 1940." Journal of Marriage and the Family 38 (1976): 233-39.

Krishnamoorthy, S. "Family Formation and the Life Cycle ." Demography 16 (1979): 121-29.

Leppel, Karen. "Household Formation and Unrelated Housemates." American Economist 31 (1987): 38-47.

MacDonald, M., and Rindfuss, R. "Earnings, Relative Income, and Family Formation." Demography 18 (1981): 123-36.

Masnick, George, and Bane, Mary Jo. The Nation's Families: 1960-1990. Boston: Auburn House, 1980.

Matthaei, J.A. "Consequences of the Rise of the Two-earner Family: The Breakdown of the Sexual Division of Labor." American Economic Review Papers and Proceedings 70 (1980): 198-213.

McAuley, W.J., and Nutty, C.L. "Residential Preferences and Moving Behavior: A Family Lifecycle Analysis." Journal of Marriage and the Family 44 (1982): 301-09.

Mcleod, P.B., and Ellis, J.R. "Housing Consumption over the Family Life Cycle: An Empirical Analysis." Urban Studies 19 (1982): 177-85.

Michael, R.T. et al. "Changes in the Propensity to Live Alone: 1950-1976." Demography 17 (1980): 39-56.

Nock, S.L. "Family Life-Cycle Transitions: Longitudinal Effects on Family Members." Journal of Marriage and the Family 43 (1981):703-14.

Rawlings, Steve W. "Household and Family Characteristics: March 1992." Current Population Reports, Series P-20 No. 467, U.S. Bureau of the Census. Washington D.C.:U.S. Government Printing Office, 1993.

Richards, Toni, White, Michael J., and Tsui, Amy O. "Changing Living Arrangements: A Hazard Model of Transitions Among Household Types." Demography 24 (1987): 77-97.

Rindfuss, Ronald R., and Jones, Jo Ann. "One Parent or Two? The Intertwining of American Marriage and Fertility Patterns." Sociological Forum 6 (1991): 311-26.

Ruggles, Steven. "The Origins of African-American Family Structure." American Sociological Review 59 (1994): 136-151.

_____ Prolonged Connections: The Rise of The Extended Family in Nineteenth-Century America. Madison: University of Wisconsin Press, 1987.

Santi, Lawrence L. "Change in the Structure and Size of American Households: 1970 to 1985." Journal of Marriage and the Family 49 (1987): 833-7.

_____ "The Demographic Context of Recent Change in the Structure of American Households." Demography 25 (1988): 509-19.

_____ "Household Headship Among Unmarried Persons in the United States, 1970-1985." Demography 27 (1990): 219-32.

Seward, Rudy R. The American Family: A Demographic History. Beverly Hills: Sage Publications, 1978.

Spanier, G.B. et al. "An Empirical Evaluation of the Family Life Cycle." Journal of Marriage and the Family 41 (1979): 27-38.

Spanier, G.B., and Glick, P.C. "The Life Cycle of American Families: An Expanded Analysis." Journal of Divorce 3 (1980): 283-98.

Sweet, James A. "Components of Change in the Number of Households 1970-1980." Demography 21 (1984): 129-40.

Sweet, James A., and Bumpass, Larry L. "American Families and Households." The Population of the United States in the 1980's: A Census Monograph Series, New York: Russell Sage, 1987.

Teachman, J., Polonko, K., and Scanzoni, J. "Demography of the Family: A Review of Recent Trends and Developments in the Field." In Handbook of Marriage and the Family. M. Sussman and S. Steinmetz (eds.). Boston: Plenum, 1982.

Treas, J. "Postwar Trends in Family Size." Demography 18 (1981): 321-34.

Tsui, Amy O. "Family Formation Process Among U.S. Marriage Cohorts." Demography 19 (1982): 1-27.

U.S. Bureau of the Census. "Home Alone in 1989." Current Housing Reports, Series H121/92-4. Washington D.C.:U.S.Government Printing Office, 1992.

_____ "Marital Status and Living Arrangements: March 1992." Current Population Reports, Series P-20 No. 468. Washington D.C.:U.S. Government Printing Office, 1992.

_____ "Population Profile of the United States: 1991." Current Population Reports, Series P-23 No. 173. Washington D.C:U.S. Government Printing Office, 1991.

_____ "Projections of the Number of Households and Families: 1986 to 2000." Current Population Reports, Series P-25 No. 986. Washington D.C.:U.S. Government Printing Office, 1986.

_____ "Studies in Marriage and the Family." Current Population Reports, Series P-23 No. 162. Washington D.C.:U.S. Government Printing Office, 1989.

Waite, Linda. "Working Wives and the Family Life Cycle." American Journal of Sociology 86 (1980): 272-94.

Waite, Linda J., Goldscheider, Frances K., and Witsberger, Christina. "Nonfamily Living and the Erosion of Traditional Family Orientations Among Young Adults." American Sociological Review 51 (1986): 541-54.

Watkins, Susan C., Menken, Jane A., and Bongaarts, John. "Demographic Foundations of Family Change." American Sociological Review 52 (1987): 346-58.

Wattenberg, E., and Reinhardt, H. "Female-Headed Families: Trends and Implications." Social Work 24 (1979): 460-67.

Wetzel, James R. "American Families: 75 years of change." Monthly Labor Review 118 (1990): 4-13.

Wojtkiewicz, Roger A., McLanahan, Sara S., and Garfinkel, Irwin. "The Growth of Families Headed by Women: 1950-1980." Demography 27 (1990): 19-30.

EDUCATIONAL ENROLLMENT AND ATTAINMENT

The recent history of the United States is one of increasing interest in, and demand for, a more educated citizenry. National interests in educational quality have become more politically significant as we become more aware of the role that an educated labor force plays in a competitive, and increasingly global, marketplace. Education is also necessary to prepare individuals for the simple tasks of daily life in what has been called 'the information age.' And the historically recognized demand for an educated citizenry in democratic societies has become more significant worldwide as democratic institutions have risen in prominence and power over the past few decades.

Education is also a personal investment of importance to all of us. Nowadays even routine tasks in factories and offices demand knowledge and skills that those with more education often command more fully than those with less. The rise of service and information industries, the professionalization of occupations, and the increasing use of technology in the workplace require, or at least benefit from, additional technical training beyond high school, either in colleges and universities or in special courses. Education increasingly plays an important role in our sense of self and shapes how we relate to our place in a rapidly advancing post-industrial society.

Because education of the adult population also has a high correlation (with causal implications) with income, with occupation, with status or social position in the community, with certain buying habits, with many attitudes and opinions, and with a great variety of other elements in human life, it is one of the most widely used population variables. It is also essential, therefore, that sociologists, economists, and analysts in other related fields comprehend the recent changes that have taken place in the level of educational attainment and the further changes that may be expected.

Finally, many policy makers, public planners and town officials have immediate practical concerns over the changing size of successively entering school cohorts, trends in the number of students dropping out of secondary educational institutions, and less well-known details of school enrollments.

In each decennial census since 1940 and in its Current Population Survey the Bureau of the Census has obtained information about the school attendance and achievement of persons of all ages (see Definition Box). These data measure only the quantity, not the quality, of school attendance and achievement, so they answer some but not all of the questions being asked about educational trends. Our growing interest in educational quality over time may lead to more consistent national level data across time. However, the most reliable longitudinal information at present concerns the quantity of education. The quantity of education can be studied from the census using both data on current school attendance, or enrollments, and on educational attainment, or achievement.

At the turn of the century only about half of the children of school age, 5-19 years, were attending school. As Figure 12-1 shows, up to 1970 school enrollment rates (the percentage of school-age children enrolled in school) rose steadily. Between 1960 and 1970 enrollments rose from over eighty to over eighty-five percent. Since 1970 enrollment rates have fluctuated but remained more or less stable. Although the percent of the population enrolled in school appears to be leveling off below ninety percent, it must be remembered that the percentage enrollment has changed, and may still change, dramatically in the future. It is also important to bear in mind that it is the percentage, not the number, of enrollments that has apparently stabilized in recent decades.

The average number of students who attend school daily is given from 1870 to 1990 in Figure 12-2 along with the pupil-teacher ratio over the same years. The average daily attendance increased steadily until the years surrounding World War II when many young adults entered military service rather than continuing with school,

Chapter 12 Definitions
Educational Enrollment and Attainment

The following definitions of educational demographic terms are generally those of the 1990 Census. Differences in definitions which may be appropriate to data from the Current Population Survey (CPS) are noted.

School Enrollment. For the 1990 Census, persons were classified as enrolled in school if they reported attending a "regular" school or college at any time between February 1, 1990, and the time of census enumeration. Regular schooling includes nursery school, kindergarten, elementary school, and schooling that leads to a high school diploma or college degree. For comparison, the CPS counts as enrolled anyone who was enrolled at any time during the current term or school year in any type of graded public, parochial, or other private school in the regular school system. Attendance may be either full time or part time and during the day or night.

Level and Year of School in Which Enrolled (CPS). The levels identified separately are nursery school, kindergarten, elementary school, high school, and college. Children in "Head Start" or similar programs were counted under "nursery school" or "kindergarten," as appropriate. Elementary school includes grades 1-8, and high school includes grades 9-12. Junior high school pupils are reported in elementary school or high school according to their grade. The term "college" includes junior or community colleges, four-year colleges, universities, and graduate or professional schools.

Years of School Completed (CPS). Data on years of school completed were derived from the combination of answers to two questions: (a) "What is the highest grade of school he (sic) has ever attended?" and (b) "Did he (sic) finish this grade?" The number in each category of highest grade of school completed represents the combination of (a) persons who reported the indicated grade as the highest grade attended and that

they had finished it, (b) those who had attended the next higher grade but had not finished it, and (c) those still attending the next higher grade. Persons who have not completed the first year of elementary school are classified as having no years of school completed.

College Enrollment (CPS). Those enrolled in college include persons reporting themselves as attending or enrolled in college, including anyone who had been enrolled at any time during the current term or school year, except those who had left for the remainder of the term. Regular college enrollment includes those persons attending a four-year or two-year college, university, or professional school (such as medical or law school), or in courses that may advance the student towards a recognized college or university degree (e.g. B.A. or M.A.). Attendance may be either full time or part time, during the day or night. The college student need not be working toward a degree, but he/she must be enrolled in a class for which credit would be applied toward a degree.

Full-Time and Part-Time Attendance (CPS). Attending college full time means taking twelve or more hours of classes during the average school week, and part time means taking less than twelve hours of classes during the average school week.

Two-Year and Four-Year Colleges (CPS). College students were asked to report whether the college in which they were enrolled was a two-year college (junior or community college) or a four-year college or university. Students enrolled in the first four years were classified by the type of college they reported.

School Enrollment Rates. The percentage of persons in a particular category of population who are enrolled in school, as defined above. Rates may be specific for sex, age, race-ethnicity, residential categories, or other traits. Rates may be computed for families that contain

members of school-going ages (ages three to thirty-four).

Public or Private School. In general, a "public" school is defined as any school controlled and supported primarily by a local, state, or Federal government agency; a "private" school is a school controlled or supported primarily by a religious organization or other private group.

Vocational School Enrollment. Enrollment in business, vocational, technical, secretarial, trade, or correspondence courses which are not counted as regular school enrollment and are not for recreation or adult education classes. Courses counted as college enrollment should not also be included as vocational.

Educational Attainment. A sample of persons 15 years old and over are classified according to the highest level of school completed or the highest degree received by the Census. The question asked included instructions to report the level of the previous grade attended or the highest degree received for persons currently enrolled in school. The question also included response categories which allowed persons to report completing the 12th grade without receiving a high school diploma, and which instructed respondents to report as "high school graduate(s)" persons who received either a high school diploma or the equivalent (e.g. passing the Test of General Educational Development) and did not attend college. Schooling completed in foreign or ungraded school systems was reported as the equivalent level of schooling in the American system. Vocational certificates or diplomas are not to be reported unless they were college level degrees, and honorary degrees are not reported.

Persons who did not report educational attainment were imputed the attainment of a person of the same age, race or Hispanic origin, and sex who resided in the same or nearby area. Persons who provided multiple responses were edited to the highest level or degree reported.

and then the children who represented the beginnings of a post-war baby boom were still too young to attend school. From the late 1940's through the early seventies the influence of the baby boom and expanded schooling across younger and adolescent ages combined to produce a dramatic rise in average attendance. In more recent years there has been a short-term downturn in average attendance reflecting declining fertility of the past several decades and the passage of the baby boom cohorts. Since 1985, however, there has been a renewed

upswing in average attendance. Since before the turn of the century the expansion of educational institutions has consistently kept pace with these rising enrollments as indicated by the more-or-less consistent decline in the number of pupils per teacher. This decline in pupils per teacher naturally slowed during the rapid expansion of attendance due to the baby boom and accelerated during more recent years of declining average attendance.

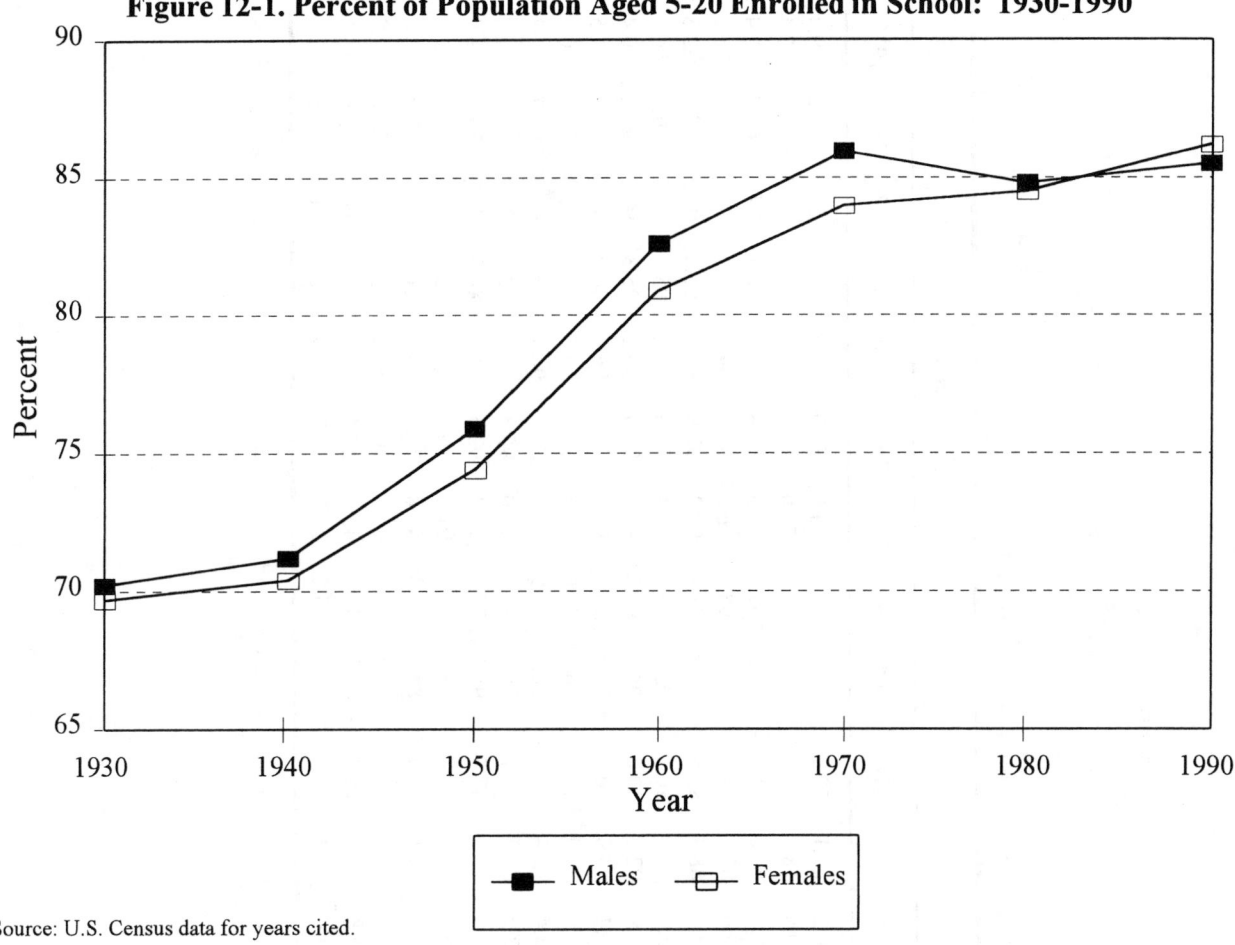

Figure 12-1. Percent of Population Aged 5-20 Enrolled in School: 1930-1990

Source: U.S. Census data for years cited.

Enrollment of Children and Adolescents

Most concern with education has historically been over the education of children and adolescents involved in compulsory education. The record of changes in school enrollment among children and adolescents is given by age and sex in Table 12-1 for censuses taken in this century. In the most recent census, nearly all children between the ages of seven and fourteen (second to eighth grade) are attending school. The law of almost every state compels school attendance at those ages, and in several states attendance is mandatory until age sixteen. Nonetheless, school enrollment has declined slightly in these ages since 1980. This decline may reflect the definition of 'regular' enrollment used in the census which excludes recently increasing in-home and alternative educational arrangements. Attendance between ages seven and fourteen has not always been so nearly universal. In 1910 parents appear to have been much less insistent than they are today that their children between six and nine years of age attend school, and at age twelve (now the age at which attendance reaches its peak rate) only 91 percent were enrolled in school. From age fourteen to age fifteen, among both boys and girls, there was a sharp drop in school attendance. At those ages children were economically useful for farm work and could help to lighten the housework attendant upon raising large families.

Preschool Enrollments

As education has become more important to a successful future and more women have entered the work force, preschool enrollments have assumed new importance and have received greater attention. At the youngest ages there has been a steady increase in school enrollment. Reliable historical data is not available for those at the earliest ages and institutionalized opportunities for such children are relatively new. However, at ages five and six, attendance in 1980 was at unprecedented high levels, having risen from much lower levels that, until 1950, were comparatively unchanging (Table 12-1). In the 1990 census the percentage of five and six year olds who were enrolled dropped rather sharply from the record 1980 levels despite remaining higher than the comparable

Table 12-1. Percent Enrolled in School by Single Years of Age and Sex for the United States: 1910-1990

Age	Males									Females								
	1990	1980	1970	1960	1950	1940	1930	1920	1910	1990	1980	1970	1960	1950	1940	1930	1920	1910
5 to 20 years, total	85.5	84.8	86.0	82.6	75.9	71.2	70.2	64.1	59.1	86.2	84.5	84.0	80.9	74.4	70.4	69.7	64.5	59.4
5 years	67.9	75.5	54.5	44.7	33.9	17.5	19.5	18.3	16.7	68.4	76.2	55.0	45.0	34.7	18.4	20.5	19.3	17.4
6 years	92.3	96.9	89.1	83.0	76.4	68.2	65.5	62.8	51.7	92.5	97.0	89.3	83.4	77.2	70.1	67.1	63.9	52.4
7 years	94.5	98.5	96.6	96.9	94.2	92.2	89.0	83.1	74.7	94.7	98.6	96.5	97.1	94.5	92.7	89.7	83.5	75.2
8 years	95.4	98.8	97.1	97.8	95.6	94.7	94.0	88.3	82.5	95.3	98.8	97.2	97.9	95.7	95.0	94.3	88.6	82.8
9 years	95.6	98.9	97.3	97.9	96.0	95.5	95.4	90.3	86.1	95.7	98.9	97.4	98.0	96.2	95.7	95.7	90.5	86.3
10 years	95.5	98.6	97.0	97.8	95.9	95.6	96.9	92.9	89.6	95.8	98.8	97.1	97.9	96.2	95.8	97.2	93.2	90.4
11 years	96.1	98.8	97.5	97.7	96.1	95.8	97.4	93.8	90.9	96.2	99.0	97.7	97.8	96.4	96.0	97.6	94.1	91.5
12 years	96.3	98.9	97.5	97.4	95.6	95.3	96.9	93.0	89.2	96.5	99.0	97.6	97.6	96.3	95.7	97.3	93.4	90.3
13 years	96.3	98.8	97.4	96.9	95.7	94.6	96.4	92.4	88.3	96.6	98.9	97.4	97.0	96.0	95.1	96.7	92.7	89.3
14 years	96.3	98.5	96.3	95.4	94.7	92.2	92.9	86.2	80.7	96.5	98.6	96.0	95.3	94.9	92.8	92.9	86.5	81.8
15 years	95.7	97.3	95.7	93.1	91.5	87.3	84.8	71.9	67.5	95.7	96.8	95.3	92.6	91.2	88.0	84.5	73.9	69.0
16 years	93.2	92.6	92.3	86.5	80.6	75.5	65.8	48.2	49.3	93.1	92.5	91.8	86.0	81.1	76.8	66.8	53.3	51.9
17 years	88.1	84.2	86.8	76.3	67.9	60.5	47.1	32.1	34.0	88.5	84.3	85.8	74.8	68.4	61.3	48.8	37.2	36.6
18 years	73.1	62.3	70.1	54.8	42.4	38.1	31.1	20.5	22.1	74.3	61.8	61.0	46.5	37.2	34.7	30.3	22.8	23.0
19 years	56.3	42.3	51.4	37.5	27.8	23.2	20.8	14.0	14.8	60.2	43.6	43.1	28.4	21.8	18.7	18.8	13.6	14.1
20 years	46.2	34.3	38.3	28.1	21.2	14.4	14.6	9.3	9.3	50.6	35.2	29.3	19.3	14.9	10.6	11.7	7.5	7.5

Source: U.S. Bureau of the Census, "Education in the United States: 1990," 1990 CP-3-4, Table 5, "Detailed Population Characteristics: United States Summary," 1980, 1970, and 1960, Tables 260, 197, and 166, U.S. Government Printing Office, Washington, D.C., 1994, 1983, 1973, and 1963. Data for 1910 from Bogue, "The Population of the United States," The Free Press, 1959.

Figure 12-2. Pupil-Teacher Ratio and Average Daily School Attendance: 1870-1990

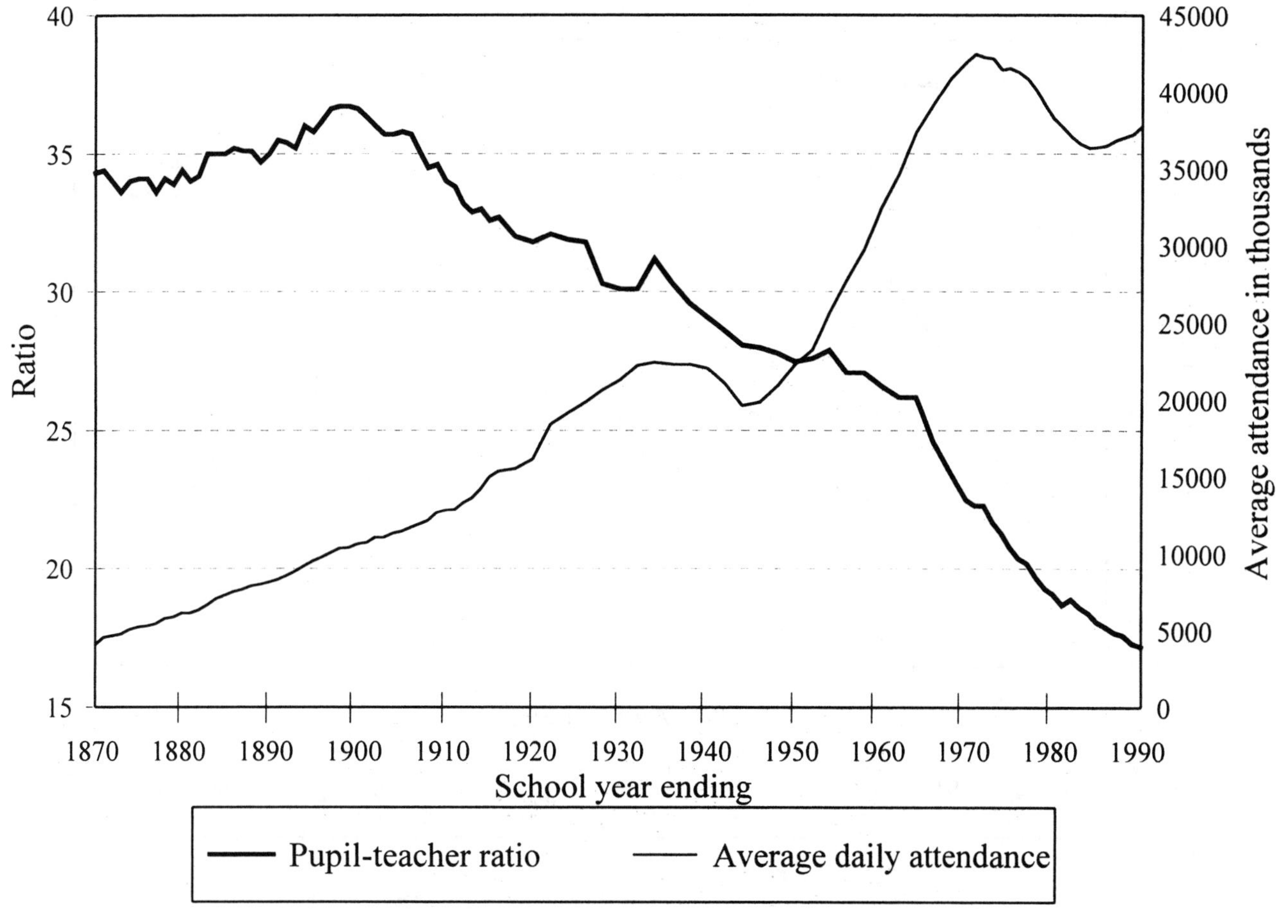

Source: National Center for Education Statistics data.

figures for 1970. This decline may again reflect a greater role of in-home and alternative education alternatives. Or the decline may reflect increasingly difficult cost burdens of sending children to school at early ages and declining social support for preschool education. Enrollment data alone is insufficient to suggest why these changes have taken place. Again, the most important fact is that enrollment at these ages remains considerably higher than it had been during the earlier years of this century. The magnitude of these differences can be seen in Figure 12-3.

Post-Compulsory Enrollments

As with schooling prior to ages of compulsory attendance, between 1910 and 1990 the proportion of children remaining in school after passing the age of compulsory attendance increased dramatically. For example, in 1910 only 34 percent of males seventeen years of age were still in school, but by 1990 the proportion had reached almost 90 percent. Similarly, the enrollment increased from 22.1 to 73.1 percent for males age 18, from 14.8 to 56.3 percent for those age 19, and from 9.3 to

46.2 percent for those age 10 between 1910 and 1990. Increases in the enrollments at these ages were even greater for women when comparing 1910 to 1990. Enrollment among men and women ages seventeen through twenty generally increased throughout the years leading up to 1970. The only exception to this trend prior to 1970 was a decreased enrollment of males of military ages between 1910 and 1920. In the decade between 1970 and 1980, however, the rates of attendance at ages sixteen to nineteen changed very little or substantially declined as the many young men and women in these ages entered the labor force and military instead of remaining in school. Over the last decade, 1980 to 1990, the percentage enrolled in school at older ages has again continued to increase. This most recent increase in enrollment came even as enrollment at the primary ages of schooling declined slightly. Moreover, the recent increase at older ages was dramatic. Those enrolled in school at ages 16 through 20 all reached record levels for both males and females in the 1990 census. The magnitude of the increase in those enrolled at older ages may be seen in Figure 12-3. The extent to which these figures are affected by genuine in-

Figure 12-3. Percent of 5-7 Year Olds and 14-18 Year Olds Enrolled in School, by Sex: 1910 and 1990

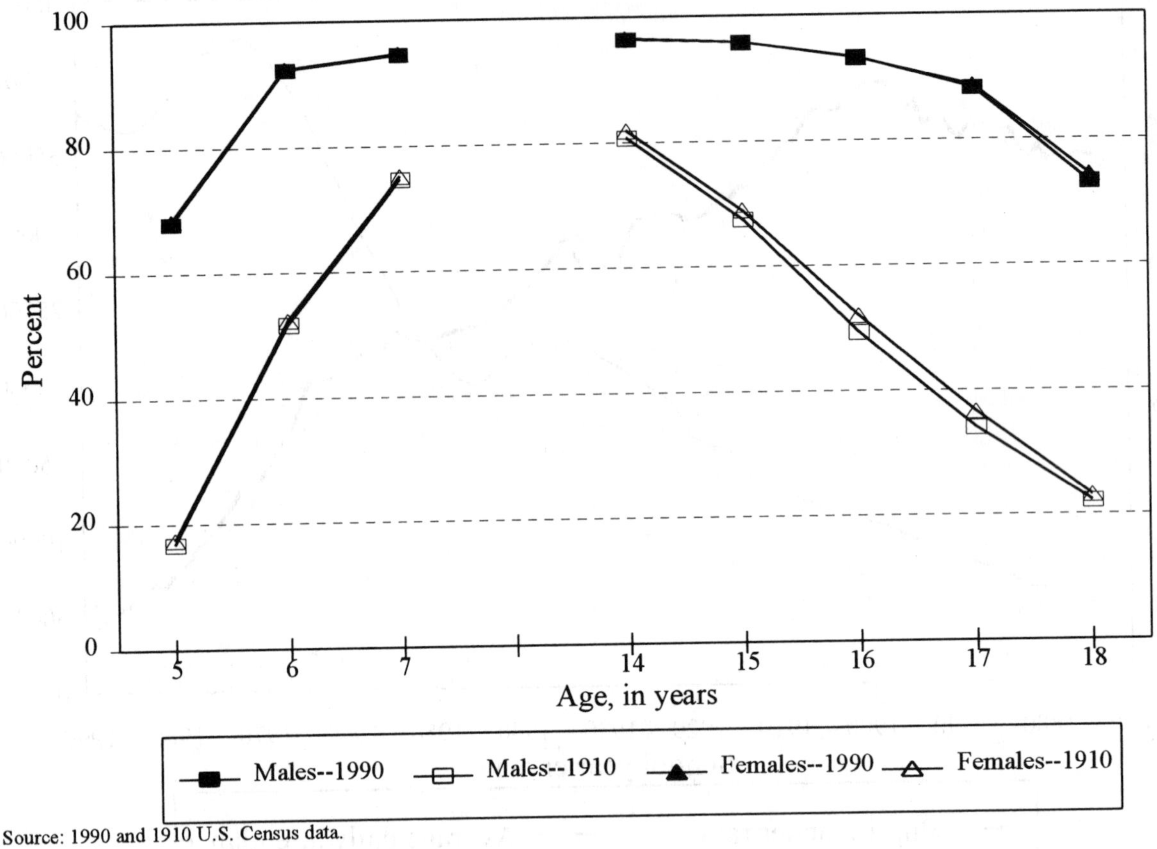

Source: 1990 and 1910 U.S. Census data.

creases in the probability individuals are more likely to remain enrolled, by the return to school of those who left at a slightly younger age, by the increasing recognition of the value of education for personal success, and by the undercounting of those most disadvantaged in the census remain open questions. It is clear, however, that despite some fluctuations in recent years, the overall trend to increased enrollment in schools is relatively consistent over time.

Declining Sex Differences in Young Adult Enrollments

Some of the most significant trends in educational enrollments over the course of the past century have involved differences in the enrollments of young men and women. Between the ages of seven and fourteen, girls have a slightly higher rate of school enrollment than boys, but the difference is small (Table 12-1). Perhaps surprisingly, these differences were small early in the century. Differences in enrollment by sex were

also small among those age 5-7 or 14-18 in both 1910 and 1990 (Figure 12-2). Increases in enrollment across ages would at first appear to have steadily increased over this century regardless of a person's sex. The greatest differences in enrollment, however, occurred in the middle of this century for those at older ages. Between 1930 and 1950, increasing enrollments of males age 18-20 created a significant gender gap in those enrolled at these ages. These trends were, in part, fueled by the entry of young men into college and young women into marriage and childbearing. It was not until 1980 that women closed the gender enrollment gap at these ages. By 1990 women had a greater percent enrolled across these ages. This trend was, again in part, fueled by the entry of young women into college and some delay of marriage and childbearing.

Mid-Life Enrollments

In more recent years, education has become increasingly important beyond the traditional years of schooling

Table 12-2. Percent of Persons 3 Years of Age and Over Enrolled in School, by Age, Sex, and Race-ethnicity: 1980 and 1990

Percent enrolled in school	Both sexes		Male		Female	
	1990	1980	1990	1980	1990	1980
All races, total	27.3	28.7	28.2	30.1	26.5	27.3
3 to 4 years	28.9	32.8	28.7	32.8	29.0	32.8
5 to 6 years	80.1	86.3	79.9	86.1	80.3	86.5
7 to 13 years	95.7	98.8	95.7	98.8	95.8	98.9
14 to 15 years	96.0	97.8	96.0	97.9	96.1	97.7
16 to 17 years	90.7	88.4	90.6	88.4	90.8	88.4
18 to 19 years	65.5	52.4	64.3	52.2	66.9	52.5
20 to 21 years	45.6	32.4	43.7	32.5	47.5	32.4
22 to 24 years	25.3	17.3	26.1	19.3	24.5	15.3
25 to 29 years	13.8	10.3	13.9	11.4	13.7	9.3
30 to 34 years	9.6	7.1	9.0	7.3	10.3	7.0
35 to 39 years	8.0	4.8	6.9	4.0	9.2	5.6
40 to 54 years	5.1	2.7	4.0	2.2	6.1	3.2
55 years and over	1.6	0.8	1.5	0.8	1.6	0.9
White, total	25.7	27.4	26.5	28.8	24.9	26.0
3 to 4 years	29.2	31.9	29.1	32.0	29.3	31.9
5 to 6 years	80.0	86.1	79.7	85.9	80.2	86.4
7 to 13 years	95.9	99.0	95.8	99.0	96.0	99.1
14 to 15 years	96.4	98.1	96.4	98.2	96.5	98.0
16 to 17 years	91.4	89.0	91.5	89.1	91.4	88.9
18 to 19 years	66.5	52.8	65.5	52.9	67.6	52.7
20 to 21 years	47.2	33.3	45.6	33.7	48.9	32.8
22 to 24 years	25.3	17.3	26.5	19.7	24.1	15.0
25 to 29 years	13.1	10.1	13.2	11.2	12.9	9.0
30 to 34 years	8.9	6.8	8.2	7.0	9.6	6.6
35 to 39 years	7.5	4.6	6.3	3.8	8.7	5.4
40 to 54 years	4.7	2.5	3.6	2.0	5.8	2.8
55 years and over	1.4	0.8	1.4	0.8	1.5	0.9
Black, total	32.8	35.3	34.0	37.0	31.8	33.8
3 to 4 years	31.0	38.8	30.8	38.7	31.3	38.9
5 to 6 years	81.3	87.2	81.3	87.1	81.3	87.4
7 to 13 years	94.9	97.9	94.9	97.8	95.0	97.9
14 to 15 years	94.9	96.9	94.6	96.8	95.1	96.9
16 to 17 years	89.1	90.4	88.6	92.5	89.7	88.4
18 to 19 years	61.8	51.7	59.8	49.8	63.9	53.5
20 to 21 years	37.0	28.4	33.6	25.6	40.4	31.0
22 to 24 years	21.7	15.8	20.4	15.8	23.0	15.9
25 to 29 years	13.8	10.6	12.7	10.8	14.9	10.4
30 to 34 years	11.1	8.5	10.0	8.1	12.1	8.8
35 to 39 years	9.6	6.1	8.3	5.1	10.8	7.0
40 to 54 years	6.4	3.8	5.3	3.3	7.2	4.2
55 years and over	2.2	1.²	2.1	1.2	2.2	1.5

Table 12-2. Percent of Persons 3 Years of Age and Over Enrolled in School, by Age, Sex, and Race-ethnicity: 1980 and 1990 (continued)

Percent enrolled in school	Both sexes		Male		Female	
	1990	1980	1990	1980	1990	1980
American, Eskimo, Aleut, total	33.5	34.9	34.0	35.6	33.1	34.2
3 to 4 years	25.2	30.8	24.3	31.2	26.2	30.4
5 to 6 years	79.6	84.7	79.7	84.7	79.4	84.6
7 to 13 years	96.0	97.5	95.9	97.5	96.1	97.6
14 to 15 years	94.9	93.8	95.3	93.6	94.5	93.9
16 to 17 years	86.5	76.9	86.5	77.2	86.5	76.6
18 to 19 years	54.2	38.5	54.6	39.2	53.7	37.8
20 to 21 years	29.6	19.3	28.4	18.3	31.0	20.2
22 to 24 years	18.4	12.6	17.9	12.6	18.9	12.7
25 to 29 years	13.1	9.6	11.5	9.2	14.6	10.0
30 to 34 years	10.8	7.8	9.0	7.3	12.4	8.3
35 to 39 years	9.6	5.8	8.0	4.7	11.0	6.9
40 to 54 years	6.5	3.6	5.3	3.0	7.6	4.1
55 years and over	2.1	1.2	1.9	1.0	2.2	1.4
Asian and Pacific Islander, total	37.1	35.3	39.6	38.6	34.7	32.2
3 to 4 years	30.4	40.4	29.8	39.8	31.1	40.9
5 to 6 years	81.3	89.5	81.4	89.7	81.2	89.4
7 to 13 years	96.0	98.2	96.0	98.2	96.1	98.2
14 to 15 years	96.6	97.9	96.5	97.9	96.6	98.0
16 to 17 years	94.4	93.4	94.3	93.8	94.4	93.0
18 to 19 years	83.7	70.7	83.2	70.6	84.3	70.8
20 to 21 years	70.8	54.1	71.2	56.2	70.4	52.0
22 to 24 years	49.9	35.9	54.0	42.6	45.6	29.6
25 to 29 years	28.2	19.9	32.6	25.9	23.8	14.8
30 to 34 years	16.8	11.6	19.5	14.6	14.4	9.1
35 to 39 years	12.1	8.1	13.0	9.2	11.4	7.1
40 to 54 years	7.8	5.2	7.9	6.0	7.7	4.5
55 years and over	3.7	1.7	4.1	1.9	3.3	1.5
Hispanic, total	34.9	35.1	34.9	36.2	34.9	34.1
3 to 4 years	21.2	26.0	21.0	26.2	21.3	25.7
5 to 6 years	78.8	84.6	78.7	84.6	78.8	84.7
7 to 13 years	95.5	98.1	95.4	98.1	95.7	98.2
14 to 15 years	94.6	95.2	94.7	95.8	94.5	94.7
16 to 17 years	84.7	80.2	84.5	80.3	85.0	80.0
18 to 19 years	55.0	43.8	52.8	43.1	57.5	44.5
20 to 21 years	33.5	23.5	31.2	23.3	36.1	23.8
22 to 24 years	21.9	14.6	21.2	15.5	22.8	13.7
25 to 29 years	15.7	9.7	15.4	10.6	16.0	8.7
30 to 34 years	12.4	7.1	11.5	7.6	13.3	6.6
35 to 39 years	10.8	5.0	9.8	4.6	11.9	5.4
40 to 54 years	7.3	3.1	6.4	2.9	8.1	3.3
55 years and over	2.9	1.4	2.9	1.4	3.0	1.4

Source: U.S. Bureau of the Census, "Education in the United States: 1990," 1990 CP-3-4, Table 5, and "Detailed Population Characteristics: United States Summary," 1980, Table 260, U.S. Government Printing Office, Washington, D.C., 1994 and 1984.

for children and adolescents. The rise of college or university training across all ages, the need for mid-life career retraining in the face of technological change, and education as a leisure pursuit among adults all illustrate the expanded influence of education across the life course. In contrast to the relatively minor changes in school enrollment since 1970 among children and adolescents, there has been an uninterrupted rise in enrollment for the 18-34 age group across the last three censuses. Table 12-2 reports data for enrollment at those ages as well as for younger ages by major race-ethnicity group and sex. These are ages which include vocational or professional schooling, college attendance and postgraduate training. At a time when older adolescents were not substantially improving their enrollment rates, there was a surge in adult education, embracing even the post-retirement years to a small extent.

Between 1970 and 1990 the enrollment rates for those age 18-19 increased by nearly nine percent, for those age 20-21 by nearly fifteen percent, and for those age 22-24 by just over ten percent. These are the primary years benefitting by increased undergraduate college enrollments. Even though fewer individuals are enrolled at even greater ages, the changes in enrollment are even more dramatic at higher ages. The percentage of those enrolled among those age 25-29 nearly doubled and the percentage enrollment more than doubled for those age 30-34 between 1970 and 1990. If this trend continues, its significance could parallel the dramatic rise in enrollment during childhood and adolescence over the past century. There are, however, alternative reactions to this trend including some desire to shorten the enrollment time required to graduate from college or obtain other educational credentials. Ultimately the continuation of these trends will likely depend upon matters somewhat beyond such policy decisions. To the extent that such trends represent increased educational demands and required instructional time, mid-career retraining, or leisure and personal pursuit of education for its own sake, enrollment may continue to rise, stabilize or decline largely independent of policy decisions concerning required enrollment.

Emerging Sex Differences in Adult Enrollments

Just as differences in enrollment of young men and women are declining, new issues may be arising from the fact that increasing adult enrollments are not distributed evenly across the sexes. Although there is a gender gap in enrollment for young adults, the difference is small (Table 12-1). And women have closed any enrollment gap at the ages of entry into college. As Table 12-2 shows, there are now higher enrollments for women up through age twenty-one. However, between age twenty-two and age twenty-nine there are slightly higher enrollment rates

for males. And the enrollment rates for women are significantly higher through most of the remaining working life span. Women's enrollment may rise as they complete childbearing and rearing, finish working while their husbands complete college, find themselves independent through divorce or decision, or simply seek to obtain training foregone earlier. Whatever the cause of these age-specific enrollment patterns, they clearly reflect what has been an emerging pattern of men and women seeking adult education at different times in their life course. Even if these patterns are temporary transitions, differences in when adult men and women choose to pursue education have many possible implications for other life course events, personal and marital satisfaction, labor force and earnings differences, etc. It remains to be seen whether these differences continue into the coming century.

Sex, Race and Ethnic Differences in Enrollments

Racial and ethnic differences of considerable concern have been manifest throughout the past century and continue to exist in American education. Total percentages enrolled are, like crude rates, heavily dependent upon age structure and do not reveal the real patterns of difference in enrollments. For many specific age groups, the percentage of school enrollment for minority populations is now nearly identical to that for the white population. Among the black population, preschool enrollment is higher at ages three to six than among the white population. However, for ages seven through twenty-four black enrollment percentages are lower than those for whites. For some ages, through fifteen, these differences are small. The differences in percentage enrolled are largest and of most concern between ages eighteen and twenty-four and are greatest in the ages of entry to college, twenty to twenty-one, where the enrollment for blacks is only eighty percent that of whites. The difference in black and white percentage enrollment is greatest among males but still very substantial among females.

Except for ages sixteen through twenty-four, indigenous peoples (e.g. American Indian, Eskimo, Aleut, etc.) have remarkable similar enrollment patterns to those of the black population. However, in the later stages of secondary schooling and early years of college these individuals have markedly lower enrollment percentages. For many of these individuals there may be less perceived gain or necessity of completing high school and college.

In contrast, the championship in school attendance rates, by a healthy margin, is held by the Asian and Pacific Island population. Their enrollment percentages are higher at all ages than those of the white population. Especially past age eighteen the percentage enrollment in the Asian population far exceed those for the white population; at ages twenty-two to thirty-four enrollment is

Table 12-3A. Level of School in Which Enrolled, by Age and Sex: All Races, 1990

Age	Males					Females				
	Elementary and high school			College		Elementary and high school			College	
	Grades 1-5	Grades 6-9	Grades 10-12	Undergraduate	Graduate	Grades 1-5	Grades 6-9	Grades 10-12	Undergraduate	Graduate
10 years	82.2	17.8	...	...	...	78.6	21.4	...	...	...
11 years	39.6	60.4	...	...	...	33.0	67.0	...	...	...
12 years	7.4	88.6	0.2	...	...	5.5	94.2	0.3	...	...
13 years	2.3	92.9	1.1	...	...	2.0	96.7	1.3	...	...
14 years	0.9	95.2	13.9	...	...	0.8	81.8	17.4	...	...
15 years	0.4	43.9	55.6	0.2	...	0.3	35.1	64.4	0.2	...
16 years	...	8.9	90.5	0.5	...	...	5.2	94.2	0.6	...
17 years	...	2.0	93.4	4.6	...	...	1.3	92.1	6.5	...
18 years	...	0.9	61.6	37.5	...	...	0.7	49.1	50.1	...
19 years	...	0.8	19.3	79.7	0.2	...	0.6	11.4	87.7	0.2
20 years	...	0.8	7.8	90.5	0.9	...	0.5	4.9	93.5	1.0
21 years	...	0.9	4.6	88.8	5.7	...	0.6	3.4	88.6	7.5
22 years	...	1.0	4.2	80.1	14.7	...	0.9	3.5	77.8	17.8
23 years	...	1.3	4.5	70.2	24.0	...	1.0	4.5	68.1	26.4
24 years	...	1.4	5.1	63.2	30.2	...	1.2	5.1	63.0	30.7
25 to 29 years	...	1.7	6.2	56.9	35.2	...	1.5	6.1	61.1	31.2
30 to 34 years	...	2.3	6.1	55.8	35.8	...	2.2	6.2	63.1	28.5
35 to 39 years	...	2.5	5.7	54.0	37.8	...	2.2	5.5	60.7	31.6
40 to 44 years	...	2.8	5.6	50.9	40.6	...	2.2	5.2	58.4	34.2
45 to 54 years	...	4.2	7.9	49.1	38.8	...	3.0	7.4	56.7	32.9
55 to 64 years	0.1	7.3	12.5	44.7	35.3	...	6.6	12.8	55.1	25.5
65 and over	0.2	14.0	18.6	42.3	24.6	0.4	15.5	19.6	48.8	15.6

Source: U.S. Bureau of the Census, "Education in the United States: 1990," 1990 CP-3-4, U.S. Government Printing Office, Washington, D.C., 1994, Table 5.

Table 12-3B. Level of School in Which Enrolled, by Age and Sex: White Students, 1990

Age	Males					Females				
	Elementary and high school			College		Elementary and high school			College	
	Grades 1-5	Grades 6-9	Grades 10-12	Undergraduate	Graduate	Grades 1-5	Grades 6-9	Grades 10-12	Undergraduate	Graduate
10 years	84.5	15.5	...	...	...	81.0	19.0	...	...	...
11 years	41.6	58.4	...	...	...	34.8	65.2	...	...	...
12 years	7.5	92.3	0.2	...	...	5.4	94.5	0.2	...	...
13 years	2.3	96.8	0.9	...	...	1.9	97.1	0.9	...	...
14 years	0.9	87.1	12.0	...	...	0.7	83.9	15.3	...	...
15 years	0.3	45.2	54.3	0.2	...	0.2	36.1	63.5	0.2	...
16 years	...	8.0	91.6	0.5	...	...	4.4	95.0	0.5	...
17 years	...	1.6	94.1	4.3	...	...	1.0	92.9	6.1	...
18 years	...	0.7	60.5	38.9	...	...	0.6	47.8	51.6	...
19 years	...	0.6	15.4	83.8	0.2	...	0.5	8.6	90.7	0.2
20 years	...	0.6	5.3	93.3	0.8	...	0.4	3.4	95.3	0.9
21 years	...	0.6	2.9	90.6	5.9	...	0.4	2.3	89.4	7.9
22 years	...	0.6	2.6	81.2	15.6	...	0.6	2.3	77.8	19.3
23 years	...	0.8	2.7	70.5	25.9	...	0.8	3.0	67.2	29.1
24 years	...	1.0	3.3	63.0	32.7	...	0.9	3.6	61.6	33.9
25 to 29 years	...	1.1	4.0	57.0	37.8	...	1.0	4.2	60.9	34.0
30 to 34 years	...	1.4	4.0	56.8	37.7	...	1.4	4.1	63.7	30.8
35 to 39 years	...	1.5	3.7	54.1	40.7	...	1.3	3.5	61.0	34.2
40 to 44 years	...	1.9	3.6	50.4	44.1	...	1.3	3.3	58.6	36.8
45 to 54 years	...	2.8	5.5	49.3	42.4	...	1.9	5.0	57.5	35.6
55 to 64 years	...	5.4	9.6	45.7	39.1	...	4.8	10.2	57.2	27.8
65 and over	0.2	12.3	17.8	43.1	26.4	0.3	14.0	18.3	50.8	16.5

Source: U.S. Bureau of the Census, "Education in the United States: 1990," 1990 CP-3-4, U.S. Government Printing Office, Washington, D.C., 1994, Table 5.

Table 12-3C. Level of School in Which Enrolled, by Age and Sex: Black Students, 1990

Age	Males					Females				
	Elementary and high school			College		Elementary and high school			College	
	Grades 1-5	Grades 6-9	Grades 10-12	Undergraduate	Graduate	Grades 1-5	Grades 6-9	Grades 10-12	Undergraduate	Graduate
10 years	74.6	25.4	...	...	...	70.3	29.7	...	...	...
11 years	34.4	65.6	...	...	...	27.7	72.3	...	...	...
12 years	8.8	90.7	0.5	...	...	6.1	93.4	0.5	...	...
13 years	2.7	95.2	2.1	...	...	2.1	95.5	2.5	...	...
14 years	1.0	79.5	19.4	...	...	0.9	75.0	24.1	...	...
15 years	0.6	41.3	57.8	0.3	...	0.5	32.3	66.9	0.4	...
16 years	...	13.0	86.3	0.7	...	...	7.8	91.3	0.9	...
17 years	...	3.3	91.6	5.0	...	...	2.2	89.8	8.0	...
18 years	...	1.5	67.2	31.2	...	...	1.1	52.3	46.5	...
19 years	...	1.3	36.5	62.1	0.1	...	0.9	20.7	78.1	0.2
20 years	...	1.3	19.4	78.6	0.6	...	0.9	10.0	88.1	1.0
21 years	...	1.6	12.5	82.3	3.6	...	0.8	7.2	86.7	5.2
22 years	...	2.2	10.8	78.6	8.4	...	1.3	7.0	80.3	11.4
23 years	...	1.6	11.0	74.7	12.6	...	1.0	8.8	74.8	15.3
24 years	...	1.9	12.9	69.8	15.4	...	1.3	9.1	72.4	17.0
25 to 29 years	...	1.8	14.6	65.4	18.1	...	1.4	11.5	68.7	18.4
30 to 34 years	...	2.2	13.9	61.0	22.7	...	2.2	12.1	66.8	18.8
35 to 39 years	...	3.0	12.6	60.0	24.4	...	2.2	11.4	64.9	21.4
40 to 44 years	...	3.6	13.1	58.4	24.8	...	3.2	11.9	61.6	23.3
45 to 54 years	...	6.7	17.9	51.3	23.9	...	4.4	17.5	55.7	22.3
55 to 64 years	0.1	14.3	27.7	39.7	17.9	...	10.7	24.5	47.4	17.4
65 and over	0.9	26.0	27.7	34.7	10.1	0.8	22.7	29.7	36.7	9.4

Source: U.S. Bureau of the Census, "Education in the United States: 1990," 1990 CP-3-4, U.S. Government Printing Office, Washington, D.C., 1994, Table 5.

Table 12-3D. Level of School in Which Enrolled, by Age and Sex: Hispanic Students, 1990

Age	Males					Females				
	Elementary and high school			College		Elementary and high school			College	
	Grades 1-5	Grades 6-9	Grades 10-12	Undergraduate	Graduate	Grades 1-5	Grades 6-9	Grades 10-12	Undergraduate	Graduate
10 years	75.7	24.3	...	...	...	71.7	28.3	...	...	...
11 years	31.7	68.3	...	...	...	27.1	72.9	...	...	...
12 years	7.4	92.1	0.5	...	...	5.3	94.2	0.4	...	...
13 years	2.4	95.5	2.1	...	...	1.7	96.2	2.1	...	...
14 years	0.8	79.5	19.6	...	...	0.7	75.6	23.7	...	...
15 years	0.6	38.0	61.0	0.4	...	0.5	31.9	67.2	0.4	...
16 years	...	11.2	87.8	1.0	...	...	7.8	91.5	0.8	...
17 years	...	3.9	90.5	5.6	...	...	2.8	89.3	7.9	...
18 years	...	2.7	66.8	30.5	...	...	1.8	57.6	40.6	...
19 years	...	3.1	34.7	61.9	0.2	...	2.0	25.3	72.2	0.4
20 years	...	4.5	22.0	72.6	0.9	...	2.2	14.6	82.2	0.9
21 years	...	4.9	15.9	75.5	3.6	...	3.1	11.2	80.7	5.1
22 years	...	5.2	16.3	71.4	7.1	...	4.2	11.8	75.1	8.9
23 years	0.1	6.9	16.1	66.2	10.7	...	4.5	12.8	69.1	13.5
24 years	...	6.9	16.5	62.2	14.4	...	4.8	13.8	65.2	16.1
25 to 29 years	0.1	8.6	17.0	57.6	16.6	0.1	6.8	15.8	60.5	16.8
30 to 34 years	0.1	11.6	15.9	54.1	18.3	0.1	11.4	15.8	57.3	15.4
35 to 39 years	0.1	12.3	15.8	52.5	19.3	...	12.4	15.4	55.6	16.5
40 to 44 years	0.1	13.9	15.7	49.5	20.7	0.2	11.8	14.7	57.2	15.9
45 to 54 years	0.2	15.4	16.8	48.8	18.9	0.1	14.7	18.1	52.3	14.7
55 to 64 years	0.4	19.0	20.9	43.9	15.6	0.2	20.8	20.2	44.8	13.7
65 and over	0.5	27.6	25.5	34.2	11.5	0.9	30.6	25.9	33.9	8.2

Source: U.S. Bureau of the Census, "Education in the United States: 1990," 1990 CP-3-4, U.S. Government Printing Office, Washington, D.C., 1994, Table 5

Table 12-3E. Level of School in Which Enrolled, by Age and Sex: American Indian Students, 1990

Age	Males					Females				
	Elementary and high school			College		Elementary and high school			College	
	Grades 1-5	Grades 6-9	Grades 10-12	Undergraduate	Graduate	Grades 1-5	Grades 6-9	Grades 10-12	Undergraduate	Graduate
10 years	83.9	16.1	...	...	...	79.8	20.2	...	...	...
11 years	43.0	57.0	...	...	...	33.4	66.6	...	...	...
12 years	11.0	88.6	0.4	...	...	6.4	93.3	0.3	...	...
13 years	2.2	95.9	1.9	...	...	2.4	95.8	1.9	...	...
14 years	0.9	85.7	13.4	...	...	1.1	82.3	16.6	...	...
15 years	0.5	47.6	51.8	0.1	...	0.4	38.0	61.5	0.1	...
16 years	...	13.5	86.3	0.2	...	...	8.8	90.5	0.7	...
17 years	...	3.7	91.8	4.5	...	...	2.5	91.5	6.0	...
18 years	...	1.6	70.3	28.1	...	...	0.7	60.7	38.5	...
19 years	...	1.8	35.9	62.1	0.2	...	1.7	23.4	74.9	...
20 years	...	1.5	18.0	80.0	0.5	...	1.1	14.4	83.7	0.7
21 years	...	1.6	11.1	84.2	3.1	...	1.8	8.7	85.1	4.5
22 years	...	2.4	13.2	78.9	5.5	...	2.5	7.9	82.3	7.3
23 years	...	1.2	12.4	75.9	10.6	...	3.0	9.9	78.9	8.2
24 years	...	2.1	9.1	72.5	16.3	...	2.4	13.8	73.3	10.5
25 to 29 years	0.2	3.2	11.3	71.9	13.6	0.1	3.0	11.0	73.1	12.8
30 to 34 years	...	2.8	12.7	66.8	17.6	...	1.9	10.5	73.8	13.8
35 to 39 years	...	2.5	9.3	64.8	23.4	...	2.1	7.6	68.3	22.0
40 to 44 years	...	3.9	9.3	56.9	29.9	...	3.1	6.6	67.7	22.6
45 to 54 years	...	6.4	10.2	60.3	23.1	...	4.0	10.5	65.9	19.7
55 to 64 years	...	14.3	12.3	43.5	28.7	...	13.2	11.0	54.9	20.9
65 and over	...	17.1	24.1	48.1	10.7	...	18.2	24.5	46.7	10.7

Source: U.S. Bureau of the Census, "Education in the United States: 1990," 1990 CP-3-4, U.S. Government Printing Office, Washington, D.C., 1994, Table 5.

Table 12-3F. Level of School in Which Enrolled, by Age and Sex: Asian/Pacific Islander Students, 1990

Age	Males					Females				
	Elementary and high school			College		Elementary and high school			College	
	Grades 1-5	Grades 6-9	Grades 10-12	Undergraduate	Graduate	Grades 1-5	Grades 6-9	Grades 10-12	Undergraduate	Graduate
10 years	74.5	25.5	...	...	...	73.0	27.0	...	...	...
11 years	30.5	69.5	...	...	...	27.1	72.9	...	...	...
12 years	6.8	92.7	0.5	...	...	5.8	93.7	0.5	...	...
13 years	2.3	95.3	2.3	...	...	2.3	95.6	2.1	...	...
14 years	1.0	77.1	21.9	...	...	0.8	75.6	23.5	...	...
15 years	0.4	33.6	65.6	0.4	...	0.3	29.6	69.6	0.5	...
16 years	...	7.7	91.2	1.1	...	...	5.6	93.4	1.0	...
17 years	...	2.0	90.9	7.1	...	...	1.7	89.8	8.4	...
18 years	...	0.6	46.9	39.5	...	...	0.9	48.3	50.8	...
19 years	...	0.8	19.8	78.0	1.3	...	0.7	15.0	83.2	1.1
20 years	...	0.4	7.7	89.0	2.8	...	0.5	6.5	90.0	3.0
21 years	...	0.6	4.8	85.9	8.7	...	0.5	4.0	86.5	9.0
22 years	...	0.7	3.8	76.3	19.2	...	1.0	3.1	75.4	20.5
23 years	...	0.7	3.5	64.3	31.5	...	0.5	3.1	62.7	33.6
24 years	...	0.8	3.0	56.2	40.1	...	1.1	3.5	53.7	41.7
25 to 29 years	...	0.9	3.5	41.0	54.5	...	1.4	4.5	44.9	49.3
30 to 34 years	...	1.5	3.7	35.3	59.5	...	2.3	6.0	46.3	45.4
35 to 39 years	...	2.3	4.6	39.0	54.1	...	3.9	7.3	47.2	41.5
40 to 44 years	...	2.7	4.8	40.8	51.6	...	3.7	7.7	46.4	42.1
45 to 54 years	...	3.5	6.5	41.8	48.2	...	4.6	7.2	48.6	39.6
55 to 64 years	...	6.0	10.0	43.8	40.4	...	6.7	11.6	55.3	26.3
65 and over	...	13.2	14.0	44.4	28.8	0.2	19.0	16.1	45.1	19.2

Source: U.S. Bureau of the Census, "Education in the United States: 1990," 1990 CP-3-4, U.S. Government Printing Office, Washington, D.C., 1994, Table 5.

nearly double that of whites. The high rates of college and postgraduate enrollment is particularly impressive in view of the fact that a substantial portion of the population in these ages is made up of recent immigrants.

The Hispanic population has a lower percentage enrolled than whites up to age twenty-five and a higher percentage thereafter. Hispanics have a lower percentage enrolled than blacks in early preschool ages up to age six, and then have enrollments roughly similar to those of blacks up to age fifteen. Between ages fifteen and twenty-one they have a lower percentage enrolled than do blacks and a higher percentage enrolled thereafter. Hispanic enrollment is most dramatically lower than both blacks and whites at seemingly critical ages. Hispanic enrollment percentages are markedly lower than those for whites or blacks in the early preschool ages of three to four and adult college entry ages of eighteen to twenty-one. Yet adult enrollment percentages are higher among Hispanics. These higher adult rates may reflect adult education among new immigrants and attempts to compensate for earlier gaps in education.

Sex, Race and Ethnic Differences in Grade in which Enrolled

Some of the race and ethnic differences in enrollments may be due to differences in the timing of educational experiences. Most students, regardless of preschooling, enter elementary school when they are five or six years of age. Although there are exceptions, it is anticipated that a typical student will complete the requirements of one grade each year. Such a student can expect to graduate from elementary school at the age of thirteen or fourteen, from high school at seventeen or eighteen, and from a four-year college at twenty-one or twenty-two. Actually, many students deviate rather markedly from this theoretical progression. A few, whose abilities demand more challenges, are "accelerated" by being enrolled in grades whose members are older than their own age group. A larger number fall behind, either because they fail to master the materials or because of illness or other factors that prevent steady attendance. Such departures from anticipated progress, of course, cumulate across the years during which a setback or advance may occur. Departures from a theoretical rate of progress also increase as students reach employable ages and enter schooling such as college where progress is more clearly subject to personal timetables and volition.

Table 12-3 (A-F) reports the actual grade distribution of students from ages ten on, enrolled in school in 1990 by sex for major race-ethnic groups. The data show marked differences from similar data for the 1980's. In Table 12-3A, for example, the percent of male students age 16 who were not in high school grades (10-12) is 8.9 percent, up from only 2.5 percent in 1980. And 5.2 per-

Table 12-4. Type of School in Which Enrolled, by Age and Race-ethnicity: 1990

Race-ethnicity and age	Type of school	
	Public	Private
All races		
3-5 years	60.6	39.4
6-13 years	89.4	10.6
14-17 years	91.5	8.5
White		
3-5 years	55.1	44.9
6-13 years	88.1	11.9
14-17 years	90.5	9.5
Black		
3-5 years	79.0	21.0
6-13 years	94.1	5.9
14-17 years	95.4	4.6
Hispanic		
3-5 years	78.7	21.3
6-13 years	92.6	7.4
14-17 years	93.2	6.8
Asian/Pacific Islander		
3-5 years	55.1	44.9
6-13 years	87.5	12.5
14-17 years	89.5	10.5
American Indian		
3-5 years	84.9	15.1
6-13 years	95.2	4.8
14-17 years	95.5	4.5

Source: U.S. Bureau of the Census, "Education in the United States:1990," 1990 CP-3-4, U.S. Government Printing Office, Washington, D.C., 1994, Table 5.

cent of female students age 16 were not in high school grades in 1990, up from only 1.6 percent in 1980. This shows a decrease in progress into high school grades. There is also declining progress into college settings. By age twenty the table shows 90.5 percent of male students in undergraduate college settings. This figure is down from 94 percent in 1980 even though there has been a slight increase in male students age twenty who have gone on to graduate work by this age.

The departures from typical progress are not necessarily to be seen in a negative light. Among male students age twenty, for example, Hispanic and then black students are less likely to have progressed to undergraduate settings and Asians are most likely to have progressed to graduate level work. Among female students, Hispanic, American Indian, and then black students are less likely to have progressed to undergraduate settings while Asians are again more likely to have progressed to graduate work. The positive light of these findings is that they show many groups remain in school at older ages seeking to remedy educational deficiencies rather than dropping out of the educational system. It is possible that a substantial share of disadvantaged minority groups are making efforts to correct past educational deficiencies by enrolling in high school even though they are well past high school age. These may be old dropouts repairing the damage to their employment potential. It is also possible that some of these departures represent new immigrants improving their educational standing at older life ages. The negative side of these findings indicates that some groups appear to suffer more delay in entering and completing college, perhaps because of economic problems. Female students also tend to advance to higher levels at earlier ages and to fall behind less than male students within each race-ethnic group, at least up to their early twenties.

Changing Public and Private School Enrollments

For a number of those with resources and access, private schooling provides an alternative to public educational systems. In 1990 roughly one pupil in ten was enrolled in a private school during primary schooling ages of six through seventeen (Table 12-4). Private schooling is, of course, more common outside the ages during which most states provide public schooling. For example, at younger ages nearly four of ten students are in private preschools. The access to private preschools mirrors the later differences in educational progress noted above. The groups with highest use of private preschools (e.g. whites and Asians) also have the fastest educational trajectories. Of course, the differential use of private education does not end with preschool. The same groups continue to have nearly twice as many students in private schools at older ages. Of the major race-ethnic groups, American Indians have the highest use of public educational institutions. This later finding likely reflects the unique role of public education among indigenous peoples.

Table 12-5 shows how the percentage enrollment in private schools has changed over time. The total enrollment in private schools has, contrary to many impres-

Table 12-5. Enrollment in Private School as a Percent of All Enrollment, by Race and Grade level: 1960 to 1990 [persons 3 years of age and older]

| Race and year | Total | Elementary school | | High school |
		Kindergarten	Grades 1-8	Grades 9-12
All races				
1990	9.0	14.5	9.1	7.1
1980	—[1]	15.3	11.1	—[1]
1970	10.9	16.8	11.6	8.0
1960	14.0	19.2	14.9	10.1
White				
1990	9.9	15.3	10.1	7.9
1980	—[1]	16.3	12.3	—[1]
1970	12.1	17.5	13.0	8.8
1960	15.4	19.7	16.7	11.0
Black				
1990	4.5	9.7	4.3	3.3
1980	—[1]	10.2	4.7	—[1]
1970	4.1	12.4	4.1	2.2
1960	4.7	15.2	4.5	3.0

[1] Data on public and private enrollments are not available for high school and college for 1980.

Source: U.S. Bureau of the Census, "School Enrollment--Social and Economic Characteristics of Students: October 1990," Current Population Reports, Series P-20, no. 460, U.S. Government Printing Office, Washington, D.C., 1992, Table A-1.

sions, decreased from the levels of 1960. This decrease has been greatest among whites and cuts across all age groups. This decline may reflect the impact of declining economic fortunes, a decrease in the use of private facilities to avoid public school integration, an increase in home schooling as an alternative to private institutions, or simply changing patterns of choice.

Nursery School and Kindergarten

It has already been noted that preschool enrollment has increased in recent years. Table 12-6 shows how preschool enrollments have changed since 1970. Although there was a dramatic increase in preschool enrollment for both white and black students between 1970 and 1980, there has been a decline in preschool enrollment for both groups since 1980. Once again, it is possible that this decline represents a return to in-home or alternative schooling either due to declining economic circumstances between 1980 and 1990 or rising concerns over curriculum content. The decline is somewhat less among whites

Education of the Disabled

by Alison Kadlec Donta

In the school year 1989-1990, there were 4,641 children from birth to age 21 served in federally-supported special education programs. This number represents 11.4% of the total public school enrollment for that year. This proportion of public school students with disabilities has been rising each year since data on the subject have been collected. In the school year 1931-1932, children with disabilities represented only 0.6% of the total public school enrollment. That proportion had increased to 1.2% by 1939-1940, to 3.7% in 1962-1963, and to 9.6% in 1979-1980. The figure below illustrates the change in relative distributions of children with various disabilities since 1977. While some categories of disabilities, such as emotionally disturbed and physically/health impaired, have remained fairly constant over time, there has been a decrease in the percentage of students classified as speech impaired or mentally retarded and an increase in the percentage classified as learning disabled. Some of these changes can be explained by different diagnostic and classification criteria over time, such as the increase in the diagnosis of children with learning disabilities. For example, during the academic year 1976-1977, children with learning disabilities represented 21.6% of all disabled children served in special education programs, and this proportion had increased

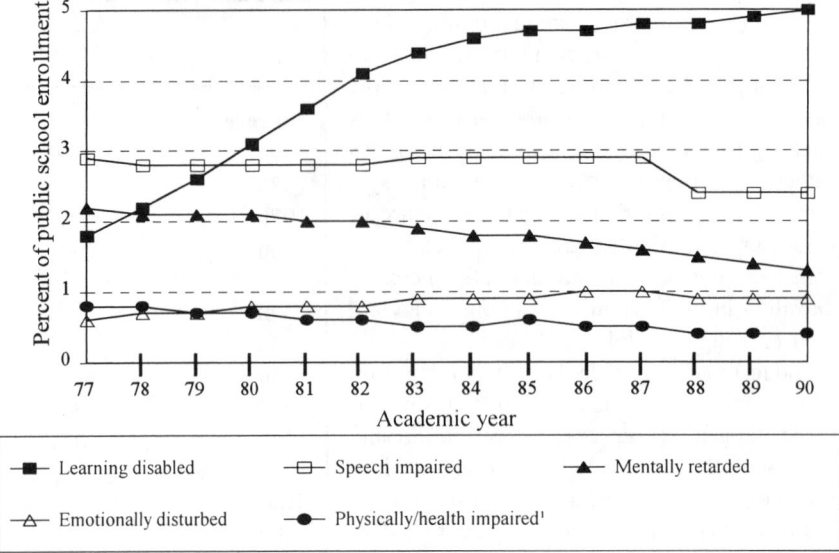

Children Served in Special Education Programs, by Type of Disability: 1977-1990

[1] This category includes children who are hard of hearing or deaf, visually handicapped, orthopedically handicapped or health impaired.

Source: National Center for Education Statistics, "120 Years of American Education: A Statistical Portrait," Table 12, 1993.

to 44.2% of disabled children by 1989-1990. There has been a simultaneous decrease in the proportion of disabled students classified as mentally retarded over the same time period. In 1976-1977, this proportion was 26.0% but it had decreased to only 11.8% by 1989-1990. The changes reflected in the figure may also

be explained by an increasing number of disabled students being served by the public education system due, in part, to changing legislation and policy regarding the education of the disabled.

In 1970, Congress passed the Education of the Handicapped Act (EHA) (Public Law No. 91-230), and the amend-

Percentage of Students Age 6-21 Served in Different Educational Environments by Disability: Academic Year 1990-1991

Disability	Educational environment					
	Regular class	Resource room	Separate class	Separate school	Residential facility	Homebound/ hospital
All disabilities	32.8	36.5	25.1	4.2	0.8	0.6
Specific learning disability	22.5	53.7	22.4	1.1	0.1	0.2
Speech or language impairments	78.9	13.9	5.7	1.4	0.1	0.2
Mental retardation	7.4	23.0	58.3	9.8	1.1	0.4
Serious emotional disturbance	16.8	29.2	35.8	13.3	3.5	1.5
Multiple disabilities	6.6	17.2	42.8	27.7	3.5	2.1
Hearing impairments	26.9	19.7	32.7	9.1	11.0	0.5
Visual impairments	42.1	23.2	19.9	5.0	8.8	1.0
Orthopedic impairments	29.6	22.2	33.0	8.9	0.7	5.6
Other health impairments	30.2	27.7	26.2	7.3	1.0	7.6
Deaf-blindness	10.5	6.4	32.3	23.5	25.2	2.2

Source: U.S. Department of Education, Office of Special Education Programs, "Fifteenth Annual Report to Congress on the Implementation of the Individuals with Disabilities Education Act," Table 1.6, 1993.

ments to this act in 1974 (Public Law No. 93-380) acknowledged the "right to education" for disabled children. It also requested that public schools integrate these children, whenever possible, into "regular" education. This act was followed in 1975 by the Education for All Handicapped Children Act (EAHCA) (Public Law No. 94-142) which required states to obtain approval of their handicapped education plans from the U.S. Office of Education in order to receive federal funds. In addition, it now required states to provide all disabled children between the ages of 5 and 21 with free and appropriate education in the least restrictive environment possible. Access was expanded to all children from age three by the EHA amendments of 1986 (Public Law No. 99-457). In 1990, additional EHA amendments (Public Law No. 101-476) changed the name of the law to the Individuals with Disabilities Education Act (IDEA) and required information on transition into the work force to be included in the Individual Education Plans (IEP) of all eligible students. Amendments to IDEA in 1991 (Public Law No. 102-119) provided for a smooth transition of services for children with disabilities from birth to age five. This series of laws represents a national focus of attention on the education of the handicapped and the shift of emphasis to serving these children in a regular classroom (mainstreaming) whenever possible.

Historically, the education of disabled children in special education programs can be described as a system of progressive inclusion. In the last century and previously, the national trend was educational neglect of the disabled who instead relied on their families for support and any education they could acquire in the course of day-to-day living. Next came the establishment of residential schools for the educable/trainable mentally retarded and other children with disabilities. This was followed by a national movement toward placement of many of these children in special day schools and classes. By the latter third of this century, resource rooms were increasingly being utilized, with disabled students spending much of their day in a regular classroom. Mainstreaming is the current mode of placement for many disabled students. Although options involving regular classrooms represented the placement of 69.3% of all disabled students age 6-21 in the school year 1990-1991, other educational environments, largely depending on the student's type of disability, are still in use. The largest proportion of children with multiple disabilities and mental retardation are placed in a separate class and 1 of every 4 deaf-blind children are educated in a residential facility. These distributions have changed even since 1988-1989 when 30.6% of all disabled students were educated in a regular class, 38.8% in a resource room, 24.2% in a separate class, 4.5% in a separate school, 0.9% in a residential facility, and 0.8% at home or in the hospital. This two-year change represents an increase in the percentage of disabled students mainstreamed, possibly as a result of the "least restrictive environment" provision of the IDEA.

The second table provides information on the educational attainment, through high school, of students with various disabilities. In the school year 1990-1991, 45.7% of all students with disabilities received their high school diploma and 13.3% left with a certificate. On the other hand, 23.3% dropped out, down from the 26.6% that dropped out in the year 1988-1989. In the past decade there has been an increasing emphasis on the transition of handicapped students from school to adulthood, and graduating high school, either through diploma or certificate, is one way to assist a smooth transition. The IDEA has increased emphasis on the transition of disabled students to the workplace as has the passage of the Americans with Disabilities Act (ADA) in 1990 which includes, among other things, nondiscrimination and greater entrance into the work-place for disabled individuals.

Additional Sources:

Hasazi, Susan B., Johnston, A.P., Liggett, Annette M., and Schattman, Richard A. "A Qualitative Policy Study of the Least Restrictive Environment Provision of the Individuals with Disabilities Education Act." Exceptional Children 60(1994):491-507.

Kauffman, James M., and Pullen, Patricia L. "An Historical Perspective: A Personal Perspective on Our History of Service to Mildly Handicapped and At-Risk Students." Remedial and Special Education 10(1989):12-14.

Lantzy, M. L. Individuals with Disabilities Education Act: An Annotated Guide to Its Literature and Resources, 1980-1991. Littleton, CO: Fred B. Rothman & Co., 1992.

Lazarus, Mitchell. Educating the Handicapped: Where We've Been, Where We're Going. Arlington, VA: National School Public Relations Association, 1980.

Reynolds, Maynard C. "An Historical Perspective: The Delivery of Special Education to Mildly Disabled and At-Risk Students." Remedial and Special Education 10(1989):7-11.

U.S. Department of Education. "To Assure the Free Appropriate Public Education of all Children with Disabilities." Fifteenth Annual Report to Congress on the Implementation of the Individuals with Disabilities Education Act. Washington, D.C.: U.S. Government Printing Office, 1993.

Wehman, Paul. "Transition for Young People with Disabilities: Challenges for the 1990's." Education and Training in Mental Retardation 27(1992):112-118.

Basis of Exit for Students with Different Disabilities: School Year 1990-1991 [percent distribution]

Disability	Total	Diploma	Certificate	Maximum age	Drop out	Status unknown
All disabilities	100.0	45.7	13.3	2.0	23.3	15.8
Specific learning disabilities	100.0	51.7	10.8	0.7	22.2	14.7
Speech or language impairments	100.0	41.3	9.1	2.3	17.1	30.3
Mental retardation	100.0	38.7	24.6	5.2	21.6	9.9
Serious emotional disturbance	100.0	30.8	7.9	1.3	37.2	22.9
Multiple disabilities	100.0	38.7	26.2	11.9	12.6	10.7
Hearing impairments	100.0	56.8	16.4	1.5	12.2	13.2
Visual impairments	100.0	60.3	14.6	2.2	12.1	10.8
Orthopedic impairments	100.0	55.3	13.0	2.7	10.1	18.9
Other health impairments	100.0	48.6	16.4	2.2	17.4	15.4
Deaf-blindness	100.0	52.8	17.6	7.0	14.1	8.5

Source: U.S. Department of Education, Office of Special Education Programs, "Fifteenth Annual Report to Congress on the Implementation of the Individuals with Disabilities Education Act," Table 1.9, 1993.

than among blacks, perhaps consistent with greater economic impacts on the ability to secure preschooling among
this group. The percentage enrollment among these students who attend for the full day has not, however, appreciably declined. In fact, the percentage of children
enrolled in full day kindergarten has continued to increase
into the 1990's. This later fact may be consistent with
increasing needs for kindergarten as a form of child care
during a full-time working day.

Table 12-7 examines preschool enrollment by residence characteristics (i.e. metropolitan area or not and
region), mother's labor force status, and mother's education for all persons, whites and blacks. Preschool enrollment is, not surprisingly, much higher among employed
mothers whose children live with them and more common in metropolitan areas. Enrollment in preschool is
much higher for children of white mothers with at least a
high school degree. The difference in preschool enrollment by mother's education is not substantial for blacks.
For both groups there are significantly more working
mothers with higher education who enroll their students
in private, as opposed to public, educational settings. For
white students the use of private schooling is greatest in
the Northeast and South. For black students the use of
private schooling is greatest in the Midwest and West.
For both blacks and whites private nursery schools but
public kindergartens are more commonly used in the West.

High School Dropouts

Perhaps the greatest concerns with the educational
system concern the adequacy of the education it provides
and its ability to retain students until their graduation from
an appropriate curriculum. The percentage of young persons who drop out of school without completing four years
of high school is a measure of insufficiency in the educational system and continues to be of great concern. Table
12-8 presents data on persons not enrolled in school, yet
not high school graduates (that is, dropouts), by age, sex,
and race-ethnicity for 1967 through 1991. This table permits more precise evaluation of the significance of the
leveling off in enrollment rates, described earlier. During
the phase of rapid improvement in enrollment, the proportion of dropouts shrank impressively. However, since
the early 1970's, progress in this direction has been somewhat less rapid. In the twenty years since 1971 the dropout rate has declined just slightly less than in the five years
prior to 1971. For the nation as a whole, about 12.5 percent of youth are dropping out of high school. For the
black non-Hispanic population the proportion is about
13.6 percent. Black non-Hispanic dropout rates have
continued to decline more rapidly into the 1990's. And
for this group the decline in male dropout rates has exceeded that of females such that since 1990 the dropout
rate for young black non-Hispanic women exceeds that
of their male counterparts for the first time in history.

**Table 12-6. Percent of Children Age 3-5
Enrolled in School, by Age and Race:
1990, 1980, and 1970**

Year and race	Age		
	3 years	4 years	5 years
1990			
Total	19.1	38.5	68.1
White	19.5	38.7	67.6
Black	20.9	41.2	71.4
1980			
Total	23.2	42.5	75.8
White	22.7	41.3	75.2
Black	27.9	49.6	79.0
1970			
Total	7.5	17.3	54.7
White	7.3	16.6	55.4
Black	8.5	19.7	49.9

Source: U.S. Bureau of the Census, "Education in the United
States: 1990," 1990 CP-3-4, Table 5, and "Detailed
Population Characteristics: United States Summary," 1980
and 1970, Tables 260 and 197, U.S. Government Printing
Office, Washington, D.C., 1994, 1984, 1973.

For the Hispanic population the dropout rate is dramatically higher at over 35 percent. Most recently, this rate
seems to have increased dramatically for Hispanic males.

College Enrollments

Increasingly, completion of a college curriculum,
in addition to a high school degree, is significant to the
probability of a successful and satisfying career. This is
reflected in a steadily growing proportion of the college-
age population enrolled in college. As of 1990, almost
18 million persons were enrolled in college. Of these
college enrollees almost 14 million were undergraduate
students and 15.5 million were under the age of thirty-
five. However, the number of college enrollees over
thirty-five years of age increased rapidly from about 1.4
million in 1980 to over 2.4 million in 1990. Tables 12-
9A through 12-9D provide information about the age,
grade level, type of college (public or private), and degree of attendance (attending full time) by sex and race-
ethnicity.

Women's college enrollment patterns are clearly
distinct from those of men, especially at older ages.
Women from twenty-two to twenty-nine years of age are
less likely to attend college full time. However, women

Table 12-7. Percent of Children Age 3-5 Enrolled in Nursery School and Kindergarten, by Residence, Mother's Labor Force Status and Education, and Race: 1990

| | Total Enrolled | | Enrolled in nursery school | | | | Enrolled in kindergarten | | | |
| | | | Public | | Private | | Public | | Private | |
	Total	Full day	Total	Full day	Total	Full day	Total	Full day	Total	Full day
All Races										
Total children	59.4	38.7	35.5	32.4	64.5	34.9	84.5	41.1	15.5	56.6
Metropolitan	60.1	38.6	34.8	32.5	65.1	37.3	83.5	38.2	16.5	60.0
Nonmetropolitan	57.0	39.0	38.5	31.4	61.7	23.5	88.1	51.2	11.9	39.3
Region										
Northeast	62.2	32.9	29.9	20.6	70.1	21.3	80.6	43.4	19.4	60.2
Midwest	62.0	22.3	37.0	16.2	63.0	25.6	87.1	21.2	13.0	32.4
South	52.2	38.7	38.4	50.9	60.7	46.6	84.1	25.1	15.8	42.0
West	56.0	31.4	31.5	23.3	68.5	43.8	85.6	20.1	14.4	59.3
Labor force status of mother										
Children living with mother	59.7	38.1	34.8	31.7	65.2	34.1	83.9	40.5	16.1	56.2
Employed	64.2	42.6	29.8	39.0	70.2	43.2	81.1	39.1	19.0	61.3
Unemployed or not in labor force	54.3	31.6	42.7	23.6	57.3	16.3	87.4	42.1	12.6	47.1
Children not living with mother	56.3	47.4	45.5	40.0	54.5	50.0	91.8	48.0	8.2	60.0
Education of mother										
Less than high school graduate	46.9	42.8	78.5	35.3	21.2	38.5	94.3	46.0	5.7	58.8
High school graduate or higher	62.6	37.3	30.1	30.7	69.9	34.0	81.5	38.9	18.6	56.3
White										
Total children	59.7	33.4	30.5	24.3	69.6	29.8	84.0	36.5	16.0	52.4
Metropolitan	60.4	33.1	29.4	24.2	70.7	31.6	83.0	33.5	17.0	55.7
Nonmetropolitan	57.3	34.5	34.9	24.6	65.1	22.3	87.1	45.9	12.9	38.5
Region										
Northeast	63.1	28.0	26.3	11.4	73.7	18.3	79.7	38.5	20.1	57.8
Midwest	62.2	17.4	34.5	10.6	65.5	21.5	87.1	16.3	12.9	21.8
South	58.5	55.8	31.4	51.0	68.6	40.9	82.4	68.0	17.6	64.0
West	55.5	29.1	28.1	21.0	71.9	39.5	86.0	18.6	14.2	58.1
Labor force status of mother										
Children living with mother	59.8	33.1	30.2	24.5	69.8	29.6	83.4	36.1	16.6	52.3
Employed	64.2	37.5	26.5	29.7	73.5	38.4	81.7	34.8	18.2	58.8
Unemployed or not in labor force	56.2	26.8	36.6	16.5	59.2	12.8	67.9	47.7	14.4	40.7
Children not living with mother	57.9	37.3	36.1	20.8	63.2	36.9	92.4	41.4	8.2	50.0
Education of mother										
Less than high school graduate	43.3	35.9	77.9	24.5	22.1	15.9	95.8	42.2	4.2	44.4
High school graduate or higher	63.1	32.7	26.3	24.2	73.6	29.9	80.7	34.5	19.3	53.1
Black										
Total children	57.8	64.8	66.0	55.8	34.0	81.5	88.4	63.0	11.4	82.0
Metropolitan	58.5	62.7	64.5	53.9	35.5	82.1	87.0	58.7	12.8	82.5
Nonmetropolitan	53.6	78.6	80.6	69.0	19.4	57.1	95.6	83.7	4.4	75.0
Region										
Northeast	52.3	65.9	69.0	55.0	31.0	61.1	89.7	73.8	10.3	85.7
Midwest	61.4	51.8	59.5	46.0	40.5	76.5	85.0	42.9	13.6	84.2
South	58.3	73.9	68.1	61.5	31.9	88.1	88.1	77.9	11.6	75.0
West	54.7	34.7	52.2	16.7	47.8	72.7	92.3	25.0	7.7	100.0
Labor force status of mother										
Children living with mother	58.1	64.3	65.2	54.5	34.8	81.4	88.0	62.8	12.0	80.4
Employed	63.1	72.9	56.3	68.4	43.8	87.9	79.4	66.9	20.6	76.7
Unemployed or not in labor force	53.8	55.7	76.7	40.8	23.3	65.8	94.9	59.8	5.1	92.3
Children not living with mother	55.7	68.5	71.2	61.9	28.8	88.2	91.2	66.1	8.8	83.3
Education of mother										
Less than high school graduate	57.8	62.3	85.2	57.3	15.9	71.4	94.8	61.8	5.2	100.0
High school graduate or higher	58.2	65.2	59.6	52.4	40.8	81.7	85.8	63.1	14.2	78.0

Source: U.S. Bureau of the Census, "School Enrollment--Social and Economic Characteristics of Students: October 1990," Current Population Reports, Series P-20, no. 460, U.S. Government Printing Office, Washington, D.C., 1992, Table 4.

Table 12-8. Percentage of High School Dropouts[1] Among Persons 16 to 24 Years Old, by Sex and Race-ethnicity: 1967 to 1991

Year	All races			White, non-Hispanic			Black, non-Hispanic			Hispanic		
	Both sexes	Males	Females	Both sexes	Males	Females	Both sexes	Males	Females	Both sexes	Males	Females
1991	12.5	13.0	11.9	8.9	8.9	8.9	13.6	13.5	13.7	35.3	39.2	31.1
1990	12.1	12.3	11.8	9.0	9.3	8.7	13.2	11.9	14.4	32.4	34.3	30.3
1989	12.6	13.6	11.7	9.4	10.3	8.5	13.9	14.9	13.0	33.0	34.4	31.6
1988	12.9	13.5	12.2	9.6	10.3	8.9	14.5	15.0	14.0	35.8	36.0	35.4
1987	12.7	13.3	12.2	10.4	10.8	10.0	14.5	15.5	13.4	28.6	29.1	28.1
1986	12.2	13.1	11.4	9.7	10.3	9.1	14.2	15.0	13.5	30.1	32.8	27.2
1985	12.6	13.4	11.8	10.4	11.1	9.8	15.2	16.1	14.3	27.6	29.9	25.2
1984	13.1	14.0	12.3	11.0	12.0	10.1	15.5	16.8	14.3	29.8	30.6	29.0
1983	13.7	14.9	12.5	11.2	12.2	10.1	18.0	19.9	16.2	31.6	34.3	29.1
1982	13.9	14.5	13.3	11.4	12.1	10.9	18.4	21.2	15.9	31.7	30.5	32.8
1981	13.9	15.1	12.8	11.4	12.5	10.2	18.4	19.9	17.1	33.2	36.0	30.4
1980	14.1	15.1	13.1	11.4	12.3	10.5	19.1	20.8	17.7	35.2	37.2	33.2
1979	14.6	15.0	14.2	12.0	12.6	11.5	21.1	22.4	20.0	33.8	33.0	34.5
1978	14.2	14.6	13.9	11.9	12.2	11.6	20.2	22.5	18.3	33.3	33.6	33.1
1977	14.1	14.5	13.8	11.9	12.6	11.2	19.8	19.5	20.0	33.0	31.6	34.3
1976	14.1	14.1	14.2	12.0	12.1	11.8	20.5	21.2	19.9	31.4	30.3	32.3
1975	13.9	13.3	14.5	11.4	11.0	11.8	22.9	13.0	22.9	29.2	26.7	31.6
1974	14.3	14.2	14.4	11.9	12.0	11.8	21.2	20.1	22.1	33.0	33.8	32.2
1973	14.1	13.7	14.5	11.6	11.5	11.8	22.2	21.5	22.8	33.5	30.4	36.4
1972	14.6	14.1	15.1	12.3	11.7	12.8	21.3	22.3	20.5	34.3	33.7	34.9
1971[2]	14.7	14.2	15.2	13.4	12.6	14.2	23.7	25.5	22.1	—	—	—
1970[2]	15.0	14.2	15.7	13.2	12.2	14.1	27.9	29.4	26.6	—	—	—
1969[2]	15.2	14.3	16.0	13.6	12.6	14.6	26.7	26.9	26.7	—	—	—
1968[2]	16.2	15.8	16.5	14.7	14.4	15.0	27.4	27.1	27.6	—	—	—
1967[2]	17.0	16.5	17.3	15.4	14.7	16.1	28.6	30.6	26.9	—	—	—

[1] Dropouts are persons who are not enrolled in school and who are not high school graduates. People who have received GED credentials are counted as graduates. Data are based on sample surveys of the civilian noninstitutional population.
[2] Includes persons of Hispanic origin.

Source: U.S. Center for Education Statistics, "Digest of Education Statistics: 1992," U.S. Government Printing Office, Washington, D.C., 1992, Table 98.

Table 12-9A. Characteristics of Persons Age 15 and Over Enrolled in College, by Sex: All Races, 1990

Characteristic	Percent distribution			Sex ratio	Percent attending full time		
	Both sexes	Male	Female		Both sexes	Male	Female
Age							
Total, age 15 and over	100.0	100.0	100.0	0.83	63.8	67.8	60.5
15 to 17 years	1.3	1.4	1.2	0.95	88.1	88.4	87.9
18 and 19 years	22.2	23.3	21.2	0.92	91.4	91.5	91.2
20 and 21 years	20.3	22.0	18.9	0.97	85.2	85.2	85.2
22 to 24 years	16.0	18.0	14.3	1.05	70.8	74.8	66.5
25 to 29 years	14.1	14.7	13.7	0.89	46.3	50.0	42.9
30 to 34 years	9.1	8.1	9.9	0.69	36.4	35.5	37.0
35 years and over	17.0	12.5	20.8	0.50	23.4	22.0	24.1
College year							
First	26.0	25.7	26.3	0.82	63.7	68.0	60.2
Second	23.4	22.9	23.8	0.80	68.5	71.2	66.3
Third	16.8	16.4	17.1	0.80	70.5	75.0	66.9
Fourth	15.4	16.2	14.6	0.93	73.8	77.2	70.7
Fifth	8.3	7.7	8.8	0.73	40.3	47.2	35.4
Sixth or higher	10.2	11.1	9.4	0.99	46.6	50.2	43.0
Control of college							
Public	78.9	77.9	79.8	0.81	62.4	66.8	58.8
Private	21.1	22.1	20.2	0.91	69.2	71.3	67.4

Source: U. S. Bureau of the Census, "School Enrollment--Social and Economic Characteristics of Students: October, 1990," Current Population Reports, Series P-20, no. 460, U.S. Government Printing Office, Washington, D.C., 1992, Tables 9 and 10.

Table 12-9B. Characteristics of Persons Age 15 and Over Enrolled in College, by Sex: White Students, 1990

Characteristic	Percent distribution			Sex ratio	Percent attending full time		
	Both sexes	Male	Female		Both sexes	Male	Female
Age							
Total, age 15 and over	100.0	100.0	100.0	0.84	63.0	66.7	59.9
15 to 17 years	1.1	1.2	1.1	0.91	88.6	90.5	84.1
18 and 19 years	22.2	23.3	21.3	0.92	92.0	92.0	91.8
20 and 21 years	20.4	22.0	19.0	0.97	85.9	86.1	85.8
22 to 24 years	15.2	17.6	13.2	1.12	70.8	74.0	67.1
25 to 29 years	14.3	14.9	13.7	0.91	43.0	46.3	40.1
30 to 34 years	9.2	8.3	10.0	0.69	34.3	32.9	35.2
35 years and over	17.6	12.7	21.7	0.49	22.7	20.2	24.0
College year							
First	25.3	25.1	25.6	0.82	62.4	66.9	58.8
Second	23.3	22.5	24.0	0.78	67.5	70.8	65.0
Third	17.1	16.7	17.5	0.80	69.8	73.5	66.8
Fourth	15.7	16.7	14.8	0.94	74.3	77.1	71.7
Fifth	8.1	7.6	8.4	0.76	38.8	43.9	35.0
Sixth or higher	10.4	11.4	9.7	0.98	44.7	48.3	41.1
Control of college							
Public	78.8	77.5	79.9	0.81	61.6	65.7	58.2
Private	21.2	22.5	20.1	0.94	68.3	70.2	66.5

Source: U. S. Bureau of the Census, "School Enrollment--Social and Economic Characteristics of Students: October, 1990," Current Population Reports, Series P-20, no. 460, U.S. Government Printing Office, Washington, D.C., 1992, Tables 9 and 10.

Table 12-9C. Characteristics of Persons Age 15 and Over Enrolled in College, by Sex: Black Students, 1990

Characteristic	Percent distribution			Sex ratio	Percent attending full time		
	Both sexes	Male	Female		Both sexes	Male	Female
Age							
Total, age 15 and over	100.0	100.0	100.0	0.73	66.1	73.1	61.2
15 to 17 years	2.5	2.7	2.4	0.84	100.0	100.0	100.0
18 and 19 years	25.1	27.9	22.9	0.89	88.5	90.9	86.5
20 and 21 years	20.6	25.7	16.9	1.11	80.1	78.8	81.6
22 to 24 years	18.5	18.9	18.1	0.76	65.1	73.9	58.9
25 to 29 years	10.8	8.9	12.1	0.53	58.0	73.1	53.1
30 to 34 years	7.8	4.4	10.2	0.32	37.0	23.1	41.5
35 years and over	14.9	11.1	17.5	0.46	26.1	33.8	22.7
College year							
First	32.9	33.6	32.3	0.75	67.9	73.6	63.6
Second	26.1	28.4	24.3	0.85	74.4	74.9	74.0
Third	14.8	14.7	14.9	0.72	72.3	83.7	65.0
Fourth	12.2	11.9	12.4	0.70	70.6	80.0	64.0
Fifth	8.3	5.3	10.5	0.36	31.0	35.5	29.4
Sixth or higher	5.7	6.1	5.5	0.82	43.8	55.6	34.1
Control of college							
Public	80.3	83.1	78.2	0.77	64.3	72.1	58.2
Private	19.7	16.9	21.8	0.57	74.5	78.8	72.0

Source: U. S. Bureau of the Census, "School Enrollment--Social and Economic Characteristics of Students: October, 1990," Current Population Reports, Series P-20, no. 460, U.S. Government Printing Office, Washington, D.C., 1992, Tables 9 and 10.

Table 12-9D. Characteristics of Persons Age 15 and Over Enrolled in College, by Sex: Hispanic Students, 1990

Characteristic	Percent distribution			Sex ratio	Percent attending full time		
	Both sexes	Male	Female		Both sexes	Male	Female
Age							
Total, age 15 and over	100.0	100.0	100.0	0.95	55.3	54.9	55.5
15 to 17 years	1.7	3.3	0.3	12.00	69.2	66.7	100.0
18 and 19 years	19.8	19.2	20.3	0.90	83.1	78.6	87.2
20 and 21 years	25.1	22.0	28.1	0.74	69.7	70.0	69.4
22 to 24 years	13.2	17.6	9.1	1.83	64.6	64.1	68.6
25 to 29 years	14.6	10.7	18.2	0.56	25.7	23.1	27.1
30 to 34 years	7.9	8.2	7.6	1.03	42.4	50.0	31.0
35 years and over	17.4	18.4	16.4	1.06	25.4	23.9	27.0
College year							
First	34.2	34.3	34.1	0.95	47.3	42.4	51.9
Second	30.2	31.0	29.4	1.00	64.2	63.7	64.6
Third	14.6	13.2	15.9	0.79	62.4	70.8	55.7
Fourth	9.6	11.5	7.8	1.40	56.9	52.4	63.3
Fifth	4.9	4.7	5.2	0.85	37.8	41.2	40.0
Sixth or higher	6.4	5.2	7.6	0.66	50.0	63.2	41.4
Control of college							
Public	84.5	82.4	86.2	0.91	52.8	53.7	52.6
Private	15.5	17.6	13.8	1.21	69.0	62.5	75.5

Source: U. S. Bureau of the Census, "School Enrollment--Social and Economic Characteristics of Students: October, 1990," Current Population Reports, Series P-20, no. 460, U.S. Government Printing Office, Washington, D.C., 1992, Tables 9 and 10.

Figure 12-4. Male:Female Ratio of High School Graduates and College Enrollees[1]: 1960-1991

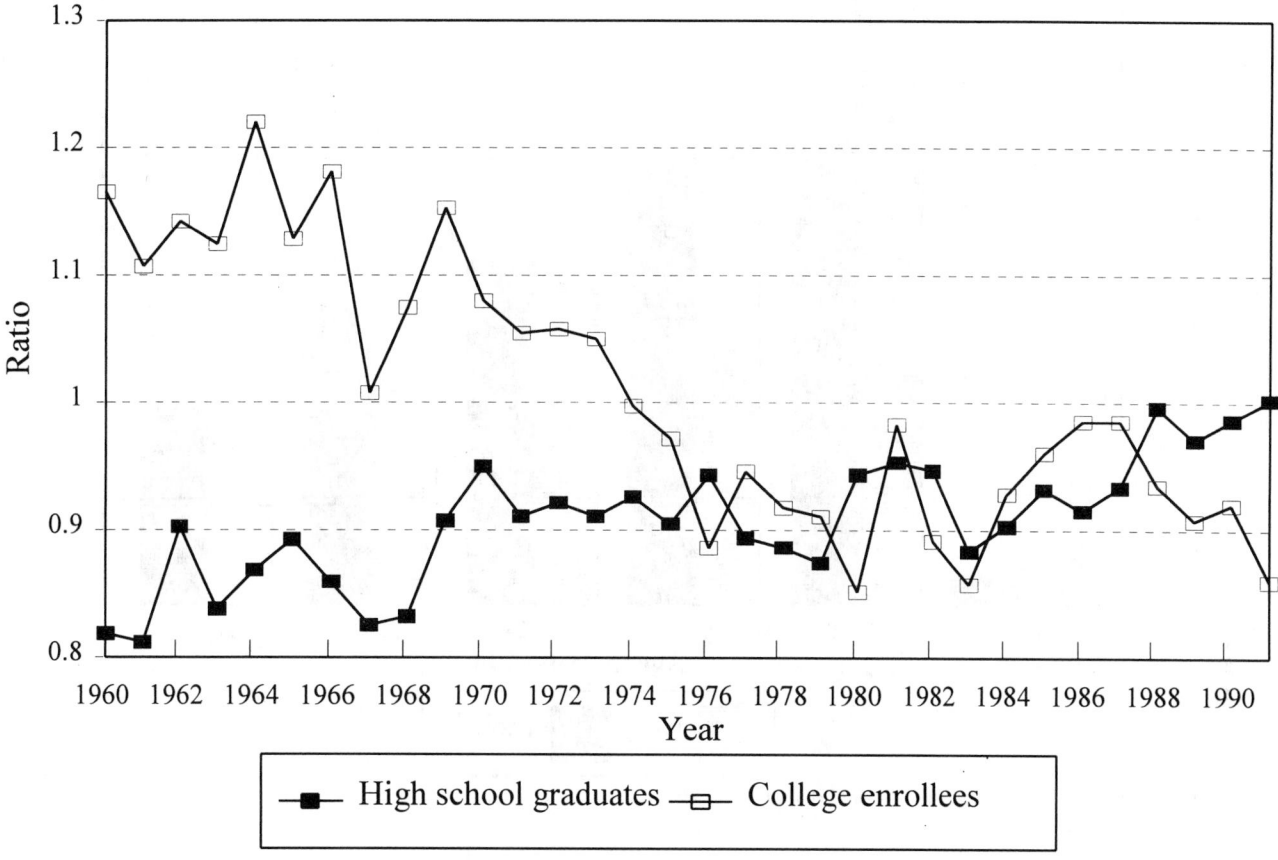

[1] Enrollment in college as of October of each year for individuals age 16 to 24 who graduated from high school during the preceding 12 months.

Source: National Center for Education Statistics, "Digest of Education Statistics: 1992," Table 171.

are a much larger percentage of college enrollments at older ages and are slightly more likely to be full-time students at these ages. Yet women are less likely to attend full time at almost all ages and across all grades. Since 1960, college enrollment of women has been increasing relative to men's (see Figure 12-4) even though women's high school graduation rates have fallen to where they are roughly the same proportion of high school graduates as are men.

The percentage of all college students at older ages has also increased (see Figure 12-5) as more older women and men are among college enrollees. The entry of these older students into college has also affected the percentage attending full time. The percentage of those enrolled in college who attend full time has declined to about 64 percent from nearly 70 percent in 1980. It is likely that older students must combine part-time schooling with the demands of a job or family. Among persons age thirty-five and over who are enrolled in college, 84.2 percent of males and 70.3 percent of females are employed while

72.4 percent of males and 61.8 percent of females are married with spouse present. Among blacks and Hispanics in this group a slightly higher percentage of males (78.5 and 76.1 percent respectively) and much lower percentage of females (40.4 and 46.0 percent respectively) are married with spouse present. Hispanic females have the highest percentage employment (82.5) of all college enrollees over thirty-five years of age.

Black students have the highest percentage attending college full time and a younger age distribution in general. A higher percentage of white and Hispanic students are over thirty-five years of age than are black students. While a higher percentage of these older Hispanic students tend to be male, women are more likely to be among these older students for blacks and whites, with white women almost twice as likely to be among the students over thirty-five years of age as are white males. The percentage of high school graduates who enroll in college has increased from just over 50 percent in the years 1980-85 to just under 60 percent for 1986-1990.

Figure 12-5. Age Distribution of College Students Age 14 to 34: All Races 1970 and 1990

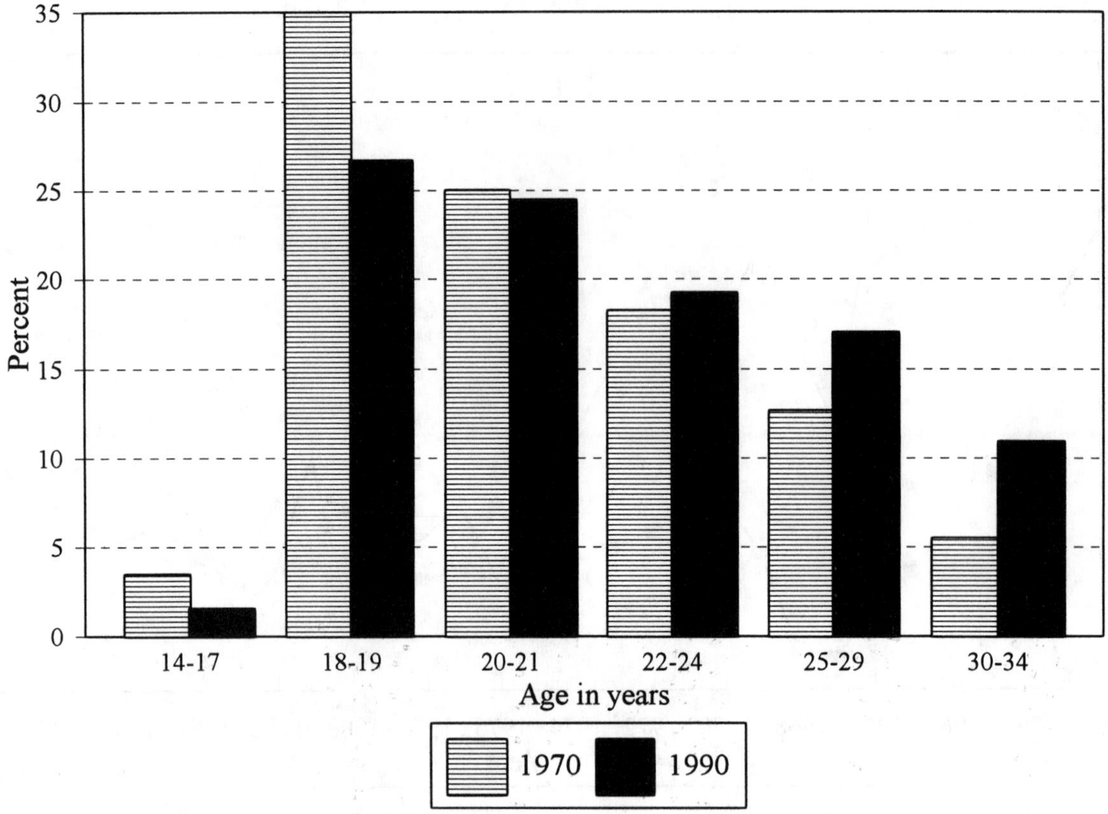

Source: Unadjusted 1990 CPS data and adjusted 1980 and 1970 CPS data.

The percentage of both black and white high school graduates who enroll in college has increased in the latter half of the 1980's while the same percentage for Hispanics has declined slightly.

Projections of Future Enrollments

Enrollments across age, race or ethnicity, sex, region, community, etc. vary a great deal over time. Projections of enrollments are important in planning for changing demands on the educational system. Increasing adult enrollments, for example, may be important in stimulating colleges to revise continuing education curricula, promote professional retraining programs, etc. Increasing enrollments at ages of compulsory schooling require planning for sufficient classroom space, teachers, equipment, etc. Although changing age-specific behavior is changing enrollment levels, the age distribution of the United States alone, twisted as it is by fluctuating birth rates and echoes of such fluctuations, can be expected to generate variability in school enrollments in future years.

Table 12-10. Percent Intercensal Change in School Enrollment, by Grade, for Persons Age 5 to 34: 1960-1990

Grade	1960-70	1970-80	1980-1990
1st-5th	10.6	-15.1	1.2
6th-9th	27.6	-8.3	-10.0
10th-12th	49.1	6.0	-5.7
Undergraduate	137.4	48.3	27.7
Graduate	137.0	79.8	45.4

Source: U.S. Bureau of the Census, "Education in the United States: 1990," Table 5, "Detailed Population Characteristics: United States Summary: 1980, 1970, and 1960" Tables 260, 197, and 168, U.S. Government Printing Office, Washington, D.C., 1992, 1983, 1973, and 1963.

Table 12-11. Projected School Enrollment for Persons Age 3 and Over for the United States, by Grade and Percent Intercensal Change: 1990-2010 [numbers in thousands]

Grade	Number enrolled			Percent change	
	1990	2000	2010	1990-2000	2000-2010
Total enrolled	64,986	72,567	75,802	11.7	4.5
Preprimary School	4,503	4,912	4,869	9.1	-0.9
1st-5th grade	18,046	20,924	20,239	15.9	-3.3
6th-9th grade	13,619	15,890	16,782	16.7	5.6
10th-12th grade	10,901	12,524	13,953	14.9	11.4
Undergraduate	13,966	14,233	15,692	1.9	10.2
Graduate	3,951	4,084	4,267	3.4	4.5

Source: Calculated from 1990 enrollment rates and distribution of enrollees by age and grade which were applied to the middle series age projections for 2000 and 2010. U.S. Bureau of the Census, "Education in the United States: 1990," 1990 CP-3-4, Table 5, and "Population Projections of the United States, by Age, Sex, Race, and Hispanic Origin:1993 to 2050," Current Population Reports, Series P-25, no. 1104, Table 2, U.S. Government Printing Office, Washington, D.C., 1994 and 1993.

A simple projection of future enrollments which does not assume any changes in age-specific behavior can be made by applying the attendance rates and the grade distribution by age proportions for 1990 to the number of persons in each age group as projected by the Bureau of the Census. These projections then show only those effects one might expect from the aging of the population through school years without any other radical changes in enrollment behavior. Table 12-11 provides the number of enrollments in 1990 and estimates of the number of students expected to be enrolled in each level by the year 2000 and 2010.

The baby boom echo, or increase in number of births since 1978, caused enrollment to increase in the first three grades during 1980-90. During the 1990-2000 decade this growth will extend to the entire range of upper elementary grades and college. The greatest increase in enrollments will be in the first through twelfth grades. By the 2000-2010 decade, enrollments at the lower elementary grades will again decline while enrollments in secondary school grades and colleges will experience the greatest increase. Overall, enrollments should increase by nearly twelve percent during the current decade with the bulk of that increase in primary and secondary grades. Enrollments should increase by at least nearly five percent the following decade with the bulk of those enrollments in secondary and college grades. It is important to remember that these projections do not include apparent trends of increase in adult schooling. Enrollments at all grades could increase substantially more than these projections if current trends of increase in adult enrollments persist into the coming decades.

Figure 12-6 provides more detail concerning anticipated changes in college enrollment during the 1990-2010s. Again, without assuming increased adult enrollment rates, the aging of the population will result in steady increases in the average age of college students. College enrollments will increase steadily for the youngest incoming students and for those students over age forty-five. There will be decreases and then subsequent increases of enrollment at the core ages of twenty through twenty-nine. A steady decrease will characterize the ages 30-34 followed by an increase and then decrease in ages 35-44. In short, as the baby boom babies pass middle age and the baby boom echo approaches college age, we should anticipate increasing enrollments at younger and older ages with some decline or level growth through the middle life course years. Of course, these mid-life trends or older enrollments might be affected by changing age-specific patterns of enrollment. If enrollment rates continue to increase at older ages we might expect either a somewhat more uniform increase in enrollments across mid-life ages or even more extreme increases in elderly enrollments.

The Income-Education Correlation in Enrollments

Unfortunately, the affordability of education and other less direct correlations between a family's income and the likelihood of enrollment among children persist as potential sources of socio-economic inequity in the United States. Table 12-12 provides the enrollment rates for children (i.e. those aged 3-17 years old) by family income level, race, and grade of school. Enrollment rates are, on average, higher for those in higher income groups. Total enrollments are higher for blacks but this is primarily limited to pre-primary school enrollments. For all three major race-ethnicity groups, enrollment appears to substantially increase with income. Although college enrollment among individuals as young as seventeen is rare, the vast majority of these exceptional enrollments are limited to the very highest income brackets. In fact, the highest such rates are among the more wealthy black and Hispanic teenagers.

College attendance among those of typical college age show even more dramatic association with income. Table 12-13 provides similar breakdowns of race-ethnicity, income group and type of college attendance for family members (excluding young couple householders) ages

Figure 12-6. College Enrollment, by Age, for 1990 and Projections for 2000 and 2010

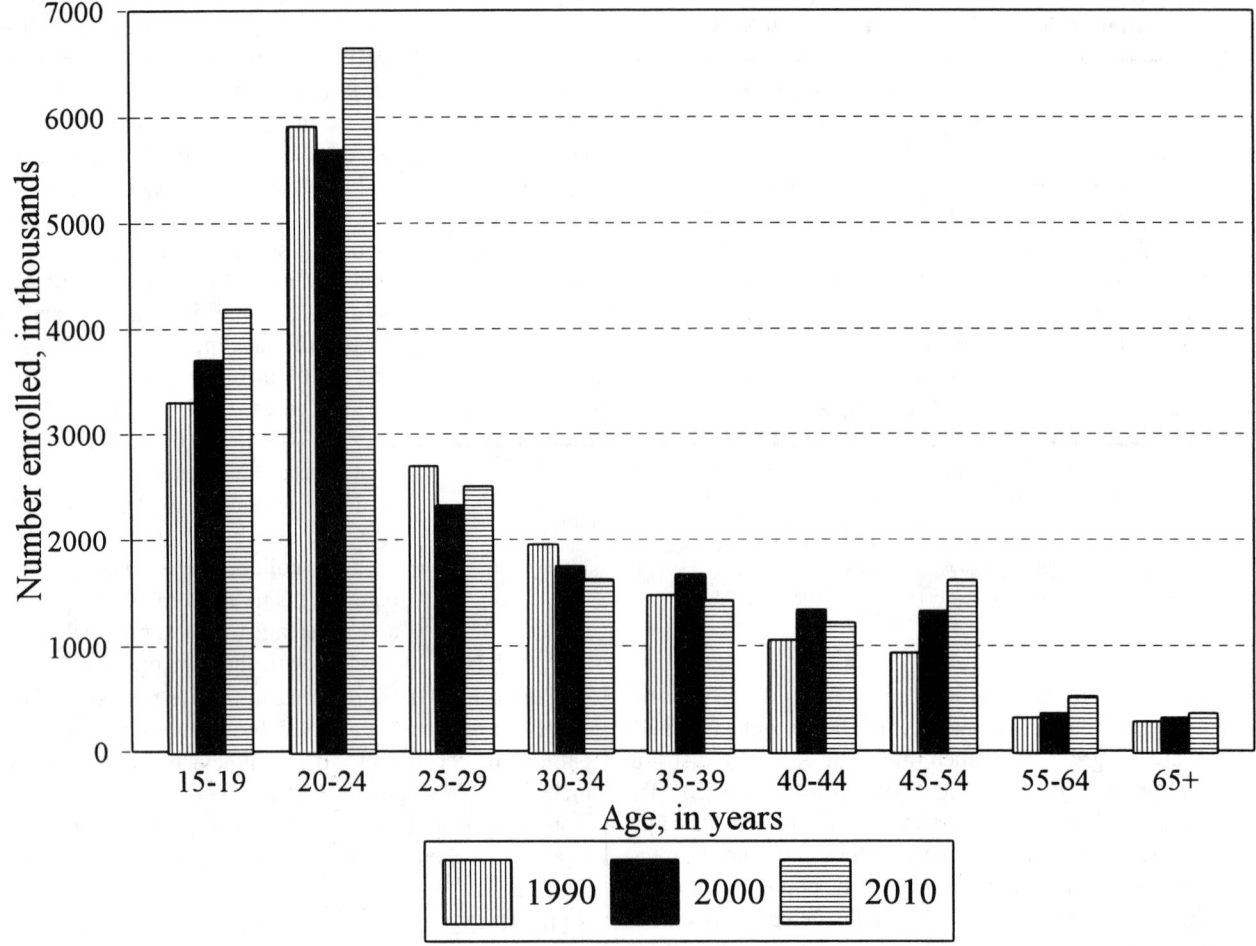

Source: 1990 U.S. Census data and 1993 CPS population projection data.

eighteen through twenty-four. The percentage of families with one or more members attending college rises from a low of around 1 in 10 of those with less than $15,000 family income to a high of nearly 2 in 3 for those families with an income of $75,000 or more. College enrollments in general are more common for whites and least common among Hispanics. Nonetheless, for all groups the increase in likelihood of college attendance with greater family income is apparent. The prospect that an individual's educational opportunities and fortunes are so clearly limited by family income is not a comforting one to the American view of equal access and opportunity. This table also shows the clearly lower percentage of families with members attending college for even the wealthiest black and Hispanic families compared to the wealthiest white families. That racial-ethnic differences persist across groups despite trends of increasing attendance with income suggests that these differences cannot be accounted for by income alone. Both racial-ethnic

and income differences suggest that educational disparities may continue, and possibly even be amplified, in the United States without active intervention efforts.

Educational Attainment

Enrollments and attendance figures provide information on the population's current educational activities. However, timing of educational experiences across the life course vary and many concerns with the cumulative educational experience provided to individuals are addressed by examining the educational level attained by a given age rather than enrollment status at that age. A question concerning educational attainment was included in a decennial census for the first time in 1940. It replaced a question on literacy, which had been abandoned because all but a very small fraction of the population was literate according to the limited standard in use. The shift from a literacy question to a "years of schooling com-

Table 12-12. Percent of Children 3-17 Years of Age Enrolled in School, by Grade, Family Income, and Race-ethnicity: 1990

Grade and race-ethnicity	Total	Family income									
		Under $10,000	$10,000-$14,999	$15,000-$19,999	$20,000-$24,999	$25,000-$29,999	$30,000-$34,999	$35,000-$39,999	$40,000-$49,999	$50,000-$74,999	$75,000 and over
All races											
Total enrolled	90.8	87.0	87.5	89.8	89.5	89.3	89.4	92.2	93.1	95.7	96.0
Preprimary school	13.8	13.8	12.8	13.4	12.8	12.8	14.3	14.8	16.2	14.3	15.1
Elementary, 1-8 years	55.2	56.8	55.3	55.3	57.1	54.6	55.3	54.9	53.7	55.2	53.1
High school, 1-4 years	21.4	16.3	19.2	20.8	19.4	21.7	19.5	22.2	22.8	25.5	27.2
College	0.3	0.2	0.1	0.3	0.3	0.2	0.3	0.2	0.4	0.7	0.6
White											
Total enrolled	89.0	85.9	86.1	89.8	89.3	89.2	88.9	92.0	92.9	95.6	96.1
Preprimary school	12.2	13.4	12.5	14.3	13.1	12.8	14.5	14.7	16.2	14.2	15.3
Elementary, 1-8 years	54.9	55.9	54.8	55.2	56.9	54.8	54.8	55.3	53.7	55.2	53.3
High school, 1-4 years	21.6	16.3	18.7	20.1	19.0	21.4	19.2	21.8	22.7	25.6	27.0
College	0.3	0.3	0.1	0.1	0.3	0.2	0.4	0.2	0.2	0.6	0.5
Black											
Total enrolled	90.5	88.9	91.4	89.9	90.1	89.7	92.4	92.3	96.8	98.6	95.8
Preprimary school	13.1	14.2	13.2	9.3	11.3	15.4	11.5	17.0	16.1	15.1	5.9
Elementary, 1-8 years	56.6	58.5	55.8	55.6	58.7	50.9	58.6	50.0	54.2	55.1	53.8
High school, 1-4 years	20.5	16.0	22.1	24.3	20.1	22.7	22.3	25.3	23.8	27.0	33.6
College	0.4	0.2	0.4	0.7	...	0.7	...	...	2.7	1.4	2.5
Hispanic											
Total enrolled	87.7	83.6	86.0	90.5	89.4	89.8	83.6	94.6	91.6	94.7	94.1
Preprimary school	12.1	11.2	10.7	15.7	11.8	11.1	13.8	9.3	20.8	8.5	10.2
Elementary, 1-8 years	55.5	55.3	56.3	55.7	58.8	53.7	49.0	59.5	54.2	58.9	57.6
High school, 1-4 years	19.8	17.0	19.0	18.9	18.8	24.6	20.8	25.9	15.9	25.2	26.3
College	0.2	0.1	...	0.1	...	0.5	...	...	0.6	2.0	...

Source: U.S. Bureau of the Census, "School Enrollment–Social and Economic Characteristics of Students: October 1990," Current Population Reports, Series P-20, no. 460, U.S. Government Printing Office, Washington, D.C., 1992, Table 6.

Table 12-13. College Attendance of Primary Family Members 18-24 Years Old, by Family Income, and Race-ethnicity: 1990
[numbers in thousands]

Families and race-ethnicity	Total	Family income									
		Under $10,000	$10,000-$14,999	$15,000-$19,999	$20,000-$24,999	$25,000-$29,999	$30,000-$34,999	$35,000-$39,999	$40,000-$49,999	$50,000-$74,999	$75,000 and over
All families											
With dependents 18 to 24 years old[1]	100.0	100.0	100.0	100.0	100.0	100.0	100.0	100.0	100.0	100.0	100.0
None attending college full time	60.3	78.5	78.7	74.4	70.4	67.0	62.5	55.6	55.6	46.5	34.7
One or more attending college full time	39.7	21.5	21.3	25.6	29.6	33.0	37.5	44.5	44.4	53.6	65.3
One attending college full time	34.4	19.5	18.5	23.3	26.8	29.9	33.6	38.2	39.1	48.0	49.9
Two attending college full time	5.3	2.0	2.8	2.3	2.8	3.0	3.9	6.3	5.2	5.6	15.4
White families											
With dependents 18 to 24 years old[1]	100.0	100.0	100.0	100.0	100.0	100.0	100.0	100.0	100.0	100.0	100.0
None attending college full time	58.5	77.7	79.7	75.3	71.6	67.0	62.8	54.8	55.6	46.0	33.4
One or more attending college full time	41.5	22.3	20.3	24.7	28.4	33.0	37.2	45.2	44.4	54.0	66.7
One attending college full time	35.9	19.9	17.4	23.0	25.1	29.5	34.2	39.4	39.3	48.1	51.0
Two attending college full time	5.7	2.4	2.9	1.7	3.3	3.5	3.0	5.7	5.1	5.9	15.7
Black families											
With dependents 18 to 24 years old[1]	100.0	100.0	100.0	100.0	100.0	100.0	100.0	100.0	100.0	100.0	100.0
None attending college full time	71.4	81.2	77.6	72.4	68.2	70.1	67.0	62.9	61.3	50.0	53.6
One or more attending college full time	28.6	18.6	22.4	26.9	32.5	29.9	33.0	37.1	38.7	50.8	46.4
One attending college full time	25.9	17.8	19.4	24.4	32.5	29.1	26.6	30.9	36.0	46.6	35.7
Two attending college full time	2.6	0.7	3.0	2.6	...	0.9	6.4	6.2	2.7	4.2	10.7
Hispanic families											
With dependents 18 to 24 years old[1]	100.0	100.0	100.0	100.0	100.0	100.0	100.0	100.0	100.0	100.0	100.0
None attending college full time	80.7	89.3	85.6	84.5	83.2	86.4	79.4	68.8	64.4	63.8	56.7
One or more attending college full time	19.3	10.3	14.4	15.5	16.8	13.6	20.6	31.3	35.6	36.2	43.3
One attending college full time	17.2	9.8	10.7	12.4	14.6	13.6	17.6	31.3	31.5	34.0	40.0
Two attending college full time	2.1	0.5	3.7	3.1	2.2	...	2.9	...	4.1	2.1	3.3

[1] Excludes families in which the only members 18 to 24 years old are the family householders, or other members who are married, spouse present.

Source: U.S. Bureau of the Census, "School Enrollment--Social and Economic Characteristics of Students: October 1990," Current Population Reports, Series P-20, no. 460, U.S. Government Printing Office, Washington, D.C., 1992, Table 16

**Figure 12-7. Trends in Educational Attainment Composition of the U.S. Population
25 Years of Age and Over: 1940-1990**

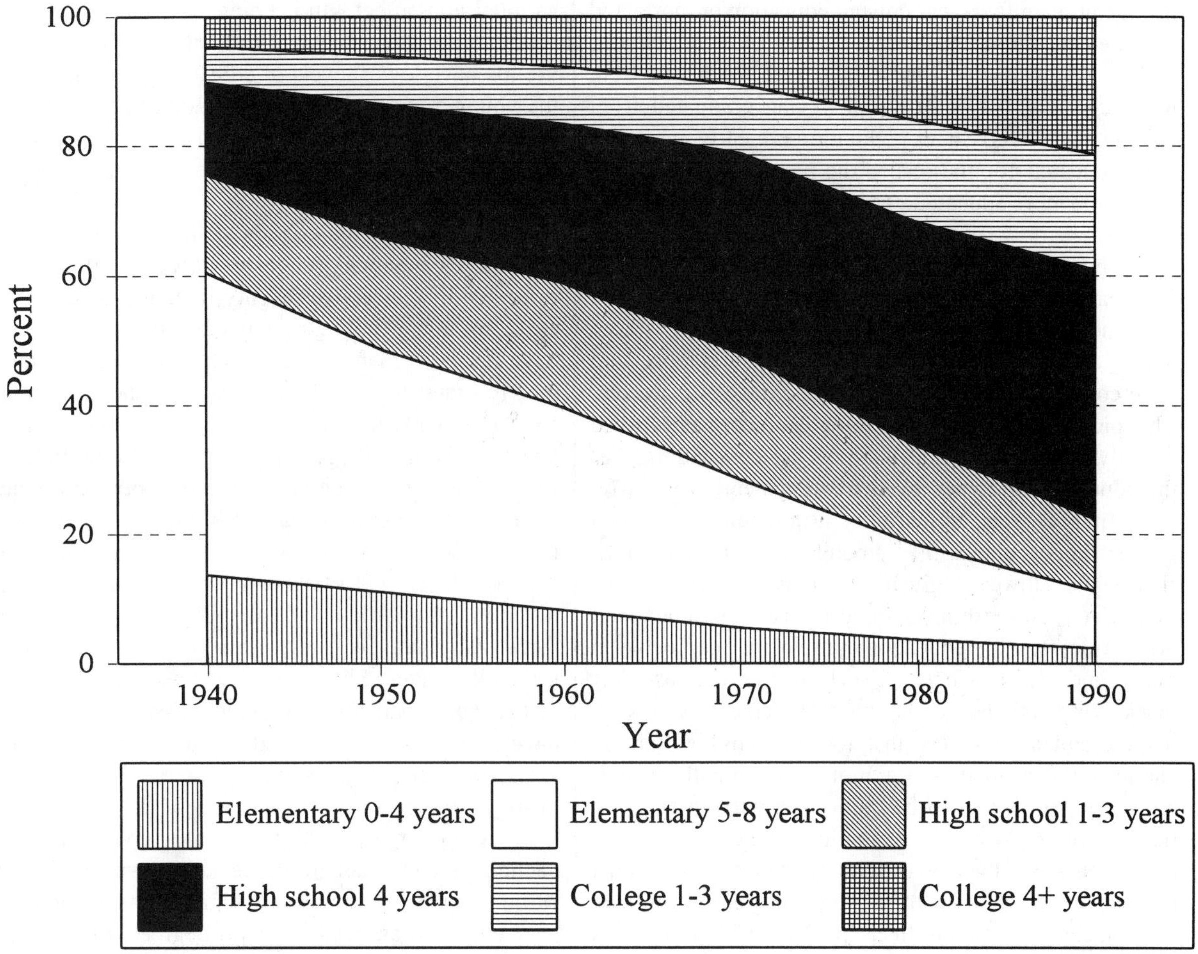

Elementary 0-4 years	Elementary 5-8 years	High school 1-3 years
High school 4 years	College 1-3 years	College 4+ years

Source: 1990 unadjusted CPS data and 1940-1980 Census data.

pleted" question provided a much richer body of information concerning the educational attainment of the population.

Despite rising adult enrollments, by the time they have reached the age of twenty-five, most persons have completed the largest part of any education to which they have aspired, could afford or were required to obtain, so they are no longer enrolled in school. Statistics on the educational attainment of the adult (out-of-school) population, therefore, are often gathered for the population age twenty-five and older. Including individuals at a younger age confounds attainment of many people who are still engaged in education with those who have terminated schooling. Still, this arbitrary cutoff point of twenty-five and older is becoming progressively less valid because of recent trends toward more postgraduate education and college enrollment at ages even beyond thirty-five, as described above. Limiting the analysis to the population age twenty-five and over is also a compromise that omits

the young persons who did not complete high school or who did not go to college but are in the labor force at ages 16-24 years.

Only a few years before 1940 the average citizen was a graduate of elementary school. By about 1965 the average citizen was a high school graduate. By the year 2000 the average adult American will have 1-3 years of college. This prospect has a variety of profound implications. Figure 12-7 illustrates the dramatic change in the proportion of the population over twenty-five that has reached each level of schooling from 1940 through 1990. The proportion of the population with less than four years of high school education has dropped dramatically and consistently. Most of this decline is in those with only elementary school educational attainment. The largest group in 1990 are those with at least four years of high school. The largest proportionate increases over the half century are in those with some college education.

Table 12-14 provides a more detailed breakdown

of these trends in educational attainment for all races and selected race groups with available historical data. In 1990, 21.3 percent of the population twenty-five and older had a complete four-year college education or more, and 17.9 percent more had completed one to three years of college. With nearly 78 percent having graduated from high school and over one-fifth having graduated from college, the United States population is clearly one of the most educated populations on the planet and continuing to become more educated. At the other end of the educational scale, only 6.4 percent had not completed elementary school in 1990, and only 2.4 percent had less than five years of schooling. The greatest concentration by far is in the groups having completed high school without having attended college, i.e. 38.4 percent, and those who have completed at least some college, i.e. 39.2 percent. This picture of high educational attainment has evolved steadily from one of high literacy but concentration of the population at lower levels of attainment.

Increases in educational attainment have been greater among blacks than among whites over the past fifty years. However, given the relative disadvantage of blacks in 1940 these more rapid increases in attainment have not closed the educational attainment gap between blacks and whites. There are still roughly twice as many blacks with less than eight years of elementary schooling, more blacks with less than four years of high school, and fewer blacks with four or more years of college. Nor are these gaps likely to be eliminated without substantially more progress. For example, despite dramatic improvements over the past fifty years, there are still almost twice as many whites with four or more years of college than blacks. And simple linear projection of past trends into the future would suggest that even by the year 2050 there will still be only roughly half as many blacks as whites with four-year college degrees. Fortunately, the situation may not be so dismal as such projections suggest. First, hope may be found in noting periods of dramatic progress. In the decade between 1970 and 1980, for example, the percentage of blacks with college degrees nearly doubled as baby boomers went through college. Second, the trends in educational attainment estimates are conservative in that these figures include all those above twenty-five; substantially greater progress in eliminating attainment gaps is apparent if one considers only these younger cohorts.

Sex and Age Patterns of Educational Attainment

The educational attainment of a particular group of persons reflects the rates of school enrollment that its members had when they were young, modified somewhat by death and migration. The level of educational attainment today is a reflection of the rising age-specific rates of past school enrollment of successive generations. According to this principle, today's differentials in school enrollment will become tomorrow's differentials in educational attainment. In keeping with the lower rates of school enrollment they had in their youth, the older age groups have lower levels of educational attainment than the younger age groups, as indicated by the summary of the educational attainment composition in 1990 by persons of each age reported in Table 12-15 and graphed in Figure 12-8.

Among both males and females, persons who never completed elementary school are now predominantly concentrated in ages above seventy-five, and hence are generally no longer in the regular labor force. Persons who have no more than an elementary school education are mostly older than sixty. Even among those over sixty-five, however, between 1 in 5 and 1 in 3, depending upon age, have some college experience. Of those under fifty years of age at least eighty percent of both males and females are high school graduates; nearly 1 in 5 females have a bachelor's degree or higher as do over 1 in 4 males. Clearly educational attainments are more heavily concentrated in this middle-aged and younger group in the labor force. Graduate and professional degrees are somewhat more likely later in life and so are most prevalent in those forty to sixty years of age for males. Because more women have pursued these advanced degrees in more recent cohorts, advanced degrees are concentrated in those thirty to fifty-five years of age for females.

A higher percentage of males continue to have bachelor's and graduate degrees above age thirty-five, while a higher percentage of females have some college with either an associate's or no degree. Enrollment of women in college surpassed that of men in the early 1980s and this is reflected in the fact that there are more women with bachelor's degrees than men for ages 25-29 and 30-34, and more women with a bachelor's or graduate degree for those ages 25-29. Because of this generational effect, future decades will likely evidence full equality or even superiority of female educational attainment at younger ages, with a progressively greater relative sex differential in educational attainment with increasing age. Yet, because of the generational effect, the upper-level educational attainment of women will be significantly below that of men for nearly half a century, but the differences will diminish with the passage of time.

Race and Ethnic Differences in Educational Attainment

The educational attainment composition of the population is reported in Table 12-16 for selected major race-ethnic groups used in the census. The most educated such group in the United States is the Asian population. Nearly 82 percent of this group have graduated from high

Table 12-14. Educational Attainment of the Population 25 Years of Age and Over, by Race: 1940-1990 [percent distribution]

Educational attainment	1990[1]	1980	1970	1960	1950	1940
All races	100.0	100.0	100.0	100.0	100.0	100.0
Elementary school						
0-4 years	2.4	3.6	5.5	8.3	11.1	13.7
5-7 years	4.0	6.7	10.0	13.8	16.4	18.5
8 years	4.8	8.0	12.8	17.5	20.8	28.2
High school						
1-3 years	11.2	15.3	19.4	19.2	17.4	15.2
4 years	38.4	34.6	31.1	24.6	20.8	14.3
College						
1-3 years	17.9	15.7	10.6	8.8	7.4	5.5
4 years and over	21.3	16.2	10.7	7.7	6.2	4.6
White	100.0	100.0	100.0	100.0	100.0	100.0
Elementary school						
0-4 years	2.0	2.6	4.5	6.7	8.9	10.9
5-7 years	3.7	5.8	9.1	12.8	15.1	17.4
8 years	4.8	8.2	13.0	18.1	21.7	29.8
High school						
1-3 years	10.5	14.6	18.8	19.3	17.8	15.8
4 years	38.9	35.7	32.2	25.8	22.0	15.3
College						
1-3 years	18.1	16.0	11.1	9.3	7.8	5.9
4 years and over	22.0	17.1	11.3	8.1	6.6	4.9
Black	100.0	100.0	100.0	100.0	100.0	100.0
Elementary school						
0-4 years	5.1	8.2	14.6	23.8	32.8	41.8
5-7 years	6.7	11.7	18.7	24.2	28.7	30.0
8 years	4.3	7.1	10.5	12.9	11.8	11.9
High school						
1-3 years	17.7	21.8	24.8	19.0	13.6	8.7
4 years	37.2	29.3	21.2	12.9	8.0	4.5
College						
1-3 years	17.6	13.5	5.9	4.1	2.9	1.9
4 years and over	11.3	8.4	4.4	3.1	2.1	1.3

[1] 1990 census data categories were inconsistent with previous years and thus 1990 CPS data are presented here.

Source: U.S. Bureau of the Census, "Educational Attainment in the United States: March 1991 and 1990," Current Population Reports, Series P-20, no. 462, Table 1, and "General Social and Economic Characteristics: 1980," Table 83, U.S. Government Printing Office, Washington, D.C, 1992 and 1983.

Table 12-15. Years of School Completed, by Sex and Age: 1990 [percent distribution]

| Age and sex | Total | Elementary | | High school | | College | | |
		0-4 years	5-8 years	1-3 years	4 years	Associate or no degree	Bachelor's degree	Graduate or professional degree
Males								
Total, 25 and over	100.0	2.8	7.6	10.3	31.3	24.7	14.4	9.0
25-29 years	100.0	1.5	2.8	9.6	35.6	28.8	17.3	4.4
30-34 years	100.0	1.6	2.8	8.4	34.2	29.0	16.5	7.5
35-39 years	100.0	1.7	3.0	6.9	29.7	30.7	17.5	10.5
40-44 years	100.0	1.8	3.7	6.8	26.8	29.4	18.3	13.4
45-49 years	100.0	2.1	5.3	9.2	30.5	25.1	14.5	13.3
50-54 years	100.0	2.7	7.4	11.0	32.7	22.6	12.5	11.2
55-59 years	100.0	3.6	10.2	11.9	32.1	20.1	12.1	10.0
60-64 years	100.0	4.1	13.0	15.1	30.8	17.7	11.1	8.3
65-69 years	100.0	4.6	14.7	15.0	31.7	17.1	9.7	7.2
70-74 years	100.0	5.1	18.3	15.8	31.6	15.7	7.6	5.9
75-79 years	100.0	6.8	24.2	16.3	27.8	13.0	6.3	5.6
80-84 years	100.0	8.8	28.6	15.6	23.1	12.0	6.2	5.8
85 years and over	100.0	13.1	34.4	13.2	18.8	10.0	5.4	5.2
Females								
Total, 25 and over	100.0	2.6	7.8	11.1	35.8	25.1	12.0	5.7
25-29 years	100.0	1.2	2.2	8.3	33.3	32.7	18.6	3.9
30-34 years	100.0	1.3	2.4	7.5	33.5	32.6	16.7	6.0
35-39 years	100.0	1.4	2.6	6.7	32.6	31.9	16.4	8.5
40-44 years	100.0	1.6	3.2	7.3	34.1	30.0	14.5	9.3
45-49 years	100.0	1.9	4.3	10.1	37.8	26.5	11.6	7.9
50-54 years	100.0	2.4	6.0	12.6	40.8	22.9	9.2	6.2
55-59 years	100.0	3.0	8.3	14.3	42.0	19.8	7.6	5.0
60-64 years	100.0	3.3	10.4	15.9	41.6	17.8	6.8	4.1
65-69 years	100.0	3.8	13.0	16.1	41.5	16.6	5.7	3.2
70-74 years	100.0	4.2	17.6	17.4	38.4	14.0	5.5	2.9
75-79 years	100.0	5.3	23.1	17.7	32.7	12.8	5.5	2.8
80-84 years	100.0	6.6	27.0	16.5	28.1	12.9	6.2	2.8
85 years and over	100.0	9.6	32.3	13.7	24.5	12.1	5.5	2.2

Source: U.S. Bureau of the Census, "Education in the United States: 1990," 1990 CP-3-4, U.S. Government Printing Office,
  Washington, D.C., 1994, Table 1.

Figure 12-8. Educational Attainment Composition of the U.S. Population, by Age: 1990

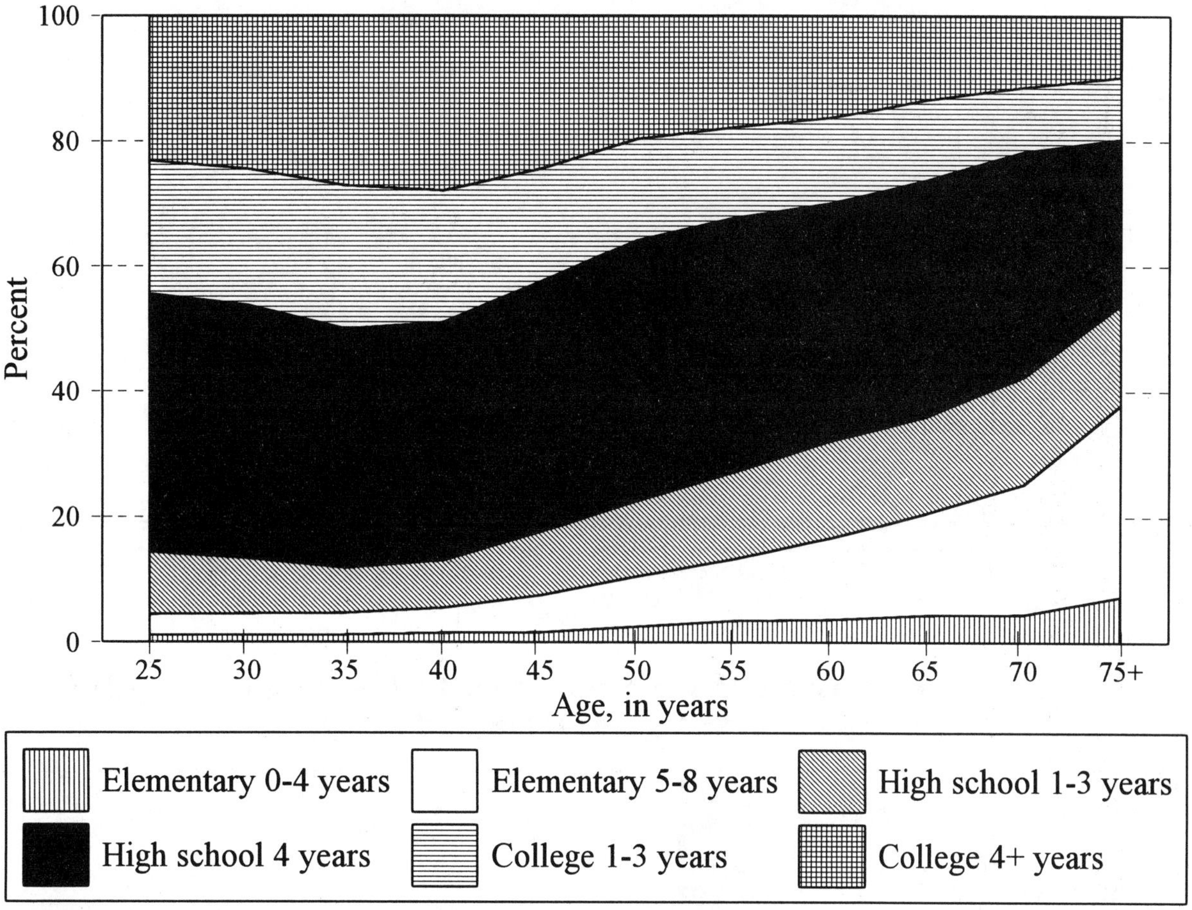

Source: 1990 unadjusted CPS data.

school and almost 37 percent have at least a four-year college degree. The majority white population occupies second place. The least educated group are Hispanics with about 56 percent high school graduates and 9 percent with at least a bachelor's degree. American Indians and the black population are much lower in educational attainment than the white, but significantly above the Hispanic population. The dramatic differences in Hispanic educational attainment are illustrated in Figure 12-9. It is very likely, of course, that the Hispanic population with lowest educational attainment includes a disproportionate number of recent immigrants. As educational enrollments reflect, adult education efforts are higher among Hispanics for similar reasons and educational attainment data which is not further broken down does not reflect the unique impacts of immigration upon Hispanic educational attainment.

Table 12-17 provides two indicators of educational attainment, by age and sex, for each racial group: graduation from high school and graduation from college with at least a bachelor's degree. The racial differentials de-

scribed above are valid for each age and sex group in general but are much diminished at the younger ages and much greater at the older ages. Asian males in the youngest age group are not yet twice as likely to have a college degree as whites and over four times more likely to have such a degree compared to any other minority group. Asian women at the youngest ages are very similar. American Indian women, as compared to men, are more clearly less educated than black women, particularly with respect to college graduation. Hispanic males over sixty years of age are more likely to be college graduates than black males, while black females over sixty are much more likely to be college graduates than Hispanic females.

The educational disadvantages that the black population suffered in the past are reflected in the race differentials for black males and females sixty and older. At those ages the percentage of persons with a high school diploma is only around half that for whites or less, and the percentage of males with a college degree is less than a third that for whites. The black-white differential is much greater for males than for females; black women have

Table 12-16. Years of School Completed by Persons 25 Years and Over, by Race-ethnicity: 1990 [percent distribution]

Educational attainment	Race-ethnicity				
	White	Black	Hispanic	American Indian	Asian/ Pacific Islander
Total	100.0	100.0	100.0	100.0	100.0
Elementary school					
None	0.8	1.9	6.2	2.6	4.7
1-4 years	1.0	2.6	7.3	2.1	2.2
5-8 years	7.1	9.2	17.2	9.3	6.1
High school					
1 year	2.9	4.1	5.3	4.4	2.0
2 years	3.9	5.8	4.3	6.0	2.0
3 years	3.1	6.6	4.1	5.7	1.3
4 years	34.2	34.5	27.3	33.4	22.7
College					
Some college, no degree	19.1	18.5	14.3	20.8	14.7
Associate degree	6.3	5.3	4.8	6.4	7.7
Bachelor's degreee	13.9	7.5	5.9	6.1	22.7
Advanced degree	7.7	3.8	3.3	3.2	13.9

Source: U.S. Bureau of the Census, "Education in the United States: 1990," 1990 CP-3-4,
  U.S. Government Printing Office, Washington, D.C., 1994, Table 1.

Figure 12-9. Educational Attainment of the White, Black, and Hispanic Population Age 25 Years and Over: 1990

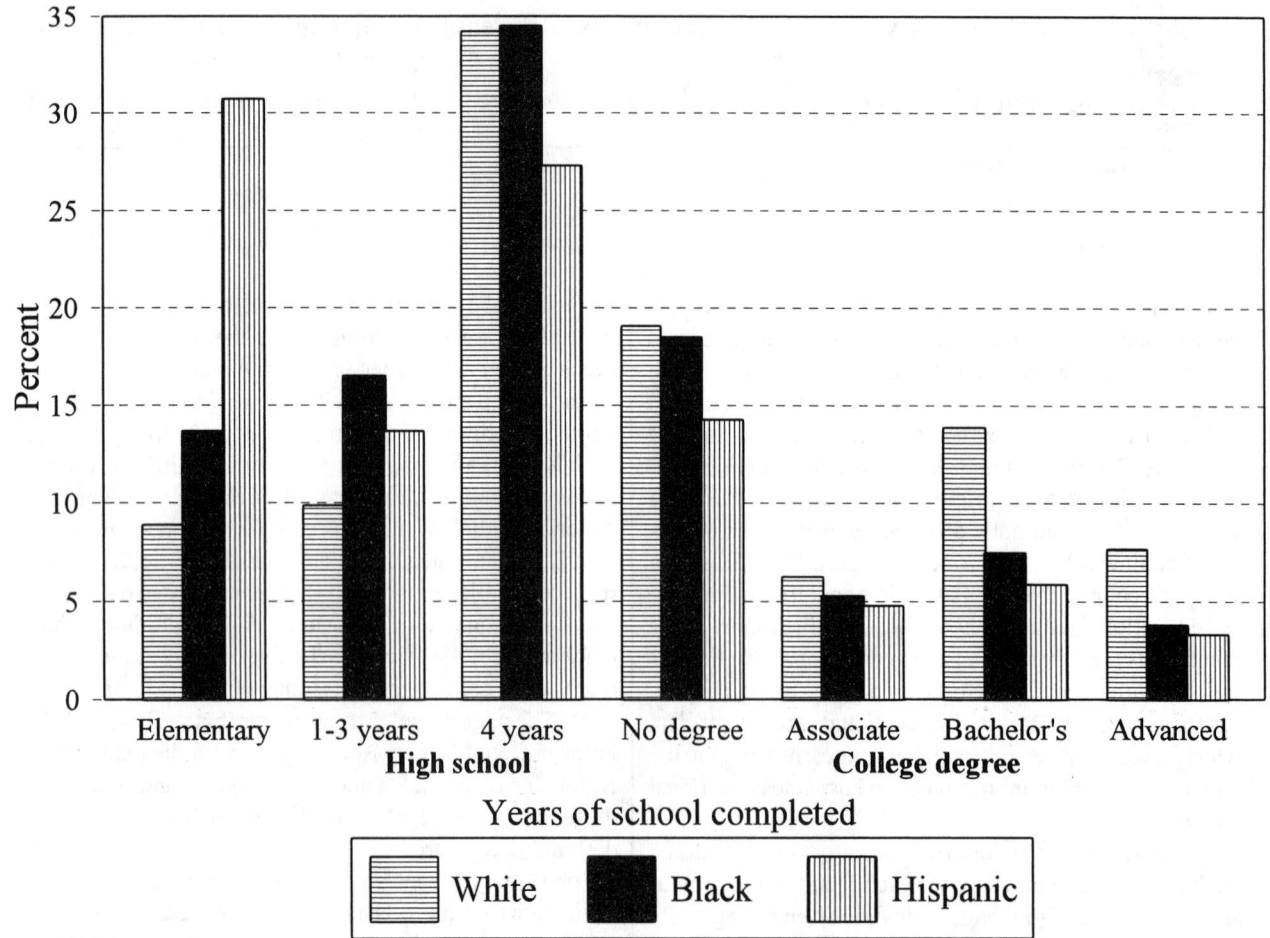

Source: 1990 Census data.

Table 12-17. Indicators of Educational Attainment of the Total Population Age 25 and Over, by Age, Sex, and Race-ethnicity: 1990

Age and sex	Percent high school graduate					Percent bachelor's degree or higher				
	White	Black	Hispanic	American Indian	Asian/ Pacific Islander	White	Black	Hispanic	American Indian	Asian/ Pacific Islander
Males										
Total	78.4	62.2	49.8	65.8	81.5	25.0	11.0	10.0	10.1	41.9
25-29 years	85.3	73.9	55.3	71.3	87.7	24.0	9.6	8.6	6.4	42.2
30-34 years	86.6	74.5	55.7	72.2	86.8	26.0	12.2	10.4	8.1	45.0
35-39 years	88.6	75.0	55.4	77.5	86.2	30.2	14.3	11.9	12.4	45.9
40-44 years	88.3	72.4	53.5	75.9	85.9	34.1	15.0	12.8	15.1	48.3
45-49 years	83.6	64.2	47.4	68.2	84.9	29.6	12.8	11.0	12.5	49.3
50-54 years	78.9	56.4	44.1	61.1	82.6	25.2	10.6	9.9	12.4	46.6
55-59 years	74.3	47.5	39.8	52.3	76.2	23.6	9.5	8.9	10.3	38.2
60-64 years	67.2	38.4	34.2	41.4	67.9	20.7	7.6	8.2	8.6	28.3
65-69 years	64.4	32.0	30.5	39.4	60.9	18.0	5.5	6.9	7.8	20.9
70-74 years	58.9	26.5	28.4	36.5	55.2	14.3	4.6	6.5	6.4	18.3
75-79 years.	50.2	21.1	21.8	30.2	46.9	12.6	4.1	5.1	5.6	15.7
80-84 years	44.3	17.3	18.4	23.4	41.5	12.8	3.6	4.5	4.1	13.8
85 years and over	37.0	14.1	15.5	19.3	35.8	11.4	3.1	3.9	3.5	11.4
Females										
Total	77.4	63.8	49.9	65.3	74.0	18.4	11.7	8.3	8.6	31.8
25-29 years	88.0	79.0	61.5	74.2	86.1	24.5	12.6	10.0	7.1	40.5
30-34 years	88.9	78.6	59.2	75.5	83.5	24.5	14.0	10.4	8.5	39.2
35-39 years	89.7	78.4	57.4	77.6	80.3	26.6	15.8	10.5	12.1	38.1
40-44 years	88.3	75.6	54.2	74.6	78.9	25.3	15.1	9.1	12.3	37.3
45-49 years	83.8	67.6	47.3	67.1	76.3	20.4	12.6	7.4	9.0	35.0
50-54 years	78.9	59.6	42.3	58.5	69.6	16.0	10.7	6.5	8.8	27.4
55-59 years	73.9	51.4	36.2	51.7	63.5	13.1	9.8	5.5	6.9	18.3
60-64 years	69.4	43.1	31.6	43.6	57.4	11.4	7.9	4.9	5.6	13.4
65-69 years	66.1	35.6	27.2	40.6	49.7	9.3	6.3	4.0	4.9	10.2
70-74 years	59.3	29.9	23.8	34.9	41.6	8.8	5.4	3.4	5.4	8.3
75-79 years.	51.8	24.6	19.9	31.1	35.7	8.8	4.8	3.2	4.8	8.5
80-84 years	47.6	21.4	17.9	28.1	30.1	9.4	4.6	3.3	4.8	7.6
85 years and over	41.9	17.9	16.5	22.1	24.6	8.1	3.6	2.6	4.2	4.9

Source: U.S. Bureau of the Census, "Education in the United States: 1990," 1990 CP-3-4, U.S. Government Printing Office, Washington, D.C., 1994, Table 1.

Table 12-18. Indicators of Educational Attainment for Regions, by Race and Year: 1940-1990

Race and year	Percent high school graduate					Percent bachelor's degree or higher				
	Total	Northeast	Midwest[1]	South	West	Total	Northeast	Midwest[1]	South	West
All races										
1990	75.2	76.2	77.2	71.2	78.6	20.3	22.8	18.4	18.7	22.7
1980	66.5	67.1	68.0	60.2	74.5	16.2	17.2	14.7	15.0	19.3
1970	52.3	52.9	53.7	45.1	62.3	10.7	11.2	9.6	9.8	13.2
1960	41.1	41.0	41.7	35.3	50.8	7.7	8.1	6.9	7.1	9.6
1950	34.3	35.7	35.4	26.7	45.6	6.0	6.6	5.5	5.3	7.7
1940	24.5	24.0	25.0	20.3	34.8	4.6	4.9	4.2	4.0	6.1
White										
1990	78.0	78.6	78.6	74.3	82.4	21.5	24.0	19.0	20.4	24.2
1980	68.8	68.7	69.3	63.5	77.2	17.1	18.0	15.2	16.3	20.2
1970	54.5	54.2	55.0	49.1	63.3	11.3	11.7	10.0	10.8	13.5
1960	43.2	41.9	42.8	39.8	51.9	8.1	8.4	7.1	7.9	9.9
1950	36.4	36.7	36.4	31.6	46.7	6.4	6.8	5.6	6.2	7.9
1940	26.1	24.4	25.4	24.6	35.4	4.9	5.1	4.3	4.8	6.2
Black										
1990	62.9	65.3	65.3	58.9	76.3	11.3	12.5	10.5	10.6	14.8
1980	51.2	56.4	54.9	44.9	68.7	8.4	8.4	7.9	8.0	11.4
1970	31.4	37.8	36.5	24.4	48.9	4.4	4.1	4.0	4.4	5.9
1960	20.1	26.9	25.3	14.7	34.3	3.1	2.9	2.9	3.1	4.1
1950	13.0	20.4	19.7	8.8	26.2	2.1	2.2	2.3	1.9	2.9
1940	7.7	11.7	12.6	5.4	18.4	1.3	1.7	1.8	1.1	2.3

[1] Designated as the North Central Region until June 1984.

Source: U.S. Bureau of the Census, "Education in the United States:1990," 1990 CP-3-4, Table 3, and "General Social and Economic
 Characteristics: United States Summary:1980," Table 83, U.S. Government Printing Office, Washington, D.C., 1994 and 1984.

sought a college education more persistently than black men for many generations, with the result that they are less disadvantaged in comparison with their white sisters than are black men in comparison with their white brothers. Although the black-white differential still exists at the youngest age groups, it is greatly reduced.

Regional Differences in Educational Attainment

Differences noted above are present in various regions of the country but there are also some interregional differences. Table 12-18 shows the trends from 1940 to 1990 in two indicators of attainment, high school graduation and completion of college with at least a bachelor's degree, for regions of the country broken down for the white and black population. The educational attainment of the population in the South remains below that of the other regions, while in the West the level of educational attainment remains generally higher than it is in other re-

gions. In the South the white-black differential is unusually large, owing to past neglect with respect to educational opportunities for blacks. Other regional differences are due in part to differences in urban-rural composition, in part to historical differences in the quality and quantity of educational facilities provided, and in part to the fact that for many years so many of the better educated persons migrated from regions of lower opportunity to regions of higher opportunity. The Northeast is notable in that high school and college graduation has risen nearly to Western levels as of 1990. However, the percent of black population graduating from high school has not risen to such levels. Again, this is partly due to the greater concentration of the urban and older black population in the Northeast.

In interpreting these interregional differences, one must keep in mind the fact that they are a net resultant of conditions that have existed over the past fifty to seventy-five years. The differences should not be used to evaluate the current educational programs of the various

Table 12-19A. Marital Status by Years of School Completed for Males Age 25 Years and Over, by Race: 1991

Marital status	Total	Elementary school			High school		College		
		0-4 years	5-7 years	8 years	1-3 years	4 years	1-3 years	4 years	5+ years
All races	100.0	100.0	100.0	100.0	100.0	100.0	100.0	100.0	100.0
Never married	16.6	20.7	13.8	10.8	15.2	16.5	18.2	19.5	14.7
Married, spouse present	68.3	52.7	62.2	68.8	65.1	68.1	67.8	70.7	75.7
Married, spouse absent	3.3	8.4	6.3	4.2	4.4	3.4	2.7	1.9	2.1
Widowed	3.2	12.5	10.1	9.4	5.1	2.2	1.8	1.4	1.4
Divorced	8.6	5.7	7.6	6.8	10.1	9.9	9.6	6.5	6.0
White	100.0	100.0	100.0	100.0	100.0	100.0	100.0	100.0	100.0
Never married	15.0	20.9	13.0	9.6	11.8	14.5	16.6	18.9	14.1
Married, spouse present	70.8	55.5	64.5	71.8	69.9	70.9	69.9	71.5	76.4
Married, spouse absent	2.6	9.5	5.3	3.0	3.2	2.6	2.2	1.6	2.0
Widowed	3.0	9.1	10.2	9.3	5.4	2.3	1.8	1.5	1.4
Divorced	8.4	5.0	7.1	6.3	9.7	9.7	9.4	6.4	6.1
Black	100.0	100.0	100.0	100.0	100.0	100.0	100.0	100.0	100.0
Never married	29.0	22.4	17.6	20.1	31.9	31.4	30.0	28.8	29.7
Married, spouse present	46.8	40.0	52.0	43.6	40.9	46.1	50.0	55.3	54.2
Married, spouse absent	8.4	6.3	11.1	14.9	10.0	8.9	6.7	4.1	3.5
Widowed	4.3	23.2	8.8	10.7	4.3	1.6	1.7	1.7	1.7
Divorced	11.5	8.1	10.5	10.7	12.9	11.9	11.7	10.1	10.8
Hispanic	100.0	100.0	100.0	100.0	100.0	100.0	100.0	100.0	100.0
Never married	20.0	17.0	16.6	17.9	18.1	22.3	23.8	23.6	18.4
Married, spouse present	62.7	57.9	64.1	62.4	65.5	61.7	62.3	63.5	69.7
Married, spouse absent	7.9	16.3	10.9	12.8	7.4	5.3	2.4	4.7	5.6
Widowed	1.9	5.1	4.4	2.4	0.6	0.8	0.7	0.6	0.4
Divorced	7.5	3.8	4.0	4.5	8.3	9.8	10.9	7.5	6.4

Source: U.S. Bureau of the Census, "Educational Attainment in the United States: March 1991 and 1990," Current Population Reports, Series P-20, no. 462, U.S. Government Printing Office, Washington, D.C., 1992, Table 3.

regions. Such programs are best evaluated from school enrollment data or recent cohort achievement data within specific schooling units.

Marital Status and Educational Attainment

Educational attainment can affect marital status in a variety of ways. It can cause persons (especially women) to remain single until they attain the amount of education they desire. It can influence the employability and hence the financial capability (particularly of males) for getting married and establishing a family. It can influence the desirability or eligibility of a person as a marriage partner. And it can provide both greater and less freedom in choosing whether, when, and with whom to marry. Both education and marital status may be influenced jointly by external factors of a physiological or environmental nature. Education can be a form of self-investment in the hope of long-term future gains at the loss of short-term income, leisure, or other benefits. Those who make such an investment tend to differ in numerous ways from those who do not, including attitudes toward marriage. Education is a somewhat rigorous attrition process in which young persons attempt (or are encouraged to attempt) to survive to the maximal extent of their intellectual, economic, and other abilities; marriage tends to occur after successful survival or as a secondary adjustment after elimination. Unforeseen events can curtail educational attainment. Important among these are premarital pregnancy followed by "forced" or "obligatory" marriage or withdrawal from school to care for a child. Death or physi-

Table 12-19B. Marital Status by Years of School Completed for Females Age 25 Years and Over, by Race: 1991

Marital status	Total	Elementary school			High school		College		
		0-4 years	5-7 years	8 years	1-3 years	4 years	1-3 years	4 years	5+ years
All races	100.0	100.0	100.0	100.0	100.0	100.0	100.0	100.0	100.0
Never married	11.5	13.1	8.2	6.5	10.2	9.0	12.0	17.7	20.5
Married, spouse present	60.3	39.9	43.7	45.4	50.7	64.3	62.8	66.0	60.5
Married, spouse absent	4.0	8.1	6.9	3.8	6.2	3.8	3.8	2.2	2.2
Widowed	13.6	34.3	33.4	37.7	21.5	11.9	8.3	6.0	4.9
Divorced	10.7	4.7	7.9	6.7	11.3	11.0	13.1	8.0	11.9
White	100.0	100.0	100.0	100.0	100.0	100.0	100.0	100.0	100.0
Never married	9.7	14.5	7.1	5.7	6.1	7.0	9.8	17.1	20.6
Married, spouse present	63.4	42.8	47.6	46.9	55.7	67.2	66.0	67.2	61.2
Married, spouse absent	3.1	6.8	5.3	3.0	5.1	3.0	2.9	2.0	1.9
Widowed	13.5	31.0	33.1	37.6	21.9	12.2	8.6	6.1	5.0
Divorced	10.3	5.0	7.0	6.9	11.2	10.6	12.7	7.7	11.3
Black	100.0	100.0	100.0	100.0	100.0	100.0	100.0	100.0	100.0
Never married	24.3	12.1	13.3	12.7	26.8	25.4	28.5	24.5	22.7
Married, spouse present	36.2	18.8	26.8	29.9	30.0	38.9	38.0	50.9	41.9
Married, spouse absent	10.3	10.5	11.2	10.2	11.1	11.0	10.7	5.4	5.6
Widowed	15.2	52.5	38.1	41.8	20.4	9.4	6.4	6.2	6.7
Divorced	13.9	6.1	10.7	5.4	11.6	15.3	16.4	12.9	23.5
Hispanic	100.0	100.0	100.0	100.0	100.0	100.0	100.0	100.0	100.0
Never married	13.5	11.6	11.2	11.4	14.6	12.8	15.6	16.9	22.3
Married, spouse present	58.5	50.9	59.2	50.5	57.4	62.3	60.3	63.8	55.3
Married, spouse absent	9.1	11.1	10.9	11.4	12.1	8.2	5.7	6.6	2.3
Widowed	8.7	20.7	11.2	13.9	5.9	5.6	5.0	3.4	7.0
Divorced	10.2	5.6	7.6	13.0	10.2	11.2	13.4	9.4	13.0

Source: U.S. Bureau of the Census, "Educational Attainment in the United States: March 1991 and 1990," Current Population Reports, Series P-20, no. 462, U.S. Government Printing Office, Washington, D.C., 1992, Table 3.

cal incapacitation of a parent and military draft are other external events that have affected education. The availability of government funds to sponsor schooling (such as veterans' educational benefits and student loans) and the willingness of one partner of a married couple to help support the education of the other are also involved.

The basic data are presented in Tables 12-19A for males of at least 25 years of age and 12-19B for females. Each table is broken down by marital status and selected major race or ethnic groups. Married with spouse present is the most common marital status for both sexes and all levels of educational attainment. Married with spouse present is also the largest group for both sexes in each racial or ethnic group. However, within sex and race groups there are some exceptions to this pattern by level of educational attainment largely related to cohort differ-

ences. Black females, for example, with an elementary school education or less are from older cohorts and more likely to be widowed. Black females with more education are the most likely to remain never married of all groups. However, as Hispanic and white women approach professional degrees with five or more years of education they have similar percentages never married as do black women. A higher percentage of women with college educations are also divorced among blacks than other groups. For males the dominance of married with spouse present is more uniform. There are higher percentages never married and divorced among all black males but these groups do not vary in relation to educational attainment to the extent that they do for black women.

A great deal of attention has been paid recently to the chances of marriage among more educated and older

Table 12-20. Education of Husband, by Education of Wife for Married Couples 18 Years of Age and Over, by age of Husband, 1991

Education and age of husband	Total	Percent distribution of education of wife							
		Elementary school			High school		College		
		0-4 years	5-7 years	8 years	1-3 years	4 years	1-3 years	4 years	5+ years
18 years old and over	100.0	1.4	2.7	3.2	10.0	44.0	19.5	12.6	6.6
Elementary									
0 to 4 years	100.0	38.4	24.7	7.7	12.6	13.7	2.3	0.5	0.1
5 to 7 years	100.0	7.8	29.1	12.1	23.3	23.2	3.6	0.8	0.3
8 years	100.0	2.2	7.6	23.2	21.9	37.3	5.9	0.9	0.9
High school									
1 to 3 years	100.0	0.7	3.8	6.2	32.0	47.5	7.9	1.5	0.5
4 years	100.0	0.3	1.0	2.0	10.2	64.4	15.3	4.6	2.1
College									
1 to 3 years	100.0	0.1	0.4	0.9	4.0	41.9	35.9	11.7	5.1
4 years	100.0	0.1	0.3	0.2	1.4	25.2	26.5	36.7	9.5
5 years or more	100.0	0.1	...	0.2	0.6	16.6	21.6	30.2	30.6
25-44 years old	100.0	0.8	1.7	1.2	7.8	41.2	22.9	16.4	7.9
Elementary									
0 to 4 years	100.0	44.6	19.8	4.1	13.1	11.7	6.8	0.5	...
5 to 7 years	100.0	11.0	41.4	7.4	20.0	16.8	2.8	0.2	0.7
8 years	100.0	3.1	10.6	20.3	26.9	33.3	5.8	0.3	...
High school									
1 to 3 years	100.0	0.4	3.7	3.8	33.2	48.3	8.4	1.7	0.6
4 years	100.0	0.3	0.7	0.9	9.3	62.9	18.2	5.6	2.1
College									
1 to 3 years	100.0	0.1	0.3	0.4	3.2	37.7	38.9	14.0	5.5
4 years	100.0	...	0.2	0.1	1.1	19.8	26.5	41.8	10.5
5 years or more	100.0	...	...	...	0.3	11.6	19.9	34.5	33.7
45-64 years old	100.0	1.6	2.8	2.8	9.8	47.7	17.5	10.9	7.0
Elementary									
0 to 4 years	100.0	39.0	24.6	6.7	13.9	14.2	1.1	0.5	0.3
5 to 7 years	100.0	7.6	23.6	8.4	24.9	30.7	4.3	0.6	...
8 years	100.0	2.4	6.6	16.2	21.9	45.7	5.1	1.0	1.0
High school									
1 to 3 years	100.0	0.8	4.0	5.7	28.9	50.7	8.3	1.6	0.1
4 years	100.0	0.4	1.2	2.1	9.6	67.3	13.1	3.7	2.5
College									
1 to 3 years	100.0	0.1	0.6	0.8	4.3	47.9	32.3	8.8	5.2
4 years	100.0	0.3	0.2	0.2	1.8	30.7	25.5	31.4	9.7
5 years or more	100.0	0.1	...	0.3	0.6	21.1	21.2	28.0	28.5
65 years old and over	100.0	2.7	5.4	9.5	15.1	43.2	13.7	6.7	3.7
Elementary									
0 to 4 years	100.0	34.3	26.3	10.9	12.0	14.8	1.3	0.4	...
5 to 7 years	100.0	6.7	28.1	19.1	22.4	19.2	3.0	1.3	0.4
8 years	100.0	1.8	6.8	29.2	20.4	33.1	6.6	1.1	1.1
High school									
1 to 3 years	100.0	1.0	3.1	10.4	32.4	43.8	7.3	1.2	0.8
4 years	100.0	0.3	2.0	5.8	13.5	62.3	11.2	3.6	1.2
College									
1 to 3 years	100.0	0.1	0.3	3.9	8.5	49.0	25.7	8.9	3.6
4 years	100.0	...	1.1	0.8	2.1	37.9	28.0	25.2	4.8
5 years or more	100.0	0.4	0.1	0.6	1.3	21.8	29.6	20.9	25.4

Source: U.S. Bureau of the Census, "Educational Attainment in the United States: March 1991 and 1990," Current Population Reports, Series P-20, no. 462, U.S. Government Printing Office, Washington, D.C., 1992, Table 5.

Table 12-21. Degrees Conferred by Institutions of Higher Education, by Level: 1961-1990

| Academic year | Bachelor's degrees | | Master's degrees | | First-professional degrees | Doctor's degrees | |
	Male:female ratio	Per 100 high school graduates 4 years earlier	Male:female ratio	Per 100 bachelor's degrees 2 years earlier	Male:female ratio	Male:female ratio	Per 1,000 bachelor's degrees x years earlier[1]
1961	1.60	25	2.16	22	36.36	8.51	27.6
1962	1.50	25	2.17	23	32.21	8.33	35.2
1963	1.42	25	2.14	27	30.77	8.33	42.3
1964	1.35	25	2.09	28	30.94	8.44	49.7
1965	1.33	25	2.04	29	27.09	8.28	57.6
1966	1.36	27	1.96	30	25.38	7.62	58.9
1967	1.37	29	1.89	32	23.49	7.40	54.3
1968	1.30	28	1.80	34	21.08	6.95	58.8
1969	1.29	27	1.68	35	22.12	6.61	71.6
1970	1.32	30	1.52	33	18.38	6.44	77.9
1971	1.31	31	1.50	32	14.80	6.01	78.0
1972	1.29	33	1.46	32	15.15	5.33	72.3
1973	1.28	33	1.42	31	13.17	4.60	70.4
1974	1.26	33	1.32	31	9.18	4.24	65.0
1975	1.21	31	1.23	32	7.03	3.69	65.5
1976	1.20	31	1.16	33	5.42	3.37	61.0
1977	1.17	30	1.12	34	4.37	3.11	52.6
1978	1.12	30	1.07	34	3.65	2.79	44.1
1979	1.07	29	1.04	33	3.25	2.56	41.3
1980	1.04	30	1.02	32	3.03	2.37	38.8
1981	1.01	30	0.99	32	2.75	2.22	37.1
1982	0.99	30	0.97	32	2.64	2.12	36.9
1983	0.98	31	1.00	31	2.35	2.01	35.5
1984	0.98	32	1.02	30	2.22	1.98	35.1
1985	0.97	32	1.00	30	2.05	1.93	35.7
1986	0.97	33	0.99	30	2.00	1.84	36.4
1987	0.94	34	0.95	30	1.88	1.84	37.1
1988	0.92	36	0.94	30	1.80	1.85	37.9
1989	0.90	38	0.93	31	1.75	1.73	38.8
1990	0.88	40	0.90	33	1.63	1.76	41.1

[1] Represents the average number of years from the receipt of the bachelor's degree to the receipt of the doctorate degree; over the period 1961-1990, this average was 9.3 years.

Source: National Center for Education Statistics, "120 Years of American Education: a Statistical Portrait," U.S. Government Printing Office, Washington, D.C., 1993, Table 28.

Table 12-22. Bachelor's Degrees Conferred by Institutions of Higher Education, by Field of Study: 1961-1990 [percent distribution]

Field of study	Academic years					
	1961-1965	1966-1970	1971-1975	1976-1980	1981-1985	1986-1990
Total	100.0	100.0	100.0	100.0	100.0	100.0
Agriculture/natural resources	1.4	1.4	1.7	2.4	2.1	1.4
Architecture/engineering/ environmental design	8.8	6.5	6.3	7.1	10.0	9.7
Business/management	12.4	12.6	13.9	17.6	22.9	24.2
Communication/public affairs	0.9	1.2	2.8	4.7	5.6	6.1
Computer/information sciences	0.0	0.1	0.4	0.8	2.7	3.5
Education	24.4	21.2	20.2	14.7	10.1	9.3
Foreign languages	2.4	2.9	2.1	1.4	1.0	1.0
Health sciences	2.7	2.8	3.9	6.4	6.7	6.1
Letters	7.3	8.1	6.5	4.0	3.5	4.0
Life sciences	4.7	5.0	4.8	5.5	4.2	3.7
Mathematics	3.9	3.7	2.5	1.4	1.3	1.6
Physical sciences	3.9	3.0	2.3	2.5	2.5	1.8
Psychology	2.7	3.8	5.1	4.9	4.2	4.6
Social sciences	15.4	18.5	16.7	12.3	10.0	10.2
Visual/performing arts	3.5	4.1	4.0	4.5	4.1	3.7
Other[1]	5.5	5.1	6.7	9.8	9.1	9.1

[1] "Other" includes degrees in area and ethnic studies, home economics, law, liberal/general studies, library sciences, military sciences, multi/interdisciplinary studies, parks and recreation, philosophy and religion, protective services, theology, and degrees not classified by field of study.

Source: National Center for Education Statistics, "120 Years of American Education: a Statistical Portrait," U.S. Government Printing Office, Washington, D.C., 1993, Table 29.

women due to mismatches in the marriage market. Table 12-20 presents the education level of wives by the age and the education level of their husbands. From this table there does appear to be considerable matching behavior in the marriage market. For those 18 years and older with less than elementary school education wives are most likely to have the same education as their husbands and are next most likely to have more education. At the other end of the spectrum, for husbands with advanced college educations wives are most likely to have similarly advanced degrees and over 80 percent of their wives have at least some college. But at these higher levels of education fewer husbands have wives with more education than they have. For those with 1-3 years of college, just under 17 percent have a wife with more education, and for those that presumably graduate with four years of college only 9.5 percent have wives with more education and over half, almost 54 percent, have wives with less education. These general patterns are surprisingly consistent across various age groups of husbands. However, an increasing percentage of college-educated husbands have wives with more education among more recent cohorts. This reflects both the increase in women with such higher education in the marriage market and perhaps a greater willingness of men to accept wives of more education and of such women to accept husbands of lesser education as educational and occupational differences continue the slow march toward equity between the sexes.

College Education and Job Market Equity

Increasingly, college education is useful for occupational advancement and success. Among some recent cohorts and certainly among selected occupations a college degree is considered essential for employment. Increasing equity in education is thus one route to increasing equity in the job market. A better indication of the trend in college degrees and the changing sex ratio of degrees awarded is given in table 12-21 for single years from 1961 through 1990. In 1961, there were 1.6 bachelor's degrees awarded to men for each awarded to a woman. By 1990 there are more such degrees being awarded to women with only 0.88 being awarded to men for each awarded to a woman. This rise parallels a rise in the number of bachelor's degrees awarded for high school

Table 12-23. Master's Degrees Conferred by Institutions of Higher Education, by Field of Study: 1961-1990 [percent distribution]

Field of study	Academic years					
	1961-1965	1966-1970	1971-1975	1976-1980	1981-1985	1986-1990
Total	100.0	100.0	100.0	100.0	100.0	100.0
Agriculture/natural resources	1.3	1.0	1.1	1.2	1.4	1.2
Architecture/engineering/ environmental design	10.2	9.0	7.0	6.3	7.8	8.8
Business/management	8.4	9.8	11.9	15.8	22.0	23.5
Communication/public affairs	3.3	3.4	5.1	6.8	7.1	7.1
Computer/information sciences	0.0	0.4	0.8	1.0	1.9	3.0
Education	38.4	36.5	40.0	38.3	29.7	26.3
Foreign languages	1.9	2.4	1.6	0.9	0.6	0.6
Health sciences	2.0	2.1	3.0	4.4	5.8	6.3
Letters	4.5	5.0	4.1	2.6	2.1	2.2
Life sciences	2.9	3.0	2.4	2.2	1.9	1.6
Mathematics	3.2	3.1	1.9	1.1	0.9	1.1
Physical sciences	4.2	3.2	2.3	1.8	1.9	1.9
Psychology	1.9	2.0	2.2	2.6	2.8	2.8
Social sciences	7.6	8.2	6.5	4.6	3.8	3.5
Visual/performing arts	3.4	3.7	2.9	2.8	3.0	2.8
Other[1]	6.8	7.3	7.3	7.6	7.4	7.4

[1] "Other" includes degrees in area and ethnic studies, home economics, law, liberal/general studies, library sciences, military sciences, multi/interdisciplinary studies, parks and recreation, philosophy and religion, protective services, theology, and degrees not classified by field of study.

Source: National Center for Education Statistics, "120 Years of American Education: a Statistical Portrait," U.S. Government Printing Office, Washington, D.C., 1993, Table 30.

graduates four years earlier. This later number is not strictly a percentage or rate but provides a similar indication of how many degrees are awarded for changing numbers of high school graduates. While only approximately 25 of 100 high school graduates went on for bachelor's degrees in 1961, that had risen to 40 of 100 by 1990. Clearly, a greater proportionate increase in the number of those going on to get college degrees were women, accounting for the changing sex ratio of college graduates. As one looks at higher level degrees the trends in the proportion going on for higher degrees are not quite as dramatic but the changing trends in sex ratio are even more dramatic. While there were 2.16 master's degrees awarded to males for each awarded to a female in 1961, there were fewer master's degrees to males in 1990 than to females (0.9 awarded to males for each to a female). First professional degrees and doctorates are still awarded to more males (1.63 and 1.76 for each awarded to a female, respectively). However, these advanced degrees have also seen the most dramatic improvements in equity. In 1961 there were over 36 professional degrees awarded to men for every one awarded to a woman. By 1990 there were only 1.63 men awarded such degrees for each woman.

Similarly the male to female ratio of doctorates has declined from 8.51 males to each female Ph.D. in 1961 down to 1.76 by 1990. Clearly this trend will continue as more of the women who have recently gone on to bachelor's and master's degrees continue on through professional degrees and doctorates. This educational equity will not itself enforce job market equity and comparable worth wages but will certainly support those trends.

Changing Fields of College Study

Areas of study are often chosen by college students for many reasons other than response to job market trends. Even when choices are intended to exploit favorable market trends the historical mismatch of training to job market demands shows that, like any market, students often forecast poorly and make individual decisions which do not necessarily result in numbers proportionate to market needs. Nonetheless, tracking areas in which students are trained provides some indication of the careers they intend to seek and provides an important inventory of the human resources available in our population. Tables 12-22, 12-23 and 12-24 show trends in the number of

Table 12-24. Doctor's Degrees Conferred by Institutions of Higher Education, by Field of Study: 1960-1990 [percent distribution]

Field of study	Academic years					
	1961-1965	1966-1970	1971-1975	1976-1980	1981-1985	1986-1990
Total	100.0	100.0	100.0	100.0	100.0	100.0
Agriculture/natural resources	3.7	2.9	3.0	2.9	3.5	3.3
Architecture/engineering/ environmental design	11.2	12.7	10.4	8.0	8.9	12.1
Business/management	1.9	2.0	2.7	2.6	2.6	3.1
Communication/public affairs	0.6	0.6	1.1	1.6	1.8	1.9
Computer/information sciences	0.0	0.2	0.5	0.7	0.8	1.3
Education	16.3	18.1	21.1	23.7	22.9	19.4
Foreign languages	2.1	2.5	2.6	2.1	1.5	1.3
Health sciences	1.2	1.2	1.6	2.0	3.2	3.8
Letters	4.4	4.7	6.0	5.0	3.8	3.4
Life sciences	11.4	11.4	10.6	10.5	10.7	10.1
Mathematics	3.8	4.1	3.2	2.4	2.1	2.1
Physical sciences	17.9	15.5	11.7	9.8	10.0	10.8
Psychology	6.2	5.7	6.3	8.1	8.9	8.9
Social sciences	11.7	11.7	12.1	11.0	9.0	8.2
Visual/performing arts	2.8	2.5	1.8	2.0	2.1	2.2
Other[1]	4.7	4.1	5.2	7.7	8.0	7.9

[1] "Other" includes degrees in area and ethnic studies, home economics, law, liberal/general studies, library sciences, military sciences, multi/interdisciplinary studies, parks and recreation, philosophy and religion, protective services, theology, and degrees not classified by field of study.

Source: National Center for Education Statistics, "120 Years of American Education: a Statistical Portrait," U.S. Government Printing Office, Washington, D.C., 1993, Table 31.

bachelor's, master's and doctorate degrees awarded in various fields of study over the years since 1961. In 1961 the largest percentage of bachelor's degrees were awarded in education followed by the social sciences. Both groups have declined over time. The proportion of bachelor's degrees which were awarded to education students in 1986-1990 was less than half of the percentage for 1961-65. Meanwhile, the percentage of degrees awarded to students of business and management has more than doubled over the same period. Some fields of study such as health science and computer science have increased dramatically but still constitute a modest proportion of all such degrees while some other areas such as psychology have had mixed or changing trends. Of some national concern, degrees in the letters, life sciences, mathematics, and physical sciences have all declined substantially over the past thirty years. Somewhat similar trends are seen in the master's degrees conferred. Education students are still the largest group among these degree students, but the decline in such degrees and the rise in master's degrees awarded to other groups such as business students is similar to those for bachelor's degrees. Again, there has been a decline in letters, life sciences,

mathematics, and physical science master's degrees. Trends are somewhat different for the more limited number of doctorates awarded. Education doctorates have had mixed trends; business Ph.D.'s have increased but are still a small fraction of all such degrees. Architecture, life sciences, physical sciences, and social sciences are somewhat larger percentages of Ph.D.'s but follow similar trends as at lower degree levels. Many of these trends will be of continuing interest as concerns mount over the proper educational mix required of the population for international competitiveness in a global economic and labor market.

Conclusion

Education has certainly been among the most rapidly changing population characteristics over the past century. The democratic ideal of an informed citizenry is approaching an unparalleled historical reality. Some of the most dramatic social and cultural divisions in education, such as those by sex, have declined dramatically over the recent past. One can anticipate that the increasing equity of education in these areas will contribute to diminished inequities in the job market and in socioeconomic power or status over time. At the same time, there are enduring differences in educational access and achievement across social strata. Dramatic improvements in educational enrollments and attainment by major minority groups belie these enduring differences and the slow speed of any process of convergence across social strata. Just as improvements in equity of education can be expected to improve equity in other areas, the persistence of inequities in education can be expected to contribute to social inequities in the marketplace and beyond. In fact, as education becomes more significant in our daily lives and work, such inequities may be amplified in their social force. Despite the great gains in democratic education of the population, it may now be more crucial than ever to ensure educational access and opportunity to all of our citizens.

Educational trends also provide information of a more practical sort with immediate policy concerns. Educational institutions have clearly had to adapt to the rapidly changing population composition of the United States. The baby boom caused an unheralded expansion of educational capacities across the country. Retrenchment of educational capacities during the baby bust has been ongoing for the past decade and a half. Now, the baby boom echo has placed strain upon secondary schools and many school systems have tried to respond with more flexible educational investment strategies (e.g. mobile classrooms, altered school years or daily shifts). This larger cohort will soon be entering colleges at the same time as an increased demand for college-level adult education and retraining becomes apparent. For all of us who have experienced the recent rapid technological changes in the workplace it is commonplace to envision continuing education as an essential part of workday activities. The extension of the educational system to fulfill these needs is among the latest innovation in education which will shape trends into the next century. The 'virtual classroom,' cooperative industry and academic training programs, and curricula increasingly directed toward adult needs are among these innovations.

At the same time as education becomes a more commonplace and continuing part of Americans' lives, it is clear that demands for education may also be increasingly oriented toward personal growth and satisfaction. Community education programs, extension courses offered through a great variety of local community and academic organizations, popular craft and non-production skill courses, tutorial software programs, and an entire variety of educational pursuits would have hardly been thought possible nor productive at the turn of the prior century. To some extent the educational exposure of our population has combined with increasing leisure time pursuits and technology to insure that continuing educational variety and experiences are integrated components

in the modern lifestyle. As dramatic as the recent past of education has been, all lifestyle trends over the next century may be increasingly influenced by educational pursuits.

At another level of policy concern, the United States' entry into a truly global market has produced a greater concern with the competitive nature of educational preparation than in the past. In the post-cold war era educational investment appears as perhaps the greatest investment in national security. The competitive skills of our labor force seem destined to play an ever greater role in maintaining a high average standard of living and solving the most immediate crises of urban industrial life. Technology has brought both great advances and difficulties to our society. Education is the surest path to navigate our future both rationally and with compassion. While educational quality is of great national concern, educational decisions made in preparation for personal success may be at odds with these needs. Increasingly students appear to have selected areas of training more compatible with their planned entry into administration and managerial positions with less selection of basic science and mathematical training. Of some concern is the rapidly declining popularity of education itself as a disciplinary choice. Many policy programs and interventions to insure training in the basic sciences and equality of access to these opportunities appear to have had limited recent success. It may well be that much stronger policy initiatives and structural changes in career compensation may be the only ways to enhance and insure the basic competitive advantages a nation finds in core scientific and technical fields. At the same time, rising education has also brought increasing technical content into fields such as business administration, health sciences, and computer science which many students are choosing in increasing numbers. Applied science and information technologies may be growing solidly but at some expense to the basic science underlying these activities.

In sum, we are the most educated population in history and it is our obligation to continue the democratic education of the citizenry and to anticipate the changes which may be required to preserve and enhance this progress. It is to our own personal and collective interests to maintain and improve the quality and directions of the education system. And our lives and those of our children will continue to be increasingly shaped by these efforts and our individual educational pursuits.

Bibliography

Ahlburg, D., Crimmins, E.M, and Easterlin, R.A. "The Outlook for Higher Education: A Cohort Size Model of Enrollment of the College Age Population, 1948-2000." Review of Public Data Use 9 (1981):211-27.

Alexander, K.L., Entwisle, D.R., and Thompson, M.S. "School Performance, Status Relations and the Structure of Sentiment: Bringing the Teacher Back In." American Sociological Review 52 (1987): 665-682.

Alexander, K.L., and Reilly, T.W. "Estimating the Effects of Marriage Timing on Educational Attainment: Some Procedural Issues and Substantive Clarifications." American Journal of Sociology 87 (1981): 143-56.

Alexander, K.L., Riordan, C., Fennessey, J., and Pallas, A.M. "Social Background, Academic Resources and College Graduation: Recent Evidence from the National Longitudinal Survey." American Journal of Education 90 (1982): 315-33.

Arrow, K.J., "Higher Education as a Filter." Journal of Public Economics 2 (1973): 193-216.

Astone, N.M., and McLanahan, S.S. "Family Structure, Parental Practices and High School Completion." American Sociological Review 56 (1991): 309-320.

_____. "Family Structure, Residential Mobility, and School Dropout: A Research Note." Demography 31 (1994): 575-584.

Ballmer, H., and Cozby, P.C. "Family Environments of Women Who Return to College." Sex Roles 7 (1981): 1019-26.

Blake, Judith. "Number of Siblings and Educational Mobility." American Sociological Review 50 (1985):84-94.

Cameron, S.V., and Heckman, J.J. "The Nonequivalence of High School Equivalents." Journal of Labor Economics 11 (1993): 1-47.

Carnegie Council on Policy Studies in Higher Education. Three Thousand Futures: The Next Twenty Years for Higher Education. San Francisco: Jossey-Bass, 1980.

Center for Educational Statistics, U.S. Dept. of Education. Who Drops out of High School? Washington, D.C.: U.S. Government Printing Office, 1987.

Clark, W.A.V. "School Desegregation and White Flight: A Reexamination and Case Study." Social Science Research 16 (1987): 211-228.

Coleman, James S., Campbell, Ernest Q., Hobson, Carol J. et al. Equality of Educational Opportunity. Washington, DC: U.S. Government Printing Office, 1966.

Coleman, James S., Hoffer, Thomas, and Kilgore, Sally. "Achievement and Segregation in Secondary Schools: A Further Look at Public and Private School Differences." Sociology of Education 55 (1982): 162-82.

College Board, Profile of SAT and Achievement Test Takers. New York: College Entrance Examination Board, 1988.

Cuban, L. How Teachers Taught: Constancy and Change in American Classrooms, 1890-1990. New York: Teachers College Press, 1993.

DiPrete, T.A., and Grusky, D.B. "Structure and Trend in the Process of Stratification for American Men and Women." American Journal of Sociology 96 (1990): 107-143.

Dreeben, R., and Gomoran, A. "Race, Instruction and Learning." American Sociological Review 51 (1986):660-669.

Entwisle, D.R., and Alexander, K.L. "Summer Setback: Race, Poverty, School Composition, and Mathematics Achievement in the First Two Years of School." American Sociological Review 57 (1992): 72-84.

_____. "Winter Setback: The Racial Composition of Schools and Learning to Read." American Sociological Review 59 (1994): 446-460.

Featherman, D.L., and Hauser, R.M. Opportunity and Change. New York: Academic Press, 1978.

Formisano, R.P. Boston Against Busing. Chapel Hill: University of North Carolina Press, 1991.

Gottfredson, D.C. "Black-White Differences in the Educational Attainment Process: What Have We Learned?" American Sociological Review 46 (1981): 542-57.

Grove, D.J. "Educational Attainment and Socioeconomic Mobility Within Ethnic Groups." Ethnic and Racial Studies 4 (1981): 466-75.

Grusky, D.B., and DiPrete, T.A. "Recent Trends in the Process of Stratification." Demography 27 (1990): 617-637.

Hauser, R.M., and Featherman, D.L. "Equality of Schooling: Trends and Prospects." Sociology of Education 49 (1976): 99-120.

Haveman, R., Wolfe, B., and Spaulding, J. "Childhood Events and Circumstances Influencing High School Completion." Demography 28 (1991): 133-157.

Hawley, W.D. (ed.). Effective School Desegregation: Equity, Quality and Feasibility. Berkeley: Sage Press, 1981.

Hernandez, P.M., Beller, A.H., and Graham, J.W. "Changes in the Relationship Between Child Support Payments and Educational Attainment of Offpring, 1979-1988." Demography 32 (1995): 249-260.

Heyns, B., and Catsambis, S. "Mother's Employment and Children's Achievement: A Critique." Sociology of Education 59 (1986): 140-151.

Hogan, D.P. Transitions and Social Change: The Early Lives of American Men. New York: Academic Press, 1981.

Hogan, D.P., and Pazul, M. "Occupational and Earnings Returns to Education Among Black Men in the North." American Journal of Sociology 87 (1982): 905-20.

Kalminjn, M. "Mother's Occupational Status and Children's Schooling." American Sociological Review 59 (1994): 257-275.

Katznelson, Ira, Gille, K., and Weir, M. "Public Schooling and Working Class Formation: The Case of the United States." American Journal of Education 90 (1982):111-43.

Kirp, D.L. Just Schools. Los Angeles: University of California Press, 1982.

Kominski, R. "Estimating the National High School Dropout Rate." Demography 27 (1990): 303-311.

Jencks, C., and Riesman, D. The Academic Revolution. Chicago: University of Chicago Press, 1977.

Levine, E.M. "The Declining Educational Achievement of Middle-Class Students, the Deterioration of Educational and Social Standards, and Parents' Negligence." Sociological Spectrum 1 (1980): 17-34.

Manski, C.F., Sadefur, G.D., McLanahan, S.S., and Powers, D. "Alternative Estimates of the Effects of Family Structure During Childhood on High School Graduation." Journal of the American Statistical Association 87 (1992): 25-37.

Mare, Robert D. "Change and Stability in Educational Stratification." American Sociological Review 46 (1981): 72-87.

Mare, Robert D., and Winship, C. "The Paradox of Lessening Racial Inequality and Joblessness Among Black Youth: Enrollment, Enlistment and Employment, 1964-1981." American Sociological Review 49 (1984): 39-55.

Mattila, J.P. "Determinants of Male School Enrollments: A Time-Series Analysis." Review of Economics and Statistics 64 (1982): 242-51.

Meyer, J.W. "The Effects of Education as an Institution." American Journal of Sociology 83 (1977): 55-77.

Monk-Turner, Elizabeth. "The Occupational Achievements of Community and Four-Year College Entrants." American Sociological Review 55 (1990): 719-725.

National Center for Education Statistics. 120 Years of American Education: A Statistical Portrait. Washington, DC: U.S. Government Printing Office, 1993.

O'Brien, N., and Fabiano, E. Core List of Books and Journals in Education. Phoenix, AZ: Oryx Press, 1991.

Olzak, S., Shanahan, S., and West, E. "School Desegregation, Interracial Exposure, and Antibusing Activity in Contemporary Urban America." American Journal of Sociology 100 (1994): 196-241.

Orfield, G., and Monofort, F. Racial Change and Desegregation in Large School Districts: Trends through the 1986-7 School Year. Washington, D.C.: National School Boards Association, 1988.

Pallas, A.M. "Conceptual and Measurement Issues in the Study of School Dropouts." Research in the Sociology of Education and Socialization V. 8. Greenwich, CT: JAI Press, 1989.

Parcel, T.L., and Menaghan, E.G. "Early Parental Work, Family Social Capital, and Early Childhood Outcomes." American Journal of Sociology 99 (1994): 972-1009.

Poole. M.E., and Low, B.C. "Who Stays? Who Leaves? An Examination of Sex Differences in Staying and Leaving." Journal of Youth and Adolescence 11 (1982): 49-63.

Portes, A., and Wilson, K.L. "Black-White Differences in Educational Attainment." American Sociological Review 41(1976): 414-31.

Prager, J., Longshore, D., and Seeman, M. School Desegregation Research. New York: Plenum, 1986.

Rossell, C. The Carrot or the Stick for School Desegregation Policy. Philadelphia: Temple University Press, 1990.

Rumberger, R.W. "The Influence of Family Background on Education, Earnings, and Wealth." Social Forces 61 (1983): 755-73.

Sandefur, G.D., McLanahan, S.S., and Wojtkiewicz, R.A. "The Effects of Parental Marital Status during Adolescence on High School Graduation." Social Forces 71 (1993): 103-121.

Sewell, W.H., and Hauser, R.M. Education, Occupation and Earnings: Achievement in the Early Career. New York: Academic Press, 1975.

Simpson, C. et al. "Conventional Failures and Unconventional Dropouts: Comparing Different Types of University Withdrawals." Sociology of Education 53 (1980): 203-14.

Sly, D.F., and Pol, L.G. "Demographic Context of School Segregation and Desegregation." Social Forces 56 (1978): 1072-86.

Spilerman, S., and Lunde T. "Features of Educational Attainment and Job Promotion Prospects." American Journal of Sociology 97 (1991): 689-720.

Steelman, L.C., and Powell, B. "Acquiring Capital for College: The Constraints of Family Configuration." American Sociological Review 54 (1989):844-855.

_____. "Sponsoring the Next Generation: Parental Willingness to Pay for Higher Education." American Journal of Sociology 96 (1991): 1505-1529.

Stephan, W.G., and Feagin, J.R. (eds.). School Desegregation: Past, Present and Future. New York: Plenum Press, 1980.

Taylor, D.G. Public Opinion and Collective Action: The Boston School Desegregation Conflict. Chicago: University of Chicago Press, 1986.

Teachman, Jay D. "Family Background, Educational Resources, and Educational Attainment." Amercian Sociological Review 52 (1987): 548-557.

U.S. Bureau of the Census. Detailed Population Characteristics: United States Summary. Washington, DC: U.S. Government Printing Office, 1963.

_____. Detailed Population Characteristics: United States Summary. Washington, DC: U.S. Government Printing Office, 1973.

_____. Detailed Population Characteristics: United States Summary. Washington, DC: U.S. Government Printing Office, 1983.

_____. General Social and Economic Characteristics: 1980. Washington, DC: U.S. Government Printing Office, 1983.

_____. Educational Attainment in the United States: March 1991 and 1990. Current Population Reports, Series P-20, No. 462. Washington, DC: U.S. Government Printing Office, 1992.

_____. School Enrollment--Social and Economic Characteristics of Students: October 1990. Current Population Reports, Series P-20, No. 460. Washington, DC: U.S. Government Printing Office, 1992.

_____. Population Projections of the United States, by Age, Race, and Hispanic Origin: 1993 to 2050. Current Population Reports. Series P-25, No. 1104. Washington, DC: U.S. Government Printing Office, 1993.

_____. Education in the United States: 1990. Washington, DC: U.S. Government Printing Office, 1994.

U.S. Center for Education Statistics. Digest of Education Statistics: 1992. Washington, DC: U.S. Government Printing Office, 1992.

U.S. Commission on Civil Rights. Reviewing a Decade of School Desegregation, 1966-1975: Report of National Survey of School Superintendents. Washington, DC: U.S. Government Printing Office, 1977.

U.S. Government Accounting Office. School Dropouts: The Nature and Extent of the Problem. Washington, D.C.: U.S. Government Printing Office, 1986.

_____. School Dropouts: Survey of Local Programs. Washington, D.C.: U.S. Government Printing Office, 1987.

Upchurch, D.M., and McCarthy, J. "The Timing of a First Birth and High School Completion."American Sociological Review 55 (1990): 224-234.

Upchurch, D.M., McCarthy, J., and Ferguson, L.R. "Childbearing and Schooling: Disentangling Temporal and Causal Mechanisms." American Sociological Review 58 (1993): 738-740.

Wojtkiewicz, R.A. "Simplicity and Complexity in the Effects of Family Strucure on High School Graduation." Demography 30 (1993): 701-718.

Wortman, P.M., and Bryant, F.B. "School Desegregation and Black Achievement." Sociological Methods and Research 13 (1985): 289-324.

THE LABOR FORCE AND EMPLOYMENT STATUS

The labor force is that part of the population engaged in the production of economic goods and services at a particular time (see Definition Box). Information about the size and distribution of the labor force and the characteristics of its members reveals how the population has organized itself to earn its livelihood. Changes in the size, distribution, or composition of the labor force reflect shifts in the level of economic well-being and disclose new patterns of economic and social organization.

Statisticians, labor economists, and others interested in the field of labor have developed definitions and procedures for obtaining detailed and continuous information. A special sample survey of the labor force is made once a month. This is the Current Population Survey (CPS) of the U.S. Bureau of the Census (described in Chapter 2). Information about each month's findings from the CPS is published by the Bureau of Labor Statistics in a monthly publication entitled Employment and Earnings and also in a statistical supplement to the Monthly Labor Review. The censuses from 1940 to 1990 all made intensive and detailed inquiries about the labor force, and they provide detailed cross-tabulations involving labor force categories and labor force data for small areas that the Current Population Survey cannot yield.

The estimates of the size of the labor force, the number of unemployed, and other labor force characteristics derived from the decennial census and from the Current Population Survey are slightly different. This chapter will use some data from the U.S. censuses to describe subgroups of the population over long historical periods. However, the data in most tables will be derived from the Current Population Survey. In some senses, the relationship between these two sources is even closer than one might think, since the decennial censuses are the basis for the ways in which the levels of stratification for the samples of the Current Population Survey are drawn. In addition, each census and Current Population Survey uses the current schemes of classification for full and part-time workers, unemployment, and so on.

This chapter and the two following chapters undertake to summarize what is known about the United States labor force. The present chapter will concentrate on labor force participation, weeks worked per year, hours worked per week, and multiple and part-time job holding as well as unemployment. In turn, the chapter establishes the groundwork for in-depth studies of occupation, industry, income, and poverty in subsequent chapters.

Labor Force Participation: Classifying the Population

Persons in the labor force are called collectively "labor force participants," and the proportion of the total noninstitutional population sixteen years or older participating in the labor force is called the "labor force participation rate." Often it is desirable to know what percentage of the population is actually employed. This statistic is called the "employment/population ratio" or simply the "employment ratio" (see Definition Box). However, since the U.S. government divides the population into several employment sub-categories, it is important to understand how these categories are related.

Figures 13-1A and 13-1B present a schematic representation of these different labor force categories for the population 16 years and over in 1980 and 1990. In 1990, according to the U.S. Census, there were 191,829,271 persons aged 16 years and over, an increase of about 20.6 million persons since the 1980 Census. The labor force, however, had increased from 106 to 125.2 million, a jump of 19.2 million over the decade. Those not in the labor force (66.6 million in 1990) increased by only about 1.5 million.

Those in the labor force are divided into those in

Chapter 13 Definitions
THE LABOR FORCE AND EMPLOYMENT STATUS

Labor Force. Persons who, during a specified week preceding the survey ("survey week"), were defined either as "employed" or "unemployed" according to the following definitions.

Employed Persons. (a) All civilians of working age who, during the survey week, did any work at all as paid employees; in their own business or profession or on their own farm; or who worked fifteen hours or more as unpaid workers in an enterprise operated by a member of the family. (b) All those who were not working but who had jobs or businesses from which they were temporarily absent because of illness, bad weather, vacation, labor-management disputes, or personal reasons, whether they were paid for the time off or were seeking other jobs. Members of the Armed Forces stationed in the United States are also included in the employed total.

Each employed person is counted only once. Those who held more than one job are counted in the job at which they worked the greatest number of hours during the survey week.

Included in the total are employed citizens of foreign countries who are temporarily in the United States but not living on the premises of an embassy. Excluded are persons whose only activity consisted of work around the house (painting, repairing, or own home housework) or volunteer work for religious, charitable, and similar organizations.

Unemployed Persons. All civilians of working age who had no employment during the survey week, were available for work, except for temporary illness, and (a) had made specific efforts to find employment sometime during the prior four weeks, (b) were waiting to be recalled to a job from which they had been laid off, or (c) were waiting to report to a new job within thirty days.

Working Age. The minimum age at which a gainfully employed child is officially recognized as being in the labor force. Before 1967 this was fourteen years. Since 1967 it has been sixteen years. There is no official upper age limit to labor force status.

Civilian Labor Force. All civilians classified as employed or unemployed in accordance with the criteria described above.

Labor Force Participation Rates. The proportion of the population that is in the labor force. The *labor force participation rate* is the ratio of the labor force, including the resident Armed Forces, to the noninstitutional population. The *civilian labor force participation rate* is the ratio of the civilian labor force to the civilian noninsti-

tutional population. Civilian labor force participation rates are usually published for age-sex groups, often cross-classified by other demographic characteristics such as race and educational attainment. They usually are reported as percents.

Employment-Population Ratios. The proportion of the noninstitutional population that is employed. The *total employment-population ratio* is total employment, including the resident Armed Forces, as a percentage of the noninstitutional population. The *civilian employment-population ratio* is the percentage of all employed civilians in the civilian noninstitutional population.

Unemployment Rates. The number unemployed as a percentage of the labor force, including members of the Armed Forces stationed in the United States. *Civilian unemployment rate* represents the number unemployed as a percentage of the civilian labor force. This measure can also be computed for groups within the labor force classified by sex, age, race, ethnic origin, martial status, and so on.

Hours of work. The actual number of hours worked during the survey week. For example, persons who normally work forty hours a week but were off because of a holiday would be reported as working thirty-two hours even though they were paid for the holiday. For persons working in more than one job, the figures relate to the number of hours worked in all jobs during the week; all the hours are credited to the major job.

The distribution of employment by hours worked relates to persons at work during the survey week. At-work data differ from data on total employment because the latter include persons in the zero-hours-worked category, with a job but not at work. Included in this latter group are persons who were on vacation, ill, involved in a labor dispute, or otherwise absent from their jobs for voluntary, noneconomic reasons.

Full-Time/Part-Time Work. Persons who worked thirty-five hours or more in the survey week are designated as working full time. Persons who worked between one and thirty-four hours are designated as working part time. Part-time workers are classified by their usual status at their present job (either full or part time) and by their reason for working part time during the survey week (economic or other reasons). Economic reasons include slack work, material shortages, repairs to plant or equipment, start or termination of a job during the week, and inability to find full-time work. Other reasons include labor dispute, bad weather, own illness, vacation, demands of home, housework, or school, no desire for full-time work, and

full-time worker only during peak season. Persons on full-time schedule include, in addition to those working thirty-five hours or more, those who worked from one to thirty-four hours for noneconomic reasons and usually work full time.

Full-Time/Part-Time Labor Force. The *full-time labor force* comprises persons working on full-time schedules, persons involuntarily working part time (part time for economic reasons), and unemployed persons seeking full-time jobs. The *part-time labor force* consists of persons working part time voluntarily and unemployed persons seeking part-time work. Persons with a job but not at work during the survey week are classified according to whether they usually work full or part time.

Weeks Worked in the Preceding Year. The number of different weeks, during the preceding calendar year, in which the person did any civilian work for pay or profit (including paid vacations and sick leave) or worked without pay on a family-operated farm or business.

Year-Round Full-Time Workers. Civilians who worked primarily at full-time jobs for fifty weeks or more during the preceding calendar year. Part-year workers are civilians who worked either full or part time for one to forty-nine weeks. These workers are further classified on the basis of their major activity during most of the weeks in which they did not work. These activities include unemployment or layoff, illness or disability (excluding paid sick leave), taking care of home, going to school, retirement, military service, etc.

Duration of Unemployment. Length of time (through the current survey week) during which persons classified as unemployed had been continuously looking for work. For persons on layoff, duration of unemployment represents the number of full weeks since the termination of their most recent employment. A period of two weeks or more during which a person was employed or ceased looking for work is considered to break the continuity of the present period of seeking work. Measurements of mean and median duration are computed from a distribution of single weeks of unemployment.

Reasons for Unemployment. Unemployment is categorized according to the status of individuals at the time they began to look for work. The reasons for unemployment are divided into four major groups. (1) Job losers are persons whose employment ended involuntarily who immediately began looking for work, and persons on layoff. (2) Job leavers are persons who quit or otherwise terminated their employment voluntarily and immediately began looking for work. (3) Reentrants are persons who previously worked at a full-time job lasting two weeks or longer but were out of the labor force prior to beginning to look for work. (4) New entrants are persons who never worked at a full-time job lasting two weeks or longer. Each of these four categories of the unemployed may be expressed as an unemployment rate or proportion of the entire civilian labor force. The sum of the four rates thus equals the unemployment rate for all civilian workers.

Jobseekers are all unemployed persons who made specific efforts to find a job sometime during the four-week period preceding the survey week. Jobseekers do not include those persons unemployed because they (a) were waiting to be called back to a job from which they had been laid off or (b) were waiting to report to a new job within thirty days. Jobseekers are grouped by the methods used to seek work, including going to a public or private employment agency or to an employer directly, seeking assistance from friends or relatives, placing or answering ads, or utilizing some other method. Examples of the "other" category include being on a union or professional register,

obtaining assistance from a community organization, or waiting at a designated labor pickup point.

Unemployed persons are civilians who had no employment during the survey week, were available for work, and had made specific efforts to find employment sometime during the prior four weeks. Persons laid off from their former jobs and awaiting recall, and those expecting to report to a job within thirty days need not be looking for work to be classified as unemployed.

Weeks of Unemployment. The number of weeks that persons with unemployment work experience were unemployed during the preceding calendar year. This is the number of weeks during that calendar year when persons sixteen and older did not work but spent any time looking for work (trying to get a job or start a business or professional practice) or on layoff from a job. Excluded are any weeks in which the person worked, even for one hour, or weeks during which the person received any wages or salary; or in which the person was on active duty in the

Armed Forces, on paid vacation, or on paid leave. The number of weeks of unemployment is the total number of weeks accumulated during the entire calendar year, regardless of whether the periods of unemployment were continuous.

Not in the Labor Force. Includes all persons sixteen years and over who are not classified as employed or unemployed. These persons are further classified as engaged in own-home housework, in school, unable to work because of long-term physical or mental illness, retired, and other. The "other" group includes individuals reported as too old or temporarily unable to work, the voluntarily idle, seasonal workers for whom the survey week fell in an off season and who were not reported as looking for work, and persons who did not look for work because they believed that no jobs were available in the area or that no jobs were available for which they could qualify—discouraged workers. Persons doing only incidental, unpaid family work (less than fifteen hours in the specified week) are also classified as not in the labor force.

---

the armed services (1.7 million in 1990) and those in the civilian labor force (123.5 million). The civilian labor force is further subdivided into the employed (115.7 million) and the unemployed (7.8 million). The unemployed are divided into the experienced unemployed (7.2 million) and the other unemployed, those without any job experience (561,601). The experienced civilian labor force (who totaled 122.9 million in 1990), another category used in labor force analysis, includes the employed and the experienced unemployed, but excludes t he other unemployed.

Between the 1980 and 1990 censuses, the civilian labor force grew by a .Ubout 19 million, while the armed services grew by less than 75,000. The employed grew by about 18 percent, the unemployed by about 14 percent during the decade.

Historical Trends

The Current Population Survey figures can be used to track annual changes in labor force participation up to 1993. From the data in Tables 13-1 and 13-2 and Figure 13-2, the following generalizations can be made about labor force participation over the past fifty years:

1. Labor force growth is linked to population growth, but changing social roles and values have had an increasing effect on it. Babies born in one year grow up to enter the labor force in late adolescence or early adulthood. Thus a wave or a trough in the birth rate results in an echo wave or trough in the labor force rates about two decades later. The rapid growth of the labor force between the early 1960s and 1989 (and especially between 1966-

1979) was caused, in part, by the maturation of the "baby boom" generation to ages at which it was seeking employment between 1960 and 1980.

2. The female component of the labor force has grown very rapidly. The female labor force participation rate rose from 25 percent in 1940 to 58 percent in 1993. During World War II, female labor force participation rose rapidly. Even though there was a large decline in female employment after the end of the war, the female labor force participation rate still rose from 25.4 percent in 1940 to 33.9 percent in 1950. The other major surge in female employment occurred from 1964 to 1989, when female labor force participation rose from 38.7 to 57.4 percent. Between 1964 and 1989, the annual rate of female labor force growth exceeded 2 percent in all but one year.

3. The labor force has tended to grow faster than population (accounting for a twenty-year lag after population change) because the rising participation of women has more than offset a slow decline in the participation rates of men. The history of labor force participation rates over the past 120 years is graphed in Figure 13-2. It may be surprising to observe that for males the participation rates rose from about 75 percent in 1870 to a high of 87 percent in 1948, following which there has been a gradual decline. In 1993 the rate stood at 75 percent--the same level as 123 years earlier. A high percentage of school-age population (due to high fertility) helped to depress the rate before 1920; prolonged school attendance and an earlier age at retirement have helped to depress it since its 1948 peak. Figure 13-2 also graphs the trend toward convergence of male and female labor force participa-

Figure 13-1A. Flow Chart of Census Employment Classifications with Total Numbers from 1990

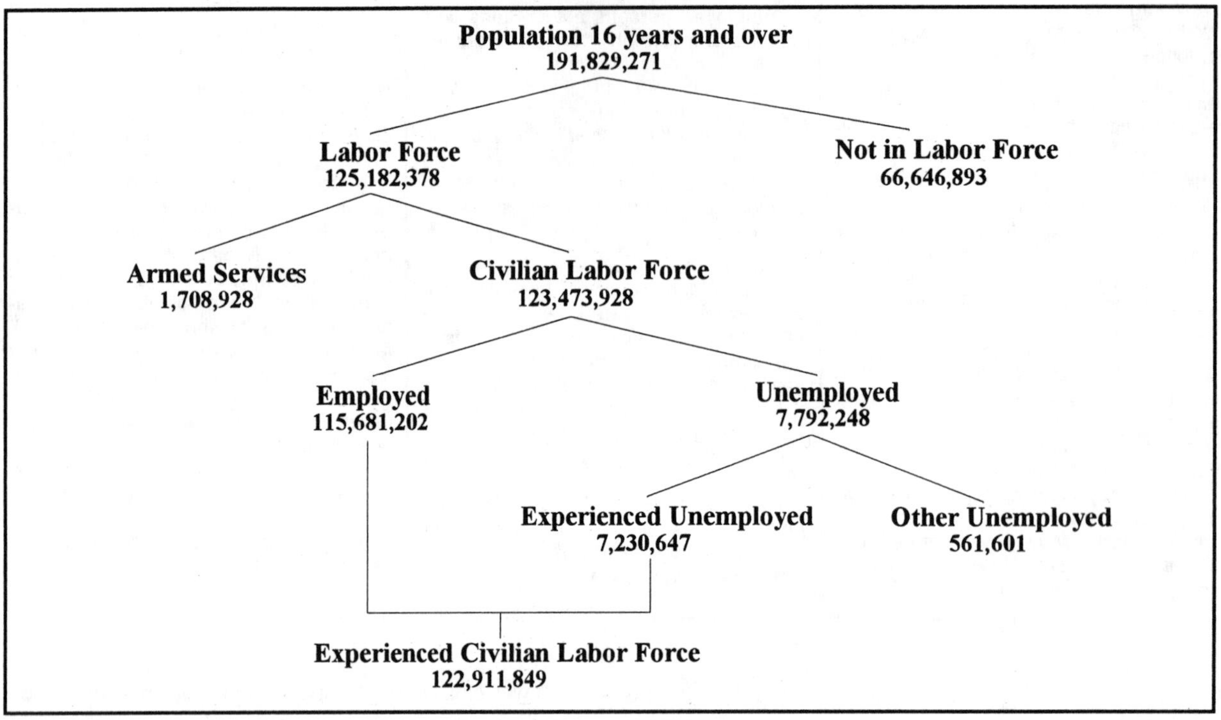

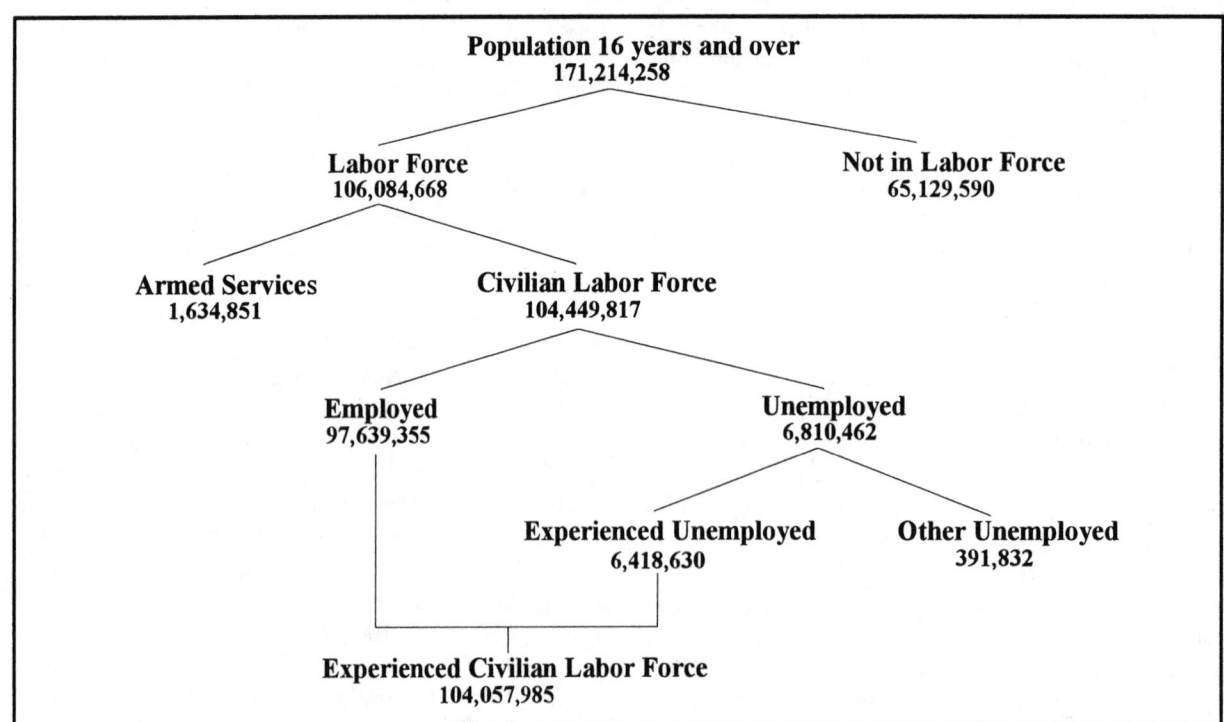

Source: 1990 U.S. Census data.

Figure 13-1B. Flow Chart of Census Employment Classifications with Total Numbers from 1980

Source: 1980 U.S. Census data.

Table 13-1. Employment Status of the Civilian Noninstitutional Population, by Sex: 1940-1993 [numbers in thousands]

Year	Labor force: both sexes				Participation rate			Employment/population			Annual labor force rate of growth			
	Total	Employed	Unemployed	Percent female	Total	Male	Female	Total	Male	Female	Year	Total	Male	Female
1993	128,040	119,306	8,734	45.6	66.2	75.2	57.9	61.6	69.9	54.1	1999-93	0.8	0.6	1.1
1992	126,982	117,598	9,384	45.5	66.3	75.6	57.8	61.4	69.7	53.8	1991-92	1.3	1.1	1.6
1991	125,304	116,877	8,427	45.4	66.0	75.5	57.3	61.6	70.2	53.7	1990-91	0.4	0.3	0.6
1990	124,788	117,914	6,874	45.3	66.4	76.1	57.5	62.7	71.9	54.3	1989-90	0.7	0.6	0.9
1989	123,870	117,342	6,528	45.2	66.5	76.4	57.4	63.0	72.5	54.3	1988-89	1.8	1.4	2.4
1988	121,669	114,969	6,700	45.0	65.9	76.2	56.6	62.3	72.0	53.4	1987-88	1.5	1.1	2.0
1987	119,865	112,441	7,424	44.8	65.6	76.2	56.0	61.5	71.5	52.5	1986-87	1.7	1.2	2.4
1986	117,835	109,598	8,237	44.5	65.3	76.3	55.3	60.7	71.0	51.4	1985-86	2.1	1.6	2.7
1985	115,461	107,150	8,311	44.2	64.8	76.3	54.5	60.1	70.9	50.4	1984-85	1.7	0.9	2.7
1984	113,544	105,006	8,538	43.8	64.4	76.4	53.6	59.5	70.7	49.5	1983-84	1.8	1.2	2.5
1983	111,550	100,834	10,717	43.5	64.0	76.4	52.9	57.9	68.8	48.0	1982-83	1.2	1.0	1.6
1982	110,204	99,526	10,678	43.3	64.0	76.6	52.6	57.8	69.0	47.7	1981-82	1.4	0.8	2.3
1981	108,670	100,397	8,273	43.0	63.9	77.0	52.1	59.0	71.3	48.0	1980-81	1.6	0.8	2.7
1980	106,940	99,303	7,637	42.5	63.8	77.4	51.5	59.2	72.0	47.7	1979-80	1.9	1.2	2.8
1979	104,962	98,824	6,137	42.1	63.7	77.8	50.9	59.9	73.8	47.5	1978-79	2.7	1.9	3.8
1978	102,251	96,048	6,202	41.7	63.2	77.9	50.0	59.3	73.8	46.4	1977-78	3.3	2.1	5.0
1977	99,009	92,017	6,991	41.0	62.3	77.7	48.4	57.9	72.8	44.5	1976-77	3.0	2.1	4.2
1976	96,158	88,752	7,406	40.5	61.6	77.5	47.3	56.8	72.0	43.2	1975-76	2.5	1.6	4.0
1975	93,775	85,846	7,929	40.0	61.2	77.9	46.3	56.1	71.7	42.0	1974-75	2.0	1.0	3.5
1974	91,949	86,794	5,156	39.4	61.3	78.7	45.7	57.8	74.9	42.6	1973-74	2.8	2.0	4.0
1973	89,429	85,064	4,365	38.9	60.8	78.8	44.7	57.8	75.5	42.0	1972-73	2.8	2.0	4.0
1972	87,034	82,153	4,882	38.5	60.4	78.9	43.9	57.0	75.0	41.0	1971-72	3.1	2.6	4.0
1971	84,382	79,367	5,016	38.2	60.2	79.1	43.4	56.6	74.9	40.4	1970-71	1.9	1.9	2.1
1970	82,771	78,678	4,093	38.1	60.4	79.7	43.3	57.4	76.2	40.8	1969-70	2.5	2.0	3.4
1969	80,734	77,902	2,832	37.8	60.1	79.8	42.7	58.0	77.6	40.7	1968-69	2.5	1.4	4.5
1968	78,737	75,920	2,817	37.1	59.6	80.1	41.6	57.5	77.8	39.6	1967-68	1.8	1.1	3.0
1967	77,347	74,372	2,975	36.7	59.6	80.4	41.1	57.3	78.0	39.0	1966-67	2.1	1.2	3.9
1966	75,770	72,895	2,875	36.0	59.2	80.4	40.3	56.9	77.9	38.3	1965-66	1.8	0.4	4.2
1965	74,455	71,088	3,366	35.2	58.9	80.7	39.3	56.2	77.5	37.1	1964-65	1.9	1.2	3.1
1964	73,091	69,305	3,786	34.8	58.7	81.0	38.7	55.7	77.3	36.3	1963-64	1.8	1.2	2.9
1963	71,833	67,762	4,070	34.4	58.7	81.4	38.3	55.4	77.1	35.8	1962-63	1.7	1.1	2.9
1962	70,614	66,702	3,911	34.0	58.8	82.0	37.9	55.5	77.7	35.6	1961-62	0.2	-0.1	0.9
1961	70,459	65,746	4,714	33.8	59.3	82.9	38.1	55.4	77.6	35.4	1960-61	1.2	0.6	2.4
1960	69,628	65,778	3,852	33.4	59.4	83.3	37.7	56.1	78.9	35.5	1950-60	11.9	5.9	26.3
1950	62,208	58,918	3,288	29.6	59.2	86.4	33.9	56.1	82.0	32.0	1940-50	18.0	10.1	42.6
1940	52,705	45,070	7,635	24.5	52.8	78.9	25.4	45.1	67.2	22.1	—	—		

Source: U. S. Bureau of Labor Statistics, "Employment and Earnings," 1994, and 1983, Table 2.   Data for 1940 from U.S. Bureau of the Census, "Historical Statistics of the United States," Series D11-25. U.S. Government Printing Office, Washington, D.C., 1994, 1983, and 1975.

Table 13-2. Civilian Labor Force Participation Rates, by Age, Sex, and Race: 1950-1993 [percent in labor force]

Year and race	Total labor force	16-19 years			20 years and over						
		Total	16-17 years	18-19 years	Total	20-24 years	25-34 years	35-44 years	45-54 years	55-64 years	65 and over
All races											
Male											
1993	75.2	53.1	41.7	65.0	76.9	83.1	93.5	93.5	90.1	66.5	15.6
1992	75.6	53.3	41.1	66.0	77.3	83.3	93.8	93.8	90.8	67.0	16.1
1990	76.1	55.7	43.7	67.0	77.8	84.3	94.2	94.4	90.7	67.7	16.4
1985	76.3	56.8	45.1	68.9	78.1	85.0	94.7	95.0	91.0	67.9	15.8
1980	77.4	60.5	50.1	71.3	79.4	85.9	95.2	95.5	91.2	72.1	19.0
1975	77.9	59.1	48.6	70.6	80.3	84.5	95.2	95.6	92.1	75.6	21.6
1970	79.7	56.1	47.0	66.7	82.6	83.3	96.4	96.9	94.3	83.0	26.8
1965	80.7	53.8	43.9	65.9	83.9	85.8	97.2	97.3	95.6	84.6	27.9
1960	83.3	56.1	46.0	69.3	86.0	88.1	97.5	97.7	95.7	86.8	33.1
1955	85.4	58.9	48.1	72.2	87.6	86.9	97.6	98.1	96.4	87.9	39.6
1950	86.4	63.2	51.3	75.8	88.4	87.9	96.0	97.6	95.8	86.9	45.8
Female											
1993	57.9	49.9	39.3	60.4	58.4	71.3	73.6	76.7	73.5	47.3	8.2
1992	57.8	49.2	39.3	59.0	58.4	71.2	74.1	76.8	72.7	46.6	8.3
1990	57.5	51.8	41.9	60.5	57.9	71.6	73.6	76.5	71.2	45.3	8.7
1985	54.5	52.1	42.1	61.7	54.7	71.8	70.9	71.8	64.4	42.0	7.3
1980	51.5	52.9	43.6	61.9	51.3	68.9	65.5	65.5	59.9	41.3	8.1
1975	46.3	49.1	40.2	58.1	46.0	64.1	54.9	55.8	54.6	40.9	8.2
1970	43.3	44.0	34.9	53.6	43.3	57.7	45.0	51.1	54.4	43.0	9.7
1965	39.3	38.0	27.7	49.3	39.4	49.9	38.5	46.1	50.9	41.1	10.0
1960	37.7	39.3	29.1	50.9	37.6	46.1	36.0	43.4	49.9	37.2	10.8
1955	35.7	39.7	28.9	50.9	35.4	45.9	34.9	41.6	43.8	32.5	10.6
1950	33.9	41.0	30.1	51.3	33.3	46.0	34.0	39.1	37.9	27.0	9.7
White											
Male											
1993	76.1	56.5	45.2	68.3	77.5	85.4	94.7	94.5	91.3	67.4	16.0
1992	76.4	56.7	44.7	69.1	77.8	85.2	94.9	94.7	91.8	67.7	16.3
1990	76.9	59.4	47.6	70.5	78.3	86.1	95.3	95.3	91.7	68.7	16.8
1985	77.0	59.7	48.5	71.2	78.5	86.4	95.7	95.7	92.0	68.8	15.9
1980	78.2	63.7	53.6	74.1	79.8	87.2	95.9	96.2	92.1	73.1	19.1
1975	78.7	61.9	51.8	72.8	80.7	85.5	95.8	96.4	92.9	76.4	21.7
1970	80.0	57.5	48.9	67.4	82.8	83.3	96.7	97.3	94.9	83.3	26.7
1965	80.8	54.1	44.6	65.8	83.9	85.3	97.4	97.7	95.9	85.2	27.9
1960	83.4	55.9	46.0	69.0	86.0	87.8	97.7	97.9	96.1	87.2	33.3
1955	85.4	58.6	48.1	71.7	87.5	86.5	97.8	98.2	96.7	88.4	39.6
Female											
1993	58.0	53.7	43.4	63.9	58.3	73.8	74.5	77.0	74.0	47.7	8.2
1992	57.8	52.6	42.6	62.4	58.1	73.8	74.6	77.1	72.9	46.9	8.3
1990	57.5	55.4	45.8	63.9	57.6	73.7	74.2	76.7	71.4	45.6	8.5
1985	54.1	55.2	45.2	64.8	54.0	73.8	70.9	71.4	64.2	41.5	7.0
1980	51.2	56.2	47.2	65.1	50.6	70.6	64.8	65.0	59.6	40.9	7.9
1975	45.9	51.5	42.7	60.4	45.3	65.5	53.8	54.9	54.3	40.6	8.0
1970	42.6	45.6	36.6	55.0	42.2	57.7	43.2	49.9	53.7	42.6	9.5
1965	38.1	39.2	28.7	50.6	38.0	49.2	36.3	44.4	49.9	40.3	9.7
1960	36.5	40.3	30.0	51.9	36.2	45.7	34.1	41.5	48.6	36.2	10.6
1955	34.5	40.7	29.9	52.0	34.0	45.8	32.8	40.0	42.7	31.8	10.5
Black											
Male											
1993	68.6	39.5	27.6	52.4	72.0	74.1	87.3	86.1	79.8	57.9	11.6
1992	69.7	40.7	27.5	54.7	73.1	75.4	88.0	86.5	81.6	59.8	13.7
1990	70.1	40.6	29.0	52.5	73.8	76.8	88.8	88.1	83.3	57.9	13.0
1985	70.8	44.6	29.8	60.0	74.4	79.0	88.8	89.8	83.0	58.9	13.9
1980	70.3	43.2	30.9	56.6	75.1	79.9	90.9	89.1	83.0	61.9	16.9
1975	70.9	42.6	29.8	57.2	76.0	78.7	91.6	89.4	83.5	67.7	20.7
Female											
1993	57.4	34.5	23.3	46.0	59.5	62.6	70.9	76.8	71.0	44.4	8.2
1992	58.0	35.2	25.0	45.3	60.1	60.7	73.1	77.1	71.5	45.2	8.6
1990	57.8	36.7	26.5	46.2	60.0	62.3	72.3	77.6	70.5	43.2	9.9
1985	56.5	37.9	27.6	47.9	58.6	62.5	72.4	74.8	65.7	45.3	9.4
1980	53.1	34.9	24.6	45.0	55.6	60.2	70.5	68.1	61.4	44.8	10.2
1975	48.8	34.2	25.0	43.8	51.1	55.9	62.8	62.0	56.6	43.1	10.7

Source: U.S. Bureau of Labor Statistics, "Employment and Earnings," 1994, 1993, and 1991, Table 3, and "Handbook of Labor Statistics," Table 5, U.S. Government Printing Office, Washington, D.C., 1994, 1993, 1991, and 1989.

**Figure 13-2. Labor Force Participation Rates[1], by Sex, and
Percent of Labor Force that is Female: 1870-1990**

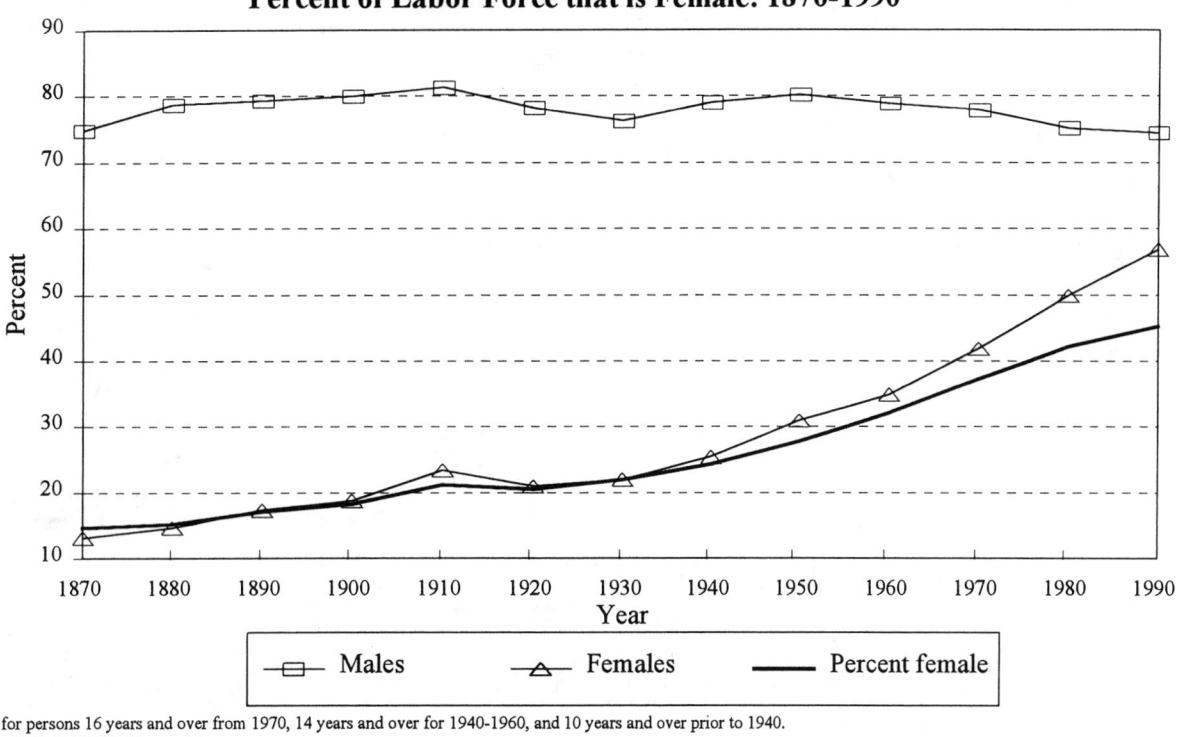

[1] Data for persons 16 years and over from 1970, 14 years and over for 1940-1960, and 10 years and over prior to 1940.
Source: 1870-1990 U.S. Census data.

tion rates and the rising female percentage of the total labor force, which stood at an all-time high of 45.6 percent in 1993.

4. Looking at statistics on the cumulative size of the labor force and at participation rates tends to mask the fact that there have been very substantial fluctuations in the annual rates of labor force growth. These rates are reported in the three right-hand columns of Table 13-1. Annual differences in labor force growth are linked to cohort size and to the business cycle. Studies by Department of Labor economists suggest that since 1970, recessions have had a much greater effect on the growth rate of the male labor force. This has been because men were more heavily concentrated in goods-producing industries, and these jobs tended to disappear during recessions and never re-appear (at least, not in the United States).

5. It is logical to expect the trends cited above to stabilize at rates of slow growth of the labor force in the very near future. It is difficult to conceive of labor force participation rates for females continuing to rise beyond the rates for males or of more than 50 percent of the labor force being female. Hence they must plateau within the next decade or two. Also, because of the "baby bust" that began in 1957 and reached major proportions in the 1960s, the labor force should already be starting to grow more slowly because of fewer new entrants each year during

the late 1980s and early 1990s. However, labor force growth rates will also be affected by the growing proportion of minorities (who have different patterns of labor force participation than whites), possible changes in immigration patterns (immigrants are concentrated in the prime working years), changes in norms about labor force participation among women, and so on.

Age Differences in Labor Force Participation

Labor force participation varies a great deal with age. Table 13-2 shows that during the years of adolescence (16-19 years) only about 53 percent of the males and 50 percent of the females are in the labor force (as of 1993). For both men and women the participation rate rises rapidly as age twenty is attained, reflecting departure from school and the shift from dependency to self-support. For each sex, the labor force participation rates have a distinctive age curve. Figure 13-3 illustrates the curves for the white population with data from the 1990 and 1950 censuses, and Figure 13-4 charts these age curves for these same years for the black population. For males the curve climbs quickly toward 100 percent and remains on a high plateau through ages twenty-five to forty-four. After that it falls slowly as disabilities gradu-

Figure 13-3. Civilian Labor Force Participation Rates of the White Population, by Age and Sex: 1950 and 1990

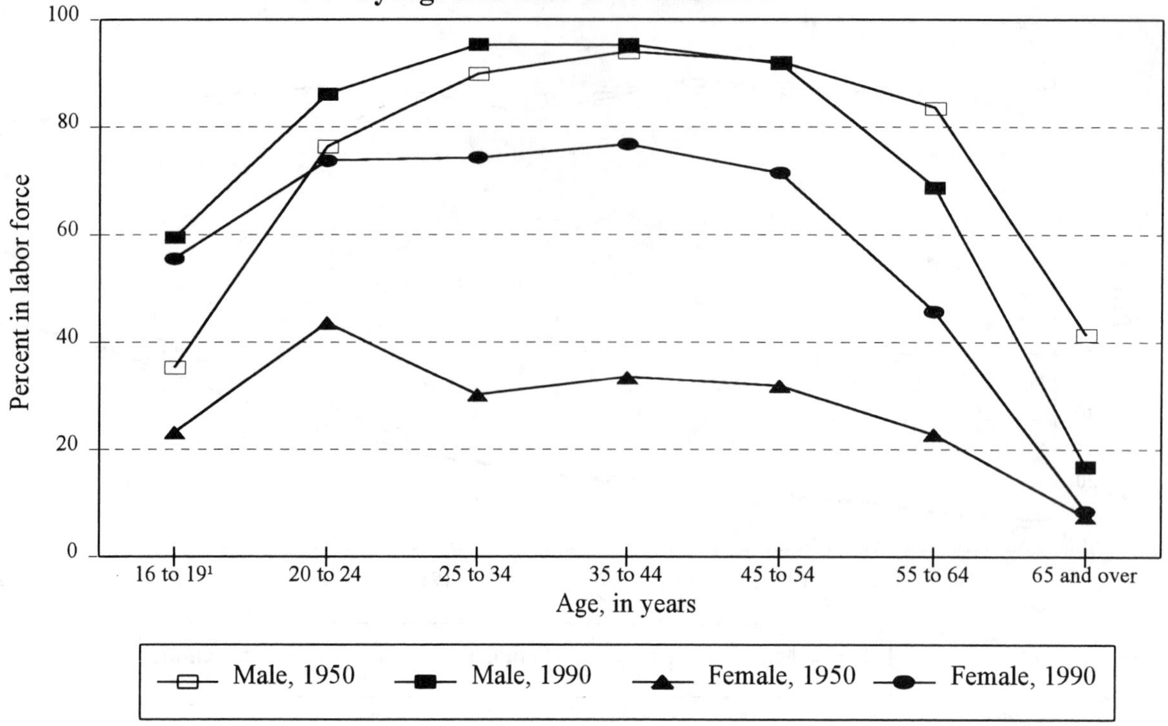

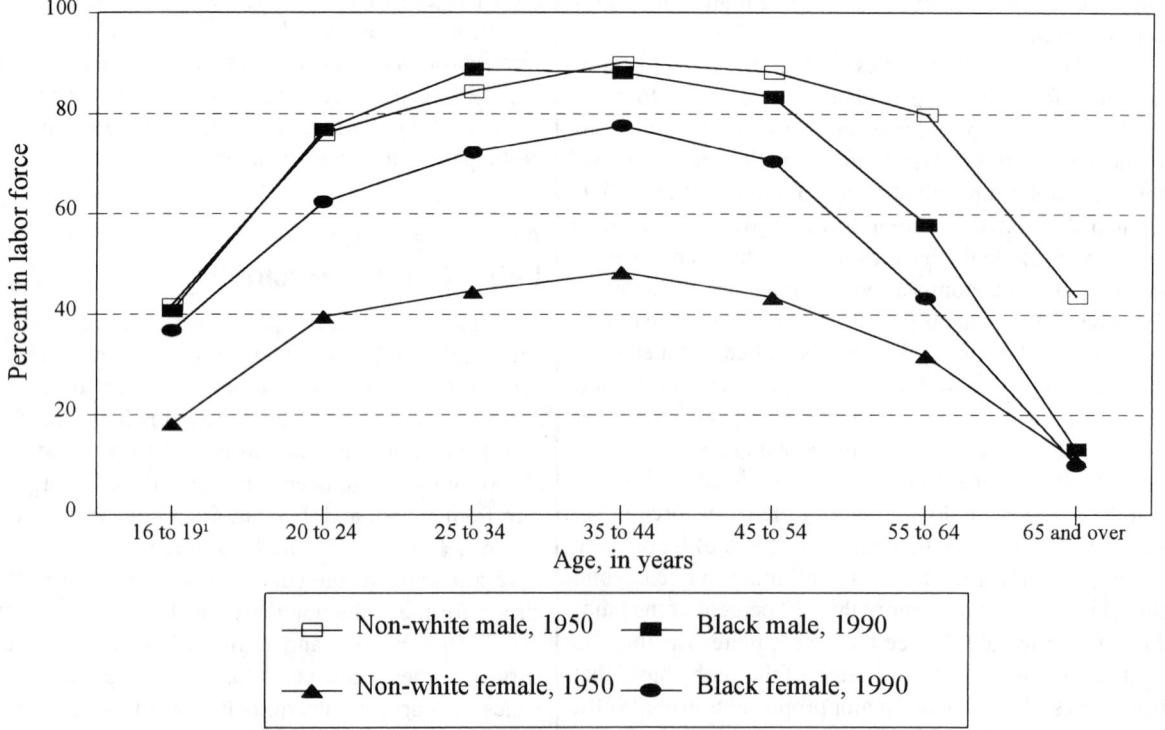

¹ Age 14 to 19 in 1950.
Source: 1950 U.S. Census data and 1990 CPS data.

Figure 13-4. Civilian Labor Force Participation Rates of the Black/Non-white Population, by Age and Sex: 1950 and 1990

¹ Age 14 to 19 in 1950.
Source: 1950 U.S. Census data and 1990 CPS data.

ally remove men from work, although it continues to be high up to age sixty. The changes in labor force participation rates of blacks and whites by age are similar over time, although usually white male participation rates are higher than those of blacks of the same age group.

Prior to about 1970, the male population appears to have largely adhered to the cultural dictum that if an adult male is not sick or disabled he should work (see Table 13-2). Yet between 1970 and 1975, male labor force participation rates for those aged 65 and over dropped by more than five percentage points, by seven percentage points for those aged 55-64, and by more than two percentage points for those aged 45-54. Since this watershed period of rapid decline in late adult male labor force participation the rates have continued to decline, albeit at a slower pace.

Women have a lower participation rate at all ages than men. Before 1980, the rate for females climbed to its highest point at about 20-24 years, dipped for the 25-34 year age group, then began a second decline after age 45-54. In more recent years the age pattern of female labor force participation has changed, with peak participation coming at age 35-44 and with increased participation for all age groups below age 65.

Trends in Labor Force Participation of Youth

When the United States was an agrarian society, and during the early phase of the industrial revolution, it was customary for children to begin work at a young age. In 1890 about 18 percent of the children ten to fifteen years of age were gainfully employed (26 percent of boys and 10 percent of girls). There has been a long-term decline in the participation of children in the work force. When the labor force definitions of 1940 were established, age fourteen was chosen as the youngest age for which it was worthwhile to collect employment data; that minimum age was raised to sixteen in 1967. As greater emphasis was placed upon attending secondary school and college, the labor force participation rates of persons under age eighteen declined. They reached a low point in the 1930s. However, this downward trend was reversed in the 1940s.

During the wartime emergency, the youth of the nation proved to be a most valuable source of labor. Many teenagers worked a shift in a factory or held some other job while attending school. In 1944, 72 percent of the boys fourteen to nineteen years old and 41 percent of the girls were in the labor force. After the war's end the young teenagers began withdrawing from the labor force; their withdrawal was gradual, however, and ceased to decline in the 1950s. Instead, it rose again in the 1970s and remained high until 1982, when it again declined. Girls reduced their labor force participation during the baby boom years of the 1950s and 1960s but reversed the decline in

the 1970s and 1980s. As with young men under twenty, the labor force participation rates of young women have declined slightly during the 1990s.

It could have been predicted that the great emphasis upon obtaining higher education would have caused a protracted withdrawal of young people from labor force participation, even at age 20-24, but this has not been the case. As will be shown later, there has been a tendency to mix school attendance with work--much of it part-time. This situation leaves the meaningfulness of labor force data for ages under twenty unclear and of a different dimension from the labor force data for the adult ages (ages twenty and above).

Trends in Labor Force Participation of Middle-Aged and Elderly Adults

For males there has been a steady decline in labor force participation rates at age 55-64 and sixty-five and beyond. Whereas fully 45.8 percent of men aged sixty-five and over were still employed in 1950, by 1993 this proportion had shrunk to only 15.6 percent. Similar (though less drastic) declines in the participation rates for ages 55-64 occurred. There was even a slight reduction at age 45-54. Programs of Social Security and disability insurance, increased prosperity, and perhaps increased employment of women have made it possible for men to retire from the labor force at younger ages than ever before. Of course, not all of the shift of older males out of the labor force has been voluntary; many older males who lost their jobs during economic downturns or from structural shifts in the economy (especially through job losses in the goods-producing and extractive industries) may have been unable to find other employment, and "retired" by ceasing to look for work.

For women the trend has been the reverse of that for men. For the age groups 24-34, 35-44 and 45-54 years, the labor force participation rates for women approximately doubled between 1950 and 1993. The rates of increase are not monotonic; instead, there seem to have been several major surges and plateaus in increases in labor force participation over time. In addition, the cohorts of women born in 1926-35 and 1936-45 appear to have been major contributors to the achievement of new and higher levels of female labor force participation after age 25, and succeeding cohorts of women have surpassed even their levels of participation. Only after age 65, an age group at which participation never exceeded 11 percent, has the rate dropped to about 8 percent by 1993. The slight drop in female labor force participation at this oldest age is probably due to the same reasons that men's participation at this age has dropped: higher Social Security payments, a greater share of the nation's wealth going to the elderly, and perhaps, to some extent, competition from younger women.

Table 13-3. Labor Force Participation Rates, by Age, Sex, and Race-ethnicity: 1980 and 1990 [percent in labor force]

Age and sex	Total		White		Black		American Indian, Eskimo, Aleut		Asian and Pacific Islander		Hispanic	
	1980	1990	1980	1990	1980	1990	1980	1990	1980	1990	1980	1990
Male												
16 years and over	75.1	74.4	76.1	75.2	66.7	66.5	69.6	69.4	76.5	75.5	78.0	78.7
16-19 years	52.4	51.5	55.5	54.5	36.5	39.3	44.1	43.7	40.4	36.6	50.8	51.5
20-24 years	82.7	80.9	84.3	82.8	73.5	71.7	76.9	75.7	69.4	66.2	83.5	84.2
25-54 years	92.5	91.4	93.8	93.1	83.7	80.4	83.2	81.3	91.1	89.9	90.4	89.0
55-64 years	71.3	67.1	72.2	67.8	62.3	58.3	56.2	54.7	77.2	74.7	72.2	69.4
65-69 years	29.2	27.9	29.5	28.2	26.1	23.0	23.3	21.7	34.2	34.5	31.7	30.2
70 years and over	13.2	11.7	13.3	11.8	12.2	10.3	11.6	8.6	16.1	12.9	13.8	12.4
Female												
16 years and over	49.9	56.8	49.4	56.3	53.3	59.5	48.1	55.1	57.7	60.1	49.3	55.9
16-19 years	45.8	49.4	49.0	52.7	30.3	38.9	35.0	40.5	39.3	36.2	39.0	42.4
20-24 years	67.8	72.1	69.5	74.3	61.4	66.4	55.8	60.6	62.4	62.0	59.1	63.7
25-54 years	63.1	74.2	62.6	74.8	69.0	75.2	57.8	66.0	66.7	71.2	56.5	65.1
55-64 years	41.6	45.6	41.4	45.6	44.1	47.3	34.1	38.7	48.8	49.4	37.4	41.8
65-69 years	15.0	16.9	14.8	16.8	16.9	18.0	13.1	15.4	16.5	18.6	12.3	15.1
70 years and over	4.9	4.8	4.8	4.7	6.7	6.4	5.0	5.8	6.4	5.7	5.2	5.2

Source: U.S. Bureau of the Census, "Social and Economic Characteristics: United States Summary," 1990 CP-2-1, Table 44, and "Detailed Population Characteristics: United States Summary," 1980 Census of Population, Table 272, U.S. Government Printing Office, Washington, D.C., 1993 and 1984.

Labor Force Participation of Women During Childbearing Years

Peak fertility comes during ages 25-29 and 30-34, and in the 1940s and 1950s it was customary for women to withdraw from the labor force to bear children and rear a family. By 1970, the decline in fertility at older ages had led to the disappearance of this decline in labor force participation for women in the 35-44 year age group. By 1990, the dip in labor force participation had also disappeared for the 25-34 year age group as well. In fact, by 1990, the age groups with the highest rates of participation (ages 25-34 and 35-44) were the same age groups that had the lowest levels of labor force participation during the 1955-70 era.

Labor Force Participation Rates by Age, Sex, Race and Hispanic Origin

The 1980-1990 decade saw a slight decline in labor force participation rates for males. Overall, this was due to a minor decline at ages 54 and below and a larger decline at ages 55 and above. However, this decline in labor force participation was distributed unevenly across race and ethnic categories (Table 13-3).

In both 1980 and 1990, Hispanics had the highest overall rate (i.e. for the total male population age 16 and above) of labor force participation, followed by Asian and Pacific Islanders, whites, American Indians, Eskimos and Aleuts, and blacks. Hispanics tended to have high rates of labor force participation during the teenage years and for the 20-24 year age group, and a high rate of participation in the oldest age groups. Asian and Pacific Islander labor force participation rates look roughly equivalent to those of whites, but with lower participation rates among younger age groups and higher participation rates in the oldest groups. American Indian, Eskimo and Aleut labor force participation rates are chiefly outstanding for a much earlier age at which participation rates decline compared to the other three groups. Black male labor force participation rates have an entirely different pattern: they lag behind those of whites by at least ten percentage points in each age group until age 64, but for the oldest ages, their labor force participation rates are much more similar to those of whites in the same age groups.

Asian and Pacific Islander women had the highest overall labor force participation rates in 1980 and 1990, followed by black, white, Hispanic and American Indian, and Eskimo and Aleut women. To some extent this overall figure is misleading; on an age-specific basis, Asian and Pacific Islander women frequently had lower labor force participation rates than white women. It is the high concentration of API women in the 25-54 year age categories (due to high rates of immigration of young adults) that gave them such a high overall level of labor force participation. In terms of specific age groups, the racial and ethnic groups with the highest rates of female labor force participation were whites for the 16-19 and 20-24 year age groups, Asian and Pacific Islanders for the 55-64 and 65-69 year age groups, and blacks for the 25-54 and 70 years and over age groups.

Age and Sex Composition of the Labor Force

The maturation of the baby boom generation, combined with comparatively high participation rates for young people and declining rates for older men, has caused the labor force to have a younger age composition in the 1990s than in the 1940s and 1950s (see Table 13-4). In fact, this change in composition has been more of a concentration of the labor force at the middle years; more than half of the labor force was found at age 25-44 in 1993. This transformation has been greater for the male than for the female labor force. As a consequence, the age compositions of the male and female labor forces are very nearly identical today, whereas in the 1950s the female labor force was considerably younger than the male.

Composition of the Civilian Labor Force by Sex and Race

What effect have rapidly increasing female and slowly declining male labor force participation rates had on the proportions of men and women in the labor force at different ages? Table 13-5 shows these overall and age-specific trends in sex composition between 1950 and 1993. In 1950, fewer than three out of every ten workers in the United States were women; by 1990, more than 45 percent were female. In 1950, only the two youngest age categories (16-19 and 20-24) were more than one-third women, but by 1990 all age groups between 16 and 54 years were at least 45 percent female. While the black and other races portion of the workforce started from a higher proportion female (except for age 16-19) in 1950, this group also saw a similar rise in proportion female. By 1990, over half of black and other race workers aged 35-54 were women.

Contrary to the perceptions of many who write about the supposed coming diversity of the United States workforce, the increase in the black proportion of the workforce has been surprisingly slow. During the 18 years for which comparable data are available from the Current Population Survey (1975-93; see Table 13-6), the black proportion of the civilian labor force has risen only one percent, from 9.9 to 10.9 percent. The black population is younger than the white population, and at the youngest ages the proportion of blacks in the labor force is increasing at a slightly faster rate. Yet lower rates of black labor force participation at most ages has tended to diminish this demographic effect; even for younger age groups,

Table 13-4. Age Composition of the Civilian Labor Force, by Sex: 1940-1993

Year and sex	Total labor force	16 to 19 years			20 years and over						
		Total	16-17 years	18-19 years	Total	20-24 years	25-34 years	35-44 years	45-54 years	55-64 years	65 and over
Total											
1993	100.0	5.3	2.1	3.2	94.7	10.6	26.9	26.8	18.4	9.3	2.7
1992	100.0	5.3	2.1	3.2	94.7	10.8	27.6	26.5	17.6	9.3	2.8
1990	100.0	5.9	2.3	3.7	94.1	11.1	28.7	25.5	16.4	9.5	2.8
1985	100.0	6.8	2.7	4.1	93.2	13.6	29.1	22.6	15.0	10.4	2.5
1980	100.0	8.8	3.6	5.1	91.2	14.9	27.3	19.1	15.8	11.2	2.9
1975	100.0	9.5	4.0	5.5	90.5	14.7	24.4	18.0	18.2	12.1	3.2
1970	100.0	8.8	3.8	5.0	91.2	12.8	20.6	19.9	20.5	13.6	3.9
1960	100.0	7.0	3.0	3.9	93.0	9.6	20.7	23.4	21.3	13.5	4.6
1950	100.0	6.8	2.7	4.1	93.2	11.7	23.5	22.4	18.4	12.3	4.9
1940	100.0	7.0	2.0	5.0	93.0	14.6	25.8	21.2	17.1	10.2	4.0
Males											
1993	100.0	5.1	2.1	3.1	94.9	10.3	27.4	26.6	18.1	9.5	2.9
1992	100.0	5.1	2.0	3.1	94.9	10.5	28.0	26.3	17.5	9.7	3.0
1990	100.0	5.7	2.2	3.5	94.3	10.7	29.0	25.3	16.4	9.9	3.0
1985	100.0	6.4	2.6	3.8	93.6	12.9	29.2	22.5	15.3	11.0	2.7
1980	100.0	8.1	3.4	4.7	91.9	14.0	27.6	19.3	16.1	11.8	3.1
1975	100.0	8.5	3.7	4.9	91.5	13.4	25.2	18.5	18.5	12.5	3.4
1970	100.0	7.8	3.5	4.3	92.2	11.2	22.1	20.4	20.3	13.9	4.2
1960	100.0	6.0	2.8	3.2	94.0	8.9	22.1	23.6	20.6	13.8	4.9
1950	100.0	5.7	2.4	3.3	94.3	10.6	24.0	22.3	18.5	13.2	5.6
1940	100.0	5.9	1.8	4.1	94.1	12.6	25.2	21.8	18.4	11.4	4.6
Females											
1993	100.0	5.6	2.2	3.4	94.4	10.9	26.4	26.9	18.7	9.0	2.5
1992	100.0	5.5	2.2	3.3	94.5	11.2	27.2	26.7	17.8	8.9	2.6
1990	100.0	6.3	2.4	3.9	93.7	11.6	28.3	25.8	16.5	9.0	2.7
1985	100.0	7.4	2.9	4.5	92.6	14.6	28.9	22.7	14.6	9.7	2.3
1980	100.0	9.6	3.9	5.7	90.4	16.1	26.9	19.0	15.4	10.4	2.6
1975	100.0	10.8	4.5	6.4	89.2	16.5	23.1	17.4	17.8	11.5	2.8
1970	100.0	10.3	4.2	6.1	89.7	15.5	18.1	18.9	20.7	13.2	3.3
1960	100.0	8.8	3.5	5.4	91.2	11.1	17.8	22.8	22.7	12.8	3.9
1950	100.0	9.3	3.3	6.0	90.7	14.5	22.3	22.6	18.1	10.0	3.2
1940	100.0	10.3	2.5	7.9	89.7	20.8	27.8	19.3	13.0	6.6	2.1

Source: U.S. Bureau of Labor Statistics, "Employment and Earnings," 1994, 1993, 1991, and 1986, Table 3, "Handbook of Labor Statistics,"
   Table 3. Data for 1940 from U.S. Bureau of the Census, "Detailed Characteristics of the Population, 1950 Census of Population," Table
   120, U.S. Government Printing Office, Washington, D.C., 1994, 1993, 1991, 1986, 1984, and 1953.

Table 13-5. Sex Composition of the Civilian Labor Force, by Race: 1950-1993 [percent female]

Year and race	Total labor force	16-19 years			20 years and over						
		Total	16-17 years	18-19 years	Total	20-24 years	25-34 years	35-44 years	45-54 years	55-64 years	65 and over
All races											
1993	45.6	47.8	47.4	48.1	45.5	47.2	44.7	45.9	46.3	44.1	42.0
1992	45.5	47.5	47.7	47.3	45.4	47.2	44.9	46.0	46.0	43.5	41.7
1990	45.3	47.8	47.9	47.8	45.2	47.3	44.7	45.8	45.5	42.8	42.5
1985	44.2	47.7	47.3	47.9	44.0	47.3	43.9	44.4	43.0	41.1	39.8
1980	42.5	46.7	45.9	47.3	42.1	45.9	41.9	42.2	41.4	39.6	38.0
1975	40.0	45.8	44.8	46.6	39.4	45.0	37.9	38.5	39.1	38.1	35.3
1970	38.1	44.7	42.3	46.6	37.5	46.1	33.5	36.3	38.5	36.8	32.8
1965	35.2	42.5	38.4	45.5	34.6	40.7	30.4	34.0	36.2	34.7	31.4
1960	33.4	42.4	38.4	45.5	32.7	38.5	28.7	32.6	35.5	31.8	28.4
1955	31.6	42.1	37.5	45.5	30.9	43.2	28.2	31.2	32.0	28.1	23.6
1950	29.6	40.6	36.8	43.1	28.8	36.6	28.0	29.8	29.1	24.1	19.2
White											
1993	45.0	47.9	47.7	48.1	44.8	47.0	44.1	45.0	45.6	43.6	41.3
1992	44.9	47.5	47.5	47.4	44.7	47.2	44.1	45.1	45.1	43.1	41.2
1990	44.7	47.8	47.8	47.7	44.5	47.1	44.0	45.0	44.7	42.2	41.5
1985	43.5	47.7	47.2	48.1	43.2	47.1	43.1	43.5	42.2	40.3	38.8
1980	41.8	46.8	46.1	47.3	41.3	45.7	40.9	41.3	40.6	38.8	37.4
1975	39.2	45.7	44.6	46.6	38.6	44.7	36.8	37.4	38.5	37.5	34.7
1970	37.4	44.9	42.3	46.9	36.7	46.0	32.2	35.2	37.9	36.5	32.5
1965	34.4	43.1	38.8	46.2	33.6	40.5	28.8	32.7	35.5	34.1	31.0
1960	32.6	43.1	39.1	46.2	31.8	38.5	27.3	31.4	34.8	31.2	28.2
1955	30.8	42.9	38.1	46.3	30.0	43.3	26.7	30.1	31.3	27.6	23.5
Black and other											
1993	49.2	46.9	44.7	47.9	49.4	48.0	48.1	50.8	51.0	47.5	49.2
1992	49.3	47.5	48.6	46.8	49.4	47.1	48.9	51.0	51.4	46.8	46.0
1990	49.3	48.1	48.0	48.1	49.3	48.7	48.6	50.6	50.1	47.2	51.2
1985	48.9	47.4	48.0	47.1	49.0	48.3	49.0	50.1	48.7	47.9	48.5
1980	48.3	46.2	44.2	47.3	48.5	48.1	49.1	49.0	48.1	48.0	46.3
1975	45.8	46.7	46.2	46.8	45.8	46.5	46.1	46.6	45.2	44.0	41.9
1970	43.6	43.4	41.8	44.4	43.7	46.4	42.6	44.8	44.7	40.8	35.6
1965	41.6	38.1	34.7	40.4	41.9	42.5	41.4	43.5	42.6	40.0	35.7
1960	39.8	37.5	33.0	40.6	39.9	38.4	38.6	42.4	42.2	37.7	31.6
1955	38.3	36.6	32.5	39.7	38.5	42.3	39.4	40.3	38.0	33.4	24.7

Source: U.S. Bureau of Labor Statistics, "Employment and Earnings," 1994, 1993, 1991, and 1986, Table 3, "Handbook of Labor Statistics,"
Table 3, U.S. Government Printing Office, Washington, D.C., 1994, 1993, 1991, 1986, and 1984.

Table 13-6. Race Composition of the Civilian Labor Force, by Age and Sex: 1975-1993 [percent black]

Year and sex	Total labor force	16 to 19 years			20 years and over						
		Total	16-17 years	18-19 years	Total	20-24 years	25-34 years	35-44 years	45-54 years	55-64 years	65 and over
Both sexes											
1993	10.9	11.4	10.1	12.2	10.9	12.5	12.1	10.9	9.4	9.3	7.3
1992	10.9	11.7	10.4	12.5	10.9	12.3	12.1	10.8	9.6	9.5	7.9
1990	10.8	11.2	10.4	11.7	10.8	12.1	11.9	10.5	9.9	8.9	7.9
1985	10.7	11.3	9.9	12.2	10.7	11.8	11.6	10.3	10.1	8.8	8.7
1980	10.2	9.5	8.4	10.3	10.2	11.3	11.2	10.2	9.4	8.2	8.4
1975	9.9	9.4	8.3	10.2	9.9	10.7	10.8	10.5	8.9	8.2	8.7
Males											
1993	9.9	11.6	10.5	12.3	9.8	11.9	11.1	9.6	8.3	8.5	6.2
1992	10.0	11.8	10.5	12.7	9.9	12.0	11.0	9.5	8.4	8.7	7.0
1990	9.8	11.2	10.6	11.6	9.7	11.7	10.9	9.3	8.8	8.2	6.4
1985	9.7	11.4	9.7	12.5	9.5	11.5	10.3	9.1	8.9	7.7	7.1
1980	9.1	9.6	8.6	10.3	9.1	10.9	9.8	9.0	8.4	7.0	7.3
1975	8.9	9.3	8.1	10.2	8.9	10.4	9.4	9.1	8.0	7.4	7.8
Females											
1993	12.0	11.1	9.6	12.1	12.1	13.1	13.3	12.4	10.7	10.3	8.9
1992	12.1	11.5	10.2	12.3	12.1	12.6	13.5	12.3	10.9	10.4	9.0
1990	12.0	11.2	10.2	11.9	12.0	12.6	13.2	12.0	11.2	10.0	9.9
1985	12.0	11.1	10.0	11.8	12.1	12.2	13.2	11.8	11.6	10.4	11.0
1980	11.5	9.4	8.1	10.3	11.8	11.9	13.1	11.8	11.0	9.9	10.2
1975	11.3	9.6	8.6	10.2	11.5	11.1	13.1	12.7	10.3	9.5	10.4

Source: U.S. Bureau of Labor Statistics, "Employment and Earnings," 1994, 1993, 1991, and 1986, Table 3, "Handbook of Labor Statistics,"
   Table 3, U.S. Government Printing Office, Washington, D.C., 1994, 1993, 1991, 1986, and 1984.

the proportion of blacks never exceeds 12.5 percent (at age 20-24) in 1993.

Labor Force Participation Rates Among the Hispanic Population

A second factor confounding the effect of the young black population on the labor force is an even younger Hispanic population that has traditionally had very high rates of labor force participation. As Table 13-7 shows, men age 20 and over with origins in Mexico, Puerto Rico or Cuba had high rates of labor force participation. Just as with white and black males, their rates of participation have dropped between 1980 and 1993, but the labor force participation rates of men of Mexican origin at age 20 and over (84.7 percent) remained far higher than those for all U.S. men (76.9 percent).

The labor force participation rates of Hispanic women at age 20 and over have shown three divergent patterns. Mexican-origin women, who were about two percentage points (at 49.1 percent) below the national level for all women in 1980, have increased their labor force participation so slowly that they are now almost five per-

cent below the national norm (53.5 to 58.4 percent). Puerto Rican-origin women, far below the national norm in 1980 (at 37.2 percent) still lag behind, but are increasing at a faster pace than the national rate of increase. Cuban-origin women, on the other hand, were above the national norm in 1980 (at 53.8 to 51.3 percent, respectively), but have declined by 1993 to a 48.5 percent labor force participation rate, a level that approximates the rate of Puerto Rican-origin women in 1993. Culture, marriage and fertility patterns, education, and job opportunities all have played a role in the patterns of labor force participation of these three Hispanic groups. These divergent trends alert us to the dangers of generalizing about "Hispanics" without also considering their specific place of origin.

Participation Rates in Metropolitan and Nonmetropolitan Areas

Labor force participation rates also vary with residence of the population within different sectors of metropolitan or nonmetropolitan areas. Table 13-8 provides labor force participation rates tabulated to show those differentials and how they affect race and ethnic groups

Table 13-7. Civilian Labor Force Participation of the Hispanic Population, by Age, Sex, and Place of Origin (In Comparison with U.S. Population, by Race): 1980-1993 [percent in labor force]

Age, sex, and year	Hispanic				United States total		
	Total	Mexican origin	Puerto Rican origin	Cuban origin	Total	White	Black
Total							
1993	65.9	67.0	56.7	59.8	66.2	66.7	62.4
1992	66.5	67.5	57.4	61.1	66.3	66.7	63.3
1990	67.0	68.3	55.6	65.1	66.4	66.8	63.3
1985	64.6	67.0	52.4	66.2	64.8	65.0	62.9
1980	64.0	66.4	56.1	66.0	63.8	64.1	61.0
Males 20 years and over							
1993	83.1	84.7	74.7	74.2	76.9	77.5	72.0
1992	83.7	85.0	74.4	74.8	77.3	77.8	73.1
1990	84.1	85.7	75.6	76.1	77.8	78.3	73.8
1985	84.0	86.5	74.8	79.9	78.1	78.5	74.4
1980	85.2	87.1	80.5	83.4	79.4	79.8	75.1
Females 20 years and over							
1993	53.6	53.5	47.0	48.5	58.4	58.3	59.5
1992	54.1	53.6	49.0	50.7	58.4	58.1	60.1
1990	54.6	54.5	43.7	56.1	57.9	57.6	60.0
1985	50.7	51.8	38.8	55.3	54.7	54.0	58.6
1980	48.9	49.1	37.2	53.8	51.3	50.6	55.6
Both sexes 16-19 years							
1993	43.6	45.8	34.9	44.3	51.5	55.1	37.0
1992	45.5	48.3	33.0	43.0	51.3	54.7	37.9
1990	47.2	50.0	34.5	50.3	53.7	57.4	38.7
1985	44.5	47.9	36.3	43.5	54.5	57.5	41.2
1980	50.4	55.9	30.8	50.0	56.7	60.0	38.9

Source: U.S. Bureau of Labor Statistics, "Employment and Earnings," 1994, 1993, 1991, and 1986, Tables 3 and 40, and "Handbook of Labor Statistics," Table 5, U.S. Government Printing Office, Washington, D.C., 1994, 1993, 1991, 1986, and 1984.

in the United States. Participation rates are higher in metropolitan than in nonmetropolitan areas. For most groups, whether classified by gender, age, race or Hispanic origin, rates are highest in the urban fringe, next highest in central places, and lag in other urban and rural areas.

Many social commentators have directed our attention to supposed low rates of labor force participation among the populations of central places, in particular to the minority teenage and young adult residents of these areas. Yet these 1990 census data indicate that among black teenagers and young adults, their labor force participation rates are higher than their black counterparts living in other urban and rural areas. Viewed in comparative perspective, among those 16-19 years of age, blacks lag behind whites by 20.5 percent (31.8 to 52.3 percent) in labor force participation rates in rural areas, compared to a lag of only 13.9 percent (39.9 to 53.8 percent) between the races in central places. While the labor force does, of course, include the unemployed (see below), these participation rates suggest that viewed in comparative perspective, the labor force attachment of black urban youth may not be as tenuous as some have suggested.

Labor Force Participation in Poverty and Nonpoverty Areas

In 1970 the U.S. Bureau of the Census identified certain counties and municipal divisions in the United States as "poverty areas" because 20 percent or more of their population received incomes insufficient to main-

Table 13-8. Labor Force Participation Rates, by Age, Race-ethnicity, Sex, and Urban-Rural Residence: 1990 [percent in labor force]

Age and sex	White					Black					Hispanic				
	Total	Central place	Urban fringe	Other urban	Rural	Total	Central place	Urban fringe	Other urban	Rural	Total	Central place	Urban fringe	Other urban	Rural
Male, 16 years and over	75.2	74.6	78.4	71.0	73.8	66.5	66.6	75.5	60.9	56.0	78.4	78.3	82.3	75.7	71.8
16 to 19 years	54.5	53.8	57.4	54.0	52.3	39.3	39.9	43.9	37.6	31.8	51.5	50.7	54.4	51.2	47.1
20 to 24 years	82.8	79.7	85.7	78.3	85.8	71.7	73.2	77.3	67.2	59.1	84.2	84.1	86.5	82.8	77.0
25 to 54 years	93.1	91.9	95.1	91.9	92.1	80.4	80.9	87.0	76.0	69.8	89.0	88.7	92.1	87.4	81.6
55 to 64 years	67.8	68.2	72.1	64.3	64.1	58.3	56.8	67.1	55.0	54.9	69.4	68.2	74.4	64.6	64.8
65 to 69 years	28.2	29.1	30.2	25.3	26.5	23.0	22.8	27.9	20.4	20.6	30.2	29.7	32.5	26.9	29.1
70 years and over	11.8	12.1	12.1	9.9	12.2	10.3	10.1	13.0	9.9	9.1	12.4	12.0	14.3	10.2	12.4
Female, 16 years and over	56.3	56.7	59.2	52.2	54.3	59.5	58.1	69.3	53.9	53.8	55.9	54.7	60.2	52.6	51.3
16 to 19 years	52.7	52.3	56.9	52.2	48.7	38.9	38.9	43.8	37.4	32.6	42.4	41.0	46.4	41.3	38.2
20 to 24 years	74.3	73.5	78.7	69.9	71.8	66.4	64.6	73.1	63.5	65.8	63.7	62.3	68.3	60.1	58.5
25 to 54 years	74.8	76.4	76.2	74.5	71.6	75.2	73.4	81.9	72.1	73.3	65.1	63.8	68.9	63.2	60.6
55 to 64 years	45.6	47.8	48.2	44.1	40.9	47.3	47.4	53.6	43.5	41.1	41.8	41.3	46.0	36.6	34.5
65 to 69 years	16.8	18.4	17.9	15.6	14.2	18.0	18.4	20.1	16.9	15.4	15.1	15.2	16.7	12.1	12.3
70 years and over	4.7	5.0	4.9	4.1	4.4	6.4	6.6	7.2	5.8	5.1	5.2	5.3	5.4	4.1	4.7

Source: U.S. Bureau of the Census, "Social and Economic Characteristics: United States Summary," 1990 CP-2-1, U.S. Government Printing Office, Washington, D.C., 1993, Tables 69, 70, and 73.

Table 13-9. Employment Status of the Civilian Noninstitutionalized Population in Poverty and Nonpoverty Areas, by Race-ethnicity: 1993

Employment status and race-ethnicity	Total United States		Metropolitan areas		Nonmetropolitan areas	
	Poverty areas	Nonpoverty areas	Poverty areas	Nonpoverty areas	Poverty areas	Nonpoverty areas
All races						
Civilian noninstitutional population	26,467	167,082	16,963	133,587	9,504	33,495
Civilian labor force	14,925	113,115	9,354	91,423	5,571	21,692
Percent of population	56.4	67.7	55.1	68.4	58.6	64.8
Employed	13,227	106,079	8,113	85,713	5,114	20,366
Unemployed	1,698	7,036	1,241	5,710	457	1,325
Unemployment rate	11.4	6.2	13.3	6.2	8.2	6.1
Men, 20 years and over	10.6	5.8	12.6	5.9	7.2	5.4
Women, 20 years and over	9.9	5.3	11.3	5.3	7.5	5.4
Both sexes, 16 to 19 years	28.8	17.5	33.1	18.0	21.8	16.0
Men	30.0	19.0	34.9	19.8	21.6	16.2
Women	27.5	16.0	30.8	16.1	22.2	15.7
Not in labor force	11,542	53,967	7,610	42,164	3,933	11,803
White						
Civilian noninstitutional population	16,173	147,748	8,990	116,222	7,183	31,525
Civilian labor force	9,477	99,882	5,183	79,452	4,294	20,430
Percent of population	58.6	67.6	57.6	68.4	59.8	64.8
Employed	8,632	94,180	4,632	74,941	4,000	19,238
Unemployed	845	5,702	551	4,511	294	1,191
Unemployment rate	8.9	5.7	10.6	5.7	6.8	5.8
Men, 20 years and over	8.3	5.4	10.0	5.4	6.3	5.2
Women, 20 years and over	7.9	4.9	9.2	4.8	6.3	5.1
Both sexes, 16 to 19 years	21.3	15.7	25.7	15.7	15.8	15.4
Men	23.8	16.9	29.3	17.3	16.2	15.9
Women	18.1	14.3	20.5	14.1	15.4	14.7
Not in labor force	6,696	47,866	3,808	36,770	2,888	11,096
Black						
Civilian noninstitutional population	9,154	13,175	7,143	11,788	2,011	1,387
Civilian labor force	4,812	9,131	3,705	8,236	1,107	894
Percent of population	52.6	69.3	51.9	69.9	55.0	64.5
Employed	4,044	8,102	3,079	7,312	965	790
Unemployed	768	1,029	627	924	141	105
Unemployment rate	16.0	11.3	16.9	11.2	12.8	11.7
Men, 20 years and over	15.5	10.4	16.9	10.5	10.6	9.4
Women, 20 years and over	13.0	9.3	13.6	9.1	10.9	11.3
Both sexes, 16 to 19 years	43.0	36.4	43.8	36.9	40.7	32.1
Men	42.9	38.5	44.2	40.0	39.1	—[1]
Women	43.1	33.8	43.3	33.1	42.5	—[1]
Not in labor force	4,342	4,044	3,438	3,552	904	493
Hispanic						
Civilian noninstitutional population	4,562	11,191	4,176	10,410	387	781
Civilian labor force	2,574	7,803	2,350	7,283	224	520
Percent of population	56.4	69.7	56.3	70.0	58.0	66.6
Employed	2,222	7,051	2,024	6,574	198	477
Unemployed	352	752	326	709	27	43
Unemployment rate	13.7	9.6	13.9	9.7	11.9	8.3
Men, 20 years and over	12.3	8.4	12.2	8.6	12.4	6.7
Women, 20 years and over	12.7	9.0	13.0	9.0	10.0	8.6
Both sexes, 16 to 19 years	29.3	24.9	30.3	25.2	—[1]	21.5
Men	31.3	23.7	32.3	24.3	—[1]	—[1]
Women	25.9	26.5	26.8	26.4	—[1]	—[1]
Not in labor force	1,988	3,388	1,826	3,127	162	261

[1] Data not shown where base is less than 35,000.

Source: U.S. Bureau of Labor Statistics, "Employment and Earnings," Government Printing Office, Washington, D.C., 1994, Table 64.

tain the family or household at or above the poverty level. (For definitions of poverty, see Chapter 15.) This delimitation has been used to identify residential areas of the nation where low income and poverty are a major problem. In 1993, 11.7 percent of the civilian labor force resided in poverty areas and 88.3 percent in nonpoverty areas. Table 13-9 shows the labor force participation rates by race of the residents of the poverty areas and the remainder of the nation.

Labor force participation rates are significantly lower in the poverty than in the nonpoverty areas for the white, black and Hispanic populations. The disparity is greater for blacks and Hispanics than for the white population. In fact, labor force participation rates for both blacks and Hispanics (at over 69 percent each) in

nonpoverty areas are higher than the rates for whites (67.6) in these areas. Rates are lower in the metropolitan poverty areas than in the nonmetropolitan poverty areas for all three groups.

Selected Facets of the Labor Force

Marital Status and Labor Force Participation

In 1955, there were striking differences in the labor force participation rates of married men and women who had a spouse present in their household. As Table 13-10 shows, in that year more than nine out of every ten married men who had a spouse present were in the labor force, as compared to fewer than three out of ten women. By

Table 13-10. Labor Force Participation Rates of the Civilian Noninstitutional Population, by Marital Status, Sex, and Race: 1955-1992
[percent in labor force]

Year and race	Male			Female		
	Single	Married, spouse present	Widowed, separated, divorced	Single	Married, spouse present	Widowed, separated, divorced
All races						
1992	72.4	77.7	68.1	64.8	59.4	46.7
1990	73.1	78.3	68.1	66.4	58.2	46.7
1985	73.8	78.7	68.7	66.6	53.8	45.1
1980	72.6	80.9	67.5	64.4	49.8	43.6
1975	68.7	83.0	63.4	59.8	44.3	40.1
1970	65.5	86.1	60.7	56.8	40.5	40.3
1965	65.1	87.4	60.4	54.5	34.9	40.7
1960	69.8	89.2	63.1	58.6	31.9	41.6
1955	72.9	90.9	64.8	61.1	28.5	40.7
White						
1992	74.8	77.6	68.8	67.9	58.8	46.3
1990	75.3	78.3	69.5	69.0	57.6	45.7
1985	75.5	78.7	69.6	69.2	53.0	44.0
1980	74.5	81.0	68.4	67.2	48.9	42.7
1975	70.4	83.1	63.3	62.0	43.5	39.2
1970	66.2	86.0	59.5	58.5	39.5	38.9
Black						
1992	63.3	77.5	63.5	55.4	66.8	48.5
1990	63.9	76.7	60.4	57.5	64.6	52.2
1985	66.1	77.4	64.1	56.5	62.4	50.5
1980	63.3	79.3	63.2	51.8	59.3	48.0
1975	58.4	81.1	63.2	46.9	54.0	44.3

Source: U.S. Bureau of the Census for the Bureau of Labor Statistics, "Current Population Survey," 1992 and 1990 (machine-readable data files), Bureau of the Census, Washington, D.C., 1992 and 1990, and U.S. Bureau of Labor Statistics, "Labor Force Statistics Derived from the Current Population Survey, 1948-87," Bulletin 2307, U.S. Government Printing Office, Washington, D.C., 1988, Table B-7.

1992, the male labor force participation rate for those with a spouse present had dropped to 77.7 percent, and the female rate had increased dramatically to 59.4 percent.

Compared to these major changes in labor force participation rates among married men and women, the changes since 1955 for single, widowed, separated and divorced men and women are surprisingly minimal. Labor force participation rates among single (i.e. never-married) men and women declined between 1955 and 1965, then swung up again, remaining relatively unchanged during the 1980-92 era. A similar pattern is found among widowed, separated and divorced men and women, except that from 1980 on, rates for both sexes rose to new levels. The recent data on labor force participation rates by marital status for whites (for 1970-92) and blacks (for 1975-92) show very similar patterns over time, although those for single black men and women lag far behind those of their white counterparts in each year.

Marital status has had relatively little effect on changes in age-specific labor force participation rates among men but some effect on women during the 1960-92 period. The data in Table 13-11 show that there were large increases in labor force participation rates for married, separated, divorced and widowed women aged 16

to 64 years between 1960 and 1992. However, the rates for single women aged 20 years and over actually decreased considerably between these two years. While increased attendance at educational institutions among single women may account for the some of the decrease in labor force participation for the 20-24 year age group, the drop among single women at age 25-44 is harder to explain.

Presence and Age of Children and Labor Force Participation

In 1950 having a preschool child in the household was a strong barrier against a wife's participation in the labor force. Not so today! Figure 13-5 demonstrates that in the four decades since 1950, labor force participation rates of married women with children under the age of six surged from about 12 percent to about 58 percent. While the labor force participation rates of married women without children and with children aged 6 to 17 years have also increased (the latter much more rapidly than the former), the increase in the rates for mothers of young children represents a profound qualitative as well as quantitative change. This major change in how society de-

Table 13-11. Labor Force Participation Rates of the Civilian Noninstitutional Population, by Marital Status, Sex, and Age: 1960-1992 [percent in labor force]

Marital status and age	Males					Females				
	1992	1990	1980	1970	1960	1992	1990	1980	1970	1960
Married, spouse present										
16-19 years	78.1	96.9	91.3	92.3	91.5	42.1	48.9	49.3	37.8	27.2
20-24 years	94.4	94.7	96.9	94.7	97.1	66.1	65.0	61.4	47.9	31.7
25-44 years	96.2	96.6	97.3	98.0	98.7	73.1	71.6	60.1	42.7	33.1
45-64 years	82.6	82.2	84.3	91.2	93.7	58.4	56.3	46.9	44.0	36.0
65 years and over	18.1	18.5	20.5	29.9	36.6	8.1	8.5	7.3	7.3	6.7
Single										
16-19 years	47.1	51.3	59.9	54.6	42.6	45.2	50.4	53.6	44.7	30.2
20-24 years	77.7	79.9	81.3	73.8	80.3	72.5	73.1	75.2	73.0	77.2
25-44 years	88.3	88.9	87.9	87.4	90.5	79.9	82.2	82.0	80.5	83.2
45-64 years	71.2	62.6	66.9	75.7	80.1	69.2	66.1	65.6	73.0	79.8
65 years and over	18.2	15.2	16.8	25.2	31.2	11.7	15.1	13.3	19.7	24.3
Separated/widowed/divorced										
16-19 years	91.4	91.5	75.0	68.8	68.8	34.6	50.8	50.0	48.5	43.8
20-24 years	88.1	89.5	92.6	90.4	96.9	69.2	65.5	68.4	60.3	58.0
25-44 years	90.7	91.9	93.1	92.3	94.7	79.3	80.0	76.8	67.2	67.2
45-64 years	76.9	75.2	73.3	78.5	83.2	65.7	64.1	60.2	61.9	60.0
65 years and over	11.9	12.4	13.7	18.3	22.7	8.6	8.6	8.2	10.0	11.4

Source: U.S. Bureau of the Census for the Bureau of Labor Statistics, "Current Population Survey," 1992 and 1990 (machine-readable data files), Bureau of the Census, Washington, D.C., 1992 and 1990, and U.S. Bureau of the Census, "Statistical Abstract of the United States: 1984-85," U.S. Government Printing Office, Washington, D.C., 1985, Table No. 682.

Table 13-12. Labor Force Participation Rates of Women¹, by Marital Status and Presence and Age of Children: 1960-1993
[percent in labor force]

| Year | All women | | | Total | | | With any children | | | | | |
| | | | | | | | Children 6 to 17 only | | | Children under 6 | | |
	Single	Married, spouse present	Widowed, separated divorced	Single	Married, spouse present	Widowed, separated divorced	Single	Married, spouse present	Widowed, separated divorced	Single	Married, spouse present	Widowed, separated divorced
1993	64.5	59.4	45.9	54.4	67.5	72.1	70.2	74.9	78.3	47.4	59.6	60.0
1990	66.4	58.2	46.8	55.2	66.3	74.2	69.7	73.6	79.7	48.7	58.9	63.6
1985	65.2	54.2	45.6	51.6	60.8	71.9	64.1	67.8	77.8	46.5	53.4	59.7
1980	61.5	50.1	44.0	52.0	54.1	69.4	67.6	61.7	74.6	44.1	45.1	60.3
1970	53.0	40.8	39.1	—	39.7	60.7	—	49.2	66.9	—	30.3	52.2
1960	44.1	30.5	40.0	—	27.6	56.0	—	39.0	65.9	—	18.6	40.5

¹ Civilian noninstitutional persons 14 years and over in 1960; 16 years and over for subsequent years.

Source: U.S. Bureau of the Census, "Statistical Abstract of the United States:1994," U.S. Government Printing Office, Washington, D.C., 1994, Table No. 626.

Figure 13-5. Civilian Labor Force Participation Rates of Women, by Marital Status, Age, and Presence and Age of Children: 1950-1990

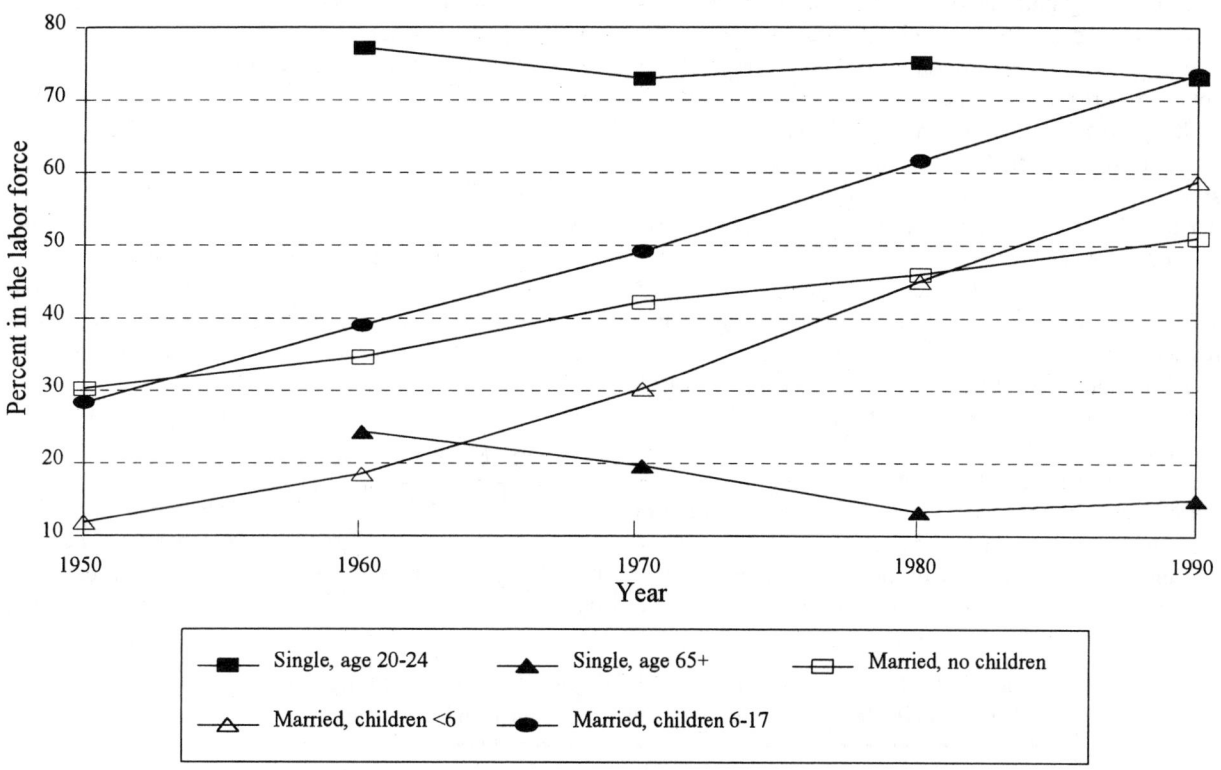

Source: 1950, 1960, 1970, 1980, and 1990 CPS data.

Table 13-13. Labor Force Participation Rates for Married Women, Spouse Present, by Age of Own Youngest Child and Race: 1993 [percent in labor force]

Presence and age of child	All races	White	Black
Married women, total	59.4	58.9	64.8
No children under 18	52.4	52.2	53.8
With children under 18	67.5	66.9	75.3
Under 6, total	59.6	58.6	70.9
Under 3	57.3	56.7	65.6
1 year or under	57.5	56.8	64.8
2 years	58.1	56.5	74.5
3 to 5 years	63.1	61.6	78.1
3 years	61.6	60.2	79.4
4 years	65.7	64.3	79.3
5 years	63.1	61.4	77.5
6 to 13 years	74.7	74.5	80.6
14 to 17 years	75.6	75.6	75.7

Source: U.S. Bureau of the Census, "Statistical Abstract of the United States:1994," U.S. Government Printing Office, Washington, D.C., 1994, Table No. 627.

fines the relationship between motherhood and employ-ment has had a number of other social effects, ranging from changing patterns of marriage and divorce to the provision of day care for children and older adults (for whom young and middle-aged mothers were often a source of care). These trends have continued into the early 1990s: Table 13-12 shows that labor force participation rates of all categories of women who are married with spouse present (i.e. those with no children, children un-der 6 years or children aged 6 to 17 years) have grown between 1990 and 1993.

Does the age of the youngest child in the house-hold of married couples have much effect on labor force participation rates of women? The 1993 data (Table 13-13) show that a majority of white (56.8 percent) and black (64.8 percent) married women with spouse present are in the work force by the time that their youngest child is one year of age or under. By the time that child is age 3, six out of ten white married women and almost eight out of ten black women are in the labor force. While labor force participation rates for married women with spouse present continue to rise for whites (peaking when their youngest

child is aged 14 to 17 years at a participation rate of 75.6 percent), black women's labor force participation rates peak when their youngest child is aged 6 to 13 years and decline slightly as their children age. Married black moth-ers with a spouse present have higher rates than white mothers no matter what the age of their youngest child.

One of the more surprising findings in Table 13-13 is that white mothers of very young children (i.e. at one year or younger) have virtually the same labor force par-ticipation rates as those with a youngest child aged two or three years (about 56 percent). Married black mothers, on the other hand, increase their labor force participation rates by almost ten percent (from 65 to 75 percent) as their youngest children move from one to two years of age.

School Enrollment and Labor Force Participation

Many analysts of trends in the labor force demog-raphy of teenagers and young adults over the past few decades have pointed to the growing proportion of young

Table 13-14. Employment Status of the Population Age 16-24, by School Enrollment, Sex, and Age: 1955-1993 [percent in labor force]

School enrollment and year	Both sexes 16 to 24 years	Male Total 16 to 24 years	16 to 19 years	20 to 24 years	Female Total 16 to 24 years	16 to 19 years	20 to 24 years
Enrolled							
1993	47.9	47.0	41.2	58.4	48.8	42.4	60.4
1990	48.4	47.7	42.9	57.6	49.1	43.5	59.9
1985	46.5	45.9	42.1	54.0	47.1	42.3	57.7
1980	47.4	47.8	44.6	55.3	47.0	42.3	58.9
1975	44.1	44.5	41.8	51.2	43.5	39.6	55.1
1970	40.7	42.9	39.7	51.2	38.0	34.8	50.5
1965	35.0	39.8	36.8	49.0	28.9	26.9	39.6
1960	31.8	36.4	34.3	44.2	26.0	24.0	40.6
1955	33.6	39.7	39.2	41.7	25.5	23.0	42.0
Not enrolled							
1993	79.5	87.3	75.0	91.9	72.0	63.1	75.1
1990	80.2	88.4	77.0	93.0	72.4	64.9	75.2
1985	80.5	89.1	78.4	93.2	72.5	65.6	75.0
1980	81.6	91.8	85.9	93.8	72.3	69.5	73.2
1975	77.8	92.1	88.6	93.5	65.8	63.3	66.6
1970	73.1	91.9	84.7	94.6	60.0	59.8	60.0
1965	70.4	94.1	88.9	96.3	54.1	59.6	51.8
1960	68.9	95.0	89.8	97.1	50.2	58.1	46.7
1955	68.5	95.5	92.9	96.7	51.6	58.1	48.6

Source: U.S. Bureau of Labor Statistics, "Employment and Earnings," 1994, 1991, and 1986, Table 6, and "Handbook of Labor Statistics," Table 63, U.S. Government Printing Office, Washington, D.C., 1994, 1991, 1986, and 1984.

people who work at the same time that they attend school. However, these trends must be examined by gender for a clearer picture of this phenomenon. As far back as 1955, almost 40 percent of all boys aged 16 to 19 years who were enrolled in school were employed, and the 1993 rate of employment for this group is only 2 percent higher than in 1955 (Table 13-14). It is teenaged schoolgirls (or college women) who have shown the major jump in employment: the labor force participation rates of those age 16-19 years rose from 25.5 percent in 1955 to 48.8 percent in 1993. Since teenage employees often receive the minimum wage and few if any benefits in their jobs (which are usually part-time), the rise in the female labor force participation rate for school enrollees ages 16-19 years (which now surpasses the male rate) raises questions about whether the "feminization of poverty" is also affecting this part of the workforce.

There has been a surge in labor force participation among school enrollees aged 20 to 24 years between 1955 and 1993, but these trends have affected men and women in much the same way. In 1955, about 42 percent of male and female school enrollees were in the labor force. By 1993, 60.4 percent of all female school enrollees and 58.4 percent of all male school enrollees were in the labor force. Undoubtedly the increase in the proportion of young Americans attending college, the rise of commuter, community and junior colleges (where students on day shifts can take courses far into the night), and the greater provi-

sion of loans for low-income students all have had an effect on the relationship between employment and school enrollment.

Not surprisingly, the labor force participation rate of young people not enrolled in school is higher than that of those enrolled in school. However, the trends in employment of young people not enrolled in school point out some of the serious problems in employment for those without advanced education over the past two decades. In 1955, 92.9 percent of all males aged 16 to 19 years not enrolled in school (i.e. including a large proportion of high school dropouts) were in the labor force. By 1993, this figure had dropped to 75 percent. In other words, about one out of every four young males who had left school was "floating," without an attachment to work in terms of either having a job or currently looking for one.

The trends for young women aged 16-19 years who were not enrolled in school were quite different. In 1955, only 58.1 percent of these young women were in the workforce. Given the historically low age at marriage in the United States and the relatively high wages paid to young male workers in the 1950s, many of these teenage women were already homemakers. Yet by 1980, the labor force participation rate of women age 16-19 not enrolled in school had risen to 69.5 percent and it fell back to 63.1 percent in 1993. The rise in this rate is easy to explain: a smaller proportion of all women were marrying by the 1960s and 1970s, and those who were marry-

Table 13-15. Labor Force Participation Rates of the Civilian Noninstitutional Population Age 25 Years and Over, by Educational Attainment, Age, and Sex: 1990 [percent in labor force]

Sex and educational attainment	Total 25 years and over	25 to 34 years	35 to 44 years	45 to 54 years	55 to 64 years	65 years and over
Males, total	77.1	94.0	94.6	90.4	67.2	17.2
High school						
Less than 4 years	53.8	88.0	82.8	79.4	54.1	11.9
Graduate	80.1	94.9	94.3	91.2	69.5	17.1
College						
1 to 3 years	84.7	94.6	96.3	92.0	69.5	21.7
4+ years	88.2	95.6	98.4	96.8	79.6	30.5
Females, total	56.3	73.6	76.4	70.6	45.3	8.9
High school						
Less than 4 years	29.2	50.0	56.6	50.1	31.9	5.1
Graduate	58.2	72.0	76.6	71.8	47.0	11.0
College						
1 to 3 years	67.5	77.8	80.4	77.5	55.6	11.2
4+ years	74.1	85.1	82.5	82.6	59.9	15.6

Source: U.S. Bureau of the Census for the Bureau of Labor Statistics, "Current Population Survey," 1990 (machine-readable data files), Bureau of the Census, Washington, D.C., 1990.

ing began doing so at older ages. The decline in the labor force participation rate among female teenagers since 1980 may be due, as with their male counterparts, to a decline in workforce attachment among those with low educational levels. Certainly, low educational attainment has a major effect on unemployment (see Table 13-33), and for teenagers, dropping out of high school may result in an inability to enter the workforce in the first place.

Educational Attainment and Labor Force Participation

For adult workers who have completed their education, there is a direct relationship between educational attainment and labor force participation. For the civilian noninstitutional population aged 25 years and over in 1990, the lowest labor force participation rates are found among those with less than four years of high school, and these rates increase with education within each age group (Table 13-15). This pattern holds true for both men and women. The highest labor force participation rates are found among males aged 35 to 44 years with four or more years of college (98.4 percent), and women aged 65 years and over with less than four years of high school have the lowest rates (5.1 percent).

The effect of education on labor force participation is particularly strong at older ages. To some extent, this is due to the nature of the kinds of employment that those with different levels of education find; a college professor is much less likely to have an early exit from the work force due to disability than is a coal miner. On the other hand, those with a higher level of education may find their employment (and their career) to be intrinsically more interesting, and to want to remain in the workforce at an older age. At age 65 years and over, men with four or more years of college are almost twice as likely to be in the work force as those with less than four years of high school, and for women this ratio is greater than three to one. Since education also leads to higher income, which should make earlier retirement possible, the effect of education on prolonging labor force participation is even more striking.

Table 13-16. Educational Attainment of the Civilian Labor Force[1], by Race-ethnicity: 1959-1990

Year and race-ethnicity	Total	Elementary		High school		College		Median school years completed
		Less than 5 years	5 to 8 years	1 to 3 years	4 years	1 to 3 years	4+ years	
All races								
1990	100.0	1.0	4.2	11.5	39.1	20.9	23.3	—
1980	100.0	1.2	7.1	15.5	40.1	17.9	18.2	12.7
1970	100.0	2.4	15.1	17.3	39.0	13.3	12.9	12.4
1959	100.0	5.3	25.2	19.8	30.7	9.3	9.6	12.0
White								
1990	100.0	1.0	4.1	11.0	39.1	20.9	24.0	—
1980	100.0	1.0	6.8	14.7	40.4	18.0	19.1	12.7
1970	100.0	1.8	14.4	16.4	40.0	13.9	13.6	12.4
1959	100.0	3.8	23.9	19.6	32.5	9.8	10.3	12.1
Black[2]								
1990	100.0	1.1	4.7	16.6	42.5	21.7	13.5	—
1980	100.0	2.7	9.7	23.1	39.3	16.1	9.1	12.4
1970	100.0	7.4	20.6	24.7	31.0	9.0	7.4	11.7
1959	100.0	17.8	35.5	21.1	16.5	4.9	4.1	8.6
Hispanic								
1990	100.0	8.0	17.8	17.3	31.7	15.8	9.5	—
1980	100.0	9.2	19.7	19.1	31.5	13.1	7.4	12.1

[1] Data for 1972 forward refer to persons 16 years and over; 18 years and over for prior years.

[2] Prior to 1977, data refer to black and other workers.

Source: U.S. Bureau of the Census for the Bureau of Labor Statistics, "Current Population Survey," 1990 (machine-readable data files), Bureau of the Census, Washington, D.C., 1990, and U.S. Bureau of Labor Statistics, "Employment and Earnings," U.S. Government Printing Office, Washington, DC, Table 61, 1985.

There has been a profound change in the educational attainment of the civilian labor force over the past four decades, especially when the changes for minority groups are examined (Table 13-16). In 1959, more than a quarter of all whites and more than half of all blacks in the civilian labor force had 8 years or less of education. By 1990, the proportion of the civilian labor force with this low level of education had dropped to less than 6 percent for both blacks and whites. At the other end of the educational spectrum, the proportion of the labor force with four or more years of college rose from 10.3 percent to 24.0 percent for whites and from 4.1 percent to 13.5 percent for blacks between 1959 and 1990. At the intermediate levels of education, both whites and blacks also showed major gains, with the latter group showing much more rapid improvement. It is seldom noted that by 1990, the educational attainment of the entire black civilian labor force (the older members of which were subjected to a systematic policy of segregation that tried to prevent them from improving their human capital) surpassed that of the educational attainment of the white civilian labor force in 1970.

The educational attainment of the Hispanic civilian labor force is quite different from that of its white or black counterparts. National-level data exist only since 1980, so it is more difficult to trace historical trends; in addition, these trends are complicated by a large-scale migration from Latin American nations over the past three decades. The Hispanic population has, relatively speaking, a larger proportion of its civilian labor force concentrated at the well-educated and very poorly- educated ends of the spectrum. By 1990, almost one in ten Hispanic workers had four or more years of college, but 8 percent had less than 5 years of education, and 17.8 percent had 5 to 8 years of elementary education. Given that many of these poorly-educated Hispanic workers are migrants who received their education in Spanish-language schools in Mexico and elsewhere, this puts them at an even greater disadvantage in most of the United States job market.

In future years, as older workers with below-average educational attainment continue to retire from the labor force and are replaced by younger persons who have completed above-average amounts of education, the educational level of the labor force will continue to rise. By 1990, almost one worker in every four was a college graduate; as recently as about 1930, the average worker was a graduate of elementary school, and only one in twenty had completed college.

The Hispanic population is the only subgroup of the population with important proportions of workers with elementary (less than eight years) education or less than a full high school education. As the number of jobs for poorly-educated workers declines, this group (and groups such as inner-city high school dropouts) could experience serious problems in obtaining employment.

Diversity in the Work Week and the Weeks Worked Per Year

Part-Time Workers

Historically, there has been a long-term decline in the average length of the work week. During the last decade of the nineteenth century the average was fifty-eight hours per week. Among non-agricultural workers in 1993, wage and salary workers worked 39.3 hours per week, the self-employed worked 40.5 hours per week, and unpaid family workers contributed an average of 34.2 hours per week. The equivalent work weeks for agricultural workers in these categories were 40.8, 46.5, and 36.9 hours per week.

Many persons who are employed do not have full-time jobs. Instead, they may work only a few hours per day or a few days each week. The U.S. Bureau of the Census, which collects data concerning hours worked as a part of its monthly survey of the labor force, defines full-time work as a total of thirty-five hours or more per week. Workers who work less than thirty-five hours per week are classed as part-time workers. The forty-hour week has come to be regarded as standard, and census statistics as to the number of workers who work forty-one hours or more per week are regarded as being a measure of the amount of "overtime" work. In assembling this information, the Bureau of the Census also asks the reason for working part time. Two categories of reasons are recognized:

- Economic reasons—slack work, inability to find full-time work, material shortages, repairs to plant or equipment, beginning or termination of job during the week
- Other reasons—labor disputes, bad weather, own illness, vacation, demands of home housework, attendance at school, no desire for full-time work, full-time worker only during peak season, legal or religious holiday, and other such reasons

The distribution of full-time and part-time workers by age and sex in 1993 is given in Table 13-17. About 12 percent of all males 16 years and over are part-time workers, compared to about 26 percent of all female workers. Of the 87.7 percent of all males who are full-time workers, a little more than half (48.8 percent) work 40 hours or less, and 38.7 percent work 41 hours or more per week. Only about one out of every five women workers is employed 41 hours or more per week. Overall, men work an average of 42.2 hours per week, and those on full-time schedules work 45.3 hours per week; the corresponding figures for women are 36.0 and 41.6 hours per week, respectively.

As Table 13-17 shows, age also has a strong effect on the propensity to work part-time, the reasons why one works part-time, and the average hours worked per week by all workers and those on full-time schedules. Among

Table 13-17. Proportional Distribution of Full-time and Part-time Work and Average Hours Worked for Persons at Work in Nonagricultural Industries, by Age and Sex: 1993

Age and sex	Total at work	Part-time schedules			Full-time schedules			Average hours worked per week	
		Total	Economic reasons	Voluntary	Total	40 hours or less	41 hours or more	Total	Full time schedules
Males, 16 and over	100.0	12.3	4.8	7.6	87.7	48.9	38.7	42.2	45.3
16 to 17 years	100.0	86.4	8.9	77.5	13.6	11.2	2.3	19.1	38.1
18 to 19 years	100.0	53.0	12.8	40.2	46.9	35.3	11.6	29.5	41.1
20 to 24 years	100.0	24.1	8.3	15.8	75.9	49.6	26.3	37.9	43.3
25 to 44 years	100.0	6.8	4.4	2.5	93.2	49.9	43.3	44.1	45.7
45 to 64 years	100.0	7.3	3.4	3.9	92.7	51.7	41.1	43.6	45.4
65 years and over	100.0	48.1	4.4	43.7	51.9	35.3	16.6	30.6	42.6
Females, 16 and over	100.0	26.4	6.4	20.0	73.6	53.6	20.0	36.0	41.6
16 to 17 years	100.0	90.6	8.7	81.8	9.4	7.9	1.4	17.6	37.8
18 to 19 years	100.0	64.0	14.1	49.9	36.0	29.1	6.9	26.5	39.8
20 to 24 years	100.0	33.2	9.2	24.0	66.8	51.3	15.5	34.2	40.8
25 to 44 years	100.0	21.2	5.7	15.5	78.8	56.6	22.2	37.4	41.7
45 to 64 years	100.0	22.1	5.7	16.4	77.9	56.6	21.3	37.2	41.7
65 years and over	100.0	60.3	6.2	54.1	39.6	30.0	9.7	27.0	41.3

Source: U.S. Bureau of Labor Statistics, "Employment and Earnings: January 1994," U.S. Government Printing Office, Washington, D.C., 1994, Table 33.

Table 13-18. Workers Doing Job-related Work at Home: 1991 [numbers in thousands]

Worker characteristics	Total at work	Persons doing job-related work at home					
		Total[1]	Worked at home for pay				
			Total	Worked 8 hours or more per week			
				Total	Percent of total at work	35 hours or more	Mean hours worked per week
Total	109,126	19,967	7,432	3,651	3.3	1,069	14.1
Age							
16 to 24 years old	16,268	862	329	122	0.7	40	12.3
25 to 34 years old	31,248	5,290	1,798	839	2.7	259	13.7
35 to 44 years old	29,500	6,755	2,430	1,144	3.9	297	13.0
45 to 54 years old	18,842	4,368	1,567	876	4.6	264	15.4
55 to 64 years old	10,291	1,995	865	462	4.5	161	16.8
65 years and over	2,977	697	445	207	7.0	47	13.3
Sex							
Male	58,794	10,731	4,210	1,894	3.2	438	12.0
Female	50,332	9,236	3,222	1,757	3.5	632	16.8
Race-ethnicity							
White	94,387	18,520	7,022	3,403	3.6	966	13.8
Black	11,020	970	239	147	1.3	76	22.8
Hispanic	7,977	667	255	137	1.7	36	13.7

[1] Includes those that did not report pay status and unpaid family members

Source: U.S. Bureau of the Census, "Statistical Abstract of the United States:1994," U.S. Government Printing Office, Washington, D.C., 1994, Table No. 636.

both men and women, those aged 25-44 years are the most likely to work full-time and to work more than 41 hours per week, and are the least likely to be working part-time for voluntary reasons. Both the young and the old are much more likely to work a lesser number of hours per week, to work part-time, and to work part-time for voluntary reasons.

Two other dimensions of employment further complicate the distinction between part-time and full-time work: whether one is working at home, and whether one is self-employed. The 1991 data in Table 13-18 show that almost 20 million Americans did job-related work at home; within this group, 7.4 million worked at home for pay. Of those who worked at home for pay, 3.651 million worked for 8 or more hours per week, and 1.069 million worked 35 or more hours per week. Whites were more than twice as likely to work at home for pay as blacks or Hispanics, and men were slightly more likely to work at home for pay than were women. Self-employment (see textbox) is another increasing trend that is complicating both the conceptualization and measurement of the nature of work in recent years.

Earlier in this chapter, the virtual revolution in fe-male labor force participation by mothers of young children was noted. Yet how much of this labor force participation was actually only part-time work? Table 13-19 demonstrates that a large proportion of all working women (and a larger proportion of working men) are working full time even if they have dependent children or have other workers in the household. For example, in the group that might be considered most likely to work only part-time, i.e. female householders with children under 6 in households with multiple workers, the proportion of part-time workers among all workers is 28.2 percent for whites, 19.1 percent for blacks, 37.5 percent for Asian/Pacific Islanders and 14.6 percent for Hispanics.

Year-Round, Part-Year, and Intermittent Workers

The number of persons who are at work during any particular week of a year is smaller than the total number of persons in the population who work at some time during the year. Many workers are employed for less than a full year. Throughout a year new workers continuously enter the labor force, and older workers retire; by defini-

Trends in Self-employment

By Alison Kadlec Donta

In 1990, there were 10.160 million self-employed workers in the United States, according to the Bureau of Labor Statistics. Of this number, 8.760 million of these workers were employed in nonagricultural industries. There were 5.618 million males self-employed in nonagricultural industries and 3.142 million women. Among white workers, 8.1% of the nonagricultural workers, or 8.022 million, were self-employed as were 434 thousand blacks. These numbers of self-employed workers represent an increase in both numbers and percent of total workers self-employed since the low self-employment rate seen in the 1970's and illustrated in the figure below.

The self-employment rate of civilian, nonagricultural workers was 13.3% in 1950, but this rate continued to fall until 1970. By 1980, however, there was evidence of a rise in self-employment among all workers, and especially among women. Since 1975, there has been a 53.5% increase in self-employment, compared to a lesser increase of 39.1% in total nonagricultural employment. For women, that change has been even more dramatic, with a 112.3% increase in self-employment since 1975 compared to a 58.1% overall increase in total nonagricultural employment. In 1975, 25.9% of self-employed nonagricultural workers were women, and that percentage had increased to 35.9% by 1990. Clearly, self-employment has become an increasingly important sector of the labor force in the United States over the past decade.

Additional characteristics of the self-employed worker in 1990 can be seen in the table below. Both male and female self-employed workers are more likely to be white than their wage-and-salary counterparts. In fact, there is a very low self-employment rate (3.7% in 1990) blacks compared to the total population employed in nonagricultural industries (8.3% in 1990). Self-employed workers in 1990 tend to be older than wage-and-salary workers, although this difference is less than it was in 1975. Another difference between the two classes of workers is marital status. While 75.2% of self-employed males are married with spouse present, only 58.2% of wage-and-salary workers are similarly married. This difference is also seen among female workers. Self-employed workers are, in general, less educated than wage-and-salary workers, although the difference in mean number of years of school completed is not great. There is a higher percentage of workers with less than a high school diploma found among self-employed workers than among those in wage-and-salary positions. The amount of time spent working is also different for these two groups. Among males, the self-employed usually work a greater mean number of hours per week than do the wage-and-salary workers (44.6 versus 40.9 hours a week). Among females, the self-employed workers work slightly fewer usual mean hours. Self-employed workers are also more likely to be part-time workers than full-time workers. This is especially evident among females, where 40.3% of the self-employed work part-time compared with the 28.8% of wage-and-salary workers who work part-time.

Self-employed workers differ not only demograhpically from their wage-and-salary counterparts, they also differ in their needs. As indicated above, self-employment may serve as a buffer against unemployment in tough economic times, but some self-employed workers, especially women, operate in a precarious, marginal arena (Devine 1994). In 1990, the median annual earnings of self-employed women was $4,783 less than women in wage-and-salary positions. The median annual earnings for self-employed men was actually $2,609 higher than those of male wage-and-salary workers. Nevertheless, 6.4% of all self-employed women and 3.3% of all self-employed men reported negative earnings in 1990 compared to less than 0.1%

Characteristics of Self-employed and Wage-and-salary Workers, by Sex: 1990

	Males		Females	
Characteristic	Self-employed	Wage-and-salary	Self-employed	Wage-and-salary
Race-ethnicity (percent)				
White	92.1	86.2	91.7	84.5
Black	4.2	10.5	3.9	12.2
Hispanic	4.7	8.3	4.4	6.8
Age				
Mean age	44.3	36.5	43.4	36.4
Percent age:				
16 to 24 years	3.7	20.4	2.9	21.1
25 to 44 years	50.9	53.5	54.8	52.7
45 to 64 years	38.0	23.6	34.9	23.6
65 years and over	7.5	2.5	6.7	2.7
Marital status (percent)				
Married, spouse present	75.2	58.2	74.7	54.1
Never married	13.2	30.3	7.3	26.1
Other[1]	11.7	11.5	18.0	19.8
Educational attainment				
Mean number of years completed	13.0	13.3	13.0	13.6
Percent with completion of:				
Less than 12 years	13.4	10.7	17.2	13.2
12 years	41.7	41.8	38.3	31.9
13 to 15 years	23.4	22.5	21.1	20.7
16 or more years	21.7	25.1	23.5	34.3
Full-time/part-time status				
Mean number of hours worked	44.6	40.9	35.3	35.5
Percent working:				
Full-time	84.6	87.9	59.7	71.2
Part-time	15.4	12.1	40.3	28.8

[1] Divorced. widowed. and married. spouse absent.

Source: Theresa J. Devine. "Characteristics of Self-employed Women in the United States." Monthly Labor Review. March 1994.

of both male and female wage-and-salary workers. In addition, self-employed workers are less likely to have health care coverage than wage-and-salary workers. Among women, 83.2% of those who were self-employed had any health plan while 87.2% of wage-and-salary workers were covered. For men, that difference is 78.7% compared to 83.9%. Even more striking is the difference in the family plan coverage between the two groups of workers. Only 5.0% of self-employed women had family coverage (compared to 22.3% for wage-and-salary workers) and only 24.7% of the male self-employed had this coverage while 41.4% of the male wage-and-salary workers had a family plan.

Additional Sources:

Bogenhold, Dieter, and Udo Staber. The Decline and Rise of Self-employment. Work, Employment, and Society 5(2):223-239, 1991.

Devine, Theresa J. Characteristics of Self-employed Wom en in the United States. Monthly Labor Review, March 1994:20-34.

U.S. Bureau of Labor Statistics. Employment and Earnings, 1991: Tables 23 and 41. Washington, D.C.: U.S. Government Printing Office, 1991.

U.S. Bureau of Labor Statistics. Handbook of Labor Statistics, 1989: Table 21. Washington, D.C.: U.S. Government Printing Office, 1989.

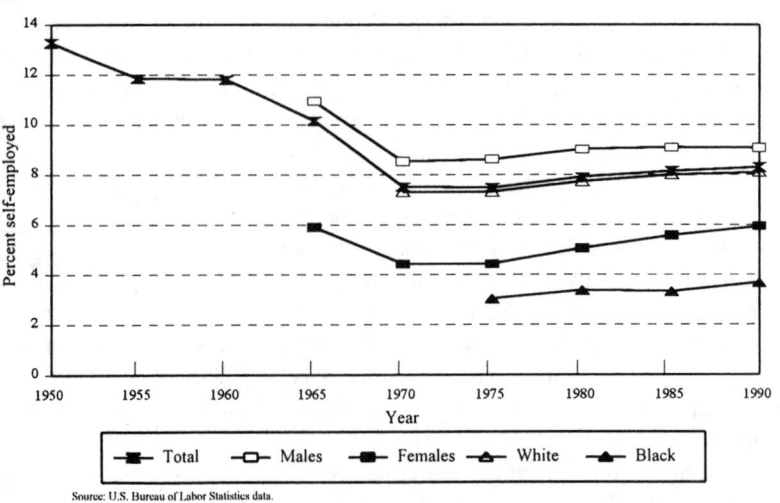

Percent of Employed Civilians in Nonagricultural Industries

Legend: ■ Total   □ Males   ■ Females   ▲ White   ▲ Black

Source: U.S. Bureau of Labor Statistics data.

Table 13-19. Percent of Working Householders Working Part-time During Past Year, by Type of Household or Family, Multiple Workers, Presence of Children, and Race-ethnicity: 1990

Type of household or family	All races	White	Black	American Indian, Eskimo, Aleut	Asian/ Pacific Islander	Hispanic
All households	10.8	10.5	12.7	13.2	10.3	8.8
Nonfamily householders	14.4	14.4	14.4	20.6	14.4	10.5
Male householder	10.4	10.4	10.2	11.1	13.0	9.6
Female householder	19.3	19.3	19.4	30.6	16.1	11.9
Family householders	9.6	9.3	12.2	10.2	9.1	8.5
Married couple, male householder	7.1	7.1	6.9	8.4	7.9	7.1
Married couple, female householder	23.9	25.9	15.9	...	14.3	12.7
Female householder	18.3	18.4	18.0	21.9	16.9	20.3
Without own children	18.2	17.2	21.4	17.2	15.9	19.4
With children under 6	23.0	24.5	20.4	19.5	23.8	22.0
With children 6-17 only	15.8	16.4	14.2	26.8	14.4	19.9
Male householder	8.8	7.6	15.9	7.4	7.7	8.3
Multiple worker households	8.4	8.4	9.1	7.8	8.6	7.6
Nonfamily householders	12.5	12.9	8.2	9.7	14.8	9.3
Male householder	9.2	9.7	4.2	12.7	9.1	9.6
Female householder	17.9	18.2	14.7	3.2	22.0	8.5
Family householders	8.0	7.9	9.1	7.6	8.0	7.5
Married couple, male householder	5.9	5.9	5.8	8.0	5.9	5.2
Married couple, female householder	23.1	24.9	15.4	...	15.7	12.2
Female householder	16.4	16.9	14.5	12.6	20.4	19.5
Without own children	16.3	16.2	15.7	13.6	19.8	17.8
With children under 6	24.6	28.2	19.1	...	37.5	14.6
With children 6-17 only	14.1	15.1	11.2	27.3	21.1	24.3
Male householder	9.2	8.4	13.5	4.9	10.3	6.7

Source: U.S. Bureau of the Census for the Bureau of Labor Statistics, "Current Population Survey," 1990 (machine-readable data files), Bureau of the Census, Washington, D.C., 1990.

Table 13-20. Persons[1] with Employment During the Preceding Year, by Sex, Weeks Worked, and Employment Status: 1950-1989

Sex and year	Total	Full time[2]				Part time[3]			
		Total	50 to 52 weeks	27 to 49 weeks	1 to 26 weeks	Total	50 to 52 weeks	27 to 49 weeks	1 to 26 weeks
Male									
1989	100.0	85.9	63.3	13.9	8.7	14.1	4.4	4.0	5.7
1985	100.0	86.5	66.8	11.5	8.2	13.5	4.8	3.2	5.5
1980	100.0	87.2	65.2	12.9	9.1	12.8	4.4	3.0	5.5
1975	100.0	87.5	63.8	13.4	10.3	12.5	4.4	3.0	5.1
1970	100.0	87.5	66.1	13.0	8.4	12.5	4.4	2.6	5.4
1965	100.0	86.9	67.3	12.0	7.5	13.1	4.4	2.3	6.4
1960	100.0	86.9	63.9	15.3	7.7	13.1	4.5	2.5	6.1
1955	100.0	89.9	67.5	15.5	7.0	10.1	4.1	2.2	3.8
1950	100.0	90.2	65.4	16.7	8.0	9.8	3.1	2.2	4.6
Female									
1989	100.0	69.4	46.4	13.9	9.1	30.6	10.8	9.1	10.7
1985	100.0	68.1	48.9	10.4	8.8	31.9	12.3	7.8	11.7
1980	100.0	67.8	44.7	12.0	11.0	32.2	11.9	8.0	12.3
1975	100.0	67.1	41.4	12.2	13.5	32.9	11.7	8.3	12.8
1970	100.0	67.9	40.7	12.8	14.4	32.1	10.0	2.5	14.6
1965	100.0	68.5	38.8	14.4	15.4	31.5	9.2	6.1	16.2
1960	100.0	67.6	36.9	14.6	16.0	32.4	10.0	6.6	15.8
1955	100.0	71.3	37.9	16.5	16.9	28.7	10.3	5.4	13.0
1950	100.0	73.4	36.8	17.9	18.7	26.6	8.2	5.1	13.2

[1] Data for 1970 forward refer to persons 16 years and over; 14 years and over for prior years.

[2] Usually worked 35 hours or more per week.

[3] Usually worked 1 to 35 hours per week.

Source: U.S. Bureau of the Census, "Social and Economic Characteristics," 1990 Census of Population, Table 22, and U.S. Bureau of Labor Statistics, "Handbook of Labor Statistics," Table 49, U.S. Government Printing Office, Washington, D.C., 1993 and 1989.

tion, such people work less than a full year. In addition, some workers are only seasonally employed and others are sporadically employed. Many students find summer jobs that they leave when school opens. As a result of these situations, the U.S. Bureau of the Census, when conducting its annual special survey of the "work experience" of the civilian population during the preceding year, finds that part-year work is very common and during any one year there is a large turnover in the labor force personnel.

Some worthwhile insights concerning this aspect of the labor force can be obtained by classifying the population according to the number of weeks worked during a year. The Bureau of the Census defines anyone who worked 50-52 weeks as a "year-round" worker and anyone who worked 1-49 weeks as a "part-year" worker. The workers may also be classified according to whether they worked primarily at full-time jobs (thirty-five hours or more per week during a majority of the weeks worked), or primarily at part-time jobs (less than thirty-five hours per week during a majority of the weeks worked). These

classifications make it possible to arrive at tabulations of the number of year-round and part-time workers. Table 13-20 is a summary of such data for the period 1950-1989.

Only slightly more than one-half of all workers who are employed during any year may be called year-round full-workers. Yet all but a small fraction of jobs are full (full workweek) jobs. For males there has been little change over recent years, but for women the trend has been toward a higher proportion of full-time, year-round employment and greater part-time, year-round employment with less part-year employment. Women's full-time, part-year employment has declined since 1950.

Intermittent and irregular workers who are on voluntary part-time schedules are primarily males under age 25 and women between 18 and 64 years (see Table 13-21). Race and marital status appear to have relatively little effect on voluntary part-time participation in the labor force, and there have been few changes in the distribution of this characteristic across gender or marital categories since 1970.

Table 13-21. Nonagricultural Workers on Voluntary Part-time Schedules, by Selected Characteristics: 1970-1993

Characteristic	1993	1990	1985	1980	1975	1970
Total						
Number	14,637	14,756	13,038	12,555	10,694	9,392
Percent	100.0	100.0	100.0	100.0	100.0	100.0
Male	30.8	29.8	29.5	30.5	31.3	32.2
16-17 years	5.2	5.4	6.2	8.0	8.7	9.2
18-24 years	10.8	10.5	10.7	10.2	10.3	11.0
25-44 years	5.6	5.1	4.5	3.8	3.5	3.0
45-64 years	4.4	4.1	3.7	3.4	3.5	3.3
65 years and over	4.8	4.7	4.5	5.0	5.3	5.8
Female	69.2	70.2	70.5	69.5	68.7	67.8
16-17 years	5.4	5.8	6.6	8.1	8.7	8.2
18-24 years	14.4	13.8	14.7	14.3	13.6	12.2
25-44 years	28.8	29.9	29.4	26.7	24.4	23.9
45-64 years	15.9	16.0	15.6	16.0	17.8	19.1
65 years and over	4.7	4.7	4.2	4.4	4.2	4.4
White	89.3	89.4	90.7	91.2	90.7	90.4
Male	26.8	26.1	26.2	27.5	28.2	29.4
Female	62.5	63.4	64.4	63.6	62.4	61.1
Black	7.3	7.5	6.8	7.1	7.8	—
Male	2.6	2.5	2.3	2.4	2.4	—
Female	4.7	5.0	4.5	4.8	5.4	—
Male						
Single (never married)	18.7	18.4	18.7	19.4	19.5	20.0
Married, spouse present	9.9	9.5	9.2	9.5	10.1	10.6
Widowed, divorced, or separated	2.1	1.9	1.5	1.6	1.7	1.5
Female						
Single (never married)	21.0	20.5	20.7	20.7	19.8	18.0
Married, spouse present	39.7	41.2	41.7	40.4	40.5	41.5
Widowed, divorced, or separated	8.5	8.4	8.2	8.3	8.5	8.6

Source: Bureau of Labor Statistics,"Employment and Earnings," 1994, 1991, and 1986, Table 33, and "Handbook of Labor Statistics," Table 19, U.S. Government Printing Office, Washington, D.C., 1994, 1991, 1986, and 1983.

Workers give several reasons for part-time work (Table 13-22), reasons that vary with sex, race, age, and urban/rural residence. Among males, unemployment or layoff is the primary reason, and illness or disability and going to school are the second and third most important reasons. Among women, taking care of the home accounts for the reason for more than one-half of all part-time work. The other reasons given by women are much the same as those given by the men workers and are ranked in the same way. Data from 1983 (when the economy was emerging from a very severe recession) on the reasons for part-time work among workers in nonagricultural industries have a very similar distribution to those found among workers in 1993, when unemployment was at an average level. There is little evidence that any particular age, sex, race, or residence group works part-time be-cause it prefers part-time work, except for persons attending school and women with home responsibilities.

A Profile of Working Wives

In 1993, 54.1 percent of all white wives living with their husbands were in the labor force. For black wives the proportion was even higher, 57 percent, and for Hispanic wives it was 49.6 percent. Tables 13-23A, 13-23B and 13-23C show some of the characteristics of married couple families where wives and husbands may or may not participate in the labor force . Among all three racial and Hispanic-origin groups, working wives are most prevalent in metropolitan areas; where there are one or two children under eighteen years of age; where children are of school age; where the husband is under forty-five

Table 13-22. Reasons for Part-Time Work for Workers in Nonagricultural Industries, by Usual Status: 1993

Reasons for working less than 35 hours a week	Numbers (in thousands)			Percent distribution		
	Total	Usually work full time	Usually work part time	Total	Usually work full time	Usually work part time
Total, 16 years and over	26,981	8,135	18,846	100.0	100.0	100.0
Economic reasons	6,106	1,896	4,210	22.6	23.3	22.3
Slack work	2,977	1,599	1,378	11.0	19.7	7.3
Material shortages or repairs to plant and equipment	48	48	...	0.2	0.6	...
New job started during week	181	181	...	0.7	2.2	...
Job terminated during week	67	67	...	0.2	0.8	...
Could find only part-time work	2,832	...	2,832	10.5	...	15.0
Other reasons	20,876	6,239	14,637	77.4	76.7	77.7
Does not want, or unavailable for, full-time work	11,865	...	11,865	44.0	...	63.0
Vacation	1,762	1,762	...	6.5	21.7	...
Illness	1,596	1,424	172	5.9	17.5	0.9
Bad weather	420	420	...	1.6	5.2	...
Industrial dispute	6	6	...	0.0	0.1	...
Legal or religious holiday	1,036	1,036	...	3.8	12.7	...
Full time for this job	1,664	...	1,664	6.2	...	8.8
All other reasons	2,526	1,590	936	9.4	19.5	5.0
Average hours						
Economic reasons	22.4	24.6	21.5	—	—	—
Other reasons	21.7	26.4	19.7	—	—	—
Worked 30-34 hours						
Economic reasons	1,971	863	1,108	7.3	10.6	5.9
Other reasons	6,483	3,483	3,000	24.0	42.8	15.9

Source: U.S. Bureau of Labor Statistics, "Employment and Earnings," Table 31, U.S. Government Printing Office, Washington, D.C., 1994.

years; and where there are no elderly persons in the household. Part-time employment and unemployment of husband were only mild stimulants, and the presence of children was only a mild deterrent.

The hours worked by husbands (measured both by hours worked per week and by weeks worked per year) have a complex relationship to the work experiences of their spouses (see Table 13-24). In general, married couple families where the husband worked 35 or more hours per week and 40 or more weeks per year also had the highest proportion of wives who did the same. Particularly among married couples with young children, the last decade has seen a major increase in full-time employment for both spouses.

Multiple Jobholding

More than one in every twenty workers holds two or more jobs simultaneously. In its survey for 1991 the Bureau of the Census estimated that 7.2 million persons (6.2 percent of all employed workers) were employed at two or more jobs during the week of the survey. This level of multiple jobholding is of long standing. It has fluctuated over the years, and has increased from 4.9 percent in 1980. Wage and salary workers in the services and public administration are more inclined to hold multiple jobs, and those least likely to hold multiple jobs are miners and self-employed and unpaid family workers.

The Status of Nonworkers

What do the people do who are not in the labor force? Why are they not working? These questions are answered, at least in part, by the data in Tables 13-25 and 13-26, which show the status of nonworkers by age, gender, race and ethnicity. Among those who do not want a job now, five categories of current activity outside of the labor force were recognized in 1993: going to school,

Table 13-23A. Characteristics of White Married-couple Families, by Labor Force Status: 1993

Characteristics	All married-couple families		Husband and wife both in labor force					Husband only in labor force			Wife only in labor force			Neither in labor force
	Number (in thousands)	Percent	Total	Both employed	Only husband employed	Only wife employed	Both unemployed	Total	Employed	Unemployed	Total	Employed	Unemployed	
Residence, total	47,601	100.0	54.1	49.7	1.9	2.2	0.3	23.4	22.3	1.1	5.0	4.8	0.2	17.5
Metropolitan areas	35,501	100.0	54.5	50.1	1.9	2.2	0.3	24.2	23.0	1.2	4.7	4.6	0.1	16.6
Central cities	10,617	100.0	52.5	48.0	1.8	2.4	0.3	23.8	22.5	1.4	5.4	5.2	0.2	18.3
Ring	24,883	100.0	55.3	50.9	1.9	2.1	0.3	24.4	23.2	1.1	4.5	4.3	0.1	15.9
Non-metropolitan areas	12,100	100.0	53.2	48.6	2.0	2.2	0.4	21.0	20.1	0.9	5.6	5.4	0.2	20.2
Own children under 18														
Without own children under 18	25,915	100.0	45.2	41.8	1.4	1.8	0.3	17.0	16.2	0.7	7.1	7.0	0.2	30.6
With own children under 18	21,686	100.0	64.8	59.2	2.6	2.7	0.4	31.0	29.5	1.6	2.4	2.3	0.1	1.8
One own child	8,256	100.0	69.6	63.8	2.3	3.1	0.4	25.5	24.4	1.1	2.8	2.7	0.1	2.1
Two own children	8,941	100.0	66.1	60.4	2.6	2.7	0.3	30.5	29.0	1.5	2.1	2.0	0.1	1.2
Three own children	3,303	100.0	56.2	51.4	2.7	2.0	0.2	39.7	37.5	2.2	2.2	2.0	0.2	1.8
Four own children	856	100.0	48.2	41.6	3.4	2.6	0.7	46.3	44.2	2.1	2.6	2.3	0.4	2.9
Five own children	231	100.0	43.7	37.2	5.2	1.3	...	53.7	48.5	4.8	0.4	0.4	...	2.6
Six or more children	98	100.0	26.5	22.4	2.0	...	2.0	61.2	55.1	6.1	2.0	...	2.0	10.2
Total own children under 18	40,543	100.0	61.8	56.3	2.7	2.5	0.3	34.0	32.2	1.8	2.2	2.1	0.2	1.9
Average per family	0.85	—	0.97	0.97	1.17	0.98	0.91	1.23	1.23	1.40	0.38	0.37	0.90	0.09
Average per family with children	1.87	—	1.78	1.78	1.94	1.76	1.82	2.05	2.04	2.19	1.76	1.73	—	1.93
Total with own children under 18	21,685	100.0	64.8	59.2	2.6	2.7	0.4	31.0	29.5	1.6	2.4	2.3	0.1	1.8
Under 6 only	5,664	100.0	59.4	53.9	3.0	2.2	0.3	37.6	35.5	2.2	1.8	1.7	...	1.2
Some under 6, some 6 to 17	4,788	100.0	54.6	49.1	3.0	2.2	0.2	41.7	39.3	2.4	1.6	1.4	0.2	2.1
6 to 17 only	11,233	100.0	71.8	66.1	2.1	3.2	0.5	23.2	22.3	0.9	3.0	2.9	0.2	2.0
Total family members	88,985	100.0	63.4	57.8	2.6	2.7	0.4	32.3	30.6	1.7	2.3	2.2	0.1	2.0
Average per family	4.10	—	4.02	4.01	4.09	4.02	4.55	4.27	4.26	4.42	4.02	3.99	—	4.50
Age of householder														
15 to 19 years	64	100.0	64.1	50.0	10.9	3.1	...	31.3	29.7	1.6	...	...	...	4.7
20 to 24 years	1,248	100.0	65.1	57.7	3.8	3.0	0.5	31.7	29.0	2.6	1.3	1.3	...	2.0
25 to 34 years	9,440	100.0	69.6	62.7	3.5	2.9	0.6	27.5	25.8	1.8	1.9	1.8	0.1	1.0
35 to 44 years	11,958	100.0	70.4	65.2	2.0	2.9	0.3	26.3	25.2	1.1	2.0	1.9	0.1	1.3
45 to 54 years	9,426	100.0	68.3	63.1	2.1	2.7	0.4	24.3	23.3	0.9	4.4	4.3	0.2	3.0
55 to 64 years	6,907	100.0	42.9	39.7	1.2	1.9	0.2	26.4	25.3	1.1	11.4	11.0	0.4	19.2
65 years and over	8,557	100.0	6.2	5.8	0.1	0.2	0.1	10.0	9.7	0.3	8.5	8.4	0.1	75.4
Median age	46.0	—	41.5	41.6	37.6	41.0	41.6	42.9	43.1	39.4	60.3	60.4	55.8	70.9

Source: U.S. Bureau of the Census, Current Population Survey, "Household and Family Characteristics: March 1993," Series P-20, No. 477, U.S. Government Printing Office, Washington, D.C., 1994, Table 15.

Table 13-23B. Characteristics of Black Married-couple Families, by Labor Force Status: 1993

Characteristics	All married-couple families		Husband and wife both in labor force					Husband only in labor force			Wife only in labor force			Neither in labor force
	Number (in thousands)	Percent	Total	Both employed	Only husband employed	Only wife employed	Both unemployed	Total	Employed	Unemployed	Total	Employed	Unemployed	
Residence, total	3,748	100.0	57.0	48.8	3.4	4.1	0.8	18.1	16.4	1.7	8.5	7.7	0.7	16.5
Metropolitan areas	3,138	100.0	58.8	50.1	3.6	4.3	0.9	17.5	15.7	1.8	8.4	7.7	0.6	15.3
Central cities	1,876	100.0	54.4	45.0	3.9	4.9	0.6	18.4	16.5	2.0	9.6	9.0	0.7	17.5
Ring	1,263	100.0	65.4	57.6	3.2	3.5	1.2	16.2	14.6	1.6	6.6	5.9	0.6	11.9
Non-metropolitan areas	610	100.0	47.9	42.3	2.1	3.0	0.5	20.8	19.8	1.0	8.7	7.5	1.1	22.6
Own children under 18														
Without own children under 18	1,803	100.0	42.2	35.8	2.2	3.3	0.9	15.7	14.5	1.2	11.9	11.3	0.7	30.2
With own children under 18	1,945	100.0	70.8	60.9	4.4	4.8	0.7	20.3	18.1	2.1	5.2	4.5	0.8	3.7
One own child	777	100.0	72.5	64.4	2.8	4.5	0.9	18.1	16.1	2.1	6.6	5.8	0.6	2.8
Two own children	669	100.0	75.5	62.6	5.4	6.6	1.0	17.6	15.8	1.8	4.5	3.4	1.0	2.2
Three own children	347	100.0	68.0	58.2	6.9	2.6	...	23.6	20.7	2.9	3.5	2.9	0.6	4.9
Four own children	110	100.0	50.9	43.6	3.6	3.6	...	36.4	36.4	...	4.5	4.5	...	9.1
Five own children	21	100.0	52.4	42.9	...	9.5	...	19.0	19.0	...	14.3	9.5	4.8	14.3
Six or more children	20	100.0	35.0	35.0	...	...	...	45.0	35.0	10.0	5.0	5.0	...	20.0
Total own children under 18	3,744	100.0	68.5	59.0	4.8	4.3	0.4	21.7	19.6	2.1	5.1	4.4	0.7	4.7
Average per family	1.00	—	1.20	1.21	1.42	1.05	—	1.20	1.20	—	0.61	0.57	—	0.28
Average per family with children	1.92	—	1.86	1.87	2.07	1.72	—	2.06	2.08	—	1.88	1.91	—	—
Total with own children under 18	1,945	100.0	70.8	60.9	4.4	4.8	0.7	20.3	18.1	2.1	5.2	4.5	0.8	3.7
Under 6 only	466	100.0	67.2	54.9	4.9	5.8	1.7	24.7	20.8	3.9	4.5	3.0	1.3	3.6
Some under 6, some 6 to 17	450	100.0	69.3	58.2	6.2	4.4	0.4	24.9	23.3	1.6	2.4	1.8	0.7	3.3
6 to 17 only	1,029	100.0	73.1	64.7	3.5	4.6	0.3	16.2	14.8	1.5	6.9	6.2	0.6	3.8
Total family members	8,377	100.0	69.6	60.3	4.4	4.4	0.6	20.6	18.6	2.0	5.7	4.9	0.7	4.1
Average per family	4.31	—	4.23	4.26	4.28	3.91	—	4.37	4.41	—	4.65	4.76	—	—
Age of householder														
15 to 19 years	6	100.0	66.7			66.7					33.3		33.3	
20 to 24 years	108	100.0	55.6	34.3	4.6	13.0	3.7	39.8	29.6	10.2	3.7	3.7	...	0.9
25 to 34 years	794	100.0	74.8	63.2	6.2	4.7	0.8	19.3	18.0	1.3	4.4	3.3	1.0	1.6
35 to 44 years	997	100.0	76.3	66.0	4.6	4.7	0.9	16.3	14.9	1.5	4.3	3.9	0.5	2.8
45 to 54 years	735	100.0	68.6	59.3	3.3	5.2	1.0	17.6	15.9	1.5	8.3	7.8	0.5	5.4
55 to 64 years	527	100.0	35.7	32.8	0.2	2.1	0.6	26.4	23.9	2.5	18.0	18.0	...	20.1
65 years and over	581	100.0	4.5	4.3	...	0.2	...	8.6	7.9	0.7	13.3	11.9	1.4	73.7
Median age	44.7	—	40.4	40.9	36.2	39.4	—	43.9	44.0	—	56.5	57.2	—	69.0

Source: U.S. Bureau of the Census, Current Population Survey, "Household and Family Characteristics: March 1993," Series P-20, No. 477, U.S. Government Printing Office, Washington, D.C., 1994, Table 15.

Table 13-23C. Characteristics of Hispanic Married-couple Families, by Labor Force Status: 1993

Characteristics	All married-couple families		Husband and wife both in labor force					Husband only in labor force			Wife only in labor force			Neither in labor force
	Number (in thousands)	Percent	Total	Both employed	Only husband employed	Only wife employed	Both unemployed	Total	Employed	Unemployed	Total	Employed	Unemployed	
Residence, total	3,673	100.0	49.6	41.6	3.8	3.7	0.6	35.1	31.7	3.4	4.2	3.6	0.6	11.1
Metropolitan areas	3,355	100.0	49.7	41.5	3.8	3.8	0.6	35.1	31.6	3.5	4.2	3.6	0.6	10.9
Central cities	1,739	100.0	45.9	38.4	3.4	3.7	0.5	37.0	33.2	3.7	4.6	4.5	0.7	12.0
Ring	1,616	100.0	53.8	44.9	4.2	3.9	0.8	33.2	29.8	3.3	3.2	2.7	0.5	9.8
Non-metropolitan areas	318	100.0	48.7	42.1	3.8	2.5	0.3	34.9	32.7	2.2	3.8	3.8	...	12.6
Own children under 18														
Without own children under 18	1,319	100.0	42.2	36.0	3.5	2.4	0.4	26.8	24.1	2.7	6.4	5.9	0.5	24.5
With own children under 18	2,355	100.0	53.8	44.7	4.0	4.4	0.7	39.7	36.0	3.8	2.9	2.3	0.6	3.6
One own child	820	100.0	56.1	46.1	4.5	4.9	0.7	35.6	33.4	2.3	2.8	2.7	0.1	5.5
Two own children	832	100.0	56.9	47.5	3.2	5.4	0.7	38.5	35.6	2.9	3.1	2.5	0.7	1.4
Three own children	447	100.0	49.4	44.1	2.2	2.7	0.4	44.7	38.0	6.7	2.9	1.8	0.9	3.1
Four own children	167	100.0	52.7	40.7	9.0	3.0	...	40.1	36.5	3.6	2.4	1.2	1.2	5.4
Five own children	58	100.0	31.0	22.4	5.2	3.4	1.7	63.8	55.2	8.6	1.7	1.7	...	3.4
Six or more children	30	100.0	16.7	3.3	6.7	...	6.7	66.7	46.7	20.0	6.7	...	6.7	10.0
Total own children under 18	4,910	100.0	51.1	42.3	4.1	3.9	0.8	42.6	37.8	4.9	2.9	2.0	0.8	3.4
Average per family	1.34	—	1.38	1.36	1.45	1.43	—	1.62	1.59	1.91	0.92	0.75	—	0.41
Average per family with children	2.08	—	1.98	1.97	2.16	1.86	—	2.24	2.19	2.68	—	—	—	1.97
Total with own children under 18	2,355	100.0	53.8	44.7	4.0	4.4	0.7	39.7	36.0	3.8	2.9	2.3	0.6	3.6
Under 6 only	617	100.0	46.7	39.1	4.4	3.9	0.8	46.8	42.1	4.7	2.3	2.1	0.2	2.6
Some under 6, some 6 to 17	691	100.0	48.0	39.4	4.6	3.6	0.4	46.3	40.1	6.4	2.6	1.7	0.7	3.0
6 to 17 only	1,047	100.0	60.6	51.5	3.3	5.1	0.8	31.2	29.7	1.5	3.6	2.7	0.8	4.5
Total family members	10,869	100.0	51.8	42.8	4.0	4.0	1.0	41.7	37.4	4.3	2.8	2.1	0.7	3.8
Average per family	4.62	—	4.45	4.42	4.65	4.16	—	4.84	4.80	5.21	—	—	—	4.9
Age of householder														
15 to 19 years	14	100.0	85.7	35.7	14.3	42.9	...	14.3	7.1	7.1	...	...	...	...
20 to 24 years	191	100.0	50.8	40.3	7.3	3.1	...	42.4	37.7	5.2	3.1	3.1	...	3.7
25 to 34 years	1,058	100.0	56.9	47.8	4.0	4.3	0.9	39.9	36.4	3.6	2.0	1.9	0.1	1.2
35 to 44 years	1,028	100.0	59.7	50.2	4.9	3.9	0.5	34.1	30.6	3.5	3.1	2.3	0.7	3.1
45 to 54 years	669	100.0	52.8	44.4	3.9	3.9	0.6	37.8	34.2	3.6	4.6	3.6	1.2	4.6
55 to 64 years	402	100.0	33.1	28.4	1.7	2.7	0.5	36.1	32.6	3.5	10.2	9.2	1.0	20.9
65 years and over	310	100.0	3.9	3.9	...	...	...	11.3	10.3	0.6	7.4	7.1	0.3	77.4
Median age	40.3	—	38.0	38.1	37.4	37.9	—	39.1	39.1	38.6	50.7	51.9	—	67.3

Source: U.S. Bureau of the Census, Current Population Survey, "Household and Family Characteristics: March 1993," Series P-20, No. 477, U.S. Government Printing Office, Washington, D.C., 1994, Table 15.

Table 13-24. Work Experience of Wives in Married-couple Families, by Work Experience of Husband, Presence and Age of Children, and Race-ethnicity: 1989

Work experience of husband and wife	With no children under 18				With children under 6 years				With children 6 to 17 years only			
	Total	White	Black	Hispanic	Total	White	Black	Hispanic	Total	White	Black	Hispanic
Husband worked 35+ hours and 40+ weeks	100.0	100.0	100.0	100.0	100.0	100.0	100.0	100.0	100.0	100.0	100.0	100.0
Wife worked 35+ hours and 40+ weeks	53.0	52.6	56.8	49.1	32.5	30.6	52.5	30.1	46.2	44.3	63.9	48.9
Wife worked 35+ hours and 1-39 weeks	6.2	6.1	5.8	7.3	10.9	10.5	14.5	11.0	7.4	7.1	10.2	8.4
Wife worked 1-34 hours and 40+ weeks	11.6	12.1	7.5	5.1	12.2	13.3	3.0	5.3	16.2	17.3	6.4	7.6
Wife worked 1-34 hours and 1-39 weeks	5.2	5.3	3.5	2.6	12.5	13.0	8.8	8.5	9.7	10.2	4.8	6.7
Wife not in labor force	24.0	23.9	26.4	36.0	31.9	32.6	21.3	45.2	20.7	21.1	14.6	28.4
Husband worked 35+ hours and 1-39 weeks	100.0	100.0	100.0	100.0	100.0	100.0	100.0	100.0	100.0	100.0	100.0	100.0
Wife worked 35+ hours and 40+ weeks	36.2	35.2	51.7	38.1	27.3	27.9	26.7	17.9	42.0	40.4	56.4	34.2
Wife worked 35+ hours and 1-39 weeks	11.1	10.7	18.5	10.3	17.4	16.6	15.6	18.9	14.9	15.0	10.6	12.3
Wife worked 1-34 hours and 40+ weeks	9.5	9.9	1.4	6.0	6.6	7.3	3.7	2.1	12.9	14.4	2.8	8.9
Wife worked 1-34 hours and 1-39 weeks	6.6	6.7	7.3	4.1	13.3	12.9	14.1	7.8	8.5	9.2	1.6	2.8
Wife not in labor force	36.6	37.6	21.0	41.6	35.5	35.4	39.9	53.4	21.6	21.1	28.6	41.9
Husband worked 1-34 hours and 40+ weeks	100.0	100.0	100.0	100.0	100.0	100.0	100.0	100.0	100.0	100.0	100.0	100.0
Wife worked 35+ hours and 40+ weeks	27.6	27.5	24.1	21.4	39.0	39.3	42.9	13.8	39.6	41.7	26.6	36.2
Wife worked 35+ hours and 1-39 weeks	3.2	2.7	12.9	5.8	11.1	11.5	4.2	21.2	2.8	3.3	...	6.6
Wife worked 1-34 hours and 40+ weeks	19.0	18.6	28.5	1.1	11.2	12.4	...	11.6	19.0	20.2	19.8	10.5
Wife worked 1-34 hours and 1-39 weeks	8.3	8.6	2.0	3.8	15.7	13.9	41.9	26.6	11.7	11.0	23.2	22.5
Wife not in labor force	41.9	42.6	32.5	67.9	23.1	22.8	11.0	26.9	26.9	23.8	30.3	24.2
Husband worked 1-34 hours and 1-39 weeks	100.0	100.0	100.0	100.0	100.0	100.0	100.0	100.0	100.0	100.0	100.0	100.0
Wife worked 35+ hours and 40+ weeks	21.6	21.3	19.5	51.0	29.7	25.1	34.5	19.1	47.7	46.9	45.4	33.1
Wife worked 35+ hours and 1-39 weeks	5.4	5.4	5.5	...	14.7	15.6	19.4	14.3	11.2	12.8	6.1	19.6
Wife worked 1-34 hours and 40+ weeks	9.6	9.1	17.6	29.4	6.6	5.3	15.6	9.7	12.6	13.9	9.2	12.3
Wife worked 1-34 hours and 1-39 weeks	12.3	13.2	3.5	11.5	13.7	15.4	9.1	9.4	10.1	12.7	...	...
Wife not in labor force	51.2	51.0	54.0	8.2	35.3	38.6	21.4	47.6	18.4	13.7	39.3	35.0
Husband not in labor force	100.0	100.0	100.0	100.0	100.0	100.0	100.0	100.0	100.0	100.0	100.0	100.0
Wife worked 35+ hours and 40+ weeks	10.5	9.7	17.4	12.3	22.4	23.9	34.6	9.6	36.2	35.8	41.6	37.6
Wife worked 35+ hours and 1-39 weeks	2.2	2.1	3.2	0.3	9.7	8.6	23.6	15.5	8.7	9.3	5.7	2.9
Wife worked 1-34 hours and 40+ weeks	4.4	4.2	6.2	3.4	6.4	7.2	7.5	3.2	8.3	7.8	11.6	7.9
Wife worked 1-34 hours and 1-39 weeks	2.7	2.7	3.4	2.3	3.8	3.8	3.9	...	4.6	5.4	...	8.2
Wife not in labor force	80.0	81.3	69.9	81.7	57.7	56.5	30.3	71.7	42.1	41.7	41.1	43.4

Source: U.S. Bureau of the Census for the Bureau of Labor Statistics, "Current Population Survey," 1990 (machine-readable data files), Bureau of the Census, Washington, D.C., 1990.

Table 13-25. Persons Not in the Labor Force, by Reason, Sex, and Age: 1993
[numbers in thousands]

Reason and sex	Total	16 to 19 years	20 to 24 years	25 to 59 years	60 years and over
Total not in labor force	65,509	6,429	4,027	21,773	33,280
Do not want a job now	90.4	81.8	78.9	83.8	97.7
Current activity:					
Going to school	10.5	66.5	40.7	4.5	0.1
Ill/disabled	8.4	0.4	3.5	14.3	6.7
Keeping house	31.9	4.8	24.2	48.1	27.5
Retired	32.2	...	...	2.4	61.9
Other activity	7.3	10.1	10.5	14.4	1.6
Want a job now	9.6	18.2	21.1	16.2	2.3
Reason for not looking:					
School attendance	2.4	13.8	7.5	1.6	...
Ill heath/disability	1.7	0.2	1.2	3.9	0.7
Home responsibility	2.0	1.0	5.7	4.5	0.2
Think cannot get a job	1.7	1.6	3.0	3.1	0.7
Job-market factors	1.1	0.9	2.2	2.3	0.3
Personal factors	0.6	0.6	0.8	0.8	0.4
Other reasons[1]	1.9	1.6	3.7	3.2	0.8
Males not in labor force	22,987	3,149	1,452	5,131	13,256
Do not want a job now	89.6	80.5	78.9	77.9	97.5
Current activity:					
Going to school	14.6	68.8	57.0	7.2	...
Ill/disabled	12.0	0.4	5.4	33.0	7.3
Keeping house	1.9	0.8	1.7	4.0	1.4
Retired	51.4	...	...	7.3	8.6
Other activity	9.7	10.4	15.0	26.5	2.4
Want a job now	10.4	19.5	21.1	22.1	2.5
Reason for not looking:					
School attendance	3.3	15.7	9.8	2.3	...
Ill heath/disability	2.4	0.2	1.8	8.5	0.7
Think cannot get a job	2.3	1.9	4.1	5.8	0.8
Other reasons[1]	2.4	1.7	5.3	5.5	1.0
Females not in labor force	42,522	3,280	2,576	16,642	20,025
Do not want a job now	90.8	83.2	78.8	85.6	97.8
Current activity:					
Going to school	8.3	64.3	31.5	3.6	0.1
Ill/disabled	6.5	0.4	2.4	8.6	6.2
Keeping house	48.1	8.7	36.9	61.7	44.7
Retired	21.8	...	...	0.9	45.6
Other activity	6.0	9.8	8.0	10.7	1.2
Want a job now	9.3	16.8	21.1	14.4	2.2
Reason for not looking:					
School attendance	1.8	12.1	6.3	1.3	...
Ill heath/disability	1.3	0.2	0.8	2.4	0.6
Home responsibility	3.1	1.9	8.9	5.8	0.3
Think cannot get a job	1.4	1.3	2.3	2.3	0.6
Other reasons[1]	1.6	1.4	2.9	2.5	0.7

[1] Includes a small number of men not looking for work because of "home responsibilities."

Source: U.S. Bureau of Labor Statistics, "Employment and Earnings, 1994," Table 35, U.S. Government Printing Office, Washington, D.C., 1994.

Table 13-26. Persons Not in the Labor Force, by Reason, Race-ethnicity, Sex, and Age: 1993
[numbers in thousands]

Reason and sex	Total	16 to 24 years	25 to 59 years	60 years and over	Sex	
					Males	Females
Whites not in labor force	54,562	7,676	17,411	29,475	18,929	35,633
Do not want a job now	91.6	82.0	85.1	97.8	90.7	92.0
Current activity:						
Going to school	9.4	57.4	4.0	0.1	13.2	7.3
Ill/disabled	7.7	1.6	13.3	5.9	11.1	5.8
Keeping house	33.1	13.1	51.0	27.8	1.7	49.9
Retired	34.5	...	2.6	62.3	55.9	23.2
Other activity	6.9	9.9	14.3	1.7	8.9	5.8
Want a job now	8.4	18.0	14.8	2.2	9.2	8.0
Reason for not looking:						
School attendance	1.9	10.7	1.3	...	2.8	1.5
Ill heath/disability	1.5	0.5	3.5	0.6	2.2	1.1
Home responsibility	1.7	2.4	4.1	0.2	...	2.7
Think cannot get a job	1.4	1.9	2.6	0.6	2.0	1.2
Other reasons[1]	1.8	2.4	3.3	0.8	2.3	1.5
Blacks not in labor force	8,386	2,119	3,242	3,025	3,167	5,220
Do not want a job now	83.2	74.7	76.5	96.4	83.9	82.8
Current activity:						
Going to school	14.5	51.0	4.2	...	17.9	12.5
Ill/disabled	13.7	1.8	21.6	13.7	17.8	11.3
Keeping house	23.8	10.1	33.2	23.4	3.3	36.3
Retired	21.5	...	1.7	57.8	31.1	15.7
Other activity	9.6	11.8	15.9	1.4	13.8	7.0
Want a job now	16.8	25.3	23.5	3.6	16.0	17.2
Reason for not looking:						
School attendance	4.6	14.2	2.5	...	5.6	3.9
Ill heath/disability	3.1	0.9	6.1	1.3	3.7	2.7
Home responsibility	3.7	4.4	6.5	0.2	...	5.9
Think cannot get a job	3.4	3.2	5.4	1.3	3.9	3.1
Other reasons[1]	2.1	2.6	3.0	0.8	2.8	1.6
Hispanics not in labor force	5,377	1,417	2,478	1,482	1,569	3,808
Do not want a job now	85.7	81.0	81.6	97.1	82.3	87.1
Current activity:						
Going to school	13.7	46.8	2.9	0.1	21.1	10.7
Ill/disabled	8.8	1.1	12.2	10.4	15.6	6.0
Keeping house	40.5	24.0	56.2	30.0	2.9	56.0
Retired	15.5	...	0.5	55.3	31.2	9.0
Other activity	7.3	9.1	9.8	1.3	11.6	5.5
Want a job now	13.9	18.3	17.7	3.5	16.6	12.8
Reason for not looking:						
School attendance	3.1	8.8	1.7	0.1	4.8	2.4
Ill heath/disability	1.9	0.4	3.3	1.2	3.6	1.3
Home responsibility	3.7	3.4	6.0	0.3	...	5.3
Think cannot get a job	2.6	2.2	3.7	1.3	3.9	2.1
Other reasons[1]	2.6	3.6	3.1	0.7	4.3	1.9

[1] Includes a small number of men not looking for work because of "home responsibilities."

Source: U.S. Bureau of Labor Statistics, "Employment and Earnings, 1994," Table 36, U.S. Government Printing Office, Washington, D.C., 1994.

keeping house, retired, ill/disabled, and other activity. Among those who want a job but are not in the labor force now, the following were the five major reasons for not looking: school attendance, ill health/disability, home responsibility, the respondent thinking he or she cannot get a job (because of job-market or personal factors), and other reasons. The Bureau of the Census has warned that the statistics for some of these categories have a low degree of reliability. For this reason only the largest differences are accepted here as being valid.

Overall, twice as many blacks who are outside the labor force (16.8 percent) want a job now as whites (8.4 percent); Hispanics fall between them at 13.7 percent. About one out of every five males at ages 16 to 59 years and females at ages 20 to 24 years not in the labor force wants a job now; other groups have lower proportions desiring employment. At ages below twenty-five, most men and unmarried women who are not in the labor force are absent from it because they are students. Among all groups, those over age 60 who are not in the labor force but want employment never total more than four percent.

Unemployment

Characteristics of the Unemployed

As was shown in Figures 13-1A and 13-1B, some members of the labor force are unemployed—that is, seeking work. A very sensitive indicator of the economy's well-being is the percentage of the labor force that is unemployed. (See the Definition Box for definitions of unemployment and unemployment rates.) Some unemployment is inevitable, and at any given moment in time a considerable number of workers will be seeking work, even in conditions of so-called full employment, due to "normal" labor turnover.

This "structural unemployment" has several causes: new workers in the labor force, migration from one community to another, quitting because of dissatisfaction, discharge for unsatisfactory performance, etc. However, this "frictional unemployment" is not very great, involving perhaps 2 to 4 percent of all workers. As soon as the unemployment rate (the percentage of the labor force that is unemployed) rises much above this minimum, it becomes a subject of immediate and serious concern. The involuntary loss of jobs due to retrenchment of operations in a firm or industry is the major cause of unemployment beyond this minimum. It is a direct indicator of significant prevalence of economic hardship that manifests itself quickly in terms of poverty and increased demands for unemployment benefits.

During the early 1990s, however, unemployment began to be watched closely by another set of observers: investors in the stock and bond markets. They theorized that if unemployment rates shrank, then firms would have to pay higher salaries to get the employees they needed. This would result in inflationary pressures in the economy, and lead the Federal Reserve Board to raise the prime lending rate in order to slow inflation by making capital more scarce. This, in turn, would make investment in the stock market less attractive. On March 8, 1996, for example, when the Labor Department announced a far greater than expected monthly rise in U.S. employment, the stock market tumbled 170 points, the third-largest one-day decline (in terms of decline in points) in stock market history. The assumed negative linkage between unemployment and inflation means that some important decision-makers may feel that unemployment can be too low as well as too high.

One of the main reasons why the Bureau of Labor Statistics and the Bureau of the Census conduct the Current Population Survey once a month is to keep a vigilant watch on the level of unemployment. Not only must this survey show the total amount of unemployment, but it must also indicate what kinds of people, and which occupations and industries, are most affected by changes in the overall unemployment level. Although the data on current unemployment collected at the time of the decennial census refer to only one week out of a total span of ten years, they are valuable in that they reveal the comparative unemployment rates of small areas and the detailed characteristics of unemployed persons.

Long-Term Trends in Unemployment

Figure 13-6 and Table 13-27 report annual rates of unemployment from an economic historian's estimates for 1900-1949 and for estimates derived from Current Population Surveys for selected years since 1950.

No one knows exactly to what heights the rate of unemployment rose during the depths of the Depression in the 1930s, or how many workers were unemployed. Using the available data, labor force experts estimate that 24.9 percent of all labor force members were unemployed in 1933. These estimates indicate that when the economic depression was at its worst, approximately one worker in four was without a job. Double-digit unemployment, hovering near 20 percent, lasted for a full decade, from 1931 to 1941, after which it plunged practically to zero because of the wartime mobilization of labor.

Various labor force experts have attempted to extend estimates of unemployment backward to years before the 1930s. Among these are the estimates made by Stanley Lebergott, which are graphed as Figure 13-6.[1] A study of this graph shows that, if the estimates are correct, rates of unemployment fluctuated more violently in the pre-Depression years than they have in the post-World War II years and that some of the economic low points that occurred earlier in the century actually were quite severe and caused extensive unemployment . For example, the "hard times" of 1908 to 1911, 1914 to 1915, and 1921 to 1922 appear to have been as severe as the 1980-83 depression.

Moreover, it appears that the average level of unemployment among nonfarm workers, even during "good times," was considerably higher than it has been in most years since World War II. Thus, the two decades from 1948 to 1968 are unique and stand out as the longest period of low unemployment during this century. The lowest recorded rates of unemployment occurred during World War II, 1942-45, when severe manpower shortages caused unemployment rates to fall almost to 1 percent. Unemployment was moderately high during the readjustment immediately after World War II.

Unemployment must also be understood in the context of long-term trends in fertility rates, in norms about employment for men and women, and in structural changes in the economy. During the period between 1967

Figure 13-6. Unemployment Rate[1]: 1900-1994

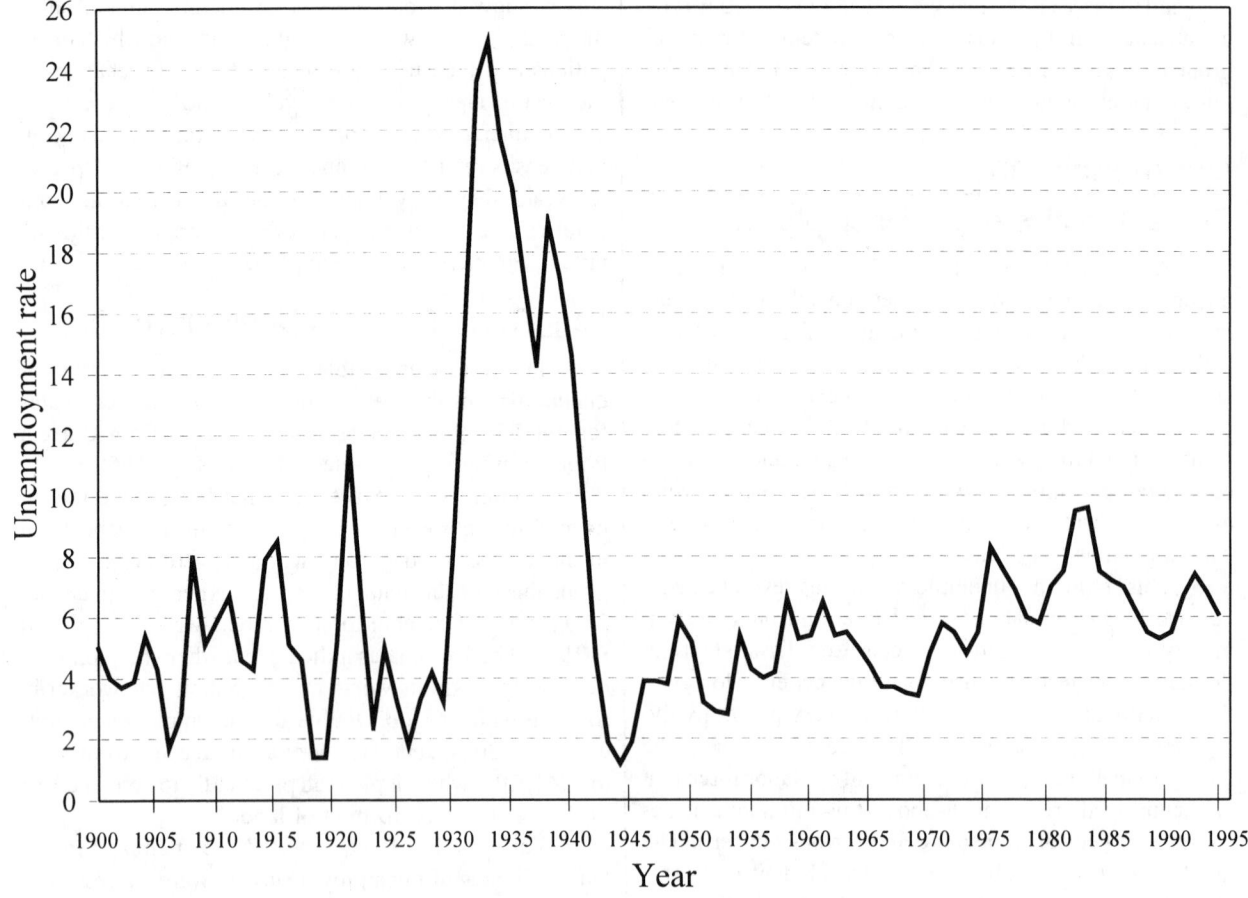

[1] Population 14 years and over prior to 1947; 16 years and over to present.
Source: 1900-1994 Bureau of Labor Statistics data.

and 1979 (see Table 13-27), unemployment rates moved upwards significantly; this was also a period during which the annual rate of growth of the labor force seldom fell below 2 percent per year (Table 13-1). By way of comparison, the labor force grew only 11.9 percent for the decade (or scarcely more than one percent per year) during the low-unemployment years of 1950-60. Rising unemployment rates were one consequence of the national economy's inability to fully absorb the baby boom cohorts as they moved into the labor market during the late 1960s and 1970s.

The rapid growth of female employment to participation rates hitherto unknown in American history (see Table 13-1) also led to a crowding of the labor market. In addition, by 1990, women's unemployment rates dropped consistently below those of men (Table 13-27). As will be shown later, this is because although women frequently have higher unemployment rates than men in the same industry, they appear to be better at picking jobs in industries with lower unemployment rates.

Unemployment is also a consequence of changing currents in the world economy and in the application of new technologies to various industries. Many low-skilled jobs have been replaced by machinery or been lost to lower-paid competition overseas. Many of the lost jobs required little skill and training, but those who lost them had characteristics (levels of education, age, region, etc.) that made it difficult for them to find similar employment elsewhere. Clerical and secretarial jobs, a key stepping stone in the upward mobility of black women out of private household service jobs, were being replaced by automated word-processing and voice- and electronic-mail systems of the 1980s and 1990s.

Unemployment During the 1980-84 Recession

During the period since 1973 a high rate of unemployment has been a serious national economic problem (Figure 13-6). In the early 1980s the unemployment rate in some months rose above ten percent, and for 1982 and 1983 it averaged 9.5 percent. This was double or triple the rate that normal labor turnover generated in conditions of relatively full employment in preceding decades.

Table 13-27. Annual Average Number of Unemployed Persons and Unemployment Rate[1], by Sex: 1950-1994

Year	Number of unemployed, in thousands			Unemployment rate		
	Total	Male	Female	Total	Male	Female
1994	7,996	4,367	3,629	6.1	6.2	6.0
1993	8,734	4,932	3,801	6.8	7.1	6.5
1992	9,384	5,380	4,005	7.4	7.8	6.9
1991	8,426	4,817	3,609	6.7	7.0	6.3
1990	6,874	3,799	3,075	5.5	5.6	5.4
1989	6,528	3,525	3,003	5.3	5.2	5.4
1988	6,701	3,655	3,046	5.5	5.5	5.6
1987	7,425	4,101	3,324	6.2	6.2	6.2
1986	8,237	4,530	3,707	7.0	6.9	7.1
1985	8,312	4,521	3,791	7.2	7.0	7.4
1984	8,539	4,744	3,794	7.5	7.4	7.6
1983	10,717	6,260	4,457	9.6	9.9	9.2
1982	10,678	6,179	4,499	9.5	9.9	9.4
1981	8,273	4,577	3,696	7.5	7.4	7.9
1980	7,637	4,267	3,370	7.0	6.9	7.4
1975	7,929	4,442	3,486	8.3	7.9	9.3
1970	4,093	2,238	1,855	4.8	4.4	5.9
1965	3,366	1,914	1,452	4.4	4.0	5.5
1960	3,852	2,486	1,366	5.4	5.4	5.9
1955	2,852	1,854	998	4.3	4.2	4.9
1950	3,288	2,239	1,049	5.2	5.1	5.7

[1] Population 14 years and over prior to 1947; 16 years and over to present.

Source: U.S. Bureau of Labor Statistics, "Employment and Earnings," U.S. Government Printing Office, Washington, D.C., 1995, Tables 1 and 2.

At its worst, the unemployment rate reached a peak of 10.7 percent when 11.9 million persons were seeking work in November of 1982. These high rates were one of the symptoms, as well as one of the causes, of the most severe economic recession since the 1930s.

In long-term perspective the rates of unemployment for 1982-83 that were widely regarded as intolerable are close to the average annual rate for the twentieth century. However, the volume of suffering involved, in terms of the number of persons unemployed (10.7 million unemployed), in 1982-83 approached the all-time record of 12.8 million set in 1933. As the labor force continues to grow in size, if the rates do not decline substantially the volume will eventually surpass the 1933 record (unemployment had already reached 9.384 million by 1992).

Seasonal Variations in Unemployment Trends

There is a seasonal cycle in unemployment; the number of jobless persons and the rate of unemployment tend to rise above the yearly average during the months of January, February, and March. These are the "slow" months with respect to employment. Retail trade is at a low ebb; winter weather hampers construction; agricultural activity and many types of manufacturing are sus-

pended or greatly curtailed because of bad weather. Unemployment drops sharply during April and May, and rises again during June, when schools close and pour out a new generation of graduates seeking jobs and a flood of students seeking part-time summer employment. By August or September a large part of the new workers have been absorbed into the labor force. Unemployment sinks to lower levels during the last quarter, when students are in school and when retail trade and other industries are at their peak in preparation for the holidays. This seasonal pattern makes it necessary for statisticians at the Bureau of Labor Statistics to adjust the measured rate of unemployment before releasing data that is comparable to that of preceding months. However, shifts in employment, such as more students combining school and employment, and shifts toward more year-round employment in service industries has led to a decline in the magnitude of seasonal swings in unemployment in recent years.

Differentials in Unemployment

Certain categories of workers are relatively secure in their jobs, whereas others lead a more precarious existence. It is useful to answer the question, "Who are the unemployed?" This may be done by examining the differences in rates of unemployment among various subgroups of the population. Differentials will be presented for age, sex and race-ethnicity, industry and occupation. Differentials in unemployment can vary widely, both from region to region and from one stage of the business cycle to another.

Age Differentials In Rates of Unemployment

The highest rates of unemployment are found among young people. Table 13-28 provides unemployment rates by age, sex, and race-ethnicity for 1994. The pattern of peak unemployment during youth, with a steady decline to age fifty-four, is consistent for all groups. At ages sixteen to twenty-five teenagers and young adults are leaving school and entering the labor force to seek their first full-time jobs. Many at these ages are searching for part-time work they can do while they attend school, or for temporary vacation work. At these ages many workers are living with parents and move from job to job, doing whatever work is available even temporarily but with frequent and sometimes prolonged unemployment between jobs. Hence among workers sixteen to nineteen years old the rates of unemployment are usually between two and three times as great as the rate for the labor force as a whole.

From one perspective, persons of this age who are seeking full-time year-round work should not be in the labor force at all, but should continue in school. The fact that they are in the labor force may mean that they in-

Table 13-28. Unemployment Rates, by Age, Sex, and Race-ethnicity: 1994

Age	All races			White			Black			Hispanic		
	Total	Male	Female	Total	Male	Female	Total	Male	Female	Total	Male	Female
16 years and over	6.1	6.2	6.0	5.3	5.4	5.2	11.5	12.0	11.0	9.9	9.4	10.7
16 to 19 years	17.6	19.0	16.2	15.1	16.3	13.8	35.2	37.6	32.6	24.5	26.3	22.2
16 and 17 years	19.9	21.0	18.7	17.6	18.5	16.6	36.1	39.3	32.9	31.7	33.3	29.7
18 and 19 years	16.0	17.6	14.3	13.3	14.7	11.8	34.6	36.5	32.5	20.6	22.5	18.1
20 to 24 years	9.7	10.2	9.2	8.1	8.8	7.4	19.5	19.4	19.6	11.8	10.8	13.5
25 to 34 years	6.0	5.9	6.2	5.2	5.2	5.1	11.1	10.6	11.7	9.0	8.4	10.1
35 to 44 years	4.6	4.5	4.7	4.0	3.9	4.2	8.5	9.1	8.0	7.7	6.6	9.2
45 to 54 years	4.0	4.0	4.0	3.7	3.7	3.7	5.6	6.5	4.9	8.1	8.1	8.0
55 to 64 years	4.1	4.4	3.9	3.9	4.1	3.7	5.4	6.0	4.9	7.3	7.4	7.1
65 years and over	4.0	4.0	4.0	3.8	3.7	3.9	6.2	8.2	4.4	7.9	10.5	3.6

Source: U.S. Bureau of Labor Statistics, "Employment and Earnings," U.S. Government Printing Office, Washington, D.C., 1995,
Tables 3 and 4.

clude school dropouts and the least educationally qualified members of their generation, hence the least employable, which could contribute to the high unemployment rates for these ages. On the demand side, however, many of the jobs available to part-time, temporary or teenage workers have little chance for advancement, and often provide no additional pay for seniority; hence it is not surprising that there is a high rate of labor turnover.

By the time they reach age twenty-five, most workers have passed through this phase of job mobility, and unemployment has more serious implications. Unemployment rates at ages 35-64 are much lower than the average for all ages; they were only 2 to 3 percent in the 1950s and 1960s, but they had risen to above 4 percent by 1994, a year of otherwise relatively low unemployment rates.

Beyond age sixty-five unemployment rates tend to be slightly higher than for ages 45-54, but remain quite low; elderly workers without jobs tend to report themselves as not being in the labor force rather than as unemployed. Until the 1980s and early 1990s, when unemployment was at a low ebb, almost everyone had a job except the very youngest and some of the very oldest people. Rising unemployment affected all age groups, but it caused the greatest relative increase in the central age groups, i.e. those 25-54 years of age. When the overall rate of unemployment rose, differentials became less sharp, because the proportional increases in joblessness were greatest among adult workers. Thus by the 1990s, even during good economic times, unemployment began to have a more even effect on workers throughout the age spectrum.

Age Differentials by Sex and Race-Ethnicity

All age groups of the black and Hispanic populations have higher unemployment rates than those of the white population, but each shows the general age differentials described above. However, the age pattern is not identical for males and females, or for all of the race-ethnic groups. Age differentials in unemployment (Table 13-28) for black workers are sharper than for either whites or Hispanics; they tend to be extremely high in youth and much lower in the later working years. Black females tend to have even sharper age differentials than black males. Hispanic workers, in contrast, have less sharp differentials overall than the white population, and Hispanic women have smaller age differentials than Hispanic men. Thus, although each race-ethnic group tends to have its own unique level of unemployment, that risk is spread most unevenly over the ages among the black and most evenly among the Hispanic populations.

Black participants in the labor force have much higher rates of unemployment than do white or Hispanic workers. All available evidence indicates that this phenomenon is so universal as to be almost a "social law" underlying the operation of American society. It applies to each age group individually, and to both males and females. It has persisted throughout the span of time for which unemployment statistics have been collected. All evidence seems to indicate that, at least on a gross basis (not considering differences in other characteristics), the cliché "Blacks are the last to be hired and the first to be fired" has a solid basis in fact. The extent to which this

Table 13-29. Unemployment Rate and Percent Distribution of the Unemployed, by Industry: 1950-1994

Industry	Unemployment rate					
	1994	1990	1980	1970	1960	1950
Total[1]	6.1	5.5	7.1	4.9	5.5	5.3
Agriculture	11.3	9.7	11.1	7.5	8.3	9.0
Mining	5.4	4.8	6.4	3.1	9.5	6.7
Construction	11.8	11.1	14.1	9.7	13.5	12.2
Manufacturing	5.6	5.8	8.5	5.6	6.2	6.2
Durables	5.2	5.8	8.9	5.7	6.4	5.7
Nondurables	6.0	5.8	7.9	5.4	6.1	6.8
Transportation/public utilities	4.8	3.8	4.9	3.2	4.6	4.7
Wholesale and retail trade	7.4	6.4	7.4	5.3	5.9	6.0
Finance/insurance/real estate	3.6	3.0	3.4	2.8	2.4	2.2
Service industries	5.9	5.0	5.9	4.7	5.1	6.4
Government	3.1	2.3	4.1	2.2	2.4	3.0
	Percent distribution					
Total	100.0	100.0	100.0	100.0	100.0	100.0
Agriculture	2.7	2.6	2.3	2.3	4.1	4.9
Mining	0.5	0.5	0.8	0.4	1.5	1.8
Construction	9.1	10.3	9.7	9.3	12.0	10.6
Manufacturing	14.4	18.4	26.2	29.2	28.6	29.8
Durables	7.9	10.9	16.6	17.6	16.3	14.2
Nondurables	6.6	7.5	9.6	11.6	12.4	15.6
Transportation/public utilities	4.3	3.6	3.7	3.7	5.0	5.7
Wholesale and retail trade	23.7	21.9	18.9	17.9	16.5	17.6
Finance/insurance/real estate	3.4	3.2	2.5	2.5	1.6	1.2
Service industries	22.5	19.3	14.0	14.0	12.1	13.7
Government	11.8	9.7	8.9	6.9	5.0	5.4
Other workers	7.6	10.5	13.0	13.8	13.6	9.3

[1] Prior to 1990, total includes the self-employed, unpaid family workers, those with no previous work experience, and those whose last job was in the Armed Forces, now shown separately. In 1990 and 1994, self-employed and unpaid family workers are classified with government workers.

Source: U.S. Bureau of Labor Statistics, "Employment and Earnings,1995," Table 26, "Employment and Earnings, 1991," Table 11, and "Handbook of Labor Statistics," Table 31, U.S. Government Printing Office, Washington, D.C., 1995, 1991, and 1989.

particular differential is due to race prejudice and how much of it is due, indirectly, to other factors associated with educational attainment, work experience, level of skill, place of residence, health, and so on is a matter still being explored.

Sex Differentials in Rates of Unemployment

During the years between 1970 and 1980 the unemployment rate for female workers was about 20 percent higher than the unemployment rate for males. A consistent pattern of higher female than male unemployment was found in each year of the three decades between 1950

and 1980. However, this differential was reversed in 1982 and 1983 during the severe recession, and during the 1980s and early 1990s, males at different ages often had higher unemployment rates than females. Studies by statisticians at the Department of Labor have shown that during the recessions of the 1980s and 1990s, male employment declined more sharply and recovered more slowly than did female employment.

By 1994, at the youngest age (16-19 years), white, black and Hispanic women had significantly lower unemployment rates than men of the same age and race-ethnicity group (Table 13-28). White males and females show little difference in age-specific unemployment rates at age 20 and above. While the unemployment rates of

Table 13-30. Unemployment Rates and Distribution of Unemployed, by Occupation, Sex, and Work Experience: 1994

Occupation and work experience	Unemployed		Unemployment rate		
	Number (in thousands)	Percent	Total	Male	Female
Total, 16 years and over	7,996	100.0	6.1	6.2	6.0
Managerial and professional specialty	907	11.3	2.6	2.4	2.8
Executive, administrative and managerial	454	5.7	2.7	2.4	3.1
Professional specialty	453	5.7	2.5	2.5	2.6
Technical, sales and administrative support	1,962	24.5	5.0	4.3	5.4
Technicians and related support	127	1.6	3.2	3.2	3.1
Sales occupations	907	11.3	5.8	4.3	7.3
Administrative support, including clerical	928	11.6	4.7	5.0	4.7
Service occupations	1,471	18.4	8.0	8.4	7.7
Private household	91	1.1	10.0	19.2	9.6
Protective service	96	1.2	4.1	3.9	4.8
Service, except private household and protective	1,285	16.1	8.5	9.9	7.7
Precision, production, craft and repair	910	11.4	6.3	6.4	6.0
Mechanics and repairers	201	2.5	4.3	4.3	5.2
Construction trades	518	6.5	9.4	9.3	11.2
Other precision production, craft, and repair	191	2.4	4.5	4.2	5.6
Operators, fabricators and laborers	1,761	22.0	9.0	8.7	9.9
Machine operators, assemblers, and inspectors	672	8.4	8.0	6.9	9.6
Transportation and material moving occupations	364	4.6	6.6	6.7	6.1
Handlers, equipment cleaners, helpers, and laborers	725	9.1	12.7	12.7	12.5
Construction laborers	172	2.2	18.9	18.9	—[1]
Other handlers, equipment cleaners, helpers, and laborers	552	6.9	11.5	11.3	12.2
Farming, forestry and fishing	333	4.2	8.4	8.3	9.0
Previous work experience					
No previous work experience	604	7.6	—	—	—
16 to 19 years	416	5.2	—	—	—
20 to 24 years	93	1.2	—	—	—
25 years and over	95	1.2	—	—	—

[1] Percent not shown where base is less than 35,000.

Source: U.S. Bureau of Labor Statistics, "Employment and Earnings," U.S. Government Printing Office, Washington, D.C., 1995, Table 25.

black women slightly exceed those of black men at ages 20-34 years, at older ages black men have higher unemployment rates. Hispanics have a different pattern: at all ages between 20 and 64 years, women's unemployment rates exceed those of men.

Economic Characteristics of the Unemployed

Asking unemployed persons a few questions about their last job, their last employer, and some of the conditions of their employment during the preceding year makes it possible to locate unemployment within the economy. This information has been collected for suffi-

cient years to permit identification of trends over time. It is particularly useful in determining how economic cycles and long-term structural changes are affecting workers in different industries and occupations.

Industry of the Unemployed

Five sectors of the industry stand out as having above-average rates of unemployment (Table 13-29):
- Agriculture
- Construction
- Manufacturing
- Wholesale and retail trade
- Service industries

Table 13-31. Duration of Unemployment: 1950-1994

Duration	1990-94	1985-89	1980-84	1975-79	1970-74	1965-69	1960-64	1955-59	1950-54
Total	100.0	100.0	100.0	100.0	100.0	100.0	100.0	100.0	100.0
Less than 5 weeks	38.3	44.2	37.9	42.3	48.9	54.4	42.6	45.6	53.9
5 to 14 weeks	29.9	30.2	30.5	30.9	30.9	28.9	29.8	29.6	29.1
5 to 10 weeks	21.3	22.2	21.6	22.3	22.8	21.6	21.1	21.2	21.4
11 to 14 weeks	8.6	8.1	8.8	8.6	8.1	7.3	8.7	8.4	7.7
15 weeks and over	31.8	25.5	31.6	26.9	20.2	16.7	27.6	24.6	17.1
15 to 26 weeks	14.5	12.2	14.4	13.4	11.6	9.7	13.6	12.9	10.0
27 weeks and over	17.3	13.3	17.2	13.5	8.6	7.0	14.0	11.7	7.1
Mean duration	16.1	14.1	15.9	13.4	10.3	9.4	14.1	12.6	10.0
Median duration[1]	7.8	6.2	8.2	7.1	5.6	3.7[2]	—	—	—

[1] Weighted average of yearly median duration.

[2] Weighted average of 1967-1969 yearly median duration.

Source: U.S. Bureau of Labor Statistics, "Employment and Earnings,1995," Table 30, "Employment and Earnings, 1993," Table 14, Employment and Earnings, 1991," Table 14, and "Handbook of Labor Statistics," Table 33, U.S. Government Printing Office, Washington, D.C., 1995, 1993, 1991, and 1989.

The sectors having below-average rates of unemployment are

- Mining
- Government
- Finance/insurance/real estate
- Transportation and public utilities

These differentials tend to be more or less stable over time. During the era of high unemployment and recession of the early 1980s, the manufacturing, mining and construction sectors had high rates of unemployment, but these rates have declined significantly since then.

The proportional distribution of the unemployed across industrial sectors shows where the unemployed are located (Table 13-29, bottom panel). In 1950, for example, almost three out of every ten unemployed workers were in the manufacturing sector. By 1994, that proportion had shrunk to 14.4 percent, and the proportion of the unemployed found in wholesale and retail trade (23.7 percent), service industries (22.5 percent) and government (11.8 percent) had all risen a great deal. While agriculture and construction have the highest rates of unemployment (both over 11 percent in 1994), they contribute only 2.7 and 9.1 percent of all of the unemployed, respectively.

Occupation of the Unemployed

Persons in some occupations are comparatively immune to unemployment, whereas persons in other occupations seem to be "sitting ducks" to both economic downturns and structural changes in the economy. Table 13-30 reports unemployment rates for broad occupational categories and sub-categories. Out of the sixteen occupational categories and sub-categories, those with below-average rates of unemployment are

- Executive, administrative and managerial
- Professional specialty
- Technicians and related support
- Administrative support, including clerical
- Protective service
- Mechanics and repairers
- Other precision production, craft and repair

Occupational categories with above-average unemployment rates are

- Private household workers
- Service, except private household and protective
- Construction trades
- Machine operators, assemblers and inspectors
- Construction laborers
- Other handlers, equipment cleaners, helpers, and laborers
- Farming, forestry and fishing

The occupations with above-average unemployment rates are blue-collar, concentrated in the "traditional" or "low technology" industries. Occupations with low levels of training and education often have the highest rates of unemployment. Low unemployment is a trait of the white-collar occupations, especially those in high technology areas. Among all white-collar occupations, only sales occupations (at 5.8 percent) have unemployment rates close to the rate of all occupations. Even though the problems of middle-aged managers who have lost their jobs through corporate mergers are a common topic of the news media, those in the executive, administrative and managerial job category have the second-lowest unemployment rate (at 2.7 percent) of all occupational categories. Farming, forestry and fishing laborers have moderately high rates of unemployment.

Table 13-32. Reasons for Unemployment, by Age, Sex, and Race:
1970-1994 [percent distribution]

Age, sex, and race	Total	Job losers	Job leavers	Reentrants	New workers
Total unemployed					
1994	100.0	47.7	9.9	34.8	7.6
1990	100.0	48.3	14.8	27.4	9.5
1985	100.0	49.8	10.6	27.1	12.5
1980	100.0	51.7	11.7	25.2	11.4
1975	100.0	55.3	10.4	23.9	10.4
1970	100.0	44.2	13.4	30.0	12.3
Both sexes, 16-19 years					
1994	100.0	14.0	6.4	48.0	31.5
1990	100.0	19.0	15.0	27.9	38.1
1985	100.0	18.7	7.7	26.6	46.9
1980	100.0	23.2	9.3	28.8	38.5
1975	100.0	25.5	8.8	29.9	35.9
1970	100.0	18.1	11.4	34.2	36.3
Male 20+ years					
1994	100.0	63.3	10.1	24.8	1.8
1990	100.0	65.0	13.2	19.3	2.4
1985	100.0	69.1	9.5	18.1	3.3
1980	100.0	71.2	10.7	15.4	2.7
1975	100.0	74.7	8.6	14.6	2.2
1970	100.0	65.1	12.8	19.4	2.7
Female 20+ years					
1994	100.0	43.8	11.1	41.1	4.0
1990	100.0	40.8	16.5	37.2	5.5
1985	100.0	41.4	13.2	38.2	7.3
1980	100.0	44.7	14.4	35.6	5.3
1975	100.0	49.9	14.0	32.0	4.2
1970	100.0	40.5	15.9	39.4	4.3
White, all ages					
1994	100.0	50.4	10.8	32.2	6.5
1990	100.0	49.8	15.5	26.4	8.3
1985	100.0	50.8	11.7	26.4	11.0
1980	100.0	52.7	12.5	24.6	10.2
1975	100.0	56.0	11.0	23.5	9.6
1970	100.0	45.0	13.7	29.4	11.9
Black, all ages					
1994	100.0	39.0	6.9	43.7	10.3
1990	100.0	44.4	12.2	30.2	13.2
1985	100.0	47.7	5.9	29.3	17.0
1980	100.0	56.6	0.7	27.3	15.4
1975	100.0	60.2	0.4	25.8	13.7

Source: U.S. Bureau of Labor Statistics, "Employment and Earnings, 1995," Tables 28 and 29,
   Employment and Earnings, 1991," Table 12, and "Handbook of Labor Statistics," Table 37,
   U.S. Government Printing Office, Washington, D.C., 1995, 1991, and 1989.

Table 13-33. Number of Unemployed and Unemployment Rates of the Population 25 Years of Age and Over, by Educational Attainment, Sex, and Race-ethnicity: 1993

Educational attainment	All races			White	Black	Hispanic
	Total	Male	Female			
Unemployed [in thousands]						
Total	6,017	3,396	2,621	4,612	1,124	740
Less than high school diploma	1,328	817	510	975	285	377
High school graduate	2,354	1,320	1,035	1,791	485	202
Some college	1,480	773	707	1,136	281	123
Bachelor's degree	855	485	370	711	73	38
Unemployment rate						
Total	5.6	5.8	5.4	5.0	9.8	9.0
Less than high school diploma	10.7	10.7	10.9	9.8	15.2	12.1
High school graduate	6.2	6.6	5.8	5.5	10.8	8.4
Some college	5.2	5.3	5.1	4.7	8.7	7.0
Bachelor's degree	2.9	2.9	3.0	2.8	3.8	3.9

Source: U.S. Bureau of the Census, "Statistical Abstract of the United States, 1994," U.S. Government Printing Office, Washington, D.C., 1994, Table No. 651.

Because of the size of this broad occupational group, as well as its high unemployment rate, operators are the largest single group of unemployed workers (22.0 percent). Among the 16 occupational categories and sub-categories, the largest proportion of all unemployed workers is found in the "service, except private household and protective" sub-category. New workers with no previous work experience constituted 7.6 percent of the unemployed in 1994. This is partially due to the small size of the "baby bust" birth cohorts of the 1970s now entering the workforce; in 1983, for example, these new workers constituted 11 percent of all unemployed.

As was noted earlier, women now have lower unemployment rates than men. Yet within all but five of fifteen occupational categories and sub-categories, women's unemployment rates exceeded those of men (Table 13-30). The reason why women had a lower overall rate of unemployment was that they were more heavily distributed in occupations with lower rates of unemployment. Women had lower rates of unemployment than men in five occupational categories:
- Technicians and related support occupations
- Administrative support, including clerical
- Private household
- Service, except private household and protective
- Transportation and material moving occupations

Within specific occupational categories, the largest margin by which male unemployment exceeded female unemployment was in private household occupations (a difference of 9.6 percent), while female unemployment exceeded male unemployment by three percent in sales occupations.

The Description of Unemployment
Duration of Unemployment

Unemployed workers may differ a great deal in how long they have been without work. Table 13-31 provides percentage distributions of duration of unemployment between the 1950-54 and 1990-94 eras. Since the 1965-69 period, there has been a steady decline in the proportion of the currently unemployed who have been jobless for less than five weeks; in 1965-69 they constituted 54.4 percent of all of the unemployed, but by 1990-94 they were only 38.3 percent of the jobless.

Labor economists sometimes divide unemployment into "short-term unemployment" (less than fifteen weeks) and "long-term unemployment" (fifteen weeks or longer). Long-term unemployment as a percentage of all unemployment increases substantially during periods of high unemployment:

Year	Percent Long-Term
1990-94	31.8
1985-89	25.5
1980-84	31.6
1975-79	26.9
1970-74	20.2
1965-69	16.7
1960-64	27.6
1955-59	24.6
1950-54	17.1

Prolonged recession causes the proportion of long-term unemployed to increase dramatically: in 1983 this proportion rose to 48 percent. Two other summary measures of the duration of unemployment are also used: the mean and median duration of unemployment (see Table 13-31, bottom panel). The rise in the mean duration of unemployment to 16.1 weeks during 1990-94 (a level that surpassed even the mean duration of unemployment during the severe 1980-84 recession) suggests that during the most recent recession many groups of workers had a very hard time finding re-employment, even while the overall unemployment rate was, by historical standards, not terribly high.

Reasons for Unemployment

The Current Population Survey classified the unemployed population into four categories, according to the reason for being unemployed:
- Job losers: persons who lost their jobs involuntarily
- Job leavers: persons who left their jobs voluntarily
- Re-entrants: persons seeking to re-enter the work force after an absence
- New workers: persons seeking to enter the labor force for the first time

The distribution of these reasons by race and sex and for young workers of both sexes are shown for selected years in Table 13-32. This table shows that:

1. For men aged 20 and above, involuntary loss of jobs is the major reason for unemployment. However, it appears to be of declining importance in recent years. For blacks, the decline in involuntary job loss as a factor in unemployment is quite striking: between 1975 and 1994, the proportion of lob losers among the black unemployed dropped from 60.2 to 39.0 percent.

2. Among young workers aged 16-19 years, new entrants and re-entrants account for the preponderant share of the unemployed, and job loss is a comparatively minor reason for unemployment. By 1994, almost half of all of the unemployed in this age group were re-entrants to the labor force.

3. Re-entrants make up a large share of unemployed women at age twenty and above. Until recently, many women left and re-entered the labor force, while men tended to enter and remain in it until retirement. This is reflected in above-average rates of female unemployment associated with re-entrance. By 1994, there were almost as many re-entrants as job losers among the female adult jobless. Bureau of Labor Statistics analysts have shown that recent recessions have had surprisingly little effect on decreasing female employment; instead, much of the burden of job loss has fallen on males, who were over-represented in the more cyclical industries heavily affected by recessions.

4. Before 1985, black workers, in comparison with white workers, seldom were job leavers. Because black workers were typically younger and a greater proportion were female, they were more likely than white workers to be new workers or re-entrants. Since 1985, however, the proportion of job leavers among the black jobless has increased significantly.

5. Among both the black and white unemployed, the proportion of new workers has been in decline since 1985. This is probably due to the small size of the "baby bust" cohorts reaching the age of entry into the labor force over the past decade, rather than to any major improvements in the youth unemployment picture.

Educational Attainment and Unemployment

Out of the slightly more than six million unemployed age 25 and over in the United States in 1993, about 1.3 million had less than a high school diploma, 2.4 million were high school graduates, 1.5 million had some college, and 855,000 had a bachelor's degree or higher level of education (Table 13-33). The modal unemployed white or black worker aged 25 or over was a high school graduate, whereas the Hispanic unemployed were most heavily concentrated among those without a high school diploma.

The unemployment rates of different educational groups attest to the power of educational attainment in helping workers to avoid unemployment. The second panel of Table 13-33 shows that for the entire U.S. population aged 25 and over, the unemployment rate of those with less than a high school diploma (10.7 percent) was more than triple the rate of those with a bachelor's degree (2.9 percent). High school graduation resulted in an unemployment rate 4.5 percent lower than that of the least-educated group, but the addition of some college lowered the unemployment rate only one percent below that of high school graduates. Possession of a bachelor's degree decreased the unemployment rate another 2.3 percent below that of the group with some college.

Some economists during the 1980s questioned whether college graduation added as much to future income as would investing the money for college in income-producing securities. Yet the unemployment figures show that attaining a college degree also decreases the possibility of unemployment throughout one's career, a fact worth considering when the mean duration of unemployment is at a high level (Table 13-31).

The effects of educational achievement on the unemployment rates of men and women are similar for racial and ethnic groups, but the levels are quite different. Blacks with less than a high school diploma are the group most at risk of unemployment (15.2 percent), followed by Hispanics at the same educational level (12.1 percent). The highest proportional differences in unemployment between racial and ethnic groups are found among high school graduates: Black graduates are almost twice as likely to suffer from unemployment as whites. Attainment of some college (and especially a bachelor's degree) benefit blacks and Hispanics more than whites in terms of providing protection from unemployment. However, there is still a significant difference in unemployment rates between whites (2.8 percent), blacks (3.8 percent) and Hispanics (3.9 percent) at the highest level of education.

Conclusion

The labor force and unemployment are large and multidimensional topics; this chapter has been able to present only some basic statuses, differentials and trends. Some of these trends are clear departures from previous patterns in American society, including the huge increase in the women's labor force, the inclusion of mothers with young children in the labor force, the declining labor force participation of men at older ages, and so on. Other aspects of the labor force and unemployment have changed relatively little, but remain significant social problems. These would include high unemployment rates among racial minorities and among those with low levels of education. Some problems are as yet difficult to evaluate, such as the new pattern of a moderately high unemployment rate coupled with a very long mean or median period of unemployment among these jobless even in good economic times.

Given the availability of annual and even monthly data on the labor force and unemployment and the known effects of the business cycles, there is sometimes a tendency to see no long-term trends, but only fluctuations in response to economic conditions. Yet as the succeeding chapter on occupations and industries will show, there has been a slow but steady overall trend towards the dominance of the service sector over the past fifty years, and a sharp decline in manufacturing employment in the last decade. This has certainly decreased the amplitude of seasonal swings in unemployment, and may affect the relationship of unemployment to the business cycle (unemployment in the manufacturing sector has typically lagged behind the swings in the business cycle) as well. Whether education will remain a key factor in high rates of labor force participation into the late adult years and a bulwark against unemployment may, in the long run, have a major effect on the solvency and survival of the Social Security system and a number of other social and economic institutions.

Unlike many other topics in demography, unemployment has no long-term "trend" but simply fluctuates in response to economic conditions. However, at any moment there are very substantial differentials associated with demographic and socioeconomic characteristics of the population. Most of the materials presented in this chapter can be updated by referring to the January issue of Employment and Earnings, the monthly bulletin published by the Bureau of Labor Statistics. This issue provides annual averages for the preceding year. Up-to-date statistics of unemployment, with rates adjusted for sea-sonal fluctuations, are presented in monthly issues of this publication, tabulated for most of the variables discussed in this chapter.

Note

1. Stanley Lebergott. "Annual Estimates of Unemployment in the United States." Pp. 213-390 in The Measurement and Behavior of Unemployment. Princeton, N.J.: National Bureau of Economic Research, Princeton University Press, 1957.

Bibliography

Abowd, John M., and Freeman, Richard B. Immigration, Trade and the Labor Market. Chicago: University of Chicago Press, 1991.
Adams, Arvil V. The Lingering Crisis of Youth Unemployment. Kalamazoo, MI: W.E. Upjohn Institute for Employment Research, 1978.
Antos, J., Mellow, W., and Triplett, J. "What Is a Current Equivalent to Unemployment Rates of the Past?" Monthly Labor Review 102 (1979):36-46.
Bancroft, Gertrude. The American Labor Force: Its Growth and Changing Composition. New York: Wiley and Sons, 1958.
Bergmann, Barbara. The Economic Emergence of Women. New York: Basic Books, 1986.
Birch, David L., Allman, Peter M., and Martin, Elizabeth A. A Model of Population and Employment Change for Metropolitan and Rural Areas in the United States. Cambridge, MA: MIT Program on Neighborhood and Regional Change, 1978.
Bluestone, Barry, and Bennett, Harrison. The Great American Job Machine: The Proliferation of Low Wage Employment in the U.S. Economy. Joint Economic Committee Report. Washington, D.C.: U.S. Government Printing Office, 1986.
Bowen, William G., and Harbison, Frederick (eds.). Unemployment in a Prosperous Economy. Princeton, NJ: Princeton University Press, 1965.
Bureau of Labor Statistics. Labor Force Statistics Derived from the Current Population Survey: A Data-book. Washington, D.C.: U.S. Government Printing Office, 1982.
Cain, C.C. "The Unemployment Rate as an Economic Indicator." Monthly Labor Review 102 (1979):24-35.
Cantrell, R.S., and Clark, R.L. "Individual Mobility, Population Growth, and Labor Force Participation." Demography 19 (1982):147-59.
Cherry, R. "What Is So Natural About the Natural Rate of Unemployment?" Journal of Economic Issues 15 (1981):729-43.
Clark, K.B., and Summers, L.H. "Demographic Differences in Cyclical Employment Variation." Journal of Human Resources 16 (1981): 61-79.
Clogg, C.C. "Cohort Analysis of Recent Trends in Labor Force Participants." Demography 19 (1982): 459-79.
Davis, R.G., and Lewis, G.M. Education and Employment. Farnborough: Lexington Books, 1975.
DiPrete, T. "Unemployment Over the Life Cycle: Differences and the Effects of Changing Economic Conditions." American Journal of Sociology 87 (1981):286-307.
Durand, John D. The Labor Force in the United States, 1890-1960. New York: Social Science Research Council, 1948.
Easterlin, Richard A. Birth and Fortune: The Impact of Numbers on Personal Welfare. Chicago: University of Chicago Press, 1987.
Felmlee, D. "Women's Job Mobility Processes." American Sociological Review 47 (1982):53-57.
Fineman, Stephen. White Collar Unemployment. New York: Wiley, 1983.
Flaim, Paul O. "The Effect of Demographic Change on the Nation's Unemployment Rate." Monthly Review 102 (1979):13-23.
Flanagan, R.J. "Discrimination Theory, Labor Turnover and Racial

Unemployment Differentials." Journal of Human Resources 13 (1978):187-207.

Freeman, Richard B., and Holtzer, Harry J. (eds.). The Black Youth Employment Crisis. Chicago: University of Chicago Press, 1986.

Fullerton, Howard N. "Evaluations of Labor Force Projection to 1990." Monthly Labor Review 115 (1992):3-14.

Garfinkle, Stuart H. The Length of Working Life for Males, 1900-1961. Washington, D.C.: U.S. Manpower Administration, 1963.

Goldstein, Harold. State and Local Labor Force Statistics. Washington, DC: National Commission of Employment and Unemployment Statistics, U.S. Government Printing Office, 1978.

Goldstein, Harvey A. Occupational Employment Projections for Labor Market Areas: An Analysis of Alternative Approaches. Washington, D.C.: U.S. Government Printing Office, 1951.

Hayghe, H. "Husbands and Wives as Earners: An Analysis of Family Data." Monthly Labor Review 104 (1981):46-59.

Hayghe, Howard V., and Bianchi, Suzanne. "Married Mothers' Work Patterns: The Job-Family Compromise." Monthly Labor Review 117 (1994):24-30.

Hogan, D.P. Transitions and Social Change: The Early Lives of American Men. New York: Academic Press, 1981.

Jennings, Jerry T. "Social and Economic Characteristics of Americans During Midlife." Current Population Reports, Series P-23 No. 111. Washington, D.C.: U.S. Government Printing Office, 1981.

Johnston, William B. Workforce 2000: Work and Workers for the 21st Century. Indianapolis, IN: Hudson Institute, 1987.

Johnston, William B. et al. Civil Service 2000. Washington, D.C.: U.S. Office of Personnel Management, 1988.

Lagerfeld, S. "Distorted Unemployment Statistics." Public Interest 56 (1979):108-11.

Lebergott, Stanley. Manpower in Economic Growth: The American Record Since 1800. New York: McGraw-Hill, 1964.

_____. Men Without Work: The Economics of Unemployment. Englewood Cliffs, NJ: Prentice-Hall, 1964.

Lichter, Daniel T., and Costanzo, Janice A. "How Do Demographic Changes Affect Labor Force Participation of Women?" Monthly Labor Review 110 (1987):23-25.

Lingle, R.C., and Jones, E.B. "Women's Increasing Unemployment: A Cross-Sectional Analysis" (with discussion). American Economic Review Papers and Proceedings 68 (1978): 84-89, 95-98.

Madden, J.F. "Why Women Work Closer to Home." Urban Studies 18 (1981):181-94.

Mare, Robert D., Winship, Christopher, and Kubitschek, Warren N. "The Transition from Youth to Adult: Understanding the Age Pattern of Employment." American Journal of Sociology 89 (1984):326-58.

Miller, Ann R. "Components of Labor Force Growth." Journal of Economic History 22 (1962):47-58.

Mishel, Lawrence, and Teixeira, Ruy A. The Myth of the Coming Labor Shortage: Jobs, Skills, and Incomes of America's Workforce 2000." Washington, D.C.: Economic Policy Institute.

Moen, P. "Measuring Unemployment: Family Considerations." Human Relations 33 (1980):183-92.

National Commission on Employment and Unemployment Statistics. Counting the Labor Force. Washington, D.C.: U.S. Government Printing Office, 1979.

O'Neill, D.M. "Racial Differentials in Teenage Unemployment: A Note on Trends." Journal of Human Resources 18 (1983):295-306.

Oppenheimer, Valerie K. The Female Labor Force in the United States. Westport, CT: Greenwood Press, 1970.

Pampel, F.C. "Changes in the Labor Force Participation and Income of the Aged in the United States 1947-1976." Social Problems 27 (1979):125-42.

Parnes, Herbert S. Unemployment Experiences of Individuals Over a Decade: Variations by Sex, Race, and Age. Kalamazoo, MI: Upjohn Institute for Employment Research, 1982.

Reskin, Barbara F. (ed.). Sex Segregation in the Workplace: Trends, Explanations, Remedies. Washington, D.C.: National Academy Press, 1984.

Rifkin, Jeremy. The End of Work: The Decline of the Global Labor Force and the Dawn of the Post-Market Era. New York: G.P. Putnam's Sons, 1995.

Rosenthal, Neal H. "Evaluating the 1990 Projections of Occupational Employment." Monthly Labor Review 115 (1992):32-48.

Rydzewski, Leo G., Demming, William G., and Rones, Philip L. "Seasonal Employment Falls over Past Three Decades." Monthly Labor Review 116 (1993):3-14.

Ryscavage, P.M. "Employment Problems and Poverty: Examining the Linkages." Monthly Labor Review 109 (1982):55-59.

Saunders, Norman C. "BLS Employment Projections for 1990: An Evaluation." Monthly Labor Review 115 (1992):15-31.

Solow, R. M. "On Theories of Unemployment." American Economic Review 70 (1980) 1-11.

Sweezy, A., and Owens, A. "Impact of Population Growth on Employment." American Economic Review Papers and Proceedings 64 (1974):45-50.

Tienda, Marta, Donato, Katherine, and Cordero-Guzman, Hector "Schooling, Color, and the Labor Force Activity of Women." Social Forces 71(1992):365.

Tinto, Vincent. "Higher Education and Occupational Attainment in Segmented Labor Markets: Recent Evidence from the United States." Higher Education 10 (1981):499-516.

Toikka, R.S., Scanlon, W.J., and Holt, C.C. "Extensions of a Structural Model of the Demographic Labor Market." Pp. 305-22 in R.G. Ehrenberg, ed. Research in Labor Economics. Greenwich, CT: JAI Press.

Treiman, D.J., and Terrell, K. "Sex and the Process of Status Attainment: A Comparison of Working Women and Men." American Sociological Review 40 (1975):174-200.

U.S. Bureau of the Census. "Detailed Population Characteristics: United States Summary." 1980 Census of Population. Washington, D.C.: U.S. Government Printing Office, 1983.

_____. "General Social and Economic Characteristics: United States Summary." 1980 Census of Population. Washington, D.C.: U.S. Government Printing Office, 1983.

_____. (Bennefield, Robert L., and McNeil, John M.). "Labor Force Status and Other Characteristics of Persons with a Work Disability." Current Population Reports, Series P-23 No. 160. Washington, D.C.: U.S. Government Printing Office, 1989.

U.S. Bureau of Economic Analysis. Area Economic Projections, 1990. Washington, D.C.: U.S. Government Printing Office, 1994.

U.S. Bureau of Labor Statistics. Handbook of Labor Statistics. Washington, D.C.: U.S. Government Printing Office, 1984.

_____. Monthly Report of Employment and Earnings. Washington, D.C.: U.S. Government Printing Office, monthly publication.

_____. Special Labor Force Reports. Washington, D.C.: U.S. Government Printing Office, periodical publication.

U.S. Department of Labor. Report on the American Workforce. Washington, D.C.: U.S. Government Printing Office, 1994.

_____. The American Work Force: 1992-2005. Bulletin 2452. Washington D.C.: Government Printing Office, 1994.

U.S. Merit Systems Protection Board. Evolving Workforce Demographics: Federal Agency Action and Reaction. Washington, D.C.: Government Printing Office, 1994.

Waite, L.J. "Working Wives and the Family Life Cycle." American Journal of Sociology 86 (1980): 272-94.

Wardwell, J.M., and Gilchrist, C.J. "Employment Deconcentration in the Nonmetropolitan Migration Turnaround." Demography 17 (1980):145-58.

Wetzel, James R. "Labor Force, Unemployment and Earnings." Pp. 59-106 in R. Farley, ed. State of the Union. New York: Russell Sage Foundation, 1995.

White, L.K. "Note on Racial Differences in the Effect of Female Economic Opportunity on Marriage Rates." Demography 18 (1981):349.54.

Wolfbein, Seymour L. Employment and Unemployment in the United States: A Study of the American Labor Force. Chicago: Science Research Associates, 1964.

OCCUPATION, INDUSTRY, AND CLASS OF WORKER

Changes in the domestic and international economy and in family formation and gender roles, and increasing levels of education are having profound effects on the nature of work in the United States. The labor force concepts of Chapter 13 separate the economically active members of the population from the inactive members and determine whether or not the economically active are employed. They do not designate the kinds of jobs performed by members of the labor force, the types of organizations in which they work, or the manner in which they obtain their income. The present chapter discusses three aspects of the economic composition of the population:

a) Occupation: What kind or kinds of work does an employed person do?

b) Industry: In what kind of business is the employed person found?

c) Class of Worker: Does the employed person work for private industry, for a non-profit organization, or for some level of government, or is he or she self-employed?

Occupational Composition and Trends

Census enumerators are instructed to record the exact kind of work performed by employed persons or (if the person is unemployed) the kind of work performed on the last job. Specially trained census clerks, supervised by occupational statisticians, classify and code these responses in terms of meaningful occupational groups. (For details see the Definition Box.)

The system of occupational classification now in use is a product of many years of experimentation, research, and critical review of the results yielded by earlier classifications. A pioneer among the statisticians responsible for the present relatively high quality and great usefulness of the occupational statistics was Dr. Alba M. Edwards. He was among the first to compile long lists of occupational names with the corresponding job descriptions in order to designate meaningful common elements on the basis of which occupational classifications could be established. During this painstaking labor Dr. Edwards did not lose sight of the immense sociological significance of the population's occupational characteristics. Today's specialists who use occupational data with narrow perspective to identify social strata and social classes or to build econometric models of the labor market might well pause to reflect on his words:

The most nearly dominant single influence in a man's [or woman's] life is probably his occupation. More than anything else, perhaps, a man's occupation determines his course and his contribution in life . . . A man's occupation not only tells, for each workday, what he does during one-half of his waking hours, but it indicates, with some degree of accuracy, his manner of life during the other half: the kind of associates he will have, the kind of clothes he will wear, the kind of house he will live in, and even, to some extent, the kind of food he will eat. And, usually, it indicates, in some degree, the cultural level of his family.

In similar manner there is probably no single set of closely related facts that tell so much about a nation as do detailed statistics of the occupations of its workers . . . And, were the figures available, the social and industrial history of a people might be traced more accurately through detailed statistics of the occupations of its gainful workers than through records of its wars, its territorial conquests, and its political struggles.[1]

In a modern industrialized nation there may be many thousands of different occupations; it would be both impossible and undesirable to tabulate statistics for each item in such a long list. Because many occupations are very similar to each other, census clerks use a classification scheme that groups similar occupations into one category.

Chapter 14 Definitions
OCCUPATION, INDUSTRY, AND CLASS OF WORKER

The materials of this chapter are based on statistics generated from responses to job description questions 28-30 in the 1990 Census, or corresponding questions from the previous censuses or the Current Population Surveys. Persons were instructed to describe the job they held during the reference week before the enumeration or if not employed, the job at which the person was most recently employed. Persons working at more than one job were instructed to describe the one at which they worked the most hours during the reference week.

Industry (question 28). "(a) For whom did this person work (last week)? (b) What kind of business or industry was this? (c) Is this mainly manufacturing, wholesale trade, retail trade, or other (agriculture, construction, service, government, etc.)?" Persons working for employers engaged in more than one activity were instructed to describe only the main activity at the place or facility where the person worked. Responses to these questions were coded into 235 categories called the "detailed industry classification." An "intermediate industrial classification" of 140 categories was arrived at by combining similar or related industries from the detailed classification. These categories, in turn, were summarized in thirteen "major industry groups." Aside from changes caused by the emergence of new industries, the death of some, and the growth and decline in others and changes in coding procedures and codebooks, industry statistics at the intermediate and major industry group levels are roughly comparable from 1940 to the present.

Occupation (question 29). "(a) What kind of work was this person doing? (b) What were this person's most important activities or duties?" These write-in responses were taken together to assign the respondent to one of 503 "detailed occupation categories," coded by specially trained coders in census processing offices. An "intermediate occupational classification" of 121 categories was arrived at by combining similar or related occupations from the detailed classification. These categories, in turn, were summarized into thirteen (sometimes fourteen) "major occupation groups." In addition, some of the intermediate and detailed occupation categories are subdivided by industry or class of worker groups. Although the enumeration procedure used in collecting occupational data in the 1990 and 1980 censuses (and since 1972 in the Current Population Survey) is similar to those used since the census of 1940, the classification system used for coding responses (1980 Census of Population: Classified Index of Industries and Occupations) was substantially different in 1990 and 1980 from the categories and coding systems used in the 1970 and prior enumerations. Segments of some occupational classifications of 1970 were moved to a different category in 1980, and the major occupational groups (and consequently the intermediate categories) are substantially different in the new system from the previous system. The changes create major problems of comparability. They were made so that the occupational classification would realistically reflect the current occupational structure of the United States, based on an assessment of the kind of work performed. The new system of occupational coding, used in the 1990 and 1980 censuses, was initiated in the Current Population Survey as early as 1972. Hence, comparable data on changes in occupational composition from 1972 to the present are available from the CPS.

Occupation Divisions. The major occupation groups are often arranged in four divisions:

- White collar—Professional technical, managers, and administrators, except farm; sales workers; and clerical and kindred workers.

- Blue collar—Craftsmen and kindred workers; operatives, except transport; transport equipment operatives; and laborers, except farm.

- Farm workers—Farmers and farm managers, farm laborers, and farm foremen.

- Service workers—Service workers, including private household.

Class of Worker (question 30). "Was this person (a) employee of a private for-profit company, business, or individual for wages, salary, or commission, (b) employee of a private not-for-profit, tax-exempt, or charitable organization, (c) federal government employee, (d) state government employee, (e) local government employee city, county, etc., (f) self-employed in own business, professional practice, or farm, or (g) working without pay in family business or farm?" Responses to these questions were classified in categories as follows:

1. For-profit private wage and salary workers— Persons who worked for a private employer for wages, salary, commission, tips, pay-in-kind, or at piece rates.

2. Non-profit private wage and salary workers—Persons employed by churches, foundations and other non-profit organizations; their wages are usually determined in much the same way as those in the for-profit private sector. Because this group is relatively small, it will be combined with the first category in the tabular results (Table 14-13).

2. Government workers—Persons who worked for any government unit, regardless of the activity of the particular agency. This category is subdivided by the level of government: (a) Federal, (b) State, (c) Local (county and its political subdivisions such as cities, villages, and townships). Employees of the United Nations, other international organizations, and foreign governments are classified as Federal government employees. Most employees of the District of Columbia government are classified as local government employees.

3. Self-employed workers—

(a) Own business not incorporated. Persons who worked for profit or fees in their own unincorporated business, profession, or trade, or who operated a farm. Included here are the owner-operators of large stores and manufacturing establishments as well as merchants, independent craftspersons and professionals, farmers, peddlers, and other persons who conducted enterprises of their own.

(b) Own business incorporated. Persons who consider themselves self-employed but work for corporations. In most cases the respondents will own or be part of a group that owns controlling interest in the corporation. Since all workers of a corporation are defined as wage and salary workers, this category is tabulated with "private wage and salary workers" and is sometimes shown as a subcategory of that group.

4. Unpaid family workers—Persons who worked without pay on a farm or in a business operated by a person to whom they are related by blood or marriage. These are usually the children or the wife of the owner of a business or farm. About one-quarter of the unpaid family workers are farm workers.

In the United States occupational data are gathered by several federal agencies as well as by private organizations; so classification must be standardized if comparability is to be achieved. In fact, the need for comparability of occupational classifications is international in scope and has led to the setting up of programs to achieve an international classification scheme. Within the federal government a multiagency task force, advised by experts from universities and the private sector, has been sponsored by the Office of Management and Budget in order to promote uniformity and comparability in the presentation of statistical data collected by various agencies. The 1980 Standard Occupational Classification (SOC) published by the U.S. Bureau of the Census is a product of this endeavor. For 1970 and earlier censuses, the occupational classification system used in the Dictionary of Occupational Titles, published by the U.S. Department of Labor, was used with some modification.

In general this system is able to present statistics on three levels of detail:

1. Detailed occupational classification. Highly specific categories of occupations, or of subgroupings of occupations, according to industry.
2. Intermediate occupational classification. Combinations of the categories of the detailed occupational classification, in which similar occupations are grouped and in which detailed occupations that contain only a few workers are merged with larger categories that they resemble.
3. Major occupational groups. Broad categories of occupation, consisting of groupings of the intermediate (and hence of the detailed) occupational categories.

New inventions, scientific discoveries, and technological progress constantly present new work tasks and need methods for performing them, causing changes in the way society is organized, so that classifications must be revised at each decennial census.

Moreover, the number and proportion of workers in each of the occupations that do continue to be recognized will change with altered conditions. The new occupations must be added and old occupations must be reevaluated to ensure that they are still in the proper groupings. Hence strict comparability cannot, and should not, be maintained from census to census. Extensive and important changes were made in the occupational classification system used in the 1980 Census in comparison with previous censuses.

Comparability of occupational categories between the 1990, 1980 and 1970 censuses has been established by the Bureau of the Census by combining and estimating classification (and data) into the nearest equivalent for the preceding or following census. Thus it is possible to discuss intercensal changes between 1970-80 and 1980-90 in terms of the new or old occupational categories.

The Bureau of Labor Statistics and the Current Population Survey continued to report occupations in terms of the "old" classification (as well as the new) until 1982, and hence it is possible to discuss long-term trends over several decades using the "old" categories. In order to provide a complete description of change, it is necessary to use both the old and the new systems of classification.

Major Occupational Groups

The most general occupational classification in the 1990 system consists of six summary categories, four of which have subdivisions, creating a total of thirteen major occupational groups. Table 14-1 lists these categories and provides indicators of relative size, demographic characteristics of workers, and change between 1980-90 for each.

Another way of approaching occupations used in many earlier scholarly works is in terms of broad occupational divisions: white collar, blue collar, service and agricultural workers. The work force in 1990, 1980 and 1970 had the following composition:

Category	1990	1980	1970	Percent Change 1980-90	Percent Change 1970-80
Total	100.0	100.0	100.0	18.5	0.0
White collar (A, B)	58.1	53.0	48.2	5.1	4.8
Blue collar (E, F)	26.2	31.2	35.3	-5.0	-4.1
Service workers (C)	13.2	12.9	12.7	0.3	0.2
Agricultural workers (D)	2.5	2.9	3.8	-0.4	-0.9

During the 1970-80 decade, white collar occupations became an absolute majority, signalling the much-heralded shift to the "postindustrial society." During the next decade, the rate of decline of blue collar jobs increased, and the decline in manufacturing jobs continued. The rate of increase in white collar jobs changed from 4.8 to 5.1 percent between 1970-80 and 1980-90. By 1990, only slightly more than one quarter of all jobs were in the blue collar sector, and almost six out of every ten jobs were white collar ones. During these two decades, agricultural workers suffered large proportional declines in numbers, while the service occupations registered small increases.

White Collar Workers

The white collar class has two major strata: the upper class and their middle class aides. The upper class group, termed by the census "Managerial and professional specialty occupations," is subdivided into two parts: administrators and professionals. The administrators are termed "Executive, administrative, and managerial occupations" (A-1). This class of workers increased rapidly-by 40.4 percent- during the 1980-90 decade (see "Percent change 1980-90" column of Table 14-1). The "Professional specialty occupations" (A-2) increased somewhat more slowly, but still more rapidly (an increase of 35.7 percent in the decade) than the labor force as a whole, which increased by 18.5 percent. Together these "elite" occupations comprised 26.4 percent of the work force by 1990.

The middle class white collar aides, who outnumber the upper occupational class (they are 31.7 percent of the work force) fall into three categories. "Technicians and related support occupations" (B-1) is a small but very rapidly growing stratum of workers; they grew by 42.8 percent between 1980 and 1990. The remaining troops of the white collar army are "Sales occupations" (B-2) and "Administrative support occupations, including clerical" (B-3). This latter group is the largest of the occupational groups, comprising 16.3 percent of the labor force. Between 1970 and 1980 the sales force grew slightly less rapidly than the work force as a whole, while the clerical-administrative support group grew slightly faster but less rapidly than the professional group. However, in the 1980-90 decade, these trends showed a marked reversal: the clerical-administrative support group grew at only 11.7 percent, while the sales force grew at a rate of 39.7 percent, a rate surpassed only by executive, administrative and managerial occupations and technicians and related support occupations.

Blue Collar Workers

These workers in shops, factories, warehouses, and on the highways and railways are divided into two subcategories, the skilled "Precision production, craft, and repair occupations" (E) and the semiskilled and unskilled "Operators, fabricators, and laborers" (F). Between 1980 and 1990 the first of these groups grew very slowly, adding only 4 percent compared to overall workforce growth of 18.5 percent (Table 14-1). It is a sizable group (11.3 percent of the work force). The second category consists of three subgroups. "Machine operators, assemblers, and inspectors" (F-1), the backbone of unskilled and semiskilled jobs in mass-production industries, declined by 13 percent. "Transportation and material moving occupations" (F-2) is a comparatively small grouping and grew at a rate of 7.7 percent for the decade. The third group, "Handlers, cleaners, helpers, and laborers" (F-3), grew by 4.1 percent. Overall, the broad category of the semiskilled and unskilled (category F) shrank by 3.7 percent as unskilled jobs moved offshore or were replaced by automation and required levels of job skills in the emerging service economy became more demanding. Only unskilled and semiskilled jobs in the transportation and material moving occupations (F-2) showed much increase,

continuing a pattern found in the 1970-80 job growth figures.

Service Workers

In this heterogeneous category, private household workers (C-1) comprise less than 1 percent of the work force and declined by nearly 12 percent during the 1980-90 decade. Protective service workers (C-2) grew quite rapidly (by 35.1 percent) during the decade, but this group is still small. The core of the service occupations is the attendants and workers who provide services in a variety of establishments. It comprises more than 10 percent of the labor force and grew at a slightly higher rate (21.0 percent) than the overall rate of labor force growth during 1980-90.

Farming, Forestry and Fishing Occupations

These occupations constituted about 2.5 percent of the total work force. They experienced a growth of about 1 percent during the 1980-90 decade, but this overall figure disguises some very divergent trends. Between 1980 and 1990, the number of farm operators and managers shrank by 16.3 percent, leaving only slightly more than a million persons in this occupational category. Other agricultural and related occupations (including farmworkers) grew by 35.6 percent in this decade. Forestry and logging occupations grew by 20.6 percent, and the number of fishers, hunters and trappers increased by 8.7 percent.

Summary

During the 1980-90 decade there was rapid growth of managerial (A-1), professional (A-2), technical (B-1), sales (B-2) and protective service occupations (C-2). The administrative support and clerical (B-3), and service occupations other than domestic (C-2), experienced moderate growth. There was slow growth in the skilled (E), transport (F-2), and agricultural occupations (D) and an absolute decline in the number of other unskilled (F-1 and F-3) and private household occupations (C-1). Occupations demanding the exercise of power, knowledge, and skill grew, while those primarily requiring the use of muscles stagnated or declined.

Long-Term Trends in Occupation

If the most recent census occupational data are reclassified using the "old" occupational classification system of the 1970 Census and before (Tables 14-2 and 14-3), it can be seen that the trends described above have been underway since 1960. White collar workers, especially the managers-administrators and professional-technical workers, have grown more rapidly than the work

Table 14-1. Occupational Composition of the Employed Labor Force, by Sex and Race-ethnicity: 1990, and Percent Change, 1980-1990

Occupation	Percent distribution, 1990				Percent composition, 1990			Percent change, 1980-90		
	Total	White	Black	Hispanic	Black	Hispanic	Female	Total	Black	Female
Total employed, 16 years and over	100.0	100.0	100.0	100.0	9.9	7.8	45.8	18.5	22.2	27.2
A. Managerial and professional specialty occupations	26.4	27.9	18.1	14.1	6.8	4.1	48.3	37.8	56.9	64.7
1. Executive, administrative, and managerial occupations	12.3	13.1	7.7	7.0	6.2	4.4	42.1	40.4	79.7	95.2
2. Professional specialty occupations	14.1	14.8	10.4	7.1	7.3	3.9	53.7	35.7	43.5	48.9
B. Technical, sales, and administrative support occupations	31.7	32.3	29.4	25.9	9.1	6.3	63.0	24.1	42.6	21.9
1. Technicians and related support occupations	3.7	3.7	3.3	2.5	8.8	5.2	46.2	42.8	50.9	50.9
2. Sales occupations	11.8	12.5	7.7	9.0	6.4	5.9	48.3	39.7	86.9	40.9
3. Administrative support occupations, including clerical	16.3	16.2	18.4	14.4	11.2	6.9	77.4	11.7	28.7	12.1
C. Service occupations	13.2	11.8	22.1	19.2	16.5	11.2	58.4	21.1	17.0	19.8
1. Private household occupations	0.5	0.3	1.2	1.3	26.2	22.9	95.0	-11.6	-43.6	-12.1
2. Protective service occupations	1.7	1.6	2.7	1.5	15.7	6.8	15.6	35.1	77.4	83.9
3. Other service occupations	11.0	9.8	18.2	16.3	16.2	11.5	63.6	21.0	19.3	20.9
D. Farming, forestry, and fishing occupations	2.5	2.5	1.5	5.0	5.8	15.7	15.8	1.0	-8.8	11.2
E. Precision production, craft, and repair occupations	11.3	11.7	8.2	13.1	7.1	9.0	9.4	4.0	11.4	26.3
F. Operators, fabricators, and laborers	14.9	13.8	20.8	22.9	13.8	11.9	26.1	-3.7	-4.9	-7.9
1. Machine operators, assemblers, and inspectors	6.8	6.2	9.7	11.7	14.0	13.2	39.2	-13.0	-12.1	-15.0
2. Transportation and material moving occupations	4.1	4.0	5.5	4.5	13.4	8.5	10.0	7.7	12.1	36.1
3. Handlers, equipment cleaners, helpers, and laborers	3.9	3.6	5.6	6.7	13.9	13.3	20.1	4.1	-5.6	4.0

Source: U. S. Bureau of the Census, "Social and Economic Characteristics: United States," 1990 CP-2-1, Table 45, and "General Social and Economic Characteristics: United States Summary," 1980 Census of Population, Tables 89 and 135, U.S. Government Printing Office, Washington, D.C., 1993 and 1983.

Table 14-2. Occupational Composition of the Employed Labor Force, by Sex: 1960-1990
[numbers in thousands]

Occupation	Number		Percent distribution			
	1990	1980	1990	1980	1970	1960
Total employed, both sexes[1]	115,681	97,639	100.0	100.0	100.0	100.0
Managerial and professional specialty occupations	30,534	22,152	26.4	22.7	19.0	18.8
Executive, administrative, and managerial occupations	14,228	10,134	12.3	10.4	7.7	9.3
Professional specialty occupations	16,306	12,018	14.1	12.3	11.3	9.6
Technical, sales, and administrative support occupations	36,718	29,594	31.7	30.3	29.2	22.7
Technicians and related support occupations	4,257	2,982	3.7	3.1	2.3	1.1
Sales occupations	13,635	9,760	11.8	10.0	10.2	8.0
Administrative support occupations, including clerical	18,826	16,851	16.3	17.3	16.7	13.7
Service occupations	15,296	12,629	13.2	12.9	12.7	10.8
Private household occupations	521	589	0.5	0.6	1.5	2.7
Protective service occupations	1,993	1,475	1.7	1.5	1.4	1.1
Other service occupations	12,782	10,565	11.0	10.8	9.8	7.0
Farming, forestry, and fishing occupations	2,839	2,811	2.5	2.9	3.8	6.7
Precision production, craft, and repair occupations	13,098	12,594	11.3	12.9	14.1	13.1
Operators, fabricators, and laborers	17,196	17,859	14.9	18.3	21.2	23.0
Machine operators, assemblers, and inspectors	7,904	9,085	6.8	9.3	10.9	12.9
Transportation and material moving occupations	4,729	4,389	4.1	4.5	4.9	5.2
Handlers, equipment cleaners, helpers, and laborers	4,563	4,385	3.9	4.5	5.4	4.9
Total males employed	62,705	56,005	100.0	100.0	100.0	100.0
Managerial and professional specialty occupations	15,781	13,197	25.2	23.6	20.2	20.1
Executive, administrative, and managerial occupations	8,235	7,063	13.1	12.6	10.1	11.7
Professional specialty occupations	7,546	6,134	12.0	11.0	10.1	8.4
Technical, sales, and administrative support occupations	13,598	10,622	21.7	19.0	19.4	14.7
Technicians and related support occupations	2,291	1,679	3.7	3.0	2.4	0.8
Sales occupations	7,050	5,089	11.2	9.1	9.7	7.2
Administrative support occupations, including clerical	4,257	3,854	6.8	6.9	7.2	6.7
Service occupations	6,366	5,178	10.2	9.2	8.2	6.1
Private household occupations	26	26	0.0	0.0	0.1	0.1
Protective service occupations	1,682	1,306	2.7	2.3	2.0	1.5
Other service occupations	4,658	3,845	7.4	6.9	6.1	4.4
Farming, forestry, and fishing occupations	2,390	2,407	3.8	4.3	5.6	9.1
Precision production, craft, and repair occupations	11,863	11,616	18.9	20.7	21.1	18.7
Operators, fabricators, and laborers	12,707	12,985	20.3	23.2	25.5	26.7
Machine operators, assemblers, and inspectors	4,803	5,439	7.7	9.7	10.8	12.6
Transportation and material moving occupations	4,256	4,042	6.8	7.2	7.5	7.6
Handlers, equipment cleaners, helpers, and laborers	3,648	3,505	5.8	6.3	7.2	6.5
Total females employed	52,977	41,635	100.0	100.0	100.0	100.0
Managerial and professional specialty occupations	14,753	8,955	27.8	21.5	17.0	16.2
Executive, administrative, and managerial occupations	5,993	3,070	11.3	7.4	3.7	4.2
Professional specialty occupations	8,759	5,885	16.5	14.1	13.2	12.0
Technical, sales, and administrative support occupations	23,120	18,971	43.6	45.6	45.3	39.1
Technicians and related support occupations	1,966	1,303	3.7	3.1	2.1	1.5
Sales occupations	6,584	4,671	12.4	11.2	10.9	9.6
Administrative support occupations, including clerical	14,570	12,997	27.5	31.2	32.3	28.0
Service occupations	8,930	7,452	16.9	17.9	20.0	20.4
Private household occupations	495	563	0.9	1.4	3.8	7.9
Protective service occupations	310	169	0.6	0.4	0.2	0.1
Other service occupations	8,124	6,720	15.3	16.1	15.9	12.4
Farming, forestry, and fishing occupations	450	404	0.8	1.0	0.9	1.7
Precision production, craft, and repair occupations	1,235	978	2.3	2.3	2.6	1.5
Operators, fabricators, and laborers	4,489	4,874	8.5	11.7	14.2	15.4
Machine operators, assemblers, and inspectors	3,101	3,646	5.9	8.8	11.2	13.4
Transportation and material moving occupations	473	348	0.9	0.8	0.5	0.2
Handlers, equipment cleaners, helpers, and laborers	915	880	1.7	2.1	2.5	1.7

[1] Persons 16 and over in 1990, 1980, and 1970, and persons 14 and over in 1960.

Source: 1990 data from U.S. Bureau of the Census, "Social and Economic Characteristics: United States," 1990-CP-2-1, Table 45, 1980 and
1970 data from "General Social and Economic Characteristics: United States Summary," 1980 Census of Population, Table 89, and 1960 data
data from "Detailed Population Characteristics," 1960 Census of Population, Table 202, U.S. Government Printing Office, Washington, D.C.,
1993, 1983, and 1964.

Table 14-3. Percent Change in Employed Labor Force, by Occupation and Sex: 1960-1990

Occupation	1980-1990			1970-1980			1960-1970		
	Both sexes	Male	Female	Both sexes	Male	Female	Both sexes	Male	Female
Total employed¹	18.5	12.0	27.2	27.5	17.6	43.9	18.4	9.6	36.6
Managerial and professional specialty occupations	37.8	19.6	64.7	52.5	37.1	82.6	19.3	10.1	42.9
Executive, administrative, and managerial occupations	40.4	16.6	95.2	72.3	47.0	184.9	-1.9	-5.9	20.5
Professional specialty occupations	35.7	23.0	48.9	39.0	27.2	53.8	40.0	32.4	50.8
Technical, sales, and administrative support occupations	24.1	28.0	21.9	32.4	15.1	44.6	52.1	44.0	58.4
Technicians and related support occupations	42.8	36.5	50.9	67.9	44.1	113.2	159.4	225.2	87.2
Sales occupations	39.7	38.6	40.9	25.6	10.2	48.1	50.5	47.2	55.4
Administrative support occupations, including clerical	11.7	10.4	12.1	31.7	11.8	39.0	44.8	18.3	57.9
Service occupations	21.1	23.0	19.8	30.1	31.9	28.8	39.3	47.8	34.1
Private household occupations	-11.6	-0.9	-12.1	-48.8	-37.1	-49.3	-33.3	-31.1	-33.3
Protective service occupations	35.1	28.8	83.9	42.3	34.7	150.9	50.4	46.4	145.4
Other service occupations	21.0	21.1	20.9	40.5	32.0	45.9	65.1	50.8	75.7
Farming, forestry, and fishing occupations	1.0	-0.7	11.2	-3.3	-9.2	59.1	-32.4	-32.6	-30.4
Precision production, craft, and repair occupations	4.0	2.1	26.3	16.6	15.8	27.9	27.8	23.5	134.6
Operators, fabricators, and laborers	-3.7	-2.1	-7.9	9.8	6.8	18.7	9.4	4.7	26.0
Machine operators, assemblers, and inspectors	-13.0	-11.7	-15.0	8.5	5.8	12.6	0.5	-6.5	14.0
Transportation and material moving occupations	7.7	5.3	36.1	17.4	12.8	123.8	11.3	8.3	204.8
Handlers, equipment cleaners, helpers, and laborers	4.1	4.1	4.0	5.7	2.1	23.3	30.6	22.3	93.9

¹ Persons 16 and over in 1990, 1980, and 1970, and persons 14 and over in 1960.

Source: 1990 data from U.S. Bureau of the Census, "Social and Economic Characteristics: United States," 1990-CP-2-1, Table 45, 1980 and 1970 data from "General Social and Economic Characteristics: United States Summary," 1980 Census of Population, Table 89, and 1960 data from "Detailed Population Characteristics," 1960 Census of Population, Table 202, U.S. Government Printing Office, Washington, D.C., 1993, 1983, and 1964.

**Figure 14-1. Trends in Occupational Composition of the
Employed Civilian Labor Force: 1950-1990**

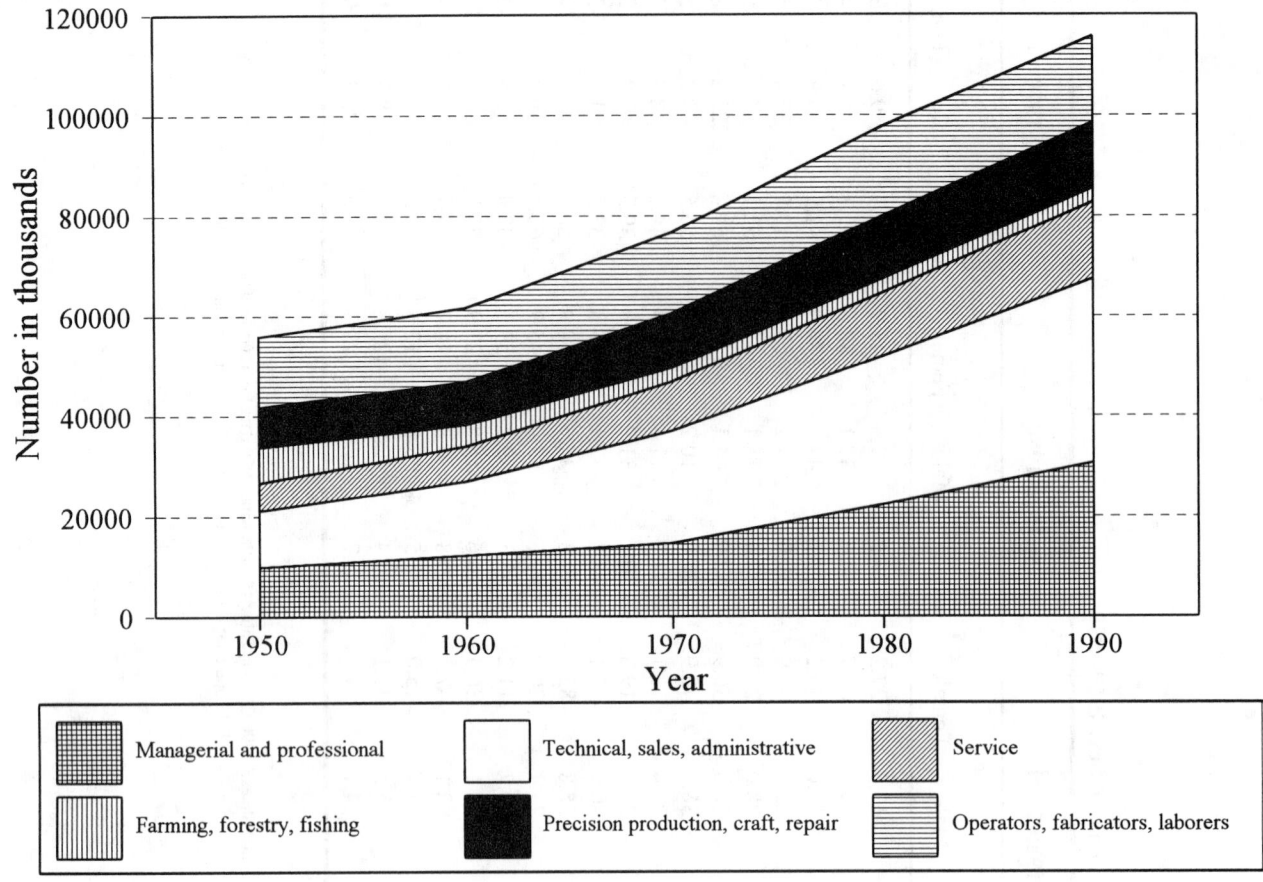

Source: 1950-1990 U.S. Census data.

force as a whole for decades. The unskilled blue collar workers (laborers) have grown more slowly, and farm workers and private household workers have declined in number. However, the skilled craft and semiskilled operative workers grew at about the same rate as the work force as a whole until 1980, after which their proportion declined. Figure 14-1 charts the long-term growth of the occupations since 1950. It shows that the drift from blue collar to white collar occupations has characterized the entire century, but has accelerated since 1960.

Occupations of Employed Women

The preceding chapter pointed out that since 1960, the female component of the work force has been growing at 2.5 to 3.0 times the rate for males. Tables 14-1, 14-2 and 14-3 show the occupations that women have entered and the rates of growth in female employment for those occupations. The main points are as follows:

1. While total employment in the workforce (i.e. for both sexes) grew by 37.7 percent between 1980 and 1990, male employment rose by only 28.4 percent, and female employment grew by 64.8 percent.

2. Women have entered the "growth occupations" at much higher rates than men. For example, between 1980 and 1990, women in executive, administrative and managerial occupations (A-1) increased by 118.2 percent, compared to an overall growth rate of 52.4 percent in the size of the occupational group over the decade. Similarly, women in professional specialty occupations increased by 70.7 percent in the same time period. Thus recent years have witnessed some feminization of the upper categories of the white collar occupational strata, even if a "glass ceiling" still prevents them from reaching the top jobs. Women's jobs in sales and administrative support occupations (B-2 and B-3), two areas where they were already strongly represented, grew only at about the same rate as the overall growth in jobs in those areas in 1980-90.

3. Since 1960 women have also entered the skilled and craft blue collar occupations at rates three to five times those of males. Women have equaled or surpassed men in their rates of entry into the expanding category of ser-

Figure 14-2. Percent Change in Occupation for Males and Females: 1950-1990

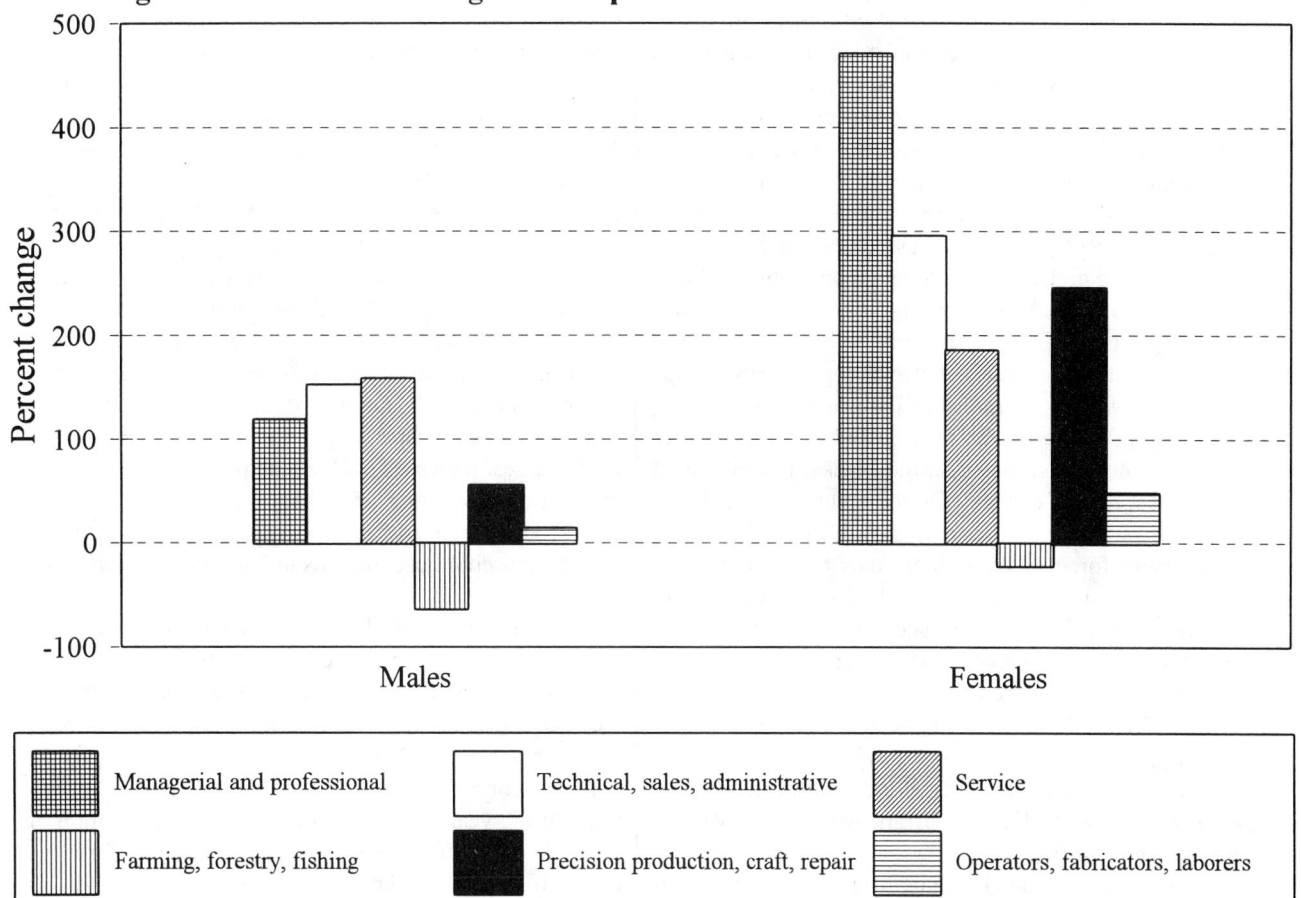

Source: 1950 and 1990 U.S. Census data.

vice industries other than domestic service. While making these gains, women have had a lower rate of growth in private household and other service jobs than men. The past decade has seen a more than doubling (133 percent) growth) of the number of women in protective service occupations, while men's employment in this area grew by only 50 percent.

4. As a consequence of this differential occupational growth between the sexes, the occupational composition of female employed workers has tended to converge on that of males. Compared to men, women still occupy proportionately fewer managerial and administrative posts and hold fewer precision craft and kindred worker jobs, while having a proportionately larger share of the clerical and service work tasks (see "percent female" column in Table 14-1 as well as Figure 14-2). As Chapter 15 on income shows, occupational titles can be deceptive, and income inequalities between men and women workers are greater than the occupational statistics might suggest.

Recent studies by researchers at the Bureau of Labor Statistics suggest that one key factor influencing the overall labor force growth and the major changes in occupational distribution of women is that economic recessions since 1980 have had very different effects on men and women in the labor force. Recessions have led to major job losses among men, particularly in the unskilled trades, that take a long time to reverse. Women's employment, however, has often suffered little decline during recessions, and women's job growth rapidly rebounds soon after recessions end. Structural changes in the economy that result in post-recession job growth appear to favor occupations where women are increasingly concentrated.

Occupation of Race and Ethnic Groups

There are still large disparities between the occupational composition of white workers on the one hand and black and Hispanic-origin workers on the other (see

Tables 14-1 and 14-4). However, recent trends have been in the direction of convergence between these groups.

There are two ways of analyzing the occupations of the black and Hispanic-origin labor force: in terms of their differential distribution across occupations, and in terms of their proportional composition of any particular occupational group. For example, 10.4 percent of all employed blacks were found in the professional specialty occupations (A-2) in 1990, and they comprised 7.3 percent of all workers in that occupational group (Table 14-1).

1. Although white workers hold a disproportionately large share of the professional, technical, and managerial jobs, the recent rates of growth for minority groups have been twice or more that of the white majority. Hispanic-origin workers, who previously held even smaller shares of these positions than did blacks, have enjoyed the highest rate of change. On the other hand, as Table 14-4 shows, the overall rate of growth of the Hispanic-origin labor force was very high: they had 64.6 percent growth in 1980-90 compared to a 14.5 percent growth in the white labor force. Hence such large changes in proportional growth of Hispanics within various occupational groups is not unexpected.

2. Meanwhile, there has been a net exodus or almost zero growth in the lowest-paying jobs of nonfarm laborer, farm laborer, and private household worker among black and Hispanic-origin workers as well as among white workers.

3. Both black and Hispanic-origin workers have entered the middle class occupations of sales workers, clerical workers, and craft and kindred workers at rates of two to seven times those of whites.

Despite these trends toward convergence, it remains true that by 1990 black and Hispanic-origin workers occupy managerial, administrative (A-1) and professional occupations (A-2) less often than whites. Blacks comprise 9.9 percent of the overall workforce, but they hold only 6.8 percent of the managerial jobs and 6.2 percent of the professional specialty occupations. Hispanics are 7.8 percent of the total workforce, and 4.1 percent and 4.4 percent of the managerial and professional specialty occupations, respectively (see Table 14-1).

Of course, the interpretation of the 1990 data on the distribution of blacks, Hispanics and women is affected by the direction of trends over the last decade as well as by their level in 1990. Between 1980 and 1990, blacks increased from 9.6 to 9.9 percent of the overall workforce, Hispanic-origin workers from 5.6 percent to 7.8 percent, and women from 42.6 to 45.8 percent. In terms of penetration of these groups into the occupational structure over the decade, we see an incremental growth (or shrinkage in occupational groups where these three groups were over-represented), but few large breakthroughs in employment. If a deviation of plus or minus 30 percent from the overall representation of the group in the specific occupational category is taken as evidence of over- or under-representation, then blacks were over-represented in three of the thirteen occupational categories and under-represented in five of these categories. Between 1980 and 1990, blacks moved to over-representation in the occupational category of protective service occupations (C-2; 12.0 percent black in 1980, 15.7 percent black in 1990).

Hispanic-origin workers were over-represented in five occupational groups and under-represented in three occupational groups. By 1990, they added another occupational group in which they were over-represented: transportation and material moving occupations (F-2, increased from 5.9 percent Hispanic to 8.5 percent Hispanic). One of the largest increases in Hispanic penetration was in an occupational grouping where they were already over-represented: they moved from comprising 9.4 percent of all private household occupations in 1980 to 22.9 percent in 1990.

Meanwhile, both blacks and Hispanics tend to be over-represented in the lower-status jobs of laborer, service worker, and operative. The proportions occupying clerical and craft jobs have already converged toward approximate equality. If the recent patterns of change that have characterized the years since 1960 were to continue to the year 2000, the occupational composition of the U.S. labor force would show reduced differences linked to race and ethnicity. Yet, as was stated for females, occupational titles do not reflect differences in real income very precisely, with the result that income differences between the race/ethnic groups are much wider than these data suggest (see Chapter 15).

Women showed no changes in the number of occupational categories where they were heavily under- or over-represented. However, in the best-paid occupational group, executive, administrative and managerial occupations (A-1), they moved from a position of marginal under-representation in 1980 (30.3 percent women) to slight under-representation in 1990 (42.1 percent women), an increase of 11.8 percent in that job category. By 1990, women had increased their degree of over-representation in the professional specialty occupations (A-2) by 4.5 percent, increasing from 49.0 percent to 53.5 percent in the decade. Women also showed large gains in the protective service occupations (C-2, rising from 11.4 to 15.6 percent), an area where they continued to be heavily under-represented. Contrary to some media speculation, the composition of administrative support occupations, including clerical (B-3) and private household occupations (C-1), showed almost no change in their proportion female during the decade; they continue to have very high proportions of female workers.

Table 14-4. Occupation of Employed Labor Force, by Race-ethnicity: 1990, 1980, and Percent Change 1980-1990 and 1970-1980

Occupation	Percent distribution, 1990			Percent distribution, 1980			Percent change, 1980-1990			Percent change, 1970-1980		
	White	Black	Hispanic	White	Black	Hispanic	White	Black	Hispanic	White	Black	Hispanic
Total employed, 16 years and over	100.0	100.0	100.0	100.0	100.0	100.0	14.5	22.2	64.6	23.1	26.8	89.0
Managerial and professional specialty occupations	27.9	18.1	14.1	23.9	14.1	12.2	33.9	56.9	89.3	46.8		80.5
Executive, administrative, and managerial occupations	13.1	7.7	7.0	11.1	5.2	5.9	35.5	79.7	93.9	65.3	180.6	91.2
Professional specialty occupations	14.8	10.4	7.1	12.8	8.9	6.3	32.6	43.5	84.9	33.8	66.2	71.4
Technical, sales, and administrative support occupations	32.3	29.4	25.9	31.1	25.2	24.5	19.0	42.6	74.0	25.9	75.5	108.2
Technicians and related support occupations	3.7	3.3	2.5	3.1	2.7	2.1	37.8	50.9	97.5	60.0	92.1	117.9
Sales occupations	12.5	7.7	9.0	10.7	5.0	7.2	33.2	86.9	105.8	20.9	78.7	118.6
Administrative support occupations, including clerical	16.2	18.4	14.4	17.3	17.5	15.2	6.9	28.7	55.7	24.4	72.4	102.5
Service occupations	11.8	22.1	19.2	11.6	23.1	16.3	16.3	17.0	93.5	30.2	5.5	106.7
Private household occupations	0.3	1.2	1.3	0.4	2.6	1.0	0.1	-43.6	115.9	-40.6	-60.3	32.9
Protective service occupations	1.6	2.7	1.5	1.5	1.9	1.2	26.0	77.4	110.1	32.7	121.0	149.7
Other service occupations	9.8	18.2	16.3	9.8	18.6	14.1	15.4	19.3	90.5	35.9	28.4	112.2
Farming, forestry, and fishing occupations	2.5	1.5	5.0	2.9	2.0	4.7	-2.7	-8.8	75.3	-4.2	-41.2	54.1
Precision production, craft, and repair occupations	11.7	8.2	13.1	13.4	8.9	14.0	0.1	11.4	54.0	12.7	17.6	93.7
Operators, fabricators, and laborers	13.8	20.8	22.9	17.1	26.7	28.4	-7.7	-4.9	32.7	4.0	9.1	74.5
Machine operators, assemblers, and inspectors	6.2	9.7	11.7	8.6	13.5	16.0	-18.0	-12.1	20.3	0.3	17.7	74.6
Transportation and material moving occupations	4.0	5.5	4.5	4.4	6.0	4.8	4.1	12.1	54.0	13.7	15.9	76.4
Handlers, equipment cleaners, helpers, and laborers	3.6	5.6	6.7	4.1	7.2	7.6	1.4	-5.6	45.6	2.4	-8.1	73.3

Source: 1990 data from U.S. Bureau of the Census, "Social and Economic Characteristics: United States," 1990-CP-2-1, Table 45, 1980 data from "Detailed Population Characteristics, 1980 Census of Population, Table 278, 1970 White and Black data from "General Social and Economic Characteristics: United States Summary," 1980 Census of Population, Table 89, and 1970 Hispanic data from "Detailed Population Characteristics," 1970 Census of Population, Table 223, U.S. Government Printing Office, Washington, D.C., 1993, 1984, 1983, and 1973.

Detailed Occupation Distribution

Any overview of occupational composition and trends provided above fails to reveal the great diversity of occupations that exists within each of the major occupation groups and the great disparities in representation of the sexes and races within them. Table 14-5, which lists the detailed occupations and provides basic demographic and socio-economic indicators for each, helps to provide the missing details, while offering a clearer picture of the occupational structure and trends of the nation.

Table 14-5 is far too lengthy and complex to be analyzed here. It is designed as a reference table explaining the detailed content of each major occupation category, showing the characteristics of workers in each. Following are some examples.

Growing and Stagnating Occupations

Between 1980 and 1990 the ten fastest-growing occupations were:

Fastest-Growing Occupations[1]

Occupation	Percent change 1980-1990
Hand engraving and printing occupations	642.7
Demonstrators, promoters, and models, sales	305.4
Inspectors, agricultural products	303.3
Health record technologists and technicians	276.7
Underwriters	271.9
Graders and sorters, agricultural products	252.7
Legal assistants	237.9
Supervisors, related agricultural occupations	231.6
Supervisors, painters, paperhangers, and plasterers	221.7
Operations and systems researchers and analysts	215.1

[1] "Not elsewhere classified" occupations are not included.

These rapidly-growing occupations are spread across a variety of occupational areas, including sales, administrative support occupations, and supervisory occupations. By contrast, the ten most slowly growing occupations during the past decade tended to be in occupations heavily affected by automation, especially in the extractive and manufacturing industries.

Most Slowly Growing Occupations

Occupation	Percent change 1980-1990
Chief communications operators	-93.5
Helpers, extractive occupations	-87.1
Patternmakers and model makers, metal	-71.9
Peripheral equipment operators	-71.4
Medical science teachers	-69.3
Lathe and turning machine operators	-67.4
Milling and planing machine operators	-66.9
Production helpers	-64.9
Drilling and boring machine operators	-64.5
Surveyors and mapping scientists	-61.7

Most and Least Gender-Segregated Occupations

In 1990 men outnumbered women by the greatest proportion mostly in occupations associated with construction and repair:

Occupations With the Lowest Proportion of Female Workers

Occupation	Percent female
Supervisors, brickmasons, stonemasons, and tile setters	0.7
Bus, truck, and stationary engine mechanics	0.9
Heavy equipment mechanics	1.1
Farm equipment mechanics	1.1
Supervisors, carpenters and related workers	1.2
Marine engineers	1.2
Brickmasons and stonemasons, except apprentices	1.2
Concrete and terrazzo finishers	1.3
Heating, air conditioning, and refrigeration mechanics	1.3
Electrical power installers and repairers	1.4

Occupations with the highest proportion of women in their workforces tended to be in the childcare, teaching, medical and clerical fields:

Occupations With the Highest Proportion of Female Workers

Occupation	Percent female
Secretaries	98.7
Family child care providers	98.6
Dental hygienists	98.4
Teachers, prekindergarten and kindergarten	97.8
Child care workers, private household	97.3
Dental assistants	97.1
Early childhood teachers' assistants	95.9
Receptionists	95.7
Typists	94.4
Registered nurses	94.3

While women have entered other occupations in large numbers in the last decade, the proportion female among these highly feminized occupations has changed hardly at all since 1980, and the categories of occupations in this group has also remained very similar. With the exception of registered nurses, the salaries of these highly feminized occupations are among the lowest of any jobs.

Occupations Dominated by Races

White workers (i.e. those categorized as white, non-Hispanic) comprised the lowest percentage of the following categories:

Occupations With the Lowest Proportion of White Workers

Occupation	Percent white
Housekeepers and butlers	46.8
Private household cleaners and servants	51.8
Graders and sorters, agricultural products	51.9
Maids and housemen	56.5
Cooks, private household	57.1
Pressing machine operators	60.3
Stevedores	60.7
Elevator operators	60.8
Garbage collectors	61.1
Parking lot attendants	61.2

Many of these occupations are poorly-paid jobs in the service industry. By contrast, the occupations with the highest proportions of white workers are frequently found in the sales, scientific, agricultural and educational sectors:

Occupations With the Highest Proportion of White Workers

Occupation	Percent white
Farmers, except horticultural	97.5
Auctioneers	97.2
Sales engineers	96.7
Airplane pilots and navigators	96.4
Geologists and geodeists	95.8
History teachers	95.5
Tool and die maker apprentices	95.5
Surveyors and mapping scientists	95.3
Dental hygienists	95.3
Theology teachers	95.0

A number of occupations have very small proportions of black workers:

Occupations With the Lowest Proportion of Black Workers

Occupation	Percent black
Earth, environmental, and marine science teachers	0.0
Sales engineers	0.9
Farmers, except horticultural	1.0
Mining engineers	1.0
Geologists and geodeists	1.1
Optometrists	1.5
Biological science teachers	1.6
Veterinarians	1.7
Airplane pilots and navigators	1.8
Nuclear engineers	1.8

Not surprisingly, the list of occupations with very low proportions of black workers looks similar to the list of occupations with very high proportions of whites. Yet in the list of occupations with the highest proportion of black workers, no occupation is more than one-third black.

Occupations With the Highest Proportion of Black Workers

Occupation	Percent black
Housekeepers and butlers	32.7
Private household cleaners and servants	32.7
Garbage collectors	31.7
Cooks, private household	31.3
Stevedores	30.1
Nursing aides, orderlies, and attendants	29.1
Maids and housemen	28.9
Winding and twisting machine operators	28.5
Postal clerks, except mail carriers	27.9
Longshore equipment operators	27.8

In 1980, the list of the top ten black occupations consisted of job categories that varied between 53.8 percent and 32.8 percent black. Thus, unlike women, blacks are reducing their concentration in some formerly segregated occupations.

Hispanic workers were least likely to be found in the following occupations, most of which tend to be in the scientific or teaching professions:

Occupations With the Lowest Proportion of Hispanic Workers

Occupation	Percent Hispanic
Theology teachers	0.8
Auctioneers	1.1
Chemical engineers	1.3
Sociology teachers	1.3
Agricultural and food scientists	1.4
Actuaries	1.4
Physics teachers	1.4
Biological and life scientists	1.6
Marine and naval architects	1.6
Agriculture and forestry teachers	1.6

While they are heavily under-represented in scientific and educational occupations, Hispanic workers are much more frequently found in agricultural, private household and construction occupations:

Occupations With the Highest Proportion of Hispanic Workers

Occupation	Percent Hispanic
Graders and sorters, agricultural products	53.6
Farm workers	33.3
Housekeepers and butlers	32.7
Supervisors, farm workers	30.7
Nursery workers	27.8
Plasterers	27.4
Private household cleaners and servants	26.7
Production samplers and weighers	26.2
Graders and sorters, except agricultural	23.1
Solderers and brazers	21.7

The 1990 data show that while there are occupations that are overwhelmingly white, there are few specific occu-

Table 14-5. Detailed Occupation of the Civilian Labor Force, by Selected Characteristics: 1990

Occupation	Number employed	Percent female	Percent white	Percent black	Percent Hispanic	Percent change in employment 1980-1990	Education 0 to 11 years	Education 16 years and over	Mean earnings Male	Mean earnings Female
Total persons, 16 years and over	123,473,450	45.7	82.2	10.6	8.1	26.5	18.3	22.5	$27,383	$18,101
Managerial and professional specialty occupations	31,266,845	48.3	87.9	6.9	4.2	41.1	3.4	58.0	$39,757	$24,619
Executive, administrative, and managerial occupations	14,619,157	42.2	88.8	6.3	4.5	44.3	5.2	43.8	$40,773	$24,196
Legislators	12,716	41.6	84.2	9.8	2.7	-29.7	4.7	57.8	$39,920	$22,851
Chief executives and general administrators, public administration	19,023	27.5	81.3	14.0	5.4	74.4	10.6	32.8	$34,939	$25,785
Administrators and officials, public administration	506,683	45.6	83.4	12.1	4.5	90.4	3.0	49.1	$39,446	$26,686
Administrators, protective services	49,273	28.6	87.3	9.2	4.2	57.6	4.0	31.1	$37,831	$22,352
Financial managers	635,911	46.0	90.6	4.8	3.9	57.6	1.8	54.9	$58,589	$30,361
Personnel and labor relations managers	275,495	48.7	85.2	8.7	6.9	28.3	6.3	42.5	$43,234	$28,750
Purchasing managers	120,775	33.6	91.1	4.9	3.4	72.6	2.1	50.2	$45,462	$29,574
Managers, marketing, advertising, and public relations	609,109	31.8	94.0	3.0	3.0	-9.7	2.3	55.0	$56,110	$31,748
Administrators, education and related fields	623,612	52.7	85.2	10.8	4.3	63.0	2.8	69.0	$42,452	$24,614
Managers, medicine and health	233,621	66.6	84.3	10.9	4.8	115.4	4.5	45.7	$44,774	$26,077
Postmasters and mail superintendents	39,846	45.8	90.0	7.0	3.1	27.9	5.5	14.9	$41,945	$28,455
Managers, food serving and lodging establishments	1,030,651	44.5	83.3	7.6	6.8	112.2	14.2	18.9	$29,525	$16,584
Managers, properties and real estate	411,466	46.1	89.5	5.9	5.7	14.3	10.5	32.4	$47,121	$21,764
Funeral directors	45,486	13.4	87.9	10.8	1.9	—	5.3	28.2	$36,328	$22,050
Managers, service organizations, n.e.c.	404,073	50.3	87.5	8.6	4.2	—	6.0	46.2	$35,598	$22,003
Managers and administrators, n.e.c., salaried	4,941,606	32.1	91.8	4.1	4.0	—	5.5	40.0	$58,539	$27,269
Managers and administrators, n.e.c., self-employed	404,387	22.5	91.8	3.0	4.4	—	13.0	24.7	$39,374	$21,535
Management related occupations	4,255,424	52.1	86.9	7.5	4.6	66.5	2.9	49.5	$37,604	$22,769
Accountants and auditors	1,590,178	52.7	86.1	6.8	4.2	60.1	0.7	64.1	$41,737	$23,333
Underwriters	67,767	67.6	88.7	7.5	3.8	271.9	2.0	41.3	$39,147	$24,770
Other financial officers	679,275	51.7	89.5	5.9	4.3	70.4	2.1	47.8	$49,347	$23,401
Management analysts	281,789	33.7	91.4	5.0	2.7	143.8	2.1	67.8	$54,701	$29,938
Personnel, training, and labor relations specialists	513,625	57.7	83.3	11.8	5.8	25.2	5.1	42.8	$36,829	$24,125
Purchasing agents and buyers, farm products	17,298	17.1	87.9	6.5	6.7	-8.9	20.4	20.3	$31,790	$16,464
Buyers, wholesale and retail trade, except farm products	228,399	53.1	91.4	4.1	4.7	40.1	7.7	27.6	$33,513	$18,913
Purchasing agents and buyers, n.e.c.	246,967	45.1	90.0	6.3	4.2	32.0	4.4	28.9	$34,205	$23,209
Business and promotion agents	36,492	46.4	89.2	6.0	5.4	85.5	7.7	42.4	$37,827	$22,981
Construction inspectors	64,284	6.5	87.5	7.3	5.6	32.4	8.0	17.5	$29,743	$21,419
Inspectors and compliance officers, except construction	161,277	30.5	80.7	13.4	7.0	5.9	5.5	40.4	$31,585	$23,865
Management related occupations, n.e.c.	368,073	77.6	84.6	9.8	5.8	1108.2	3.8	25.9	$30,820	$20,807
Professional specialty occupations	16,647,688	53.7	87.1	7.4	3.9	38.5	1.8	70.6	$39,479	$24,735
Engineers, architects, and surveyors	1,876,523	9.6	88.4	3.5	3.3	23.7	0.7	70.6	$44,073	$30,681
Architects	156,874	15.1	90.5	2.8	5.1	49.3	0.7	80.2	$43,537	$26,242
Engineers	1,708,244	9.1	88.1	3.5	3.2	23.6	0.7	70.1	$44,901	$31,723
Aerospace	143,434	8.1	87.2	3.2	3.9	63.3	0.4	77.2	$47,300	$34,601
Metallurgical and materials	19,230	11.5	89.9	3.5	2.6	-20.5	0.8	68.6	$43,964	$28,546
Mining	6,478	6.4	94.2	1.0	2.8	-33.8	1.0	67.1	$44,252	$21,918
Petroleum	24,565	6.7	93.4	2.2	3.1	7.7	1.0	82.6	$53,560	$39,920
Chemical	64,320	11.1	88.8	3.5	1.3	13.0	0.3	84.7	$48,795	$35,488
Nuclear	10,801	6.4	90.7	1.8	2.3	17.6	0.1	77.9	$48,472	$34,259
Civil	252,808	7.0	87.3	3.2	3.7	26.1	0.8	74.9	$44,377	$31,301
Agricultural	2,148	6.3	93.1	2.1	3.9	-52.1	0.6	75.0	$40,104	$25,835
Electrical and electronic	467,023	10.0	86.6	4.2	3.2	46.1	0.5	70.5	$44,801	$35,084
Industrial	176,333	13.9	90.8	3.7	3.3	-7.7	0.9	54.3	$39,198	$28,925
Mechanical	185,872	5.3	90.3	2.8	2.4	-4.7	1.0	63.6	$42,464	$32,928
Marine and naval architects	13,269	3.7	91.8	2.8	1.6	-16.3	2.8	58.3	$42,560	$32,627
Engineers, n.e.c.	341,963	9.8	87.8	3.5	3.0	39.6	0.6	71.6	$43,861	$30,968
Surveyors and mapping scientists	11,405	7.8	95.3	2.1	3.0	-61.7	0.5	56.5	$33,849	$21,572
Mathematical and computer scientists	779,507	35.4	86.1	6.3	3.2	138.8	0.9	63.9	$45,984	$31,196
Computer systems analysts and scientists	471,290	30.7	86.2	5.4	2.8	134.8	0.7	67.2	$41,702	$33,041
Operations and systems researchers and analysts	251,818	42.6	85.7	8.2	4.1	215.1	1.4	54.7	$40,224	$35,985
Actuaries	18,732	33.7	83.5	8.8	1.4	83.8		90.6	$65,493	$30,162
Statisticians	31,852	50.6	90.5	2.2	4.0	8.4	0.2	68.1	$37,801	$25,541
Mathematical scientists, n.e.c.	5,815	25.5	87.0	6.3	2.0	-7.8		86.9	$44,701	$31,252

Table 14-5. Detailed Occupation of the Civilian Labor Force, by Selected Characteristics: 1990 (continued)

Occupation	Number employed	Percent female	Percent white	Percent black	Percent Hispanic	Percent change in employment 1980-1990	Education 0 to 11 years	Education 16 years and over	Mean earnings Male	Mean earnings Female
Natural scientists	408,675	26.5	87.7	4.2	3.0	33.0	0.6	82.9	$38,821	$26,532
Physicists and astronomers	27,842	12.9	90.6	2.5	2.4	24.8	0.1	86.3	$49,942	$33,423
Chemists, except biochemists	141,255	27.4	82.8	6.2	3.2	40.6	0.2	81.9	$38,267	$27,469
Atmospheric and space scientists	8,354	12.9	92.0	3.7	2.1	1.3	0.3	67.5	$37,396	$26,603
Geologists and geodesists	53,129	14.4	95.8	1.1	2.4	17.2	...	92.5	$45,008	$29,513
Physical scientists, n.e.c.	18,782	29.0	91.0	4.6	1.9	120.8	0.2	88.0	$37,008	$27,480
Agricultural and food scientists	34,842	26.7	90.6	4.2	1.4	46.6	1.6	63.0	$30,265	$19,525
Biological and life scientists	62,137	41.7	87.5	3.9	1.6	37.9	0.1	89.9	$33,400	$24,896
Forestry and conservation scientists	34,815	13.2	93.2	3.2	2.5	2.8	4.5	64.2	$31,579	$20,205
Medical scientists	27,519	42.7	80.6	4.0	3.7	39.4		99.5	$46,524	$29,676
Health diagnosing occupations	874,525	19.9	86.8	3.3	4.1	35.9	0.4	98.1	$80,153	$37,737
Physicians	586,715	20.7	84.2	3.7	4.9	36.0	0.2	99.2	$126,002	$60,447
Dentists	155,529	12.8	90.5	3.1	2.6	24.7	0.3	99.1	$84,659	$38,716
Veterinarians	48,744	26.6	94.7	1.7	2.0	43.1	0.3	99.0	$58,847	$29,608
Optometrists	27,515	14.7	93.7	1.5	2.1	12.6	0.3	98.4	$60,823	$34,679
Podiatrists	8,908	11.3	92.8	3.4	2.1	15.3	0.2	98.7	$83,374	$38,972
Health diagnosing practitioners, n.e.c.	47,114	31.6	92.8	1.9	2.8	121.3	2.4	79.2	$67,212	$24,002
Health assessment and treating occupations	2,514,340	87.2	85.4	8.7	3.1	48.3	1.0	51.1	$33,621	$24,219
Registered nurses	1,885,129	94.3	85.2	8.9	2.9	48.8	0.8	45.0	$35,221	$25,898
Pharmacists	181,798	36.8	88.1	4.3	3.1	26.7	0.2	87.9	$42,693	$28,117
Dieticians	90,223	89.3	74.0	19.3	4.8	38.3	10.9	51.2	$22,949	$18,642
Therapists	331,621	76.4	88.4	7.3	3.7	74.3	2.3	69.8	$32,619	$22,517
Respiratory therapists	65,589	60.1	83.3	10.8	4.9	37.8	1.1	21.8	$28,035	$21,995
Occupational therapists	37,895	89.6	89.6	5.4	3.1	116.3	1.8	79.9	$29,910	$24,186
Physical therapists	92,022	75.5	89.7	5.6	3.6	116.7	2.6	73.4	$44,408	$25,102
Speech therapists	64,713	91.1	93.5	4.4	2.3	58.3	0.5	96.4	$38,251	$24,604
Therapists, n.e.c.	71,402	72.3	86.2	9.9	4.2	71.0	3.0	68.9	$25,522	$19,608
Physicians' assistants	25,569	49.3	84.4	8.7	6.2	-13.9	5.6	30.7	$29,587	$19,609
Teachers, postsecondary	786,233	40.5	86.8	4.9	3.4	25.6	8.5	88.2	$37,582	$22,469
Earth, environmental, and marine science teachers	1,253	29.1	94.3	0.0	3.4			93.8	$36,470	$18,241
Biological science teachers	6,101	33.9	93.2	1.6	3.1	-35.5		93.6	$40,791	$21,042
Chemistry teachers	5,446	25.6	88.8	2.8	1.9	-34.0		91.3	$37,098	$19,081
Physics teachers	4,432	12.5	87.5	3.5	1.4	-17.3	0.2	91.7	$42,074	$16,822
Natural science teachers, n.e.c.	389	24.9	90.5	4.1	2.1		4.4	88.9	$28,528	$18,184
Psychology teachers	4,518	46.7	92.4	4.0	2.7	-21.0	0.2	93.1	$44,383	$26,277
Economics teachers	3,426	22.7	89.0	2.7	2.7	-30.7	0.5	96.7	$43,167	$30,276
History teachers	4,121	27.3	95.5	3.4	2.2	-25.0		96.7	$36,007	$23,866
Political science teachers	1,005	25.2	89.6	5.3	4.5		0.7	93.8	$34,434	$22,039
Sociology teachers	1,457	37.9	88.0	5.4	1.3			92.7	$40,413	$30,428
Social science teachers, n.e.c.	860	36.3	84.8	8.8	2.1		0.1	95.2	$34,836	$28,378
Engineering teachers	7,777	16.6	87.7	4.4	3.3	-27.7	0.3	76.2	$37,612	$19,784
Mathematical science teachers	17,357	38.7	87.2	5.1	2.7		0.1	81.0	$28,040	$15,911
Computer science teachers	4,384	38.9	85.6	4.3	4.7	14.8		61.1	$22,269	$14,814
Medical science teachers	2,743	28.0	91.2	3.9	1.9	-69.3	0.2	91.1	$81,858	$37,873
Health specialties teachers	15,711	75.9	89.6	6.6	2.3	-17.9	0.5	85.4	$40,855	$26,403
Business, commerce, and marketing teachers	5,063	54.8	87.3	6.8	2.5	-32.0	0.1	85.0	$41,223	$19,027
Agriculture and forestry teachers	1,061	28.5	94.9	2.5	1.6			84.5	$34,881	$18,388
Art, drama, and music teachers	21,393	50.5	91.4	4.3	3.1	-23.2	0.2	85.4	$29,708	$15,511
Physical education teachers	4,115	50.4	85.6	10.2	3.0		0.4	62.0	$23,589	$11,918
Education teachers	1,455	48.7	86.9	11.1	5.4			89.1	$38,719	$26,463
English teachers	24,276	57.8	92.1	4.4	3.2	6.8	0.3	90.6	$30,637	$18,436
Foreign language teachers	10,025	70.4	86.2	2.4	17.2	5.1	0.4	81.8	$21,268	$13,405
Law teachers	4,555	30.7	92.5	5.3	1.9		0.4	96.6	$77,511	$42,314
Social work teachers	308	66.6	95.0	7.8	7.1			92.2	$40,360	$27,397
Theology teachers	2,616	23.5	86.2	2.9	0.8		0.4	92.1	$29,114	$22,220
Trade and industrial teachers	1,270	47.4	90.1	6.4	2.7		1.8	56.2	$27,946	$21,340
Home economics teachers	593	84.1	78.4	18.9	6.1		1.5	74.0	$29,927	$24,550

Table 14-5. Detailed Occupation of the Civilian Labor Force, by Selected Characteristics: 1990 (continued)

Occupation	Number employed	Percent female	Percent white	Percent black	Percent Hispanic	Percent change in employment 1980-1990	Education 0 to 11 years	Education 16 years and over	Mean earnings Male	Mean earnings Female
Teachers, postsecondary, n.e.c.	13,455	34.8	88.7	4.2	3.9	—¹	0.4	86.9	$37,820	$22,712
Postsecondary teachers, subject not specified	615,068	39.2	86.0	5.0	3.4	47.0	0.5	88.8	$35,917	$20,972
Teachers, except postsecondary	4,559,526	74.6	86.9	9.7	4.3	24.6	1.3	83.0	$26,595	$17,406
Teachers, prekindergarten and kindergarten	269,330	97.8	81.9	13.2	5.8	52.3	5.8	35.6	$16,794	$9,008
Teachers, elementary school	3,024,189	78.4	86.3	10.4	4.4	32.3	0.2	86.2	$30,432	$21,745
Teachers, secondary school	624,400	56.8	91.1	6.3	3.4	-26.5	0.1	89.4	$30,762	$22,939
Teachers, special education	62,216	82.2	86.4	10.5	3.7	94.9	3.6	67.9	$29,206	$19,740
Teachers, n.e.c.	579,391	62.2	87.6	7.5	4.5	84.3	5.5	52.5	$25,782	$13,598
Counselors, educational and vocational	238,533	61.5	81.0	14.0	5.5	23.3	1.7	74.7	$27,968	$22,538
Librarians, archivists, and curators	228,456	78.2	87.6	7.5	3.2	15.2	0.9	64.1	$25,123	$18,664
Librarians	200,881	81.3	87.4	7.8	3.1	9.5	0.6	63.8	$22,435	$18,800
Archivists and curators	27,575	55.5	89.5	5.5	4.3	85.5	3.3	66.5	$27,811	$18,528
Social scientists and urban planners	385,238	50.9	90.6	5.8	3.3	81.3	0.2	85.5	$39,379	$25,905
Economists	152,237	43.9	91.2	4.7	2.8	62.9	0.2	78.1	$50,622	$29,794
Psychologists	191,962	58.6	90.5	6.5	3.5	111.2	0.2	92.4	$43,286	$28,528
Sociologists	2,211	47.9	81.5	7.7	7.6	-10.4		83.0	$33,871	$22,073
Social scientists, n.e.c.	20,297	47.5	91.2	5.0	3.6	60.5	0.3	78.5	$31,820	$21,341
Urban planners	18,531	32.7	87.4	7.6	5.0	42.3	1.1	82.4	$37,297	$27,789
Social, recreation, and religious workers	1,133,394	51.2	80.0	15.0	5.4	40.5	4.7	64.9	$20,876	$14,955
Social workers	658,919	68.9	73.8	20.5	6.8	48.8	3.9	64.9	$25,488	$20,098
Recreation workers	50,779	70.8	79.9	15.1	5.7	50.2	12.3	25.6	$15,132	$11,408
Clergy	324,889	10.4	89.3	6.7	3.0	15.6	4.5	73.6	$22,073	$16,013
Religious workers, n.e.c.	98,807	57.3	90.9	5.5	4.0	102.3	6.1	56.8	$20,809	$12,300
Lawyers and judges	779,471	24.4	94.2	3.6	2.5	48.5	0.2	98.5	$74,738	$41,608
Lawyers	747,077	24.5	94.4	3.4	2.5	50.2	0.1	99.5	$88,324	$45,862
Judges	32,394	22.8	90.6	7.0	3.4	17.5	2.4	76.5	$61,152	$37,354
Writers, artists, entertainers, and athletes	2,083,267	47.9	89.8	5.2	5.0	59.2	5.9	46.9	$30,641	$18,403
Authors	106,730	49.5	94.4	3.0	1.9	142.4	1.7	74.0	$38,312	$22,058
Technical writers	74,292	49.8	92.4	4.6	2.0	54.6	1.0	64.6	$35,205	$26,232
Designers	596,802	55.5	90.2	3.6	5.4	83.5	7.1	36.1	$33,558	$17,771
Musicians and composers	148,020	32.8	87.4	7.5	6.5	14.9	9.5	41.7	$21,406	$11,298
Actors and directors	109,573	38.1	89.5	7.3	4.9	93.3	2.9	59.3	$44,657	$29,603
Painters, sculptors, craft-artists, and artist printmakers	212,762	52.5	90.9	3.6	4.9	45.6	5.2	40.2	$25,180	$14,440
Photographers	143,520	30.2	88.9	5.7	5.8	58.8	7.2	32.8	$26,306	$14,416
Dancers	21,913	76.7	85.1	7.4	7.3	89.7	20.6	16.9	$16,825	$12,607
Artists, preformers, and related workers, n.e.c.	93,421	49.8	84.8	5.4	11.1	103.9	10.5	36.4	$26,687	$15,912
Editors and reporters	266,543	50.7	91.4	5.3	3.1	31.4	1.9	70.7	$34,874	$22,497
Public relations specialists	167,568	58.8	89.3	7.2	4.4	45.6	2.8	61.0	$41,475	$24,833
Announcers	60,269	20.8	87.2	9.0	5.5	35.1	10.4	26.2	$22,508	$15,945
Athletes	81,854	26.7	87.6	8.3	5.0	65.7	10.7	38.7	$31,339	$11,631
Technical, sales, and administrative support occupations	38,525,740	63.2	84.1	9.7	6.5	30.2	11.1	17.7	$25,899	$16,908
Technicians and related support occupations	4,387,408	46.1	83.6	9.0	5.3	47.1	4.8	30.5	$30,990	$20,990
Health technologists and technicians	1,429,097	81.0	80.1	13.3	5.6	47.9	5.4	21.9	$25,118	$18,582
Clinical laboratory technologists and technicians	329,892	75.1	77.4	13.1	5.5	38.4	3.4	43.8	$25,840	$20,975
Dental hygienists	72,394	98.4	95.3	2.1	2.8	59.3	0.7	31.7	$26,379	$21,248
Health record technologists and technicians	55,764	91.6	76.2	15.8	7.3	276.7	5.7	12.9	$17,941	$15,200
Radiologic technicians	130,383	72.3	87.2	7.8	5.5	38.2	2.3	15.3	$30,351	$21,624
Licensed practical nurses	429,473	93.6	76.3	18.6	4.6	1.1	8.2	10.7	$25,236	$17,260
Health technologists and technicians, n.e.c.	411,191	71.0	81.9	11.4	7.2	176.8	5.6	17.5	$24,960	$15,186
Technologists and technicians, except health	2,958,311	29.2	85.3	6.9	5.1	46.8	4.5	34.7	$32,244	$21,893
Engineering and related technologists and technicians	1,104,435	18.6	86.2	6.3	5.7	20.2	5.4	21.9	$30,592	$21,241
Electrical and electronic technicians	401,463	13.9	83.8	7.4	5.9	53.8	4.2	15.5	$29,782	$22,541
Industrial engineering technicians	15,324	21.8	89.2	6.6	4.2	48.8	10.1	43.8	$33,895	$23,887
Mechanical engineering technicians	30,109	8.4	88.5	4.4	4.5	99.0	7.9	49.3	$38,324	$25,316
Engineering technicians, n.e.c.	239,680	30.5	85.1	7.7	5.2	-9.2	6.2	30.7	$28,528	$18,583
Drafting technicians	324,764	18.7	88.0	4.7	6.0	1.7	4.4	21.2	$27,913	$20,626
Surveying and mapping technicians	93,095	10.1	91.2	4.1	5.1	90.6	9.9	16.5	$25,108	$16,496

Table 14-5. Detailed Occupation of the Civilian Labor Force, by Selected Characteristics: 1990 (continued)

Occupation	Number employed	Percent female	Percent white	Percent black	Percent Hispanic	Percent change in employment 1980-1990	Education 0 to 11 years	Education 16 years and over	Mean earnings Male	Mean earnings Female
Science technicians	208,988	32.5	82.4	8.8	6.4	12.7	9.9	28.4	$28,117	$19,233
Biological technicians	56,723	42.8	82.6	7.8	8.5	29.5	15.2	28.8	$25,204	$17,967
Chemical technicians	76,639	24.7	82.6	10.8	5.0	7.2	8.7	23.9	$30,966	$22,761
Science technicians, n.e.c.	75,626	32.8	82.2	7.5	6.2	7.8	7.2	32.6	$28,180	$16,971
Technicians, except health, engineering, and science	1,644,888	35.8	85.1	7.0	4.6	80.5	3.2	44.1	$35,429	$23,591
Airplane pilots and navigators	109,826	3.5	96.4	1.8	2.1	48.2	1.6	56.2	$57,019	$30,199
Air traffic controllers	47,163	22.3	86.5	10.0	4.8	17.5	3.3	21.9	$37,080	$24,295
Broadcast equipment operators	35,519	23.3	83.7	10.8	5.8	-49.1	6.2	22.1	$26,471	$17,426
Computer programmers	662,759	32.5	85.4	6.0	3.4	111.6	1.3	57.5	$35,068	$28,516
Tool programmers, numerical control	3,670	14.4	89.1	6.6	3.7	-56.4	3.9	14.8	$36,204	$23,744
Legal assistants	258,152	75.9	87.0	7.7	6.2	237.9	3.5	33.7	$27,350	$21,168
Technicians, n.e.c.	527,799	29.3	81.3	8.3	5.6	60.3	5.5	33.4	$28,810	$19,791
Sales occupations	14,432,769	49.2	87.0	7.1	6.1	47.9	2.4	21.4	$29,101	$15,881
Supervisors and proprietors, sales occupations, salaried	3,015,374	34.8	89.9	5.1	5.3	175.1	9.2	24.6	$38,887	$19,502
Supervisors and proprietors, sales occupations, self-employed	436,087	34.5	88.1	2.6	4.8	-1.9	14.9	21.7	$32,377	$14,978
Sales representatives, finance and business services	2,488,640	40.7	91.7	4.7	3.8	38.0	4.3	41.2	$47,082	$25,376
Insurance sales occupations	666,542	35.3	90.4	6.1	4.0	19.4	3.4	39.2	$48,222	$23,039
Real estate sales occupations	801,238	50.4	92.8	3.1	3.6	24.4	4.1	37.6	$42,603	$24,956
Securities and financial services sales occupations	297,548	27.8	92.2	4.0	3.3	127.9	2.0	63.0	$71,822	$33,100
Advertising and related sales occupations	174,065	51.7	91.5	5.6	3.9	58.2	4.8	43.0	$35,046	$23,626
Sales occupations, other business services	549,247	36.7	91.5	5.4	4.0	52.7	6.9	36.4	$37,716	$22,161
Sales representatives, commodities, except retail	1,571,432	22.3	93.3	3.0	4.5	23.9	7.6	35.4	$43,618	$27,781
Sales engineers	43,616	5.1	96.7	0.9	1.9	0.3	1.5	61.5	$48,289	$33,004
Sales representatives, mining, manufacturing, and wholesale	1,527,816	22.8	93.2	3.1	4.6	24.7	7.8	34.7	$38,946	$22,557
Sales workers, retail and personal services	6,848,281	65.5	82.6	10.2	7.9	33.7	25.4	9.7	$18,435	$10,637
Sales workers, motor vehicles and boats	352,279	10.6	91.0	5.1	5.7	31.3	14.2	14.0	$26,275	$15,672
Sales workers, apparel	444,577	81.3	83.4	9.2	8.4	7.7	24.4	10.2	$15,337	$7,455
Sales workers, shoes	117,767	62.2	79.8	12.5	9.9	8.5	26.8	7.1	$12,285	$7,074
Sales workers, furniture and home furnishings	187,120	45.2	91.6	4.5	5.4	30.1	13.5	16.4	$24,038	$13,486
Sales workers, radio, TV, hi-fi, and appliances	170,872	28.6	88.9	5.8	5.7	57.6	11.6	26.6	$24,656	$15,306
Sales workers, hardware and building supplies	175,187	22.6	92.8	3.5	5.3	-5.8	15.5	12.7	$19,717	$11,610
Sales workers, parts	132,093	9.9	90.8	4.2	7.3	-30.5	17.1	4.5	$18,842	$13,512
Sales workers, other commodities	1,857,857	66.3	86.6	7.2	6.7	16.5	19.3	14.0	$19,710	$9,303
Sales counter clerks	210,073	65.5	83.8	7.9	7.5	134.5	28.5	8.4	$17,387	$8,400
Cashiers	2,855,680	79.1	76.3	14.6	9.4	66.4	33.5	4.2	$11,180	$7,182
Street and door-to-door sales workers	230,927	66.5	86.8	8.8	5.6	12.5	16.0	22.1	$20,684	$10,645
News vendors	113,849	39.0	87.2	6.9	6.3	15.8	37.6	7.7	$11,111	$7,997
Sales related occupations	72,955	65.8	91.6	4.5	4.7	181.3	16.8	16.9	$27,766	$12,196
Demonstrators, promoters, and models, sales	45,265	81.6	90.5	5.2	5.3	305.4	20.7	12.6	$16,451	$8,429
Auctioneers	8,372	13.9	97.2	1.8	1.1	23.1	17.8	15.6	$34,191	$12,891
Sales support occupations, n.e.c.	19,318	51.3	91.5	4.1	4.8	142.3	7.2	27.3	$32,655	$15,267
Administrative support occupations, including clerical	19,705,563	77.3	82.1	11.7	7.0	16.9	8.9	12.1	$22,742	$15,723
Supervisors, administrative support occupations	924,326	56.0	82.4	12.3	6.5	-12.5	6.1	22.3	$37,302	$24,471
Supervisors, general office	579,625	63.0	81.6	12.9	6.8	-8.2	5.9	21.1	$34,002	$21,761
Supervisors, computer equipment operators	34,548	36.6	85.6	9.9	4.9	-18.0	2.3	28.9	$37,218	$27,283
Supervisors, financial records processing	110,386	69.8	86.9	8.1	5.0	-29.9	2.8	33.5	$40,407	$25,590
Chief communications operators	4,373	60.7	84.7	10.8	5.5	-93.5	6.2	21.6	$43,369	$23,428
Supervisors, distribution, scheduling, and adjusting clerks	195,394	30.9	81.3	13.4	6.7	22.8	8.9	18.3	$31,513	$24,295
Computer equipment operators	667,213	61.6	79.3	13.9	6.4	63.3	5.9	14.7	$22,922	$15,677
Computer operators	660,318	61.7	79.4	13.8	6.4	71.8	5.8	14.8	$25,549	$16,950
Peripheral equipment operators	6,895	53.7	70.4	19.7	10.5	-71.4	16.6	8.9	$20,296	$14,404
Secretaries, stenographers, and typists	4,761,326	98.0	86.4	8.9	5.8	2.2	5.2	8.8	$26,018	$17,739
Secretaries	4,018,671	98.7	88.2	7.5	5.6	3.8	5.0	8.6	$19,328	$15,885
Stenographers	79,880	90.5	89.3	7.1	4.1	-6.9	2.1	13.5	$43,137	$23,623
Typists	662,775	94.4	75.2	17.9	7.2	-5.4	6.8	9.5	$15,587	$13,710

Table 14-5. Detailed Occupation of the Civilian Labor Force, by Selected Characteristics: 1990 (continued)

Occupation	Number employed	Percent female	Percent white	Percent black	Percent Hispanic	Percent change in employment 1980-1990	Education 0 to 11 years	Education 16 years and over	Mean earnings Male	Mean earnings Female
Information clerks	1,578,646	85.4	82.9	10.4	8.0	76.5	10.4	12.7	$16,595	$12,274
Interviewers	205,958	75.8	78.8	14.5	7.5	53.7	8.5	18.2	$15,255	$12,378
Hotel clerks	96,390	72.0	81.4	10.3	7.0	57.5	13.0	11.2	$11,503	$9,753
Transportation ticket and reservation agents	269,951	70.5	83.8	8.8	7.9	171.4	4.3	23.2	$26,635	$17,058
Receptionists	822,093	95.7	84.5	9.2	8.4	59.2	11.6	8.1	$12,686	$10,720
Information clerks, n.e.c.	184,254	78.8	79.6	13.8	7.2	122.0	15.0	12.5	$16,898	$11,461
Records processing occupations, except financial	884,211	78.2	77.2	15.4	7.7	-8.4	12.2	13.3	$19,922	$14,316
Classified-ad clerks	5,282	82.8	89.4	7.4	5.5	-61.0	7.5	18.1	$18,765	$14,714
Correspondence clerks	12,521	83.1	79.6	16.5	4.6	-35.2	4.5	19.3	$28,981	$17,127
Order clerks	229,122	71.8	78.4	15.4	8.1	-26.4	10.9	11.3	$21,899	$17,456
Personnel clerks, except payroll and timekeeping	80,893	85.4	79.3	13.8	7.8	7.5	5.8	13.8	$25,919	$16,634
Library clerks	150,475	78.8	80.4	11.2	6.1	6.9	12.9	21.2	$7,217	$8,563
File clerks	267,946	80.6	72.2	18.9	9.0	-3.5	18.2	7.9	$11,835	$9,805
Records clerks	137,972	78.6	79.8	14.1	6.6	8.3	6.8	17.7	$24,836	$15,913
Financial records processing occupations	2,401,529	89.0	88.0	6.6	5.4	6.5	7.0	11.2	$22,724	$15,424
Bookkeepers, accounting, and auditing clerks	1,921,952	89.6	89.1	5.7	5.2	5.1	6.7	11.3	$21,667	$15,384
Payroll and timekeeping clerks	179,480	88.7	84.8	9.6	5.8	12.7	6.3	9.5	$23,015	$16,959
Billing clerks	168,476	90.6	84.5	9.3	6.5	30.2	7.2	9.3	$19,528	$14,955
Cost and rate clerks	78,267	74.2	82.1	10.4	7.5	-8.8	13.3	17.7	$27,711	$16,107
Billing, posting, and calculating machine operators	53,354	85.8	78.5	13.0	7.8	3.3	8.5	9.3	$21,697	$13,714
Duplicating, mail, and other office machine operators	68,788	58.8	72.3	17.8	9.5	17.2	17.0	7.0	$17,170	$11,522
Duplicating machine operators	27,866	53.3	71.7	17.4	9.8	48.1	12.9	8.3	$15,630	$11,087
Mail preparing and paper handling machine operators	6,196	57.9	73.8	15.8	10.5	-12.1	28.6	6.1	$18,040	$11,596
Office machine operators, n.e.c.	34,726	63.4	72.6	18.6	9.0	5.9	18.2	5.7	$17,839	$11,883
Communications equipment operators	244,115	86.2	75.5	19.3	7.0	-20.9	12.8	5.5	$23,762	$13,943
Telephone operators	233,257	87.3	75.6	19.3	6.9	-20.2	12.7	5.5	$19,572	$14,939
Communications equipment operators, n.e.c.	10,858	62.0	73.5	20.3	8.6	41.3	15.4	9.3	$27,952	$12,947
Mail and message distributing occupations	1,033,277	37.4	71.2	20.9	7.5	33.5	10.8	10.0	$22,376	$17,709
Postal clerks, except mail carriers	350,565	45.0	62.9	27.9	6.9	31.3	7.1	11.3	$29,278	$24,344
Mail carriers, postal service	328,241	26.8	79.9	13.9	6.5	27.9	5.9	11.0	$29,640	$23,083
Mail clerks, except postal service	211,709	49.9	68.7	22.9	9.1	26.0	18.8	6.1	$14,756	$10,973
Messengers	142,762	24.8	75.5	16.8	9.2	—	19.5	10.2	$15,831	$12,438
Material recording, scheduling, and distributing clerks	2,220,906	40.0	79.8	12.7	9.5	33.6	19.0	8.7	$22,738	$15,272
Dispatchers	204,947	47.4	86.0	10.1	5.9	116.1	13.2	7.6	$24,860	$16,553
Production coordinators	252,659	47.2	86.0	8.0	6.6	-0.8	8.6	22.4	$30,664	$20,124
Traffic, shipping, and receiving clerks	648,602	29.0	77.0	13.9	12.5	34.6	22.2	5.4	$18,555	$14,407
Stock and inventory clerks	711,772	36.6	77.6	14.2	9.7	24.7	22.0	6.5	$16,699	$14,036
Meter readers	49,536	14.1	79.4	15.4	8.3	19.6	11.6	5.2	$22,787	$19,273
Weighers, measurers, checkers, and samplers	80,746	46.6	77.4	14.2	9.9	8.3	26.9	7.0	$20,946	$12,802
Expediters	238,789	65.5	83.5	10.6	7.2	125.0	16.1	10.9	$19,606	$12,705
Material recording, scheduling, and distributing clerks, n.e.c.	33,855	67.9	77.8	14.1	9.2	-10.4	19.0	14.4	$27,790	$12,275
Adjusters and investigators	1,139,087	72.5	82.3	12.2	6.4	120.9	5.3	22.8	$24,855	$17,093
Insurance adjusters, examiners, and investigators	344,639	70.7	83.2	12.4	4.5	110.7	3.1	30.8	$30,084	$19,611
Investigators and adjusters, except insurance	581,830	73.9	82.5	11.7	6.7	138.8	5.8	20.3	$25,952	$16,996
Eligibility clerks, social welfare	49,506	89.6	76.0	15.6	9.9	105.2	4.2	20.4	$22,773	$15,730
Bill and account collectors	163,112	66.2	81.3	12.9	8.1	93.4	8.7	15.2	$20,612	$16,036
Miscellaneous administrative support occupations	3,782,139	82.0	79.0	13.6	7.9	14.7	8.7	13.3	$19,209	$13,617
General office clerks	1,491,116	82.3	78.6	13.9	8.2	-9.6	10.8	10.6	$19,172	$13,733
Bank tellers	509,023	89.8	83.5	9.2	7.1	2.9	6.4	7.7	$14,342	$11,323
Proofreaders	30,326	75.9	87.7	8.3	3.4	11.0	6.0	35.7	$19,124	$13,568
Data-entry keyers	639,265	87.0	73.4	18.1	8.1	69.1	7.0	9.5	$16,382	$13,782
Statistical clerks	148,578	67.2	80.4	13.5	5.6	6.8	6.5	20.9	$26,930	$17,331
Teachers' aides	275,543	89.2	75.9	13.9	13.0	33.3	10.6	14.6	$10,110	$8,020
Administrative support occupations, n.e.c.	688,288	71.6	82.1	11.9	6.2	71.3	7.2	23.9	$28,406	$17,561

Table 14-5. Detailed Occupation of the Civilian Labor Force, by Selected Characteristics: 1990 (continued)

Occupation	Number employed	Percent female	Percent white	Percent black	Percent Hispanic	Percent change in employment 1980-1990	Education 0 to 11 years	Education 16 years and over	Mean earnings Male	Mean earnings Female
Service occupations	16,567,557	58.2	73.2	17.4	11.4	31.2	32.5	6.4	$17,373	$11,847
Private household occupations	563,918	94.8	59.8	26.2	23.2	-4.3	49.3	4.2	$13,423	$6,738
Launderers and ironers	1,687	82.8	71.0	17.0	13.7	-23.1	50.3	6.8	$25,978	$5,506
Cooks, private household	9,212	89.1	57.1	31.3	12.8	-18.9	48.4	5.8	$12,230	$8,465
Housekeepers and butlers	34,416	93.9	46.8	32.7	32.7	-47.6	55.6	3.6	$13,969	$7,448
Child care workers, private household	164,252	97.3	79.7	10.8	14.3	11.7	36.7	5.8	$4,587	$5,460
Private household cleaners and servants	354,351	94.0	51.8	32.7	26.7	-2.4	54.6	3.5	$10,350	$6,810
Protective service occupations	2,084,775	15.8	78.4	16.4	6.9	41.3	11.9	14.6	$25,777	$18,787
Supervisors, protective service occupations	135,206	10.5	84.1	12.4	5.1	42.9	5.7	22.1	$35,457	$25,524
Supervisors, firefighting and fire prevention occupations	29,298	2.8	93.1	4.4	3.3	41.9	4.1	15.4	$42,342	$27,872
Supervisors, police and detectives	61,222	11.5	85.2	11.8	4.6	20.6	2.9	28.8	$38,695	$27,740
Supervisors, guards	44,686	14.0	76.7	18.5	6.9	92.5	10.5	17.2	$29,335	$20,959
Firefighting and fire prevention occupations	241,486	3.4	86.7	9.0	4.9	14.9	5.3	10.0	$29,891	$18,755
Fire inspection and fire prevention occupations	16,725	13.9	85.1	10.7	4.6	-21.0	11.2	16.9	$27,079	$16,119
Firefighting occupations	224,761	2.7	86.8	8.9	4.9	18.9	4.9	9.5	$32,702	$21,391
Police and detectives	822,283	14.6	81.2	14.4	6.4	47.4	3.6	19.5	$28,140	$22,737
Police and detectives, public service	519,184	12.0	84.1	11.6	6.5	26.7	2.5	23.6	$32,930	$26,063
Sheriffs, bailiffs, and other law enforcement officers	118,432	19.3	83.5	12.5	5.8	92.6	6.1	16.4	$26,911	$21,754
Correctional institution officers	184,667	18.9	71.7	23.8	6.4	113.2	5.4	9.8	$24,579	$20,395
Guards	885,800	21.2	72.6	20.9	8.3	44.6	22.2	10.1	$10,990	$8,123
Crossing guards	45,313	71.7	77.8	18.7	6.5	0.6	36.4	2.9	$7,597	$5,548
Guards and police, except public service	785,511	16.6	71.0	22.1	8.6	47.2	20.8	10.8	$17,187	$14,003
Protective service occupations, n.e.c.	54,976	45.7	90.6	5.3	5.4	61.7	31.1	7.5	$8,186	$4,819
Service occupations, except protective and household	13,918,864	63.1	73.0	17.2	11.5	31.7	34.9	5.3	$14,867	$10,095
Food preparation and service occupations	5,738,958	58.7	76.0	12.9	11.7	30.9	40.0	4.3	$10,450	$7,582
Supervisors, food preparation and service occupations	276,420	57.5	79.0	11.6	8.5	18.4	24.2	8.9	$21,223	$10,699
Bartenders	330,710	49.6	91.0	3.6	5.8	14.3	19.6	9.0	$13,135	$9,502
Waiters and waitresses	1,488,253	80.5	86.1	5.4	7.9	9.2	28.8	6.6	$10,692	$7,354
Cooks	2,073,260	47.6	68.2	18.7	13.4	58.1	46.1	2.7	$9,714	$7,817
Food counter, fountain, and related occupations	236,480	72.3	80.9	11.1	8.7	25.5	54.7	2.5	$6,202	$4,529
Kitchen workers, food preparation	211,500	75.3	79.3	13.0	9.5	118.1	36.6	3.0	$9,744	$7,657
Waiters'/waitresses' assistants	378,558	42.6	73.0	13.2	18.3	44.0	51.7	3.0	$6,081	$6,094
Miscellaneous food preparation occupations	743,777	49.8	69.0	17.2	16.6	16.2	50.5	2.3	$6,810	$7,001
Health service occupations	2,261,958	87.3	66.5	26.5	7.8	31.0	24.0	6.8	$19,111	$11,823
Dental assistants	179,287	97.1	87.5	5.4	8.5	18.1	7.3	5.9	$21,622	$12,252
Health aides, except nursing	222,977	79.8	71.1	22.2	6.5	-20.3	22.3	11.0	$17,535	$11,652
Nursing aides, orderlies, and attendants	1,859,694	87.2	63.9	29.1	7.8	43.6	25.8	6.3	$18,177	$11,566
Cleaning and building services, except household	3,423,701	41.2	66.4	22.2	15.8	24.7	43.4	3.1	$18,501	$11,544
Supervisors, cleaning and building service workers	167,475	29.6	73.6	18.1	11.9	48.2	25.9	7.4	$24,365	$14,115
Maids and housemen	712,789	80.7	56.5	28.9	18.7	16.4	50.4	2.1	$13,289	$8,591
Janitors and cleaners	2,481,545	31.5	68.4	20.9	15.3	26.3	43.0	3.1	$14,833	$8,880
Elevator operators	11,411	15.1	60.8	26.5	20.6	-43.7	43.0	3.8	$20,284	$12,015
Pest control occupations	50,481	6.1	86.0	8.5	8.5	43.9	22.7	7.0	$19,734	$14,121
Personal service occupations	2,494,247	81.4	81.0	11.7	8.8	46.1	21.3	9.0	$15,207	$10,686
Supervisors, personal service occupations	62,932	69.3	81.2	12.1	7.6	126.9	12.7	17.2	$24,082	$13,532
Barbers	84,626	21.2	80.9	13.0	8.9	-18.4	27.9	3.5	$17,073	$11,646
Hairdressers and cosmetologists	733,576	89.6	84.6	8.5	8.1	34.8	14.8	4.5	$21,026	$11,217
Attendants, amusement and recreation facilities	137,153	37.1	79.2	9.9	8.0	50.1	28.1	9.2	$12,658	$10,742
Guides	41,286	53.3	76.2	13.5	6.0	61.3	15.2	19.4	$13,930	$9,967
Ushers	29,611	33.0	79.2	13.1	9.0	36.1	44.7	8.1	$6,036	$6,036
Public transportation attendants	105,949	79.4	81.0	13.2	5.8	56.3	6.3	29.5	$25,601	$23,084
Baggage porters and bellhops	38,763	10.8	62.3	26.0	8.5	96.9	21.5	8.3	$14,292	$13,264
Welfare service aides	48,190	83.7	65.9	24.9	11.2	-14.1	22.8	18.3	$19,668	$11,252
Family child care providers	434,643	98.6	86.5	7.2	8.6	[1]	22.2	8.8	$10,176	$6,161
Early childhood teachers' assistants	338,928	95.9	79.0	15.1	8.0	[1]	20.7	9.3	$9,405	$6,611
Child care workers, n.e.c.	211,351	89.1	74.8	17.6	10.2	34.2	34.2	8.6	$11,164	$6,713
Personal service occupations, n.e.c.	227,239	69.2	76.1	13.9	12.3	33.9	30.3	10.3	$12,584	$8,494

Table 14-5. Detailed Occupation of the Civilian Labor Force, by Selected Characteristics: 1990 (continued)

Occupation	Number employed	Percent female	Percent white	Percent black	Percent Hispanic	Percent change in employment 1980-1990	Education		Mean earnings	
							0 to 11 years	16 years and over	Male	Female
Farming, forestry, and fishing occupations	3,105,395	16.3	81.8	6.5	17.0	10.5	40.5	7.6	$20,372	$11,836
Farm operators and managers	1,087,365	14.1	95.4	1.8	3.5	-16.3	25.1	12.3	$23,908	$11,786
Farmers, except horticultural	795,187	14.4	97.5	1.0	1.7	-29.9	24.2	11.4	$22,148	$11,025
Horticultural specialty farmers	34,732	10.0	87.4	5.2	9.8	158.4	23.2	16.4	$21,239	$10,058
Managers, farms, except horticultural	238,884	12.9	90.3	3.6	8.1	74.1	28.5	14.1	$26,085	$13,823
Managers, horticultural specialty farms	18,562	25.0	86.7	4.7	11.5	35.1	21.4	21.8	$26,161	$12,237
Other agricultural and related occupations	1,809,415	18.9	73.5	9.1	26.5	35.6	49.5	5.0	$15,820	$10,394
Farm occupations, except managerial	842,073	20.9	71.0	7.6	32.9	-3.8	57.4	4.0	$15,352	$8,968
Supervisors, farm workers	43,435	14.2	74.7	5.0	30.7	-15.1	40.7	9.8	$22,968	$13,617
Farm workers	759,669	19.8	70.6	7.8	33.3	-4.1	58.9	3.5	$10,997	$7,096
Marine life cultivation workers	1,233	28.7	82.6	7.5	8.2	2.6	32.8	8.1	$16,333	$7,729
Nursery workers	37,736	49.2	74.1	6.7	27.8	23.8	47.6	7.0	$11,109	$7,429
Related agricultural occupations	967,342	17.3	75.6	10.5	20.9	110.8	42.6	6.0	$16,195	$11,534
Supervisors, related agricultural occupations	65,607	7.9	86.7	4.7	12.2	231.6	23.7	13.8	$23,688	$13,797
Groundskeepers and gardeners, except farm	735,556	7.4	74.0	11.8	21.4	107.1	45.2	5.0	$12,365	$9,237
Animal caretakers, except farm	107,205	62.6	91.5	4.3	6.2	59.5	24.6	9.9	$14,172	$9,537
Graders and sorters, agricultural products	54,659	69.5	51.9	11.7	53.6	252.7	67.6	1.3	$9,826	$6,894
Inspectors, agricultural products	4,315	46.3	73.6	15.2	18.4	303.3	32.6	12.7	$20,926	$18,207
Forestry and logging occupations	148,023	5.1	83.0	11.1	5.4	20.6	44.5	5.1	$22,813	$14,528
Supervisors, forestry and logging workers	12,068	4.5	89.7	6.3	3.3	56.2	29.8	11.6	$35,024	$20,320
Forestry workers, except logging	20,431	17.5	79.8	7.0	15.1	-7.9	35.0	13.6	$15,409	$11,001
Timber cutting and logging occupations	115,524	3.0	82.9	12.3	3.9	24.4	47.7	3.0	$18,005	$12,264
Fishers, hunters, and trappers	60,592	6.4	86.1	4.1	5.4	8.7	37.8	7.3	$26,872	$13,540
Captains and other officers, fishing vessels	6,341	3.0	92.0	1.8	5.4	2.1	29.2	10.6	$38,336	$13,708
Fishers	52,152	6.4	85.5	4.3	6.1	9.8	39.2	6.6	$23,005	$13,246
Hunters and trappers	2,099	15.8	85.1	5.4	5.4	4.8	29.1	14.3	$19,276	$13,667
Precision production, craft, and repair occupations	14,031,300	9.5	85.4	7.5	9.2	11.4	24.7	5.6	$24,622	$17,882
Mechanics and repairers	4,271,166	4.3	86.7	7.3	7.9	12.4	22.0	4.5	$26,101	$19,843
Supervisors, mechanics and repairers	270,582	8.4	90.8	5.7	4.7	70.8	12.3	9.5	$35,327	$30,805
Mechanics and repairers, except supervisors	4,000,584	4.1	86.5	7.4	8.1	9.9	22.7	4.1	$25,747	$19,421
Vehicle and mobile equipment mechanics and repairers	1,865,678	1.9	86.0	7.3	9.2	17.6	27.4	3.5	$23,044	$18,024
Automobile mechanics, except apprentices	954,623	1.8	84.8	7.9	9.9	5.2	29.3	2.9	$20,685	$18,081
Automobile mechanic apprentices	1,591	3.8	83.0	10.5	8.0		27.4	1.4	$17,056	$15,053
Bus, truck, and stationary engine mechanics	266,142	0.9	87.6	7.3	7.2	82.0	27.7	1.9	$24,176	$20,394
Aircraft engine mechanics	134,672	4.0	85.1	7.9	8.9	51.0[a]	6.7	6.4	$29,898	$22,293
Small engine repairers	62,022	1.8	90.9	4.8	6.1	83.2	29.2	3.5	$18,689	$15,978
Automobile body and related repairers	228,710	2.1	85.4	6.0	12.4	18.5	35.1	2.0	$20,267	$16,197
Aircraft mechanics, except engine	31,814	7.5	82.1	9.4	8.6	—[a]	10.5	5.5	$29,787	$23,508
Heavy equipment mechanics	157,495	1.1	89.8	5.6	6.5	5.1	24.9	2.7	$27,001	$20,511
Farm equipment mechanics	28,609	1.1	92.0	3.5	6.4	-35.5	26.8	3.5	$19,833	$10,203
Industrial machinery repairers	332,779	4.1	87.5	7.3	6.7	-28.8	25.2	2.8	$26,970	$18,883
Machinery maintenance occupations	25,273	4.5	83.2	11.2	9.9	-40.9	30.9	2.6	$26,079	$18,819
Electrical and electronic equipment repairers	635,525	9.8	86.2	8.2	6.5	0.9	8.9	8.7	$28,702	$22,660
Electronic repairers, communications/industrial equipment	179,229	8.1	85.1	8.4	7.5	12.9	10.3	8.6	$24,338	$21,896
Data processing equipment repairers	91,657	13.0	85.6	7.9	5.6	96.6	3.6	16.4	$30,891	$22,813
Household appliance and power tool repairers	53,125	4.1	89.1	5.4	7.0	-33.5	17.3	4.6	$22,204	$16,120
Telephone line installers and repairers	50,633	6.8	88.6	6.8	6.0	-17.1	7.8	4.0	$32,888	$27,091
Telephone installers and repairers	190,927	13.9	86.4	9.4	5.5	-24.4	6.2	5.3	$32,370	$26,652
Miscellaneous electrical and electronic equipment repairers	69,954	5.5	85.3	8.0	7.6	124.7	14.4	5.5	$29,522	$21,391
Heating, air conditioning, and refrigeration mechanics	192,983	1.3	90.2	5.1	6.9	34.4	18.9	3.2	$24,086	$18,937
Miscellaneous mechanics and repairers	948,346	4.9	86.5	7.5	7.7	23.2	22.1	4.8	$26,584	$18,766
Camera, watch, and musical instrument repairers	31,097	12.2	89.1	4.0	3.3	-20.6	14.9	15.9	$21,881	$16,643
Locksmiths and safe repairers	27,137	6.5	90.5	4.9	6.0	44.6	17.9	6.4	$22,730	$18,379
Office machine repairers	41,888	5.6	86.2	7.9	6.5	10.1	7.6	6.0	$23,315	$17,765
Mechanical controls and valve repairers	20,408	5.0	82.1	12.6	7.7	-26.1	16.3	3.6	$28,011	$21,508
Elevator installers and repairers	25,634	1.7	90.7	5.0	5.8	27.0	12.3	4.5	$37,566	$21,448
Millwrights	96,140	3.4	92.2	5.3	3.1	-22.7	20.3	2.3	$32,931	$19,570

Table 14-5. Detailed Occupation of the Civilian Labor Force, by Selected Characteristics: 1990 (continued)

Occupation	Number employed	Percent female	Percent white	Percent black	Percent Hispanic	Percent change in employment 1980-1990	Education 0 to 11 years	Education 16 years and over	Mean earnings Male	Mean earnings Female
Specified mechanics and repairers, n.e.c.	213,949	6.9	86.9	7.2	7.4	-27.3	22.4	5.7	$22,381	$15,778
Not specified mechanics and repairers	492,093	4.0	84.8	8.4	9.1	137.6	25.0	4.2	$23,855	$19,037
Construction trades	5,318,000	2.8	86.3	7.0	9.7	25.2	28.0	5.2	$22,899	$17,123
Supervisors, construction occupations	838,000	2.7	90.6	4.9	6.4	13.0	21.1	10.3	$31,510	$21,046
Supervisors, brickmasons, stonemasons, and tile setters	12,968	0.7	85.7	9.1	7.4	178.6	31.2	5.2	$28,232	$18,115
Supervisors, carpenters and related workers	45,625	1.2	92.8	2.2	7.0	39.4	21.7	5.7	$29,028	$17,572
Supervisors, electricians and power transmission installers	73,556	2.2	93.2	3.6	4.5	103.8	10.1	8.9	$38,754	$28,514
Supervisors, painters, paperhangers, and plasterers	32,369	5.0	87.3	6.5	8.5	221.7	32.0	7.0	$24,711	$14,110
Supervisors, plumbers, pipefitters, and steamfitters	20,518	2.0	92.7	3.8	4.7	22.2	19.9	5.0	$34,182	$22,551
Supervisors, construction, n.e.c.	652,964	2.8	90.4	5.1	6.6	1.8	21.5	11.3	$34,150	$25,413
Construction trades, except supervisors	4,480,000	2.8	85.5	7.4	10.3	27.8	29.3	4.2	$20,746	$16,142
Brickmasons and stonemasons, except apprentices	196,939	1.2	78.6	14.8	10.4	19.1	41.0	2.2	$20,775	$15,426
Brickmason and stonemason apprentices	727	5.8	82.7	12.9	7.6		37.1	2.1	$12,479	$21,635
Tile setters, hard and soft	55,642	2.3	84.9	5.7	16.6	88.0	34.8	4.4	$21,972	$16,186
Carpet installers	111,836	2.2	86.8	5.8	12.1	38.6	35.7	2.3	$20,499	$12,970
Carpenters, except apprentices	1,360,707	1.7	88.7	5.1	8.9	24.0	28.7	5.5	$19,968	$14,694
Carpenter apprentices	4,853	5.2	85.0	6.2	9.1		22.9	3.1	$13,205	$13,663
Drywall installers	150,554	2.5	83.3	6.3	15.4	86.5	41.6	2.0	$19,720	$12,864
Electricians, except apprentices	635,017	2.5	89.2	6.0	6.0	5.2	13.2	4.5	$28,048	$21,061
Electrician apprentices	15,572	4.4	89.8	6.2	5.8		11.4	3.3	$15,704	$16,214
Electrical power installers and repairers	120,232	1.4	88.4	8.3	4.3	17.9	12.7	2.8	$33,283	$26,498
Painters, construction and maintenance	559,026	7.8	80.6	9.1	15.6	54.0	37.8	5.7	$17,379	$11,537
Paperhangers	17,210	25.6	93.7	2.0	5.8	7.8	19.8	9.3	$22,456	$12,394
Plasterers	43,109	2.0	72.2	13.2	27.4	71.7	46.6	2.0	$21,172	$16,119
Plumbers, pipefitters, and steamfitters, except apprentices	488,858	1.5	87.5	7.1	7.8	7.4	23.5	3.2	$26,145	$19,646
Plumber, pipefitter, and steamfitter apprentices	6,579	2.3	89.6	5.4	6.3		14.2	2.9	$16,056	$17,351
Concrete and terrazzo finishers	75,945	1.3	67.6	20.3	18.8	33.3	45.7	1.7	$19,325	$14,242
Glaziers	45,595	5.4	89.7	4.7	8.7	46.1	25.5	3.0	$22,873	$13,996
Insulation workers	74,412	4.0	78.4	10.9	15.6	54.3	30.5	3.0	$20,659	$17,029
Paving, surfacing, and tamping equipment operators	13,110	2.5	78.7	14.5	11.3	158.4	45.9	1.4	$19,975	$17,566
Roofers	197,183	1.6	80.4	9.7	14.6	93.1	46.9	2.1	$15,824	$13,096
Sheetmetal duct installers	29,962	1.4	91.2	5.0	5.9	14.0	23.0	1.5	$22,925	$16,624
Structural metal workers	75,338	1.9	88.5	5.7	6.9	-1.6	26.6	3.1	$25,614	$17,269
Drillers, earth	20,491	2.5	89.7	4.8	8.2	-1.0	34.1	3.4	$22,711	$14,136
Construction trades, n.e.c.	181,103	3.1	80.8	11.4	10.9	46.6	36.1	3.1	$19,136	$15,187
Extractive occupations	192,862	2.8	90.2	4.4	8.0	-34.1	30.4	6.1	$28,790	$23,786
Supervisors, extractive occupations	49,319	3.5	93.4	2.8	5.2	-38.8	18.8	14.6	$41,677	$33,999
Drillers, oil well	37,072	1.4	88.4	4.6	10.6	-45.9	35.7	4.5	$21,993	$21,340
Explosives workers	9,377	5.4	85.6	8.4	7.5	-4.1	30.3	2.5	$25,525	$17,890
Mining machine operators	62,318	2.7	91.3	4.6	6.2	-26.7	32.9	2.8	$29,411	$23,439
Mining occupations, n.e.c.	34,776	2.7	86.7	5.1	12.4	-28.9	36.7	3.0	$25,343	$22,261
Precision production occupations	4,249,272	23.3	82.7	8.4	10.0	-0.2	22.9	20.7	$24,396	$21,852
Supervisors, production occupations	1,299,637	17.7	85.9	8.0	8.2	-29.3	18.3	12.1	$34,289	$21,681
Precision metal working occupations	1,052,374	7.5	86.9	6.1	7.7	6.6	20.4	3.3	$24,716	$17,981
Tool and die makers, except apprentices	142,814	2.3	94.5	2.7	3.8	-22.6	13.3	2.9	$33,482	$21,967
Tool and die maker apprentices	2,376	4.6	95.5	2.1	2.8		8.4	3.7	$19,457	$24,873
Precision assemblers, metal	40,959	22.1	74.4	13.7	12.7	85.4	27.2	3.4	$24,861	$16,510
Machinists, except apprentices	569,081	4.6	86.7	6.5	12.0	11.6	20.3	2.6	$26,381	$17,727
Machinist apprentices	1,543	6.9	88.7	4.9	7.3		19.5	4.2	$18,444	$17,129
Boilermakers	24,293	2.4	86.5	9.1	5.9	-26.4	22.8	2.2	$27,453	$18,753
Precision grinders, filers, and tool sharpeners	23,069	7.3	91.8	4.3	4.7	21.7	22.7	2.3	$27,039	$18,155
Patternmakers and model makers, metal	5,442	4.9	94.4	3.7	4.1	-71.9	11.1	6.5	$36,278	$24,540
Lay-out workers	16,987	12.7	80.5	14.2	4.4	-20.6	23.5	3.5	$23,407	$20,873
Precious stones and metals workers (jewelers)	61,830	33.7	76.6	4.1	19.5	80.0	28.5	11.5	$22,233	$12,326
Engravers, metal	17,158	37.9	89.7	4.6	7.6	17.8	19.8	8.8	$23,864	$13,074

Table 14-5. Detailed Occupation of the Civilian Labor Force, by Selected Characteristics: 1990 (continued)

Occupation	Number employed	Percent female	Percent white	Percent black	Percent Hispanic	Percent change in employment 1980-1990	Education 0 to 11 years	Education 16 years and over	Mean earnings Male	Mean earnings Female
Sheet metal workers, except apprentices	143,491	5.6	87.7	5.8	7.9	18.1	21.4	3.0	$25,219	$19,114
Sheet metal worker apprentices	951	9.0	82.5	8.8	10.5		12.6	1.5	$15,670	$11,648
Miscellaneous precision metal workers	2,380	21.1	87.5	7.6	5.9	5.8	33.6	1.7	$22,237	$15,049
Precision woodworking occupations	110,659	12.3	86.9	6.3	10.2	0.3	29.4	6.8	$22,958	$13,510
Patternmakers and model makers, wood	3,299	9.8	91.9	3.9	4.8	-24.9	16.4	4.6	$38,612	$17,742
Cabinetmakers and bench carpenters	71,871	6.4	89.5	4.4	9.5	-0.0	26.4	6.8	$19,761	$12,902
Furniture and wood finishers	33,431	25.1	80.9	10.4	12.4	13.6	37.0	7.2	$16,688	$11,275
Miscellaneous precision woodworkers	2,058	14.8	83.9	7.8	7.7	-55.6	32.3	5.5	$16,771	$12,122
Precision textile, apparel, and furnishings machine workers	272,520	56.1	73.4	9.7	17.5	4.3	41.1	5.6	$18,197	$11,386
Dressmakers	97,258	93.4	71.1	9.9	16.2	0.5	38.8	7.3	$16,465	$9,180
Tailors	56,807	48.0	66.8	11.4	21.3	-1.2	47.6	5.2	$19,426	$11,926
Upholsterers	73,938	22.7	80.7	8.1	17.6	13.5	39.9	3.1	$18,191	$11,456
Shoe repairers	28,028	28.0	74.3	10.4	15.7	-5.8	41.7	4.6	$16,599	$11,094
Miscellaneous precision apparel and fabric workers	16,489	62.2	75.3	9.9	14.1	35.8	36.0	9.4	$20,305	$13,271
Precision workers, assorted materials	568,371	53.3	75.1	9.9	12.9	85.5	25.8	5.3	$24,251	$15,567
Hand molders and shapers, except jewelers	20,057	15.8	85.1	5.7	13.2	-41.5	32.0	7.4	$21,995	$15,314
Patternmakers, lay-out workers, and cutters	22,890	24.0	86.7	4.2	7.8	158.5	15.5	10.3	$31,882	$20,062
Optical goods workers	74,907	55.7	86.2	6.3	8.3	67.1	12.2	9.4	$24,403	$14,301
Dental laboratory and medical appliance technicians	56,964	39.6	82.4	6.4	9.4	21.2	10.2	12.4	$28,824	$16,069
Bookbinders	29,933	53.3	79.3	12.3	10.4	6.1	29.0	4.5	$21,873	$12,963
Electrical and electronic equipment assemblers	309,406	66.4	68.0	12.2	15.0	196.1	31.0	2.9	$18,698	$15,204
Miscellaneous precision workers, n.e.c.	54,214	16.3	81.2	7.5	14.9	39.9	31.4	3.0	$22,082	$15,056
Precision food production occupations	491,912	32.6	75.4	12.0	15.7	19.4	34.8	3.1	$18,782	$10,675
Butchers and meat cutters	278,902	19.6	74.7	12.7	15.6	0.5	34.9	2.1	$20,287	$10,996
Bakers	159,172	45.9	75.5	12.0	15.6	44.5	35.1	4.7	$18,438	$10,587
Food batchmakers	53,838	60.2	79.1	8.4	16.1	122.7	33.1	3.9	$17,622	$10,443
Precision inspectors, testers, and related workers	140,655	24.8	83.5	9.0	7.2	41.1	15.1	7.4	$29,026	$17,691
Inspectors, testers, and graders	131,905	24.3	83.6	9.0	7.0	36.6	15.0	7.5	$29,325	$19,603
Adjusters and calibrators	8,750	31.9	83.1	8.9	9.2	182.8	16.4	5.6	$28,727	$15,779
Plant and system operators	313,144	5.5	86.3	8.6	5.6	30.1	12.5	11.0	$32,136	$23,700
Water and sewage treatment plant operators	61,269	5.1	86.7	9.3	5.0	88.2	12.5	7.8	$25,042	$20,386
Power plant operators	37,012	6.1	88.2	7.5	5.0	35.3	6.2	8.0	$38,033	$27,749
Stationary engineers	161,241	4.7	86.8	8.0	4.9	24.0	12.7	14.1	$33,776	$24,206
Miscellaneous plant and system operators	53,622	7.8	83.2	10.5	8.8	5.6	16.0	7.7	$31,691	$22,461
Operators, fabricators, and laborers	18,976,662	26.3	76.2	14.5	12.2	6.3	34.9	3.4	$21,504	$15,093
Machine operators, assemblers, and inspectors	8,635,504	40.0	74.3	14.6	13.6	-4.9	34.6	3.3	$20,938	$13,993
Machine operators and tenders, except precision	5,408,726	41.3	73.6	15.1	14.1	-9.3	36.3	3.1	$21,203	$14,163
Metal working and plastic working machine operators	388,032	18.2	83.1	7.4	9.3	-45.8	33.1	1.9	$24,731	$16,732
Lathe and turning machine set-up operators	29,460	9.1	86.9	5.9	8.8	-44.6	30.5	1.7	$25,428	$19,449
Lathe and turning machine operators	36,530	12.2	89.1	6.8	6.0	-67.4	24.4	3.6	$24,229	$18,552
Milling and planing machine operators	6,789	14.5	87.3	11.6	6.6	-66.9	27.7	5.5	$24,267	$17,246
Punching and stamping press machine operators	110,466	28.2	81.7	11.6	8.9	-26.6	34.8	1.4	$22,354	$16,532
Rolling machine operators	13,743	14.4	84.5	11.3	7.4	-24.1	29.9	1.8	$27,727	$16,471
Drilling and boring machine operators	21,576	20.3	87.0	8.3	6.3	-64.5	32.4	1.5	$21,714	$15,486
Grinding, abrading, buffing, and polishing machine operators	125,458	15.6	80.1	10.8	12.5	-50.2	37.2	1.7	$21,606	$14,915
Forging machine operators	17,046	5.7	84.1	10.8	6.4	17.0	31.4	1.6	$25,920	$17,321
Numerical control machine operators	1,636	16.7	83.7	6.7	9.5	-38.3	15.8	4.3	$27,628	$15,858
Misc. metal, plastic, stone, glass working machine operators	25,328	17.4	85.2	9.2	7.2	-18.1	26.5	2.4	$26,433	$15,488
Fabricating machine operators, n.e.c.	26,662	32.0	77.8	12.5	12.4	-16.2	36.3	2.4	$20,293	$12,985
Metal and plastic processing machine operators	162,367	18.3	79.8	11.2	12.0	-25.6	34.0	2.1	$22,151	$15,015
Molding and casting machine operators	89,468	23.7	81.5	11.1	11.1	-36.3	32.7	1.9	$22,976	$13,496
Metal plating machine operators	35,397	12.1	75.2	10.2	17.8	-13.0	36.1	2.4	$20,891	$16,894
Heat treating equipment operators	18,543	6.6	84.9	10.9	6.5	-20.3	27.4	3.1	$27,572	$17,143
Miscellaneous metal and plastic processing machine operators	18,959	15.7	75.3	14.1	15.1	36.3	42.2	1.5	$17,166	$12,529
Woodworking machine operators	155,637	15.1	82.9	10.6	7.7	9.6	40.3	3.4	$17,690	$12,131
Wood lathe, routing, and planing machine operators	8,211	12.8	87.2	8.0	5.2	13.7	34.8	4.3	$19,308	$13,677
Sawing machine operators	94,905	12.8	81.7	11.8	7.6	0.8	43.9	1.7	$15,940	$12,553
Shaping and joining machine operators	6,044	30.8	85.0	8.3	7.7	-25.7	37.9	2.8	$15,771	$11,318

Table 14-5. Detailed Occupation of the Civilian Labor Force, by Selected Characteristics: 1990 (continued)

Occupation	Number employed	Percent female	Percent white	Percent black	Percent Hispanic	Percent change in employment 1980-1990	Education 0 to 11 years	Education 16 years and over	Mean earnings Male	Mean earnings Female
Nailing and tacking machine operators	3,219	27.2	78.3	11.2	13.7	-20.6	50.6	2.8	$21,274	$12,313
Miscellaneous woodworking machine operators	43,258	17.4	84.9	8.6	8.2	51.8	33.2	7.0	$16,158	$10,813
Printing machine operators	532,145	29.6	85.6	7.7	8.4	26.0	16.9	6.7	$25,041	$15,357
Printing press operators	359,781	18.4	83.7	8.8	9.6	25.4	19.3	4.9	$23,856	$14,531
Photoengravers and lithographers	49,106	27.0	90.7	4.8	6.8	95.7	10.9	6.9	$31,552	$18,048
Typesetters and compositors	72,353	70.1	91.4	4.3	4.4	7.2	6.1	14.8	$24,813	$15,428
Miscellaneous printing machine operators	50,905	54.1	85.9	7.7	7.4	18.2	21.3	8.1	$19,943	$13,423
Textile, apparel, and furnishings machine operators	1,417,572	75.9	64.9	20.0	16.7	-4.7	48.3	1.9	$16,116	$11,432
Winding and twisting machine operators	70,620	72.3	68.9	28.5	1.7	-31.0	48.5	0.7	$18,286	$13,551
Knitting, looping, taping, and weaving machine operators	60,223	64.7	70.6	23.4	6.2	-12.4	44.0	3.1	$17,200	$13,729
Textile cutting machine operators	7,839	42.0	70.1	19.6	16.4	-8.4	45.7	1.5	$15,905	$10,787
Textile sewing machine operators	783,799	88.1	63.4	18.0	19.9	-5.5	50.1	1.6	$15,108	$10,269
Shoe machine operators	34,244	70.6	87.6	7.5	8.9	-49.9	43.0	1.1	$13,115	$10,980
Pressing machine operators	148,411	63.2	60.3	25.4	17.7	52.7	48.3	1.6	$16,782	$10,108
Laundering and dry cleaning machine operators	219,097	62.2	63.6	21.3	16.9	26.5	46.2	3.4	$15,199	$9,434
Miscellaneous textile machine operators	93,339	40.7	72.5	21.0	8.8	-33.3	42.7	2.1	$17,330	$12,600
Machine operators, assorted materials	2,726,311	31.7	73.6	15.1	15.1	-7.4	34.3	3.3	$21,429	$14,130
Cementing and gluing machine operators	32,386	38.0	71.8	16.9	15.0	1.9	41.7	2.0	$18,758	$12,641
Packaging and filling machine operators	281,245	60.0	65.7	18.9	20.7	176.8	42.7	2.2	$17,020	$12,100
Extruding and forming machine operators	27,901	15.2	84.8	9.7	7.5	21.3	29.9	2.4	$22,378	$15,972
Mixing and blending machine operators	111,141	11.8	73.2	18.4	11.0	6.9	31.7	3.5	$21,657	$15,356
Separating, filtering, and clarifying machine operators	69,630	11.2	80.9	12.8	8.5	-0.1	18.9	6.7	$30,653	$19,646
Compressing and compacting machine operators	22,353	22.4	76.9	15.9	9.6	10.5	35.7	2.2	$21,326	$14,139
Painting and paint spraying machine operators	136,177	14.6	77.6	11.1	17.3	-11.2	37.2	2.1	$21,014	$14,049
Roasting and baking machine operators	4,748	20.1	75.7	16.3	14.2	-28.9	32.6	3.9	$21,616	$14,786
Washing, cleaning, and pickling machine operators	10,438	30.7	76.1	13.3	15.3	27.2	38.4	1.7	$18,556	$13,551
Folding machine operators	20,429	67.2	72.0	18.6	12.5	-32.8	40.7	1.9	$20,906	$11,508
Furnace, kiln, and oven operators, except food	96,276	6.1	82.0	13.3	6.2	-33.2	27.4	2.5	$26,973	$18,701
Crushing and grinding machine operators	45,207	19.1	79.6	12.5	11.1	-6.2	40.7	1.7	$19,992	$12,853
Slicing and cutting machine operators	187,949	28.8	73.5	13.8	17.5	-0.9	41.1	2.0	$18,202	$11,515
Motion picture projectionists	10,357	14.9	90.6	4.8	6.0	-24.6	22.7	15.5	$20,320	$12,090
Photographic process machine operators	101,939	51.7	81.8	9.1	8.5	20.4	14.2	13.6	$19,688	$12,285
Miscellaneous machine operators, n.e.c.	611,270	32.7	72.6	15.7	15.6	-4.5	33.7	3.1	$21,769	$14,216
Manufacturing, nondurable goods	236,820	30.4	72.6	17.1	13.9	—	32.3	2.6	$24,855	$15,030
Manufacturing, durable goods	277,112	31.6	71.9	14.7	17.9	—	36.5	2.2	$21,319	$15,036
Nonmanufacturing industries	97,338	41.1	74.7	15.0	12.9	—	29.0	6.8	$19,133	$12,583
Machine operators, not specified	956,865	30.7	72.9	15.4	15.7	-24.9	34.3	3.0	$21,888	$14,299
Manufacturing, nondurable goods	309,226	38.4	71.8	17.0	15.6	—	33.7	2.8	$22,411	$14,758
Manufacturing, durable goods	439,484	28.5	73.7	14.3	15.6	—	35.5	2.4	$21,937	$15,204
Nonmanufacturing industries	208,155	24.0	72.8	15.3	15.9	—	32.9	4.7	$21,316	$12,935
Fabricators, assemblers, and hand working occupations	2,392,653	32.6	75.4	13.9	13.1	4.1	33.1	2.7	$18,875	$12,724
Welders and cutters	643,978	4.7	82.6	9.0	11.1	-9.6	30.7	1.7	$22,894	$16,237
Solderers and brazers	28,237	67.0	73.3	9.7	21.7	-7.5	37.7	2.0	$16,456	$14,102
Assemblers	1,573,979	43.3	72.2	16.2	13.8	7.9	34.0	2.9	$19,745	$13,955
Hand cutting and trimming occupations	16,505	37.1	63.2	19.6	19.5	5.0	47.2	2.2	$14,416	$10,801
Hand molding, casting, and forming occupations	26,409	28.8	81.2	9.5	11.7	55.8	30.2	8.9	$23,018	$11,436
Hand painting, coating, and decorating occupations	45,058	31.5	82.4	8.6	11.6	19.3	28.4	7.0	$18,200	$11,154
Hand engraving and printing occupations	14,854	43.3	85.7	6.3	10.7	642.7	24.9	5.3	$17,301	$12,630
Miscellaneous hand working occupations	43,633	36.3	75.2	13.9	13.1	77.2	36.8	3.6	$18,971	$11,474
Production inspectors, testers, samplers, and weighers	834,125	52.4	75.9	14.1	11.5	1.1	27.9	5.9	$21,550	$14,282
Production inspectors, checkers, and examiners	625,008	53.0	78.1	13.6	9.1	-6.7	24.8	6.2	$26,075	$15,545
Production testers	60,144	32.9	79.5	9.8	7.4	8.0	16.4	11.1	$26,286	$17,937
Production samplers and weighers	10,790	51.0	73.6	11.1	26.2	23.4	41.3	5.1	$19,158	$13,590
Graders and sorters, except agricultural	138,183	58.6	64.6	18.5	23.1	51.9	45.9	2.6	$14,679	$10,057

Table 14-5. Detailed Occupation of the Civilian Labor Force, by Selected Characteristics: 1990 (continued)

Occupation	Number employed	Percent female	Percent white	Percent black	Percent Hispanic	Percent change in employment 1980-1990	Education 0 to 11 years	Education 16 years and over	Mean earnings Male	Mean earnings Female
Transportation and material moving occupations	5,098,974	9.9	80.3	13.7	8.6	16.2	31.1	3.9	$26,922	$19,686
Motor vehicle operators	3,837,900	11.6	79.7	14.2	8.7	27.2	30.6	4.1	$20,599	$13,421
Supervisors, motor vehicle operators	80,351	15.7	84.3	11.2	6.6	152.3	13.8	13.6	$30,157	$20,510
Truck drivers	2,908,952	6.0	81.7	12.5	8.7	30.8	32.6	3.2	$22,245	$12,998
Driver-sales workers	143,353	10.1	89.5	6.2	6.4	-19.2	18.0	6.2	$23,547	$12,037
Bus drivers	447,570	48.1	71.8	23.5	6.3	19.8	24.4	4.9	$19,315	$10,599
Taxicab drivers and chauffeurs	207,333	10.8	63.7	23.8	14.5	18.9	29.4	10.3	$16,823	$11,251
Parking lot attendants	46,559	10.3	61.2	23.2	19.7	39.1	34.5	6.0	$11,835	$9,838
Motor transportation occupations, n.e.c.	3,789	4.8	71.5	17.4	15.0	12.9	39.1	2.1	$20,269	$16,725
Transportation occupations, except motor vehicle	191,107	3.9	88.3	8.8	3.7	-29.5	17.9	8.5	$33,105	$23,517
Rail transportation occupations	121,846	3.7	87.5	10.1	3.7	-40.0	12.5	6.8	$37,660	$28,383
Railroad conductors and yardmasters	37,573	6.5	89.2	8.3	3.3	-18.5	12.1	8.1	$41,978	$25,654
Locomotive operating occupations	45,966	2.7	86.3	11.3	3.5	-35.2	11.7	7.8	$40,632	$28,619
Railroad brake, signal, and switch operators	33,259	1.7	87.6	10.0	4.2	-57.0	14.1	4.2	$36,140	$30,737
Rail vehicle operators, n.e.c.	5,048	6.0	83.8	13.8	5.1	-42.6	13.1	4.5	$31,890	$28,521
Water transportation occupations	69,261	4.1	89.8	6.5	3.8	1.8	27.5	11.6	$28,549	$18,651
Ship captains and mates, except fishing boats	32,997	3.2	94.6	2.7	2.4	6.2	25.8	16.5	$33,737	$25,652
Sailors and deckhands	25,945	3.7	84.0	10.8	5.7	-9.2	31.5	6.5	$21,891	$15,928
Marine engineers	4,152	1.2	92.3	5.0	2.6	23.6	17.1	13.2	$34,283	$17,167
Bridge, lock, and lighthouse tenders	6,167	13.1	86.4	10.4	3.7	22.9	26.6	5.3	$24,285	$15,855
Material moving equipment operators	1,069,960	4.9	80.8	12.6	9.1	-2.7	35.5	2.2	$26,345	$21,154
Supervisors, material moving equipment operators	23,803	6.0	87.4	8.3	5.9	-19.2	20.1	9.9	$30,284	$26,711
Operating engineers	241,812	2.0	87.5	7.2	6.5	24.2	33.5	2.4	$25,661	$19,202
Longshore equipment operators	4,403	1.6	64.4	27.8	10.3	10.9	32.0	5.5	$37,914	$33,716
Hoist and winch operators	20,300	2.3	84.3	6.7	12.3	-28.8	37.7	2.1	$21,703	$19,226
Crane and tower operators	81,825	2.4	82.3	13.3	6.0	-32.2	33.1	1.5	$29,162	$25,356
Excavating and loading machine operators	95,983	1.6	90.6	5.7	4.9	32.5	38.2	2.0	$25,256	$17,851
Grader, dozer, and scraper operators	64,880	1.7	90.0	6.4	4.0	-3.0	44.5	1.4	$22,834	$15,696
Industrial truck and tractor equipment operators	441,859	6.3	73.2	18.2	12.6	13.7	36.5	1.6	$20,363	$18,747
Miscellaneous material moving equipment operators	95,095	13.4	80.2	13.0	9.5	-51.2	32.9	3.5	$23,927	$13,883
Handlers, equipment cleaners, helpers, and laborers	5,242,184	19.8	75.3	15.1	13.4	19.5	39.1	3.1	$16,843	$13,154
Supervisors, handlers, equipment cleaners, and laborers, n.e.c.	15,668	10.7	75.8	15.3	11.4	59.0	22.4	10.9	$27,122	$21,151
Helpers, mechanics, and repairers	21,871	5.8	75.3	12.0	19.9	-11.8	42.7	1.9	$14,246	$13,291
Helpers, construction and extractive occupations	92,712	5.0	78.2	11.5	16.9	-26.4	40.7	2.5	$15,987	$13,981
Helpers, construction trades	85,604	4.5	77.3	12.0	17.9	-12.4	42.1	2.2	$11,564	$10,597
Helpers, surveyor	4,675	9.7	90.9	4.8	4.0	-50.7	20.0	6.6	$15,315	$8,710
Helpers, extractive occupations	2,433	16.0	85.2	9.0	7.6	-87.1	31.2	6.5	$21,083	$22,634
Construction laborers	1,149,780	4.0	75.5	13.5	16.8	73.8	40.4	3.9	$17,352	$12,155
Production helpers	37,983	21.5	70.3	14.8	19.9	-64.9	39.2	1.9	$15,092	$11,298
Freight, stock, and material handlers	1,761,920	22.6	77.4	15.5	11.3	39.9	37.8	3.1	$19,063	$13,899
Garbage collectors	59,909	4.2	61.1	31.7	14.6	-14.1	45.8	2.2	$18,536	$12,754
Stevedores	11,483	3.0	60.7	30.1	14.6	-43.0	38.2	4.8	$32,778	$21,026
Stock handlers and baggers	1,030,362	29.5	80.9	12.1	8.8	58.1	41.6	2.8	$9,668	$9,069
Machine feeders and offbearers	87,209	34.7	74.2	18.5	9.3	-12.5	37.7	2.3	$17,802	$12,262
Freight, stock, and material handlers, n.e.c.	572,957	10.6	73.5	19.1	10.2	37.1	30.3	3.6	$16,533	$14,383
Garage and service station related occupations	270,227	10.7	82.8	10.0	9.2	-10.7	42.0	2.8	$11,902	$10,358
Vehicle washers and equipment cleaners	232,516	12.4	69.6	19.5	16.3	82.5	47.4	1.9	$11,277	$10,813
Hand packers and packagers	368,341	64.7	68.4	16.5	20.4	-32.2	42.1	2.3	$13,521	$11,387
Laborers, except construction	1,291,166	22.0	73.6	16.3	13.7	5.6	36.8	2.9	$16,613	$12,237
Manufacturing, nondurable goods	230,549	32.2	70.7	18.2	14.6	-0.6	39.2	2.1	$17,055	$12,475
Manufacturing, durable goods	307,855	22.6	76.5	14.3	13.1	-0.2	37.6	2.0	$18,064	$14,103
Transportation, communications, and other public utilities	133,611	10.8	76.9	20.0	12.5	-8.1	30.5	3.2	$19,683	$14,438
Wholesale and retail trade	348,823	20.1	76.7	13.4	13.4	13.3	34.1	3.3	$15,004	$10,803
All other industries	270,328	20.5	70.3	18.6	14.7	25.2	40.4	4.1	$13,257	$9,363
Experienced unemployed not classified by occupation Unemployed, no recent civilian work experience	999,951	55.4	53.3	31.9	19.0	194.2	57.3	4.7	$12,964	$9,283

1 Data not available due to a change in occupation classification between 1980 and 1990.
2 Number represents the percent change in both aircraft mechanic occupations combined.

Source: 1990 Census Supplemental Reports, "Detailed Occupation and Other Characteristics from the EEO File for the United States," U.S. Government Printing Office, Washington, D.C., 1992, Tables 1 and 2, "Equal Opportunity Supplemental Tabulations File," Part I (ICPSR 6223), The Bureau Producer and Distributor, Washington, D.C., 1993, Tables P1 and P2, and 1980 Census of Population, "Detailed Population Characteristics," U.S. Government Printing Office, Washington, DC, 1983, Table 276.

Occupational Segregation Since 1940

Sociologists who study social stratification have been particularly interested in the occupational segregation between black and white men and women over the past five decades. Since the choice of occupation (or the inability to choose one's occupation) can have a major effect on income, residence, and a variety of other life chances, it has been seen as a key variable in the American system of social stratification. Historically, the U.S. occupational system has included various formal and informal rules that discriminated against minorities and women, and changes in such rules—whether to help or hinder minorities and women—should be reflected in different patterns of occupational segregation.

The most commonly-used measure of occupational segregation is the dissimilarity index, a measure developed by Otis Dudley Duncan and Beverly Duncan. Basically, this index measures how many workers would have to move between occupations if each occupation were to reflect the overall proportion of two groups in a population. For example, if it was used for a population of ninety percent white men and ten percent black men, it would show how many male workers would have to move between occupations so that the men in each occupation would reflect this ninety-ten racial distribution. A dissimilarity index of 44, the level of ra-

cial segregation for males in the United States in 1940, shows that 44 percent of all black and white males would have to switch jobs for the males in each occupation to be balanced in the same way as the racial composition of the overall male population.

The figure below, created by combining the work of Mary C. King and Joyce P. Jocobsen, shows the changes over time in the dissimilarity index between 1940 and 1990. For 1940 through 1980, the data are based on data from the Public Use Microdata Samples for each census year (a 1 percent sample of the total population); the 1990 data are based on the Current Population Survey, a large-scale survey. King's 1940 and 1950 data are based on comparisons of blacks and whites, while Jocobsen's 1960-1990 data compare whites and non-whites. Both analysts use the total number of occupations in the census year (which increase from 226 job titles in 1940 to 503 titles in 1980 and 1990) to compute the dissimilarity index.

During the 1940-50 and 1970-80 periods, there were large declines in the dissimilarity index for men and women of both races, indicating that occupational racial barriers were falling. Yet for men, the dissimilarity index actually increased between 1950 and 1960 and between 1980 and 1990, indicating a slight rise in

racial job segregation. The decline in sex segregation in occupations has been slower but steadier; the dissimilarity index by sex drops from 71 to 56 for non-whites and from 67 to 56 for whites between 1940 and 1990. However, the current level of sex segregation by race (56 for whites and non-whites) is still well above the 1940 level of race segregation for men (when such racial segregation was in many cases enforced by law or union contract) and is above the 1960 racial segregation level for women (50).

These recent historical data on occupational segregation suggest that these groups confronted very different challenges in the labor market over time. "Further work, which focuses more tightly on the years since 1960, is needed to disentangle the possible effects of improving education for black women, tight labor markets, the civil rights movement and consequent legislation, the women's movement, and widening opportunities for white women" (King, 1992:36). The use of more occupational categories in computing the dissimilarity in later years may understate some of the progress made in decreasing sex- and race-based occupational segregation: more job categories gives more opportunity for job segregation. Yet the relatively small declines in the dissimilarity index between 1980 and 1990 (and the actual increase in the index for non-white and white men from 28 to 31 in the decade) during a period of very rapid growth in female employment and great structural change in the economy suggest that many old patterns of occupational race and sex segregation are being replicated, or that new ones are being invented.

Additional Sources:

Jacobs, Jerry A. "Long-term trends in occupational segregation by sex." American Journal of Sociology 95 (1989): 160-73.

Jacobsen, Joyce P. "Trends in work force segregation, 1960-90." Social Science Quarterly 75(1994): 204-11.

King, Mary C. "Occupational segregation by race and sex, 1940-88." Monthly Labor Review, 115, 4 (1992):30-37.

Reskin, Barbara, ed. Sex Segregation in the Workplace: Trends, Explanations, Remedies. Washington, D.C.: National Academy Press, 1984.

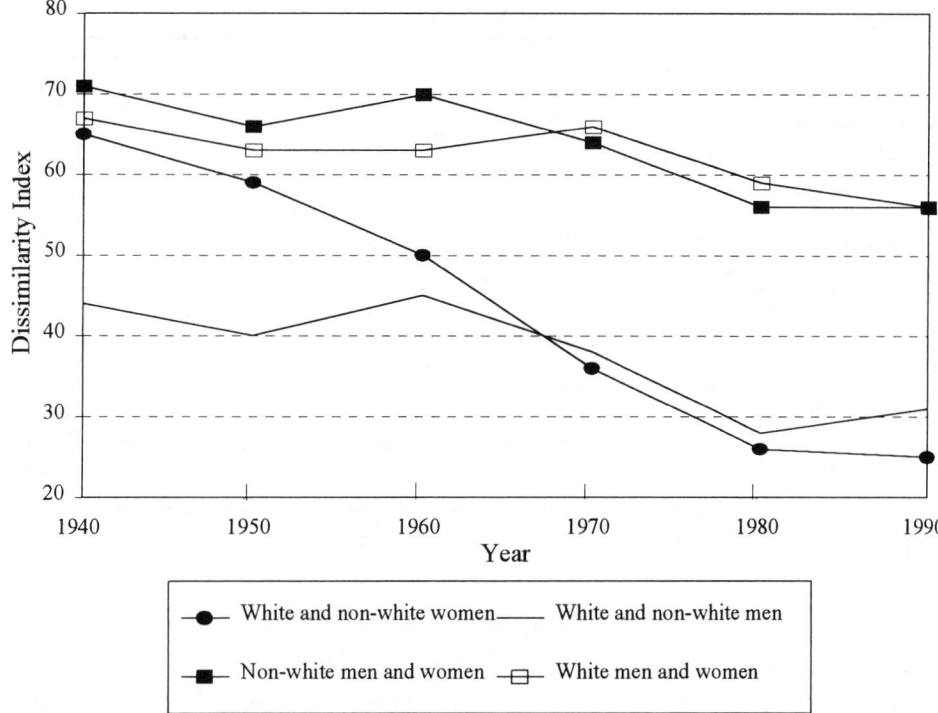

Dissimilarity Indexes of Occupational Differentiation: 1940-1990

Legend:
- White and non-white women
- White and non-white men
- Non-white men and women
- White men and women

Source: 1940, 1950, 1960, 1970, and 1980 PUMS data and 1990 CPS data.

pations where minorities constitute a majority. In this sense minorities are different from women, who constitute an overwhelming majority in a number of occupations. On the other hand, when sex and race are examined jointly, new patterns of occupational segregation emerge (see Textbox).

Occupations with Highest and Lowest Educational Requirements

There are two different ways of looking at the effects of education on occupation: the degree to which highly-educated workers avoid or are attracted to certain occupations, and the degree to which poorly-educated workers are excluded from some occupations and attracted to others. The ten occupations with the lowest proportion of workers with 16 or more years of education (college graduates) were:

Occupations with the Lowest Proportion of Workers with Education Level 16 Years and Over

Occupation	Proportion with education 16+ years
Winding and twisting machine operators	0.7
Shoe machine operators	1.1
Graders and sorters, agricultural products	1.3
Punching and stamping press machine operators	1.4
Grader, dozer, and scraper operators	1.4
Automobile mechanic apprentices	1.4
Paving, surfacing, and tamping equipment operators	1.4
Textile cutting machine operators	1.5
Sheet metal worker apprentices	1.5
Drilling and boring machine operators	1.5
Crane and tower operators	1.5
Miscellaneous metal and plastic processing machine operators	1.5
Sheetmetal duct installers	1.5

The ten occupations with the highest proportion of workers with more than 16 years of education are:

Occupations with the Highest Proportion of Workers with Education Level 16 Years and Over

Occupation	Proportion with education 16+ years
Law teachers	96.6
Economics teachers	96.7
History teachers	96.7
Optometrists	98.4
Podiatrists	98.7
Veterinarians	99.0
Dentists	99.1
Physicians	99.2
Lawyers	99.5
Medical scientists	99.5

A lack of advanced education appears to be a major handicap in the educational and scientific fields:

Occupations with the Lowest Proportion of Workers with Education Level 0 to 11 Years

Occupation[1]	Percent with education 0 to 11 years
Sociology teachers	0.0
Computer science teachers	0.0
Earth, environmental, and marine science teachers	0.0
History teachers	0.0
Agriculture and forestry teachers	0.0
Medical scientists	0.0
Chemistry teachers	0.0
Social work teachers	0.0
Sociologists	0.0
Biological science teachers	0.0
Geologists and geodeists	0.0
Education teachers	0.0
Actuaries	0.0
Biological and life scientists	0.1
Lawyers	0.1
Business, commerce, and marketing teachers	0.1
Physicists and astronomers	0.1
Teachers, secondary school	0.1
Mathematical science teachers	0.1
Nuclear engineers	0.1

[1] "Not elsewhere classified" occupations not included.

On the other hand, workers with less than a high school education (education level 0 to 11 years) appear to be scattered among a variety of occupations. The top ten occupations with low educational levels vary from 50.3 to 67.6 percent of all workers with 11 or fewer years of education:

Occupations with the Highest Proportion of Workers with Education Level 0 to 11 Years

Occupation	Percent with education 0 to 11 years
Launderers and ironers	50.3
Maids and housemen	50.4
Miscellaneous food preparation occupations	50.5
Nailing and tacking machine operators	50.6
Waiters'/waitresses' assistants	51.7
Private household cleaners and servants	54.6
Food counter, fountain, and related occupations	54.7
Housekeepers and butlers	55.6
Farm workers	58.9
Graders and sorters, agricultural products	67.6

Thus while low education clearly excludes workers from a number of jobs, there appears to be a greater interpenetration of schooled and largely unschooled workers in the lower levels of the occupational structure.

Occupations with the Lowest and Highest Income

The ten occupations with the lowest mean income for men were as follows:

Occupations with the Lowest Mean Male Earnings

Occupation[1]	Mean male earnings
Child care workers, private household	$4,587
Ushers	$6,036
Waiters'/waitresses' assistants	$6,081
Food counter, fountain, and related occupations	$6,202
Miscellaneous food preparation occupations	$6,810
Library clerks	$7,217
Crossing guards	$7,597
Early childhood teachers' assistants	$9,405
Stock handlers and baggers	$9,668
Cooks	$9,714

[1] "Not elsewhere classified" occupations not included.

While the lowest-income jobs for men were concentrated in the service sector, the male occupations with the highest incomes were those in the fields of medicine, law and finance:

Occupations with the Highest Mean Male Earnings

Occupation[1]	Mean male earnings
Optometrists	$60,823
Judges	$61,152
Actuaries	$65,493
Securities and financial services sales occupations	$71,822
Law teachers	$77,511
Medical science teachers	$81,858
Podiatrists	$83,374
Dentists	$84,659
Lawyers	$88,324
Physicians	$126,002

[1] "Not elsewhere classified" occupations not included.

The occupations where women received the lowest incomes were also in the service sector:

Occupations with the Lowest Mean Female Earnings

Occupation[1]	Mean female earnings
Food counter, fountain, and related occupations	$4,529
Child care workers, private household	$5,460
Launderers and ironers	$5,506
Crossing guards	$5,548
Waiters'/waitresses' assistants	$6,094
Family child care providers	$6,161
Ushers	$6,236
Early childhood teachers' assistants	$6,611
Private household cleaners and servants	$6,810
Graders and sorters, agricultural products	$6,894

[1] "Not elsewhere classified" occupations not included.

While women's high-income occupations were heavily in the fields of law and medicine, they also included engineering and teaching:

Occupations with the Highest Mean Female Earnings

Occupation[1]	Mean female earnings
Chemical engineers	$35,488
Actuaries	$35,985
Judges	$37,354
Medical science teachers	$37,873
Dentists	$38,716
Podiatrists	$38,972
Petroleum engineers	$39,920
Law teachers	$42,314
Lawyers	$45,862
Physicians	$60,447

Differences in Earnings Between Men and Women in the Same Occupations

While much has been written about the aggregate differences in income between the sexes, an examination of the actual income differentials **within the same occupation** can be instructive as well. There are two ways of looking at this: a) the occupations with the largest or smallest **absolute** (in dollar terms) differences in income between the sexes, and b) the occupations with the largest or smallest **percentage** difference in incomes of men and women.

Which occupations have the largest absolute differences in income between the sexes? Physicians win hands down here, with the average male doctor making over $65,000 more than his female counterpart in 1989.

Ten Occupations with the Greatest Absolute Difference in Mean Earnings

Occupation	Male-female difference
Physicians	$65,556
Dentists	$45,944
Podiatrists	$44,403
Medical science teachers	$43,985
Lawyers	$42,461
Securities and financial services sales occupations	$38,722
Law teachers	$35,197
Actuaries	$29,508
Veterinarians	$29,239
Financial managers	$28,227

Dentists, podiatrists and medical science teachers lag here, followed by a variety of legal and financial occupations. By contrast, the occupations where women have larger mean incomes than men tend to be in different forms of apprenticeships, and the gap between the sexes is not usually very large at all:

Occupations in Which Women Have Greater Mean Earnings than Men

Occupation[1]	Absolute female male difference
Brickmason and stonemason apprentices	$9,156
Tool and die maker apprentices	$5,416
Helpers, extractive occupations	$1,551
Library clerks	$1,346
Plumber, pipefitter, and steamfitter apprentices	$1,295
Child care workers, private household	$873
Electrician apprentices	$511
Carpenter apprentices	$458
Ushers	$200
Miscellaneous food preparation occupations	$191
Waiters'/waitresses' assistants	$13

[1] "Not elsewhere classified" occupations not included.

The occupations where women make the least as a percentage of men's mean earnings are a potpourri of jobs ranging from dentists to athletes to captains and other officers of fishing vessels:

Ten Occupations with the Lowest Female Mean Earnings as Percent of Male Earnings

Occupation	Female earnings as % of male
Launderers and ironers	21.2
Captains and other officers, fishing vessels	35.8
Athletes	37.1
Auctioneers	37.7
Physics teachers	40.0
Dentists	45.7
Patternmakers and model makers, wood	45.9
Securities and financial services sales occupations	46.1
Business, commerce, and marketing teachers	46.2
Managers, properties, and real estate	46.2

On the other hand, jobs where women make proportionally almost as much money as men are often found (much to the authors' surprise) in a variety of blue-collar construction and service trades:

Ten Occupations with the Highest Female Mean Earnings as Percent of Male Earnings

Occupation	Female earnings as % of male
Electronic repairers, communications/industrial equipment	90.0
Public transportation attendants	90.2
Helpers, construction trades	91.6
Industrial truck and tractor equipment operators	92.1
Baggage porters and bellhops	92.8
Machinist apprentices	92.9
Helpers, mechanics, and repairers	93.3
Stock handlers and baggers	93.8
Vehicle washers and equipment cleaners	95.9
Drillers, oil well	97.0

While it is hard to account for all of these trends, one possibility is that once women can enter these occupa-

tions, their strong unions and specific rules about seniority and job assignment help to prevent discrimination against women within them. However, as a number of researchers have shown, the interpretation of the substantial gains in income made by women during the 1980s is a complex process involving a number of unique historical factors.

Occupational Composition of Urban and Rural Areas

Table 14-6 provides data on the place of residence of those with different occupations among urban and rural areas (with urban subdivided into three categories). The occupational classification is somewhat more detailed than that of Table 14-1. It shows that the highest socioeconomic status occupations are concentrated in urban fringes (with regard to the worker's place of residence, not necessarily to his or her place of work), and this is also the major area of residence of those in technical, sales, and administrative support occupations. Central cities of urbanized areas tend to have concentrations of service workers, but a plurality of skilled (precision production, craft and repair occupations) and unskilled workers (operators, fabricators, and laborers) as well as those in the farming, forestry and fishing occupations now live in rural areas.

Yet this table shows some surprising trends in place of residence by occupation between 1980 and 1990. Overall, the largest growth in number of employed residents aged 16 years and over was found in central places, with a 24.2 percent increase for the decade. Those with the highest status occupations have not been deserting the central cities over the past decade; the growth of number of residents with managerial and professional specialty occupations increased by 44.6 percent in central places between 1980 and 1990, outstripping the growth rates of any of the other three levels of the urban hierarchy for this occupational category. Among this high status group, only those in the health assessment and treating occupations show a pronounced shift toward rural (or perhaps, more accurately, "exurb") residence over the last decade. Dire warnings of an abandonment of central places for urban fringe and rural residence among those with highly-paid employment appear to be somewhat overstated.

Occupational Composition of Regions and MSAs, by Sex

Do different regions of the United States have a different occupational composition? Certainly this was true fifty years ago, but Table 14-7 shows the surprising degree of similarity in occupational distribution for both men and women by 1990. No region of the nation has a male work force that has a greater than 4.7 percent con-

Table 14-6. Occupational Composition by Urban and Rural Residence of Employed Persons: 1990 and Percent Change 1980-1990 [numbers in thousands]

Occupation	1990					Percent Change 1980-1990				
	Total	Central place	Urban fringe	Other urban	Rural	Total	Central place	Urban fringe	Other urban	Rural
Employed persons, 16 years and over	115,681	31.2	34.4	10.6	23.9	18.5	24.2	19.2	7.7	15.6
Managerial and professional specialty occupations	30,534	32.3	40.0	6.0	18.4	37.8	44.6	39.3	-23.9	35.5
Executive, administrative, and managerial occupations	14,228	30.8	42.2	8.7	18.3	40.4	46.5	42.7	18.7	37.7
Officials and administrators, public administration	578	30.0	36.5	11.1	22.4	60.0	72.7	71.3	31.7	45.3
Management and related occupations	4,141	33.2	43.6	7.6	15.5	62.0	64.6	65.1	38.9	61.1
Professional specialty occupations	16,306	33.6	38.0	9.8	18.6	35.7	43.1	36.2	16.5	33.7
Engineers and natural scientists	3,001	29.9	47.8	6.8	15.5	39.5	53.9	40.1	12.3	28.3
Engineers	1,673	27.4	49.1	7.1	16.3	21.0	31.3	20.9	1.1	15.9
Health diagnosing occupations	870	34.2	42.1	8.4	15.3	35.1	36.4	37.8	14.5	38.3
Health assessment and treating occupations	2,483	31.5	38.5	9.5	20.5	46.4	41.8	47.7	30.2	61.3
Teachers, librarians, and counselors	5,714	31.4	33.5	12.6	22.5	22.2	31.1	21.1	8.7	20.8
Teachers, elementary and secondary schools	3,861	28.1	34.1	12.6	25.1	16.6	22.9	16.4	4.8	16.7
Technical, sales, and administrative support occupations	36,718	32.5	38.0	9.7	19.8	24.1	24.9	23.1	13.0	30.9
Health technologists and technicians	1,397	33.2	34.2	10.8	21.8	44.6	38.5	51.6	28.8	52.8
Technologists and technicians, except health	2,860	32.9	40.4	8.5	18.2	41.9	50.5	38.9	24.0	43.6
Sales occupations	13,635	30.7	38.8	10.3	20.2	39.7	45.0	39.4	22.9	42.3
Supervisors and proprietors, sales occupations	3,352	28.2	38.6	10.8	22.5	117.6	134.6	141.4	67.3	94.9
Sales representatives, commodities and finance	3,942	30.5	44.3	8.0	17.1	28.4	30.9	29.6	13.3	28.8
Other sales occupations	6,341	32.2	35.5	11.5	20.9	23.2	30.2	17.8	12.3	29.3
Cashiers	2,534	32.9	32.6	12.3	22.2	47.6	55.3	35.9	44.4	58.0
Administrative support occupations, including clerical	18,826	33.6	37.4	9.4	19.7	11.7	11.2	9.9	4.0	20.8
Computer equipment operators	641	34.8	38.2	8.5	18.4	56.9	48.9	48.5	70.3	92.2
Secretaries, stenographers, and typists	4,582	31.1	38.0	9.8	21.0	-1.6	-4.0	-3.8	-7.7	10.4
Financial records processing occupations	2,315	29.5	36.6	10.4	23.5	2.7	-0.2	3.1	-8.4	12.1
Mail and message distributing occupations	990	38.3	35.4	7.4	19.0	28.0	25.5	33.1	13.7	30.2
Service occupations	15,296	35.9	29.5	12.4	22.2	21.1	27.5	17.3	12.5	21.7
Private household occupations	521	41.8	26.3	11.0	20.9	-11.6	-3.4	-0.3	-33.4	-22.3
Protective service occupations	1,993	34.7	34.0	11.0	20.3	35.1	38.8	29.5	31.0	41.2
Police and firefighters	733	32.1	37.0	11.0	19.9	22.3	22.2	19.0	16.4	33.2
Service occupations, except protective and household	12,782	35.9	28.9	12.7	22.5	21.0	27.9	16.1	13.1	21.9
Food service occupations	5,167	35.6	29.8	12.9	21.7	17.8	28.4	9.8	11.7	17.6
Cleaning and building service occupations	3,128	38.4	25.9	12.4	23.3	13.9	19.6	9.6	5.7	14.8
Farming, forestry, and fishing occupations	2,839	13.7	13.5	10.3	62.5	1.0	63.7	36.5	13.7	-12.8
Farm operators and managers	1,067	3.7	4.4	5.3	86.7	-17.8	37.8	21.5	-0.5	-21.3
Farm workers and related occupations	1,590	20.8	20.1	13.1	46.0	19.2	73.0	41.2	19.5	-1.5
Precision production, craft, and repair occupations	13,098	26.1	31.9	11.1	30.9	4.0	8.9	0.7	-4.3	6.9
Mechanics and repairers	4,080	25.2	32.4	10.9	31.4	7.4	11.5	5.1	-1.6	10.2
Construction trades	4,794	26.3	32.1	10.4	31.2	12.9	20.9	13.3	-0.4	11.2
Precision production occupations	4,047	27.5	32.1	11.5	28.9	-4.9	-3.0	-13.9	-4.3	5.1
Operators, fabricators, and laborers	17,196	28.8	26.6	12.6	32.0	-3.7	-0.2	-8.9	-6.1	-1.2
Machine operators and tenders, except precision	4,982	29.0	24.0	13.5	33.5	-16.4	-13.9	-23.9	-15.4	-12.9
Fabricators, assemblers, inspectors, and samplers	2,922	28.1	26.5	13.1	32.3	-6.5	-3.1	-17.8	-3.0	0.4
Transportation occupations	3,761	28.9	29.3	10.9	30.9	14.3	19.9	13.4	5.3	13.8
Motor vehicle operators	3,580	29.1	29.3	10.7	30.9	18.6	24.3	18.1	10.4	17.1
Material moving equipment operators	968	20.8	23.1	13.7	42.4	-12.0	-15.1	-18.4	-14.0	-5.6
Handlers, equipment cleaners, helpers, and laborers	4,563	30.5	28.0	12.6	28.8	4.1	8.1	1.5	-1.0	4.9
Construction laborers	949	30.3	27.7	11.1	30.8	43.4	54.5	51.4	21.2	36.4
Freight, stock, and material handlers	1,577	30.0	30.0	12.9	27.2	25.2	26.8	20.9	20.1	31.3

Source: U. S. Bureau of the Census, "Social and Economic Characteristics: United States," 1990 CP-2-1, Table 20, and "General Social and Economic Characteristics: United States Summary," 1980 Census of Population, Table 104, U.S. Government Printing Office, Washington, D.C., 1993 and 1983.

centration in agricultural (farming, forestry and fishing) occupations, and none of the regional differences between major occupational groupings exceed six percent (the largest gap is the 23.0 percent of Midwestern employed males found in the operators, fabricators and laborers category, an occupational category constituting only 17.7 percent of Western male workers). Among women workers, the effect of region on distribution of occupation is even less pronounced.

Yet the percent changes between regions in occupational growth over the past decade show some interesting patterns of differentiation. Between 1980-90, job growth for employed males ranged from only 2.7 percent in the Midwest to 24.1 percent in the West. Job growth for women was much more even across regions, ranging from a 19.2 percent increase in the Midwest to a 36.0 percent increase in the West during the 1980-90 period.

As was shown in Table 14-1, various occupational categories grew at considerably different rates during the 1980-90 era, and the regional data show that there were pronounced regional effects here as well. For example, for men between 1980-90, job growth in managerial and professional specialty occupations occurred at a rate twice that of overall job growth in the Northeast (15.9 percent growth for managerial and professional to 7.0 percent growth for all jobs) and triple the overall job growth rate (9.4 to 2.7 percent) in the Midwest, but it exceeded the overall job creation rate by only 40 percent in the South (25.0 to 15.5 percent) and by about 10 percent in the West (27.7 to 24.1 percent). The disparity of growth rates indicates that for men in the Northeast and Midwest, there has been a massive drop in unskilled jobs (which accounts for the very low rate of overall job growth in these two regions) and a transition toward better-paid managerial and professional occupations. At the other end of the job spectrum, three of the regions have witnessed little change or substantial decreases in the size of the private household occupations for both sexes. Yet in the West, this traditionally poorly-paid occupational category grew by 30.1 percent for males and 31.4 percent for females during 1980-90.

Occupational Composition of Employed Persons by Race-Ethnicity, Sex and Urban-Rural Residence

While the gains in the reduction in occupational segregation for minorities over the last several decades have been documented in this chapter, Table 14-8 shows that there are still great differences in the places of residence by race and ethnicity for men and women in each occupation. In a society unaffected by race or ethnicity, we might expect that the concentration of jobs in certain locations (lawyers around courthouses, operatives near factories, professors near colleges) would also lead to a

similar set of choices about the most convenient places of residence. Yet no matter what the occupation, blacks (and in most cases Hispanics as well) are about twice as likely to be residents of a central place (i.e. cities) and about half as likely to be rural dwellers as whites. Men and women of the same race and occupation, on the other hand, show few differences in area of residence. This segregation of residence by race within occupations may have important implications for workers' life chances because occupations grow at different rates in various parts of the urban hierarchy.

Summary

Since 1900, there has been a major shift in occupational distribution away from agricultural pursuits and, since about 1960 on, away from the skilled (precision production) and unskilled (operators, fabricators and laborers) occupations associated with manufacturing. While service jobs have increased by better than one-half in each decade since 1970, the 1970's saw a surge in technical, sales and administrative support occupations, and managerial and professional specialty occupations grew rapidly during the 1980's. Throughout each decade since 1960, the growth rate of women exceeded that of men in most occupations (especially in white-collar jobs), as did the growth rate of blacks and Hispanics.

While occupational segregation across occupations has declined for women and blacks, a wide variety of occupations still remain largely segregated by sex or race. Within many occupations, women's earnings lag behind those of men, although younger women have closed some of this gap. The major regions of the United States increasingly resemble each other in terms of their occupational distribution, and (with the exception of farming, forestry and fishing occupations) most occupations have a similar distribution by residence across urban and rural areas. However, blacks and Hispanics within the same occupations as whites have a much greater concentration of central city residence.

Industrial Composition and Trends

Introduction

Whereas occupation refers to the work activity of each individual worker, the industry classification refers to the establishment or organization (employer) for which the worker carries out his or her occupational tasks (for details see the Definition Box). Industry statistics reveal how a nation is organized to earn its livelihood. Often the economy is divided into "sectors": primary (extractive), secondary (industrial), and tertiary (services) industries. At other times it is dichotomized into agricultural and

Table 14-7. Occupational Composition of Employed Persons, by Region: 1990 and Percent Change 1980-1990

Occupation	1990				Percent Change 1980-1990			
	Northeast	Midwest[1]	South	West	Northeast	Midwest[1]	South	West
Employed males, 16 years and over (in thousands)	13,018	15,106	20,943	13,638	—	—	—	—
Employed males, 16 years and over (percent)	100.0	100.0	100.0	100.0	7.0	2.7	15.5	24.1
Managerial and professional specialty occupations	28.2	23.4	23.6	26.6	15.9	9.4	25.0	27.7
Executive, administrative, and managerial occupations	14.6	12.3	12.6	13.5	15.5	6.1	20.6	24.3
Professional specialty occupations	13.6	11.2	11.0	13.2	16.4	13.2	30.5	31.4
Technical, sales, and administrative support occupations	22.8	20.5	21.4	22.4	19.9	20.1	32.9	38.9
Health technologists and technicians	0.4	0.4	0.4	0.4	59.8	52.0	78.1	73.3
Technologists and technicians, except health	3.3	2.9	3.2	3.5	27.1	25.7	39.2	39.0
Sales occupations	11.2	10.8	11.4	11.5	35.2	30.6	42.8	44.5
Administrative support occupations, including clerical	7.8	6.4	6.4	6.9	0.0	2.7	14.3	28.9
Service occupations	11.1	9.5	9.6	10.7	13.1	12.1	32.0	34.6
Private household occupations	...	...	...	0.1	0.2	-10.6	-16.2	30.1
Protective service occupations	3.2	2.2	3.2	2.6	18.1	14.8	63.4	41.6
Service occupations, except protective and household	7.8	7.3	6.8	8.1	11.2	11.5	29.4	32.6
Farming, forestry, and fishing occupations	1.9	4.7	3.9	4.5	8.4	-16.5	1.6	17.0
Precision production, craft, and repair occupations	17.7	18.8	20.3	18.0	-1.4	-4.7	4.4	10.0
Operators, fabricators, and laborers	18.3	23.0	21.2	17.7	-11.2	-8.5	0.6	15.1
Machine operators and tenders, except precison	4.5	5.9	4.7	3.8	-32.4	-20.7	-9.8	6.0
Fabricators, assemblers, inspectors, and samplers	2.3	4.0	2.9	2.4	-17.5	-9.3	6.4	14.9
Transportation occupations	5.1	5.5	5.7	4.7	9.9	3.9	11.5	22.3
Material moving occupations	1.1	1.5	1.7	1.3	-20.3	-19.9	-5.7	-0.5
Handlers, equipment cleaners, helpers, and laborers	5.3	6.0	6.2	5.5	2.9	-0.2	-0.2	20.5
Employed females, 16 years and over (in thousands)	11,294	12,879	17,844	10,959	—	—	—	—
Employed females, 16 years and over (percent)	100.0	100.0	100.0	100.0	22.4	19.2	31.8	36.0
Managerial and professional specialty occupations	30.0	25.9	27.0	29.3	64.6	52.5	68.0	74.2
Executive, administrative, and managerial occupations	11.7	10.0	11.0	12.9	108.2	83.8	97.6	91.5
Professional specialty occupations	18.3	15.9	16.0	16.4	45.1	37.8	52.4	62.6
Technical, sales, and administrative support occupations	44.3	43.5	43.1	44.0	16.8	14.9	28.5	26.2
Health technologists and technicians	2.1	2.4	2.2	1.7	34.1	36.2	45.0	45.4
Technologists and technicians, except health	1.6	1.3	1.6	1.8	73.9	51.7	71.9	74.9
Sales occupations	11.7	12.2	12.9	12.7	39.2	28.8	49.5	44.4
Administrative support occupations, including clerical	28.9	27.6	26.4	27.8	6.8	7.1	17.5	16.4
Service occupations	15.5	18.1	17.0	16.5	17.8	10.2	25.3	26.8
Private household occupations	0.7	0.6	1.1	1.1	-19.6	-23.1	-20.6	31.4
Protective service occupations	0.7	0.5	0.1	0.6	64.3	60.3	-79.3	103.3
Service occupations, except protective and household	14.1	16.9	15.3	14.8	19.2	11.0	28.8	24.6
Farming, forestry, and fishing occupations	0.5	1.0	0.8	1.1	22.2	-6.9	13.0	29.9
Precision production, craft, and repair occupations	2.1	2.4	2.4	2.4	20.2	31.4	28.4	23.0
Operators, fabricators, and laborers	7.6	9.1	9.8	6.6	-25.7	-6.5	-4.1	10.4
Machine operators and tenders, except precison	3.5	3.5	5.0	2.6	-35.0	-13.1	-13.1	9.9
Fabricators, assemblers, inspectors, and samplers	1.8	2.6	2.1	1.6	-30.1	-14.0	-0.5	-6.4
Transportation occupations	0.7	0.8	0.9	0.8	54.0	34.3	56.2	52.5
Material moving occupations	0.1	0.1	0.1	0.1	-52.3	-20.0	-14.0	-1.8
Handlers, equipment cleaners, helpers, and laborers	1.5	2.0	1.7	1.6	-9.4	7.0	3.4	17.7

[1] North Central in 1980.

Source: U. S. Bureau of the Census, "Social and Economic Characteristics: United States," 1990 CP-2-1, Table 85, and "General Social and Economic Characteristics: United States Summary," 1980 Census of Population, Table 188, U.S. Government Printing Office, Washington, D.C., 1993 and 1983.

Table 14-8. Occupational Composition of Employed Persons, by Urban-rural Residence, Race-ethnicity, and Sex: 1990 [numbers in thousands]

Occupation	White					Black					Hispanic				
	Total	Central place	Urban fringe	Other urban	Rural	Total	Central place	Urban fringe	Other urban	Rural	Total	Central place	Urban fringe	Other urban	Rural
Employed males, 16 years and over	52,722	26.2	35.3	10.9	27.7	5,393	55.8	24.6	7.3	12.4	5,312	51.3	32.4	8.2	8.1
Managerial and professional specialty occupations	14,136	29.6	41.7	9.6	19.2	782	55.9	32.7	5.0	6.4	638	48.3	39.1	6.2	6.4
Executive, administrative, and managerial occupations	7,449	27.1	43.5	9.3	20.1	391	55.3	33.8	4.6	6.3	349	47.2	40.6	6.0	6.2
Professional specialty occupations	6,687	32.3	39.6	10.0	18.2	391	56.4	31.6	5.5	6.5	289	49.6	37.3	6.5	6.6
Technical, sales, and administrative support occupations	11,667	29.4	40.2	10.0	20.4	1,024	60.0	29.6	4.3	6.1	887	52.8	36.1	6.0	5.0
Health technologists and technicians	203	34.3	35.3	11.2	19.2	34	61.0	29.4	4.4	5.2	263	4.7	94.5	0.5	0.4
Technologists and technicians, except health	1,757	29.3	40.6	9.4	20.7	114	53.4	34.3	4.8	7.5	101	47.8	38.8	6.8	6.6
Sales occupations	6,351	27.9	41.1	10.2	20.8	324	57.7	31.5	4.6	6.2	391	50.6	37.5	6.5	5.4
Administrative support occupations, including clerical	3,356	32.1	38.5	9.7	19.7	551	62.6	27.6	4.1	5.8	372	56.3	34.1	5.4	4.2
Service occupations	10,653	13.8	70.9	5.5	9.9	1,014	62.8	22.0	6.8	8.4	5,387	9.4	89.3	0.5	0.8
Private household occupations	16	35.8	31.4	10.3	22.5	6	61.6	18.9	8.8	10.7	6	63.4	27.9	3.9	4.7
Protective service occupations	1,356	28.0	35.9	12.1	24.0	241	61.4	25.9	5.5	7.1	115	53.0	30.6	8.7	7.7
Service occupations, except protective and household	3,281	33.0	32.3	12.7	22.0	766	63.3	20.8	7.2	8.7	736	59.7	29.2	6.5	4.6
Farming, forestry, and fishing occupations	1,987	10.3	12.6	8.9	68.2	145	31.2	13.9	12.2	42.7	386	30.9	20.9	17.7	30.5
Precision production, craft, and repair occupations	10,300	21.9	32.6	11.4	34.1	786	52.4	24.1	8.1	15.3	1,049	50.8	33.4	8.4	7.4
Operators, fabricators, and laborers	9,979	22.6	28.6	13.1	35.8	1,642	52.6	20.4	9.6	17.5	1,495	53.0	31.1	8.6	7.3
Machine operators and tenders, except precison	2,296	22.8	27.3	13.8	36.1	366	47.7	17.7	12.2	22.4	401	56.0	31.7	6.9	5.3
Fabricators, assemblers, inspectors, and samplers	1,454	21.4	27.8	13.5	37.3	208	53.5	19.8	10.4	16.3	221	52.9	32.4	8.1	6.5
Transportation occupations	2,685	23.2	30.1	11.9	34.8	448	56.6	23.7	6.5	13.2	292	52.4	32.3	7.8	7.6
Material moving occupations	750	15.6	23.4	13.7	47.3	112	45.3	19.0	11.6	24.1	83	40.6	29.5	15.7	14.2
Handlers, equipment cleaners, helpers, and laborers	2,794	24.5	29.9	13.1	32.5	508	53.6	19.9	9.7	16.8	498	53.0	29.6	9.5	7.8
Employed females, 16 years and over	43,515	27.3	35.9	11.5	25.4	6,015	57.3	24.4	7.4	10.8	3,669	51.7	33.7	7.9	6.7
Managerial and professional specialty occupations	12,741	29.9	39.1	10.0	20.9	1,284	57.3	30.1	5.3	7.3	624	48.9	37.4	7.0	6.7
Executive, administrative, and managerial occupations	5,202	30.0	41.7	9.0	19.3	485	57.3	33.2	4.1	5.4	279	47.9	40.2	6.2	5.7
Professional specialty occupations	7,539	29.9	37.3	10.8	22.0	799	57.3	28.3	6.0	8.4	345	49.6	35.2	7.6	7.5
Technical, sales, and administrative support occupations	19,455	27.5	38.4	10.8	23.4	2,331	61.2	27.7	4.8	6.3	1,435	50.6	36.2	7.1	6.1
Health technologists and technicians	921	26.0	35.1	12.1	26.8	149	60.8	25.4	6.1	7.8	56	51.1	34.4	7.5	6.9
Technologists and technicians, except health	689	32.0	40.3	8.5	19.2	77	55.1	34.0	4.6	6.4	42	51.1	37.1	5.7	6.1
Sales occupations	5,633	27.2	37.9	11.5	23.3	551	58.3	25.8	7.1	8.8	418	49.5	35.4	8.3	6.8
Administrative support occupations, including clerical	12,212	27.4	38.7	10.5	23.4	1,554	62.6	28.3	3.9	5.2	920	51.1	36.7	6.5	5.7
Service occupations	6,701	26.0	30.1	14.6	29.2	1,508	58.9	19.2	9.5	12.4	893	51.9	28.5	12.4	7.2
Private household occupations	297	31.7	29.9	12.2	26.1	131	54.2	16.2	11.9	17.6	114	59.6	30.8	4.7	4.9
Protective service occupations	224	30.6	36.2	12.2	21.0	71	63.3	24.5	5.6	6.7	20	52.5	32.0	8.7	6.7
Service occupations, except protective and household	6,180	25.6	29.9	14.8	29.7	1,307	59.1	19.2	9.5	12.2	729	52.8	29.2	10.1	7.8
Farming, forestry, and fishing occupations	383	11.1	14.4	8.3	66.3	21	26.4	12.4	16.7	44.5	60	28.5	17.5	26.5	27.4
Precision production, craft, and repair occupations	957	24.6	30.9	12.3	32.3	144	51.3	20.8	10.3	17.6	129	54.3	34.0	6.4	5.3
Operators, fabricators, and laborers	3,277	21.0	24.5	14.5	40.0	728	43.9	15.4	14.3	26.3	559	56.5	31.0	6.9	5.6
Machine operators and tenders, except precison	1,410	20.9	21.2	15.0	42.9	356	39.1	12.1	16.9	31.9	284	60.0	29.6	5.8	4.6
Fabricators, assemblers, inspectors, and samplers	782	20.8	25.2	15.1	38.8	175	46.2	17.4	13.5	22.9	141	54.3	33.4	6.9	5.4
Transportation occupations	345	19.4	30.5	11.0	39.1	64	53.4	24.4	6.4	15.7	22	48.2	33.0	9.0	9.8
Material moving occupations	36	19.3	24.1	14.7	41.8	8	46.9	18.9	12.4	21.8	4	55.0	29.7	9.0	6.3
Handlers, equipment cleaners, helpers, and laborers	704	22.2	27.4	14.4	36.0	125	49.4	17.3	12.5	20.8	107	52.1	30.9	9.6	7.4

Source: U. S. Bureau of the Census, "Social and Economic Characteristics: United States," 1990 CP-2-1, U.S. Government Printing Office, Washington, D.C., 1993, Tables 81, 82, and 85

nonagricultural sectors. Both of these systems are summary ways of looking at the industrial composition which need to be refined.

In order to produce statistics on industry composition, standardized classifications of establishments and organizations have been developed for use not only in taking censuses, but in publishing a wide variety of other trade and economic statistics. As in the case of occupational classification, industrial classification is made at three levels:

- Major industrial group: 12 categories
- Intermediate industrial classification: 150 categories
- Detailed industrial classification: 231 categories

Space limitations have made it necessary to confine this chapter to only the first. Readers who wish data on the more detailed levels are referred to the volumes of the 1990 and 1980 censuses and to the "Special Reports" issued on occupation and industry on the basis of detailed cross-tabulations of census data.

Major Industry Groups

Table 14-9 provides data about long-term trends in industrial composition of the employed civilian labor force between 1900 and 1990. Several trends are found here. The first is the shift from a predominantly agricultural to a nonagricultural economy. In 1860 nearly 60 percent of the labor force was employed in agriculture. The crossover point at which non-agricultural workers outnumbered agricultural came about in 1880. By the start of the present century, more than one-third of the work force was still in agriculture, but by 1990 the agricultural work force had shrunk to less than 3 percent of the total. Table 14-9 shows the rapid decline in the agricultural sector during this century.

The second aspect of industrial compositional change has been the changing "mix" of industries within the nonagricultural sector. Table 14-9 and Figure 14-3 illustrate this remarkable change.

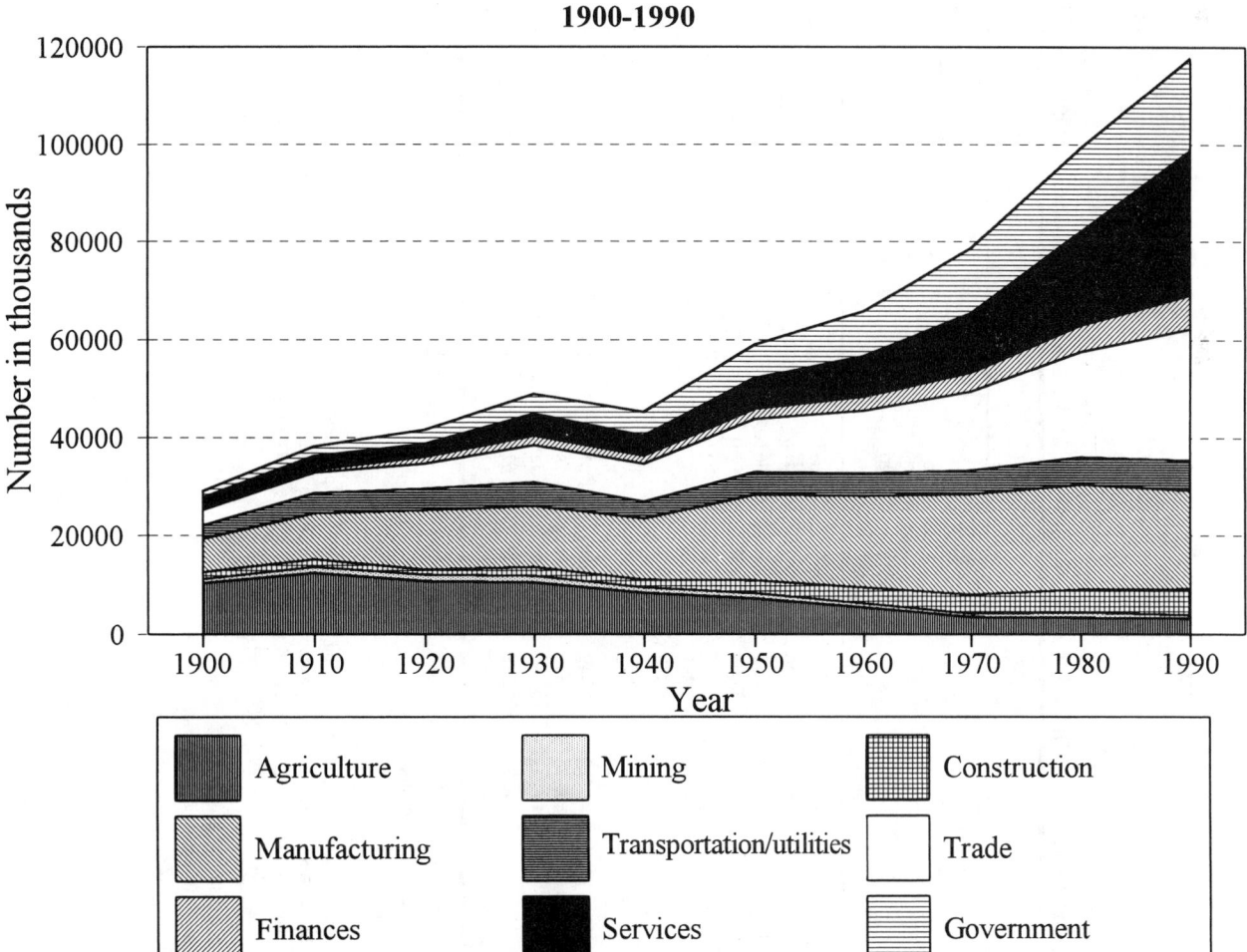

Figure 14-3. Trends in Industrial Composition of the Employed Civilian Labor Force: 1900-1990

Source: 1900-1990 U.S. Census and U.S. Labor Statistics data.

Table 14-9. Trends in Industrial Composition of the Employed Civilian Labor Force: 1900-1990 [numbers in thousands]

Year	Total employed[1]	Agricultural	Nonagricultural	Percent nonagricultural	Mining	Construction	Manufacturing Total	Durable goods	Non-durable goods	Transportation/utilities	Wholesale trade	Retail trade	Finance/insurance/real estate	Services	Government total
1990	117,914	3,186	114,728	97.3	0.6	4.7	17.4	10.1	7.3	5.3	5.6	17.8	6.1	25.7	16.7
1985	107,150	3,179	103,971	97.0	1.0	4.8	19.9	11.8	8.0	5.4	5.9	17.8	6.1	22.4	16.7
1980	99,303	3,364	95,935	96.6	1.1	4.8	22.4	13.5	9.0	5.7	5.8	16.6	5.7	19.8	18.0
1975	85,846	3,408	82,438	96.0	1.0	4.6	23.8	13.9	9.9	5.9	5.7	16.4	5.4	18.1	19.1
1970	78,678	3,463	75,215	95.6	0.9	5.1	27.3	15.8	11.5	6.4	5.6	15.6	5.1	16.3	17.7
1965	71,088	4,361	66,726	93.9	1.0	5.3	29.7	17.1	12.6	6.6	5.7	15.2	4.9	14.9	16.6
1960	65,778	5,458	60,318	91.7	1.3	5.4	31.0	17.5	13.5	7.4	5.8	15.2	4.9	13.6	15.4
1955	62,170	6,450	55,722	89.6	1.5	5.6	33.3	18.8	14.5	8.2	5.8	15.0	4.5	12.3	13.7
1950	58,918	7,160	51,758	87.8	2.0	5.2	33.7	17.9	15.8	8.9	5.8	14.9	4.2	11.9	13.3
1940[2]	47,520	8,449	36,621	81.3	2.9	4.1	33.9	16.6	17.4	9.4	5.7	15.2	4.6	11.3	13.0
1930[2]	44,183	10,472[3]	38,358	78.6	3.4	4.7	32.5	—	—	12.5	19.7		5.0	11.4	10.7
1920[2]	39,208	10,666[3]	30,948	74.4	4.5	3.2	39.0	—	—	14.6	16.3		4.2	8.6	9.5
1910[2]	34,559	12,388[3]	25,779	67.5	4.9	6.2	36.1	—	—	15.5	16.5		2.0	11.1	7.5
1900[2]	26,956	10,382[3]	18,691	64.3	4.2	7.6	36.0	—	—	15.0	16.5		2.0	11.5	7.2

[1] Data for total employed for 1940 and prior years are designed to be comparable with the Current Population Survey and hence are not consistent with census counts, especially for 1940.

[2] Data are from decennial census.

[3] Data are for gainful workers.

Source: Data for total, agricultural, and nonagricultural employment from U. S. Bureau of the Census, "Statistical Abstract of the United States," pages 126-127, U.S. Government Printing Office, Washington, D.C., 1992 and 1975. Distribution by industries from U.S. Bureau of Labor Statistics, "Monthly Labor Review," December 1991 and June 1986, Table 13, "Handbook of Labor Statistics: 1983," Table 67, and U.S. Bureau of the Census, "Historical Statistics of the United States," page 137, U.S. Government Printing Office, Washington, D.C., 1991, 1986, 1983, and 1975.

1. Early in this century, manufacturing dominated the nonagricultural sector, contributing almost 40 percent of all such workers. Manufacturing's share of the employed civilian labor force peaked in 1920 at 39 percent. Between 1950 and 1990, manufacturing employment has varied in a relatively narrow range, usually in response to economic cycles; in 1950, manufacturing employment was 19.8 million, and by 1990, it stood at 20.5 million. Yet because of the lack of growth of manufacturing employment, its proportion of all nonagricultural workers dropped by almost half (from 33.7 to 17.4 percent) between 1950 and 1990.

2. The transformation of the nation's transportation system from one based on railroads to roads and the change from coal to other power sources (including hydroelectric, natural gas, oil, and nuclear power) led to important changes in the sectoral distribution of employment. Between 1900 and 1990, mining employment declined from 4.2 to 0.6 percent of total employment, and employment in the transportation and utilities sector declined from 15.0 to 5.3 percent of all employment. Of course, part of this decline in employment in these industries was due to automation; construction, another field where the use of machinery has become more widespread, has declined from 7.6 to 4.7 percent of total employment between 1900 and 1990.

3. Since 1955 manufacturing employment has been replaced by "tertiary" industries, including finance, insurance, real estate and services (except domestic). The 1980-90 decade appears to have continued these trends with a few modifications:

a. There was expansion of growth in the personal service, business service, professional service, and entertainment and recreational service sectors (see Table 14-10).

b. Retail trade, wholesale trade, construction, and personal services were stable, growing at rates close to the national growth rate of employment for the decade (18.5 percent).

Race-Ethnicity and Industry of Employment

Unlike occupations, the race-ethnicity groups tend to have a more similar industrial composition (see Table 14-10). That is, while discrimination against blacks and Hispanics exists, it is no longer found at the industry level, but rather in specific occupations. The Hispanic-origin population deviates more from the average than does the black population (with an excess of agriculture workers and a deficit of professional workers). Black workers are less likely to be found in wholesale and retail trade, agriculture, mining and construction, and have surpluses in public administration, professional services, personal services and transport, communication, and public utilities.

Table 14-10. Industry of the Employed Labor Force, by Sex and Race-ethnicity: 1990, and Percent Change, 1980-1990

Industry	Percent distribution, 1990				Percent composition, 1990			Percent change, 1980-90		
	Total	White	Black	Hispanic	Black	Hispanic	Female	Total	Black	Female
Total employed, 16 years and over	100.0	100.0	100.0	100.0	9.9	7.8	45.8	18.5	22.2	27.2
Agriculture, forestry, and fisheries	2.7	2.8	1.3	5.1	4.8	14.8	20.8	6.9	-6.4	24.3
Mining	0.6	0.7	0.3	0.5	4.4	6.6	14.7	-29.6	-25.1	-14.4
Construction	6.2	6.5	4.2	7.4	6.6	9.2	10.0	25.7	17.9	51.1
Manufacturing	17.7	17.6	17.2	20.0	9.6	8.8	33.2	-6.6	-9.3	-3.0
Nondurable goods	7.0	6.7	8.0	8.6	11.4	9.6	42.0	-4.5	-2.5	-3.1
Durable goods	10.7	10.8	9.2	11.4	8.4	8.3	27.4	-7.9	-14.6	-2.9
Transportation, communication, public utilities	7.1	6.9	9.3	6.2	12.9	6.8	29.2	15.8	27.9	36.9
Wholesale and retail trade	21.2	21.6	17.0	22.7	7.9	8.3	46.9	23.2	49.7	26.0
Wholesale trade	4.4	4.6	2.9	4.6	6.5	8.2	30.4	20.2	26.4	36.2
Retail trade	16.8	17.0	14.1	18.1	8.3	8.4	51.2	24.0	55.6	24.5
Finance, insurance, and real estate	6.9	7.1	5.9	5.1	8.4	5.8	59.6	35.4	49.1	39.1
Business and repair services	4.8	4.8	4.9	5.9	10.1	9.4	36.7	36.6	65.2	48.4
Personal services	3.2	2.8	4.6	5.3	14.5	13.0	68.5	19.3	-7.2	16.0
Entertainment and recreation services	1.4	1.5	1.1	1.4	7.5	7.7	42.2	62.5	60.5	69.7
Professional and related services	23.3	23.3	26.8	16.5	11.3	5.5	68.2	36.3	32.9	40.1
Public administration	4.8	4.5	7.4	0.3	15.3	0.4	42.9	7.6	20.7	13.1

Source: U.S. Bureau of the Census, "Social and Economic Characteristics: United States," 1990 CP-2-1, Table 46, and "General Social and Economic Characteristics: United States Summary," 1980 Census of Population, Table 90, U.S. Government Printing Office, Washington, D.C., 1993 and 1983.

Gender and Industry of Employment

Industries with the lowest proportion female among their workers in 1990 (see Table 14-10) include mining (14.7 percent), construction (10.0 percent), and agriculture, forestry and fisheries (20.8 percent). All other industries had workforces that were at least a quarter female. The industries with the largest proportion of female workers were personal services (68.5 percent), professional and related services (68.2 percent), finance, insurance and real estate (59.6 percent), and retail trade (51.2 percent). All of the remaining industries had workforces that were between 25 and 50 percent female.

The changes in employment in different industries between 1980 and 1990 show that while growing industries appear to provide opportunities for employment for both blacks and women, their rates of employment growth are often quite different. For example, while overall growth in construction employment was 25.7 percent in the decade, women's employment in this industry grew by 51.1 percent, while blacks' employment growth (17.9 percent) lagged behind the industry's growth rate. In retail trade, however, blacks' job growth (55.6 percent) was more than double that of the industry (24.0 percent), and women only matched the industry rate of growth (24.5 percent). Of course, since a large proportion of all blacks in different industries are women, these figures cannot show any conclusive trends.

Industrial Composition of Metropolitan and Nonmetropolitan Areas by Race and Ethnicity

Table 14-11 shows that, aside from the obvious (but still small) differences linked to agriculture and mining, the industrial composition of urban and rural areas are very much alike. Central cities tend to contain a disproportionate share of finance, business and repair, entertainment, and professional services, but all of these are found in urban fringe, other urban, and rural areas in only moderately smaller proportions. Yet black and Hispanic populations have a heavy residential concentration in central places and urban fringe areas. For some kinds of jobs, especially those found in urban fringe areas and so-called "edge cities," these minority groups are at a significant disadvantage because of the distance they would have to commute or the difficulty in finding low-cost housing in these places.

Regional Composition of Industries by Sex

When trends in job growth are looked at in terms of both sex and region, some interesting patterns emerge (Table 14-12). Job growth between 1980 and 1990 was almost nine times greater for men and twice as great for women in the West than in the Midwest. Yet in the field of transportation, communication and public utilities, the growth of jobs for women was much more similar for the two regions, a 29.0 percent increase in the Midwest and a 34.6 percent increase in the West. While the Northeast was a region of only moderate overall job growth for women (22.4 percent), women in construction in that region increased by 95.2 percent, compared to only a 51.9 percent increase in the West. As with blacks and Hispanics, women are increasing their proportion in all industries, but their rate of penetration into a region's industries is usually linked to the overall rate of job growth in the region.

Class of Worker

Class of worker identifies the source from which individuals in the labor force receive income or benefits. There are seven categories, including three government sectors (federal, state, and local employees) and four nongovernment sectors (private wage and salary workers, wage workers in the non-profit sector, self-employed workers, and unpaid family workers). The distribution of the employed labor force among these categories and the percentage change 1970-80 are shown in Table 14-13. This table shows that more than three-fourths of employed persons are private wage and salary workers (workers in the non-profit sector in 1990 were added in here to make this category comparable to the 1980 Census classification). An additional one-sixth of the workers are employees of governments (federal, state, or local; this does not include about 1.2 million active-duty U.S. military personnel in 1990). Only 7 percent of all workers are self-employed, and 0.4 percent are unpaid family workers. While much has been made in the media about a trend towards self-employment, home-based employment, the "electronic cottage" and so on, the growth rate of self-employed workers between 1980 and 1990 (20.8 percent) was actually slightly lower than the growth rate of employment of private wage and salary workers (21.4 percent).

Black workers tend to be more concentrated than white workers in government employment and are less likely to be private wage or salary workers or to be self-employed. The Hispanic population, however, is underrepresented in government employment and even more concentrated than whites in wage and salary work.

What is the racial, ethnic and sex composition of various classes of employment? The second panel of Table 14-13 shows what proportion of each class of worker is contributed by each group. For example, while 9.9 percent of all workers are black, 18.4 percent of all federal, 14.1 percent of all state and 14.9 percent of all local government workers are black. Conversely, Hispanics are

Class of Worker:
Which Level of Government Has Grown Most Rapidly?

Much of the political rhetoric of the late 1980's and early 1990's has been aimed at the supposed rapid growth of the federal government, and particularly the growth of its work force. When the state and local work forces are mentioned, it is usually to point out how much more efficient they are in meeting local needs than the bloated federal bureaucracy inside the Washington Beltway that spends much of its time sending memos to itself while attempting to administer the failed policies of the past.

An examination of the rates of growth of the federal, state, and local work forces provides little support for this stereotype, however. While the size of all three sectors of the governmental work force have grown between 1970 and 1990, the growth rate of the federal work force lagged far behind the explosive growth of the other two sectors during the 1970-80 decade, and federal employment only grew by 4.8 percent during 1980-1990.

Since governments do serve people, one reason for this growth in governmental work force might be population growth. Another way of measuring the growth of government is to measure trends in the ratio of federal, state, and local employees per thousand population.

Number of Government Workers: 1970, 1980, and 1990, and Percent Change 1970-1980 and 1980-1990

Level of government	Year			Percent Change	
	1970	1980	1990	1970-1980	1980-1990
Federal	3,284	3,762	3,941	14.5	4.8
State	3,016	4,474	5,381	48.3	20.3
Local	6,020	8,454	8,245	40.4	-2.5

Source: U. S. Bureau of the Census, "Social and Economic Characteristics: United States Summary," 1990 CP-2-1, Table 47, and "General Social and Economic Characteristics: United States Summary," 1980 Census of Population, Table 90, U.S. Government Printing Office, Washington, D.C., 1993 and 1983.

As the figure below shows, there has been a small decline in the ratio of federal employees per thousand population since 1970, a steady increase in this ratio for state employees, and a rise-and-fall pattern for the ratio of local government employment to population. The ratio of federal government employees per thousand population actually decreased by 12.1 percent (from 14.1 to 12.4 per 1,000 population) from 1970 to 1990. During the same twenty-year period, this ratio increased by 34.4 percent for state workers (from 13.4 to 18.0 per 1,000 population), and by 19.7 percent (from 36.0 to 43.1 per 1,000 population) for local government workers. When examined from the point of view of either overall growth or growth as a ratio of governmental work force to population, the growth of federal employment lagged behind that of the other two levels of government (and behind the overall rate of population growth) during the last two decades.

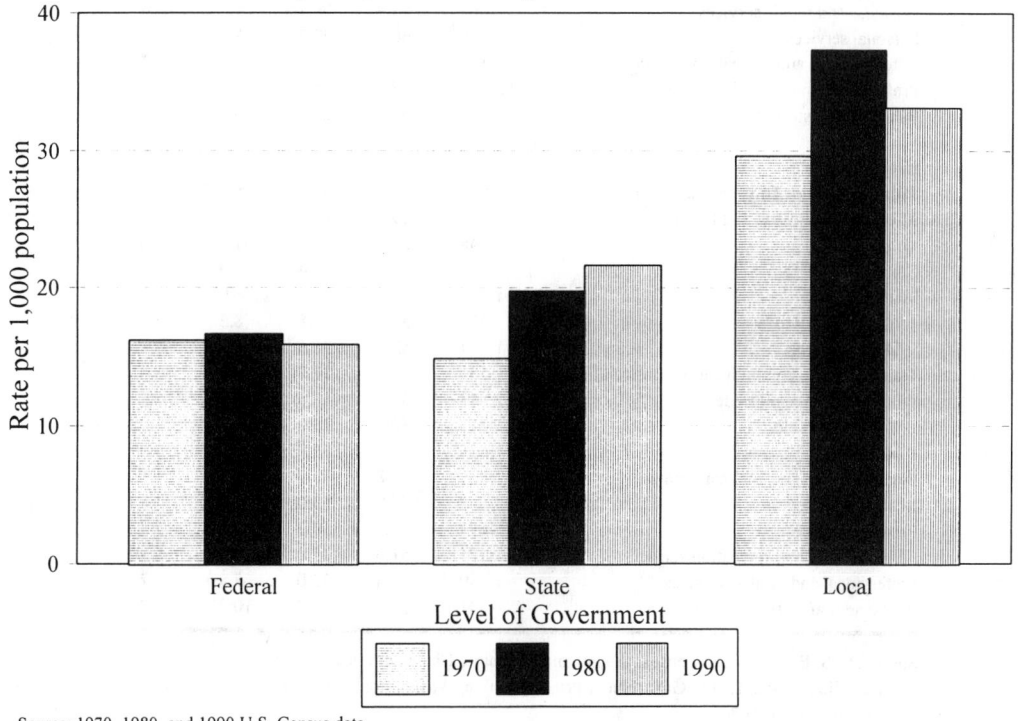

Rate of Federal, State, and Local Government Workers per 1,000 U.S. Population: 1970-1990

Source: 1970, 1980, and 1990 U.S. Census data.

Table 14-11. Industry of Employed Persons, by Race-ethnicity and Urban-rural Residence: 1990 [numbers in thousands]

Industry	Total	Central place	Urban fringe	Other urban	Rural
White					
Total employed, 16 years and over	96,218	26.7	35.6	11.2	26.6
Agriculture, forestry, and fisheries	2,648	10.6	13.8	9.2	66.4
Mining	657	16.8	16.3	18.9	47.9
Construction	6,264	22.5	34.1	10.3	33.0
Manufacturing	16,890	22.2	33.9	11.9	32.0
Nondurable goods	6,483	23.0	31.3	12.9	32.8
Durable goods	10,407	21.7	35.5	11.3	31.5
Transportation, communication, public utilities	6,669	25.7	37.6	10.0	26.7
Wholesale and retail trade	20,759	27.2	36.9	11.7	24.2
Wholesale trade	4,395	26.8	41.7	8.8	22.7
Retail trade	16,364	27.3	35.6	12.5	24.5
Finance, insurance, and real estate	6,861	31.3	42.6	8.4	17.7
Business and repair services	4,598	30.6	39.9	8.5	20.9
Personal services	2,727	29.9	33.2	12.6	24.3
Entertainment and recreation services	1,406	34.1	37.5	10.0	18.4
Professional and related services	22,391	29.9	35.5	11.8	22.8
Public administration	4,368	28.0	35.3	12.1	24.5
Black					
Total employed, 16 years and over	11,408	56.6	24.5	7.4	11.6
Agriculture, forestry, and fisheries	151	27.7	13.2	13.5	45.6
Mining	31	39.4	19.1	14.9	26.5
Construction	476	51.8	22.6	8.3	17.3
Manufacturing	1,961	45.8	20.0	12.1	22.1
Nondurable goods	917	42.0	17.6	13.9	26.5
Durable goods	1,045	49.2	22.0	10.5	18.3
Transportation, communication, public utilities	3,898	16.1	80.9	1.1	1.9
Wholesale and retail trade	1,940	57.6	25.0	7.6	9.8
Wholesale trade	329	55.9	28.2	5.8	10.2
Retail trade	1,611	58.0	24.4	7.9	9.7
Finance, insurance, and real estate	671	64.4	29.3	2.6	3.7
Business and repair services	562	63.4	26.1	4.2	6.4
Personal services	530	60.5	20.3	8.0	11.3
Entertainment and recreation services	123	62.4	25.5	5.0	7.1
Professional and related services	3,057	60.2	24.1	6.9	8.8
Public administration	848	57.7	29.1	5.6	7.6
Hispanic					
Total employed, 16 years and over	8,982	51.5	32.9	8.1	7.6
Agriculture, forestry, and fisheries	462	29.0	19.9	19.8	31.3
Mining	48	28.6	16.6	31.9	23.0
Construction	667	51.1	33.4	7.9	7.6
Manufacturing	1,794	53.0	34.5	6.9	5.6
Nondurable goods	770	53.8	31.8	8.3	6.1
Durable goods	1,024	52.4	36.6	5.9	5.1
Transportation, communication, public utilities	559	49.8	37.2	6.6	6.4
Wholesale and retail trade	2,043	52.5	33.8	7.7	6.0
Wholesale trade	415	50.7	36.9	6.5	5.9
Retail trade	1,628	52.9	33.0	8.1	6.0
Finance, insurance, and real estate	459	53.8	37.7	4.4	4.1
Business and repair services	527	56.9	33.0	5.3	4.8
Personal services	477	57.3	30.7	6.6	5.4
Entertainment and recreation services	125	51.6	35.0	6.5	6.9
Professional and related services	1,480	52.4	32.0	8.4	7.2
Public administration	341	50.4	30.7	10.3	8.7

Source: U. S. Bureau of the Census, "Social and Economic Characteristics: United States," 1990 CP-2-1, U.S. Government Printing Office, Washington, D.C., 1993, Tables 63, 64, and 67.

Table 14-12. Industry of Employed Persons, by Sex and Region: 1990 and Percent Change 1980-1990

Industry	1990				Percent Change 1980-1990			
	Northeast	Midwest[1]	South	West	Northeast	Midwest[1]	South	West
Employed males, 16 years and over (in thousands)	13,018	15,106	20,943	13,638	—	—	—	—
Employed males, 16 years and over (percent)	100.0	100.0	100.0	100.0	7.0	2.7	15.5	24.1
Agriculture, forestry, and fisheries	1.9	4.9	3.9	4.8	19.7	-11.9	2.7	21.1
Mining	0.3	0.6	1.7	1.0	-32.4	-33.5	-31.4	-31.1
Construction	9.7	8.7	11.7	10.8	46.2	15.1	14.2	32.0
Manufacturing	21.4	27.3	20.2	18.7	-22.5	-13.5	-0.3	9.7
Nondurable goods	7.6	8.1	8.4	5.1	-19.7	-3.2	-3.6	11.9
Durable goods	13.8	19.2	11.7	13.6	-24.0	-17.3	2.2	8.9
Transportation, communication, public utilities	9.7	8.9	9.7	8.7	5.1	-0.5	13.7	17.2
Wholesale and retail trade	20.5	20.5	21.0	21.1	15.9	12.8	24.6	29.8
Wholesale trade	5.6	5.8	5.6	5.4	11.9	7.9	15.0	25.0
Retail trade	14.9	14.7	15.4	15.7	17.4	14.9	28.6	31.6
Finance, insurance, and real estate	6.6	4.5	4.6	5.2	31.6	20.6	33.3	34.7
Business and repair services	5.6	5.1	5.6	6.3	16.1	29.4	38.8	35.5
Personal services	1.8	1.4	1.8	2.4	15.7	17.3	28.6	42.3
Entertainment and recreation services	1.5	1.2	1.4	2.1	44.1	52.8	68.1	60.6
Professional and related services	16.1	13.1	12.5	13.8	25.3	18.1	34.9	37.3
Public administration	5.0	3.9	5.9	5.1	-0.8	-3.3	7.9	7.8
Employed females, 16 years and over (in thousands)	11,294	12,879	17,844	10,959	—	—	—	—
Employed females, 16 years and over (percent)	100.0	100.0	100.0	100.0	22.4	19.2	31.8	36.0
Agriculture, forestry, and fisheries	0.7	1.4	1.2	1.7	42.8	7.9	24.3	37.0
Mining	0.1	0.1	0.4	0.2	-3.7	-8.2	-16.9	-13.1
Construction	1.2	1.1	1.5	1.6	95.2	39.5	41.0	51.9
Manufacturing	13.1	13.8	13.0	11.0	-18.7	-4.1	1.6	15.9
Nondurable goods	6.7	6.0	7.7	4.4	-20.0	7.5	-3.8	19.6
Durable goods	6.4	7.8	5.3	6.6	-17.3	-11.4	10.7	13.6
Transportation, communication, public utilities	4.5	4.2	4.6	4.9	36.0	29.0	45.1	34.6
Wholesale and retail trade	20.0	23.1	21.9	21.6	22.5	17.0	33.8	29.5
Wholesale trade	3.0	2.9	2.8	3.1	32.0	27.8	39.6	46.1
Retail trade	17.0	20.2	19.1	18.5	21.0	15.7	33.0	27.0
Finance, insurance, and real estate	10.2	8.5	8.4	9.3	41.6	30.5	46.9	35.4
Business and repair services	3.9	3.5	3.8	4.4	30.9	44.4	63.9	50.6
Personal services	3.9	4.2	5.1	5.7	18.9	5.7	11.0	33.9
Entertainment and recreation services	1.2	1.1	1.1	1.9	61.2	59.6	79.0	74.5
Professional and related services	37.3	35.5	33.7	33.0	38.6	29.6	44.8	49.2
Public administration	3.9	3.6	5.3	4.7	7.4	4.9	17.0	19.4

[1] North Central in 1980.

Source: U.S. Bureau of the Census, "Social and Economic Characteristics: United States," 1990 CP-2-1, Table 151, and "General Social and Economic Characteristics: United States Summary," 1980 Census of Population, Table 189, U.S. Government Printing Office, Washington, D.C., 1993 and 1983.

Table 14-13. Class of Worker of the Employed Labor Force, by Sex and Race-ethnicity: 1990, and Percent Change, 1980-1990

Class of worker	Percent distribution, 1990				Percent composition, 1990			Percent change, 1980-1990		
	Total	White	Black	Hispanic	Black	Hispanic	Female	Total	Black	Female
Total employed, 16 years and over	100.0	100.0	100.0	100.0	9.9	7.8	45.8	18.5	22.2	27.2
Private wage and salary workers	77.4	77.6	73.2	82.4	9.3	8.3	45.4	21.4	27.2	30.3
Federal government workers	3.4	3.0	6.4	2.8	18.4	6.4	42.2	4.8	4.7	12.1
State government workers	4.7	4.4	6.6	3.3	14.1	5.6	55.8	20.3	22.6	27.0
Local government workers	7.1	6.8	10.8	6.4	14.9	7.0	56.0	-2.5	0.9	-1.7
Self-employed workers	7.0	7.6	2.8	4.7	4.0	5.2	33.6	20.8	43.7	77.1
Unpaid family workers	0.4	0.5	0.2	0.4	3.4	6.3	57.6	1.2	40.9	-15.1

Source: U. S. Bureau of the Census, "Social and Economic Characteristics: United States Summary," 1990 CP-2-1, Table 47,
   and "General Social and Economic Characteristics: United States Summary," 1980 Census of Population, Table 90,
   U.S. Government Printing Office, Washington, D.C., 1993 and 1983

Table 14-14. Projected Employment in Selected Occupations: 2005 and Percent Change, 1992-2005
[numbers in thousands]

Occupation	Employment		Percent distribution		Percent change 1992-2005		Total Job Openings
	1992	2005	1992	2005	Percent	Ratio to nation	
Employed persons, 16 years and over	121,099	147,482	100.0	100.0	21.8	1.00	49,631
Managerial and professional specialty occupations	28,658	37,996	23.7	25.8	32.6	1.50	13,220
Executive, administrative, and managerial occupations	12,066	15,195	10.0	10.3	25.9	1.19	4,844
Professional specialty occupations	16,592	22,801	13.7	15.5	37.4	1.72	8,376
Technical, sales, and administrative support occupations	39,624	46,734	32.7	31.7	17.9	0.82	15,495
Technicians and related support occupations	4,282	5,664	3.5	3.8	32.3	1.48	1,798
Marketing and sales occupations	12,993	15,664	10.7	10.6	20.6	0.94	6,706
Administrative support occupations, including clerical	22,349	25,406	18.5	17.2	13.7	0.63	6,991
Service occupations	19,358	25,820	16.0	17.5	33.4	1.53	9,813
Private household occupations	869	583	0.7	0.4	-32.9	—	245
Protective service occupations	3,200	4,386	2.6	3.0	37.1	1.70	1,514
Service occupations, except protective and household	15,289	20,851	12.6	14.1	36.4	1.67	8,054
Farming, forestry, and fishing occupations	3,530	3,650	2.9	2.5	3.4	0.16	988
Precision production, craft, and repair occupations	13,580	15,380	11.2	10.4	13.3	0.61	4,489
Construction trades	3,510	4,295	2.9	2.9	22.4	1.03	1,183
Mechanics, installers, and repairers	4,819	5,581	4.0	3.8	15.8	0.73	1,950
Precision production occupations	2,965	2,965	2.4	2.0	...	...	730
Other precision production, craft, and repair occupations	2,286	2,539	1.9	1.7	11.1	0.51	626
Operators, fabricators, and laborers	16,349	17,902	13.5	12.1	9.5	0.44	5,626
Machine operators and tenders, except precision	4,676	4,326	3.9	2.9	-7.5	—	1,353
Hand workers, including assemblers and fabricators	2,528	2,630	2.1	1.8	4.0	0.19	784
Transportation, material moving machine and vehicle operators	4,694	5,719	3.9	3.9	21.8	1.00	1,434
Helpers, laborers, and material movers, hand	4,451	5,227	3.7	3.5	17.4	0.80	2,056

Source: U.S. Bureau of Labor Statistics, "Occupational Projections and Training Data," 1994 Edition, U.S. Government Printing Office,
   Washington, D.C., 1994, Table 1.

somewhat underrepresented (relative to their size in the total workforce) in government employment.

Women comprised 45.8 percent of the nation's workforce in 1990, and were a majority of workers in three classes: state government workers (55.8 percent), local government workers (56.0 percent) and unpaid family workers (57.6 percent). Women were heavily underrepresented only among self-employed workers, where they contributed only 33.6 percent of the workforce. While women are slightly underrepresented in the federal government (42.2 percent of all workers), between 1980 and 1990 they increased their rate of employment there almost twice as fast (12.1 percent) as the overall rate of growth in federal government employment (7.1 percent).

Conclusion: The Future Occupational Composition

It is over-simplistic to assume that the dynamic changes in occupational composition characterizing recent decades will continue with the same differentials and momentum. Alternatively, an equilibrium may be reached between agricultural and nonagricultural sectors, between the manufacturing and nonmanufacturing industries of the nonagricultural sector, and between governmental and nongovernmental employment. The slowdown in the labor force growth (now underway), coupled with the convergence of differentials in labor force participation of the sexes, of the races, and of the age groups, may also have a stabilizing effect on future occupational composition. A possible major problem for the near future will be to find suitable employment (both by occupation and industry) for the labor force that will exist. The phenomenon of chronic high unemployment may continue to shadow large numbers of workers who lack the education and skills to meet the opportunities offered by high technology, or who are victims during their youth of a combination of race, poverty, and low education.

An attempt to foresee the future occupational structure of the U.S. labor force has been made by the Bureau of Labor Statistics. In a report entitled Occupational Projections and Training Data: 1994 Edition, the Bureau has estimated the number of persons employed in each of the detailed occupations in the year 2005, with measures of percent change 1992-2005. These projections were made using an economic growth model which combines assumptions about future productivity of the U.S. economy, the division of this productivity among the industrial sectors, the employment required to fulfill the necessary production in each industry, and the occupational composition of the workers in each of the industries. The future size of the labor force is taken into account. When such a series of unknowns are chained, all of them interacting in ways neither well understood nor easily predictable, the

resulting predictions must be viewed with caution.

Table 14-14 presents the projections of the Bureau of Labor Statistics for the major occupational groups. (For projections for the individual detailed occupations, the reader should consult the source, which is revised biennially.) It is plausible that the Bureau's methodology has built-in assumptions about continuation of past trends, so that the amount of rapid growth in some occupations may be underpredicted (a fact recognized by the Bureau of Labor Statistics analysts in their evaluations of past predictions). Despite their cautions and limitations, these projections contain some startling predictions.

The model predicts that the total size of the workforce will grow from 121.1 to 147.5 million workers between 1992 and 2005. Certain occupations (see the "Ratio to nation" column) will grow far faster than the overall rate of growth in the workforce (which will gain about 21.8 percent over this period). The most rapidly-growing occupations will include professional specialty occupations, protective service occupations, service occupations except protective and household, and technicians and related support occupations. Jobs in precision production, craft and repair occupations, and operators, fabricators, and laborers, the backbone of employment for those with educational levels of high school and below, will grow at rates of only about half (0.61 and 0.44, respectively) that of the workforce as a whole. The future demand for highly-educated workers and the lack of demand for those with low levels of education may continue to exacerbate the growing gap in income distribution between these two parts of the labor force.

Notes

1. Edwards, Alba M. "Preface." Comparative Occupation Statistics for the United States, 1870 to 1940. Washington, DC: U.S. Census of Population, 1940, p.xi.
2. The data on industrial composition, shown in Table 14-9, are Bureau of Labor Statistics tabulations of workers on nonagricultural payrolls, used because the census enumerations before 1940 employed definitions not consistent with the present classifications. Because the payroll data are known to be incomplete, especially for early years, the trends are roughly, not precisely, indicative of long-term shifts in the nonagricultural sectors of the economy.

Bibliography

Albelda, Randy P. "Occupational segregation by race and gender, 1958-81." Industrial and Labor Relations Review, (1986):404-411.

Bianchi, Suzanne. "Changing Economic Roles of Women and Men." Pp. 107-154 in Reynolds Farley, ed. State of the Union: America in the 1990s. New York: Russell Sage Foundation, 1995.

Blau, Peter M., and Duncan, Otis Dudley. The American Occupational Structure. New York: The Free Press, 1978.

Bureau of Labor Statistics. Occupational Employment Patterns for 1960 and 1975. Washington, DC: U.S. Government Printing Office, 1968.

Choldin, H.M., and Hanson, C. "Status Shifts within the City." American Sociological Review 47 (1982):129-41.

Conroy, M.E. "Concept and Measurement of Regional Industrial Diversification." Southern Economic Journal 41 (1975):492-505.

Curry, L. "Division of Labor from Geographical Competition." Association of American Geographers Annual 71 (1981):133-65.

Duncan, Otis Dudley. "The Trend of Occupational Mobility in the United States." American Sociological Review 30 (1965): 491-98.

Edwards, Alba M. A Social-Economic Grouping of the Gainful Workers of the United States. Washington, D.C,: U.S. Government Printing Office, 1938.

England, Paula. "Assessing trends in occupational sex segregation, 1900-1976." In Ivar Berg, ed. Sociological Perspectives on Labor Markets. New York: Academic Press, 1981.

Featherman, David L., and Hauser, Robert M. Opportunity and Change. New York: Academic Press, 1978.

Fossett, M., and Swicegood, G. "Rediscovering City Differences in Racial Occupational Inequality." American Sociological Review 47 (1982):681-89.

Fullerton, H.N. "The 1995 Labor Force: A First Look." Monthly Labor Review 103 (1980):11-21.

Gittleman, Maury. "Earnings in the 1980's: an occupational perspective." Monthly Labor Review, 117, 7 (1994):16-27.

Goldin, Claudia. Understanding the Gender Gap: An Economic History of American Women. New York: Oxford University Press, 1990.

Goodman, Leo A. "Multiplicative models for the analysis of occupational mobility tables and other kinds of cross-classification tables." American Journal of Sociology 84(1979):804-819.

Goodman, William. "Women and jobs in recoveries: 1970-93." Monthly Labor Review, 117, 7 (1994):28-36.

Goodman, William, Stephen Antczak, and Laura Freeman. "Women and jobs in recessions: 1969-92." Monthly Labor Review 116, 7 (1993):26-35.

Gory, M. la, and Magnani, R.J. "Structural Correlates of Black-White Occupational Differentiation: Will Regional Differences in Status Remain?" Social Problems 27 (1979):157-69.

Hauser, Robert M. The Process of Stratification: Trends and Analysis. New York: Academic Press, 1977.

Hauser, Robert M. et al. Social Structure and Behavior: Essays in Honor of William Hamilton Sewell. New York: Academic Press, 1982.

Hodge, Robert W. "Perspectives on Occupational Mobility." PhD. thesis, University of Chicago, Department of Sociology, 1967.

Hodge, Robert, and Duncan, Otis Dudley. "Educational and Occupational Mobility: A Regression Analysis." American Journal of Sociology 68 (1963):629-44.

Hout, Michael. "More universalism, less structural mobility: The American occupational structure in the 1980s." American Journal of Sociology 93(6)(1988):1358-1400.

Hyman, D.N., and Fearn, R.M. "Influence of City Size on Labor Economics." Quarterly Review of Economics and Business 18 (1978):63-73.

Jaffe, A.J., and Carleton, R.O. Occupational Mobility in the United States, 1930-1960. New York: King's Crown Press, Columbia University, 1954.

Kasarda, Jolin. "The Changing Occupational Structure of the American Metropolis." In the Changing Face of the Suburbs. Barry Schwartz (ed.). Chicago: University of Chicago Press, 1976.

King, P.E. "Mobility of Manufacturing and the Interstate Redistribution of Employment." Professional Geography 27(1975):441-48.

Landecker, Werner S. Class Crystallization. New Brunswick, NJ: Rutgers University Press, 1981.

Lonsdale, Richard E., and Seyler, H.L. (eds.). Nonmetropolitan Industrialization. Washington, DC: Winston and Sons, 1979.

McKenzie, R.B. "Myths of Sunbelt and Frostbelt." Policy Review 20 (1982):103-14.

Mickens, A. "Regional Defense Demand and Racial Response Differences in the Net Migration of Workers." Quarterly Review of Economics and Business 17 (1977):65-82.

Morgan, B.S. "Occupational Segregation in Metropolitan Areas in the U.S., 1970." Urban Studies 17 (1980):63-69.

National Research Council, Committee on Occupational Classification and Analysis (edited by Ann R. Miller et al.). Work Jobs and Occupations: A Critical Review of the Dictionary of Occupational Titles. Washington, DC: National Academy Press, 1980.

Newman, R.J. "Industry Migration and Growth in the South." Review of Economics and Statistics 65 (1983):76-86.

Parnes, Herbert S. Research in Labor Mobility: An Appraisal of Research Findings in the United States. New York: Social Science Research Council, 1954.

Personnick, V.A. "Outlook for Industry Output, and Employment through 1990." Monthly Labor Review 104 (1981):28-41.

Pullum, Thomas. Measuring Occupational Inheritance. New York: Elsivere Press, 1975.

Rodriguez, O. "Occupational Shifts and Educational Upgrading in the American Labor Force Between 1950 and 1970." Sociology of Education 51 (1978):55-67.

Rosenthal, Neal H. "Evaluating the 1990 projections of occupational employment." Monthly Labor Review, 115, 8 (1992):32-48.

Rytina, Steve. "Scaling intergenerational continuity: is occupational inheritance ascriptive after all?" American Journal of Sociology 97(6)(1992):1658-88.

Saunders, Norman C. "BLS employment projections for 1990: an evaluation." Monthly Labor Review, 115, 8 (1992):15-31.

Scott, A.J. "Production System Dynamics and Metropolitan Development." Association of American Geographers Annual 72 (1982):185-200.

Sell, R.R. "Research Note on the Demography of Occupational Relocation." Social Forces 60 (1982):859-65.

Serow, W.J. "Alternative Demographic Futures and the Composition of the Demand for Labor, by Industry and by Occupation." Research in Population Economics 3 (1981):209-23.

Siegel, Paul M. Prestige in the American Occupational Structure. Chicago: University of Chicago Press, 1971.

Singelmann, J., and Browning, H.L. "Industrial Transformation and Occupational Change in the U.S., 1960-1970." Social Forces 59 (1980):246-64.

Spilerman, S., and Miller, R.E. "City Nondifferences Revisited." American Sociological Review 42 (1977):979-83.

Stolzenberg, R.M., and D'Amico, R.J. "City Differences and Nondifferences in the Effect of Race and Sex on Occupational Distribution." American Sociological Review 42(1977):937-50.

U.S. Bureau of the Census (Littman, Mark S.). "Social and Economic Characteristics of the Metropolitan and Nonmetropolitan Population: 1977 and 1970." Current Population Reports (Series P-23, no. 75). Washington, DC: U.S. Government Printing Office, 1978.

U.S. Bureau of the Census. The Relationship Between the 1970 and 1980 Industry and Occupation Classification Systems(Technical Paper No. 59). Washington, D.C.: U.S. Department of Commerce, Bureau of the Census, 1989.

_____. 1980 Industry and Occupation Categories that had Title or Code Changes for the 1990 Census of Population (Mimeo, 27 May 1992; Revised 18 August 1993). Washington, D.C.: U.S. Department of Commerce, Bureau of the Census, 1993.

U.S. Department of Labor (Goldstein, Harvey A.). Occupational Employment Projections for Labor Market Areas: An Alternative Approach. Washington, DC: U.S. Government Printing Office, 1981.

Wetzel, James R. "Labor Force, Unemployment and Earnings." pp. 59-106 in Reynolds Farley, ed. State of the Union: America in the 1990s. New York: Russell Sage Foundation, 1995.

Williams, Gregory. "The changing U.S. labor force and occupational differentiation by sex." Demography (1979):73-87.

Zuiches, James J. Economic Function and Population Age in Nonmetropolitan Cities. Madison, WI:University of Wisconsin, 1973.

INCOME, WEALTH AND POVERTY

In sociology and economics, income, wealth and poverty are often considered as three different concepts or areas of study. However, social and economic trends in the 1980s and 1990s have made us more aware that the trends in these three areas are linked, and that trends in one area have ramifications for the others. For this reason, this chapter will treat all three areas of social stratification.

Trends in Income in the United States

In the United States, as in all technologically advanced nations, money income is a sensitive measure of economic well-being. Income received is usually expended in a patterned way to provide for the current and future needs of individuals, families and households. Income distribution is, therefore, one of the best measures of the economic status of different parts of the population.

The income of the American population has been a topic of serious academic study only since the late 1930s. When President Franklin Roosevelt made his famous statement in the depths of the Depression in the early 1930s that one-third of the nation was ill-fed, ill-clothed and ill-housed, it was little more than an educated guess. However, since that time, various federal agencies have developed measures of household, family and individual income that are as sophisticated as those of any of the world's nations.

These measures are pointing toward a historic shift in the distribution of income and wealth in the United States over the last two decades. Reversing the trends of the previous two decades (i.e. since World War II), the lower classes now capture an increasingly smaller pro-

portion of income. There is a "hollowing out" of the income structure, with the proportion of those in the middle of the income distribution declining a great deal. In terms of wealth, there has been an even more radical concentration of wealth among the rich over the past two decades. Poverty rates have also risen over the past twenty years. Finally, there has been little convergence of racial groups: there is still a major difference in income between racial and ethnic groups in the United States, and a striking difference in wealth. These racial and ethnic differences in income and wealth and the lack of convergence between groups over time are so well known that scholars no longer even debate their existence, only their possible origins, such as a changing industrial structure, racial discrimination, changing family structures, and so on.

International Comparisons of Income

The most commonly-used measure in international comparisons of personal income is the Gross National Product per capita measure. This measure simply takes the estimate of a nation's gross national product (GNP) and divides it by the total population to create an estimate of the mean income available to the average citizen. Of course, this measure has significant defects, the most important of which is that it does not measure the actual distribution of income within nations.

In 1993, the United States stood fifth among all nations in terms of Gross National Product per capita, surpassed only by Switzerland, Japan, Denmark and Norway (Table 15-1). Nations within $2,000 of GNP per capita in the United States included Sweden (tied for fifth place with the United States), Germany and Austria. In terms of average annual per capita income growth between 1980 and 1993, the United States was in the middle,

629

Chapter 15 Definitions
INCOME, WEALTH AND POVERTY

Income. Total income is the algebraic sum of the amounts reported separately for wage or salary income; net nonfarm self-employment income; net farm self-employment income; interest, dividend, or net rental or royalty income; Social Security or railroad retirement income; public assistance or welfare income; retirement or disability income; and all other income.

Earnings. This represents the amount of income received regularly before deductions for personal income taxes, Social Security, bond purchases, union dues, Medicare deductions, etc.

Income Year. The twelve-month interval for which the respondent is asked to report income. In most cases this refers to the calendar year preceding the survey.

Individual Income. Total income received by persons aged fifteen years or older.

Income of Households. Includes the income of the householder and all other persons fifteen years old and over in the household, whether related to the householder or not. Because many households consist of only one person, average household income is usually less than average family income.

Income of Families. Includes the total incomes of all members fifteen years old and over in each family. Although income statistics generally cover the previous calendar year, the composition of families refers to the time of enumeration (current year). Thus, the income of the family does not include amounts received by persons who were members of the family during all or part of the previous calendar year if these persons no longer resided with the family at the time of enumeration.

Zero or Negative Income. The income tabulations for families and unrelated individuals included in the lowest income group (under $2,500), those who were classified as having no income in the income year, and those reporting a loss in net income from farm and nonfarm self-employment or in rental income.

Government Transfer Payments. The sum of income from the following sources: Social Security or railroad retirement; public assistance or welfare payments; Supplemental Security income; retirement and annuities paid from government funds; veterans' payments; and unemployment and worker's compensation.

Receipts Not Counted as Income. Receipts from the sale of property (unless the recipient was engaged in the business of selling such property); the value "in kind" from food stamps, public housing subsidies, medical care, employer contributions for persons, etc.; withdrawal of bank deposits; money borrowed; tax refunds; exchange of money between relatives living in the same household; gifts and lump-sum inheritances, insurance payments, and other types of lump-sum receipts are not included as income.

Median Income. The amount that divides the income distribution into two equal parts, one having incomes above the median and the other having incomes below the median. The medians for households and families are based on the distribution of the total number of units including those with no income. The median for persons is based on persons with income.

Mean Income. This amount is obtained by dividing the total aggregate income of a group by the total number of units in that group.

Per Capita Income. This is the mean income computed for every man, woman, and child in a particular group. It is derived by dividing the total income of a particular group by the total population in that group.

Index of Income Concentration or Gini Index. This is a statistical measure of income inequality, or the extent to which income is differentially distributed in such a way that a comparatively small proportion of the population receives a disproportionately large share of the income. The Gini Index is a measure in which a value of 0 indicates perfect equality, i.e. all persons having equal shares of the income, and a value of 1 indicates perfect inequality, i.e. one person has all the income and the rest have none.

Average Income-to-Poverty Ratios. These ratios represent the average ratio of family or unrelated individual income to their appropriate poverty threshold. Ratios below 1.00 mean that the average income of the respective families or unrelated individuals is below the official poverty definition, while a ratio of 1.00 or

---

at 1.7 percent growth per year, or thirteenth out of the 29 most prosperous nations in the world.

Trends in Personal Income over Time in the United States

The economic well-being of the population cannot be measured solely in terms of the average income available per citizen; the distribution of this income must also be discovered. Many analysts of income feel that median rather than mean income is a more accurate representation of the distribution of income within the population and the condition of the average person or family. In addition, most analysts prefer using constant rather than current dollars in such comparisons of changes in income over time to discount the effects of periods of rapid inflation.

In the late 1930s the Bureau of the Census began to collect statistics on the income received from all sources by individuals, and it is these data that provide detailed information about income distribution. The questions asked are illustrated by questions 32 and 33 in the 1990 Census questionnaire (see Technical Appendix 2-1); the Current Population Surveys ask similar questions of respondents. This chapter's Definition Box explains the concepts and terms employed in tabulating and reporting the results. Similar questions about income were included in all censuses from 1940 on and in the Current Population Surveys from the late 1940s on.

Not included as income in these inquiries was the value of food produced and consumed in the home, the economic benefits of home ownership, the consumption of funds from savings, borrowed money, tax refunds, gifts or lump-sum inheritances, and insurance benefits. Also not included were goods and social services provided gratis or at subsidized prices through social welfare programs for low income persons, such as food stamps, Medicaid, public housing, aid to families with dependent children, senior citizens programs, and so on. Recent surveys developed by the Bureau of the Census include ques-

greater means that income is above the poverty level.

Poverty. Persons and families defined as living in poverty received money income below a threshold amount adjusted for family or household size, age of householder, and number of children under eighteen, during the year preceding the enumeration. The threshold amount is based on a definition developed by the Social Security Administration in 1964 and revised in 1969 and 1981 by interagency committees.

Extreme Poverty. While poverty is defined as income ratio below 1.00 of the poverty threshold, extreme poverty is defined as income ratio below 0.50 of the poverty threshold.

Poverty Rate. The percent of individuals, families, or households that received incomes below the specified thresholds.

Poverty Areas. Defined in terms of census tracts (in metropolitan areas) or minor civil divisions (townships, districts, etc. in nonmetropolitan areas) in which 20 percent or more of the population was below the poverty threshold.

Income Deficit. This represents the difference between the total income of families and unrelated individuals below the poverty level and their respective poverty thresholds. In computing the income deficit, families reporting a net income loss are assigned zero dollars and for such cases the deficit is equal to the poverty threshold.

This measure provides an estimate of the amount which would be required to raise the incomes of all poor families and unrelated individuals to their respective poverty thresholds. The income deficit is thus a measure of the degree of impoverishment of a family or unrelated individual. However, caution must be used in comparing the average deficits of families with different characteristics. Apparent differences in average income deficits may, to some extent, be a function of differences in family size.

Median Income Deficit. The median income deficit is the dollar amount at the midpoint of the range of all income deficits. Half of the households showing an income deficit will have one greater than the median and the other half will have one smaller than the median.

Mean Income Deficit. This is the amount obtained by dividing the total income deficit of a group below the poverty level by the total number of families or unrelated individuals in that group.

Computation of Constant Dollar Distributions. For the years since 1967, adjustments for price change have been made by converting the incomes (in current dollars) of households, families, or persons into constant dollars on the basis of the Consumer Price Index (CPI-U-X1).

This index is designed to measure changes in family purchasing power.

Income Quintiles and Deciles. Suppose all income-producing individuals in the United States are ordered by income. If the population is then divided into five (for quintiles) or ten (for deciles) equal numbers of individuals, and the total income of the individuals in each quintile or decile is summed, then the distribution of total income among those groups of equal size can be compared.

Non-cash Benefits. These are benefits that households, families, or individuals receive that are not in the form of money. These may include food stamps, health benefits, rent-subsidized or free housing, etc.

Progressive Taxes. These are forms of taxation where as income or consumption go up, a higher percentage of tax is paid. These include federal income taxes and income taxes in some states.

Regressive Taxes. These are forms of taxation whereby the same percentage of tax is paid regardless of the amount of income or consumption. These taxes include state and local sales taxes, many state income taxes and especially the Social Security payroll tax (where those with high incomes pay no tax at all on the bulk of their income). They are called regressive because those with lower incomes pay a higher proportion of their income in such taxes than do those with higher incomes.

Net Worth. This represents the sum of the market value of assets owned by every household member minus secured or unsecured liabilities owed by these members. This concept does not include the value of pension plans, cash value of life insurance or value of home furnishings or jewelry.

Median Net Worth. The amount which divides the net worth distribution into two equal groups, one-half of all households having more and one-half having less than this median value.

Mean Net Worth. The average obtained by dividing the total net worth of a group by the total number of households in that group.

---

tions on these topics. The Bureau of the Census has also developed several alternative definitions of income that take these factors into account, and that also account for the negative effects of taxation on income. These topics will be explored later in this chapter.

Income information is tabulated and published in two principal forms: as income of *individuals* and as income of *families* or *households*. Both of these types of data are reviewed below. Most of the materials in this section on income are based on annual data from the *Current Population Reports* (CPS) from 1994 and earlier. Because of their greater frequency of administration, their large sample size, and their comparability, these CPS income reports provide a good framework with which to study trends and variations. Results from the decennial censuses are used to provide details not available from the *Current Population Reports*.

Table 15-2 and Figure 15-1 show the trends in median income for persons 15 years and over by race and sex between 1947 and 1992. In 1947, males 14 years and over had an annual income of $14,140 (in 1992-equivalent dollars), and women had an income of $6,449. By 1973, male income rose to almost $24,000, and female income had risen to $8,311. However, after 1973, male incomes declined, dropping to $20,654 for those 15 years and over in 1992. Women's incomes continued to rise after 1973, increasing $2,463 to $10,774 in 1992.

The decline in male median incomes after 1973 was found among both blacks and whites, and was particularly severe for Hispanics. In 1973, Hispanic males had a median income of $18,429 (in 1992 dollars), but by 1992 this figure had dropped to only $13,810, a decline of more than $4,600. This large decline in median male Hispanic earnings is due to a number of factors, including structural shifts in the economy, declining labor market opportunities and salaries for those with little education, and a large international influx of poorly-educated Hispanic migrants.

Declines in male income were particularly sharp in recent recessions: real male income dropped sharply in

Table 15-1. Per Capita GNP and Average Annual Growth for the 30 Richest Nations: 1993

Country	GNP per capita	
	Dollars 1993	Average annual growth (%) 1980-1993
World	4,420	1.2
Switzerland	35,760	1.1
Japan	31,490	3.4
Denmark	26,730	2.0
Norway	25,970	2.2
United States	24,740	1.7
Sweden	24,740	1.3
Germany	23,560	2.1*
Austria	23,510	2.0
France	22,490	1.6
Belgium	21,650	1.9
United Arab Emirates[1]	21,430	-4.4
Netherlands	20,950	1.7
Canada	19,970	1.4
Singapore[1]	19,850	6.1
Italy	19,840	2.1
Kuwait[1]	19,360	-4.3
Finland	19,300	1.5
United Kingdom	18,060	2.3
Hong Kong[1]	18,060[2]	5.4[2]
Australia	17,500	1.6
Israel[1]	13,920	2.0
Spain	13,590	2.7
Ireland	13,000	3.6
New Zealand	12,600	0.7
Portugal	9,130[3]	3.3
Korea, Republic	7,660	8.2
Greece	7,390	0.9
Argentina	7,220	-0.5
Puerto Rico	7,000	1.0
Slovenia	6,490	—

[1] Economies classified by the United Nations or otherwise regarded by their authorities as developing.
[2] Data refer to GDP.
[3] Reflect recent revision of 1993 GNP per capita from $7,890 to $9,130.
* Refers to the Federal Republic of Germany before unification.

Source: World Bank, "World Development Report 1995: Workers in an Integrating World," Oxford University Press, Oxford, 1995, Table 1.

the recessions of the mid-1970s, the early 1980s and the early 1990s. These recessions had less of an effect on the income of women. For example, between 1978 and 1982, the real income of all men dropped over $2,000 (from $22,729 to $20,473). Yet during the same time period, the income of white women rose $200, the income of black women rose $19, and the income of Hispanic women dropped $330. The most recent recession had almost no effect on white and black women, and only a minor effect on Hispanic women, whose incomes declined sharply from 1989 to 1990 but rebounded in 1991 and 1992.

Much of the decline in real (or constant dollar) male income is obscured when income data are presented in current dollars. Figure 15-2 presents the same data as that given in Figure 15-1, but in current rather than constant dollars. Due to the high rates of inflation during the 1970s and 1980s, the decline in real income is obscured; even when real income declines, measuring income in current dollars makes it appear that it is increasing. The rise in income for white males in current dollars between 1947 and 1992 was a more than six-fold increase (from less than $3,000 to almost $22,000), but in real terms, the increase was only about 46 percent (from $14,140 to $20,654).

Proportion of American Adults Receiving Income

Income distribution is a function of the proportion of the population receiving income and how much income they are receiving. While the latter topic receives most attention from scholars of the subject, demographers are interested in the former topic as well. Demographic factors, including the age distribution of the population, age at accession to or retirement from the workforce, and marriage rates, all can affect whether individuals received income in a particular year.

Table 15-3 shows that there has been a gradual rise in the proportion of men and a sharp increase in the proportion of women receiving income between 1947 and 1992. In the late 1940s, about 90 percent of men age 14 years and over received income; by the late 1980s that proportion had risen to 95 percent. Several contradictory factors were probably responsible for this increase: a larger proportion of students engaged in part-time or full-time work, more retirees qualifying for earlier Social Security payments, and a one-year rise in the minimum age boundary for this measure in 1980 to those fifteen years and older.

For women, of course, the rise in the percent receiving income is much more rapid. In the late 1940s only about 40 percent of all women age 14 or over received income. Contrary to the portrait that is sometimes painted of the 1950s, women made significant gains in employment and in income reception; by 1959 almost 54 percent of women received income. By 1980 this figure had risen to almost 89 percent, or to about the same level as the proportion of all men receiving income in the late 1940s. In 1992 the proportion of all women aged 15 years and over receiving income stood at 91 percent. Explanations for this striking rise in the proportion of women receiving income mirror those used to explain their increases in labor force participation: greater education, lower rates of marriage and fertility, higher divorce rates, and less discrimination against women in the labor market.

Racial and ethnic groups vary with regard to the proportion receiving income. In 1953 (the first time such

Table 15-2. Median Income for Persons[1], by Sex and Race-ethnicity: 1947-1992
[in constant 1992 dollars]

Year	All races Male	All races Female	White Male	White Female	Black[2] Male	Black[2] Female	Hispanic Male	Hispanic Female
1992	20,654	10,774	21,645	11,036	12,754	8,857	13,810	8,357
1991	21,085	10,791	22,039	11,044	13,352	9,081	14,234	8,254
1990	21,784	10,810	22,725	11,075	13,813	8,940	14,459	8,085
1989	22,508	10,889	23,605	11,102	14,266	8,910	15,161	8,652
1988	22,424	10,536	23,671	10,796	14,284	8,716	15,453	8,290
1987	21,966	10,245	23,348	10,506	13,851	8,582	15,104	8,188
1986	21,908	9,742	23,119	9,934	13,853	8,405	14,762	8,113
1985	21,268	9,410	22,311	9,593	14,040	8,185	14,909	7,849
1984	21,065	9,274	22,236	9,383	12,758	8,323	14,990	7,872
1983	20,652	9,022	21,727	9,180	12,706	7,845	15,271	7,566
1982	20,473	8,640	21,644	8,757	12,970	7,724	15,367	7,543
1981	20,980	8,499	22,261	8,594	13,237	7,635	15,888	7,879
1980	21,360	8,387	22,721	8,433	13,653	7,808	16,466	7,509
1979	22,332	8,251	23,330	8,329	14,441	7,580	16,819	7,868
1978	22,729	8,455	23,805	8,557	14,261	7,705	17,418	7,873
1977	22,472	8,749	23,538	8,882	13,968	7,670	17,309	8,145
1976	22,264	8,446	23,471	8,517	14,132	8,026	16,652	7,934
1975	22,101	8,450	23,217	8,538	13,880	7,756	16,918	7,994
1974	22,848	8,331	23,935	8,426	14,830	7,607	17,417	8,131
1973	23,946	8,311	25,126	8,391	15,198	7,574	18,429	7,883
1972	23,541	8,213	24,692	8,266	14,956	7,723	18,283	8,364
1971	22,471	7,839	23,558	7,969	14,050	6,982	—	—
1970	22,659	7,599	23,817	7,698	14,122	7,008	—	—
1969	22,893	7,592	24,090	7,770	14,012	6,552	—	—
1968	22,254	7,514	23,323	7,737	13,836	6,137	—	—
1967	21,462	6,961	22,595	7,170	12,932	5,643	—	—
1966	23,160	7,151	24,407	7,486	13,519	5,697	—	—
1965	22,552	6,829	23,753	7,244	12,783	5,270	—	—
1964	21,221	6,617	22,543	6,931	12,780	4,866	—	—
1963	20,870	6,349	22,235	6,655	11,556	4,456	—	—
1962	20,474	6,286	21,807	6,619	10,740	4,442	—	—
1961	19,837	6,058	20,972	6,422	10,838	4,306	—	—
1960	19,517	6,033	20,550	6,468	10,812	4,002	—	—
1959	19,426	5,944	20,454	6,374	9,629	3,927	—	—
1958	18,337	5,762	19,482	6,268	9,707	3,819	—	—
1957	18,505	6,041	19,668	6,610	10,414	3,823	—	—
1956	18,772	5,988	19,897	6,592	10,439	3,789	—	—
1955	17,764	5,925	18,750	6,622	9,868	3,455	—	—
1954	16,829	6,115	17,728	6,792	8,822	3,685	—	—
1953	17,059	6,176	17,959	6,848	9,921	4,012	—	—
1952	16,569	6,120	17,372	7,144	9,520	2,761	—	—
1951	16,096	5,697	16,912	6,657	9,313	2,827	—	—
1950	15,122	5,608	15,941	6,239	8,657	2,791	—	—
1949	13,940	5,706	14,685	6,356	7,109	2,941	—	—
1948	14,096	5,941	14,770	6,666	8,020	2,896	—	—
1947	14,140	6,449	—	—	—	—	—	—

[1] Persons 15 years and over beginning in 1980; persons 14 and over prior to that date.
[2] Data refer to black and other prior to 1967.

Source: U.S. Bureau of the Census, Current Population Reports, "Money Income of Households, Families, and Persons in the United States: 1992," Tables B-1 and B-14, and "Money Income of Households, Families, and Persons in the United States: 1982," Table 40 (data prior to 1967), U.S. Government Printing Office, Washington, D.C., 1993 and 1984.

Figure 15-1. Median Income for Persons[1], by Sex and Race-ethnicity:
1947-1992 [in constant 1992 dollars]

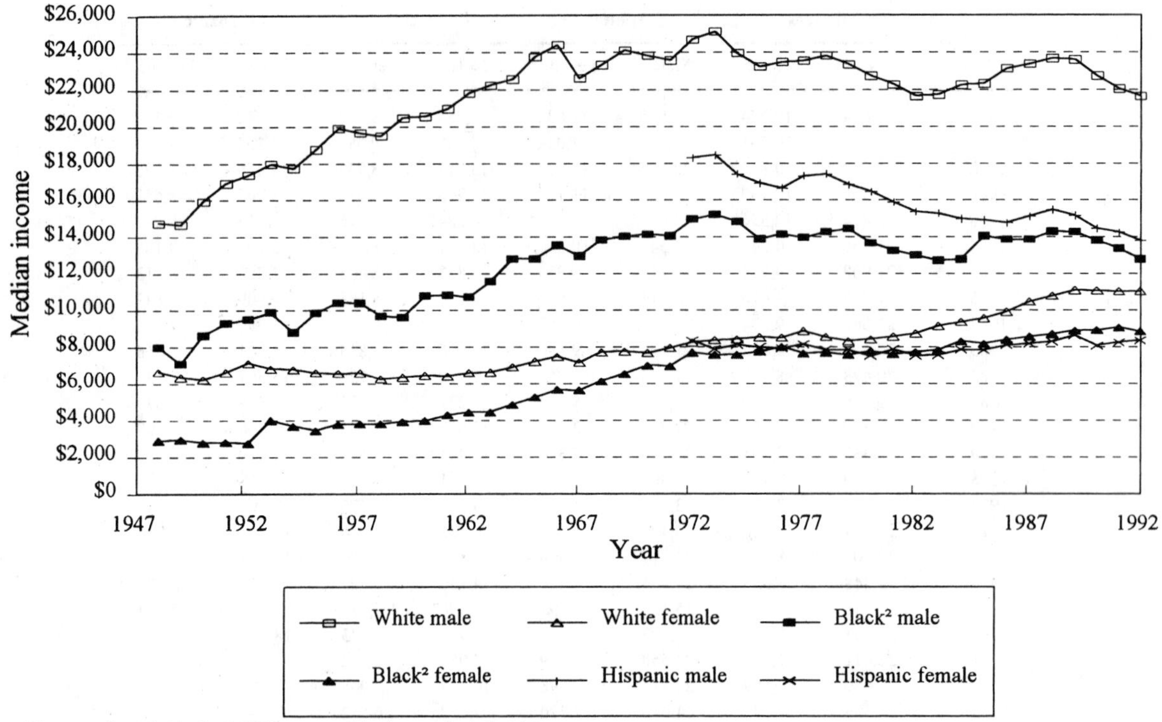

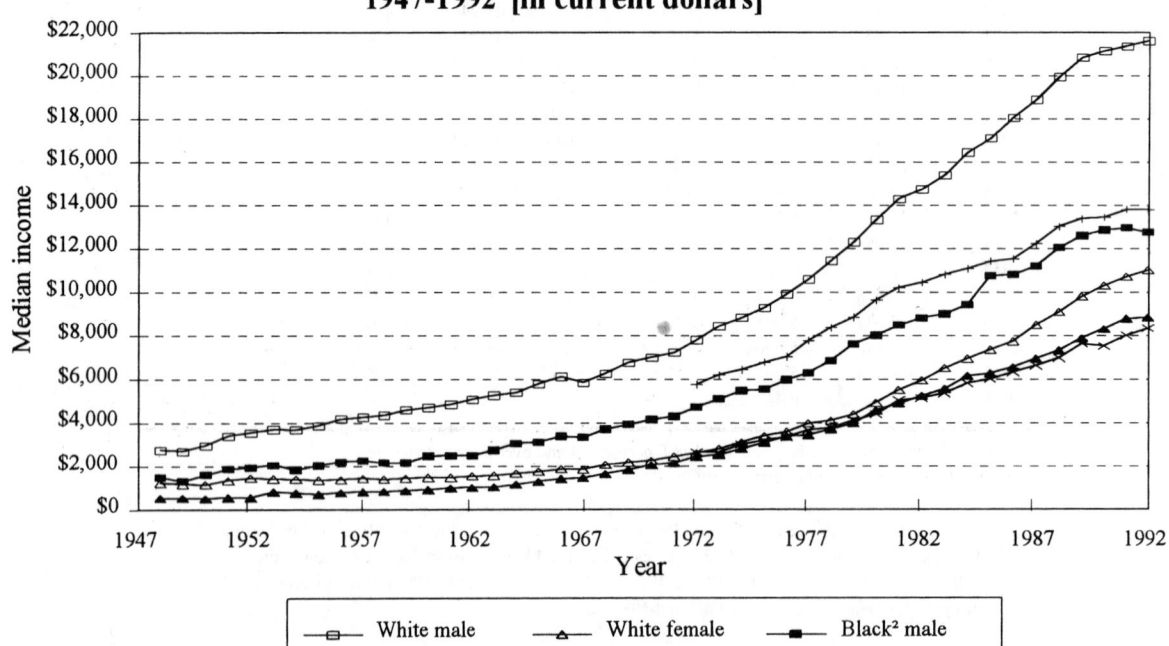

[1] Persons 15 years and over beginning in 1980; persons 14 and over prior to that date.
[2] Data refer to black and other prior to 1967.
Source: 1947-1992 CPS data.

Figure 15-2. Median Income for Persons[1], by Sex and Race-ethnicity:
1947-1992 [in current dollars]

[1] Persons 15 years and over beginning in 1980; persons 14 and over prior to that date.
[2] Data refer to black and other prior to 1967.
Source: 1947-1992 CPS data.

Table 15-3. Percent Receiving Income for Persons[1], by Sex and Race-ethnicity: 1947-1992 [in constant 1992 dollars]

Year	All races		White		Black[2]		Hispanic	
	Male	Female	Male	Female	Male	Female	Male	Female
1992	94.5	91.0	95.6	91.8	87.3	87.6	89.9	76.7
1991	94.6	91.2	95.7	92.1	87.2	87.3	89.7	77.9
1990	95.0	91.6	96.1	92.4	87.6	88.1	90.2	78.1
1989	95.1	91.5	96.1	92.2	88.5	88.4	90.9	77.5
1988	95.1	91.5	96.2	92.2	87.8	88.1	90.4	78.5
1987	95.0	91.3	96.0	92.1	87.8	87.1	90.2	78.4
1986	94.5	90.2	95.6	91.1	87.5	85.8	90.1	77.4
1985	94.5	89.8	95.6	90.6	87.3	85.3	88.6	76.1
1984	94.1	89.8	95.6	90.7	85.9	85.3	89.1	77.4
1983	93.9	88.9	95.2	89.8	84.4	83.5	75.2	70.8
1982	93.8	88.6	95.2	89.5	83.2	83.5	89.1	74.9
1981	94.9	89.1	96.0	89.9	86.6	84.0	90.7	76.4
1980	94.8	88.7	95.8	89.6	87.4	83.3	90.2	76.4
1979	95.3	88.9	96.3	89.7	87.9	84.4	91.8	77.6
1978	93.4	81.1	94.3	81.3	85.6	80.4	88.8	70.6
1977	92.7	74.8	93.7	74.6	84.1	78.1	87.7	66.0
1976	92.4	73.3	93.4	73.1	84.0	75.8	87.9	65.5
1975	91.8	71.6	92.8	71.2	84.0	75.2	86.2	63.0
1974	92.8	71.3	93.7	71.0	85.4	74.9	86.7	62.9
1973	92.5	69.3	93.3	68.8	86.2	73.7	83.5	57.4
1972	91.7	67.4	92.6	66.7	83.9	72.8	84.6	54.9
1971	91.7	66.1	92.4	65.4	85.6	73.0	—	—
1970	92.1	66.5	92.8	65.8	86.0	72.7	—	—
1969	92.5	65.8	93.0	65.0	88.4	73.1	—	—
1968	92.4	64.8	92.9	63.8	88.5	73.7	—	—
1967	92.4	63.7	92.9	62.7	88.2	72.3	—	—
1966	92.0	61.0	92.4	60.1	88.2	68.0	—	—
1965	91.5	59.4	92.0	58.5	87.7	66.8	—	—
1964	91.4	59.7	91.9	58.8	87.6	67.3	—	—
1963	91.4	58.7	91.8	57.9	87.9	66.1	—	—
1962	91.1	57.7	91.5	56.7	87.0	65.8	—	—
1961	91.4	57.3	91.9	56.1	87.1	67.5	—	—
1960	91.4	56.0	91.8	54.8	88.3	66.2	—	—
1959	91.4	53.7	91.7	52.6	88.3	63.4	—	—
1958	91.7	52.9	92.0	51.6	89.0	64.2	—	—
1957	91.8	52.6	92.1	51.3	89.5	63.4	—	—
1956	91.9	51.9	92.1	50.4	90.1	64.8	—	—
1955	92.1	49.3	92.3	47.9	89.8	62.3	—	—
1954	90.2	46.4	90.5	45.2	87.6	57.6	—	—
1953	91.3	46.4	91.5	44.8	89.4	61.2	—	—
1952	91.3	46.5	—	—	—	—	—	—
1951	93.9	43.7	—	—	—	—	—	—
1950	90.5	43.3	—	—	—	—	—	—
1949	90.3	41.8	—	—	—	—	—	—
1948	89.9	40.9	—	—	—	—	—	—
1947	89.2	39.1	—	—	—	—	—	—

[1] Persons 15 years and over beginning in 1980; persons 14 and over prior to that date.
[2] Data refer to black and other prior to 1967.

Source: U.S. Bureau of the Census, Current Population Reports, "Money Income of Households, Families, and Persons in the United States: 1992," Table B-14, and "Money Income of Households, Families, and Persons in the United States: 1982," Table 40 (data prior to 1967), U.S. Government Printing Office, Washington, D.C., 1993 and 1984.

Table 15-4. Income Distribution of Persons 15 Years of Age and Over Receiving Income, by Sex and Race-ethnicity: 1992 [in 1992 dollars]

Total money income	All races Male	Female	White Male	Female	Black Male	Female	Hispanic Male	Female
Total								
Median income	$20,654	$10,774	$21,645	$11,036	$12,754	$8,857	$13,810	$8,357
Mean income	$27,049	$14,999	$28,245	$15,279	$17,340	$12,767	$18,066	$11,746
Percent with income	94.5	91.0	95.6	91.8	87.3	87.6	89.9	76.7
Income total	100.0	100.0	100.0	100.0	100.0	100.0	100.0	100.0
$1 to $2,499 or loss	6.9	14.6	6.4	14.7	10.8	13.0	7.6	16.9
$2,500 to $4,999	5.1	11.2	4.5	10.7	9.7	15.1	7.1	14.1
$5,000 to $7,499	6.9	12.5	6.2	12.0	12.5	17.1	11.2	15.3
$7,500 to $9,999	6.1	8.9	5.9	9.0	7.8	8.9	9.8	11.1
$10,000 to $12,499	7.0	8.7	6.7	8.7	8.6	8.6	10.6	10.1
$12,500 to $14,999	5.4	5.9	5.4	6.0	5.3	5.5	7.2	5.7
$15,000 to $17,499	6.4	6.1	6.3	6.1	7.0	6.0	8.7	5.0
$17,500 to $19,999	4.7	4.4	4.8	4.6	4.5	3.3	5.0	3.5
$20,000 to $22,499	5.9	4.8	5.8	4.9	6.2	4.2	6.1	3.5
$22,500 to $24,999	3.7	3.3	3.9	3.4	3.0	3.0	3.4	2.8
$25,000 to $29,999	8.2	6.1	8.4	6.2	6.6	5.9	6.5	4.3
$30,000 to $34,999	7.0	4.3	7.2	4.4	5.2	3.5	4.8	2.7
$35,000 to $39,999	5.9	2.8	6.2	2.9	4.1	1.9	3.3	1.8
$40,000 to $44,999	4.8	1.9	5.0	2.0	3.0	1.6	2.6	1.2
$45,000 to $49,999	3.3	1.3	3.5	1.3	1.7	0.9	1.9	0.8
$50,000 to $54,999	3.0	0.8	3.2	0.8	1.1	0.6	1.2	0.3
$55,000 to $64,999	3.3	0.8	3.6	0.8	1.1	0.7	1.2	0.3
$65,000 to $74,999	1.9	0.4	2.1	0.5	0.5	0.1	0.7	0.2
$75,000 to $84,999	1.3	0.3	1.4	0.3	0.4	0.1	0.4	0.2
$85,000 to $99,999	1.0	0.2	1.1	0.2	0.2	...	0.3	...
$100,000 and over	2.3	0.3	2.5	0.4	0.4	...	0.6	0.2
Year-round, full-time workers								
Percent of total with income	53.9	35.6	54.9	35.3	45.7	37.2	52.4	34.9
Median income	$31,012	$22,167	$31,737	$22,423	$22,943	$20,299	$20,312	$17,743
Mean income	$37,469	$25,337	$38,533	$25,727	$26,921	$22,031	$24,976	$20,335

Source: U.S. Bureau of the Census, Current Population Reports, "Money Income of Households, Families, and Persons in the United States: 1992," U.S. Government Printing Office, Washington, D.C., 1993, Table 26.

data were available), about 89 percent of all black men received income, compared to about 91 percent of all white men. There were larger differences between black and white women: more than six out of ten of the former received income, compared to less than 45 percent of the latter. By 1992, the proportions of black men and women receiving income were almost exactly the same (slightly more than 87 percent). The proportion of black men receiving income was about 7 percent lower than their white counterparts, while black women lagged behind white women by about 3 percent.

Data on Hispanics (beginning in 1972) show a third pattern of income reception. Roughly the same proportion of Hispanic and black men received income in 1972, but by 1992 almost 90 percent of Hispanic men received income. During the 1972-92 period the proportion of Hispanic women rose from about 55 percent to more than 76 percent. However, both in 1972 and 1992, Hispanic women lagged behind their black and white counterparts in proportion receiving income. To a large extent, the figures on proportions receiving income among both genders and the race and ethnic groups reflect trends in labor force participation rates.

Income Distribution of Those Receiving Income in 1992

Among all Americans 15 years and over who received income in 1992, the median income was $20,654 for males and $10,774 for females; their mean incomes were $27,049 and $14,999, respectively (see Table 15-4 and Figure 15-3). There is a wide range of incomes; 6.9 percent of all males (and 14.6 percent of all females) received incomes of $2,499 or less, while 2.3 percent of all men (and 0.3 percent of all women) had incomes of $100,000 or more. A chart of income distribution for males (Figure 15-3) shows that while incomes are heavily concentrated at below $20,000, there is a secondary peak in the $30,000 to $39,999 category. Women show a much more systematic and progressive decline in numbers as their incomes rise; there is only a small rise in numbers in the $30,000 to $39,999 category.

At the high end of the income distribution, 5 percent of all white males had incomes of $75,000 or more in 1992, compared to 1 percent of black and 1.3 percent of Hispanic males. Only 0.9 percent of white women, 0.1 percent of black women and 0.4 percent of Hispanic women reached this level of income in that year.

Factors Affecting Income Distribution

Age

Age has a major effect on income (Table 15-5). Income for both men and women is lowest at ages 15-24 years (when many workers are still in school), peaks at age 45 to 49 years, and then declines at older ages. There are several reasons for the decline in income at older ages, including a less-educated older workforce, fewer hours worked per week among older workers, and lower incomes after retirement. Hispanic men and black and Hispanic women reach their peak income at age 40 to 44 years, which may reflect how younger, better-educated minority workers have been able to take more advantage of declining discrimination in employment in the United States than their elders in recent decades.

Marital Status

While marital status has some direct effect on income distribution among individuals, much of it is due to the effect of age on both marital status and income. Those who are married and have a spouse present (Table 15-6) have the highest income; yet they are also those most likely to be in middle age, when both labor force participation rates and salaries are likely to be high. For white men, income of persons who are married is the highest, followed by the divorced, the widowed and the single. Among blacks and Hispanic men, the order of these last two categories is reversed, probably reflecting the low levels of pension income among these two groups.

Among women, the income of the divorced is highest, reflecting high rates of labor force participation, lower rates of part-time employment, and more years in the labor force. For white women, there is surprisingly little difference between the income levels of married, single and widowed women. These groups of women each have different characteristics, however: single women have lower income because they are younger, have little seniority, but are often in better-paid occupations; married women often work part-time or have interrupted job histories; and widowed women often benefit from their late husbands' pensions (which were usually based on larger salaries than they themselves earned). Among black and Hispanic women, married women trail divorced women, but their incomes are higher than those of women who are single or widowed.

Educational Attainment

One of the strongest and best-established relationships in the study of social stratification in the United States is that between education and income. As Table 15-7 shows, there is a monotonic relationship within each racial or ethnic group between the level of education achieved and the income received by the civilian population age 18 years and over in 1989 (i.e. from 1990 Census results). Those who were high school graduates made about $3,000 more than those with less than a ninth-grade education; those who were college graduates made almost $14,000 more than high school graduates. A master's degree added almost $7,000 in annual income, and those with doctoral degrees made about $12,000 more per year than those with master's degrees. A graduate of a professional school had mean earnings of $71,083, more than $20,000 per year more than those with doctorates and about $53,000 more than high school graduates.

When the categories of race, ethnicity and education are compared, there is an almost ten-fold range in incomes. The highest mean incomes were found among white male graduates of professional schools ($86,676), and the lowest incomes were those of Hispanic women with less than ninth-grade education ($8,670). There are a few interesting anomalies in these data. Among black and American Indian men, those with less than a ninth-grade education had higher mean incomes than did those with some high school education but no diploma. For all groups of women except Asian or Pacific Islanders, those with doctoral degrees made more money than did those with professional school degrees; for men, the reverse is true (except for American Indian men).

Some of these apparent anomalies are probably due to a differential distribution of education across age groups. Table 15-8, which reports income data by age, sex and race-ethnicity, shows that education has a curvilinear (rise and fall) effect on income across age groups. For each succeeding age group, however, the ratio of income between its well- and poorly-educated members expands.

Figure 15-3. Income Distribution of Persons 15 Years of Age and Over Receiving Income, by Sex and Race-ethnicity: 1992 [in 1992 dollars]

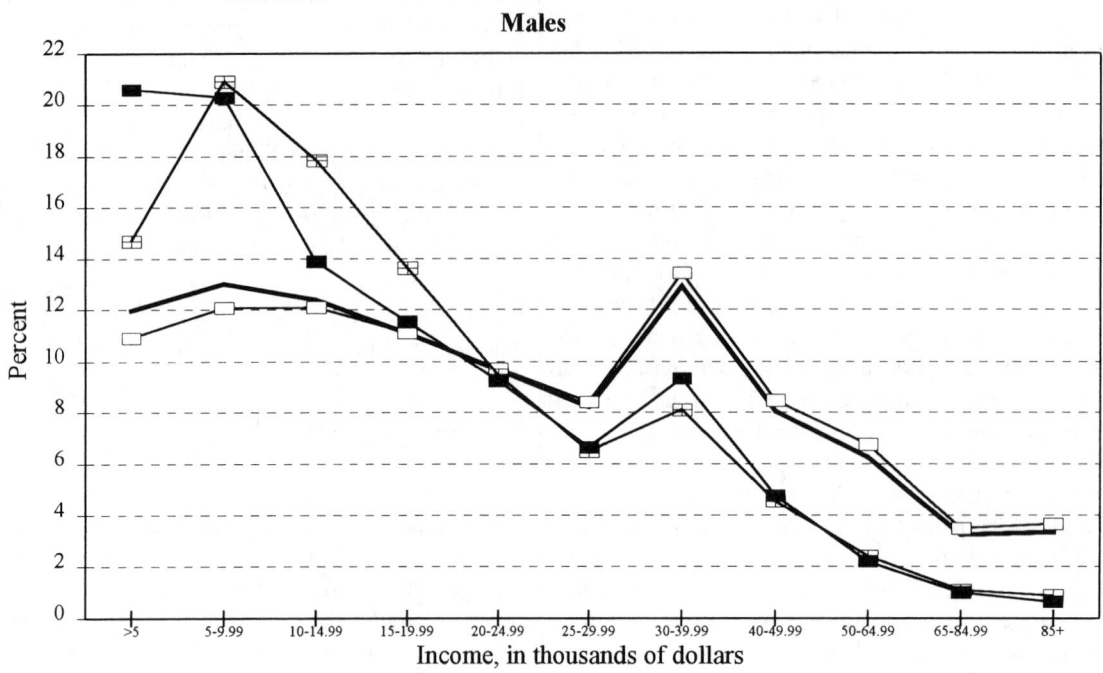

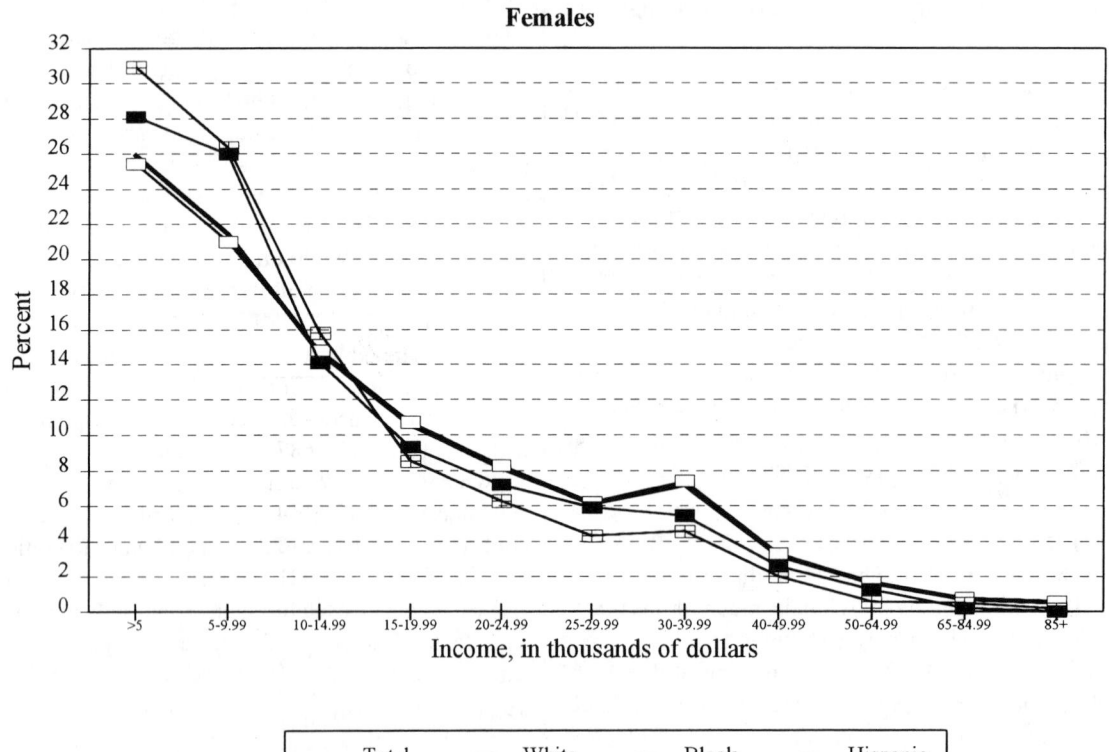

Source: 1992 CPS data.

Table 15-5. Indices of Income of Persons, by Age, Sex, and Race-ethnicity: 1992
[in 1992 dollars] [Index: Total males, all ages=1.00]

Age	Males				Females			
	Total	White	Black	Hispanic	Total	White	Black	Hispanic
Median income, all ages	$20,654	$21,645	$12,754	$13,810	$10,774	$11,036	$8,857	$8,357
Indices, all ages	1.00	1.05	0.62	0.67	0.52	0.53	0.43	0.40
15 to 24 years	0.30	0.31	0.22	0.34	0.25	0.26	0.21	0.25
25 to 29 years	0.95	0.99	0.71	0.68	0.65	0.70	0.46	0.49
30 to 34 years	1.18	1.24	0.78	0.79	0.68	0.70	0.57	0.54
35 to 39 years	1.34	1.45	0.84	0.88	0.72	0.73	0.70	0.54
40 to 44 years	1.51	1.56	1.06	0.96	0.78	0.79	0.71	0.56
45 to 49 years	1.59	1.67	1.14	0.90	0.80	0.82	0.70	0.52
50 to 54 years	1.55	1.63	0.84	0.88	0.73	0.73	0.69	0.53
55 to 59 years	1.37	1.45	0.82	0.89	0.56	0.57	0.48	0.39
60 to 64 years	1.08	1.16	0.62	0.71	0.44	0.46	0.34	0.27
65 to 69 years	0.82	0.87	0.41	0.48	0.41	0.42	0.31	0.30
70 to 74 years	0.70	0.74	0.41	0.53	0.39	0.41	0.31	0.29
75 years and over	0.62	0.65	0.36	0.39	0.39	0.41	0.29	0.28

Source: U.S. Bureau of the Census, Current Population Reports, "Money Income of Households, Families, and Persons in the United States: 1992," Series P-60, No.184, U.S. Government Printing Office, Washington, D.C., 1993, Table 26.

Table 15-6. Median Income of Persons 18 Years Old and Over, by
Marital Status, Sex, and Race-ethnicity: 1992 [in 1992 dollars]

Sex and marital status	Total	White	Black	Hispanic
Male	$21,287	$22,288	$13,485	$14,256
Single (never married)	$11,736	$12,337	$8,687	$9,929
Married	$26,291	$26,997	$19,151	$16,547
Spouse present	$26,689	$27,306	$20,114	$17,150
Spouse absent	$17,071	$18,535	$13,018	$10,719
Widowed	$12,850	$14,275	$8,021	$9,679
Divorced	$20,989	$21,979	$15,046	$17,702
Female	$11,121	$11,389	$9,135	$8,610
Single (never married)	$10,063	$10,792	$7,479	$7,584
Married	$11,062	$11,043	$10,931	$8,937
Spouse present	$11,149	$11,073	$11,736	$9,002
Spouse absent	$9,997	$10,552	$8,175	$8,598
Widowed	$9,781	$10,332	$6,909	$7,039
Divorced	$16,554	$17,046	$13,287	$12,201

Source: U.S. Bureau of the Census, Current Population Reports, "Money Income of Households, Families, and Persons in the United States: 1992," Series P-60, No.184, U.S. Government Printing Office, Washington, D.C., 1993, Table 28.

Table 15-7. Mean Earnings in 1989 of the Civilian Population Age 18 Years and Over, by Educational Attainment, Sex, and Race-ethnicity: 1990 [in 1989 dollars]

Sex and educational attainment	Total	White	Black	American Indian, Eskimo, Aleut	Asian or Pacific Islander	Hispanic
Civilian persons 18 years and over	$22,378	$23,378	$16,806	$15,596	$23,791	$16,400
Less than 9th grade	$13,586	$14,341	$12,410	$12,103	$12,930	$12,042
High school, no diploma	$14,092	$14,736	$12,095	$11,255	$13,630	$12,754
High school graduate	$17,952	$18,483	$14,967	$14,062	$16,438	$15,608
Some college	$19,747	$20,319	$16,640	$15,957	$17,265	$17,799
Associate degree	$22,655	$23,076	$19,931	$18,312	$22,483	$20,368
Bachelor's degree	$31,808	$32,581	$25,385	$24,634	$28,063	$26,372
Master's degree	$38,686	$39,438	$32,445	$31,215	$35,349	$34,040
Professional school degree	$71,083	$72,411	$46,541	$40,155	$75,820	$51,087
Doctorate degree	$51,058	$51,790	$43,043	$53,288	$48,244	$45,627
Civilian males 18 years and over	$28,495	$30,097	$19,112	$18,740	$28,961	$19,035
Less than 9th grade	$16,000	$16,977	$14,552	$14,556	$15,210	$13,819
High school, no diploma	$17,222	$18,266	$13,913	$13,561	$15,729	$14,711
High school graduate	$22,923	$23,879	$17,384	$17,106	$19,477	$18,469
Some college	$25,289	$26,230	$19,587	$19,742	$20,018	$21,458
Associate degree	$28,794	$29,623	$23,345	$21,828	$25,961	$24,596
Bachelor's degree	$40,517	$41,683	$29,048	$29,418	$33,232	$31,299
Master's degree	$47,916	$49,230	$36,107	$35,247	$40,243	$39,335
Professional school degree	$85,438	$86,676	$57,390	$49,298	$90,242	$61,397
Doctorate degree	$55,626	$56,545	$45,853	$62,069	$51,007	$50,485
Civilian females 18 years and over	$15,311	$15,462	$14,692	$11,987	$17,969	$12,746
Less than 9th grade	$9,122	$9,107	$9,153	$7,881	$10,980	$8,670
High school, no diploma	$9,715	$9,659	$9,957	$8,057	$11,382	$9,442
High school graduate	$12,720	$12,754	$12,684	$10,609	$13,463	$12,219
Some college	$13,993	$13,971	$14,383	$12,281	$14,211	$13,779
Associate degree	$17,203	$17,152	$17,596	$15,019	$19,044	$16,080
Bachelor's degree	$21,351	$21,181	$22,620	$19,571	$22,758	$20,698
Master's degree	$27,789	$27,639	$30,081	$26,670	$26,311	$27,731
Professional school degree	$35,884	$35,261	$33,942	$26,807	$48,896	$28,708
Doctorate degree	$36,682	$36,705	$38,400	$34,570	$35,362	$35,005

Source: U.S. Bureau of the Census, "Education in the United States," 1990 Census of Population, U.S. Government Printing Office, Washington, D.C., 1994, Table 4.

Table 15-8. Median Income of Persons Age 25 Years and Over, by Educational Attainment, Age, and Race-ethnicity: 1992 [in 1992 dollars]

Age and educational attainment	Total		White		Black		Hispanic	
	Male	Female	Male	Female	Male	Female	Male	Female
25 to 34 years	$21,692	$16,022	$22,487	$16,344	$16,138	$13,265	$15,091	$11,987
Less than 9th grade	$10,235	$7,503	$10,400	$7,514	—	—	$10,882	$8,355
High school, no diploma	$13,449	$9,205	$14,279	$9,574	$9,607	$7,891	$12,301	$9,578
High school graduate	$20,016	$12,261	$20,923	$12,447	$14,596	$11,102	$17,093	$11,938
Some college	$21,537	$15,588	$22,146	$15,715	$16,616	$14,017	$19,929	$15,381
Associate degree	$25,489	$18,427	$25,531	$18,807	$25,528	$15,816	$23,724	—
Bachelor's degree	$31,119	$23,604	$31,669	$23,620	$24,416	$22,717	$26,258	$23,094
Master's degree	$35,555	$27,088	$36,163	$27,488	—	—	—	—
Professional school degree	$39,342	$35,667	$41,460	$35,764	—	—	—	—
Doctorate degree	$36,485	—	$36,027	—	—	—	—	—
35 to 44 years	$30,306	$17,286	$31,170	$17,304	$20,445	$17,069	$19,495	$12,647
Less than 9th grade	$14,366	$8,392	$14,713	$8,599	—	—	$15,006	$8,884
High school, no diploma	$16,606	$9,558	$17,868	$9,621	$13,659	$9,585	$15,085	$9,464
High school graduate	$25,587	$14,145	$26,510	$14,104	$16,632	$14,519	$20,367	$12,747
Some college	$30,536	$17,174	$30,989	$17,057	$25,016	$17,294	$23,764	$17,162
Associate degree	$31,270	$20,415	$31,832	$20,257	$26,006	$21,632	$25,024	$22,018
Bachelor's degree	$40,903	$25,245	$41,526	$25,096	$30,252	$26,217	$34,305	$19,713
Master's degree	$45,831	$30,850	$46,411	$30,451	—	$34,080	—	—
Professional school degree	$85,870	$40,000	$85,990	$40,834	—	—	—	—
Doctorate degree	$54,527	$40,218	$55,160	$39,521	—	—	—	—
45 to 54 years	$32,817	$17,977	$34,462	$18,079	$23,031	$17,637	$19,516	$13,575
Less than 9th grade	$15,317	$9,845	$15,365	$9,579	$14,992	—	$13,406	$9,671
High school, no diploma	$20,674	$11,395	$21,458	$11,483	$16,318	$11,366	$14,827	$9,801
High school graduate	$28,084	$15,240	$28,747	$15,263	$24,518	$15,349	$21,281	$16,155
Some college	$34,243	$19,324	$35,259	$19,504	$28,345	$20,203	$28,615	$15,837
Associate degree	$36,542	$21,112	$36,915	$20,848	—	$25,850	—	—
Bachelor's degree	$41,898	$25,818	$42,259	$25,513	—	$30,894	$35,025	—
Master's degree	$51,104	$34,669	$51,379	$35,120	—	—	—	—
Professional school degree	$78,822	$44,824	$79,407	$39,950	—	—	—	—
Doctorate degree	$59,155	$41,490	$58,951	$41,061	—	—	—	—
55 to 64 years	$26,703	$14,017	$27,442	$14,061	$18,839	$13,551	$19,595	$9,712
Less than 9th grade	$15,971	$7,906	$16,898	$7,915	$11,699	—	$12,248	$8,083
High school, no diploma	$20,352	$10,064	$21,434	$10,083	$16,902	$9,520	—	—
High school graduate	$23,934	$12,805	$24,983	$12,805	$18,411	$12,407	$22,076	$10,253
Some college	$29,633	$16,825	$30,178	$16,746	—	$18,607	—	—
Associate degree	$30,462	$20,227	$31,474	$19,427	—	—	—	—
Bachelor's degree	$40,467	$21,757	$41,610	$20,946	—	—	—	—
Master's degree	$37,429	$33,037	$37,157	$32,543	—	—	—	—
Professional school degree	$80,185	—	$80,972	—	—	—	—	—
Doctorate degree	$55,179	—	$56,803	—	—	—	—	—
65 years and over	$9,093	$6,292	$9,152	$6,234	$8,458	$6,316	$10,363	—
Less than 9th grade	$4,817	$4,665	$4,916	$4,680	$4,710	—	—	—
High school, no diploma	$6,941	$4,993	$6,512	$4,936	—	—	—	—
High school graduate	$8,307	$6,768	$8,144	$6,647	—	—	—	—
Some college	$9,257	$6,010	$8,914	$5,924	—	—	—	—
Associate degree	$11,247	$6,894	$11,052	$7,143	—	—	—	—
Bachelor's degree	$16,333	$6,593	$17,465	$6,560	—	—	—	—
Master's degree	$12,406	$9,078	$13,304	$9,173	—	—	—	—
Professional school degree	$48,318	—	$50,181	—	—	—	—	—
Doctorate degree	$37,440	—	—	—	—	—	—	—

Source: U.S. Bureau of the Census, Current Population Reports, "Money Income of Households, Families, and Persons in the United States: 1992," Series P-60, No.184, U.S. Government Printing Office, Washington, D.C., 1993, Table 29.

The Income of Households and Families

In one sense, income is an individual characteristic: individuals earn salaries, pensions, and so on. Yet in terms of consumption, income is a household or family characteristic: families usually pool their incomes to make different kinds of purchases. Thus looking at the income distribution of households and families (Table 15-9) is a much better gauge of the purchasing power and the economic resources available to most Americans.

The Census Bureau defines households as all individuals living in a dwelling, and families as all related individuals sharing a dwelling (i.e. excluding non-family members who may share the same household). Before 1980 only secondary attention was paid to household income data. With the rapidly changing patterns of living arrangements, wherein more persons are living alone or two or more unrelated individuals form households or live as consumption units, analysts now pay more attention to household as well as family income data.

In 1992, almost 5 percent of all households and 6.2 percent of all families had an income of $100,000 or more. By contrast, 4.6 percent of all households and 3.7 percent of all families had an income of less than $5,000. Family income is higher than household income because the numerous one-person households, with a maximum of one earner, are excluded from family tabulations.

Household and family incomes differ by the amount workers earn, the size of returns on investment, and other sources of income, such as pensions. They can also differ by the number of household or family members receiving income. Blacks and Hispanics are relatively similar in terms of their median individual incomes (see Table 15-4), but the larger number of wage earners in Hispanic households and families means that both of these units have higher incomes than their black equivalents.

Table 15-9. Income Distribution of Households and Families, by Race-ethnicity: 1992
[in 1992 dollars]

Total money income	Households				Families			
	Total	White	Black	Hispanic	Total	White	Black	Hispanic
Median income	$30,786	$32,368	$18,660	$22,848	$36,812	$38,909	$21,161	$23,901
Mean income	$39,020	$40,780	$25,409	$29,102	$44,483	$46,674	$28,050	$30,332
Income total	100.0	100.0	100.0	100.0	100.0	100.0	100.0	100.0
Less than $5,000	4.6	3.6	11.8	6.6	3.7	2.7	11.3	6.0
$5,000 to $9,999	10.0	8.9	18.7	13.8	5.8	4.5	15.0	11.7
$10,000 to $14,999	9.5	9.1	12.2	12.6	7.3	6.6	11.8	12.6
$15,000 to $19,999	8.8	8.7	9.8	11.2	7.9	7.6	9.7	11.8
$20,000 to $24,999	8.1	8.0	8.5	9.7	7.7	7.6	9.1	9.9
$25,000 to $29,999	7.8	7.9	7.4	9.3	7.6	7.7	7.1	9.4
$30,000 to $34,999	7.0	7.2	5.8	7.0	7.4	7.5	5.9	6.9
$35,000 to $39,999	6.5	6.7	5.1	6.1	7.0	7.3	5.3	6.1
$40,000 to $44,999	5.6	5.7	4.6	4.4	6.4	6.6	5.2	4.8
$45,000 to $49,999	5.0	5.3	3.2	3.9	5.8	6.1	3.5	4.1
$50,000 to $54,999	4.5	4.7	2.8	3.4	5.3	5.7	3.4	3.8
$55,000 to $59,999	3.8	4.0	2.2	2.3	4.6	4.9	2.6	2.4
$60,000 to $64,999	3.1	3.3	1.8	2.1	3.9	5.7	2.2	2.2
$65,000 to $69,999	2.6	2.7	1.1	1.7	3.2	3.4	1.4	1.7
$70,000 to $74,999	2.1	2.2	1.0	1.0	2.6	2.8	1.2	1.2
$75,000 to $79,999	1.6	1.8	0.7	0.9	2.1	2.2	1.0	0.9
$80,000 to $84,999	1.4	1.5	0.6	0.7	1.8	1.9	0.8	0.7
$85,000 to $89,999	1.2	1.3	0.5	0.5	1.5	1.6	0.6	0.5
$90,000 to $94,999	1.1	1.1	0.6	0.6	1.4	1.4	0.7	0.7
$95,000 to $99,999	0.8	0.9	0.3	0.5	1.0	1.1	0.3	0.6
$100,000 and over	4.9	5.3	1.5	1.8	6.2	6.7	1.8	2.0

Source: U.S. Bureau of the Census, Current Population Reports, "Money Income of Households, Families, and Persons in the United States: 1992," Series P-60, No. 184, U.S. Government Printing Office, Washington, D.C., 1993, Tables 5 and 17.

Trends in Income Distribution among Families and Households

Earlier, we have seen that males have suffered a significant decline in income over the last two decades, while women have experienced a great increase in the proportion receiving income (due largely to increased rates of labor force participation) and a moderate rise in income. How has this translated into trends in household and family income distribution? In 1970 (Table 15-10), the median income of all U.S. households was $29,670; it rose to $32,142 by 1990. Both white and black households showed increases in income between 1970 and 1990; Hispanic households showed a slight increase in income between 1980 and 1990. The trends in family income across racial and ethnic groups are roughly similar to those of households.

While median household and family incomes have increased since 1970, so has the proportion of black and Hispanic households and families with incomes of less than $5,000 per year. This has been offset by a large jump in the proportion of households and families with incomes of $100,000 and over among the racial and ethnic groups. The largest increase was registered among black families: in 1970, only 0.4 percent of all black families had incomes of $100,000 or more, but by 1990, 1.8 percent had reached this income level.

Household Structure and Income

One important predictor of household income in the United States is household and family structure. As Table 15-11 shows, married-couple family households have the highest median incomes ($42,140 in 1992), while female householders living alone have the lowest ($12,944). Almost 40 percent of this latter group had incomes under $10,000 in 1992, compared to only 4.4 percent of the former group.

Among non-family households, which have a high proportion of the elderly living alone, there is a heavy concentration of persons living at just above the poverty level (i.e. with incomes of between about $7,000 and $20,000). Most scholars of trends in income distribution in the United States agree that the most successful part of government anti-poverty measures was lifting a large proportion of the elderly above the poverty level.

Income-to-Poverty Ratios of Households

Analysts of income distribution have developed several measures of how to conceive of change. The income-to-poverty ratio takes the median income of an income quintile and compares it to the poverty line at the time. Figure 15-4 shows that for the lowest income quintile (the lowest fifth) of families, the ratio has remained around one since 1967. In other words, the median income of this quintile has been just about at the poverty line, with no significant progress above the pov-

erty line. For the middle quintile of families, there has been a slight improvement, with the ratio of their median income rising from about 2.7 to 3.25 times the poverty line. The top fifth of all families have seen their median income rise from 6 to 8.4 times the poverty line between 1967 and 1992, with most of the increase coming between 1981-89.

Among black and Hispanic families, the income-to-poverty ratio of the lowest income quintile has declined, and the ratio of the middle income quintile has changed little. While the income-to-poverty ratio of the top fifth of black and Hispanic families has risen, it has failed to match the increase in this ratio for the top income quintile of white families. The distribution of income to those near or below the poverty line will be discussed in more detail later in this chapter.

Household Income by Quintile Distribution

The distribution of aggregate household income across income quintiles is given in Table 15-12. By 1990, the proportion of all income going to the top quintile of all households had risen to 46.6; in other words, almost half of all of the nation's income was going to the top twenty percent of all households. The distribution of income was becoming more unequal over time, and was more unequal among black and Hispanic households than among white households. The Gini ratio, a summary measure of distribution often used in studies of income inequality, also reflects these temporal changes and differences between racial and ethnic groups.

Regional Distribution of Family Income

Another measure of income distribution is the ratio of median income level by region for various groups to the overall national median income level. Table 15-13 shows these ratios for whites, blacks and Hispanics in 1992 and for whites and blacks in 1955. In 1955, the median income of families in the West was 9 percent above the national average, and the income of families in the South lagged by 19 percent (a score of 0.81). By 1992, Southern families cut this income gap almost in half (rising to a score of 0.90), and the Northeast replaced the West as the region with the highest level of family income (1.11).

The median income level of whites in 1955 was 1.04 times (or 4 percent higher) than the level of all families in the United States, and the ratio for black families was 0.58. Given the remarkable change in the social and legal situation of blacks in the United States over the past forty years, it is surprising to find that the ratio of black family income to total income actually declined to 0.57 by 1992. Gains in the ratio for black families in the South between 1955 to 1992 (from 0.42 to 0.55) were offset by declines in this ratio among blacks in the Northeast, Midwest, and West. Hispanic families also lag on this mea-

Table 15-10. Income Distribution of Households and Families, by Race-ethnicity: 1970-1990 [in constant 1992 dollars]

Income	All races 1990	All races 1980	All races 1970	White 1990	White 1980	White 1970	Black 1990	Black 1980	Black 1970	Hispanic 1990	Hispanic 1980
Households											
Median income	$32,142	$30,191	$29,670	$33,525	$31,851	$30,903	$20,048	$18,350	$18,810	$23,970	$23,271
Income	100.0	100.0	100.0	100.0	100.0	100.0	100.0	100.0	100.0	100.0	100.0
Less than $5,000	4.4	4.3	5.9	3.4	3.5	5.3	12.0	10.6	11.5	6.4	5.9
$5,000 to $9,999	9.4	10.4	9.6	8.4	9.4	8.9	16.9	18.4	16.4	12.9	12.9
$10,000 to $14,999	8.7	9.3	8.7	8.4	8.8	8.2	11.5	13.5	13.4	12.6	12.5
$15,000 to $24,999	16.9	17.7	17.5	16.8	17.4	16.9	18.5	20.4	22.4	20.0	22.5
$25,000 to $34,999	15.1	16.1	18.5	15.4	16.3	18.8	13.4	13.8	15.5	16.3	16.7
$35,000 to $49,999	17.6	18.7	20.0	18.2	19.5	20.9	13.5	12.4	12.2	16.2	15.3
$50,000 to $74,999	16.1	15.6	14.0	16.9	16.5	14.7	9.3	8.3	7.2	10.0	10.6
$75,000 to $99,999	6.5	5.0	3.7	6.8	5.4	3.9	3.4	1.9	1.1	3.4	2.2
$100,000 and over	5.2	3.0	2.2	5.6	3.2	2.4	1.5	0.6	0.4	2.1	1.3
Families											
Median income	$37,950	$35,839	$33,519	$39,626	$37,341	$34,773	$22,997	$21,606	$21,330	$25,152	$25,087
Income	100.0	100.0	100.0	100.0	100.0	100.0	100.0	100.0	100.0	100.0	100.0
Less than $5,000	3.2	2.6	2.7	2.2	2.0	2.3	10.3	7.3	6.7	5.6	4.3
$5,000 to $9,999	5.4	5.7	5.9	4.3	4.7	5.0	13.5	14.2	14.1	11.2	10.8
$10,000 to $14,999	6.7	7.4	7.5	6.2	6.6	6.9	11.2	13.7	13.5	12.3	12.5
$15,000 to $24,999	15.4	16.5	17.4	14.9	16.0	16.7	18.9	21.3	24.1	20.7	22.7
$25,000 to $34,999	15.2	16.8	20.2	15.4	17.1	20.5	13.6	14.8	17.4	16.2	17.8
$35,000 to $49,999	20.0	21.8	23.1	20.7	22.7	24.1	15.3	14.8	14.0	17.0	16.6
$50,000 to $74,999	19.4	19.2	16.3	20.5	20.2	17.2	11.2	10.5	8.5	10.9	11.6
$75,000 to $99,999	8.2	6.3	4.3	8.6	6.7	4.6	4.3	2.5	1.3	3.9	2.3
$100,000 and over	6.6	3.7	2.5	7.1	4.0	2.7	1.8	0.7	0.4	2.2	1.5

Source: U.S. Bureau of the Census, Current Population Reports, "Money Income of Households, Families, and Persons in the United States: 1992," Series P-60, No. 184, U.S. Government Printing Office, Washington, D.C., 1993, Tables B-2 and B-6.

Table 15-11. Income Distribution of Households, by Type of Household: 1992 [in 1992 dollars]

Income	Total households	Family households				Total	Nonfamily households			
		Total	Married couple	Male householder, no spouse present	Female householder, no spouse present		Male householder		Female householder	
							Total	Living alone	Total	Living alone
Households [in thousands]	96,391	68,144	53,171	3,026	11,947	28,247	12,254	9,436	15,993	14,206
Median income	$30,786	$37,222	$42,140	$30,492	$18,587	$17,711	$23,168	$20,011	$14,438	$12,944
Mean income	$39,020	$44,951	$50,062	$37,308	$24,138	$24,713	$30,243	$26,648	$20,476	$17,871
Income total	100.0	100.0	100.0	100.0	100.0	100.0	100.0	100.0	100.0	100.0
Less than $5,000	4.6	3.4	1.4	3.6	12.6	7.4	5.8	6.7	8.7	9.5
$5,000 to $9,999	10.0	5.5	3.0	7.0	16.2	20.9	13.9	16.5	26.3	29.0
$10,000 to $14,999	9.5	7.2	5.7	8.6	13.1	15.0	12.9	14.8	16.6	17.6
$15,000 to $19,999	8.8	7.8	6.9	10.5	11.0	11.2	11.1	12.0	11.2	11.7
$20,000 to $24,999	8.1	7.7	7.1	10.1	9.9	8.9	9.1	9.4	8.7	8.8
$25,000 to $29,999	7.8	7.7	7.5	9.5	8.1	8.1	9.1	9.0	7.3	7.0
$30,000 to $34,999	7.0	7.4	7.5	8.2	6.7	6.2	7.3	6.7	5.5	5.1
$35,000 to $39,999	6.5	7.1	7.5	8.4	4.8	5.0	6.4	6.2	3.9	3.3
$40,000 to $44,999	5.6	6.5	7.0	5.4	4.4	3.5	4.6	4.1	2.7	2.2
$45,000 to $49,999	5.0	5.9	6.5	5.8	3.0	3.0	3.9	3.0	2.4	1.7
$50,000 to $54,999	4.5	5.4	6.1	4.7	2.6	2.3	3.0	2.4	1.7	1.3
$55,000 to $59,999	3.8	4.7	5.4	3.4	1.8	1.7	2.6	2.1	0.9	0.6
$60,000 to $64,999	3.1	3.9	4.6	2.3	1.3	1.3	2.0	1.6	0.8	0.4
$65,000 to $69,999	2.6	3.2	3.8	2.5	1.0	1.0	1.3	0.7	0.7	0.3
$70,000 to $74,999	2.1	2.6	3.1	1.8	0.6	0.9	1.3	0.9	0.6	0.3
$75,000 to $79,999	1.6	2.1	2.5	0.7	0.5	0.5	0.8	0.6	0.3	0.2
$80,000 to $84,999	1.4	1.8	2.2	1.5	0.4	0.5	0.7	0.5	0.3	0.2
$85,000 to $89,999	1.2	1.5	1.8	0.8	0.4	0.4	0.6	0.3	0.3	0.1
$90,000 to $94,999	1.1	1.4	1.6	1.1	0.3	0.4	0.6	0.4	0.2	0.0
$95,000 to $99,999	0.8	1.0	1.2	0.6	0.2	0.3	0.3	0.2	0.3	0.2
$100,000 and over	4.9	6.3	7.6	3.7	1.1	1.6	2.8	2.1	0.7	0.4

Source: U.S. Bureau of the Census, Current Population Reports, "Money Income of Households, Families, and Persons in the United States: 1992," Series P-60, No. 184, U.S. Government Printing Office, Washington, D.C., 1993, Table 6.

Figure 15-4. Income-to-poverty Ratios for Families, by Income Quintile and Race-ethnicity: 1967-1992

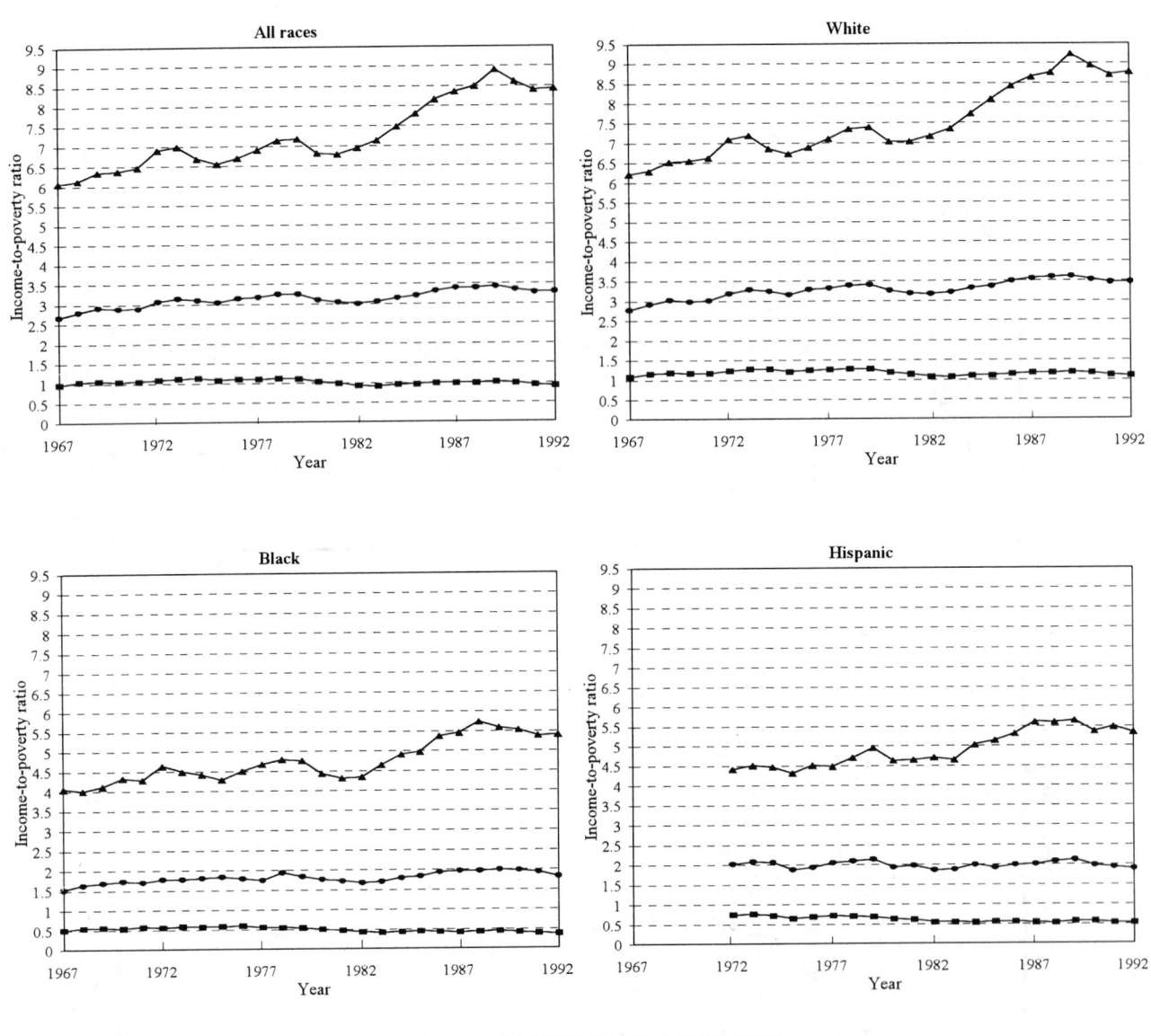

Source: 1967-1992 CPS data.

Table 15-12. Share of Aggregate Household Income, by Income Quintile and Race-ethnicity: 1970-1990

Year and race-ethnicity	Households (in thousands)	Percent distribution of aggregate income						Gini ratio
		Total	Lowest fifth	Second fifth	Middle fifth	Fourth fifth	Highest fifth	
All races								
1990	94,312	100.0	3.9	9.6	15.9	24.0	46.6	0.428
1980	82,368	100.0	4.2	10.2	16.8	24.8	44.1	0.403
1970	64,374	100.0	4.1	10.8	17.4	24.5	43.3	0.394
White								
1990	80,968	100.0	4.2	9.9	16.0	23.9	46.0	0.419
1980	71,872	100.0	4.4	10.5	17.0	24.6	43.5	0.394
1970	57,575	100.0	4.2	11.1	17.5	24.3	42.9	0.387
Black								
1990	10,671	100.0	3.1	7.9	15.0	25.1	49.0	0.464
1980	8,847	100.0	3.7	8.7	15.3	25.2	47.1	0.439
1970	6,180	100.0	3.7	9.3	16.3	25.2	45.5	0.422
Hispanic								
1990	6,220	100.0	4.0	9.5	15.9	24.3	46.3	0.425
1980	3,906	100.0	4.3	10.1	16.4	24.8	44.5	0.405

Source: U.S. Bureau of the Census, Current Population Reports, "Money Income of Households, Families, and Persons in the United States: 1990," Series P-60, No. 174, U.S. Government Printing Office, Washington, D.C., 1991, Table B.

Table 15-13. Index of Family Median Income Levels, by Region and Race-ethnicity: 1955 and 1992 [total (year)=1.00]

Region	1992				1955		
	Total	White	Black	Hispanic	Total	White	Black
Total	1.00	1.06	0.57	0.65	1.00	1.04	0.58
Northeast	1.11	1.15	0.63	0.55	1.07	1.10	0.75
Midwest[1]	1.01	1.06	0.55	0.65	1.07	1.09	0.84
South	0.90	0.99	0.55	0.62	0.81	0.92	0.42
West	1.06	1.07	0.67	0.70	1.09	1.12	0.82

[1] North Central in 1955.

Source: U.S. Bureau of the Census, Current Population Reports, "Money Income of Households, Families, and Persons in the United States: 1992," Series P-60, No. 184, U.S. Government Printing Office, Washington, D.C., 1993, Table 13. 1955 data from Donald Bogue, "The Population of the United States: Historical Trends and Future Projections," The Free Press, New York, 1985, page 567.

Table 15-14. Median Income of Families, by Race-ethnicity: 1947-1992
[in constant 1992 dollars] [Index: 1992 Total=1.00]

Year	Family income				Index			
	Total	White	Black	Hispanic	Total	White	Black	Hispanic
1992	36,812	46,674	21,161	23,901	1.00	1.27	0.57	0.65
1991	37,021	46,637	22,197	24,614	1.01	1.27	0.60	0.67
1990	37,950	47,803	22,997	25,152	1.03	1.30	0.62	0.68
1989	38,710	49,108	22,866	26,528	1.05	1.33	0.62	0.72
1988	38,177	47,809	22,924	25,817	1.04	1.30	0.62	0.70
1987	38,249	47,585	22,732	25,071	1.04	1.29	0.62	0.68
1986	37,709	46,616	22,535	25,596	1.02	1.27	0.61	0.70
1985	36,164	44,822	21,887	24,809	0.98	1.22	0.59	0.67
1984	35,693	43,781	20,837	25,430	0.97	1.19	0.57	0.69
1983	34,757	42,353	20,511	23,848	0.94	1.15	0.56	0.65
1982	34,390	41,977	19,956	23,814	0.93	1.14	0.54	0.65
1981	34,862	41,941	20,657	25,539	0.95	1.14	0.56	0.69
1980	35,839	42,514	21,606	25,087	0.97	1.15	0.59	0.68
1979	37,136	44,047	21,944	26,864	1.01	1.20	0.60	0.73
1978	36,665	43,358	22,612	26,119	1.00	1.18	0.61	0.71
1977	35,539	42,172	21,229	25,354	0.97	1.15	0.58	0.69
1976	35,330	41,393	21,829	24,231	0.96	1.12	0.59	0.66
1975	34,249	40,220	21,916	23,844	0.93	1.09	0.60	0.65
1974	34,878	41,230	21,642	25,789	0.95	1.12	0.59	0.70
1973	35,821	42,099	21,607	25,905	0.97	1.14	0.59	0.70
1972	35,126	41,414	21,690	25,858	0.95	1.13	0.59	0.70
1971	33,480	39,053	20,964	—	0.91	1.06	0.57	—
1970	33,519	38,050	21,330	—	0.91	1.03	0.58	—
1969	33,590	39,003	21,362	—	0.91	1.06	0.58	—
1968	32,124	37,222	19,947	—	0.87	1.01	0.54	—
1967	30,661	35,233	18,842	—	0.83	0.96	0.51	—
1966	32,877	34,156	20,476	—	0.89	0.93	0.56	—
1965	31,234	32,555	17,928	—	0.85	0.88	0.49	—
1964	30,000	31,321	17,529	—	0.81	0.85	0.48	—
1963	28,913	30,297	16,032	—	0.79	0.82	0.44	—
1962	27,891	29,208	15,584	—	0.76	0.79	0.42	—
1961	27,156	28,321	15,110	—	0.74	0.77	0.41	—
1960	26,882	27,910	15,451	—	0.73	0.76	0.42	—
1959	26,327	27,425	14,166	—	0.72	0.74	0.38	—
1958	24,922	25,966	13,302	—	0.68	0.71	0.36	—
1957	24,993	26,010	13,905	—	0.68	0.71	0.38	—
1956	24,915	26,071	13,719	—	0.68	0.71	0.37	—
1955	23,373	24,404	13,458	—	0.63	0.66	0.37	—
1954	21,962	22,863	12,734	—	0.60	0.62	0.35	—
1953	22,469	23,295	13,061	—	0.61	0.63	0.35	—
1952	20,760	21,955	12,477	—	0.56	0.60	0.34	—
1951	20,226	21,045	11,082	—	0.55	0.57	0.30	—
1950	19,530	20,272	10,998	—	0.53	0.55	0.30	—
1949	18,462	19,205	9,805	—	0.50	0.52	0.27	—
1948	18,754	19,478	10,404	—	0.51	0.53	0.28	—
1947	19,222	20,022	10,236	—	0.52	0.54	0.28	—

Source: U.S. Bureau of the Census, Current Population Reports, "Money Income of Households,
   Families, and Persons in the United States: 1992," Tables B-1 and B-6, and "Money Income of
   Households, Families, and Persons in the United States: 1982," Table 15 (data prior to 1967), U.S.
   Government Printing Office, Washington, D.C., 1993 and 1984.

Table 15-15. Indices of Income Level of Families, by Residence and Race-ethnicity: 1989
[Index: Total all families=1.00]

Residence	Total	White	Black	American Indian, Eskimo, Aleut	Asian, Pacific Islander	Hispanic
All families, median income	$35,225	$37,152	$22,429	$21,750	$41,251	$25,064
All families, indices	1.00	1.05	0.64	0.62	1.17	0.71
Urban and rural residence						
Urban	1.04	1.12	0.66	0.70	1.17	0.72
Central place	0.91	1.04	0.61	0.65	0.98	0.64
Urban fringe	1.24	1.28	0.92	0.92	1.40	0.91
Other urban	—	0.89	0.44	0.57	1.01	0.58
Rural	0.89	0.92	0.53	0.53	1.17	0.61
Metropolitan area						
Inside metropolitan area	1.08	1.15	0.69	0.75	1.18	0.73
Central city	0.91	1.04	0.61	0.65	0.97	0.64
Not in central city	1.18	1.20	0.87	0.84	1.39	0.86
Outside metropolitan area	0.78	0.82	0.45	0.49	0.97	0.55

Source: U.S. Bureau of the Census, "Social and Economic Characteristics: United States Summary," 1990 Census of Population, U.S. Government Printing Office, Washington, D.C., 1993, Tables 23, 37, 48, and 87-91.

sure (especially in the Northeast, where Hispanic families have a ratio of only 0.55). The regional differences in the family incomes of whites that were so apparent in 1955 shrank significantly by 1992.

Median Income of Families over Time

Have families in different racial and ethnic groups improved in terms of median income over time? In Table 15-14, the median income of all families in 1992 is taken as the standard, and the ratio of median family income of whites and blacks in each prior year back to 1947 (for Hispanics, back to 1972) is computed. In 1947, the ratios were 0.54 for whites and 0.28 for blacks. In that year the median income of white families was only about one-half and the income of black families was a little more than one-quarter of the income of all U.S. families in 1992. By this measure, black families have made little or no progress in converging on 1992 median family income since 1969, and the ratio of Hispanic families has actually declined (falling from 0.70 to 0.65) since 1972. Only white families have shown a significant increase in this ratio since the late 1960s. These differences may partially account for the very different perceptions of the amount of economic progress by minorities: whites are usually convinced that blacks and Hispanics have made great progress, while members of these minority groups are far less enthusiastic.

Income of Families by Urban-and-Rural Residence

In Table 15-15, this same approach of comparing the median income of sub-groups of families to the national median income of all U.S. families is applied to their place of residence. Race and ethnicity combine with place of residence in establishing a hierarchy of family incomes; for each racial or ethnic group, family median income (and the ratio of family income) is usually highest in the urban fringe area, and lowest in the other urban area. This same pattern holds true for racial and ethnic groups in the metropolitan area hierarchy; the ratios of family incomes are highest in the non-central city (suburban) areas of metropolitan areas, and lowest outside metropolitan areas.

Age of Householder and Income

Age of householder and type of family both play important parts in determining family income. As Table 15-16 shows, the families with the highest median incomes are those of white married couples where the householder is between 45 and 54 years of age (this group had a ratio of 1.52 times the national median family income). Families with the lowest incomes are those with a female householder aged 15 to 24 years with no spouse present (with a ratio of 0.17). Race has surprisingly little effect on family income for this group: the ratios of white, black and

Table 15-16. Indices of Family Income, by Age of Householder, Type of Family, and Race-ethnicity of Householder: 1992 [in 1992 dollars] [Index: Total families, all ages=1.00]

Age and race-ethnicity of householder	All families	Married couple	Male householder, no spouse	Female householder, no spouse
Total				
Median income, all ages	$36,812	$42,064	$27,821	$17,221
Indices, all ages	1.00	1.14	0.76	0.47
15 to 24 years	0.43	0.61	0.51	0.17
25 to 34 years	0.89	1.08	0.66	0.30
35 to 44 years	1.16	1.35	0.81	0.52
45 to 54 years	1.36	1.49	1.03	0.74
55 to 64 years	1.13	1.21	0.93	0.70
65 years and over	0.69	0.70	0.70	0.60
White				
Median income, all ages	$38,909	$42,738	$29,671	$20,130
Indices, all ages	1.06	1.16	0.81	0.55
15 to 24 years	0.49	0.61	0.51	0.18
25 to 34 years	0.96	1.09	0.70	0.34
35 to 44 years	1.23	1.37	0.84	0.57
45 to 54 years	1.41	1.52	1.07	0.80
55 to 64 years	1.18	1.24	1.02	0.83
65 years and over	0.71	0.71	0.76	0.66
Black				
Median income, all ages	$21,161	$34,196	$20,678	$11,956
Indices, all ages	0.57	0.93	0.56	0.32
15 to 24 years	0.19	0.53	—	0.15
25 to 34 years	0.44	0.87	0.53	0.23
35 to 44 years	0.68	1.14	0.64	0.40
45 to 54 years	0.88	1.19	—	0.57
55 to 64 years	0.72	1.02	—	0.41
65 years and over	0.45	0.48	—	0.37
Hispanic				
Median income, all ages	$23,901	$28,515	$19,468	$12,894
Indices, all ages	0.65	0.77	0.53	0.35
15 to 24 years	0.36	0.44	—	0.18
25 to 34 years	0.59	0.74	0.52	0.26
35 to 44 years	0.73	0.89	0.53	0.37
45 to 54 years	0.80	0.98	—	0.55
55 to 64 years	0.75	0.87	—	0.56
65 years and over	0.52	0.52	—	0.44

Source: U.S. Bureau of the Census, Current Population Reports, "Money Income of Households, Families, and Persons in the United States: 1992," Series P-60, No.184, U.S. Government Printing Office, Washington, D.C., 1993, Table 17.

Figure 15-5. Median Income of Married-couple Families, by Labor Force Status of the Wife and Race-ethnicity: 1992 [in 1992 dollars]

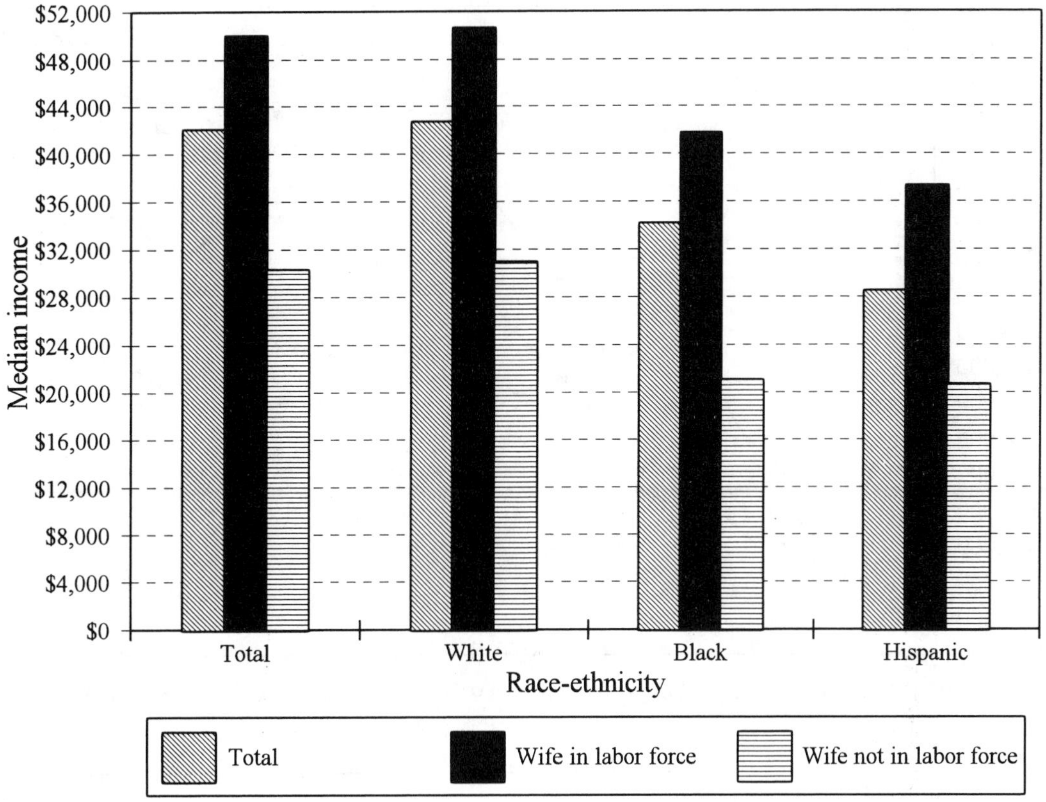

Source: 1992 CPS data.

Hispanic female householders with these characteristics are 0.18, 0.15 and 0.18 of the income of all families in 1992, respectively.

Participation of women in the labor force has a major effect on the income of families (Figure 15-5). In black families, for example, the labor force participation of a wife almost doubles the family's income. Figure 15-6 shows how the effect of a wife's labor force participation on total family income has been increasing over time. In addition, as analysts at the Bureau of Labor Statistics have pointed out, women's employment rates and salary gains over the last two decades have been far less affected by economic cycles than have been those of their husbands (Figure 15-6). The differential distribution of husbands and wives across occupations and industries means that it is relatively infrequent that they will both lose their jobs at the same time. As a result, women's employment has played an important role in cushioning the effect of recent economic downturns on individual married-couple families.

Family Size, Composition and Income

Four-person families had the most total income in 1992 ($44,615), but two-person families had the highest mean income per person ($19,521; see Table 15-17).

When family size reached five or more persons, there was a decline in median family income; this held true for whites, blacks and Hispanics. Not surprisingly, in families of five persons or more, there was also a sharp drop-off in the mean income per person as well. The individual living in a two-person white family had more than six times the mean income of an individual living in a black family of 7 or more persons ($20,501 to $3,355).

Family income also varied by type of family and presence of related children under 18 years old (Table 15-18). As with household income, married-couple families had the highest incomes in 1992, followed by male householder families (with no wife) and female householder families (with no husband). The income of married-couple families was almost two and one-half times that of female householder families. Among all families, the highest incomes were found among those with two or more related children aged 6 to 17 years. However, among married-couple families, the highest incomes were found among those families that had only a single child aged 6 to 17 years. Given the strong impact of wives' employment on family income in recent years, couples may find that they can maximize their incomes only if they "trade-off" lower fertility for more hours spent at the plant or office and the resultant higher income. These data also

Figure 15-6. Median Income of Married-couple Families, by Labor Force Status of the Wife: 1950-1992 [in constant 1992 dollars]

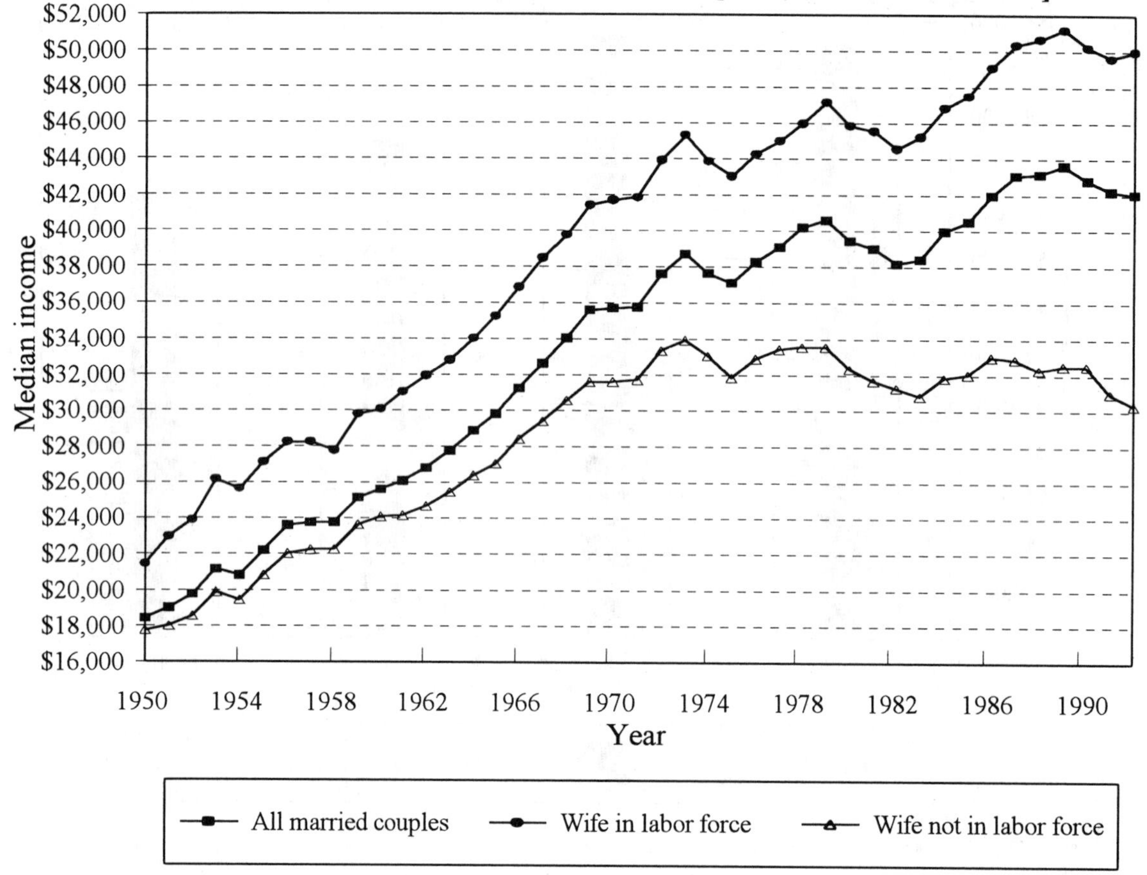

Source: 1950-1992 CPS data.

Table 15-17. Median Family Income and Mean Income per Family Member, by Size and Race-ethnicity: 1992 [in 1992 dollars]

Size of family	Total	White	Black	Hispanic
Median income	$36,812	$38,909	$21,161	$23,901
2 persons	$31,098	$32,502	$17,583	$19,663
3 persons	$38,564	$41,176	$21,148	$21,554
4 persons	$44,615	$46,693	$26,555	$27,452
5 persons	$42,605	$45,366	$24,118	$26,613
6 persons	$38,093	$41,284	$23,672	$27,393
7 or more persons	$34,917	$40,124	$12,858	$26,254
Mean income per person	$14,065	$15,027	$8,133	$8,024
2 persons	$19,521	$20,501	$11,148	$12,452
3 persons	$14,885	$15,838	$8,918	$9,512
4 persons	$12,654	$13,282	$8,344	$8,351
5 persons	$9,785	$10,299	$6,184	$6,591
6 persons	$7,935	$8,561	$5,298	$5,336
7 or more persons	$5,710	$6,337	$3,355	$4,500

Source: U.S. Bureau of the Census, Current Population Reports, "Money Income of
Households, Families, and Persons in the United States: 1992," Series P-60, No.184,
U.S. Government Printing Office, Washington, D.C., 1993, Table 20.

Table 15-18. Median Family Income, by Type of Family and Presence of Related Children Under 18 Years: 1992 [in 1992 dollars]

Number of related children under 18 years	All families	Married couples	Male householder, no wife	Female householder, no husband
Total	$36,812	$42,064	$27,821	$17,221
No related children	$37,819	$39,768	$34,245	$27,495
One related child	$35,071	$45,534	$20,889	$15,625
Under 6 years	$31,768	$40,938	$17,200	$11,243
6 to 17 years	$37,217	$48,869	$24,371	$18,050
Two or more related children	$36,429	$43,818	$25,472	$11,591
All under 6 years	$33,754	$40,952	$22,205	$6,948
Some under 6, some 6 to 17 years	$32,323	$40,815	$21,937	$9,742
All 6 to 17 years	$40,345	$47,429	$30,178	$16,330

Source: U.S. Bureau of the Census, Current Population Reports, "Money Income of Households, Families, and Persons in the United States: 1992," Series P-60, No.184, U.S. Government Printing Office, Washington, D.C., 1993, Table 18.

Table 15-19. Median Family Income, by Number of Earners and Race-ethnicity: 1992 [in 1992 dollars]

Number of earners	Total	White	Black	Hispanic
Total	$36,812	$38,909	$21,161	$23,901
No earners	$15,536	$17,880	$6,532	$8,166
One earner	$26,292	$28,666	$16,131	$17,134
Two earners	$45,779	$46,895	$34,950	$32,402
Three earners	$56,550	$57,440	$50,770	$39,393
Four or more earners	$69,923	$70,224	$67,700	$50,292

Source: U.S. Bureau of the Census, Current Population Reports, "Money Income of Households, Families, and Persons in the United States: 1992," Series P-60, No.184, U.S. Government Printing Office, Washington, D.C., 1993, Table 21.

show the huge disparities in the standard of living of different children: married couples raising two or more related children under 6 years had a median income of $40,952, compared to a median income of $6,948 for female householders with no husband present attempting to raise two or more children under 6 years. For the latter group, this difference in income results in lots of missing vacations, sports lessons, personal computers, and so on, not to mention missed immunizations, medical care and proper nutrition.

Many American families now cling to a middle-class lifestyle primarily by having more than one wage earner in the family. Overall (see Table 15-19), families with one wage earner make more than $10,000 more than those without a wage earner, and the presence of a second wage earner boosts family income by almost $20,000 per year more. A third wage earner adds about $10,000 more in income, and families with four or more members producing income raise

annual income to almost $70,000. Of course, such families are relatively uncommon; American families in recent years have been dividing, not combining (although more unmarried adult children appear to be leaving the parental nest at an older age, or returning there after divorce). However, they are found more often among Asian and other immigrant groups with strong traditions of family co-residence, and may partially account for their ability to mobilize large amounts of capital for investment in small businesses or the purchase of housing soon after their arrival.

How Should Income be Measured?

During the late 1980s and early 1990s, the measurement of income changed from being an obscure topic of interest to only a handful of scholars and government statisticians to a topic of intense interest among conservative economists and ideologues. Briefly, these conser-

Table 15-20. Median Household Income, by Income Definition: 1990 [in 1990 dollars]

Household characteristics	Offical	Private sector	After tax	After transfer	All inclusive
Race-ethnicity					
All races	$29,943	$28,779	$23,947	$27,720	$29,615
White	$31,231	$30,330	$25,069	$28,812	$30,828
Black	$18,676	$16,757	$14,966	$19,391	$20,391
Hispanic	$22,330	$21,802	$19,072	$22,087	$23,193
Type of household					
All households	$29,943	$28,779	$23,947	$27,720	$29,615
Married-couple	$39,996	$40,217	$33,108	$36,328	$38,721
Female householder, no spouse present	$18,069	$15,929	$14,609	$19,399	$20,423
Gini index	0.426	0.490	0.463	0.384	0.383

Source: U.S. Bureau of the Census, Current Population Reports, "Income, Poverty, and Wealth in the United States: A Chartbook," Series P-60, No. 179, U.S. Government Printing Office, Washington, D.C., 1992, Table 5.

vatives said that income distribution in the United States appeared to be far less equal than it really was. This, they said, was because the measures of income did not take into account benefits that the poor received (such as food stamps and Medicaid) and some benefits that accrued to the middle class (such as employer-provided health care) that were not given in cash. In addition, they contended, since the rich pay more taxes than the poor, a true measure of usable income should measure after-tax income. This would be a more realistic measure of the income individuals and families had available to spend or invest.

If these factors are taken into account, how much do they change the income distribution picture? Table 15-20 presents five alternative ways of computing income, and demonstrates the effect of alternative computations on the median household income of racial and ethnic groups and of households of different types:

1. The *official* definition is the one used in the prior tables in this chapter; it is money income excluding capital gains before taxes.
2. *Private sector income* is official money income minus government cash transfers, plus capital gains and the value of employer-provided health insurance supplements to wage or salary income.
3. *After-tax income* deducts all payroll and income taxes from private sector income.
4. *After-transfer income* includes all money income after taxes plus the value of noncash transfer benefits (including both means-tested and non-means-tested government programs) such as food stamps, rent subsidies, Medicaid, veterans' or Social Security payments, free school lunches, and so on.
5. The *all-inclusive* definition adds in the net imputed return on home equity to the value of after-transfer income.

What Difference do Alternative Definitions of Income Make?

The median official household income in 1990 was $29,943. When government cash transfers are excluded and the value of health insurance is added, private sector income drops to $28,779. When all taxes are factored in, the median after-tax household income of all races drops to a median income of $23,947. After government transfer payments (after transfer income) are added to the official definition, the median household income is $27,720. Since transfer payments are thought to be heavily concentrated in helping society's poorest members, it is surprising to find that the median income of households after transfers is actually below the original official figure ($27,720 to $29,943). Yet the government's non-cash transfer payments are not simply aimed at the poor; the largest non-cash program, Medicare, pays out equally to the rich or poor over age 65.

When all of these modifications to income are included (the all-inclusive definition), the median household income changes only by a little more than $300 dollars ($29,615) from the original official figure. In addition, the slight decline in median income between the official and all-inclusive median incomes suggests that when all of these factors are taken into account, the half of the American population with lower incomes is benefiting less from taxes, transfer programs increasing home equity, and so on. And what of blacks and Hispanics, who are thought by many to be great beneficiaries of non-cash government programs? Blacks increase their median household income by less than $2,000 and Hispanics increase theirs by slightly more than $1,000 when the all-inclusive rather than the official definition of income is used. Yet there is still a gap of more than $10,000 in the median household income of whites and blacks, and a difference of more than $7,000 in the incomes of white and Hispanic households when the all-inclusive definition of income is used. Similarly, the median income of married-couple households drops by slightly more than $1,000 and that of female householders with no spouse present increases by a little more than $2,000 when the all-inclusive definition is used, but there is still a large gap (of more than $18,000) in median income between the two groups.

The Changing Income Distribution

Between 1990 and 1993, the proportion of national income going to the bottom 80 percent of the population shrank, and the amount of inequality in income grew. By 1993, 48.6 percent of the nation's income (official definition) was going to the top 20 percent of the population. If measured by the second definition , private sector income (see Table 15-20), the top quintile's income was 53.1 percent. When measured as after-tax income (definition 3), the top quintile got almost exactly half (50.3 percent) of the nation's income. Only when after-transfer income was factored in (definition 4, 44.8 percent of income) or when the all-inclusive definition was used (44.6 percent) did the top quintile's income subside below one-half of the nation's total income. Incidentally, when the private sector definition of income is used (definition 2), the bottom quintile of the population received less than 1 percent (0.8 percent) of the nation's income in 1993.

Changes in Income Distribution among Families over Time

Those who study international trends in income distribution often look at the proportion of all income that goes to the lowest fifth (bottom quintile) and the top 5 percent of all families. Data from the Current Population Survey show that in 1947, 5 percent of all income went to the bottom 20 percent of all families. By the early 1970s this proportion rose to 5.5 percent, but since that time it has steadily dropped to 4.2 percent in 1994. The top 5 percent of all families received 17.5 percent of all income in 1947; their proportion sunk to a low of 15.3 percent in 1981, but by 1994, they were receiving 20.1 of all income, a higher figure than at any time since World War II.

When compared to the distribution of income within the other 21 high-income OECD nations (the World Bank's definition of the advanced industrial states), the bottom income quintile in the U.S. receives less than that of any other nation. The proportion of national income received by the top income quintile in the United States is rivaled only by the proportion of income received by the rich in Hong Kong and Singapore.

Measuring Income Inequality by the Gini Ratio

The commonly-used summary measure of income distribution, the Gini distribution, shows how income inequality has increased (Figure 15-7). In 1967, the Gini ratio for all households stood at just below 0.400; by 1992 it had risen to more than 0.430. By 1993, the Gini ratio had risen to .448, and even if the all-inclusive rather than the official definition is used, the Gini ratio is 0.395 (up from 0.383 in 1990).

The change in income distribution within the black and Hispanic groups was even more striking. In 1967, black households had a greater degree of income inequality than did white ones; the Gini ratio declined between 1968-72, then rose steadily. By 1992, the Gini ratio for black households had risen to a very unequal ratio of 0.470. Hispanic households had a more equal distribution of income in 1972 (at about 0.370 in the first year such data were available) than did white or black households, but by 1979 the Hispanic Gini ratio had become more unequal than that of whites. Economic and social changes in the United States over the past several decades have increased the overall degree of income inequality, and they have had a particularly strong effect on increasing income inequality within minority groups.

Economists no longer debate whether income has become more unequally divided in the United States over the past two decades; it is an established fact. What is more debatable, of course, is why income inequality is increasing. Is it a function of the new economic forces at work in our nation and throughout the industrialized world? Is it due to long-term trends in household composition, fertility and marriage patterns, and investment in human capital? Is it affected by various social and political choices that we are making? Finally, if income inequality is widening in relatively good times (as it is now), what will happen to it if there are moderate or severe (as in the early 1980s) economic downturns?

Cross-sectional income differences (what we have measured so far) could take different paths over the lifetimes of individuals. Some economists argue that when income is measured for individuals over longer time periods, income distribution looks more equal. Yet, over time, differences in income distribution can also become differences in wealth. Wealth, as well as income, has important influences on a number of demographic variables, including place of residence, life expectancy, length of education, nuptiality, and occupation. Since wealth is distributed in a different way from income, it is useful to explore how wealth is related to other key demographic variables.

Figure 15-7. Household Gini Ratios, by Race-ethnicity: 1967-1992

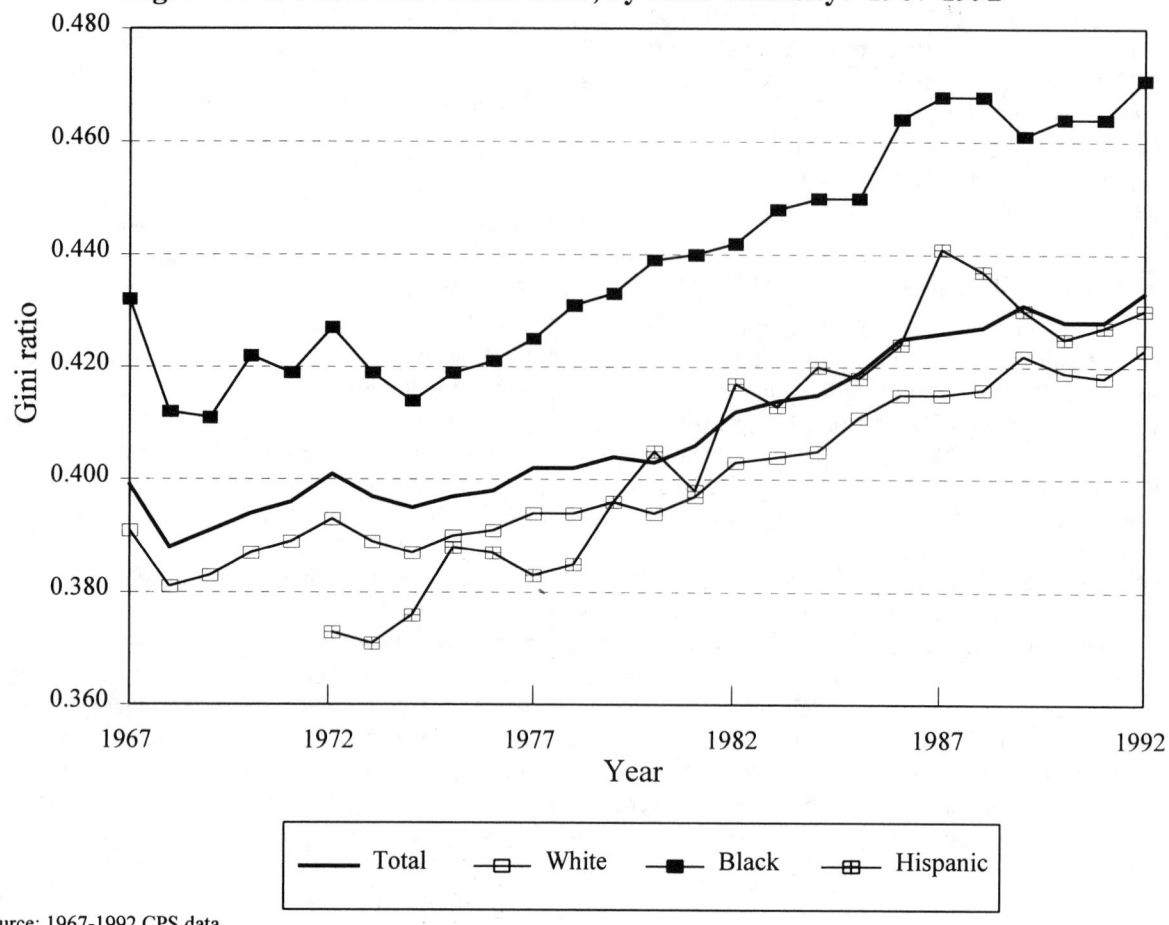

Source: 1967-1992 CPS data.

The Distribution of Wealth in the United States

While earnings differentials can be huge, they are inherently limited, since everyone has the same inherently limited number of hours that they can work. Wealth, however, is not similarly constrained. It has no upper limit. Wealth can generate wealth and the process is not limited by the individual's personal time (Lester C. Thurow, *The Future of Capitalism*, p. 244).

Household Net Worth

Until recently, the Bureau of the Census made few efforts to measure wealth. However, during the 1980s and early 1990s, the Survey of Income and Program Participation (SIPP) asked a series of detailed questions about assets (such as money in checking accounts, savings accounts, IRAs, stocks and bonds, ownership of homes or rental property, value of motor vehicles, and so on) and liabilities (outstanding mortgages, student loans, vehicle loans, credit card or medical bills, and so on). Household net worth is the sum of all assets held by household members minus the sum of all of their liabilities. The major categories not included in net worth are the value of equity in pension plans, the cash value of life insurance and the value of home furnishings and jewelry.

Effects of Age, Type of Household and Race-Ethnicity on Household Net Worth

In 1991, the 94.7 million households in the United States had a median net worth of $36,623 (Table 15-21). The 81.4 million white households had a median net worth of $44,408; the 10.8 million black households had a median net worth ($4,604) that was only a little more than a tenth of this figure. The 6.4 million Hispanic households' median net worth of $5,345 was only slightly higher than the black figure.

Both marital status and age have strong influences on net worth. Net worth increases with age, and married-couple households have a higher net worth than do male or female householders. The 9 million married-couple households where the householder is age 65 or over have a median net worth of $147,904, while the 7 million households where the female householder is under age 35 have a median net worth of only $1,360.

In fact, younger households (those with a householder under age 35) as a group do not have much in the way of assets: overall, their median net worth stands at $5,565; married-couple households have $12,036 in assets, and male householders have $5,014. A large proportion of younger American households are only one prolonged spell of unemployment or one serious accident or illness away from exhausting their net assets in very short order (see this chapter's later section on "Social Mobility and Poverty"). Almost 22 percent of the population aged 15-44 years in 1993 was medically uninsured; this proportion had risen by 50 percent since 1980 (see Textbox).

Effects of Income on Household Net Worth

In theory, if households have higher incomes, then they can save more, and increase their net worth. On the other hand, Americans are known to have one of the lowest savings rates in the world; as they increase their incomes, they tend to increase their levels of consumption as well. How close is the relationship between income and the acquisition of net worth? Table 15-22 shows the median net worth of each income quintile of the population. The fifth of the population with the lowest incomes had a median net worth of $5,224 in 1991, while the fifth of all households with the highest incomes had a median net worth of $123,166.

Racial and ethnic differences in available resources become even more apparent when income and wealth are cross-classified. The median income of white households in 1991 (in 1991 dollars) was $31,569; of black households, $18,807; and of Hispanic households, $22,691. Yet the median net worth of black households in the lowest income quintile in 1991 was $1, of Hispanics, $645, and of whites, $10,257. Similarly, the net worth of white households in the highest income quintile was more than twice as much as the top-earning quintile of black households and almost twice as much as Hispanic households in the highest income quintile. These differences reflect both the differences in levels of income between the top quintiles of the race-ethnic groups and the much longer time (often over several generations) that white families have had to build up their household wealth. As the old joke goes, most of those at the pinnacle of wealth in the United States got it the old-fashioned way—they inherited it.

Short-term Trends in Net Worth, 1984-1993

The distribution of median net worth across income quintiles appears to have remained relatively steady between 1984 and 1993 (Table 15-23). Yet it is important to remember that, over time, the distribution of income

Table 15-21. Median Net Worth of Households, by Type of Household, Age, and Race-ethnicity of Householder: 1991 [in 1991 dollars]

Household characteristics	Number of households (in thousands)	Net worth
Total households	94,692	$36,623
Race-ethnicity		
White	81,409	$44,408
Black	10,768	$4,604
Hispanic	6,407	$5,345
Type of household		
Total	94,692	$36,623
Less than 35 years	25,031	$5,565
35 to 44 years	21,514	$31,148
45 to 54 years	14,934	$58,250
55 to 64 years	12,575	$83,041
65 years and over	20,638	$88,192
Married-couple	52,216	$60,065
Less than 35 years	12,247	$12,036
35 to 54 years	23,080	$60,505
55 to 64 years	7,849	$128,782
65 years and over	9,040	$147,904
Male householder	15,297	$11,986
Less than 35 years	5,746	$5,014
35 to 54 years	5,409	$17,740
55 to 64 years	1,514	$30,857
65 years and over	2,627	$64,381
Female householder	27,179	$14,762
Less than 35 years	7,038	$1,360
35 to 54 years	7,959	$10,684
55 to 64 years	3,211	$39,591
65 years and over	8,972	$59,521

Source: U.S. Bureau of the Census, Current Population Reports, "Household Wealth and Asset Ownership: 1991," Series P-70, No. 34, U.S. Government Printing Office, Washington, D.C., 1994, Tables 1 and 2..

Table 15-22. Median Net Worth, by Monthly Household Income and Race-ethnicity of Householder: 1991 [in 1991 dollars]

Income quintile	Total	White	Black	Hispanic
Lowest quintile	$5,224	$10,257	$1	$645
Second quintile	$19,191	$25,602	$3,299	$3,182
Middle quintile	$28,859	$33,503	$7,987	$7,150
Fourth quintile	$49,204	$52,767	$20,547	$19,413
Highest quintile	$123,166	$129,394	$54,449	$67,435

Source: U.S. Bureau of the Census, Current Population Reports, "Household Wealth and Asset Ownership: 1991," Series P-70, No. 34, U.S. Government Printing Office, Washington, D.C., 1994, Table H.

The Growing Uninsured Population

by Alison Kadlec Donta

The number of uninsured Americans has risen steadily since 1987, the first year for which comprehensive national insurance information was obtained. According to the U.S. Bureau of the Census, in 1992 there were 37.4 million uninsured, a 20.6% increase over the 31.0 million uninsured in 1987. This represents 14.7% and 12.9% of the population for those years, respectively. The Survey of Income and Program Participation estimates that 22.6% of the population did not have continuous insurance coverage for the 32 months of the survey during the 1991-1993 period. Another large segment of the insured population is estimated to be underinsured due to increasing co-payments and deductibles in many policies.

Most of this rise in the uninsured population has been seen among working-age adults and reflects the reduction in employment-related health insurance coverage from 1987 to 1992. In 1987, 75.5% of the population had employment-related coverage. By 1992, this was reduced to only 71.1% of the population. The primary explanation for this reduction in employment-related health insurance coverage is the rising cost of insurance, both for employers and employees. In addition, when changing employers, many Americans are forced to change insurance coverage and have subsequently been denied health insurance due to a pre-existing health condition clause.

People in all occupational categories are experiencing a reduction in employment-related health insurance coverage, but some workers are more affected than others. Those in the household service (38.1% uninsured), forestry/fishing (32.5%), agriculture (30.6%), and construction (30.0%) industries were most likely to be uninsured in 1990. Persons working in the utilities/sanitation industry had only a 5.3% uninsured rate and those in public administration had 5.5% of their population uninsured. Different types of workers are also differentially affected. The accompanying table illustrates that, for the 1991-1993 period, full-time, full-period workers were more likely to have continuous health coverage from any source than were either part-time, full-period workers or workers with one or more job interruptions. This difference is seen most clearly in coverage through employment-related health insurance. While 64.3% of full-time, full-period workers had employment-provided coverage, only 21.4% of part-time, full-period workers and 14.1% of workers with one or more job interruptions had that type of continuous coverage.

During the 1991-1993 period, 73.5% of the population had continuous coverage through private or government health insurance. Only 63.6% of the black population, however, and 50.5% of the Hispanic population had the same coverage. Females were more likely to have continuous coverage (75.3%) than males (71.7%) during this time period. Persons aged 18 to 21 years were least likely to be continuously covered for 32 months, with only 51.1% of that age group covered. In contrast, 75.7% of those aged 35 to 44 years, 80.1% of those aged 45 to 64, and 99.3% of those aged 65 and over had continuous coverage. High rates of coverage for the oldest segment of the population result, in large part, from the Medicare program.

Contrary to many popular notions, the uninsured are not limited

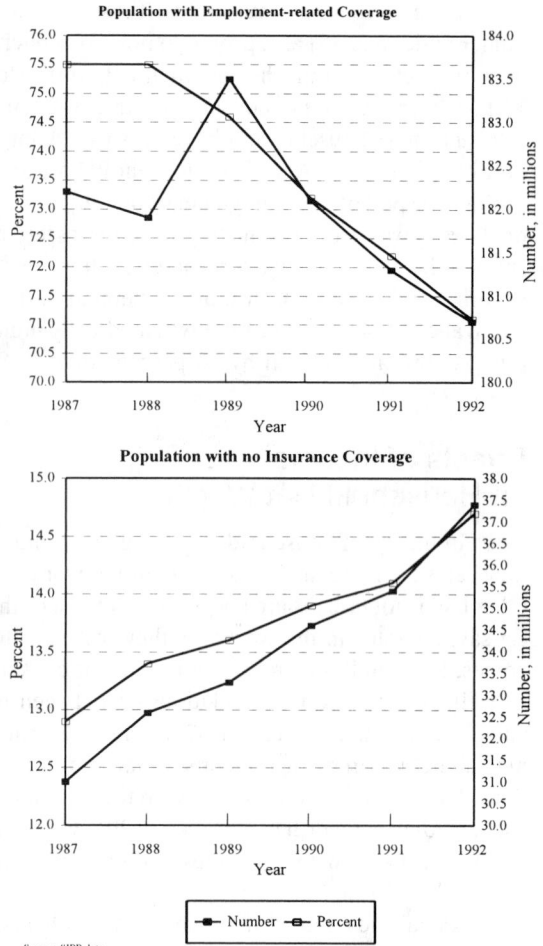

Source: SIPP data

to those living below the poverty line. In fact, 71.9% of the 37.4 million uninsured in 1992 were above the poverty line. Those below the poverty line are much more likely to qualify for Medicaid and thus be covered through that program. Of the 28.4 million Medicaid recipients in 1992, 61.3% of them had incomes below the poverty line. Although the eligibility requirements for Medicaid were changed slightly in 1990 to allow more people to receive coverage, the proportion of the population on Medicaid has remained fairly steady over the past decade. Most of the uninsured and/or underinsured population is ineligible for Medicaid and other government support programs. This fact, combined with the continued reduction in employment-related health insurance coverage, points to an increasingly bleak prospect for health insurance coverage in the United States without major social initiatives.

Additional Sources:

Himmelstein, David U., Woolhandler, Steffie, and Wolfe, Sidney M. "The Vanishing Health Care Safety Net: New Data on Uninsured Americans." International Journal of Health Services 22(1992):381-96.

Snider, Sarah. "Characteristics of the Part-time Work Force and Part-time Employee Participation in Health and Pension Benefits." Journal of Labor Research 16(1995):239-48.

Summer, Laura. "The Escalating Number of Uninsured in the United States." International Journal of Health Services 24(1994):409-13.

U.S. Bureau of the Census. Poverty in the United States: 1992. Current Population Reports Series P-60, Number 185. Washington, D.C.: U.S. Government Printing Office, 1993.

————. Health Insurance, 1991 to 1993. Current Population Reports Series P-70, Number 43. Washington, D.C.: U.S. Government Printing Office, 1995.

U.S. Centers for Disease Control and Prevention. Health Insurance Coverage--U.S. Morbidity and Mortality Weekly Report 44(1995):219-25.

Percent of Wage and Salary Workers Age 18 to 64 Continuously Covered[1] by Health Insurance, by Sex, Race-ethnicity, and Labor Force Status: 1991 to 1993 [numbers in thousands]

Health insurance type and labor force status	Sex			Race-ethnicity		
	Total	Male	Female	White	Black	Hispanic
Full-time, full-period workers	53,232	31,938	21,295	45,610	5,731	3,868
Private or government insurance	86.7	86.2	87.4	88.0	76.6	67.0
Private health insurance	86.0	85.4	86.9	87.4	75.4	65.5
Employer-provided health insurance	64.3	67.6	59.4	65.4	57.7	48.9
Part-time, full-period workers	5,092	1,140	3,952	4,544	328	242
Private or government insurance	72.5	61.5	75.6	75.2	39.9	52.0
Private health insurance	70.3	56.0	74.5	73.2	38.5	49.1
Employer-provided health insurance	21.4	29.6	19.1	22.1	21.0	26.3
Workers with one or more job interruptions	77,034	31,619	45,416	63,769	9,727	7,790
Private or government insurance	59.9	51.5	65.7	61.7	50.1	38.6
Private health insurance	50.7	45.1	54.6	54.4	28.9	26.2
Employer-provided health insurance	14.1	20.8	9.5	14.7	11.4	8.3

[1] Continuous coverage represents 32 months of coverage during this time period.

Source: U.S. Bureau of the Census, Current Population Reports, "Health Insurance, 1991 to 1993," Series P-70, No. 43, U.S. Government Printing Office, Washington, D.C., 1995, Table I.

**Table 15-23. Distribution of Median Net Worth, by Monthly
Household Income Quintile: 1984-1993**

Monthly income quintile	1993	1991	1988	1984[1]
Total	100.0	100.0	100.0	100.0
Lowest quintile	7.2	7.0	7.0	7.2
Second quintile	12.2	12.2	12.3	11.9
Middle quintile	15.9	15.8	15.7	14.0
Fourth quintile	20.6	20.4	20.6	19.4
Highest quintile	44.1	44.7	44.4	47.5
Gini ratio	—	0.428	0.427	0.415

[1] In constant 1988 dollars.

Source: U.S. Bureau of the Census, Current Population Reports, "Money Income
of Households, Families, and Persons in the United States: 1992," Table B-3,
"Asset Ownership of Housholds: 1993," Series P-70, No. 47, Table B,
"Household Wealth and Asset Ownership: 1991," Series P-70, No. 34, Table B,
and Household Wealth and Asset Ownership: 1988," Series P-70, No. 47,
Table B, U.S. Government Printing Office, Washington, D.C., 1993, 1995,
1994, and 1990.

between income quintiles has become more unequal (Table 15-12). The Gini ratio for the net worth of households continued to increase slightly between 1984 and 1991, indicating increasing inequality in the distribution of net worth across all households. Contrary to the expectations of many economists and sociologists, increasing levels of education, technology and the increasing importance of human capital in the generation of national income have had no leveling effect on the distribution of either income or wealth in the United States in recent years.

Net Worth by Region

Over the past several decades there has been a convergence in the distribution of the population across industries and occupations in different regions. As industry has moved South and West, incomes in those regions rose. While significant differences in median family incomes still remain (Table 15-13), they are shrinking. There are also differences in the net worth of households across regions of the United States (Table 15-24). The median net worth of households in the Northeast is more than $30,000 greater than the net worth of those residing in the South.

There are several reasons for these regional differentials. The most obvious one is age: the population of the Northeast is older than the population in the South or West, and hence has had more time to accumulate wealth. A differential distribution of education, racial and ethnic groups, occupations and other population characteristics also plays a part in regional differences in wealth. Even such factors as the favorable tax treatment of capital gains

for the elderly (those over 55 years have a one-time exclusion from capital gains taxes on the sale of a house) can affect the regional distribution of wealth. The even larger regional differences in mean household net worth (where the West leads at $131,727, and the South lags at $80,409) indicate that the very rich are clustered in some regions of the nation.

The Composition of Net Worth

For the majority of Americans, the key element in their net worth is their ownership (or lack) of housing. As Table 15-25 shows, the value of equity in home ownership (the current estimated selling price of a house mi-

**Table 15-24. Net Worth of Holdings for Asset
Owners, by Region: 1991 [in 1991 dollars]**

Region	Number of households (in thousands)	Median net worth	Mean net worth
Total	94,692	$36,623	$102,118
Northeast	19,007	$57,294	$123,971
Midwest	24,376	$38,677	$90,225
South	32,049	$26,775	$80,409
West	19,260	$39,735	$131,727

Source: U.S. Bureau of the Census, Current Population Reports,
"Household Wealth and Asset Ownership: 1991," Series P-70,
No. 34, U.S. Government Printing Office, Washington, D.C.,
1994, Tables 1, 2, and 5.

Table 15-25. Distribution of Net Worth, by Asset Type, Race-ethnictiy, and Age of Householder: 1991

Age and race-ethnicity	Total net worth	Own home	Vehicles	Business or profession	Real estate	Interest-earning assets	Other
Total	100.0	41.9	6.4	7.3	12.2	19.2	13.0
White	100.0	41.1	6.2	7.2	12.2	19.7	13.6
Black	100.0	63.3	10.2	6.7	11.5	10.1	-1.8
Hispanic	100.0	54.9	9.8	8.8	15.1	9.6	1.8
Age of householder							
Under 35 years	100.0	42.1	18.1	13.5	12.3	14.1	-0.1
35 to 44 years	100.0	45.1	8.7	11.5	13.4	12.6	8.7
45 to 54 years	100.0	40.8	6.4	10.8	16.2	13.2	12.6
55 to 64 years	100.0	40.9	5.2	6.8	13.4	17.2	16.5
65 years and over	100.0	41.5	3.5	2.1	8.6	28.3	16.0

Source: U.S. Bureau of the Census, Current Population Reports, "Household Wealth and Asset Ownership: 1991," Series P-70, No. 34, U.S. Government Printing Office, Washington, D.C., 1994, Tables G and I.

nus any outstanding mortgages) comprised 41.1 percent of the net worth of white households, 63.3 percent of the net worth of black households, and 54.9 percent of the net worth of Hispanic households. Regional differences in the value of housing had a strong effect on the large regional differences in net worth (Table 15-24): in 1991 the median selling price for an existing single-family house in the Northeast was $141,900, compared to only $88,900 in the South.

Interest-earning assets (including certificates of deposit, bonds, savings accounts, and so on) contributed another fifth of the net worth of white households and about another tenth of the net worth of black and Hispanic households. The proportional distribution of net worth across businesses and professions and real estate are roughly similar for the three racial and ethnic groups, although, of course, white households had a far higher absolute median net worth. The "other" category includes checking accounts, stocks and mutual funds, U.S. savings bonds, IRA and Keogh plan investments, and so on; they comprise 13 percent of net worth of the general population, but 16 percent or more of the net worth of those in the 55-64 and 65-years-and-over age categories.

The proportion of net worth accounted for by home ownership does not change much with age. Young families often sacrifice to buy a house, and concentrate their available resources in a down payment; older householders get the benefit of a shrinking mortgage and the gradual appreciation of their property. The major change in the distribution of net worth with age is a shift away from its concentration in vehicles, business or professional assets and real estate and into interest-earning assets. Those who are 55 years of age and older shift their wealth into more liquid and interest-generating assets.

Poverty in the United States

A significant proportion of the population lives in a state of poverty, with an annual money income less than the minimum required to maintain basic nutritional, health, housing, and consumption needs and services according to American consumption patterns at what would be widely accepted as a minimal socially acceptable level. Such a concept of poverty is not easy to quantify or define precisely, because the income that would define the poverty threshold varies with size of family and the characteristics of family members. Such a definition was developed in 1964 by the Social Security Administration (SSA) and was subsequently accepted--with refinements and modifications--for general use in publishing federal statistics. The history of that definition is explained in detail in the technical appendix to this chapter.

Once each year the Bureau of the Census publishes a report, "Characteristics of the Population Below the Poverty Level," in the Current Population Reports (Series P-60) on consumer income. These reports, as well as the decennial censuses of 1970, 1980, and 1990, use the poverty threshold definitions to provide data about the population facing economic hardship. The Bureau of the Census emphasizes that the definition of poverty has limitations because it is based on average consumption patterns. Since individual circumstances or consumption patterns differ, the dollar value of the poverty threshold for a given family size may not represent the cash income required by any particular family of that size to maintain a level of economic well-being equivalent to other families of the same size with similar incomes. Table 15-26 shows the poverty thresholds in terms of annual income and size and composition of family that would place a family above or below the poverty line in 1992.

Table 15-26. Poverty Thresholds in 1992, by Size of Family and Number of Related Children Under 18 Years [in 1992 dollars]

Size of family unit	Weighted average thresholds	Number of related children under 18 years								
		None	One	Two	Three	Four	Five	Six	Seven	Eight or more
One person (unrelated individual)	$7,143	—	—	—	—	—	—	—	—	—
Under 65 years	$7,299	$7,299	—	—	—	—	—	—	—	—
65 years and over	$6,729	$6,729	—	—	—	—	—	—	—	—
Two persons	$9,137	—	—	—	—	—	—	—	—	—
Householder under 65 years	$9,443	$9,395	$9,670	—	—	—	—	—	—	—
Householder 65 years and over	$8,487	$8,480	$9,634	—	—	—	—	—	—	—
Three persons	$11,186	$10,974	$11,293	$11,304	—	—	—	—	—	—
Four persons	$14,335	$14,471	$14,708	$14,228	$14,277	—	—	—	—	—
Five persons	$16,592	$17,451	$17,705	$17,163	$16,743	$16,487	—	—	—	—
Six persons	$19,137	$20,072	$20,152	$19,737	$19,339	$18,747	$18,396	—	—	—
Seven persons	$21,594	$23,096	$23,240	$22,743	$22,396	$21,751	$20,998	$20,171	—	—
Eight persons	$24,053	$25,831	$26,059	$25,590	$25,179	$24,596	$23,855	$23,085	$22,889	—
Nine persons or more	$28,745	$31,073	$31,223	$30,808	$30,459	$29,887	$29,099	$28,387	$28,211	$27,124

Source: U.S. Bureau of the Census, Current Population Reports, "Poverty in the United States: 1992," Series P-60, No. 185, U.S. Government Printing Office, Washington, D.C., 1993, Table A-3.

Number and Proportion of Persons in Poverty

According to the Current Population Survey conducted in March, 1993, a total of 36.9 million persons were below the poverty level during 1992. This represented 14.5 percent of all individuals, and is called the "poverty rate" (see Definition Box). This total was also the largest number of people in poverty since the early 1960s.

The Bureau of the Census has recently begun to adjust its estimates for poverty, income and other characteristics of the population to take account of the differential undercount of the U.S. population in the 1990 Census (see Chapter 2). The 1990 Census missed a significant proportion of racial minorities and low-income respondents. If the sampling frame for the Current Population Survey is not re-weighted to take account of these errors, then the size of these groups will be underestimated throughout the decade following the 1990 Census, and the errors will increase in each succeeding year. Using these adjustments for undercount, the Bureau of the Census estimates that there were actually about 38 million Americans in poverty in 1992, and a poverty rate of 14.8 (about 0.3 percent higher than the rate based on the unadjusted 1990 Census figures). In order to retain consistency with prior data (which were not adjusted for census undercounts), the non-adjusted 1992 data will be used here.

Alternative Definitions of Poverty

Some organizations that use poverty statistics believe the SSA thresholds are too low in the light of current living standards. They prefer an alternative threshold that is 125 percent of the official poverty thresholds. By the alternative indicator, the population below the poverty level numbered 49.17 million in 1992, making a poverty rate of 19.4 percent.

On the other hand, some analysts contend that various kinds of means-tested and non-means-tested benefits should be included in the definition of income of those in poverty. The 1993 and 1994 Current Population Survey findings on poverty have been analyzed by Bureau of the Census researchers using the same framework of alternative definitions of income used in Table 15-20. Their results show that if all of the adjustments to income are included (the "all-inclusive" measure, including taxes, government transfer payments, and imputed home equity), then the poverty rate drops from the official rate of 15.1 in 1994 to a rate of 11.2 (comparable figures for 1993 were 14.5 and 10.0). Whether or not one out of every ten residents of the United States remains in poverty even after almost all public and private and cash and non-cash programs to ameliorate their condition are taken into account is a good or acceptable condition probably depends on one's point of view of the role of poverty in American life.

Extreme Poverty

A significant proportion of the population of the United States lives at a level of income that is less than half of the poverty threshold income. Out of the total of 14.5 percent of the population below the poverty line, more than one out of every three (5.9 percent) families had incomes that were below 0.5 of the poverty line. Over 15 million people in the United States, or 5.9 percent of the population, lived in such extreme poverty in 1992. Extreme poverty has an even more uneven distribution across population groups than does poverty as defined by the conventional definition (see Table 15-27).

Changes in Poverty Rates over Time

In 1959, the poverty rate stood at 22.4 percent of the population (Figure 15-8). It fell steadily (with a small rise in 1970-71) until 1973, when it reached a historic low of 11.1 percent. This was almost certainly the lowest rate of poverty in the history of the United States population. After that date, it began an uneven rise, with a post-recession peak in 1983 at 15.2 percent. It then dropped back to 12.8 percent in 1989, but rose during the early 1990s, reaching 14.5 percent in both 1992 and 1994.

There is a popular and widespread mythology that the anti-poverty programs of the 1960s "failed." From a demographic perspective, this is clearly false. The size of the population in poverty decreased from almost 39.5 million in 1959 to 25.4 million in 1970. Due to the increase in the size of the overall population, the poverty rate declined from 22.4 to 12.6 percent, or a relative decline of more than 43 percent. This decade's decline in poverty was relatively evenly distributed between blacks (a population with more than 55 percent of its members in poverty in 1959) and whites. The black poverty rate declined from 55.1 to 33.5 percent by 1970, a relative decline of 39.2 percent over this eleven-year period; the white decline in the poverty rate was from 18.1 to 9.9 percent, a relative decline of 45.3 percent over the same era.

The decline in poverty among the white population in the 1960s is the reason why the ratio of the proportion of blacks to whites in poverty grew from 3.04 in 1959 to 3.38 in 1970. Many of the anti-poverty programs of the 1960s were an attempt to address the problems of the "other America" (Michael Harrington's phrase for the large white and minority populations in poverty in the late 1950s), and for the white population, they were fairly successful. Since that time, the proportion of whites and Hispanics in poverty has risen, and blacks have failed to make any further progress in lowering their high rates of poverty.

Table 15-27. Percent of the Population Below the Threshold of Poverty and Extreme Poverty, by Selected Characteristics and Sex: 1992

Characteristics of persons	Poverty		Extreme poverty	
	Male	Female	Male	Female
Total population	12.7	16.3	5.2	6.6
Age				
Under 18 years	21.4	22.3	10.1	10.4
65 years and over	12.9	15.7	2.3	2.6
Race-ethnicity				
White	10.1	13.0	3.7	4.8
Black	29.3	36.8	14.5	18.0
Hispanic	27.0	31.6	9.7	12.1
Marital status, persons 18 years and over				
Never married	13.3	22.4	5.5	11.0
Married, spouse present	6.3	6.4	1.9	1.9
Married, spouse absent	22.4	21.0	9.3	11.2
Divorced	13.0	23.4	5.3	9.5
Separated	16.6	44.0	6.0	20.4
Widowed	16.2	22.1	3.2	4.2
Residence				
Metropolitan area	12.0	15.7	5.0	6.5
Central cities	18.0	22.8	7.7	9.9
Not in central cities	8.3	11.1	3.3	4.3
Outside metropolitan area	15.0	18.4	5.8	7.0
Region				
Northeast	10.5	13.9	4.5	5.5
Midwest	11.3	14.8	5.0	6.2
South	14.6	19.0	6.1	8.3
West	13.1	15.7	4.5	5.6
Educational attainment, persons 25 years and over				
No high school diploma	25.6		8.2	
High school diploma	7.5		2.8	
Bachelor's degree or higher	3.0		1.3	

Source: U.S. Bureau of the Census, "Poverty in the United States: 1992," Current Population Reports, Series P-60, No. 185, U.S. Government Printing Office, Washington, D.C., 1993, Tables 6 and 17.

Poverty and Economic Cycles

It seems almost axiomatic that the number of poor should increase and that the poverty rate should rise during times of economic recession. Yet as we have already seen with regard to family incomes, a number of different factors (including number of wage earners in a family, size of Social Security payments, level of the minimum wage, and so on) can affect whether families remain in or slip into poverty. The recessions of 1960, 1970, and 1974 appear to have had only transitory effects on the poverty rate, whereas the two most recent recessions (the very severe recession of 1980-82 and the recession of 1990) both led to large increases in the poverty rate. In addition, the long but relatively weak expansion of the economy during the first half of the 1990s has had little effect on reducing the proportion of Americans in destitution.

Components of Poverty

Poverty is highly concentrated in particular race-ethnic groups and among families of particular types. Tables 15-27 through 15-30, and Figure 15-8, provide data demonstrating these fundamental components of poverty. While specific topics will be considered later, the following general observations can be made:

1. Poverty rates are consistently higher among females than among males. This is true at all ages and for all races and ethnic groups.

Figure 15-8. Trend in Poverty Rates, by Race-ethnicity: 1959-1992

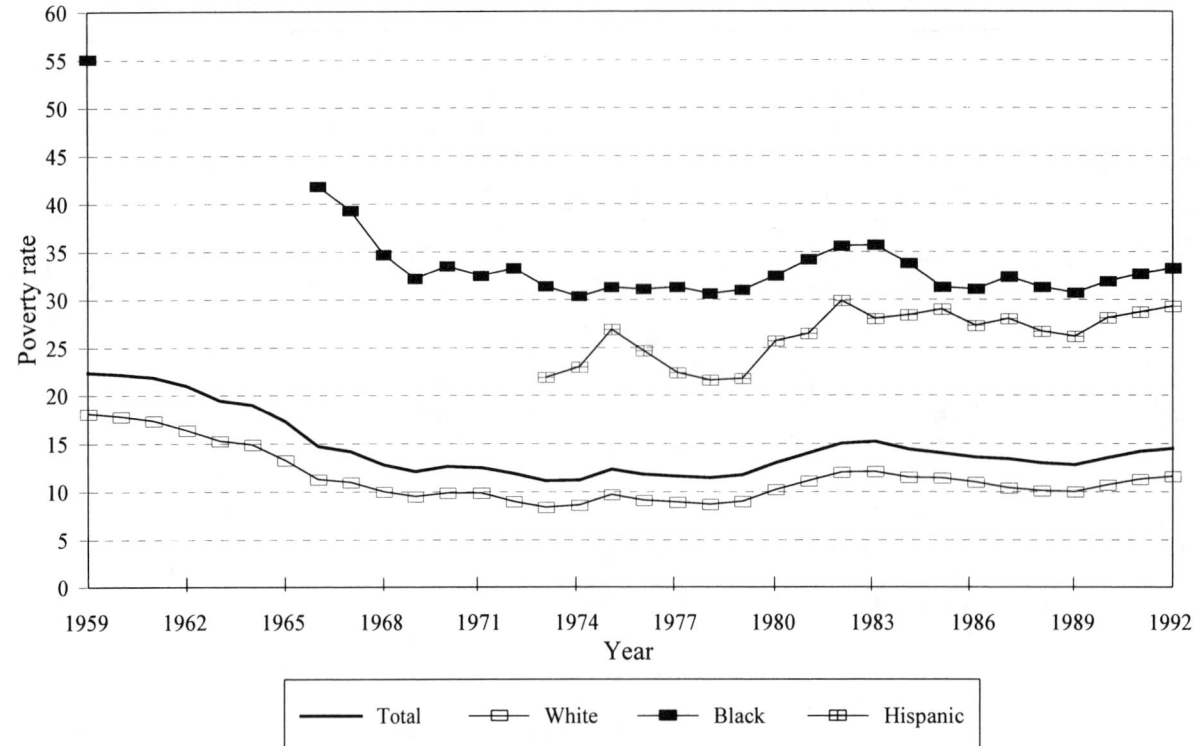

Source: 1959-1992 CPS data.

2. Poverty rates are highest at the childhood ages; a disproportionate share of the nation's poor are children.

3. The sex difference in poverty is small at the childhood ages, but as soon as females reach adulthood they suffer a differential increase in poverty, which persists for the rest of their lives. The size of this sex differential is very great for all three race-ethnic groups. This "feminization of poverty" is increasingly due to high rates of non-marital fertility, separation and divorce; children typically live in the household of the mother, and women's incomes usually lag behind those of men.

4. The sex difference in poverty is far greater among the black population than among the white or Hispanic population. This becomes particularly great at the mature adult ages. However, the disparity in poverty rates between black men and women in the late adult years has been shrinking in recent years.

5. Young adults are poorer than mature adults. For both sexes and in all racial and ethnic groups, poverty rates reach their lowest level at ages 45-54.

6. Poverty rises moderately as people pass into retirement ages. However, poverty rates among those sixty-five and over are lower than those for young adults under twenty-five years of age among whites, lower than those under 18 years among blacks, and lower than those under 35 years among Hispanics. As was noted in the section on wealth, the elderly have a much higher net worth than

do the young, so that they have greater financial resources with which to protect themselves from the immediate effects of impoverishment. On the other hand, there is a high concentration of the elderly at levels of income just above the poverty level; this is the result of major increases in the levels of Social Security pensions during the 1960s and 1970s.

Race-Ethnicity

Poverty rates among the black population are approximately three times as great as among the white population in 1992 (33.3 as against 11.6 percent). The Hispanic population has a poverty rate of 29.3 percent, 2.5 times that of the white population but somewhat lower than that of the black population. The poverty rate for "Other races" was 17.0 percent; this included the Asian and Pacific Islander racial group, whose poverty rate was 12.5 percent.

The race differentials have persisted in roughly the same ratios since 1959, the earliest year for which poverty statistics have been prepared (Table 15-28). Even though the percentage of the poverty-level population that is black and Hispanic is much higher than their percentage in the total population, the majority (66.5 percent) of the population living below the poverty level is white (they comprised 73.9 percent of the general population in 1992). The poverty level population is 28.8 percent black (as

Table 15-28. Poverty Status of Persons, by Type of Family and Race-ethnicity: 1959-1992

Year and type of family	Persons below poverty level (in thousands)	Poverty rate				Percent of total poor		
		Total	White	Black	Hispanic	White	Black	Hispanic
All persons								
1992	36,880	14.5	11.6	33.3	29.3	66.5	28.8	18.0
1990	33,585	13.5	10.7	31.9	28.1	66.5	29.3	17.9
1985	33,064	14.0	11.4	31.3	29.0	69.1	27.0	15.8
1980	29,272	13.0	10.2	32.5	25.7	67.3	29.3	11.9
1975	25,877	12.3	9.7	31.3	26.9	68.7	29.2	11.6
1970	25,420	12.6	9.9	33.5	—	68.8	29.7	—
1965	33,185	17.3	13.3	—	—	67.8	—	—
1959	39,490	22.4	18.1	55.1	—	72.1	25.1	—
Persons in families								
All families								
1992	27,947	13.0	9.8	32.7	28.1	63.1	31.9	20.2
1990	25,232	12.0	9.0	31.0	26.9	63.1	32.3	20.2
1985	25,729	12.6	9.9	30.5	28.3	66.6	29.2	17.9
1980	22,601	11.5	8.6	31.1	25.1	64.5	31.8	13.9
1975	20,789	10.9	8.3	30.1	26.3	66.4	31.4	13.3
1970	20,330	10.9	8.1	32.2	—	65.5	32.9	—
1965	28,358	15.8	11.7	—	—	65.3	—	—
1959	34,562	20.8	16.5	54.9	—	70.7	26.4	—
Families with female householder, no spouse present								
1992	13,716	38.5	30.2	53.7	51.2	48.5	48.2	15.7
1990	12,578	37.2	29.8	50.6	53.0	49.4	47.7	16.8
1985	11,600	37.6	29.8	53.2	55.7	51.6	46.1	17.1
1980	10,120	36.7	28.0	53.4	54.5	48.8	49.2	13.0
1975	9,846	37.5	29.4	54.3	57.2	46.5	42.3	10.7
1970	7,503	38.1	28.4	58.7	—	50.1	48.7	—
1965	7,524	46.0	35.4	—	—	54.4	—	—
1959	7,014	49.4	40.2	70.6	—	60.3	34.4	—

Source: U.S. Bureau of the Census, Current Population Reports, "Poverty in the United States: 1992," Series P-60, No. 185, U.S. Government Printing Office, Washington, D.C., 1993, Table 2.

against 12.4 percent of the general population), and the Hispanic poverty population is 18.0 percent of the whole poverty population (as against 8.8 percent of the general population). Asian and Pacific Islanders comprise about 2.8 percent of the general population and 2.4 percent of the poverty population.

Race-Ethnicity and Extreme Poverty

Race and ethnicity have strong influences on the proportion of the population in extreme poverty (below .5 of the poverty line). Out of the total of 15 million persons in extreme poverty in 1992, 4.3 percent of whites (9.1 million persons), 16.3 percent of blacks (5.2 million persons) and 10.9 percent of Hispanics (2.5 million persons) lived in families (or as unrelated individuals) in extreme poverty. Thus the extreme poverty population is about 60.7 percent white, 34.7 percent black and 16.7 percent Hispanic (the racial and Hispanic categories can overlap), or somewhat more black and less white or Hispanic than the poverty population in general.

Educational Attainment

Educational attainment is strongly linked to the avoidance of poverty. Not only is there a strong inverse relationship between poverty status and educational attainment, but a high school diploma or a college education stand as a bulwark against poverty. Among the population 25 years and over in 1992, the poverty rate of those with no high school diploma was 25.6 percent (22.0 percent for whites, 42.7 percent for blacks, and 32.4 percent for Hispanics). With each increment of educational attainment, the poverty rate declines; for those with a bachelor's degree or higher the poverty rate shrank to 3.0 percent in 1992. Yet educational attainment is not able to wipe out the sex and race differentials in poverty. Females have a higher poverty rate than males at all educational levels. The black population has a far higher poverty rate at each educational level than does the white population. Within both the white and the black populations, females have higher poverty rates than males. Thus sex and race differentials remain intact while reflecting the fundamental importance of education.

To a large extent, the poverty rates simply reflect the lower end of the income spectrum shown in Table 15-8 (where the incomes of the population by educational attainment, age and race-ethnicity were reported). Attainment of higher education also keeps people out of penury: only a little more than 1 percent of those with bachelor's degrees live in extreme poverty, compared to more than 8 percent of those with no high school diploma.

Marital Status

Next to high educational attainment, the most important factor in avoiding poverty is being married and living with a spouse. Both wives and husbands in married-couple families had a very low poverty rate of 6.2 percent in 1992 (Table 15-29). By comparison, female householders with no spouse present have a poverty rate of 34.9 percent. Among blacks, husbands and wives with

a spouse present have a poverty rate of 13.0 percent, and roughly half (49.8 percent) of all black female householders without a spouse live in poverty. For Hispanics, more husbands (18.6 percent) and wives (17.7 percent) with spouses present live in poverty than among blacks, but the poverty rate is slightly lower (48.8 percent) among female householders with no spouse present.

The sex difference in poverty is particularly striking when looking at the never married, divorced or separated populations (Table 15-27). In 1992, never married men age 18 years and over had a poverty rate of 13.3 percent, compared to 22.4 percent for their female counterparts. This gender disparity in poverty is similar among the divorced, but among the separated, women had a poverty rate of 44.0 percent, compared to a male poverty rate of 16.6 percent.

Family Type

Poverty rates are far higher in families where the householder is a female living with children or other relatives without a husband present (third panel of Table 15-28, and Table 15-29). This generalization holds true for the white, black, and Hispanic populations. Only 7.5 percent of the population living in married-couple families lives below the poverty level. For families with a female householder with no spouse present, the poverty rate is 38.5 percent, or 5.1 times higher than for married-couple families.

A similar disparity is seen among families with chil-

Table 15-29. Poverty Status of Persons, by Family Status and Race-ethnicity: 1992

Year and type of family	Persons below poverty level (in thousands)	Poverty rate				Percent of total poor		
		Total	White	Black	Hispanic	White	Black	Hispanic
All persons	36,880	14.5	11.6	33.3	29.3	66.5	28.8	18.0
In families	27,947	13.0	9.8	32.7	28.1	63.1	31.9	20.2
Householder	7,960	11.7	8.9	30.9	26.2	64.8	30.6	17.5
Own children under 18 years	12,422	20.3	15.6	46.3	39.2	62.0	32.7	21.3
In married-couple families	12,830	7.5	6.7	14.3	21.4	78.4	15.1	24.4
Householder	3,318	6.2	5.5	13.0	18.5	79.3	14.6	20.5
Own children under 18 years	4,862	10.5	9.6	17.2	28.3	79.5	13.2	27.8
In familes with female								
Householder, no spouse present	13,716	38.5	30.2	53.7	51.2	48.5	48.2	15.7
Householder	4,171	34.9	28.1	49.8	48.8	52.8	44.0	14.5
Own children under 18 years	7,092	55.6	46.6	69.6	69.1	49.2	47.1	16.6
In unrelated subfamilies	943	54.8	54.7	58.9	67.9	83.9	12.8	23.5
Children under 18 years	556	59.9	59.6	63.4	75.4	84.0	12.8	22.1
Unrelated individuals	7,991	21.8	19.5	35.8	34.1	76.2	19.8	9.7

Source: U.S. Bureau of the Census, Current Population Reports, "Poverty in the United States: 1992," Series P-60, No. 185, U.S. Government Printing Office, Washington, D.C., 1993, Table 5.

dren under 18 years (a subset of all families). Married-couple households with children have a poverty rate of 10.5 percent, but families with children and a female householder but no spouse present have a poverty rate that is 5.3 times greater (55.6 percent). Such a high rate of insufficiency of income means that persons living in female-headed families make up nearly one-half (47.5 percent) of the entire poverty-level population.

The highest rate of poverty (59.9 percent) is found among "unrelated subfamilies with children under 18 years." These units are families with children who are living (or who have been forced to live) with another unrelated family (or individual) in a dwelling unit. Such unrelated subfamilies comprise almost one million of the almost 37 million Americans below the poverty line, and the unrelated subfamilies with children under 18 years comprise more than half (556,000) of this nearly one million. Not surprisingly, these children under age 18 living in unrelated subfamilies have very high rates of extreme poverty (36.1 percent in 1992) as well. Unrelated individuals living by themselves comprise almost 8 million of those living in poverty; their poverty rate is 21.8 percent.

Interaction of Race and Family Type

The effects of race-ethnicity and family type on poverty are almost independent of each other, with the result that the poverty rates are extremely high among black and Hispanic populations living in families with a female householder with own children under 18 years (69.6 percent for blacks and 69.1 percent for Hispanics). By contrast, they are low among white married-couple families (6.7 percent). The poverty rates among the two former groups are more than ten times the poverty rate in the latter group.

The last panel of Table 15-28 shows that there was progress in reducing poverty during the 1960s and 1970s among families with a female householder with no spouse present. The poverty rate for this group dropped from 40.2 to 28.0 percent for whites between 1959 and 1980, and from 70.6 to 53.4 percent among blacks during the same period. The growth of the poverty population since 1980 can be explained by the increase in the number of households with female householders as well as by the rise (since 1980) in poverty rates for households of all types.

The Poverty Status of Children

Children, more than adults, tend to be the victims of poverty. This is consistent with the fact that poverty rates are often lowest in families where there are no children and highest in families with many children. This is the well-known dependency effect. Children are not earners but tend to claim a share of the income; the more children, the less income per capita in the family, so that a higher proportion of families with children are pushed below the poverty line. The concentration of children

below the poverty line is especially strong for families with female householders who have no husband present.

For example, all persons in families in 1992 had a poverty rate of 13.0 percent, but the children (own children under 18 years) of these families had a poverty rate of 20.3 percent. Almost half (46.3 percent) of black children in families were in poverty. While Hispanic children in families had a lower rate of poverty (39.2 percent) than did black children, their poverty rate in married-couple families was higher (28.3 percent for Hispanics compared to 17.2 percent for blacks and 9.6 percent for whites).

Since women more commonly raise children from non-marital unions or after divorce or separation, the gender disparity in poverty for these groups described above (in the "Marital Status" section) has a profound effect on children. Almost nine out of every ten children (88.0 percent) who were raised by never-married women who had two or more children under age six were being raised in poverty in 1992, and the equivalent poverty rate for the children of divorced or separated mothers with two or more children was more than three out of four (76.5 percent).

Unrelated Adult Individuals

Unrelated individuals, who by definition do not live as members of a family, have substantially higher poverty rates than do persons who live in families (Table 15-29). At all ages, those who live outside families have higher poverty rates than persons of the same sex, race, and age who are married and living with a spouse, although the gap between these two statuses for blacks and those of Hispanic origin is not very large.

These persons who live outside families either live alone or live in households with one or more persons unrelated to them. Poverty rates are lower for those who live alone than for those who live with others. White males who live alone tend to have relatively low poverty rates. Even at ages of retirement, only 14.5 percent of white males are defined as living in poverty in 1992. The rates are much higher for females and for blacks of both sexes.

The Elderly in Poverty

As Table 15-30 shows, the poverty rates of the white elderly in 1992 (7.1 percent for males 65 years and over and 13.6 percent for females) were slightly higher than those of people in their middle ages, but below those of people in their twenties or younger. Although black and Hispanic elderly had considerably higher poverty rates than whites (especially black women, at 37.7 percent), the age pattern of poverty across age was much the same as among whites.

To a great extent, however, the elderly are now able to avoid extreme poverty (an income below half of the poverty threshold). In 1992, 14.5 percent of the general

Table 15-30. Poverty Rates, by Age, Sex, and Race-ethnicity: 1992

Age	All races			White			Black			Hispanic		
	Total	Male	Female	Total	Male	Female	Total	Male	Female	Total	Male	Female
Total	14.5	12.7	16.3	11.6	10.1	13.0	33.3	29.3	36.8	29.3	27.0	31.6
Under 18 years	21.9	21.5	22.3	16.9	16.6	17.2	46.6	45.9	47.3	39.9	39.2	40.7
18 to 24 years	18.0	14.2	21.6	15.3	12.4	18.2	31.7	24.2	38.5	30.0	25.4	34.7
25 to 34 years	13.2	9.8	16.6	10.8	8.5	13.2	28.2	17.7	37.1	25.2	20.9	29.9
35 to 44 years	9.8	8.3	11.2	7.8	6.9	8.7	23.3	18.4	27.3	21.6	19.5	23.7
45 to 54 years	7.9	7.0	8.7	6.5	5.7	7.2	18.7	17.1	20.0	17.1	16.5	17.8
55 to 59 years	10.0	8.7	11.3	8.4	7.4	9.3	22.9	18.2	26.8	20.2	18.1	21.7
60 to 64 years	10.6	7.8	13.1	8.7	6.4	10.8	25.2	17.5	31.5	26.2	19.9	31.3
65 years and over	12.9	8.9	15.7	10.9	7.1	13.6	33.3	26.9	37.7	22.0	17.4	25.3

Source: U.S. Bureau of the Census, Current Population Reports, "Poverty in the United States: 1992," Series P-60, No. 185, U.S. Government Printing Office, Washington, D.C., 1993, Table 5.

population was in poverty, and 5.9 percent was in extreme poverty. Among the elderly, 12.9 percent were in poverty, but the proportion in extreme poverty was only 2.6 percent. For blacks this comparison is even more striking: 33.3 percent of the overall black population was in poverty, and 16.3 percent were in extreme poverty. Among the black elderly, poverty was as common as in the rest of the black population (33.3 percent), but extreme poverty was found only among 5.2 percent of the black elderly.

Not all the elderly are living in splendor; in 1992 41.5 percent of the elderly were living at incomes that were below twice the poverty level, and for minorities this proportion was even higher (68.3 percent for blacks and 59.6 percent for Hispanics). The 1994 Current Population Report on Consumer Income showed that without non-means-tested cash transfers (the largest of which is the Social Security program), the poverty rate would have risen from 14.5 percent to 21.9 percent. Any future changes in the payment of Social Security or Medicare benefits will have a major effect on the elderly, many of whose members are perched just above the poverty line.

Residential Differentials in Poverty

Metropolitan-Nonmetropolitan

The poverty rate of nonmetropolitan areas (16.8 percent in 1992; see Table 15-27) is significantly higher than that of metropolitan areas (13.9 percent). Yet within metropolitan areas, central cities had the highest poverty rates (20.5 percent), and the portion of metropolitan areas not in central cities had the lowest poverty rate (9.7 percent). Further, extreme poverty was most commonly found in central cities (8.9 percent), followed by nonmetropolitan areas (6.4 percent) and the non-central city portion of metropolitan areas (only 3.8 percent).

While the analysis of American poverty often focuses on urban minorities, the poverty rates of black and Hispanics outside of metropolitan areas still remain the highest. Blacks have poverty rates of 35.2 in central cities, of 25.4 percent in non-central city metropolitan areas, and of 40.8 percent in areas outside of metropolitan areas (as of 1992). The equivalent figures for Hispanics are 33.7 percent, 22.2 percent, and 36.7 percent. On the other hand, extreme poverty is more likely to be concentrated in the central city: only 30.1 percent of the U.S. population lives in the central city, but 45.1 percent of those suffering from extreme poverty lives there. By contrast, 22.3 percent of the population lives in nonmetropolitan areas, compared to 24.2 percent of the extreme poverty population--a roughly even balance of population and proportion in extreme poverty.

Poverty Areas

Within poverty areas (see Definition Box) poverty rates are far higher than in non-poverty areas. Poverty rates are substantially higher in poverty areas within central cities than in poverty areas outside central cities. Throughout the nation, the poverty rate in poverty areas (34.2 percent) was about two and one-half times the national average in 1992. The poverty rate within poverty areas also differed by level of urbanization: 39.5 percent of those in poverty areas of central cities were poor, compared to 31.7 percent in the suburbs and 27.3 in non-metropolitan areas. While this was due to the concentration of poverty in various areas of large cities, the use of smaller areas (census tracts) in the measurement of central city poverty areas also contributed to the apparent high levels of concentration of poverty there. This may partially explain why the Northeast region, an area of lower overall poverty rates (but high levels of urbanization and a high proportion of its population in census tracts) had the highest level of poverty (36.9 percent) among its population living in poverty areas.

The poverty rate of those living outside of poverty areas was less than one-third that of those living in poverty areas in 1992 (11.1 to 34.2 percent). These figures are exacerbated when we look at children under age 18: 48.5 percent of children in poverty areas are poor themselves, compared to 16.4 percent who live outside poverty areas. Since most children attend schools in their own neighborhoods, this leads to a high concentration of poor children in some schools, and very few in others.

Regions

Poverty rates (Table 15-27) are much higher in the South (16.9 percent in 1992), followed by the West (14.4 percent), the Midwest (13.1 percent) and the Northeast (12.3 percent). The black population has higher rates of poverty in the North Central region (35.7 percent) than in the South (34.2 percent), and its poverty rates are lowest in the Northeast (31.6 percent) and the West (24.4 percent). Among whites, the West has higher poverty rates (13.5 percent), followed by the South (12.4 percent), the Midwest (10.1 percent), and the Northeast (9.9 percent). Hispanics show a third pattern of poverty distribution: their poverty rates are highest in the Northeast (34.5 percent), medium in the South and West (both at 28.5 percent), and lowest in the Midwest (27.3 percent).

Even within regions, the poverty rates of racial and ethnic groups can differ considerably: for example, within the Midwest region, the poverty rate of Hispanics in 1992 in the East North Central division is only 24.9 percent, but their poverty rate in the West North Central division (where they are far fewer in number) is 39.4 percent. Among states, Louisiana, Mississippi, New Mexico, West Virginia and the District of Columbia all had overall poverty rates of over 20 percent in 1992, and Connecticut, Delaware, New Hampshire, Utah and Virginia had poverty rates below 10 percent.

Social Mobility and Poverty

One of the key questions of public life in the United States is how much "opportunity" there is. Politicians and other opinion leaders proclaim it; many immigrants are attracted to this nation because they perceive greater opportunity for mobility (particularly income mobility) here than elsewhere. Yet numerous opinion surveys show that a good number of Americans (especially minority Americans) feel that the deck is stacked against them. Some academics talk of a "culture of poverty," and give the impression that poverty (and its supposed negative psychological attributes) is handed down as an old family tradition. Yet in the writings of most of those interested in the subject, there is surprisingly little attention paid to the empirical question of how difficult it is to rise out of or fall into poverty.

In order to measure the social mobility of individuals and families, it is necessary to have repeated measures of the income of the same people over time (panel surveys). Only two such major surveys exist: the Panel Study of Income Dynamics (the PSID, which has existed since the late 1960s) and the U.S. government's Survey of Income and Program Participation (the SIPP, which has been generating data since the early 1980s).

The Panel Study of Income Dynamics generated important data (analyzed by Greg Duncan and others) that showed that there was considerable movement of the population between different levels of income and movement of families into and out of poverty during the 1970s and early 1980s. The more recent data from the PSID and from the SIPP show that while there appears to be a long-term trend towards less income mobility and more class crystallization, the amount of income mobility is still sufficient to call into question whether there really is an "underclass" (in the sense of a permanently poor, self-reproducing group) in the United States.

In 1993, SIPP data reveal, about 14.6 percent of the U.S. population (37.6 million people) fell below the poverty line in an average month. However, 20.8 percent of the U.S. population (52.9 million people) fell into poverty for two or more months during that year. This group of people who were below the poverty threshold for two or more months in 1993 included half (50.8 percent) of all the unemployed, 46.5 percent of all people in female-householder families, more than 40 percent of all blacks and Hispanics, almost a third (30.3 percent) of everyone under 18 years, and 28.6 percent of all unrelated individuals. Because of the low levels of wealth of much of the population and the decrease in wage levels over the last two decades, a surprisingly large proportion of the population frequently finds itself close to financial disaster.

What about the other side? Is there a permanent underclass, mired in poverty? The SIPP data show that for the 24 months of 1992 and 1993, 4.8 percent of the population were chronically poor (below the poverty line in all 24 months). The key groups of chronically poor people included blacks (15.1 percent of whom were chronically poor), people in female householder families (17.2 percent), Hispanics (10.3 percent), those under 18 years, the unemployed, those not in the labor force, and unrelated individuals (between 8-10 percent of whom were chronically poor).

According to the SIPP interviews, there were about 22.7 million people who were poor in both 1992 and 1993. Yet about 6.3 million people moved out of poverty between those two years; they were replaced by another 6.5 million people who entered poverty (or about 3 percent of the total population) in 1993. There appear to be a number of factors (family composition, race, age, employment status) which account for people having longer or shorter "spells" of poverty. In the lives of many Americans, falling above or below the poverty line is not a condition to which one is assigned on a long-term basis, but rather is a month-to-month struggle.

Conclusion

The combination of high unemployment, inflation, economic recession, and other economic problems that plagued the American economy in the late 1970s and early 1980s brought income growth to a halt for most Americans and reversed the reduction of poverty. At the end of the deep recession of the early 1980s, it seemed likely that long-term trends in income growth, a more even distribution of wealth and the reduction of poverty would resume as the business cycle turned upward again. Rising levels of educational and occupational attainment, a stronger positive correlation between education and income, and prospects for greater family stability, smaller families, and for greater socioeconomic equality among the race-ethnic groups all seemed to point in this direction.

Instead, the economic upturn of the mid 1980s to mid 1990s (broken only by a short recession between July of 1990 and March of 1991) has led to a dramatic increase in national product that has produced little if any gain for the bottom 80 percent of the population. Even with large increases in human capital (i.e. added education), median male earnings in 1992 were more than $3,000 *less* (in constant dollars) than in 1973 (Table 15-2). This male income decline has hit college graduates in their forties as well as high school dropouts in their twenties.

Women's earnings gained only less than $2,500 over the 1973-92 period. As a result, median family earnings grew only by about 3 percent between these dates, with all of the income growth concentrated among white families (black and Hispanic family income declined; Table 15-14). The increasing household income Gini ratios between 1968 and the present (Figure 15-7) show the increasing inequalities in income distribution both between and within racial and ethnic groups. Taxes and government transfer programs have only a minor effect in terms of narrowing income disparities among various population groups (Table 15-20).

Large-scale, high-quality data on wealth has become available only during the last decade, so it is somewhat harder to interpret long-term trends. Yet between 1988 and 1991, the net worth of the lowest income quintile rose less than $1,000 dollars (from $4,324 to $5,224) while the net worth of the highest income quintile rose by almost $11,500 (from $111,700 to $123,166). While the percentage increase may actually be higher for the lowest income quintile, the highest income quintile gained about $10,500 more in net worth than the lowest quintile in this three-year interval.

The lack of net worth of the lowest income quintile of the population is tied to continuing high rates of poverty in the population, particularly among blacks and Hispanics. This population has failed to benefit from the economic expansion of the 1980s and 1990s. Poverty is heavily influenced by age, education, marital status and family type. On the other hand, a large proportion of the U.S. population cycles in and out of poverty; probably less than one out of 20 Americans is "chronically poor." Yet data from the Panel Study of Income Dynamics and the SIPP both suggest that over the last decade mobility between income classes is declining, particularly for those at the bottom and at the top of the income distribution. We may be seeing, for the first time since the first decades of this century, the re-emergence of a self-replicating elite and a working class that teeters on the edge of poverty.

What is perhaps most disturbing about trends in poverty is the increase in children in poverty. In 1969, their rate of poverty dropped below 15 percent, but by 1992 it stood at almost 22 percent. Poverty among children appears to have two major roots: family instability and the concentration of poverty among minority children (and within poverty areas). Children in extreme poverty (those whose family income was less than half the poverty threshold) included over 3.2 million white, 2.8 million black and 1.1 million Hispanic (who could be of any race) children. The differences in life chances now apportioned to various groups of children in the United States have reached a gulf of Dickensian proportions. How the United States plans to compete in the twenty-first century against other economic powers (such as the nations of the European Union and Japan, or even Korea or Taiwan) who are raising far smaller proportions of their offspring in poverty remains a mystery.

Technical Appendix 15-1
The SSA Poverty Threshold

At the core of the poverty index developed by the Social Security Administration (SSA) in 1964 was the economy food plan, the least costly of four nutritionally adequate food plans designed by the Department of Agriculture. It was determined from the Department of Agriculture's 1955 survey of food consumption that families of three or more spent approximately one-third of their income on food; the poverty level for such families was therefore set at three times the cost of the economy food plan. For smaller families and persons living alone, the cost of the economy food plan was multiplied by slightly higher coefficients to compensate for the relatively larger fixed expenses of smaller households. Annual revisions of the SSA poverty cutoffs were based on price changes of the items in the economy food budget.

As a result of deliberations of a Federal Interagency

Committee in 1969, the following two modifications to the original SSA definitions of poverty were recommended: (1) that the SSA thresholds for non-farm families be retained for the base year 1963, but annual adjustments in the levels be based on changes in the Consumer Price Index (CPI) rather than changes in the cost of food included in the economy food plan; and (2) that the farm thresholds be raised from 70 to 85 percent of the corresponding nonfarm levels. The combined impact of these two modifications resulted in an increase of 360,000 poor families and 1.6 million poor persons in 1967.

The poverty thresholds change each year by the same percentage as the annual average Consumer Price Index. Thus in current dollars, the poverty threshold for a family of four (of whom two were children) rose from $2,973 in 1959 to $9,862 in 1982 and to $14,228 in 1992.

In 1980 another interagency committee recommended three additional modifications that were implemented in the March, 1982, Current Population Survey as well as in the 1980 Census: (1) elimination of separate thresholds for farm families, (2) averaging of thresholds for female-householder and "all other" families, and (3) extension of the poverty matrix to families with nine or more members. During the early 1990s, Bureau of the Census statisticians began to compute the alternative definitions of income shown in Table 15-20 and to apply them to the formulation of alternative measures of the poverty line. The latest major change came in 1994, when the Bureau of the Census began to adjust for the undercount in the 1990 Census (which excluded a larger proportion of the poor) in the computation of the population below the poverty line.

Size-Composition Matrix. The poverty cutoffs used by the Bureau of the Census to determine the poverty status of families and unrelated individuals consist of a set of forty-eight thresholds arranged in a two-dimensional matrix consisting of family size (from one person-unrelated individuals to nine or more persons) cross-classified by presence and number of family members under eighteen years old (from no children present to eight or more children present). Unrelated individuals and two-person families are further differentiated by the age of the individual or family householder (under sixty-five and sixty-five and over). The total family income of each family in the sample is tested against the appropriate dollar threshold to determine the poverty status of that family. If the family's total income is less than its corresponding cutoff, the family is classified as below the poverty level. The average thresholds were weighted by the number of children. For a given size of family, the weighted average threshold for that group is obtained by multiplying the threshold for each presence and the number of children category within the given family size by the number of families in that category (see Table 15-26 for the 1992 threshold values). These products are then aggregated across the entire range of presence and number of children categories, and the total aggregate is divided by the total number of families in the group to yield the weighted average threshold at the poverty level for that size family.

Bibliography

Aldrich, H., and Weiss, J. "Differentiation Within the United States Capitalist Class: Workforce Size and Income Differences." American Sociological Review 46(1981): 279-90.

Anderson, Claud. Black Labor, White Wealth: The Search for Power and Economic Justice. Edgewood, MD: Duncan and Duncan. 1994.

Avery, Robert B., Elliehausen, Gregory E., Canner, Glenn B., and Gustafson, Thomas. "Survey of Consumer Finances, 1983." Federal Reserve Bulletin 70(1986):679-92.

Barlett, Donald L., and Steele, James B. America: Who Really Pays the Taxes? New York: Touchstone. 1994.

Beck, Elwood M., Horan, Patrick, and Tolbert, Charles. "Stratification in a Dual Economy: A Sectoral Model of Earnings Determination." American Sociological Review 43(1978): 704-20.

Bianchi, Suzanne M. "Racial Differences in Per Capita Income, 1960-1976: The Importance of Household Size, Headship and Labor Force Participation." Demography 17(1980): 129-43.

Blau, Francine D., and Graham, John W. "Black-White Differences in Wealth and Asset Composition." Quarterly Journal of Economics, 105(1990): 321-39.

Blau, Peter M., and Duncan, Otis D. The American Occupational Structure. New York: Wiley. 1965.

Bluestone, Barry, and Harrison, Bennett. The Deindustrializing of America. New York: Basic Books. 1982.

Bonacich, Edna. "Advanced Capitalism and Black-White Relations in the United States: A Split Labor Market Interpretation." American Sociological Review 37(1976): 547-59.

Bound, John, and Freeman, Richard. "What Went Wrong? The Erosion of Relative Earnings and Employment of Young Black Men in the 1980s." Quarterly Journal of Economics 107(1992): 201-32.

Braun, Denny. The Rich Get Richer: The Rise of Income Inequality in the United States and the World. Chicago: Nelson-Hall. 1991.

Brimmer, Andrew F. "Income, Wealth and Investment Behavior in the Black Community." American Economic Review Papers and Proceedings 15(1988): 1-5.

Brittain, John A. Inheritance and the Inequality of Material Wealth. Washington, D.C.: Brookings Institution. 1978.

Butler, John Sibley. Entrepreneurship and Self-Help among Black Americans: A Reconsideration of Race and Economics. Albany, NY: State University of New York Press. 1991.

Card, David, and Kreuger, Alan B. "Trends in Relative Black-White Earnings Revisited." American Economic Review 83(1993): 85-93.

Carnoy, Martin. Faded Dreams: The Politics and Economics of Race in America. Cambridge: Cambridge University Press. 1994.

Citro, Constance F., and Kalton, Graham. The Future of the Survey of Income and Program Participation. Washington, D.C.: National Academy Press. 1993.

Citro, Constance F., and Michael, Robert T. (eds.). Measuring Poverty: A New Approach. Washington, D.C.: National Academy Press. 1995.

Crystal, Graef S. In Search of Excess: The Overcompensation of American Executives. New York: Norton. 1992.

Danziger, Sheldon, and Gottschalk, Peter (eds.). Uneven Tides: Rising Inequality in America. New York: Russell Sage Foundation. 1993.

Danziger, Sheldon, and Gottschalk, Peter. America Unequal. Cambridge, MA: Harvard University Press. 1995.

Duncan, Greg J., and Hill, Martha S. "Conceptions of Longitudinal Households: Fertile and Futile." Journal of Economic and Social Measurements 13(1985): 361-76.

Ellwood, David T. Poor Support: Poverty in the American Family. New York: Basic Books. 1988.

Ericksen Eugene P. "Estimating the Concentration of Wealth in America." Public Opinion Quarterly 52(1988):243-53.

Farley, Reynolds (ed.). State of the Union: America in the 1990s. Volume One: Economic Trends. New York: Russell Sage Foundation. 1995.

Farley, Reynolds, and Allen, Walter R. The Color Line and the Quality of American Life. New York: Russell Sage Foundation. 1987.

Federman, Mary, Garner, Thesia I., Short, Kathleen, Cutler, W. Bowman IV, Kiely, John, Levine, David, McGough, Duane, and McMillen, Marilyn. "What Does it Mean to be Poor in America?" Monthly Labor Review 119(1996): 3-17.

Feenberg, Daniel R., and Poterba, James M. Income Inequality and the Incomes of Very High Income Taxpayers, National Bureau of Economic Research Working Paper No. 4229. Cambridge, MA: National Bureau of Economic Research. 1992.

Fitzgerald, Hiram E., Lester, Barry M., and Zuckerman, Barry (eds.). Children of Poverty: Research, Health Care, and Policy Issues. New York: Garland. 1995.

Freeman, Richard. Working Under Different Rules. New York: Russell Sage Foundation. 1994.

Gittleman, Maury B., and Howell, David R. Job Quality, Labor Market Segmentation and Earnings Inequality: Effects of the Economic Restructuring in the 1980s. Annandale-on-Hudson, NY: Jerome Levy Economics Institute. 1992.

Hacker, Andrew. Two Nations: Black and White, Separate, Hostile, Unequal. New York: Scribner's. 1992.

Harrison, Bennett, and Bluestone, Barry. The Great U-Turn: Corporate Restructuring and the Polarizing of America. New York: Basic Books. 1988.

Henretta, John C. and Campbell, Richard T. "Net Worth as an Aspect of Status." American Jornal of Sociology, 83 (1978):1204-23.

Hout, Michael, Lucas, Samuel R., Fischer, Claude S., Janowski, Martin S., Swidler, Ann, and Voss, Kim. Inequality by Design. Princeton, NJ: Princeton University Press. 1996.

Hungerford, Thomas L. "U.S. Income Mobility in the Seventies and Eighties." Review of Income and Wealth 39(1993):403-17.

Jenks, Christopher, and Paul Peterson (eds.). The Urban Underclass. Washington, D.C.:Brookings Institution. 1991.

Karoly, Lynn A., and Burtless, Gary. "Demographic Change, Rising Earnings Inequality and the Distribution of Personal Well-Being, 1959-89." Demography 32(1995):379-405.

Katz, Lawrence F., and Murphy, Kevin M. "Changes in Relative Wages, 1963-1987: Supply and Demand Factors." The Quarterly Journal of Economics 107 (1992):35-78.

Kaus, Mickey. The End of Equality. New York: Basic Books. 1992.

Klein, Bruce W., and Philip L. Rones. "A Profile of the Working Poor." Monthly Labor Review 112(1989):3-13.

Kolikoff, Laurence, and Summers, Lawrence. "The Role of Intergenerational Transfers in Aggregate Capital Accumulation." Journal of Political Economy 89(1981):706-32.

Kuznets, Simon S. Growth, Population and Income Distribution: Selected Essays. New York: W.W. Norton. 1979.

Landry, Bart. The New Black Middle Class. Berkeley, CA: University of California Press. 1987.

Lebergott, Stanley. Consumer Expenditures: New Measures and Old Motives. Princeton, NJ: Princeton University Press. 1996.

Levy, Frank S. Dollars and Dreams: The Changing American Income Distribution. New York: Norton. 1987.

_____. "Income and Inequality." In State of the Union: America in the 1990s. Volume One: Economic Trends. Reynolds Farley (ed.). New York: Russell Sage Foundation. 1995.

Levy, Frank S., and Michel, Richard. The Economic Future of American Families: Income and Wealth Trends. Washington, D.C.: Urban Institute Press. 1991.

Lieberson, Stanley. A Piece of the Pie: Blacks and White Immigrants Since 1880. Berkeley, CA: University of California Press. 1980.

Lipset, Seymour Martin, and Bendix, Reinhard. Social Mobility in Industrial Society. Berkeley: University of California Press. 1959.

Long, James E., and Caudill, Steven B. "Racial Differences in Home Ownership and Housing Wealth, 1970-1986." Economic Inquiry 30(1992):83-100.

Massey, Douglas S., and Denton, Nancy A. American Apartheid: Segregation and the Making of the Underclass. Cambridge, MA: Harvard University Press. 1993.

Mayer, Susan, and Jenks, Christopher. "Recent Trends in Economic Inequality in the United States: Income versus Expenditure versus Material Well-being." In Poverty and Prosperity in the USA in the Late Twentieth Century. Dimitri Papadimitriou and Edward N. Wolff (eds.) New York: St. Martin's Press. 1993.

Murray, Charles. Losing Ground: American Social Policy, 1950-1980. New York: Basic Books. 1984.

Oliver, Melvin L. and Shapiro, Thomas M. Black Wealth/White Wealth. New York: Routledge. 1995.

Rainwater, Lee. What Money Buys: Inequality and the Social Meaning of Income. New York: Basic Books. 1974.

Ryscavage, Paul. "A Surge in Growing Income Inequality?" Monthly Labor Review 118(1995):51-61.

Ryscavage, Paul, and Henle, Peter. "Earnings Inequality Accelerates in the 1980s." Monthly Labor Review 113(1990):3-16.

Shea, Martin. "Dynamics of Economic Well-Being: Poverty, 1990-92." Current Population Reports Series P70-42. 1995.

Squires, Gregory D., Bennett, Larry, McCourt, Kathleen, and Nyden, Philip. Chicago: Race, Class and the Response to Urban Decline. Philadelphia: Temple University Press. 1987.

Steckel, Richard H., and Krishnan, Jayanthi. "Wealth Mobility in America: A Long View from the National Longitudinal Survey." National Bureau of Economic Research Working Paper No. 4137. Cambridge, MA: National Bureau of Economic Research. 1992.

Thurow, Lester C. Generating Inequality: Mechanisms of Inequality in the U.S. Economy. New York: Basic Books. 1975.

_____. The Future of Capitalism. New York: William Morrow and Co. 1996.

Treas, Judith. "U.S. Income Stratification: Bringing Families Back In." Sociology and Social Research 66(1982):231-51.

U.S. Bureau of the Census. Poverty in the United States: 1992. Current Population Reports, Consumer Income Series, P60-185. Washington, D.C.: U.S. Government Printing Office. 1993.

_____. Income, Poverty and Valuation of Noncash Benefits: 1993. Current Population Reports, P60-188. Washington, D.C.: U.S. Government Printing Office. 1995.

_____. A Brief Look at Postwar U.S. Economic Inequality. Current Population Reports, Household Economic Studies, P60-191. Washington, D.C.: U.S. Government Printing Office. 1996.

_____. Income, Poverty and Valuation of Noncash Benefits: 1994. Current Population Reports, P60-189. Washington, D.C.: U.S. Government Printing Office. 1996.

_____. Who Stays Poor? Who Doesn't? Current Population Reports, Household Economic Studies, P70-55. Washington, D.C.: U.S. Government Printing Office. 1996.

Villemez, Wayne J., and Kasarda, John D. "Impact of Regional Destination on Black Migrant Income." Social Science Quarterly 57(1977):767:83.

Welch, Finis. "Effect of Cohort Size on Earnings: The Baby Boom Babies' Financial Bust." Journal of Political Economy 87 (1979):65-97.

Wilson, William J. The Truly Disadvantaged: The Inner City, the Underclass and Public Policy. Chicago: University of Chicago Press. 1987.

Wolff, Edward N. "Estimates of Household Wealth Inequality in the U.S., 1962-1983." Review of Income and Wealth 35(1987): 231-42.

_____. "How the Pie is Sliced: America's Growing Concentration of Wealth." American Prospect, Summer (1995):58-64.

_____. "The Rich Get Increasingly Richer: Latest Data on Household Wealth During the 1980s." In Research in Politics and Society Vol. 5. Richard E. Ratcliff, Melvin L. Oliver, and Thomas M. Shapiro (eds.). Greenwich, CT: JAI Press. 1995.

INDEX